Collins

Collins
Spanish
Dictionary

HarperCollins Publishers
Westerhill Road
Bishopbriggs
Glasgow
G64 2QT
Great Britain

Second Edition 2009

Reprint 10 9 8 7 6 5 4 3 2 1

© HarperCollins Publishers 2006, 2009

ISBN 978-0-00-729884-6

Collins® is a registered trademark of
HarperCollins Publishers Limited

www.collinslanguage.com

A catalogue record for this book is
available from the British Library

Typeset by Wordcraft, Glasgow

Printed and bound in Great Britain by
Clays Ltd, St Ives, plc

Acknowledgements
We would like to thank those
authors and publishers who kindly
gave permission for copyright
material to be used in the Collins
Word Web. We would also like to
thank Times Newspapers Ltd for
providing valuable data.

MANAGING EDITOR
Gaëlle Amiot-Cadey

CONTRIBUTORS
José Martín Galera
Wendy Lee
José María Ruiz Vaca
Cordelia Lilly

EDITORIAL COORDINATION
Susie Beattie

SERIES EDITOR
Rob Scriven

ÍNDICE

CONTENTS

MARCAS REGISTRADAS

Las marcas que creemos que constituyen marcas registradas las denominamos como tales. Sin embargo, no debe considerarse que la presencia o la ausencia de esta designación tenga que ver con la situación legal de ninguna marca.

NOTE ON TRADEMARKS

Words which we have reason to believe constitute trademarks have been designated as such. However, neither the presence nor the absence of such designation should be regarded as affecting the legal status of any trademark.

William Collins' dream of knowledge for all began with the publication of his first book in 1819. A self-educated mill worker, he not only enriched millions of lives, but also founded a flourishing publishing house. Today, staying true to this spirit, Collins books are packed with inspiration, innovation, and practical expertise. They place you at the centre of a world of possibility and give you exactly what you need to explore it.

Language is the key to this exploration, and at the heart of Collins Dictionaries is language as it is really used. New words, phrases, and meanings spring up every day, and all of them are captured and analysed by the Collins Word Web. Constantly updated, and with over 2.5 billion entries, this living language resource is unique to our dictionaries.

Words are tools for life. And a Collins Dictionary makes them work for you.

Collins. Do more

INTRODUCCIÓN

Estamos muy satisfechos de que hayas decidido comprar este diccionario y esperamos que lo disfrutes y que te sirva de gran ayuda ya sea en el colegio, en el trabajo, en tus vacaciones o en casa.

INTRODUCTION

We are delighted that you have decided to buy this Spanish dictionary and hope you will enjoy and benefit from using it at school, at home, on holiday or at work.

ABREVIATURAS

ABBREVIATIONS

abreviatura	*ab(b)r*	abbreviation
adjetivo, locución adjetiva	*adj*	adjective, adjectival phrase
administración	*Admin*	administration
adverbio, locución adverbial	*adv*	adverb, adverbial phrase
agricultura	*Agr*	agriculture
anatomía	*Anat*	anatomy
Argentina	*Arg*	Argentina
arquitectura	*Arq, Arch*	architecture
el automóvil	*Aut(o)*	the motor car and motoring
aviación, viajes aéreos	*Aviac, Aviat*	flying, air travel
biología	*Bio(l)*	biology
botánica, flores	*Bot*	botany
inglés británico	BRIT	British English
Centroamérica	CAM	Central America
química	*Chem*	chemistry
comercio, finanzas, banca	*Com(m)*	commerce, finance, banking
informática	*Comput*	computing
conjunción	*conj*	conjunction
construcción	*Constr*	building
compuesto	*cpd*	compound element
Cono Sur	CS	Southern Cone
cocina	*Culin*	cookery
economía	*Econ*	economics
eletricidad, electrónica	*Elec*	electricity, electronics
enseñanza, sistema escolar y universitario	*Escol*	schooling, schools and universities
España	ESP	Spain
especialmente	*esp*	especially
exclamación, interjección	*excl*	exclamation, interjection
femenino	*f*	feminine
lengua familiar (! vulgar)	*fam(!)*	colloquial usage (! particularly offensive)
ferrocarril	*Ferro*	railways
uso figurado	*fig*	figurative use
fotografía	*Foto*	photography
(verbo inglés) del cual la partícula es inseparable	*fus*	(phrasal verb) where the particle is inseparable
generalmente	*gen*	generally
geografía, geología	*Geo*	geography, geology
geometría	*Geom*	geometry
historia	*Hist*	history
uso familiar (! vulgar)	*inf(!)*	colloquial usage (! particularly offensive)
infinitivo	*infin*	infinitive
informática	*Inform*	computing
invariable	*inv*	invariable
irregular	*irreg*	irregular
lo jurídico	*Jur*	law
América Latina	LAM	Latin America
gramática, lingüística	*Ling*	grammar, linguistics

ABREVIATURAS

ABBREVIATIONS

masculino	m	masculine
matemáticas	Mat(h)	mathematics
masculino/femenino	m/f	masculine/feminine
medicina	Med	medicine
México	MÉX, MEX	Mexico
lo militar, ejército	Mil	military matters
música	Mús, Mus	music
substantivo, nombre	n	noun
navegación, náutica	Náut, Naut	sailing, navigation
sustantivo numérico	num	numeral noun
complemento	obj	(grammatical) object
	o.s.	oneself
peyorativo	pey, pej	derogatory, pejorative
fotografía	Phot	photography
fisiología	Physiol	physiology
plural	pl	plural
política	Pol	politics
participio de pasado	pp	past participle
preposición	prep	preposition
pronombre	pron	pronoun
psicología, psiquiatría	Psico, Psych	psychology, psychiatry
tiempo pasado	pt	past tense
química	Quím	chemistry
ferrocarril	Rail	railways
religión	Rel	religion
Río de la Plata	RPL	River Plate
	sb	somebody
Cono Sur	SC	Southern Cone
enseñanza, sistema escolar y universitario	Scol	schooling, schools and universities
singular	sg	singular
España	SP	Spain
	sth	something
sujeto	su(b)j	(grammatical) subject
subjuntivo	subjun	subjunctive
tauromaquia	Taur	bullfighting
también	tb	also
técnica, tecnología	Tec(h)	technical term, technology
telecomunicaciones	Telec, Tel	telecommunications
imprenta, tipografía	Tip, Typ	typography, printing
televisión	TV	television
universidad	Univ	university
inglés norteamericano	US	American English
verbo	vb	verb
verbo intransitivo	vi	intransitive verb
verbo pronominal	vr	reflexive verb
verbo transitivo	vt	transitive verb
zoología	Zool	zoology
marca registrada	®	registered trademark
indica un equivalente cultural	≈	introduces a cultural equivalent

SPANISH PRONUNCIATION

VOWELS

a	[a]	pata	not as long as *a* in f*a*r. When followed by a consonant in the same syllable (i.e. in a closed syllable), as in *a*mante, the *a* is short, as in b*a*t
e	[e]	me	like *e* in th*e*y. In a closed syllable, as in g*e*nte, the *e* is short as in p*e*t
i	[i]	pino	as in m*ea*n or mach*i*ne
o	[o]	lo	as in l*o*cal. In a closed syllable, as in c*o*ntrol, the *o* is short as in c*o*t
u	[u]	lunes	as in r*u*le. It is silent after q, and in g*u*e, g*u*i, unless marked güe, güi e.g. antigüedad, when it is pronounced like *w* in *w*olf

SEMIVOWELS

i, y	[j]	bien hielo yunta	pronounced like *y* in *y*es
u	[w]	huevo fuento antigüedad	unstressed *u* between consonant and vowel is pronounced like *w* in *w*ell. See notes on *u* above.

DIPHTHONGS

ai, ay	[ai]	baile	as *i* in r*i*de
au	[au]	auto	as *ou* in sh*ou*t
ei, ey	[ei]	buey	as *ey* in gr*ey*
eu	[eu]	deuda	both elements pronounced independently [e] + [u]
oi, oy	[oi]	hoy	as *oy* in t*oy*

CONSONANTS

b	[b,β]	boda bomba labor	see notes on *v* below
c ce, ci	[k] [θe,θi]	caja cero cielo	*c* before *a, o, u* is pronounced as in *c*at *c* before *e* or *i* is pronounced as in *th*in
ch	[tʃ]	chiste	*ch* is pronounced as *ch* in *ch*air
d	[d,ð]	danés ciudad	at the beginning of a phrase or after *l* or *n*, *d* is pronounced as in English. In any other position it is pronounced like *th* in *th*e

g	[g,ɣ]	**g**afas	*g* before *a, o* or *u* is pronounced as in
		pa**g**a	*g*ap, if at the beginning of a phrase
			or after *n*. In other positions the sound
			is softened
ge, gi	[xe, xi]	**g**ente	*g* before *e* or *i* is pronounced similar
		girar	to *ch* in Scottish lo*ch*
h		**h**aber	*h* is always silent in Spanish
j	[x]	**j**ugar	*j* is pronounced similar to *ch* in
			Scottish lo*ch*
ll	[ʎ]	ta**ll**e	*ll* is pronounced like the *y* in *y*et or the
			lli in mi*lli*on
ñ	[ʃ]	ni**ñ**o	*ñ* is pronounced like the *ni* in o*ni*on
q	[k]	**q**ue	*q* is pronounced as *k* in *k*ing
r, rr	[r, rr]	qui**t**ar	*r* is always pronounced in Spanish,
		ga**rr**a	unlike the silent *r* in dance*r*. *rr* is trilled,
			like a Scottish *r*
s	[s]	quizá**s**	*s* is usually pronounced as in pa**s**s,
		i**s**la	but before *b, d, g, l, m* or *n* it is
			pronounced as in ro**s**e
v	[b,β]	**v**ía	*v* is pronounced something like *b*.
			At the beginning of a phrase or after
			m or *n* it is pronounced as *b* in *b*oy.
			In any other position the sound is
			softened
z	[θ]	tena**z**	*z* is pronounced as *th* in *th*in

f, k, l, m, n, p, t and x are pronounced as in English.

STRESS

The rules of stress in Spanish are as follows:

(a) when a word ends in a vowel or in *n* or *s*, the second last syllable is stressed:
pa*ta*ta, pa*ta*tas; *co*me, *co*men

(b) when a word ends in a consonant other than *n* or *s*, the stress falls on the last syllable:
pa*red*, ha*blar*

(c) when the rules set out in (a) and (b) are not applied, an acute accent appears over the stressed vowel:
co*mún*, geogra*fía*, in*glés*

In the phonetic transcription, the symbol [¹] precedes the syllable on which the stress falls.

LA PRONUNCIACIÓN INGLESA

VOCALES

	Ejemplo inglés	Explicación
[ɑː]	father	Entre *a* de padre y *o* de noche
[ʌ]	but, come	*a* muy breve
[æ]	man, cat	Con los labios en la posición de *e* en pena y luego se pronuncia el sonido *a* parecido a la *a* de carro
[ə]	father, ago	Vocal neutra parecida a una *e* u *o* casi muda
[əː]	bird, heard	Entre *e* abierta y *o* cerrada, sonido alargado
[ɛ]	get, bed	Como en perro
[ɪ]	it, big	Más breve que en sí
[iː]	tea, see	Como en fino
[ɔ]	hot, wash	Como en torre
[ɔː]	saw, all	Como en por
[u]	put, book	Sonido breve, más cerrado que burro
[uː]	too, you	Sonido largo, como en uno

DIPTONGOS

	Ejemplo inglés	Explicación
[aɪ]	fly, high	Como en fraile
[au]	how, house	Como en pausa
[ɛə]	there, bear	Casi como en vea, pero el sonido *a* se mezcla con el indistinto [ə]
[eɪ]	day, obey	*e* cerrada seguida por una *i* débil
[ɪə]	here, hear	Como en manía, mezclándose el sonido *a* con el indistinto [ə]
[əu]	go, note	[ə] seguido por una breve *u*
[ɔɪ]	boy, oil	Como en voy
[uə]	poor, sure	*u* bastante larga más el sonido indistinto [ə]

CONSONANTES

	Ejemplo inglés	Explicación
[b]	big, lobby	Como en tumban
[d]	mended	Como en conde, andar
[g]	go, get, big	Como en grande, gol
[dʒ]	gin, judge	Como en la ll andaluza y en Generalitat (catalán)
[ŋ]	sing	Como en vínculo
[h]	house, he	Como la jota hispanoamericana
[j]	young, yes	Como en ya
[k]	come, mock	Como en caña, Escocia
[r]	red, tread	Se pronuncia con la punta de la lengua hacia atrás y sin hacerla vibrar
[s]	sand, yes	Como en casa, sesión
[z]	rose, zebra	Como en desde, mismo
[ʃ]	she, machine	Como en chambre (francés), roxo (portugués)
[tʃ]	chin, rich	Como en chocolate
[v]	valley	Como f, pero se retiran los dientes superiores vibrándolos contra el labio inferior
[w]	water, which	Como la u de huevo, puede
[ʒ]	vision	Como en journal (francés)
[θ]	think, myth	Como en receta, zapato
[ð]	this, the	Como en hablado, verdad

f, l, m, n, p, t y x iguales que en español.

El signo [*] indica que la r final escrita apenas se pronuncia en inglés británico cuando la palabra siguiente empieza con vocal. El signo [¹] indica la sílaba acentuada.

SPANISH VERB TABLES

1 Gerund 2 Imperative 3 Present 4 Preterite 5 Future 6 Present subjunctive 7 Imperfect subjunctive 8 Past participle 9 Imperfect

Etc indicates that the irregular root is used for all persons of the tense, e.g. oír: 6 oiga, oigas, oigamos, oigáis, oigan

agradecer 3 agradezco 6 agradezca *etc*

aprobar 2 aprueba 3 apruebo, apruebas, aprueba, aprueban 6 apruebe, apruebes, apruebe, aprueben

atravesar 2 atraviesa 3 atravieso, atraviesas, atraviesa, atraviesan 6 atraviese, atravieses, atraviese, atraviesen

caber 3 quepo 4 cupe, cupiste, cupo, cupimos, cupisteis, cupieron 5 cabré *etc* 6 quepa *etc* 7 cupiera *etc*

caer 1 cayendo 3 caigo 4 cayó, cayeron 6 caiga *etc* 7 cayera *etc*

cerrar 2 cierra 3 cierro, cierras, cierra, cierran 6 cierre, cierres, cierre, cierren

COMER 1 comiendo 2 come, comed 3 como, comes, come, comemos, coméis, comen 4 comí, comiste, comió, comimos, comisteis, comieron 5 comeré, comerás, comerá, comeremos, comeréis, comerán 6 coma, comas, coma, comamos, comáis, coman 7 comiera, comieras, comiera, comiéramos, comierais, comieran 8 comido 9 comía, comías, comía, comíamos, comíais, comían

conocer 3 conozco 6 conozca *etc*

contar 2 cuenta 3 cuento, cuentas, cuenta, cuentan 6 cuente, cuentes, cuente, cuenten

dar 3 doy 4 di, diste, dio, dimos, disteis, dieron 7 diera *etc*

decir 2 di 3 digo 4 dije, dijiste, dijo, dijimos, dijisteis, dijeron 5 diré *etc* 6 diga *etc* 7 dijera *etc* 8 dicho

despertar 2 despierta 3 despierto, despiertas, despierta, despiertan 6 despierte, despiertes, despierte, despierten

divertir 1 divirtiendo 2 divierte 3 divierto, diviertes, divierte, divierten 4 divirtió, divirtieron 6 divierta, diviertas, divierta, divirtamos, divirtáis, diviertan 7 divirtiera *etc*

dormir 1 durmiendo 2 duerme 3 duermo, duermes, duerme, duermen 4 durmió, durmieron 6 duerma, duermas, duerma, durmamos, durmáis, duerman 7 durmiera *etc*

empezar 2 empieza 3 empiezo, empiezas, empieza, empiezan 4 empecé 6 empiece, empieces, empiece, empecemos, empecéis, empiecen

entender 2 entiende 3 entiendo, entiendes, entiende, entienden 6 entienda, entiendas, entienda, entiendan

ESTAR 2 está 3 estoy, estás, está, están 4 estuve, estuviste, estuvo, estuvimos, estuvisteis, estuvieron **6** esté, estés, esté, estén **7** estuviera *etc*

HABER 3 he, has, ha, hemos, han **4** hube, hubiste, hubo, hubimos, hubisteis, hubieron **5** habré *etc* **6** haya *etc* **7** hubiera *etc*

HABLAR 1 hablando **2** habla, hablad **3** hablo, hablas, habla, hablamos, habláis, hablan **4** hablé, hablaste, habló, hablamos, hablasteis, hablaron **5** hablaré, hablarás, hablará, hablaremos, hablaréis, hablarán **6** hable, hables, hable, hablemos, habléis, hablen **7** hablara, hablaras, hablara, habláramos, hablarais, hablaran **8** hablado **9** hablaba, hablabas, hablaba, hablábamos, hablabais, hablaban

hacer 2 haz **3** hago **4** hice, hiciste, hizo, hicimos, hicisteis, hicieron **5** haré *etc* **6** haga *etc* **7** hiciera *etc* **8** hecho

instruir 1 instruyendo **2** instruye **3** instruyo, instruyes, instruye, instruyen **4** instruyó, instruyeron **6** instruya *etc* **7** instruyera *etc*

ir 1 yendo **2** ve **3** voy, vas, va, vamos, vais, van **4** fui, fuiste, fue, fuimos, fuisteis, fueron **6** vaya, vayas, vaya, vayamos, vayáis, vayan **7** fuera *etc* **9** iba, ibas, iba, íbamos, ibais, iban

jugar 2 juega **3** juego, juegas, juega, juegan **4** jugué **6** juegue *etc*

leer 1 leyendo **4** leyó, leyeron **7** leyera *etc*

morir 1 muriendo **2** muere **3** muero, mueres, muere, mueren **4** murió, murieron

6 muera, mueras, muera, muramos, muráis, mueran **7** muriera *etc* **8** muerto

mover 2 mueve **3** muevo, mueves, mueve, mueven **6** mueva, muevas, mueva, muevan

negar 2 niega **3** niego, niegas, niega, niegan **4** negué **6** niegue, niegues, niegue, neguemos, neguéis, nieguen

ofrecer 3 ofrezco **6** ofrezca *etc*

oír 1 oyendo **2** oye **3** oigo, oyes, oye, oyen **4** oyó, oyeron **6** oiga *etc* **7** oyera *etc*

oler 2 huele **3** huelo, hueles, huele, huelen **6** huela, huelas, huela, huelan

parecer 3 parezco **6** parezca *etc*

pedir 1 pidiendo **2** pide **3** pido, pides, pide, piden **4** pidió, pidieron **6** pida *etc* **7** pidiera *etc*

pensar 2 piensa **3** pienso, piensas, piensa, piensan **6** piense, pienses, piense, piensen

perder 2 pierde **3** pierdo, pierdes, pierde, pierden **6** pierda, pierdas, pierda, pierdan

poder 1 pudiendo **2** puede **3** puedo, puedes, puede, pueden **4** pude, pudiste, pudo, pudimos, pudisteis, pudieron **5** podré *etc* **6** pueda, puedas, pueda, puedan **7** pudiera *etc*

poner 2 pon **3** pongo **4** puse, pusiste, puso, pusimos, pusisteis, pusieron **5** pondré *etc* **6** ponga *etc* **7** pusiera *etc* **8** puesto

preferir 1 prefiriendo **2** prefiere **3** prefiero, prefieres, prefiere, prefirió, prefirieron **6** prefiera, prefieras, prefiera, prefiramos, prefiráis, prefieran **7** prefiriera *etc*

querer 2 quiere 3 quiero, quieres, quiere, quieren 4 quise, quisiste, quiso, quisimos, quisisteis, quisieron 5 querré *etc* 6 quiera, quieras, quiera, quieran 7 quisiera *etc*

reír 2 ríe 3 río, ríes, ríe, ríen 4 reí, rieron 6 ría, rías, ría, riamos, riáis, rían 7 riera *etc*

repetir 1 repitiendo 2 repite 3 repito, repites, repite, repiten 4 repitió, repitieron 6 repita *etc* 7 repitiera *etc*

rogar 2 ruega 3 ruego, ruegas, ruega, ruegan 4 rogué 6 ruegue, ruegues, ruegue, roguemos, roguéis, rueguen

saber 3 sé 4 supe, supiste, supo, supimos, supisteis, supieron 5 sabré *etc* 6 sepa *etc* 7 supiera *etc*

salir 2 sal 3 salgo 5 saldré *etc* 6 salga *etc*

seguir 1 siguiendo 2 sigue 3 sigo, sigues, sigue, siguen 4 siguió, siguieron 6 siga *etc* 7 siguiera *etc*

sentar 2 sienta 3 siento, sientas, sienta, sientan 6 siente, sientes, siente, sienten

sentir 1 sintiendo 2 siente 3 siento, sientes, siente, sienten 4 sintió, sintieron 6 sienta, sientas, sienta, sintamos, sintáis, sientan 7 sintiera *etc*

SER 2 sé 3 soy, eres, es, somos, sois, son 4 fui, fuiste, fue, fuimos, fuisteis, fueron 6 sea *etc* 7 fuera *etc* 9 era, eras, era, éramos, erais, eran

servir 1 sirviendo 2 sirve 3 sirvo, sirves, sirve, sirven 4 sirvió, sirvieron 6 sirva *etc* 7 sirviera *etc*

soñar 2 sueña 3 sueño, sueñas, sueña, sueñan 6 sueñe, sueñes, sueñe, sueñen

tener 2 ten 3 tengo, tienes, tiene, tienen 4 tuve, tuviste, tuvo, tuvimos, tuvisteis, tuvieron 5 tendré *etc* 6 tenga *etc* 7 tuviera *etc*

traer 2 trayendo 3 traigo 4 traje, trajiste, trajo, trajimos, trajisteis, trajeron 6 traiga *etc* 7 trajera *etc*

valer 2 vale 3 valgo 5 valdré *etc* 6 valga *etc*

venir 2 ven 3 vengo, vienes, viene, vienen 4 vine, viniste, vino, vinimos, vinisteis, vinieron 5 vendré *etc* 6 venga *etc* 7 viniera *etc*

ver 3 veo 6 vea 8 visto 9 veía *etc*

vestir 1 vistiendo 2 viste 3 visto, vistes, viste, visten 4 vistió, vistieron 6 vista *etc* 7 vistiera *etc*

VIVIR 1 viviendo 2 vive, vivid 3 vivo, vives, vive, vivimos, vivís, viven 4 viví, viviste, vivió, vivimos, vivisteis, vivieron 5 viviré, vivirás, vivirá, viviremos, viviréis, vivirán 6 viva, vivas, viva, vivamos, viváis, vivan 7 viviera, vivieras, viviera, viviéramos, vivierais, vivieran 8 vivido 9 vivía, vivías, vivía, vivíamos, vivías, vivían

volver 2 vuelve 3 vuelvo, vuelves, vuelve, vuelven 6 vuelva, vuelvas, vuelva, vuelvan 8 vuelto

VERBOS IRREGULARES EN INGLÉS

PRESENTE	PASADO	PARTICIPIO	PRESENTE	PASADO	PARTICIPIO
arise	arose	arisen	fall	fell	fallen
awake	awoke	awoken	feed	fed	fed
be (am, is, are; being)	was, were	been	feel	felt	felt
			fight	fought	fought
bear	bore	born(e)	find	found	found
beat	beat	beaten	flee	fled	fled
become	became	become	fling	flung	flung
begin	began	begun	fly	flew	flown
bend	bent	bent	forbid	forbad(e)	forbidden
bet	bet, betted	bet, betted	forecast	forecast	forecast
			forget	forgot	forgotten
bid (at auction, cards)	bid	bid	forgive	forgave	forgiven
			forsake	forsook	forsaken
bid (say)	bade	bidden	freeze	froze	frozen
bind	bound	bound	get	got	got, (us) gotten
bite	bit	bitten			
bleed	bled	bled	give	gave	given
blow	blew	blown	go (goes)	went	gone
break	broke	broken	grind	ground	ground
breed	bred	bred	grow	grew	grown
bring	brought	brought	hang	hung	hung
build	built	built	hang (suspend) (execute)	hanged	hanged
burn	burnt, burned	burnt, burned	have	had	had
burst	burst	burst	hear	heard	heard
buy	bought	bought	hide	hid	hidden
can	could	(been able)	hit	hit	hit
cast	cast	cast	hold	held	held
catch	caught	caught	hurt	hurt	hurt
choose	chose	chosen	keep	kept	kept
cling	clung	clung	kneel	knelt, kneeled	knelt, kneeled
come	came	come			
cost (be valued at)	cost	cost	know	knew	known
			lay	laid	laid
cost (work out price of)	costed	costed	lead	led	led
			lean	leant, leaned	leant, leaned
creep	crept	crept			
cut	cut	cut	leap	leapt, leaped	leapt, leaped
deal	dealt	dealt			
dig	dug	dug	learn	learnt, learned	learnt, learned
do (does)	did	done			
draw	drew	drawn	leave	left	left
dream	dreamed, dreamt	dreamed, dreamt	lend	lent	lent
			let	let	let
drink	drank	drunk	lie (lying)	lay	lain
drive	drove	driven	light	lit, lighted	lit, lighted
dwell	dwelt	dwelt			
eat	ate	eaten	lose	lost	lost

XV

PRESENTE	PASADO	PARTICIPIO	PRESENTE	PASADO	PARTICIPIO
make	made	made	speed	sped,	sped,
may	might	–		speeded	speeded
mean	meant	meant	spell	spelt,	spelt,
meet	met	met		spelled	spelled
mistake	mistook	mistaken	spend	spent	spent
mow	mowed	mown,	spill	spilt,	spilt,
		mowed		spilled	spilled
must	(had to)	(had to)	spin	spun	spun
pay	paid	paid	spit	spat	spat
put	put	put	spoil	spoiled,	spoiled,
quit	quit,	quit,		spoilt	spoilt
	quitted	quitted	spread	spread	spread
read	read	read	spring	sprang	sprung
rid	rid	rid	stand	stood	stood
ride	rode	ridden	steal	stole	stolen
ring	rang	rung	stick	stuck	stuck
rise	rose	risen	sting	stung	stung
run	ran	run	stink	stank	stunk
saw	sawed	sawed,	stride	strode	stridden
		sawn	strike	struck	struck
say	said	said	strive	strove	striven
see	saw	seen	swear	swore	sworn
seek	sought	sought	sweep	swept	swept
sell	sold	sold	swell	swelled	swollen,
send	sent	sent			swelled
set	set	set	swim	swam	swum
sew	sewed	sewn	swing	swung	swung
shake	shook	shaken	take	took	taken
shear	sheared	shorn,	teach	taught	taught
		sheared	tear	tore	torn
shed	shed	shed	tell	told	told
shine	shone	shone	think	thought	thought
shoot	shot	shot	throw	threw	thrown
show	showed	shown	thrust	thrust	thrust
shrink	shrank	shrunk	tread	trod	trodden
shut	shut	shut	wake	woke,	woken,
sing	sang	sung		waked	waked
sink	sank	sunk	wear	wore	worn
sit	sat	sat	weave (on	wove	woven
slay	slew	slain	loom)		
sleep	slept	slept	weave (wind)	weaved	weaved
slide	slid	slid	wed	wedded,	wedded,
sling	slung	slung		wed	wed
slit	slit	slit	weep	wept	wept
smell	smelt,	smelt,	win	won	won
	smelled	smelled	wind	wound	wound
sow	sowed	sown,	wring	wrung	wrung
		sowed	write	wrote	written
speak	spoke	spoken			

a

a [a] (*a + el = al*) *prep* **1** (*dirección*) to; **fueron a Madrid/Grecia** they went to Madrid/Greece; **me voy a casa** I'm going home
2 (*distancia*): **está a 15 km de aquí** it's 15 kms from here
3 (*posición*): **estar a la mesa** to be at table; **al lado de** next to, beside; *V tb* **puerta**
4 (*tiempo*): **a las 10/a medianoche** at 10/midnight; **a la mañana siguiente** the following morning; **a los pocos días** after a few days; **estamos a 9 de julio** it's the ninth of July; **a los 24 años** at the age of 24; **al año/a la semana** a year/week later
5 (*manera*): **a la francesa** the French way; **a caballo** on horseback; **a oscuras** in the dark
6 (*medio, instrumento*): **a lápiz** in pencil; **a mano** by hand; **cocina a gas** gas stove
7 (*razón*): **a 30 céntimos el kilo** at 30 cents a kilo; **a más de 50 km/h** at more than 50 kms per hour
8 (*dativo*): **se lo di a él** I gave it to him; **vi al policía** I saw the policeman; **se lo compré a él** I bought it from him
9 (*tras ciertos verbos*): **voy a verle** I'm going to see him; **empezó a trabajar** he started working o to work
10 (+ *infin*): **al verlo, lo reconocí inmediatamente** when I saw him I recognized him at once; **el camino a recorrer** the distance we *etc* have to travel; **¡a callar!** keep quiet!; **¡a comer!** let's eat!

abad, esa [a'βað, 'ðesa] *nm/f* abbot/abbess; **abadía** *nf* abbey
abajo [a'βaxo] *adv* (*situación*) (down) below, underneath; (*en edificio*) downstairs; (*dirección*) down, downwards; **el piso de ~** the downstairs flat; **la parte de ~** the lower part; **¡~ el gobierno!** down with the government!; **cuesta/río ~** downhill/downstream; **de arriba ~** from top to bottom; **el ~ firmante** the undersigned; **más ~** lower o further down
abalanzarse [aβalan'θarse] *vr*: **~ sobre** o **contra** to throw o.s. at
abanderado, -a [aβande'raðo] *nm/f* (*portaestandarte*) standard bearer; (*de un movimiento*) champion, leader; (*MÉX*: linier) linesman, assistant referee
abandonado, -a [aβando'naðo, a] *adj* derelict; (*desatendido*) abandoned; (*desierto*) deserted; (*descuidado*) neglected
abandonar [aβando'nar] *vt* to leave; (*persona*) to abandon, desert; (*cosa*) to abandon, leave behind; (*descuidar*) to neglect; (*renunciar a*) to give up; (*Inform*) to quit; **abandonarse** *vr*: **~se a** to abandon o.s. to; **abandono** *nm* (*acto*) desertion, abandonment; (*estado*) abandon, neglect; (*renuncia*) withdrawal, retirement; **ganar por abandono** to win by default
abanico [aβa'niko] *nm* fan; (*Náut*) derrick
abarcar [aβar'kar] *vt* to include, embrace; (*LAM*: *acaparar*) to monopolize
abarrotado, -a [aβarro'taðo, a] *adj* packed
abarrotar [aβarro'tar] *vt* (*local, estadio, teatro*) to fill, pack
abarrotero, -a [aβarro'tero, a] (*MÉX*) *nm/f* grocer; **abarrotes** (*MÉX*) *nmpl* groceries; **tienda de abarrotes** (*MÉX, CAM*) grocery store
abastecer [aβaste'θer] *vt*: **~ (de)** to supply (with); **abastecimiento** *nm* supply
abasto [a'βasto] *nm* supply; **no dar ~ a** to be unable to cope with
abatible [aβa'tiβle] *adj*: **asiento ~** tip-up seat; (*Auto*) reclining seat
abatido, -a [aβa'tiðo, a] *adj* dejected, downcast
abatir [aβa'tir] *vt* (*muro*) to demolish; (*pájaro*) to shoot o bring down; (*fig*) to depress
abdicar [aβði'kar] *vi* to abdicate
abdomen [aβ'ðomen] *nm* abdomen; **abdominales** *nmpl* (*tb*: **ejercicios abdominales**) sit-ups
abecedario [aβeθe'ðarjo] *nm* alphabet
abedul [aβe'ðul] *nm* birch
abeja [a'βexa] *nf* bee
abejorro [aβe'xorro] *nm* bumblebee
abertura [aβer'tura] *nf* = **apertura**
abeto [a'βeto] *nm* fir
abierto, -a [a'βjerto, a] *pp de* **abrir** ▷ *adj* open
abismal [aβis'mal] *adj* (*fig*) vast, enormous

abismo [a'βismo] nm abyss

ablandar [aβlan'dar] vt to soften; **ablandarse** vr to get softer

abocado, -a [aβo'kaðo, a] adj (vino) smooth, pleasant

abochornar [aβotʃor'nar] vt to embarrass

abofetear [aβofete'ar] vt to slap (in the face)

abogado, -a [aβo'ɣaðo, a] nm/f lawyer; (notario) solicitor; (en tribunal) barrister (BRIT), attorney (US); **abogado defensor** defence lawyer o (US) attorney

abogar [aβo'ɣar] vi: ~ **por** to plead for; (fig) to advocate

abolir [aβo'lir] vt to abolish; (cancelar) to cancel

abolladura [aβoʎa'ðura] nf dent

abollar [aβo'ʎar] vt to dent

abombarse [aβom'barse] (LAM) vr to go bad

abominable [aβomi'naβle] adj abominable

abonado, -a [aβo'naðo, a] adj (deuda) paid(-up) ⊳ nm/f subscriber

abonar [aβo'nar] vt (deuda) to settle; (terreno) to fertilize; (idea) to endorse; **abonarse** vr to subscribe; **abono** nm payment; fertilizer; subscription

abordar [aβor'ðar] vt (barco) to board; (asunto) to broach

aborigen [aβo'rixen] nmf aborigine

aborrecer [aβorre'θer] vt to hate, loathe

abortar [aβor'tar] vi (malparir) to have a miscarriage; (deliberadamente) to have an abortion; **aborto** nm miscarriage; abortion

abovedado, -a [aβoβe'ðaðo, a] adj vaulted, domed

abrasar [aβra'sar] vt to burn (up); (Agr) to dry up, parch

abrazar [aβra'θar] vt to embrace, hug

abrazo [a'βraθo] nm embrace, hug; **un ~** (en carta) with best wishes

abrebotellas [aβreβo'teʎas] nm inv bottle opener

abrecartas [aβre'kartas] nm inv letter opener

abrelatas [aβre'latas] nm inv tin (BRIT) o can opener

abreviatura [aβreβja'tura] nf abbreviation

abridor [aβri'ðor] nm bottle opener; (de latas) tin (BRIT) o can opener

abrigador, a [aβriɣa'ðor, a] (MÉX) adj warm

abrigar [aβri'ɣar] vt (proteger) to shelter; (ropa) to keep warm; (fig) to cherish

abrigo [a'βriɣo] nm (prenda) coat, overcoat; (lugar protegido) shelter

abril [a'βril] nm April

abrillantador [aβriʎanta'ðor] nm polish

abrillantar [aβriʎan'tar] vt to polish

abrir [a'βrir] vt to open (up) ⊳ vi to open; **abrirse** vr to open (up); (extenderse) to open out; (cielo) to clear; **~se paso** to find o force a way through

abrochar [aβro'tʃar] vt (con botones) to button (up); (zapato, con broche) to do up

abrupto, -a [a'βrupto, a] adj abrupt; (empinado) steep

absoluto, -a [aβso'luto, a] adj absolute; **en ~** adv not at all

absolver [aβsol'βer] vt to absolve; (Jur) to pardon; (: acusado) to acquit

absorbente [aβsor'βente] adj absorbent; (interesante) absorbing

absorber [aβsor'βer] vt to absorb; (embeber) to soak up

absorción [aβsor'θjon] nf absorption; (Com) takeover

abstemio, -a [aβs'temjo, a] adj teetotal

abstención [aβsten'θjon] nf abstention

abstenerse [aβste'nerse] vr: ~ **(de)** to abstain o refrain (from)

abstinencia [aβsti'nenθja] nf abstinence; (ayuno) fasting

abstracto, -a [aβs'trakto, a] adj abstract

abstraer [aβstra'er] vt to abstract; **abstraerse** vr to be o become absorbed

abstraído, -a [aβstra'iðo, a] adj absent-minded

absuelto [aβ'swelto] pp de **absolver**

absurdo, -a [aβ'surðo, a] adj absurd

abuchear [aβutʃe'ar] vt to boo

abuelo, -a [a'βwelo, a] nm/f grandfather(-mother); **abuelos** nmpl grandparents

abultado, -a [aβul'taðo, a] adj bulky

abultar [aβul'tar] vi to be bulky

abundancia [aβun'danθja] nf: **una ~ de** plenty of; **abundante** adj abundant, plentiful

abundar [aβun'dar] vi to abound, be plentiful

aburrido, -a [aβu'rriðo, a] adj (hastiado) bored; (que aburre) boring; **aburrimiento** nm boredom, tedium

aburrir [aβu'rrir] vt to bore; **aburrirse** vr to be bored, get bored

abusado, -a [aβu'saðo, a] (MÉX: fam) adj (astuto) sharp, cunning ⊳ excl: ¡~! (inv) look out!, careful!

abusar [aβu'sar] vi to go too far; ~ **de** to abuse

abusivo, -a [aβu'siβo, a] adj (precio)

exorbitant

abuso [a'βuso] *nm* abuse

acá [a'ka] *adv (lugar)* here

acabado, -a [aka'βaðo, a] *adj* finished, complete; *(perfecto)* perfect; *(agotado)* worn out; *(fig)* masterly ▷ *nm* finish

acabar [aka'βar] *vt (llevar a su fin)* to finish, complete; *(consumir)* to use up; *(rematar)* to finish off ▷ *vi* to finish, end; **acabarse** *vr* to finish, stop; *(terminarse)* to be over; *(agotarse)* to run out; **~ con** to put an end to; **~ de llegar** to have just arrived; **~ por hacer** to end (up) by doing; **¡se acabó!** it's all over!; *(¡basta!)* that's enough!

acabóse [aka'βose] *nm*: **esto es el ~** this is the last straw

academia [aka'ðemja] *nf* academy; **academia de idiomas** language school; **académico, -a** *adj* academic

acalorado, -a [akalo'raðo, a] *adj (discusión)* heated

acampar [akam'par] *vi* to camp

acantilado [akanti'laðo] *nm* cliff

acaparar [akapa'rar] *vt* to monopolize; *(acumular)* to hoard

acariciar [akari'θjar] *vt* to caress; *(esperanza)* to cherish

acarrear [akarre'ar] *vt* to transport; *(fig)* to cause, result in

acaso [a'kaso] *adv* perhaps, maybe; **(por) si ~** (just) in case

acatar [aka'tar] *vt* to respect; *(ley)* obey

acatarrarse [akata'rrarse] *vr* to catch a cold

acceder [akθe'ðer] *vi*: **~ a** *(petición etc)* to agree to; *(tener acceso a)* to have access to; *(Inform)* to access

accesible [akθe'siβle] *adj* accessible

acceso [ak'θeso] *nm* access, entry; *(camino)* access, approach; *(Med)* attack, fit

accesorio, -a [akθe'sorjo, a] *adj, nm* accessory

accidentado, -a [akθiðen'taðo, a] *adj* uneven; *(montañoso)* hilly; *(azaroso)* eventful ▷ *nm/f* accident victim

accidental [akθiðen'tal] *adj* accidental

accidente [akθi'ðente] *nm* accident; **accidentes** *nmpl (de terreno)* unevenness *sg*; **accidente laboral** *o* **de trabajo/de tráfico** industrial/road *o* traffic accident

acción [ak'θjon] *nf* action; *(acto)* action, act; *(Com)* share; *(Jur)* action, lawsuit; **accionar** *vt* to work, operate; *(Inform)* to drive

accionista [akθjo'nista] *nmf* shareholder, stockholder

acebo [a'θeβo] *nm* holly; *(árbol)* holly tree

acechar [aθe'tʃar] *vt* to spy on; *(aguardar)*

to lie in wait for; **acecho** *nm*: **estar al acecho (de)** to lie in wait (for)

aceite [a'θeite] *nm* oil; **aceite de girasol/oliva** sunflower/olive oil; **aceitera** *nf* oilcan; **aceitoso, -a** *adj* oily

aceituna [aθei'tuna] *nf* olive; **aceituna rellena** stuffed olive

acelerador [aθelera'ðor] *nm* accelerator

acelerar [aθele'rar] *vt* to accelerate

acelga [a'θelɣa] *nf* chard, beet

acento [a'θento] *nm* accent; *(acentuación)* stress

acentuar [aθen'twar] *vt* to accent; to stress; *(fig)* to accentuate

acepción [aθep'θjon] *nf* meaning

aceptable [aθep'taβle] *adj* acceptable

aceptación [aθepta'θjon] *nf* acceptance; *(aprobación)* approval

aceptar [aθep'tar] *vt* to accept; *(aprobar)* to approve; **~ hacer algo** to agree to do sth

acequia [a'θekja] *nf* irrigation ditch

acera [a'θera] *nf* pavement (BRIT), sidewalk (US)

acerca [a'θerka]: **~ de** *prep* about, concerning

acercar [aθer'kar] *vt* to bring *o* move nearer; **acercarse** *vr* to approach, come near

acero [a'θero] *nm* steel

acérrimo, -a [a'θerrimo, a] *adj (partidario)* staunch; *(enemigo)* bitter

acertado, -a [aθer'taðo, a] *adj* correct; *(apropiado)* apt; *(sensato)* sensible

acertar [aθer'tar] *vt (blanco)* to hit; *(solución)* to get right; *(adivinar)* to guess ▷ *vi* to get it right, be right; **~ a** to manage to; **~ con** to happen *o* hit on

acertijo [aθer'tixo] *nm* riddle, puzzle

achacar [atʃa'kar] *vt* to attribute

achacoso, -a [atʃa'koso, a] *adj* sickly

achicar [atʃi'kar] *vt* to reduce; *(Náut)* to bale out

achicharrar [atʃitʃa'rrar] *vt* to scorch, burn

achichincle [atʃi'tʃinkle] *(MÉX: fam)* *nmf* minion

achicoria [atʃi'korja] *nf* chicory

achuras [a'tʃuras] *(RPL)* *nfpl* offal *sg*

acicate [aθi'kate] *nm* spur

acidez [aθi'ðeθ] *nf* acidity

ácido, -a ['aθiðo, a] *adj* sour, acid ▷ *nm* acid

acierto *etc* [a'θjerto] *vb* V **acertar** ▷ *nm* success; *(buen paso)* wise move; *(solución)* solution; *(habilidad)* skill, ability

acitronar [aθitro'nar] *(MÉX: fam)* *vt* to brown

aclamar [akla'mar] *vt* to acclaim;

(*aplaudir*) to applaud

aclaración [aklara'θjon] *nf* clarification, explanation

aclarar [akla'rar] *vt* to clarify, explain; (*ropa*) to rinse ▷ *vi* to clear up; **aclararse** *vr* (*explicarse*) to understand; **~se la garganta** to clear one's throat

aclimatación [aklimata'θjon] *nf* acclimatization

aclimatar [aklima'tar] *vt* to acclimatize; **aclimatarse** *vr* to become acclimatized

acné [ak'ne] *nm* acne

acobardar [akoβar'ðar] *vt* to intimidate

acogedor, a [akoxe'ðor, a] *adj* welcoming; (*hospitalario*) hospitable

acoger [ako'xer] *vt* to welcome; (*abrigar*) to shelter

acogida [ako'xiða] *nf* reception; refuge

acomedido, -a [akome'ðiðo, a] (*MÉX*) *adj* helpful, obliging

acometer [akome'ter] *vt* to attack; (*emprender*) to undertake; **acometida** *nf* attack, assault

acomodado, -a [akomo'ðaðo, a] *adj* (*persona*) well-to-do

acomodador, a [akomoða'ðor, a] *nm/f* usher(ette)

acomodar [akomo'ðar] *vt* to adjust; (*alojar*) to accommodate; **acomodarse** *vr* to conform; (*instalarse*) to install o.s.; (*adaptarse*): **~se (a)** to adapt (to)

acompañar [akompa'ɲar] *vt* to accompany; (*documentos*) to enclose

acondicionar [akondiθjo'nar] *vt* to arrange, prepare; (*pelo*) to condition

aconsejar [akonse'xar] *vt* to advise, counsel; **~ a algn que haga algo** to advise sb to do sth

acontecer [akonte'θer] *vi* to happen, occur; **acontecimiento** *nm* event

acopio [a'kopjo] *nm* store, stock

acoplar [ako'plar] *vt* to fit; (*Elec*) to connect; (*vagones*) to couple

acorazado, -a [akora'θaðo, a] *adj* armour-plated, armoured ▷ *nm* battleship

acordar [akor'ðar] *vt* (*resolver*) to agree, resolve; (*recordar*) to remind; **acordarse** *vr* to agree; **~ hacer algo** to agree to do sth; **~se (de algo)** to remember (sth); **acorde** *adj* (*Mús*) harmonious; **acorde con** (*medidas etc*) in keeping with ▷ *nm* chord

acordeón [akorðe'on] *nm* accordion

acordonado, -a [akorðo'naðo, a] *adj* (*calle*) cordoned-off

acorralar [akorra'lar] *vt* to round up, corral

acortar [akor'tar] *vt* to shorten; (*duración*) to cut short; (*cantidad*) to reduce; **acortarse**

vr to become shorter

acosar [ako'sar] *vt* to pursue relentlessly; (*fig*) to hound, pester; **acoso** *nm* harassment; **acoso sexual** sexual harassment

acostar [akos'tar] *vt* (*en cama*) to put to bed; (*en suelo*) to lay down; **acostarse** *vr* to go to bed; to lie down; **~se con algn** to sleep with sb

acostumbrado, -a [akostum'braðo, a] *adj* usual; **~ a** used to

acostumbrar [akostum'brar] *vt*: **~ a algn a algo** to get sb used to sth ▷ *vi*: **~ (a) hacer** to be in the habit of doing; **acostumbrarse** *vr*: **~se a** to get used to

acotación [akota'θjon] *nf* marginal note; (*Geo*) elevation mark; (*de límite*) boundary mark; (*Teatro*) stage direction

acotamiento [akota'mjento] (*MÉX*) *nm* hard shoulder (*BRIT*), berm (*US*)

acre ['akre] *adj* (*olor*) acrid; (*fig*) biting ▷ *nm* acre

acreditar [akreði'tar] *vt* (*garantizar*) to vouch for, guarantee; (*autorizar*) to authorize; (*dar prueba de*) to prove; (*Com: abonar*) to credit; (*embajador*) to accredit

acreedor, a [akree'ðor, a] *nm/f* creditor

acribillar [akriβi'ʎar] *vt*: **~ a balazos** to riddle with bullets

acróbata [a'kroβata] *nmf* acrobat

acta ['akta] *nf* certificate; (*de comisión*) minutes *pl*, record; **acta de matrimonio/ nacimiento** (*MÉX*) marriage/birth certificate; **acta notarial** affidavit

actitud [akti'tuð] *nf* attitude; (*postura*) posture

activar [akti'βar] *vt* to activate; (*acelerar*) to speed up

actividad [aktiβi'ðað] *nf* activity

activo, -a [ak'tiβo, a] *adj* active; (*vivo*) lively ▷ *nm* (*Com*) assets *pl*

acto ['akto] *nm* act, action; (*ceremonia*) ceremony; (*Teatro*) act; **en el ~** immediately

actor [ak'tor] *nm* actor; (*Jur*) plaintiff ▷ *adj*: **parte ~a** prosecution

actriz [ak'triθ] *nf* actress

actuación [aktwa'θjon] *nf* action; (*comportamiento*) conduct, behaviour; (*Jur*) proceedings *pl*; (*desempeño*) performance

actual [ak'twal] *adj* present(-day), current

▌No confundir **actual** con la palabra inglesa *actual*.

actualidad *nf* present; **actualidades** *nfpl* (*noticias*) news *sg*; **en la actualidad** at present; (*hoy día*) nowadays; **actualizar** [aktwali'θar] *vt* to update, modernize; **actualmente** [aktwal'mente] *adv* at present; (*hoy día*) nowadays

No confundir **actualmente** con la palabra inglesa *actually*.

actuar [ak'twar] *vi* (*obrar*) to work, operate; (*actor*) to act, perform ▷ *vt* to work, operate; **~ de** to act as

acuarela [akwa'rela] *nf* watercolour

acuario [a'kwarjo] *nm* aquarium; (*Astrología*): **A~** Aquarius

acuático, -a [a'kwatiko, a] *adj* aquatic

acudir [aku'ðir] *vi* (*asistir*) to attend; (*ir*) to go; **~ a** (*tip*) to turn to; **~ a una cita** to keep an appointment; **~ en ayuda de** to go to the aid of

acuerdo *etc* [a'kwerðo] *vb* V **acordar** ▷ *nm* agreement; **¡de ~!** agreed!; **de ~ con** (*persona*) in agreement with; (*acción, documento*) in accordance with; **estar de ~** to be agreed, agree

acumular [akumu'lar] *vt* to accumulate, collect

acuñar [aku'ɲar] *vt* (*moneda*) to mint; (*frase*) to coin

acupuntura [akupun'tura] *nf* acupuncture

acurrucarse [akurru'karse] *vr* to crouch; (*ovillarse*) to curl up

acusación [akusa'θjon] *nf* accusation

acusar [aku'sar] *vt* to accuse; (*revelar*) to reveal; (*denunciar*) to denounce

acuse [a'kuse] *nm*: **~ de recibo** acknowledgement of receipt

acústica [a'kustika] *nf* acoustics *pl*

acústico, -a [a'kustiko, a] *adj* acoustic

adaptación [aðapta'θjon] *nf* adaptation

adaptador [aðapta'ðor] *nm* (*Elec*) adapter, adaptor; **adaptador universal** universal adapter *o* adaptor

adaptar [aðap'tar] *vt* to adapt; (*acomodar*) to fit

adecuado, -a [aðe'kwaðo, a] *adj* (*apto*) suitable; (*oportuno*) appropriate

a. de J.C. *abr* (= *antes de Jesucristo*) B.C.

adelantado, -a [aðelan'taðo, a] *adj* advanced; (*reloj*) fast; **pagar por ~** to pay in advance

adelantamiento [aðelanta'mjento] *nm* (*Auto*) overtaking

adelantar [aðelan'tar] *vt* to move forward; (*avanzar*) to advance; (*acelerar*) to speed up; (*Auto*) to overtake ▷ *vi* to go forward, advance; **adelantarse** *vr* to go forward, advance

adelante [aðe'lante] *adv* forward(s), ahead ▷ *excl* come in!; **de hoy en ~** from now on; **más ~** later on; (*más allá*) further on

adelanto [aðe'lanto] *nm* advance; (*mejora*) improvement; (*progreso*) progress

adelgazar [aðelɣa'θar] *vt* to thin (down) ▷ *vi* to get thin; (*con régimen*) to slim down, lose weight

ademán [aðe'man] *nm* gesture; **ademanes** *nmpl* manners

además [aðe'mas] *adv* besides; (*por otra parte*) moreover; (*también*) also; **~ de** besides, in addition to

adentrarse [aðen'trarse] *vr*: **~ en** to go into, get inside; (*penetrar*) to penetrate (into)

adentro [a'ðentro] *adv* inside, in; **mar ~** out at sea; **tierra ~** inland

adepto, -a [a'ðepto, a] *nm/f* supporter

aderezar [aðere'θar] *vt* (*ensalada*) to dress; (*comida*) to season; **aderezo** *nm* dressing; seasoning

adeudar [aðeu'ðar] *vt* to owe

adherirse [aðe'rirse] *vr*: **~ a** to adhere to; (*partido*) to join

adhesión [aðe'sjon] *nf* adhesion; (*fig*) adherence

adicción [aðik'θjon] *nf* addiction

adición [aði'θjon] *nf* addition

adicto, -a [a'ðikto, a] *adj*: **~ a** addicted to; (*dedicado*) devoted to ▷ *nm/f* supporter, follower; (*toxicómano*) addict

adiestrar [aðjes'trar] *vt* to train, teach; (*conducir*) to guide, lead

adinerado, -a [aðine'raðo, a] *adj* wealthy

adiós [a'ðjos] *excl* (*para despedirse*) goodbye!, cheerio!; (*al pasar*) hello!

aditivo [aði'tiβo] *nm* additive

adivinanza [aðiβi'nanθa] *nf* riddle

adivinar [aðiβi'nar] *vt* to prophesy; (*conjeturar*) to guess; **adivino, -a** *nm/f* fortune-teller

adj *abr* (= *adjunto*) encl

adjetivo [aðxe'tiβo] *nm* adjective

adjudicar [aðxuði'kar] *vt* to award; **adjudicarse** *vr*: **~se algo** to appropriate sth

adjuntar [aðxun'tar] *vt* to attach, enclose; **adjunto, -a** *adj* attached, enclosed ▷ *nm/f* assistant

administración [aðministra'θjon] *nf* administration; (*dirección*) management; **administrador, a** *nm/f* administrator, manager(ess)

administrar [aðminis'trar] *vt* to administer; **administrativo, -a** *adj* administrative

admirable [aðmi'raβle] *adj* admirable

admiración [aðmira'θjon] *nf* admiration; (*asombro*) wonder; (*Ling*) exclamation mark

admirar [aðmi'rar] *vt* to admire; (*extrañar*) to surprise

admisible [aðmi'siβle] *adj* admissible

admisión [aðmi'sjon] nf admission;
(reconocimiento) acceptance

admitir [aðmi'tir] vt to admit; (aceptar)
to accept

adobar [aðo'βar] vt (Culin) to season

adobe [a'ðoβe] nm adobe, sun-dried brick

adolecer [aðole'θer] vi: ~ **de** to suffer from

adolescente [aðoles'θente] nmf
adolescent, teenager

adonde [a'ðonðe] conj (to) where

adónde [a'ðonðe] adv = **dónde**

adopción [aðop'θjon] nf adoption

adoptar [aðop'tar] vt to adopt

adoptivo, -a [aðop'tiβo, a] adj (padres)
adoptive; (hijo) adopted

adoquín [aðo'kin] nm paving stone

adorar [aðo'rar] vt to adore

adornar [aðor'nar] vt to adorn

adorno [a'ðorno] nm ornament;
(decoración) decoration

adosado, -a [aðo'saðo, a] adj: **casa
adosada** semi-detached house

adosar [aðo'sar] (MÉX) vt (adjuntar) to
attach, enclose (with a letter)

adquiero etc vb V **adquirir**

adquirir [aðki'rir] vt to acquire, obtain

adquisición [aðkisi'θjon] nf acquisition

adrede [a'ðreðe] adv on purpose

ADSL nm abr broadband

aduana [a'ðwana] nf customs pl

aduanero, -a [aðwa'nero, a] adj customs
cpd ▷ nm/f customs officer

adueñarse [aðwe'narse] vr: ~ **de** to take
possession of

adular [aðu'lar] vt to flatter

adulterar [aðulte'rar] vt to adulterate

adulterio [aðul'terjo] nm adultery

adúltero, -a [a'ðultero, a] adj adulterous
▷ nm/f adulterer/adulteress

adulto, -a [a'ðulto, a] adj, nm/f adult

adverbio [að'βerβjo] nm adverb

adversario, -a [aðβer'sarjo, a] nm/f
adversary

adversidad [aðβersi'ðað] nf adversity;
(contratiempo) setback

adverso, -a [að'βerso, a] adj adverse

advertencia [aðβer'tenθja] nf warning;
(prefacio) preface, foreword

advertir [aðβer'tir] vt to notice; (avisar): ~
a algn to warn sb about o of

Adviento [að'βjento] nm Advent

advierto etc vb V **advertir**

aéreo, -a [a'ereo, a] adj aerial

aerobic [ae'roβik] nm aerobics sg;
aerobics (MÉX) nmpl aerobics sg

aeromozo, -a [aero'moθo, a] (LAM) nm/f
air steward(ess)

aeronáutica [aero'nautika] nf
aeronautics sg

aeronave [aero'naβe] nm spaceship

aeroplano [aero'plano] nm aeroplane

aeropuerto [aero'pwerto] nm airport

aerosol [aero'sol] nm aerosol

afamado, -a [afa'maðo, a] adj famous

afán [a'fan] nm hard work; (deseo) desire

afanador, a [afana'ðor, a] (MÉX) nm/f (de
limpieza) cleaner

afanar [afa'nar] vt to harass; (fam) to
pinch

afear [afe'ar] vt to disfigure

afección [afek'θjon] nf (Med) disease

afectado, -a [afek'taðo, a] adj affected

afectar [afek'tar] vt to affect

afectísimo, -a [afek'tisimo, a] adj
affectionate; **suyo** ~ yours truly

afectivo, -a [afek'tiβo, a] adj (problema
etc) emotional

afecto [a'fekto] nm affection; **tenerle** ~ **a
algn** to be fond of sb

afectuoso, -a [afek'twoso, a] adj
affectionate

afeitar [afei'tar] vt to shave; **afeitarse**
vr to shave

afeminado, -a [afemi'naðo, a] adj
effeminate

Afganistán [afɣanis'tan] nm
Afghanistan

afianzar [afjan'θar] vt to strengthen;
to secure; **afianzarse** vr to become
established

afiche [a'fitʃe] (RPL) nm poster

afición [afi'θjon] nf fondness, liking; **la** ~
the fans pl; **pinto por** ~ I paint as a hobby;

aficionado, -a adj keen, enthusiastic; (no
profesional) amateur ▷ nm/f enthusiast, fan;
amateur; **ser aficionado a algo** to be very
keen on o fond of sth

aficionar [afiθjo'nar] vt: ~ **a algn a algo** to
make sb like sth; **aficionarse** vr: ~**se a algo**
to grow fond of sth

afilado, -a [afi'laðo, a] adj sharp

afilar [afi'lar] vt to sharpen

afiliarse [afi'ljarse] vr to affiliate

afín [a'fin] adj (parecido) similar; (conexo)
related

afinar [afi'nar] vt (Tec) to refine; (Mús) to
tune ▷ vi (tocar) to play in tune; (cantar) to
sing in tune

afincarse [afin'karse] vr to settle

afinidad [afini'ðað] nf affinity;
(parentesco) relationship; **por** ~ by marriage

afirmación [afirma'θjon] nf affirmation

afirmar [afir'mar] vt to affirm, state;
afirmativo, -a adj affirmative

afligir [afli'xir] vt to afflict; (apenar) to
distress

aflojar [aflo'xar] vt to slacken; (desatar) to loosen, undo; (relajar) to relax ▷ vi to drop; (bajar) to go down; **aflojarse** vr to relax

afluente [aflu'ente] adj flowing ▷ nm tributary

afmo, -a abr (= afectísimo(a) suyo(a)) Yours

afónico, -a [a'foniko, a] adj: **estar ~** to have a sore throat; to have lost one's voice

aforo [a'foro] nm (de teatro etc) capacity

afortunado, -a [afortu'naðo, a] adj fortunate, lucky

África ['afrika] nf Africa; **África del Sur** South Africa; **africano, -a** adj, nm/f African

afrontar [afron'tar] vt to confront; (poner cara a cara) to bring face to face

afrutado, -a [afru'taðo, a] adj fruity

after ['after] (pl ~s) nm after-hours club; **afterhours** [after'aurs] nm inv = **after**

afuera [a'fwera] adv out, outside; **afueras** nfpl outskirts

agachar [aɣa'tʃar] vt to bend, bow; **agacharse** vr to stoop, bend

agalla [a'ɣaʎa] nf (Zool) gill; **tener ~s** (fam) to have guts

agarradera [aɣarra'ðera] (MÉX) nf handle

agarrado, -a [aɣa'rraðo, a] adj mean, stingy

agarrar [aɣa'rrar] vt to grasp, grab; (LAM: tomar) to take, catch; (recoger) to pick up ▷ vi (planta) to take root; **agarrarse** vr to hold on (tightly)

agencia [a'xenθja] nf agency; **agencia de viajes** travel agency; **agencia inmobiliaria** estate (BRIT) o real estate (US) agent's (office)

agenciarse [axen'θjarse] vr to obtain, procure

agenda [a'xenda] nf diary; **~ electronica** PDA

▎No confundir **agenda** con la palabra inglesa agenda.

agente [a'xente] nmf agent; (tb: **~ de policía**) policeman/policewoman; **agente de seguros** insurance agent; **agente de tránsito** (MÉX) traffic cop; **agente inmobiliario** estate agent (BRIT), realtor (US)

ágil ['axil] adj agile, nimble; **agilidad** nf agility, nimbleness

agilizar [axili'θar] vt (trámites) to speed up

agiotista [axjo'tista] (MÉX) nmf (usurero) usurer

agitación [axita'θjon] nf (de mano etc) shaking, waving; (de líquido etc) stirring; (fig) agitation

agitado, -a [axi'aðo, a] adj hectic; (viaje) bumpy

agitar [axi'tar] vt to wave, shake; (líquido) to stir; (fig) to stir up, excite; **agitarse** vr

to get excited; (inquietarse) to get worried o upset

aglomeración [aɣlomera'θjon] nf agglomeration; **aglomeración de gente/tráfico** mass of people/traffic jam

agnóstico, -a [aɣ'nostiko, a] adj, nm/f agnostic

agobiar [aɣo'βjar] vt to weigh down; (oprimir) to oppress; (cargar) to burden

agolparse [aɣol'parse] vr to crowd together

agonía [aɣo'nia] nf death throes pl; (fig) agony, anguish

agonizante [aɣoni'θante] adj dying

agonizar [aɣoni'θar] vi to be dying

agosto [a'ɣosto] nm August

agotado, -a [aɣo'taðo, a] adj (persona) exhausted; (libros) out of print; (acabado) finished; (Com) sold out; **agotador, a** [aɣota'ðor, a] adj exhausting

agotamiento [aɣota'mjento] nm exhaustion

agotar [aɣo'tar] vt to exhaust; (consumir) to drain; (recursos) to use up, deplete; **agotarse** vr to be exhausted; (acabarse) to run out; (libro) to go out of print

agraciado, -a [aɣra'θjaðo, a] adj (atractivo) attractive; (en sorteo etc) lucky

agradable [aɣra'ðaβle] adj pleasant, nice

agradar [aɣra'ðar] vt: **él me agrada** I like him

agradecer [aɣraðe'θer] vt to thank; (favor etc) to be grateful for; **agradecido, -a** adj grateful; **¡muy agradecido!** thanks a lot!; **agradecimiento** nm thanks pl; gratitude

agradezco etc vb V **agradecer**

agrado [a'ɣraðo] nm: **ser de tu ~** to be to your etc liking

agrandar [aɣran'dar] vt to enlarge; (fig) to exaggerate; **agrandarse** vr to get bigger

agrario, -a [a'ɣrarjo, a] adj agrarian, land cpd; (política) agricultural, farming

agravante [aɣra'βante] adj aggravating ▷ nm: **con el ~ de que ...** with the further difficulty that ...

agravar [aɣra'βar] vt (pesar sobre) to make heavier; (irritar) to aggravate; **agravarse** vr to worsen, get worse

agraviar [aɣra'βjar] vt to offend; (ser injusto con) to wrong

agredir [aɣre'ðir] vt to attack

agregado, -a [aɣre'ɣaðo, a] nm/f: **A~** ≈ teacher (who is not head of department) ▷ nm aggregate; (persona) attaché

agregar [aɣre'ɣar] vt to gather; (añadir) to add; (persona) to appoint

agresión [aɣre'sjon] nf aggression

agresivo, -a [aɣre'siβo, a] adj aggressive

agriar [a'ɣrjar] vt to (turn) sour

agrícola [a'ɣrikola] adj farming cpd, agricultural

agricultor, a [aɣrikul'tor, a] nm/f farmer

agricultura [aɣrikul'tura] nf agriculture, farming

agridulce [aɣri'ðulθe] adj bittersweet; (Culin) sweet and sour

agrietarse [aɣrje'tarse] vr to crack; (piel) to chap

agrio, -a ['aɣrjo, a] adj bitter

agrupación [aɣrupa'θjon] nf group; (acto) grouping

agrupar [aɣru'par] vt to group

agua ['aɣwa] nf water; (Náut) wake; (Arq) slope of a roof; **aguas** nfpl (de piedra) water sg, sparkle sg; (Med) water sg, urine sg; (Náut) waters; **agua bendita/destilada/ potable** holy/distilled/drinking water; **agua caliente** hot water; **agua corriente** running water; **agua de colonia** eau de cologne; **agua mineral (con/sin gas)** (sparkling/still) mineral water; **agua oxigenada** hydrogen peroxide; **aguas abajo/arriba** downstream/upstream; **aguas jurisdiccionales** territorial waters

aguacate [aɣwa'kate] nm avocado (pear)

aguacero [aɣwa'θero] nm (heavy) shower, downpour

aguado, -a [a'ɣwaðo, a] adj watery, watered down

aguafiestas [aɣwa'fjestas] nmf inv spoilsport, killjoy

aguamiel [aɣwa'mjel] (MÉX) nf fermented maguey o agave juice

aguanieve [aɣwa'njeβe] nf sleet

aguantar [aɣwan'tar] vt to bear, put up with; (sostener) to hold up ▷ vi to last; **aguantarse** vr to restrain o.s.; **aguante** nm (paciencia) patience; (resistencia) endurance

aguar [a'ɣwar] vt to water down

aguardar [aɣwar'ðar] vt to wait for

aguardiente [aɣwar'ðjente] nm brandy, liquor

aguarrás [aɣwa'rras] nm turpentine

aguaviva [aɣwa'biβa] (RPL) nf jellyfish

agudeza [aɣu'ðeθa] nf sharpness; (ingenio) wit

agudo, -a [a'ɣuðo, a] adj sharp; (voz) high-pitched, piercing; (dolor, enfermedad) acute

agüero [a'ɣwero] nm: **buen/mal ~** good/ bad omen

aguijón [aɣi'xon] nm sting; (fig) spur

águila ['aɣila] nf eagle; (fig) genius

aguileño, -a [aɣi'leɲo, a] adj (nariz) aquiline; (rostro) sharp-featured

aguinaldo [aɣi'naldo] nm Christmas box

aguja [a'ɣuxa] nf needle; (de reloj) hand; (Arq) spire; (Tec) firing-pin; **agujas** nfpl (Zool) ribs; (Ferro) points

agujerear [aɣuxere'ar] vt to make holes in

agujero [aɣu'xero] nm hole

agujetas [aɣu'xetas] nfpl stitch sg; (rigidez) stiffness sg

ahí [a'i] adv there; **de ~ que** so that, with the result that; **~ llega** here he comes; **por ~** that way; (allá) over there; **200 o por ~** 200 or so

ahijado, -a [ai'xaðo, a] nm/f godson/ daughter

ahogar [ao'ɣar] vt to drown; (asfixiar) to suffocate, smother; (fuego) to put out; **ahogarse** vr (en el agua) to drown; (por asfixia) to suffocate

ahogo [a'oxo] nm breathlessness; (fig) financial difficulty

ahondar [aon'dar] vt to deepen, make deeper; (fig) to study thoroughly ▷ vi: **~ en** to study thoroughly

ahora [a'ora] adv now; (hace poco) a moment ago, just now; (dentro de poco) in a moment; **~ voy** I'm coming; **~ mismo** right now; **~ bien** now then; **por ~** for the present

ahorcar [aor'kar] vt to hang

ahorita [ao'rita] (fam) adv (LAM: en este momento) right now; (MÉX: hace poco) just now; (: dentro de poco) in a minute

ahorrar [ao'rrar] vt (dinero) to save; (esfuerzos) to save, avoid; **ahorro** nm (acto) saving; **ahorros** nmpl (dinero) savings

ahuecar [awe'kar] vt to hollow (out); (voz) to deepen; **ahuecarse** vr to give o.s. airs

ahumar [au'mar] vt to smoke, cure; (llenar de humo) to fill with smoke ▷ vi to smoke; **ahumarse** vr to fill with smoke

ahuyentar [aujen'tar] vt to drive off, frighten off; (fig) to dispel

aire ['aire] nm air; (viento) wind; (corriente) draught; (Mús) tune; **al ~ libre** in the open air; **aire acondicionado** air conditioning; **airear** vt to air; **airearse** vr (persona) to go out for a breath of fresh air; **airoso, -a** adj windy; draughty; (fig) graceful

aislado, -a [ais'laðo, a] adj isolated; (incomunicado) cut-off; (Elec) insulated

aislar [ais'lar] vt to isolate; (Elec) to insulate

ajardinado, -a [axarði'naðo, a] adj landscaped

ajedrez [axe'ðreθ] nm chess

ajeno, -a [a'xeno, a] adj (que pertenece a otro) somebody else's; **~ a** foreign to

ajetreado, -a [axetre'aðo, a] adj busy

ajetreo [axe'treo] *nm* bustle

ají [a'xi] (*cs*) *nm* chil(l)i, red pepper; (*salsa*) chil(l)i sauce

ajillo [a'xiʎo] *nm*: **gambas al ~** garlic prawns

ajo ['axo] *nm* garlic

ajuar [a'xwar] *nm* household furnishings *pl*; (*de novia*) trousseau; (*de niño*) layette

ajustado, -a [axus'taðo, a] *adj* (*tornillo*) tight; (*cálculo*) right; (*ropa*) tight(-fitting); (*resultado*) close

ajustar [axus'tar] *vt* (*adaptar*) to adjust; (*encajar*) to fit; (*Tec*) to engage; (*Imprenta*) to make up; (*apretar*) to tighten; (*concertar*) to agree (on); (*reconciliar*) to reconcile; (*cuentas, deudas*) to settle ▷ *vi* to fit; **ajustarse** *vr*: **~se a** (*precio etc*) to be in keeping with, fit in with; **~ las cuentas a algn** to get even with sb

ajuste [a'xuste] *nm* adjustment; (*Costura*) fitting; (*acuerdo*) compromise; (*de cuenta*) settlement

al [al] = **a** + **el**; V **a**

ala ['ala] *nf* wing; (*de sombrero*) brim; winger; **ala delta** *nf* hang-glider

alabanza [ala'βanθa] *nf* praise

alabar [ala'βar] *vt* to praise

alacena [ala'θena] *nf* kitchen cupboard (*BRIT*) o closet (*US*)

alacrán [ala'kran] *nm* scorpion

alambrada [alam'braða] *nf* wire fence; (*red*) wire netting

alambre [a'lambre] *nm* wire; **alambre de púas** barbed wire

alameda [ala'meða] *nf* (*plantío*) poplar grove; (*lugar de paseo*) avenue, boulevard

álamo ['alamo] *nm* poplar

alarde [a'larðe] *nm* show, display; **hacer ~ de** to boast of

alargador [alarɣa'ðor] *nm* (*Elec*) extension lead

alargar [alar'ɣar] *vt* to lengthen, extend; (*paso*) to hasten; (*brazo*) to stretch out; (*cuerda*) to pay out; (*conversación*) to spin out; **alargarse** *vr* to get longer

alarma [a'larma] *nf* alarm; **alarma de incendios** fire alarm; **alarmar** *vt* to alarm; **alarmarse** to get alarmed; **alarmante** [alar'mante] *adj* alarming

alba ['alβa] *nf* dawn

albahaca [al'βaka] *nf* basil

Albania [al'βanja] *nf* Albania

albañil [alβa'nil] *nm* bricklayer; (*cantero*) mason

albarán [alβa'ran] *nm* (*Com*) delivery note, invoice

albaricoque [alβari'koke] *nm* apricot

albedrío [alβe'ðrio] *nm*: **libre ~** free will

alberca [al'βerka] *nf* reservoir; (*MÉX: piscina*) swimming pool

albergar [alβer'ɣar] *vt* to shelter

albergue *etc* [al'βerɣe] *vb* V **albergar** ▷ *nm* shelter, refuge; **albergue juvenil** youth hostel

albóndiga [al'βondiɣa] *nf* meatball

albornoz [alβor'noθ] *nm* (*de los árabes*) burnous; (*para el baño*) bathrobe

alborotar [alβoro'tar] *vi* to make a row ▷ *vt* to agitate, stir up; **alborotarse** *vr* to get excited; (*mar*) to get rough; **alboroto** *nm* row, uproar

álbum ['alβum] (*pl* **~s, ~es**) *nm* album; **álbum de recortes** scrapbook

albur [al'βur] (*MÉX*) *nm* (*juego de palabras*) pun; (*doble sentido*) double entendre

alcachofa [alka'tʃofa] *nf* artichoke

alcalde, -esa [al'kalde, esa] *nm/f* mayor(ess)

alcaldía [alkal'dia] *nf* mayoralty; (*lugar*) mayor's office

alcance *etc* [al'kanθe] *vb* V **alcanzar** ▷ *nm* reach; (*Com*) adverse balance; **al ~ de algn** available to sb

alcancía [alkan'θia] (*LAM*) *nf* (*para ahorrar*) money box; (*para colectas*) collection box

alcantarilla [alkanta'riʎa] *nf* (*de aguas cloacales*) sewer; (*en la calle*) gutter

alcanzar [alkan'θar] *vt* (*algo: con la mano, el pie*) to reach; (*alguien: en el camino etc*) to catch up (with); (*autobús*) to catch; (*bala*) to hit, strike ▷ *vi* (*ser suficiente*) to be enough; **~ a hacer** to manage to do

alcaparra [alka'parra] *nf* caper

alcayata [alka'jata] *nf* hook

alcázar [al'kaθar] *nm* fortress; (*Náut*) quarter-deck

alcoba [al'koβa] *nf* bedroom

alcohol [al'kol] *nm* alcohol; **alcohol metílico** methylated spirits *pl* (*BRIT*), wood alcohol (*US*); **alcohólico, -a** *adj, nm/f* alcoholic; **alcoholímetro** [alko'limetro] *nm* Breathalyser® (*BRIT*), drunkometer (*US*); **alcoholismo** [alko'lismo] *nm* alcoholism

alcornoque [alkor'noke] *nm* cork tree; (*fam*) idiot

aldea [al'dea] *nf* village; **aldeano, -a** *adj* village *cpd* ▷ *nm/f* villager

aleación [alea'θjon] *nf* alloy

aleatorio, -a [alea'torjo, a] *adj* random

aleccionar [alekθjo'nar] *vt* to instruct; (*adiestrar*) to train

alegar [ale'ɣar] *vt* to claim; (*Jur*) to plead ▷ *vi* (*LAM: discutir*) to argue

alegoría [aleɣo'ria] *nf* allegory

alegrar [ale'ɣrar] *vt* (*causar alegría*) to cheer (up); (*fuego*) to poke; (*fiesta*) to liven

up; **alegrarse** *vr* (*fam*) to get merry o tight;
~se de to be glad about
alegre [a'leɣre] *adj* happy, cheerful; (*fam*)
merry, tight; (*chiste*) risqué, blue; **alegría** *nf*
happiness; merriment
alejar [ale'xar] *vt* to remove; (*fig*) to
estrange; **alejarse** *vr* to move away
alemán, -ana [ale'man, ana] *adj*, *nm/f*
German ⊳ *nm* (*Ling*) German
Alemania [ale'manja] *nf* Germany
alentador, a [alenta'ðor, a] *adj*
encouraging
alentar [alen'tar] *vt* to encourage
alergia [a'lerxja] *nf* allergy
alero [a'lero] *nm* (*de tejado*) eaves pl;
(*guardabarros*) mudguard
alerta [a'lerta] *adj*, *adv* alert
aleta [a'leta] *nf* (*de pez*) fin; (*ala*) wing; (*de
foca*, *Deporte*) flipper; (*Auto*) mudguard
aletear [alete'ar] *vi* to flutter
alevín [ale'βin] *nm* fry, young fish
alevosía [aleβo'sia] *nf* treachery
alfabeto [alfa'βeto] *nm* alphabet
alfalfa [al'falfa] *nf* alfalfa, lucerne
alfarería [alfare'ria] *nf* pottery; (*tienda*)
pottery shop; **alfarero, -a** *nm/f* potter
alféizar [al'feiθar] *nm* window-sill
alférez [al'fereθ] *nm* (*Mil*) second
lieutenant; (*Náut*) ensign
alfil [al'fil] *nm* (*Ajedrez*) bishop
alfiler [alfi'ler] *nm* pin; (*broche*) clip
alfombra [al'fombra] *nf* carpet; (*más
pequeña*) rug; **alfombrilla** *nf* rug, mat;
(*Inform*) mouse mat o pad
alforja [al'forxa] *nf* saddlebag
algas ['alɣas] *nfpl* seaweed
álgebra [al'xeβra] *nf* algebra
algo ['alɣo] *pron* something; anything
⊳ *adv* somewhat, rather; **¿~ más?** anything
else?; (*en tienda*) is that all?; **por ~ será** there
must be some reason for it
algodón [alɣo'ðon] *nm* cotton; (*planta*)
cotton plant; **algodón de azúcar** candy
floss (BRIT), cotton candy (US); **algodón
hidrófilo** cotton wool (BRIT), absorbent
cotton (US)
alguien ['alɣjen] *pron* someone,
somebody; (*en frases interrogativas*) anyone,
anybody
alguno, -a [al'ɣuno, a] *adj* (*delante de
nm*): **algún** some; (*después de n*): **no tiene
talento ~** he has no talent, he doesn't
have any talent ⊳ *pron* (*alguien*) someone,
somebody; **algún que otro libro** some book
or other; **algún día iré** I'll go one o some day;
sin interés ~ without the slightest interest;
~ que otro an occasional one; **~s piensan**
some (people) think

alhaja [a'laxa] *nf* jewel; (*tesoro*) precious
object, treasure
alhelí [ale'li] *nm* wallflower, stock
aliado, -a [a'ljaðo, a] *adj* allied
alianza [a'ljanθa] *nf* alliance; (*anillo*)
wedding ring
aliar [a'ljar] *vt* to ally; **aliarse** *vr* to form
an alliance
alias ['aljas] *adv* alias
alicatado [alika'taðo] (ESP) *nm* tiling
alicates [ali'kates] *nmpl* pliers
aliciente [ali'θjente] *nm* incentive;
(*atracción*) attraction
alienación [aljena'θjon] *nf* alienation
aliento [a'ljento] *nm* breath; (*respiración*)
breathing; **sin ~** breathless
aligerar [alixe'rar] *vt* to lighten; (*reducir*)
to shorten; (*aliviar*) to alleviate; (*mitigar*) to
ease; (*paso*) to quicken
alijo [a'lixo] *nm* consignment
alimaña [ali'maɲa] *nf* pest
alimentación [alimenta'θjon] *nf*
(*comida*) food; (*acción*) feeding; (*tienda*)
grocer's (shop)
alimentar [alimen'tar] *vt* to feed; (*nutrir*)
to nourish; **alimentarse** *vr* to feed
alimenticio, -a [alimen'tiθjo, a] *adj* food
cpd; (*nutritivo*) nourishing, nutritious
alimento [ali'mento] *nm* food; (*nutrición*)
nourishment
alineación [alinea'θjon] *nf* alignment;
(*Deporte*) line-up
alinear [aline'ar] *vt* to align; (*Deporte*) to
select, pick
aliñar [ali'ɲar] *vt* (*Culin*) to season; **aliño**
nm (*Culin*) dressing
alioli [ali'oli] *nm* garlic mayonnaise
alisar [ali'sar] *vt* to smooth
alistarse [alis'tarse] *vr* to enlist;
(*inscribirse*) to enrol
aliviar [ali'βjar] *vt* (*carga*) to lighten;
(*persona*) to relieve; (*dolor*) to relieve,
alleviate
alivio [a'liβjo] *nm* alleviation, relief
aljibe [al'xiβe] *nm* cistern
allá [a'ʎa] *adv* (*lugar*) there; (*por ahí*) over
there; (*tiempo*) then; **~ abajo** down there;
más ~ further on; **más ~ de** beyond; **¡~ tú!**
that's your problem!; **¡~ voy!** I'm coming!
allanamiento [aʎana'mjento] *nm*
(LAM: *de policía*) raid; **allanamiento de
morada** burglary
allanar [aʎa'nar] *vt* to flatten, level (out);
(*igualar*) to smooth (out); (*fig*) to subdue;
(*Jur*) to burgle, break into
allegado, -a [aʎe'xaðo, a] *adj* near, close
⊳ *nm/f* relation
allí [a'ʎi] *adv* there; **~ mismo** right there;

por ~ over there; (*por ese camino*) that way

alma ['alma] *nf* soul; (*persona*) person

almacén [alma'θen] *nm* (*depósito*) warehouse, store; (*Mil*) magazine; (*cs: de comestibles*) grocer's (shop); **grandes almacenes** department store *sg*; **almacenaje** *nm* storage

almacenar [almaθe'nar] *vt* to store, put in storage; (*proveerse*) to stock up with

almanaque [alma'nake] *nm* almanac

almeja [al'mexa] *nf* clam

almendra [al'mendra] *nf* almond; **almendro** *nm* almond tree

almíbar [al'miβar] *nm* syrup

almidón [almi'ðon] *nm* starch

almirante [almi'rante] *nm* admiral

almohada [almo'aða] *nf* pillow; (*funda*) pillowcase; **almohadilla** *nf* cushion; (*para alfileres*) pincushion; (*Tec*) pad

almohadón [almoa'ðon] *nm* large pillow; bolster

almorranas [almo'rranas] *nfpl* piles, haemorrhoids

almorzar [almor'θar] *vt*: **~ una tortilla** to have an omelette for lunch ▷ *vi* to (have) lunch

almuerzo *etc* [al'mwerθo] *vb* V **almorzar** ▷ *nm* lunch

alocado, -a [alo'kaðo, a] *adj* crazy

alojamiento [aloxa'mjento] *nm* lodging(s) *pl*; (*viviendas*) housing

alojar [alo'xar] *vt* to lodge; **alojarse** *vr* to lodge, stay

alondra [a'londra] *nf* lark, skylark

alpargata [alpar'ɣata] *nf* rope-soled sandal, espadrille

Alpes ['alpes] *nmpl*: **los ~** the Alps

alpinismo [alpi'nismo] *nm* mountaineering, climbing; **alpinista** *nmf* mountaineer, climber

alpiste [al'piste] *nm* birdseed

alquilar [alki'lar] *vt* (*propietario: inmuebles*) to let, rent (out); (: *coche*) to hire out; (: *TV*) to rent (out); (*alquilador: inmuebles, TV*) to rent; (: *coche*) to hire; **"se alquila casa"** "house to let (*BRIT*) o for rent (*US*)"

alquiler [alki'ler] *nm* renting; letting; hiring; (*arriendo*) rent; hire charge; **de ~** for hire; **alquiler de automóviles** o **coches** car hire

alquimia [al'kimja] *nf* alchemy

alquitrán [alki'tran] *nm* tar

alrededor [alreðe'ðor] *adv* around, about; **~ de** around, about; **mirar a su ~** to look (round) about one; **alrededores** *nmpl* surroundings

alta ['alta] *nf* (certificate of) discharge

altar [al'tar] *nm* altar

altavoz [alta'βoθ] *nm* loudspeaker; (*amplificador*) amplifier

alteración [altera'θjon] *nf* alteration; (*alboroto*) disturbance

alterar [alte'rar] *vt* to alter; to disturb; **alterarse** *vr* (*persona*) to get upset

altercado [alter'kaðo] *nm* argument

alternar [alter'nar] *vt* to alternate ▷ *vi* to alternate; (*turnar*) to take turns; **alternarse** *vr* to alternate; to take turns; **~ con** to mix with; **alternativa** *nf* alternative; (*elección*) choice; **alternativo, -a** *adj* alternative; (*alterno*) alternating; **alterno, -a** *adj* alternate; (*Elec*) alternating

Alteza [al'teθa] *nf* (*tratamiento*) Highness

altibajos [alti'βaxos] *nmpl* ups and downs

altiplano [alti'plano] *nm* = **altiplanicie**

altisonante [altiso'nante] *adj* high-flown, high-sounding

altitud [alti'tuð] *nf* height; (*Aviac, Geo*) altitude

altivo, -a [al'tiβo, a] *adj* haughty, arrogant

alto, -a ['alto, a] *adj* high; (*persona*) tall; (*sonido*) high, sharp; (*noble*) high, lofty ▷ *nm* halt; (*Mús*) alto; (*Geo*) hill ▷ *adv* (*de sitio*) high; (*de sonido*) loud, loudly ▷ *excl* halt!; **la pared tiene 2 metros de ~** the wall is 2 metres high; **en alta mar** on the high seas; **en voz alta** in a loud voice; **las altas horas de la noche** the small o wee hours; **en lo ~ de** at the top of; **pasar por ~** to overlook; **altoparlante** [altopar'lante] (*LAM*) *nm* loudspeaker

altura [al'tura] *nf* height; (*Náut*) depth; (*Geo*) latitude; **la pared tiene 1.80 de ~** the wall is 1 metre 80cm high; **a estas ~s** at this stage; **a estas ~s del año** at this time of the year

alubia [a'luβja] *nf* bean

alucinación [aluθina'θjon] *nf* hallucination

alucinar [aluθi'nar] *vi* to hallucinate ▷ *vt* to deceive; (*fascinar*) to fascinate

alud [a'luð] *nm* avalanche; (*fig*) flood

aludir [alu'ðir] *vi*: **~ a** to allude to; **darse por aludido** to take the hint

alumbrado [alum'braðo] *nm* lighting

alumbrar [alum'brar] *vt* to light (up) ▷ *vi* (*Med*) to give birth

aluminio [alu'minjo] *nm* aluminium (*BRIT*), aluminum (*US*)

alumno, -a [a'lumno, a] *nm/f* pupil, student

alusión [alu'sjon] *nf* allusion

alusivo, -a [alu'siβo, a] *adj* allusive

aluvión [alu'βjon] *nm* alluvium; (*fig*) flood

alverja [al'βerxa] (*LAM*) *nf* pea

alza ['alθa] *nf* rise; (*Mil*) sight
alzamiento [alθa'mjento] *nm* (*rebelión*)
rising
alzar [al'θar] *vt* to lift (up); (*precio, muro*)
to raise; (*cuello de abrigo*) to turn up; (*Agr*) to
gather in; (*Imprenta*) to gather; **alzarse** *vr*
to get up, rise; (*rebelarse*) to revolt; (*Com*) to
go fraudulently bankrupt; (*Jur*) to appeal
ama ['ama] *nf* lady of the house; (*dueña*)
owner; (*institutriz*) governess; (*madre
adoptiva*) foster mother; **ama de casa**
housewife; **ama de llaves** housekeeper
amabilidad [amaβili'ðað] *nf* kindness;
(*simpatía*) niceness; **amable** *adj* kind; nice;
es usted muy amable that's very kind of
you
amaestrado, -a [amaes'traðo, a] *adj*
(*animal: en circo etc*) performing
amaestrar [amaes'trar] *vt* to train
amago [a'maxo] *nm* threat; (*gesto*)
threatening gesture; (*Med*) symptom
amainar [amai'nar] *vi* (*viento*) to die
down
amamantar [amaman'tar] *vt* to suckle,
nurse
amanecer [amane'θer] *vi* to dawn ▷ *nm*
dawn; **~ afiebrado** to wake up with a fever
amanerado, -a [amane'raðo, a] *adj*
affected
amante [a'mante] *adj*: **~ de** fond of ▷ *nmf*
lover
amapola [ama'pola] *nf* poppy
amar [a'mar] *vt* to love
amargado, -a [amar'xaðo, a] *adj* bitter
amargar [amar'xar] *vt* to make bitter;
(*fig*) to embitter; **amargarse** *vr* to become
embittered
amargo, -a [a'marxo, a] *adj* bitter
amarillento, -a [amari'Δento, a] *adj*
yellowish; (*tez*) sallow; **amarillo, -a** *adj*,
nm yellow
amarrado, -a [ama'rraðo, a] (*MÉX: fam*)
adj mean, stingy
amarrar [ama'rrar] *vt* to moor; (*sujetar*)
to tie up
amarras [a'marras] *nfpl*: **soltar ~** to set
sail
amasar [ama'sar] *vt* (*masa*) to knead;
(*mezclar*) to mix, prepare; (*confeccionar*) to
concoct
amateur [ama'ter] *nmf* amateur
amazona [ama'θona] *nf* horsewoman;
Amazonas *nm*: **el Amazonas** the Amazon
ámbar ['ambar] *nm* amber
ambición [ambi'θjon] *nf* ambition;
ambicionar *vt* to aspire to; **ambicioso, -a**
adj ambitious
ambidextro, -a [ambi'ðekstro, a] *adj*
ambidextrous
ambientación [ambjenta'θjon] *nf* (*Cine,
Teatro etc*) setting; (*Radio*) sound effects
ambiente [am'bjente] *nm* atmosphere;
(*medio*) environment
ambigüedad [ambixwe'ðað] *nf*
ambiguity; **ambiguo, -a** *adj* ambiguous
ámbito ['ambito] *nm* (*campo*) field; (*fig*)
scope
ambos, -as ['ambos, as] *adj pl, pron pl*
both
ambulancia [ambu'lanθja] *nf*
ambulance
ambulante [ambu'lante] *adj* travelling
cpd, itinerant
ambulatorio [ambula'torio] *nm* state
health-service clinic
amén [a'men] *excl* amen; **~ de** besides
amenaza [ame'naθa] *nf* threat;
amenazar [amena'θar] *vt* to threaten
▷ *vi*: **amenazar con hacer** to threaten to do
ameno, -a [a'meno, a] *adj* pleasant
América [a'merika] *nf* America; **América
Central/Latina** Central/Latin America;
América del Norte/del Sur North/South
America; **americana** *nf* coat, jacket; V
tb **americano**; **americano, -a** *adj*, *nm/f*
American
ametralladora [ametraΔa'ðora] *nf*
machine gun
amigable [ami'xaβle] *adj* friendly
amígdala [a'mixðala] *nf* tonsil;
amigdalitis *nf* tonsillitis
amigo, -a [a'mixo, a] *adj* friendly ▷ *nm/f*
friend; (*amante*) lover; **ser ~ de algo** to be
fond of sth; **ser muy ~s** to be close friends
aminorar [amino'rar] *vt* to diminish;
(*reducir*) to reduce; **~ la marcha** to slow
down
amistad [amis'tað] *nf* friendship;
amistades *nfpl* (*amigos*) friends; **amistoso,
-a** *adj* friendly
amnesia [am'nesja] *nf* amnesia
amnistía [amnis'tia] *nf* amnesty
amo ['amo] *nm* owner; (*jefe*) boss
amolar [amo'lar] (*MÉX: fam*) *vt* to ruin,
damage
amoldar [amol'dar] *vt* to mould; (*adaptar*)
to adapt
amonestación [amonesta'θjon] *nf*
warning; **amonestaciones** *nfpl* (*Rel*)
marriage banns
amonestar [amones'tar] *vt* to warn; (*Rel*)
to publish the banns of
amontonar [amonto'nar] *vt* to collect,
pile up; **amontonarse** *vr* to crowd
together; (*acumularse*) to pile up
amor [a'mor] *nm* love; (*amante*) lover;

hacer el ~ to make love; **amor propio**
self-respect
amoratado, -a [amora'taðo, a] *adj*
purple
amordazar [amorða'θar] *vt* to muzzle;
(fig) to gag
amorfo, -a [a'morfo, a] *adj* amorphous,
shapeless
amoroso, -a [amo'roso, a] *adj*
affectionate, loving
amortiguador [amortigwa'ðor] *nm*
shock absorber; *(parachoques)* bumper;
amortiguadores *nmpl (Auto)* suspension
sg
amortiguar [amorti'ɣwar] *vt* to deaden;
(ruido) to muffle; *(color)* to soften
amotinar [amoti'nar] *vt* to stir up, incite
(to riot); **amotinarse** *vr* to mutiny
amparar [ampa'rar] *vt* to protect;
ampararse *vr* to seek protection; *(de la
lluvia etc)* to shelter; **amparo** *nm* help,
protection; **al amparo de** under the
protection of
amperio [am'perjo] *nm* ampère, amp
ampliación [amplja'θjon] *nf*
enlargement; *(extensión)* extension
ampliar [am'pljar] *vt* to enlarge; to
extend
amplificador [amplifika'ðor] *nm*
amplifier
amplificar [amplifi'kar] *vt* to amplify
amplio, -a ['ampljo, a] *adj* spacious; *(de
falda etc)* full; *(extenso)* extensive; *(ancho)*
wide; **amplitud** *nf* spaciousness; extent;
(fig) amplitude
ampolla [am'poʎa] *nf* blister; *(Med)*
ampoule
amputar [ampu'tar] *vt* to cut off,
amputate
amueblar [amwe'βlar] *vt* to furnish
anales [a'nales] *nmpl* annals
analfabetismo [analfaβe'tismo]
nm illiteracy; **analfabeto, -a** *adj, nm/f*
illiterate
analgésico [anal'xesiko] *nm* painkiller,
analgesic
análisis [a'nalisis] *nm inv* analysis
analista [ana'lista] *nmf (gen)* analyst
analizar [anali'θar] *vt* to analyse
analógico, -a [ana'loxiko, a] *adj (Inform)*
analog; *(reloj)* analogue *(BRIT)*, analog *(US)*
análogo, -a [a'naloɣo, a] *adj* analogous,
similar
ananá [ana'na] *(RPL) nm* pineapple
anarquía [anar'kia] *nf* anarchy;
anarquista *nmf* anarchist
anatomía [anato'mia] *nf* anatomy
anca ['anka] *nf* rump, haunch; **ancas** *nfpl*

(fam) behind *sg*
ancho, -a ['antʃo, a] *adj* wide; *(falda)*
full; *(fig)* liberal ▷ *nm* width; *(Ferro)* gauge;
ponerse ~ to get conceited; **estar a sus
anchas** to be at one's ease
anchoa [an'tʃoa] *nf* anchovy
anchura [an'tʃura] *nf* width; *(extensión)*
wideness
anciano, -a [an'θjano, a] *adj* old, aged
▷ *nm/f* old man/woman; elder
ancla ['ankla] *nf* anchor
Andalucía [andalu'θia] *nf* Andalusia;
andaluz, -a *adj, nm/f* Andalusian
andamio [an'damjo] *nm* scaffold(ing)
andar [an'dar] *vt* to go, cover, travel
▷ *vi* to go, walk, travel; *(funcionar)* to go,
work; *(estar)* to be ▷ *nm* walk, gait, pace;
andarse *vr* to go away; **~ a pie/a caballo/
en bicicleta** to go on foot/on horseback/
by bicycle; **~ haciendo algo** to be doing sth;
¡anda! *(sorpresa)* go on!; **anda por** *o* **en los
40** he's about 40
andén [an'den] *nm (Ferro)* platform; *(Náut)*
quayside; *(CAM: de la calle)* pavement *(BRIT)*,
sidewalk *(US)*
Andes ['andes] *nmpl*: **los ~** the Andes
andinismo [andi'nismo] *(LAM) nm*
mountaineering, climbing
Andorra [an'dorra] *nf* Andorra
andrajoso, -a [andra'xoso, a] *adj* ragged
anduve *etc vb* V **andar**
anécdota [a'nekðota] *nf* anecdote, story
anegar [ane'ɣar] *vt* to flood; *(ahogar)* to
drown
anemia [a'nemja] *nf* anaemia
anestesia [anes'tesja] *nf (sustancia)*
anaesthetic; *(proceso)* anaesthesia;
anestesia general/local general/local
anaesthetic
anexar [anek'sar] *vt* to annex; *(documento)*
to attach; **anexión** *nf* annexation; **anexo,
-a** *adj* attached ▷ *nm* annexe
anfibio, -a [an'fiβjo, a] *adj* amphibious
▷ *nm* amphibian
anfiteatro [anfite'atro] *nm*
amphitheatre; *(Teatro)* dress circle
anfitrión, -ona [anfi'trjon, ona] *nm/f*
host(ess)
ánfora ['anfora] *nf (cántaro)* amphora;
(MÉX Pol) ballot box
ángel ['anxel] *nm* angel; **ángel de la
guarda** guardian angel
angina [an'xina] *nf (Med)* inflammation
of the throat; **tener ~s** to have tonsillitis;
angina de pecho angina
anglicano, -a [angli'kano, a] *adj, nm/f*
Anglican
anglosajón, -ona [anglosa'xon, ona] *adj*

Anglo-Saxon
anguila [an'gila] *nf* eel
angula [an'gula] *nf* elver, baby eel
ángulo ['angulo] *nm* angle; (*esquina*)
corner; (*curva*) bend
angustia [an'gustja] *nf* anguish
anhelar [ane'lar] *vt* to be eager for;
(*desear*) to long for, desire ▷ *vi* to pant, gasp;
anhelo *nm* eagerness; desire
anidar [ani'ðar] *vi* to nest
anillo [a'niʎo] *nm* ring; **anillo de boda/
compromiso** wedding/engagement ring
animación [anima'θjon] *nf* liveliness;
(*vitalidad*) life; (*actividad*) activity; bustle
animado, -a [ani'maðo, a] *adj* lively;
(*vivaz*) animated; **animador, a** *nm/f* (TV)
host(ess), compère; (*Deporte*) cheerleader
animal [ani'mal] *adj* animal; (*fig*) stupid
▷ *nm* animal; (*fig*) fool; (*bestia*) brute
animar [ani'mar] *vt* (*Bio*) to animate, give
life to; (*fig*) to liven up, brighten up, cheer
up; (*estimular*) to stimulate; **animarse** *vr* to
cheer up; to feel encouraged; (*decidirse*) to
make up one's mind
ánimo ['animo] *nm* (*alma*) soul; (*mente*)
mind; (*valentía*) courage ▷ *excl* cheer up!
animoso, -a [ani'moso, a] *adj* brave;
(*vivo*) lively
aniquilar [aniki'lar] *vt* to annihilate,
destroy
anís [a'nis] *nm* aniseed; (*licor*) anisette
aniversario [aniβer'sarjo] *nm*
anniversary
anoche [a'notʃe] *adv* last night; **antes de
~** the night before last
anochecer [anotʃe'θer] *vi* to get dark
▷ *nm* nightfall, dark; **al ~** at nightfall
anodino, -a [ano'ðino, a] *adj* dull,
anodyne
anomalía [anoma'lia] *nf* anomaly
anonadado, -a [anona'ðaðo, a]
adj: **estar ~** to be overwhelmed *o* amazed
anonimato [anoni'mato] *nm* anonymity
anónimo, -a [a'nonimo, a] *adj*
anonymous; (*Com*) limited ▷ *nm* (*carta
anónima*) anonymous letter; (: *maliciosa*)
poison-pen letter
anormal [anor'mal] *adj* abnormal
anotación [anota'θjon] *nf* note;
annotation
anotar [ano'tar] *vt* to note down;
(*comentar*) to annotate
ansia ['ansja] *nf* anxiety; (*añoranza*)
yearning; **ansiar** *vt* to long for
ansiedad [ansje'ðað] *nf* anxiety
ansioso, -a [an'sjoso, a] *adj* anxious;
(*anhelante*) eager; **~ de** *o* **por algo** greedy
for sth

antaño [an'taɲo] *adv* long ago, formerly
Antártico [an'tartiko] *nm*: **el ~** the
Antarctic
ante ['ante] *prep* before, in the presence of;
(*problema etc*) faced with ▷ *nm* (*piel*) suede;
~ todo above all
anteanoche [antea'notʃe] *adv* the night
before last
anteayer [antea'jer] *adv* the day before
yesterday
antebrazo [ante'βraθo] *nm* forearm
antecedente [anteθe'ðente] *adj* previous
▷ *nm* antecedent; **antecedentes** *nmpl*
(*historial*) record *sg*; **antecedentes penales**
criminal record
anteceder [anteθe'ðer] *vt* to precede,
go before
antecesor, a [anteθe'sor, a] *nm/f*
predecessor
antelación [antela'θjon] *nf*: **con ~** in
advance
antemano [ante'mano] **de ~** *adv*
beforehand, in advance
antena [an'tena] *nf* antenna; (*de televisión
etc*) aerial; **antena parabólica** satellite dish
antenoche [ante'notʃe] *adv* (LAM) the
night before last
anteojo [ante'oxo] *nm* eyeglass; **anteojos**
nmpl (LAM): *gafas*) glasses, spectacles
antepasados [antepa'saðos] *nmpl*
ancestors
anteponer [antepo'ner] *vt* to place in
front; (*fig*) to prefer
anterior [ante'rjor] *adj* preceding,
previous; **anterioridad** *nf*: **con
anterioridad a** prior to, before
antes ['antes] *adv* (*con prioridad*) before
▷ *prep*: **~ de** before ▷ *conj*: **~ de ir/de que te
vayas** before going/before you go; **~ bien**
(but) rather; **dos días ~** two days before
o previously; **no quiso venir ~** she didn't
want to come any earlier; **tomo el avión ~
que el barco** I take the plane rather than the
boat; **~ de o que nada** (*en el tiempo*) first of
all; (*indicando preferencia*) above all; **~ que yo**
before me; **lo ~ posible** as soon as possible;
cuanto ~ mejor the sooner the better
antibalas [anti'βalas] *adj inv*: **chaleco ~**
bullet-proof jacket
antibiótico [anti'βjotiko] *nm* antibiotic
anticaspa [anti'kaspa] *adj inv* anti-
dandruff *cpd*
anticipación [antiθipa'θjon] *nf*
anticipation; **con 10 minutos de ~** 10
minutes early
anticipado, -a [antiθi'paðo, a] *adj* (*pago*)
advance; **por ~** in advance
anticipar [antiθi'par] *vt* to anticipate;

(adelantar) to bring forward; *(Com)* to advance; **anticiparse** *vr*: **~se a su época** to be ahead of one's time

anticipo [anti'θipo] *nm* (*Com*) advance

anticonceptivo, -a [antikonθep'tiβo, a] *adj, nm* contraceptive

anticongelante [antikonxe'lante] *nm* antifreeze

anticuado, -a [anti'kwaðo, a] *adj* out-of-date, old-fashioned; (*desusado*) obsolete

anticuario [anti'kwarjo] *nm* antique dealer

anticuerpo [anti'kwerpo] *nm* (*Med*) antibody

antidepresivo [antiðepre'siβo] *nm* antidepressant

antidóping [anti'dopin] *adj inv*: **control ~** drugs test

antídoto [an'tiðoto] *nm* antidote

antiestético, -a [anties'tetiko, a] *adj* unsightly

antifaz [anti'faθ] *nm* mask; (*velo*) veil

antiglobalización [antigloβaliθa'θjon] *nf* anti-globalization; **antiglobalizador, a** *adj* anti-globalization *cpd*

antiguamente [antixwa'mente] *adv* formerly; (*hace mucho tiempo*) long ago

antigüedad [antixwe'ðað] *nf* antiquity; (*artículo*) antique; (*rango*) seniority

antiguo, -a [an'tixwo, a] *adj* old, ancient; (*que fue*) former

Antillas [an'tiʎas] *nfpl*: **las ~** the West Indies

antílope [an'tilope] *nm* antelope

antinatural [antinatu'ral] *adj* unnatural

antipatía [antipa'tia] *nf* antipathy, dislike; **antipático, -a** *adj* disagreeable, unpleasant

antirrobo [anti'rroβo] *adj inv* (*alarma etc*) anti-theft

antisemita [antise'mita] *adj* anti-Semitic ▷ *nmf* anti-Semite

antiséptico, -a [anti'septiko, a] *adj* antiseptic ▷ *nm* antiseptic

antivirus [anti'birus] *nm inv* (*Comput*) antivirus program

antojarse [anto'xarse] *vr* (*desear*): **se me antoja comprarlo** I have a mind to buy it; (*pensar*): **se me antoja que ...** I have a feeling that ...

antojitos [anto'xitos] (*MÉX*) *nmpl* snacks, nibbles

antojo [an'toxo] *nm* caprice, whim; (*rosa*) birthmark; (*lunar*) mole

antología [antolo'xia] *nf* anthology

antorcha [an'tortʃa] *nf* torch

antro ['antro] *nm* cavern

antropología [antropolo'xia] *nf* anthropology

anual [a'nwal] *adj* annual

anuario [a'nwarjo] *nm* yearbook

anulación [anula'θjon] *nf* annulment; (*cancelación*) cancellation

anular [anu'lar] *vt* (*contrato*) to annul, cancel; (*ley*) to revoke, repeal; (*suscripción*) to cancel ▷ *nm* ring finger

anunciar [anun'θjar] *vt* to announce; (*proclamar*) to proclaim; (*Com*) to advertise

anuncio [a'nunθjo] *nm* announcement; (*señal*) sign; (*Com*) advertisement; (*cartel*) poster

anzuelo [an'θwelo] *nm* hook; (*para pescar*) fish hook

añadidura [aɲaði'ðura] *nf* addition, extra; **por ~** besides, in addition

añadir [aɲa'ðir] *vt* to add

añejo, -a [a'ɲexo, a] *adj* old; (*vino*) mellow

añicos [a'ɲikos] *nmpl*: **hacer ~** to smash, shatter

año ['aɲo] *nm* year; **¡Feliz A~ Nuevo!** Happy New Year!; **tener 15 ~s** to be 15 (years old); **los ~s 90** the nineties; **el ~ que viene** next year; **año bisiesto/escolar/fiscal/ sabático** leap/school/tax/sabbatical year

añoranza [aɲo'ranθa] *nf* nostalgia; (*anhelo*) longing

apa ['apa] (*MÉX*) *excl* goodness me!, good gracious!

apabullar [apaβu'ʎar] *vt* to crush, squash

apacible [apa'θiβle] *adj* gentle, mild

apaciguar [apaθi'ɣwar] *vt* to pacify, calm (down)

apadrinar [apaðri'nar] *vt* to sponsor, support; (*Rel*) to be godfather to

apagado, -a [apa'ɣaðo, a] *adj* (*volcán*) extinct; (*color*) dull; (*voz*) quiet; (*sonido*) muted, muffled; (*persona: apático*) listless; **estar ~** (*fuego, luz*) to be out; (*Radio, TV etc*) to be off

apagar [apa'ɣar] *vt* to put out; (*Elec, Radio, TV*) to turn off; (*sonido*) to silence, muffle; (*sed*) to quench

apagón [apa'ɣon] *nm* blackout; power cut

apalabrar [apala'βrar] *vt* to agree to; (*contratar*) to engage

apalear [apale'ar] *vt* to beat, thrash

apantallar [apanta'ʎar] (*MÉX*) *vt* to impress

apañar [apa'ɲar] *vt* to pick up; (*asir*) to take hold of, grasp; (*reparar*) to mend, patch up; **apañarse** *vr* to manage, get along

apapachar [apapa'tʃar] (*MÉX: fam*) *vt* to cuddle, hug

aparador [apara'ðor] *nm* sideboard; (*MÉX: escaparate*) shop window

aparato [apa'rato] *nm* apparatus;

(*máquina*) machine; (*doméstico*) appliance; (*boato*) ostentation; **aparato digestivo** (*Anat*) digestive system; **aparatoso, -a** *adj* showy, ostentatious

aparcamiento [aparka'mjento] *nm* car park (BRIT), parking lot (US)

aparcar [apar'kar] *vt, vi* to park

aparear [apare'ar] *vt* (*objetos*) to pair, match; (*animales*) to mate; **aparearse** *vr* to make a pair; to mate

aparecer [apare'θer] *vi* to appear; **aparecerse** *vr* to appear

aparejador, a [aparexa'ðor, a] *nm/f* (*Arq*) master builder

aparejo [apa'rexo] *nm* harness; rigging; (*de poleas*) block and tackle

aparentar [aparen'tar] *vt* (*edad*) to look; (*fingir*): **~ tristeza** to pretend to be sad

aparente [apa'rente] *adj* apparent; (*adecuado*) suitable

aparezco *etc vb* V **aparecer**

aparición [apari'θjon] *nf* appearance; (*de libro*) publication; (*espectro*) apparition

apariencia [apa'rjenθja] *nf* (outward) appearance; **en ~** outwardly, seemingly

apartado, -a [apar'taðo, a] *adj* separate; (*lejano*) remote ▷ *nm* (*tipográfico*) paragraph; **apartado de correos** (ESP) post office box; **apartado postal** (LAM) post office box

apartamento [aparta'mento] *nm* apartment, flat (BRIT)

apartar [apar'tar] *vt* to separate; (*quitar*) to remove; **apartarse** *vr* to separate, part; (*irse*) to move away; to keep away

aparte [a'parte] *adv* (*separadamente*) separately; (*además*) besides ▷ *nm* aside; (*tipográfico*) new paragraph

aparthotel [aparto'tel] *nm* serviced apartments

apasionado, -a [apasjo'naðo, a] *adj* passionate

apasionar [apasjo'nar] *vt* to excite; **le apasiona el fútbol** she's crazy about football; **apasionarse** *vr* to get excited

apatía [apa'tia] *nf* apathy

apático, -a [a'patiko, a] *adj* apathetic

Apdo *abr* (= *Apartado (de Correos)*) PO Box

apeadero [apea'ðero] *nm* halt, stop, stopping place

apearse [ape'arse] *vr* (*jinete*) to dismount; (*bajarse*) to get down o out; (*Auto, Ferro*) to get off o out

apechugar [apetʃu'ɣar] *vr*: **~ con algo** to face up to sth

apegarse [ape'ɣarse] *vr*: **~ a** to become attached to; **apego** *nm* attachment, devotion

apelar [ape'lar] *vi* to appeal; **~ a** (*fig*) to resort to

apellidar [apeʎi'ðar] *vt* to call, name; **apellidarse** *vr*: **se apellida Pérez** her (sur)name's Pérez

apellido [ape'ʎiðo] *nm* surname

apenar [ape'nar] *vt* to grieve, trouble; (LAM: *avergonzar*) to embarrass; **apenarse** *vr* to grieve; (LAM: *avergonzarse*) to be embarrassed

apenas [a'penas] *adv* scarcely, hardly ▷ *conj* as soon as, no sooner

apéndice [a'pendiθe] *nm* appendix; **apendicitis** *nf* appendicitis

aperitivo [aperi'tiβo] *nm* (*bebida*) aperitif; (*comida*) appetizer

apertura [aper'tura] *nf* opening; (*Pol*) liberalization

apestar [apes'tar] *vt* to infect ▷ *vi*: **~ (a)** to stink (of)

apetecer [apete'θer] *vt*: **¿te apetece un café?** do you fancy a (cup of) coffee?; **apetecible** *adj* desirable; (*comida*) appetizing

apetito [ape'tito] *nm* appetite; **apetitoso, -a** *adj* appetizing; (*fig*) tempting

apiadarse [apja'ðarse] *vr*: **~ de** to take pity on

ápice ['apiθe] *nm* whit, iota

apilar [api'lar] *vt* to pile o heap up

apiñarse [api'ɲarse] *vr* to crowd o press together

apio ['apjo] *nm* celery

apisonadora [apisona'ðora] *nf* steamroller

aplacar [apla'kar] *vt* to placate

aplastante [aplas'tante] *adj* overwhelming; (*lógica*) compelling

aplastar [aplas'tar] *vt* to squash (flat); (*fig*) to crush

aplaudir [aplau'ðir] *vt* to applaud

aplauso [a'plauso] *nm* applause; (*fig*) approval, acclaim

aplazamiento [aplaθa'mjento] *nm* postponement

aplazar [apla'θar] *vt* to postpone, defer

aplicación [aplika'θjon] *nf* application; (*esfuerzo*) effort

aplicado, -a [apli'kaðo, a] *adj* diligent, hard-working

aplicar [apli'kar] *vt* (*ejecutar*) to apply; **aplicarse** *vr* to apply o.s.

aplique *etc* [a'plike] *vb* V **aplicar** ▷ *nm* wall light

aplomo [a'plomo] *nm* aplomb, self-assurance

apodar [apo'ðar] *vt* to nickname

apoderado [apoðe'raðo] *nm* agent,

representative

apoderarse [apoðe'rarse] *vr:* **~ de** to take possession of

apodo [a'poðo] *nm* nickname

apogeo [apo'xeo] *nm* peak, summit

apoquinar [apoki'nar] *(fam) vt* to fork out, cough up

aporrear [aporre'ar] *vt* to beat (up)

aportar [apor'tar] *vt* to contribute ▷ *vi* to reach port; **aportarse** *vr* (LAM: *llegar*) to arrive, come

aposta [a'posta] *adv* deliberately, on purpose

apostar [apos'tar] *vt* to bet, stake; (*tropas etc*) to station, post ▷ *vi* to bet

apóstol [a'postol] *nm* apostle

apóstrofo [a'postrofo] *nm* apostrophe

apoyar [apo'jar] *vt* to lean, rest; (*fig*) to support, back; **apoyarse** *vr:* **~se en** to lean on; **apoyo** *nm* (*gen*) support; backing, help

apreciable [apre'θjaβle] *adj* considerable; (*fig*) esteemed

apreciar [apre'θjar] *vt* to evaluate, assess; (*Com*) to appreciate, value; (*persona*) to respect; (*tamaño*) to gauge, assess; (*detalles*) to notice

aprecio [a'preθjo] *nm* valuation, estimate; (*fig*) appreciation

aprehender [apreen'der] *vt* to apprehend, detain

apremio [a'premjo] *nm* urgency

aprender [apren'der] *vt, vi* to learn; **~ algo de memoria** to learn sth (off) by heart

aprendiz, a [apren'diθ, a] *nm/f* apprentice; (*principiante*) learner; **aprendizaje** *nm* apprenticeship

aprensión [apren'sjon] *nm* apprehension, fear; **aprensivo, -a** *adj* apprehensive

apresar [apre'sar] *vt* to seize; (*capturar*) to capture

apresurado, -a [apresu'raðo, a] *adj* hurried, hasty

apresurar [apresu'rar] *vt* to hurry, accelerate; **apresurarse** *vr* to hurry, make haste

apretado, -a [apre'taðo, a] *adj* tight; (*escritura*) cramped

apretar [apre'tar] *vt* to squeeze; (*Tec*) to tighten; (*presionar*) to press together, pack ▷ *vi* to be too tight

apretón [apre'ton] *nm* squeeze; **apretón de manos** handshake

aprieto [a'prjeto] *nm* squeeze; (*dificultad*) difficulty; **estar en un ~** to be in a fix

aprisa [a'prisa] *adv* quickly, hurriedly

aprisionar [aprisjo'nar] *vt* to imprison

aprobación [aproβa'θjon] *nf* approval

aprobar [apro'βar] *vt* to approve (of); (*examen, materia*) to pass ▷ *vi* to pass

apropiado, -a [apro'pjaðo, a] *adj* suitable

apropiarse [apro'pjarse] *vr:* **~ de** to appropriate

aprovechado, -a [aproβe'tʃaðo, a] *adj* industrious, hard-working; (*económico*) thrifty; (*pey*) unscrupulous

aprovechar [aproβe'tʃar] *vt* to use; (*explotar*) to exploit; (*experiencia*) to profit from; (*oferta, oportunidad*) to take advantage of ▷ *vi* to progress, improve; **aprovecharse** *vr:* **~se de** to make use of; to take advantage of; **¡que aproveche!** enjoy your meal!

aproximación [aproksima'θjon] *nf* approximation; (*de lotería*) consolation prize

aproximar [aproksi'mar] *vt* to bring nearer; **aproximarse** *vr* to come near, approach

apruebo *etc vb* V **aprobar**

aptitud [apti'tuð] *nf* aptitude

apto, -a ['apto, a] *adj* suitable

apuesta [a'pwesta] *nf* bet, wager

apuesto, -a [a'pwesto, a] *adj* neat, elegant

apuntar [apun'tar] *vt* (*con arma*) to aim at; (*con dedo*) to point at o to; (*anotar*) to note (down); (*Teatro*) to prompt; **apuntarse** *vr* (*Deporte: tanto, victoria*) to score; (*Escol*) to enrol

▌ No confundir **apuntar** con la palabra inglesa *appoint*.

apunte [a'punte] *nm* note

apuñalar [apuɲa'lar] *vt* to stab

apurado, -a [apu'raðo, a] *adj* needy; (*difícil*) difficult; (*peligroso*) dangerous; (LAM: *con prisa*) hurried, rushed

apurar [apu'rar] *vt* (*agotar*) to drain; (*recursos*) to use up; (*molestar*) to annoy; **apurarse** *vr* (*preocuparse*) to worry; (LAM: *darse prisa*) to hurry

apuro [a'puro] *nm* (*aprieto*) fix, jam; (*escasez*) want, hardship; (*vergüenza*) embarrassment; (LAM: *prisa*) haste, urgency

aquejado, -a [ake'xaðo, a] *adj:* **~ de** (*Med*) afflicted by

aquel, aquella [a'kel, a'keʎa] *adj* that; **~los(as)** those

aquél, aquélla [a'kel, a'keʎa] *pron* that (one); **~los(as)** those (ones)

aquello [a'keʎo] *pron* that, that business

aquí [a'ki] *adv* (*lugar*) here; (*tiempo*) now; **~ arriba** up here; **~ mismo** right here; **~ yace** here lies; **de ~ a siete días** a week from now

ara ['ara] *nf:* **en ~s de** for the sake of

árabe ['araβe] *adj, nmf* Arab ▷ *nm* (*Ling*) Arabic

Arabia [a'raβja] nf Arabia; **Arabia Saudí**o **Saudita** Saudi Arabia

arado [a'raðo] nm plough

Aragón [ara'ɣon] nm Aragon; **aragonés, -esa** adj, nm/f Aragonese

arancel [aran'θel] nm tariff, duty

arandela [aran'dela] nf (Tec) washer

araña [a'raɲa] nf (Zool) spider; (lámpara) chandelier

arañar [ara'ɲar] vt to scratch

arañazo [ara'ɲaθo] nm scratch

arbitrar [arβi'trar] vt to arbitrate in; (Deporte) to referee ▷ vi to arbitrate

arbitrario, -a [arβi'trarjo, a] adj arbitrary

árbitro ['arβitro] nm arbitrator; (Deporte) referee; (Tenis) umpire

árbol ['arβol] nm (Bot) tree; (Náut) mast; (Tec) axle, shaft; **árbol de Navidad** Christmas tree

arboleda [arβo'leða] nf grove, plantation

arbusto [ar'βusto] nm bush, shrub

arca ['arka] nf chest, box

arcada [ar'kaða] nf arcade; (de puente) arch, span; **arcadas** nfpl (náuseas) retching sg

arcaico, -a [ar'kaiko, a] adj archaic

arce ['arθe] nm maple tree

arcén [ar'θen] nm (de autopista) hard shoulder; (de carretera) verge

archipiélago [artʃi'pjelaɣo] nm archipelago

archivador [artʃiβa'ðor] nm filing cabinet

archivar [artʃi'βar] vt to file (away); **archivo** nm file, archive(s) pl; **archivo adjunto** (Inform) attachment; **archivo de seguridad** (Inform) backup file

arcilla [ar'θiʎa] nf clay

arco ['arko] nm arch; (Mat) arc; (Mil, Mús) bow; **arco iris** rainbow

arder [ar'ðer] vi to burn; **estar que arde** (persona) to fume

ardid [ar'ðið] nm ploy, trick

ardiente [ar'ðjente] adj burning, ardent

ardilla [ar'ðiʎa] nf squirrel

ardor [ar'ðor] nm (calor) heat; (fig) ardour; **ardor de estómago** heartburn

arduo, -a ['arðwo, a] adj arduous

área ['area] nf area; (Deporte) penalty area

arena [a'rena] nf sand; (de una lucha) arena; **arenas movedizas** quicksand sg; **arenal** [are'nal] nm (terreno arenoso) sandy spot

arenisca [are'niska] nf sandstone; (cascajo) grit

arenoso, -a [are'noso, a] adj sandy

arenque [a'renke] nm herring

arete [a'rete] (MÉx) nm earring

Argel [ar'xel] n Algiers; **Argelia** nf Algeria; **argelino, -a** adj, nm/f Algerian

Argentina [arxen'tina] nf (tb: **la ~**) Argentina

argentino, -a [arxen'tino, a] adj Argentinian; (de plata) silvery ▷ nm/f Argentinian

argolla [ar'ɣoʎa] nf (large) ring

argot [ar'ɣo] (pl **~s**) nm slang

argucia [ar'ɣuθja] nf subtlety, sophistry

argumentar [arɣumen'tar] vt, vi to argue

argumento [arɣu'mento] nm argument; (razonamiento) reasoning; (de novela etc) plot; (Cine, TV) storyline

aria ['arja] nf aria

aridez [ari'ðeθ] nf aridity, dryness

árido, -a ['ariðo, a] adj arid, dry

Aries ['arjes] nm Aries

arisco, -a [a'risko, a] adj surly; (insociable) unsociable

aristócrata [aris'tokrata] nmf aristocrat

arma ['arma] nf arm; **armas** nfpl arms; **arma blanca** blade, knife; **arma de doble filo** double-edged sword; **arma de fuego** firearm; **armas de destrucción masiva** weapons of mass destruction

armada [ar'maða] nf armada; (flota) fleet

armadillo [arma'ðiʎo] nm armadillo

armado, -a [ar'maðo, a] adj armed; (Tec) reinforced

armadura [arma'ðura] nf (Mil) armour; (Tec) framework; (Zool) skeleton; (Física) armature

armamento [arma'mento] nm armament; (Náut) fitting-out

armar [ar'mar] vt (soldado) to arm; (máquina) to assemble; (navío) to fit out; **~la, ~ un lío** to start a row, kick up a fuss

armario [ar'marjo] nm wardrobe; (de cocina, baño) cupboard; **armario empotrado** built-in cupboard

armatoste [arma'toste] nm (mueble) monstrosity; (máquina) contraption

armazón [arma'θon] nf o m body, chassis; (de mueble etc) frame; (Arq) skeleton

armiño [ar'miɲo] nm stoat; (piel) ermine

armisticio [armis'tiθjo] nm armistice

armonía [armo'nia] nf harmony

armónica [ar'monika] nf harmonica

armonizar [armoni'θar] vt to harmonize; (diferencias) to reconcile

aro ['aro] nm ring; (tejo) quoit; (cs: pendiente) earring

aroma [a'roma] nm aroma, scent; **aromaterapia** n aromatherapy; **aromático, -a** [aro'matiko, a] adj aromatic

arpa ['arpa] nf harp

arpía [ar'pia] *nf* shrew

arpón [ar'pon] *nm* harpoon

arqueología [arkeolo'xia] *nf* archaeology; **arqueólogo, -a** *nm/f* archaeologist

arquetipo [arke'tipo] *nm* archetype

arquitecto [arki'tekto] *nm* architect; **arquitectura** *nf* architecture

arrabal [arra'βal] *nm* poor suburb, slum; **arrabales** *nmpl* (*afueras*) outskirts

arraigar [arrai'ɣar] *vt* to establish ▷ *vi* to take root

arrancar [arran'kar] *vt* (*sacar*) to extract, pull out; (*arrebatar*) to snatch (away); (*Inform*) to boot; (*fig*) to extract ▷ *vi* (*Auto, máquina*) to start; (*ponerse en marcha*) to get going; **~ de** to stem from

arranque *etc* [a'rranke] *vb* V **arrancar** ▷ *nm* sudden start; (*Auto*) start; (*fig*) fit, outburst

arrasar [arra'sar] *vt* (*aplanar*) to level, flatten; (*destruir*) to demolish

arrastrar [arras'trar] *vt* to drag (along); (*fig*) to drag down, degrade; (*agua, viento*) to carry away ▷ *vi* to drag, trail on the ground; **arrastrarse** *vr* to crawl; (*fig*) to grovel; **llevar algo arrastrado** to drag sth along

arrear [arre'ar] *vt* to drive on, urge on ▷ *vi* to hurry along

arrebatar [arreβa'tar] *vt* to snatch (away), seize; (*fig*) to captivate

arrebato [arre'βato] *nm* fit of rage, fury; (*éxtasis*) rapture

arrecife [arre'θife] *nm* reef

arreglado, -a [arre'ɣlaðo, a] *adj* (*ordenado*) neat, orderly; (*moderado*) moderate, reasonable

arreglar [arre'ɣlar] *vt* (*poner orden*) to tidy up; (*algo roto*) to fix, repair; (*problema*) to solve; **arreglarse** *vr* to reach an understanding; **arreglárselas** (*fam*) to get by, manage

arreglo [a'rreɣlo] *nm* settlement; (*orden*) order; (*acuerdo*) agreement; (*Mús*) arrangement, setting

arremangar [arreman'gar] *vt* to roll up, turn up; **arremangarse** *vr* to roll up one's sleeves

arremeter [arreme'ter] *vi*: **~ contra** to attack, rush at

arrendamiento [arrenda'mjento] *nm* letting; (*alquilar*) hiring; (*contrato*) lease; (*alquiler*) rent; **arrendar** *vt* to let, lease; to rent; **arrendatario, -a** *nm/f* tenant

arreos [a'rreos] *nmpl* (*de caballo*) harness *sg*, trappings

arrepentimiento [arrepenti'mjento] *nm* regret, repentance

arrepentirse [arrepen'tirse] *vr* to repent; **~ de** to regret

arresto [a'rresto] *nm* arrest; (*Mil*) detention; (*audacia*) boldness, daring; **arresto domiciliario** house arrest

arriar [a'rrjar] *vt* (*velas*) to haul down; (*bandera*) to lower, strike; (*cable*) to pay out

○ **PALABRA CLAVE**

arriba [a'rriβa] *adv* **1** (*posición*) above; **desde arriba** from above; **arriba de todo** at the very top, right on top; **Juan está arriba** Juan is upstairs; **lo arriba mencionado** the aforementioned

2 (*dirección*): **calle arriba** up the street

3 **de arriba abajo** from top to bottom; **mirar a algn de arriba abajo** to look sb up and down

4 **para arriba: de 5000 euros para arriba** from 5000 euros up(wards)

▷ *adj*: **de arriba: el piso de arriba** the upstairs (*BRIT*) flat o apartment; **la parte de arriba** the top o upper part

▷ *prep*: **arriba de** (*LAM: por encima de*) above; **arriba de 200 dólares** more than 200 dollars

▷ *excl*: **¡arriba!** up!; **¡manos arriba!** hands up!; **¡arriba España!** long live Spain!

arribar [arri'βar] *vi* to put into port; (*llegar*) to arrive

arriendo *etc* [a'rrjendo] *vb* V **arrendar** ▷ *nm* = **arrendamiento**

arriesgado, -a [arrjes'ɣaðo, a] *adj* (*peligroso*) risky; (*audaz*) bold, daring

arriesgar [arrjes'ɣar] *vt* to risk; (*poner en peligro*) to endanger; **arriesgarse** *vr* to take a risk

arrimar [arri'mar] *vt* (*acercar*) to bring close; (*poner de lado*) to set aside; **arrimarse** *vr* to come close o closer; **~se a** to lean on

arrinconar [arrinko'nar] *vt* (*colocar*) to put in a corner; (*enemigo*) to corner; (*fig*) to put on one side; (*abandonar*) to push aside

arroba [a'rroβa] *nf* (*Internet*) at (sign)

arrodillarse [arroði'ʎarse] *vr* to kneel (down)

arrogante [arro'ɣante] *adj* arrogant

arrojar [arro'xar] *vt* to throw, hurl; (*humo*) to emit, give out; (*Com*) to yield, produce; **arrojarse** *vr* to throw o hurl o.s.

arrojo [a'rroxo] *nm* daring

arrollador, a [arroʎa'ðor, a] *adj* overwhelming

arrollar [arro'ʎar] *vt* (*Auto etc*) to run over, knock down; (*Deporte*) to crush

arropar [arro'par] *vt* to cover, wrap up;

arroparse vr to wrap o.s. up

arroyo [a'rrojo] nm stream; (de la calle) gutter

arroz [a'rroθ] nm rice; **arroz con leche** rice pudding

arruga [a'rruɣa] nf (de cara) wrinkle; (de vestido) crease; **arrugar** [arru'ɣar] vt to wrinkle; to crease; **arrugarse** vr to get creased

arruinar [arrwi'nar] vt to ruin, wreck; **arruinarse** vr to be ruined, go bankrupt

arsenal [arse'nal] nm naval dockyard; (Mil) arsenal

arte ['arte] (gen m en sg y siempre f en pl) nm art; (maña) skill, guile; **artes** nfpl (bellas artes) arts

artefacto [arte'fakto] nm appliance

arteria [ar'terja] nf artery

artesanía [artesa'nia] nf craftsmanship; (artículos) handicrafts pl; **artesano, -a** nm/f artisan, craftsman(-woman)

ártico, -a ['artiko, a] adj Arctic ▷ nm: **el Á~** the Arctic

articulación [artikula'θjon] nf articulation; (Med, Tec) joint

artículo [ar'tikulo] nm article; (cosa) thing, article; **artículos** nmpl (Com) goods; **artículos de escritorio** stationery

artífice [ar'tifiθe] nmf (fig) architect

artificial [artifi'θjal] adj artificial

artillería [artiʎe'ria] nf artillery

artilugio [arti'luxjo] nm gadget

artimaña [arti'maɲa] nf trap, snare; (astucia) cunning

artista [ar'tista] nmf (pintor) artist, painter; (Teatro) artist, artiste; **artista de cine** film actor/actress; **artístico, -a** adj artistic

artritis [ar'tritis] nf arthritis

arveja [ar'βexa] (LAM) nf pea

arzobispo [arθo'βispo] nm archbishop

as [as] nm ace

asa ['asa] nf handle; (fig) lever

asado [a'saðo] nm roast (meat); (LAM: barbacoa) barbecue

asador [asa'ðor] nm spit

asadura [asa'ðura] nf entrails pl, offal

asalariado, -a [asala'rjaðo, a] adj paid, salaried ▷ nm/f wage earner

asaltar [asal'tar] vt to attack, assault; (fig) to assail; **asalto** nm attack, assault; (Deporte) round

asamblea [asam'blea] nf assembly; (reunión) meeting

asar [a'sar] vt to roast

ascendencia [asθen'denθja] nf ancestry; (LAM: influencia) ascendancy; **de ~ francesa** of French origin

ascender [asθen'der] vi (subir) to ascend, rise; (ser promovido) to gain promotion ▷ vt to promote; **~ a** to amount to; **ascendiente** nm influence ▷ nmf ancestor

ascensión [asθen'sjon] nf ascent; (Rel): **la A~** the Ascension

ascenso [as'θenso] nm ascent; (promoción) promotion

ascensor [asθen'sor] nm lift (BRIT), elevator (US)

asco ['asko] nm: **¡qué ~!** how revolting o disgusting; **el ajo me da ~** I hate o loathe garlic; **estar hecho un ~** to be filthy

ascua ['askwa] nf ember

aseado, -a [ase'aðo, a] adj clean; (arreglado) tidy; (pulcro) smart

asear [ase'ar] vt to clean, wash; to tidy (up)

asediar [ase'ðjar] vt (Mil) to besiege, lay siege to; (fig) to chase, pester; **asedio** nm siege; (Com) run

asegurado, -a [aseɣu'raðo, a] adj insured

asegurador, a [aseɣura'ðor, a] nm/f insurer

asegurar [aseɣu'rar] vt (consolidar) to secure, fasten; (dar garantía de) to guarantee; (preservar) to safeguard; (afirmar, dar por cierto) to assure, affirm; (tranquilizar) to reassure; (tomar un seguro) to insure; **asegurarse** vr to assure o.s., make sure

asemejarse [aseme'xarse] vr to be alike; **~ a** to be like, resemble

asentado, -a [asen'taðo, a] adj established, settled

asentar [asen'tar] vt (sentar) to seat, sit down; (poner) to place, establish; (alisar) to level, smooth down o out; (anotar) to note down ▷ vi to be suitable, suit

asentir [asen'tir] vi to assent, agree; **~ con la cabeza** to nod (one's head)

aseo [a'seo] nm cleanliness; **aseos** nmpl (servicios) toilet sg (BRIT), cloakroom sg (BRIT), restroom sg (US)

aséptico, -a [a'septiko, a] adj germ-free,

free from infection

asequible [ase'kiβle] *adj (precio)* reasonable; *(meta)* attainable; *(persona)* approachable

asesinar [asesi'nar] *vt* to murder; *(Pol)* to assassinate; **asesinato** *nm* murder; assassination

asesino, -a [ase'sino, a] *nm/f* murderer, killer; *(Pol)* assassin

asesor, a [ase'sor, a] *nm/f* adviser, consultant; **asesorar** [aseso'rar] *vt (Jur)* to advise, give legal advice to; *(Com)* to act as consultant to; **asesorarse** *vr*: **asesorarse con** *o* **de** to take advice from, consult; **asesoría** *nf (cargo)* consultancy; *(oficina)* consultant's office

asestar [ases'tar] *vt (golpe)* to deal, strike

asfalto [as'falto] *nm* asphalt

asfixia [as'fiksja] *nf* asphyxia, suffocation; **asfixiar** [asfik'sjar] *vt* to asphyxiate, suffocate; **asfixiarse** *vr* to be asphyxiated, suffocate

así [a'si] *adv (de esta manera)* in this way, like this, thus; *(aunque)* although; *(tan pronto como)* as soon as; **~ que** so; **~ como** as well as; **~ y todo** even so; **¿no es ~?** isn't it?, didn't you? *etc*; **~ de grande** this big

Asia ['asja] *nf* Asia; **asiático, -a** *adj, nm/f* Asian, Asiatic

asiduo, -a [a'siðwo, a] *adj* assiduous; *(frecuente)* frequent ▷ *nm/f* regular (customer)

asiento [a'sjento] *nm (mueble)* seat, chair; *(de coche, en tribunal etc)* seat; *(localidad)* seat, place; *(fundamento)* site; **asiento delantero/ trasero** front/back seat

asignación [asiɣna'θjon] *nf (atribución)* assignment; *(reparto)* allocation; *(sueldo)* salary; **asignación (semanal)** pocket money

asignar [asiɣ'nar] *vt* to assign, allocate

asignatura [asiɣna'tura] *nf* subject; course

asilo [a'silo] *nm (refugio)* asylum, refuge; *(establecimiento)* home, institution; **asilo político** political asylum

asimilar [asimi'lar] *vt* to assimilate

asimismo [asi'mismo] *adv* in the same way, likewise

asistencia [asis'tenθja] *nf* audience; *(Med)* attendance; *(ayuda)* assistance; **asistencia en carretera** roadside assistance; **asistente** *nmf* assistant; **los asistentes** those present; **asistente social** social worker

asistido, -a [asis'tiðo, a] *adj*: **~ por ordenador** computer-assisted

asistir [asis'tir] *vt* to assist, help ▷ *vi*: **~ a**

asma ['asma] *nf* asthma

asno ['asno] *nm* donkey; *(fig)* ass

asociación [asoθja'θjon] *nf* association; *(Com)* partnership; **asociado, -a** *adj* associate ▷ *nm/f* associate; *(Com)* partner

asociar [aso'θjar] *vt* to associate

asomar [aso'mar] *vt* to show, stick out ▷ *vi* to appear; **asomarse** *vr* to appear, show up; **~ la cabeza por la ventana** to put one's head out of the window

asombrar [asom'brar] *vt* to amaze, astonish; **asombrarse** *vr (sorprenderse)* to be amazed; *(asustarse)* to get a fright; **asombro** *nm* amazement, astonishment; *(susto)* fright; **asombroso, -a** *adj* astonishing, amazing

asomo [a'somo] *nm* hint, sign

aspa ['aspa] *nf (cruz)* cross; *(de molino)* sail; **en ~** X-shaped

aspaviento [aspa'βjento] *nm* exaggerated display of feeling; *(fam)* fuss

aspecto [as'pekto] *nm (apariencia)* look, appearance; *(fig)* aspect

áspero, -a ['aspero, a] *adj* rough; bitter; sour; harsh

aspersión [asper'sjon] *nf* sprinkling

aspiración [aspira'θjon] *nf* breath, inhalation; *(Mús)* short pause; **aspiraciones** *nfpl (ambiciones)* aspirations

aspirador [aspira'ðor] *nm* = **aspiradora**

aspiradora [aspira'ðora] *nf* vacuum cleaner, Hoover®

aspirante [aspi'rante] *nmf (candidato)* candidate; *(Deporte)* contender

aspirar [aspi'rar] *vt* to breathe in ▷ *vi*: **~ a** to aspire to

aspirina [aspi'rina] *nf* aspirin

asqueroso, -a [aske'roso, a] *adj* disgusting, sickening

asta ['asta] *nf* lance; *(arpón)* spear; *(mango)* shaft, handle; *(Zool)* horn; **a media ~** at half mast

asterisco [aste'risko] *nm* asterisk

astilla [as'tiʎa] *nf* splinter; *(pedacito)* chip; **astillas** *nfpl (leña)* firewood *sg*

astillero [asti'ʎero] *nm* shipyard

astro ['astro] *nm* star

astrología [astrolo'xia] *nf* astrology; **astrólogo, -a** *nm/f* astrologer

astronauta [astro'nauta] *nmf* astronaut

astronomía [astrono'mia] *nf* astronomy

astucia [as'tuθja] *nf* astuteness; *(ardid)* clever trick

asturiano, -a [astu'rjano, a] *adj, nm/f* Asturian

astuto, -a [as'tuto, a] *adj* astute; *(taimado)* cunning

asumir [asu'mir] *vt* to assume

asunción [asun'θjon] *nf* assumption; *(Rel):* **A~** Assumption

asunto [a'sunto] *nm (tema)* matter, subject; *(negocio)* business

asustar [asus'tar] *vt* to frighten; **asustarse** *vr* to be (*o* become) frightened

atacar [ata'kar] *vt* to attack

atadura [ata'ðura] *nf* bond, tie

atajar [ata'xar] *vt (enfermedad, mal)* to stop ▷ *vi (persona)* to take a short cut

atajo [a'taxo] *nm* short cut

atañer [ata'ɲer] *vi:* **~ a** to concern

ataque *etc* [a'take] *vb* V **atacar** ▷ *nm* attack; **ataque cardíaco** heart attack

atar [a'tar] *vt* to tie, tie up

atarantado, -a [ataran'taðo, a] *(MÉX) adj (aturdido)* dazed

atardecer [atarðe'θer] *vi* to get dark ▷ *nm* evening; *(crepúsculo)* dusk

atareado, -a [atare'aðo, a] *adj* busy

atascar [atas'kar] *vt* to clog up; *(obstruir)* to jam; *(fig)* to hinder; **atascarse** *vr* to stall; *(cañería)* to get blocked up; **atasco** *nm* obstruction; *(Auto)* traffic jam

ataúd [ata'uð] *nm* coffin

ataviar [ata'βjar] *vt* to deck, array

atemorizar [atemori'θar] *vt* to frighten, scare

Atenas [a'tenas] *n* Athens

atención [aten'θjon] *nf* attention; *(bondad)* kindness ▷ *excl* (be) careful!, look out!

atender [aten'der] *vt* to attend to, look after; *(Tel)* to answer ▷ *vi* to pay attention

atenerse [ate'nerse] *vr:* **~ a** to abide by, adhere to

atentado [aten'taðo] *nm* crime, illegal act; *(asalto)* assault; *(tb:* **~ terrorista)** terrorist attack; **~ contra la vida de algn** attempt on sb's life; **atentado suicida** suicide bombing

atentamente [atenta'mente] *adv:* **Le saluda ~** Yours faithfully

atentar [aten'tar] *vi:* **~ a** *o* **contra** to commit an outrage against

atento, -a [a'tento, a] *adj* attentive, observant; *(cortés)* polite, thoughtful; **estar ~ a** *(explicación)* to pay attention to

atenuar [ate'nwar] *vt (disminuir)* to lessen, minimize

ateo, -a [a'teo, a] *adj* atheistic ▷ *nm/f* atheist

aterrador, a [aterra'ðor, a] *adj* frightening

aterrizaje [aterri'θaxe] *nm* landing; **aterrizaje forzoso** emergency *o* forced landing

aterrizar [aterri'θar] *vi* to land

aterrorizar [aterrori'θar] *vt* to terrify

atesorar [ateso'rar] *vt* to hoard

atestar [ates'tar] *vt* to pack, stuff; *(Jur)* to attest, testify to

atestiguar [atesti'ɣwar] *vt* to testify to, bear witness to

atiborrar [atiβo'rrar] *vt* to fill, stuff; **atiborrarse** *vr* to stuff o.s.

ático ['atiko] *nm (desván)* attic; *(apartamento)* penthouse

atinado, -a [ati'naðo, a] *adj (sensato)* wise; *(correcto)* right, correct

atinar [ati'nar] *vi (al disparar):* **~ al blanco** to hit the target; *(fig)* to be right

atizar [ati'θar] *vt* to poke; *(horno etc)* to stoke; *(fig)* to stir up, rouse

atlántico, -a [at'lantiko, a] *adj* Atlantic ▷ *nm:* **el (océano) A~** the Atlantic (Ocean)

atlas ['atlas] *nm inv* atlas

atleta [at'leta] *nm* athlete; **atlético, -a** *adj* athletic; **atletismo** *nm* athletics *sg*

atmósfera [at'mosfera] *nf* atmosphere

atolladero [atoʎa'ðero] *nm (fig)* jam, fix

atómico, -a [a'tomiko, a] *adj* atomic

átomo ['atomo] *nm* atom

atónito, -a [a'tonito, a] *adj* astonished, amazed

atontado, -a [aton'taðo, a] *adj* stunned; *(bobo)* silly, daft

atormentar [atormen'tar] *vt* to torture; *(molestar)* to torment; *(acosar)* to plague, harass

atornillar [atorni'ʎar] *vt* to screw on *o* down

atosigar [atosi'ɣar] *vt* to harass, pester

atracador, a [atraka'ðor, a] *nm/f* robber

atracar [atra'kar] *vt (Náut)* to moor; *(robar)* to hold up, rob ▷ *vi* to moor; **atracarse** *vr:* **~se (de)** to stuff o.s. (with)

atracción [atrak'θjon] *nf* attraction

atraco [a'trako] *nm* holdup, robbery

atracón [atra'kon] *nm:* **darse** *o* **pegarse un ~ (de)** *(fam)* to stuff o.s. (with)

atractivo, -a [atrak'tiβo, a] *adj* attractive ▷ *nm* appeal

atraer [atra'er] *vt* to attract

atragantarse [atraɣan'tarse] *vr:* **~ (con)** to choke (on); **se me ha atragantado el chico** I can't stand the boy

atrancar [atran'kar] *vt (puerta)* to bar, bolt

atrapar [atra'par] *vt* to trap; *(resfriado etc)* to catch

atrás [a'tras] *adv (movimiento)* back(-wards); *(lugar)* behind; *(tiempo)* previously; **ir hacia ~** to go back(wards), to go to the rear; **estar ~** to be behind *o* at the back

atrasado, -a [atra'saðo, a] *adj* slow;

(*pago*) overdue, late; (*país*) backward

atrasar [atra'sar] *vi* to be slow; **atrasarse** *vr* to remain behind; (*tren*) to be o run late; **atraso** *nm* slowness; lateness, delay; (*de país*) backwardness; **atrasos** *nmpl* (*Com*) arrears

atravesar [atraβe'sar] *vt* (*cruzar*) to cross (over); (*traspasar*) to pierce; to go through; (*poner al través*) to lay o put across; **atravesarse** *vr* to come in between; (*intervenir*) to interfere

atravieso *etc vb* V **atravesar**

atreverse [atre'βerse] *vr* to dare; (*insolentarse*) to be insolent; **atrevido, -a** *adj* daring; insolent; **atrevimiento** *nm* daring; insolence

atribución [atriβu'θjon] *nf* attribution; **atribuciones** *nfpl* (*Pol*) powers; (*Admin*) responsibilities

atribuir [atriβu'ir] *vt* to attribute; (*funciones*) to confer

atributo [atri'βuto] *nm* attribute

atril [a'tril] *nm* (*para libro*) lectern; (*Mús*) music stand

atropellar [atrope'ʎar] *vt* (*derribar*) to knock over o down; (*empujar*) to push (aside); (*Auto*) to run over, run down; (*agraviar*) to insult; **atropello** *nm* (*Auto*) accident; (*empujón*) push; (*agravio*) wrong; (*atrocidad*) outrage

atroz [a'troθ] *adj* atrocious, awful

ATS *nmf abr* (= *Ayudante Técnico Sanitario*) nurse

atuendo [a'twendo] *nm* attire

atún [a'tun] *nm* tuna

aturdir [atur'ðir] *vt* to stun; (*de ruido*) to deafen; (*fig*) to dumbfound, bewilder

audacia [au'ðaθja] *nf* boldness, audacity; **audaz** *adj* bold, audacious

audición [auði'θjon] *nf* hearing; (*Teatro*) audition

audiencia [au'ðjenθja] *nf* audience; (*Jur: tribunal*) court

audífono [au'ðifono] *nm* (*para sordos*) hearing aid

auditor [auði'tor] *nm* (*Jur*) judge advocate; (*Com*) auditor

auditorio [auði'torjo] *nm* audience; (*sala*) auditorium

auge [auxe] *nm* boom; (*clímax*) climax

augurar [auxu'rar] *vt* to predict; (*presagiar*) to portend

augurio [au'xurjo] *nm* omen

aula ['aula] *nf* classroom; (*en universidad etc*) lecture room

aullar [au'ʎar] *vi* to howl, yell

aullido [au'ʎiðo] *nm* howl, yell

aumentar [aumen'tar] *vt* to increase;

(*precios*) to put up; (*producción*) to step up; (*con microscopio, anteojos*) to magnify ▷ *vi* to increase, be on the increase; **aumentarse** *vr* to increase, be on the increase; **aumento** *nm* increase; rise

aun [a'un] *adv* even; **~ así** even so; **~ más** even o yet more

aún [a'un] *adv*: **~ está aquí** he's still here; **~ no lo sabemos** we don't know yet; **¿no ha venido ~?** hasn't she come yet?

aunque [a'unke] *conj* though, although, even though

aúpa [a'upa] *excl* come on!

auricular [auriku'lar] *nm* (*Tel*) receiver; **auriculares** *nmpl* (*cascos*) headphones

aurora [au'rora] *nf* dawn

ausencia [au'senθja] *nf* absence

ausentarse [ausen'tarse] *vr* to go away; (*por poco tiempo*) to go out

ausente [au'sente] *adj* absent

austero, -a [aus'tero, a] *adj* austere

austral [aus'tral] *adj* southern ▷ *nm* monetary unit of Argentina

Australia [aus'tralja] *nf* Australia; **australiano, -a** *adj, nm/f* Australian

Austria ['austrja] *nf* Austria; **austríaco, -a** *adj, nm/f* Austrian

auténtico, -a [au'tentiko, a] *adj* authentic

auto ['auto] *nm* (*Jur*) edict, decree; (: *orden*) writ; (*Auto*) car; **autos** *nmpl* (*Jur*) proceedings; (: *acta*) court record *sg*

autoadhesivo [autoaðe'siβo] *adj* self-adhesive; (*sobre*) self-sealing

autobiografía [autoβjoɤra'fia] *nf* autobiography

autobomba [auto'bomba] (*RPL*) *nm* fire engine

autobronceador [autoβronθea'ðor] *adj* self-tanning

autobús [auto'βus] *nm* bus; **autobús de línea** long-distance coach

autocar [auto'kar] *nm* coach (*BRIT*), (passenger) bus (*US*)

autóctono, -a [au'toktono, a] *adj* native, indigenous

autodefensa [autoðe'fensa] *nf* self-defence

autodidacta [autoði'ðakta] *adj* self-taught

autoescuela [autoes'kwela] (*ESP*) *nf* driving school

autógrafo [au'toɤrafo] *nm* autograph

autómata [au'tomata] *nm* automaton

automático, -a [auto'matiko, a] *adj* automatic ▷ *nm* press stud

automóvil [auto'moβil] *nm* (motor) car (*BRIT*), automobile (*US*); **automovilismo** *nm*

(actividad) motoring; (Deporte) motor racing;
automovilista nmf motorist, driver
autonomía [auto'nomia] nf autonomy;
autónomo, -a (ESP), **autonómico, -a** (ESP)
adj (Pol) autonomous
autopista [auto'pista] nf motorway
(BRIT), freeway (US); **autopista de cuota**
(ESP) o **peaje** (MÉX) toll (BRIT) o turnpike
(US) road
autopsia [au'topsja] nf autopsy,
postmortem
autor, a [au'tor, a] nm/f author
autoridad [autori'ðað] nf authority;
autoritario, -a adj authoritarian
autorización [autoriθa'θjon] nf
authorization; **autorizado, -a** adj
authorized; (aprobado) approved
autorizar [autori'θar] vt to authorize;
(aprobar) to approve
autoservicio [autoser'βiθjo] nm (tienda)
self-service shop (BRIT) o store (US);
(restaurante) self-service restaurant
autostop [auto'stop] nm hitch-hiking;
hacer ~ to hitch-hike; **autostopista** nmf
hitch-hiker
autovía [auto'βia] nf ≈ A-road (BRIT), dual
carriageway (BRIT), ≈ state highway (US)
auxiliar [auksi'ljar] vt to help ▷ nmf
assistant; **auxilio** nm assistance, help;
primeros auxilios first aid sg
Av abr (= Avenida) Av(e)
aval [a'βal] nm guarantee; (persona)
guarantor
avalancha [aβa'lantʃa] nf avalanche
avance [a'βanθe] nm advance; (pago)
advance payment; (Cine) trailer
avanzar [aβan'θar] vt, vi to advance
avaricia [aβa'riθja] nf avarice, greed;
avaricioso, -a adj avaricious, greedy
avaro, -a [a'βaro, a] adj miserly, mean
▷ nm/f miser
Avda abr (= Avenida) Av(e)
AVE ['aβe] nm abr (= Alta Velocidad Española)
≈ bullet train
ave ['aβe] nf bird; **ave de rapiña** bird of
prey
avecinarse [aβeθi'narse] vr (tormenta: fig)
to be on the way
avellana [aβe'ʎana] nf hazelnut;
avellano nm hazel tree
avemaría [aβema'ria] nm Hail Mary,
Ave Maria
avena [a'βena] nf oats pl
avenida [aβe'niða] nf (calle) avenue
aventajar [aβenta'xar] vt (sobrepasar) to
surpass, outstrip
aventón [aβen'ton] (MÉX: fam) nm ride;
dar ~ a algn to give sb a ride

aventura [aβen'tura] nf adventure;
aventurero, -a adj adventurous
avergonzar [aβerɣon'θar] vt to shame;
(desconcertar) to embarrass; **avergonzarse**
vr to be ashamed; to be embarrassed
avería [aβe'ria] nf (Tec) breakdown, fault
averiado, -a [aβe'rjaðo, a] adj broken
down; "**~**" "out of order"
averiguar [aβeri'ɣwar] vt to investigate;
(descubrir) to find out, ascertain
avestruz [aβes'truθ] nm ostrich
aviación [aβja'θjon] nf aviation; (fuerzas
aéreas) air force
aviador, a [aβja'ðor, a] nm/f aviator,
airman(-woman)
ávido, -a ['aβiðo, a] adj avid, eager
avinagrado, -a [aβina'ɣraðo, a] adj
sour, acid
avión [a'βjon] nm aeroplane; (ave) martin;
avión de reacción jet (plane)
avioneta [aβjo'neta] nf light aircraft
avisar [aβi'sar] vt (advertir) to warn,
notify; (informar) to tell; (aconsejar) to advise,
counsel; **aviso** nm warning; (noticia) notice
avispa [a'βispa] nf wasp
avispado, -a [aβis'paðo, a] adj sharp,
clever
avivar [aβi'βar] vt to strengthen, intensify
axila [ak'sila] nf armpit
ay [ai] excl (dolor) ow!, ouch!; (aflicción) oh!,
oh dear!; **¡~ de mi!** poor me!
ayer [a'jer] adv, nm yesterday; **antes de**
~ the day before yesterday; **~ mismo** only
yesterday
ayote [a'jote] (CAM) nm pumpkin
ayuda [a'juða] nf help, assistance ▷ nm
page; **ayudante** nmf assistant, helper;
(Escol) assistant; (Mil) adjutant
ayudar [aju'ðar] vt to help, assist
ayunar [aju'nar] vi to fast; **ayunas**
nfpl: **estar en ayunas** to be fasting; **ayuno**
nm fast; fasting
ayuntamiento [ajunta'mjento] nm
(consejo) town (o city) council; (edificio) town
(o city) hall
azafata [aθa'fata] nf air stewardess
azafrán [aθa'fran] nm saffron
azahar [aθa'ar] nm orange/lemon
blossom
azar [a'θar] nm (casualidad) chance, fate;
(desgracia) misfortune, accident; **por ~** by
chance; **al ~** at random
Azores [a'θores] nfpl: **las ~** the Azores
azotar [aθo'tar] vt to whip, beat; (pegar)
to spank; **azote** nm (látigo) whip; (latigazo)
lash, stroke; (en las nalgas) spank; (calamidad)
calamity
azotea [aθo'tea] nf (flat) roof

azteca [aθ'teka] *adj, nmf* Aztec
azúcar [a'θukar] *nm* sugar; **azucarado, -a** *adj* sugary, sweet
azucarero, -a [aθuka'rero, a] *adj* sugar *cpd* ▷ *nm* sugar bowl
azucena [aθu'θena] *nf* white lily
azufre [a'θufre] *nm* sulphur
azul [a'θul] *adj, nm* blue; **azul celeste/ marino** sky/navy blue
azulejo [aθu'lexo] *nm* tile
azuzar [aθu'θar] *vt* to incite, egg on

b

B.A. *abr* (= *Buenos Aires*) B.A.
baba ['baβa] *nf* spittle, saliva; **babear** *vi* to drool, slaver
babero [ba'βero] *nm* bib
babor [ba'βor] *nm* port (side)
babosada [baβo'saða] (*MÉX, CAM: fam*) *nf* drivel; **baboso, -a** [ba'βoso, a] (*LAM: fam*) *adj* silly
baca ['baka] *nf* (*Auto*) luggage *o* roof rack
bacalao [baka'lao] *nm* cod (fish)
bache ['batʃe] *nm* pothole, rut; (*fig*) bad patch
bachillerato [batʃiʎe'rato] *nm* higher secondary school course
bacinica [baθi'nika] (*LAM*) *nf* potty
bacteria [bak'terja] *nf* bacterium, germ
Bahama [ba'ama]: **las (Islas) ~** *nfpl* the Bahamas
bahía [ba'ia] *nf* bay
bailar [bai'lar] *vt, vi* to dance; **bailarín, -ina** *nm/f* (ballet) dancer; **baile** *nm* dance; (*formal*) ball
baja ['baxa] *nf* drop, fall; (*Mil*) casualty; **dar de ~** (*soldado*) to discharge; (*empleado*) to dismiss
bajada [ba'xaða] *nf* descent; (*camino*) slope; (*de aguas*) ebb
bajar [ba'xar] *vi* to go down, come down; (*temperatura, precios*) to drop, fall ▷ *vt* (*cabeza*) to bow; (*escalera*) to go down, come down; (*precio, voz*) to lower; (*llevar abajo*) to take down; **bajarse** *vr* (*de coche*) to get out; (*de autobús, tren*) to get off; **~ de** (*coche*) to get out of; (*autobús, tren*) to get off; **~se algo de Internet** to download sth from the Internet
bajío [ba'xio] (*LAM*) *nm* lowlands *pl*
bajo, -a ['baxo] *adj* (*mueble, número, precio*) low; (*piso*) ground; (*de estatura*) small, short; (*color*) pale; (*sonido*) faint, soft, low; (*voz: en tono*) deep; (*metal*) base; (*humilde*) low, humble ▷ *adv* (*hablar*) softly, quietly; (*volar*)

low ▷ *prep* under, below, underneath ▷ *nm* (*Mús*) bass; **~ la lluvia** in the rain
bajón [ba'xon] *nm* fall, drop
bakalao [baka'lao] (*ESP: fam*) *nm* rave (music)
bala ['bala] *nf* bullet
balacear [balaθe'ar] (*MÉX, CAM*) *vt* to shoot
balance [ba'lanθe] *nm* (*Com*) balance; (: *libro*) balance sheet; (: *cuenta general*) stocktaking
balancear [balanθe'ar] *vt* to balance ▷ *vi* to swing (to and fro); (*vacilar*) to hesitate; **balancearse** *vr* to swing (to and fro), to hesitate
balanza [ba'lanθa] *nf* scales *pl*, balance; **balanza comercial** balance of trade; **balanza de pagos** balance of payments
balaustrada [balaus'traða] *nf* balustrade; (*pasamanos*) banisters *pl*
balazo [ba'laθo] *nm* (*golpe*) shot; (*herida*) bullet wound
balbucear [balβuθe'ar] *vi, vt* to stammer, stutter
balcón [bal'kon] *nm* balcony
balde ['balde] *nm* bucket, pail; **de ~** (for) free, for nothing; **en ~** in vain
baldosa [bal'dosa] *nf* (*azulejo*) floor tile; (*grande*) flagstone; **baldosín** *nm* (small) tile
Baleares [bale'ares] *nfpl*: **las (Islas) ~** the Balearic Islands
balero [ba'lero] (*LAM*) *nm* (*juguete*) cup-and-ball toy
baliza [ba'liθa] *nf* (*Aviac*) beacon; (*Náut*) buoy
ballena [ba'ʎena] *nf* whale
ballet [ba'le] (*pl* **~s**) *nm* ballet
balneario [balne'arjo] *nm* spa; (*cs: en la costa*) seaside resort
balón [ba'lon] *nm* ball
baloncesto [balon'θesto] *nm* basketball
balonmano [balon'mano] *nm* handball
balsa ['balsa] *nf* raft; (*Bot*) balsa wood
bálsamo ['balsamo] *nm* balsam, balm
baluarte [ba'lwarte] *nm* bastion, bulwark
bambú [bam'bu] *nm* bamboo
banana [ba'nana] (*LAM*) *nf* banana; **banano** *nm* (*LAM: árbol*) banana tree; (*CAM: fruta*) banana
banca ['banka] *nf* (*Com*) banking
bancario, -a [ban'karjo, a] *adj* banking *cpd*, bank *cpd*
bancarrota [banka'rrota] *nf* bankruptcy; **hacer ~** to go bankrupt
banco ['banko] *nm* bench; (*Escol*) desk; (*Com*) bank; (*Geo*) stratum; **banco de arena** sandbank; **banco de crédito** credit bank; **banco de datos** databank

banda ['banda] *nf* band; (*pandilla*) gang; (*Náut*) side, edge; **banda ancha** broadband; **banda sonora** soundtrack
bandada [ban'daða] *nf* (*de pájaros*) flock; (*de peces*) shoal
bandazo [ban'daθo] *nm*: **dar ~s** to sway from side to side
bandeja [ban'dexa] *nf* tray
bandera [ban'dera] *nf* flag
banderilla [bande'riʎa] *nf* banderilla
bandido [ban'diðo] *nm* bandit
bando ['bando] *nm* (*edicto*) edict, proclamation; (*facción*) faction; **bandos** *nmpl* (*Rel*) banns
bandolera [bando'lera] *nf*: **llevar en ~** to wear across one's chest
banquero [ban'kero] *nm* banker
banqueta [ban'keta] *nf* stool; (*MÉX: en calle*) pavement (*BRIT*), sidewalk (*US*)
banquete [ban'kete] *nm* banquet; (*para convidados*) formal dinner; **banquete de boda(s)** wedding reception
banquillo [ban'kiʎo] *nm* (*Jur*) dock, prisoner's bench; (*banco*) bench; (*para los pies*) footstool
banquina [ban'kina] (*RPL*) *nf* hard shoulder (*BRIT*), berm (*US*)
bañadera [baɲa'ðera] (*RPL*) *nf* bathtub
bañador [baɲa'ðor] (*ESP*) *nm* swimming costume (*BRIT*), bathing suit (*US*)
bañar [ba'ɲar] *vt* to bath, bathe; (*objeto*) to dip; (*de barniz*) to coat; **bañarse** *vr* (*en el mar*) to bathe, swim; (*en la bañera*) to have a bath
bañera [ba'ɲera] (*ESP*) *nf* bath(tub)
bañero, -a [ba'ɲero, a] (*cs*) *nm/f* lifeguard
bañista [ba'ɲista] *nmf* bather
baño ['baɲo] *nm* (*en bañera*) bath; (*en río*) dip, swim; (*cuarto*) bathroom; (*bañera*) bath(tub); (*capa*) coating; **darse** *o* **tomar un ~** (*en bañera*) to have *o* take a bath; (*en mar, piscina*) to have a swim; **baño María** bain-marie
bar [bar] *nm* bar
barahúnda [bara'unda] *nf* uproar, hubbub
baraja [ba'raxa] *nf* pack (of cards); **barajar** *vt* (*naipes*) to shuffle; (*fig*) to jumble up
baranda [ba'randa] *nf* = **barandilla**
barandilla [baran'diʎa] *nf* rail, railing
barata [ba'rata] (*MÉX*) *nf* (*bargain*) sale
baratillo [bara'tiʎo] *nm* (*tienda*) junkshop; (*subasta*) bargain sale; (*conjunto de cosas*) secondhand goods *pl*
barato, -a [ba'rato, a] *adj* cheap ▷ *adv* cheap, cheaply
barba ['barβa] *nf* (*mentón*) chin; (*pelo*) beard

barbacoa [barβa'koa] nf (parrilla)
barbecue; (carne) barbecued meat
barbaridad [barβari'ðað] nf barbarity;
(acto) barbarism; (atrocidad) outrage; **una ~**
(fam) loads; **¡qué ~!** (fam) how awful!
barbarie [bar'βarje] nf barbarism,
savagery; (crueldad) barbarity
bárbaro, -a ['barβaro, a] adj barbarous,
cruel; (grosero) rough, uncouth ▷ nm/f
barbarian ▷ adv: **lo pasamos ~** (fam) we had
a great time; **¡qué ~!** (fam) how marvellous!;
un éxito ~ (fam) a terrific success; **es un
tipo ~** (fam) he's a great bloke
barbero [bar'βero] nm barber, hairdresser
barbilla [bar'βiʎa] nf chin, tip of the chin
barbudo, -a [bar'βuðo, a] adj bearded
barca ['barka] nf (small) boat; **barcaza**
nf barge
Barcelona [barθe'lona] n Barcelona
barco ['barko] nm boat; (grande) ship;
barco de carga/pesca cargo/fishing boat;
barco de vela sailing ship
barda ['barða] (MÉX) nf (de madera) fence
baremo [ba'remo] nm (Mat: fig) scale
barítono [ba'ritono] nm baritone
barman ['barman] nm barman
barniz [bar'niθ] nm varnish; (en loza) glaze;
(fig) veneer; **barnizar** vt to varnish; (loza)
to glaze
barómetro [ba'rometro] nm barometer
barquillo [bar'kiʎo] nm cone, cornet
barra ['barra] nf bar, rod; (de un bar, café)
bar; (de pan) French stick; (palanca) lever;
barra de labios lipstick; **barra libre** free bar
barraca [ba'rraka] nf hut, cabin
barranco [ba'rranko] nm ravine; (fig)
difficulty
barrena [ba'rrena] nf drill
barrer [ba'rrer] vt to sweep; (quitar) to
sweep away
barrera [ba'rrera] nf barrier
barriada [ba'rrjaða] nf quarter, district
barricada [barri'kaða] nf barricade
barrida [ba'rriða] nf sweep, sweeping
barriga [ba'rriɣa] nf belly; (panza) paunch;
barrigón, -ona adj potbellied; **barrigudo,
-a** adj potbellied
barril [ba'rril] nm barrel, cask
barrio ['barrjo] nm (vecindad) area,
neighborhood (US); (en afueras) suburb;
barrio chino (ESP) red-light district
barro ['barro] nm (lodo) mud; (objetos)
earthenware; (Med) pimple
barroco, -a [ba'rroko, a] adj, nm baroque
barrote [ba'rrote] nm (de ventana) bar
bartola [bar'tola] nf: **tirarse** o **tumbarse a
la ~** to take it easy, be lazy
bártulos ['bartulos] nmpl things,

belongings
barullo [ba'ruʎo] nm row, uproar
basar [ba'sar] vt to base; **basarse** vr: **~se
en** to be based on
báscula ['baskula] nf (platform) scales
base ['base] nf base; **a ~ de** on the basis
of; (mediante) by means of; **base de datos**
(Inform) database
básico, -a ['basiko, a] adj basic
basílica [ba'silika] nf basilica
básquetbol ['basketbol] (LAM) nm
basketball

○ **PALABRA CLAVE**

bastante [bas'tante] adj **1** (suficiente)
enough; **bastante dinero** enough o
sufficient money; **bastantes libros** enough
books
2 (valor intensivo): **bastante gente** quite a
lot of people; **tener bastante calor** to be
rather hot
▷ adv: **bastante bueno/malo** quite good/
rather bad; **bastante rico** pretty rich; **(lo)
bastante inteligente (como) para hacer
algo** clever enough o sufficiently clever to
do sth

bastar [bas'tar] vi to be enough o
sufficient; **bastarse** vr to be self-sufficient;
~ para to be enough to; **¡basta!** (that's)
enough!
bastardo, -a [bas'tarðo, a] adj, nm/f
bastard
bastidor [basti'ðor] nm frame; (de coche)
chassis; (Teatro) wing; **entre ~es** (fig) behind
the scenes
basto, -a ['basto, a] adj coarse, rough;
bastos nmpl (Naipes) ≈ clubs
bastón [bas'ton] nm stick, staff; (para
pasear) walking stick
bastoncillo [baston'θiʎo] nm cotton bud
basura [ba'sura] nf rubbish (BRIT),
garbage (US) ▷ adj: **comida/televisión ~**
junk food/TV
basurero [basu'rero] nm (hombre)
dustman (BRIT), garbage man (US); (lugar)
dump; (cubo) (rubbish) bin (BRIT), trash
can (US)
bata ['bata] nf (gen) dressing gown;
(cubretodo) smock, overall; (Med, Tec etc)
lab(oratory) coat
batalla [ba'taʎa] nf battle; **de ~** (fig) for
everyday use; **batalla campal** pitched
battle
batallón [bata'ʎon] nm battalion
batata [ba'tata] nf sweet potato
batería [bate'ria] nf battery; (Mús) drums;

batería de cocina kitchen utensils
batido, -a [ba'tiðo, a] *adj* (*camino*) beaten, well-trodden ▷ *nm* (*Culin: de leche*) milk shake
batidora [bati'ðora] *nf* beater, mixer; **batidora eléctrica** food mixer, blender
batir [ba'tir] *vt* to beat, strike; (*vencer*) to beat, defeat; (*revolver*) to beat, mix; **batirse** *vr* to fight; **~ palmas** to applaud
batuta [ba'tuta] *nf* baton; **llevar la ~** (*fig*) to be the boss, be in charge
baúl [ba'ul] *nm* trunk; (*Auto*) boot (*BRIT*), trunk (*US*)
bautismo [bau'tismo] *nm* baptism, christening
bautizar [bauti'θar] *vt* to baptize, christen; (*fam: diluir*) to water down; **bautizo** *nm* baptism, christening
bayeta [ba'jeta] *nf* floorcloth
baza ['baθa] *nf* trick; **meter ~** to butt in
bazar [ba'θar] *nm* bazaar
bazofia [ba'θofja] *nf* trash
be [be] *nf name of the letter B*; **be chica/grande** (*MÉX*) V/B; **be larga** (*LAM*) B
beato, -a [be'ato, a] *adj* blessed; (*piadoso*) pious
bebé [be'ße] (*pl* ~**s**) *nm* baby
bebedero [beße'ðero, a] (*MÉX, CS*) *nm* drinking fountain
bebedor, a [beße'ðor, a] *adj* hard-drinking
beber [be'ßer] *vt, vi* to drink
bebida [be'ßiða] *nf* drink; **bebido, -a** *adj* drunk
beca ['beka] *nf* grant, scholarship; **becario, -a** [be'karjo, a] *nm/f* scholarship holder, grant holder
bedel [be'ðel] *nm* (*Escol*) janitor; (*Univ*) porter
béisbol ['beisßol] *nm* baseball
Belén [be'len] *nm* Bethlehem; **belén** *nm* (*de Navidad*) nativity scene, crib
belga ['belɣa] *adj, nmf* Belgian
Bélgica ['belxika] *nf* Belgium
bélico, -a ['beliko, a] *adj* (*actitud*) warlike
belleza [be'ʎeθa] *nf* beauty
bello, -a ['beʎo, a] *adj* beautiful, lovely; **Bellas Artes** Fine Art
bellota [be'ʎota] *nf* acorn
bemol [be'mol] *nm* (*Mús*) flat; **esto tiene ~es** (*fam*) this is a tough one
bencina [ben'θina] *nf* (*Quím*) benzine
bendecir [bende'θir] *vt* to bless
bendición [bendi'θjon] *nf* blessing
bendito, -a [ben'dito, a] *pp de* **bendecir** ▷ *adj* holy; (*afortunado*) lucky; (*feliz*) happy; (*sencillo*) simple ▷ *nm/f* simple soul
beneficencia [benefi'θenθja] *nf* charity

beneficiario, -a [benefi'θjarjo, a] *nm/f* beneficiary
beneficio [bene'fiθjo] *nm* (*bien*) benefit, advantage; (*ganancia*) profit, gain; **a ~ de algn** in aid of sb; **beneficioso, -a** *adj* beneficial
benéfico, -a [be'nefiko, a] *adj* charitable
beneplácito [bene'plaθito] *nm* approval, consent
benévolo, -a [be'neßolo, a] *adj* benevolent, kind
benigno, -a [be'niɣno, a] *adj* kind; (*suave*) mild; (*Med: tumor*) benign, non-malignant
berberecho [berße'retʃo] *nm* (*Zool, Culin*) cockle
berenjena [beren'xena] *nf* aubergine (*BRIT*), eggplant (*US*)
Berlín [ber'lin] *n* Berlin
berlinesa [berli'nesa] (*RPL*) *nf* doughnut, donut (*US*)
bermudas [ber'muðas] *nfpl* Bermuda shorts
berrido [be'rriðo] *nm* bellow(ing)
berrinche [be'rrintʃe] (*fam*) *nm* temper, tantrum
berro ['berro] *nm* watercress
berza ['berθa] *nf* cabbage
besamel [besa'mel] *nf* (*Culin*) white sauce, bechamel sauce
besar [be'sar] *vt* to kiss; (*fig: tocar*) to graze; **besarse** *vr* to kiss (one another); **beso** *nm* kiss
bestia ['bestja] *nf* beast, animal; (*fig*) idiot; **bestia de carga** beast of burden; **bestial** [bes'tjal] *adj* bestial; (*fam*) terrific; **bestialidad** *nf* bestiality; (*fam*) stupidity
besugo [be'suxo] *nm* sea bream; (*fam*) idiot
besuquear [besuke'ar] *vt* to cover with kisses; **besuquearse** *vr* to kiss and cuddle
betabel [beta'bel] (*MÉX*) *nm* beetroot (*BRIT*), beet (*US*)
betún [be'tun] *nm* shoe polish; (*Quím*) bitumen
biberón [biße'ron] *nm* feeding bottle
Biblia ['bißlja] *nf* Bible
bibliografía [bißljoɣra'fia] *nf* bibliography
biblioteca [bißljo'teka] *nf* library; (*mueble*) bookshelves; **biblioteca de consulta** reference library; **bibliotecario, -a** *nm/f* librarian
bicarbonato [bikarßo'nato] *nm* bicarbonate
bicho ['bitʃo] *nm* (*animal*) small animal; (*sabandija*) bug, insect; (*Taur*) bull
bici ['biθi] (*fam*) *nf* bike
bicicleta [biθi'kleta] *nf* bicycle, cycle; **ir**

en ~ to cycle
bidé [bi'ðe] (pl **~s**) nm bidet
bidón [bi'ðon] nm (de aceite) drum; (de gasolina) can

○ **PALABRA CLAVE**

bien [bjen] nm **1** (bienestar) good; **te lo digo por tu bien** I'm telling you for your own good; **el bien y el mal** good and evil
2 (posesión): **bienes** goods; **bienes de consumo** consumer goods; **bienes inmuebles** o **raíces/bienes muebles** real estate sg/personal property sg ▷ adv
1 (de manera satisfactoria, correcta etc) well; **trabaja/come bien** she works/eats well; **contestó bien** he answered correctly; **me siento bien** I feel fine; **no me siento bien** I don't feel very well; **se está bien aquí** it's nice here
2 (frases): **hiciste bien en llamarme** you were right to call me
3 (valor intensivo) very; **un cuarto bien caliente** a nice warm room; **bien se ve que ...** it's quite clear that ...
4 estar bien: estoy muy bien aquí I feel very happy here; **está bien que vengan** it's all right for them to come; **¡está bien! lo haré** oh all right, I'll do it
5 (de buena gana): **yo bien que iría pero ...** I'd gladly go but ... ▷ excl: **¡bien!** (aprobación) O.K.!; **¡muy bien!** well done! ▷ adj inv (matiz despectivo): **gente bien** posh people ▷ conj
1 bien ... bien: bien en coche bien en tren either by car or by train
2 (LAM): **no bien: no bien llegue te llamaré** as soon as I arrive I'll call you
3 si bien even though; V tb **más**

bienal [bje'nal] adj biennial
bienestar [bjenes'tar] nm well-being, welfare
bienvenida [bjembe'niða] nf welcome; **dar la ~ a algn** to welcome sb
bienvenido [bjembe'niðo] excl welcome!
bife ['bife] (cs) nm steak
bifurcación [bifurka'θjon] nf fork
bígamo, -a ['bixamo, a] adj bigamous ▷ nm/f bigamist
bigote [bi'xote] nm moustache; **bigotudo, -a** adj with a big moustache
bikini [bi'kini] nm bikini; (Culin) toasted ham and cheese sandwich
bilingüe [bi'lingwe] adj bilingual
billar [bi'ʎar] nm billiards sg; **billares** nmpl (lugar) billiard hall; (sala de juegos) amusement arcade; **billar americano** pool
billete [bi'ʎete] nm ticket; (de banco)

(bank)note (BRIT), bill (US); (carta) note; **~ de 20 libras** £20 note; **billete de ida y vuelta** return (BRIT) o round-trip (US) ticket; **billete sencillo** o **de ida** single (BRIT) o one-way (US) ticket; **billete electrónico** e-ticket
billetera [biʎe'tera] nf wallet
billón [bi'ʎon] nm billion
bimensual [bimen'swal] adj twice monthly
bingo ['bingo] nm bingo
biodegradable [bioðexra'ðaβle] adj biodegradable
biografía [bjoxra'fia] nf biography
biología [bjolo'xia] nf biology; **biológico, -a** adj biological; (cultivo, producto) organic; **biólogo, -a** nm/f biologist
biombo ['bjombo] nm (folding) screen
bioterrorismo [bjoterro'rismo] nm bioterrorism
biquini [bi'kini] nm o (RPL) f bikini
birlar [bir'lar] (fam) vt to pinch
Birmania [bir'manja] nf Burma
birome [bi'rome] (RPL) nf ballpoint (pen)
birria ['birrja] nf: **ser una ~** (película, libro) to be rubbish
bis [bis] excl encore!
bisabuelo, -a [bisa'βwelo, a] nm/f great-grandfather(-mother)
bisagra [bi'saxra] nf hinge
bisiesto [bi'sjesto] adj: **año ~** leap year
bisnieto, -a [bis'njeto, a] nm/f great-grandson/daughter
bisonte [bi'sonte] nm bison
bisté [bis'te] nm **= bistec**
bistec [bis'tek] nm steak
bisturí [bistu'ri] nm scalpel
bisutería [bisute'ria] nf imitation o costume jewellery
bit [bit] nm (Inform) bit
bizco, -a ['biθko, a] adj cross-eyed
bizcocho [biθ'kotʃo] nm (Culin) sponge cake
blanca ['blanka] nf (Mús) minim; **estar sin ~** (ESP: fam) to be broke; V tb **blanco**
blanco, -a ['blanko, a] adj white ▷ nm/f white man/woman, white ▷ nm (color) white; (en texto) blank; (Mil, fig) target; **en ~** blank; **noche en ~** sleepless night
blandir [blan'dir] vt to brandish
blando, -a ['blando, a] adj soft; (tierno) tender, gentle; (carácter) mild; (fam) cowardly
blanqueador [blankea'ðor] (MÉX) nm bleach
blanquear [blanke'ar] vt to whiten; (fachada) to whitewash; (paño) to bleach ▷ vi to turn white
blanquillo [blan'kiʎo] (MÉX, CAM) nm egg

blasfemar [blasfe'mar] vi to blaspheme, curse

bledo ['bleðo] nm: **me importa un ~ I** couldn't care less

blindado, -a [blin'daðo, a] adj (Mil) armour-plated; (antibala) bullet-proof; **coche** (ESP) o **carro** (LAM) ~ armoured car

bloc [blok] (pl **~s**) nm writing pad

blof [blof] (MÉX) nm bluff; **blofear** (MÉX) vi to bluff

blog [bloɣ] (pl **~s**) nm blog

bloque ['bloke] nm block; (Pol) bloc

bloquear [bloke'ar] vt to blockade; **bloqueo** nm blockade; (Com) freezing, blocking; **bloqueo mental** mental block

blusa ['blusa] nf blouse

bobada [bo'βaða] nf foolish action; foolish statement; **decir ~s** to talk nonsense

bobina [bo'βina] nf (Tec) bobbin; (Foto) spool; (Elec) coil

bobo, -a ['boβo, a] adj (tonto) daft, silly; (cándido) naôve ▷ nm/f fool, idiot ▷ nm (Teatro) clown, funny man

boca ['boka] nf mouth; (de crustáceo) pincer; (de cañón) muzzle; (entrada) mouth, entrance; **bocas** nfpl (de río) mouth sg; **~ abajo/arriba** face down/up; **se me hace la ~ agua** my mouth is watering; **boca de incendios** hydrant; **boca del estómago** pit of the stomach; **boca de metro** underground (BRIT) o subway (US) entrance

bocacalle [boka'kaʎe] nf (entrance to a) street; **la primera ~** the first turning o street

bocadillo [boka'ðiʎo] nm sandwich

bocado [bo'kaðo] nm mouthful, bite; (de caballo) bridle

bocajarro [boka'xarro]: **a ~** adv (disparar) point-blank

bocanada [boka'naða] nf (de vino) mouthful, swallow; (de aire) gust, puff

bocata [bo'kata] (fam) nm sandwich

bocazas [bo'kaθas] (fam) nm inv bigmouth

boceto [bo'θeto] nm sketch, outline

bochorno [bo'tʃorno] nm (vergüenza) embarrassment; (color) **hace ~** it's very muggy

bocina [bo'θina] nf (Mús) trumpet; (Auto) horn; (para hablar) megaphone

boda ['boða] nf (tb: **~s**) wedding, marriage; (fiesta) wedding reception; **bodas de oro/ plata** golden/silver wedding sg

bodega [bo'ðeɣa] nf (de vino) (wine) cellar; (depósito) storeroom; (de barco) hold

bodegón [boðe'ɣon] nm (Arte) still life

bofetada [bofe'taða] nf slap (in the face)

boga ['boɣa] nf: **en ~** (fig) in vogue

Bogotá [boɣo'ta] n Bogotá

bohemio, -a [bo'emjo, a] adj, nm/f Bohemian

bohío [bo'io] (CAM) nm shack, hut

boicot [boi'kot] (pl **~s**) nm boycott; **boicotear** vt to boycott

bóiler ['boiler] (MÉX) nm boiler

boina ['boina] nf beret

bola ['bola] nf ball; (canica) marble; (Naipes) (grand) slam; (betún) shoe polish; (mentira) tale, story; **bolas** nfpl (LAM: caza) bolas sg; **bola de billar** billiard ball; **bola de nieve** snowball

boleadoras [bolea'ðoras] nfpl bolas sg

bolear [bole'ar] (MÉX) vt (zapatos) to polish, shine

bolera [bo'lera] nf skittle o bowling alley

bolero, -a (MÉX) [bo'lero] nm/f (limpiabotas) shoeshine boy/girl

boleta [bo'leta] (LAM) nf (de rifa) ticket; (cs: recibo) receipt; **boleta de calificaciones** (MÉX) report card

boletería [bolete'ria] (LAM) nf ticket office

boletín [bole'tin] nm bulletin; (periódico) journal, review; **boletín de noticias** news bulletin

boleto [bo'leto] nm (LAM) ticket; **boleto de ida y vuelta** (LAM) round trip ticket; **boleto electrónico** (LAM) e-ticket; **boleto redondo** (MÉX) round trip ticket

boli ['boli] (fam) nm Biro®

bolígrafo [bo'liɣrafo] nm ball-point pen, Biro®

bolilla [bo'liʎa] (RPL) nf topic

bolillo [bo'liʎo] (MÉX) nm (bread) roll

bolita [bo'lita] (cs) nf marble

bolívar [bo'liβar] nm monetary unit of Venezuela

Bolivia [bo'liβja] nf Bolivia; **boliviano, -a** adj, nm/f Bolivian

bollería [boʎe'ria] nf cakes pl and pastries pl

bollo ['boʎo] nm (pan) roll; (bulto) bump, lump; (abolladura) dent

bolo ['bolo] nm skittle; (píldora) (large) pill; **(juego de) bolos** nmpl skittles sg

bolsa ['bolsa] nf (para llevar algo) bag; (MÉX, CAM: bolsillo) pocket; (MÉX: de mujer) handbag; (Anat) cavity, sac; (Com) stock exchange; (Minería) pocket; **de ~** pocket cpd; **bolsa de agua caliente** hot water bottle; **bolsa de aire** air pocket; **bolsa de dormir** (MÉX, RPL) sleeping bag; **bolsa de la compra** shopping bag; **bolsa de papel/plástico** paper/plastic bag

bolsear [bolse'ar] (MÉX, CAM) vt: **~ a algn** to pick sb's pocket

bolsillo [bol'siʎo] nm pocket; (cartera) purse; **de ~** pocket(-size)

bolso ['bolso] nm (bolsa) bag; (de mujer)

handbag

bomba ['bomba] nf (Mil) bomb; (Tec) pump ▷ adj (fam): **noticia ~** bombshell ▷ adv (fam): **pasarlo ~** to have a great time; **bomba atómica/de efecto retardado/de humo** atomic/time/smoke bomb

bombacha [bom'batʃa] (RPL) nf panties pl

bombardear [bombarðe'ar] vt to bombard; (Mil) to bomb; **bombardeo** nm bombardment; bombing

bombazo [bom'baθo] (MÉX) nm (explosión) explosion; (fam: notición) bombshell; (: éxito) smash hit

bombear [bombe'ar] vt (agua) to pump (out o up)

bombero [bom'bero] nm fireman

bombilla [bom'biʎa] (ESP) nf (light) bulb

bombita [bom'bita] (RPL) nf (light) bulb

bombo ['bombo] nm (Mús) bass drum; (Tec) drum

bombón [bom'bon] nm chocolate; (MÉX: de caramelo) marshmallow

bombona [bom'bona] (ESP) nf (de butano, oxígeno) cylinder

bonachón, -ona [bona'tʃon, ona] adj good-natured, easy-going

bonanza [bo'nanθa] nf (Náut) fair weather; (fig) bonanza; (Minería) rich pocket o vein

bondad [bon'dað] nf goodness, kindness; **tenga la ~ de** (please) be good enough to

bonito, -a [bo'nito, a] adj pretty; (agradable) nice ▷ nm (atún) tuna (fish)

bono ['bono] nm voucher; (Finanzas) bond

bonobús [bono'βus] (ESP) nm bus pass

bonoloto [bono'loto] nf state-run weekly lottery

boquerón [boke'ron] nm (pez) (kind of) anchovy; (agujero) large hole

boquete [bo'kete] nm gap, hole

boquiabierto, -a [bokia'βjerto, a] adj: **quedarse ~** to be amazed o flabbergasted

boquilla [bo'kiʎa] nf (para riego) nozzle; (para cigarro) cigarette holder; (Mús) mouthpiece

borbotón [borβo'ton] nm: **salir a borbotones** to gush out

borda ['borða] nf (Náut) (ship's) rail; **tirar algo/caerse por la ~** to throw sth/fall overboard

bordado [bor'ðaðo] nm embroidery

bordar [bor'ðar] vt to embroider

borde ['borðe] nm edge, border; (de camino etc) side; (en la costura) hem; **al ~ de** (fig) on the verge o brink of; **ser ~** (ESP: fam) to be rude; **bordear** vt to border

bordillo [bor'ðiʎo] nm kerb (BRIT), curb (US)

bordo ['borðo] nm (Náut) side; **a ~** on board

borlote [bor'lote] (MÉX) nm row, uproar

borrachera [borra'tʃera] nf (ebriedad) drunkenness; (orgía) spree, binge

borracho, -a [bo'rratʃo, a] adj drunk ▷ nm/f (habitual) drunkard, drunk; (temporal) drunk, drunk man/woman

borrador [borra'ðor] nm (escritura) first draft, rough sketch; (goma) rubber (BRIT), eraser

borrar [bo'rrar] vt to erase, rub out

borrasca [bo'rraska] nf storm

borrego, -a [bo'rreɣo, a] nm/f (Zool: joven) (yearling) lamb; (adulto) sheep ▷ nm (MÉX: fam) false rumour

borrico, -a [bo'rriko, a] nm/f donkey/ she-donkey; (fig) stupid man/woman

borrón [bo'rron] nm (mancha) stain

borroso, -a [bo'rroso, a] adj vague, unclear; (escritura) illegible

bosque ['boske] nm wood; (grande) forest

bostezar [boste'θar] vi to yawn; **bostezo** nm yawn

bota ['bota] nf (calzado) boot; (para vino) leather wine bottle; **botas de agua** o **goma** Wellingtons

botana [bo'tana] (MÉX) nf snack, appetizer

botánica [bo'tanika] nf (ciencia) botany; V tb **botánico**

botánico, -a [bo'taniko, a] adj botanical ▷ nm/f botanist

botar [bo'tar] vt to throw, hurl; (Náut) to launch; (LAM: echar) to throw out ▷ vi (ESP: saltar) to bounce

bote ['bote] nm (salto) bounce; (golpe) thrust; (ESP: envase) tin, can; (embarcación) boat; (MÉX, CAM: pey: cárcel) jail; **de ~ en ~** packed, jammed full; **bote de la basura** (MÉX) dustbin (BRIT), trashcan (US); **bote salvavidas** lifeboat

botella [bo'teʎa] nf bottle; **botellín** nm small bottle; **botellón** nm (ESP: fam) outdoor drinking session

botijo [bo'tixo] nm (earthenware) jug

botín [bo'tin] nm (calzado) half boot; (polaina) spat; (Mil) booty

botiquín [boti'kin] nm (armario) medicine cabinet; (portátil) first-aid kit

botón [bo'ton] nm button; (Bot) bud

botones [bo'tones] nm inv bellboy (BRIT), bellhop (US)

bóveda ['boβeða] nf (Arq) vault

boxeador [boksea'ðor] nm boxer

boxeo [bok'seo] nm boxing

boya ['boja] nf (Náut) buoy; (de caña) float

boyante [bo'jante] adj prosperous

bozal [bo'θal] nm (para caballos) halter; (de

perro) muzzle

bragas ['braɣas] *nfpl* (*de mujer*) panties, knickers (BRIT)

bragueta [bra'ɣeta] *nf* fly, flies *pl*

braille [breil] *nm* braille

brasa ['brasa] *nf* live *o* hot coal

brasero [bra'sero] *nm* brazier

brasier [bra'sjer] (MÉX) *nm* bra

Brasil [bra'sil] *nm* (tb: **el ~**) Brazil; **brasileño, -a** *adj, nm/f* Brazilian

brassier [bra'sjer] (MÉX) *nm* V **brasier**

bravo, -a ['braβo, a] *adj* (*valiente*) brave; (*feroz*) ferocious; (*salvaje*) wild; (*mar etc*) rough, stormy ▷ *excl* bravo!; **bravura** *nf* bravery; ferocity

braza ['braθa] *nf* fathom; **nadar a ~** to swim breast-stroke

brazalete [braθa'lete] *nm* (*pulsera*) bracelet; (*banda*) armband

brazo ['braθo] *nm* arm; (*Zool*) foreleg; (*Bot*) limb, branch; **luchar a ~ partido** to fight hand-to-hand; **ir cogidos del ~** to walk arm in arm

brebaje [bre'βaxe] *nm* potion

brecha ['bretʃa] *nf* (*hoyo, vacío*) gap, opening; (*Mil, fig*) breach

brega ['breɣa] *nf* (*lucha*) struggle; (*trabajo*) hard work

breva ['breβa] *nf* early fig

breve ['breβe] *adj* short, brief ▷ *nf* (*Mús*) breve; **en ~** (*pronto*) shortly, before long; **brevedad** *nf* brevity, shortness

bribón, -ona [bri'βon, ona] *adj* idle, lazy ▷ *nm/f* (*pícaro*) rascal, rogue

bricolaje [briko'laxe] *nm* do-it-yourself, DIY

brida ['briða] *nf* bridle, rein; (*Tec*) clamp

bridge [britʃ] *nm* bridge

brigada [bri'ɣaða] *nf* (*unidad*) brigade; (*de trabajadores*) squad, gang ▷ *nm* ≈ staff-sergeant, sergeant-major

brillante [bri'ʎante] *adj* brilliant ▷ *nm* diamond

brillar [bri'ʎar] *vi* to shine; (*joyas*) to sparkle

brillo ['briʎo] *nm* shine; (*brillantez*) brilliance; (*fig*) splendour; **sacar ~ a** to polish

brincar [brin'kar] *vi* to skip about, hop about, jump about

brinco ['brinko] *nm* jump, leap

brindar [brin'dar] *vi*: **~ a** *o* **por** to drink (a toast) to ▷ *vt* to offer, present

brindis ['brindis] *nm inv* toast

brío ['brio] *nm* spirit, dash

brisa ['brisa] *nf* breeze

británico, -a [bri'taniko, a] *adj* British

▷ *nm/f* Briton, British person

brizna [bri'θna] *nf* (*de hierba, paja*) blade; (*de tabaco*) leaf

broca ['broka] *nf* (*Tec*) drill, bit

brocha ['brotʃa] *nf* (*large*) paintbrush; **brocha de afeitar** shaving brush

broche ['brotʃe] *nm* brooch

broma ['broma] *nf* joke; **de** *o* **en ~** in fun, as a joke; **broma pesada** practical joke; **bromear** *vi* to joke

bromista [bro'mista] *adj* fond of joking ▷ *nmf* joker, wag

bronca ['bronka] *nf* row; **echar una ~ a algn** to tick sb off

bronce ['bronθe] *nm* bronze; **bronceado, -a** *adj* bronze; (*por el sol*) tanned ▷ *nm* (sun) tan; (*Tec*) bronzing

bronceador [bronθea'ðor] *nm* suntan lotion

broncearse [bronθe'arse] *vr* to get a suntan

bronquio ['bronkjo] *nm* (*Anat*) bronchial tube

bronquitis [bron'kitis] *nf inv* bronchitis

brotar [bro'tar] *vi* (*Bot*) to sprout; (*aguas*) to gush (forth); (*Med*) to break out

brote ['brote] *nm* (*Bot*) shoot; (*Med, fig*) outbreak

bruces ['bruθes]: **de bruces** *adv*: **caer** *o* **dar de ~** to fall headlong, fall flat

bruja ['bruxa] *nf* witch; **brujería** *nf* witchcraft

brujo ['bruxo] *nm* wizard, magician

brújula ['bruxula] *nf* compass

bruma ['bruma] *nf* mist

brusco, -a ['brusko, a] *adj* (*súbito*) sudden; (*áspero*) brusque

Bruselas [bru'selas] *n* Brussels

brutal [bru'tal] *adj* brutal; **brutalidad** [brutali'ðað] *nf* brutality

bruto, -a ['bruto, a] *adj* (*idiota*) stupid; (*bestial*) brutish; (*peso*) gross; **en ~** raw, unworked

Bs.As. *abr* (= *Buenos Aires*) B.A.

bucal [bu'kal] *adj* oral; **por vía ~** orally

bucear [buθe'ar] *vi* to dive ▷ *vt* to explore; **buceo** *nm* diving

bucle ['bukle] *nm* curl

budismo [bu'ðismo] *nm* Buddhism

buen [bwen] *adj m* V **bueno**

buenamente [bwena'mente] *adv* (*fácilmente*) easily; (*voluntariamente*) willingly

buenaventura [bwenaβen'tura] *nf* (*suerte*) good luck; (*adivinación*) fortune

buenmozo [bwen'moθo] (MÉX) *adj* handsome

○ **PALABRA CLAVE**

bueno, -a ['bweno, a] (antes de nmsg: **buen**) adj **1** (excelente etc) good; **es un libro bueno, es un buen libro** it's a good book; **hace bueno, hace buen tiempo** the weather is fine, it is fine; **el bueno de Paco** good old Paco; **fue muy bueno conmigo** he was very nice o kind to me **2** (apropiado): **ser bueno para** to be good for; **creo que vamos por buen camino** I think we're on the right track **3** (irónico): **le di un buen rapapolvo** I gave him a good o real ticking off; **¡buen conductor estás hecho!** some o a fine driver you are!; **¡estaría bueno que ...!** a fine thing it would be if ...! **4** (atractivo, sabroso): **está bueno este bizcocho** this sponge is delicious; **Carmen está muy buena** Carmen is gorgeous **5** (saludos): **¡buen día!, ¡buenos días!** (good) morning!; **¡buenas (tardes)!** (good) afternoon!; (más tarde) (good) evening!; **¡buenas noches!** good night! **6** (otras locuciones): **estar de buenas** to be in a good mood; **por las buenas o por las malas** by hook or by crook; **de buenas a primeras** all of a sudden ▷ excl: **¡bueno!** all right!; **bueno, ¿y qué?** well, so what?

Buenos Aires [bweno'saires] nm Buenos Aires
buey [bwei] nm ox
búfalo ['bufalo] nm buffalo
bufanda [bu'fanda] nf scarf
bufete [bu'fete] nm (despacho de abogado) lawyer's office
bufón [bu'fon] nm clown
buhardilla [buar'ðiʎa] nf attic
búho ['buo] nm owl; (fig) hermit, recluse
buitre ['bwitre] nm vulture
bujía [bu'xia] nf (vela) candle; (Elec) candle (power); (Auto) spark plug
bula ['bula] nf (papal) bull
bulbo ['bulβo] nm bulb
bulevar [bule'βar] nm boulevard
Bulgaria [bul'ɣarja] nf Bulgaria; **búlgaro, -a** adj, nm/f Bulgarian
bulla ['buʎa] nf (ruido) uproar; (de gente) crowd
bullicio [bu'ʎiθjo] nm (ruido) uproar; (movimiento) bustle
bulto ['bulto] nm (paquete) package; (fardo) bundle; (tamaño) size, bulkiness; (Med) swelling, lump; (silueta) vague shape
buñuelo [bu'ɲwelo] nm ≈ doughnut (BRIT), ≈ donut (US); (fruta de sartén) fritter
buque ['buke] nm ship, vessel; **buque de guerra** warship
burbuja [bur'βuxa] nf bubble
burdel [bur'ðel] nm brothel
burgués, -esa [bur'ɣes, esa] adj middle-class, bourgeois; **burguesía** nf middle class, bourgeoisie
burla ['burla] nf (mofa) gibe; (broma) joke; (engaño) trick; **burlar** [bur'lar] vt (engañar) to deceive ▷ vi to joke; **burlarse** vr to joke; **burlarse de** to make fun of
burlón, -ona [bur'lon, ona] adj mocking
buró [bu'ro] (MÉX) nm bedside table
burocracia [buro'kraθja] nf civil service
burrada [bu'rraða] nf: **decir o soltar ~s** to talk nonsense; **hacer ~s** to act stupid; **una ~** (ESP: mucho) a (hell of a) lot
burro, -a ['burro, a] nm/f donkey/she-donkey; (fig) ass, idiot
bursátil [bur'satil] adj stock-exchange cpd
bus [bus] nm bus
busca ['buska] nf search, hunt ▷ nm (Tel) bleeper; **en ~ de** in search of
buscador [buska'ðor] nm (Internet) search engine
buscar [bus'kar] vt to look for, search for, seek ▷ vi to look, search, seek; **se busca secretaria** secretary wanted
busque etc vb V **buscar**
búsqueda ['buskeða] nf = **busca**
busto ['busto] nm (Anat, Arte) bust
butaca [bu'taka] nf armchair; (de cine, teatro) stall, seat
butano [bu'tano] nm butane (gas)
buzo ['buθo] nm diver
buzón [bu'θon] nm (en puerta) letter box; (en calle) pillar box

C

C. abr (= centígrado) C; (compañía) Co.

C/ abr (= calle) St

cabal [ka'βal] adj (exacto) exact; (correcto) right, proper; (acabado) finished, complete; **cabales** nmpl: **no está en sus cabales** she isn't in her right mind

cábalas ['kaβalas] nfpl: **hacer ~** to guess

cabalgar [kaβal'ɣar] vt, vi to ride

cabalgata [kaβal'ɣata] nf procession

caballa [ka'βaʎa] nf mackerel

caballería [kaβaʎe'ria] nf mount; (Mil) cavalry

caballero [kaβa'ʎero] nm gentleman; (de la orden de caballería) knight; (trato directo) sir

caballete [kaβa'ʎete] nm (Arte) easel; (Tec) trestle

caballito [kaβa'ʎito] nm (caballo pequeño) small horse, pony; **caballitos** nmpl (en verbena) roundabout, merry-go-round

caballo [ka'βaʎo] nm horse; (Ajedrez) knight; (Naipes) queen; **ir en ~** to ride; **caballo de carreras** racehorse; **caballo de fuerza** o **vapor** horsepower

cabaña [ka'βaɲa] nf (casita) hut, cabin

cabecear [kaβeθe'ar] vt, vi to nod

cabecera [kaβe'θera] nf head; (Imprenta) headline

cabecilla [kaβe'θiʎa] nm ringleader

cabellera [kaβe'ʎera] nf (head of) hair; (de cometa) tail

cabello [ka'βeʎo] nm (tb: ~**s**) hair; **cabello de ángel** confectionery and pastry filling made of pumpkin and syrup

caber [ka'βer] vi (entrar) to fit, go; **caben 3 más** there's room for 3 more

cabestrillo [kaβes'triʎo] nm sling

cabeza [ka'βeθa] nf head; (Pol) chief, leader; **cabeza de ajo** bulb of garlic; **cabeza de familia** head of the household; **cabeza rapada** skinhead; **cabezada** nf (golpe) butt; **dar cabezadas** to nod off; **cabezón, -ona**

adj (vino) heady; (fam: persona) pig-headed

cabida [ka'βiða] nf space

cabina [ka'βina] nf cabin; (de avión) cockpit; (de camión) cab; **cabina telefónica** telephone (BRIT) box o booth

cabizbajo, -a [kaβiθ'βaxo, a] adj crestfallen, dejected

cable ['kaβle] nm cable

cabo ['kaβo] nm (de objeto) end, extremity; (Mil) corporal; (Náut) rope, cable; (Geo) cape; **al ~ de 3 días** after 3 days; **llevar a ~** to carry out

cabra ['kaβra] nf goat

cabré etc vb V **caber**

cabrear [kaβre'ar] (fam) vt to bug; **cabrearse** vr (enfadarse) to fly off the handle

cabrito [ka'βrito] nm kid

cabrón [ka'βron] nm cuckold; (fam!) bastard (!)

caca ['kaka] (fam) nf pooh

cacahuete [kaka'wete] (ESP) nm peanut

cacao [ka'kao] nm cocoa; (Bot) cacao

cacarear [kakare'ar] vi (persona) to boast; (gallina) to crow

cacería [kaθe'ria] nf hunt

cacarizo, -a [kaka'riθo, a] (MÉX) adj pockmarked

cacerola [kaθe'rola] nf pan, saucepan

cachalote [katʃa'lote] nm (Zool) sperm whale

cacharro [ka'tʃarro] nm earthenware pot; **cacharros** nmpl pots and pans

cachear [katʃe'ar] vt to search, frisk

cachemir [katʃe'mir] nm cashmere

cachetada [katʃe'taða] (LAM: fam) nf (bofetada) slap

cachete [ka'tʃete] nm (Anat) cheek; (ESP: bofetada) slap (in the face)

cachivache [katʃi'βatʃe] nm (trasto) piece of junk; **cachivaches** nmpl junk sg

cacho ['katʃo] nm (small) bit; (LAM: cuerno) horn

cachondeo [katʃon'deo] (ESP: fam) nm farce, joke

cachondo, -a [ka'tʃondo, a] adj (Zool) on heat; (fam: sexualmente) randy; (: gracioso) funny

cachorro, -a [ka'tʃorro, a] nm/f (perro) pup, puppy; (león) cub

cachucha [ka'tʃutʃa] (MÉX: fam) nf cap

cacique [ka'θike] nm chief, local ruler; (Pol) local party boss

cactus ['kaktus] nm inv cactus

cada ['kaða] adj inv each; (antes de número) every; **~ día** each day, every day; **~ dos días** every other day; **~ uno/a** each one, every one; **~ vez más/menos** more and more/less and less; **~ vez que ...** whenever, every time (that) ...; **uno de ~ diez** one out of every ten

cadáver [ka'ðaβer] nm (dead) body, corpse

cadena [ka'ðena] nf chain; (TV) channel; **trabajo en ~** assembly line work; **cadena montañosa** mountain range; **cadena perpetua** (Jur) life imprisonment

cadera [ka'ðera] nf hip

cadete [ka'ðete] nm cadet

caducar [kaðu'kar] vi to expire; **caduco, -a** adj expired; (persona) very old

caer [ka'er] vi to fall (down); **caerse** vr to fall (down); **me cae bien/mal** I get on well with him/I can't stand him; **~ en la cuenta** to realize; **dejar ~** to drop; **su cumpleaños cae en viernes** her birthday falls on a Friday

café [ka'fe] (pl **~s**) nm (bebida, planta) coffee; (lugar) café ▷ adj (MÉX: color) brown, tan; **café con leche** white coffee; **café negro** (LAM) black coffee; **café solo** (ESP) black coffee

cafetera [kafe'tera] nf coffee pot

cafetería [kafete'ria] nf (gen) café

cafetero, -a [kafe'tero, a] adj coffee cpd; **ser muy ~** to be a coffee addict

cafishio [ka'fiʃo] (CS) nm pimp

cagar [ka'ɣar] (fam!) vt to bungle, mess up ▷ vi to have a shit (!)

caída [ka'iða] nf fall; (declive) slope; (disminución) fall, drop

caído, -a [ka'iðo, a] adj drooping

caiga etc vb V **caer**

caimán [kai'man] nm alligator

caja ['kaxa] nf box; (para reloj) case; (de ascensor) shaft; (Com) cashbox; (donde se hacen los pagos) cashdesk; (: en supermercado) checkout, till; **caja de ahorros** savings bank; **caja de cambios** gearbox; **caja de fusibles** fuse box; **caja fuerte** o **de caudales** safe, strongbox

cajero, -a [ka'xero, a] nm/f cashier; **cajero automático** cash dispenser

cajetilla [kaxe'tiʎa] nf (de cigarrillos) packet

cajón [ka'xon] nm big box; (de mueble) drawer

cajuela (MÉX) nf (Auto) boot (BRIT), trunk (US)

cal [kal] nf lime

cala ['kala] nf (Geo) cove, inlet; (de barco) hold

calabacín [kalaβa'θin] nm (Bot) baby marrow; (: más pequeño) courgette (BRIT), zucchini (US)

calabacita [kalaβa'θita] (MÉX) nf courgette (BRIT), zucchini (US)

calabaza [kala'βaθa] nf (Bot) pumpkin

calabozo [kala'βoθo] nm (cárcel) prison; (celda) cell

calada [ka'laða] (ESP) nf (de cigarrillo) puff

calado, -a [ka'laðo, a] adj (prenda) lace cpd ▷ nm (Náut) draught

calamar [kala'mar] nm squid no pl

calambre [ka'lambre] nm (Elec) shock

calar [ka'lar] vt to soak, drench; (penetrar) to pierce, penetrate; (comprender) to see through; (vela) to lower; **calarse** vr (Auto) to stall; **~se las gafas** to stick one's glasses on

calavera [kala'βera] nf skull

calcar [kal'kar] vt (reproducir) to trace; (imitar) to copy

calcetín [kalθe'tin] nm sock

calcio ['kalθjo] nm calcium

calcomanía [kalkoma'nia] nf transfer

calculador, a [kalkula'ðor, a] adj (persona) calculating; **calculadora** [kalkula'ðora] nf calculator

calcular [kalku'lar] vt (Mat) to calculate, compute; **~ que ...** to reckon that ...

caldera [kal'dera] nf boiler

calderilla [kalde'riʎa] nf (moneda) small change

caldo ['kaldo] nm stock; (consomé) consommé

calefacción [kalefak'θjon] nf heating; **calefacción central** central heating

calefón [kale'fon] (RPL) nm boiler

calendario [kalen'darjo] nm calendar

calentador [kalenta'ðor] nm heater

calentamiento [kalenta'mjento] nm (Deporte) warm-up; **calentamiento global** global warming

calentar [kalen'tar] vt to heat (up); **calentarse** vr to heat up, warm up; (fig: discusión etc) to get heated

calentón [kalen'ton] (RPL: fam) adj (sexualmente) horny, randy (BRIT)

calentura [kalen'tura] nf (Med) fever, (high) temperature

calesita [kale'sita] (RPL) nf merry-go-round, carousel

calibre [ka'liβre] nm (de cañón) calibre, bore; (diámetro) diameter; (fig) calibre

calidad [kali'ðað] nf quality; **de ~** quality cpd; **en ~ de** in the capacity of, as

cálido, -a ['kaliðo, a] adj hot; (fig) warm

caliente etc [ka'ljente] vb V **calentar** ▷ adj hot; (fig) fiery; (disputa) heated; (fam: cachondo) randy

calificación [kalifika'θjon] nf qualification; (de alumno) grade, mark

calificado, -a [kalifi'kaðo, a] (LAM) adj (competente) qualified; (obrero) skilled

calificar [kalifi'kar] vt to qualify; (alumno) to grade, mark; **~ de** to describe as

calima [ka'lima] *nf* (*cerca del mar*) mist

cáliz ['kaliθ] *nm* chalice

caliza [ka'liθa] *nf* limestone

callado, -a [ka'ʎaðo, a] *adj* quiet

callar [ka'ʎar] *vt* (*asunto delicado*) to keep quiet about, say nothing about; (*persona, opinión*) to silence ▷ *vi* to keep quiet, be silent; **callarse** *vr* to keep quiet, be silent; **¡cállate!** be quiet!, shut up!

calle ['kaʎe] *nf* street; (*Deporte*) lane; **~ arriba/abajo** up/down the street; **calle de sentido único** one-way street; **calle mayor** (*ESP*) high (*BRIT*) o main (*US*) street; **calle peatonal** pedestrianized o pedestrian street; **calle principal** (*LAM*) high (*BRIT*) o main (*US*) street; **callejear** *vi* to wander (about) the streets; **callejero, -a** *adj* street *cpd* ▷ *nm* street map; **callejón** *nm* alley, passage; **callejón sin salida** cul-de-sac; **callejuela** *nf* side-street, alley

callista [ka'ʎista] *nmf* chiropodist

callo ['kaʎo] *nm* callus; (*en el pie*) corn; **callos** *nmpl* (*Culin*) tripe *sg*

calma ['kalma] *nf* calm

calmante [kal'mante] *nm* sedative, tranquillizer

calmar [kal'mar] *vt* to calm, calm down ▷ *vi* (*tempestad*) to abate; (*mente etc*) to become calm

calor [ka'lor] *nm* heat; (*agradable*) warmth; **hace ~** it's hot; **tener ~** to be hot

caloría [kalo'ria] *nf* calorie

calumnia [ka'lumnja] *nf* calumny, slander

caluroso, -a [kalu'roso, a] *adj* hot; (*sin exceso*) warm; (*fig*) enthusiastic

calva ['kalβa] *nf* bald patch; (*en bosque*) clearing

calvario [kal'βarjo] *nm* stations *pl* of the cross

calvicie [kal'βiθje] *nf* baldness

calvo, -a ['kalβo, a] *adj* bald; (*terreno*) bare, barren; (*tejido*) threadbare

calza ['kalθa] *nf* wedge, chock

calzada [kal'θaða] *nf* roadway, highway

calzado, -a [kal'θaðo, a] *adj* shod ▷ *nm* footwear

calzador [kalθa'ðor] *nm* shoehorn

calzar [kal'θar] *vt* (*zapatos etc*) to wear; (*mueble*) to put a wedge under; **calzarse** *vr*: **~se los zapatos** to put on one's shoes; **¿qué (número) calza?** what size do you take?

calzón [kal'θon] *nm* (*ESP: pantalón corto*) shorts; (*LAM: ropa interior: de hombre*) underpants, pants (*BRIT*), shorts (*US*); (: *de mujer*) panties, knickers (*BRIT*)

calzoncillos [kalθon'θiʎos] *nmpl* underpants

cama ['kama] *nf* bed; **hacer la ~** to make the bed; **cama individual/de matrimonio** single/double bed

camaleón [kamale'on] *nm* chameleon

cámara ['kamara] *nf* chamber; (*habitación*) room; (*sala*) hall; (*Cine*) cine camera; (*fotográfica*) camera; **cámara de aire** (*ESP*) inner tube; **cámara de comercio** chamber of commerce; **cámara de gas** gas chamber; **cámara digital** digital camera; **cámara frigorífica** cold-storage room

camarada [kama'raða] *nmf* comrade, companion

camarera [kama'rera] *nf* (*en restaurante*) waitress; (*en casa, hotel*) maid

camarero [kama'rero] *nm* waiter

camarógrafo, -a [kama'rografo, a] (*LAM*) *nm/f* cameraman/camerawoman

camarón [kama'ron] *nm* shrimp

camarote [kama'rote] *nm* cabin

cambiable [kam'bjaβle] *adj* (*variable*) changeable, variable; (*intercambiable*) interchangeable

cambiante [kam'bjante] *adj* variable

cambiar [kam'bjar] *vt* to change; (*dinero*) to exchange ▷ *vi* to change; **cambiarse** *vr* (*mudarse*) to move; (*de ropa*) to change; **~ de idea** u **opinión** to change one's mind; **~se de ropa** to change (one's clothes)

cambio ['kambjo] *nm* change; (*trueque*) exchange; (*Com*) rate of exchange; (*oficina*) bureau de change; (*dinero menudo*) small change; **a ~ de** in return o exchange for; **en ~** on the other hand; (*en lugar de*) instead; **cambio climático** climate change; **cambio de divisas** foreign exchange; **cambio de marchas** o **velocidades** gear lever

camelar [kame'lar] *vt* to sweet-talk

camello [ka'meʎo] *nm* camel; (*fam: traficante*) pusher

camerino [kame'rino] *nm* dressing room

camilla [ka'miʎa] *nf* (*Med*) stretcher

caminar [kami'nar] *vi* (*marchar*) to walk, go ▷ *vt* (*recorrer*) to cover, travel

caminata [kami'nata] *nf* long walk; (*por el campo*) hike

camino [ka'mino] *nm* way, road; (*sendero*) track; **a medio ~** halfway (there); **en el ~** on the way, en route; **~ de** on the way to; **Camino de Santiago** Way of St James; **camino particular** private road

● **CAMINO DE SANTIAGO**

The **Camino de Santiago** is a medieval pilgrim route stretching from the Pyrenees to Santiago de Compostela

● in north-west Spain, where tradition
● has it the body of the Apostle James is
● buried. Nowadays it is a popular tourist
● route as well as a religious one.

camión [ka'mjon] nm lorry (BRIT), truck (US); (MÉX: autobús) bus; **camión cisterna** tanker; **camión de la basura** dustcart, refuse lorry; **camión de mudanzas** removal (BRIT) o moving (US) van; **camionero, -a** nm/f lorry o truck driver

camioneta [kamjo'neta] nf van, light truck

camisa [ka'misa] nf shirt; (Bot) skin; **camisa de fuerza** straitjacket

camiseta [kami'seta] nf (prenda) tee-shirt; (ropa interior) vest; (de deportista) top

camisón [kami'son] nm nightdress, nightgown

camorra [ka'morra] nf: **buscar ~** to look for trouble

camote [ka'mote] nm (MÉX, CS: batata) sweet potato, yam; (MÉX: bulbo) tuber, bulb; (CS: fam: enamoramiento) crush

campamento [kampa'mento] nm camp

campana [kam'pana] nf bell; **campanada** nf peal; **campanario** nm belfry

campanilla [kampa'niʎa] nf small bell

campaña [kam'paɲa] nf (Mil, Pol) campaign; **campaña electoral** election campaign

campechano, -a [kampe'tʃano, a] adj (franco) open

campeón, -ona [kampe'on, ona] nm/f champion; **campeonato** nm championship

cámper ['kamper] (LAM) nm o f caravan (BRIT), trailer (US)

campera [kam'pera] (RPL) nf anorak

campesino, -a [kampe'sino, a] adj country cpd, rural; (gente) peasant cpd ▷ nm/f countryman/woman; (agricultor) farmer

campestre [kam'pestre] adj country cpd, rural

camping ['kampin] (pl ~s) nm camping; (lugar) campsite; **ir** o **estar de ~** to go camping

campo ['kampo] nm (fuera de la ciudad) country, countryside; (Agr, Elec) field; (de fútbol) pitch; (de golf) course; (Mil) camp; **campo de batalla** battlefield; **campo de concentración** concentration camp; **campo de deportes** sports ground, playing field; **campo visual** field of vision, visual field

camuflaje [kamu'flaxe] nm camouflage

cana ['kana] nf white o grey hair; **tener ~s**

to be going grey

Canadá [kana'ða] nm Canada; **canadiense** adj, nmf Canadian ▷ nf fur-lined jacket

canal [ka'nal] nm canal; (Geo) channel, strait; (de televisión) channel; (de tejado) gutter; **canal de Panamá** Panama Canal

canaleta [kana'leta] (LAM) nf (de tejado) gutter

canalizar [kanali'θar] vt to channel

canalla [ka'naʎa] nf rabble, mob ▷ nm swine

canapé [kana'pe] (pl ~s) nm sofa, settee; (Culin) canapé

Canarias [ka'narjas] nfpl (tb: **las Islas ~**) the Canary Islands, the Canaries

canario, -a [ka'narjo, a] adj, nm/f (native) of the Canary Isles ▷ nm (Zool) canary

canasta [ka'nasta] nf (round) basket

canasto [ka'nasto] nm large basket

cancela [kan'θela] nf gate

cancelación [kanθela'θjon] nf cancellation

cancelar [kanθe'lar] vt to cancel; (una deuda) to write off

cáncer ['kanθer] nm (Med) cancer; **C~** (Astrología) Cancer

cancha ['kantʃa] nf (de baloncesto) court; (LAM: campo) pitch; **cancha de tenis** (LAM) tennis court

canciller [kanθi'ʎer] nm chancellor

canción [kan'θjon] nf song; **canción de cuna** lullaby

candado [kan'daðo] nm padlock

candente [kan'dente] adj red-hot; (fig: tema) burning

candidato, -a [kandi'ðato, a] nm/f candidate

cándido, -a ['kandiðo, a] adj simple; naive

▌ No confundir **cándido** con la palabra inglesa candid.

candil [kan'dil] nm oil lamp; **candilejas** nfpl (Teatro) footlights

canela [ka'nela] nf cinnamon

canelones [kane'lones] nmpl cannelloni

cangrejo [kan'grexo] nm crab

canguro [kan'guro] nm kangaroo; **hacer de ~** to babysit

caníbal [ka'niβal] adj, nmf cannibal

canica [ka'nika] nf marble

canijo, -a [ka'nixo, a] adj frail, sickly

canilla [ka'niʎa] (RPL) nf tap (BRIT), faucet (US)

canjear [kanxe'ar] vt to exchange

canoa [ka'noa] nf canoe

canon ['kanon] nm canon; (pensión) rent;

(Com) tax

canonizar [kanoni'θar] vt to canonize

canoso, -a [ka'noso, a] adj grey-haired

cansado, -a [kan'saðo, a] adj tired, weary; (tedioso) tedious, boring

cansancio [kan'sanθjo] nm tiredness, fatigue

cansar [kan'sar] vt (fatigar) to tire, tire out; (aburrir) to bore; (fastidiar) to bother; **cansarse** vr to tire, get tired; (aburrirse) to get bored

cantábrico, -a [kan'taβriko, a] adj Cantabrian

cantante [kan'tante] adj singing ⊳ nmf singer

cantar [kan'tar] vt (fatigar) to sing ⊳ vi to sing; (insecto) to chirp ⊳ nm (acción) singing; (canción) song; (poema) poem

cántaro ['kantaro] nm pitcher, jug; **llover a ~s** to rain cats and dogs

cante ['kante] nm (Mús) Andalusian folk song; **cante jondo** flamenco singing

cantera [kan'tera] nf quarry

cantero [kan'tero] (RPL) nm (arriate) border

cantidad [kanti'ðað] nf quantity, amount; **~ de** lots of

cantimplora [kantim'plora] nf (frasco) water bottle, canteen

cantina [kan'tina] nf canteen; (de estación) buffet; (LAM: bar) bar

cantinero, -a [kanti'nero, a] (MÉX) nm/f barman/barmaid, bartender (US)

canto ['kanto] nm singing; (canción) song; (borde) edge, rim; (de cuchillo) back; **canto rodado** boulder

cantor, a [kan'tor, a] nm/f singer

canturrear [kanturre'ar] vi to sing softly

canuto [ka'nuto] nm (tubo) small tube; (fam: droga) joint

caña ['kaɲa] nf (Bot: tallo) stem, stalk; (carrizo) reed; (vaso) tumbler; (de cerveza) glass of beer; (Anat) shinbone; **caña de azúcar** sugar cane; **caña de pescar** fishing rod

cañada [ka'ɲaða] nf (entre dos montañas) gully, ravine; (camino) cattle track

cáñamo ['kaɲamo] nm hemp

cañería [kaɲe'ria] nf (tubo) pipe

caño ['kaɲo] nm (tubo) tube, pipe; (de albañal) sewer; (Mús) pipe; (de fuente) jet

cañón [ka'ɲon] nm (Mil) cannon; (de fusil) barrel; (Geo) canyon, gorge

caoba [ka'oβa] nf mahogany

caos ['kaos] nm chaos

capa ['kapa] nf cloak, cape; (Geo) layer, stratum; **capa de ozono** ozone layer

capacidad [kapaθi'ðað] nf (medida) capacity; (aptitud) capacity, ability

caparazón [kapara'θon] nm shell

capataz [kapa'taθ] nm foreman

capaz [ka'paθ] adj able, capable; (amplio) capacious, roomy

capellán [kape'ʎan] nm chaplain; (sacerdote) priest

capicúa [kapi'kua] adj inv (número, fecha) reversible

capilla [ka'piʎa] nf chapel

capital [kapi'tal] adj capital ⊳ nm (Com) capital ⊳ nf (ciudad) capital; **capital social** share o authorized capital

capitalismo [kapita'lismo] nm capitalism; **capitalista** adj, nmf capitalist

capitán [kapi'tan] nm captain

capítulo [ka'pitulo] nm chapter

capó [ka'po] nm (Auto) bonnet

capón [ka'pon] nm (gallo) capon

capota [ka'pota] nf (de mujer) bonnet; (Auto) hood (BRIT), top (US)

capote [ka'pote] nm (abrigo: de militar) greatcoat; (de torero) cloak

capricho [ka'pritʃo] nm whim, caprice; **caprichoso, -a** adj capricious

Capricornio [kapri'kornjo] nm Capricorn

cápsula ['kapsula] nf capsule

captar [kap'tar] vt (comprender) to understand; (Radio) to pick up; (atención, apoyo) to attract

captura [kap'tura] nf capture; (Jur) arrest; **capturar** vt to capture; to arrest

capucha [ka'putʃa] nf hood, cowl

capuchón [kapu'tʃon] (ESP) nm (de bolígrafo) cap

capullo [ka'puʎo] nm (Bot) bud; (Zool) cocoon; (fam) idiot

caqui ['kaki] nm khaki

cara ['kara] nf (Anat: de moneda) face; (de disco) side; (descaro) boldness; **~ a** facing; **de ~** opposite, facing; **dar la ~** to face the consequences; **¿~ o cruz?** heads or tails?; **¡qué ~ (más dura)!** what a nerve!

Caracas [ka'rakas] n Caracas

caracol [kara'kol] nm (Zool) snail; (concha) (sea) shell

carácter [ka'rakter] (pl **caracteres**) nm character; **tener buen/mal ~** to be good natured/bad tempered

característica [karakte'ristika] nf characteristic

característico, -a [karakte'ristiko, a] adj characteristic

caracterizar [karakteri'θar] vt to characterize, typify

caradura [kara'ðura] nmf: **es un ~** he's got a nerve

carajillo [kara'xiʎo] nm coffee with a dash

of brandy

carajo [ka'raxo] (fam!) nm: ¡~! shit! (!)

caramba [ka'ramba] excl good gracious!

caramelo [kara'melo] nm (dulce) sweet; (azúcar fundida) caramel

caravana [kara'βana] nf caravan; (fig) group; (Auto) tailback

carbón [kar'βon] nm coal; **papel ~** carbon paper

carbono [kar'βono] nm carbon

carburador [karβura'ðor] nm carburettor

carburante [karβu'rante] nm (para motor) fuel

carcajada [karka'xaða] nf (loud) laugh, guffaw

cárcel ['karθel] nf prison, jail; (Tec) clamp

carcoma [kar'koma] nf woodworm

cardar [kar'ðar] vt (pelo) to backcomb

cardenal [karðe'nal] nm (Rel) cardinal; (Med) bruise

cardíaco, -a [kar'ðiako, a] adj cardiac, heart cpd

cardinal [karði'nal] adj cardinal

cardo ['karðo] nm thistle

carecer [kare'θer] vi: ~ **de** to lack, be in need of

carencia [ka'renθja] nf lack; (escasez) shortage; (Med) deficiency

careta [ka'reta] nf mask

carga ['karxa] nf (peso, Elec) load; (de barco) cargo, freight; (Mil) charge; (responsabilidad) duty, obligation

cargado, -a [kar'xaðo, a] adj loaded; (Elec) live; (café, té) strong; (cielo) overcast

cargamento [karxa'mento] nm (acción) loading; (mercancías) load, cargo

cargar [kar'xar] vt (barco, arma) to load; (Elec) to charge; (Com: algo en cuenta) to charge; (Inform) to load ▷ vi (Mil) to charge; (Auto) to load (up); **~ con** to pick up, carry away; (peso: fig) to shoulder, bear; **cargarse** vr (fam: estropear) to break; (: matar) to bump off

cargo ['karxo] nm (puesto) post, office; (responsabilidad) duty, obligation; (Jur) charge; **hacerse ~ de** to take charge of o responsibility for

carguero [kar'xero] nm freighter, cargo boat; (avión) freight plane

Caribe [ka'riβe] nm: **el ~ the** Caribbean; **del ~** Caribbean; **caribeño, -a** [kari'βeɲo, a] adj Caribbean

caricatura [karika'tura] nf caricature

caricia [ka'riθja] nf caress

caridad [kari'ðað] nf charity

caries ['karjes] nf inv tooth decay

cariño [ka'riɲo] nm affection, love; (caricia) caress; (en carta) love ...; **tener ~ a** to be fond

of; **cariñoso, -a** adj affectionate

carisma [ka'risma] nm charisma

caritativo, -a [karita'tiβo, a] adj charitable

cariz [ka'riθ] nm: **tener** o **tomar buen/mal ~** to look good/bad

carmín [kar'min] nm lipstick

carnal [kar'nal] adj carnal; **primo ~** first cousin

carnaval [karna'βal] nm carnival

carne ['karne] nf flesh; (Culin) meat; **se me pone la ~ de gallina sólo verlo** I get the creeps just seeing it; **carne de cerdo/ cordero/ternera/vaca** pork/lamb/veal/ beef; **carne de gallina** (fig) gooseflesh; **carne molida** (LAM) mince (BRIT), ground meat (US); **carne picada** (ESP, RPL) mince (BRIT), ground meat (US)

carné [kar'ne] (ESP) (pl ~s) nm: ~ **de conducir** driving licence (BRIT), driver's license (US); ~ **de identidad** identity card; ~ **de socio** membership card

carnero [kar'nero] nm sheep, ram; (carne) mutton

carnet [kar'ne] (ESP) (pl ~s) nm = **carné**

carnicería [karniθe'ria] nf butcher's (shop); (fig: matanza) carnage, slaughter

carnicero, -a [karni'θero, a] adj carnivorous ▷ nm/f butcher; (carnívoro) carnivore

carnívoro, -a [kar'niβoro, a] adj carnivorous

caro, -a ['karo, a] adj dear; (Com) dear, expensive ▷ adv dear, dearly

carpa ['karpa] nf (pez) carp; (de circo) big top; (LAM: tienda de campaña) tent

carpeta [kar'peta] nf folder, file; **carpeta de anillas** ring binder

carpintería [karpinte'ria] nf carpentry, joinery; **carpintero** nm carpenter

carraspear [karraspe'ar] vi to clear one's throat

carraspera [karras'pera] nf hoarseness

carrera [ka'rrera] nf (acción) run(ning); (espacio recorrido) run; (competición) race; (trayecto) course; (profesión) career; (licenciatura) degree; **a la ~** at (full) speed; **carrera de obstáculos** (Deporte) steeplechase

carrete [ka'rrete] nm reel, spool; (Tec) coil

carretera [karre'tera] nf (main) road, highway; **carretera de circunvalación** ring road; **carretera nacional** ≈ A road (BRIT), ≈ state highway (US)

carretilla [karre'tiʎa] nf trolley; (Agr) (wheel)barrow

carril [ka'rril] nm furrow; (de autopista) lane; (Ferro) rail; **carril-bici** cycle lane

carrito [ka'rrito] nm trolley

carro ['karro] nm cart, wagon; (Mil) tank; (LAM: coche) car; **carro patrulla** (LAM) patrol o panda (BRIT) car

carrocería [karroθe'ria] nf bodywork, coachwork

carroña [ka'rroɲa] nf carrion no pl

carroza [ka'rroθa] nf (carruaje) coach

carrusel [karru'sel] nm merry-go-round, roundabout

carta ['karta] nf letter; (Culin) menu; (naipe) card; (mapa) map; (Jur) document; **carta certificada/urgente** registered/special-delivery letter

cartabón [karta'βon] nm set square

cartel [kar'tel] nm (anuncio) poster, placard; (Escol) wall chart; (Com) cartel; **cartelera** nf hoarding, billboard; (en periódico etc) entertainments guide; **"en cartelera"** "showing"

cartera [kar'tera] nf (de bolsillo) wallet; (de colegial, cobrador) satchel; (de señora) handbag; (para documentos) briefcase; (Com) portfolio; **ocupa la ~ de Agricultura** she is Minister of Agriculture

carterista [karte'rista] nmf pickpocket

cartero [kar'tero] nm postman

cartilla [kar'tiʎa] nf primer, first reading book; **cartilla de ahorros** savings book

cartón [kar'ton] nm cardboard; **cartón piedra** papier-mâché

cartucho [kar'tutʃo] nm (Mil) cartridge

cartulina [kartu'lina] nf card

casa ['kasa] nf house; (hogar) home; (Com) firm, company; **en ~** at home; **casa consistorial** town hall; **casa de campo** country house; **casa de huéspedes** boarding house; **casa de socorro** first aid post; **casa rodante** (CS) caravan (BRIT), trailer (US)

casado, -a [ka'saðo, a] adj married ▷ nm/f married man/woman

casar [ka'sar] vt to marry; (Jur) to quash, annul; **casarse** vr to marry, get married

cascabel [kaska'βel] nm (small) bell

cascada [kas'kaða] nf waterfall

cascanueces [kaska'nweθes] nm inv nutcrackers pl

cascar [kas'kar] vt to crack, split, break (open); **cascarse** vr to crack, split, break (open)

cáscara ['kaskara] nf (de huevo, fruta seca) shell; (de fruta) skin; (de limón) peel

casco ['kasko] nm (de bombero, soldado) helmet; (Náut: de barco) hull; (Zool: de caballo) hoof; (botella) empty bottle; (de ciudad): **el ~ antiguo** the old part; **el ~ urbano** the town centre; **los ~s azules** the UN peace-keeping force, the blue berets

cascote [kas'kote] nm rubble

caserío [kase'rio] (ESP) nm farmhouse; (casa) country mansion

casero, -a [ka'sero, a] adj (pan etc) home-made ▷ nm/f (propietario) landlord/lady; **ser muy ~** to be home-loving; **"comida casera"** "home cooking"

caseta [ka'seta] nf hut; (para bañista) cubicle; (de feria) stall

casete [ka'sete] nm o f cassette

casi ['kasi] adv almost, nearly; **~ nada** hardly anything; **~ nunca** hardly ever, almost never; **~ te caes** you almost fell

casilla [ka'siʎa] nf (casita) hut, cabin; (Ajedrez) square; (para cartas) pigeonhole; **casilla de correo** (CS) P.O. Box; **casillero** nm (para cartas) pigeonholes pl

casino [ka'sino] nm club; (de juego) casino

caso ['kaso] nm case; **en ~ de** in case of; **en ~ de que ...** in case ...; **el ~ es que ...** the fact is that ...; **en ese/todo ~** in that/any case; **hacer ~ a** to pay attention to; **venir al ~** to be relevant

caspa ['kaspa] nf dandruff

cassette [ka'sete] nm o f = **casete**

castaña [kas'taɲa] nf chestnut

castaño, -a [kas'taɲo, a] adj chestnut(-coloured), brown ▷ nm chestnut tree

castañuelas [kasta'ɲwelas] nfpl castanets

castellano, -a [kaste'ʎano, a] adj, nm/f Castilian ▷ nm (Ling) Castilian, Spanish

castigar [kasti'ɣar] vt to punish; (Deporte) to penalize; **castigo** nm punishment; (Deporte) penalty

Castilla [kas'tiʎa] nf Castille

castillo [kas'tiʎo] nm castle

castizo, -a [kas'tiθo, a] adj (Ling) pure

casto, -a ['kasto, a] adj chaste, pure

castor [kas'tor] nm beaver

castrar [kas'trar] vt to castrate

casual [ka'swal] *adj* chance, accidental

▌No confundir **casual** con la palabra
inglesa *casual*.

casualidad *nf* chance, accident;
(combinación de circunstancias) coincidence;
da la casualidad de que ... it (just) so
happens that ...; **¡qué casualidad!** what a
coincidence!

cataclismo [kata'klismo] *nm* cataclysm

catador, a [kata'ðor, a] *nm/f* wine taster

catalán, -ana [kata'lan, ana] *adj, nm/f*
Catalan ▷ *nm* (*Ling*) Catalan

catalizador [kataliθa'ðor] *nm* catalyst;
(Auto) catalytic convertor

catalogar [katalo'xar] *vt* to catalogue; **~**
a algn (de) *(fig)* to categorize sb (as)

catálogo [ka'taloxo] *nm* catalogue

Cataluña [kata'luɲa] *nf* Catalonia

catar [ka'tar] *vt* to taste, sample

catarata [kata'rata] *nf* (*Geo*) waterfall;
(Med) cataract

catarro [ka'tarro] *nm* catarrh; *(constipado)*
cold

catástrofe [ka'tastrofe] *nf* catastrophe

catear [kate'ar] *(fam) vt (examen, alumno)*
to fail

cátedra ['kateðra] *nf* (*Univ*) chair,
professorship

catedral [kate'ðral] *nf* cathedral

catedrático, -a [kate'ðratiko, a] *nm/f*
professor

categoría [katexo'ria] *nf* category; *(rango)*
rank, standing; *(calidad)* quality; **de ~** *(hotel)*
top-class

cateto, -a ['kateto, a] *(ESP: pey) nm/f*
peasant

catolicismo [katoli'θismo] *nm*
Catholicism

católico, -a [ka'toliko, a] *adj, nm/f*
Catholic

catorce [ka'torθe] *num* fourteen

cauce ['kauθe] *nm* (*de río*) riverbed; *(fig)*
channel

caucho ['kautʃo] *(ESP) nm* rubber

caudal [kau'ðal] *nm* (*de río*) volume, flow;
(fortuna) wealth; *(abundancia)* abundance

caudillo [kau'ðiʎo] *nm* leader, chief

causa ['kausa] *nf* cause; *(razón)* reason;
(Jur) lawsuit, case; **a ~ de** because of; **causar**
[kau'sar] *vt* to cause

cautela [kau'tela] *nf* caution,
cautiousness; **cauteloso, -a** *adj* cautious,
wary

cautivar [kauti'βar] *vt* to capture; *(atraer)*
to captivate

cautiverio [kauti'βerjo] *nm* captivity

cautividad [kautiβi'ðað] *nf* = **cautiverio**

cautivo, -a [kau'tiβo, a] *adj, nm/f* captive

cauto, -a ['kauto, a] *adj* cautious, careful

cava ['kaβa] *nm* champagne-type wine

cavar [ka'βar] *vt* to dig

caverna [ka'βerna] *nf* cave, cavern

cavidad [kaβi'ðað] *nf* cavity

cavilar [kaβi'lar] *vt* to ponder

cayendo *etc vb* V **caer**

caza ['kaθa] *nf* (*acción: gen*) hunting; *(: con
fusil)* shooting; *(una caza)* hunt, chase; *(de
animales)* game ▷ *nm* (*Aviac*) fighter; **ir de ~**
to go hunting; **caza mayor** game hunting;
cazador, a [kaθa'ðor, a] *nm/f* hunter;
cazadora *nf* jacket; **cazar** [ka'θar] *vt* to
hunt; *(perseguir)* to chase; *(prender)* to catch

cazo ['kaθo] *nm* saucepan

cazuela [ka'θwela] *nf* (*vasija*) pan;
(guisado) casserole

CD *nm abr (= compact disc)* CD

CD-ROM [θeðe'rom] *nm abr* CD-ROM

CE *nf abr (= Comunidad Europea)* EC

cebada [θe'βaða] *nf* barley

cebar [θe'βar] *vt (animal)* to fatten (up);
(anzuelo) to bait; *(Mil, Tec)* to prime

cebo ['θeβo] *nm (para animales)* feed, food;
(para peces, fig) bait; *(de arma)* charge

cebolla [θe'βoʎa] *nf* onion; **cebolleta** *nf*
spring onion

cebra ['θeβra] *nf* zebra

cecear [θeθe'ar] *vi* to lisp

ceder [θe'ðer] *vt* to hand over, give up,
part with ▷ *vi (renunciar)* to give in, yield;
(disminuir) to diminish, decline; *(romperse)*
to give way

cedro ['θeðro] *nm* cedar

cédula ['θeðula] *nf* certificate, document;
cédula de identidad *(LAM)* identity card;
cédula electoral *(LAM)* ballot

cegar [θe'xar] *vt* to blind; *(tubería etc)* to
block up, stop up ▷ *vi* to go blind; **cegarse**
vr: **~se (de)** to be blinded (by)

ceguera [θe'xera] *nf* blindness

ceja ['θexa] *nf* eyebrow

cejar [θe'xar] *vi (fig)* to back down

celador, a [θela'ðor, a] *nm/f (de edificio)*
watchman; *(de museo etc)* attendant

celda ['θelda] *nf* cell

celebración [θeleβra'θjon] *nf* celebration

celebrar [θele'βrar] *vt* to celebrate;
(alabar) to praise ▷ *vi* to be glad; **celebrarse**
vr to occur, take place

célebre ['θeleβre] *adj* famous

celebridad [θeleβri'ðað] *nf* fame;
(persona) celebrity

celeste [θe'leste] *adj (azul)* sky-blue

celestial [θeles'tjal] *adj* celestial, heavenly

celo¹ ['θelo] *nm* zeal; *(Rel)* fervour; *(Zool)*: **en**
~ on heat; **celos** *nmpl* jealousy *sg*; **dar ~s**
a algn to make sb jealous; **tener ~s** to be

jealous

celo²® ['θelo] nm Sellotape®

celofán [θelo'fan] nm cellophane

celoso, -a [θe'loso, a] adj jealous; (trabajador) zealous

celta ['θelta] adj Celtic ▷ nmf Celt

célula ['θelula] nf cell

celulitis [θelu'litis] nf cellulite

cementerio [θemen'terjo] nm cemetery, graveyard

cemento [θe'mento] nm cement; (hormigón) concrete; (LAM: cola) glue

cena ['θena] nf evening meal, dinner; **cenar** [θe'nar] vt to have for dinner ▷ vi to have dinner

cenicero [θeni'θero] nm ashtray

ceniza [θe'niθa] nf ash, ashes pl

censo ['θenso] nm census; **censo electoral** electoral roll

censura [θen'sura] nf (Pol) censorship; **censurar** [θensu'rar] vt (idea) to censure; (cortar: película) to censor

centella [θen'teʎa] nf spark

centenar [θente'nar] nm hundred

centenario, -a [θente'narjo, a] adj centenary; hundred-year-old ▷ nm centenary

centeno [θen'teno] nm (Bot) rye

centésimo, -a [θen'tesimo, a] adj hundredth

centígrado [θen'tixraðo] adj centigrade

centímetro [θen'timetro] nm centimetre (BRIT), centimeter (US)

céntimo ['θentimo] nm cent

centinela [θenti'nela] nm sentry, guard

centollo [θen'toʎo] nm spider crab

central [θen'tral] adj central ▷ nf head office; (Tec) plant; (Tel) exchange; **central eléctrica** power station; **central nuclear** nuclear power station; **central telefónica** telephone exchange

centralita [θentra'lita] nf switchboard

centralizar [θentrali'θar] vt to centralize

centrar [θen'trar] vt to centre

céntrico, -a ['θentriko, a] adj central

centrifugar [θentrifu'xar] vt to spin-dry

centro ['θentro] nm centre; **centro comercial** shopping centre; **centro de atención al cliente** call centre; **centro de salud** health centre; **centro escolar** school; **centro juvenil** youth club; **centro turístico** (lugar muy visitado) tourist centre; **centro urbano** urban area, city

centroamericano, -a [θentroameri'kano, a] adj, nm/f Central American

ceñido, -a [θe'ɲiðo, a] adj (chaqueta, pantalón) tight(-fitting)

ceñir [θe'ɲir] vt (rodear) to encircle, surround; (ajustar) to fit (tightly)

ceño ['θeɲo] nm frown, scowl; **fruncir el ~** to frown, knit one's brow

cepillar [θepi'ʎar] vt to brush; (madera) to plane (down)

cepillo [θe'piʎo] nm brush; (para madera) plane; **cepillo de dientes** toothbrush

cera ['θera] nf wax

cerámica [θe'ramika] nf pottery; (arte) ceramics

cerca ['θerka] nf fence ▷ adv near, nearby, close; **~ de** near, close to

cercanías [θerka'nias] nfpl (afueras) outskirts, suburbs

cercano, -a [θer'kano, a] adj close, near

cercar [θer'kar] vt to fence in; (rodear) to surround

cerco ['θerko] nm (Agr) enclosure; (LAM: valla) fence; (Mil) siege

cerdo, -a ['θerðo, a] nm/f pig/sow

cereal [θere'al] nm cereal; **cereales** nmpl cereals, grain sg

cerebro [θe'reβro] nm brain; (fig) brains pl

ceremonia [θere'monja] nf ceremony; **ceremonioso, -a** adj ceremonious

cereza [θe'reθa] nf cherry

cerilla [θe'riʎa] nf (fósforo) match

cerillo [θe'riʎo] (MÉX) nm match

cero ['θero] nm nothing, zero

cerquillo [θer'kiʎo] nm (CAM, RPL) fringe (BRIT), bangs pl (US)

cerrado, -a [θe'rraðo, a] adj closed, shut; (con llave) locked; (tiempo) cloudy, overcast; (curva) sharp; (acento) thick, broad

cerradura [θerra'ðura] nf (acción) closing; (mecanismo) lock

cerrajero [θerra'xero] nm locksmith

cerrar [θe'rrar] vt to close, shut; (paso, carretera) to close; (grifo) to turn off; (cuenta, negocio) to close ▷ vi to close, shut; (noche) to come down; **cerrarse** vr to close, shut; **~ con llave** to lock; **~ un trato** to strike a bargain

cerro ['θerro] nm hill

cerrojo [θe'rroxo] nm (herramienta) bolt; (de puerta) latch

certamen [θer'tamen] nm competition, contest

certero, -a [θer'tero, a] adj (gen) accurate

certeza [θer'teθa] nf certainty

certidumbre [θerti'ðumbre] nf = **certeza**

certificado, -a [θertifi'kaðo, a] adj (carta, paquete) registered; (aprobado) certified ▷ nm certificate; **certificado médico** medical certificate

certificar [θertifi'kar] vt (asegurar, atestar) to certify

cervatillo [θerβa'tiʎo] *nm* fawn

cervecería [θerβeθe'ria] *nf (fábrica)* brewery; *(bar)* public house, pub

cerveza [θer'βeθa] *nf* beer

cesar [θe'sar] *vi* to cease, stop ▷ *vt (funcionario)* to remove from office

cesárea [θe'sarea] *nf (Med)* Caesarean operation *o* section

cese ['θese] *nm (de trabajo)* dismissal; *(de pago)* suspension

césped ['θespeð] *nm* grass, lawn

cesta ['θesta] *nf* basket

cesto ['θesto] *nm (large)* basket, hamper

cfr *abr (=confróntese)* cf.

chabacano, -a [tʃaβa'kano, a] *adj* vulgar, coarse

chabola [tʃa'βola] *(ESP) nf* shack; **barrio de chabolas** shanty town

chacal [tʃa'kal] *nm* jackal

chacha ['tʃatʃa] *(fam) nf* maid

cháchara ['tʃatʃara] *nf* chatter; **estar de ~** to chatter away

chacra ['tʃakra] *(CS) nf* smallholding

chafa ['tʃafa] *(MÉX: fam) adj* useless, dud

chafar [tʃa'far] *vt (aplastar)* to crush; *(plan etc)* to ruin

chal [tʃal] *nm* shawl

chalado, -a [tʃa'lado, a] *(fam) adj* crazy

chalé [tʃa'le] *(pl* **~s***) nm* villa, ≈ detached house

chaleco [tʃa'leko] *nm* waistcoat, vest *(US)*; **chaleco de seguridad** *(Aut)* reflective safety vest; **chaleco salvavidas** life jacket

chalet [tʃa'le] *(pl* **~s***) nm* = **chalé**

chamaco, -a *(MÉX)* [tʃa'mako, a] *nm/f (niño)* kid

chambear [tʃambe'ar] *(MÉX: fam) vi* to earn one's living

champán [tʃam'pan] *nm* champagne

champiñón [tʃampi'non] *nm* mushroom

champú [tʃam'pu] *(pl* **~es, ~s***) nm* shampoo

chamuscar [tʃamus'kar] *vt* to scorch, sear, singe

chance ['tʃanθe] *(LAM) nm* chance

chancho, -a ['tʃantʃo, a] *(LAM) nm/f* pig

chanchullo [tʃan'tʃuʎo] *(fam) nm* fiddle

chandal [tʃan'dal] *nm* tracksuit

chantaje [tʃan'taxe] *nm* blackmail

chapa ['tʃapa] *nf (de metal)* plate, sheet; *(de madera)* board, panel; *(RPL Auto)* number *(BRIT) o* license *(US)* plate; **chapado, -a** *adj*: **chapado en oro** gold-plated

chaparrón [tʃapa'rron] *nm* downpour, cloudburst

chaperón [tʃape'ron] *(MÉX) nm*: **hacer de ~** to play gooseberry; **chaperona** *(LAM) nf*: **hacer de chaperona** to play gooseberry

chapopote [tʃapo'pote] *(MÉX) nm* tar

chapulín [tʃapu'lin] *(MÉX, CAM) nm* grasshopper

chapurrear [tʃapurre'ar] *vt (idioma)* to speak badly

chapuza [tʃa'puθa] *nf* botched job

chapuzón [tʃapu'θon] *nm*: **darse un ~** to go for a dip

chaqueta [tʃa'keta] *nf* jacket

chaquetón [tʃake'ton] *nm* long jacket

charca ['tʃarka] *nf* pond, pool

charco ['tʃarko] *nm* pool, puddle

charcutería [tʃarkute'ria] *nf (tienda)* shop selling chiefly pork meat products; *(productos)* cooked pork meats *pl*

charla ['tʃarla] *nf* talk, chat; *(conferencia)* lecture; **charlar** [tʃar'lar] *vi* to talk, chat; **charlatán, -ana** [tʃarla'tan, ana] *nm/f (hablador)* chatterbox; *(estafador)* trickster

charol [tʃa'rol] *nm* varnish; *(cuero)* patent leather

charola [tʃa'rola] *(MÉX) nf* tray

charro, -a ['tʃarro, a] *(MÉX) nm* typical Mexican

chasco ['tʃasko] *nm (desengaño)* disappointment

chasis ['tʃasis] *nm inv* chassis

chasquido [tʃas'kiðo] *nm* crack; click

chat [tʃat] *nm (Internet)* chat room

chatarra [tʃa'tarra] *nf* scrap (metal)

chatear [tʃate'ar] *vi (Internet)* to chat

chato, -a ['tʃato, a] *adj* flat; *(nariz)* snub

chaucha ['tʃautʃa] *(RPL) nf* runner *(BRIT) o* pole *(US)* bean

chaval, a [tʃa'βal, a] *(ESP) nm/f* kid, lad/ lass

chavo, -a ['tʃaβo] *(MÉX: fam) nm/f* guy/girl

checar [tʃe'kar] *(MÉX) vt*: **~ tarjeta** *(al entrar)* to clock in *o* on; *(: al salir)* to clock off *o* out

checo, -a ['tʃeko, a] *adj, nm/f* Czech ▷ *nm (Ling)* Czech

checoslovaco, -a [tʃekoslo'βako, a] *adj, nm/f* Czech, Czechoslovak

Checoslovaquia [tʃekoslo'βakja] *nf (Hist)* Czechoslovakia

cheque ['tʃeke] *nm* cheque *(BRIT)*, check *(US)*; **cobrar un ~** to cash a cheque; **cheque al portador** cheque payable to bearer; **cheque de viaje** traveller's cheque *(BRIT)*, traveler's check *(US)*; **cheque en blanco** blank cheque

chequeo [tʃe'keo] *nm (Med)* check-up; *(Auto)* service

chequera [tʃe'kera] *(LAM) nf* chequebook *(BRIT)*, checkbook *(US)*

chévere ['tʃeβere] *(LAM: fam) adj* great

chícharo ['tʃitʃaro] *(MÉX, CAM) nm* pea

chichón [tʃi'tʃon] *nm* bump, lump

chicle ['tʃikle] *nm* chewing gum

chico, -a ['tʃiko, a] *adj* small, little ▷ *nm/f* (*niño*) child; (*muchacho*) boy/girl

chiflado, -a [tʃi'flaðo, a] *adj* crazy

chiflar [tʃi'flar] *vt* to hiss, boo

chilango, -a [tʃi'lango, a] (*MÉX*) *adj* of o from Mexico City

Chile ['tʃile] *nm* Chile; **chileno, -a** *adj*, *nm/f* Chilean

chile ['tʃile] *nm* chilli pepper

chillar [tʃi'ʎar] *vi* (*persona*) to yell, scream; (*animal salvaje*) to howl; (*cerdo*) to squeal

chillido [tʃi'ʎiðo] *nm* (*de persona*) yell, scream; (*de animal*) howl

chimenea [tʃime'nea] *nf* chimney; (*hogar*) fireplace

China ['tʃina] *nf* (*tb*: **la ~**) China

chinche ['tʃintʃe] *nf* (*insecto*) (bed)bug; (*Tec*) drawing pin (*BRIT*), thumbtack (*US*) ▷ *nmf* nuisance, pest

chincheta [tʃin'tʃeta] *nf* drawing pin (*BRIT*), thumbtack (*US*)

chingada [tʃin'gaða] (*MÉX: fam!*) *nf*: **hijo de la ~** bastard

chino, -a ['tʃino, a] *adj*, *nm/f* Chinese ▷ *nm* (*Ling*) Chinese

chipirón [tʃipi'ron] *nm* (*Zool, Culin*) squid

Chipre ['tʃipre] *nf* Cyprus; **chipriota** *adj*, *nmf* Cypriot

chiquillo, -a [tʃi'kiʎo, a] *nm/f* (*fam*) kid

chirimoya [tʃiri'moja] *nf* custard apple

chiringuito [tʃirin'xito] *nm* small open-air bar

chiripa [tʃi'ripa] *nf* fluke

chirriar [tʃi'rrjar] *vi* to creak, squeak

chirrido [tʃi'rriðo] *nm* creak(ing), squeak(ing)

chisme ['tʃisme] *nm* (*habladurías*) piece of gossip; (*fam: objeto*) thingummyjig

chismoso, -a [tʃis'moso, a] *adj* gossiping ▷ *nm/f* gossip

chispa ['tʃispa] *nf* spark; (*fig*) sparkle; (*ingenio*) wit; (*fam*) drunkenness

chispear [tʃispe'ar] *vi* (*lloviznar*) to drizzle

chiste ['tʃiste] *nm* joke, funny story

chistoso, -a [tʃis'toso, a] *adj* funny, amusing

chivo, -a ['tʃiβo, a] *nm/f* (billy-/nanny-) goat; **chivo expiatorio** scapegoat

chocante [tʃo'kante] *adj* startling; (*extraño*) odd; (*ofensivo*) shocking

chocar [tʃo'kar] *vi* (*coches etc*) to collide, crash ▷ *vt* to shock; (*sorprender*) to startle; **~ con** to collide with; (*fig*) to run into, run up against; **¡chócala!** (*fam*) put it there!

chochear [tʃotʃe'ar] *vi* to be senile

chocho, -a ['tʃotʃo, a] *adj* doddering,

senile; (*fig*) soft, doting

choclo ['tʃoklo] (*cs*) *nm* (*grano*) sweet corn; (*mazorca*) corn on the cob

chocolate [tʃoko'late] *adj*, *nm* chocolate; **chocolatina** *nf* chocolate

chofer [tʃo'fer] *nm* = **chófer**

chófer ['tʃofer] *nm* driver

chollo ['tʃoʎo] (*ESP: fam*) *nm* bargain, snip

choque *etc* ['tʃoke] *vb* V **chocar** ▷ *nm* (*impacto*) impact; (*golpe*) jolt; (*Auto*) crash; (*fig*) conflict; **choque frontal** head-on collision

chorizo [tʃo'riθo] *nm* hard pork sausage, (type of) salami

chorrada [tʃo'rraða] (*ESP: fam*) *nf*: **¡es una ~!** that's crap! (*!*); **decir ~s** to talk crap (*!*)

chorrear [tʃorre'ar] *vi* to gush (out), spout (out); (*gotear*) to drip, trickle

chorro ['tʃorro] *nm* jet; (*fig*) stream

choza ['tʃoθa] *nf* hut, shack

chubasco [tʃu'βasko] *nm* squall

chubasquero [tʃuβas'kero] *nm* lightweight raincoat

chuchería [tʃutʃe'ria] *nf* trinket

chuleta [tʃu'leta] *nf* chop, cutlet

chulo ['tʃulo] *nm* (*de prostituta*) pimp

chupaleta [tʃupa'leta] (*MÉX*) *nf* lollipop

chupar [tʃu'par] *vt* to suck; (*absorber*) to absorb; **chuparse** *vr* to grow thin

chupete [tʃu'pete] (*ESP, cs*) *nm* dummy (*BRIT*), pacifier (*US*)

chupetín [tʃupe'tin] (*RPL*) *nf* lollipop

chupito [tʃu'pito] (*fam*) *nm* shot

chupón [tʃu'pon] *nm* (*piruleta*) lollipop; (*LAM: chupete*) dummy (*BRIT*), pacifier (*US*)

churro ['tʃurro] *nm* (type of) fritter

chusma ['tʃusma] *nf* rabble, mob

chutar [tʃu'tar] *vi* to shoot (at goal)

Cía *abr* (= *compañía*) Co.

cianuro [θja'nuro] *nm* cyanide

cibercafé [θiβerka'fe] *nm* cybercafé

cibernauta [θiβer'nauta] *nmf* web surfer, Internet user

ciberterrorista [θiβerterro'rista] *nmf* cyberterrorist

cicatriz [θika'triθ] *nf* scar; **cicatrizarse** *vr* to heal (up), form a scar

ciclismo [θi'klismo] *nm* cycling

ciclista [θi'klista] *adj* cycle *cpd* ▷ *nmf* cyclist

ciclo ['θiklo] *nm* cycle; **cicloturismo** *nm* touring by bicycle

ciclón [θi'klon] *nm* cyclone

ciego, -a ['θjeɣo, a] *adj* blind ▷ *nm/f* blind man/woman

cielo ['θjelo] *nm* sky; (*Rel*) heaven; **¡~s!** good heavens!

ciempiés [θjem'pjes] *nm inv* centipede

cien [θjen] *num* V **ciento**

ciencia ['θjenθja] *nf* science; **ciencias** *nfpl* (*Escol*) science *sg*; **ciencia-ficción** *nf* science fiction

científico, -a [θjen'tifiko, a] *adj* scientific ▷ *nm/f* scientist

ciento ['θjento] *num* hundred; **pagar al 10 por ~** to pay at 10 per cent; V tb **cien**

cierre *etc* ['θjerre] *vb* V **cerrar** ▷ *nm* closing, shutting; (*con llave*) locking; (*LAM: cremallera*) zip (fastener)

cierro *etc* *vb* V **cerrar**

cierto, -a ['θjerto, a] *adj* sure, certain; (*un tal*) a certain; (*correcto*) right, correct; **por ~** by the way; **~ hombre** a certain man; **ciertas personas** certain *o* some people; **sí, es ~** yes, that's correct

ciervo ['θjerβo] *nm* deer; (*macho*) stag

cifra ['θifra] *nf* number; (*secreta*) code; **cifrar** [θi'frar] *vt* to code, write in code

cigala [θi'xala] *nf* Norway lobster

cigarra [θi'xarra] *nf* cicada

cigarrillo [θixa'rriʎo] *nm* cigarette

cigarro [θi'xarro] *nm* cigarette; (*puro*) cigar

cigüeña [θi'xweɲa] *nf* stork

cilíndrico, -a [θi'lindriko, a] *adj* cylindrical

cilindro [θi'lindro] *nm* cylinder

cima ['θima] *nf* (*de montaña*) top, peak; (*de árbol*) top; (*fig*) height

cimentar [θimen'tar] *vt* to lay the foundations of; (*fig: fundar*) to found

cimiento [θi'mjento] *nm* foundation

cincel [θin'θel] *nm* chisel

cinco ['θinko] *num* five

cincuenta [θin'kwenta] *num* fifty

cine ['θine] *nm* cinema; **cinematográfico, -a** [θinemato'xrafiko, a] *adj* cine-, film *cpd*

cínico, -a ['θiniko, a] *adj* cynical ▷ *nm/f* cynic

cinismo [θi'nismo] *nm* cynicism

cinta ['θinta] *nf* band, strip; (*de tela*) ribbon; (*película*) reel; (*de máquina de escribir*) ribbon; **cinta adhesiva/aislante** sticky/insulating tape; **cinta de vídeo** videotape; **cinta magnetofónica** tape; **cinta métrica** tape measure

cintura [θin'tura] *nf* waist

cinturón [θintu'ron] *nm* belt; **cinturón de seguridad** safety belt

ciprés [θi'pres] *nm* cypress (tree)

circo ['θirko] *nm* circus

circuito [θir'kwito] *nm* circuit

circulación [θirkula'θjon] *nf* circulation; (*Auto*) traffic

circular [θirku'lar] *adj, nf* circular ▷ *vi*, *vt* to circulate ▷ *vi* (*Auto*) to drive; **"circule por la derecha"** "keep (to the) right"

círculo ['θirkulo] *nm* circle; **círculo vicioso** vicious circle

circunferencia [θirkunfe'renθja] *nf* circumference

circunstancia [θirkuns'tanθja] *nf* circumstance

cirio ['θirjo] *nm* (wax) candle

ciruela [θi'rwela] *nf* plum; **ciruela pasa** prune

cirugía [θiru'xia] *nf* surgery; **cirugía estética** *o* **plástica** plastic surgery

cirujano [θiru'xano] *nm* surgeon

cisne ['θisne] *nm* swan

cisterna [θis'terna] *nf* cistern, tank

cita ['θita] *nf* appointment, meeting; (*de novios*) date; (*referencia*) quotation

citación [θita'θjon] *nf* (*Jur*) summons *sg*

citar [θi'tar] *vt* (*gen*) to make an appointment with; (*Jur*) to summons; (*un autor, texto*) to quote; **citarse** *vr*: **se ~on en el cine** they arranged to meet at the cinema

cítricos ['θitrikos] *nmpl* citrus fruit(s)

ciudad [θju'ðað] *nf* town; (*más grande*) city; **ciudadano, -a** *nm/f* citizen

cívico, -a ['θiβiko, a] *adj* civic

civil [θi'βil] *adj* civil ▷ *nm* (*guardia*) policeman; **civilización** [θiβiliθa'θjon] *nf* civilization; **civilizar** [θiβili'θar] *vt* to civilize

cizaña [θi'θaɲa] *nf* (*fig*) discord

cl. *abr* (= *centilitro*) cl.

clamor [kla'mor] *nm* clamour, protest

clandestino, -a [klandes'tino, a] *adj* clandestine; (*Pol*) underground

clara ['klara] *nf* (*de huevo*) egg white

claraboya [klara'βoja] *nf* skylight

clarear [klare'ar] *vi* (*el día*) to dawn; (*el cielo*) to clear up, brighten up; **clarearse** *vr* to be transparent

claridad [klari'ðað] *nf* (*de día*) brightness; (*de estilo*) clarity

clarificar [klarifi'kar] *vt* to clarify

clarinete [klari'nete] *nm* clarinet

claro, -a ['klaro, a] *adj* clear; (*luminoso*) bright; (*color*) light; (*evidente*) clear, evident; (*poco espeso*) thin ▷ *nm* (*en bosque*) clearing ▷ *adv* clearly ▷ *excl*: **¡~ que sí!** of course!; **¡~ que no!** of course not!

clase ['klase] *nf* class; **dar ~(s)** to teach; **clase alta/media/obrera** upper/middle/working class; **clases particulares** private lessons *o* tuition *sg*

clásico, -a ['klasiko, a] *adj* classical

clasificación [klasifika'θjon] *nf* classification; (*Deporte*) league (table)

clasificar [klasifi'kar] *vt* to classify

claustro ['klaustro] *nm* cloister

cláusula ['klausula] nf clause
clausura [klau'sura] nf closing, closure
clavar [kla'βar] vt (clavo) to hammer in;
  (cuchillo) to stick, thrust
clave ['klaβe] nf key; (Mús) clef; **clave de**
  acceso password; **clave lada** (MÉX) dialling
  (BRIT) o area (US) code
clavel [kla'βel] nm carnation
clavícula [kla'βikula] nf collar bone
clavija [kla'βixa] nf peg, dowel, pin; (Elec)
  plug
clavo ['klaβo] nm (de metal) nail; (Bot) clove
claxon ['klakson] (pl ~s) nm horn
clérigo ['klerixo] nm priest
clero ['klero] nm clergy
clicar [kli'kar] vi (Internet) to click; **~ en**
  el icono to click on an icon; **~ dos veces** to
  double-click
cliché [kli'tʃe] nm cliché; (Foto) negative
cliente, -a ['kljente, a] nm/f client,
  customer; **clientela** [kljen'tela] nf
  clientele, customers pl
clima ['klima] nm climate; **climatizado,**
  -a [klimati'θaðo, a] adj air-conditioned
clímax ['klimaks] nm inv climax
clínica ['klinika] nf clinic; (particular)
  private hospital
clip [klip] (pl ~s) nm paper clip
clítoris ['klitoris] nm inv (Anat) clitoris
cloaca [klo'aka] nf sewer
clonar [klo'nar] vt to clone
cloro ['kloro] nm chlorine
clóset ['kloset] (MÉX) nm cupboard
club [klub] (pl ~s o ~es) nm club; **club**
  nocturno night club
cm abr (= centímetro, centímetros) cm
coágulo [ko'aɣulo] nm clot
coalición [koali'θjon] nf coalition
coartada [koar'taða] nf alibi
coartar [koar'tar] vt to limit, restrict
coba ['koβa] nf: **dar ~ a algn** (adular) to
  suck up to sb
cobarde [ko'βarðe] adj cowardly ▷ nm
  coward; **cobardía** nf cowardice
cobaya [ko'βaja] nf guinea pig
cobertizo [koβer'tiθo] nm shelter
cobertura [koβer'tura] nf cover; **aquí no**
  hay ~ (Tel) I can't get a signal
cobija [ko'βixa] (LAM) nf blanket; **cobijar**
  [koβi'xar] vt (cubrir) to cover; (proteger) to
  shelter; **cobijo** nm shelter
cobra ['koβra] nf cobra
cobrador, a [koβra'ðor, a] nm/f (de
  autobús) conductor/conductress; (de
  impuestos, gas) collector
cobrar [ko'βrar] vt (cheque) to cash; (sueldo)
  to collect, draw; (objeto) to recover; (precio)
  to charge; (deuda) to collect ▷ vi to be paid;

cóbrese al entregar cash on delivery; **¿me**
  cobra, por favor? how much do I owe you?,
  can I have the bill, please?
cobre ['koβre] nm copper; **cobres** nmpl
  (Mús) brass instruments
cobro ['koβro] nm (de cheque) cashing;
  presentar al ~ to cash
cocaína [koka'ina] nf cocaine
cocción [kok'θjon] nf (Culin) cooking; (en
  agua) boiling
cocer [ko'θer] vt, vi to cook; (en agua) to
  boil; (en horno) to bake
coche ['kotʃe] nm (Auto) car (BRIT),
  automobile (US); (de tren, de caballos) coach,
  carriage; (para niños) pram (BRIT), baby
  carriage (US); **ir en ~** to drive; **coche celular**
  police van; **coche de bomberos** fire engine;
  coche de carreras racing car; **coche**
  fúnebre hearse; **coche-cama** (pl **coches-**
  cama) nm (Ferro) sleeping car, sleeper
cochera [ko'tʃera] nf garage; (de autobuses,
  trenes) depot
coche restaurante (pl **coches**
  restaurante) nm (Ferro) dining car, diner
cochinillo [kotʃi'niʎo] nm (Culin) suckling
  pig, sucking pig
cochino, -a [ko'tʃino, a] adj filthy, dirty
  ▷ nm/f pig
cocido [ko'θiðo] nm stew
cocina [ko'θina] nf kitchen; (aparato)
  cooker, stove; (acto) cookery; **cocina**
  eléctrica/de gas electric/gas cooker;
  cocina francesa French cuisine; **cocinar**
  vt, vi to cook
cocinero, -a [koθi'nero, a] nm/f cook
coco ['koko] nm coconut
cocodrilo [koko'ðrilo] nm crocodile
cocotero [koko'tero] nm coconut palm
cóctel ['koktel] nm cocktail; **cóctel**
  molotov petrol bomb, Molotov cocktail
codazo [ko'ðaθo] nm: **dar un ~ a algn** to
  nudge sb
codicia [ko'ðiθja] nf greed; **codiciar** vt
  to covet
código ['koðixo] nm code; **código civil**
  common law; **código de barras** bar code;
  código de circulación highway code;
  código de la zona (LAM) dialling (BRIT) o
  area (US) code; **código postal** postcode
codillo [ko'ðiʎo] nm (Zool) knee; (Tec)
  elbow (joint)
codo ['koðo] nm (Anat, de tubo) elbow;
  (Zool) knee
codorniz [koðor'niθ] nf quail
coexistir [koe(k)sis'tir] vi to coexist
cofradía [kofra'ðia] nf brotherhood,
  fraternity
cofre ['kofre] nm (de joyas) case; (de dinero)

chest

coger [ko'xer] (ESP) vt to take (hold of); (objeto caído) to pick up; (frutas) to pick, harvest; (resfriado, ladrón, pelota) to catch ▷ vi: **~ por el buen camino** to take the right road; **cogerse** vr (el dedo) to catch; **~se a algo** to get hold of sth

cogollo [ko'xoʎo] nm (de lechuga) heart

cogote [ko'xote] nm back o nape of the neck

cohabitar [koaβi'tar] vi to live together, cohabit

coherente [koe'rente] adj coherent

cohesión [koe'sjon] nm cohesion

cohete [ko'ete] nm rocket

cohibido, -a [koi'βiðo, a] adj (Psico) inhibited; (tímido) shy

coincidencia [koinθi'ðenθja] nf coincidence

coincidir [koinθi'ðir] vi (en idea) to coincide, agree; (en lugar) to coincide

coito ['koito] nm intercourse, coitus

coja etc vb V **coger**

cojear [koxe'ar] vi (persona) to limp, hobble; (mueble) to wobble, rock

cojera [ko'xera] nf limp

cojín [ko'xin] nm cushion

cojo, -a etc ['koxo, a] vb V **coger** ▷ adj (que no puede andar) lame, crippled; (mueble) wobbly ▷ nm/f lame person, cripple

cojón [ko'xon] (fam!) nm: **¡cojones!** shit! (!); **cojonudo, -a** (fam) adj great, fantastic

col [kol] nf cabbage; **coles de Bruselas** Brussels sprouts

cola ['kola] nf tail; (de gente) queue; (lugar) end, last place; (para pegar) glue, gum; **hacer ~** to queue (up)

colaborador, a [kolaβora'ðor, a] nm/f collaborator

colaborar [kolaβo'rar] vi to collaborate

colada [ko'laða] (ESP) nf: **hacer la ~** to do the washing

colador [kola'ðor] nm (para líquidos) strainer; (para verduras etc) colander

colapso [ko'lapso] nm collapse

colar [ko'lar] vt (líquido) to strain off; (metal) to cast ▷ vi to ooze, seep (through); **colarse** vr to jump the queue; **~se en** to get into without paying; (fiesta) to gatecrash

colcha ['koltʃa] nf bedspread

colchón [kol'tʃon] nm mattress; **colchón inflable** air bed o mattress

colchoneta [koltʃo'neta] nf (en gimnasio) mat; (de playa) air bed

colección [kolek'θjon] nf collection; **coleccionar** vt to collect; **coleccionista** nmf collector

colecta [ko'lekta] nf collection

colectivo, -a [kolek'tiβo, a] adj collective, joint ▷ nm (ARG: autobús) (small) bus

colega [ko'leɣa] nmf colleague; (ESP: amigo) mate

colegial, a [kole'xjal, a] nm/f schoolboy(-girl)

colegio [ko'lexjo] nm college; (escuela) school; (de abogados etc) association; **colegio electoral** polling station; **colegio mayor** (ESP) hall of residence

● **COLEGIO**
●
● A **colegio** is normally a private primary
● or secondary school. In the state system
● it means a primary school although
● these are also called **escuelas**. State
● secondary schools are called **institutos**.

cólera ['kolera] nf (ira) anger; (Med) cholera

colesterol [koleste'rol] nm cholesterol

coleta [ko'leta] nf pigtail

colgante [kol'ɣante] adj hanging ▷ nm (joya) pendant

colgar [kol'ɣar] vt to hang (up); (ropa) to hang out ▷ vi to hang; (Tel) to hang up

cólico ['koliko] nm colic

coliflor [koli'flor] nf cauliflower

colilla [ko'liʎa] nf cigarette end, butt

colina [ko'lina] nf hill

colisión [koli'sjon] nf collision; **colisión frontal** head-on crash

collar [ko'ʎar] nm necklace; (de perro) collar

colmar [kol'mar] vt to fill to the brim; (fig) to fulfil, realize

colmena [kol'mena] nf beehive

colmillo [kol'miʎo] nm (diente) eye tooth; (de elefante) tusk; (de perro) fang

colmo ['kolmo] nm: **¡es el ~!** it's the limit!

colocación [koloka'θjon] nf (acto) placing; (empleo) job, position

colocar [kolo'kar] vt to place, put, position; (dinero) to invest; (poner en empleo) to find a job for; **colocarse** vr to get a job

Colombia [ko'lombja] nf Colombia; **colombiano, -a** adj, nm/f Colombian

colonia [ko'lonja] nf colony; (agua de colonia) cologne; (MÉX: de casas) residential area; **colonia proletaria** (MÉX) shantytown

colonización [koloniθa'θjon] nf colonization; **colonizador, a** [koloniθa'ðor, a] adj colonizing ▷ nm/f colonist, settler

colonizar [koloni'θar] vt to colonize

coloquio [ko'lokjo] nm conversation; (congreso) conference

color [ko'lor] *nm* colour

colorado, -a [kolo'raðo, a] *adj (rojo)* red; *(MÉX: chiste)* smutty, rude

colorante [kolo'rante] *nm* colouring

colorear [kolore'ar] *vt* to colour

colorete [kolo'rete] *nm* blusher

colorido [kolo'riðo] *nm* colouring

columna [ko'lumna] *nf* column; *(pilar)* pillar; *(apoyo)* support; *(tb:* **~ vertebral)** spine, spinal column; *(fig)* backbone

columpiar [kolum'pjar] *vt* to swing; **columpiarse** *vr* to swing; **columpio** *nm* swing

coma ['koma] *nf* comma ▷ *nm (Med)* coma

comadre [ko'maðre] *nf (madrina)* godmother; *(chismosa)* gossip; **comadrona** *nf* midwife

comal [ko'mal] *(MÉX, CAM) nm* griddle

comandante [koman'dante] *nm* commandant

comarca [ko'marka] *nf* region

comba ['komba] *(ESP) nf (cuerda)* skipping rope; **saltar a la ~** to skip

combate [kom'bate] *nm* fight

combatir [komba'tir] *vt* to fight, combat

combinación [kombina'θjon] *nf* combination; *(Quím)* compound; *(prenda)* slip

combinar [kombi'nar] *vt* to combine

combustible [kombus'tiβle] *nm* fuel

comedia [ko'meðja] *nf* comedy; *(Teatro)* play, drama; **comediante** [kome'ðjante] *nmf (comic)* actor/actress

comedido, -a [kome'ðiðo, a] *adj* moderate

comedor, a [kome'ðor, a] *nm (habitación)* dining room; *(cantina)* canteen

comensal [komen'sal] *nmf* fellow guest *(o diner)*

comentar [komen'tar] *vt* to comment on; **comentario** [komen'tarjo] *nm* comment, remark; *(literario)* commentary; **comentarios** *nmpl (chismes)* gossip *sg*; **comentarista** [komenta'rista] *nmf* commentator

comenzar [komen'θar] *vt, vi* to begin, start; **~ a hacer algo** to begin *o* start doing sth

comer [ko'mer] *vt* to eat; *(Damas, Ajedrez)* to take, capture ▷ *vi* to eat; *(ESP, MÉX: almorzar)* to have lunch; **comerse** *vr* to eat up

comercial [komer'θjal] *adj* commercial; *(relativo al negocio)* business *cpd*; **comercializar** *vt (producto)* to market; *(pey)* to commercialize

comerciante [komer'θjante] *nmf* trader, merchant

comerciar [komer'θjar] *vi* to trade, do business

comercio [ko'merθjo] *nm* commerce, trade; *(tienda)* shop, store; *(negocio)* business; *(fig)* dealings *pl*; **comercio electrónico** e-commerce; **comercio exterior/interior** foreign/domestic trade

comestible [komes'tiβle] *adj* eatable, edible; **comestibles** *nmpl* food *sg*, foodstuffs

cometa [ko'meta] *nm* comet ▷ *nf* kite

cometer [kome'ter] *vt* to commit

cometido [kome'tiðo] *nm* task, assignment

cómic ['komik] *nm* comic

comicios [ko'miθjos] *nmpl* elections

cómico, -a ['komiko, a] *adj* comic(al) ▷ *nm/f* comedian

comida [ko'miða] *nf (alimento)* food; *(almuerzo, cena)* meal; *(de mediodía)* lunch; **comida basura** junk food; **comida chatarra** *(MÉX)* junk food

comidilla [komi'ðiʎa] *nf*: **ser la ~ del barrio** *o* **pueblo** to be the talk of the town

comienzo *etc* [ko'mjenθo] *vb* V **comenzar** ▷ *nm* beginning, start

comillas [ko'miʎas] *nfpl* quotation marks

comilona [komi'lona] *(fam) nf* blow-out

comino [ko'mino] *nm*: **(no) me importa un ~** I don't give a damn

comisaría [komisa'ria] *nf (de policía)* police station; *(Mil)* commissariat

comisario [komi'sarjo] *nm (Mil etc)* commissary; *(Pol)* commissar

comisión [komi'sjon] *nf* commission; **Comisiones Obreras** *(ESP)* Communist trade union

comité [komi'te] *(pl* **~s)** *nm* committee

comitiva [komi'tiβa] *nf* retinue

como ['komo] *adv* as; *(tal* **~)** like; *(aproximadamente)* about, approximately ▷ *conj (ya que, puesto que)* as, since; **¡~ no!** of course!; **~ no lo haga hoy** unless he does it today; **~ si** as if; **es tan alto ~ ancho** it is as high as it is wide

cómo ['komo] *adv* how?, why? ▷ *excl* what?, I beg your pardon? ▷ *nm*: **el ~ y el porqué** the whys and wherefores

cómoda ['komoða] *nf* chest of drawers

comodidad [komoði'ðað] *nf* comfort

comodín [komo'ðin] *nm* joker

cómodo, -a ['komoðo, a] *adj* comfortable; *(práctico, de fácil uso)* convenient

compact [kom'pakt] *(pl* **~s)** *nm (tb:* **~ disc)** compact disk player

compacto, -a [kom'pakto, a] *adj*

compact
compadecer [kompaðe'θer] vt to pity, be
sorry for; **compadecerse** vr: **~se de** to pity,
be o feel sorry for
compadre [kom'paðre] nm (padrino)
godfather; (amigo) friend, pal
compañero, -a [kompa'ɲero, a]
nm/f companion; (novio) boy/girlfriend;
compañero de clase classmate
compañía [kompa'ɲia] nf company;
hacer ~ a algn to keep sb company
comparación [kompara'θjon] nf
comparison; **en ~ con** in comparison with
comparar [kompa'rar] vt to compare
comparecer [kompare'θer] vi to appear
(in court)
comparsa [kom'parsa] nmf (Teatro) extra
compartimiento [komparti'mjento] nm
(Ferro) compartment
compartir [kompar'tir] vt to share;
(dinero, comida etc) to divide (up), share (out)
compás [kom'pas] nm (Mús) beat, rhythm;
(Mat) compasses pl; (Náut etc) compass
compasión [kompa'sjon] nf compassion,
pity
compasivo, -a [kompa'siβo, a] adj
compassionate
compatible [kompa'tiβle] adj
compatible
compatriota [kompa'trjota] nmf
compatriot, fellow countryman/woman
compenetrarse [kompene'trarse] vr to
be in tune
compensación [kompensa'θjon] nf
compensation
compensar [kompen'sar] vt to
compensate
competencia [kompe'tenθja] nf
(incumbencia) domain, field; (Jur, habilidad)
competence; (rivalidad) competition
competente [kompe'tente] adj
competent
competición [kompeti'θjon] nf
competition
competir [kompe'tir] vi to compete
compinche [kom'pintʃe] (LAM) nmf mate,
buddy (US)
complacer [kompla'θer] vt to please;
complacerse vr to be pleased
complaciente [kompla'θjente] adj kind,
obliging, helpful
complejo, -a [kom'plexo, a] adj, nm
complex
complementario, -a [komplemen'tarjo,
a] adj complementary
completar [komple'tar] vt to complete
completo, -a [kom'pleto, a] adj
complete; (perfecto) perfect; (lleno) full ▷ nm

full complement
complicado, -a [kompli'kaðo, a] adj
complicated; **estar ~ en** to be mixed up in
cómplice ['kompliθe] nmf accomplice
complot [kom'plo(t)] (pl **~s**) nm plot
componer [kompo'ner] vt (Mús,
Literatura, Imprenta) to compose; (algo
roto) to mend, repair; (arreglar) to arrange;
componerse vr: **~se de** to consist of
comportamiento [komporta'mjento]
nm behaviour, conduct
comportarse [kompor'tarse] vr to
behave
composición [komposi'θjon] nf
composition
compositor, a [komposi'tor, a] nm/f
composer
compostura [kompos'tura] nf (actitud)
composure
compra ['kompra] nf purchase; **hacer la ~**
to do the shopping; **ir de ~s** to go shopping;
comprador, a nm/f buyer, purchaser;
comprar [kom'prar] vt to buy, purchase
comprender [kompren'der] vt to
understand; (incluir) to comprise, include
comprensión [kompren'sjon] nf
understanding; **comprensivo, -a** adj
(actitud) understanding
compresa [kom'presa] nf (para mujer)
sanitary towel (BRIT) o napkin (US)
comprimido, -a [kompri'miðo, a] adj
compressed ▷ nm (Med) pill, tablet
comprimir [kompri'mir] vt to compress;
(Internet) to zip
comprobante [kompro'βante] nm proof;
(Com) voucher; **comprobante de compra**
proof of purchase
comprobar [kompro'βar] vt to check;
(probar) to prove; (Tec) to check, test
comprometer [komprome'ter] vt to
compromise; (poner en peligro) to endanger;
comprometerse vr (involucrarse) to get
involved
compromiso [kompro'miso] nm
(obligación) obligation; (cometido)
commitment; (convenio) agreement; (apuro)
awkward situation
compuesto, -a [kom'pwesto, a] adj: **~ de**
composed of, made up of ▷ nm compound
computadora [komputa'ðora] (LAM)
nf computer; **computadora central**
mainframe (computer); **computadora**
personal personal computer
cómputo ['komputo] nm calculation
comulgar [komul'ɣar] vi to receive
communion
común [ko'mun] adj common ▷ nm: **el ~**
the community

comunicación [komunika'θjon] *nf*
communication; (*informe*) report
comunicado [komuni'kaðo] *nm*
announcement; **comunicado de prensa**
press release
comunicar [komuni'kar] *vt, vi* to
communicate; **comunicarse** *vr* to
communicate; **está comunicando** (*Tel*)
the line's engaged (*BRIT*) o busy (*US*);
comunicativo, -a *adj* communicative
comunidad [komuni'ðað] *nf*
community; **comunidad autónoma**
(*ESP*) autonomous region; **Comunidad
(Económica) Europea** European
(Economic) Community; **comunidad de
vecinos** residents' association
comunión [komu'njon] *nf* communion
comunismo [komu'nismo] *nm*
communism; **comunista** *adj, nmf*
communist

○ **PALABRA CLAVE**

con [kon] *prep* **1** (*medio, compañía*) with;
comer con cuchara to eat with a spoon;
pasear con algn to go for a walk with sb
2 (*a pesar de*): **con todo, merece nuestros
respetos** all the same, he deserves our
respect
3 (*para con*): **es muy bueno para con los
niños** he's very good with (the) children
4 (+ *infin*): **con llegar a las seis estará bien**
if you come by six it will be fine ▷ *conj*: **con
que: será suficiente con que le escribas** it
will be sufficient if you write to her

concebir [konθe'βir] *vt, vi* to conceive
conceder [konθe'ðer] *vt* to concede
concejal, a [konθe'xal, a] *nm/f* town
councillor
concentración [konθentra'θjon] *nf*
concentration
concentrar [konθen'trar] *vt* to
concentrate; **concentrarse** *vr* to
concentrate
concepto [kon'θepto] *nm* concept
concernir [konθer'nir] *vi* to concern;
en lo que concierne a ... as far as ... is
concerned; **en lo que a mí concierne** as far
as I'm concerned
concertar [konθer'tar] *vt* (*Mús*) to
harmonize; (*acordar: precio*) to agree;
(: *tratado*) to conclude; (*trato*) to arrange, fix
up; (*combinar: esfuerzos*) to coordinate ▷ *vi*
to harmonize, be in tune
concesión [konθe'sjon] *nf* concession
concesionario [konθesjo'narjo] *nm*
(licensed) dealer, agent

concha ['kontʃa] *nf* shell
conciencia [kon'θjenθja] *nf* conscience;
tomar ~ de to become aware of; **tener la ~
tranquila** to have a clear conscience
concienciar [konθjen'θjar] *vt* to make
aware; **concienciarse** *vr* to become aware
concienzudo, -a [konθjen'θuðo, a] *adj*
conscientious
concierto *etc* [kon'θjerto] *vb* V **concertar**
▷ *nm* concert; (*obra*) concerto
conciliar [konθi'ljar] *vt* to reconcile; **~ el
sueño** to get to sleep
concilio [kon'θiljo] *nm* council
conciso, -a [kon'θiso, a] *adj* concise
concluir [konklu'ir] *vt, vi* to conclude;
concluirse *vr* to conclude
conclusión [konklu'sjon] *nf* conclusion
concordar [konkor'ðar] *vt* to reconcile
▷ *vi* to agree, tally
concordia [kon'korðja] *nf* harmony
concretar [konkre'tar] *vt* to make
concrete, make more specific; **concretarse**
vr to become more definite
concreto, -a [kon'kreto, a] *adj, nm*
(*LAM: hormigón*) concrete; **en ~** (*en resumen*)
to sum up; (*específicamente*) specifically; **no
hay nada en ~** there's nothing definite
concurrido, -a [konku'rriðo, a] *adj* (*calle*)
busy; (*local, reunión*) crowded
concursante [konkur'sante] *nmf*
competitor
concurso [kon'kurso] *nm* (*de público*)
crowd; (*Escol, Deporte, competencia*)
competition; (*ayuda*) help,
cooperation
condal [kon'dal] *adj*: **la Ciudad C~**
Barcelona
conde ['konde] *nm* count
condecoración [kondekora'θjon] *nf*
(*Mil*) medal
condena [kon'dena] *nf* sentence;
condenación [kondena'θjon] *nf*
condemnation; (*Rel*) damnation; **condenar**
[konde'nar] *vt* to condemn; (*Jur*) to convict;
condenarse *vr* (*Rel*) to be damned
condesa [kon'desa] *nf* countess
condición [kondi'θjon] *nf* condition; **a ~
de que ...** on condition that ...; **condicional**
adj conditional
condimento [kondi'mento] *nm*
seasoning
condominio [kondo'minjo] (*LAM*) *nm*
condominium
condón [kon'don] *nm* condom
conducir [kondu'θir] *vt* to take, convey;
(*Auto*) to drive ▷ *vi* to drive; (*fig*) to lead;
conducirse *vr* to behave
conducta [kon'dukta] *nf* conduct,

behaviour

conducto [kon'dukto] *nm* pipe, tube; *(fig)* channel

conductor, a [konduk'tor, a] *adj* leading, guiding ▷ *nm (Física)* conductor; *(de vehículo)* driver

conduje *etc vb* V **conducir**

conduzco *etc vb* V **conducir**

conectado, -a [konek'taðo, a] *adj (Inform)* on-line

conectar [konek'tar] *vt* to connect (up); *(enchufar)* plug in

conejillo [kone'xiʎo] *nm:* **~ de Indias** guinea pig

conejo [ko'nexo] *nm* rabbit

conexión [konek'sjon] *nf* connection

confección [konfe(k)'θjon] *nf* preparation; *(industria)* clothing industry

confeccionar [konfekθjo'nar] *vt* to make (up)

conferencia [konfe'renθja] *nf* conference; *(lección)* lecture; *(ESP Tel)* call; **conferencia de prensa** press conference

conferir [konfe'rir] *vt* to award

confesar [konfe'sar] *vt* to confess, admit

confesión [konfe'sjon] *nf* confession

confesionario [konfesjo'narjo] *nm* confessional

confeti [kon'feti] *nm* confetti

confiado, -a [kon'fjaðo, a] *adj (crédulo)* trusting; *(seguro)* confident

confianza [kon'fjanθa] *nf* trust; *(seguridad)* confidence; *(familiaridad)* intimacy, familiarity

confiar [kon'fjar] *vt* to entrust ▷ *vi* to trust; **~ en algn** to trust sb; **~ en que ...** to hope that ...

confidencial [konfiðen'θjal] *adj* confidential

confidente [konfi'ðente] *nmf* confidant/e; *(policial)* informer

configurar [konfiɣu'rar] *vt* to shape, form

confín [kon'fin] *nm* limit; **confines** *nmpl* confines, limits

confirmar [konfir'mar] *vt* to confirm

confiscar [konfis'kar] *vt* to confiscate

confite [kon'fite] *nm* sweet *(BRIT)*, candy *(US)*; **confitería** [konfite'ria] *nf (tienda)* confectioner's (shop)

confitura [konfi'tura] *nf* jam

conflictivo, -a [konflik'tiβo, a] *adj (asunto, propuesta)* controversial; *(país, situación)* troubled

conflicto [kon'flikto] *nm* conflict; *(fig)* clash

confluir [kon'flwir] *vi (ríos)* to meet; *(gente)* to gather

conformar [konfor'mar] *vt* to shape, fashion ▷ *vi* to agree; **conformarse** *vr* to conform; *(resignarse)* to resign o.s.; **~se con algo** to be happy with sth

conforme [kon'forme] *adj (correspondiente):* **~ con** in line with; *(de acuerdo):* **estar ~s (con algo)** to be in agreement (with sth) ▷ *adv* as ▷ *excl* agreed! ▷ *prep:* **~ a** in accordance with; **quedarse ~ (con algo)** to be satisfied (with sth)

confortable [konfor'taβle] *adj* comfortable

confortar [konfor'tar] *vt* to comfort

confrontar [konfron'tar] *vt* to confront; *(dos personas)* to bring face to face; *(cotejar)* to compare

confundir [konfun'dir] *vt (equivocar)* to mistake, confuse; *(turbar)* to confuse; **confundirse** *vr (turbarse)* to get confused; *(equivocarse)* to make a mistake; *(mezclarse)* to mix

confusión [konfu'sjon] *nf* confusion

confuso, -a [kon'fuso, a] *adj* confused

congelado, -a [konxe'laðo, a] *adj* frozen; **congelados** *nmpl* frozen food(s); **congelador** *nm (aparato)* freezer, deep freeze

congelar [konxe'lar] *vt* to freeze; **congelarse** *vr (sangre, grasa)* to congeal

congeniar [konxe'njar] *vi* to get on *(BRIT)* o along *(US)* well

congestión [konxes'tjon] *nf* congestion

congestionar [konxestjo'nar] *vt* to congest

congraciarse [kongra'θjarse] *vr* to ingratiate o.s.

congratular [kongratu'lar] *vt* to congratulate

congregar [kongre'ɣar] *vt* to gather together; **congregarse** *vr* to gather together

congresista [kongre'sista] *nmf* delegate, congressman/woman

congreso [kon'greso] *nm* congress

conjetura [konxe'tura] *nf* guess; **conjeturar** *vt* to guess

conjugar [konxu'ɣar] *vt* to combine, fit together; *(Ling)* to conjugate

conjunción [konxun'θjon] *nf* conjunction

conjunto, -a [kon'xunto, a] *adj* joint, united ▷ *nm* whole; *(Mús)* band; **en ~** as a whole

conmemoración [konmemora'θjon] *nf* commemoration

conmemorar [konmemo'rar] *vt* to commemorate

conmigo [kon'miɣo] *pron* with me

conmoción [konmo'θjon] *nf* shock; (*fig*) upheaval; **conmoción cerebral** (*Med*) concussion

conmovedor, a [konmoβe'ðor, a] *adj* touching, moving; (*emocionante*) exciting

conmover [konmo'βer] *vt* to shake, disturb; (*fig*) to move

conmutador [konmuta'ðor] *nm* switch; (*LAM: centralita*) switchboard; (: *central*) telephone exchange

cono ['kono] *nm* cone; **Cono Sur** Southern Cone

conocedor, a [konoθe'ðor, a] *adj* expert, knowledgeable ▷ *nm/f* expert

conocer [kono'θer] *vt* to know; (*por primera vez*) to meet, get to know; (*entender*) to know about; (*reconocer*) to recognize; **conocerse** *vr* (*una persona*) to know o.s.; (*dos personas*) to (get to) know each other; **~ a algn de vista** to know sb by sight

conocido, -a [kono'θiðo, a] *adj* (well-)known ▷ *nm/f* acquaintance

conocimiento [konoθi'mjento] *nm* knowledge; (*Med*) consciousness; **conocimientos** *nmpl* (*saber*) knowledge *sg*

conozco *etc vb* V **conocer**

conque ['konke] *conj* and so, so then

conquista [kon'kista] *nf* conquest; **conquistador, a** *adj* conquering ▷ *nm* conqueror; **conquistar** [konkis'tar] *vt* to conquer

consagrar [konsa'ɣrar] *vt* (*Rel*) to consecrate; (*fig*) to devote

consciente [kons'θjente] *adj* conscious

consecución [konseku'θjon] *nf* acquisition; (*de fin*) attainment

consecuencia [konse'kwenθja] *nf* consequence, outcome; (*coherencia*) consistency

consecuente [konse'kwente] *adj* consistent

consecutivo, -a [konseku'tiβo, a] *adj* consecutive

conseguir [konse'ɣir] *vt* to get, obtain; (*objetivo*) to attain

consejero, -a [konse'xero, a] *nm/f* adviser, consultant; (*Pol*) councillor

consejo [kon'sexo] *nm* advice; (*Pol*) council; **consejo de administración** (*Com*) board of directors; **consejo de guerra** court martial; **consejo de ministros** cabinet meeting

consenso [kon'senso] *nm* consensus

consentimiento [konsenti'mjento] *nm* consent

consentir [konsen'tir] *vt* (*permitir, tolerar*) to consent to; (*mimar*) to pamper, spoil; (*aguantar*) to put up with ▷ *vi* to agree, consent; **~ que algn haga algo** to allow sb to do sth

conserje [kon'serxe] *nm* caretaker; (*portero*) porter

conservación [konserβa'θjon] *nf* conservation; (*de alimentos, vida*) preservation

conservador, a [konserβa'ðor, a] *adj* (*Pol*) conservative ▷ *nm/f* conservative

conservante [konser'βante] *nm* preservative

conservar [konser'βar] *vt* to conserve, keep; (*alimentos, vida*) to preserve; **conservarse** *vr* to survive

conservas [kon'serβas] *nfpl* canned food(s) *pl*

conservatorio [konserβa'torjo] *nm* (*Mús*) conservatoire, conservatory

considerable [konsiðe'raβle] *adj* considerable

consideración [konsiðera'θjon] *nf* consideration; (*estimación*) respect

considerado, -a [konsiðe'raðo, a] *adj* (*atento*) considerate; (*respetado*) respected

considerar [konsiðe'rar] *vt* to consider

consigna [kon'siɣna] *nf* (*orden*) order, instruction; (*para equipajes*) left-luggage office

consigo *etc* [kon'siɣo] *vb* V **conseguir** ▷ *pron* (*m*) with him; (*f*) with her; (*Vd*) with you; (*reflexivo*) with o.s.

consiguiendo *etc vb* V **conseguir**

consiguiente [konsi'ɣjente] *adj* consequent; **por ~** and so, therefore, consequently

consistente [konsis'tente] *adj* consistent; (*sólido*) solid, firm; (*válido*) sound

consistir [konsis'tir] *vi*: **~ en** (*componerse de*) to consist of

consola [kon'sola] *nf* (*mueble*) console table; (*de videojuegos*) console

consolación [konsola'θjon] *nf* consolation

consolar [konso'lar] *vt* to console

consolidar [konsoli'ðar] *vt* to consolidate

consomé [konso'me] (*pl* **~s**) *nm* consommé, clear soup

consonante [konso'nante] *adj* consonant, harmonious ▷ *nf* consonant

consorcio [kon'sorθjo] *nm* consortium

conspiración [konspira'θjon] *nf* conspiracy

conspirar [konspi'rar] *vi* to conspire

constancia [kon'stanθja] *nf* constancy; **dejar ~ de** to put on record

constante [kons'tante] *adj, nf* constant

constar [kons'tar] *vi* (*evidenciarse*) to be

clear o evident; **~ de** to consist of

constipado, -a [konsti'paðo, a] *adj*: **estar ~** to have a cold ▷ *nm* cold

■ No confundir **constipado** con la palabra inglesa *constipated*.

constitución [konstitu'θjon] *nf* constitution

constituir [konstitu'ir] *vt* (*formar, componer*) to constitute, make up; (*fundar, erigir, ordenar*) to constitute, establish

construcción [konstruk'θjon] *nf* construction, building

constructor, a [konstruk'tor, a] *nm/f* builder

construir [konstru'ir] *vt* to build, construct

construyendo *etc vb* V **construir**

consuelo [kon'swelo] *nm* consolation, solace

cónsul ['konsul] *nm* consul; **consulado** *nm* consulate

consulta [kon'sulta] *nf* consultation; (*Med*): **horas de ~** surgery hours; **consultar** [konsul'tar] *vt* to consult; **consultar algo con algn** to discuss sth with sb; **consultorio** [konsul'torjo] *nm* (*Med*) surgery

consumición [konsumi'θjon] *nf* consumption; (*bebida*) drink; (*comida*) food; **consumición mínima** cover charge

consumidor, a [konsumi'ðor, a] *nm/f* consumer

consumir [konsu'mir] *vt* to consume; **consumirse** *vr* to be consumed; (*persona*) to waste away

consumismo [konsu'mismo] *nm* consumerism

consumo [kon'sumo] *nm* consumption

contabilidad [kontaβili'ðað] *nf* accounting, book-keeping; (*profesión*) accountancy; **contable** *nmf* accountant

contacto [kon'takto] *nm* contact; (*Auto*) ignition; **estar/ponerse en ~ con algn** to be/to get in touch with sb

contado, -a [kon'taðo, a] *adj*: **~s** (*escasos*) numbered, scarce, few ▷ *nm*: **pagar al ~** to pay (in) cash

contador [konta'ðor] *nm* (ESP: *aparato*) meter ▷ *nmf* (LAM Com) accountant

contagiar [konta'xjar] *vt* (*enfermedad*) to pass on, transmit; (*persona*) to infect; **contagiarse** *vr* to become infected

contagio [kon'taxjo] *nm* infection; **contagioso, -a** *adj* infectious; (*fig*) catching

contaminación [kontamina'θjon] *nf* contamination; (*polución*) pollution

contaminar [kontami'nar] *vt* to contaminate; (*aire, agua*) to pollute

contante [kon'tante] *adj*: **dinero ~ (y sonante)** cash

contar [kon'tar] *vt* (*páginas, dinero*) to count; (*anécdota, chiste etc*) to tell ▷ *vi* to count; **~ con** to rely on, count on

contemplar [kontem'plar] *vt* to contemplate; (*mirar*) to look at

contemporáneo, -a [kontempo'raneo, a] *adj, nm/f* contemporary

contenedor [kontene'ðor] *nm* container

contener [konte'ner] *vt* to contain, hold; (*retener*) to hold back, contain; **contenerse** *vr* to control o restrain o.s.

contenido, -a [konte'niðo, a] *adj* (*moderado*) restrained; (*risa etc*) suppressed ▷ *nm* contents *pl*, content

contentar [konten'tar] *vt* (*satisfacer*) to satisfy; (*complacer*) to please; **contentarse** *vr* to be satisfied

contento, -a [kon'tento, a] *adj* (*alegre*) pleased; (*feliz*) happy

contestación [kontesta'θjon] *nf* answer, reply

contestador [kontesta'ðor] *nm* (*tb*: **~ automático**) answering machine

contestar [kontes'tar] *vt* to answer, reply; (*Jur*) to corroborate, confirm

■ No confundir **contestar** con la palabra inglesa *contest*.

contexto [kon'te(k)sto] *nm* context

contigo [kon'tixo] *pron* with you

contiguo, -a [kon'tixwo, a] *adj* adjacent, adjoining

continente [konti'nente] *adj, nm* continent

continuación [kontinwa'θjon] *nf* continuation; **a ~** then, next

continuar [konti'nwar] *vt* to continue, go on with ▷ *vi* to continue, go on; **~ hablando** to continue talking o to talk

continuidad [kontinwi'ðað] *nf* continuity

continuo, -a [kon'tinwo, a] *adj* (*sin interrupción*) continuous; (*acción perseverante*) continual

contorno [kon'torno] *nm* outline; (*Geo*) contour; **contornos** *nmpl* neighbourhood *sg*, surrounding area *sg*

contra ['kontra] *prep, adv* against ▷ *nm inv* con ▷ *nf*: **la C~** (*de Nicaragua*) the Contras *pl*

contraataque [kontraa'take] *nm* counter-attack

contrabajo [kontra'βaxo] *nm* double bass

contrabandista [kontraβan'dista] *nmf* smuggler

contrabando [kontra'βando] *nm* (*acción*)

smuggling; (*mercancías*) contraband

contracción [kontrak'θjon] *nf* contraction

contracorriente [kontrako'rrjente] *nf* cross-current

contradecir [kontraðe'θir] *vt* to contradict

contradicción [kontraðik'θjon] *nf* contradiction

contradictorio, -a [kontraðik'torjo, a] *adj* contradictory

contraer [kontra'er] *vt* to contract; (*limitar*) to restrict; **contraerse** *vr* to contract; (*limitarse*) to limit o.s.

contraluz [kontra'luθ] *nm* view against the light

contrapartida [kontrapar'tiða] *nf*: **como ~ (de)** in return (for)

contrapelo [kontra'pelo]: **a ~** *adv* the wrong way

contrapeso [kontra'peso] *nm* counterweight

contraportada [kontrapor'taða] *nf* (*de revista*) back cover

contraproducente [kontraproðu'θente] *adj* counterproductive

contrario, -a [kon'trarjo, a] *adj* contrary; (*persona*) opposed; (*sentido, lado*) opposite ▷ *nm/f* enemy, adversary; (*Deporte*) opponent; **al o por el ~** on the contrary; **de lo ~** otherwise

contrarreloj [kontrarre'lo] *nf* (*tb*: **prueba ~**) time trial

contrarrestar [kontrarres'tar] *vt* to counteract

contrasentido [kontrasen'tiðo] *nm* (*contradicción*) contradiction

contraseña [kontra'seɲa] *nf* (*Inform*) password

contrastar [kontras'tar] *vt, vi* to contrast

contraste [kon'traste] *nm* contrast

contratar [kontra'tar] *vt firmar un acuerdo para*, to contract for; (*empleados, obreros*) to hire, engage

contratiempo [kontra'tjempo] *nm* setback

contratista [kontra'tista] *nmf* contractor

contrato [kon'trato] *nm* contract

contraventana [kontraβen'tana] *nf* shutter

contribución [kontriβu'θjon] *nf* (*municipal etc*) tax; (*ayuda*) contribution

contribuir [kontriβu'ir] *vt, vi* to contribute; (*Com*) to pay (in taxes)

contribuyente [kontriβu'jente] *nmf* (*Com*) taxpayer; (*que ayuda*) contributor

contrincante [kontrin'kante] *nmf* opponent

control [kon'trol] *nm* control; (*inspección*) inspection, check; **control de pasaportes** passport inspection; **controlador, a** *nm/f* controller; **controlador aéreo** air-traffic controller; **controlar** [kontro'lar] *vt* to control; (*inspeccionar*) to inspect, check

contundente [kontun'dente] *adj* (*instrumento*) blunt; (*argumento, derrota*) overwhelming

contusión [kontu'sjon] *nf* bruise

convalecencia [kombale'θenθja] *nf* convalescence

convalecer [kombale'θer] *vi* to convalesce, get better

convalidar [kombali'ðar] *vt* (*título*) to recognize

convencer [komben'θer] *vt* to convince; **~ a algn (de o para hacer algo)** to persuade sb (to do sth)

convención [komben'θjon] *nf* convention

conveniente [kombe'njente] *adj* suitable; (*útil*) useful

convenio [kom'benjo] *nm* agreement, treaty

convenir [kombe'nir] *vi* (*estar de acuerdo*) to agree; (*venir bien*) to suit, be suitable

▌ No confundir **convenir** con la palabra inglesa *convene*.

convento [kom'bento] *nm* convent

convenza *etc vb* V **convencer**

convergir [komber'xir] *vi* = **converger**

conversación [kombersa'θjon] *nf* conversation

conversar [komber'sar] *vi* to talk, converse

conversión [komber'sjon] *nf* conversion

convertir [komber'tir] *vt* to convert

convidar [kombi'ðar] *vt* to invite; **~ a algn a una cerveza** to buy sb a beer

convincente [kombin'θente] *adj* convincing

convite [kom'bite] *nm* invitation; (*banquete*) banquet

convivencia [kombi'βenθja] *nf* coexistence, living together

convivir [kombi'βir] *vi* to live together

convocar [kombo'kar] *vt* to summon, call (together)

convocatoria [komboka'torja] *nf* (*de oposiciones, elecciones*) notice; (*de huelga*) call

cónyuge ['konjuxe] *nmf* spouse

coñac [ko'na(k)] (*pl* **~s**) *nm* cognac, brandy

coño ['koɲo] (*fam!*) *excl* (*enfado*) shit! (*!*); (*sorpresa*) bloody hell! (*!*)

cool [kul] *adj* (*fam*) cool

cooperación [koopera'θjon] *nf* cooperation

cooperar [koope'rar] vi to cooperate

cooperativa [koopera'tiβa] nf cooperative

coordinadora [koorðina'ðora] nf (comité) coordinating committee

coordinar [koorði'nar] vt to coordinate

copa ['kopa] nf cup; (vaso) glass; (bebida): **tomar una ~** (to have a) drink; (de árbol) top; (de sombrero) crown; **copas** nfpl (Naipes) ≈ hearts

copia ['kopja] nf copy; **copia de respaldo** o **seguridad** (Inform) back-up copy; **copiar** vt to copy

copla ['kopla] nf verse; (canción) (popular) song

copo ['kopo] nm: **~ de nieve** snowflake; **~s de maíz** cornflakes

coqueta [ko'keta] adj flirtatious, coquettish; **coquetear** vi to flirt

coraje [ko'raxe] nm courage; (ánimo) spirit; (ira) anger

coral [ko'ral] adj choral ▷ nf (Mús) choir ▷ nm (Zool) coral

coraza [ko'raθa] nf (armadura) armour; (blindaje) armour-plating

corazón [kora'θon] nm heart

corazonada [koraθo'naða] nf impulse; (presentimiento) hunch

corbata [kor'βata] nf tie

corchete [kor'tʃete] nm catch, clasp

corcho ['kortʃo] nm cork; (Pesca) float

cordel [kor'ðel] nm cord, line

cordero [kor'ðero] nm lamb

cordial [kor'ðjal] adj cordial

cordillera [korði'ʎera] nf range (of mountains)

Córdoba ['korðoβa] n Cordova

cordón [kor'ðon] nm (cuerda) cord, string; (de zapatos) lace; (Mil etc) cordon; **cordón umbilical** umbilical cord

cordura [kor'ðura] nf: **con ~** (obrar, hablar) sensibly

corneta [kor'neta] nf bugle

cornisa [kor'nisa] nf (Arq) cornice

coro ['koro] nm chorus; (conjunto de cantores) choir

corona [ko'rona] nf crown; (de flores) garland

coronel [koro'nel] nm colonel

coronilla [koro'niʎa] nf (Anat) crown (of the head)

corporal [korpo'ral] adj corporal, bodily

corpulento, -a [korpu'lento, a] adj (persona) heavily-built

corral [ko'rral] nm farmyard

correa [ko'rrea] nf strap; (cinturón) belt; (de perro) lead, leash; **correa del ventilador** (Auto) fan belt

corrección [korrek'θjon] nf correction; (reprensión) rebuke; **correccional** nm reformatory

correcto, -a [ko'rrekto, a] adj correct; (persona) well-mannered

corredizo, -a [korre'ðiθo, a] adj (puerta etc) sliding

corredor, a [korre'ðor, a] nm (pasillo) corridor; (balcón corrido) gallery; (Com) agent, broker ▷ nm/f (Deporte) runner

corregir [korre'xir] vt (error) to correct; **corregirse** vr to reform

correo [ko'rreo] nm post, mail; (persona) courier; **Correos** nmpl (ESP) Post Office sg; **correo aéreo** airmail; **correo basura** (Inform) spam; **correo electrónico** e-mail, electronic mail; **correo web** webmail

correr [ko'rrer] vt to run; (cortinas) to draw; (cerrojo) to shoot ▷ vi to run; (líquido) to run, flow; **correrse** vr to slide, move; (colores) to run

correspondencia [korrespon'denθja] nf correspondence; (Ferro) connection

corresponder [korrespon'der] vi to correspond; (convenir) to be suitable; (pertenecer) to belong; (concernir) to concern; **corresponder** vr (por escrito) to correspond; (amarse) to love one another

correspondiente [korrespon'djente] adj corresponding

corresponsal [korrespon'sal] nmf correspondent

corrida [ko'rriða] nf (de toros) bullfight

corrido, -a [ko'rriðo, a] adj (avergonzado) abashed; **un kilo ~** a good kilo

corriente [ko'rrjente] adj (agua) running; (dinero etc) current; (común) ordinary, normal ▷ nf current ▷ nm current month; **estar al ~ de** to be informed about; **corriente eléctrica** electric current

corrija etc vb V **corregir**

corro ['korro] nm ring, circle (of people)

corromper [korrom'per] vt (madera) to rot; (fig) to corrupt

corrosivo, -a [korro'siβo, a] adj corrosive

corrupción [korrup'θjon] nf rot, decay; (fig) corruption

corsé [kor'se] nm corset

cortacésped [korta'θespeð] nm lawn mower

cortado, -a [kor'taðo, a] adj (gen) cut; (leche) sour; (tímido) shy; (avergonzado) embarrassed ▷ nm coffee (with a little milk)

cortafuegos [korta'fweɣos] nm inv (en el bosque) firebreak, fire lane (us); (Internet) firewall

cortar [kor'tar] vt to cut; (suministro) to

cut off; (*un pasaje*) to cut out ▷ *vi* to cut;
cortarse *vr* (*avergonzarse*) to become
embarrassed; (*leche*) to turn, curdle; **~se el
pelo** to have one's hair cut

cortauñas [korta'uɲas] *nm inv* nail
clippers *pl*

corte ['korte] *nm* cut, cutting; (*de tela*)
piece, length ▷ *nf*: **las C~s** the Spanish
Parliament; **corte de luz** power cut; **corte y
confección** dressmaking

cortejo [kor'texo] *nm* entourage; **cortejo
fúnebre** funeral procession

cortés [kor'tes] *adj* courteous, polite

cortesía [korte'sia] *nf* courtesy

corteza [kor'teθa] *nf* (*de árbol*) bark; (*de
pan*) crust

cortijo [kor'tixo] (*ESP*) *nm* farm,
farmhouse

cortina [kor'tina] *nf* curtain

corto, -a ['korto, a] *adj* (*breve*) short;
(*tímido*) bashful; **~ de luces** not very bright;
~ de vista short-sighted; **estar ~ de fondos**
to be short of funds; **cortocircuito** *nm*
short circuit; **cortometraje** *nm* (*Cine*) short

cosa ['kosa] *nf* thing; **~ de** about; **eso es ~
mía** that's my business

coscorrón [kosko'rron] *nm* bump on
the head

cosecha [ko'setʃa] *nf* (*Agr*) harvest; (*de
vino*) vintage; **cosechar** [kose'tʃar] *vt* to
harvest, gather (in)

coser [ko'ser] *vt* to sew

cosmético, -a [kos'metiko, a] *adj, nm*
cosmetic

cosquillas [kos'kiʎas] *nfpl*: **hacer ~** to
tickle; **tener ~** to be ticklish

costa ['kosta] *nf* (*Geo*) coast; **a toda ~** at
all costs; **Costa Brava** Costa Brava; **Costa
Cantábrica** Cantabrian Coast; **Costa del
Sol** Costa del Sol

costado [kos'taðo] *nm* side

costanera [kosta'nera] (*cs*) *nf*
promenade, sea front

costar [kos'tar] *vt* (*valer*) to cost; **me
cuesta hablarle** I find it hard to talk to him

Costa Rica [kosta'rika] *nf* Costa Rica;
costarricense *adj, nmf* Costa Rican;
costarriqueño, -a *adj, nm/f* Costa Rican

coste ['koste] *nm* = **costo**

costear [koste'ar] *vt* to pay for

costero, -a [kos'tero, a] *adj* (*pueblecito,
camino*) coastal

costilla [kos'tiʎa] *nf* rib; (*Culin*) cutlet

costo ['kosto] *nm* cost, price; **costo de (la)
vida** cost of living; **costoso, -a** *adj* costly,
expensive

costra ['kostra] *nf* (*corteza*) crust; (*Med*)
scab

costumbre [kos'tumbre] *nf* custom,
habit

costura [kos'tura] *nf* sewing, needlework;
(*zurcido*) seam

costurera [kostu'rera] *nf* dressmaker

costurero [kostu'rero] *nm* sewing box
o case

cotidiano, -a [koti'ðjano, a] *adj* daily,
day to day

cotilla [ko'tiʎa] (*ESP: fam*) *nmf* gossip;
cotillear (*ESP*) *vi* to gossip; **cotilleo** (*ESP*)
nm gossip(ing)

cotizar [koti'θar] *vt* (*Com*) to quote, price;
cotizarse *vr*: **~se a** to sell at, fetch; (*Bolsa*) to
stand at, be quoted at

coto ['koto] *nm* (*terreno cercado*) enclosure;
(*de caza*) reserve

cotorra [ko'torra] *nf* parrot

coyote [ko'jote] *nm* coyote, prairie wolf

coz [koθ] *nf* kick

crack [krak] *nm* (*droga*) crack

cráneo ['kraneo] *nm* skull, cranium

cráter ['krater] *nm* crater

crayón [kra'jon] (*MÉX, RPL*) *nm* crayon,
chalk

creación [krea'θjon] *nf* creation

creador, a [krea'ðor, a] *adj* creative
▷ *nm/f* creator

crear [kre'ar] *vt* to create, make

crecer [kre'θer] *vi* to grow; (*precio*) to rise

creces ['kreθes] : **con ~** *adv* amply, fully

crecido, -a [kre'θiðo, a] *adj* (*persona,
planta*) full-grown; (*cantidad*) large

crecimiento [kreθi'mjento] *nm* growth;
(*aumento*) increase

credencial [kreðen'θjal] *nf* (*LAM: tarjeta*)
card; **credenciales** *nfpl* credentials;
credencial de socio (*LAM*) membership card

crédito ['kreðito] *nm* credit

credo ['kreðo] *nm* creed

creencia [kre'enθja] *nf* belief

creer [kre'er] *vt, vi* to think, believe;
creerse *vr* to believe o.s. (to be); **~ en** to
believe in; **creo que sí/no** I think/don't
think so; **¡ya lo creo!** I should think so!

creído, -a [kre'iðo, a] *adj* (*engreído*)
conceited

crema ['krema] *nf* cream; **crema batida**
(*LAM*) whipped cream; **crema pastelera**
(confectioner's) custard

cremallera [krema'ʎera] *nf* zip (fastener)

crepe ['krepe] (*ESP*) *nf* pancake

cresta ['kresta] *nf* (*Geo, Zool*) crest

creyendo *etc vb* V **creer**

creyente [kre'jente] *nmf* believer

creyó *etc vb* V **creer**

crezco *etc vb* V **crecer**

cría *etc* ['kria] *vb* V **criar** ▷ *nf* (*de animales*) rearing, breeding; (*animal*) young; V tb **crío**

criadero [kria'ðero] nm (*Zool*) breeding place

criado, -a [kri'aðo, a] nm servant ▷ nf servant, maid

criador [kria'ðor] nm breeder

crianza [kri'anθa] nf rearing, breeding; (*fig*) breeding

criar [kri'ar] vt (*educar*) to bring up; (*producir*) to grow, produce; (*animales*) to breed

criatura [kria'tura] nf creature; (*niño*) baby, (small) child

cribar [kri'βar] vt to sieve

crimen ['krimen] nm crime

criminal [krimi'nal] adj, nmf criminal

crines ['krines] nfpl mane

crío, -a ['krio, a] (*fam*) nm/f (*niño*) kid

crisis ['krisis] nf inv crisis; **crisis nerviosa** nervous breakdown

crismas ['krismas] (*ESP*) nm inv Christmas card

cristal [kris'tal] nm crystal; (*de ventana*) glass, pane; (*lente*) lens; **cristalino, -a** adj crystalline; (*fig*) clear ▷ nm lens (of the eye)

cristianismo [kristja'nismo] nm Christianity

cristiano, -a [kris'tjano, a] adj, nm/f Christian

Cristo ['kristo] nm Christ; (*crucifijo*) crucifix

criterio [kri'terjo] nm criterion; (*juicio*) judgement

crítica ['kritika] nf criticism; V tb **crítico**

criticar [kriti'kar] vt to criticize

crítico, -a ['kritiko, a] adj critical ▷ nm/f critic

Croacia [kro'aθja] nf Croatia

cromo ['kromo] nm chrome

crónica ['kronika] nf chronicle, account

crónico, -a ['kroniko, a] adj chronic

cronómetro [kro'nometro] nm stopwatch

croqueta [kro'keta] nf croquette

cruce etc ['kruθe] vb V **cruzar** ▷ nm (*para peatones*) crossing; (*de carreteras*) crossroads

crucero [kru'θero] nm (*viaje*) cruise

crucificar [kruθifi'kar] vt to crucify

crucifijo [kruθi'fixo] nm crucifix

crucigrama [kruθi'ɣrama] nm crossword (puzzle)

cruda ['kruða] (*MÉX, CAM: fam*) nf hangover

crudo, -a ['kruðo, a] adj raw; (*no maduro*) unripe; (*petróleo*) crude; (*rudo, cruel*) cruel ▷ nm crude (oil)

cruel [krwel] adj cruel; **crueldad** nf cruelty

crujiente [kru'xjente] adj (*galleta etc*) crunchy

crujir [kru'xir] vi (*madera etc*) to creak; (*dedos*) to crack; (*dientes*) to grind; (*nieve, arena*) to crunch

cruz [kruθ] nf cross; (*de moneda*) tails sg; **cruz gamada** swastika

cruzada [kru'θaða] nf crusade

cruzado, -a [kru'θaðo, a] adj crossed ▷ nm crusader

cruzar [kru'θar] vt to cross; **cruzarse** vr (*líneas etc*) to cross; (*personas*) to pass each other

Cruz Roja nf Red Cross

cuaderno [kwa'ðerno] nm notebook; (*de escuela*) exercise book; (*Náut*) logbook

cuadra ['kwaðra] nf (*caballeriza*) stable; (*LAM: entre calles*) block

cuadrado, -a [kwa'ðraðo, a] adj square ▷ nm (*Mat*) square

cuadrar [kwa'ðrar] vt to square ▷ vi: ~ **con** to square with, tally with; **cuadrarse** vr (*soldado*) to stand to attention

cuadrilátero [kwaðri'latero] nm (*Deporte*) boxing ring; (*Geom*) quadrilateral

cuadrilla [kwa'ðriʎa] nf party, group

cuadro ['kwaðro] nm square; (*Arte*) painting; (*Teatro*) scene; (*diagrama*) chart; (*Deporte, Med*) team; **tela a ~s** checked (*BRIT*) o chequered (*US*) material

cuajar [kwa'xar] vt (*leche*) to curdle; (*sangre*) to congeal; (*Culin*) to set; **cuajarse** vr to curdle; to congeal; to set; (*llenarse*) to fill up

cuajo ['kwaxo] nm: **de ~** (*arrancar*) by the roots; (*cortar*) completely

cual [kwal] adv like, as ▷ pron: **el** etc ~ which; (*persona sujeto*) who; (: *objeto*) whom ▷ adj such as; **cada ~** each one; **déjalo tal ~** leave it just as it is

cuál [kwal] pron interr which (one)

cualesquier, a [kwales'kjer(a)] pl de **cualquier(a)**

cualidad [kwali'ðað] nf quality

cualquier [kwal'kjer] adj V **cualquiera**

cualquiera [kwal'kjera] (pl **cualesquiera**) adj (*delante de nm y f* **cualquier**) any ▷ pron anybody; any car will do; **no es un hombre ~** he isn't just anybody; **cualquier día/libro** any day/book; **eso ~ lo sabe hacer** anybody can do that; **es un ~** he's a nobody

cuando ['kwando] adv when; (*aún si*) if, even if ▷ conj (*puesto que*) since ▷ prep: **yo, ~ niño ...** when I was a child ...; ~ **no sea así** even if it is not so; ~ **más** at (the) most; ~ **menos** at least; ~ **no** if not, otherwise; **de ~ en ~** from time to time

cuándo ['kwando] adv when; **¿desde ~?**

since when?

cuantía [kwan'tia] *nf* extent

○ **PALABRA CLAVE**

cuanto, -a ['kwanto, a] *adj* **1** (*todo*):
tiene todo cuanto desea he's got
everything he wants; **le daremos cuantos
ejemplares necesite** we'll give him as many
copies as *o* all the copies he needs; **cuantos
hombres la ven** all the men who see her
**2 unos cuantos: había unos cuantos
periodistas** there were a few journalists
3 (+ *más*): **cuanto más vino bebes peor te
sentirás** the more wine you drink the worse
you'll feel
▷ *pron*: **tiene cuanto desea** he has
everything he wants; **tome cuanto/
cuantos quiera** take as much/many as
you want
▷ *adv*: **en cuanto: en cuanto profesor** as
a teacher; **en cuanto a mí** as for me; *V tb*
antes
▷ *conj* **1 cuanto más gana menos gasta**
the more he earns the less he spends;
cuanto más joven más confiado the
younger you are the more trusting you are
2 en cuanto: en cuanto llegue/llegué as
soon as I arrive/arrived

cuánto, -a ['kwanto, a] *adj* (*exclamación*)
what a lot of; (*interr: sg*) how much?; (: *pl*)
how many? ▷ *pron, adv* how; (: *interr: sg*)
how much?; (: *pl*) how many?; **¡cuánta
gente!** what a lot of people!; **¿~ cuesta?**
how much does it cost?; **¿a ~s estamos?**
what's the date?

cuarenta [kwa'renta] *num* forty
cuarentena [kwaren'tena] *nf* quarantine
cuaresma [kwa'resma] *nf* Lent
cuarta ['kwarta] *nf* (*Mat*) quarter, fourth;
(*palmo*) span
cuartel [kwar'tel] *nm* (*Mil*) barracks *pl*;
cuartel de bomberos (*RPL*) fire station;
cuartel general headquarters *pl*
cuarteto [kwar'teto] *nm* quartet
cuarto, -a ['kwarto, a] *adj* fourth ▷ *nm*
(*Mat*) quarter, fourth; (*habitación*) room;
cuarto de baño bathroom; **cuarto de estar**
living room; **cuarto de hora** quarter (of an)
hour; **cuarto de kilo** quarter kilo; **cuartos
de final** quarter finals
cuatro ['kwatro] *num* four
Cuba ['kuβa] *nf* Cuba
cuba ['kuβa] *nf* cask, barrel
cubano, -a [ku'βano, a] *adj, nm/f* Cuban
cubata [ku'βata] *nm* (*fam*) large drink (*of
rum and coke etc*)

cubeta [ku'βeta] (*ESP, MÉX*) *nf* (*balde*)
bucket, tub
cúbico, -a ['kuβiko, a] *adj* cubic
cubierta [ku'βjerta] *nf* cover, covering;
(*neumático*) tyre; (*Náut*) deck
cubierto, -a [ku'βjerto, a] *pp de* **cubrir**
▷ *adj* covered ▷ *nm* cover; (*lugar en la mesa*)
place; **cubiertos** *nmpl* cutlery *sg*; **a ~** under
cover
cubilete [kuβi'lete] *nm* (*en juegos*) cup
cubito [ku'βito] *nm* (*tb*: **~ de hielo**)
ice-cube
cubo ['kuβo] *nm* (*Mat*) cube; (*ESP: balde*)
bucket, tub; (*Tec*) drum; **cubo de (la) basura**
dustbin (*BRIT*), trash can (*US*)
cubrir [ku'βrir] *vt* to cover; **cubrirse** *vr*
(*cielo*) to become overcast
cucaracha [kuka'ratʃa] *nf* cockroach
cuchara [ku'tʃara] *nf* spoon; (*Tec*) scoop;
cucharada *nf* spoonful; **cucharadita** *nf*
teaspoonful
cucharilla [kutʃa'riʎa] *nf* teaspoon
cucharón [kutʃa'ron] *nm* ladle
cuchilla [ku'tʃiʎa] *nf* (*large*) knife; (*de
arma blanca*) blade; **cuchilla de afeitar**
razor blade
cuchillo [ku'tʃiʎo] *nm* knife
cuchitril [kutʃi'tril] *nm* hovel
cuclillas [ku'kliʎas] *nfpl*: **en ~** squatting
cuco, -a ['kuko, a] *adj* pretty; (*astuto*)
sharp ▷ *nm* cuckoo
cucurucho [kuku'rutʃo] *nm* cornet
cueca ['kweka] *nf* Chilean national dance
cuello ['kweʎo] *nm* (*Anat*) neck; (*de vestido,
camisa*) collar
cuenca ['kwenka] *nf* (*Anat*) eye socket;
(*Geo*) bowl, deep valley
cuenco ['kwenko] *nm* bowl
cuenta *etc* ['kwenta] *vb* V **contar**
▷ *nf* (*cálculo*) count, counting; (*en café,
restaurante*) bill (*BRIT*), check (*US*); (*Com*)
account; (*de collar*) bead; **a fin de ~s** in the
end; **caer en la ~** to catch on; **darse ~ de** to
realize; **tener en ~** to bear in mind; **echar
~s** to take stock; **cuenta atrás** countdown;
cuenta corriente/de ahorros current/
savings account; **cuenta de correo
(electrónica)** (*Inform*) email account;
cuentakilómetros *nm inv* ≈ milometer; (*de
velocidad*) speedometer
cuento *etc* ['kwento] *vb* V **contar** ▷ *nm*
story; **cuento chino** tall story; **cuento de
hadas** a fairy tale
cuerda ['kwerða] *nf* rope; (*fina*) string;
(*de reloj*) spring; **dar ~ a un reloj** to wind up
a clock; **cuerda floja** tightrope; **cuerdas
vocales** vocal cords
cuerdo, -a ['kwerðo, a] *adj* sane;

(*prudente*) wise, sensible

cuerno ['kwerno] *nm* horn

cuero ['kwero] *nm* leather; **en ~s** stark naked; **cuero cabelludo** scalp

cuerpo ['kwerpo] *nm* body

cuervo ['kwerβo] *nm* crow

cuesta *etc* ['kwesta] *vb* V **costar** ▷ *nf* slope; (*en camino etc*) hill; **~ arriba/abajo** uphill/downhill; **a ~s** on one's back

cueste *etc vb* V **costar**

cuestión [kwes'tjon] *nf* matter, question

cuete ['kwete] *adj* (*MÉX: fam*) drunk ▷ *nm* (*LAM: cohete*) rocket; (*MÉX,RPL: fam: embriaguez*) drunkenness; (*MÉX: Culin*) steak

cueva ['kweβa] *nf* cave

cuidado [kwi'ðaðo] *nm* care, carefulness; (*preocupación*) care, worry ▷ *excl* careful!, look out!; **eso me tiene sin ~** I'm not worried about that

cuidadoso, -a [kwiða'ðoso, a] *adj* careful; (*preocupado*) anxious

cuidar [kwi'ðar] *vt* (*Med*) to care for; (*ocuparse de*) to take care of, look after ▷ *vi*: **~ de** to take care of, look after; **cuidarse** *vr* to look after o.s.; **~se de hacer algo** to take care to do sth

culata [ku'lata] *nf* (*de fusil*) butt

culebra [ku'leβra] *nf* snake

culebrón [kule'βron] (*fam*) *nm* (*TV*) soap(-opera)

culo ['kulo] *nm* bottom, backside; (*de vaso, botella*) bottom

culpa ['kulpa] *nf* fault; (*Jur*) guilt; **por ~ de** because of; **echar la ~ a algn** to blame sb for sth; **tener la ~ (de)** to be to blame (for); **culpable** *adj* guilty ▷ *nmf* culprit; **culpar** [kul'par] *vt* to blame; (*acusar*) to accuse

cultivar [kulti'βar] *vt* to cultivate

cultivo [kul'tiβo] *nm* (*acto*) cultivation; (*plantas*) crop

culto, -a ['kulto, a] *adj* (*que tiene cultura*) cultured, educated ▷ *nm* (*homenaje*) worship; (*religión*) cult

cultura [kul'tura] *nf* culture

culturismo [kultu'rismo] *nm* bodybuilding

cumbia ['kumbja] *nf* popular Colombian dance

cumbre ['kumbre] *nf* summit, top

cumpleaños [kumple'aɲos] *nm inv* birthday

cumplido, -a [kum'pliðo, a] *adj* (*abundante*) plentiful; (*cortés*) courteous ▷ *nm* compliment; **visita de ~** courtesy call

cumplidor, a [kumpli'ðor, a] *adj* reliable

cumplimiento [kumpli'mjento] *nm* (*de un deber*) fulfilment; (*acabamiento*) completion

cumplir [kum'plir] *vt* (*orden*) to carry out, obey; (*promesa*) to carry out, fulfil; (*condena*) to serve ▷ *vi*: **~ con** (*deber*) to carry out, fulfil; **cumplirse** *vr* (*plazo*) to expire; **hoy cumple dieciocho años** he is eighteen today

cuna ['kuna] *nf* cradle, cot

cundir [kun'dir] *vi* (*noticia, rumor, pánico*) to spread; (*rendir*) to go a long way

cuneta [ku'neta] *nf* ditch

cuña ['kuɲa] *nf* wedge

cuñado, -a [ku'ɲaðo, a] *nm/f* brother-/ sister-in-law

cuota ['kwota] *nf* (*parte proporcional*) share; (*cotización*) fee, dues *pl*

cupe *etc vb* V **caber**

cupiera *etc vb* V **caber**

cupo ['kupo] *vb* V **caber** ▷ *nm* quota

cupón [ku'pon] *nm* coupon

cúpula ['kupula] *nf* dome

cura ['kura] *nf* (*curación*) cure; (*método curativo*) treatment ▷ *nm* priest

curación [kura'θjon] *nf* cure

curandero, -a [kuran'dero, a] *nm/f* quack

curar [ku'rar] *vt* (*Med: herida*) to treat, dress; (*: enfermo*) to cure; (*Culin*) to cure, salt; (*cuero*) to tan; **curarse** *vr* to get well, recover

curiosear [kurjose'ar] *vt* to glance at, look over ▷ *vi* to look round, wander round; (*explorar*) to poke about

curiosidad [kurjosi'ðað] *nf* curiosity

curioso, -a [ku'rjoso, a] *adj* curious ▷ *nm/f* bystander, onlooker

curita [ku'rita] (*LAM*) *nf* (sticking) plaster (*BRIT*), Bandaid® (*US*)

currante [ku'rrante] (*ESP: fam*) *nmf* worker

currar [ku'rrar] (*ESP: fam*) *vi* to work

currículo [ku'rrikulo] = **curriculum**

curriculum [ku'rrikulum] *nm* curriculum vitae

cursi ['kursi] (*fam*) *adj* affected

cursillo [kur'siʎo] *nm* short course

cursiva [kur'siβa] *nf* italics *pl*

curso ['kurso] *nm* course; **en ~** (*año*) current; (*proceso*) going on, under way

cursor [kur'sor] *nm* (*Inform*) cursor

curul [ku'rul] (*MÉX*) *nm* (*escaño*) seat

curva ['kurβa] *nf* curve, bend

custodia [kus'toðja] *nf* safekeeping; custody

cutis ['kutis] *nm inv* skin, complexion

cutre ['kutre] (*ESP: fam*) *adj* (*lugar*) grotty

cuyo, -a ['kujo, a] *pron* (*de quien*) whose; (*de que*) whose, of which; **en ~ caso** in which case

C.V. *abr* (= *caballos de vapor*) H.P.

d

D. *abr* (= *Don*) Esq

dado, -a ['daðo, a] *pp de* **dar** ▷ *nm* die;
dados *nmpl* dice; **~ que** given that

daltónico, -a [dal'toniko, a] *adj* colour-blind

dama ['dama] *nf* (*gen*) lady; (*Ajedrez*)
queen; **damas** *nfpl* (*juego*) draughts *sg*;
dama de honor bridesmaid

damasco [da'masko] (*RPL*) *nm* apricot

danés, -esa [da'nes, esa] *adj* Danish
▷ *nm/f* Dane

dañar [da'ɲar] *vt* (*objeto*) to damage;
(*persona*) to hurt; **dañarse** *vr* (*objeto*) to get
damaged

dañino, -a [da'ɲino, a] *adj* harmful

daño ['daɲo] *nm* (*objeto*) damage; (*persona*)
harm, injury; **~s y perjuicios** (*Jur*) damages;
hacer ~ a to damage; (*persona*) to hurt,
injure; **hacerse ~** to hurt o.s.

dar [dar] *vt* **1** (*gen*) to give; (*obra de teatro*)
to put on; (*film*) to show; (*fiesta*) to hold; **dar
algo a algn** to give sb sth *o* sth to sb; **dar de
beber a algn** to give sb a drink

2 (*producir: intereses*) to yield; (*fruta*) to
produce

3 (*locuciones + n*): **da gusto escucharle** it's a
pleasure to listen to him; *V tb* **paseo**

4 (*+ n: = perífrasis de verbo*): **me da asco** it
sickens me

5 (*considerar*): **dar algo por descontado/
entendido** to take sth for granted/as read;
dar algo por concluido to consider sth
finished

6 (*hora*): **el reloj dio las 6** the clock struck
6 (o'clock)

7: **me da lo mismo** it's all the same to me; *V
tb* **igual, más**

▷ *vi* **1** **dar con**: **dimos con él dos horas**
más tarde we came across him two hours
later; **al final di con la solución** I eventually
came up with the answer

2: **dar en** (*blanco, suelo*) to hit; **el sol me
da en la cara** the sun is shining (right) on
my face

3: **dar de sí** (*zapatos etc*) to stretch, give

darse *vr* **1**: **darse por vencido** to give up

2 (*ocurrir*): **se han dado muchos casos** there
have been a lot of cases

3: **darse a**: **se ha dado a la bebida** he's
taken to drinking

4: **se me dan bien/mal las ciencias** I'm
good/bad at science

5: **dárselas de**: **se las da de experto** he
fancies himself *o* poses as an expert

dardo ['darðo] *nm* dart

dátil ['datil] *nm* date

dato ['dato] *nm* fact, piece of information;
datos personales personal details

dcha. *abr* (= *derecha*) r.h.

d. de C. *abr* (= *después de Cristo*) A.D.

de [de] (*de + el = del*) *prep* **1** (*posesión*) of; **la
casa de Isabel/mis padres** Isabel's/my
parents' house; **es de ellos** it's theirs

2 (*origen, distancia, con números*) from; **soy
de Gijón** I'm from Gijón; **de 8 a 20** from 8
to 20; **salir del cine** to go out *o* leave the
cinema; **de 2 en 2** 2 by 2, 2 at a time

3 (*valor descriptivo*): **una copa de vino** a glass
of wine; **la mesa de la cocina** the kitchen
table; **un billete de 10 euros** a 10 euro note;
un niño de tres años a three-year-old
(child); **una máquina de coser** a sewing
machine; **ir vestido de gris** to be dressed in
grey; **la niña del vestido azul** the girl in the
blue dress; **trabaja de profesora** she works
as a teacher; **de lado** sideways; **de atrás/
delante** rear/front

4 (*hora, tiempo*): **a las 8 de la mañana** at 8
o'clock in the morning; **de día/noche** by
day/night; **de hoy en ocho días** a week
from now; **de niño era gordo** as a child he
was fat

5 (*comparaciones*): **más/menos de cien
personas** more/less than a hundred
people; **el más caro de la tienda** the most
expensive in the shop; **menos/más de lo
pensado** less/more than expected

6 (*causa*): **del calor** from the heat

7 (*tema*) about; **clases de inglés** English
classes; **¿sabes algo de él?** do you know
anything about him?; **un libro de física** a
physics book

8 (*adj + de + infin*): **fácil de entender** easy to understand

9 (*oraciones pasivas*): **fue respetado de todos** he was loved by all

10 (*condicional + infin*) if; **de ser posible** if possible; **de no terminarlo hoy** if I *etc* don't finish it today

dé [de] *vb* V **dar**

debajo [de'βaxo] *adv* underneath; **~ de** below, under; **por ~ de** beneath

debate [de'βate] *nm* debate; **debatir** *vt* to debate

deber [de'βer] *nm* duty ▷*vt* to owe ▷*vi*: **debe (de)** it must, it should; **deberes** *nmpl* (*Escol*) homework; **deberse** *vr*: **~se a** to be owing o due to; **debo hacerlo** I must do it; **debe de ir** he should go

debido, -a [de'βiðo, a] *adj* proper, just; **~ a** due to, because of

débil ['deβil] *adj* (*persona, carácter*) weak; (*luz*) dim; **debilidad** *nf* weakness; dimness

debilitar [deβili'tar] *vt* to weaken; **debilitarse** *vr* to grow weak

débito ['deβito] *nm* debit; **débito bancario** (*LAM*) direct debit (*BRIT*) o billing (*US*)

debutar [deβu'tar] *vi* to make one's debut

década ['dekaða] *nf* decade

decadencia [deka'ðenθja] *nf* (*estado*) decadence; (*proceso*) decline, decay

decaído, -a [deka'iðo, a] *adj*: **estar ~** (*abatido*) to be down

decano, -a [de'kano, a] *nm/f* (*de universidad etc*) dean

decena [de'θena] *nf*: **una ~** ten (or so)

decente [de'θente] *adj* decent

decepción [deθep'θjon] *nf* disappointment

> No confundir **decepción** con la palabra inglesa *deception*.

decepcionar [deθepθjo'nar] *vt* to disappoint

decidir [deθi'ðir] *vt, vi* to decide; **decidirse** *vr*: **~se a** to make up one's mind to

décimo, -a ['deθimo, a] *adj* tenth ▷*nm* tenth

decir [de'θir] *vt* to say; (*contar*) to tell; (*hablar*) to speak ▷*nm* saying; **decirse** *vr*: **se dice que** it is said that; **es ~** that is (to say); **~ para sí** to say to o.s.; **querer ~** to mean; **¡dígame!** (*Tel*) hello!; (*en tienda*) can I help you?

decisión [deθi'sjon] *nf* (*resolución*) decision; (*firmeza*) decisiveness

decisivo, -a [deθi'siβo, a] *adj* decisive

declaración [deklara'θjon] *nf* (*manifestación*) statement; (*de amor*) declaration; **declaración fiscal** o **de la renta** income-tax return

declarar [dekla'rar] *vt* to declare ▷*vi* to declare; (*Jur*) to testify; **declararse** *vr* to propose

decoración [dekora'θjon] *nf* decoration

decorado [deko'raðo] *nm* (*Cine, Teatro*) scenery, set

decorar [deko'rar] *vt* to decorate; **decorativo, -a** *adj* ornamental, decorative

decreto [de'kreto] *nm* decree

dedal [de'ðal] *nm* thimble

dedicación [deðika'θjon] *nf* dedication

dedicar [deði'kar] *vt* (*libro*) to dedicate; (*tiempo, dinero*) to devote; (*palabras: decir, consagrar*) to dedicate, devote; **dedicatoria** *nf* (*de libro*) dedication

dedo ['deðo] *nm* finger; **hacer ~** (*fam*) to hitch (a lift); **dedo anular** ring finger; **dedo corazón** middle finger; **dedo (del pie)** toe; **dedo gordo** (*de la mano*) thumb; (*del pie*) big toe; **dedo índice** index finger; **dedo meñique** little finger; **dedo pulgar** thumb

deducción [deðuk'θjon] *nf* deduction

deducir [deðu'θir] *vt* (*concluir*) to deduce, infer; (*Com*) to deduct

defecto [de'fekto] *nm* defect, flaw; **defectuoso, -a** *adj* defective, faulty

defender [defen'der] *vt* to defend; **defenderse** *vr* (*desenvolverse*) to get by

defensa [de'fensa] *nf* defence ▷*nm* (*Deporte*) defender, back; **defensivo, -a** *adj* defensive; **a la defensiva** on the defensive

defensor, a [defen'sor, a] *adj* defending ▷*nm/f* (*abogado defensor*) defending counsel; (*protector*) protector

deficiencia [defi'θjenθja] *nf* deficiency

deficiente [defi'θjente] *adj* (*defectuoso*) defective; **~ en** lacking o deficient in; **ser un ~ mental** to be mentally handicapped

déficit ['defiθit] (*pl* **~s**) *nm* deficit

definición [defini'θjon] *nf* definition

definir [defi'nir] *vt* (*determinar*) to determine, establish; (*decidir*) to define; (*aclarar*) to clarify; **definitivo, -a** *adj* definitive; **en definitiva** definitively; (*en resumen*) in short

deformación [deforma'θjon] *nf* (*alteración*) deformation; (*Radio etc*) distortion

deformar [defor'mar] *vt* (*gen*) to deform; **deformarse** *vr* to become deformed; **deforme** *adj* (*informe*) deformed; (*feo*) ugly; (*malhecho*) misshapen

defraudar [defrau'ðar] *vt* (*decepcionar*) to disappoint; (*estafar*) to defraud

defunción [defun'θjon] *nf* death, demise

degenerar [dexene'rar] *vi* to degenerate

degradar [deɣra'ðar] *vt* to debase,

degrade; **degradarse** *vr* to demean o.s.
degustación [deɣusta'θjon] *nf* sampling,
tasting
dejar [de'xar] *vt* to leave; (*permitir*) to
allow, let; (*abandonar*) to abandon, forsake;
(*beneficios*) to produce, yield ▷ *vi*: **~ de** (*parar*)
to stop; (*no hacer*) to fail to; **~ a un lado** to
leave *o* set aside; **~ entrar/salir** to let in/
out; **~ pasar** to let through
del [del] (= **de** + **el**) ∨ **de**
delantal [delan'tal] *nm* apron
delante [de'lante] *adv* in front; (*enfrente*)
opposite; (*adelante*) ahead; **~ de** in front of,
before
delantera [delan'tera] *nf* (*de vestido, casa
etc*) front part; (*Deporte*) forward line; **llevar
la ~ (a algn)** to be ahead (of sb)
delantero, -a [delan'tero, a] *adj* front
▷ *nm* (*Deporte*) forward, striker
delatar [dela'tar] *vt* to inform on *o*
against, betray; **delator, a** *nm/f* informer
delegación [deleɣa'θjon] *nf* (*acción,
delegados*) delegation; (*Com: oficina*) office,
branch; **delegación de policía** (*MÉX*) police
station
delegado, -a [dele'ɣaðo, a] *nm/f*
delegate; (*Com*) agent
delegar [dele'ɣar] *vt* to delegate
deletrear [deletre'ar] *vt* to spell (out)
delfín [del'fin] *nm* dolphin
delgado, -a [del'ɣaðo, a] *adj* thin;
(*persona*) slim, thin; (*tela etc*) light, delicate
deliberar [deliβe'rar] *vt* to debate, discuss
delicadeza [delika'ðeθa] *nf* (*gen*) delicacy;
(*refinamiento, sutileza*) refinement
delicado, -a [deli'kaðo, a] *adj* (*gen*)
delicate; (*sensible*) sensitive; (*quisquilloso*)
touchy
delicia [de'liθja] *nf* delight
delicioso, -a [deli'θjoso, a] *adj* (*gracioso*)
delightful; (*exquisito*) delicious
delimitar [delimi'tar] *vt* (*función,
responsabilidades*) to define
delincuencia [delin'kwenθja] *nf*
delinquency; **delincuente** *nmf* delinquent;
(*criminal*) criminal
delineante [deline'ante] *nmf*
draughtsman/woman
delirante [deli'rante] *adj* delirious
delirar [deli'rar] *vi* to be delirious, rave
delirio [de'lirjo] *nm* (*Med*) delirium;
(*palabras insensatas*) ravings *pl*
delito [de'lito] *nm* (*gen*) crime; (*infracción*)
offence
delta ['delta] *nm* delta
demacrado, -a [dema'krado, a]
adj: **estar ~** to look pale and drawn, be
wasted away

demanda [de'manda] *nf* (*pedido, Com*)
demand; (*petición*) request; (*Jur*) action,
lawsuit; **demandar** [deman'dar] *vt* (*gen*)
to demand; (*Jur*) to sue, file a lawsuit against
demás [de'mas] *adj*: **los ~ niños** the other
o remaining children ▷ *pron*: **los/las ~** the
others, the rest (of them); **lo ~** the rest (of it)
demasía [dema'sia] *nf* (*exceso*) excess,
surplus; **comer en ~** to eat to excess
demasiado, -a [dema'sjaðo, a] *adj*: **~
vino** too much wine ▷ *adv* (*antes de adj, adv*)
too; **~s libros** too many books; **¡esto es ~!**
that's the limit!; **hace ~ calor** it's too hot; **~
despacio** too slowly; **~s** too many
demencia [de'menθja] *nf* (*locura*)
madness
democracia [demo'kraθja] *nf* democracy
demócrata [de'mokrata] *nmf* democrat;
democrático, -a *adj* democratic
demoler [demo'ler] *vt* to demolish;
demolición *nf* demolition
demonio [de'monjo] *nm* devil, demon;
¡~s! hell!, damn!; **¿cómo ~s?** how the hell?
demora [de'mora] *nf* delay
demos ['demos] *vb* ∨ **dar**
demostración [demostra'θjon] *nf* (*Mat*)
proof; (*de afecto*) show, display
demostrar [demos'trar] *vt* (*probar*) to
prove; (*mostrar*) to show; (*manifestar*) to
demonstrate
den [den] *vb* ∨ **dar**
denegar [dene'xar] *vt* (*rechazar*) to refuse;
(*Jur*) to reject
denominación [denomina'θjon] *nf*
(*acto*) naming; **Denominación de Origen**
see below

- **DENOMINACIÓN DE ORIGEN**
-
- The **Denominación de Origen**,
- abbreviated to **D.O.**, is a prestigious
- classification awarded to food products
- such as wines, cheeses, sausages
- and hams which meet the stringent
- quality and production standards of the
- designated region. **D.O.** labels serve as a
- guarantee of quality.

---

densidad [densi'ðað] *nf* density; (*fig*)
thickness
denso, -a ['denso, a] *adj* dense; (*espeso,
pastoso*) thick; (*fig*) heavy
dentadura [denta'ðura] *nf* (set of) teeth
pl; **dentadura postiza** false teeth *pl*
dentera [den'tera] *nf* (*grima*): **dar ~ a algn**
to set sb's teeth on edge
dentífrico, -a [den'tifriko, a] *adj* dental
▷ *nm* toothpaste

dentista [den'tista] nmf dentist

dentro ['dentro] adv inside ▷ prep: **~ de** in, inside, within; **por ~** (on the) inside; **mirar por ~** to look inside; **~ de tres meses** within three months

denuncia [de'nunθja] nf (delación) denunciation; (acusación) accusation; (de accidente) report; **denunciar** vt to report; (delatar) to inform on o against

departamento [departa'mento] nm sección administrativa, department, section; (LAM: apartamento) flat (BRIT), apartment

depender [depen'der] vi: **~ de** to depend on; **depende** it (all) depends

dependienta [depen'djenta] nf saleswoman, shop assistant

dependiente [depen'djente] adj dependent ▷ nm salesman, shop assistant

depilar [depi'lar] vt (con cera) to wax; (cejas) to pluck

deportar [depor'tar] vt to deport

deporte [de'porte] nm sport; **hacer ~** to play sports; **deportista** adj sports cpd ▷ nmf sportsman/woman; **deportivo, -a** adj (club, periódico) sports cpd ▷ nm sports car

depositar [deposi'tar] vt (dinero) to deposit; (mercancías) to put away, store; **depositarse** vr to settle

depósito [de'posito] nm (gen) deposit; (almacén) warehouse, store; (de agua, gasolina etc) tank; **depósito de cadáveres** mortuary

depredador, a [depreða'ðor, a] adj predatory ▷ nm predator

depresión [depre'sjon] nf depression; **depresión nerviosa** nervous breakdown

deprimido, -a [depri'miðo, a] adj depressed

deprimir [depri'mir] vt to depress; **deprimirse** vr (persona) to become depressed

deprisa [de'prisa] adv quickly, hurriedly

depurar [depu'rar] vt to purify; (purgar) to purge

derecha [de'retʃa] nf right(-hand) side; (Pol) right; **a la ~** (estar) on the right; (torcer etc) (to the) right

derecho, -a [de'retʃo, a] adj right, right-hand ▷ nm (privilegio) right; (lado) right(-hand) side; (leyes) law ▷ adv straight, directly; **derechos** nmpl (de aduana) duty sg; (de autor) royalties; **tener ~ a** to have a right to; **derechos de autor** royalties

deriva [de'riβa] nf: **ir o estar a la ~** to drift, be adrift

derivado [deri'βaðo] nm (Com) by-product

derivar [deri'βar] vt to derive; (desviar) to direct ▷ vi to derive, be derived; (Náut) to drift; **derivarse** vr to derive, be derived; to drift

derramamiento [derrama'mjento] nm (dispersión) spilling; **derramamiento de sangre** bloodshed

derramar [derra'mar] vt to spill; (verter) to pour out; (esparcir) to scatter; **derramarse** vr to pour out

derrame [de'rrame] nm (de líquido) spilling; (de sangre) shedding; (de tubo etc) overflow; (pérdida) leakage; **derrame cerebral** brain haemorrhage

derredor [derre'ðor] adv: **al o en ~ de** around, about

derretir [derre'tir] vt (gen) to melt; (nieve) to thaw; **derretirse** vr to melt

derribar [derri'βar] vt to knock down; (construcción) to demolish; (persona, gobierno, político) to bring down

derrocar [derro'kar] vt (gobierno) to bring down, overthrow

derrochar [derro'tʃar] vt to squander; **derroche** nm (despilfarro) waste, squandering

derrota [de'rrota] nf (Náut) course; (Mil, Deporte etc) defeat, rout; **derrotar** vt (gen) to defeat; **derrotero** nm (rumbo) course

derrumbar [derrum'bar] vt (edificio) to knock down; **derrumbarse** vr to collapse

des etc vb V **dar**

desabrochar [desaβro'tʃar] vt (botones, broches) to undo, unfasten; **desabrocharse** vr (ropa etc) to come undone

desacato [desa'kato] nm (falta de respeto) disrespect; (Jur) contempt

desacertado, -a [desaθer'taðo, a] adj (equivocado) mistaken; (inoportuno) unwise

desacierto [desa'θjerto] nm mistake, error

desaconsejar [desakonse'xar] vt to advise against

desacreditar [desakreði'tar] vt (desprestigiar) to discredit, bring into disrepute; (denigrar) to run down

desacuerdo [desa'kwerðo] nm disagreement, discord

desafiar [desa'fjar] vt (retar) to challenge; (enfrentarse a) to defy

desafilado, -a [desafi'laðo, a] adj blunt

desafinado, -a [desafi'naðo, a] adj: **estar ~** to be out of tune

desafinar [desafi'nar] vi (al cantar) to be o go out of tune

desafío etc [desa'fio] vb V **desafiar** ▷ nm (reto) challenge; (combate) duel; (resistencia) defiance

desafortunado, -a [desafortu'naðo, a]

adj (desgraciado) unfortunate, unlucky

desagradable [desaɣra'ðaβle] *adj (fastidioso, enojoso)* unpleasant; *(irritante)* disagreeable

desagradar [desaɣra'ðar] *vi (disgustar)* to displease; *(molestar)* to bother

desagradecido, -a [desaɣraðe'θiðo, a] *adj* ungrateful

desagrado [desa'ɣraðo] *nm (disgusto)* displeasure; *(contrariedad)* dissatisfaction

desagüe [des'aɣwe] *nm (de un líquido)* drainage; *(cañería)* drainpipe; *(salida)* outlet, drain

desahogar [desao'ɣar] *vt (aliviar)* to ease, relieve; *(ira)* to vent; **desahogarse** *vr (relajarse)* to relax; *(desfogarse)* to let off steam

desahogo [desa'oɣo] *nm (alivio)* relief; *(comodidad)* comfort, ease

desahuciar [desau'θjar] *vt (enfermo)* to give up hope for; *(inquilino)* to evict

desairar [desai'rar] *vt (menospreciar)* to slight, snub

desalentador, a [desalenta'ðor, a] *adj* discouraging

desaliño [desa'liɲo] *nm* slovenliness

desalmado, -a [desal'maðo, a] *adj (cruel)* cruel, heartless

desalojar [desalo'xar] *vt (expulsar, echar)* to eject; *(abandonar)* to move out of ▷ *vi* to move out

desamor [desa'mor] *nm (frialdad)* indifference; *(odio)* dislike

desamparado, -a [desampa'raðo, a] *adj (persona)* helpless; *(lugar: expuesto)* exposed; *(desierto)* deserted

desangrar [desaŋ'grar] *vt* to bleed; *(fig: persona)* to bleed dry; **desangrarse** *vr* to lose a lot of blood

desanimado, -a [desani'maðo, a] *adj (persona)* downhearted; *(espectáculo, fiesta)* dull

desanimar [desani'mar] *vt (desalentar)* to discourage; *(deprimir)* to depress; **desanimarse** *vr* to lose heart

desapacible [desapa'θiβle] *adj (gen)* unpleasant

desaparecer [desapare'θer] *vi (gen)* to disappear; *(el sol, el luz)* to vanish; **desaparecido, -a** *adj* missing; **desaparición** *nf* disappearance

desapercibido, -a [desaperθi'βiðo, a] *adj (desprevenido)* unprepared; **pasar ~** to go unnoticed

desaprensivo, -a [desapren'siβo, a] *adj* unscrupulous

desaprobar [desapro'βar] *vt (reprobar)* to disapprove of; *(condenar)* to condemn; *(no consentir)* to reject

desaprovechado, -a [desaproβe'tʃaðo, a] *adj (oportunidad, tiempo)* wasted; *(estudiante)* slack

desaprovechar [desaproβe'tʃar] *vt* to waste

desarmador [desarma'ðor] *(MÉX) nm* screwdriver

desarmar [desar'mar] *vt (Mil, fig)* to disarm; *(Tec)* to take apart, dismantle; **desarme** *nm* disarmament

desarraigar [desarrai'xar] *vt* to uproot; **desarraigo** *nm* uprooting

desarreglar [desarre'xlar] *vt (desordenar)* to disarrange; *(trastocar)* to upset, disturb

desarrollar [desarro'ʎar] *vt (gen)* to develop; **desarrollarse** *vr* to develop; *(ocurrir)* to take place; *(Foto)* to develop; **desarrollo** *nm* development

desarticular [desartiku'lar] *vt (hueso)* to dislocate; *(objeto)* to take apart; *(fig)* to break up

desasosegar [desasose'xar] *vt (inquietar)* to disturb, make uneasy

desasosiego *etc* [desaso'sjeɣo] *vb* V **desasosegar** ▷ *nm (intranquilidad)* uneasiness, restlessness; *(ansiedad)* anxiety

desastre [de'sastre] *nm* disaster; **desastroso, -a** *adj* disastrous

desatar [desa'tar] *vt (nudo)* to untie; *(paquete)* to undo; *(separar)* to detach; **desatarse** *vr (zapatos)* to come untied; *(tormenta)* to break

desatascar [desatas'kar] *vt (cañería)* to unblock, clear

desatender [desaten'der] *vt no prestar atención a*, to disregard; *(abandonar)* to neglect

desatino [desa'tino] *nm (idiotez)* foolishness, folly; *(error)* blunder

desatornillar [desatorni'ʎar] *vt* to unscrew

desatrancar [desatran'kar] *vt (puerta)* to unbolt; *(cañería)* to clear, unblock

desautorizado, -a [desautori'θaðo, a] *adj* unauthorized

desautorizar [desautori'θar] *vt (oficial)* to deprive of authority; *(informe)* to deny

desayunar [desaju'nar] *vi* to have breakfast ▷ *vt* to have for breakfast; **desayuno** *nm* breakfast

desazón [desa'θon] *nf* anxiety

desbarajuste [desβara'xuste] *nm* confusion, disorder

desbaratar [desβara'tar] *vt (deshacer, destruir)* to ruin

desbloquear [desβloke'ar] *vt (negociaciónes, tráfico)* to get going again;

(Com: *cuenta*) to unfreeze

desbordar [desβor'ðar] *vt* (*sobrepasar*) to go beyond; (*exceder*) to exceed; **desbordarse** *vr* (*río*) to overflow; (*entusiasmo*) to erupt

descabellado, -a [deskaβe'ʎaðo, a] *adj* (*disparatado*) wild, crazy

descafeinado, -a [deskafei'naðo, a] *adj* decaffeinated ▷ *nm* decaffeinated coffee

descalabro [deska'laβro] *nm* blow; (*desgracia*) misfortune

descalificar [deskalifi'kar] *vt* to disqualify; (*desacreditar*) to discredit

descalzar [deskal'θar] *vt* (*zapato*) to take off; **descalzo, -a** *adj* barefoot(ed)

descambiar [deskam'bjar] *vt* to exchange

descaminado, -a [deskami'naðo, a] *adj* (*equivocado*) on the wrong road; (*fig*) misguided

descampado [deskam'paðo] *nm* open space

descansado, -a [deskan'saðo, a] *adj* (*gen*) rested; (*que tranquiliza*) restful

descansar [deskan'sar] *vt* (*gen*) to rest ▷ *vi* to rest, have a rest; (*echarse*) to lie down

descansillo [deskan'siʎo] *nm* (*de escalera*) landing

descanso [des'kanso] *nm* (*reposo*) rest; (*alivio*) relief; (*pausa*) break; (*Deporte*) interval, half time

descapotable [deskapo'taβle] *nm* (*tb: coche ~*) convertible

descarado, -a [deska'raðo, a] *adj* shameless; (*insolente*) cheeky

descarga [des'karɣa] *nf* (*Arq, Elec, Mil*) discharge; (*Náut*) unloading; **descargar** [deskar'ɣar] *vt* to unload; (*golpe*) to let fly; **descargarse** *vr* to unburden o.s.; **descargarse algo de Internet** to download sth from the Internet

descaro [des'karo] *nm* nerve

descarriar [deska'rrjar] *vt* (*descaminar*) to misdirect; (*fig*) to lead astray; **descarriarse** *vr* (*perderse*) to lose one's way; (*separarse*) to stray; (*pervertirse*) to err, go astray

descarrilamiento [deskarrila'mjento] *nm* (*de tren*) derailment

descarrilar [deskarri'lar] *vi* to be derailed

descartar [deskar'tar] *vt* (*rechazar*) to reject; (*eliminar*) to rule out; **descartarse** *vr* (*Naipes*) to discard; **~se de** to shirk

descendencia [desθen'denθja] *nf* (*origen*) origin, descent; (*hijos*) offspring

descender [desθen'der] *vt* (*bajar: escalera*) to go down ▷ *vi* to descend; (*temperatura, nivel*) to fall, drop; **~ de** to be descended from

descendiente [desθen'djente] *nmf* descendant

descenso [des'θenso] *nm* descent; (*de temperatura*) drop

descifrar [desθi'frar] *vt* to decipher; (*mensaje*) to decode

descolgar [deskol'ɣar] *vt* (*bajar*) to take down; (*teléfono*) to pick up; **descolgarse** *vr* to let o.s. down

descolorido, -a [deskolo'riðo, a] *adj* faded; (*pálido*) pale

descompasado, -a [deskompa'saðo, a] *adj* (*sin proporción*) out of all proportion; (*excesivo*) excessive

descomponer [deskompo'ner] *vt* (*desordenar*) to disarrange, disturb; (*Tec*) to put out of order; (*dividir*) to break down (into parts); (*fig*) to provoke; **descomponerse** *vr* (*corromperse*) to rot, decompose; (*LAM Tec*) to break down

descomposición [deskomposi'θjon] *nf* (*de un objeto*) breakdown; (*de fruta etc*) decomposition; **descomposición de vientre** (*ESP*) stomach upset, diarrhoea

descompostura [deskompos'tura] *nf* (*MÉX: avería*) breakdown, fault; (*LAM: diarrea*) diarrhoea

descomprimir [deskompri'mir] (*Internet*) to unzip

descompuesto, -a [deskom'pwesto, a] *adj* (*corrompido*) decomposed; (*roto*) broken

desconcertado, -a [deskonθer'taðo, a] *adj* disconcerted, bewildered

desconcertar [deskonθer'tar] *vt* (*confundir*) to baffle; (*incomodar*) to upset, put out; **desconcertarse** *vr* (*turbarse*) to be upset

desconchado, -a [deskon't∫aðo, a] *adj* (*pintura*) peeling

desconcierto *etc* [deskon'θjerto] *vb* ∨ **desconcertar** ▷ *nm* (*gen*) disorder; (*desorientación*) uncertainty; (*inquietud*) uneasiness

desconectar [deskonek'tar] *vt* to disconnect

desconfianza [deskon'fjanθa] *nf* distrust

desconfiar [deskon'fjar] *vi* to be distrustful; **~ de** to distrust, suspect

descongelar [deskonxe'lar] *vt* to defrost; (*Com, Pol*) to unfreeze

descongestionar [deskonxestjo'nar] *vt* (*cabeza, tráfico*) to clear

desconocer [deskono'θer] *vt* (*ignorar*) not to know, be ignorant of

desconocido, -a [deskono'θiðo, a] *adj* unknown ▷ *nm/f* stranger

desconocimiento [deskonoθi'mjento]

nm falta de conocimientos, ignorance

desconsiderado, -a [deskonsiðe'raðo, a] *adj* inconsiderate; (*insensible*) thoughtless

desconsuelo *etc* [deskon'swelo] *vb* V

desconsolar ▷ *nm* (*tristeza*) distress; (*desesperación*) despair

descontado, -a [deskon'taðo, a] *adj*: **dar por ~ (que)** to take (it) for granted (that)

descontar [deskon'tar] *vt* (*deducir*) to take away, deduct; (*rebajar*) to discount

descontento, -a [deskon'tento, a] *adj* dissatisfied ▷ *nm* dissatisfaction, discontent

descorchar [deskor'tʃar] *vt* to uncork

descorrer [desko'rrer] *vt* (*cortinas, cerrojo*) to draw back

descortés [deskor'tes] *adj* (*mal educado*) discourteous; (*grosero*) rude

descoser [desko'ser] *vt* to unstitch; **descoserse** *vr* to come apart (at the seams)

descosido, -a [desko'siðo, a] *adj* (*Costura*) unstitched

descreído, -a [deskre'iðo, a] *adj* (*incrédulo*) incredulous; (*falto de fe*) unbelieving

descremado, -a [deskre'maðo, a] *adj* skimmed

describir [deskri'βir] *vt* to describe; **descripción** [deskrip'θjon] *nf* description

descrito [des'krito] *pp de* **describir**

descuartizar [deskwarti'θar] *vt* (*animal*) to cut up

descubierto, -a [desku'βjerto, a] *pp de* **descubrir** ▷ *adj* uncovered, bare; (*persona*) bareheaded ▷ *nm* (*bancario*) overdraft; **al ~** in the open

descubrimiento [deskuβri'mjento] *nm* (*hallazgo*) discovery; (*revelación*) revelation

descubrir [desku'βrir] *vt* to discover, find; (*inaugurar*) to unveil; (*vislumbrar*) to detect; (*revelar*) to reveal, show; (*destapar*) to uncover; **descubrirse** *vr* to reveal o.s.; (*quitarse sombrero*) to take off one's hat; (*confesar*) to confess

descuento *etc* [des'kwento] *vb* V

descontar ▷ *nm* discount

descuidado, -a [deskwi'ðaðo, a] *adj* (*sin cuidado*) careless; (*desordenado*) untidy; (*olvidadizo*) forgetful; (*dejado*) neglected; (*desprevenido*) unprepared

descuidar [deskwi'ðar] *vt* (*dejar*) to neglect; (*olvidar*) to overlook; **descuidarse** *vr* (*distraerse*) to be careless; (*abandonarse*) to let o.s. go; (*desprevenirse*) to drop one's guard; **¡descuida!** don't worry!; **descuido** *nm*

(*dejadez*) carelessness; (*olvido*) negligence

○ **PALABRA CLAVE**

desde ['desðe] *prep* **1** (*lugar*) from; **desde Burgos hasta mi casa hay 30 km** it's 30 km from Burgos to my house

2 (*posición*): **hablaba desde el balcón** she was speaking from the balcony

3 (*tiempo: + adv, n*): **desde ahora** from now on; **desde la boda** since the wedding; **desde niño** since I *etc* was a child; **desde 3 años atrás** since 3 years ago

4 (*tiempo: + vb, fecha*) since; for; **nos conocemos desde 1992/desde hace 20 años** we've known each other since 1992/ for 20 years; **no le veo desde 1997/desde hace 5 años** I haven't seen him since 1997/ for 5 years

5 (*gama*): **desde los más lujosos hasta los más económicos** from the most luxurious to the most reasonably priced

6: **desde luego (que no)** of course (not)

▷ *conj*: **desde que: desde que recuerdo** for as long as I can remember; **desde que llegó no ha salido** he hasn't been out since he arrived

desdén [des'ðen] *nm* scorn

desdeñar [desðe'ɲar] *vt* (*despreciar*) to scorn

desdicha [des'ðitʃa] *nf* (*desgracia*) misfortune; (*infelicidad*) unhappiness; **desdichado, -a** *adj* (*sin suerte*) unlucky; (*infeliz*) unhappy

desear [dese'ar] *vt* to want, desire, wish for

desechar [dese'tʃar] *vt* (*basura*) to throw out o away; (*ideas*) to reject, discard; **desechos** *nmpl* rubbish *sg*, waste *sg*

desembalar [desemba'lar] *vt* to unpack

desembarazar [desembara'θar] *vt* (*desocupar*) to clear; (*desenredar*) to free; **desembarazarse** *vr*: **~se de** to free o.s. of, get rid of

desembarcar [desembar'kar] *vt* (*mercancías etc*) to unload ▷ *vi* to disembark

desembocadura [desemboka'ðura] *nf* (*de río*) mouth; (*de calle*) opening

desembocar [desembo'kar] *vi* (*río*) to flow into; (*fig*) to result in

desembolso [desem'bolso] *nm* payment

desembrollar [desembro'ʎar] *vt* (*madeja*) to unravel; (*asunto, malentendido*) to sort out

desemejanza [deseme'xanθa] *nf* dissimilarity

desempaquetar [desempake'tar] *vt* (*regalo*) to unwrap; (*mercancía*) to unpack

desempate [desem'pate] nm (Fútbol) replay, play-off; (Tenis) tie-break(er)

desempeñar [desempe'ɲar] vt (cargo) to hold; (papel) to perform; (lo empeñado) to redeem; **~ un papel** (fig) to play (a role)

desempleado, -a [desemple'aðo, a] nm/f unemployed person; **desempleo** nm unemployment

desencadenar [desenkaðe'nar] vt to unchain; (ira) to unleash; **desencadenarse** vr to break loose; (tormenta) to burst; (guerra) to break out

desencajar [desenka'xar] vt (hueso) to dislocate; (mecanismo, pieza) to disconnect, disengage

desencanto [desen'kanto] nm disillusionment

desenchufar [desentʃu'far] vt to unplug

desenfadado, -a [desenfa'ðaðo, a] adj (desenvuelto) uninhibited; (descarado) forward; **desenfado** nm (libertad) freedom; (comportamiento) free and easy manner; (descaro) forwardness

desenfocado, -a [desenfo'kaðo, a] adj (Foto) out of focus

desenfreno [desen'freno] nm wildness; (de las pasiones) lack of self-control

desenganchar [desengan'tʃar] vt (gen) to unhook; (Ferro) to uncouple

desengañar [desenga'ɲar] vt to disillusion; **desengañarse** vr to become disillusioned; **desengaño** nm disillusionment; (decepción) disappointment

desenlace [desen'laθe] nm outcome

desenmascarar [desenmaska'rar] vt to unmask

desenredar [desenre'ðar] vt (pelo) to untangle; (problema) to sort out

desenroscar [desenros'kar] vt to unscrew

desentenderse [desenten'derse] vr: **~ de** to pretend not to know about; (apartarse) to have nothing to do with

desenterrar [desente'rrar] vt to exhume; (tesoro, fig) to unearth, dig up

desentonar [desento'nar] vi (Mús) to sing (o play) out of tune; (color) to clash

desentrañar [desentra'ɲar] vt (misterio) to unravel

desenvoltura [desenβol'tura] nf ease

desenvolver [desenβol'βer] vt (paquete) to unwrap; (fig) to develop; **desenvolverse** vr (desarrollarse) to unfold, develop; (arreglárselas) to cope

deseo [de'seo] nm desire, wish; **deseoso, -a** adj: **estar deseoso de** to be anxious to

desequilibrado, -a [desekili'βraðo, a] adj unbalanced

desertar [deser'tar] vi to desert

desértico, -a [de'sertiko, a] adj desert cpd

desesperación [desespera'θjon] nf (impaciencia) desperation, despair; (irritación) fury

desesperar [desespe'rar] vt to drive to despair; (exasperar) to drive to distraction ▷ vi: **~ de** to despair of; **desesperarse** vr to despair, lose hope

desestabilizar [desestaβili'θar] vt to destabilize

desestimar [desesti'mar] vt (menospreciar) to have a low opinion of; (rechazar) to reject

desfachatez [desfatʃa'teθ] nf (insolencia) impudence; (descaro) rudeness

desfalco [des'falko] nm embezzlement

desfallecer [desfaʎe'θer] vi (perder las fuerzas) to become weak; (desvanecerse) to faint

desfasado, -a [desfa'saðo, a] adj (anticuado) old-fashioned; **desfase** nm (diferencia) gap

desfavorable [desfaβo'raβle] adj unfavourable

desfigurar [desfixu'rar] vt (cara) to disfigure; (cuerpo) to deform

desfiladero [desfila'ðero] nm gorge

desfilar [desfi'lar] vi to parade; **desfile** nm procession; **desfile de modelos** fashion show

desgana [des'xana] nf (falta de apetito) loss of appetite; (apatía) unwillingness; **desganado, -a** adj: **estar desganado** (sin apetito) to have no appetite; (sin entusiasmo) to have lost interest

desgarrar [desxa'rrar] vt to tear (up); (fig) to shatter; **desgarro** nm (en tela) tear; (aflicción) grief

desgastar [desxas'tar] vt (deteriorar) to wear away o down; (estropear) to spoil; **desgastarse** vr to get worn out; **desgaste** nm wear (and tear)

desglosar [desxlo'sar] vt (factura) to break down

desgracia [des'xraθja] nf misfortune; (accidente) accident; (vergüenza) disgrace; (contratiempo) setback; **por ~** unfortunately; **desgraciado, -a** [desxra'θjaðo, a] adj (sin suerte) unlucky, unfortunate; (miserable) wretched; (infeliz) miserable

desgravar [desxra'βar] vt (impuestos) to reduce the tax o duty on

desguace [des'xwaθe] (ESP) nm junkyard

deshabitado, -a [desaβi'taðo, a] adj uninhabited

deshacer [desa'θer] *vt* (*casa*) to break up; (*Tec*) to take apart; (*enemigo*) to defeat; (*diluir*) to melt; (*contrato*) to break; (*intriga*) to solve; **deshacerse** *vr* (*disolverse*) to melt; (*despedazarse*) to come apart o undone; **~se de** to get rid of; **~se en lágrimas** to burst into tears

deshecho, -a [des'etʃo, a] *adj* undone; (*roto*) smashed; (*persona*): **estar ~** to be shattered

desheredar [desere'ðar] *vt* to disinherit

deshidratar [desiðra'tar] *vt* to dehydrate

deshielo [des'jelo] *nm* thaw

deshonesto, -a [deso'nesto, a] *adj* indecent

deshonra [des'onra] *nf* (*deshonor*) dishonour; (*vergüenza*) shame

deshora [des'ora]: **a ~** *adv* at the wrong time

deshuesadero [deswesa'ðero] (*MÉX*) *nm* junkyard

deshuesar [deswe'sar] *vt* (*carne*) to bone; (*fruta*) to stone

designar [desix'nar] *vt* (*nombrar*) to designate; (*indicar*) to fix

desigual [desi'ɣwal] *adj* (*terreno*) uneven; (*lucha etc*) unequal

desilusión [desilu'sjon] *nf* disillusionment; (*decepción*) disappointment; **desilusionar** *vt* to disillusion; to disappoint; **desilusionarse** *vr* to become disillusioned

desinfectar [desinfek'tar] *vt* to disinfect

desinflar [desin'flar] *vt* to deflate

desintegración [desinteɣra'θjon] *nf* disintegration

desinterés [desinte'res] *nm* (*desgana*) lack of interest; (*altruismo*) unselfishness

desintoxicarse [desintoksi'karse] *vr* (*drogadicto*) to undergo detoxification

desistir [desis'tir] *vi* (*renunciar*) to stop, desist

desleal [desle'al] *adj* (*infiel*) disloyal; (*Com: competencia*) unfair; **deslealtad** *nf* disloyalty

desligar [desli'ɣar] *vt* (*desatar*) to untie, undo; (*separar*) to separate; **desligarse** *vr* (*de un compromiso*) to extricate o.s.

desliz [des'liθ] *nm* lapse; (*fig*) failing; **deslizar** *vt* to slip, slide

deslumbrar [deslum'brar] *vt* to dazzle

desmadrarse [desma'ðrarse] (*fam*) *vr* (*descontrolarse*) to run wild; (*divertirse*) to let one's hair down; **desmadre** (*fam*) *nm* (*desorganización*) chaos; (*jaleo*) commotion

desmán [des'man] *nm* (*exceso*) outrage; (*abuso de poder*) abuse

desmantelar [desmante'lar] *vt* (*deshacer*) to dismantle; (*casa*) to strip

desmaquillador [desmakiʎa'ðor] *nm* make-up remover

desmayar [desma'jar] *vi* to lose heart; **desmayarse** *vr* (*Med*) to faint; **desmayo** *nm* (*Med: acto*) faint; (*: estado*) unconsciousness

desmemoriado, -a [desmemo'rjado, a] *adj* forgetful

desmentir [desmen'tir] *vt* (*contradecir*) to contradict; (*refutar*) to deny

desmenuzar [desmenu'θar] *vt* (*deshacer*) to crumble; (*carne*) to chop; (*examinar*) to examine closely

desmesurado, -a [desmesu'raðo, a] *adj* disproportionate

desmontable [desmon'taβle] *adj* (*que se quita: pieza*) detachable; (*plegable*) collapsible, folding

desmontar [desmon'tar] *vt* (*deshacer*) to dismantle; (*tierra*) to level ▷ *vi* to dismount

desmoralizar [desmorali'θar] *vt* to demoralize

desmoronar [desmoro'nar] *vt* to wear away, erode; **desmoronarse** *vr* (*edificio*, *dique*) to collapse; (*economía*) to decline

desnatado, -a [desna'taðo, a] *adj* skimmed

desnivel [desni'βel] *nm* (*de terreno*) unevenness

desnudar [desnu'ðar] *vt* (*desvestir*) to undress; (*despojar*) to strip; **desnudarse** *vr* (*desvestirse*) to get undressed; **desnudo, -a** *adj* naked ▷ *nm/f* nude; **desnudo de** devoid o bereft of

desnutrición [desnutri'θjon] *nf* malnutrition; **desnutrido, -a** *adj* undernourished

desobedecer [desoβeðe'θer] *vt, vi* to disobey; **desobediencia** *nf* disobedience

desocupado, -a [desoku'paðo, a] *adj* at leisure; (*desempleado*) unemployed; (*deshabitado*) empty, vacant

desodorante [desoðo'rante] *nm* deodorant

desolación [desola'θjon] *nf* (*de lugar*) desolation; (*fig*) grief

desolar [deso'lar] *vt* to ruin, lay waste

desorbitado, -a [desorβi'taðo, a] *adj* (*excesivo: ambición*) boundless; (*deseos*) excessive; (*: precio*) exorbitant

desorden [des'orðen] *nm* confusion; (*político*) disorder, unrest

desorganización [desorɣaniθa'θjon] *nf* (*de persona*) disorganization; (*en empresa*, *oficina*) disorder, chaos

desorientar [desorjen'tar] vt (extraviar) to mislead; (confundir, desconcertar) to confuse; **desorientarse** vr (perderse) to lose one's way

despabilado, -a [despaβi'laðo, a] adj (despierto) wide-awake; (fig) alert, sharp

despachar [despa'tʃar] vt (negocio) to do, complete; (enviar) to send, dispatch; (vender) to sell, deal in; (billete) to issue; (mandar ir) to send away

despacho [des'patʃo] nm (oficina) office; (de paquetes) dispatch; (venta) sale; (comunicación) message

despacio [des'paθjo] adv slowly

desparpajo [despar'paxo] nm self-confidence; (pey) nerve

desparramar [desparra'mar] vt (esparcir) to scatter; (líquido) to spill

despecho [des'petʃo] nm spite

despectivo, -a [despek'tiβo, a] adj (despreciativo) derogatory; (Ling) pejorative

despedida [despe'ðiða] nf (adiós) farewell; (de obrero) sacking

despedir [despe'ðir] vt (visita) to see off, show out; (empleado) to dismiss; (inquilino) to evict; (objeto) to hurl; (olor etc) to give out o off; **despedirse** vr: **~se de** to say goodbye to

despegar [despe'ɣar] vt to unstick ▷ vi (avión) to take off; **despegarse** vr to come loose, come unstuck; **despego** nm detachment

despegue etc [des'peɣe] vb V **despegar** ▷ nm takeoff

despeinado, -a [despei'naðo, a] adj dishevelled, unkempt

despejado, -a [despe'xaðo, a] adj (lugar) clear, free; (cielo) clear; (persona) wide-awake, bright

despejar [despe'xar] vt (gen) to clear; (misterio) to clear up ▷ vi (el tiempo) to clear; **despejarse** vr (tiempo, cielo) to clear (up); (misterio) to become clearer; (cabeza) to clear

despensa [des'pensa] nf larder

despeñarse [despe'ɲarse] vr to hurl o.s. down; (coche) to tumble over

desperdicio [desper'ðiθjo] nm (despilfarro) squandering; **desperdicios** nmpl (basura) rubbish sg (BRIT), garbage sg (US); (residuos) waste sg

desperezarse [despere'θarse] vr to stretch

desperfecto [desper'fekto] nm (deterioro) slight damage; (defecto) flaw, imperfection

despertador [desperta'ðor] nm alarm clock

despertar [desper'tar] nm awakening ▷ vt (persona) to wake up; (recuerdos) to revive; (sentimiento) to arouse ▷ vi to awaken, wake up; **despertarse** vr to awaken, wake up

despido etc [des'piðo] vb V **despedir** ▷ nm dismissal, sacking

despierto, -a etc [des'pjerto, a] vb V **despertar** ▷ adj awake; (fig) sharp, alert

despilfarro [despil'farro] nm (derroche) squandering; (lujo desmedido) extravagance

despistar [despis'tar] vt to throw off the track o scent; (confundir) to mislead, confuse; **despistarse** vr to take the wrong road; (confundirse) to become confused

despiste [des'piste] nm absent-mindedness; **un ~ a** mistake o slip

desplazamiento [desplaθa'mjento] nm displacement

desplazar [despla'θar] vt to move; (Náut) to displace; (Inform) to scroll; (fig) to oust; **desplazarse** vr (persona) to travel

desplegar [desple'ɣar] vt (tela, papel) to unfold, open out; (bandera) to unfurl; **despliegue** etc [des'pleɣe] vb V **desplegar** ▷ nm display

desplomarse [desplo'marse] vr (edificio, gobierno, persona) to collapse

desplumar [desplu'mar] vt (ave) to pluck; (fam: estafar) to fleece

despoblado, -a [despo'βlaðo, a] adj (sin habitantes) uninhabited

despojar [despo'xar] vt (alguien: de sus bienes) to divest of, deprive of; (casa) to strip, leave bare; (alguien: de su cargo) to strip of

despojo [des'poxo] nm (acto) plundering; (objetos) plunder, loot; **despojos** nmpl (de ave, res) offal sg

desposado, -a [despo'saðo, a] adj, nm/f newly-wed

despreciar [despre'θjar] vt (desdeñar) to despise, scorn; (afrentar) to slight; **desprecio** nm scorn, contempt; slight

desprender [despren'der] vt (broche) to unfasten; (olor) to give off; **desprenderse** vr (botón: caerse) to fall off; (broche) to come unfastened; (olor, perfume) to be given off; **~se de algo que ...** to draw from sth that ...

desprendimiento [desprendi'mjento] nm (gen) loosening; (generosidad) disinterestedness; (de tierra, rocas) landslide; **desprendimiento de retina** detachment of the retina

despreocupado, -a [despreoku'paðo, a] adj (sin preocupación) unworried, nonchalant; (negligente) careless

despreocuparse [despreoku'parse] vr not to worry; **~ de** to have no interest in

desprestigiar [despresti'xjar] vt (criticar) to run down; (desacreditar) to discredit

desprevenido, -a [despreβe'niðo, a] adj
(no preparado) unprepared, unready

desproporcionado, -a
[despropor θjo'naðo, a] adj
disproportionate, out of proportion

desprovisto, -a [despro'βisto, a] adj: ~
de devoid of

después [des'pwes] adv afterwards,
later; (próximo paso) next; **~ de comer** after
lunch; **un año ~** a year later; **~ se debatió el
tema** next the matter was discussed; **~ de
corregido el texto** after the text had been
corrected; **~ de todo** after all

desquiciado, -a [deski'θjaðo, a] adj
deranged

destacar [desta'kar] vt to emphasize,
point up; (Mil) to detach, detail ▷ vi
(resaltarse) to stand out; (persona) to be
outstanding o exceptional; **destacarse**
vr to stand out; to be outstanding o
exceptional

destajo [des'taxo] nm: **trabajar a ~** to do
piecework

destapar [desta'par] vt (botella) to open;
(cacerola) to take the lid off; (descubrir) to
uncover; **destaparse** vr (revelarse) to reveal
one's true character

destartalado, -a [destarta'laðo, a] adj
(desordenado) untidy; (ruinoso) tumbledown

destello [des'teʎo] nm (de estrella) twinkle;
(de faro) signal light

destemplado, -a [destem'plaðo, a] adj
(Mús) out of tune; (voz) harsh; (Med) out of
sorts; (tiempo) unpleasant, nasty

desteñir [deste'ɲir] vt to fade ▷ vi to
fade; **desteñirse** vr to fade; **esta tela no
destiñe** this fabric will not run

desternillarse [desterni'ʎarse] vr: **~ de
risa** to split one's sides laughing

desterrar [deste'rrar] vt (exiliar) to exile;
(fig) to banish, dismiss

destiempo [des'tjempo]: **a ~** adv out of
turn

destierro etc [des'tjerro] vb V **desterrar**
▷ nm exile

destilar [desti'lar] vt to distil; **destilería**
nf distillery

destinar [desti'nar] vt (funcionario) to
appoint, assign; (fondos): **~ (a)** to set aside
(for)

destinatario, -a [destina'tarjo, a] nm/f
addressee

destino [des'tino] nm (suerte) destiny; (de
avión, viajero) destination; **con ~ a Londres**
(barco) (bound) for London; (avión, carta) to
London

destituir [destitu'ir] vt to dismiss

destornillador [destorniʎa'ðor] nm

screwdriver

destornillar [destorni'ʎar] vt (tornillo) to
unscrew; **destornillarse** vr to unscrew

destreza [des'treθa] nf (habilidad) skill;
(maña) dexterity

destrozar [destro'θar] vt (romper) to
smash, break (up); (estropear) to ruin;
(nervios) to shatter

destrozo [des'troθo] nm (acción)
destruction; (desastre) smashing; **destrozos**
nmpl (pedazos) pieces; (daños) havoc sg

destrucción [destruk'θjon] nf
destruction

destruir [destru'ir] vt to destroy

desuso [des'uso] nm disuse; **caer en ~** to
become obsolete

desvalijar [desvali'xar] vt (persona) to rob;
(casa, tienda) to burgle; (coche) to break into

desván [des'βan] nm attic

desvanecer [desβane'θer] vt (disipar) to
dispel; (borrar) to blur; **desvanecerse** vr
(humo etc) to vanish, disappear; (color) to
fade; (recuerdo, sonido) to fade away; (Med) to
pass out; (duda) to be dispelled

desvariar [desβa'rjar] vi (enfermo) to be
delirious

desvelar [desβe'lar] vt to keep awake;
desvelarse vr (no poder dormir) to stay
awake; (preocuparse) to be vigilant o
watchful

desventaja [desβen'taxa] nf
disadvantage

desvergonzado, -a [desβerɣon'θaðo, a]
adj shameless

desvestir [desβes'tir] vt to undress;
desvestirse vr to undress

desviación [desβja'θjon] nf deviation;
(Auto) diversion, detour

desviar [des'βjar] vt to turn aside; (río)
to alter the course of; (navío) to divert, re-
route; (conversación) to sidetrack; **desviarse**
vr (apartarse del camino) to turn aside;
(: barco) to go off course

desvío etc [des'βio] vb V **desviar**
▷ nm (desviación) detour, diversion; (fig)
indifference

desvivirse [desβi'βirse] vr: **~ por** (anhelar)
to long for, crave for; (hacer lo posible por) to
do one's utmost for

detallar [deta'ʎar] vt to detail

detalle [de'taʎe] nm detail; (gesto) gesture,
token; **al ~** in detail; (Com) retail

detallista [deta'ʎista] nmf (Com) retailer

detective [detek'tiβe] nmf detective;
detective privado private detective

detener [dete'ner] vt (gen) to stop; (Jur)
to arrest; (objeto) to keep; **detenerse** vr
to stop; (demorarse): **~se en** to delay over,

linger over

detenidamente [deteniða'mente] *adv*
(*minuciosamente*) carefully; (*extensamente*) at
great length

detenido, -a [dete'niðo, a] *adj* (*arrestado*)
under arrest ▷ *nm/f* person under arrest,
prisoner

detenimiento [deteni'mjento] *nm*: **con ~**
thoroughly; (*observar, considerar*) carefully

detergente [deter'xente] *nm* detergent

deteriorar [deterjo'rar] *vt* to spoil,
damage; **deteriorarse** *vr* to deteriorate;
deterioro *nm* deterioration

determinación [determina'θjon] *nf*
(*empeño*) determination; (*decisión*) decision;
determinado, -a *adj* specific

determinar [determi'nar] *vt* (*plazo*) to
fix; (*precio*) to settle; **determinarse** *vr* to
decide

detestar [detes'tar] *vt* to detest

detractor, a [detrak'tor, a] *nm/f*
slanderer, libeller

detrás [de'tras] *adv* (*tb*: **por ~**) behind;
(*atrás*) at the back; **~ de** behind

detrimento [detri'mento] *nm*: **en ~ de** to
the detriment of

deuda ['deuða] *nf* debt; **deuda exterior/
pública** foreign/national debt

devaluación [deβalwa'θjon] *nf*
devaluation

devastar [deβas'tar] *vt* (*destruir*) to
devastate

deveras [de'βeras] (*MÉX*) *nf inv*: **un amigo
de (a) ~** a true o real friend

devoción [deβo'θjon] *nf* devotion

devolución [deβolu'θjon] *nf* (*reenvío*)
return, sending back; (*reembolso*)
repayment; (*Jur*) devolution

devolver [deβol'βer] *vt* to return; (*lo
extraviado, lo prestado*) to give back; (*carta al
correo*) to send back; (*Com*) to repay, refund
▷ *vi* (*vomitar*) to be sick

devorar [deβo'rar] *vt* to devour

devoto, -a [de'βoto, a] *adj* devout ▷ *nm/f*
admirer

devuelto *pp de* **devolver**

devuelva *etc vb* V **devolver**

di *etc vb* V **dar; decir**

día ['dia] *nm* day; **¿qué ~ es?** what's the
date?; **estar/poner al ~** to be/keep up
to date; **el ~ de hoy/de mañana** today/
tomorrow; **al ~ siguiente** (on) the following
day; **vivir al ~** to live from hand to mouth;
de ~ by day, in daylight; **en pleno ~** in
full daylight; **Día de la Independencia**
Independence Day; **Día de los Muertos**
(*MÉX*) All Souls' Day; **Día de Reyes** Epiphany;
día feriado (*LAM*) holiday; **día festivo** (*ESP*)

holiday; **día lectivo** teaching day; **día libre**
day off

diabetes [dja'βetes] *nf* diabetes

diablo ['djaβlo] *nm* devil; **diablura** *nf*
prank

diadema [dja'ðema] *nf* tiara

diafragma [dja'fraɣma] *nm* diaphragm

diagnóstico [djax'nostiko] *nm* =
diagnosis

diagonal [djaxo'nal] *adj* diagonal

diagrama [dja'ɣrama] *nm* diagram

dial [djal] *nm* dial

dialecto [dja'lekto] *nm* dialect

dialogar [djalo'ɣar] *vi*: **~ con** (*Pol*) to hold
talks with

diálogo ['djaloxo] *nm* dialogue

diamante [dja'mante] *nm* diamond

diana ['djana] *nf* (*Mil*) reveille; (*de blanco*)
centre, bull's-eye

diapositiva [djaposi'tiβa] *nf* (*Foto*) slide,
transparency

diario, -a ['djarjo, a] *adj* daily ▷ *nm*
newspaper; **a ~** daily; **de ~** everyday

diarrea [dja'rrea] *nf* diarrhoea

dibujar [diβu'xar] *vt* to draw, sketch;
dibujo *nm* drawing; **dibujos animados**
cartoons

diccionario [dikθjo'narjo] *nm* dictionary

dice *etc vb* V **decir**

dicho, -a ['ditʃo, a] *pp de* **decir** ▷ *adj*: **en
~s países** in the aforementioned countries
▷ *nm* saying

dichoso, -a [di'tʃoso, a] *adj* happy

diciembre [di'θjembre] *nm* December

dictado [dik'taðo] *nm* dictation

dictador [dikta'ðor] *nm* dictator;
dictadura *nf* dictatorship

dictar [dik'tar] *vt* (*carta*) to dictate;
(*Jur: sentencia*) to pronounce; (*decreto*) to
issue; (*LAM: clase*) to give

didáctico, -a [di'ðaktiko, a] *adj*
educational

diecinueve [djeθi'nweβe] *num* nineteen

dieciocho [djeθi'otʃo] *num* eighteen

dieciséis [djeθi'seis] *num* sixteen

diecisiete [djeθi'sjete] *num* seventeen

diente ['djente] *nm* (*Anat, Tec*) tooth; (*Zool*)
fang; (: *de elefante*) tusk; (*de ajo*) clove

diera *etc vb* V **dar**

diesel ['disel] *adj*: **motor ~** diesel engine

diestro, -a ['djestro, a] *adj* (*derecho*) right;
(*hábil*) skilful

dieta ['djeta] *nf* diet; **estar a ~** to be on
a diet

diez [djeθ] *num* ten

diferencia [dife'renθja] *nf* difference; **a
~ de** unlike; **diferenciar** *vt* to differentiate
between ▷ *vi* to differ; **diferenciarse**

vr to differ, be different; (*distinguirse*) to distinguish o.s.

diferente [dife'rente] *adj* different

diferido [dife'riðo] *nm*: **en ~** (*TV etc*) recorded

difícil [di'fiθil] *adj* difficult

dificultad [difikul'taθ] *nf* difficulty; (*problema*) trouble

dificultar [difikul'tar] *vt* (*complicar*) to complicate, make difficult; (*estorbar*) to obstruct

difundir [difun'dir] *vt* (*calor, luz*) to diffuse; (*Radio, TV*) to broadcast; **~ una noticia** to spread a piece of news; **difundirse** *vr* to spread (out)

difunto, -a [di'funto, a] *adj* dead, deceased ▷ *nm/f* deceased (person)

difusión [difu'sjon] *nf* (*Radio, TV*) broadcasting

diga *etc vb* V **decir**

digerir [dixe'rir] *vt* to digest; (*fig*) to absorb; **digestión** *nf* digestion; **digestivo, -a** *adj* digestive

digital [dixi'tal] *adj* digital

dignarse [diɣ'narse] *vr* to deign to

dignidad [diɣni'ðaθ] *nf* dignity

digno, -a ['diɣno, a] *adj* worthy

digo *etc vb* V **decir**

dije *etc vb* V **decir**

dilatar [dila'tar] *vt* (*cuerpo*) to dilate; (*prolongar*) to prolong

dilema [di'lema] *nm* dilemma

diluir [dilu'ir] *vt* to dilute

diluvio [di'luβjo] *nm* deluge, flood

dimensión [dimen'sjon] *nf* dimension

diminuto, -a [dimi'nuto, a] *adj* tiny, diminutive

dimitir [dimi'tir] *vi* to resign

dimos *vb* V **dar**

Dinamarca [dina'marka] *nf* Denmark

dinámico, -a [di'namiko, a] *adj* dynamic

dinamita [dina'mita] *nf* dynamite

dínamo ['dinamo] *nf* dynamo

dineral [dine'ral] *nm* large sum of money, fortune

dinero [di'nero] *nm* money; **dinero en efectivo** *o* **metálico** cash; **dinero suelto** (loose) change

dio *vb* V **dar**

dios [djos] *nm* god; **¡D~ mío!** (oh,) my God!; **¡por D~!** for heaven's sake!; **diosa** ['djosa] *nf* goddess

diploma [di'ploma] *nm* diploma

diplomacia [diplo'maθja] *nf* diplomacy; (*fig*) tact

diplomado, -a [diplo'maðo, a] *adj* qualified

diplomático, -a [diplo'matiko, a] *adj*

diplomatic ▷ *nm/f* diplomat

diputación [diputa'θjon] *nf* (*tb:* **~ provincial**) ≈ county council

diputado, -a [dipu'taðo, a] *nm/f* delegate; (*Pol*) ≈ member of parliament (*BRIT*) ≈ representative (*US*)

dique ['dike] *nm* dyke

diré *etc vb* V **decir**

dirección [direk'θjon] *nf* direction; (*señas*) address; (*Auto*) steering; (*gerencia*) management; (*Pol*) leadership; **dirección única/prohibida** one-way street/no entry

direccional [direkθjo'nal] (*MÉX*) *nf* (*Auto*) indicator

directa [di'rekta] *nf* (*Auto*) top gear

directiva [direk'tiβa] *nf* (*tb:* **junta ~**) board of directors

directo, -a [di'rekto, a] *adj* direct; (*Radio, TV*) live; **transmitir en ~** to broadcast live

director, a [direk'tor, a] *adj* leading ▷ *nm/f* director; (*Escol*) head(teacher) (*BRIT*), principal (*US*); (*gerente*) manager/ess; (*Prensa*) editor; **director de cine** film director; **director general** managing director

directorio [direk'torjo] (*MÉX*) *nm* (*telefónico*) phone book

dirigente [diri'xente] *nmf* (*Pol*) leader

dirigir [diri'xir] *vt* to direct; (*carta*) to address; (*obra de teatro, film*) to direct; (*Mús*) to conduct; (*negocio*) to manage; **dirigirse** *vr*: **~se a** to go towards, make one's way towards; (*hablar con*) to speak to

dirija *etc vb* V **dirigir**

disciplina [disθi'plina] *nf* discipline

discípulo, -a [dis'θipulo, a] *nm/f* disciple

Discman® ['diskman] *nm* Discman®

disco ['disko] *nm* disc; (*Deporte*) discus; (*Tel*) dial; (*Auto: semáforo*) light; (*Mús*) record; **disco compacto/de larga duración** compact disc/long-playing record; **disco de freno** brake disc; **disco flexible/duro** *o* **rígido** (*Inform*) floppy/hard disk

disconforme [diskon'forme] *adj* differing; **estar ~ (con)** to be in disagreement (with)

discordia [dis'korðja] *nf* discord

discoteca [disko'teka] *nf* disco(theque)

discreción [diskre'θjon] *nf* discretion; (*reserva*) prudence; **comer a ~** to eat as much as one wishes

discreto, -a [dis'kreto, a] *adj* discreet

discriminación [diskrimina'θjon] *nf* discrimination

disculpa [dis'kulpa] *nf* excuse; (*pedir perdón*) apology; **pedir ~s a/por** to apologize to/for; **disculpar** *vt* to excuse, pardon; **disculparse** *vr* to excuse o.s.; to apologize

discurso [dis'kurso] nm speech

discusión [disku'sjon] nf (diálogo) discussion; (riña) argument

discutir [disku'tir] vt (debatir) to discuss; (pelear) to argue about; (contradecir) to argue against ▷ vi (debatir) to discuss; (pelearse) to argue

disecar [dise'kar] vt (conservar: animal) to stuff; (: planta) to dry

diseñar [dise'ɲar] vt, vi to design

diseño [di'seɲo] nm design

disfraz [dis'fraθ] nm (máscara) disguise; (excusa) pretext; **disfrazar** vt to disguise; **disfrazarse** vr: **disfrazarse de** to disguise o.s. as

disfrutar [disfru'tar] vt to enjoy ▷ vi to enjoy o.s.; **~ de** to enjoy, possess

disgustar [disɣus'tar] vt (no gustar) to displease; (contrariar, enojar) to annoy, upset; **disgustarse** vr (enfadarse) to get upset; (dos personas) to fall out

⬛ No confunda **disgustar** con la palabra inglesa disgust.

disgusto [dis'ɣusto] nm (contrariedad) annoyance; (tristeza) grief; (riña) quarrel

disimular [disimu'lar] vt (ocultar) to hide, conceal ▷ vi to dissemble

dislocarse [dislo'karse] vr (articulación) to sprain, dislocate

disminución [disminu'θjon] nf decrease, reduction

disminuido, -a [disminu'iðo, a] nm/f: **~ mental/físico** mentally/physically handicapped person

disminuir [disminu'ir] vt to decrease, diminish

disolver [disol'βer] vt (gen) to dissolve; **disolverse** vr to dissolve; (Com) to go into liquidation

dispar [dis'par] adj different

disparar [dispa'rar] vt, vi to shoot, fire

disparate [dispa'rate] nm (tontería) foolish remark; (error) blunder; **decir ~s** to talk nonsense

disparo [dis'paro] nm shot

dispersar [disper'sar] vt to disperse; **dispersarse** vr to scatter

disponer [dispo'ner] vt (arreglar) to arrange; (ordenar) to put in order; (preparar) to prepare, get ready ▷ vi: **~ de** to have, own; **disponerse** vr: **~se a** o **para hacer** to prepare to do

disponible [dispo'niβle] adj available

disposición [disposi'θjon] nf arrangement, disposition; (voluntad) willingness; (Inform) layout; **a su ~** at your service

dispositivo [disposi'tiβo] nm device, mechanism

dispuesto, -a [dis'pwesto, a] pp de **disponer** ▷ adj (arreglado) arranged; (preparado) disposed

disputar [dispu'tar] vt (carrera) to compete in

disquete [dis'kete] nm floppy disk, diskette

distancia [dis'tanθja] nf distance; **distanciar** [distan'θjar] vt to space out; **distanciarse** vr to become estranged; **distante** [dis'tante] adj distant

diste vb V **dar**

disteis vb V **dar**

distinción [distin'θjon] nf distinction; (elegancia) elegance; (honor) honour

distinguido, -a [distin'giðo, a] adj distinguished

distinguir [distin'gir] vt to distinguish; (escoger) to single out; **distinguirse** vr to be distinguished

distintivo [distin'tiβo] nm badge; (fig) characteristic

distinto, -a [dis'tinto, a] adj different; (claro) clear

distracción [distrak'θjon] nf distraction; (pasatiempo) hobby, pastime; (olvido) absent-mindedness, distraction

distraer [distra'er] vt (atención) to distract; (divertir) to amuse; (fondos) to embezzle; **distraerse** vr (entretenerse) to amuse o.s.; (perder la concentración) to allow one's attention to wander

distraído, -a [distra'iðo, a] adj (gen) absent-minded; (entretenido) amusing

distribuidor, a [distriβui'ðor, a] nm/f distributor; **distribuidora** nf (Com) dealer, agent; (Cine) distributor

distribuir [distriβu'ir] vt to distribute

distrito [dis'trito] nm (sector, territorio) region; (barrio) district; **Distrito Federal** (MÉX) Federal District; **distrito postal** postal district

disturbio [dis'turβjo] nm disturbance; (desorden) riot

disuadir [diswa'ðir] vt to dissuade

disuelto [di'swelto] pp de **disolver**

DIU nm abr (= dispositivo intrauterino) IUD

diurno, -a ['djurno, a] adj day cpd

divagar [diβa'ɣar] vi (desviarse) to digress

diván [di'βan] nm divan

diversidad [diβersi'ðað] nf diversity, variety

diversión [diβer'sjon] nf (gen) entertainment; (actividad) hobby, pastime

diverso, -a [di'βerso, a] adj diverse; **~s libros** several books; **diversos** nmpl sundries

divertido, -a [diβer'tiðo, a] *adj* (*chiste*) amusing; (*fiesta etc*) enjoyable

divertir [diβer'tir] *vt* (*entretener, recrear*) to amuse; **divertirse** *vr* (*pasarlo bien*) to have a good time; (*distraerse*) to amuse o.s.

dividendos [diβi'ðendos] *nmpl* (*Com*) dividends

dividir [diβi'ðir] *vt* (*gen*) to divide; (*distribuir*) to distribute, share out

divierta *etc vb* V **divertir**

divino, -a [di'βino, a] *adj* divine

divirtiendo *etc vb* V **divertir**

divisa [di'βisa] *nf* (*emblema*) emblem, badge; **divisas** *nfpl* foreign exchange *sg*

divisar [diβi'sar] *vt* to make out, distinguish

división [diβi'sjon] *nf* (*gen*) division; (*de partido*) split; (*de país*) partition

divorciar [diβor'θjar] *vt* to divorce; **divorciarse** *vr* to get divorced; **divorcio** *nm* divorce

divulgar [diβul'xar] *vt* (*ideas*) to spread; (*secreto*) to divulge

DNI (*ESP*) *nm abr* (= *Documento Nacional de Identidad*) *national identity card*

● **DNI**
●
●
● The **Documento Nacional de**
● **Identidad** is a Spanish ID card
● which must be carried at all times
● and produced on request for the
● police. It contains the holder's photo,
● fingerprints and personal details. It
● is also known as the **DNI** or "carnet de
● identidad".

Dña. *abr* (= *doña*) Mrs

do [do] *nm* (*Mús*) do, C

dobladillo [doβla'ðiʎo] *nm* (*de vestido*) hem; (*de pantalón: vuelta*) turn-up (BRIT), cuff (US)

doblar [do'βlar] *vt* to double; (*papel*) to fold; (*caño*) to bend; (*la esquina*) to turn, go round; (*film*) to dub ▷ *vi* to turn; (*campana*) to toll; **doblarse** *vr* (*plegarse*) to fold (up), crease; (*encorvarse*) to bend; **~ a la derecha/izquierda** to turn right/left

doble ['doβle] *adj* double; (*de dos aspectos*) dual; (*fig*) two-faced ▷ *nm* double ▷ *nmf* (*Teatro*) double, stand-in; **dobles** *nmpl* (*Deporte*) doubles *sg*; **con ~ sentido** with a double meaning

doce [do'θe] *num* twelve; **docena** *nf* dozen

docente [do'θente] *adj*: **centro/personal ~** teaching establishment/staff

dócil ['doθil] *adj* (*pasivo*) docile; (*obediente*) obedient

doctor, a [dok'tor, a] *nm/f* doctor

doctorado [dokto'raðo] *nm* doctorate

doctrina [dok'trina] *nf* doctrine, teaching

documentación [dokumenta'θjon] *nf* documentation, papers *pl*

documental [dokumen'tal] *adj*, *nm* documentary

documento [doku'mento] *nm* (*certificado*) document; **documento adjunto** (*Inform*) attachment; **documento nacional de identidad** identity card

dólar ['dolar] *nm* dollar

doler [do'ler] *vt*, *vi* to hurt; (*fig*) to grieve; **dolerse** *vr* (*de su situación*) to grieve, feel sorry; (*de las desgracias ajenas*) to sympathize; **me duele el brazo** my arm hurts

dolor [do'lor] *nm* pain; (*fig*) grief, sorrow; **dolor de cabeza/estómago/muelas** headache/stomachache/toothache

domar [do'mar] *vt* to tame

domesticar [domesti'kar] *vt* = **domar**

doméstico, -a [do'mestiko, a] *adj* (*vida, servicio*) home; (*tareas*) household; (*animal*) tame, pet

domicilio [domi'θiljo] *nm* home; **servicio a ~** home delivery service; **sin ~ fijo** of no fixed abode; **domicilio particular** private residence

dominante [domi'nante] *adj* dominant; (*persona*) domineering

dominar [domi'nar] *vt* (*gen*) to dominate; (*idiomas*) to be fluent in ▷ *vi* to dominate, prevail

domingo [do'mingo] *nm* Sunday; **Domingo de Ramos/Resurrección** Palm/Easter Sunday

dominio [do'minjo] *nm* (*tierras*) domain; (*autoridad*) power, authority; (*de las pasiones*) grip, hold; (*de idiomas*) command

don [don] *nm* (*talento*) gift; **~ Juan Gómez** Mr Juan Gómez, Juan Gómez Esq (BRIT)

● **DON/DOÑA**
●
● The term **don/doña** often abbreviated
● to **D./Dña** is placed before the first
● name as a mark of respect to an older
● or more senior person – eg Don Diego,
● Doña Inés. Although becoming rarer
● in Spain it is still used with names and
● surnames on official documents and
● formal correspondence – eg "Sr. D. Pedro
● Rodríguez Hernández", "Sra. Dña. Inés
● Rodríguez Hernández".

dona ['dona] (MÉX) nf doughnut, donut (US)

donar [do'nar] vt to donate

donativo [dona'tiβo] nm donation

donde ['donde] adv where ▷ prep: **el coche está allí ~ el farol** the car is over there by the lamppost o where the lamppost is; **en ~** where, in which

dónde ['donde] adv where?; **¿a ~ vas?** where are you going (to)?; **¿de ~ vienes?** where have you been?; **¿por ~?** where?, whereabouts?

dondequiera [donde'kjera] adv anywhere; **por ~** everywhere, all over the place ▷ conj: **~ que** wherever

donut® [do'nut] (ESP) nm doughnut, donut (US)

doña ['doɲa] nf: **~ Alicia** Alicia; **~ Victoria Benito** Mrs Victoria Benito

dorado, -a [do'raðo, a] adj (color) golden; (Tec) gilt

dormir [dor'mir] vt: **~ la siesta** to have an afternoon nap ▷ vi to sleep; **dormirse** vr to fall asleep

dormitorio [dormi'torjo] nm bedroom

dorsal [dor'sal] nm (Deporte) number

dorso ['dorso] nm (de mano) back; (de hoja) other side

dos [dos] num two

dosis ['dosis] nf inv dose, dosage

dotado, -a [do'taðo, a] adj gifted; **~ de** endowed with

dotar [do'tar] vt to endow; **dote** nf dowry; **dotes** nfpl (talentos) gifts

doy [doj] vb V **dar**

drama ['drama] nm drama; **dramaturgo** [drama'turɣo] nm dramatist, playwright

drástico, -a ['drastiko, a] adj drastic

drenaje [dre'naxe] nm drainage

droga ['droɣa] nf drug; **drogadicto, -a** [droɣa'ðikto, a] nm/f drug addict

droguería [droɣe'ria] nf hardware shop (BRIT) o store (US)

ducha ['dutʃa] nf (baño) shower; (Med) douche; **ducharse** vr to take a shower

duda ['duða] nf doubt; **no cabe ~** there is no doubt about it; **dudar** vt, vi to doubt; **dudoso, -a** [du'ðoso, a] adj (incierto) hesitant; (sospechoso) doubtful

duela etc vb V **doler**

duelo ['dwelo] vb V **doler** ▷ nm (combate) duel; (luto) mourning

duende ['dwende] nm imp, goblin

dueño, -a ['dweɲo, a] nm/f (propietario) owner; (de pensión, taberna) landlord/lady; (empresario) employer

duermo etc vb V **dormir**

dulce ['dulθe] adj sweet ▷ adv gently, softly ▷ nm sweet

dulcería [dulθe'ria] (LAM) nf confectioner's (shop)

dulzura [dul'θura] nf sweetness; (ternura) gentleness

dúo ['duo] nm duet

duplicar [dupli'kar] vt (hacer el doble de) to duplicate

duque ['duke] nm duke; **duquesa** nf duchess

duración [dura'θjon] nf (de película, disco etc) length; (de pila etc) life; (curso: de acontecimientos etc) duration

duradero, -a [dura'ðero, a] adj (tela etc) hard-wearing; (fe, paz) lasting

durante [du'rante] prep during

durar [du'rar] vi to last; (recuerdo) to remain

durazno [du'raθno] (LAM) nm (fruta) peach; (árbol) peach tree

durex ['dureks] (MÉX, ARG) nm (tira adhesiva) Sellotape® (BRIT), Scotch tape® (US)

dureza [du'reθa] nf (calidad) hardness

duro, -a ['duro, a] adj hard; (carácter) tough ▷ adv hard ▷ nm (moneda) five-peseta coin o piece

DVD nm abr (= disco de vídeo digital) DVD

e

E *abr* (=*este*) E

e [e] *conj* and

ébano ['eβano] *nm* ebony

ebrio, -a ['eβrjo, a] *adj* drunk

ebullición [eβuʎi'θjon] *nf* boiling

echar [e'tʃar] *vt* to throw; (*agua, vino*) to pour (out); (*empleado: despedir*) to fire, sack; (*hojas*) to sprout; (*cartas*) to post; (*humo*) to emit, give out ▷ *vi*: **~ a correr** to run off; **echarse** *vr* to lie down; **~ llave a** to lock (up); **~ abajo** (*gobierno*) to overthrow; (*edificio*) to demolish; **~ mano a** to lay hands on; **~ una mano a algn** (*ayudar*) to give sb a hand; **~ de menos** to miss; **~se atrás** (*fig*) to back out

eclesiástico, -a [ekle'sjastiko, a] *adj* ecclesiastical

eco ['eko] *nm* echo; **tener ~** to catch on

ecología [ekolo'xia] *nf* ecology; **ecológico, -a** *adj* (*producto, método*) environmentally-friendly; (*agricultura*) organic; **ecologista** *adj* ecological, environmental ▷ *nmf* environmentalist

economía [ekono'mia] *nf* (*sistema*) economy; (*carrera*) economics

económico, -a [eko'nomiko, a] *adj* (*barato*) cheap, economical; (*ahorrativo*) thrifty; (*Com: año etc*) financial; (: *situación*) economic

economista [ekono'mista] *nmf* economist

Ecuador [ekwa'ðor] *nm* Ecuador; **ecuador** *nm* (*Geo*) equator

ecuatoriano, -a [ekwato'rjano, a] *adj, nm/f* Ecuadorian

ecuestre [e'kwestre] *adj* equestrian

edad [e'ðað] *nf* age; **¿qué ~ tienes?** how old are you?; **tiene ocho años de ~** he's eight (years old); **de ~ mediana/avanzada** middle-aged/advanced in years; **la E~ Media** the Middle Ages

edición [eði'θjon] *nf* (*acto*) publication; (*ejemplar*) edition

edificar [eðifi'kar] *vt, vi* to build

edificio [eði'fiθjo] *nm* building; (*fig*) edifice, structure

Edimburgo [eðim'burxo] *nm* Edinburgh

editar [eði'tar] *vt* (*publicar*) to publish; (*preparar textos*) to edit

editor, a [eði'tor, a] *nm/f* (*que publica*) publisher; (*redactor*) editor ▷ *adj* publishing *cpd*; **editorial** *adj* editorial ▷ *nm* leading article, editorial; **casa editorial** publisher

edredón [eðre'ðon] *nm* duvet

educación [eðuka'θjon] *nf* education; (*crianza*) upbringing; (*modales*) (good) manners *pl*

educado, -a [eðu'kaðo, a] *adj*: **bien/mal ~** well/badly behaved

educar [eðu'kar] *vt* to educate; (*criar*) to bring up; (*voz*) to train

EE. UU. *nmpl abr* (=*Estados Unidos*) US(A)

efectivamente [efectiβa'mente] *adv* (*como respuesta*) exactly, precisely; (*verdaderamente*) really; (*de hecho*) in fact

efectivo, -a [efek'tiβo, a] *adj* effective; (*real*) actual, real ▷ *nm*: **pagar en ~** to pay (in) cash; **hacer ~ un cheque** to cash a cheque

efecto [e'fekto] *nm* effect, result; **efectos** *nmpl* (*efectos personales*) effects; (*bienes*) goods; (*Com*) assets; **en ~** in fact; (*respuesta*) exactly, indeed; **efecto invernadero** greenhouse effect; **efectos especiales/secundarios/sonoros** special/side/sound effects

efectuar [efek'twar] *vt* to carry out; (*viaje*) to make

eficacia [efi'kaθja] *nf* (*de persona*) efficiency; (*de medicamento etc*) effectiveness

eficaz [efi'kaθ] *adj* (*persona*) efficient; (*acción*) effective

eficiente [efi'θjente] *adj* efficient

egipcio, -a [e'xipθjo, a] *adj, nm/f* Egyptian

Egipto [e'xipto] *nm* Egypt

egoísmo [exo'ismo] *nm* egoism

egoísta [exo'ista] *adj* egoistical, selfish ▷ *nmf* egoist

Eire ['eire] *nm* Eire

ej. *abr* (=*ejemplo*) eg

eje ['exe] *nm* (*Geo, Mat*) axis; (*de rueda*) axle; (*de máquina*) shaft, spindle

ejecución [exeku'θjon] *nf* execution; (*cumplimiento*) fulfilment; (*Mús*) performance; (*Jur: embargo de deudor*) attachment

ejecutar [exeku'tar] *vt* to execute, carry out; (*matar*) to execute; (*cumplir*) to fulfil;

(*Mús*) to perform; (*Jur: embargar*) to attach, distrain (on)

ejecutivo, -a [exeku'tiβo, a] *adj* executive; **el (poder) ~** the executive (power)

ejemplar [exem'plar] *adj* exemplary ▷ *nm* example; (*Zool*) specimen; (*de libro*) copy; (*de periódico*) number, issue

ejemplo [e'xemplo] *nm* example; **por ~** for example

ejercer [exer'θer] *vt* to exercise; (*influencia*) to exert; (*un oficio*) to practise ▷ *vi* (*practicar*): **~ (de)** to practise (as)

ejercicio [exer'θiθjo] *nm* exercise; (*período*) tenure; **hacer ~** to take exercise; **ejercicio comercial** financial year

ejército [e'xerθito] *nm* army; **entrar en el ~** to join the army, join up; **ejército del aire/ de tierra** Air Force/Army

ejote [e'xote] (*MÉX*) *nm* green bean

○ **PALABRA CLAVE**

el [el] (*f* **la**, *pl* **los, las**, *neutro* **lo**) *art def* **1** the; **el libro/la mesa/los estudiantes** the book/table/students

2 (*con n abstracto: no se traduce*): **el amor/la juventud** love/youth

3 (*posesión: se traduce a menudo por adj posesivo*): **romperse el brazo** to break one's arm; **levantó la mano** he put his hand up; **se puso el sombrero** she put her hat on

4 (*valor descriptivo*): **tener la boca grande/ los ojos azules** to have a big mouth/blue eyes

5 (*con días*) on; **me iré el viernes** I'll leave on Friday; **los domingos suelo ir a nadar** on Sundays I generally go swimming

6 (*lo +adj*): **lo difícil/caro** what is difficult/ expensive; (*cuán*): **no se da cuenta de lo pesado que es** he doesn't realise how boring he is

▷ *pron demos* **1**: **mi libro y el de usted** my book and yours; **las de Pepe son mejores** Pepe's are better; **no la(s) blanca(s) sino la(s) gris(es)** not the white one(s) but the grey one(s)

2: **lo de: lo de ayer** what happened yesterday; **lo de las facturas** that business about the invoices

▷ *pron relativo* **1** (*indef*): **el que: el (los) que quiera(n) que se vaya(n)** anyone who wants to can leave; **llévese el que más le guste** take the one you like best

2 (*def*): **el que: el que compré ayer** the one I bought yesterday; **los que se van** those who leave

3: **lo que: lo que pienso yo/más me gusta** what I think/like most

▷ *conj*: **el que: el que lo diga** the fact that he says so; **el que sea tan vago me molesta** his being so lazy bothers me

▷ *excl*: **¡el susto que me diste!** what a fright you gave me!

▷ *pron personal* **1** (*persona: m*) him; (: *f*) her; (: *pl*) them; **lo/las veo** I can see him/them **2** (*animal, cosa: sg*) it; (: *pl*) them; **lo** (*o* **la**) **veo** I can see it; **los** (*o* **las**) **veo** I can see them **3** (*como sustituto de frase*): **lo: no lo sabía** I didn't know; **ya lo entiendo** I understand now

él [el] *pron* (*persona*) he; (*cosa*) it; (*después de prep: persona*) him; (: *cosa*) it; **de ~** his

elaborar [elaβo'rar] *vt* (*producto*) to make, manufacture; (*preparar*) to prepare; (*madera, metal etc*) to work; (*proyecto etc*) to work on *o* out

elástico, -a [e'lastiko, a] *adj* elastic; (*flexible*) flexible ▷ *nm* elastic; (*un elástico*) elastic band

elección [elek'θjon] *nf* election; (*selección*) choice, selection; **elecciones generales** general election *sg*

electorado [elekto'raðo] *nm* electorate, voters *pl*

electricidad [elektriθi'ðað] *nf* electricity

electricista [elektri'θista] *nmf* electrician

eléctrico, -a [e'lektriko, a] *adj* electric

electro... [elektro] *prefijo* electro...; **electrocardiograma** *nm* electrocardiogram; **electrocutar** *vt* to electrocute; **electrodo** *nm* electrode; **electrodomésticos** *nmpl* (electrical) household appliances

electrónica [elek'tronika] *nf* electronics *sg*

electrónico, -a [elek'troniko, a] *adj* electronic

elefante [ele'fante] *nm* elephant

elegancia [ele'xanθja] *nf* elegance, grace; (*estilo*) stylishness

elegante [ele'xante] *adj* elegant, graceful; (*estiloso*) stylish, fashionable

elegir [ele'xir] *vt* (*escoger*) to choose, select; (*optar*) to opt for; (*presidente*) to elect

elemental [elemen'tal] *adj* (*claro, obvio*) elementary; (*fundamental*) elemental, fundamental

elemento [ele'mento] *nm* element; (*fig*) ingredient; **elementos** *nmpl* elements, rudiments

elevación [eleβa'θjon] *nf* elevation; (*acto*) raising, lifting; (*de precios*) rise; (*Geo etc*) height, altitude

elevar [ele'βar] *vt* to raise, lift (up); (*precio*)

to put up; **elevarse** *vr* (*edificio*) to rise; (*precios*) to go up

eligiendo *etc vb* V **elegir**

elija *etc vb* V **elegir**

eliminar [elimi'nar] *vt* to eliminate, remove

eliminatoria [elimina'torja] *nf* heat, preliminary (round)

élite ['elite] *nf* elite

ella ['eʎa] *pron* (*persona*) she; (*cosa*) it; (*después de prep: persona*) her; (: *cosa*) it; **de ~** hers

ellas ['eʎas] *pron* (*personas y cosas*) they; (*después de prep*) them; **de ~** theirs

ello ['eʎo] *pron* it

ellos ['eʎos] *pron* they; (*después de prep*) them; **de ~** theirs

elogiar [elo'xjar] *vt* to praise; **elogio** *nm* praise

elote [e'lote] (*MÉX*) *nm* corn on the cob

eludir [elu'ðir] *vt* to avoid

email [i'mel] *nm* email; (*dirección*) email address; **mandar un ~ a algn** to email sb, send sb an email

embajada [emba'xaða] *nf* embassy

embajador, a [embaxa'ðor, a] *nm/f* ambassador/ambassadress

embalar [emba'lar] *vt* to parcel, wrap (up); **embalarse** *vr* to go fast

embalse [em'balse] *nm* (*presa*) dam; (*lago*) reservoir

embarazada [embara'θaða] *adj* pregnant ▷ *nf* pregnant woman

▌ No confundir **embarazada** con la palabra inglesa *embarrassed*.

embarazo [emba'raθo] *nm* (*de mujer*) pregnancy; (*impedimento*) obstacle, obstruction; (*timidez*) embarrassment; **embarazoso, -a** *adj* awkward, embarrassing

embarcación [embarka'θjon] *nf* (*barco*) boat, craft; (*acto*) embarkation, boarding

embarcadero [embarka'ðero] *nm* pier, landing stage

embarcar [embar'kar] *vt* (*cargamento*) to ship, stow; (*persona*) to embark, put on board; **embarcarse** *vr* to embark, go on board

embargar [embar'xar] *vt* (*Jur*) to seize, impound

embargo [em'barxo] *nm* (*Jur*) seizure; (*Com, Pol*) embargo

embargue *etc vb* V **embargar**

embarque *etc* [em'barke] *vb* V **embarcar** ▷ *nm* shipment, loading

embellecer [embeʎe'θer] *vt* to embellish, beautify

embestida [embes'tiða] *nf* attack,

onslaught; (*carga*) charge

embestir [embes'tir] *vt* to attack, assault; to charge, attack ▷ *vi* to attack

emblema [em'blema] *nm* emblem

embobado, -a [embo'βaðo, a] *adj* (*atontado*) stunned, bewildered

embolia [em'bolja] *nf* (*Med*) clot

émbolo ['embolo] *nm* (*Auto*) piston

emborrachar [emborra'tʃar] *vt* to make drunk, intoxicate; **emborracharse** *vr* to get drunk

emboscada [embos'kaða] *nf* ambush

embotar [embo'tar] *vt* to blunt, dull

embotellamiento [emboteʎa'mjento] *nm* (*Auto*) traffic jam

embotellar [embote'ʎar] *vt* to bottle

embrague [em'braxe] *nm* (*tb:* **pedal de ~**) clutch

embrión [em'brjon] *nm* embryo

embrollo [em'broʎo] *nm* (*enredo*) muddle, confusion; (*aprieto*) fix, jam

embrujado, -a [embru'xaðo, a] *adj* bewitched; **casa embrujada** haunted house

embrutecer [embrute'θer] *vt* (*atontar*) to stupefy

embudo [em'buðo] *nm* funnel

embuste [em'buste] *nm* (*mentira*) lie; **embustero, -a** *adj* lying, deceitful ▷ *nm/f* (*mentiroso*) liar

embutido [embu'tiðo] *nm* (*Culin*) sausage; (*Tec*) inlay

emergencia [emer'xenθja] *nf* emergency; (*surgimiento*) emergence

emerger [emer'xer] *vi* to emerge, appear

emigración [emixra'θjon] *nf* emigration; (*de pájaros*) migration

emigrar [emi'xrar] *vi* (*personas*) to emigrate; (*pájaros*) to migrate

eminente [emi'nente] *adj* eminent, distinguished; (*elevado*) high

emisión [emi'sjon] *nf* (*acto*) emission; (*Com etc*) issue; (*Radio, TV: acto*) broadcasting; (: *programa*) broadcast, programme (*BRIT*), program (*US*)

emisora [emi'sora] *nf* radio o broadcasting station

emitir [emi'tir] *vt* (*olor etc*) to emit, give off; (*moneda etc*) to issue; (*opinión*) to express; (*Radio*) to broadcast

emoción [emo'θjon] *nf* emotion; (*excitación*) excitement; (*sentimiento*) feeling

emocionante [emoθjo'nante] *adj* (*excitante*) exciting, thrilling

emocionar [emoθjo'nar] *vt* (*excitar*) to excite, thrill; (*conmover*) to move, touch; (*impresionar*) to impress

emoticón [emoti'kon], **emoticono**

[emoti'kono] *nm* smiley

emotivo, -a [emo'tiβo, a] *adj* emotional

empacho [em'patʃo] *nm* (*Med*) indigestion; (*fig*) embarrassment

empalagoso, -a [empala'ɣoso, a] *adj* cloying; (*fig*) tiresome

empalmar [empal'mar] *vt* to join, connect ▷ *vi* (*dos caminos*) to meet, join; **empalme** *nm* joint, connection; junction; (*de trenes*) connection

empanada [empa'naða] *nf* pie, pasty

empañarse [empa'ɲarse] *vr* (*cristales etc*) to steam up

empapar [empa'par] *vt* (*mojar*) to soak, saturate; (*absorber*) to soak up, absorb; **empaparse** *vr*: **~se de** to soak up

empapelar [empape'lar] *vt* (*paredes*) to paper

empaquetar [empake'tar] *vt* to pack, parcel up

empastar [empas'tar] *vt* (*embadurnar*) to paste; (*diente*) to fill

empaste [em'paste] *nm* (*de diente*) filling

empatar [empa'tar] *vi* to draw, tie; **~on a dos** they drew two-all; **empate** *nm* draw, tie

empecé *etc vb* V **empezar**

empedernido, -a [empeðer'niðo, a] *adj* hard, heartless; (*fumador*) inveterate

empeine [em'peine] *nm* (*de pie, zapato*) instep

empeñado, -a [empe'ɲaðo, a] *adj* (*persona*) determined; (*objeto*) pawned

empeñar [empe'ɲar] *vt* (*objeto*) to pawn, pledge; (*persona*) to compel; **empeñarse** *vr* (*endeudarse*) to get into debt; **~se en** to be set on, be determined to

empeño [em'peɲo] *nm* (*determinación, insistencia*) determination, insistence; **casa de ~s** pawnshop

empeorar [empeo'rar] *vt* to make worse, worsen ▷ *vi* to get worse, deteriorate

empezar [empe'θar] *vt, vi* to begin, start

empiece *etc vb* V **empezar**

empiezo *etc vb* V **empezar**

emplasto [em'plasto] *nm* (*Med*) plaster

emplazar [empla'θar] *vt* (*ubicar*) to site, place, locate; (*Jur*) to summons; (*convocar*) to summon

empleado, -a [emple'aðo, a] *nm/f* (*gen*) employee; (*de banco etc*) clerk

emplear [emple'ar] *vt* (*usar*) to use, employ; (*dar trabajo a*) to employ; **emplearse** *vr* (*conseguir trabajo*) to be employed; (*ocuparse*) to occupy o.s.

empleo [em'pleo] *nm* (*puesto*) job; (*puestos: colectivamente*) employment; (*uso*) use, employment

empollar [empo'ʎar] (*ESP: fam*) *vt, vi* to swot (up); **empollón, -ona** (*ESP: fam*) *nm/f* swot

emporio [em'porjo] (*LAM*) *nm* (*gran almacén*) department store

empotrado, -a [empo'traðo, a] *adj* (*armario etc*) built-in

emprender [empren'der] *vt* (*empezar*) to begin, embark on; (*acometer*) to tackle, take on

empresa [em'presa] *nf* (*de espíritu etc*) enterprise; (*Com*) company, firm; **empresariales** *nfpl* business studies; **empresario, -a** *nm/f* (*Com*) businessman(-woman)

empujar [empu'xar] *vt* to push, shove

empujón [empu'xon] *nm* push, shove

empuñar [empu'ɲar] *vt* (*asir*) to grasp, take (firm) hold of

○ **PALABRA CLAVE**

en [en] *prep* **1** (*posición*) in; (: *sobre*) on; **está en el cajón** it's in the drawer; **en Argentina/La Paz** in Argentina/La Paz; **en la oficina/el colegio** at the office/school; **está en el suelo/quinto piso** it's on the floor/the fifth floor

2 (*dirección*) into; **entró en el aula** she went into the classroom; **meter algo en el bolso** to put sth into one's bag

3 (*tiempo*) in; on; **en 1605/3 semanas/ invierno** in 1605/3 weeks/winter; **en (el mes de) enero** in (the month of) January; **en aquella ocasión/época** on that occasion/at that time

4 (*precio*) for; **lo vendió en 20 dólares** he sold it for 20 dollars

5 (*diferencia*) by; **reducir/aumentar en una tercera parte/un 20 por ciento** to reduce/ increase by a third/20 per cent

6 (*manera*): **en avión/autobús** by plane/ bus; **escrito en inglés** written in English

7 (*después de vb que indica gastar etc*) on; **han cobrado demasiado en dietas** they've charged too much to expenses; **se le va la mitad del sueldo en comida** he spends half his salary on food

8 (*tema, ocupación*): **experto en la materia** expert on the subject; **trabaja en la construcción** he works in the building industry

9 (*adj + en + infin*): **lento en reaccionar** slow to react

enaguas [e'naɣwas] *nfpl* petticoat *sg*, underskirt *sg*

enajenación [enaxena'θjon] *nf* (*Psico: tb*:

~ mental) mental derangement

enamorado, -a [enamo'raðo, a] *adj* in love ▷ *nm/f* lover; **estar ~ (de)** to be in love (with)

enamorar [enamo'rar] *vt* to win the love of; **enamorarse** *vr*: **~se de algn** to fall in love with sb

enano, -a [e'nano, a] *adj* tiny ▷ *nm/f* dwarf

encabezamiento [enkaβeθa'mjento] *nm* (*de carta*) heading; (*de periódico*) headline

encabezar [enkaβe'θar] *vt* (*movimiento, revolución*) to lead, head; (*lista*) to head, be at the top of; (*carta*) to put a heading to

encadenar [enkaðe'nar] *vt* to chain (together); (*poner grilletes a*) to shackle

encajar [enka'xar] *vt* (*ajustar*): **~ (en)** to fit (into); (*fam: golpe*) to take ▷ *vi* to fit (well); (*fig: corresponder a*) to match

encaje [en'kaxe] *nm* (*labor*) lace

encallar [enka'ʎar] *vi* (*Náut*) to run aground

encaminar [enkami'nar] *vt* to direct, send

encantado, -a [enkan'taðo, a] *adj* (*hechizado*) bewitched; (*muy contento*) delighted; **¡~!** how do you do, pleased to meet you

encantador, a [enkanta'ðor, a] *adj* charming, lovely ▷ *nm/f* magician, enchanter/enchantress

encantar [enkan'tar] *vt* (*agradar*) to charm, delight; (*hechizar*) to bewitch, cast a spell on; **me encanta eso** I love that; **encanto** *nm* (*hechizo*) spell, charm; (*fig*) charm, delight

encarcelar [enkarθe'lar] *vt* to imprison, jail

encarecer [enkare'θer] *vt* to put up the price of; **encarecerse** *vr* to get dearer

encargado, -a [enkar'ɣaðo, a] *adj* in charge ▷ *nm/f* agent, representative; (*responsable*) person in charge

encargar [enkar'ɣar] *vt* to entrust; (*recomendar*) to urge, recommend; **encargarse** *vr*: **~se de** to look after, take charge of; **~ algo a algn** to put sb in charge of sth; **~ a algn que haga algo** to ask sb to do sth

encargo [en'karɣo] *nm* (*tarea*) assignment, job; (*responsabilidad*) responsibility; (*Com*) order

encariñarse [enkari'narse] *vr*: **~ con** to grow fond of, get attached to

encarnación [enkarna'θjon] *nf* incarnation, embodiment

encarrilar [enkarri'lar] *vt* (*tren*) to put back on the rails; (*fig*) to correct, put on the right track

encasillar [enkasi'ʎar] *vt* (*fig*) to pigeonhole; (*actor*) to typecast

encendedor [enθende'ðor] *nm* lighter

encender [enθen'der] *vt* (*con fuego*) to light; (*luz, radio*) to put on, switch on; (*avivar: pasión*) to inflame; **encenderse** *vr* to catch fire; (*excitarse*) to get excited; (*de cólera*) to flare up; (*el rostro*) to blush

encendido [enθen'diðo] *nm* (*Auto*) ignition

encerado [enθe'raðo] *nm* (*Escol*) blackboard

encerrar [enθe'rrar] *vt* (*confinar*) to shut in, shut up; (*comprender, incluir*) to include, contain

encharcado, -a [entʃar'kaðo, a] *adj* (*terreno*) flooded

encharcarse [entʃar'karse] *vr* to get flooded

enchufado, -a [entʃu'faðo, a] (*fam*) *nm/f* well-connected person

enchufar [entʃu'far] *vt* (*Elec*) to plug in; (*Tec*) to connect, fit together; **enchufe** *nm* (*Elec: clavija*) plug; (: *toma*) socket; (*do dos tubos*) joint, connection; (*fam: influencia*) contact, connection; (: *puesto*) cushy job

encía [en'θia] *nf* gum

encienda *etc vb* V **encender**

encierro *etc* [en'θjerro] *vb* V **encerrar** ▷ *nm* shutting in, shutting up; (*calabozo*) prison

encima [en'θima] *adv* (*sobre*) above, over; (*además*) besides; **~ de** (*en*) on, on top of; (*sobre*) above, over; (*además de*) besides, on top of; **por ~ de** over; **¿llevas dinero ~?** have you (got) any money on you?; **se me vino ~** it took me by surprise

encina [en'θina] *nf* holm oak

encinta [en'θinta] *adj* pregnant

enclenque [en'klenke] *adj* weak, sickly

encoger [enko'xer] *vt* to shrink, contract; **encogerse** *vr* to shrink, contract; (*fig*) to cringe; **~se de hombros** to shrug one's shoulders

encomendar [enkomen'dar] *vt* to entrust, commend; **encomendarse** *vr*: **~se a** to put one's trust in

encomienda *etc* [enko'mjenda] *vb* V **encomendar** ▷ *nf* (*encargo*) charge, commission; (*elogio*) tribute; **encomienda postal** (*LAM*) package

encontrar [enkon'trar] *vt* (*hallar*) to find; (*inesperadamente*) to meet, run into; **encontrarse** *vr* to meet (each other); (*situarse*) to be (situated); **~se con** to meet; **~se bien (de salud)** to feel well

encrucijada [enkruθi'xaða] *nf*

crossroads sg

encuadernación [enkwaðerna'θjon] nf binding

encuadrar [enkwa'ðrar] vt (retrato) to frame; (ajustar) to fit, insert; (contener) to contain

encubrir [enku'βrir] vt (ocultar) to hide, conceal; (criminal) to harbour, shelter

encuentro etc [en'kwentro] vb V **encontrar** ▷ nm (de personas) meeting; (Auto etc) collision, crash; (Deporte) match, game; (Mil) encounter

encuerado, -a (MÉX) [enkwe'raðo, a] adj nude, naked

encuesta [en'kwesta] nf inquiry, investigation; (sondeo) (public) opinion poll

encumbrar [enkum'brar] vt (persona) to exalt

endeble [en'deβle] adj (persona) weak; (argumento, excusa, persona) weak

endemoniado, -a [endemo'njaðo, a] adj possessed (of the devil); (travieso) devilish

enderezar [endere'θar] vt (poner derecho) to straighten (out); (: verticalmente) to set upright; (situación) to straighten o sort out; (dirigir) to direct; **enderezarse** vr (persona sentada) to straighten up

endeudarse [endeu'ðarse] vr to get into debt

endiablado, -a [endja'βlaðo, a] adj devilish, diabolical; (travieso) mischievous

endilgar [endil'xar] (fam) vt: **~le algo a algn** to lumber sb with sth

endiñar [endi'nar] (ESP: fam) vt (bofetón) to land, belt

endosar [endo'sar] vt (cheque etc) to endorse

endulzar [endul'θar] vt to sweeten; (suavizar) to soften

endurecer [endure'θer] vt to harden; **endurecerse** vr to harden, grow hard

enema [e'nema] nm (Med) enema

enemigo, -a [ene'miχo, a] adj enemy, hostile ▷ nm/f enemy

enemistad [enemis'tað] nf enmity

enemistar [enemis'tar] vt to make enemies of, cause a rift between; **enemistarse** vr to become enemies; (amigos) to fall out

energía [ener'χia] nf (vigor) energy, drive; (empuje) push; (Tec, Elec) energy, power; **energía eólica** wind power; **energía solar** solar energy o power

enérgico, -a [e'nerχiko, a] adj (gen) energetic; (voz, modales) forceful

energúmeno, -a [ener'χumeno, a] (fam) nm/f (fig) madman(-woman)

enero [e'nero] nm January

enfadado, -a [enfa'ðaðo, a] adj angry, annoyed

enfadar [enfa'ðar] vt to anger, annoy; **enfadarse** vr to get angry o annoyed

enfado [en'faðo] nm (enojo) anger, annoyance; (disgusto) trouble, bother

énfasis ['enfasis] nm emphasis, stress

enfático, -a [en'fatiko, a] adj emphatic

enfermar [enfer'mar] vt to make ill ▷ vi to fall ill, be taken ill

enfermedad [enferme'ðað] nf illness; **enfermedad venérea** venereal disease

enfermera [enfer'mera] nf nurse

enfermería [enferme'ria] nf infirmary; (de colegio etc) sick bay

enfermero [enfer'mero] nm (male) nurse

enfermizo, -a [enfer'miθo, a] adj (persona) sickly, unhealthy; (fig) unhealthy

enfermo, -a [en'fermo, a] adj ill, sick ▷ nm/f invalid, sick person; (en hospital) patient; **caer o ponerse ~** to fall ill

enfocar [enfo'kar] vt (foto etc) to focus; (problema etc) to approach

enfoque etc [en'foke] vb V **enfocar** ▷ nm focus

enfrentar [enfren'tar] vt (peligro) to face (up to), confront; (oponer) to bring face to face; **enfrentarse** vr (dos personas) to face o confront each other; (Deporte: dos equipos) to meet; **~se con** to face up to, confront

enfrente [en'frente] adv opposite; **la casa de ~** the house opposite, the house across the street; **~ de** opposite, facing

enfriamiento [enfria'mjento] nm chilling, refrigeration; (Med) cold, chill

enfriar [enfri'ar] vt (alimentos) to cool, chill; (algo caliente) to cool down; **enfriarse** vr to cool down; (Med) to catch a chill; (amistad) to cool

enfurecer [enfure'θer] vt to enrage, madden; **enfurecerse** vr to become furious, fly into a rage; (mar) to get rough

enganchar [engan'tʃar] vt to hook; (dos vagones) to hitch up; (Tec) to couple, connect; (Mil) to recruit; **engancharse** vr (Mil) to enlist, join up

enganche [en'gantʃe] nm hook; (ESP Tec) coupling, connection; (acto) hooking (up); (Mil) recruitment, enlistment; (MÉX: depósito) deposit

engañar [enga'nar] vt to deceive; (estafar) to cheat, swindle; **engañarse** vr (equivocarse) to be wrong; (disimular la verdad) to deceive o.s.

engaño [en'gano] nm deceit; (estafa) trick, swindle; (error) mistake, misunderstanding; (ilusión) delusion; **engañoso, -a** adj (tramposo) crooked; (mentiroso) dishonest, deceitful; (*aspecto*) deceptive; (*consejo*) misleading

engatusar [engatu'sar] (*fam*) *vt* to coax

engendro [en'xendro] *nm* (*Bio*) foetus; (*fig*) monstrosity

englobar [englo'βar] *vt* to include, comprise

engordar [engor'ðar] *vt* to fatten ▷ *vi* to get fat, put on weight

engorroso, -a [engo'rroso, a] *adj* bothersome, trying

engranaje [engra'naxe] *nm* (*Auto*) gear

engrasar [engra'sar] *vt* (*Tec: poner grasa*) to grease; (: *lubricar*) to lubricate, oil; (*manchar*) to make greasy

engreído, -a [engre'iðo, a] *adj* vain, conceited

enhebrar [ene'βrar] *vt* to thread

enhorabuena [enora'βwena] *excl* ¡~! congratulations! ▷ *nf*: **dar la ~ a** to congratulate

enigma [e'niɣma] *nm* enigma; (*problema*) puzzle; (*misterio*) mystery

enjambre [en'xambre] *nm* swarm

enjaular [enxau'lar] *vt* (to put in a) cage; (*fam*) to jail, lock up

enjuagar [enxwa'ɣar] *vt* (*ropa*) to rinse (out)

enjuague *etc* [en'xwaxe] *vb* V **enjuagar** ▷ *nm* (*Med*) mouthwash; (*de ropa*) rinse, rinsing

enlace [en'laθe] *nm* link, connection; (*relación*) relationship; (*tb*: **~ matrimonial**) marriage; (*de carretera, trenes*) connection; **enlace sindical** shop steward

enlatado, -a [enla'taðo, a] *adj* (*alimentos, productos*) tinned, canned

enlazar [enla'θar] *vt* (*unir con lazos*) to bind together; (*atar*) to tie; (*conectar*) to link, connect; (*LAM: caballo*) to lasso

enloquecer [enloke'θer] *vt* to drive mad ▷ *vi* to go mad

enmarañar [enmara'ɲar] *vt* (*enredar*) to tangle (up), entangle; (*complicar*) to complicate; (*confundir*) to confuse

enmarcar [enmar'kar] *vt* (*cuadro*) to frame

enmascarar [enmaska'rar] *vt* to mask; **enmascararse** *vr* to put on a mask

enmendar [enmen'dar] *vt* to emend, correct; (*constitución etc*) to amend; (*comportamiento*) to reform; **enmendarse** *vr* to reform, mend one's ways; **enmienda** *nf* correction; amendment; reform

enmudecer [enmuðe'θer] *vi* (*perder el habla*) to fall silent; (*guardar silencio*) to remain silent

ennoblecer [ennoβle'θer] *vt* to ennoble

enojado, -a [eno'xaðo, a] (*LAM*) *adj* angry

enojar [eno'xar] *vt* (*encolerizar*) to anger; (*disgustar*) to annoy, upset; **enojarse** *vr* to get angry; to get annoyed

enojo [e'noxo] *nm* (*cólera*) anger; (*irritación*) annoyance

enorme [e'norme] *adj* enormous, huge; (*fig*) monstrous

enredadera [enreða'ðera] *nf* (*Bot*) creeper, climbing plant

enredar [enre'ðar] *vt* (*cables, hilos etc*) to tangle (up), entangle; (*situación*) to complicate, confuse; (*meter cizaña*) to sow discord among o between; (*implicar*) to embroil, implicate; **enredarse** *vr* to get entangled, get tangled (up); (*situación*) to get complicated; (*persona*) to get embroiled; (*LAM: fam*) to meddle

enredo [en'reðo] *nm* (*maraña*) tangle; (*confusión*) mix-up, confusion; (*intriga*) intrigue

enriquecer [enrike'θer] *vt* to make rich, enrich; **enriquecerse** *vr* to get rich

enrojecer [enroxe'θer] *vt* to redden ▷ *vi* (*persona*) to blush; **enrojecerse** *vr* to blush

enrollar [enro'ʎar] *vt* to roll (up), wind (up)

ensalada [ensa'laða] *nf* salad; **ensaladilla (rusa)** *nf* Russian salad

ensanchar [ensan'tʃar] *vt* (*hacer más ancho*) to widen; (*agrandar*) to enlarge, expand; (*Costura*) to let out; **ensancharse** *vr* to get wider, expand

ensayar [ensa'jar] *vt* to test, try (out); (*Teatro*) to rehearse

ensayo [en'sajo] *nm* test, trial; (*Quím*) experiment; (*Teatro*) rehearsal; (*Deporte*) try; (*Escol, Literatura*) essay

enseguida [ense'ɣiða] *adv* at once, right away

ensenada [ense'naða] *nf* inlet, cove

enseñanza [ense'ɲanθa] *nf* (*educación*) education; (*acción*) teaching; (*doctrina*) teaching, doctrine; **enseñanza (de) primaria/secundaria** elementary/ secondary education

enseñar [ense'ɲar] *vt* (*educar*) to teach; (*mostrar, señalar*) to show

enseres [en'seres] *nmpl* belongings

ensuciar [ensu'θjar] *vt* (*manchar*) to dirty, soil; (*fig*) to defile; **ensuciarse** *vr* to get dirty; (*bebé*) to dirty one's nappy

entablar [enta'βlar] *vt* (*recubrir*) to board (up); (*Ajedrez, Damas*) to set up; (*conversación*) to strike up; (*Jur*) to file ▷ *vi* to draw

ente ['ente] *nm* (*organización*) body, organization; (*fam: persona*) odd character

entender [enten'der] *vt* (*comprender*) to

understand; (*darse cuenta*) to realize ▷ *vi* to understand; (*creer*) to think, believe; **entenderse** *vr* (*comprenderse*) to be understood; (*ponerse de acuerdo*) to agree, reach an agreement; **~ de** to know all about; **~ algo de** to know a little about; **~ en** to deal with, have to do with; **~ mal** to misunderstand; **~se con algn** (*llevarse bien*) to get on *o* along with sb; **~se mal** (*dos personas*) to get on badly

entendido, -a [enten'diðo, a] *adj* (*comprendido*) understood; (*hábil*) skilled; (*inteligente*) knowledgeable ▷ *nm/f* (*experto*) expert ▷ *excl* agreed!; **entendimiento** *nm* (*comprensión*) understanding; (*inteligencia*) mind, intellect; (*juicio*) judgement

enterado, -a [ente'raðo, a] *adj* well-informed; **estar ~ de** to know about, be aware of

enteramente [entera'mente] *adv* entirely, completely

enterar [ente'rar] *vt* (*informar*) to inform, tell; **enterarse** *vr* to find out, get to know

enterito [ente'rito] (RPL) *nm* boiler suit (BRIT), overalls (US)

entero, -a [en'tero, a] *adj* (*total*) whole, entire; (*fig: honesto*) honest; (: *firme*) firm, resolute ▷ *nm* (Com: *punto*) point

enterrar [ente'rrar] *vt* to bury

entidad [enti'ðað] *nf* (*empresa*) firm, company; (*organismo*) body; (*sociedad*) society; (*Filosofía*) entity

entiendo *etc vb* V **entender**

entierro [en'tjerro] *nm* (*acción*) burial; (*funeral*) funeral

entonación [entona'θjon] *nf* (Ling) intonation

entonar [ento'nar] *vt* (*canción*) to intone; (*colores*) to tone; (*Med*) to tone up ▷ *vi* to be in tune

entonces [en'tonθes] *adv* then, at that time; **desde ~** since then; **en aquel ~** at that time; **(pues) ~** and so

entornar [entor'nar] *vt* (*puerta, ventana*) to half-close, leave ajar; (*los ojos*) to screw up

entorpecer [entorpe'θer] *vt* (*entendimiento*) to dull; (*impedir*) to obstruct, hinder; (: *tránsito*) to slow down, delay

entrada [en'traða] *nf* (*acción*) entry, access; (*sitio*) entrance, way in; (*Inform*) input; (Com) receipts *pl*, takings *pl*; (Culin) starter; (*Deporte*) innings *sg*; (*Teatro*) house, audience; (*billete*) ticket; **~s y salidas** (Com) income and expenditure; **de ~** from the outset; **entrada de aire** (Tec) air intake *o* inlet

entrado, -a [en'traðo, a] *adj*: **~ en años** elderly; **una vez ~ el verano** in the summer(time), when summer comes

entramparse [entram'parse] *vr* to get into debt

entrante [en'trante] *adj* next, coming; **mes/año ~** next month/year; **entrantes** *nmpl* starters

entraña [en'traɲa] *nf* (*fig: centro*) heart, core; (*raíz*) root; **entrañas** *nfpl* (Anat) entrails; (*fig*) heart *sg*; **entrañable** *adj* close, intimate; **entrañar** *vt* to entail

entrar [en'trar] *vt* (*introducir*) to bring in; (*Inform*) to input ▷ *vi* (*meterse*) to go in, come in, enter; (*comenzar*): **~ diciendo** to begin by saying; **hacer ~** to show in; **me entró sed/sueño** I started to feel thirsty/sleepy; **no me entra** I can't get the hang of it

entre ['entre] *prep* (*dos*) between; (*más de dos*) among(st)

entreabrir [entrea'βrir] *vt* to half-open, open halfway

entrecejo [entre'θexo] *nm*: **fruncir el ~** to frown

entredicho [entre'ðitʃo] *nm* (Jur) injunction; **poner en ~** to cast doubt on; **estar en ~** to be in doubt

entrega [en'treɣa] *nf* (*de mercancías*) delivery; (*de novela etc*) instalment; **entregar** [entre'ɣar] *vt* (*dar*) to hand (over), deliver; **entregarse** *vr* (*rendirse*) to surrender, give in, submit; (*dedicarse*) to devote o.s.

entremeses [entre'meses] *nmpl* hors d'œuvres

entremeter [entreme'ter] *vt* to insert, put in; **entremeterse** *vr* to meddle, interfere; **entremetido, -a** *adj* meddling, interfering

entremezclar [entremeθ'klar] *vt* to intermingle; **entremezclarse** *vr* to intermingle

entrenador, a [entrena'ðor, a] *nm/f* trainer, coach

entrenarse [entre'narse] *vr* to train

entrepierna [entre'pjerna] *nf* crotch

entresuelo [entre'swelo] *nm* mezzanine

entretanto [entre'tanto] *adv* meanwhile, meantime

entretecho [entre'tetʃo] (CS) *nm* attic

entretejer [entrete'xer] *vt* to interweave

entretener [entrete'ner] *vt* (*divertir*) to entertain, amuse; (*detener*) to hold up, delay; **entretenerse** *vr* (*divertirse*) to amuse o.s.; (*retrasarse*) to delay, linger; **entretenido, -a** *adj* entertaining, amusing; **entretenimiento** *nm* entertainment, amusement

entrever [entre'βer] *vt* to glimpse, catch a glimpse of

entrevista [entre'βista] *nf* interview;

entrevistar vt to interview; **entrevistarse** vr to have an interview

entristecer [entriste'θer] vt to sadden, grieve; **entristecerse** vr to grow sad

entrometerse [entrome'terse] vr: **~ (en)** to interfere (in o with)

entumecer [entume'θer] vt to numb, benumb; **entumecerse** vr (por el frío) to go o become numb

enturbiar [entur'βjar] vt (el agua) to make cloudy; (fig) to confuse; **enturbiarse** vr (oscurecerse) to become cloudy; (fig) to get confused, become obscure

entusiasmar [entusjas'mar] vt to excite, fill with enthusiasm; (gustar mucho) to delight; **entusiasmarse** vr: **~se con** o **por** to get enthusiastic o excited about

entusiasmo [entu'sjasmo] nm enthusiasm; (excitación) excitement

entusiasta [entu'sjasta] adj enthusiastic ▷ nmf enthusiast

enumerar [enume'rar] vt to enumerate

envainar [embai'nar] vt to sheathe

envalentonar [embalento'nar] vt to give courage to; **envalentonarse** vr (pey: jactarse) to boast, brag

envasar [emba'sar] vt (empaquetar) to pack, wrap; (enfrascar) to bottle; (enlatar) to can; (embolsar) to pocket

envase [em'base] nm (en paquete) packing, wrapping; (en botella) bottling; (en lata) canning; (recipiente) container; (paquete) package; (botella) bottle; (lata) tin (BRIT), can

envejecer [embexe'θer] vt to make old, age ▷ vi (volverse viejo) to grow old; (parecer viejo) to age

envenenar [embene'nar] vt to poison; (fig) to embitter

envergadura [emberɤa'ðura] nf (fig) scope, compass

enviar [em'bjar] vt to send; **~ un mensaje a algn** (por movil) to text sb, to send sb a text message

enviciarse [embi'θjarse] vr: **~ (con)** to get addicted (to)

envidia [em'biðja] nf envy; **tener ~ a** to envy, be jealous of; **envidiar** vt to envy

envío [em'bio] nm (acción) sending; (de mercancías) consignment; (de dinero) remittance

enviudar [embju'ðar] vi to be widowed

envoltura [embol'tura] nf (cobertura) cover; (embalaje) wrapper, wrapping; **envoltorio** nm package

envolver [embol'βer] vt to wrap (up); (cubrir) to cover; (enemigo) to surround; (implicar) to involve, implicate

envuelto [em'bwelto] pp de **envolver**

enyesar [enje'sar] vt (pared) to plaster; (Med) to put in plaster

enzarzarse [enθar'θarse] vr: **~ en** (pelea) to get mixed up in; (disputa) to get involved in

épica ['epika] nf epic

epidemia [epi'ðemja] nf epidemic

epilepsia [epi'lepsja] nf epilepsy

episodio [epi'soðjo] nm episode

época ['epoka] nf period, time; (Hist) age, epoch; **hacer ~** to be epoch-making

equilibrar [ekili'βrar] vt to balance; **equilibrio** nm balance, equilibrium; **mantener/perder el equilibrio** to keep/lose one's balance; **equilibrista** nmf (funámbulo) tightrope walker; (acróbata) acrobat

equipaje [eki'paxe] nm luggage; (avíos): **hacer el ~** to pack; **equipaje de mano** hand luggage

equipar [eki'par] vt (proveer) to equip

equipararse [ekipa'rarse] vr: **~ con** to be on a level with

equipo [e'kipo] nm (conjunto de cosas) equipment; (Deporte) team; (de obreros) shift

equis ['ekis] nf inv (the letter) X

equitación [ekita'θjon] nf horse riding

equivalente [ekiβa'lente] adj, nm equivalent

equivaler [ekiβa'ler] vi to be equivalent o equal

equivocación [ekiβoka'θjon] nf mistake, error

equivocado, -a [ekiβo'kaðo, a] adj wrong, mistaken

equivocarse [ekiβo'karse] vr to be wrong, make a mistake; **~ de camino** to take the wrong road

era ['era] vb V **ser** ▷ nf era, age

erais vb V **ser**

éramos vb V **ser**

eran vb V **ser**

eras vb V **ser**

erección [erek'θjon] nf erection

eres vb V **ser**

erigir [eri'xir] vt to erect, build; **erigirse** vr: **~se en** to set o.s. up as

erizo [e'riθo] nm (Zool) hedgehog; **erizo de mar** sea-urchin

ermita [er'mita] nf hermitage; **ermitaño, -a** [ermi'taɲo, a] nm/f hermit

erosión [ero'sjon] nf erosion

erosionar [erosjo'nar] vt to erode

erótico, -a [e'rotiko, a] adj erotic; **erotismo** nm eroticism

errante [e'rrante] adj wandering, errant

erróneo, -a [e'rroneo, a] adj (equivocado) wrong, mistaken

error [e'rror] nm error, mistake; (Inform)

bug; **error de imprenta** misprint

eructar [eruk'tar] *vt* to belch, burp

erudito, -a [eru'ðito, a] *adj* erudite, learned

erupción [erup'θjon] *nf* eruption; (*Med*) rash

es *vb* V **ser**

esa ['esa] (*pl* ~**s**) *adj* demos V **ese**

ésa ['esa] (*pl* ~**s**) *pron* V **ése**

esbelto, -a [es'βelto, a] *adj* slim, slender

esbozo [es'βoθo] *nm* sketch, outline

escabeche [eska'βetʃe] *nm* brine; (*de aceitunas etc*) pickle; **en ~** pickled

escabullirse [eskaβu'ʎirse] *vr* to slip away, to clear out

escafandra [eska'fandra] *nf* (*buzo*) diving suit; (*escafandra espacial*) space suit

escala [es'kala] *nf* (*proporción, Mús*) scale; (*de mano*) ladder; (*Aviac*) stopover; **hacer ~ en** to stop o call in at

escalafón [eskala'fon] *nm* (*escala de salarios*) salary scale, wage scale

escalar [eska'lar] *vt* to climb, scale

escalera [eska'lera] *nf* stairs *pl*, staircase; (*escala*) ladder; (*Naipes*) run; **escalera de caracol** spiral staircase; **escalera de incendios** fire escape; **escalera mecánica** escalator

escalfar [eskal'far] *vt* (*huevos*) to poach

escalinata [eskali'nata] *nf* staircase

escalofriante [eskalo'frjante] *adj* chilling

escalofrío [eskalo'frio] *nm* (*Med*) chill; **escalofríos** *nmpl* (*fig*) shivers

escalón [eska'lon] *nm* step, stair; (*de escalera*) rung

escalope [eska'lope] *nm* (*Culin*) escalope

escama [es'kama] *nf* (*de pez, serpiente*) scale; (*de jabón*) flake; (*fig*) resentment

escampar [eskam'par] *vb impers* to stop raining

escandalizar [eskandali'θar] *vt* to scandalize, shock; **escandalizarse** *vr* to be shocked; (*ofenderse*) to be offended

escándalo [es'kandalo] *nm* scandal; (*alboroto, tumulto*) row, uproar; **escandaloso, -a** *adj* scandalous, shocking

escandinavo, -a [eskandi'naβo, a] *adj*, *nm/f* Scandinavian

escanear [eskane'ar] *vt* to scan

escaño [es'kaɲo] *nm* bench; (*Pol*) seat

escapar [eska'par] *vi* (*gen*) to escape, run away; (*Deporte*) to break away; **escaparse** *vr* to escape, get away; (*agua, gas*) to leak (out)

escaparate [eskapa'rate] *nm* shop window

escape [es'kape] *nm* (*de agua, gas*) leak; (*de motor*) exhaust

escarabajo [eskara'βaxo] *nm* beetle

escaramuza [eskara'muθa] *nf* skirmish

escarbar [eskar'βar] *vt* (*tierra*) to scratch

escarceos [eskar'θeos] *nmpl*: **en mis ~ con la política ...** in my dealings with politics ...; **escarceos amorosos** love affairs

escarcha [es'kartʃa] *nf* frost; **escarchado, -a** [eskar'tʃaðo, a] *adj* (*Culin: fruta*) crystallized

escarlatina [eskarla'tina] *nf* scarlet fever

escarmentar [eskarmen'tar] *vt* to punish severely ▷ *vi* to learn one's lesson

escarmiento *etc* [eskar'mjento] *vb* V **escarmentar** ▷ *nm* (*ejemplo*) lesson; (*castigo*) punishment

escarola [eska'rola] *nf* endive

escarpado, -a [eskar'paðo, a] *adj* (*pendiente*) sheer, steep; (*rocas*) craggy

escasear [eskase'ar] *vi* to be scarce

escasez [eska'seθ] *nf* (*falta*) shortage, scarcity; (*pobreza*) poverty

escaso, -a [es'kaso, a] *adj* (*poco*) scarce; (*raro*) rare; (*ralo*) thin, sparse; (*limitado*) limited

escatimar [eskati'mar] *vt* to skimp (on), be sparing with

escayola [eska'jola] *nf* plaster

escena [es'θena] *nf* scene; **escenario** [esθe'narjo] *nm* (*Teatro*) stage; (*Cine*) set; (*fig*) scene

No confundir **escenario** con la palabra inglesa *scenery*.

escenografía [esθeno] *nf* set design

escéptico, -a [es'θeptiko, a] *adj* sceptical ▷ *nm/f* sceptic

esclarecer [esklare'θer] *vt* (*misterio, problema*) to shed light on

esclavitud [esklaβi'tuð] *nf* slavery

esclavizar [esklaβi'θar] *vt* to enslave

esclavo, -a [es'klaβo, a] *nm/f* slave

escoba [es'koβa] *nf* broom; **escobilla** *nf* brush

escocer [esko'θer] *vi* to burn, sting; **escocerse** *vr* to chafe, get chafed

escocés, -esa [esko'θes, esa] *adj* Scottish ▷ *nm/f* Scotsman(-woman), Scot

Escocia [es'koθja] *nf* Scotland

escoger [esko'xer] *vt* to choose, pick, select; **escogido, -a** *adj* chosen, selected

escolar [esko'lar] *adj* school *cpd* ▷ *nmf* schoolboy(-girl), pupil

escollo [es'koʎo] *nm* (*obstáculo*) pitfall

escolta [es'kolta] *nf* escort; **escoltar** *vt* to escort

escombros [es'kombros] *nmpl* (*basura*) rubbish *sg*; (*restos*) debris *sg*

esconder [eskon'der] *vt* to hide, conceal; **esconderse** *vr* to hide; **escondidas** (*LAM*) *nfpl*: **a escondidas** secretly; **escondite** *nm* hiding place; (*ESP: juego*) hide-and-seek; **escondrijo** *nm* hiding place, hideout

escopeta [esko'peta] *nf* shotgun

escoria [es'korja] *nf* (*de alto horno*) slag; (*fig*) scum, dregs *pl*

Escorpio [es'korpjo] *nm* Scorpio

escorpión [eskor'pjon] *nm* scorpion

escotado, -a [esko'taðo, a] *adj* low-cut

escote [es'kote] *nm* (*de vestido*) low neck; **pagar a ~** to share the expenses

escotilla [esko'tiʎa] *nf* (*Náut*) hatch(way)

escozor [esko'θor] *nm* (*dolor*) sting(ing)

escribible [eskri'βiβle] *adj* writable

escribir [eskri'βir] *vt, vi* to write; **~ a máquina** to type; **¿cómo se escribe?** how do you spell it?

escrito, -a [es'krito, a] *pp de* **escribir** ▷ *nm* (*documento*) document; (*manuscrito*) text, manuscript; **por ~** in writing

escritor, a [eskri'tor, a] *nm/f* writer

escritorio [eskri'torjo] *nm* desk

escritura [eskri'tura] *nf* (*acción*) writing; (*caligrafía*) (hand)writing; (*Jur: documento*) deed

escrúpulo [es'krupulo] *nm* scruple; (*minuciosidad*) scrupulousness; **escrupuloso, -a** *adj* scrupulous

escrutinio [eskru'tinjo] *nm* (*examen atento*) scrutiny; (*Pol: recuento de votos*) count(ing)

escuadra [es'kwaðra] *nf* (*Mil etc*) squad; (*Náut*) squadron; (*flota: de coches etc*) fleet; **escuadrilla** *nf* (*de aviones*) squadron; (*LAM: de obreros*) gang

escuadrón [eskwa'ðron] *nm* squadron

escuálido, -a [es'kwaliðo, a] *adj* skinny, scraggy; (*sucio*) squalid

escuchar [esku'tʃar] *vt* to listen to ▷ *vi* to listen

escudo [es'kuðo] *nm* shield

escuela [es'kwela] *nf* school; **escuela de artes y oficios** (*ESP*) ≈ technical college; **escuela de choferes** (*LAM*) driving school; **escuela de manejo** (*MÉX*) driving school

escueto, -a [es'kweto, a] *adj* plain; (*estilo*) simple

escuincle, -a [es'kwinkle, a] (*MÉX: fam*) *nm/f* kid

esculpir [eskul'pir] *vt* to sculpt; (*grabar*) to engrave; (*tallar*) to carve; **escultor, a** *nm/f* sculptor(-tress); **escultura** *nf* sculpture

escupidera [eskupi'ðera] *nf* spittoon

escupir [esku'pir] *vt, vi* to spit (out)

escurreplatos [eskurre'platos] (*ESP*) *nm inv* draining board (*BRIT*), drainboard (*US*)

escurridero [eskurri'ðero] (*LAM*) *nm* draining board (*BRIT*), drainboard (*US*)

escurridizo, -a [eskurri'ðiθo, a] *adj* slippery

escurridor [eskurri'ðor] *nm* colander

escurrir [esku'rrir] *vt* (*ropa*) to wring out; (*verduras, platos*) to drain ▷ *vi* (*líquidos*) to drip; **escurrirse** *vr* (*secarse*) to drain; (*resbalarse*) to slip, slide; (*escaparse*) to slip away

ese ['ese] (*f* **esa**, *pl* **esos, esas**) *adj demos* (*sg*) that; (*pl*) those

ése ['ese] (*f* **ésa**, *pl* **ésos, ésas**) *pron* (*sg*) that (one); (*pl*) those (ones); **~ ... éste ...** the former ... the latter ...; **no me vengas con ésas** don't give me any more of that nonsense

esencia [e'senθja] *nf* essence; **esencial** *adj* essential

esfera [es'fera] *nf* sphere; (*de reloj*) face; **esférico, -a** *adj* spherical

esforzarse [esfor'θarse] *vr* to exert o.s., make an effort

esfuerzo *etc* [es'fwerθo] *vb* V **esforzarse** ▷ *nm* effort

esfumarse [esfu'marse] *vr* (*apoyo, esperanzas*) to fade away

esgrima [es'ɣrima] *nf* fencing

esguince [es'ɣinθe] *nm* (*Med*) sprain

eslabón [esla'βon] *nm* link

eslip [ez'lip] *nm* pants *pl* (*BRIT*), briefs *pl*

eslovaco, -a [eslo'βako, a] *adj, nm/f* Slovak, Slovakian ▷ *nm* (*Ling*) Slovak, Slovakian

Eslovaquia [eslo'βakja] *nf* Slovakia

esmalte [es'malte] *nm* enamel; **esmalte de uñas** nail varnish o polish

esmeralda [esme'ralda] *nf* emerald

esmerarse [esme'rarse] *vr* (*aplicarse*) to take great pains, exercise great care; (*afanarse*) to work hard

esmero [es'mero] *nm* (great) care

esnob [es'nob] (*pl* **~s**) *adj* (*persona*) snobbish ▷ *nmf* snob

eso ['eso] *pron* that, that thing o matter; **~ de su coche** that business about his car; **~ de ir al cine** all that about going to the cinema; **a ~ de las cinco** at about five o'clock; **en ~** thereupon, at that point; **~ es** that's it; **¡~ sí que es vida!** now that is really living!; **por ~ te lo dije** that's why I told you; **y ~ que llovía** in spite of the fact it was raining

esos *adj demos* V **ese**

ésos *pron* V **ése**

espabilar *etc* [espaβi'lar] = **despabilar** *etc*

espacial [espa'θjal] *adj* (*del espacio*) space *cpd*

espaciar [espa'θjar] *vt* to space (out)

espacio [es'paθjo] *nm* space; (*Mús*)

interval; (*Radio, TV*) programme (BRIT),
program (US); **el ~** space; **espacio aéreo/
exterior** air/outer space; **espacioso, -a** *adj*
spacious, roomy

espada [es'paða] *nf* sword; **espadas** *nfpl*
(*Naipes*) spades

espaguetis [espa'ɣetis] *nmpl* spaghetti *sg*

espalda [es'palda] *nf* (*gen*) back; **espaldas**
nfpl (*hombros*) shoulders; **a ~s de algn**
behind sb's back; **estar de ~s** to have one's
back turned; **tenderse de ~s** to lie (down)
on one's back; **volver la ~ a algn** to cold-
shoulder sb

espantajo [espan'taxo] *nm* =
espantapájaros

espantapájaros [espanta'paxaros] *nm
inv* scarecrow

espantar [espan'tar] *vt* (*asustar*) to
frighten, scare; (*ahuyentar*) to frighten off;
(*asombrar*) to horrify, appal; **espantarse** *vr*
to get frightened *o* scared; to be appalled

espanto [es'panto] *nm* (*susto*) fright;
(*terror*) terror; (*asombro*) astonishment;
espantoso, -a *adj* frightening; terrifying;
astonishing

España [es'paɲa] *nf* Spain; **español, a**
adj Spanish ▷*nm/f* Spaniard ▷*nm* (*Ling*)
Spanish

esparadrapo [espara'ðrapo] *nm*
(sticking) plaster (BRIT), adhesive tape (US)

esparcir [espar'θir] *vt* to spread;
(*diseminar*) to scatter; **esparcirse** *vr* to
spread (out), to scatter; (*divertirse*) to enjoy
o.s.

espárrago [es'parraxo] *nm* asparagus

esparto [es'parto] *nm* esparto (grass)

espasmo [es'pasmo] *nm* spasm

espátula [es'patula] *nf* spatula

especia [es'peθja] *nf* spice

especial [espe'θjal] *adj* special;
especialidad *nf* speciality (BRIT), specialty
(US)

especie [es'peθje] *nf* (*Bio*) species; (*clase*)
kind, sort; **en ~** in kind

especificar [espeθifi'kar] *vt* to specify;
específico, -a *adj* specific

espécimen [es'peθimen] (*pl
especímenes*) *nm* specimen

espectáculo [espek'takulo] *nm* (*gen*)
spectacle; (*Teatro etc*) show

espectador, a [espekta'ðor, a] *nm/f*
spectator

especular [espeku'lar] *vt, vi* to speculate

espejismo [espe'xismo] *nm* mirage

espejo [es'pexo] *nm* mirror; **(espejo)
retrovisor** rear-view mirror

espeluznante [espeluθ'nante] *adj*
horrifying, hair-raising

espera [es'pera] *nf* (*pausa, intervalo*) wait;
(*Jur: plazo*) respite; **en ~ de** waiting for; (*con
expectativa*) expecting

esperanza [espe'ranθa] *nf* (*confianza*)
hope; (*expectativa*) expectation; **hay pocas
~s de que venga** there is little prospect
of his coming; **esperanza de vida** life
expectancy

esperar [espe'rar] *vt* (*aguardar*) to wait
for; (*tener expectativa de*) to expect; (*desear*)
to hope for ▷*vi* to wait; to expect; to hope;
hacer ~ a algn to keep sb waiting; **~ un
bebé** to be expecting (a baby)

esperma [es'perma] *nf* sperm

espeso, -a [es'peso, a] *adj* thick; **espesor**
nm thickness

espía [es'pia] *nmf* spy; **espiar** *vt* (*observar*)
to spy on

espiga [es'piɣa] *nf* (*Bot: de trigo etc*) ear

espigón [espi'ɣon] *nm* (*Bot*) ear; (*Náut*)
breakwater

espina [es'pina] *nf* thorn; (*de pez*) bone;
espina dorsal (*Anat*) spine

espinaca [espi'naka] *nf* spinach

espinazo [espi'naθo] *nm* spine, backbone

espinilla [espi'niʎa] *nf* (*Anat: tibia*)
shin(bone); (*grano*) blackhead

espinoso, -a [espi'noso, a] *adj* (*planta*)
thorny, prickly; (*asunto*) difficult

espionaje [espjo'naxe] *nm* spying,
espionage

espiral [espi'ral] *adj, nf* spiral

espirar [espi'rar] *vt* to breathe out, exhale

espiritista [espiri'tista] *adj, nmf*
spiritualist

espíritu [es'piritu] *nm* spirit; **Espíritu
Santo** Holy Ghost *o* Spirit; **espiritual** *adj*
spiritual

espléndido, -a [es'plendiðo, a] *adj*
(*magnífico*) magnificent, splendid; (*generoso*)
generous

esplendor [esplen'dor] *nm* splendour

espolvorear [espolβore'ar] *vt* to dust,
sprinkle

esponja [es'ponxa] *nf* sponge; (*fig*)
sponger; **esponjoso, -a** *adj* spongy

espontaneidad [espontanei'ðað]
nf spontaneity; **espontáneo, -a** *adj*
spontaneous

esposa [es'posa] *nf* wife; **esposas** *nfpl*
handcuffs; **esposar** *vt* to handcuff

esposo [es'poso] *nm* husband

espray [es'prai] *nm* spray

espuela [es'pwela] *nf* spur

espuma [es'puma] *nf* foam; (*de cerveza*)
froth, head; (*de jabón*) lather; **espuma de
afeitar** shaving foam; **espumadera** *nf*
(*utensilio*) skimmer; **espumoso, -a** *adj*

frothy, foamy; (*vino*) sparkling

esqueleto [eske'leto] *nm* skeleton

esquema [es'kema] *nm* (*diagrama*) diagram; (*dibujo*) plan; (*Filosofía*) schema

esquí [es'ki] (*pl* **~s**) *nm* (*objeto*) ski; (*Deporte*) skiing; **esquí acuático** water-skiing; **esquiar** *vi* to ski

esquilar [eski'lar] *vt* to shear

esquimal [eski'mal] *adj, nmf* Eskimo

esquina [es'kina] *nf* corner; **esquinazo** [eski'naθo] *nm*: **dar esquinazo a algn** to give sb the slip

esquirol [eski'rol] (*ESP*) *nm* strikebreaker, scab

esquivar [eski'βar] *vt* to avoid

esta ['esta] *adj demos* V **este²**

está *vb* V **estar**

ésta *pron* V **éste**

estabilidad [estaβili'ðað] *nf* stability; **estable** *adj* stable

establecer [estaβle'θer] *vt* to establish; **establecerse** *vr* to establish o.s.; (*echar raíces*) to settle (down); **establecimiento** *nm* establishment

establo [es'taβlo] *nm* (*Agr*) stable

estaca [es'taka] *nf* stake, post; (*de tienda de campaña*) peg

estacada [esta'kaða] *nf* (*cerca*) fence, fencing; (*palenque*) stockade

estación [esta'θjon] *nf* station; (*del año*) season; **estación balnearia** seaside resort; **estación de autobuses** bus station; **estación de servicio** service station

estacionamiento [estaθjona'mjento] *nm* (*Auto*) parking; (*Mil*) stationing

estacionar [estaθjo'nar] *vt* (*Auto*) to park; (*Mil*) to station

estadía [esta'ðia] (*LAM*) *nf* stay

estadio [es'taðjo] *nm* (*fase*) stage, phase; (*Deporte*) stadium

estadista [esta'ðista] *nm* (*Pol*) statesman; (*Mat*) statistician

estadística [esta'ðistika] *nf* figure, statistic; (*ciencia*) statistics *sg*

estado [es'taðo] *nm* (*Pol: condición*) state; **estar en ~** to be pregnant; **estado civil** marital status; **estado de ánimo** state of mind; **estado de cuenta** bank statement; **estado de sitio** state of siege; **estado mayor** staff; **Estados Unidos** United States (of America)

estadounidense [estaðouni'ðense] *adj* United States *cpd*, American ▷ *nmf* American

estafa [es'tafa] *nf* swindle, trick; **estafar** *vt* to swindle, defraud

estáis *vb* V **estar**

estallar [esta'ʎar] *vi* to burst; (*bomba*) to explode, go off; (*epidemia, guerra, rebelión*) to break out; **~ en llanto** to burst into tears; **estallido** *nm* explosion; (*fig*) outbreak

estampa [es'tampa] *nf* print, engraving; **estampado, -a** [estam'paðo, a] *adj* printed ▷ *nm* (*impresión: acción*) printing; (*: efecto*) print; (*marca*) stamping

estampar [estam'par] *vt* (*imprimir*) to print; (*marcar*) to stamp; (*metal*) to engrave; (*poner sello en*) to stamp; (*fig*) to stamp, imprint

estampida [estam'piða] *nf* stampede

estampido [estam'piðo] *nm* bang, report

estampilla [estam'piʎa] (*LAM*) *nf* (postage) stamp

están *vb* V **estar**

estancado, -a [estan'kaðo, a] *adj* stagnant

estancar [estan'kar] *vt* (*aguas*) to hold up, hold back; (*Com*) to monopolize; (*fig*) to block, hold up; **estancarse** *vr* to stagnate

estancia [es'tanθja] *nf* (*ESP, MÉX: permanencia*; *tb*: *sala*) room; (*RPL: de ganado*) farm, ranch; **estanciero** (*RPL*) *nm* farmer, rancher

estanco, -a [es'tanko, a] *adj* watertight ▷ *nm* tobacconist's (shop), cigar store (*US*)

● ESTANCO

Cigarettes, tobacco, postage stamps and official forms are all sold under state monopoly in shops called **estancos**. Although tobacco products can also be bought in bars and quioscos they are generally more expensive.

---

estándar [es'tandar] *adj, nm* standard

estandarte [estan'darte] *nm* banner, standard

estanque [es'tanke] *nm* (*lago*) pool, pond; (*Agr*) reservoir

estanquero, -a [estan'kero, a] *nm/f* tobacconist

estante [es'tante] *nm* (*armario*) rack, stand; (*biblioteca*) bookcase; (*anaquel*) shelf; **estantería** *nf* shelving, shelves *pl*

○ PALABRA CLAVE

estar [es'tar] *vi* **1** (*posición*) to be; **está en la plaza** it's in the square; **¿está Juan?** is Juan in?; **estamos a 30 km de Junín** we're 30 kms from Junín

2 (+ *adj: estado*) to be; **estar enfermo** to be ill; **está muy elegante** he's looking very smart; **¿cómo estás?** how are you keeping?

3 (+ *gerundio*) to be; **estoy leyendo** I'm

reading

4 (*uso pasivo*): **está condenado a muerte** he's been condemned to death; **está envasado en ...** it's packed in ...

5 (*con fechas*): **¿a cuántos estamos?** what's the date today?; **estamos a 5 de mayo** it's the 5th of May

6 (*locuciones*): **¿estamos?** (*¿de acuerdo?*) okay?; (*¿listo?*) ready?

7: **estar de**: **estar de vacaciones/viaje** to be on holiday/away o on a trip; **está de camarero** he's working as a waiter

8: **estar para**: **está para salir** he's about to leave; **no estoy para bromas** I'm not in the mood for jokes

9: **estar por** (*propuesta etc*) to be in favour of; (*persona etc*) to support, side with; **está por limpiar** it still has to be cleaned

10: **estar sin**: **estar sin dinero** to have no money; **está sin terminar** it isn't finished yet

estarse *vr*: **se estuvo en la cama toda la tarde** he stayed in bed all afternoon

estas ['estas] *adj demos* V **este²**

éstas *pron* V **éste**

estatal [esta'tal] *adj* state *cpd*

estático, -a [es'tatiko, a] *adj* static

estatua [es'tatwa] *nf* statue

estatura [esta'tura] *nf* stature, height

este¹ ['este] *nm* east

este² ['este] (*f* **esta**, *pl* **estos, estas**) *adj demos* (*sg*) this; (*pl*) these

esté *etc vb* V **estar**

éste ['este] (*f* **ésta**, *pl* **éstos, éstas**) *pron* (*sg*) this (one); (*pl*) these (ones); **ése ... ~ ...** the former ... the latter ...

estén *etc vb* V **estar**

estepa [es'tepa] *nf* (*Geo*) steppe

estera [es'tera] *nf* mat(ting)

estéreo [es'tereo] *adj inv, nm* stereo; **estereotipo** *nm* stereotype

estéril [es'teril] *adj* sterile, barren; (*fig*) vain, futile; **esterilizar** *vt* to sterilize

esterlina [ester'lina] *adj*: **libra ~** pound sterling

estés *etc vb* V **estar**

estética [es'tetika] *nf* aesthetics *sg*

estético, -a [es'tetiko, a] *adj* aesthetic

estiércol [es'tjerkol] *nm* dung, manure

estigma [es'tiɣma] *nm* stigma

estilo [es'tilo] *nm* style; (*Tec*) stylus; (*Natación*) stroke; **algo por el ~** something along those lines

estima [es'tima] *nf* esteem, respect; **estimación** [estima'θjon] *nf* (*evaluación*) estimation; (*aprecio, afecto*) esteem, regard; **estimado, a** *adj* esteemed; **E~ señor** Dear

Sir

estimar [esti'mar] *vt* (*evaluar*) to estimate; (*valorar*) to value; (*apreciar*) to esteem, respect; (*pensar, considerar*) to think, reckon

estimulante [estimu'lante] *adj* stimulating ▷ *nm* stimulant

estimular [estimu'lar] *vt* to stimulate; (*excitar*) to excite

estímulo [es'timulo] *nm* stimulus; (*ánimo*) encouragement

estirar [esti'rar] *vt* to stretch; (*dinero, suma etc*) to stretch out; **estirarse** *vr* to stretch

estirón [esti'ron] *nm* pull, tug; (*crecimiento*) spurt, sudden growth; **dar** o **pegar un ~** (*fam: niño*) to shoot up (*inf*)

estirpe [es'tirpe] *nf* stock, lineage

estival [esti'βal] *adj* summer *cpd*

esto ['esto] *pron* this, this thing o matter; **~ de la boda** this business about the wedding

Estocolmo [esto'kolmo] *nm* Stockholm

estofado [esto'faðo] *nm* stew

estómago [es'tomaxo] *nm* stomach; **tener ~** to be thick-skinned

estorbar [estor'βar] *vt* to hinder, obstruct; (*molestar*) to bother, disturb ▷ *vi* to be in the way; **estorbo** *nm* (*molestia*) bother, nuisance; (*obstáculo*) hindrance, obstacle

estornudar [estornu'ðar] *vi* to sneeze

estos ['estos] *adj demos* V **este²**

éstos *pron* V **éste**

estoy *vb* V **estar**

estrado [es'traðo] *nm* platform

estrafalario, -a [estrafa'larjo, a] *adj* odd, eccentric

estrago [es'traxo] *nm* ruin, destruction; **hacer ~s en** to wreak havoc among

estragón [estra'xon] *nm* tarragon

estrambótico, -a [estram'botiko, a] *adj* (*persona*) eccentric; (*peinado, ropa*) outlandish

estrangular [estrangu'lar] *vt* (*persona*) to strangle; (*Med*) to strangulate

estratagema [estrata'xema] *nf* (*Mil*) stratagem; (*astucia*) cunning

estrategia [estra'texja] *nf* strategy; **estratégico, -a** *adj* strategic

estrato [es'trato] *nm* stratum, layer

estrechar [estre'tʃar] *vt* (*reducir*) to narrow; (*Costura*) to take in; (*abrazar*) to hug, embrace; **estrecharse** *vr* (*reducirse*) to narrow, grow narrow; (*abrazarse*) to embrace; **~ la mano** to shake hands

estrechez [estre'tʃeθ] *nf* narrowness; (*de ropa*) tightness; **estrecheces** *nfpl* (*dificultades económicas*) financial difficulties

estrecho, -a [es'tretʃo, a] *adj* narrow; (*apretado*) tight; (*íntimo*) close, intimate; (*miserable*) mean ▷ *nm* strait; **~ de miras**

narrow-minded
estrella [es'treʎa] nf star; **estrella de mar**
(Zool) starfish; **estrella fugaz** shooting star
estrellar [estre'ʎar] vt (hacer añicos)
to smash (to pieces); (huevos) to fry;
estrellarse vr to smash; (chocarse) to crash;
(fracasar) to fail
estremecer [estreme'θer] vt to shake;
estremecerse vr to shake, tremble
estrenar [estre'nar] vt (vestido) to wear for
the first time; (casa) to move into; (película,
obra de teatro) to première; **estrenarse** vr
(persona) to make one's début; **estreno** nm
(Cine etc) première
estreñido, -a [estre'niðo, a] adj
constipated
estreñimiento [estreni'mjento] nm
constipation
estrepitoso, -a [estrepi'toso, a] adj
noisy; (fiesta) rowdy
estría [es'tria] nf groove
estribar [estri'βar] vi: ~ **en** to lie on
estribillo [estri'βiʎo] nm (Literatura)
refrain; (Mús) chorus
estribo [es'triβo] nm (de jinete) stirrup; (de
coche, tren) step; (de puente) support; (Geo)
spur; **perder los ~s** to fly off the handle
estribor [estri'βor] nm (Náut) starboard
estricto, -a [es'trikto, a] adj (riguroso)
strict; (severo) severe
estridente [estri'ðente] adj (color) loud;
(voz) raucous
estropajo [estro'paxo] nm scourer
estropear [estrope'ar] vt to spoil; (dañar)
to damage; **estropearse** vr (objeto) to get
damaged; (persona, piel) to be ruined
estructura [estruk'tura] nf structure
estrujar [estru'xar] vt (apretar) to squeeze;
(aplastar) to crush; (fig) to drain, bleed
estuario [es'twarjo] nm estuary
estuche [es'tutʃe] nm box, case
estudiante [estu'ðjante] nmf student;
estudiantil adj student cpd
estudiar [estu'ðjar] vt to study
estudio [es'tuðjo] nm study; (Cine, Arte,
Radio) studio; **estudios** nmpl studies;
(erudición) learning sg; **estudioso, -a** adj
studious
estufa [es'tufa] nf heater, fire
estupefaciente [estupefa'θjente] nm
drug, narcotic
estupefacto, -a [estupe'fakto, a] adj
speechless, thunderstruck
estupendo, -a [estu'pendo, a] adj
wonderful, terrific; (fam) great; ¡~! that's
great!, fantastic!
estupidez [estupi'ðeθ] nf (torpeza)
stupidity; (acto) stupid thing (to do)

estúpido, -a [es'tupiðo, a] adj stupid,
silly
estuve etc vb V **estar**
ETA ['eta] (ESP) nf abr (= Euskadi ta
Askatasuna) ETA
etapa [e'tapa] nf (de viaje) stage; (Deporte)
leg; (parada) stopping place; (fase) stage,
phase
etarra [e'tarra] nmf member of ETA
etc. abr (= etcétera) etc
etcétera [et'θetera] adv etcetera
eternidad [eterni'ðað] nf eternity;
eterno, -a adj eternal, everlasting
ética ['etika] nf ethics pl
ético, -a ['etiko, a] adj ethical
etiqueta [eti'keta] nf (modales) etiquette;
(rótulo) label, tag
Eucaristía [eukaris'tia] nf Eucharist
euforia [eu'forja] nf euphoria
euro ['euro] nm (moneda) euro
eurodiputado, -a [euroðipu'taðo, a]
nm/f Euro MP, MEP
Europa [eu'ropa] nf Europe; **europeo, -a**
adj, nm/f European
Euskadi [eus'kaði] nm the Basque
Country o Provinces pl
euskera [eus'kera] nm (Ling) Basque
evacuación [eβakwa'θjon] nf evacuation
evacuar [eβa'kwar] vt to evacuate
evadir [eβa'ðir] vt to evade, avoid;
evadirse vr to escape
evaluar [eβa'lwar] vt to evaluate
evangelio [eβan'xeljo] nm gospel
evaporar [eβapo'rar] vt to evaporate;
evaporarse vr to vanish
evasión [eβa'sjon] nf escape, flight; (fig)
evasion; **evasión de capitales** flight of
capital
evasiva [eβa'siβa] nf (pretexto) excuse
evento [e'βento] nm event
eventual [eβen'twal] adj possible,
conditional (upon circumstances);
(trabajador) casual, temporary

▌No confundir **eventual** con la palabra
inglesa eventual.

evidencia [eβi'ðenθja] nf evidence, proof
evidente [eβi'ðente] adj obvious, clear,
evident
evitar [eβi'tar] vt (evadir) to avoid; (impedir)
to prevent; ~ **hacer algo** to avoid doing sth
evocar [eβo'kar] vt to evoke, call forth
evolución [eβolu'θjon] nf (desarrollo)
evolution, development; (cambio) change;
(Mil) manoeuvre; **evolucionar** vi to evolve;
to manoeuvre
ex [eks] adj ex-; **el ~ ministro** the former
minister, the ex-minister
exactitud [eksakti'tuð] nf exactness;

(*precisión*) accuracy; (*puntualidad*) punctuality; **exacto, -a** *adj* exact; accurate; punctual; **¡exacto!** exactly!

exageración [eksaxeraˈθjon] *nf* exaggeration

exagerar [eksaxeˈrar] *vt, vi* to exaggerate

exaltar [eksalˈtar] *vt* to exalt, glorify; **exaltarse** *vr* (*excitarse*) to get excited o worked up

examen [ekˈsamen] *nm* examination; **examen de conducir** driving test; **examen de ingreso** entrance examination

examinar [eksamiˈnar] *vt* to examine; **examinarse** *vr* to be examined, take an examination

excavadora [ekskaβaˈðora] *nf* excavator

excavar [ekskaˈβar] *vt* to excavate

excedencia [eksθeˈðenθja] *nf*: **estar en ~** to be on leave; **pedir** o **solicitar la ~** to ask for leave

excedente [eksθeˈðente] *adj, nm* excess, surplus

exceder [eksθeˈðer] *vt* to exceed, surpass; **excederse** *vr* (*extralimitarse*) to go too far

excelencia [eksθeˈlenθja] *nf* excellence; **su E~** his Excellency; **excelente** *adj* excellent

excéntrico, -a [eksˈθentriko, a] *adj, nm/f* eccentric

excepción [eksθepˈθjon] *nf* exception; **a ~ de** with the exception of, except for; **excepcional** *adj* exceptional

excepto [eksˈθepto] *adv* excepting, except (for)

exceptuar [eksθepˈtwar] *vt* to except, exclude

excesivo, -a [eksθeˈsiβo, a] *adj* excessive

exceso [eksˈθeso] *nm* (*gen*) excess; (*Com*) surplus; **exceso de equipaje/peso** excess luggage/weight; **exceso de velocidad** speeding

excitado, -a [eksθiˈtaðo, a] *adj* excited; (*emociónes*) aroused

excitar [eksθiˈtar] *vt* to excite; (*incitar*) to urge; **excitarse** *vr* to get excited

exclamación [eksklamaˈθjon] *nf* exclamation

exclamar [eksklaˈmar] *vi* to exclaim

excluir [ekskluˈir] *vt* to exclude; (*dejar fuera*) to shut out; (*descartar*) to reject

exclusiva [ekskluˈsiβa] *nf* (*Prensa*) exclusive, scoop; (*Com*) sole right

exclusivo, -a [ekskluˈsiβo, a] *adj* exclusive; **derecho ~** sole o exclusive right

Excmo. *abr* = **excelentísimo**

excomulgar [ekskomulˈɣar] *vt* (*Rel*) to excommunicate

excomunión [ekskomuˈnjon] *nf* excommunication

excursión [ekskurˈsjon] *nf* excursion, outing; **excursionista** *nmf* (*turista*) sightseer

excusa [eksˈkusa] *nf* excuse; (*disculpa*) apology; **excusar** [ekskuˈsar] *vt* to excuse

exhaustivo, -a [eksausˈtiβo, a] *adj* (*análisis*) thorough; (*estudio*) exhaustive

exhausto, -a [ekˈsausto, a] *adj* exhausted

exhibición [eksiβiˈθjon] *nf* exhibition, display, show

exhibir [eksiˈβir] *vt* to exhibit, display, show

exigencia [eksiˈxenθja] *nf* demand, requirement; **exigente** *adj* demanding

exigir [eksiˈxir] *vt* (*gen*) to demand, require; **~ el pago** to demand payment

exiliado, -a [eksiˈljaðo, a] *adj* exiled ▷ *nm/f* exile

exilio [ekˈsiljo] *nm* exile

eximir [eksiˈmir] *vt* to exempt

existencia [eksisˈtenθja] *nf* existence; **existencias** *nfpl* stock(s) *pl*

existir [eksisˈtir] *vi* to exist, be

éxito [ˈeksito] *nm* (*triunfo*) success; (*Mús etc*) hit; **tener ~** to be successful

> ❚ No confundir **éxito** con la palabra inglesa *exit*.

exorbitante [eksorβiˈtante] *adj* (*precio*) exorbitant; (*cantidad*) excessive

exótico, -a [ekˈsotiko, a] *adj* exotic

expandir [ekspanˈdir] *vt* to expand

expansión [ekspanˈsjon] *nf* expansion

expansivo, -a [ekspanˈsiβo, a] *adj*: **onda expansiva** shock wave

expatriarse [ekspaˈtrjarse] *vr* to emigrate; (*Pol*) to go into exile

expectativa [ekspektaˈtiβa] *nf* (*espera*) expectation; (*perspectiva*) prospect

expedición [ekspeðiˈθjon] *nf* (*excursión*) expedition

expediente [ekspeˈðjente] *nm* expedient; (*Jur: procedimiento*) action, proceedings *pl*; (*: papeles*) dossier, file, record

expedir [ekspeˈðir] *vt* (*despachar*) to send, forward; (*pasaporte*) to issue

expensas [eksˈpensas] *nfpl*: **a ~ de** at the expense of

experiencia [ekspeˈrjenθja] *nf* experience

experimentado, -a [eksperimenˈtaðo, a] *adj* experienced

experimentar [eksperimenˈtar] *vt* (*en laboratorio*) to experiment with; (*probar*) to test, try out; (*notar, observar*) to experience; (*deterioro, pérdida*) to suffer; **experimento** *nm* experiment

experto, -a [eks'perto, a] adj expert, skilled ▷ nm/f expert

expirar [ekspi'rar] vi to expire

explanada [ekspla'naða] nf (llano) plain

explayarse [ekspla'jarse] vr (en discurso) to speak at length; ~ **con algn** to confide in sb

explicación [eksplika'θjon] nf explanation

explicar [ekspli'kar] vt to explain; **explicarse** vr to explain (o.s.)

explícito, -a [eks'pliθito, a] adj explicit

explique etc vb V **explicar**

explorador, a [eksplora'ðor, a] nm/f (pionero) explorer; (Mil) scout ▷ nm (Med) probe; (Tec) (radar) scanner

explorar [eksplo'rar] vt to explore; (Med) to probe; (radar) to scan

explosión [eksplo'sjon] nf explosion; **explosivo, -a** adj explosive

explotación [eksplota'θjon] nf exploitation; (de planta etc) running

explotar [eksplo'tar] vt to exploit to run, operate ▷ vi to explode

exponer [ekspo'ner] vt to expose; (cuadro) to display; (vida) to risk; (idea) to explain; **exponerse** vr: ~**se a (hacer) algo** to run the risk of (doing) sth

exportación [eksporta'θjon] nf (acción) export; (mercancías) exports pl

exportar [ekspor'tar] vt to export

exposición [eksposi'θjon] nf (gen) exposure; (de arte) show, exhibition; (explicación) explanation; (declaración) account, statement

expresamente [ekspresa'mente] adv (decir) clearly; (a propósito) expressly

expresar [ekspre'sar] vt to express; **expresión** nf expression

expresivo, -a [ekspre'siβo, a] adj (persona, gesto, palabras) expressive; (cariñoso) affectionate

expreso, -a [eks'preso, a] pp de **expresar** ▷ adj (explícito) express; (claro) specific, clear; (tren) fast ▷ adv: **enviar** ~ to send by express (delivery)

express [eks'pres] (LAM) adv: **enviar algo** ~ to send sth special delivery

exprimidor [eksprimi'ðor] nm squeezer

exprimir [ekspri'mir] vt (fruta) to squeeze; (zumo) to squeeze out

expuesto, -a [eks'pwesto, a] pp de **exponer** ▷ adj exposed; (cuadro etc) on show, on display

expulsar [ekspul'sar] vt (echar) to eject, throw out; (alumno) to expel; (despedir) to sack, fire; (Deporte) to send off; **expulsión** nf expulsion; sending-off

exquisito, -a [ekski'sito, a] adj exquisite; (comida) delicious

éxtasis ['ekstasis] nm ecstasy

extender [eksten'der] vt to extend; (los brazos) to stretch out, hold out; (mapa, tela) to spread (out), open (out); (mantequilla) to spread; (certificado) to issue; (cheque, recibo) to make out; (documento) to draw up; **extenderse** vr (gen) to extend; (persona: en el suelo) to stretch out; (epidemia) to spread; **extendido, -a** adj (abierto) spread out, open; (brazos) outstretched; (costumbre) widespread

extensión [eksten'sjon] nf (de terreno, mar) expanse, stretch; (de tiempo) length, duration; (Tel) extension; **en toda la ~ de la palabra** in every sense of the word

extenso, -a [eks'tenso, a] adj extensive

exterior [ekste'rjor] adj (de fuera) external; (afuera) outside, exterior; (apariencia) outward; (deuda, relaciones) foreign ▷ nm (gen) exterior, outside; (aspecto) outward appearance; (Deporte) winger; (países extranjeros) abroad; **en el** ~ abroad; **al** ~ outwardly, on the surface

exterminar [ekstermi'nar] vt to exterminate

externo, -a [eks'terno, a] adj (exterior) external, outside; (superficial) outward ▷ nm/f day pupil

extinguir [ekstin'gir] vt (fuego) to extinguish, put out; (raza, población) to wipe out; **extinguirse** vr (fuego) to go out; (Bio) to die out, become extinct

extintor [ekstin'tor] nm (fire) extinguisher

extirpar [ekstir'par] vt (Med) to remove (surgically)

extra ['ekstra] adj inv (tiempo) extra; (chocolate, vino) good-quality ▷ nmf extra ▷ nm extra; (bono) bonus

extracción [ekstrak'θjon] nf extraction; (en lotería) draw

extracto [eks'trakto] nm extract

extradición [ekstraði'θjon] nf extradition

extraer [ekstra'er] vt to extract, take out

extraescolar [ekstraesko'lar] adj: **actividad** ~ extracurricular activity

extranjero, -a [ekstran'xero, a] adj foreign ▷ nm/f foreigner ▷ nm foreign countries pl; **en el** ~ abroad

▌ No confundir **extranjero** con la palabra inglesa *stranger*.

extrañar [ekstra'nar] vt (sorprender) to find strange o odd; (echar de menos) to miss; **extrañarse** vr (sorprenderse) to be amazed, be surprised; **me extraña** I'm surprised

extraño, -a [eks'traɲo, a] *adj (extranjero)* foreign; *(raro, sorprendente)* strange, odd
extraordinario, -a [ekstraorði'narjo, a] *adj* extraordinary; *(edición, número)* special ▷ *nm (de periódico)* special edition; **horas extraordinarias** overtime *sg*
extrarradio [ekstra'rraðjo] *nm* suburbs
extravagante [ekstraβa'ɣante] *adj (excéntrico)* eccentric; *(estrafalario)* outlandish
extraviado, -a [ekstra'βjaðo, a] *adj* lost, missing
extraviar [ekstra'βjar] *vt (persona: desorientar)* to mislead, misdirect; *(perder)* to lose, misplace; **extraviarse** *vr* to lose one's way, get lost
extremar [ekstre'mar] *vt* to carry to extremes
extremaunción [ekstremaun'θjon] *nf* extreme unction
extremidad [ekstremi'ðað] *nf (punta)* extremity; **extremidades** *nfpl (Anat)* extremities
extremo, -a [eks'tremo, a] *adj* extreme; *(último)* last ▷ *nm* end; *(límite, grado sumo)* extreme; **en último ~** as a last resort
extrovertido, -a [ekstroβer'tiðo, a] *adj, nm/f* extrovert
exuberante [eksuβe'rante] *adj* exuberant; *(fig)* luxuriant, lush
eyacular [ejaku'lar] *vt, vi* to ejaculate

f

fa [fa] *nm (Mús)* fa, F
fabada [fa'βaða] *nf* bean and sausage stew
fábrica ['faβrika] *nf* factory; **marca de ~** trademark; **precio de ~** factory price
⬛ No confundir **fábrica** con la palabra inglesa *fabric*.
fabricación [faβrika'θjon] *nf (manufactura)* manufacture; *(producción)* production; **de ~ casera** home-made; **fabricación en serie** mass production
fabricante [faβri'kante] *nmf* manufacturer
fabricar [faβri'kar] *vt (manufacturar)* to manufacture, make; *(construir)* to build; *(cuento)* to fabricate, devise
fábula ['faβula] *nf (cuento)* fable; *(chisme)* rumour; *(mentira)* fib
fabuloso, -a [faβu'loso, a] *adj (oportunidad, tiempo)* fabulous, great
facción [fak'θjon] *nf (Pol)* faction; **facciones** *nfpl (de rostro)* features
faceta [fa'θeta] *nf* facet
facha ['fatʃa] *(fam) nf (aspecto)* look; *(cara)* face
fachada [fa'tʃaða] *nf (Arq)* façade, front
fácil ['faθil] *adj (simple)* easy; *(probable)* likely
facilidad [faθili'ðað] *nf (capacidad)* ease; *(sencillez)* simplicity; *(de palabra)* fluency; **facilidades** *nfpl* facilities; **facilidades de pago** credit facilities
facilitar [faθili'tar] *vt (hacer fácil)* to make easy; *(proporcionar)* to provide
factor [fak'tor] *nm* factor
factura [fak'tura] *nf (cuenta)* bill; **facturación** *nf (de equipaje)* check-in; **facturar** *vt (Com)* to invoice, charge for; *(equipaje)* to check in
facultad [fakul'tað] *nf (aptitud, Escol etc)* faculty; *(poder)* power

faena [fa'ena] *nf* (*trabajo*) work; (*quehacer*) task, job

faisán [fai'san] *nm* pheasant

faja ['faxa] *nf* (*para la cintura*) sash; (*de mujer*) corset; (*de tierra*) strip

fajo ['faxo] *nm* (*de papeles*) bundle; (*de billetes*) wad

falda ['falda] *nf* (*prenda de vestir*) skirt; **falda pantalón** culottes *pl*, split skirt

falla ['faʎa] *nf* (*defecto*) fault, flaw; **falla humana** (*LAM*) human error

fallar [fa'ʎar] *vt* (*Jur*) to pronounce sentence on ▷ *vi* (*memoria*) to fail; (*motor*) to miss

Fallas ['faʎas] *nfpl* *Valencian celebration of the feast of St Joseph*

* **FALLAS**
*
* In the week of 19 March (the feast
* of San José), Valencia honours its
* patron saint with a spectacular fiesta
* called **Las Fallas**. The **Fallas** are huge
* papier-mâché, cardboard and wooden
* sculptures which are built by competing
* teams throughout the year. They depict
* politicians and well-known public
* figures and are thrown onto bonfires
* and set alight once a jury has judged
* them – only the best sculpture escapes
* the flames.

fallecer [faʎe'θer] *vi* to pass away, die; **fallecimiento** *nm* decease, demise

fallido, -a [fa'ʎiðo, a] *adj* (*gen*) frustrated, unsuccessful

fallo ['faʎo] *nm* (*Jur*) verdict, ruling; (*fracaso*) failure; **fallo cardíaco** heart failure; **fallo humano** (*ESP*) human error

falsificar [falsifi'kar] *vt* (*firma etc*) to forge; (*moneda*) to counterfeit

falso, -a ['falso, a] *adj* false; (*documento, moneda etc*) fake; **en ~** falsely

falta ['falta] *nf* (*defecto*) fault, flaw; (*privación*) lack, want; (*ausencia*) absence; (*carencia*) shortage; (*equivocación*) mistake; (*Deporte*) foul; **echar en ~** to miss; **hacer ~ hacer algo** to be necessary to do sth; **me hace ~ una pluma** I need a pen; **falta de educación** bad manners *pl*; **falta de ortografía** spelling mistake

faltar [fal'tar] *vi* (*escasear*) to be lacking, be wanting; (*ausentarse*) to be absent, be missing; **faltan 2 horas para llegar** there are 2 hours to go till arrival; **~ al respeto a algn** to be disrespectful to sb; **¡no faltaba más!** (*no hay de qué*) don't mention it

fama ['fama] *nf* (*renombre*) fame; (*reputación*) reputation

familia [fa'milja] *nf* family; **familia numerosa** large family; **familia política** in-laws *pl*

familiar [fami'ljar] *adj* (*relativo a la familia*) family *cpd*; (*conocido, informal*) familiar ▷ *nm* relative, relation

famoso, -a [fa'moso, a] *adj* (*renombrado*) famous

fan [fan] (*pl* **~s**) *nmf* fan

fanático, -a [fa'natiko, a] *adj* fanatical ▷ *nm/f* fanatic; (*Cine, Deporte*) fan

fanfarrón, -ona [fanfa'rron, ona] *adj* boastful

fango ['fango] *nm* mud

fantasía [fanta'sia] *nf* fantasy, imagination; **joyas de ~** imitation jewellery *sg*

fantasma [fan'tasma] *nm* (*espectro*) ghost, apparition; (*fanfarrón*) show-off

fantástico, -a [fan'tastiko, a] *adj* fantastic

farmacéutico, -a [farma'θeutiko, a] *adj* pharmaceutical ▷ *nm/f* chemist (*BRIT*), pharmacist

farmacia [far'maθja] *nf* chemist's (shop) (*BRIT*), pharmacy; **farmacia de guardia** all-night chemist

fármaco ['farmako] *nm* drug

faro ['faro] *nm* (*Náut: torre*) lighthouse; (*Auto*) headlamp; **faros antiniebla** fog lamps; **faros delanteros/traseros** headlights/rear lights

farol [fa'rol] *nm* lantern, lamp

farola [fa'rola] *nf* street lamp (*BRIT*) o light (*US*)

farra ['farra] (*LAM: fam*) *nf* party; **ir de ~** to go on a binge

farsa ['farsa] *nf* (*gen*) farce

farsante [far'sante] *nmf* fraud, fake

fascículo [fas'θikulo] *nm* (*de revista*) part, instalment

fascinar [fasθi'nar] *vt* (*gen*) to fascinate

fascismo [fas'θismo] *nm* fascism; **fascista** *adj, nmf* fascist

fase ['fase] *nf* phase

fashion ['faʃon] *adj* (*fam*) trendy

fastidiar [fasti'ðjar] *vt* (*molestar*) to annoy, bother; (*estropear*) to spoil; **fastidiarse** *vr*: **¡que se fastidie!** (*fam*) he'll just have to put up with it!

fastidio [fas'tiðjo] *nm* (*molestia*) annoyance; **fastidioso, -a** *adj* (*molesto*) annoying

fatal [fa'tal] *adj* (*gen*) fatal; (*desgraciado*) ill-fated; (*fam: malo, pésimo*) awful; **fatalidad** *nf* (*destino*) fate; (*mala suerte*) misfortune

fatiga [fa'tiɣa] *nf* (*cansancio*) fatigue,

weariness

fatigar [fati'ɣar] vt to tire, weary

fatigoso, -a [fati'ɣoso, a] adj (cansador) tiring

fauna ['fauna] nf fauna

favor [fa'βor] nm favour; **estar a ~ de** to be in favour of; **haga el ~ de ...** would you be so good as to ..., kindly ...; **por ~** please; **favorable** adj favourable

favorecer [faβore'θer] vt to favour; (vestido etc) to become, flatter; **este peinado le favorece** this hairstyle suits him

favorito, -a [faβo'rito, a] adj, nm/f favourite

fax [faks] nm inv fax; **mandar por ~** to fax

fe [fe] nf (Rel) faith; (documento) certificate; **actuar con buena/mala ~** to act in good/bad faith

febrero [fe'βrero] nm February

fecha ['fetʃa] nf date; **con ~ adelantada** postdated; **en ~ próxima** soon; **hasta la ~** to date, so far; **poner ~** to date; **fecha de caducidad** (de producto alimenticio) sell-by date; (de contrato etc) expiry date; **fecha de nacimiento** date of birth; **fecha límite** o **tope** deadline

fecundo, -a [fe'kundo, a] adj (fértil) fertile; (fig) prolific; (productivo) productive

federación [feðera'θjon] nf federation

felicidad [feliθi'ðað] nf happiness; **¡~es!** (deseos) best wishes, congratulations!; (en cumpleaños) happy birthday!

felicitación [feliθita'θjon] nf (tarjeta) greeting(s) card

felicitar [feliθi'tar] vt to congratulate

feliz [fe'liθ] adj happy

felpudo [fel'puðo] nm doormat

femenino, -a [feme'nino, a] adj, nm feminine

feminista [femi'nista] adj, nmf feminist

fenómeno [fe'nomeno] nm phenomenon; (fig) freak, accident ▷ adj great ▷ excl great!, marvellous!; **fenomenal** adj = **fenómeno**

feo, -a ['feo, a] adj (gen) ugly; (desagradable) bad, nasty

féretro ['feretro] nm (ataúd) coffin; (sarcófago) bier

feria ['ferja] nf (gen) fair; (descanso) holiday, rest day; (MÉX: cambio) small o loose change; (cs: mercado) village market

feriado [fe'rjaðo] (LAM) nm holiday

fermentar [fermen'tar] vi to ferment

feroz [fe'roθ] adj (cruel) cruel; (salvaje) fierce

férreo, -a ['ferreo, a] adj iron

ferretería [ferrete'ria] nf (tienda) ironmonger's (shop) (BRIT), hardware

store (US)

ferrocarril [ferroka'rril] nm railway

ferroviario, -a [ferro'βjarjo, a] adj rail cpd

ferry ['ferri] (pl ~s o **ferries**) nm ferry

fértil ['fertil] adj (productivo) fertile; (rico) rich; **fertilidad** nf (gen) fertility; (productividad) fruitfulness

fervor [fer'βor] nm fervour

festejar [feste'xar] vt (celebrar) to celebrate

festejo [fes'texo] nm celebration; **festejos** nmpl (fiestas) festivals

festín [fes'tin] nm feast, banquet

festival [festi'βal] nm festival

festividad [festiβi'ðað] nf festivity

festivo, -a [fes'tiβo, a] adj (de fiesta) festive; (Cine, Literatura) humorous; **día ~** holiday

feto ['feto] nm foetus

fiable ['fjaβle] adj (persona) trustworthy; (máquina) reliable

fiambre ['fjambre] nm cold meat

fiambrera [fjam'brera] nf (para almuerzo) lunch box

fianza ['fjanθa] nf surety; (Jur): **libertad bajo ~** release on bail

fiar [fi'ar] vt (salir garante de) to guarantee; (vender a crédito) to sell on credit ▷ vi to trust; **fiarse** vr to trust (in), rely on; **~ a** (secreto) to confide (to); **~se de algn** to rely on sb

fibra ['fiβra] nf fibre; **fibra óptica** optical fibre

ficción [fik'θjon] nf fiction

ficha ['fitʃa] nf (Tel) token; (en juegos) counter, marker; (tarjeta) (index) card; **fichaje** nm (Deporte) signing; **fichar** vt (archivar) to file, index; (Deporte) to sign; **estar fichado** to have a record; **fichero** nm box file; (Inform) file

ficticio, -a [fik'tiθjo, a] adj (imaginario) fictitious; (falso) fabricated

fidelidad [fiðeli'ðað] nf (lealtad) fidelity, loyalty; **alta ~** high fidelity, hi-fi

fideos [fi'ðeos] nmpl noodles

fiebre ['fjeβre] nf (Med) fever; (fig) fever, excitement; **tener ~** to have a temperature; **fiebre aftosa** foot-and-mouth disease

fiel [fjel] adj (leal) faithful, loyal; (fiable) reliable; (exacto) accurate, faithful ▷ nm: **los ~es** the faithful

fieltro ['fjeltro] nm felt

fiera ['fjera] nf (animal feroz) wild animal o beast; (fig) dragon; V tb **fiero**

fiero, -a ['fjero, a] adj (cruel) cruel; (feroz) fierce; (duro) harsh

fierro ['fjerro] (LAM) nm (hierro) iron

fiesta ['fjesta] nf party; (de pueblo) festival; (vacaciones: tb: ~s) holiday sg; **fiesta mayor** annual festival; **fiesta patria** (LAM) independence day

● **FIESTAS**
●
● **Fiestas** can be official public holidays
● or holidays set by each autonomous
● region, many of which coincide with
● religious festivals. There are also
● many **fiestas** all over Spain for a local
● patron saint or the Virgin Mary. These
● often last several days and can include
● religious processions, carnival parades,
● bullfights and dancing.

figura [fi'ɣura] nf (gen) figure; (forma, imagen) shape, form; (Naipes) face card
figurar [fiɣu'rar] vt (representar) to represent; (fingir) to figure ▷ vi to figure; **figurarse** vr (imaginarse) to imagine; (suponer) to suppose
fijador [fixa'ðor] nm (Foto etc) fixative; (de pelo) gel
fijar [fi'xar] vt (gen) to fix; (estampilla) to affix, stick (on); **fijarse** vr: **~se en** to notice
fijo, -a ['fixo, a] adj (gen) fixed; (firme) firm; (permanente) permanent ▷ adv: **mirar ~** to stare
fila ['fila] nf row; (Mil) rank; **ponerse en ~** to line up, get into line; **fila india** single file
filatelia [fila'telja] nf philately, stamp collecting
filete [fi'lete] nm (de carne) fillet steak; (de pescado) fillet
filiación [filja'θjon] nf (Pol) affiliation
filial [fi'ljal] adj filial ▷ nf subsidiary
Filipinas [fili'pinas] nfpl: **las (Islas) ~** the Philippines; **filipino, -a** adj, nm/f Philippine
filmar [fil'mar] vt to film, shoot
filo ['filo] nm (gen) edge; **sacar ~ a** to sharpen; **al ~ del mediodía** at about midday; **de doble ~** double-edged
filología [filolo'ɣia] nf philology; **filología inglesa** (Univ) English Studies
filón [fi'lon] nm (Minería) vein, lode; (fig) goldmine
filosofía [filoso'fia] nf philosophy; **filósofo, -a** nm/f philosopher
filtrar [fil'trar] vt, vi to filter, strain; **filtrarse** vr to filter; **filtro** nm (Tec, utensilio) filter
fin [fin] nm end; (objetivo) aim, purpose; **al ~ y al cabo** when all's said and done; **a ~ de** in order to; **por ~** finally; **en ~** in short; **fin de semana** weekend

final [fi'nal] adj final ▷ nm end, conclusion ▷ nf final; **al ~** in the end; **a ~es de** at the end of; **finalidad** nf (propósito) purpose, intention; **finalista** nmf finalist; **finalizar** vt to end, finish; (Inform) to log out o off ▷ vi to end, come to an end
financiar [finan'θjar] vt to finance; **financiero, -a** adj financial ▷ nm/f financier
finca ['finka] nf (casa de campo) country house; (ESP: bien inmueble) property, land; (LAM: granja) farm
finde ['finde] nm abr (fam: fin de semana) weekend
fingir [fin'xir] vt (simular) to simulate, feign ▷ vi (aparentar) to pretend
finlandés, -esa [finlan'des, esa] adj Finnish ▷ nm/f Finn ▷ nm (Ling) Finnish
Finlandia [fin'landja] nf Finland
fino, -a ['fino, a] adj fine; (delgado) slender; (de buenas maneras) polite, refined; (jerez) fino, dry
firma ['firma] nf signature; (Com) firm, company
firmamento [firma'mento] nm firmament
firmar [fir'mar] vt to sign
firme ['firme] adj firm; (estable) stable; (sólido) solid; (constante) steady; (decidido) resolute ▷ nm road (surface); **firmeza** nf firmness; (constancia) steadiness; (solidez) solidity
fiscal [fis'kal] adj fiscal ▷ nmf public prosecutor; **año ~** tax o fiscal year
fisgonear [fisɣone'ar] vt to poke one's nose into ▷ vi to pry, spy
física ['fisika] nf physics sg; V tb **físico**
físico, -a ['fisiko, a] adj physical ▷ nm physique ▷ nm/f physicist
fisura [fi'sura] nf crack; (Med) fracture
flác(c)ido, -a ['fla(k)θiðo, a] adj flabby
flaco, -a ['flako, a] adj (muy delgado) skinny, thin; (débil) weak, feeble
flagrante [fla'ɣrante] adj flagrant
flama ['flama] (MÉX) nf flame; **flamable** (MÉX) adj flammable
flamante [fla'mante] (fam) adj brilliant; (nuevo) brand-new
flamenco, -a [fla'menko, a] adj (de Flandes) Flemish; (baile, música) flamenco ▷ nm (baile, música) flamenco; (Zool) flamingo
flamingo [fla'mingo] (MÉX) nm flamingo
flan [flan] nm creme caramel
▌ No confundir **flan** con la palabra inglesa *flan*.
flash [flaʃ] (pl ~ o ~**es**) nm (Foto) flash
flauta ['flauta] nf (Mús) flute

flecha ['fletʃa] nf arrow
flechazo [fle'tʃaθo] nm love at first sight
fleco ['fleko] nm fringe
flema ['flema] nm phlegm
flequillo [fle'kiʎo] nm (pelo) fringe
flexible [flek'siβle] adj flexible
flexión [flek'sjon] nf press-up
flexo ['flekso] nm adjustable table-lamp
flirtear [flirte'ar] vi to flirt
flojera [flo'xera] (LAM: fam) nf: **me da ~** I
can't be bothered
flojo, -a ['floxo, a] adj (gen) loose; (sin
fuerzas) limp; (débil) weak
flor [flor] nf flower; **a ~ de** on the surface
of; **flora** nf flora; **florecer** vi (Bot) to flower,
bloom; (fig) to flourish; **florería** (LAM) nf
florist's (shop); **florero** nm vase; **floristería**
nf florist's (shop)
flota ['flota] nf fleet
flotador [flota'ðor] nm (gen) float; (para
nadar) rubber ring
flotar [flo'tar] vi (gen) to float; **flote** nm: **a
flote** afloat; **salir a flote** (fig) to get back on
one's feet
fluidez [flui'ðeθ] nf fluidity; (fig) fluency
fluido, -a [flu'iðo, a] adj, nm fluid
fluir [flu'ir] vi to flow
flujo ['fluxo] nm flow; **flujo y reflujo** ebb
and flow
flúor ['fluor] nm fluoride
fluorescente [flwores'θente] adj
fluorescent ▷ nm fluorescent light
fluvial [fluβi'al] adj (navegación, cuenca)
fluvial, river cpd
fobia ['fobja] nf phobia; **fobia a las
alturas** fear of heights
foca ['foka] nf seal
foco ['foko] nm focus; (Elec) floodlight;
(MÉX: bombilla) (light) bulb
fofo, -a ['fofo, a] adj soft, spongy; (carnes)
flabby
fogata [fo'ɣata] nf bonfire
fogón [fo'ɣon] nm (de cocina) ring, burner
folio ['foljo] nm folio, page
follaje [fo'ʎaxe] nm foliage
folleto [fo'ʎeto] nm (Pol) pamphlet
follón [fo'ʎon] (ESP: fam) nm (lío) mess;
(conmoción) fuss; **armar un ~** to kick up a
row
fomentar [fomen'tar] vt (Med) to foment
fonda ['fonda] nf inn
fondo ['fondo] nm (de mar) bottom; (de
coche, sala) back; (Arte etc) background;
(reserva) fund; **fondos** nmpl (Com) funds,
resources; **una investigación a ~** a
thorough investigation; **en el ~** at bottom,
deep down
fonobuzón [fonoβu'θon] nm voice mail

fontanería [fontane'ria] nf plumbing;
fontanero, -a nm/f plumber
footing ['futin] nm jogging; **hacer ~** to
jog, go jogging
forastero, -a [foras'tero, a] nm/f
stranger
forcejear [forθexe'ar] vi (luchar) to
struggle
forense [fo'rense] nmf pathologist
forma ['forma] nf (figura) form, shape;
(Med) fitness; (método) way, means; **las ~s**
the conventions; **estar en ~** to be fit; **de ~
que ...** so that ...; **de todas ~s** in any case
formación [forma'θjon] nf (gen)
formation; (educación) education;
formación profesional vocational training
formal [for'mal] adj (gen) formal; (fig: serio)
serious; (: de fiar) reliable; **formalidad** nf
formality; seriousness; **formalizar** vt (Jur)
to formalize; (situación) to put in order,
regularize; **formalizarse** vr (situación) to be
put in order, be regularized
formar [for'mar] vt (componer) to form,
shape; (constituir) to make up, constitute;
(Escol) to train, educate; **formarse** vr (Escol)
to be trained, educated; (cobrar forma) to
form, take form; (desarrollarse) to develop
formatear [formate'ar] vt to format
formato [for'mato] nm format
formidable [formi'ðaβle] adj (temible)
formidable; (estupendo) tremendous
fórmula ['formula] nf formula
formulario [formu'larjo] nm form
fornido, -a [for'niðo, a] adj well-built
foro ['foro] nm (Pol, Inform etc) forum
forrar [fo'rrar] vt (abrigo) to line; (libro)
to cover; **forro** nm (de cuaderno) cover;
(Costura) lining; (de sillón) upholstery; **forro
polar** fleece
fortalecer [fortale'θer] vt to strengthen
fortaleza [forta'leθa] nf (Mil) fortress,
stronghold; (fuerza) strength; (determinación)
resolution
fortuito, -a [for'twito, a] adj accidental
fortuna [for'tuna] nf (suerte) fortune,
(good) luck; (riqueza) fortune, wealth
forzar [for'θar] vt (puerta) to force (open);
(compeler) to compel
forzoso, -a [for'θoso, a] adj necessary
fosa ['fosa] nf (sepultura) grave; (en tierra)
pit; **fosas nasales** nostrils
fósforo ['fosforo] nm (Quím) phosphorus;
(cerilla) match
fósil ['fosil] nm fossil
foso ['foso] nm ditch; (Teatro) pit; (Auto)
inspection pit
foto ['foto] nf photo, snap(shot); **sacar
una ~** to take a photo o picture; **foto (de)**

carné passport(-size) photo

fotocopia [foto'kopja] nf photocopy; **fotocopiadora** nf photocopier; **fotocopiar** vt to photocopy

fotografía [fotoɤra'fia] nf (Arte) photography; (una fotografía) photograph; **fotografiar** vt to photograph

fotógrafo, -a [fo'toɤrafo, a] nm/f photographer

fotomatón [fotoma'ton] nm photo booth

FP (ESP) nf abr (= Formación Profesional) vocational courses for 14- to 18-year-olds

fracasar [fraka'sar] vi (gen) to fail

fracaso [fra'kaso] nm failure

fracción [frak'θjon] nf fraction

fractura [frak'tura] nf fracture, break

fragancia [fra'ɣanθja] nf (olor) fragrance, perfume

frágil ['fraxil] adj (débil) fragile; (Com) breakable

fragmento [fraɤ'mento] nm (pedazo) fragment

fraile ['fraile] nm (Rel) friar; (: monje) monk

frambuesa [fram'bwesa] nf raspberry

francés, -esa [fran'θes, esa] adj French ▷ nm/f Frenchman(-woman) ▷ nm (Ling) French

Francia ['franθja] nf France

franco, -a ['franko, a] adj (cándido) frank, open; (Com: exento) free ▷ nm (moneda) franc

francotirador, a [frankotira'ðor, a] nm/f sniper

franela [fra'nela] nf flannel

franja ['franxa] nf fringe

franquear [franke'ar] vt (camino) to clear; (carta, paquete postal) to frank, stamp; (obstáculo) to overcome

franqueo [fran'keo] nm postage

franqueza [fran'keθa] nf (candor) frankness

frasco ['frasko] nm bottle, flask

frase ['frase] nf sentence; **frase hecha** set phrase; (pey) stock phrase

fraterno, -a [fra'terno, a] adj brotherly, fraternal

fraude ['frauðe] nm (cualidad) dishonesty; (acto) fraud

frazada [fra'saða] (LAM) nf blanket

frecuencia [fre'kwenθja] nf frequency; **con ~** frequently, often

frecuentar [frekwen'tar] vt to frequent

frecuente [fre'kwente] adj (gen) frequent

fregadero [freɤa'ðero] nm (kitchen) sink

fregar [fre'ɤar] vt (frotar) to scrub; (platos) to wash (up); (LAM: fam: fastidiar) to annoy; (: malograr) to screw up

fregona [fre'ɤona] nf mop

freír [fre'ir] vt to fry

frenar [fre'nar] vt to brake; (fig) to check

frenazo [fre'naθo] nm: **dar un ~** to brake sharply

frenesí [frene'si] nm frenzy

freno ['freno] nm (Tec, Auto) brake; (de cabalgadura) bit; (fig) check; **freno de mano** handbrake

frente ['frente] nm (Arq, Pol) front; (de objeto) front part ▷ nf forehead, brow; **~ a** in front of; (en situación opuesta de) opposite; **al ~ de** (fig) at the head of; **chocar de ~** to crash head-on; **hacer ~ a** to face up to

fresa ['fresa] (ESP) nf strawberry

fresco, -a ['fresko, a] adj (nuevo) fresh; (frío) cool; (descarado) cheeky ▷ nm (aire) fresh air; (Arte) fresco; (LAM: jugo) fruit drink ▷ nm/f (fam): **ser un ~** to have a nerve; **tomar el ~** to get some fresh air; **frescura** nf freshness; (descaro) cheek, nerve

frialdad [frial'daθ] nf (gen) coldness; (indiferencia) indifference

frigidez [frixi'ðeθ] nf frigidity

frigorífico [friɤo'rifiko] nm refrigerator

frijol [fri'xol] nm kidney bean

frío, -a etc ['frio, a] vb V **freír** ▷ adj cold; (indiferente) indifferent ▷ nm cold; indifference; **hace ~** it's cold; **tener ~** to be cold

frito, -a ['frito, a] adj fried; **me trae ~ ese hombre** I'm sick and tired of that man; **fritos** nmpl fried food

frívolo, -a ['friβolo, a] adj frivolous

frontal [fron'tal] adj frontal; **choque ~** head-on collision

frontera [fron'tera] nf frontier; **fronterizo, -a** adj frontier cpd; (contiguo) bordering

frontón [fron'ton] nm (Deporte: cancha) pelota court; (: juego) pelota

frotar [fro'tar] vt to rub; **frotarse** vr: **~se las manos** to rub one's hands

fructífero, -a [fruk'tifero, a] adj fruitful

fruncir [frun'θir] vt to pucker; (Costura) to pleat; **~ el ceño** to knit one's brow

frustrar [frus'trar] vt to frustrate

fruta ['fruta] nf fruit; **frutería** nf fruit shop; **frutero, -a** adj fruit cpd ▷ nm/f fruiterer ▷ nm fruit bowl

frutilla [fru'tiʎa] (cs) nf strawberry

fruto ['fruto] nm fruit; (fig: resultado) result; (: beneficio) benefit; **frutos secos** nuts and dried fruit pl

fucsia ['fuksja] nf fuchsia

fue [fwe] vb V **ser**; **ir**

fuego ['fweɤo] nm fire; **a ~ lento** on a low heat; **¿tienes ~?** have you (got) a light?; **fuego amigo** friendly fire; **fuegos artificiales** fireworks

fuente ['fwente] nf fountain; (manantial: fig) spring; (origen) source; (plato) large dish

fuera etc ['fwera] vb V **ser; ir** ⊳ adv out(side); (en otra parte) away; (excepto, salvo) except, save ⊳ prep: ~ **de** outside; (fig) besides; ~ **de sí** beside o.s.; **por ~** (on the) outside

fuera-borda [fwera'βorða] nm speedboat

fuerte ['fwerte] adj strong; (golpe) hard; (ruido) loud; (comida) rich; (lluvia) heavy; (dolor) intense ⊳ adv strongly; hard; loud(ly)

fuerza etc ['fwerθa] vb V **forzar** ⊳ nf (fortaleza) strength; (Tec, Elec) power; (coacción) force; (Mil, Pol) force; **a ~ de** by dint of; **cobrar ~s** to recover one's strength; **tener ~s para** to have the strength to; **a la ~** forcibly, by force; **por ~** of necessity; **fuerza de voluntad** willpower; **fuerzas aéreas** air force sg; **fuerzas armadas** armed forces

fuga ['fuxa] nf (huida) flight, escape; (de gas etc) leak

fugarse [fu'xarse] vr to flee, escape

fugaz [fu'xaθ] adj fleeting

fugitivo, a [fuxi'tiβo, a] adj, nm/f fugitive

fui [fwi] vb V **ser; ir**

fulano, -a [fu'lano, a] nm/f so-and-so, what's-his-name/what's-her-name

fulminante [fulmi'nante] adj (fig: mirada) fierce; (Med: enfermedad, ataque) sudden; (fam: éxito, golpe) sudden

fumador, a [fuma'ðor, a] nm/f smoker

fumar [fu'mar] vt, vi to smoke; ~ **en pipa** to smoke a pipe

función [fun'θjon] nf function; (en trabajo) duties pl; (espectáculo) show; **entrar en funciones** to take up one's duties

funcionar [funθjo'nar] vi (gen) to function; (máquina) to work; **"no funciona"** "out of order"

funcionario, -a [funθjo'narjo, a] nm/f civil servant

funda ['funda] nf (gen) cover; (de almohada) pillowcase

fundación [funda'θjon] nf foundation

fundamental [fundamen'tal] adj fundamental, basic

fundamento [funda'mento] nm (base) foundation

fundar [fun'dar] vt to found; **fundarse** vr: ~**se en** to be founded on

fundición [fundi'θjon] nf fusing; (fábrica) foundry

fundir [fun'dir] vt (gen) to fuse; (metal) to smelt, melt down; (nieve etc) to melt; (Com) to merge; (estatua) to cast; **fundirse** vr (colores etc) to merge, blend; (unirse) to fuse together; (Elec: fusible, lámpara etc) to fuse, blow; (nieve etc) to melt

fúnebre ['funeβre] adj funeral cpd, funereal

funeral [fune'ral] nm funeral; **funeraria** nf undertaker's

funicular [funiku'lar] nm (tren) funicular; (teleférico) cable car

furgón [fur'xon] nm wagon; **furgoneta** nf (Auto, Com) (transit) van (BRIT), pick-up (truck) (US)

furia ['furja] nf (ira) fury; (violencia) violence; **furioso, -a** adj (iracundo) furious; (violento) violent

furtivo, -a [fur'tiβo, a] adj furtive ⊳ nm poacher

fusible [fu'siβle] nm fuse

fusil [fu'sil] nm rifle; **fusilar** vt to shoot

fusión [fu'sjon] nf (gen) melting; (unión) fusion; (Com) merger

fútbol ['futβol] nm football (BRIT), soccer (US); **fútbol americano** American football (BRIT), football (US); **fútbol sala** indoor football (BRIT) o soccer (US); **futbolín** nm table football; **futbolista** nmf footballer

futuro, -a [fu'turo, a] adj, nm future

g

gabardina [gaβar'ðina] nf raincoat, gabardine

gabinete [gaβi'nete] nm (Pol) cabinet; (estudio) study; (de abogados etc) office

gachas ['gatʃas] nfpl porridge sg

gafas ['gafas] nfpl glasses; **gafas de sol** sunglasses

gafe ['gafe] (ESP) nmf jinx

gaita ['gaita] nf bagpipes pl

gajes ['gaxes] nmpl: ~ **del oficio** occupational hazards

gajo ['gaxo] nm (de naranja) segment

gala ['gala] nf (traje de etiqueta) full dress; **galas** nfpl (ropa) finery sg; **estar de** ~ to be in one's best clothes; **hacer** ~ **de** to display

galápago [ga'lapaxo] nm (Zool) turtle

galardón [galar'ðon] nm award, prize

galaxia [ga'laksja] nf galaxy

galera [ga'lera] nf (nave) galley; (carro) wagon; (Imprenta) galley

galería [gale'ria] nf (gen) gallery; (balcón) veranda(h); (pasillo) corridor; **galería comercial** shopping mall

Gales ['gales] nm (tb: **País de** ~) Wales; **galés, -esa** adj Welsh ▷ nm/f Welshman(-woman) ▷ nm (Ling) Welsh

galgo, -a ['galxo, a] nm/f greyhound

gallego, -a [ga'ʎexo, a] adj, nm/f Galician

galleta [ga'ʎeta] nf biscuit (BRIT), cookie (US)

gallina [ga'ʎina] nf hen ▷ nmf (fam: cobarde) chicken; **gallinero** nm henhouse; (Teatro) top gallery

gallo ['gaʎo] nm cock, rooster

galopar [galo'par] vi to gallop

gama ['gama] nf (fig) range

gamba ['gamba] nf prawn (BRIT), shrimp (US)

gamberro, -a [gam'berro, a] (ESP) nm/f hooligan, lout

gamuza [ga'muθa] nf chamois

gana ['gana] nf (deseo) desire, wish; (apetito) appetite; (voluntad) will; (añoranza) longing; **de buena** ~ willingly; **de mala** ~ reluctantly; **me da ~s de** I feel like, I want to; **no me da la** ~ I don't feel like it; **tener ~s de** to feel like

ganadería [ganaðe'ria] nf (ganado) livestock; (ganado vacuno) cattle pl; (cría, comercio) cattle raising

ganadero, -a [gana'ðero, a] (ESP) nm/f (hacendado) rancher

ganado [ga'naðo] nm livestock; **ganado porcino** pigs pl

ganador, a [gana'ðor, a] adj winning ▷ nm/f winner

ganancia [ga'nanθja] nf (lo ganado) gain; (aumento) increase; (beneficio) profit; **ganancias** nfpl (ingresos) earnings; (beneficios) profit sg, winnings

ganar [ga'nar] vt (obtener) to get, obtain; (sacar ventaja) to gain; (salario etc) to earn; (Deporte, premio) to win; (derrotar a) to beat; (alcanzar) to reach ▷ vi (Deporte) to win; **ganarse** vr: ~**se la vida** to earn one's living

ganchillo [gan'tʃiʎo] nm crochet

gancho ['gantʃo] nm (gen) hook; (colgador) hanger

gandul, a [gan'dul, a] adj, nm/f good-for-nothing, layabout

ganga ['ganga] nf bargain

gangrena [gan'grena] nf gangrene

ganso, -a ['ganso, a] nm/f (Zool) goose; (fam) idiot

ganzúa [gan'θua] nf skeleton key

garabato [gara'βato] nm (escritura) scrawl, scribble

garaje [ga'raxe] nm garage

garantía [garan'tia] nf guarantee

garantizar [garanti'θar] vt to guarantee

garbanzo [gar'βanθo] nm chickpea (BRIT), garbanzo (US)

garfio ['garfjo] nm grappling iron

garganta [gar'xanta] nf (Anat) throat; (de botella) neck; **gargantilla** nf necklace

gárgaras ['garxaras] nfpl: **hacer** ~ to gargle

gargarear [garxare'ar] (LAM) vi to gargle

garita [ga'rita] nf cabin, hut; (Mil) sentry box

garra ['garra] nf (de gato, Tec) claw; (de ave) talon; (fam: mano) hand, paw

garrafa [ga'rrafa] nf carafe, decanter

garrapata [garra'pata] nf tick

gas [gas] nm gas; **gases lacrimógenos** tear gas sg

gasa ['gasa] nf gauze

gaseosa [gase'osa] nf lemonade

gaseoso, -a [gase'oso, a] adj gassy, fizzy

gasoil [ga'soil] nm diesel (oil)

gasóleo [ga'soleo] nm = **gasoil**

gasolina [gaso'lina] nf petrol (BRIT), gas(oline) (US); **gasolinera** nf petrol (BRIT) o gas (US) station

gastado, -a [gas'taðo, a] adj (dinero) spent; (ropa) worn out; (usado: frase etc) trite

gastar [gas'tar] vt (dinero, tiempo) to spend; (fuerzas) to use up; (desperdiciar) to waste; (llevar) to wear; **gastarse** vr to wear out; (estropearse) to waste; **~ en** to spend on; **~ bromas** to crack jokes; **¿qué número gastas?** what size (shoe) do you take?

gasto ['gasto] nm (desembolso) expenditure, spending; (consumo, uso) use; **gastos** nmpl (desembolsos) expenses; (cargos) charges, costs

gastronomía [gastrono'mia] nf gastronomy

gatear [gate'ar] vi (andar a gatas) to go on all fours

gatillo [ga'tiʎo] nm (de arma de fuego) trigger; (de dentista) forceps

gato, -a ['gato, a] nm/f cat ▷ nm (Tec) jack; **andar a gatas** to go on all fours

gaucho ['gautʃo] nm gaucho

● **GAUCHO**
●
● **Gauchos** are the herdsmen or riders of
● the Southern Cone plains. Although
● popularly associated with Argentine
● folklore, **gauchos** belong equally to the
● cattle-raising areas of Southern Brazil
● and Uruguay. **Gauchos'** traditions and
● clothing reflect their mixed ancestry
● and cultural roots. Their baggy trousers
● are Arabic in origin, while the horse and
● guitar are inherited from the Spanish
● conquistadors; the poncho, maté and
● **boleadoras** (strips of leather weighted
● at either end with stones) form part of
● the Indian tradition.

gaviota [ga'βjota] nf seagull

gay [ge] adj inv, nm gay, homosexual

gazpacho [gaθ'patʃo] nm gazpacho

gel [xel] nm: **~ de baño/ducha** bath/shower gel

gelatina [xela'tina] nf jelly; (polvos etc) gelatine

gema ['xema] nf gem

gemelo, -a [xe'melo, a] adj, nm/f twin; **gemelos** nmpl (de camisa) cufflinks; (prismáticos) field glasses, binoculars

gemido [xe'miðo] nm (quejido) moan, groan; (aullido) howl

Géminis ['xeminis] nm Gemini

gemir [xe'mir] vi (quejarse) to moan, groan; (aullar) to howl

generación [xenera'θjon] nf generation

general [xene'ral] adj general ▷ nm general; **por lo** o **en ~** in general; **Generalitat** nf Catalan parliament; **generalizar** vt to generalize; **generalizarse** vr to become generalized, spread

generar [xene'rar] vt to generate

género ['xenero] nm (clase) kind, sort; (tipo) type; (Bio) genus; (Ling) gender; (Com) material; **género humano** human race

generosidad [xenerosi'ðað] nf generosity; **generoso, -a** adj generous

genial [xe'njal] adj inspired; (idea) brilliant; (estupendo) wonderful

genio ['xenjo] nm (carácter) nature, disposition; (humor) temper; (facultad creadora) genius; **de mal ~** bad-tempered

genital [xeni'tal] adj genital; **genitales** nmpl genitals

genoma [xe'noma] nm genome

gente ['xente] nf (personas) people pl; (parientes) relatives pl

gentil [xen'til] adj (elegante) graceful; (encantador) charming

▌ No confundir **gentil** con la palabra inglesa gentle.

genuino, -a [xe'nwino, a] adj genuine

geografía [xeoɣra'fia] nf geography

geología [xeolo'xia] nf geology

geometría [xeome'tria] nf geometry

gerente [xe'rente] nmf (supervisor) manager; (jefe) director

geriatría [xeria'tria] nf (Med) geriatrics sg

germen ['xermen] nm germ

gesticular [xestiku'lar] vi to gesticulate; (hacer muecas) to grimace; **gesticulación** nf gesticulation; (mueca) grimace

gestión [xes'tjon] nf management; (diligencia, acción) negotiation

gesto ['xesto] nm (mueca) grimace; (ademán) gesture

Gibraltar [xiβral'tar] nm Gibraltar; **gibraltareño, -a** adj, nm/f Gibraltarian

gigante [xi'xante] adj, nmf giant; **gigantesco, -a** adj gigantic

gilipollas [xili'poʎas] (fam) adj inv daft ▷ nmf inv wally

gimnasia [xim'nasja] nf gymnastics pl; **gimnasio** nm gymnasium; **gimnasta** nmf gymnast

ginebra [xi'neβra] nf gin

ginecólogo, -a [xine'koloɣo, a] nm/f gynaecologist

gira ['xira] nf tour, trip

girar [xi'rar] vt (dar la vuelta) to turn

(around); (: *rápidamente*) to spin; (*Com: giro postal*) to draw; (: *letra de cambio*) to issue ▷ *vi* to turn (round); (*rápido*) to spin

girasol [xira'sol] *nm* sunflower

giratorio, -a [xira'torjo, a] *adj* revolving

giro ['xiro] *nm* (*movimiento*) turn, revolution; (*Ling*) expression; (*Com*) draft; **giro bancario/postal** bank draft/money order

gis [xis] (*MÉX*) *nm* chalk

gitano, -a [xi'tano, a] *adj, nm/f* gypsy

glacial [gla'θjal] *adj* icy, freezing

glaciar [gla'θjar] *nm* glacier

glándula ['glandula] *nf* gland

global [glo'βal] *adj* global; **globalización** *nf* globalization

globo ['gloβo] *nm* (*esfera*) globe, sphere; (*aerostato, juguete*) balloon

glóbulo ['gloβulo] *nm* globule; (*Anat*) corpuscle

gloria ['glorja] *nf* glory

glorieta [glo'rjeta] *nf* (*de jardín*) bower, arbour; (*plazoleta*) roundabout (*BRIT*), traffic circle (*US*)

glorioso, -a [glo'rjoso, a] *adj* glorious

glotón, -ona [glo'ton, ona] *adj* gluttonous, greedy ▷ *nm/f* glutton

glucosa [glu'kosa] *nf* glucose

gobernador, a [goβerna'ðor, a] *adj* governing ▷ *nm/f* governor; **gobernante** *adj* governing

gobernar [goβer'nar] *vt* (*dirigir*) to guide, direct; (*Pol*) to rule, govern ▷ *vi* to govern; (*Náut*) to steer

gobierno *etc* [go'βjerno] *vb* V **gobernar** ▷ *nm* (*Pol*) government; (*dirección*) guidance, direction; (*Náut*) steering

goce *etc* ['goθe] *vb* V **gozar** ▷ *nm* enjoyment

gol [gol] *nm* goal

golf [golf] *nm* golf

golfa ['golfa] (*fam!*) *nf* (*mujer*) slut, whore

golfo, -a ['golfo, a] *nm* (*Geo*) gulf ▷ *nm/f* (*fam: niño*) urchin; (*gamberro*) lout

golondrina [golon'drina] *nf* swallow

golosina [golo'sina] *nf* (*dulce*) sweet; **goloso, -a** *adj* sweet-toothed

golpe ['golpe] *nm* blow; (*de puño*) punch; (*de mano*) smack; (*de remo*) stroke; (*fig: choque*) clash; **no dar ~** to be bone idle; **de un ~** with one blow; **de ~** suddenly; **golpe (de estado)** coup (d'état); **golpear** *vt, vi* to strike, knock; (*asestar*) to beat; (*de puño*) to punch; (*golpetear*) to tap

goma ['goma] *nf* (*caucho*) rubber; (*elástico*) elastic; (*una goma*) elastic band; **goma de borrar** eraser, rubber (*BRIT*); **goma espuma** foam rubber

gomina [go'mina] *nf* hair gel

gomita [go'mita] (*RPL*) *nf* rubber band

gordo, -a ['gorðo, a] *adj* (*gen*) fat; (*fam*) enormous; **el (premio) ~** (*en lotería*) first prize

gorila [go'rila] *nm* gorilla

gorra ['gorra] *nf* cap; (*de bebé*) bonnet; (*militar*) bearskin; **entrar de ~** (*fam*) to gatecrash; **ir de ~** to sponge

gorrión [go'rrjon] *nm* sparrow

gorro ['gorro] *nm* (*gen*) cap; (*de bebé, mujer*) bonnet

gorrón, -ona [go'rron, ona] *nm/f* scrounger; **gorronear** (*fam*) *vi* to scrounge

gota ['gota] *nf* (*gen*) drop; (*de sudor*) bead; (*Med*) gout; **gotear** *vi* to drip; (*lloviznar*) to drizzle; **gotera** *nf* leak

gozar [go'θar] *vi* to enjoy o.s.; **~ de** (*disfrutar*) to enjoy; (*poseer*) to possess

gr. *abr* (= *gramo, gramos*) g

grabación [graβa'θjon] *nf* recording

grabado [gra'βaðo] *nm* print, engraving

grabadora [graβa'ðora] *nf* tape-recorder; **grabadora de CD/DVD** CD/DVD writer

grabar [gra'βar] *vt* to engrave; (*discos, cintas*) to record

gracia ['graθja] *nf* (*encanto*) grace, gracefulness; (*humor*) humour, wit; **¡(muchas) ~s!** thanks (very much)!; **~s a** thanks to; **dar las ~s a algn por algo** to thank sb for sth; **tener ~** (*chiste etc*) to be funny; **no me hace ~** I am not keen; **gracioso, -a** *adj* (*divertido*) funny, amusing; (*cómico*) comical ▷ *nm/f* (*Teatro*) comic character

grada ['graða] *nf* (*de escalera*) step; (*de anfiteatro*) tier, row; **gradas** *nfpl* (*Deporte: de estadio*) terraces

grado ['graðo] *nm* degree; (*de aceite, vino*) grade; (*grada*) step; (*Mil*) rank; **de buen ~** willingly; **grado centígrado/Fahrenheit** degree centigrade/Fahrenheit

graduación [graðwa'θjon] *nf* (*del alcohol*) proof, strength; (*Escol*) graduation; (*Mil*) rank

gradual [gra'ðwal] *adj* gradual

graduar [gra'ðwar] *vt* (*gen*) to graduate; (*Mil*) to commission; **graduarse** *vr* to graduate; **~se la vista** to have one's eyes tested

gráfica ['grafika] *nf* graph

gráfico, -a ['grafiko, a] *adj* graphic ▷ *nm* diagram; **gráficos** *nmpl* (*Inform*) graphics

grajo ['graxo] *nm* rook

gramática [gra'matika] *nf* grammar

gramo ['gramo] *nm* gramme (*BRIT*), gram (*US*)

gran [gran] *adj* V **grande**

grana ['grana] nf (color, tela) scarlet

granada [gra'naða] nf pomegranate; (Mil) grenade

granate [gra'nate] adj deep red

Gran Bretaña [-bre'taṇa] nf Great Britain

grande ['grande] (antes de nmsg **gran**) adj (de tamaño) big, large; (alto) tall; (distinguido) great; (impresionante) grand ▷ nm grandee

granel [gra'nel]: **a ~** adv (Com) in bulk

granero [gra'nero] nm granary, barn

granito [gra'nito] nm (Agr) small grain; (roca) granite

granizado [grani'θaðo] nm iced drink

granizar [grani'θar] vi to hail; **granizo** nm hail

granja ['granxa] nf (gen) farm; **granjero, -a** nm/f farmer

grano ['grano] nm grain; (semilla) seed; (de café) bean; (Med) pimple, spot

granuja [gra'nuxa] nmf rogue; (golfillo) urchin

grapa ['grapa] nf staple; (Tec) clamp; **grapadora** nf stapler

grasa ['grasa] nf (gen) grease; (de cocinar) fat, lard; (sebo) suet; (mugre) filth; **grasiento, -a** adj greasy; (de aceite) oily; **graso, -a** adj (leche, queso, carne) fatty; (pelo, piel) greasy

gratinar [grati'nar] vt to cook au gratin

gratis ['gratis] adv free

grato, -a ['grato, a] adj (agradable) pleasant, agreeable

gratuito, -a [gra'twito, a] adj (gratis) free; (sin razón) gratuitous

grave ['graβe] adj heavy; (serio) grave, serious; **gravedad** nf gravity

Grecia ['greθja] nf Greece

gremio ['gremjo] nm trade, industry

griego, -a ['grjeɣo, a] adj, nm/f Greek

grieta ['grjeta] nf crack

grifo ['grifo] (ESP) nm tap (BRIT), faucet (US)

grillo ['griʎo] nm (Zool) cricket

gripa ['gripa] (MÉX) nf flu, influenza

gripe ['gripe] nf flu, influenza; **gripe aviar** bird flu

gris [gris] adj (color) grey

gritar [gri'tar] vt, vi to shout, yell; **grito** nm shout, yell; (de horror) scream

grosella [gro'seʎa] nf (red)currant

grosero, -a [gro'sero, a] adj (poco cortés) rude, bad-mannered; (ordinario) vulgar, crude

grosor [gro'sor] nm thickness

grúa ['grua] nf (Tec) crane; (de petróleo) derrick

grueso, -a ['grweso, a] adj thick; (persona) stout ▷ nm bulk; **el ~ de** the bulk of

grulla ['gruʎa] nf crane

grumo ['grumo] nm clot, lump

gruñido [gru'ṇiðo] nm grunt; (de persona) grumble

gruñir [gru'ṇir] vi (animal) to growl; (persona) to grumble

grupo ['grupo] nm group; (Tec) unit, set; **grupo de presión** pressure group; **grupo sanguíneo** blood group

gruta ['gruta] nf grotto

guacho, -a ['gwatʃo, a] (CS) nm/f homeless child

guajolote [gwaxo'lote] (MÉX) nm turkey

guante ['gwante] nm glove; **guantes de goma** rubber gloves; **guantera** nf glove compartment

guapo, -a ['gwapo, a] adj good-looking, attractive; (elegante) smart

guarda ['gwarða] nmf (persona) guard, keeper ▷ nf (acto) guarding; (custodia) custody; **guarda jurado** (armed) security guard; **guardabarros** nm inv mudguard (BRIT), fender (US); **guardabosques** nm inv gamekeeper; **guardacostas** nm inv coastguard vessel ▷ nmf guardian, protector; **guardaespaldas** nmf inv bodyguard; **guardameta** nmf goalkeeper; **guardar** vt (gen) to keep; (vigilar) to guard, watch over; (dinero: ahorrar) to save; **guardarse** vr (preservarse) to protect o.s.; (evitar) to avoid; **guardar cama** to stay in bed; **guardarropa** nm (armario) wardrobe; (en establecimiento público) cloakroom

guardería [gwarðe'ria] nf nursery

guardia ['gwarðja] nf (Mil) guard; (cuidado) care, custody ▷ nmf guard; (policía) policeman(-woman); **estar de ~** to be on guard; **montar ~** to mount guard; **Guardia Civil** Civil Guard

guardián, -ana [gwar'ðjan, ana] nm/f (gen) guardian, keeper

guarida [gwa'riða] nf (de animal) den, lair; (refugio) refuge

guarnición [gwarni'θjon] nf (de vestimenta) trimming; (de piedra) mount; (Culin) garnish; (arneses) harness; (Mil) garrison

guarro, -a ['gwarro, a] nm/f pig

guasa ['gwasa] nf joke; **guasón, -ona** adj (bromista) joking ▷ nm/f wit; joker

Guatemala [gwate'mala] nf Guatemala

guay [gwai] (fam) adj super, great

güero, -a ['gwero, a] (MÉX) adj blond(e)

guerra ['gerra] nf war; **dar ~** to annoy; **guerra civil** civil war; **guerra fría** cold war; **guerrero, -a** adj fighting; (carácter) warlike ▷ nm/f warrior

guerrilla [ge'rriʎa] nf guerrilla warfare; (tropas) guerrilla band o group

guía etc ['gia] vb V **guiar** ▷ nmf (persona)

guide; (*nf: libro*) guidebook; **guía telefónica** telephone directory; **guía turística** tourist guide

guiar [gi'ar] *vt* to guide, direct; (*Auto*) to steer; **guiarse** *vr*: **~se por** to be guided by

guinda ['ginda] *nf* morello cherry

guindilla [gin'diʎa] *nf* chilli pepper

guiñar [gi'ɲar] *vt* to wink

guión [gi'on] *nm* (*Ling*) hyphen, dash; (*Cine*) script; **guionista** *nmf* scriptwriter

guiri ['giri] (*ESP: fam, pey*) *nmf* foreigner

guirnalda [gir'nalda] *nf* garland

guisado [gi'saðo] *nm* stew

guisante [gi'sante] *nm* pea

guisar [gi'sar] *vt, vi* to cook; **guiso** *nm* cooked dish

guitarra [gi'tarra] *nf* guitar

gula ['gula] *nf* gluttony, greed

gusano [gu'sano] *nm* worm; (*lombriz*) earthworm

gustar [gus'tar] *vt* to taste, sample ▷ *vi* to please, be pleasing; **~ de algo** to like o enjoy sth; **me gustan las uvas** I like grapes; **le gusta nadar** she likes o enjoys swimming

gusto ['gusto] *nm* (*sentido, sabor*) taste; (*placer*) pleasure; **tiene ~ a menta** it tastes of mint; **tener buen ~** to have good taste; **coger el** o **tomar ~ a algo** to take a liking to sth; **sentirse a ~** to feel at ease; **mucho ~ (en conocerle)** pleased to meet you; **el ~ es mío** the pleasure is mine; **con ~** willingly, gladly

ha *vb* V **haber**

haba ['aβa] *nf* bean

Habana [a'βana] *nf*: **la ~** Havana

habano [a'βano] *nm* Havana cigar

habéis *vb* V **haber**

○ **PALABRA CLAVE**

haber [a'βer] *vb aux* **1** (*tiempos compuestos*) to have; **había comido** I had eaten; **antes/ después de haberlo visto** before seeing/ after seeing o having seen it

2: **¡haberlo dicho antes!** you should have said so before!

3: **haber de: he de hacerlo** I have to do it; **ha de llegar mañana** it should arrive tomorrow

▷ *vb impers* **1** (*existencia: sg*) there is; (*: pl*) there are; **hay un hermano/dos hermanos** there is one brother/there are two brothers; **¿cuánto hay de aquí a Sucre?** how far is it from here to Sucre?

2 (*obligación*): **hay que hacer algo** something must be done; **hay que apuntarlo para acordarse** you have to write it down to remember

3: **¡hay que ver!** well I never!

4: **¡no hay de** o **por** (*LAM*) **qué!** don't mention it!, not at all!

5: **¿qué hay?** (*¿qué pasa?*) what's up?, what's the matter?; (*¿qué tal?*) how's it going?

▷ *vt*: **he aquí unas sugerencias** here are some suggestions; **no hay cintas blancas pero sí las hay rojas** there aren't any white ribbons but there are some red ones

▷ *nm* (*en cuenta*) credit side; **haberes** *nmpl* assets; **¿cuánto tengo en el haber?** how much do I have in my account?; **tiene varias novelas en su haber** he has several novels to his credit

haberse *vr*: **habérselas con algn** to have

it out with sb

habichuela [aβi'tʃwela] *nf* kidney bean
hábil ['aβil] *adj* (*listo*) clever, smart; (*capaz*)
fit, capable; (*experto*) expert; **día ~** working
day; **habilidad** *nf* skill, ability
habitación [aβita'θjon] *nf* (*cuarto*) room;
(*Bio: morada*) habitat; **habitación doble** *o*
de matrimonio double room; **habitación**
individual *o* **sencilla** single room
habitante [aβi'tante] *nmf* inhabitant
habitar [aβi'tar] *vt* (*residir en*) to inhabit;
(*ocupar*) to occupy ▷ *vi* to live
hábito ['aβito] *nm* habit
habitual [aβi'twal] *adj* usual
habituar [aβi'twar] *vt* to accustom;
habituarse *vr*: **~se a** to get used to
habla ['aβla] *nf* (*capacidad de hablar*)
speech; (*idioma*) language; (*dialecto*) dialect;
perder el ~ to become speechless; **de ~**
francesa French-speaking; **estar al ~** to be
in contact; (*Tel*) to be on the line; **¡González**
al ~! (*Tel*) González speaking!
hablador, a [aβla'ðor, a] *adj* talkative
▷ *nm/f* chatterbox
habladuría [aβlaðu'ria] *nf* rumour;
habladurías *nfpl* gossip *sg*
hablante [a'βlante] *adj* speaking ▷ *nmf*
speaker
hablar [a'βlar] *vt* to speak, talk ▷ *vi* to
speak; **hablarse** *vr* to speak to each other;
~ con to speak to; **~ de** to speak of o about;
¡ni ~! it's out of the question!; **"se habla**
inglés" "English spoken here"
habré *etc* [a'βre] *vb* V **haber**
hacendado [aθen'daðo] (*LAM*) *nm*
rancher, farmer
hacendoso, -a [aθen'doso, a] *adj*
industrious

○ **PALABRA CLAVE**

hacer [a'θer] *vt* **1** (*fabricar, producir*) to
make; (*construir*) to build; **hacer una**
película/un ruido to make a film/noise;
el guisado lo hice yo I made o cooked the
stew
2 (*ejecutar: trabajo etc*) to do; **hacer la colada**
to do the washing; **hacer la comida** to do
the cooking; **¿qué haces?** what are you
doing?; **hacer el malo** o **el papel del malo**
(*Teatro*) to play the villain
3 (*estudios, algunos deportes*) to do; **hacer**
español/económicas to do o study
Spanish/economics; **hacer yoga/**
gimnasia to do yoga/go to gym
4 (*transformar, incidir en*): **esto lo hará más**
difícil this will make it more difficult; **salir**

te hará sentir mejor going out will make
you feel better
5 (*cálculo*): **2 y 2 hacen 4** 2 and 2 make 4; **éste**
hace 100 this one makes 100
6 (+ *sub*): **esto hará que ganemos** this will
make us win; **harás que no quiera venir**
you'll stop him wanting to come
7 (*como sustituto de vb*) to do; **él bebió y yo**
hice lo mismo he drank and I did likewise
8 no hace más que criticar all he does is
criticize
▷ *vb semi-aux* (*directo*): **hacer +infin**: **les**
hice venir I made o had them come; **hacer**
trabajar a los demás to get others to work
▷ *vi* **1 haz como que no lo sabes** act as if
you don't know
2 (*ser apropiado*): **si os hace** if it's alright
with you
3 hacer de: hacer de Otelo to play Othello
▷ *vb impers* **1 hace calor/frío** it's hot/cold;
V tb **bueno, sol, tiempo**
2 (*tiempo*): **hace 3 años** 3 years ago; **hace**
un mes que no voy/no voy I've been going/I
haven't been for a month
3 ¿cómo has hecho para llegar tan
rápido? how did you manage to get here
so quickly?
hacerse *vr* **1** (*volverse*) to become; **se**
hicieron amigos they became friends
2 (*acostumbrarse*): **hacerse a** to get used to
3 se hace con huevos y leche it's made
out of eggs and milk; **eso no se hace** that's
not done
4 (*obtener*): **hacerse de** o **con algo** to get
hold of sth
5 (*fingirse*): **hacerse el sueco** to turn a deaf
ear

hacha ['atʃa] *nf* axe; (*antorcha*) torch
hachís [a'tʃis] *nm* hashish
hacia ['aθja] *prep* (*en dirección de*)
towards; (*cerca de*) near; (*actitud*) towards;
~ adelante/atrás forwards/backwards; **~**
arriba/abajo up(wards)/down(wards); **~**
mediodía/las cinco about noon/five
hacienda [a'θjenda] *nf* (*propiedad*)
property; (*finca*) farm; (*LAM: rancho*) ranch;
(Ministerio de) H~ Exchequer (*BRIT*),
Treasury Department (*US*); **hacienda**
pública public finance
hada ['aða] *nf* fairy
hago *etc vb* V **hacer**
Haití [ai'ti] *nm* Haiti
halagar [ala'ɣar] *vt* to flatter
halago [a'laɣo] *nm* flattery
halcón [al'kon] *nm* falcon, hawk
hallar [a'ʎar] *vt* (*gen*) to find; (*descubrir*) to
discover; (*toparse con*) to run into; **hallarse**

vr to be (situated)

halterofilia [altero'filja] nf weightlifting
hamaca [a'maka] nf hammock
hambre ['ambre] nf hunger; (plaga)
famine; (deseo) longing; **tener ~** to be
hungry; **¡me muero de ~!** I'm starving!;
hambriento, -a adj hungry, starving
hamburguesa [ambur'ɣesa] nf
hamburger; **hamburguesería** nf burger
bar
han vb V **haber**
harapos [a'rapos] nmpl rags
haré vb V **hacer**
harina [a'rina] nf flour; **harina de maíz**
cornflour (BRIT), cornstarch (US); **harina de
trigo** wheat flour
hartar [ar'tar] vt to satiate, glut; (fig) to
tire, sicken; **hartarse** vr (de comida) to fill
o.s., gorge o.s.; (cansarse): **~se (de)** to get fed
up (with); **harto, -a** adj (lleno) full; (cansado)
fed up ▷ adv (bastante) enough; (muy) very;
estar harto de hacer algo/de algn to be
fed up of doing sth/with sb
has vb V **haber**
hasta ['asta] adv even ▷ prep (alcanzando
a) as far as; up to; down to; (de tiempo: a tal
hora) till, until; (antes de) before ▷ conj: **~ que
... until; ~ luego/el sábado** see you soon/
on Saturday; **~ ahora** (al despedirse) see you
in a minute; **~ pronto** see you soon
hay vb V **haber**
Haya ['aja] nf: **la ~** The Hague
haya etc ['aja] vb V **haber** ▷ nf beech tree
haz [aθ] vb V **hacer** ▷ nm (de luz) beam
hazaña [a'θaɲa] nf feat, exploit
hazmerreír [aθmerre'ir] nm inv laughing
stock
he vb V **haber**
hebilla [e'βiʎa] nf buckle, clasp
hebra ['eβra] nf thread; (Bot: fibra) fibre,
grain
hebreo, -a [e'βreo, a] adj, nm/f Hebrew
▷ nm (Ling) Hebrew
hechizar [etʃi'θar] vt to cast a spell on,
bewitch
hechizo [e'tʃiθo] nm witchcraft, magic;
(acto de magia) spell, charm
hecho, -a ['etʃo, a] pp de **hacer** ▷ adj
(carne) done; (Costura) ready-to-wear ▷ nm
deed, act; (dato) fact; (cuestión) matter;
(suceso) event ▷ excl agreed!, done!; **de ~** in
fact, as a matter of fact; **el ~ es que ...** the
fact is that ...; **¡bien ~!** well done!
hechura [e'tʃura] nf (forma) form, shape;
(de persona) build
hectárea [ek'tarea] nf hectare
helada [e'laða] nf frost
heladera [ela'ðera] (LAM) nf (refrigerador)

refrigerator
helado, -a [e'laðo, a] adj frozen; (glacial)
icy; (fig) chilly, cold ▷ nm ice cream
helar [e'lar] vt to freeze, ice (up); (dejar
atónito) to amaze; (desalentar) to discourage
▷ vi to freeze; **helarse** vr to freeze
helecho [e'letʃo] nm fern
hélice ['eliθe] nf (Tec) propeller
helicóptero [eli'koptero] nm helicopter
hembra ['embra] nf (Bot, Zool) female;
(mujer) woman; (Tec) nut
hemorragia [emo'rraxja] nf
haemorrhage
hemorroides [emo'rroiðes] nfpl
haemorrhoids, piles
hemos vb V **haber**
heno ['eno] nm hay
heredar [ere'ðar] vt to inherit; **heredero,
-a** nm/f heir(ess)
hereje [e'rexe] nmf heretic
herencia [e'renθja] nf inheritance
herida [e'riða] nf wound, injury; V tb
herido
herido, -a [e'riðo, a] adj injured,
wounded ▷ nm/f casualty
herir [e'rir] vt to wound, injure; (fig) to
offend
hermanastro, -a [erma'nastro, a] nm/f
stepbrother/sister
hermandad [erman'dað] nf brotherhood
hermano, -a [er'mano, a] nm/f brother/
sister; **hermano(-a) gemelo(-a)**, twin
brother/sister; **hermano(-a) político(-a)**,
brother-in-law/sister-in-law
hermético, -a [er'metiko, a] adj
hermetic; (fig) watertight
hermoso, -a [er'moso, a] adj beautiful,
lovely; (estupendo) splendid; (guapo)
handsome; **hermosura** nf beauty
hernia ['ernja] nf hernia; **hernia discal**
slipped disc
héroe ['eroe] nm hero
heroína [ero'ina] nf (mujer) heroine;
(droga) heroin
herradura [erra'ðura] nf horseshoe
herramienta [erra'mjenta] nf tool
herrero [e'rrero] nm blacksmith
hervidero [erβi'ðero] nm (fig) swarm; (Pol
etc) hotbed
hervir [er'βir] vi to boil; (burbujear) to
bubble; **~ a fuego lento** to simmer; **hervor**
nm boiling; (fig) ardour, fervour
heterosexual [eterosek'swal] adj
heterosexual
hice etc vb V **hacer**
hidratante [iðra'tante] adj: **crema ~**
moisturizing cream, moisturizer; **hidratar**
vt (piel) to moisturize; **hidrato** nm hydrate;

hidratos de carbono carbohydrates
hidráulico, -a [i'ðrauliko, a] adj hydraulic
hidro... [iðro] prefijo hydro..., water-...;
hidroeléctrico, -a adj hydroelectric;
hidrógeno nm hydrogen
hiedra ['jeðra] nf ivy
hiel [jel] nf gall, bile; (fig) bitterness
hiela etc vb V **helar**
hielo ['jelo] nm (gen) ice; (escarcha) frost; (fig) coldness, reserve
hiena ['jena] nf hyena
hierba ['jerβa] nf (pasto) grass; (Culin, Med: planta) herb; **mala ~** weed; (fig) evil influence; **hierbabuena** nf mint
hierro ['jerro] nm (metal) iron; (objeto) iron object
hígado ['iɣaðo] nm liver
higiene [i'xjene] nf hygiene; **higiénico, -a** adj hygienic
higo ['iɣo] nm fig; **higo seco** dried fig; **higuera** nf fig tree
hijastro, -a [i'xastro, a] nm/f stepson/daughter
hijo, -a ['ixo, a] nm/f son/daughter, child; **hijos** nmpl children, sons and daughters; **hijo adoptivo** adopted child; **hijo de papá/mamá** daddy's/mummy's boy; **hijo de puta** (fam!) bastard (!), son of a bitch (!); **hijo/a político/a** son-/daughter-in-law
hilera [i'lera] nf row, file
hilo ['ilo] nm thread; (Bot) fibre; (metal) wire; (de agua) trickle, thin stream
hilvanar [ilβa'nar] vt (Costura) to tack (BRIT), baste (US); (fig) to do hurriedly
himno ['imno] nm hymn; **himno nacional** national anthem
hincapié [inka'pje] nm: **hacer ~ en** to emphasize
hincar [in'kar] vt to drive (in), thrust (in)
hincha ['intʃa] (fam) nmf fan
hinchado, -a [in'tʃaðo, a] adj (gen) swollen; (persona) pompous
hinchar [in'tʃar] vt (gen) to swell; (inflar) to blow up, inflate; (fig) to exaggerate; **hincharse** vr (inflarse) to swell up; (fam: de comer) to stuff o.s.; **hinchazón** nf (Med) swelling; (altivez) arrogance
hinojo [i'noxo] nm fennel
hipermercado [ipermer'kaðo] nm hypermarket, superstore
hípico, -a ['ipiko, a] adj horse cpd
hipnotismo [ipno'tismo] nm hypnotism; **hipnotizar** vt to hypnotize
hipo ['ipo] nm hiccups pl
hipocresía [ipokre'sia] nf hypocrisy; **hipócrita** adj hypocritical ▷ nmf hypocrite
hipódromo [i'poðromo] nm racetrack

hipopótamo [ipo'potamo] nm hippopotamus
hipoteca [ipo'teka] nf mortgage
hipótesis [i'potesis] nf inv hypothesis
hispánico, -a [is'paniko, a] adj Hispanic
hispano, -a [is'pano, a] adj Hispanic, Spanish, Hispano- ▷ nm/f Spaniard; **Hispanoamérica** nf Latin America; **hispanoamericano, -a** adj, nm/f Latin American
histeria [is'terja] nf hysteria
historia [is'torja] nf history; (cuento) story, tale; **historias** nfpl (chismes) gossip sg; **dejarse de ~s** to come to the point; **pasar a la ~** to go down in history; **historiador, a** nm/f historian; **historial** nm (profesional) curriculum vitae, C.V.; (Med) case history; **histórico, -a** adj historical; (memorable) historic
historieta [isto'rjeta] nf tale, anecdote; (dibujos) comic strip
hito ['ito] nm (fig) landmark
hizo vb V **hacer**
hocico [o'θiko] nm snout
hockey ['xokei] nm hockey; **hockey sobre hielo/patines** ice/roller hockey
hogar [o'ɣar] nm fireplace, hearth; (casa) home; (vida familiar) home life; **hogareño, -a** adj home cpd; (persona) home-loving
hoguera [o'ɣera] nf (gen) bonfire
hoja ['oxa] nf (gen) leaf; (de flor) petal; (de papel) sheet; (página) page; **hoja de afeitar** (LAM) razor blade; **hoja electrónica** o **de cálculo** spreadsheet; **hoja informativa** leaflet, handout
hojalata [oxa'lata] nf tin(plate)
hojaldre [o'xaldre] nm (Culin) puff pastry
hojear [oxe'ar] vt to leaf through, turn the pages of
hojuela [o'xwela] (MÉX) nf flake
hola ['ola] excl hello!
holá [o'la] (RPL) excl hello!
Holanda [o'landa] nf Holland; **holandés, -esa** adj Dutch ▷ nm/f Dutchman(-woman) ▷ nm (Ling) Dutch
holgado, -a [ol'ɣaðo, a] adj (ropa) loose, baggy; (rico) comfortable
holgar [ol'ɣar] vi (descansar) to rest; (sobrar) to be superfluous
holgazán, -ana [olɣa'θan, ana] adj idle, lazy ▷ nm/f loafer
hollín [o'ʎin] nm soot
hombre ['ombre] nm (gen) man; (raza humana): **el ~** man(kind) ▷ excl: **¡sí ~!** (claro) of course!; (para énfasis) man, old boy; **hombre de negocios** businessman; **hombre de pro** honest man; **hombre-rana** frogman

hombrera [om'brera] nf shoulder strap

hombro ['ombro] nm shoulder

homenaje [ome'naxe] nm (gen) homage; (tributo) tribute

homicida [omi'θiða] adj homicidal ▷ nmf murderer; **homicidio** nm murder, homicide

homologar [omolo'ðar] vt (Com: productos, tamaños) to standardize

homólogo, -a [o'moloxo, a] nm/f: **su** etc ~ his etc counterpart o opposite number

homosexual [omosek'swal] adj, nmf homosexual

honda ['onda] (cs) nf catapult

hondo, -a ['ondo, a] adj deep; **lo ~** the depth(s) pl, the bottom; **hondonada** nf hollow, depression; (cañón) ravine

Honduras [on'duras] nf Honduras

hondureño, -a [ondu'reno, a] adj, nm/f Honduran

honestidad [onesti'ðað] nf purity, chastity; (decencia) decency; **honesto, -a** adj chaste; decent; honest; (justo) just

hongo ['ongo] nm (Bot: gen) fungus; (: comestible) mushroom; (: venenoso) toadstool

honor [o'nor] nm (gen) honour; **en ~ a la verdad** to be fair; **honorable** adj honourable

honorario, -a [ono'rarjo, a] adj honorary; **honorarios** nmpl fees

honra ['onra] nf (gen) honour; (renombre) good name; **honradez** nf honesty; (de persona) integrity; **honrado, -a** adj honest, upright; **honrar** [on'rar] vt to honour

hora ['ora] nf (una hora) hour; (tiempo) time; **¿qué ~ es?** what time is it?; **¿a qué ~?** at what time?; **media ~** half an hour; **a la ~ de recreo** at playtime; **a primera ~** first thing (in the morning); **a última ~** at the last moment; **a altas ~s** in the small hours; **¡a buena ~!** about time too!; **pedir ~** to make an appointment; **dar la ~** to strike the hour; **horas de oficina/trabajo** office/working hours; **horas de visita** visiting times; **horas extras o extraordinarias** overtime sg; **horas pico** (LAM) rush o peak hours; **horas punta** (ESP) rush hours

horario, -a [o'rarjo, a] adj hourly, hour cpd ▷ nm timetable; **horario comercial** business hours pl

horca ['orka] nf gallows sg

horcajadas [orka'xaðas]: **a ~** adv astride

horchata [or'tʃata] nf cold drink made from tiger nuts and water, tiger nut milk

horizontal [oriθon'tal] adj horizontal

horizonte [ori'θonte] nm horizon

horma ['orma] nf mould

hormiga [or'mixa] nf ant; **hormigas** nfpl (Med) pins and needles

hormigón [ormi'xon] nm concrete; **hormigón armado/pretensado** reinforced/prestressed concrete; **hormigonera** nf cement mixer

hormigueo [ormi'xeo] nm (comezón) itch

hormona [or'mona] nf hormone

hornillo [or'niʎo] nm (cocina) portable stove; **hornillo de gas** gas ring

horno ['orno] nm (Culin) oven; (Tec) furnace; **alto ~** blast furnace

horóscopo [o'roskopo] nm horoscope

horquilla [or'kiʎa] nf hairpin; (Agr) pitchfork

horrendo, -a [o'rrendo, a] adj horrendous, frightful

horrible [o'rriβle] adj horrible, dreadful

horripilante [orripi'lante] adj hair-raising, horrifying

horror [o'rror] nm horror, dread; (atrocidad) atrocity; **¡qué ~!** (fam) how awful!; **horrorizar** vt to horrify, frighten; **horrorizarse** vr to be horrified; **horroroso, -a** adj horrifying, ghastly

hortaliza [orta'liθa] nf vegetable

hortelano, -a [orte'lano, a] nm/f (market) gardener

hortera [or'tera] (fam) adj tacky

hospedar [ospe'ðar] vt to put up; **hospedarse** vr to stay, lodge

hospital [ospi'tal] nm hospital

hospitalario, -a [ospita'larjo, a] adj (acogedor) hospitable; **hospitalidad** nf hospitality

hostal [os'tal] nm small hotel

hostelería [ostele'ria] nf hotel business o trade

hostia ['ostja] nf (Rel) host, consecrated wafer; (fam!: golpe) whack, punch ▷ excl (fam!): **¡~(s)!** damn!

hostil [os'til] adj hostile

hotdog [ot'dog] (LAM) nm hot dog

hotel [o'tel] nm hotel; **hotelero, -a** adj hotel cpd ▷ nm/f hotelier

● **HOTEL**
●
● In Spain you can choose from
● the following categories of
● accommodation, in descending order of
● quality and price: **hotel** (from 5 stars to
● 1), **hostal**, **pensión**, **casa de huéspedes**,
● **fonda**. The State also runs luxury hotels
● called **paradores**, which are usually
● sited in places of particular historical
● interest and are often historic buildings
● themselves.

hoy [oi] adv (este día) today; (la actualidad) now(adays) ▷ nm present time; **~ (en) día** now(adays)

hoyo ['ojo] nm hole, pit

hoz [oθ] nf sickle

hube etc vb V **haber**

hucha ['utʃa] nf money box

hueco, -a ['weko, a] adj (vacío) hollow, empty; (resonante) booming ▷ nm hollow, cavity

huelga etc ['welɣa] vb V **holgar** ▷ nf strike; **declararse en ~** to go on strike, come out on strike; **huelga de hambre** hunger strike; **huelga general** general strike

huelguista [wel'ɣista] nmf striker

huella ['weʎa] nf (pisada) tread; (marca del paso) footprint, footstep; (: de animal, máquina) track; **huella dactilar** fingerprint

huelo etc vb V **oler**

huérfano, -a ['werfano, a] adj orphan(ed) ▷ nm/f orphan

huerta ['werta] nf market garden; (en Murcia y Valencia) irrigated region

huerto ['werto] nm kitchen garden; (de árboles frutales) orchard

hueso ['weso] nm (Anat) bone; (de fruta) stone

huésped ['wespeð] nmf guest

hueva ['weβa] nf roe

huevera [we'βera] nf eggcup

huevo ['weβo] nm egg; **huevo a la copa** (cs) soft-boiled egg; **huevo duro/escalfado** hard-boiled/poached egg; **huevo estrellado** (LAM) fried egg; **huevo frito** (ESP) fried egg; **huevo pasado por agua** soft-boiled egg; **huevos revueltos** scrambled eggs; **huevo tibio** (MÉX) soft-boiled egg

huida [u'iða] nf escape, flight

huir [u'ir] vi (escapar) to flee, escape; (evitar) to avoid

hule ['ule] nm oilskin; (MÉX: goma) rubber

hulera [u'lera] (MÉX) nf catapult

humanidad [umani'ðað] nf (género humano) man(kind); (cualidad) humanity

humanitario, -a [umani'tarjo, a] adj humanitarian

humano, -a [u'mano, a] adj (gen) human; (humanitario) humane ▷ nm human; **ser ~** human being

humareda [uma'reða] nf cloud of smoke

humedad [ume'ðað] nf (de clima) humidity; (de pared etc) dampness; **a prueba de ~** damp-proof; **humedecer** vt to moisten, wet; **humedecerse** vr to get wet

húmedo, -a ['umeðo, a] adj (mojado) damp, wet; (tiempo etc) humid

humilde [u'milde] adj humble, modest

humillación [umiʎa'θjon] nf humiliation; **humillante** adj humiliating

humillar [umi'ʎar] vt to humiliate

humo ['umo] nm (de fuego) smoke; (gas nocivo) fumes pl; (vapor) steam, vapour; **humos** nmpl (fig) conceit sg

humor [u'mor] nm (disposición) mood, temper; (lo que divierte) humour; **de buen/mal ~** in a good/bad mood; **humorista** nmf comic; **humorístico, -a** adj funny, humorous

hundimiento [undi'mjento] nm (gen) sinking; (colapso) collapse

hundir [un'dir] vt to sink; (edificio, plan) to ruin, destroy; **hundirse** vr to sink, collapse

húngaro, -a ['ungaro, a] adj, nm/f Hungarian

Hungría [un'gria] nf Hungary

huracán [ura'kan] nm hurricane

huraño, -a [u'raɲo, a] adj (antisocial) unsociable

hurgar [ur'ɣar] vt to poke, jab; (remover) to stir (up); **hurgarse** vr: **~se (las narices)** to pick one's nose

hurón, -ona [u'ron, ona] nm (Zool) ferret

hurtadillas [urta'ðiʎas]: **a ~** adv stealthily, on the sly

hurtar [ur'tar] vt to steal; **hurto** nm theft, stealing

husmear [usme'ar] vt (oler) to sniff out, scent; (fam) to pry into

huyo etc vb V **huir**

I

iba etc vb V **ir**

ibérico, -a [i'βeriko, a] adj Iberian

iberoamericano, -a [iβeroameri'kano, a] adj, nm/f Latin American

Ibiza [i'βiθa] nf Ibiza

iceberg [iθe'βer] nm iceberg

icono [i'kono] nm ikon, icon

ida ['iða] nf going, departure; **~ y vuelta** round trip, return

idea [i'ðea] nf idea; **no tengo la menor ~** I haven't a clue

ideal [iðe'al] adj, nm ideal; **idealista** nmf idealist; **idealizar** vt to idealize

ídem ['iðem] pron ditto

idéntico, -a [i'ðentiko, a] adj identical

identidad [iðenti'ðað] nf identity

identificación [iðentifika'θjon] nf identification

identificar [iðentifi'kar] vt to identify; **identificarse** vr: **~se con** to identify with

ideología [iðeolo'xia] nf ideology

idilio [i'ðiljo] nm love-affair

idioma [i'ðjoma] nm (gen) language

┃ No confundir **idioma** con la palabra inglesa *idiom*.

idiota [i'ðjota] adj idiotic ▷ nmf idiot

ídolo ['iðolo] nm (tb fig) idol

idóneo, -a [i'ðoneo, a] adj suitable

iglesia [i'ɣlesja] nf church

ignorante [iɣno'rante] adj ignorant, uninformed ▷ nmf ignoramus

ignorar [iɣno'rar] vt not to know, be ignorant of; (no hacer caso a) to ignore

igual [i'ɣwal] adj (gen) equal; (similar) like, similar; (mismo) (the) same; (constante) constant; (temperatura) even ▷ nmf equal; **~ que** like, the same as; **me da o es ~** I don't care; **son ~es** they're the same; **al ~ que** (prep, conj) like, just like

igualar [iɣwa'lar] vt (gen) to equalize, make equal; (allanar, nivelar) to level (off), even (out); **igualarse** vr (platos de balanza) to balance out

igualdad [iɣwal'dað] nf equality; (similaridad) sameness; (uniformidad) uniformity

igualmente [iɣwal'mente] adv equally; (también) also, likewise ▷ excl the same to you!

ilegal [ile'ɣal] adj illegal

ilegítimo, -a [ile'xitimo, a] adj illegitimate

ileso, -a [i'leso, a] adj unhurt

ilimitado, -a [ilimi'taðo, a] adj unlimited

iluminación [ilumina'θjon] nf illumination; (alumbrado) lighting

iluminar [ilumi'nar] vt to illuminate, light (up); (fig) to enlighten

ilusión [ilu'sjon] nf illusion; (quimera) delusion; (esperanza) hope; **hacerse ilusiones** to build up one's hopes; **ilusionado, -a** adj excited; **ilusionar** vi: **le ilusiona ir de vacaciones** he's looking forward to going on holiday; **ilusionarse** vr: **ilusionarse (con)** to get excited (about)

iluso, -a [i'luso, a] adj easily deceived ▷ nm/f dreamer

ilustración [ilustra'θjon] nf illustration; (saber) learning, erudition; **la I~** the Enlightenment; **ilustrado, -a** adj illustrated; learned

ilustrar [ilus'trar] vt to illustrate; (instruir) to instruct; (explicar) to explain, make clear

ilustre [i'lustre] adj famous, illustrious

imagen [i'maxen] nf (gen) image; (dibujo) picture

imaginación [imaxina'θjon] nf imagination

imaginar [imaxi'nar] vt (gen) to imagine; (idear) to think up; (suponer) to suppose; **imaginarse** vr to imagine; **imaginario, -a** adj imaginary; **imaginativo, -a** adj imaginative

imán [i'man] nm magnet

imbécil [im'beθil] nmf imbecile, idiot

imitación [imita'θjon] nf imitation; **de ~** imitation cpd

imitar [imi'tar] vt to imitate; (parodiar, remedar) to mimic, ape

impaciente [impa'θjente] adj impatient; (nervioso) anxious

impacto [im'pakto] nm impact

impar [im'par] adj odd

imparcial [impar'θjal] adj impartial, fair

impecable [impe'kaβle] adj impeccable

impedimento [impeði'mento] nm impediment, obstacle

impedir [impe'ðir] vt (obstruir) to impede, obstruct; (estorbar) to prevent; **~ a algn**

hacer *o* **que algn haga algo** to prevent sb (from) doing sth, stop sb doing sth
imperativo, -a [impera'tiβo, a] *adj* (*urgente*, *Ling*) imperative
imperdible [imper'ðiβle] *nm* safety pin
imperdonable [imperðo'naβle] *adj* unforgivable, inexcusable
imperfecto, -a [imper'fekto, a] *adj* imperfect
imperio [im'perjo] *nm* empire; (*autoridad*) rule, authority; (*fig*) pride, haughtiness
impermeable [imperme'aβle] *adj* waterproof ▷ *nm* raincoat, mac (BRIT)
impersonal [imperso'nal] *adj* impersonal
impertinente [imperti'nente] *adj* impertinent
ímpetu ['impetu] *nm* (*impulso*) impetus, impulse; (*impetuosidad*) impetuosity; (*violencia*) violence
implantar [implan'tar] *vt* to introduce
implemento [imple'mento] (LAM) *nm* tool, implement
implicar [impli'kar] *vt* to involve; (*entrañar*) to imply
implícito, -a [im'pliθito, a] *adj* (*tácito*) implicit; (*sobreentendido*) implied
imponente [impo'nente] *adj* (*impresionante*) impressive, imposing; (*solemne*) grand
imponer [impo'ner] *vt* (*gen*) to impose; (*exigir*) to exact; **imponerse** *vr* to assert o.s.; (*prevalecer*) to prevail; **imponible** *adj* (*Com*) taxable
impopular [impopu'lar] *adj* unpopular
importación [importa'θjon] *nf* (*acto*) importing; (*mercancías*) imports *pl*
importancia [impor'tanθja] *nf* importance; (*valor*) value, significance; (*extensión*) size, magnitude; **no tiene ~** it's nothing; **importante** *adj* important; valuable, significant
importar [impor'tar] *vt* (*del extranjero*) to import; (*costar*) to amount to ▷ *vi* to be important, matter; **me importa un rábano** I couldn't care less; **no importa** it doesn't matter; **¿le importa que fume?** do you mind if I smoke?
importe [im'porte] *nm* (*total*) amount; (*valor*) value
imposible [impo'siβle] *adj* (*gen*) impossible; (*insoportable*) unbearable, intolerable
imposición [imposi'θjon] *nf* imposition; (*Com: impuesto*) tax; (: *inversión*) deposit
impostor [impos'tor, a] *nm/f* impostor
impotencia [impo'tenθja] *nf* impotence; **impotente** *adj* impotent
impreciso, -a [impre'θiso, a] *adj*

imprecise, vague
impregnar [impreɣ'nar] *vt* to impregnate; **impregnarse** *vr* to become impregnated
imprenta [im'prenta] *nf* (*acto*) printing; (*aparato*) press; (*casa*) printer's; (*letra*) print
imprescindible [impresθin'diβle] *adj* essential, vital
impresión [impre'sjon] *nf* (*gen*) impression; (*Imprenta*) printing; (*edición*) edition; (*Foto*) print; (*marca*) imprint; **impresión digital** fingerprint
impresionante [impresjo'nante] *adj* impressive; (*tremendo*) tremendous; (*maravilloso*) great, marvellous
impresionar [impresjo'nar] *vt* (*conmover*) to move; (*afectar*) to impress, strike; (*película fotográfica*) to expose; **impresionarse** *vr* to be impressed; (*conmoverse*) to be moved
impreso, -a [im'preso, a] *pp de* **imprimir** ▷ *adj* printed; **impresos** *nmpl* printed matter; **impresora** *nf* printer
imprevisto, -a [impre'βisto, a] *adj* (*gen*) unforeseen; (*inesperado*) unexpected
imprimir [impri'mir] *vt* to imprint, impress, stamp; (*textos*) to print; (*Inform*) to output, print out
improbable [impro'βaβle] *adj* improbable; (*inverosímil*) unlikely
impropio, -a [im'propjo, a] *adj* improper
improvisado, -a [improβi'saðo, a] *adj* improvised
improvisar [improβi'sar] *vt* to improvise
improviso, -a [impro'βiso, a] *adj*: **de ~** unexpectedly, suddenly
imprudencia [impru'ðenθja] *nf* imprudence; (*indiscreción*) indiscretion; (*descuido*) carelessness; **imprudente** *adj* unwise, imprudent; (*indiscreto*) indiscreet
impuesto, -a [im'pwesto, a] *adj* imposed ▷ *nm* tax; **impuesto al valor agregado** *o* **añadido** (LAM) value added tax (BRIT) ≈ sales tax (US); **impuesto sobre el valor añadido** (ESP) value added tax (BRIT) ≈ sales tax (US)
impulsar [impul'sar] *vt* to drive; (*promover*) to promote, stimulate
impulsivo, -a [impul'siβo, a] *adj* impulsive; **impulso** *nm* impulse; (*fuerza*, *empuje*) thrust, drive; (*fig*: *sentimiento*) urge, impulse
impureza [impu're θa] *nf* impurity; **impuro, -a** *adj* impure
inaccesible [inakθe'siβle] *adj* inaccessible
inaceptable [inaθep'taβle] *adj* unacceptable
inactivo, -a [inak'tiβo, a] *adj* inactive
inadecuado, -a [inaðe'kwaðo, a] *adj*

(*insuficiente*) inadequate; (*inapto*) unsuitable

inadvertido, -a [inaðβer'tiðo, a] *adj* (*no visto*) unnoticed

inaguantable [inaxwan'taβle] *adj* unbearable

inanimado, -a [inani'maðo, a] *adj* inanimate

inaudito, -a [inau'ðito, a] *adj* unheard-of

inauguración [inauxura'θjon] *nf* inauguration; opening

inaugurar [inauxu'rar] *vt* to inaugurate; (*exposición*) to open

inca ['inka] *nmf* Inca

incalculable [inkalku'laβle] *adj* incalculable

incandescente [inkandes'θente] *adj* incandescent

incansable [inkan'saβle] *adj* tireless, untiring

incapacidad [inkapaθi'ðað] *nf* incapacity; (*incompetencia*) incompetence; **incapacidad física/mental** physical/mental disability

incapacitar [inkapaθi'tar] *vt* (*inhabilitar*) to incapacitate, render unfit; (*descalificar*) to disqualify

incapaz [inka'paθ] *adj* incapable

incautarse [inkau'tarse] *vr*: **~ de** to seize, confiscate

incauto, -a [in'kauto, a] *adj* (*imprudente*) incautious, unwary

incendiar [inθen'djar] *vt* to set fire to; (*fig*) to inflame; **incendiarse** *vr* to catch fire; **incendiario, -a** *adj* incendiary

incendio [in'θendjo] *nm* fire

incentivo [inθen'tiβo] *nm* incentive

incertidumbre [inθerti'ðumbre] *nf* (*inseguridad*) uncertainty; (*duda*) doubt

incesante [inθe'sante] *adj* incessant

incesto [in'θesto] *nm* incest

incidencia [inθi'ðenθja] *nf* (*Mat*) incidence

incidente [inθi'ðente] *nm* incident

incidir [inθi'ðir] *vi* (*influir*) to influence; (*afectar*) to affect

incienso [in'θjenso] *nm* incense

incierto, -a [in'θjerto, a] *adj* uncertain

incineración [inθinera'θjon] *nf* incineration; (*de cadáveres*) cremation

incinerar [inθine'rar] *vt* to burn; (*cadáveres*) to cremate

incisión [inθi'sjon] *nf* incision

incisivo, -a [inθi'siβo, a] *adj* sharp, cutting; (*fig*) incisive

incitar [inθi'tar] *vt* to incite, rouse

inclemencia [inkle'menθja] *nf* (*severidad*) harshness, severity; (*del tiempo*) inclemency

inclinación [inklina'θjon] *nf* (*gen*) inclination; (*de tierras*) slope, incline; (*de cabeza*) nod, bow; (*fig*) leaning, bent

inclinar [inkli'nar] *vt* to incline; (*cabeza*) to nod, bow ▷ *vi* to lean, slope; **inclinarse** *vr* to bow; (*encorvarse*) to stoop; **~se a** (*parecerse a*) to take after, resemble; **~se ante** to bow down to; **me inclino a pensar que ...** I'm inclined to think that ...

incluir [inklu'ir] *vt* to include; (*incorporar*) to incorporate; (*meter*) to enclose

inclusive [inklu'siβe] *adv* inclusive ▷ *prep* including

incluso [in'kluso] *adv* even

incógnita [in'koɣnita] *nf* (*Mat*) unknown quantity

incógnito [in'koɣnito] *nm*: **de ~** incognito

incoherente [inkoe'rente] *adj* incoherent

incoloro, -a [inko'loro, a] *adj* colourless

incomodar [inkomo'ðar] *vt* to inconvenience; (*molestar*) to bother, trouble; (*fastidiar*) to annoy

incomodidad [inkomoði'ðað] *nf* inconvenience; (*fastidio, enojo*) annoyance; (*de vivienda*) discomfort

incómodo, -a [in'komoðo, a] *adj* (*inconfortable*) uncomfortable; (*molesto*) annoying; (*inconveniente*) inconvenient

incomparable [inkompa'raβle] *adj* incomparable

incompatible [inkompa'tiβle] *adj* incompatible

incompetente [inkompe'tente] *adj* incompetent

incompleto, -a [inkom'pleto, a] *adj* incomplete, unfinished

incomprensible [inkompren'siβle] *adj* incomprehensible

incomunicado, -a [inkomuni'kaðo, a] *adj* (*aislado*) cut off, isolated; (*confinado*) in solitary confinement

incondicional [inkondiθjo'nal] *adj* unconditional; (*apoyo*) wholehearted; (*partidario*) staunch

inconfundible [inkonfun'diβle] *adj* unmistakable

incongruente [inkon'grwente] *adj* incongruous

inconsciente [inkons'θjente] *adj* unconscious; thoughtless

inconsecuente [inkonse'kwente] *adj* inconsistent

inconstante [inkons'tante] *adj* inconstant

incontable [inkon'taβle] *adj* countless, innumerable

inconveniencia [inkombe'njenθja] *nf* unsuitability, inappropriateness;

(*descortesía*) impoliteness; **inconveniente** *adj* unsuitable; impolite ▷ *nm* obstacle; (*desventaja*) disadvantage; **el inconveniente es que ...** the trouble is that ...

incordiar [inkor'ðjar] (*fam*) *vt* to bug, annoy

incorporar [inkorpo'rar] *vt* to incorporate; **incorporarse** *vr* to sit up; **~se a** to join

incorrecto, -a [inko'rrekto, a] *adj* (*gen*) incorrect, wrong; (*comportamiento*) bad-mannered

incorregible [inkorre'xiβle] *adj* incorrigible

incrédulo, -a [in'kreðulo, a] *adj* incredulous, unbelieving; sceptical

increíble [inkre'iβle] *adj* incredible

incremento [inkre'mento] *nm* increment; (*aumento*) rise, increase

increpar [inkre'par] *vt* to reprimand

incruento, -a [in'krwento, a] *adj* bloodless

incrustar [inkrus'tar] *vt* to incrust; (*piedras: en joya*) to inlay

incubar [inku'βar] *vt* to incubate

inculcar [inkul'kar] *vt* to inculcate

inculto, -a [in'kulto, a] *adj* (*persona*) uneducated; (*grosero*) uncouth ▷ *nm/f* ignoramus

incumplimiento [inkumpli'mjento] *nm* non-fulfilment; **incumplimiento de contrato** breach of contract

incurrir [inku'rrir] *vi*: **~ en** to incur; (*crimen*) to commit

indagar [inda'ɣar] *vt* to investigate; to search; (*averiguar*) to ascertain

indecente [inde'θente] *adj* indecent, improper; (*lascivo*) obscene

indeciso, -a [inde'θiso, a] *adj* (*por decidir*) undecided; (*vacilante*) hesitant

indefenso, -a [inde'fenso, a] *adj* defenceless

indefinido, -a [indefi'niðo, a] *adj* indefinite; (*vago*) vague, undefined

indemne [in'demne] *adj* (*objeto*) undamaged; (*persona*) unharmed, unhurt

indemnizar [indemni'θar] *vt* to indemnify; (*compensar*) to compensate

independencia [indepen'denθja] *nf* independence

independiente [indepen'djente] *adj* (*libre*) independent; (*autónomo*) self-sufficient

indeterminado, -a [indetermi'naðo, a] *adj* indefinite; (*desconocido*) indeterminate

India ['indja] *nf*: **la ~** India

indicación [indika'θjon] *nf* indication;

(*señal*) sign; (*sugerencia*) suggestion, hint

indicado, -a [indi'kaðo, a] *adj* (*momento, método*) right; (*tratamiento*) appropriate; (*solución*) likely

indicador [indika'ðor] *nm* indicator; (*Tec*) gauge, meter

indicar [indi'kar] *vt* (*mostrar*) to indicate, show; (*termómetro etc*) to read, register; (*señalar*) to point to

índice ['indiθe] *nm* index; (*catálogo*) catalogue; (*Anat*) index finger, forefinger; **índice de materias** table of contents

indicio [in'diθjo] *nm* indication, sign; (*en pesquisa etc*) clue

indiferencia [indife'renθja] *nf* indifference; (*apatía*) apathy; **indiferente** *adj* indifferent

indígena [in'dixena] *adj* indigenous, native ▷ *nm/f* native

indigestión [indixes'tjon] *nf* indigestion

indigesto, -a [indi'xesto, a] *adj* (*alimento*) indigestible; (*fig*) turgid

indignación [indiɣna'θjon] *nf* indignation

indignar [indiɣ'nar] *vt* to anger, make indignant; **indignarse** *vr*: **~se por** to get indignant about

indigno, -a [in'diɣno, a] *adj* (*despreciable*) low, contemptible; (*inmerecido*) unworthy

indio, -a ['indjo, a] *adj, nm/f* Indian

indirecta [indi'rekta] *nf* insinuation, innuendo; (*sugerencia*) hint

indirecto, -a [indi'rekto, a] *adj* indirect

indiscreción [indiskre'θjon] *nf* (*imprudencia*) indiscretion; (*irreflexión*) tactlessness; (*acto*) gaffe, faux pas

indiscreto, -a [indis'kreto, a] *adj* indiscreet

indiscutible [indisku'tiβle] *adj* indisputable, unquestionable

indispensable [indispen'saβle] *adj* indispensable, essential

indispuesto, -a [indis'pwesto, a] *adj* (*enfermo*) unwell, indisposed

indistinto, -a [indis'tinto, a] *adj* indistinct; (*vago*) vague

individual [indiβi'ðwal] *adj* individual; (*habitación*) single ▷ *nm* (*Deporte*) singles *sg*

individuo, -a [indi'βiðwo, a] *adj, nm* individual

índole ['indole] *nf* (*naturaleza*) nature; (*clase*) sort, kind

inducir [indu'θir] *vt* to induce; (*inferir*) to infer; (*persuadir*) to persuade

indudable [indu'ðaβle] *adj* undoubted; (*incuestionable*) unquestionable

indultar [indul'tar] *vt* (*perdonar*) to pardon, reprieve; (*librar de pago*) to exempt;

indulto *nm* pardon; exemption
industria [in'dustrja] *nf* industry;
(*habilidad*) skill; **industrial** *adj* industrial
▷ *nm* industrialist
inédito, -a [in'eðito, a] *adj* (*texto*)
unpublished; (*nuevo*) new
ineficaz [inefi'kaθ] *adj* (*inútil*) ineffective;
(*ineficiente*) inefficient
ineludible [inelu'ðiβle] *adj* inescapable,
unavoidable
ineptitud [inepti'tuð] *nf* ineptitude,
incompetence; **inepto, -a** *adj* inept,
incompetent
inequívoco, -a [ine'kiβoko, a] *adj*
unequivocal; (*inconfundible*) unmistakable
inercia [in'erθja] *nf* inertia; (*pasividad*)
passivity
inerte [in'erte] *adj* inert; (*inmóvil*)
motionless
inesperado, -a [inespe'raðo, a] *adj*
unexpected, unforeseen
inestable [ines'taβle] *adj* unstable
inevitable [ineβi'taβle] *adj* inevitable
inexacto, -a [inek'sakto, a] *adj*
inaccurate; (*falso*) untrue
inexperto, -a [inek'sperto, a] *adj*
(*novato*) inexperienced
infalible [infa'liβle] *adj* infallible; (*plan*)
foolproof
infame [in'fame] *adj* infamous; (*horrible*)
dreadful; **infamia** *nf* infamy; (*deshonra*)
disgrace
infancia [in'fanθja] *nf* infancy, childhood
infantería [infante'ria] *nf* infantry
infantil [infan'til] *adj* (*pueril, aniñado*)
infantile; (*cándido*) childlike; (*literatura, ropa
etc*) children's
infarto [in'farto] *nm* (*tb: ~ de miocardio*)
heart attack
infatigable [infati'ɣaβle] *adj* tireless,
untiring
infección [infek'θjon] *nf* infection;
infeccioso, -a *adj* infectious
infectar [infek'tar] *vt* to infect;
infectarse *vr* to become infected
infeliz [infe'liθ] *adj* unhappy, wretched
▷ *nmf* wretch
inferior [infe'rjor] *adj* inferior; (*situación*)
lower ▷ *nmf* inferior, subordinate
inferir [infe'rir] *vt* (*deducir*) to infer,
deduce; (*causar*) to cause
infidelidad [infiðeli'ðað] *nf* (*gen*)
infidelity, unfaithfulness
infiel [in'fjel] *adj* unfaithful, disloyal;
(*erróneo*) inaccurate ▷ *nmf* infidel,
unbeliever
infierno [in'fjerno] *nm* hell
infiltrarse [infil'trarse] *vr*: ~ **en** to

infiltrate in(to); (*persona*) to work one's
way in(to)
ínfimo, -a ['infimo, a] *adj* (*más bajo*)
lowest; (*despreciable*) vile, mean
infinidad [infini'ðað] *nf* infinity;
(*abundancia*) great quantity
infinito, -a [infi'nito, a] *adj, nm* infinite
inflación [infla'θjon] *nf* (*hinchazón*)
swelling; (*monetaria*) inflation; (*fig*) conceit
inflamable [infl'maβle] *adj* flammable
inflamar [infla'mar] *vt* (*Med: fig*) to
inflame; **inflamarse** *vr* to catch fire; to
become inflamed
inflar [in'flar] *vt* (*hinchar*) to inflate, blow
up; (*fig*) to exaggerate; **inflarse** *vr* to swell
(up); (*fig*) to get conceited
inflexible [inflek'siβle] *adj* inflexible; (*fig*)
unbending
influencia [influ'enθja] *nf* influence
influir [influ'ir] *vt* to influence
influjo [in'fluxo] *nm* influence
influya *etc vb* V **influir**
influyente [influ'jente] *adj* influential
información [informa'θjon] *nf*
information; (*noticias*) news *sg*; (*Jur*) inquiry;
I~ (*oficina*) Information Office; (*mostrador*)
Information Desk; (*Tel*) Directory Enquiries
informal [infor'mal] *adj* (*gen*) informal
informar [infor'mar] *vt* (*gen*) to inform;
(*revelar*) to reveal, make known ▷ *vi* (*Jur*) to
plead; (*denunciar*) to inform; (*dar cuenta de*)
to report on; **informarse** *vr* to find out; **~se
de** to inquire into
informática [infor'matika] *nf* computer
science, information technology
informe [in'forme] *adj* shapeless ▷ *nm*
report
infracción [infrak'θjon] *nf* infraction,
infringement
infravalorar [infrabalo'rar] *vt* to
undervalue, underestimate
infringir [infrin'xir] *vt* to infringe,
contravene
infundado, -a [infun'daðo, a] *adj*
groundless, unfounded
infundir [infun'dir] *vt* to infuse, instil
infusión [infu'sjon] *nf* infusion; **infusión
de manzanilla** camomile tea
ingeniería [inxenje'ria] *nf* engineering;
ingeniería genética genetic engineering;
ingeniero, -a *nm/f* engineer; **ingeniero
civil** *o* **de caminos** civil engineer
ingenio [in'xenjo] *nm* (*talento*) talent;
(*agudeza*) wit; (*habilidad*) ingenuity,
inventiveness; **ingenio azucarero** (*LAM*)
sugar refinery; **ingenioso, -a** [inxe'njoso,
a] *adj* ingenious, clever; (*divertido*) witty;
ingenuo, -a *adj* ingenuous

ingerir [inxe'rir] vt to ingest; (tragar) to swallow; (consumir) to consume

Inglaterra [ingla'terra] nf England

ingle ['ingle] nf groin

inglés, -esa [in'gles, esa] adj English ▷ nm/f Englishman(-woman) ▷ nm (Ling) English

ingrato, -a [in'grato, a] adj (gen) ungrateful

ingrediente [ingre'ðjente] nm ingredient

ingresar [ingre'sar] vt (dinero) to deposit ▷ vi to come in; **~ en el hospital** to go into hospital

ingreso [in'greso] nm (entrada) entry; (en hospital etc) admission; **ingresos** nmpl (dinero) income sg; (Com) takings pl

inhabitable [inaβi'taβle] adj uninhabitable

inhalar [ina'lar] vt to inhale

inhibir [ini'βir] vt to inhibit

inhóspito, -a [i'nospito, a] adj (región, paisaje) inhospitable

inhumano, -a [inu'mano, a] adj inhuman

inicial [ini'θjal] adj, nf initial

iniciar [ini'θjar] vt (persona) to initiate; (empezar) to begin, commence; (conversación) to start up

iniciativa [iniθja'tiβa] nf initiative; **iniciativa privada** private enterprise

ininterrumpido, -a [ininterrum'piðo, a] adj uninterrupted

injertar [inxer'tar] vt to graft; **injerto** nm graft

injuria [in'xurja] nf (agravio, ofensa) offence; (insulto) insult

▎ No confundir **injuria** con la palabra inglesa **injury**.

injusticia [inxus'tiθja] nf injustice

injusto, -a [in'xusto, a] adj unjust, unfair

inmadurez [inmaðu're θ] nf immaturity

inmediaciones [inmeðja'θjones] nfpl neighbourhood sg, environs

inmediato, -a [inme'ðjato, a] adj immediate; (contiguo) adjoining; (rápido) prompt; (próximo) neighbouring, next; **de ~** immediately

inmejorable [inmexo'raβle] adj unsurpassable; (precio) unbeatable

inmenso, -a [in'menso, a] adj immense, huge

inmigración [inmixra'θjon] nf immigration

inmobiliaria [inmoβi'ljarja] nf estate agency

inmolar [inmo'lar] vt to immolate, sacrifice

inmoral [inmo'ral] adj immoral

inmortal [inmor'tal] adj immortal; **inmortalizar** vt to immortalize

inmóvil [in'moβil] adj immobile

inmueble [in'mweβle] adj: **bienes ~s** real estate, landed property ▷ nm property

inmundo, -a [in'mundo, a] adj filthy

inmune [in'mune] adj: **~ (a)** (Med) immune (to)

inmunidad [inmuni'ðað] nf immunity

inmutarse [inmu'tarse] vr to turn pale; **no se inmutó** he didn't turn a hair

innato, -a [in'nato, a] adj innate

innecesario, -a [inneθe'sarjo, a] adj unnecessary

innovación [innoβa'θjon] nf innovation

innovar [inno'βar] vt to introduce

inocencia [ino'θenθja] nf innocence

inocentada [inoθen'taða] nf practical joke

inocente [ino'θente] adj (ingenuo) naive, innocent; (inculpable) innocent; (sin malicia) harmless ▷ nmf simpleton; **el día de los (Santos) I~s =** April Fools' Day

● **DÍA DE LOS (SANTOS)**
● **INOCENTES**
●
● The 28th December, **el día de los**
● **(Santos) Inocentes**, is when the
● Church commemorates the story of
● Herod's slaughter of the innocent
● children of Judaea. On this day
● Spaniards play **inocentadas** (practical
● jokes) on each other, much like our April
● Fool's Day pranks.

inodoro [ino'ðoro] nm toilet, lavatory (BRIT)

inofensivo, -a [inofen'siβo, a] adj inoffensive, harmless

inolvidable [inolβi'ðaβle] adj unforgettable

inoportuno, -a [inopor'tuno, a] adj untimely; (molesto) inconvenient

inoxidable [inoksi'ðaβle] adj: **acero ~** stainless steel

inquietar [inkje'tar] vt to worry, trouble; **inquietarse** vr to worry, get upset; **inquieto, -a** adj anxious, worried; **inquietud** nf anxiety, worry

inquilino, -a [inki'lino, a] nm/f tenant

insaciable [insa'θjaβle] adj insatiable

inscribir [inskri'βir] vt to inscribe; **~ a algn en** (lista) to put sb on; (censo) to register sb on

inscripción [inskrip'θjon] nf inscription; (Escol etc) enrolment; (en censo) registration

insecticida [insekti'θiða] nm insecticide

insecto [in'sekto] nm insect
inseguridad [inseɣuri'ðað] nf insecurity;
inseguridad ciudadana lack of safety in
the streets
inseguro, -a [inse'ɣuro, a] adj insecure;
(inconstante) unsteady; (incierto) uncertain
insensato, -a [insen'sato, a] adj foolish,
stupid
insensible [insen'siβle] adj (gen)
insensitive; (movimiento) imperceptible; (sin
sentido) numb
insertar [inser'tar] vt to insert
inservible [inser'βiβle] adj useless
insignia [in'siɣnja] nf (señal distintiva)
badge; (estandarte) flag
insignificante [insiɣnifi'kante] adj
insignificant
insinuar [insi'nwar] vt to insinuate,
imply
insípido, -a [in'sipiðo, a] adj insipid
insistir [insis'tir] vi to insist; **~ en algo** to
insist on sth; (enfatizar) to stress sth
insolación [insola'θjon] nf (Med)
sunstroke
insolente [inso'lente] adj insolent
insólito, -a [in'solito, a] adj unusual
insoluble [inso'luβle] adj insoluble
insomnio [in'somnjo] nm insomnia
insonorizado, -a [insonori'θaðo, a] adj
(cuarto etc) soundproof
insoportable [insopor'taβle] adj
unbearable
inspección [inspek'θjon] nf inspection,
check; **inspeccionar** vt (examinar) to
inspect, examine; (controlar) to check
inspector, a [inspek'tor, a] nm/f
inspector
inspiración [inspira'θjon] nf inspiration
inspirar [inspi'rar] vt to inspire; (Med) to
inhale; **inspirarse** vr: **~se en** to be inspired
by
instalación [instala'θjon] nf (equipo)
fittings pl, equipment; **instalación
eléctrica** wiring
instalar [insta'lar] vt (establecer) to instal;
(erguir) to set up, erect; **instalarse** vr to
establish o.s.; (en una vivienda) to move into
instancia [ins'tanθja] nf (Jur) petition;
(ruego) request; **en última ~** as a last resort
instantáneo, -a [instan'taneo, a] adj
instantaneous; **café ~** instant coffee
instante [ins'tante] nm instant, moment;
al ~ right now
instar [ins'tar] vt to press, urge
instaurar [instau'rar] vt (costumbre)
to establish; (normas, sistema) to bring in,
introduce; (gobierno) to instal
instigar [insti'ɣar] vt to instigate

instinto [ins'tinto] nm instinct; **por ~**
instinctively
institución [institu'θjon] nf institution,
establishment
instituir [institu'ir] vt to establish;
(fundar) to found; **instituto** nm (gen)
institute; (ESP Escol) ≈ comprehensive (BRIT)
o high (US) school
institutriz [institu'triθ] nf governess
instrucción [instruk'θjon] nf instruction
instruir [instru'ir] vt (gen) to instruct;
(enseñar) to teach, educate
instrumento [instru'mento] nm (gen)
instrument; (herramienta) tool, implement
insubordinarse [insuβorði'narse] vr to
rebel
insuficiente [insufi'θjente] adj
(gen) insufficient; (Escol: calificación)
unsatisfactory
insular [insu'lar] adj insular
insultar [insul'tar] vt to insult; **insulto**
nm insult
insuperable [insupe'raβle] adj
(excelente) unsurpassable; (problema etc)
insurmountable
insurrección [insurrek'θjon] nf
insurrection, rebellion
intachable [inta't∫aβle] adj
irreproachable
intacto, -a [in'takto, a] adj intact
integral [inte'ɣral] adj integral; (completo)
complete; **pan ~** wholemeal (BRIT) o
wholewheat (US) bread
integrar [inte'ɣrar] vt to make up,
compose; (Mat: fig) to integrate
integridad [inteɣri'ðað] nf wholeness;
(carácter) integrity; **íntegro, -a** adj whole,
entire; (honrado) honest
intelectual [intelek'twal] adj, nmf
intellectual
inteligencia [inteli'xenθja] nf
intelligence; (ingenio) ability; **inteligente**
adj intelligent
intemperie [intem'perje] nf: **a la ~** out in
the open, exposed to the elements
intención [inten'θjon] nf (gen) intention,
purpose; **con segundas intenciones**
maliciously; **con ~** deliberately
intencionado, -a [intenθjo'naðo, a] adj
deliberate; **mal ~** ill-disposed, hostile
intensidad [intensi'ðað] nf (gen)
intensity; (Elec, Tec) strength; **llover con ~**
to rain hard
intenso, -a [in'tenso, a] adj intense;
(sentimiento) profound, deep
intentar [inten'tar] vt (tratar) to try,
attempt; **intento** nm attempt
interactivo, -a [interak'tiβo, a] adj

(*Inform*) interactive

intercalar [interka'lar] *vt* to insert

intercambio [inter'kambjo] *nm*
exchange, swap

interceder [interθe'ðer] *vi* to intercede

interceptar [interθep'tar] *vt* to intercept

interés [inte'res] *nm* (*gen*) interest; (*parte*)
share, part; (*pey*) self-interest; **intereses
creados** vested interests

interesado, -a [intere'saðo, a] *adj*
interested; (*prejuiciado*) prejudiced; (*pey*)
mercenary, self-seeking

interesante [intere'sante] *adj*
interesting

interesar [intere'sar] *vt*, *vi* to interest, be
of interest to; **interesarse** *vr*: **~se en** *o* **por**
to take an interest in

interferir [interfe'rir] *vt* to interfere with;
(*Tel*) to jam ▷ *vi* to interfere

interfón [inter'fon] (*MÉX*) *nm* entry
phone

interino, -a [inte'rino, a] *adj* temporary
▷ *nm/f* temporary holder of a post; (*Med*)
locum; (*Escol*) supply teacher

interior [inte'rjor] *adj* inner, inside;
(*Com*) domestic, internal ▷ *nm* interior,
inside; (*fig*) soul, mind; **Ministerio del I~**
≈ Home Office (*BRIT*), ≈ Department of the
Interior (*US*); **interiorista** (*ESP*) *nmf* interior
designer

interjección [interxek'θjon] *nf*
interjection

interlocutor, a [interloku'tor, a] *nm/f*
speaker

intermedio, -a [inter'meðjo, a] *adj*
intermediate ▷ *nm* interval

interminable [intermi'naβle] *adj*
endless

intermitente [intermi'tente] *adj*
intermittent ▷ *nm* (*Auto*) indicator

internacional [internaθjo'nal] *adj*
international

internado [inter'naðo] *nm* boarding
school

internar [inter'nar] *vt* to intern; (*en
un manicomio*) to commit; **internarse** *vr*
(*penetrar*) to penetrate

internauta [inter'nauta] *nmf* web surfer,
Internet user

Internet, internet [inter'net] *nm o f*
Internet

interno, -a [in'terno, a] *adj* internal,
interior; (*Pol etc*) domestic ▷ *nm/f* (*alumno*)
boarder

interponer [interpo'ner] *vt* to interpose,
put in; **interponerse** *vr* to intervene

interpretación [interpreta'θjon] *nf*
interpretation

interpretar [interpre'tar] *vt* to interpret;
(*Teatro, Mús*) to perform, play; **intérprete**
nmf (*Ling*) interpreter, translator; (*Mús,
Teatro*) performer, artist(e)

interrogación [interroɣa'θjon] *nf*
interrogation; (*Ling: tb*: **signo de ~**)
question mark

interrogar [interro'ɣar] *vt* to interrogate,
question

interrumpir [interrum'pir] *vt* to
interrupt

interrupción [interrup'θjon] *nf*
interruption

interruptor [interrup'tor] *nm* (*Elec*)
switch

intersección [intersek'θjon] *nf*
intersection

interurbano, -a [interur'βano, a]
adj: **llamada interurbana** long-distance
call

intervalo [inter'βalo] *nm* interval;
(*descanso*) break

intervenir [interβe'nir] *vt* (*controlar*) to
control, supervise; (*Med*) to operate on ▷ *vi*
(*participar*) to take part, participate; (*mediar*)
to intervene

interventor, a [interβen'tor, a] *nm/f*
inspector; (*Com*) auditor

intestino [intes'tino] *nm* (*Med*) intestine

intimar [inti'mar] *vi* to become friendly

intimidad [intimi'ðað] *nf* intimacy;
(*familiaridad*) familiarity; (*vida privada*)
private life; (*Jur*) privacy

íntimo, -a ['intimo, a] *adj* intimate

intolerable [intole'raβle] *adj* intolerable,
unbearable

intoxicación [intoksika'θjon] *nf*
poisoning; **intoxicación alimenticia** food
poisoning

intranet [intra'net] *nf* intranet

intranquilo, -a [intran'kilo, a] *adj*
worried

intransitable [intransi'taβle] *adj*
impassable

intrépido, -a [in'trepiðo, a] *adj* intrepid

intriga [in'triɣa] *nf* intrigue; (*plan*) plot;
intrigar *vt*, *vi* to intrigue

intrínseco, -a [in'trinseko, a] *adj*
intrinsic

introducción [introðuk'θjon] *nf*
introduction

introducir [introðu'θir] *vt* (*gen*) to
introduce; (*moneda etc*) to insert; (*Inform*) to
input, enter

intromisión [intromi'sjon] *nf*
interference, meddling

introvertido, -a [introβer'tiðo, a] *adj*,
nm/f introvert

intruso, -a [in'truso, a] *adj* intrusive
▷ *nm/f* intruder
intuición [intwi'θjon] *nf* intuition
inundación [inunda'θjon] *nf* flood(ing);
inundar *vt* to flood; (*fig*) to swamp,
inundate
inusitado, -a [inusi'taðo, a] *adj* unusual,
rare
inútil [in'util] *adj* useless; (*esfuerzo*) vain,
fruitless
inutilizar [inutili'θar] *vt* to make o render
useless
invadir [imba'ðir] *vt* to invade
inválido, -a [im'baliðo, a] *adj* invalid
▷ *nm/f* invalid
invasión [imba'sjon] *nf* invasion
invasor, a [imba'sor, a] *adj* invading
▷ *nm/f* invader
invención [imben'θjon] *nf* invention
inventar [imben'tar] *vt* to invent
inventario [imben'tarjo] *nm* inventory
invento [im'bento] *nm* invention
inventor, a [imben'tor, a] *nm/f* inventor
invernadero [imberna'ðero] *nm*
greenhouse
inverosímil [imbero'simil] *adj*
implausible
inversión [imber'sjon] *nf* (*Com*)
investment
inverso, -a [im'berso, a] *adj* inverse,
opposite; **en el orden ~** in reverse order; **a la
inversa** inversely, the other way round
inversor, a [imber'sor, a] *nm/f* (*Com*)
investor
invertir [imber'tir] *vt* (*Com*) to invest;
(*volcar*) to turn upside down; (*tiempo etc*)
to spend
investigación [imbestiɣa'θjon]
nf investigation; (*Escol*) research;
investigación y desarrollo research and
development
investigar [imbesti'ɣar] *vt* to investigate;
(*Escol*) to do research into
invierno [im'bjerno] *nm* winter
invisible [imbi'siβle] *adj* invisible
invitado, -a [imbi'taðo, a] *nm/f* guest
invitar [imbi'tar] *vt* to invite; (*incitar*) to
entice; (*pagar*) to buy, pay for
invocar [imbo'kar] *vt* to invoke, call on
involucrar [imbolu'krar] *vt*: **~ en** to
involve in; **involucrarse** *vr* (*persona*): **~se
en** to get mixed up in
involuntario, -a [imbolun'tarjo, a]
adj (*movimiento, gesto*) involuntary; (*error*)
unintentional
inyección [injek'θjon] *nf* injection
inyectar [injek'tar] *vt* to inject
iPod® ['ipoð] (*pl* **~s**) *nm* iPod ®

○ **PALABRA CLAVE**

ir [ir] *vi* 1 to go; (*a pie*) to walk; (*viajar*) to
travel; **ir caminando** to walk; **fui en tren** I
went o travelled by train; **¡(ahora) voy!** (I'm
just) coming!
2: **ir (a) por**: **ir (a) por el médico** to fetch
the doctor
3 (*progresar: persona, cosa*) to go; **el trabajo
va muy bien** work is going very well; **¿cómo
te va?** how are things going?; **me va muy
bien** I'm getting on very well; **le fue fatal** it
went awfully badly for him
4 (*funcionar*): **el coche no va muy bien** the
car isn't running very well
5: **te va estupendamente ese color** that
colour suits you fantastically well
6 (*locuciones*): **¿vino? – ¡que va!** did he come?
– of course not!; **vamos, no llores** come on,
don't cry; **¡vaya coche!** what a car!, that's
some car!
7: **no vaya a ser: tienes que correr, no
vaya a ser que pierdas el tren** you'll have
to run so as not to miss the train
8 (*+ pp*): **iba vestido muy bien** he was very
well dressed
9: **ni me** *etc* **va ni me** *etc* **viene** I *etc* don't
care
▷ *vb aux* 1 **ir a**: **voy/iba a hacerlo hoy** I am/
was going to do it today
2 (*+ gerundio*): **iba anocheciendo** it was
getting dark; **todo se me iba aclarando**
everything was gradually becoming clearer
to me
3 (*+ pp*: = *pasivo*): **van vendidos 300
ejemplares** 300 copies have been sold so far
irse *vr* 1: **¿por dónde se va al zoológico?**
which is the way to the zoo?
2 (*marcharse*) to leave; **ya se habrán ido** they
must already have left o gone

ira ['ira] *nf* anger, rage
Irak [i'rak] *nm* = Iraq
Irán [i'ran] *nm* Iran; **iraní** *adj*, *nmf* Iranian
Iraq [i'rak] *nm* Iraq; **iraquí** *adj*, *nmf* Iraqi
iris ['iris] *nm inv* (*tb*: **arco ~**) rainbow;
(*Anat*) iris
Irlanda [ir'landa] *nf* Ireland; **irlandés,
-esa** *adj* Irish ▷ *nm/f* Irishman(-woman);
los irlandeses the Irish
ironía [iro'nia] *nf* irony; **irónico, -a** *adj*
ironic(al)
IRPF *nm abr* (= *Impuesto sobre la Renta de las
Personas Físicas*) (personal) income tax
irreal [irre'al] *adj* unreal
irregular [irreɣu'lar] *adj* (*gen*) irregular;
(*situación*) abnormal
irremediable [irreme'ðjaβle] *adj*

irremediable; (vicio) incurable

irreparable [irrepaˈraβle] adj (daños)
irreparable; (pérdida) irrecoverable

irrespetuoso, -a [irrespeˈtwoso, a] adj
disrespectful

irresponsable [irresponˈsaβle] adj
irresponsible

irreversible [irreβerˈsiβle] adj irreversible

irrigar [irriˈɣar] vt to irrigate

irrisorio, -a [irriˈsorjo, a] adj derisory,
ridiculous

irritar [irriˈtar] vt to irritate, annoy

irrupción [irrupˈθjon] nf irruption;
(invasión) invasion

isla [ˈisla] nf island

Islam [isˈlam] nm Islam; **las enseñanzas
del ~** the teachings of Islam; **islámico, -a**
adj Islamic

islandés, -esa [islanˈdes, esa] adj
Icelandic ▷ nm/f Icelander

Islandia [isˈlandja] nf Iceland

isleño, -a [isˈleɲo, a] adj island cpd ▷ nm/f
islander

Israel [israˈel] nm Israel; **israelí** adj, nmf
Israeli

istmo [ˈistmo] nm isthmus

Italia [iˈtalja] nf Italy; **italiano, -a** adj,
nm/f Italian

itinerario [itineˈrarjo] nm itinerary, route

ITV (ESP) nf abr (= inspección técnica de
vehículos) roadworthiness test, ≈ MOT (BRIT)

IVA [ˈiβa] nm abr (= impuesto sobre el valor
añadido) VAT

izar [iˈθar] vt to hoist

izdo, -a abr (= izquierdo, a) l

izquierda [iθˈkjerda] nf left; (Pol) left
(wing); **a la ~** (estar) on the left; (torcer etc)
(to the) left

izquierdo, -a [iθˈkjerðo, a] adj left

J

jabalí [xaβaˈli] nm wild boar

jabalina [xaβaˈlina] nf javelin

jabón [xaˈβon] nm soap

jaca [ˈxaka] nf pony

jacal [xaˈkal] (MÉX) nm shack

jacinto [xaˈθinto] nm hyacinth

jactarse [xakˈtarse] vr to boast, brag

jadear [xaðeˈar] vi to pant, gasp for breath

jaguar [xaˈɣwar] nm jaguar

jaiba [ˈxaiβa] (LAM) nf crab

jalar [xaˈlar] (LAM) vt to pull

jalea [xaˈlea] nf jelly

jaleo [xaˈleo] nm racket, uproar; **armar un
~** to kick up a racket

jalón [xaˈlon] (LAM) nm tug

jamás [xaˈmas] adv never

jamón [xaˈmon] nm ham; **jamón dulce**
o **de York** cooked ham; **jamón serrano**
cured ham

Japón [xaˈpon] nm Japan; **japonés, -esa**
adj, nm/f Japanese ▷ nm (Ling) Japanese

jaque [ˈxake] nm (Ajedrez) check; **jaque
mate** checkmate

jaqueca [xaˈkeka] nf (very bad) headache,
migraine

jarabe [xaˈraβe] nm syrup

jardín [xarˈðin] nm garden; **jardín infantil**
o **de infancia** nursery (school); **jardinería**
nf gardening; **jardinero, -a** nm/f gardener

jarra [ˈxarra] nf jar; (jarro) jug

jarro [ˈxarro] nm jug

jarrón [xaˈrron] nm vase

jaula [ˈxaula] nf cage

jauría [xauˈria] nf pack of hounds

jazmín [xaθˈmin] nm jasmine

J.C. abr (= Jesucristo) J.C.

jeans [jins, dʒins] (LAM) nmpl jeans,
denims; **unos ~** a pair of jeans

jefatura [xefaˈtura] nf (tb: **~ de policía**)
police headquarters sg

jefe, -a [ˈxefe, a] nm/f (gen) chief, head;

(*patrón*) boss; **jefe de cocina** chef; **jefe de estación** stationmaster; **jefe de Estado** head of state; **jefe de estudios** (*Escol*) director of studies; **jefe de gobierno** head of government

jengibre [xen'xiβre] *nm* ginger

jeque ['xeke] *nm* sheik

jerárquico, -a [xe'rarkiko, a] *adj* hierarchic(al)

jerez [xe'reθ] *nm* sherry

jerga ['xerɣa] *nf* jargon

jeringa [xe'ringa] *nf* syringe; (*LAM: molestia*) annoyance, bother; **jeringuilla** *nf* syringe

jeroglífico [xero'ɣlifiko] *nm* hieroglyphic

jersey [xer'sei] (*pl* **~s**) *nm* jersey, pullover, jumper

Jerusalén [xerusa'len] *n* Jerusalem

Jesucristo [xesu'kristo] *nm* Jesus Christ

jesuita [xe'swita] *adj, nm* Jesuit

Jesús [xe'sus] *nm* Jesus; **¡~!** good heavens!; (*al estornudar*) bless you!

jinete [xi'nete] *nmf* horseman(-woman), rider

jipijapa [xipi'xapa] (*LAM*) *nm* straw hat

jirafa [xi'rafa] *nf* giraffe

jirón [xi'ron] *nm* rag, shred

jitomate [xito'mate] (*MÉX*) *nm* tomato

joder [xo'ðer] (*fam!*) *vt, vi* to fuck (!)

jogging ['joxin] (*RPL*) *nm* tracksuit (*BRIT*), sweat suit (*US*)

jornada [xor'naða] *nf* (*viaje de un día*) day's journey; (*camino o viaje entero*) journey; (*día de trabajo*) working day

jornal [xor'nal] *nm* (day's) wage; **jornalero** *nm* (day) labourer

joroba [xo'roβa] *nf* hump, hunched back; **jorobado, -a** *adj* hunchbacked ▷ *nm/f* hunchback

jota ['xota] *nf* (the letter) J; (*danza*) Aragonese dance; **no saber ni ~** to have no idea

joven ['xoβen] (*pl* **jóvenes**) *adj* young ▷ *nm* young man, youth ▷ *nf* young woman, girl

joya ['xoja] *nf* jewel, gem; (*fig: persona*) gem; **joyas de fantasía** costume *o* imitation jewellery; **joyería** *nf* (*joyas*) jewellery; (*tienda*) jeweller's (shop); **joyero** *nm* (*persona*) jeweller; (*caja*) jewel case

juanete [xwa'nete] *nm* (*del pie*) bunion

jubilación [xuβila'θjon] *nf* (*retiro*) retirement

jubilado, -a [xuβi'laðo, a] *adj* retired ▷ *nm/f* pensioner (*BRIT*), senior citizen

jubilar [xuβi'lar] *vt* to pension off, retire; (*fam*) to discard; **jubilarse** *vr* to retire

júbilo ['xuβilo] *nm* joy, rejoicing; **jubiloso,**

-a *adj* jubilant

judía [xu'ðia] (*ESP*) *nf* (*Culin*) bean; **judía blanca/verde** haricot/French bean; V tb **judío**

judicial [xuði'θjal] *adj* judicial

judío, -a [xu'ðio, a] *adj* Jewish ▷ *nm/f* Jew(ess)

judo ['juðo] *nm* judo

juego *etc* ['xweɣo] *vb* V**jugar** ▷ *nm* (*gen*) play; (*pasatiempo, partido*) game; (*en casino*) gambling; (*conjunto*) set; **fuera de ~** (*Deporte: persona*) offside; (*: pelota*) out of play; **juego de palabras** pun, play on words; **Juegos Olímpicos** Olympic Games

juerga ['xwerɣa] (*ESP: fam*) *nf* binge; (*fiesta*) party; **ir de ~** to go out on a binge

jueves ['xweβes] *nm inv* Thursday

juez [xweθ] *nmf* judge; **juez de instrucción** examining magistrate; **juez de línea** linesman; **juez de salida** starter

jugada [xu'ɣaða] *nf* play; **buena ~** good move *o* shot *o* stroke *etc*

jugador, a [xuɣa'ðor, a] *nm/f* player; (*en casino*) gambler

jugar [xu'ɣar] *vt, vi* to play; (*en casino*) to gamble; (*apostar*) to bet; **~ al fútbol** to play football

juglar [xu'ɣlar] *nm* minstrel

jugo ['xuɣo] *nm* (*Bot*) juice; (*fig*) essence, substance; **jugo de naranja** (*LAM*) orange juice; **jugoso, -a** *adj* juicy; (*fig*) substantial, important

juguete [xu'ɣete] *nm* toy; **juguetear** *vi* to play; **juguetería** *nf* toyshop

juguetón, -ona [xuɣe'ton, ona] *adj* playful

juicio ['xwiθjo] *nm* judgement; (*razón*) sanity, reason; (*opinión*) opinion

julio ['xuljo] *nm* July

jumper ['dʒumper] (*LAM*) *nm* pinafore dress (*BRIT*), jumper (*US*)

junco ['xunko] *nm* rush, reed

jungla ['xungla] *nf* jungle

junio ['xunjo] *nm* June

junta ['xunta] *nf* (*asamblea*) meeting, assembly; (*comité, consejo*) council, committee; (*Com, Finanzas*) board; (*Tec*) joint; **junta directiva** board of directors

juntar [xun'tar] *vt* to join, unite; (*maquinaria*) to assemble, put together; (*dinero*) to collect; **juntarse** *vr* to join, meet; (*reunirse: personas*) to meet, assemble; (*arrimarse*) to approach, draw closer; **~se con algn** to join sb

junto, -a ['xunto, a] *adj* joined; (*unido*) united; (*anexo*) near, close; (*contiguo, próximo*) next, adjacent ▷ *adv*: **todo ~** all at once; **~s** together; **~ a** near (to), next to; **~**

con (together) with

jurado [xu'raðo] *nm* (*Jur: individuo*) juror; (*: grupo*) jury; (*de concurso: grupo*) panel (of judges); (*: individuo*) member of a panel

juramento [xura'mento] *nm* oath; (*maldición*) oath, curse; **prestar ~** to take the oath; **tomar ~ a** to swear in, administer the oath to

jurar [xu'rar] *vt, vi* to swear; **~ en falso** to commit perjury; **tenérsela jurada a algn** to have it in for sb

jurídico, -a [xu'riðiko, a] *adj* legal

jurisdicción [xurisðik'θjon] *nf* (*poder, autoridad*) jurisdiction; (*territorio*) district

justamente [xusta'mente] *adv* justly, fairly; (*precisamente*) just, exactly

justicia [xus'tiθja] *nf* justice; (*equidad*) fairness, justice

justificación [xustifika'θjon] *nf* justification; **justificar** *vt* to justify

justo, -a ['xusto, a] *adj* (*equitativo*) just, fair, right; (*preciso*) exact, correct; (*ajustado*) tight ▷ *adv* (*precisamente*) exactly, precisely; (LAM: *apenas a tiempo*) just in time

juvenil [xuβe'nil] *adj* youthful

juventud [xuβen'tuð] *nf* (*adolescencia*) youth; (*jóvenes*) young people *pl*

juzgado [xuθ'ɣaðo] *nm* tribunal; (*Jur*) court

juzgar [xuθ'ɣar] *vt* to judge; **a ~ por ...** to judge by ..., judging by ...

kárate ['karate] *nm* karate

kg *abr* (= *kilogramo*) kg

kilo ['kilo] *nm* kilo; **kilogramo** *nm* kilogramme; **kilometraje** *nm* distance in kilometres ≈ mileage; **kilómetro** *nm* kilometre; **kilovatio** *nm* kilowatt

kiosco ['kjosko] *nm* = **quiosco**

kleenex® [kli'neks] *nm* paper handkerchief, tissue

Kosovo [ko'soβo] *nm* Kosovo

km *abr* (= *kilómetro*) km

kv *abr* (= *kilovatio*) kw

l abr (= litro) l

la [la] art def the ▷ pron her; (Ud.) you; (cosa) it ▷ nm (Mús) la; **~ del sombrero rojo** the girl in the red hat; V tb **el**

laberinto [laβe'rinto] nm labyrinth

labio ['laβjo] nm lip

labor [la'βor] nf labour; (Agr) farm work; (tarea) job, task; (Costura) needlework; **labores domésticas** o **del hogar** household chores; **laborable** adj (Agr) workable; **día laborable** working day; **laboral** adj (accidente) at work; (jornada) working

laboratorio [laβora'torjo] nm laboratory

laborista [laβo'rista] adj: **Partido L~** Labour Party

labrador, a [laβra'ðor, a] adj farming cpd ▷ nm/f farmer

labranza [la'βranθa] nf (Agr) cultivation

labrar [la'βrar] vt (gen) to work; (madera etc) to carve; (fig) to cause, bring about

laca ['laka] nf lacquer

lacio, -a ['laθjo, a] adj (pelo) straight

lacón [la'kon] nm shoulder of pork

lactancia [lak'tanθja] nf lactation

lácteo, -a ['lakteo, a] adj: **productos ~s** dairy products

ladear [laðe'ar] vt to tip, tilt ▷ vi to tilt; **ladearse** vr to lean

ladera [la'ðera] nf slope

lado ['laðo] nm (gen) side; (fig) protection; (Mil) flank; **al ~ de** beside; **poner de ~** to put on its side; **poner a un ~** to put aside; **por todos ~s** on all sides, all round (BRIT)

ladrar [la'ðrar] vi to bark; **ladrido** nm bark, barking

ladrillo [la'ðriʎo] nm (gen) brick; (azulejo) tile

ladrón, -ona [la'ðron, ona] nm/f thief

lagartija [laɣar'tixa] nf (Zool) (small) lizard

lagarto [la'ɣarto] nm (Zool) lizard

lago ['laɣo] nm lake

lágrima ['laɣrima] nf tear

laguna [la'ɣuna] nf (lago) lagoon; (hueco) gap

lamentable [lamen'taβle] adj lamentable, regrettable; (miserable) pitiful

lamentar [lamen'tar] vt (sentir) to regret; (deplorar) to lament; **lamentarse** vr to lament; **lo lamento mucho** I'm very sorry

lamer [la'mer] vt to lick

lámina ['lamina] nf (plancha delgada) sheet; (para estampar, estampa) plate

lámpara ['lampara] nf lamp; **lámpara de alcohol/gas** spirit/gas lamp; **lámpara de pie** standard lamp

lana ['lana] nf wool

lancha ['lantʃa] nf launch; **lancha motora** motorboat, speedboat

langosta [lan'gosta] nf (crustáceo) lobster; (: de río) crayfish; **langostino** nm Dublin Bay prawn

lanza ['lanθa] nf (arma) lance, spear

lanzamiento [lanθa'mjento] nm (gen) throwing; (Náut, Com) launch, launching; **lanzamiento de peso** putting the shot

lanzar [lan'θar] vt (gen) to throw; (Deporte: pelota) to bowl; (Náut, Com) to launch; (Jur) to evict; **lanzarse** vr to throw o.s.

lapa ['lapa] nf limpet

lapicero [lapi'θero] (CAM) nm (bolígrafo) ballpoint pen, Biro®

lápida ['lapiða] nf stone; **lápida mortuoria** headstone

lápiz ['lapiθ] nm pencil; **lápiz de color** coloured pencil; **lápiz de labios** lipstick; **lápiz de ojos** eyebrow pencil

largar [lar'ɣar] vt (soltar) to release; (aflojar) to loosen; (lanzar) to launch; (fam) to let fly; (velas) to unfurl; (LAM: lanzar) to throw; **largarse** vr (fam) to beat it; **~se a** (CS: empezar) to start to

largo, -a ['larɣo, a] adj (longitud) long; (tiempo) long; (fig) generous ▷ nm length; (Mús) largo; **dos años ~s** two long years; **tiene 9 metros de ~** it is 9 metres long; **a la larga** in the long run; **a lo ~ de** along; (tiempo) all through, throughout

▌ No confundir **largo** con la palabra inglesa large.

largometraje nm feature film

laringe [la'rinxe] nf larynx; **laringitis** nf laryngitis

las [las] art def the ▷ pron them; **~ que cantan** the ones o women o girls who sing; V tb **el**

lasaña [la'saɲa] nf lasagne, lasagna

láser ['laser] nm laser

lástima ['lastima] nf (pena) pity; **dar ~** to be pitiful; **es una ~ que ...** it's a pity that ...; **¡qué ~!** what a pity!; **está hecha una ~** she looks pitiful

lastimar [lasti'mar] vt (herir) to wound; (ofender) to offend; **lastimarse** vr to hurt o.s.

lata ['lata] nf (metal) tin; (caja) tin (BRIT), can; (fam) nuisance; **en ~** tinned (BRIT), canned; **dar la ~** to be a nuisance

latente [la'tente] adj latent

lateral [late'ral] adj side cpd, lateral ▷ nm (Teatro) wings

latido [la'tiðo] nm (de corazón) beat

latifundio [lati'fundjo] nm large estate

latigazo [lati'xaθo] nm (golpe) lash; (sonido) crack

látigo ['latixo] nm whip

latín [la'tin] nm Latin

latino, -a [la'tino, a] adj Latin; **latinoamericano, -a** adj, nm/f Latin-American

latir [la'tir] vi (corazón, pulso) to beat

latitud [lati'tuð] nf (Geo) latitude

latón [la'ton] nm brass

laurel [lau'rel] nm (Bot) laurel; (Culin) bay

lava ['laβa] nf lava

lavabo [la'βaβo] nm (pila) washbasin; (tb: ~s) toilet

lavado [la'βaðo] nm washing; (de ropa) laundry; (Arte) wash; **lavado de cerebro** brainwashing; **lavado en seco** dry-cleaning

lavadora [laβa'ðora] nf washing machine

lavanda [la'βanda] nf lavender

lavandería [laβande'ria] nf laundry; (automática) launderette

lavaplatos [laβa'platos] nm inv dishwasher

lavar [la'βar] vt to wash; (borrar) to wipe away; **lavarse** vr to wash o.s.; **~se las manos** to wash one's hands; **~se los dientes** to brush one's teeth; **~ y marcar** (pelo) to shampoo and set; **~ en seco** to dry-clean; **~ los platos** to wash the dishes

lavarropas [laβa'rropas] (RPL) nm inv washing machine

lavavajillas [laβaβa'xiʎas] nm inv dishwasher

laxante [lak'sante] nm laxative

lazarillo [laθa'riʎo] nm (tb: **perro ~**) guide dog

lazo ['laθo] nm knot; (lazada) bow; (para animales) lasso; (trampa) snare; (vínculo) tie

le [le] pron (directo) to him (o her); (: usted) you; (indirecto) to him (o her o to you); (: usted) to you

leal [le'al] adj loyal; **lealtad** nf loyalty

lección [lek'θjon] nf lesson

leche ['letʃe] nf milk; **tiene mala ~** (fam!) he's a swine (!); **leche condensada** condensed milk; **leche desnatada** skimmed milk

lecho ['letʃo] nm (cama: de río) bed; (Geo) layer

lechón [le'tʃon] nm sucking (BRIT) o suckling (US) pig

lechoso, -a [le'tʃoso, a] adj milky

lechuga [le'tʃuxa] nf lettuce

lechuza [le'tʃuθa] nf owl

lector, a [lek'tor, a] nm/f reader ▷ nm: **~ de discos compactos** CD player

lectura [lek'tura] nf reading

leer [le'er] vt to read

legado [le'xaðo] nm (don) bequest; (herencia) legacy; (enviado) legate

legajo [le'xaxo] nm file

legal [le'xal] adj (gen) legal; (persona) trustworthy; **legalizar** [lexali'θar] vt to legalize; (documento) to authenticate

legaña [le'xaɲa] nf sleep (in eyes)

legión [le'xjon] nf legion; **legionario, -a** adj legionary ▷ nm legionnaire

legislación [lexisla'θjon] nf legislation

legislar [lexis'lar] vi to legislate

legislatura [lexisla'tura] nf (Pol) period of office

legítimo, -a [le'xitimo, a] adj (genuino) authentic; (legal) legitimate

legua ['lexwa] nf league

legumbres [le'xumbres] nfpl pulses

leído, -a [le'iðo, a] adj well-read

lejanía [lexa'nia] nf distance; **lejano, -a** adj far-off; (en el tiempo) distant; (fig) remote

lejía [le'xia] nf bleach

lejos ['lexos] adv far, far away; **a lo ~** in the distance; **de o desde ~** from afar; **~ de** far from

lema ['lema] nm motto; (Pol) slogan

lencería [lenθe'ria] nf linen, drapery

lengua ['lengwa] nf tongue; (Ling) language; **morderse la ~** to hold one's tongue

lenguado [len'gwaðo] nm sole

lenguaje [len'gwaxe] nm language; **lenguaje de programación** program(m)ing language

lengüeta [len'gweta] nf (Anat) epiglottis; (zapatos) tongue; (Mús) reed

lente ['lente] nf lens; (lupa) magnifying glass; **lentes** nfpl lenses ▷ nmpl (LAM: gafas) glasses; **lentes bifocales/de sol** (LAM) bifocals/sunglasses; **lentes de contacto** contact lenses

lenteja [len'texa] nf lentil; **lentejuela** nf sequin

lentilla [len'tiʎa] nf contact lens

lentitud [lenti'tuð] nf slowness; **con ~**

slowly
lento, -a ['lento, a] *adj* slow
leña ['leɲa] *nf* firewood; **leñador, a** *nm/f* woodcutter
leño ['leɲo] *nm* (*trozo de árbol*) log; (*madero*) timber; (*fig*) blockhead
Leo ['leo] *nm* Leo
león [le'on] *nm* lion; **león marino** sea lion
leopardo [leo'parðo] *nm* leopard
leotardos [leo'tarðos] *nmpl* tights
lepra ['lepra] *nf* leprosy; **leproso, -a** *nm/f* leper
les [les] *pron* (*directo*) them; (: *ustedes*) you; (*indirecto*) to them; (: *ustedes*) to you
lesbiana [les'βjana] *adj, nf* lesbian
lesión [le'sjon] *nf* wound, lesion; (*Deporte*) injury; **lesionado, -a** *adj* injured ▷ *nm/f* injured person
letal [le'tal] *adj* lethal
letanía [leta'nia] *nf* litany
letra ['letra] *nf* letter; (*escritura*) handwriting; (*Mús*) lyrics *pl*; **letra de cambio** bill of exchange; **letra de imprenta** print; **letrado, -a** *adj* learned ▷ *nm/f* lawyer; **letrero** *nm* (*cartel*) sign; (*etiqueta*) label
letrina [le'trina] *nf* latrine
leucemia [leu'θemja] *nf* leukaemia
levadura [leβa'ðura] *nf* (*para el pan*) yeast; (*de cerveza*) brewer's yeast
levantar [leβan'tar] *vt* (*gen*) to raise; (*del suelo*) to pick up; (*hacia arriba*) to lift (up); (*plan*) to make, draw up; (*mesa*) to clear; (*campamento*) to strike; (*fig*) to cheer up, hearten; **levantarse** *vr* to get up; (*enderezarse*) to straighten up; (*rebelarse*) to rebel; **~ el ánimo** to cheer up
levante [le'βante] *nm* east coast; **el L~** *region of Spain extending from Castellón to Murcia*
levar [le'βar] *vt* to weigh
leve ['leβe] *adj* light; (*fig*) trivial
levita [le'βita] *nf* frock coat
léxico ['leksiko] *nm* (*vocabulario*) vocabulary
ley [lei] *nf* (*gen*) law; (*metal*) standard
leyenda [le'jenda] *nf* legend
leyó *etc vb* V **leer**
liar [li'ar] *vt* to tie (up); (*unir*) to bind; (*envolver*) to wrap (up); (*enredar*) to confuse; (*cigarrillo*) to roll; **liarse** *vr* (*fam*) to get involved; **~se a palos** to get involved in a fight
Líbano ['liβano] *nm*: **el ~** the Lebanon
libélula [li'βelula] *nf* dragonfly
liberación [liβera'θjon] *nf* liberation; (*de la cárcel*) release
liberal [liβe'ral] *adj, nmf* liberal

liberar [liβe'rar] *vt* to liberate
libertad [liβer'tað] *nf* liberty, freedom; **libertad bajo fianza** bail; **libertad bajo palabra** parole; **libertad condicional** probation; **libertad de culto/de prensa/de comercio** freedom of worship/of the press/of trade
libertar [liβer'tar] *vt* (*preso*) to set free; (*de una obligación*) to release; (*eximir*) to exempt
libertino, -a [liβer'tino, a] *adj* permissive ▷ *nm/f* permissive person
libra ['liβra] *nf* pound; **L~** (*Astrología*) Libra; **libra esterlina** pound sterling
libramiento [liβra'mjento] (*MÉX*) *nm* ring road (*BRIT*), beltway (*US*)
librar [li'βrar] *vt* (*de peligro*) to save; (*batalla*) to wage, fight; (*de impuestos*) to exempt; (*cheque*) to make out; (*Jur*) to exempt; **librarse** *vr*: **~se de** to escape from, free o.s. from
libre ['liβre] *adj* free; (*lugar*) unoccupied; (*asiento*) vacant; (*de deudas*) free of debts; **~ de impuestos** free of tax; **tiro ~** free kick; **los 100 metros ~s** the 100 metres free-style (race); **al aire ~** in the open air
librería [liβre'ria] *nf* (*tienda*) bookshop

> No confundir **librería** con la palabra inglesa *library*.

librero, -a *nm/f* bookseller
libreta [li'βreta] *nf* notebook
libro ['liβro] *nm* book; **libro de bolsillo** paperback; **libro de texto** textbook; **libro electrónico** e-book
Lic. *abr* = **licenciado, a**
licencia [li'θenθja] *nf* (*gen*) licence; (*permiso*) permission; **licencia de caza** game licence; **licencia por enfermedad** (*MÉX*, *RPL*) sick leave; **licenciado, -a** *adj* licensed ▷ *nm/f* graduate; **licenciar** *vt* (*empleado*) to dismiss; (*permitir*) to permit, allow; (*soldado*) to discharge; (*estudiante*) to confer a degree upon; **licenciarse** *vr*: **licenciarse en Derecho** to graduate in law
lícito, -a ['liθito, a] *adj* (*legal*) lawful; (*justo*) fair, just; (*permisible*) permissible
licor [li'kor] *nm* spirits *pl* (*BRIT*), liquor (*US*); (*de frutas etc*) liqueur
licuadora [likwa'ðora] *nf* blender
líder ['liðer] *nmf* leader; **liderato** *nm* leadership; **liderazgo** *nm* leadership
lidia ['liðja] *nf* bullfighting; (*una lidia*) bullfight; **toros de ~** fighting bulls; **lidiar** *vt, vi* to fight
liebre ['ljeβre] *nf* hare
lienzo ['ljenθo] *nm* linen; (*Arte*) canvas; (*Arq*) wall
liga ['liɣa] *nf* (*de medias*) garter, suspender; (*LAM*: *goma*) rubber band; (*confederación*)

league
ligadura [liɣaˈðura] nf bond, tie; (Med, Mús) ligature
ligamento [liɣaˈmento] nm ligament
ligar [liˈɣar] vt (atar) to tie; (unir) to join; (Med) to bind up; (Mús) to slur ▷ vi to mix, blend; (fam): **(él) liga mucho** he pulls a lot of women; **ligarse** vr to commit o.s.
ligero, -a [liˈxero, a] adj (de peso) light; (tela) thin; (rápido) swift, quick; (ágil) agile, nimble; (de importancia) slight; (de carácter) flippant, superficial ▷ adv: **a la ligera** superficially
liguero [liˈɣero] nm suspender (BRIT) o garter (US) belt
lija [ˈlixa] nf (Zool) dogfish; (tb: **papel de ~**) sandpaper
lila [ˈlila] nf lilac
lima [ˈlima] nf file; (Bot) lime; **lima de uñas** nailfile; **limar** vt to file
limitación [limitaˈθjon] nf limitation, limit
limitar [limiˈtar] vt to limit; (reducir) to reduce, cut down ▷ vi: **~ con** to border on; **limitarse** vr: **~se a** to limit o.s. to
límite [ˈlimite] nm (gen) limit; (fin) end; (frontera) border; **límite de velocidad** speed limit
limítrofe [liˈmitrofe] adj neighbouring
limón [liˈmon] nm lemon ▷ adj: **amarillo ~** lemon-yellow; **limonada** nf lemonade
limosna [liˈmosna] nf alms pl; **vivir de ~** to live on charity
limpiador [limpjaˈðor] (MÉX) nm = **limpiaparabrisas**
limpiaparabrisas [limpjaparaˈβrisas] nm inv windscreen (BRIT) o windshield (US) wiper
limpiar [limˈpjar] vt to clean; (con trapo) to wipe; (quitar) to wipe away; (zapatos) to shine, polish; (fig) to clean up
limpieza [limˈpjeθa] nf (estado) cleanliness; (acto) cleaning; (: de las calles) cleansing; (: de zapatos) polishing; (habilidad) skill; (fig: Policía) clean-up; (pureza) purity; (Mil): **operación de ~** mopping-up operation; **limpieza en seco** dry cleaning
limpio, -a [ˈlimpjo, a] adj clean; (moralmente) pure; (Com) clear, net; (fam) honest ▷ adv: **jugar ~** to play fair; **pasar a** (ESP) o **en** (LAM) **~** to make a clean copy of
lince [ˈlinθe] nm lynx
linchar [linˈtʃar] vt to lynch
lindar [linˈdar] vi to adjoin; **~ con** to border on
lindo, -a [ˈlindo, a] adj pretty, lovely ▷ adv: **nos divertimos de lo ~** we had a marvellous time; **canta muy ~** (LAM) he

sings beautifully
línea [ˈlinea] nf (gen) line; **en ~** (Inform) on line; **línea aérea** airline; **línea de meta** goal line; (en carrera) finishing line; **línea discontinua** (Auto) broken line; **línea recta** straight line
lingote [linˈgote] nm ingot
lingüista [linˈgwista] nmf linguist; **lingüística** nf linguistics sg
lino [ˈlino] nm linen; (Bot) flax
linterna [linˈterna] nf torch (BRIT), flashlight (US)
lío [ˈlio] nm bundle; (fam) fuss; (desorden) muddle, mess; **armar un ~** to make a fuss
liquen [ˈliken] nm lichen
liquidación [likiðaˈθjon] nf liquidation; **venta de ~** clearance sale
liquidar [likiˈðar] vt (mercancías) to liquidate; (deudas) to pay off; (empresa) to wind up
líquido, -a [ˈlikiðo, a] adj liquid; (ganancia) net ▷ nm liquid; **líquido imponible** net taxable income
lira [ˈlira] nf (Mús) lyre; (moneda) lira
lírico, -a [ˈliriko, a] adj lyrical
lirio [ˈlirjo] nm (Bot) iris
lirón [liˈron] nm (Zool) dormouse; (fig) sleepyhead
Lisboa [lisˈβoa] n Lisbon
lisiar [liˈsjar] vt to maim
liso, -a [ˈliso, a] adj (terreno) flat; (cabello) straight; (superficie) even; (tela) plain
lista [ˈlista] nf list; (de alumnos) school register; (de libros) catalogue; (de platos) menu; (de precios) price list; **pasar ~** to call the roll; **tela de ~s** striped material; **lista de espera** waiting list; **lista de precios** price list; **listín** nm (tb: **listín telefónico** o **de teléfonos**) telephone directory
listo, -a [ˈlisto, a] adj (perspicaz) smart, clever; (preparado) ready
listón [lisˈton] nm (de madera, metal) strip
litera [liˈtera] nf (en barco, tren) berth; (en dormitorio) bunk, bunk bed
literal [liteˈral] adj literal
literario, -a [liteˈrarjo, a] adj literary
literato, -a [liteˈrato, a] adj literary ▷ nm/f writer
literatura [literaˈtura] nf literature
litigio [liˈtixjo] nm (Jur) lawsuit; (fig): **en ~ con** in dispute with
litografía [litoɣraˈfia] nf lithography; (una litografía) lithograph
litoral [litoˈral] adj coastal ▷ nm coast, seaboard
litro [ˈlitro] nm litre
lívido, -a [ˈliβiðo, a] adj livid
llaga [ˈʎaɣa] nf wound

llama ['ʎama] nf flame; (Zool) llama

llamada [ʎa'maða] nf call; **llamada a cobro revertido** reverse-charge (BRIT) o collect (US) call; **llamada al orden** call to order; **llamada de atención** warning; **llamada local** (LAM) local call; **llamada metropolitana** (ESP) local call; **llamada por cobrar** (MÉX) reverse-charge (BRIT) o collect (US) call

llamamiento [ʎama'mjento] nm call

llamar [ʎa'mar] vt to call; (atención) to attract ▷ vi (por teléfono) to telephone; (a la puerta) to knock (o ring); (por señas) to beckon; (Mil) to call up; **llamarse** vr to be called, be named; **¿cómo se llama (usted)?** what's your name?

llamativo, -a [ʎama'tiβo, a] adj showy; (color) loud

llano, -a ['ʎano, a] adj (superficie) flat; (persona) straightforward; (estilo) clear ▷ nm plain, flat ground

llanta ['ʎanta] nf (ESP) (wheel) rim; **llanta (de goma)** (LAM: neumático) tyre; (: cámara) inner (tube); **llanta de repuesto** (LAM) spare tyre

llanto ['ʎanto] nm weeping

llanura [ʎa'nura] nf plain

llave ['ʎaβe] nf key; (del agua) tap; (Mecánica) spanner; (de la luz) switch; (Mús) key; **echar la ~ a** to lock up; **llave de contacto** (ESP Auto) ignition key; **llave de encendido** (LAM Auto) ignition key; **llave de paso** stopcock; **llave inglesa** monkey wrench; **llave maestra** master key; **llavero** nm keyring

llegada [ʎe'ɣaða] nf arrival

llegar [ʎe'ɣar] vi to arrive; (alcanzar) to reach; (bastar) to be enough; **llegarse** vr: **~se a** to approach; **~ a** to manage to, succeed in; **~ a saber** to find out; **~ a ser** to become; **~ a las manos de** to come into the hands of

llenar [ʎe'nar] vt to fill; (espacio) to cover; (formulario) to fill in o up; (fig) to heap

lleno, -a ['ʎeno, a] adj full, filled; (repleto) full up ▷ nm (Teatro) full house; **dar de ~ contra un muro** to hit a wall head-on

llevadero, -a [ʎeβa'ðero, a] adj bearable, tolerable

llevar [ʎe'βar] vt to take; (ropa) to wear; (cargar) to carry; (quitar) to take away; (en coche) to drive; (transportar) to transport; (traer: dinero) to carry; (conducir) to lead; (Mat) to carry ▷ vi (suj: camino etc) to lead to; **llevarse** vr to carry off, take away; **llevamos dos días aquí** we have been here for two days; **él me lleva 2 años** he's 2 years older than me; **~ los libros** (Com) to keep the

books; **~se bien** to get on well (together)

llorar [ʎo'rar] vt, vi to cry, weep; **~ de risa** to cry with laughter

llorón, -ona [ʎo'ron, ona] adj tearful ▷ nm/f cry-baby

lloroso, -a [ʎo'roso, a] adj (gen) weeping, tearful; (triste) sad, sorrowful

llover [ʎo'βer] vi to rain

llovizna [ʎo'βiθna] nf drizzle; **lloviznar** vi to drizzle

llueve etc vb V **llover**

lluvia ['ʎuβja] nf rain; **lluvia radioactiva** (radioactive) fallout; **lluvioso, -a** adj rainy

lo [lo] art def: **~ bel~** the beautiful, what is beautiful, that which is beautiful ▷ pron (persona) him; (cosa) it; **~ que sea** whatever; V tb **el**

loable [lo'aβle] adj praiseworthy

lobo ['loβo] nm wolf; **lobo de mar** (fig) sea dog

lóbulo ['loβulo] nm lobe

local [lo'kal] adj local ▷ nm place, site; (oficinas) premises pl; **localidad** nf (barrio) locality; (lugar) location; (Teatro) seat, ticket; **localizar** vt (ubicar) to locate, find; (restringir) to localize; (situar) to place

loción [lo'θjon] nf lotion

loco, -a ['loko, a] adj mad ▷ nm/f lunatic, mad person; **estar ~ con** o **por algo/por algn** to be mad about sth/sb

locomotora [lokomo'tora] nf engine, locomotive

locuaz [lo'kwaθ] adj loquacious

locución [loku'θjon] nf expression

locura [lo'kura] nf madness; (acto) crazy act

locutor, a [loku'tor, a] nm/f (Radio) announcer; (comentarista) commentator; (TV) newsreader

locutorio [loku'torjo] nm (en telefónica) telephone booth

lodo ['loðo] nm mud

lógica ['loxika] nf logic

lógico, -a [lo'xiko, a] adj logical

login ['loxin] nm login

logística [lo'xistika] nf logistics sg

logotipo [loðo'tipo] nm logo

logrado, -a [lo'ðraðo, a] adj (interpretación, reproducción) polished, excellent

lograr [lo'ɣrar] vt to achieve; (obtener) to get, obtain; **~ hacer** to manage to do; **~ que algn venga** to manage to get sb to come

logro ['loɣro] nm achievement, success

lóker ['loker] nm (LAM) locker

loma ['loma] nf hillock (BRIT), small hill

lombriz [lom'briθ] nf worm

lomo ['lomo] nm (de animal) back; (Culin: de

cerdo) pork loin; (: *de vaca*) rib steak; (*de libro*) spine

lona ['lona] *nf* canvas

loncha ['lontʃa] *nf* =**lonja**

lonchería [lontʃe'ria] (LAM) *nf* snack bar, diner (US)

Londres ['londres] *n* London

longaniza [longa'niθa] *nf* pork sausage

longitud [lonxi'tuð] *nf* length; (Geo) longitude; **tener 3 metros de ~** to be 3 metres long; **longitud de onda** wavelength

lonja ['lonxa] *nf* slice; (*de tocino*) rasher; **lonja de pescado** fish market

loro ['loro] *nm* parrot

los [los] *art def* the ▷ *pron* them; (*ustedes*) you; **mis libros y ~ tuyos** my books and yours; *V tb* **el**

losa ['losa] *nf* stone

lote ['lote] *nm* portion; (Com) lot

lotería [lote'ria] *nf* lottery; (*juego*) lotto

loza ['loθa] *nf* crockery

lubina [lu'βina] *nf* sea bass

lubricante [luβri'kante] *nm* lubricant

lubricar [luβri'kar] *vt* to lubricate

lucha ['lutʃa] *nf* fight, struggle; **lucha de clases** class struggle; **lucha libre** wrestling; **luchar** *vi* to fight

lúcido, -a ['luθiðo, a] *adj* (*persona*) lucid; (*mente*) logical; (*idea*) crystal-clear

luciérnaga [lu'θjernaxa] *nf* glow-worm

lucir [lu'θir] *vt* to illuminate, light (up); (*ostentar*) to show off ▷ *vi* (*brillar*) to shine; **lucirse** *vr* (*irónico*) to make a fool of o.s.

lucro ['lukro] *nm* profit, gain

lúdico, -a ['ludiko, a] *adj* (*aspecto*, *actividad*) play *cpd*

luego ['lweɣo] *adv* (*después*) next; (*más tarde*) later, afterwards

lugar [lu'ɣar] *nm* place; (*sitio*) spot; **en primer ~** in the first place, firstly; **en ~ de** instead of; **hacer ~** to make room; **fuera de ~** out of place; **sin ~ a dudas** without doubt, undoubtedly; **dar ~ a** to give rise to; **tener ~** to take place; **yo en su ~** if I were him; **lugar común** commonplace

lúgubre ['luɣuβre] *adj* mournful

lujo ['luxo] *nm* luxury; (*fig*) profusion, abundance; **de ~** luxury *cpd*, de luxe; **lujoso, -a** *adj* luxurious

lujuria [lu'xurja] *nf* lust

lumbre ['lumbre] *nf* fire; (*para cigarrillo*) light

luminoso, -a [lumi'noso, a] *adj* luminous, shining

luna ['luna] *nf* moon; (*de un espejo*) glass; (*de gafas*) lens; (*fig*) crescent; **estar en la ~** to have one's head in the clouds; **luna de miel** honeymoon; **luna llena/nueva** full/new moon

lunar [lu'nar] *adj* lunar ▷ *nm* (Anat) mole; **tela de ~es** spotted material

lunes ['lunes] *nm inv* Monday

lupa ['lupa] *nf* magnifying glass

lustre ['lustre] *nm* polish; (*fig*) lustre; **dar ~ a** to polish

luto ['luto] *nm* mourning; **llevar el o vestirse de ~** to be in mourning

Luxemburgo [luksem'burxo] *nm* Luxembourg

luz [luθ] (*pl* **luces**) *nf* light; **dar a ~ un niño** to give birth to a child; **sacar a la ~** to bring to light; **dar o encender** (ESP) **o prender** (LAM)**/apagar la ~** to switch the light on/off; **tener pocas luces** to be dim o stupid; **traje de luces** bullfighter's costume; **luces de tráfico** traffic lights; **luz de freno** brake light; **luz roja/verde** red/green light

m

m *abr* (= *metro*) m; (= *minuto*) m

macana [ma'kana] (MÉX) *nf* truncheon (BRIT), billy club (US)

macarrones [maka'rrones] *nmpl* macaroni *sg*

macedonia [maθe'ðonja] *nf* (*tb*: **~ de frutas**) fruit salad

maceta [ma'θeta] *nf* (*de flores*) pot of flowers; (*para plantas*) flowerpot

machacar [matʃa'kar] *vt* to crush, pound ▷ *vi* (*insistir*) to go on, keep on

machete [ma'tʃete] *nm* machete, (large) knife

machetear [matʃete'ar] (MÉX) *vt* to swot (BRIT), grind away (US)

machismo [ma'tʃismo] *nm* male chauvinism; **machista** *adj, nm* sexist

macho ['matʃo] *adj* male; (*fig*) virile ▷ *nm* male; (*fig*) he-man

macizo, -a [ma'θiθo, a] *adj* (*grande*) massive; (*fuerte, sólido*) solid ▷ *nm* mass, chunk

madeja [ma'ðexa] *nf* (*de lana*) skein, hank; (*de pelo*) mass, mop

madera [ma'ðera] *nf* wood; (*fig*) nature, character; **una ~** a piece of wood

madrastra [ma'ðrastra] *nf* stepmother

madre ['maðre] *adj* mother *cpd* ▷ *nf* mother; (*de vino etc*) dregs *pl*; **madre política/soltera** mother-in-law/unmarried mother

Madrid [ma'ðrið] *n* Madrid

madriguera [maðri'xera] *nf* burrow

madrileño, -a [maðri'leɲo, a] *adj* of o from Madrid ▷ *nm/f* native of Madrid

madrina [ma'ðrina] *nf* godmother; (*Arq*) prop, shore; (*Tec*) brace; (*de boda*) bridesmaid

madrugada [maðru'xaða] *nf* early morning; (*alba*) dawn, daybreak

madrugador, a [maðruxa'ðor, a] *adj* early-rising

madrugar [maðru'xar] *vi* to get up early; (*fig*) to get ahead

madurar [maðu'rar] *vt, vi* (*fruta*) to ripen; (*fig*) to mature; **madurez** *nf* ripeness; maturity; **maduro, -a** *adj* ripe; mature

maestra *nf* V **maestro**

maestría [maes'tria] *nf* mastery; (*habilidad*) skill, expertise

maestro, -a [ma'estro, a] *adj* masterly; (*principal*) main ▷ *nm/f* master/mistress; (*profesor*) teacher ▷ *nm* (*autoridad*) authority; (*Mús*) maestro; (*experto*) master; **maestro albañil** master mason

magdalena [maxða'lena] *nf* fairy cake

magia ['maxja] *nf* magic; **mágico, -a** *adj* magic(al) ▷ *nm/f* magician

magisterio [maxis'terjo] *nm* (*enseñanza*) teaching; (*profesión*) teaching profession; (*maestros*) teachers *pl*

magistrado [maxis'traðo] *nm* magistrate

magistral [maxis'tral] *adj* magisterial; (*fig*) masterly

magnate [max'nate] *nm* magnate, tycoon

magnético, -a [max'netiko, a] *adj* magnetic

magnetofón [maxneto'fon] *nm* tape recorder

magnetófono [maxne'tofono] *nm* = **magnetofón**

magnífico, -a [max'nifiko, a] *adj* splendid, magnificent

magnitud [maxni'tuð] *nf* magnitude

mago, -a ['maxo, a] *nm/f* magician; **los Reyes M~s** the Three Wise Men

magro, -a ['maxro, a] *adj* (*carne*) lean

mahonesa [mao'nesa] *nf* mayonnaise

maître ['metre] *nm* head waiter

maíz [ma'iθ] *nm* maize (BRIT), corn (US); sweet corn

majestad [maxes'tað] *nf* majesty

majo, -a ['maxo, a] *adj* nice; (*guapo*) attractive, good-looking; (*elegante*) smart

mal [mal] *adv* badly; (*equivocadamente*) wrongly ▷ *adj* = **malo** ▷ *nm* evil; (*desgracia*) misfortune; (*daño*) harm, damage; (*Med*) illness; **~ que bien** rightly or wrongly; **ir de ~ en peor** to get worse and worse

malabarista [malaβa'rista] *nmf* juggler

malaria [ma'larja] *nf* malaria

malcriado, -a [mal'krjaðo, a] *adj* spoiled

maldad [mal'dað] *nf* evil, wickedness

maldecir [malde'θir] *vt* to curse

maldición [maldi'θjon] *nf* curse

maldito, -a [mal'dito, a] *adj* (*condenado*) damned; (*perverso*) wicked; **¡~ sea!** damn it!

malecón [male'kon] (LAM) *nm* sea front,

promenade

maleducado, -a [maleðu'kaðo, a] *adj* bad-mannered, rude

malentendido [malenten'diðo] *nm* misunderstanding

malestar [males'tar] *nm* (*gen*) discomfort; (*fig: inquietud*) uneasiness; (*Pol*) unrest

maleta [ma'leta] *nf* case, suitcase; (*Auto*) boot (BRIT), trunk (US); **hacer las ~s** to pack; **maletero** *nm* (*Auto*) boot (BRIT), trunk (US); **maletín** *nm* small case, bag

maleza [ma'leθa] *nf* (*malas hierbas*) weeds *pl*; (*arbustos*) thicket

malgastar [malɣas'tar] *vt* (*tiempo, dinero*) to waste; (*salud*) to ruin

malhechor, a [male'tʃor, a] *nm/f* delinquent

malhumorado, -a [malumo'raðo, a] *adj* bad-tempered

malicia [ma'liθja] *nf* (*maldad*) wickedness; (*astucia*) slyness, guile; (*mala intención*) malice, spite; (*carácter travieso*) mischievousness

maligno, -a [ma'liɣno, a] *adj* evil; (*malévolo*) malicious; (*Med*) malignant

malla ['maʎa] *nf* mesh; (*de baño*) swimsuit; (*de ballet, gimnasia*) leotard; **mallas** *nfpl* tights; **malla de alambre** wire mesh

Mallorca [ma'ʎorka] *nf* Majorca

malo, -a ['malo, a] *adj* bad, false ▷ *nm/f* villain; **estar ~** to be ill

malograr [malo'ɣrar] *vt* to spoil; (*plan*) to upset; (*ocasión*) to waste

malparado, -a [malpa'raðo, a] *adj*: **salir ~** to come off badly

malpensado, -a [malpen'saðo, a] *adj* nasty

malteada [malte'aða] (LAM) *nf* milkshake

maltratar [maltra'tar] *vt* to ill-treat, mistreat

malvado, -a [mal'βaðo, a] *adj* evil, villainous

Malvinas [mal'βinas] *nfpl* (*tb:* **Islas ~**) Falklands, Falkland Islands

mama ['mama] *nf* (*de animal*) teat; (*de mujer*) breast

mamá [ma'ma] (*pl* **~s**) (*fam*) *nf* mum, mummy

mamar [ma'mar] *vt*, *vi* to suck

mamarracho [mama'rratʃo] *nm* sight, mess

mameluco [mame'luko] (RPL) *nm* dungarees *pl* (BRIT), overalls *pl* (US)

mamífero [ma'mifero] *nm* mammal

mampara [mam'para] *nf* (*entre habitaciones*) partition; (*biombo*) screen

mampostería [mamposte'ria] *nf* masonry

manada [ma'naða] *nf* (*Zool*) herd; (*: de leones*) pride; (*: de lobos*) pack

manantial [manan'tjal] *nm* spring

mancha ['mantʃa] *nf* stain, mark; (*Zool*) patch; **manchar** *vt* (*gen*) to stain, mark; (*ensuciar*) to soil, dirty

manchego, -a [man'tʃeɣo, a] *adj* of o from La Mancha

manco, -a ['manko, a] *adj* (*de un brazo*) one-armed; (*de una mano*) one-handed; (*fig*) defective, faulty

mancuernas [man'kwernas] (MÉX) *nfpl* cufflinks

mandado [man'daðo] (LAM) *nm* errand

mandamiento [manda'mjento] *nm* (*orden*) order, command; (*Rel*) commandment

mandar [man'dar] *vt* (*ordenar*) to order; (*dirigir*) to lead, command; (*enviar*) to send; (*pedir*) to order, ask for ▷ *vi* to be in charge; (*pey*) to be bossy; **¿mande?** (MÉX: ¿*cómo dice?*) pardon?, excuse me?; **~ hacer un traje** to have a suit made

mandarina [manda'rina] (ESP) *nf* tangerine, mandarin (orange)

mandato [man'dato] *nm* (*orden*) order; (*Pol: período*) term of office; (*: territorio*) mandate

mandíbula [man'diβula] *nf* jaw

mandil [man'dil] *nm* apron

mando ['mando] *nm* (*Mil*) command; (*de país*) rule; (*el primer lugar*) lead; (*Pol*) term of office; (*Tec*) control; **~ a la izquierda** left-hand drive; **mando a distancia** remote control

mandón, -ona [man'don, ona] *adj* bossy, domineering

manejar [mane'xar] *vt* to manage; (*máquina*) to work, operate; (*caballo etc*) to handle; (*casa*) to run, manage; (LAM: *coche*) to drive; **manejarse** *vr* (*comportarse*) to act, behave; (*arreglárselas*) to manage; **manejo** *nm* (*de bicicleta*) handling; (*de negocio*) management, running; (LAM *Auto*) driving; (*facilidad de trato*) ease, confidence; **manejos** *nmpl* (*intrigas*) intrigues

manera [ma'nera] *nf* way, manner, fashion; **maneras** *nfpl* (*modales*) manners; **su ~ de ser** the way he is; (*aire*) his manner; **de ninguna ~** no way, by no means; **de otra ~** otherwise; **de todas ~s** at any rate; **no hay ~ de persuadirle** there's no way of convincing him

manga ['manga] *nf* (*de camisa*) sleeve; (*de riego*) hose

mango ['mango] *nm* handle; (*Bot*) mango

manguera [man'gera] *nf* hose

maní [ma'ni] (LAM) *nm* peanut

m

manía [ma'nia] nf (Med) mania; (fig: moda) rage, craze; (disgusto) dislike; (malicia) spite; **coger ~ a algn** to take a dislike to sb; **tener ~ a algn** to dislike sb; **maníaco, -a** adj maniac(al) ▷ nm/f maniac

maniático, -a [ma'njatiko, a] adj maniac(al) ▷ nm/f maniac

manicomio [mani'komjo] nm mental hospital (BRIT), insane asylum (US)

manifestación [manifesta'θjon] nf (declaración) statement, declaration; (de emoción) show, display; (Pol: desfile) demonstration; (: concentración) mass meeting

manifestar [manifes'tar] vt to show, manifest; (declarar) to state, declare; **manifiesto, -a** adj clear, manifest ▷ nm manifesto

manillar [mani'ʎar] nm handlebars pl

maniobra [ma'njoβra] nf manoeuvre; **maniobras** nfpl (Mil) manoeuvres; **maniobrar** vt to manoeuvre

manipulación [manipula'θjon] nf manipulation

manipular [manipu'lar] vt to manipulate; (manejar) to handle

maniquí [mani'ki] nm dummy ▷ nmf model

manivela [mani'βela] nf crank

manjar [man'xar] nm (tasty) dish

mano ['mano] nf hand; (Zool) foot, paw; (de pintura) coat; (serie) lot, series; **a ~** by hand; **a ~ derecha/izquierda** on the right(-hand side)/left(-hand side); **de primera ~** (at) first hand; **de segunda ~** (at) second hand; **robo a ~ armada** armed robbery; **estrechar la ~ a algn** to shake sb's hand; **mano de obra** labour, manpower; **manos libres** adj inv (teléfono, dispositivo) hands-free ▷ nm inv hands-free kit

manojo [ma'noxo] nm handful, bunch; (de llaves) bunch

manopla [ma'nopla] nf mitten

manosear [manose'ar] vt (tocar) to handle, touch; (desordenar) to mess up, rumple; (insistir en) to overwork; (LAM: acariciar) to caress, fondle

manotazo [mano'taθo] nm slap, smack

mansalva [man'salβa] **a ~** adv indiscriminately

mansión [man'sjon] nf mansion

manso, -a ['manso, a] adj gentle, mild; (animal) tame

manta ['manta] (ESP) nf blanket

manteca [man'teka] nf fat; (cs: mantequilla) butter; **manteca de cerdo** lard

mantecado [mante'kaðo] (ESP) nm Christmas sweet made from flour, almonds and lard

mantel [man'tel] nm tablecloth

mantendré etc vb V **mantener**

mantener [mante'ner] vt to support, maintain; (alimentar) to sustain; (conservar) to keep; (Tec) to maintain, service; **mantenerse** vr (seguir de pie) to be still standing; (no ceder) to hold one's ground; (subsistir) to sustain o.s., keep going; **mantenimiento** nm maintenance; sustenance; (sustento) support

mantequilla [mante'kiʎa] nf butter

mantilla [man'tiʎa] nf mantilla; **mantillas** nfpl (de bebé) baby clothes

manto ['manto] nm (capa) cloak; (de ceremonia) robe, gown

mantuve etc vb V **mantener**

manual [ma'nwal] adj manual ▷ nm manual, handbook

manuscrito, -a [manus'krito, a] adj handwritten ▷ nm manuscript

manutención [manuten'θjon] nf maintenance; (sustento) support

manzana [man'θana] nf apple; (Arq) block (of houses)

manzanilla [manθa'niʎa] nf (planta) camomile; (infusión) camomile tea

manzano [man'θano] nm apple tree

maña ['maɲa] nf (gen) skill, dexterity; (pey) guile; (destreza) trick, knack

mañana [ma'ɲana] adv tomorrow ▷ nm future ▷ nf morning; **de o por la ~** in the morning; **¡hasta ~!** see you tomorrow!; **~ por la ~** tomorrow morning

mapa ['mapa] nm map

maple ['maple] (LAM) nm maple

maqueta [ma'keta] nf (scale) model

maquiladora [makila'ðora] (MÉX) nf (Com) bonded assembly plant

maquillaje [maki'ʎaxe] nm make-up; (acto) making up

maquillar [maki'ʎar] vt to make up; **maquillarse** vr to put on (some) make-up

máquina ['makina] nf machine; (de tren) locomotive, engine; (Foto) camera; (fig) machinery; **escrito a ~** typewritten; **máquina de coser** sewing machine; **máquina de escribir** typewriter; **máquina fotográfica** camera

maquinaria [maki'narja] nf (máquinas) machinery; (mecanismo) mechanism, works pl

maquinilla [maki'niʎa] (ESP) nf (tb: **~ de afeitar**) razor

maquinista [maki'nista] nmf (de tren) engine driver; (Tec) operator; (Náut) engineer

mar [mar] nm of sea; **~ adentro** out at sea; **en alta ~** on the high seas; **la ~ de** (fam) lots of; **el Mar Negro/Báltico** the Black/Baltic Sea

maraña [ma'raɲa] nf (maleza) thicket; (confusión) tangle

maravilla [mara'βiʎa] nf marvel, wonder; (Bot) marigold; **maravillar** vt to astonish, amaze; **maravillarse** vr to be astonished, be amazed; **maravilloso, -a** adj wonderful, marvellous

marca ['marka] nf (gen) mark; (sello) stamp; (Com) make, brand; **de ~** excellent, outstanding; **marca de fábrica** trademark; **marca registrada** registered trademark

marcado, -a [mar'kaðo, a] adj marked, strong

marcador [marka'ðor] nm (Deporte) scoreboard; (: persona) scorer

marcapasos [marka'pasos] nm inv pacemaker

marcar [mar'kar] vt (gen) to mark; (número de teléfono) to dial; (gol) to score; (números) to record, keep a tally of; (pelo) to set ▷ vi (Deporte) to score; (Tel) to dial

marcha ['martʃa] nf march; (Tec) running, working; (Auto) gear; (velocidad) speed; (fig) progress; (dirección) course; **poner en ~** to put into gear; (fig) to set in motion, get going; **dar ~ atrás** to reverse, put into reverse; **estar en ~** to be under way, be in motion

marchar [mar'tʃar] vi (ir) to go; (funcionar) to work, go; **marcharse** vr to go (away), leave

marchitar [martʃi'tar] vt to wither, dry up; **marchitarse** vr (Bot) to wither; (fig) to fade away; **marchito, -a** adj withered, faded; (fig) in decline

marciano, -a [mar'θjano, a] adj, nm/f Martian

marco ['marko] nm frame; (moneda) mark; (fig) framework

marea [ma'rea] nf tide; **marea negra** oil slick

marear [mare'ar] vt (fig) to annoy, upset; (Med): **~ a algn** to make sb feel sick; **marearse** vr (tener náuseas) to feel sick; (desvanecerse) to feel faint; (aturdirse) to feel dizzy; (fam: emborracharse) to get tipsy

maremoto [mare'moto] nm tidal wave

mareo [ma'reo] nm (náusea) sick feeling; (en viaje) travel sickness; (aturdimiento) dizziness; (fam: lata) nuisance

marfil [mar'fil] nm ivory

margarina [marɣa'rina] nf margarine

margarita [marɣa'rita] nf (Bot) daisy; (Tip) daisywheel

margen ['marxen] nm (borde) edge, border; (fig) margin, space ▷ nf (de río etc) bank; **dar ~ para** to give an opportunity for; **mantenerse al ~** to keep out (of things)

marginar [marxi'nar] vt (socialmente) to marginalize, ostracize

mariachi [ma'rjatʃi] nm (persona) mariachi musician; (grupo) mariachi band

● **MARIACHI**
●
● Mariachi music is the musical style
● most characteristic of Mexico. From the
● state of Jalisco in the 19th century, this
● music spread rapidly throughout the
● country, until each region had its own
● particular style of the Mariachi "sound".
● A Mariachi band can be made up of
● several singers, up to eight violins, two
● trumpets, guitars, a "vihuela" (an old
● form of guitar), and a harp. The dance
● associated with this music is called the
● "zapateado".

marica [ma'rika] (fam) nm sissy

maricón [mari'kon] (fam) nm queer

marido [ma'riðo] nm husband

marihuana [mari'wana] nf marijuana, cannabis

marina [ma'rina] nf navy; **marina mercante** merchant navy

marinero, -a [mari'nero, a] adj sea cpd ▷ nm sailor, seaman

marino, -a [ma'rino, a] adj sea cpd, marine ▷ nm sailor

marioneta [marjo'neta] nf puppet

mariposa [mari'posa] nf butterfly

mariquita [mari'kita] nf ladybird (BRIT), ladybug (US)

marisco [ma'risko] (ESP) nm shellfish inv, seafood; **mariscos** (LAM) nmpl = **marisco**

marítimo, -a [ma'ritimo, a] adj sea cpd, maritime

mármol ['marmol] nm marble

marqués, -esa [mar'kes, esa] nm/f marquis/marchioness

marrón [ma'rron] adj brown

marroquí [marro'ki] adj, nmf Moroccan ▷ nm Morocco (leather)

Marruecos [ma'rrwekos] nm Morocco

martes ['martes] nm inv Tuesday; **~ y trece** ≈ Friday 13th

● **MARTES Y TRECE**
●
● According to Spanish superstition
● Tuesday is an unlucky day, even more so
● if it falls on the 13th of the month.

m

martillo [mar'tiʎo] *nm* hammer

mártir ['martir] *nmf* martyr; **martirio** *nm* martyrdom; (*fig*) torture, torment

marxismo [mark'sismo] *nm* Marxism

marzo ['marθo] *nm* March

○ **PALABRA CLAVE**

más [mas] *adj, adv* **1**: **más (que** *o* **de)** (*compar*) more (than), ...+ er (than); **más grande/inteligente** bigger/more intelligent; **trabaja más (que yo)** he works more (than me); V *tb* **cada**

2 (*superl*): **el más** the most, ...+ est; **el más grande/inteligente (de)** the biggest/most intelligent (in)

3 (*negativo*): **no tengo más dinero** I haven't got any more money; **no viene más por aquí** he doesn't come round here any more

4 (*adicional*): **no le veo más solución que ...** I see no other solution than to ...; **¿quién más?** anybody else?

5 (+ *adj: valor intensivo*): **¡qué perro más sucio!** what a filthy dog!; **¡es más tonto!** he's so stupid!

6 (*locuciones*): **más o menos** more or less; **los más** most people; **es más** furthermore; **más bien** rather; **¡qué más da!** what does it matter!; V *tb* **no**

7: **por más: por más que te esfuerces** no matter how hard you try; **por más que quisiera ...** much as I should like to ...

8: **de más: veo que aquí estoy de más** I can see I'm not needed here; **tenemos uno de más** we've got one extra ▷ *prep*: **2 más 2 son 4** 2 and 0 plus 2 are 4

▷ *nm inv*: **este trabajo tiene sus más y sus menos** this job's got its good points and its bad points

mas [mas] *conj* but

masa ['masa] *nf* (*mezcla*) dough; (*volumen*) volume, mass; (*Física*) mass; **en ~** en masse; **las ~s** (*Pol*) the masses

masacre [ma'sakre] *nf* massacre

masaje [ma'saxe] *nm* massage

máscara ['maskara] *nf* mask; **máscara antigás/de oxígeno** gas/oxygen mask; **mascarilla** *nf* (*de belleza, Med*) mask

masculino, -a [masku'lino, a] *adj* masculine; (*Bio*) male

masía [ma'sia] *nf* farmhouse

masivo, -a [ma'siβo, a] *adj* mass *cpd*

masoquista [maso'kista] *nmf* masochist

máster ['master] (*ESP*) *nm* master

masticar [masti'kar] *vt* to chew

mástil ['mastil] *nm* (*de navío*) mast; (*de guitarra*) neck

mastín [mas'tin] *nm* mastiff

masturbarse [mastur'βarse] *vr* to masturbate

mata ['mata] *nf* (*arbusto*) bush, shrub; (*de hierba*) tuft

matadero [mata'ðero] *nm* slaughterhouse, abattoir

matamoscas [mata'moskas] *nm inv* (*pala*) fly swat

matanza [ma'tanθa] *nf* slaughter

matar [ma'tar] *vt, vi* to kill; **matarse** *vr* (*suicidarse*) to kill o.s., commit suicide; (*morir*) to be *o* get killed; **~ el hambre** to stave off hunger

matasellos [mata'seʎos] *nm inv* postmark

mate ['mate] *adj* matt ▷ *nm* (*en ajedrez*) (check)mate; (*LAM: hierba*) maté; (: *vasija*) gourd

matemáticas [mate'matikas] *nfpl* mathematics; **matemático, -a** *adj* mathematical ▷ *nm/f* mathematician

materia [ma'terja] *nf* (*gen*) matter; (*Tec*) material; (*Escol*) subject; **en ~ de** on the subject of; **materia prima** raw material; **material** *adj* material ▷ *nm* material; (*Tec*) equipment; **materialista** *adj* materialist(ic); **materialmente** *adv* materially; (*fig*) absolutely

maternal [mater'nal] *adj* motherly, maternal

maternidad [materni'ðað] *nf* motherhood, maternity; **materno, -a** *adj* maternal; (*lengua*) mother *cpd*

matinal [mati'nal] *adj* morning *cpd*

matiz [ma'tiθ] *nm* shade; **matizar** *vt* (*variar*) to vary; (*Arte*) to blend; **matizar de** to tinge with

matón [ma'ton] *nm* bully

matorral [mato'rral] *nm* thicket

matrícula [ma'trikula] *nf* (*registro*) register; (*Auto*) registration number; (: *placa*) number plate; **matrícula de honor** (*Univ*) top marks in a subject at university with the right to free registration the following year; **matricular** *vt* to register, enrol

matrimonio [matri'monjo] *nm* (*pareja*) (married) couple; (*unión*) marriage

matriz [ma'triθ] *nf* (*Anat*) womb; (*Tec*) mould

matrona [ma'trona] *nf* (*persona de edad*) matron; (*comadrona*) midwife

matufia [ma'tufja] (*RPL: fam*) *nf* put-up job

maullar [mau'ʎar] *vi* to mew, miaow

maxilar [maksi'lar] *nm* jaw(bone)

máxima ['maksima] *nf* maxim

máximo, -a ['maksimo, a] *adj*

maximum; (*más alto*) highest; (*más grande*) greatest ▷ *nm* maximum; **como ~** at most
mayo ['majo] *nm* May
mayonesa [majo'nesa] *nf* mayonnaise
mayor [ma'jor] *adj* main, chief; (*adulto*) adult; (*de edad avanzada*) elderly; (*Mús*) major; (*compar: de tamaño*) bigger; (: *de edad*) older; (*superl: de tamaño*) biggest; (: *de edad*) oldest ▷ *nm* (*adulto*) adult; **mayores** *nmpl* (*antepasados*) ancestors; **al por ~** wholesale; **mayor de edad** adult
mayoral [majo'ral] *nm* foreman
mayordomo [major'ðomo] *nm* butler
mayoría [majo'ria] *nf* majority, greater part
mayorista [majo'rista] *nmf* wholesaler
mayoritario, -a [majori'tarjo, a] *adj* majority *cpd*
mayúscula [ma'juskula] *nf* capital letter
mazapán [maθa'pan] *nm* marzipan
mazo ['maθo] *nm* (*martillo*) mallet; (*de flores*) bunch; (*Deporte*) bat
me [me] *pron* (*directo*) me; (*indirecto*) (to) me; (*reflexivo*) (to) myself; **¡dá~lo!** give it to me!
mear [me'ar] (*fam*) *vi* to pee, piss (!)
mecánica [me'kanika] *nf* (*Escol*) mechanics *sg*; (*mecanismo*) mechanism; *V tb* **mecánico**
mecánico, -a [me'kaniko, a] *adj* mechanical ▷ *nm/f* mechanic
mecanismo [meka'nismo] *nm* mechanism; (*marcha*) gear
mecanografía [mekanoɣra'fia] *nf* typewriting; **mecanógrafo, -a** *nm/f* typist
mecate [me'kate] (*MÉX, CAM*) *nm* rope
mecedora [meθe'ðora] *nf* rocking chair
mecer [me'θer] *vt* (*cuna*) to rock; **mecerse** *vr* to rock; (*rama*) to sway
mecha ['metʃa] *nf* (*de vela*) wick; (*de bomba*) fuse
mechero [me'tʃero] *nm* (cigarette) lighter
mechón [me'tʃon] *nm* (*gen*) tuft; (*de pelo*) lock
medalla [me'ðaʎa] *nf* medal
media ['meðja] *nf* stocking; (*LAM: calcetín*) sock; (*promedio*) average
mediado, -a [me'ðjaðo, a] *adj* half-full; (*trabajo*) half-completed; **a ~s de** in the middle of, halfway through
mediano, -a [me'ðjano, a] *adj* (*regular*) medium, average; (*mediocre*) mediocre
medianoche [meðja'notʃe] *nf* midnight
mediante [me'ðjante] *adv* by (means of), through
mediar [me'ðjar] *vi* (*interceder*) to mediate, intervene
medicamento [meðika'mento] *nm* medicine, drug
medicina [meði'θina] *nf* medicine
médico, -a ['meðiko, a] *adj* medical ▷ *nm/f*
medida [me'ðiða] *nf* measure; (*medición*) measurement; (*prudencia*) moderation, prudence; **en cierta/gran ~** up to a point/ to a great extent; **un traje a la ~** a made-to-measure suit; **~ de cuello** collar size; **a ~ de** in proportion to; (*de acuerdo con*) in keeping with; **a ~ que** (*conforme*) as; **medidor** (*LAM*) *nm* meter
medio, -a ['meðjo, a] *adj* half (a); (*punto*) mid, middle; (*promedio*) average ▷ *adv* half ▷ *nm* (*centro*) middle, centre; (*promedio*) average; (*método*) means, way; (*ambiente*) environment; **medios** *nmpl*, means, resources; **~ litro** half a litre; **las tres y media** half past three; **a ~ terminar** half finished; **pagar a medias** to share the cost; **medio ambiente** environment; **medio de transporte** means of transport; **Medio Oriente** Middle East; **medios de comunicación** media; **medioambiental** *adj* (*política, efectos*) environmental
mediocre [me'ðjokre] *adj* mediocre
mediodía [meðjo'ðia] *nm* midday, noon
medir [me'ðir] *vt, vi* (*gen*) to measure
meditar [meði'tar] *vt* to ponder, think over, meditate on; (*planear*) to think out
mediterráneo, -a [meðite'rraneo, a] *adj* Mediterranean ▷ *nm*: **el M~** the Mediterranean
médula ['meðula] *nf* (*Anat*) marrow; **médula espinal** spinal cord
medusa [me'ðusa] (*ESP*) *nf* jellyfish
megáfono [me'ɣafono] *nm* megaphone
megapíxel [meɣa'piksel] (*pl* **megapixels** *or* **~es**) *nm* megapixel
mejilla [me'xiʎa] *nf* cheek
mejillón [mexi'ʎon] *nm* mussel
mejor [me'xor] *adj, adv* (*compar*) better; (*superl*) best; **a lo ~** probably; (*quizá*) maybe; **~ dicho** rather; **tanto ~** so much the better
mejora [me'xora] *nf* improvement; **mejorar** *vt* to improve, make better ▷ *vi* to improve, get better; **mejorarse** *vr* to improve, get better
melancólico, -a [melan'koliko, a] *adj* (*triste*) sad, melancholy; (*soñador*) dreamy
melena [me'lena] *nf* (*de persona*) long hair; (*Zool*) mane
mellizo, -a [me'ʎiθo, a] *adj, nm/f* twin
melocotón [meloko'ton] (*ESP*) *nm* peach
melodía [melo'ðia] *nf* melody, tune
melodrama [melo'ðrama] *nm* melodrama; **melodramático, -a** *adj* melodramatic

m

melón [me'lon] *nm* melon
membrete [mem'brete] *nm* letterhead
membrillo [mem'briʎo] *nm* quince;
(**carne de**) **~** quince jelly
memoria [me'morja] *nf* (*gen*) memory;
memorias *nfpl* (*de autor*) memoirs;
memorizar *vt* to memorize
menaje [me'naxe] *nm* (*tb:* **artículos de ~**)
household items
mencionar [menθjo'nar] *vt* to mention
mendigo, -a [men'diɣo, a] *nm/f* beggar
menear [mene'ar] *vt* to move; **menearse**
vr to shake; (*balancearse*) to sway; (*moverse*)
to move; (*fig*) to get a move on
menestra [me'nestra] *nf* (*tb:* **~ de
verduras**) vegetable stew
menopausia [meno'pausja] *nf*
menopause
menor [me'nor] *adj* (*más pequeño: compar*)
smaller; (: *superl*) smallest; (*más
joven: compar*) younger; (: *superl*) youngest;
(*Mús*) minor ▷ *nmf* (*joven*) young person,
juvenile; **no tengo la ~ idea** I haven't the
faintest idea; **al por ~** retail; **menor de edad**
person under age
Menorca [me'norka] *nf* Minorca

○ **PALABRA CLAVE**

menos [menos] *adj* **1**: **menos (que** *o* **de)**
(*compar: cantidad*) less (than); (: *número*)
fewer (than); **con menos entusiasmo**
with less enthusiasm; **menos gente** fewer
people; *V tb* **cada**
2 (*superl*): **es el que menos culpa tiene** he is
the least to blame
▷ *adv* **1** (*compar*): **menos (que** *o* **de)** less
(than); **me gusta menos que el otro** I like it
less than the other one
2 (*superl*): **es el menos listo (de su clase)**
he's the least bright in his class; **de todas
ellas es la que menos me agrada** out of all
of them she's the one I like least
3 (*locuciones*): **no quiero verle y menos
visitarle** I don't want to see him, let alone
visit him; **tenemos siete de menos** we're
seven short; **(por) lo menos** at (the very)
least; **¡menos mal!** thank goodness!
▷ *prep* except; (*cifras*) minus; **todos menos
él** everyone except (for) him; **5 menos 2** 5
minus 2
▷ *conj*: **a menos que: a menos que venga
mañana** unless he comes tomorrow

menospreciar [menospre'θjar] *vt* to
underrate, undervalue; (*despreciar*) to scorn,
despise
mensaje [men'saxe] *nm* message; **enviar**

un ~ a algn (*por móvil*) to text sb, send sb
a text message; **mensaje de texto** text
message; **mensajero, -a** *nm/f* messenger
menso, -a ['menso, a] (*MÉX: fam*) *adj*
stupid
menstruación [menstrua'θjon] *nf*
menstruation
mensual [men'swal] *adj* monthly; **100
euros ~es** 100 euros a month; **mensualidad**
nf (*salario*) monthly salary; (*Com*) monthly
payment, monthly instalment
menta ['menta] *nf* mint
mental [men'tal] *adj* mental; **mentalidad**
nf mentality; **mentalizar** *vt* (*sensibilizar*) to
make aware; (*convencer*) to convince; (*padres*)
to prepare (mentally); **mentalizarse**
vr (*concienciarse*) to become aware;
mentalizarse (de) to get used to the idea
(of); **mentalizarse de que ...** (*convencerse*)
to get it into one's head that ...
mente ['mente] *nf* mind
mentir [men'tir] *vi* to lie
mentira [men'tira] *nf* (*una mentira*) lie;
(*acto*) lying; (*invención*) fiction; **parece
mentira que ...** it seems incredible that
..., I can't believe that ...; **mentiroso, -a**
[menti'roso, a] *adj* lying ▷ *nm/f* liar
menú [me'nu] (*pl* **~s**) *nm* menu; **menú del
día** set menu; **menú turístico** tourist menu
menudencias [menu'ðenθjas] (*LAM*)
nfpl giblets
menudo, -a [me'nuðo, a] *adj* (*pequeño*)
small, tiny; (*sin importancia*) petty,
insignificant; **¡~ negocio!** (*fam*) some deal!;
a ~ often, frequently
meñique [me'ɲike] *nm* little finger
mercadillo [merka'ðiʎo] (*ESP*) *nm* flea
market
mercado [mer'kaðo] *nm* market;
mercado de pulgas (*LAM*) flea market
mercancía [merkan'θia] *nf* commodity;
mercancías *nfpl* goods, merchandise *sg*
mercenario, -a [merθe'narjo, a] *adj, nm*
mercenary
mercería [merθe'ria] *nf* haberdashery
(*BRIT*), notions *pl* (*US*); (*tienda*) haberdasher's
(*BRIT*), notions store (*US*)
mercurio [mer'kurjo] *nm* mercury
merecer [mere'θer] *vt* to deserve, merit
▷ *vi* to be deserving, be worthy; **merece
la pena** it's worthwhile; **merecido, -a** *adj*
(well) deserved; **llevar su merecido** to get
one's deserts
merendar [meren'dar] *vt* to have for
tea ▷ *vi* to have tea; (*en el campo*) to have a
picnic; **merendero** *nm* open-air cafe
merengue [me'renge] *nm* meringue
meridiano [meri'ðjano] *nm* (*Geo*)

meridian

merienda [me'rjenda] nf (light) tea, afternoon snack; (de campo) picnic

mérito ['merito] nm merit; (valor) worth, value

merluza [mer'luθa] nf hake

mermelada [merme'laða] nf jam

mero, -a ['mero, a] adj mere; (MÉX, CAM: fam) very

merodear [meroðe'ar] vi: ~ **por** to prowl about

mes [mes] nm month

mesa ['mesa] nf table; (de trabajo) desk; (Geo) plateau; **poner/quitar la** ~ to lay/clear the table; **mesa electoral** officials in charge of a polling station; **mesa redonda** (reunión) round table; **mesero, -a** (LAM) nm/f waiter/ waitress

meseta [me'seta] nf (Geo) plateau, tableland

mesilla [me'siʎa] nf (tb: ~ **de noche**) bedside table

mesón [me'son] nm inn

mestizo, -a [mes'tiθo, a] adj half-caste, of mixed race ⊳ nm/f half-caste

meta ['meta] nf goal; (de carrera) finish

metabolismo [metaβo'lismo] nm metabolism

metáfora [me'tafora] nf metaphor

metal [me'tal] nm (materia) metal; (Mús) brass; **metálico, -a** adj metallic; (de metal) metal ⊳ nm (dinero contante) cash

meteorología [meteorolo'xia] nf meteorology

meter [me'ter] vt (colocar) to put, place; (introducir) to put in, insert; (involucrar) to involve; (causar) to make, cause; **meterse** vr: ~**se en** to go into, enter; (fig) to interfere in, meddle in; ~**se a** to start; ~**se a escritor** to become a writer; ~**se con uno** to provoke sb, pick a quarrel with sb

meticuloso, -a [metiku'loso, a] adj meticulous, thorough

metódico, -a [me'toðiko, a] adj methodical

método ['metoðo] nm method

metralleta [metra'ʎeta] nf sub-machine-gun

métrico, -a ['metriko, a] adj metric

metro ['metro] nm metre; (tren) underground (BRIT), subway (US)

metrosexual [metrosek'swal] adj, nm metrosexual

mexicano, -a [mexi'kano, a] adj, nm/f Mexican

México ['mexiko] nm Mexico; **Ciudad de ~** Mexico City

mezcla ['meθkla] nf mixture; **mezcladora** (MÉX) nf (tb: **mezcladora de cemento**) cement mixer; **mezclar** vt to mix (up); **mezclarse** vr to mix, mingle; **mezclarse en** to get mixed up in, get involved in

mezquino, -a [meθ'kino, a] adj mean

mezquita [meθ'kita] nf mosque

mg. abr (= miligramo) mg

mi [mi] adj pos my ⊳ nm (Mús) E

mí [mi] pron me; myself

mía pron V **mío**

michelín [mitʃe'lin] (fam) nm (de grasa) spare tyre

microbio [mi'kroβjo] nm microbe

micrófono [mi'krofono] nm microphone

microondas [mikro'ondas] nm inv (tb: **horno ~**) microwave (oven)

microscopio [mikro'skopjo] nm microscope

miedo ['mjeðo] nm fear; (nerviosismo) apprehension, nervousness; **tener ~** to be afraid; **de ~** wonderful, marvellous; **hace un frío de ~** (fam) it's terribly cold; **miedoso, -a** adj fearful, timid

miel [mjel] nf honey

miembro ['mjembro] nm limb; (socio) member; **miembro viril** penis

mientras ['mjentras] conj while; (duración) as long as ⊳ adv meanwhile; ~ **tanto** meanwhile

miércoles ['mjerkoles] nm inv Wednesday

mierda ['mjerða] (fam!) nf shit (!)

miga ['miɣa] nf crumb; (fig: meollo) essence; **hacer buenas ~s** (fam) to get on well

mil [mil] num thousand; **dos ~ libras** two thousand pounds

milagro [mi'laɣro] nm miracle; **milagroso, -a** adj miraculous

milésima [mi'lesima] nf (de segundo) thousandth

mili ['mili] (ESP: fam) nf: **hacer la ~** to do one's military service

milímetro [mi'limetro] nm millimetre

militante [mili'tante] adj militant

militar [mili'tar] adj military ⊳ nmf soldier ⊳ vi (Mil) to serve; (en un partido) to be a member

milla ['miʎa] nf mile

millar [mi'ʎar] nm thousand

millón [mi'ʎon] num million; **millonario, -a** nm/f millionaire

milusos [mi'lusos] (MÉX) nm inv odd-job man

mimar [mi'mar] vt to spoil, pamper

mimbre ['mimbre] nm wicker

mímica ['mimika] nf (para comunicarse) sign language; (imitación) mimicry

mimo ['mimo] nm (caricia) caress; (de niño)

spoiling; (*Teatro*) mime; (: *actor*) mime artist

mina ['mina] *nf* mine

mineral [mine'ral] *adj* mineral ▷ *nm* (Geo) mineral; (*mena*) ore

minero, -a [mi'nero, a] *adj* mining *cpd* ▷ *nm/f* miner

miniatura [minja'tura] *adj inv, nf* miniature

minidisco [mini'disko] *nm* MiniDisc®

minifalda [mini'falda] *nf* miniskirt

mínimo, -a ['minimo, a] *adj, nm* minimum

minino, -a [mi'nino, a] (*fam*) *nm/f* puss, pussy

ministerio [minis'terjo] *nm* Ministry; **Ministerio de Hacienda/de Asuntos Exteriores** Treasury (BRIT), Treasury Department (US)/Foreign Office (BRIT), State Department (US)

ministro, -a [mi'nistro, a] *nm/f* minister

minoría [mino'ria] *nf* minority

minúscula [mi'nuskula] *nf* small letter

minúsculo, -a [mi'nuskulo, a] *adj* tiny, minute

minusválido, -a [minus'βaliðo, a] *adj* (physically) handicapped ▷ *nm/f* (physically) handicapped person

minuta [mi'nuta] *nf* (*de comida*) menu

minutero [minu'tero] *nm* minute hand

minuto [mi'nuto] *nm* minute

mío, -a ['mio, a] *pron*: **el ~/la mía** mine; **un amigo ~** a friend of mine; **lo ~** what is mine

miope [mi'ope] *adj* short-sighted

mira ['mira] *nf* (*de arma*) sight(s) (*pl*); (*fig*) aim, intention

mirada [mi'raða] *nf* look, glance; (*expresión*) look, expression; **clavar la ~ en** to stare at; **echar una ~ a** to glance at

mirado, -a [mi'raðo, a] *adj* (*sensato*) sensible; (*considerado*) considerate; **bien/ mal ~** (*estimado*) well/not well thought of; **bien ~...** all things considered...

mirador [mira'ðor] *nm* viewpoint, vantage point

mirar [mi'rar] *vt* to look at; (*observar*) to watch; (*considerar*) to consider, think over; (*vigilar, cuidar*) to watch, look after ▷ *vi* to look; (*Arq*) to face; **mirarse** *vr* (*dos personas*) to look at each other; **~ bien/mal** to think highly of/have a poor opinion of; **~se al espejo** to look at o.s. in the mirror

mirilla [mi'riλa] *nf* spyhole, peephole

mirlo ['mirlo] *nm* blackbird

misa ['misa] *nf* mass

miserable [mise'raβle] *adj* (*avaro*) mean, stingy; (*nimio*) miserable, paltry; (*lugar*) squalid; (*fam*) vile, despicable ▷ *nmf* (*malvado*) rogue

miseria [mi'serja] *nf* (*pobreza*) poverty; (*tacañería*) meanness, stinginess; (*condiciones*) squalor; **una ~** a pittance

misericordia [miseri'korðja] *nf* (*compasión*) compassion, pity; (*piedad*) mercy

misil [mi'sil] *nm* missile

misión [mi'sjon] *nf* mission; **misionero, -a** *nm/f* missionary

mismo, -a ['mismo, a] *adj* (*semejante*) same; (*después de pron*) -self; (*para énfasis*) very ▷ *adv*: **aquí/hoy ~** right here/this very day; **ahora ~** right now ▷ *conj*: **lo ~ que** just like *o* as; **el ~ traje** the same suit; **en ese ~ momento** at that very moment; **vino el ~ ministro** the minister himself came; **yo ~ lo vi** I saw it myself; **lo ~** the same (thing); **da lo ~** it's all the same; **quedamos en las mismas** we're no further forward; **por lo ~** for the same reason

misterio [mis'terjo] *nm* mystery; **misterioso, -a** *adj* mysterious

mitad [mi'tað] *nf* (*medio*) half; (*centro*) middle; **a ~ de precio** (at) half-price; **en** *o* **a ~ del camino** halfway along the road; **cortar por la ~** to cut through the middle

mitin ['mitin] (*pl* **mítines**) *nm* meeting

mito ['mito] *nm* myth

mixto, -a ['miksto, a] *adj* mixed

ml. *abr* (= *mililitro*) ml

mm. *abr* (= *milímetro*) mm

mobiliario [moβi'ljarjo] *nm* furniture

mochila [mo'tʃila] *nf* rucksack (BRIT), back-pack

moco ['moko] *nm* mucus; **mocos** *nmpl* (*fam*) snot; **limpiarse los ~s de la nariz** (*fam*) to wipe one's nose

moda ['moða] *nf* fashion; (*estilo*) style; **a la** *o* **de ~** in fashion, fashionable; **pasado de ~** out of fashion

modales [mo'ðales] *nmpl* manners

modelar [moðe'lar] *vt* to model

modelo [mo'ðelo] *adj inv, nmf* model

módem ['moðem] *nm* (*Inform*) modem

moderado, -a [moðe'raðo, a] *adj* moderate

moderar [moðe'rar] *vt* to moderate; (*violencia*) to restrain, control; (*velocidad*) to reduce; **moderarse** *vr* to restrain o.s., control o.s.

modernizar [moðerni'θar] *vt* to modernize

moderno, -a [mo'ðerno, a] *adj* modern; (*actual*) present-day

modestia [mo'ðestja] *nf* modesty; **modesto, -a** *adj* modest

modificar [moðifi'kar] *vt* to modify

modisto, -a [mo'ðisto, a] *nm/f* (*diseñador*) couturier, designer; (*que confecciona*) dressmaker

modo ['moðo] nm way, manner; (Mús) mode; **modos** nmpl manners; **de ningún ~** in no way; **de todos ~s** at any rate; **modo de empleo** directions pl (for use)

mofarse [mo'farse] vr: **~ de** to mock, scoff at

mofle ['mofle] (MÉX, CAM) nm silencer (BRIT), muffler (US)

mogollón [moɣo'ʎon] (ESP: fam) adv a hell of a lot

moho ['moo] nm mould, mildew; (en metal) rust

mojar [mo'xar] vt to wet; (humedecer) to damp(en), moisten; (calar) to soak; **mojarse** vr to get wet

molcajete [molka'xete] (MÉX) nm mortar

molde ['molde] nm mould; (Costura) pattern; (fig) model; **moldeado** nm soft perm; **moldear** vt to mould

mole ['mole] nf mass, bulk; (edificio) pile

moler [mo'ler] vt to grind, crush

molestar [moles'tar] vt to bother; (fastidiar) to annoy; (incomodar) to inconvenience, put out ▷ vi to be a nuisance; **molestarse** vr to bother; (incomodarse) to go to trouble; (ofenderse) to take offence; **¿(no) te molesta si ...?** do you mind if ...?

▌ No confundir **molestar** con la palabra inglesa molest.

molestia [mo'lestja] nf bother, trouble; (incomodidad) inconvenience; (Med) discomfort; **es una ~** it's a nuisance; **molesto, -a** adj (que fastidia) annoying; (incómodo) inconvenient; (inquieto) uncomfortable, ill at ease; (enfadado) annoyed

molido, -a [mo'liðo, a] adj: **estar ~** (fig) to be exhausted o dead beat

molinillo [moli'niʎo] nm hand mill; **molinillo de café** coffee grinder

molino [mo'lino] nm (edificio) mill; (máquina) grinder

momentáneo, -a [momen'taneo, a] adj momentary

momento [mo'mento] nm moment; **de ~** at o for the moment

momia ['momja] nf mummy

monarca [mo'narka] nmf monarch, ruler; **monarquía** nf monarchy

monasterio [monas'terjo] nm monastery

mondar [mon'dar] vt to peel; **mondarse** vr (ESP): **~se de risa** (fam) to split one's sides laughing

mondongo [mon'dongo] (LAM) nm tripe

moneda [mo'neða] nf (tipo de dinero) currency, money; (pieza) coin; **una ~ de 2 euros** a 2 euro piece; **monedero** nm purse

monitor, a [moni'tor, a] nm/f instructor, coach ▷ nm (TV) set; (Inform) monitor

monja ['monxa] nf nun

monje ['monxe] nm monk

mono, -a ['mono, a] adj (bonito) lovely, pretty; (gracioso) nice, charming ▷ nm/f monkey, ape ▷ nm dungarees pl; (overoles) overalls pl

monopatín [monopa'tin] nm skateboard

monopolio [mono'poljo] nm monopoly; **monopolizar** vt to monopolize

monótono, -a [mo'notono, a] adj monotonous

monstruo ['monstrwo] nm monster ▷ adj inv fantastic; **monstruoso, -a** adj monstrous

montaje [mon'taxe] nm assembly; (Teatro) décor; (Cine) montage

montaña [mon'taɲa] nf (monte) mountain; (sierra) mountains pl, mountainous area; **montaña rusa** roller coaster; **montañero, -a** nm/f mountaineer; **montañismo** nm mountaineering

montar [mon'tar] vt (subir a) to mount, get on; (Tec) to assemble, put together; (negocio) to set up; (arma) to cock; (colocar) to lift on to; (Culin) to beat ▷ vi to mount, get on; (sobresalir) to overlap; **~ en bicicleta** to ride a bicycle; **~ en cólera** to get angry; **~ a caballo** to ride, go horseriding

monte ['monte] nm (montaña) mountain; (bosque) woodland; (área sin cultivar) wild area, wild country; **monte de piedad** pawnshop

montón [mon'ton] nm heap, pile; (fig): **un ~ de** heaps o lots of

monumento [monu'mento] nm monument

moño ['moɲo] nm bun

moqueta [mo'keta] nf fitted carpet

mora ['mora] nf blackberry; V tb **moro**

morado, -a [mo'raðo, a] adj purple, violet ▷ nm bruise

moral [mo'ral] adj moral ▷ nf (ética) ethics pl; (moralidad) morals pl, morality; (ánimo) morale

moraleja [mora'lexa] nf moral

morboso, -a [mor'βoso, a] adj morbid

morcilla [mor'θiʎa] nf blood sausage ≈ black pudding (BRIT)

mordaza [mor'ðaθa] nf (para la boca) gag; (Tec) clamp

morder [mor'ðer] vt to bite; (fig: consumir) to eat away, eat into; **mordisco** nm bite

moreno, -a [mo'reno, a] adj (color) (dark) brown; (de tez) dark; (de pelo moreno) dark-

m

haired; (*negro*) black

morfina [mor'fina] *nf* morphine

moribundo, -a [mori'βundo, a] *adj*
dying

morir [mo'rir] *vi* to die; (*fuego*) to die
down; (*luz*) to go out; **morirse** *vr* to die;
(*fig*) to be dying; **murió en un accidente** he
was killed in an accident; **~se por algo** to be
dying for sth

moro, -a ['moro, a] *adj* Moorish ▷ *nm/f*
Moor

moroso, -a [mo'roso, a] *nm/f* bad debtor,
defaulter

morraña [mo'rraɲa] (*MÉX*) *nf* (*cambio*)
small o loose change

morro ['morro] *nm* (*Zool*) snout, nose;
(*Auto, Aviac*) nose

morsa ['morsa] *nf* walrus

mortadela [morta'ðela] *nf* mortadella

mortal [mor'tal] *adj* mortal; (*golpe*)
deadly; **mortalidad** *nf* mortality

mortero [mor'tero] *nm* mortar

mosca ['moska] *nf* fly

Moscú [mos'ku] *n* Moscow

mosquearse [moske'arse] (*fam*) *vr*
(*enojarse*) to get cross; (*ofenderse*) to take
offence

mosquitero [moski'tero] *nm* mosquito
net

mosquito [mos'kito] *nm* mosquito

mostaza [mos'taθa] *nf* mustard

mosto ['mosto] *nm* (unfermented) grape
juice

mostrador [mostra'ðor] *nm* (*de tienda*)
counter; (*de café*) bar

mostrar [mos'trar] *vt* to show; (*exhibir*)
to display, exhibit; (*explicar*) to explain;
mostrarse *vr*: **~se amable** to be kind;
to prove to be kind; **no se muestra muy
inteligente** he doesn't seem (to be) very
intelligent

mota ['mota] *nf* speck, tiny piece; (*en
diseño*) dot

mote ['mote] *nm* nickname

motín [mo'tin] *nm* (*del pueblo*) revolt,
rising; (*del ejército*) mutiny

motivar [moti'βar] *vt* (*causar*) to cause,
motivate; (*explicar*) to explain, justify;
motivo *nm* motive, reason

moto ['moto] (*fam*) *nf* = **motocicleta**

motocicleta [motoθi'kleta] *nf* motorbike
(*BRIT*), motorcycle

motoneta [moto'neta] (*cs*) *nf* scooter

motor [mo'tor] *nm* motor, engine; **motor
a chorro** o **de reacción/de explosión** jet
engine/internal combustion engine

motora [mo'tora] *nf* motorboat

movedizo, -a *adj* V **arena**

mover [mo'βer] *vt* to move; (*cabeza*) to
shake; (*accionar*) to drive; (*fig*) to cause,
provoke; **moverse** *vr* to move; (*fig*) to get
a move on

móvil ['moβil] *adj* mobile; (*pieza de
máquina*) moving; (*mueble*) movable ▷ *nm*
(*motivo*) motive; (*teléfono*) mobile

movimiento [moβi'mjento] *nm*
movement; (*Tec*) motion; (*actividad*) activity

mozo, -a ['moθo, a] *adj* (*joven*) young
▷ *nm/f* youth, young man/girl; (*cs: mesero*)
waiter/waitress

MP3 *nm* MP3; **reproductor (de) ~** MP3
player

mucama [mu'kama] (*RPL*) *nf* maid

muchacho, -a [mu'tʃatʃo, a] *nm/f* (*niño*)
boy/girl; (*criado*) servant; (*criada*) maid

muchedumbre [mutʃe'ðumbre] *nf*
crowd

Ｏ PALABRA CLAVE

mucho, -a ['mutʃo, a] *adj* **1** (*cantidad*) a
lot of, much; (*número*) lots of, a lot of, many;
mucho dinero a lot of money; **hace mucho
calor** it's very hot; **muchas amigas** lots o a
lot of friends

2 (*sg: grande*): **ésta es mucha casa para él**
this house is much too big for him

▷ *pron*: **tengo mucho que hacer** I've got
a lot to do; **muchos dicen que ...** a lot of
people say that ...; V *tb* **tener**

▷ *adv* **1** **me gusta mucho** I like it a lot; **lo
siento mucho** I'm very sorry; **come mucho**
he eats a lot; **¿te vas a quedar mucho?** are
you going to be staying long?

2 (*respuesta*) very; **¿estás cansado? –
¡mucho!** are you tired? – very!

3 (*locuciones*): **como mucho** at (the) most;
con mucho: el mejor con mucho by far
the best; **ni mucho menos: no es rico ni
mucho menos** he's far from being rich

4: **por mucho que: por mucho que le
creas** no matter how o however much you
believe her

---

muda ['muða] *nf* change of clothes

mudanza [mu'ðanθa] *nf* (*de casa*) move

mudar [mu'ðar] *vt* to change; (*Zool*) to
shed ▷ *vi* to change; **mudarse** *vr* (*ropa*) to
change; **~se de casa** to move house

mudo, -a ['muðo, a] *adj* dumb; (*callado,
Cine*) silent

mueble ['mweβle] *nm* piece of furniture;
muebles *nmpl* furniture *sg*

mueca ['mweka] *nf* face, grimace; **hacer
~s a** to make faces at

muela ['mwela] *nf* back tooth; **muela del**

juicio wisdom tooth
muelle ['mweʎe] nm spring; (Náut) wharf;
(malecón) pier
muero etc vb V **morir**
muerte ['mwerte] nf death; (homicidio)
murder; **dar ~ a** to kill
muerto, -a ['mwerto, a] pp de **morir**
▷ adj dead ▷ nm/f dead man/woman;
(difunto) deceased; (cadáver) corpse; **estar
~ de cansancio** to be dead tired; **Día de los
Muertos** (MÉX) All Souls' Day

● **DÍA DE LOS MUERTOS**
●
●
● All Souls' Day (or "Day of the Dead")
● in Mexico coincides with All Saints'
● Day, which is celebrated in the
● Catholic countries of Latin America on
● November 1st and 2nd. All Souls' Day
● is actually a celebration which begins
● in the evening of October 31st and
● continues until November 2nd. It is a
● combination of the Catholic tradition
● of honouring the Christian saints and
● martyrs, and the ancient Mexican or
● Aztec traditions, in which death was
● not something sinister. For this reason
● all the dead are honoured by bringing
● offerings of food, flowers and candles to
● the cemetery.

---

muestra ['mwestra] nf (señal) indication,
sign; (demostración) demonstration; (prueba)
proof; (estadística) sample; (modelo) model,
pattern; (testimonio) token
muestro etc vb V **mostrar**
muevo etc vb V **mover**
mugir [mu'xir] vi (vaca) to moo
mugre ['muɣre] nf dirt, filth
mujer [mu'xer] nf woman; (esposa) wife;
mujeriego nm womanizer
mula ['mula] nf mule
muleta [mu'leta] nf (para andar) crutch;
(Taur) stick with red cape attached
multa ['multa] nf fine; **poner una ~ a** to
fine; **multar** vt to fine
multicines [multi'θines] nmpl
multiscreen cinema sg
multinacional [multinaθjo'nal] nf
multinational
múltiple ['multiple] adj multiple; (pl)
many, numerous
multiplicar [multipli'kar] vt (Mat) to
multiply; (fig) to increase; **multiplicarse**
vr (Bio) to multiply; (fig) to be everywhere
at once
multitud [multi'tuð] nf (muchedumbre)
crowd; **~ de** lots of

mundial [mun'djal] adj world-wide,
universal; (guerra, récord) world cpd
mundo ['mundo] nm world; **todo el ~**
everybody; **tener ~** to be experienced, know
one's way around
munición [muni'θjon] nf ammunition
municipal [muniθi'pal] adj municipal,
local
municipio [muni'θipjo] nm
(ayuntamiento) town council, corporation;
(territorio administrativo) town, municipality
muñeca [mu'ɲeka] nf (Anat) wrist;
(juguete) doll
muñeco [mu'ɲeko] nm (figura) figure;
(marioneta) puppet; (fig) puppet, pawn
mural [mu'ral] adj mural, wall cpd ▷ nm
mural
muralla [mu'raʎa] nf (city) wall(s) (pl)
murciélago [mur'θjelaɣo] nm bat
murmullo [mur'muʎo] nm murmur(ing);
(cuchicheo) whispering
murmurar [murmu'rar] vi to murmur,
whisper; (cotillear) to gossip
muro ['muro] nm wall
muscular [musku'lar] adj muscular
músculo ['muskulo] nm muscle
museo [mu'seo] nm museum; **museo de
arte** art gallery
musgo ['musɣo] nm moss
música ['musika] nf music; V tb **músico**
músico, -a ['musiko, a] adj musical
▷ nm/f musician
muslo ['muslo] nm thigh
musulmán, -ana [musul'man, ana]
nm/f Moslem
mutación [muta'θjon] nf (Bio) mutation;
(cambio) (sudden) change
mutilar [muti'lar] vt to mutilate; (a una
persona) to maim
mutuo, -a ['mutwo, a] adj mutual
muy [mwi] adv very; (demasiado) too; **M~
Señor mío** Dear Sir; **~ de noche** very late at
night; **eso es ~ de él** that's just like him

m

n

N *abr* (= norte) N

nabo ['naβo] *nm* turnip

nacer [na'θer] *vi* to be born; (de huevo) to hatch; (vegetal) to sprout; (río) to rise; **nací en Barcelona** I was born in Barcelona; **nacido, -a** *adj* born; **recién nacido** newborn; **nacimiento** *nm* birth; (de Navidad) Nativity; (de río) source

nación [na'θjon] *nf* nation; **nacional** *adj* national; **nacionalismo** *nm* nationalism

nada ['naða] *pron* nothing ▷ *adv* not at all, in no way; **no decir ~** to say nothing, not to say anything; **~ más** nothing else; **de ~** don't mention it

nadador, a [naða'ðor, a] *nm/f* swimmer

nadar [na'ðar] *vi* to swim

nadie ['naðje] *pron* nobody, no-one; **~ habló** nobody spoke; **no había ~** there was nobody there, there wasn't anybody there

nado ['naðo] **a nado** *adv*: **pasar a ~** to swim across

nafta ['nafta] (RPL) *nf* petrol (BRIT), gas (US)

naipe ['naipe] *nm* (playing) card; **naipes** *nmpl* cards

nalgas ['nalɣas] *nfpl* buttocks

nalguear [nalɣe'ar] (MÉX, CAM) *vt* to spank

nana ['nana] (ESP) *nf* lullaby

naranja [na'ranxa] *adj inv, nf* orange; **media ~** (fam) better half; **naranjada** *nf* orangeade; **naranjo** *nm* orange tree

narciso [nar'θiso] *nm* narcissus

narcótico, -a [nar'kotiko, a] *adj, nm* narcotic; **narcotizar** *vt* to drug; **narcotráfico** *nm* drug trafficking *o* running

nariz [na'riθ] *nf* nose; **nariz chata/respingona** snub/turned-up nose

narración [narra'θjon] *nf* narration

narrar [na'rrar] *vt* to narrate, recount; **narrativa** *nf* narrative

nata ['nata] *nf* cream; **nata montada** whipped cream

natación [nata'θjon] *nf* swimming

natal [na'tal] *adj*: **ciudad ~** home town; **natalidad** *nf* birth rate

natillas [na'tiʎas] *nfpl* custard *sg*

nativo, -a [na'tiβo, a] *adj, nm/f* native

natural [natu'ral] *adj* natural; (fruta etc) fresh ▷ *nmf* native ▷ *nm* (disposición) nature

naturaleza [natura'leθa] *nf* nature; (género) nature, kind; **naturaleza muerta** still life

naturalmente [natural'mente] *adv* (de modo natural) in a natural way; **¡~!** of course!

naufragar [naufra'ɣar] *vi* to sink; **naufragio** *nm* shipwreck

nauseabundo, -a [nausea'βundo, a] *adj* nauseating, sickening

náuseas ['nauseas] *nfpl* nausea *sg*; **me da ~** it makes me feel sick

náutico, -a ['nautiko, a] *adj* nautical

navaja [na'βaxa] *nf* knife; (de barbero, peluquero) razor

naval [na'βal] *adj* naval

Navarra [na'βarra] *n* Navarre

nave ['naβe] *nf* (barco) ship, vessel; (Arq) nave; **nave espacial** spaceship; **nave industrial** factory premises *pl*

navegador [naβeɣa'ðor] *nm* (Inform) browser

navegante [naβe'ɣante] *nmf* navigator

navegar [naβe'ɣar] *vi* (barco) to sail; (avión) to fly; **~ por Internet** to surf the Net

Navidad [naβi'ðað] *nf* Christmas; **Navidades** *nfpl* Christmas time; **¡Feliz ~!** Merry Christmas!; **navideño, -a** *adj* Christmas *cpd*

nazca *etc vb* V **nacer**

nazi ['naθi] *adj, nmf* Nazi

NE *abr* (= nor(d)este) NE

neblina [ne'βlina] *nf* mist

necesario, -a [neθe'sarjo, a] *adj* necessary

neceser [neθe'ser] *nm* toilet bag; (bolsa grande) holdall

necesidad [neθesi'ðað] *nf* need; (lo inevitable) necessity; (miseria) poverty; **en caso de ~** in case of need *o* emergency; **hacer sus ~es** to relieve o.s.

necesitado, -a [neθesi'taðo, a] *adj* needy, poor; **~ de** in need of

necesitar [neθesi'tar] *vt* to need, require

necio, -a ['neθjo, a] *adj* foolish

nectarina [nekta'rina] *nf* nectarine

nefasto, -a [ne'fasto, a] *adj* ill-fated, unlucky

negación [neɣa'θjon] *nf* negation;

(rechazo) refusal, denial

negar [ne'ɣar] vt (renegar, rechazar) to refuse; (prohibir) to refuse, deny; (desmentir) to deny; **negarse** vr: **~se a** to refuse to

negativa [neɣa'tiβa] nf negative; (rechazo) refusal, denial

negativo, -a [neɣa'tiβo, a] adj, nm negative

negociante [neɣo'θjante] nmf businessman/woman

negociar [neɣo'θjar] vt, vi to negotiate; **~ en** to deal o trade in

negocio [ne'ɣoθjo] nm (Com) business; (asunto) affair, business; (operación comercial) deal, transaction; (lugar) place of business; **los ~s** sg; **hacer ~** to do business

negra ['neɣra] nf (Mús) crotchet; V tb **negro**

negro, -a ['neɣro, a] adj black; (suerte) awful ▷ nm black ▷ nm/f black man/ woman

nene, -a ['nene, a] nm/f baby, small child

neón [ne'on] nm: **luces/lámpara de ~** neon lights/lamp

neoyorquino, -a [neojor'kino, a] adj (of) New York

nervio ['nerβjo] nm nerve; **nerviosismo** nm nervousness, nerves pl; **nervioso, -a** adj nervous

neto, -a ['neto, a] adj net

neumático, -a [neu'matiko, a] adj pneumatic ▷ nm (ESP) tyre (BRIT), tire (US); **neumático de recambio** spare tyre

neurólogo, -a [neu'roloɣo, a] nm/f neurologist

neurona [neu'rona] nf nerve cell

neutral [neu'tral] adj neutral; **neutralizar** vt to neutralize; (contrarrestar) to counteract

neutro, -a ['neutro, a] adj (Bio, Ling) neuter

neutrón [neu'tron] nm neutron

nevada [ne'βaða] nf snowstorm; (caída de nieve) snowfall

nevar [ne'βar] vi to snow

nevera [ne'βera] (ESP) nf refrigerator (BRIT), icebox (US)

nevería [neβe'ria] (MÉX) nf ice-cream parlour

nexo ['nekso] nm link, connection

ni [ni] conj nor, neither; (tb: **~ siquiera**) not ... even; **~ aunque** not even if; **~ blanco ~ negro** neither white nor black

Nicaragua [nika'raɣwa] nf Nicaragua; **nicaragüense** adj, nmf Nicaraguan

nicho ['nitʃo] nm niche

nicotina [niko'tina] nf nicotine

nido ['niðo] nm nest

niebla ['njeβla] nf fog; (neblina) mist

niego etc vb V **negar**

nieto, -a ['njeto, a] nm/f grandson/ daughter; **nietos** nmpl grandchildren

nieve etc ['njeβe] vb V **nevar** ▷ nf snow; (MÉX: helado) ice cream

NIF nm abr (= Número de Identificación Fiscal) personal identification number used for financial and tax purposes

ninfa ['ninfa] nf nymph

ningún adj V **ninguno**

ninguno, -a [nin'guno, a] (adj **ningún**) no pron (nadie) nobody; (ni uno) none, not one; (ni uno ni otro) neither; **de ninguna manera** by no means, not at all

niña ['niɲa] nf (Anat) pupil; V tb **niño**

niñera [ni'ɲera] nf nursemaid, nanny

niñez [ni'ɲeθ] nf childhood; (infancia) infancy

niño, -a ['niɲo, a] adj (joven) young; (inmaduro) immature ▷ nm/f child, boy/girl

nipón, -ona [ni'pon, ona] adj, nm/f Japanese

níquel ['nikel] nm nickel

níspero ['nispero] nm medlar

nítido, -a ['nitiðo, a] adj clear; sharp

nitrato [ni'trato] nm nitrate

nitrógeno [ni'troxeno] nm nitrogen

nivel [ni'βel] nm (Geo) level; (norma) level, standard; (altura) height; **nivel de aceite** oil level; **nivel de aire** spirit level; **nivel de vida** standard of living; **nivelar** vt to level out; (fig) to even up; (Com) to balance

no [no] adv no; not; (con verbo) not ▷ excl no!; **~ tengo nada** I don't have anything, I have nothing; **~ es el mío** it's not mine; **ahora ~** not now; **¿~ lo sabes?** don't you know?; **~ mucho** not much; **~ bien termine, lo entregaré** as soon as I finish, I'll hand it over; **~ más: ayer ~ más** just yesterday; **¡pase ~ más!** come in!; **¡a que ~ lo sabes!** I bet you don't know!; **¡cómo ~!** of course!; **la ~ intervención** non-intervention

noble ['noβle] adj, nmf noble; **nobleza** nf nobility

noche ['notʃe] nf night, night-time; (la tarde) evening; **de ~, por la ~** at night; **es de ~** it's dark; **Noche de San Juan** see below

● **NOCHE DE SAN JUAN**
●
● The **Noche de San Juan** on the 24th June
● is a **fiesta** coinciding with the summer
● solstice and which has taken the
● place of other ancient pagan festivals.
● Traditionally fire plays a major part in
● these festivities with celebrations and
● dancing taking place around bonfires
● in towns and villages across the country.

n

nochebuena [notʃeˈβwena] nf Christmas Eve

nochevieja [notʃeˈβjexa] nf New Year's Eve

nocivo, -a [noˈθiβo, a] adj harmful

noctámbulo, -a [nokˈtambulo, a] nm/f sleepwalker

nocturno, -a [nokˈturno, a] adj (de la noche) nocturnal, night cpd; (de la tarde) evening cpd ▷ nm nocturne

nogal [noˈɣal] nm walnut tree

nómada [ˈnomaða] adj nomadic ▷ nmf nomad

nombrar [nomˈbrar] vt (designar) to name; (mencionar) to mention; (dar puesto a) to appoint

nombre [ˈnombre] nm name; (sustantivo) noun; ~ **y apellidos** name in full; **poner ~ a** to call, name; **nombre común/propio** common/proper noun; **nombre de pila/de soltera** Christian/maiden name

nómina [ˈnomina] nf (lista) payroll; (hoja) payslip

nominal [nomiˈnal] adj nominal

nominar [nomiˈnar] vt to nominate

nominativo, -a [nominaˈtiβo, a] adj (Com): **cheque ~ a X** cheque made out to X

nordeste [norˈðeste] adj north-east, north-eastern, north-easterly ▷ nm north-east

nórdico, -a [ˈnorðiko, a] adj Nordic

noreste [noˈreste] adj, nm = **nordeste**

noria [ˈnorja] nf (Agr) waterwheel; (de carnaval) big (BRIT) o Ferris (US) wheel

norma [ˈnorma] nf rule (of thumb)

normal [norˈmal] adj (corriente) normal; (habitual) usual, natural; **normalizarse** vr to return to normal; **normalmente** adv normally

normativa [normaˈtiβa] nf (set of) rules pl, regulations pl

noroeste [noroˈeste] adj north-west, north-western, north-westerly ▷ nm north-west

norte [ˈnorte] adj north, northern, northerly ▷ nm north; (fig) guide

norteamericano, -a [norteameriˈkano, a] adj, nm/f (North) American

Noruega [noˈrweɣa] nf Norway

noruego, -a [noˈrweɣo, a] adj, nm/f Norwegian

nos [nos] pron (directo) us; (indirecto) us; to us; for us; from us; (reflexivo) (to) ourselves; (recíproco) (to) each other; ~ **levantamos a las 7** we get up at 7

nosotros, -as [noˈsotros, as] pron (sujeto) we; (después de prep) us

nostalgia [nosˈtalxja] nf nostalgia

nota [ˈnota] nf note; (Escol) mark

notable [noˈtaβle] adj notable; (Escol) outstanding

notar [noˈtar] vt to notice, note; **notarse** vr to be obvious; **se nota que ...** one observes that ...

notario [noˈtarjo] nm notary

noticia [noˈtiθja] nf (información) piece of news; **las ~s** the news sg; **tener ~s de algn** to hear from sb

▌ No confundir **noticia** con la palabra inglesa notice.

noticiero [notiˈθjero] (LAM) nm news bulletin

notificar [notifiˈkar] vt to notify, inform

notorio, -a [noˈtorjo, a] adj (público) well-known; (evidente) obvious

novato, -a [noˈβato, a] adj inexperienced ▷ nm/f beginner, novice

novecientos, -as [noβeˈθjentos, as] num nine hundred

novedad [noβeˈðað] nf (calidad de nuevo) newness; (noticia) piece of news; (cambio) change, (new) development

novel [noˈβel] adj new; (inexperto) inexperienced ▷ nmf beginner

novela [noˈβela] nf novel

noveno, -a [noˈβeno, a] adj ninth

noventa [noˈβenta] num ninety

novia nf V **novio**

novicio, -a [noˈβiθjo, a] nm/f novice

noviembre [noˈβjembre] nm November

novillada [noβiˈʎaða] nf (Taur) bullfight with young bulls; **novillero** nm novice bullfighter; **novillo** nm young bull, bullock; **hacer novillos** (fam) to play truant

novio, -a [ˈnoβjo, a] nm/f boyfriend/girlfriend; (prometido) fiancé/fiancée; (recién casado) bridegroom/bride; **los ~s** the newly-weds

nube [ˈnuβe] nf cloud

nublado, -a [nuˈβlaðo, a] adj cloudy; **nublarse** vr to grow dark

nubosidad [nuβosiˈðað] nf cloudiness;

había mucha ~ it was very cloudy
nuca ['nuka] nf nape of the neck
nuclear [nukle'ar] adj nuclear
núcleo ['nukleo] nm (centro) core; (Física) nucleus; **núcleo urbano** city centre
nudillo [nu'ðiʎo] nm knuckle
nudista [nu'ðista] adj nudist
nudo ['nuðo] nm knot; (de carreteras) junction
nuera ['nwera] nf daughter-in-law
nuestro, -a ['nwestro, a] adj pos our ▷ pron ours; **~ padre** our father; **un amigo ~** a friend of ours; **es el ~** it's ours
Nueva York [-jɔrk] n New York
Nueva Zelanda [-θe'landa] nf New Zealand
nueve ['nweβe] num nine
nuevo, -a ['nweβo, a] adj (gen) new; **de ~** again
nuez [nweθ] nf walnut; (Anat) Adam's apple; **nuez moscada** nutmeg
nulo, -a ['nulo, a] adj (inepto, torpe) useless; (inválido) (null and) void; (Deporte) drawn, tied
núm. abr (= número) no.
numerar [nume'rar] vt to number
número ['numero] nm (gen) number; (tamaño: de zapato) size; (ejemplar: de diario) number, issue; **sin ~** numberless, unnumbered; **número atrasado** back number; **número de matrícula/teléfono** registration/telephone number; **número impar/par** odd/even number; **número romano** Roman numeral
numeroso, -a [nume'roso, a] adj numerous
nunca ['nunka] adv (jamás) never; **~ lo pensé** I never thought it; **no viene ~** he never comes; **~ más** never again; **más que ~** more than ever
nupcias ['nupθjas] nfpl wedding sg, nuptials
nutria ['nutrja] nf otter
nutrición [nutri'θjon] nf nutrition
nutrir [nu'trir] vt (alimentar) to nourish; (dar de comer) to feed; (fig) to strengthen; **nutritivo, -a** adj nourishing, nutritious
nylon [ni'lon] nm nylon

ñ

ñango, -a ['nango, a] (MÉX) adj puny
ñapa ['napa] (LAM) nf extra
ñata ['nata] (LAM: fam) nf nose; V tb **ñato**
ñato, -a ['nato, a] (LAM) adj snub-nosed
ñoñería [none'ria] nf insipidness
ñoño, -a ['nono, a] adj (fam: tonto) silly, stupid; (soso) insipid; (persona) spineless; (ESP: película, novela) sentimental

O

O *abr* (= *oeste*) W

o [o] *conj* or

oasis [o'asis] *nm inv* oasis

obcecarse [oβθe'karse] *vr* to get o become stubborn

obedecer [oβeðe'θer] *vt* to obey; **obediente** *adj* obedient

obertura [oβer'tura] *nf* overture

obeso, -a [o'βeso, a] *adj* obese

obispo [o'βispo] *nm* bishop

obituario [oβɪ'twarjo] (*LAM*) *nm* obituary

objetar [oβxe'tar] *vt, vi* to object

objetivo, -a [oβxe'tiβo, a] *adj, nm* objective

objeto [oβ'xeto] *nm* (*cosa*) object; (*fin*) aim

objetor, a [oβxe'tor, a] *nm/f* objector

obligación [oβlixa'θjon] *nf* obligation; (*Com*) bond

obligar [oβli'ɣar] *vt* to force; **obligarse** *vr* to bind o.s.; **obligatorio, -a** *adj* compulsory, obligatory

oboe [o'βoe] *nm* oboe

obra ['oβra] *nf* work; (*Arq*) construction, building; (*Teatro*) play; **por ~ de** thanks to (the efforts of); **obra maestra** masterpiece; **obras públicas** public works; **obrar** *vt* to work; (*tener efecto*) to have an effect on ▷ *vi* to act, behave; (*tener efecto*) to have an effect; **la carta obra en su poder** the letter is in his/her possession

obrero, -a [o'βrero, a] *adj* (*clase*) working; (*movimiento*) labour *cpd* ▷ *nm/f* (*gen*) worker; (*sin oficio*) labourer

obsceno, -a [oβs'θeno, a] *adj* obscene

obscu... = oscu...

obsequiar [oβse'kjar] *vt* (*ofrecer*) to present with; (*agasajar*) to make a fuss of, lavish attention on; **obsequio** *nm* (*regalo*) gift; (*cortesía*) courtesy, attention

observación [oβserβa'θjon] *nf* observation; (*reflexión*) remark

observador, a [oβserβa'ðor, a] *nm/f* observer

observar [oβser'βar] *vt* to observe; (*anotar*) to notice; **observarse** *vr* to keep to, observe

obsesión [oβse'sjon] *nf* obsession; **obsesivo, -a** *adj* obsessive

obstáculo [oβs'takulo] *nm* obstacle; (*impedimento*) hindrance, drawback

obstante [oβs'tante]: **no ~** *adv* nevertheless

obstinado, -a [oβsti'naðo, a] *adj* obstinate, stubborn

obstinarse [oβsti'narse] *vr* to be obstinate; **~ en** to persist in

obstruir [oβstru'ir] *vt* to obstruct

obtener [oβte'ner] *vt* (*gen*) to obtain; (*premio*) to win

obturador [oβtura'ðor] *nm* (*Foto*) shutter

obvio, -a ['oββjo, a] *adj* obvious

oca ['oka] *nf* (*animal*) goose; (*juego*) ≈ snakes and ladders

ocasión [oka'sjon] *nf* (*oportunidad*) opportunity, chance; (*momento*) occasion, time; (*causa*) cause; **de ~** secondhand; **ocasionar** *vt* to cause

ocaso [o'kaso] *nm* (*fig*) decline

occidente [okθi'ðente] *nm* west

OCDE *nf abr* (= *Organización de Cooperación y Desarrollo Económico*) OECD

océano [o'θeano] *nm* ocean; **Océano Índico** Indian Ocean

ochenta [o'tʃenta] *num* eighty

ocho ['otʃo] *num* eight; **dentro de ~ días** within a week

ocio ['oθjo] *nm* (*tiempo*) leisure; (*pey*) idleness

octavilla [okta'viʎa] *nf* leaflet, pamphlet

octavo, -a [ok'taβo, a] *adj* eighth

octubre [ok'tuβre] *nm* October

oculista [oku'lista] *nmf* oculist

ocultar [okul'tar] *vt* (*esconder*) to hide; (*callar*) to conceal; **oculto, -a** *adj* hidden; (*fig*) secret

ocupación [okupa'θjon] *nf* occupation

ocupado, -a [oku'paðo, a] *adj* (*persona*) busy; (*plaza*) occupied, taken; (*teléfono*) engaged; **ocupar** *vt* (*gen*) to occupy; **ocuparse** *vr*: **ocuparse de** o **en** (*gen*) to concern o.s. with; (*cuidar*) to look after

ocurrencia [oku'rrenθja] *nf* (*idea*) bright idea

ocurrir [oku'rrir] *vi* to happen; **ocurrirse** *vr*: **se me ocurrió que ...** it occurred to me that ...

odiar [o'ðjar] *vt* to hate; **odio** *nm* hate, hatred; **odioso, -a** *adj* (*gen*) hateful; (*malo*) nasty

odontólogo, -a [oðon'toloxo, a] *nm/f* dentist, dental surgeon

oeste [o'este] *nm* west; **una película del ~** a western

ofender [ofen'der] *vt* (*agraviar*) to offend; (*insultar*) to insult; **ofenderse** *vr* to take offence; **ofensa** *nf* offence; **ofensiva** *nf* offensive; **ofensivo, -a** *adj* offensive

oferta [o'ferta] *nf* offer; (*propuesta*) proposal; **la ~ y la demanda** supply and demand; **artículos en ~** goods on offer

oficial [ofi'θjal] *adj* official ▷ *nm* (*Mil*) officer

oficina [ofi'θina] *nf* office; **oficina de correos** post office; **oficina de información** information bureau; **oficina de turismo** tourist office; **oficinista** *nmf* clerk

oficio [o'fiθjo] *nm* (*profesión*) profession; (*puesto*) post; (*Rel*) service; **ser del ~** to be an old hand; **tener mucho ~** to have a lot of experience; **oficio de difuntos** funeral service

ofimática [ofi'matika] *nf* office automation

ofrecer [ofre'θer] *vt* (*dar*) to offer; (*proponer*) to propose; **ofrecerse** *vr* (*persona*) to offer o.s., volunteer; (*situación*) to present itself; **¿qué se le ofrece?, ¿se le ofrece algo?** what can I do for you?, can I get you anything?

ofrecimiento [ofreθi'mjento] *nm* offer

oftalmólogo, -a [oftal'moloxo, a] *nm/f* ophthalmologist

oída [o'iða] *nf*: **de ~s** by hearsay

oído [o'iðo] *nm* (*Anat*) ear; (*sentido*) hearing

oigo *etc vb* V **oír**

oír [o'ir] *vt* (*gen*) to hear; (*atender a*) to listen to; **¡oiga!** listen!; **~ misa** to attend mass

OIT *nf abr* (= *Organización Internacional del Trabajo*) ILO

ojal [o'xal] *nm* buttonhole

ojalá [oxa'la] *excl* if only (it were so)!, some hope! ▷ *conj* if only ...!, would that ...!; **~ (que) venga hoy** I hope he comes today

ojeada [oxe'aða] *nf* glance

ojera [o'xera] *nf*: **tener ~s** to have bags under one's eyes

ojo ['oxo] *nm* eye; (*de puente*) span; (*de cerradura*) keyhole ▷ *excl* carefully!; **tener ~ para** to have an eye for; **ojo de buey** porthole

okey ['okei] (*LAM*) *excl* O.K.

okupa [o'kupa] (*ESP: fam*) *nmf* squatter

ola ['ola] *nf* wave

olé [o'le] *excl* bravo!, olé!

oleada [ole'aða] *nf* big wave, swell; (*fig*) wave

oleaje [ole'axe] *nm* swell

óleo ['oleo] *nm* oil; **oleoducto** *nm* (oil) pipeline

oler [o'ler] *vt* (*gen*) to smell; (*inquirir*) to pry into; (*fig: sospechar*) to sniff out ▷ *vi* to smell; **~ a** to smell of

olfatear [olfate'ar] *vt* to smell; (*inquirir*) to pry into; **olfato** *nm* sense of smell

olimpiada [olim'pjaða] *nf*: **las O~s** the Olympics; **olímpico, -a** [o'limpiko, a] *adj* Olympic

oliva [o'liβa] *nf* (*aceituna*) olive; **aceite de ~** olive oil; **olivo** *nm* olive tree

olla ['oʎa] *nf* pan; (*comida*) stew; **olla exprés** *o* **a presión** (*ESP*) pressure cooker; **olla podrida** type of Spanish stew

olmo ['olmo] *nm* elm (tree)

olor [o'lor] *nm* smell; **oloroso, -a** *adj* scented

olvidar [olβi'ðar] *vt* to forget; (*omitir*) to omit; **olvidarse** *vr* (*fig*) to forget o.s.; **se me olvidó** I forgot

olvido [ol'βiðo] *nm* oblivion; (*despiste*) forgetfulness

ombligo [om'bliɣo] *nm* navel

omelette [ome'lete] (*LAM*) *nf* omelet(te)

omisión [omi'sjon] *nf* (*abstención*) omission; (*descuido*) neglect

omiso, -a [o'miso, a] *adj*: **hacer caso ~ de** to ignore, pass over

omitir [omi'tir] *vt* to omit

omnipotente [omnipo'tente] *adj* omnipotent

omóplato [o'moplato] *nm* shoulder blade

OMS *nf abr* (= *Organización Mundial de la Salud*) WHO

once ['onθe] *num* eleven; **onces** (*CS*) *nfpl* tea break *sg*

onda ['onda] *nf* wave; **onda corta/larga/ media** short/long/medium wave; **ondear** *vt, vi* to wave; (*tener ondas*) to be wavy; (*agua*) to ripple

ondulación [ondula'θjon] *nf* undulation; **ondulado, -a** *adj* wavy

ONG *nf abr* (= *organización no gubernamental*) NGO

ONU ['onu] *nf abr* (= *Organización de las Naciones Unidas*) UNO

opaco, -a [o'pako, a] *adj* opaque

opción [op'θjon] *nf* (*gen*) option; (*derecho*) right, option

OPEP ['opep] *nf abr* (= *Organización de Países Exportadores de Petróleo*) OPEC

ópera ['opera] *nf* opera; **ópera bufa** *o* **cómica** comic opera

operación [opera'θjon] *nf* (*gen*) operation; (*Com*) transaction, deal

operador, a [opera'ðor, a] *nm/f* operator; (*Cine: de proyección*) projectionist; (: *de rodaje*)

cameraman
operar [ope'rar] vt (*producir*) to produce, bring about; (*Med*) to operate on ▷ vi (*Com*) to operate, deal; **operarse** vr to occur; (*Med*) to have an operation
opereta [ope'reta] nf operetta
opinar [opi'nar] vt to think ▷ vi to give one's opinion; **opinión** nf (*creencia*) belief; (*criterio*) opinion
opio ['opjo] nm opium
oponer [opo'ner] vt (*resistencia*) to put up, offer; **oponerse** vr (*objetar*) to object; (*estar frente a frente*) to be opposed; (*dos personas*) to oppose each other; **~ A a B** to set A against B; **me opongo a pensar que ...** I refuse to believe o think that ...
oportunidad [oportuni'ðað] nf (*ocasión*) opportunity; (*posibilidad*) chance
oportuno, -a [opor'tuno, a] adj (*en su tiempo*) opportune, timely; (*respuesta*) suitable; **en el momento ~** at the right moment
oposición [oposi'θjon] nf opposition; **oposiciones** nfpl (*Escol*) public examinations
opositor, a [oposi'tor, a] nm/f (*adversario*) opponent; (*candidato*) **~ (a)** candidate (for)
opresión [opre'sjon] nf oppression; **opresor, a** nm/f oppressor
oprimir [opri'mir] vt to squeeze; (*fig*) to oppress
optar [op'tar] vi (*elegir*) to choose; **~ por** to opt for; **optativo, -a** adj optional
óptico, -a [l'optiko, a] adj optic(al) ▷ nm/f optician; **óptica** nf optician's (shop); **desde esta óptica** from this point of view
optimismo [opti'mismo] nm optimism; **optimista** nmf optimist
opuesto, -a [o'pwesto, a] adj (*contrario*) opposite; (*antagónico*) opposing
oración [ora'θjon] nf (*Rel*) prayer; (*Ling*) sentence
orador, a [ora'ðor, a] nm/f (*conferenciante*) speaker, orator
oral [o'ral] adj oral
orangután [orangu'tan] nm orangutan
orar [o'rar] vi to pray
oratoria [ora'torja] nf oratory
órbita ['orβita] nf orbit
orden ['orðen] nm (*gen*) order ▷ nf (*gen*) order; (*Inform*) command; **en ~ de prioridad** in order of priority; **orden del día** agenda
ordenado, -a [orðe'naðo, a] adj (*metódico*) methodical; (*arreglado*) orderly
ordenador [orðena'ðor] nm computer; **ordenador central** mainframe computer
ordenar [orðe'nar] vt (*mandar*) to order; (*poner orden*) to put in order, arrange;

ordenarse vr (*Rel*) to be ordained
ordeñar [orðe'nar] vt to milk
ordinario, -a [orði'narjo, a] adj (*común*) ordinary, usual; (*vulgar*) vulgar, common
orégano [o'reɣano] nm oregano
oreja [o'rexa] nf ear; (*Mecánica*) lug, flange
orfanato [orfa'nato] nm orphanage
orfebrería [orfeβre'ria] nf gold/silver work
orgánico, -a [or'ɣaniko, a] adj organic
organismo [orɣa'nismo] nm (*Bio*) organism; (*Pol*) organization
organización [orɣaniθa'θjon] nf organization; **organizar** vt to organize
órgano ['orɣano] nm organ
orgasmo [or'ɣasmo] nm orgasm
orgía [or'xia] nf orgy
orgullo [or'ɣuʎo] nm pride; **orgulloso, -a** adj (*gen*) proud; (*altanero*) haughty
orientación [orjenta'θjon] nf (*posición*) position; (*dirección*) direction
oriental [orjen'tal] adj eastern; (*del Extremo Oriente*) oriental
orientar [orjen'tar] vt (*situar*) to orientate; (*señalar*) to point; (*dirigir*) to direct; (*guiar*) to guide; **orientarse** vr to get one's bearings
oriente [o'rjente] nm east; **el O~ Medio** the Middle East; **el Próximo/Extremo O~** the Near/Far East
origen [o'rixen] nm origin
original [orixi'nal] adj (*nuevo*) original; (*extraño*) odd, strange; **originalidad** nf originality
originar [orixi'nar] vt to start, cause; **originarse** vr to originate; **originario, -a** adj original; **originario de** native of
orilla [o'riʎa] nf (*borde*) border; (*de río*) bank; (*de bosque, tela*) edge; (*de mar*) shore
orina [o'rina] nf urine; **orinal** nm (*chamber*) pot; **orinar** vi to urinate; **orinarse** vr to wet o.s.
oro ['oro] nm gold; **oros** nmpl (*Naipes*) hearts
orquesta [or'kesta] nf orchestra; **orquesta sinfónica** symphony orchestra
orquídea [or'kiðea] nf orchid
ortiga [or'tixa] nf nettle
ortodoxo, -a [orto'ðokso, a] adj orthodox
ortografía [ortoɣra'fia] nf spelling
ortopedia [orto'peðja] nf orthopaedics sg; **ortopédico, -a** adj orthopaedic
oruga [o'ruxa] nf caterpillar
orzuelo [or'θwelo] nm stye
os [os] pron (*gen*) you; (*a vosotros*) to you
osa ['osa] nf (she-)bear; **Osa Mayor/ Menor** Great/Little Bear

osadía [osa'ðia] *nf* daring

osar [o'sar] *vi* to dare

oscilación [osθila'θjon] *nf* (*movimiento*) oscillation; (*fluctuación*) fluctuation

oscilar [osθi'lar] *vi* to oscillate; to fluctuate

oscurecer [oskure'θer] *vt* to darken ▷ *vi* to grow dark; **oscurecerse** *vr* to grow o get dark

oscuridad [oskuri'ðað] *nf* obscurity; (*tinieblas*) darkness

oscuro, -a [os'kuro, a] *adj* dark; (*fig*) obscure; **a oscuras** in the dark

óseo, -a ['oseo, a] *adj* bone *cpd*

oso ['oso] *nm* bear; **oso de peluche** teddy bear; **oso hormiguero** anteater

ostentar [osten'tar] *vt* (*gen*) to show; (*pey*) to flaunt, show off; (*poseer*) to have, possess

ostión [os'tjon] (*MÉX*) *nm* = **ostra**

ostra ['ostra] *nf* oyster

OTAN ['otan] *nf abr* (= *Organización del Tratado del Atlántico Norte*) NATO

otitis [o'titis] *nf* earache

otoñal [oto'ɲal] *adj* autumnal

otoño [o'toɲo] *nm* autumn

otorgar [otor'ɣar] *vt* (*conceder*) to concede; (*dar*) to grant

otorrino, -a [oto'rrino, a], **otorrinolaringólogo, -a** [otorrinolarin'goloxo, a] *nm/f* ear, nose and throat specialist

○ **PALABRA CLAVE**

otro, -a ['otro, a] *adj* **1** (*distinto: sg*) another; (: *pl*) other; **con otros amigos** with other o different friends

2 (*adicional*): **tráigame otro café (más), por favor** can I have another coffee please; **otros diez días más** another ten days

▷ *pron* **1** **el otro** the other one; **(los) otros** (the) others; **de otro** somebody else's; **que lo haga otro** let somebody else do it

2 (*recíproco*): **se odian (la) una a (la) otra** they hate one another o each other

3: **otro tanto: comer otro tanto** to eat the same o as much again; **recibió una decena de telegramas y otras tantas llamadas** he got about ten telegrams and as many calls

ovación [oβa'θjon] *nf* ovation

oval [o'βal] *adj* oval; **ovalado, -a** *adj* oval; **óvalo** *nm* oval

ovario [o'βario] *nm* ovary

oveja [o'βexa] *nf* sheep

overol [oβe'rol] (*LAM*) *nm* overalls *pl*

ovillo [o'βiʎo] *nm* (*de lana*) ball of wool

OVNI ['oβni] *nm abr* (= *objeto volante no identificado*) UFO

ovulación [oβula'θjon] *nf* ovulation; **óvulo** *nm* ovum

oxidación [oksiða'θjon] *nf* rusting

oxidar [oksi'ðar] *vt* to rust; **oxidarse** *vr* to go rusty

óxido ['oksiðo] *nm* oxide

oxigenado, -a [oksixe'naðo, a] *adj* (*Quím*) oxygenated; (*pelo*) bleached

oxígeno [ok'sixeno] *nm* oxygen

oyente [o'jente] *nmf* listener

oyes *etc vb* V **oír**

ozono [o'θono] *nm* ozone

P

pabellón [paβe'ʎon] nm bell tent; (Arq) pavilion; (de hospital etc) block, section; (bandera) flag

pacer [pa'θer] vi to graze

paciencia [pa'θjenθja] nf patience

paciente [pa'θjente] adj, nmf patient

pacificación [paθifika'θjon] nf pacification

pacífico, -a [pa'θifiko, a] adj (persona) peaceable; (existencia) peaceful; **el (Océano) P~** the Pacific (Ocean)

pacifista [paθi'fista] nmf pacifist

pacotilla [pako'tiʎa] nf: **de ~** (actor, escritor) third-rate

pactar [pak'tar] vt to agree to o on ▷ vi to come to an agreement

pacto ['pakto] nm (tratado) pact; (acuerdo) agreement

padecer [paðe'θer] vt (sufrir) to suffer; (soportar) to endure, put up with; **padecimiento** nm suffering

padrastro [pa'ðrastro] nm stepfather

padre ['paðre] nm father ▷ adj (fam): **un éxito ~** a tremendous success; **padres** nmpl parents; **padre político** father-in-law

padrino [pa'ðrino] nm (Rel) godfather; (tb: **~ de boda**) best man; (fig) sponsor, patron; **padrinos** nmpl godparents

padrón [pa'ðron] nm (censo) census, roll

padrote [pa'ðrote] (MÉX: fam) nm pimp

paella [pa'eʎa] nf paella, dish of rice with meat, shellfish etc

paga ['paɣa] nf (pago) payment; (sueldo) pay, wages pl

pagano, -a [pa'ɣano, a] adj, nm/f pagan, heathen

pagar [pa'ɣar] vt to pay; (las compras, crimen) to pay for; (fig: favor) to repay ▷ vi to pay; **~ al contado/a plazos** to pay (in) cash/ in instalments

pagaré [paɣa're] nm I.O.U.

página ['paxina] nf page; **página de inicio** (Inform) home page; **página web** (Inform) web page

pago ['paɣo] nm (dinero) payment; **en ~ de** in return for; **pago anticipado/a cuenta/ contra reembolso/en especie** advance payment/payment on account/cash on delivery/payment in kind

pág(s). abr (= página(s)) p(p).

pague etc vb V **pagar**

país [pa'is] nm (gen) country; (región) land; **los P~es Bajos** the Low Countries; **el P~ Vasco** the Basque Country

paisaje [pai'saxe] nm landscape, scenery

paisano, -a [pai'sano, a] adj of the same country ▷ nm/f (compatriota) fellow countryman/woman; **vestir de ~** (soldado) to be in civvies; (guardia) to be in plain clothes

paja ['paxa] nf straw; (fig) rubbish (BRIT), trash (US)

pajarita [paxa'rita] nf (corbata) bow tie

pájaro ['paxaro] nm bird; **pájaro carpintero** woodpecker

pajita [pa'xita] nf (drinking) straw

pala ['pala] nf spade, shovel; (raqueta etc) bat; (: de tenis) racquet; (Culin) slice; **pala mecánica** power shovel

palabra [pa'laβra] nf word; (facultad) (power of) speech; (derecho de hablar) right to speak; **tomar la ~** (en mitin) to take the floor

palabrota [pala'βrota] nf swearword

palacio [pa'laθjo] nm palace; (mansión) mansion, large house; **palacio de justicia** courthouse; **palacio municipal** town o city hall

paladar [pala'ðar] nm palate; **paladear** vt to taste

palanca [pa'lanka] nf lever; (fig) pull, influence

palangana [palan'gana] nf washbasin

palco ['palko] nm box

Palestina [pales'tina] nf Palestine; **palestino, -a** nm/f Palestinian

paleta [pa'leta] nf (de pintor) palette; (de albañil) trowel; (de ping-pong) bat; (MÉX, CAM: helado) ice lolly (BRIT), Popsicle® (US)

palidecer [paliðe'θer] vi to turn pale; **palidez** nf paleness; **pálido, -a** adj pale

palillo [pa'liʎo] nm (mondadientes) toothpick; (para comer) chopstick

palito [pa'lito] (RPL) nm (helado) ice lolly (BRIT), Popsicle® (US)

paliza [pa'liθa] nf beating, thrashing

palma ['palma] nf (Anat) palm; (árbol) palm tree; **batir o dar ~s** to clap, applaud; **palmada** nf slap; **palmadas** nfpl clapping

sg, applause *sg*
palmar [pal'mar] *(fam)* vi *(tb:* **~la**) to die, kick the bucket
palmear [palme'ar] vi to clap
palmera [pal'mera] *nf (Bot)* palm tree
palmo ['palmo] *nm (medida)* span; *(fig)* small amount; **~ a ~** inch by inch
palo ['palo] *nm* stick; *(poste)* post; *(de tienda de campaña)* pole; *(mango)* handle, shaft; *(golpe)* blow, hit; *(de golf)* club; *(de béisbol)* bat; *(Náut)* mast; *(Naipes)* suit
paloma [pa'loma] *nf* dove, pigeon
palomitas [palo'mitas] *nfpl* popcorn *sg*
palpar [pal'par] *vt* to touch, feel
palpitar [palpi'tar] vi to palpitate; *(latir)* to beat
palta ['palta] *(cs) nf* avocado
paludismo [palu'ðismo] *nm* malaria
pamela [pa'mela] *nf* picture hat, sun hat
pampa ['pampa] *nf* pampas, prairie
pan [pan] *nm* bread; *(una barra)* loaf; **pan integral** wholemeal *(BRIT)* o wholewheat *(US)* bread; **pan rallado** breadcrumbs *pl*; **pan tostado** *(MÉX: tostada)* toast
pana ['pana] *nf* corduroy
panadería [pana.ðe'ria] *nf* baker's (shop); **panadero, -a** *nm/f* baker
Panamá [pana'ma] *nm* Panama; **panameño, -a** *adj* Panamanian
pancarta [pan'karta] *nf* placard, banner
panceta [pan'θeta] *(ESP, RPL) nf* bacon
pancho ['pantʃo] *(RPL) nm* hot dog
pancito [pan'θito] *nm* (bread) roll
panda ['panda] *nm (Zool)* panda
pandereta [pande'reta] *nf* tambourine
pandilla [pan'diʎa] *nf* set, group; *(de criminales)* gang; *(pey: camarilla)* clique
panecillo [pane'θiʎo] *(ESP) nm* (bread) roll
panel [pa'nel] *nm* panel; **panel solar** solar panel
panfleto [pan'fleto] *nm* pamphlet
pánico ['paniko] *nm* panic
panorama [pano'rama] *nm* panorama; *(vista)* view
panqueque [pan'keke] *(LAM) nm* pancake
pantalla [pan'taʎa] *nf (de cine)* screen; *(de lámpara)* lampshade
pantalón [panta'lon] *nm* trousers; **pantalones** *nmpl* trousers; **pantalones cortes** shorts
pantano [pan'tano] *nm (ciénaga)* marsh, swamp; *(depósito: de agua)* reservoir; *(fig)* jam, difficulty
panteón [pante'on] *nm (monumento)* pantheon
pantera [pan'tera] *nf* panther
pantimedias [panti'meðjas] *(MÉX) nfpl*

= **pantis**
pantis ['pantis] *nmpl* tights *(BRIT)*, pantyhose *(US)*
pantomima [panto'mima] *nf* pantomime
pantorrilla [panto'rriʎa] *nf* calf (of the leg)
pants [pants] *(MÉX) nmpl* tracksuit *(BRIT)*, sweat suit *(US)*
pantufla [pan'tufla] *nf* slipper
panty(s) ['panti(s)] *nm(pl)* tights *(BRIT)*, pantyhose *(US)*
panza ['panθa] *nf* belly, paunch
pañal [pa'nal] *nm* nappy *(BRIT)*, diaper *(US)*; **pañales** *nmpl (fig)* early stages, infancy *sg*
paño ['paɲo] *nm (tela)* cloth; *(pedazo de tela)* (piece of) cloth; *(trapo)* duster, rag; **paños menores** underclothes
pañuelo [pa'ɲwelo] *nm* handkerchief, hanky; *(fam: para la cabeza)* (head)scarf
papa ['papa] *nm:* **el P~** the Pope ▷ *nf (LAM: patata)* potato; **papas fritas** *(LAM)* French fries, chips *(BRIT)*; *(de bolsa)* crisps *(BRIT)*, potato chips *(US)*
papá [pa'pa] *(fam) nm* dad(dy), pa *(US)*
papada [pa'paða] *nf* double chin
papagayo [papa'ɣajo] *nm* parrot
papalote [papa'lote] *(MÉX, CAM) nm* kite
papanatas [papa'natas] *(fam) nm inv* simpleton
papaya [pa'paja] *nf* papaya
papear [pape'ar] *(fam)* vt, vi to scoff
papel [pa'pel] *nm* paper; *(hoja de papel)* sheet of paper; *(Teatro: fig)* role; **papel de aluminio** aluminium *(BRIT)* o aluminum *(US)* foil; **papel de arroz/envolver/fumar** rice/wrapping/cigarette paper; **papel de estaño** o **plata** tinfoil; **papel de lija** sandpaper; **papel higiénico** toilet paper; **papel moneda** paper money; **papel secante** blotting paper
papeleo [pape'leo] *nm* red tape
papelera [pape'lera] *nf* wastepaper basket; *(en la calle)* litter bin; **papelera (de reciclaje)** *(Inform)* wastebasket
papelería [papele'ria] *nf* stationer's (shop)
papeleta [pape'leta] *(ESP) nf (Pol)* ballot paper
paperas [pa'peras] *nfpl* mumps *sg*
papilla [pa'piʎa] *nf (de bebé)* baby food
paquete [pa'kete] *nm (de cigarrillos etc)* packet; *(Correos etc)* parcel
par [par] *adj (igual)* like, equal; *(Mat)* even ▷ *nm* equal; *(de guantes)* pair; *(de veces)* couple; *(Pol)* peer; *(Golf, Com)* par; **abrir de ~ en ~** to open wide

P

para ['para] *prep* for; **no es ~ comer** it's not for eating; **decir ~ sí** to say to o.s.; **¿~ qué lo quieres?** what do you want it for?; **se casaron ~ separarse otra vez** they married only to separate again; **lo tendré ~ mañana** I'll have it (for) tomorrow; **ir ~ casa** to go home, head for home; **~ profesor es muy estúpido** he's very stupid for a teacher; **¿quién es usted ~ gritar así?** who are you to shout like that?; **tengo bastante ~ vivir** I have enough to live on; *V tb* **con**

parabién [para'βjen] *nm* congratulations *pl*

parábola [pa'raβola] *nf* parable; (*Mat*) parabola; **parabólica** *nf* (*tb*: **antena parabólica**) satellite dish

parabrisas [para'βrisas] *nm inv* windscreen (*BRIT*), windshield (*US*)

paracaídas [paraka'iðas] *nm inv* parachute; **paracaidista** *nmf* parachutist; (*Mil*) paratrooper

parachoques [para'tʃokes] *nm inv* (*Auto*) bumper; (*Mecánica etc*) shock absorber

parada [pa'raða] *nf* stop; (*acto*) stopping; (*de industria*) shutdown, stoppage; (*lugar*) stopping place; **parada de autobús** bus stop; **parada de taxis** taxi stand *o* rank (*BRIT*)

paradero [para'ðero] *nm* stopping-place; (*situación*) whereabouts

parado, -a [pa'raðo, a] *adj* (*persona*) motionless, standing still; (*fábrica*) closed, at a standstill; (*coche*) stopped; (*LAM: de pie*) standing (up); (*ESP: sin empleo*) unemployed, idle

paradoja [para'ðoxa] *nf* paradox

parador [para'ðor] *nm* parador, state-run hotel

paragolpes [para'golpes] (*RPL*) *nm inv* (*Auto*) bumper, fender (*US*)

paraguas [pa'raɣwas] *nm inv* umbrella

Paraguay [para'ɣwai] *nm* Paraguay; **paraguayo, -a** *adj, nm/f* Paraguayan

paraíso [para'iso] *nm* paradise, heaven

paraje [pa'raxe] *nm* place, spot

paralelo, -a [para'lelo, a] *adj* parallel

parálisis [pa'ralisis] *nf inv* paralysis; **paralítico, -a** *adj, nm/f* paralytic

paralizar [parali'θar] *vt* to paralyse; **paralizarse** *vr* to become paralysed; (*fig*) to come to a standstill

páramo ['paramo] *nm* bleak plateau

paranoico, -a [para'noiko, a] *nm/f* paranoiac

parapente [para'pente] *nm* (*deporte*) paragliding; (*aparato*) paraglider

parapléjico, -a [para'plexiko, a] *adj, nm/f* paraplegic

parar [pa'rar] *vt* to stop; (*golpe*) to ward off ▷ *vi* to stop; **pararse** *vr* to stop; (*LAM: ponerse de pie*) to stand up; **ha parado de llover** it has stopped raining; **van a ir a ~ a comisaría** they're going to end up in the police station; **~se en** to pay attention to

pararrayos [para'rrajos] *nm inv* lightning conductor

parásito, -a [pa'rasito, a] *nm/f* parasite

parcela [par'θela] *nf* plot, piece of ground

parche ['partʃe] *nm* (*gen*) patch

parchís [par'tʃis] *nm* ludo

parcial [par'θjal] *adj* (*pago*) part-; (*eclipse*) partial; (*Jur*) prejudiced, biased; (*Pol*) partisan

parecer [pare'θer] *nm* (*opinión*) opinion, view; (*aspecto*) looks *pl* ▷ *vi* (*tener apariencia*) to seem, look; (*asemejarse*) to look *o* seem like; (*aparecer, llegar*) to appear; **parecerse** *vr* to look alike, resemble each other; **al ~** apparently; **según parece** evidently, apparently; **~se a** to look like, resemble; **me parece que** I think (that), it seems to me that

parecido, -a [pare'θiðo, a] *adj* similar ▷ *nm* similarity, likeness, resemblance; **bien ~** good-looking, nice-looking

pared [pa'reð] *nf* wall

pareja [pa'rexa] *nf* (*par*) pair; (*dos personas*) couple; (*otro: de un par*) other one (of a pair); (*persona*) partner

parentesco [paren'tesko] *nm* relationship

paréntesis [pa'rentesis] *nm inv* parenthesis; (*en escrito*) bracket

parezco *etc vb V* **parecer**

pariente [pa'rjente] *nmf* relative, relation

⬛ No confundir **pariente** con la palabra inglesa *parent*.

parir [pa'rir] *vt* to give birth to ▷ *vi* (*mujer*) to give birth, have a baby

París [pa'ris] *n* Paris

parka ['parka] (*LAM*) *nf* anorak

parking ['parkin] *nm* car park (*BRIT*), parking lot (*US*)

parlamentar [parlamen'tar] *vi* to parley

parlamentario, -a [parlamen'tarjo, a] *adj* parliamentary ▷ *nm/f* member of parliament

parlamento [parla'mento] *nm* parliament

parlanchín, -ina [parlan'tʃin, ina] *adj* indiscreet ▷ *nm/f* chatterbox

parlar [par'lar] *vi* to chatter (away)

paro ['paro] *nm* (*huelga*) stoppage (of work), strike; (*ESP: desempleo*) unemployment; (: *subsidio*) unemployment benefit; **estar en ~** (*ESP*) to be unemployed;

paro cardíaco cardiac arrest

parodia [pa'roðja] nf parody; **parodiar**
vt to parody

parpadear [parpaðe'ar] vi (ojos) to blink;
(luz) to flicker

párpado ['parpaðo] nm eyelid

parque ['parke] nm (lugar verde) park;
(MÉX: munición) ammunition; **parque
de atracciones** fairground; **parque de
bomberos** (ESP) fire station; **parque
infantil/temático/zoológico** playground/
theme park/zoo

parqué [par'ke] nm parquet (flooring)

parquímetro [par'kimetro] nm parking
meter

parra ['parra] nf (grape)vine

párrafo ['parrafo] nm paragraph; **echar
un ~** (fam) to have a chat

parranda [pa'rranda] (fam) nf spree,
binge

parrilla [pa'rriʎa] nf (Culin) grill; (de coche)
grille; **(carne a la) ~** barbecue; **parrillada**
nf barbecue

párroco ['parroko] nm parish priest

parroquia [pa'rrokja] nf parish; (iglesia)
parish church; (Com) clientele, customers pl;
parroquiano, -a nm/f parishioner; (Com)
client, customer

parte ▷ ['parte] nm message; (informe)
report ▷ nf part; (lado, cara) side; (de reparto)
share; (Jur) party; **en alguna ~ de Europa**
somewhere in Europe; **en o por todas ~s**
everywhere; **en gran ~** to a large extent; **la
mayor ~ de los españoles** most Spaniards;
de un tiempo a esta ~ for some time past;
de ~ de algn on sb's behalf; **¿de ~ de quién?**
(Tel) who is speaking?; **por ~ de** on the part
of; **yo por mi ~** I for my part; **por otra ~** on
the other hand; **dar ~** to inform; **tomar ~** to
take part; **parte meteorológico** weather
forecast o report

participación [partiθipa'θjon] nf (acto)
participation, taking part; (parte, Com)
share; (de lotería) shared prize; (aviso) notice,
notification

participante [partiθi'pante] nmf
participant

participar [partiθi'par] vt to notify,
inform ▷ vi to take part, participate

partícipe [par'tiθipe] nmf participant

particular [partiku'lar] adj (especial)
particular, special; (individual, personal)
private, personal ▷ nm (punto, asunto)
particular, point; (individuo) individual;
tiene coche ~ he has a car of his own

partida [par'tiða] nf (salida) departure;
(Com) entry, item; (juego) game; (grupo de
personas) band, group; **mala ~** dirty trick;

**partida de nacimiento/matrimonio/
defunción** (ESP) birth/marriage/death
certificate

partidario, -a [parti'ðarjo, a] adj
partisan ▷ nm/f supporter, follower

partido [par'tiðo] nm (Pol) party; (Deporte)
game, match; **sacar ~ de** to profit o benefit
from; **tomar ~** to take sides

partir [par'tir] vt (dividir) to split, divide;
(compartir, distribuir) to share (out),
distribute; (romper) to break open, split
open; (rebanada) to cut (off) ▷ vi (ponerse en
camino) to set off o out; (comenzar) to start
(off o out); **partirse** vr to crack o split o
break (in two etc); **a ~ de** (starting) from

partitura [parti'tura] nf (Mús) score

parto ['parto] nm birth; (fig) product,
creation; **estar de ~** to be in labour

parvulario [parβu'larjo] (ESP) nm
nursery school, kindergarten

pasa ['pasa] nf raisin; **pasa de Corinto**
currant

pasacintas [pasa'θintas] (LAM) nm
cassette player

pasada [pa'saða] nf passing, passage;
de ~ in passing, incidentally; **una mala ~** a
dirty trick

pasadizo [pasa'ðiθo] nm (pasillo) passage,
corridor; (callejuela) alley

pasado, -a [pa'saðo, a] adj past;
(malo: comida, fruta) bad; (muy cocido)
overdone; (anticuado) out of date ▷ nm past;
~ mañana the day after tomorrow; **el mes
~** last month

pasador [pasa'ðor] nm (cerrojo) bolt; (de
pelo) hair slide; (horquilla) grip

pasaje [pa'saxe] nm passage; (pago de
viaje) fare; (los pasajeros) passengers pl;
(pasillo) passageway

pasajero, -a [pasa'xero, a] adj passing;
(situación, estado) temporary; (amor,
enfermedad) brief ▷ nm/f passenger

pasamontañas [pasamon'taɲas] nm inv
balaclava helmet

pasaporte [pasa'porte] nm passport

pasar [pa'sar] vt to pass; (tiempo) to spend;
(desgracias) to suffer, endure; (noticia) to
give, pass on; (río) to cross; (barrera) to
pass through; (falta) to overlook, tolerate;
(contrincante) to surpass, do better than;
(coche) to overtake; (Cine) to show;
(enfermedad) to give, infect with ▷ vi (gen)
to pass; (terminarse) to be over; (ocurrir) to
happen; **pasarse** vr (flores) to fade; (comida)
to go bad o off; (fig) to overdo it, go too far;
~ de to go beyond, exceed; **~ por** (LAM) to
fetch; **~lo bien/mal** to have a good/bad
time; **¡pase!** come in!; **hacer ~** to show in;

P

lo que pasa es que ... the thing is ...; **~se al enemigo** to go over to the enemy; **se me pasó** I forgot; **no se le pasa nada** he misses nothing; **pase lo que pase** come what may; **¿qué pasa?** what's going on?, what's up?; **¿qué te pasa?** what's wrong?

pasarela [pasa'rela] nf footbridge; (en barco) gangway

pasatiempo [pasa'tjempo] nm pastime, hobby

Pascua ['paskwa] nf (en Semana Santa) Easter; **Pascuas** nfpl Christmas (time); **¡felices ~s!** Merry Christmas!

pase ['pase] nm pass; (Cine) performance, showing

pasear [pase'ar] vt to take for a walk; (exhibir) to parade, show off ▷ vi to walk, go for a walk; **pasearse** vr to walk, go for a walk; **~ en coche** to go for a drive; **paseo** nm (avenida) avenue; (distancia corta) walk, stroll; **dar un** o **ir de paseo** to go for a walk; **paseo marítimo** (ESP) promenade

pasillo [pa'siʎo] nm passage, corridor

pasión [pa'sjon] nf passion

pasivo, -a [pa'siβo, a] adj passive; (inactivo) inactive ▷ nm (Com) liabilities pl, debts pl

pasmoso, -a [pas'moso, a] adj amazing, astonishing

paso, -a ['paso, a] adj dried ▷ nm step; (modo de andar) walk; (huella) footprint; (rapidez) speed, pace, rate; (camino accesible) way through, passage; (cruce) crossing; (pasaje) passing, passage; (Geo) pass; (estrecho) strait; **a ese ~** (fig) at that rate; **salir al ~ de** o **a** to waylay; **estar de ~** to be passing through; **prohibido el ~** no entry; **ceda el ~** give way; **paso a nivel** (Ferro) level-crossing; **paso (de) cebra** (ESP) zebra crossing; **paso de peatones** pedestrian crossing; **paso elevado** flyover

pasota [pa'sota] (ESP: fam) adj, nmf ≈ dropout; **ser un ~** to be a bit of a dropout; (ser indiferente) not to care about anything

pasta ['pasta] nf paste; (Culin: masa) dough; (: de bizcochos etc) pastry; (fam) dough; **pastas** nfpl (bizcochos) pastries, small cakes; (fideos, espaguetis etc) pasta; **pasta dentífrica** o **de dientes** toothpaste

pastar [pas'tar] vt, vi to graze

pastel [pas'tel] nm (dulce) cake; (Arte) pastel; **pastel de carne** meat pie; **pastelería** nf cake shop

pastilla [pas'tiʎa] nf (de jabón, chocolate) bar; (píldora) tablet, pill

pasto ['pasto] nm (hierba) grass; (lugar) pasture, field; **pastor, a** [pas'tor, a] nm/f shepherd/ess ▷ nm (Rel) clergyman, pastor;

pastor alemán Alsatian

pata ['pata] nf (pierna) leg; (pie) foot; (de muebles) leg; **~s arriba** upside down; **metedura de ~** (fam) gaffe; **meter la ~** (fam) to put one's foot in it; **tener buena/mala ~** to be lucky/unlucky; **pata de cabra** (Tec) crowbar; **patada** nf kick; (en el suelo) stamp

patata [pa'tata] nf potato; **patatas fritas** chips, French fries; (de bolsa) crisps

paté [pa'te] nm pâté

patente [pa'tente] adj obvious, evident; (Com) patent ▷ nf patent

paternal [pater'nal] adj fatherly, paternal; **paterno, -a** adj paternal

patético, -a [pa'tetiko, a] adj pathetic, moving

patilla [pa'tiʎa] nf (de gafas) side(piece); **patillas** nfpl sideburns

patín [pa'tin] nm skate; (de trineo) runner; **patín de ruedas** roller skate; **patinaje** nm skating; **patinar** vi to skate; (resbalarse) to skid, slip; (fam) to slip up, blunder

patineta [pati'neta] nf (MÉX: patinete) scooter; (CS: monopatín) skateboard

patinete [pati'nete] nm scooter

patio ['patjo] nm (de casa) patio, courtyard; **patio de recreo** playground

pato ['pato] nm duck; **pagar el ~** (fam) to take the blame, carry the can

patoso, -a [pa'toso, a] (fam) adj clumsy

patotero [pato'tero] (cs) nm hooligan, lout

patraña [pa'traɲa] nf story, fib

patria ['patrja] nf native land, mother country

patrimonio [patri'monjo] nm inheritance; (fig) heritage

patriota [pa'trjota] nmf patriot

patrocinar [patroθi'nar] vt to sponsor

patrón, -ona [pa'tron, ona] nm/f (jefe) boss, chief, master(mistress); (propietario) landlord/lady; (Rel) patron saint ▷ nm (Tec, Costura) pattern

patronato [patro'nato] nm sponsorship; (acto) patronage; (fundación benéfica) trust, foundation

patrulla [pa'truʎa] nf patrol

pausa ['pausa] nf pause, break

pauta ['pauta] nf line, guide line

pava ['paβa] (RPL) nf kettle

pavimento [paβi'mento] nm (de losa) pavement, paving

pavo ['paβo] nm turkey; **pavo real** peacock

payaso, -a [pa'jaso, a] nm/f clown

payo, -a [pa'jo, a] nm/f non-gipsy

paz [paθ] nf peace; (tranquilidad) peacefulness, tranquillity; **hacer las paces** to make peace; (fig) to make up; **¡déjame en**

~! leave me alone!

PC nm PC, personal computer

P.D. abr (= posdata) P.S., p.s.

peaje [pe'axe] nm toll

peatón [pea'ton] nm pedestrian; **peatonal** adj pedestrian

peca ['peka] nf freckle

pecado [pe'kaðo] nm sin; **pecador, a** adj sinful ▷ nm/f sinner

pecaminoso, -a [pekami'noso, a] adj sinful

pecar [pe'kar] vi (Rel) to sin; **peca de generoso** he is generous to a fault

pecera [pe'θera] nf fish tank; (redonda) goldfish bowl

pecho ['petʃo] nm (Anat) chest; (de mujer) breast; **dar el ~ a** to breast-feed; **tomar algo a ~** to take sth to heart

pechuga [pe'tʃuxa] nf breast

peculiar [peku'ljar] adj special, peculiar; (característico) typical, characteristic

pedal [pe'ðal] nm pedal; **pedalear** vi to pedal

pedante [pe'ðante] adj pedantic ▷ nmf pedant

pedazo [pe'ðaθo] nm piece, bit; **hacerse ~s** to smash, shatter

pediatra [pe'ðjatra] nmf paediatrician

pedido [pe'ðiðo] nm (Com) order; (petición) request

pedir [pe'ðir] vt to ask for, request; (comida, Com: mandar) to order; (necesitar) to need, demand, require ▷ vi to ask; **me pidió que cerrara la puerta** he asked me to shut the door; **¿cuánto piden por el coche?** how much are they asking for the car?

pedo ['peðo] (fam!) nm fart

pega ['pexa] nf snag; **poner ~s (a)** to complain (about)

pegadizo, -a [pexa'ðiθo, a] adj (Mús) catchy

pegajoso, -a [pexa'xoso, a] adj sticky, adhesive

pegamento [pexa'mento] nm gum, glue

pegar [pe'xar] vt (papel, sellos) to stick (on); (cartel) to stick up; (coser) to sew (on); (unir: partes) to join, fix together; (Comput) to paste; (Med) to give, infect with; (dar: golpe) to give, deal ▷ vi (adherirse) to stick, adhere; (ir juntos: colores) to match, go together; (golpear) to hit; (quemar: el sol) to strike hot, burn; **pegarse** vr (gen) to stick; (dos personas) to hit each other, fight; (fam): **~ un grito** to let out a yell; **~ un salto** to jump (with fright); **~ en** to touch; **~se un tiro** to shoot o.s.

pegatina [pexa'tina] nf sticker

pegote [pe'xote] (fam) nm eyesore, sight

peinado [pei'naðo] nm hairstyle

peinar [pei'nar] vt to comb; (hacer estilo) to style; **peinarse** vr to comb one's hair

peine ['peine] nm comb; **peineta** nf ornamental comb

p.ej. abr (= por ejemplo) e.g.

Pekín [pe'kin] n Pekin(g)

pelado, -a [pe'laðo, a] adj (fruta, patata etc) peeled; (cabeza) shorn; (campo, fig) bare; (fam: sin dinero) broke

pelar [pe'lar] vt (fruta, patatas etc) to peel; (cortar el pelo a) to cut the hair of; (quitar la piel: animal) to skin; **pelarse** vr (la piel) to peel off; **voy a ~me** I'm going to get my hair cut

peldaño [pel'daɲo] nm step

pelea [pe'lea] nf (lucha) fight; (discusión) quarrel, row; **peleado, -a** [pele'aðo, a] adj: **estar peleado (con algn)** to have fallen out (with sb); **pelear** [pele'ar] vi to fight; **pelearse** vr to fight; (reñirse) to fall out, quarrel

pelela [pe'lela] (cs) nf potty

peletería [pelete'ria] nf furrier's, fur shop

pelícano [pe'likano] nm pelican

película [pe'likula] nf film; (cobertura ligera) thin covering; (Foto: rollo) roll o reel of film; **película de dibujos (animados)/del oeste** cartoon/western

peligro [pe'lixro] nm danger; (riesgo) risk; **correr ~ de** to run the risk of; **peligroso, -a** adj dangerous; risky

pelirrojo, -a [peli'rroxo, a] adj red-haired, red-headed ▷ nm/f redhead

pellejo [pe'ʎexo] nm (de animal) skin, hide

pellizcar [peʎiθ'kar] vt to pinch, nip

pelma ['pelma] (esp: fam) nmf pain (in the neck)

pelmazo [pel'maθo] (fam) nm = **pelma**

pelo ['pelo] nm (cabellos) hair; (de barba, bigote) whisker; (de animal: pellejo) hair, fur, coat; **venir al ~** to be exactly what one needs; **un hombre de ~ en pecho** a brave man; **por los ~s** by the skin of one's teeth; **no tener ~s en la lengua** to be outspoken, not to mince one's words; **con ~s y señales** in minute detail; **tomar el ~ a algn** to pull sb's leg

pelota [pe'lota] nf ball; **en ~** stark naked; **hacer la ~ (a algn)** (esp: fam) to creep (to sb); **pelota vasca** pelota

pelotón [pelo'ton] nm (Mil) squad, detachment

peluca [pe'luka] nf wig

peluche [pe'lutʃe] nm: **oso/muñeco de ~** teddy bear/soft toy

peludo, -a [pe'luðo, a] adj hairy, shaggy

peluquería [peluke'ria] nf hairdresser's;

P

peluquero, -a *nm/f* hairdresser
pelusa [pe'lusa] *nf* (*Bot*) down; (*en tela*) fluff
pena ['pena] *nf* (*congoja*) grief, sadness; (*remordimiento*) regret; (*dificultad*) trouble; (*dolor*) pain; (*Jur*) sentence; **merecer** *o* **valer la ~** to be worthwhile; **a duras ~s** with great difficulty; **¡qué ~!** what a shame!; **pena capital** capital punishment; **pena de muerte** death penalty
penal [pe'nal] *adj* penal ▷ *nm* (*cárcel*) prison
penalidad [penali'ðað] *nf* (*problema*, *dificultad*) trouble, hardship; (*Jur*) penalty, punishment; **penalidades** *nfpl* trouble *sg*, hardship *sg*
penalti [pe'nalti] *nm* = **penalty**
penalty [pe'nalti] (*pl* **~s** *o* **penalties**) *nm* penalty (kick)
pendiente [pen'djente] *adj* pending, unsettled ▷ *nm* earring ▷ *nf* hill, slope
pene ['pene] *nm* penis
penetrante [pene'trante] *adj* (*herida*) deep; (*persona, arma*) sharp; (*sonido*) penetrating, piercing; (*mirada*) searching; (*viento, ironía*) biting
penetrar [pene'trar] *vt* to penetrate, pierce; (*entender*) to grasp ▷ *vi* to penetrate, go in; (*entrar*) to enter, go in; (*líquido*) to soak in; (*fig*) to pierce
penicilina [peniθi'lina] *nf* penicillin
península [pe'ninsula] *nf* peninsula; **peninsular** *adj* peninsular
penique [pe'nike] *nm* penny
penitencia [peni'tenθja] *nf* penance
penoso, -a [pe'noso, a] *adj* (*lamentable*) distressing; (*difícil*) arduous, difficult
pensador, a [pensa'ðor, a] *nm/f* thinker
pensamiento [pensa'mjento] *nm* thought; (*mente*) mind; (*idea*) idea
pensar [pen'sar] *vt* to think; (*considerar*) to think over, think out; (*proponerse*) to intend, plan; (*imaginarse*) to think up, invent ▷ *vi* to think; **~ en** to aim at, aspire to; **pensativo, -a** *adj* thoughtful, pensive
pensión [pen'sjon] *nf* (*casa*) boarding *o* guest house; (*dinero*) pension; (*cama y comida*) board and lodging; **media ~** half-board; **pensión completa** full board; **pensionista** *nmf* (*jubilado*) (old-age) pensioner; (*huésped*) lodger
penúltimo, -a [pe'nultimo, a] *adj* penultimate, last but one
penumbra [pe'numbra] *nf* half-light
peña ['peɲa] *nf* (*roca*) rock; (*cuesta*) cliff, crag; (*grupo*) group, circle; (*LAM: club*) folk club
peñasco [pe'ɲasko] *nm* large rock, boulder

peñón [pe'ɲon] *nm* wall of rock; **el P~** the Rock (of Gibraltar)
peón [pe'on] *nm* labourer; (*LAM Agr*) farm labourer, farmhand; (*Ajedrez*) pawn
peonza [pe'onθa] *nf* spinning top
peor [pe'or] *adj* (*comparativo*) worse; (*superlativo*) worst ▷ *adv* worse; worst; **de mal en ~** from bad to worse
pepinillo [pepi'niʎo] *nm* gherkin
pepino [pe'pino] *nm* cucumber; **(no) me importa un ~** I don't care one bit
pepita [pe'pita] *nf* (*Bot*) pip; (*Minería*) nugget
pepito [pe'pito] (*ESP*) *nm* (*tb:* **~ de ternera**) steak sandwich
pequeño, -a [pe'keɲo, a] *adj* small, little
pera ['pera] *nf* pear; **peral** *nm* pear tree
percance [per'kanθe] *nm* setback, misfortune
percatarse [perka'tarse] *vr*: **~ de** to notice, take note of
percebe [per'θeβe] *nm* barnacle
percepción [perθep'θjon] *nf* (*vista*) perception; (*idea*) notion, idea
percha ['pertʃa] *nf* (*coat*) hanger; (*ganchos*) coat hooks *pl*; (*de ave*) perch
percibir [perθi'βir] *vt* to perceive, notice; (*Com*) to earn, get
percusión [perku'sjon] *nf* percussion
perdedor, a [perðe'ðor, a] *adj* losing ▷ *nm/f* loser
perder [per'ðer] *vt* to lose; (*tiempo, palabras*) to waste; (*oportunidad*) to lose, miss; (*tren*) to miss ▷ *vi* to lose; **perderse** *vr* (*extraviarse*) to get lost; (*desaparecer*) to disappear, be lost to view; (*arruinarse*) to be ruined; **echar a ~** (*comida*) to spoil, ruin; (*oportunidad*) to waste
pérdida ['perðiða] *nf* loss; (*de tiempo*) waste; **pérdidas** *nfpl* (*Com*) losses
perdido, -a [per'ðiðo, a] *adj* lost
perdiz [per'ðiθ] *nf* partridge
perdón [per'ðon] *nm* (*disculpa*) pardon, forgiveness; (*clemencia*) mercy; **¡~!** sorry!, I beg your pardon!; **perdonar** *vt* to pardon, forgive; (*la vida*) to spare; (*excusar*) to exempt, excuse; **¡perdone (usted)!** sorry!, I beg your pardon!
perecedero, -a [pereθe'ðero, a] *adj* perishable
perecer [pere'θer] *vi* to perish, die
peregrinación [pereɣrina'θjon] *nf* (*Rel*) pilgrimage
peregrino, -a [pere'ɣrino, a] *adj* (*idea*) strange, absurd ▷ *nm/f* pilgrim
perejil [pere'xil] *nm* parsley
perenne [pe'renne] *adj* everlasting, perennial

pereza [pe'reθa] nf laziness, idleness;
perezoso, -a adj lazy, idle
perfección [perfek'θjon] nf perfection;
perfeccionar vt to perfect; (mejorar) to
improve; (acabar) to complete, finish
perfecto, -a [per'fekto, a] adj perfect;
(total) complete
perfil [per'fil] nm profile; (contorno)
silhouette, outline; (Arq) (cross) section;
perfiles nmpl features
perforación [perfora'θjon] nf
perforation; (con taladro) drilling;
perforadora nf punch
perforar [perfo'rar] vt to perforate;
(agujero) to drill, bore; (papel) to punch a hole
in ▷ vi to drill, bore
perfume [per'fume] nm perfume, scent
periferia [peri'ferja] nf periphery; (de
ciudad) outskirts pl
periférico [peri'feriko] (LAM) nm ring road
(BRIT), beltway (US)
perilla [pe'riʎa] nf (barba) goatee; (LAM: de
puerta) doorknob, door handle
perímetro [pe'rimetro] nm perimeter
periódico, -a [pe'rjoðiko, a] adj
periodic(al) ▷ nm newspaper
periodismo [perjo'ðismo] nm
journalism; **periodista** nmf journalist
periodo [pe'rjoðo] nm period
período [pe'rjoðo] nm = **periodo**
periquito [peri'kito] nm budgerigar,
budgie
perito, -a [pe'rito, a] adj (experto) expert;
(diestro) skilled, skilful ▷ nm/f expert;
skilled worker; (técnico) technician
perjudicar [perxuði'kar] vt (gen) to
damage, harm; **perjudicial** adj damaging,
harmful; (en detrimento) detrimental;
perjuicio nm damage, harm
perjurar [perxu'rar] vi to commit perjury
perla ['perla] nf pearl; **me viene de ~s** it
suits me fine
permanecer [permane'θer] vi (quedarse)
to stay, remain; (seguir) to continue to be
permanente [perma'nente] adj
permanent, constant ▷ nf perm
permiso [per'miso] nm permission;
(licencia) permit, licence; **con ~** excuse me;
estar de ~ (Mil) to be on leave; **permiso de
conducir** driving licence (BRIT), driver's
license (US); **permiso por enfermedad**
(LAM) sick leave
permitir [permi'tir] vt to permit, allow
pernera [per'nera] nf trouser leg
pero ['pero] conj but; (aún) yet ▷ nm
(defecto) flaw, defect; (reparo) objection
perpendicular [perpendiku'lar] adj
perpendicular

perpetuo, -a [per'petwo, a] adj perpetual
perplejo, -a [per'plexo, a] adj perplexed,
bewildered
perra ['perra] nf (Zool) bitch; **estar sin una
~** (ESP: fam) to be flat broke
perrera [pe'rrera] nf kennel
perrito [pe'rrito] nm (tb: ~ **caliente**) hot
dog
perro ['perro] nm dog
persa ['persa] adj, nmf Persian
persecución [perseku'θjon] nf pursuit,
chase; (Rel, Pol) persecution
perseguir [perse'ɣir] vt to pursue, hunt;
(cortejar) to chase after; (molestar) to pester,
annoy; (Rel, Pol) to persecute
persiana [per'sjana] nf (Venetian) blind
persistente [persis'tente] adj persistent
persistir [persis'tir] vi to persist
persona [per'sona] nf person; **persona
mayor** elderly person
personaje [perso'naxe] nm important
person, celebrity; (Teatro etc) character
personal [perso'nal] adj (particular)
personal; (para una persona) single, for
one person ▷ nm personnel, staff;
personalidad nf personality
personarse [perso'narse] vr to appear
in person
personificar [personifi'kar] vt to
personify
perspectiva [perspek'tiβa] nf
perspective; (vista, panorama) view,
panorama; (posibilidad futura) outlook,
prospect
persuadir [perswa'ðir] vt (gen) to
persuade; (convencer) to convince;
persuadirse vr to become convinced;
persuasión nf persuasion
pertenecer [pertene'θer] vi to
belong; (fig) to concern; **perteneciente**
adj: **perteneciente a** belonging to;
pertenencia nf ownership; **pertenencias**
nfpl (bienes) possessions, property sg
pertenezca etc vb V **pertenecer**
pértiga ['pertiɣa] nf: **salto de ~** pole vault
pertinente [perti'nente] adj relevant,
pertinent; (apropiado) appropriate; **~ a**
concerning, relevant to
perturbación [perturβa'θjon] nf (Pol)
disturbance; (Med) upset, disturbance
Perú [pe'ru] nm Peru; **peruano, -a** adj,
nm/f Peruvian
perversión [perβer'sjon] nf perversion;
perverso, -a adj perverse; (depravado)
depraved
pervertido, -a [perβer'tiðo, a] adj
perverted ▷ nm/f pervert
pervertir [perβer'tir] vt to pervert,

corrupt

pesa ['pesa] nf weight; (Deporte) shot

pesadez [pesa'ðeθ] nf (peso) heaviness; (lentitud) slowness; (aburrimiento) tediousness

pesadilla [pesa'ðiʎa] nf nightmare, bad dream

pesado, -a [pe'saðo, a] adj heavy; (lento) slow; (difícil, duro) tough, hard; (aburrido) boring, tedious; (tiempo) sultry

pésame ['pesame] nm expression of condolence, message of sympathy; **dar el ~** to express one's condolences

pesar [pe'sar] vt to weigh ▷ vi to weigh; (ser pesado) to weigh a lot, be heavy; (fig: opinión) to carry weight; **no pesa mucho** it's not very heavy ▷ nm (arrepentimiento) regret; (pena) grief, sorrow; **a ~ de** o **pese a (que)** in spite of, despite

pesca ['peska] nf (acto) fishing; (lo pescado) catch; **ir de ~** to go fishing

pescadería [peskaðe'ria] nf fish shop, fishmonger's (BRIT)

pescadilla [peska'ðiʎa] nf whiting

pescado [pes'kaðo] nm fish

pescador, a [peska'ðor, a] nm/f fisherman/woman

pescar [pes'kar] vt (tomar) to catch; (intentar tomar) to fish for; (conseguir: trabajo) to manage to get ▷ vi to fish, go fishing

pesebre [pe'seβre] nm manger

peseta [pe'seta] nf (Hist) peseta

pesimista [pesi'mista] adj pessimistic ▷ nmf pessimist

pésimo, -a ['pesimo, a] adj awful, dreadful

peso ['peso] nm weight; (balanza) scales pl; (moneda) peso; **vender al ~** to sell by weight; **peso bruto/neto** gross/net weight; **peso pesado/pluma** heavyweight/featherweight

pesquero, -a [pes'kero, a] adj fishing cpd

pestaña [pes'taɲa] nf (Anat) eyelash; (borde) rim

peste ['peste] nf plague; (mal olor) stink, stench

pesticida [pesti'θiða] nm pesticide

pestillo [pes'tiʎo] nm (cerrojo) bolt; (picaporte) door handle

petaca [pe'taka] nf (de cigarros) cigarette case; (de pipa) tobacco pouch; (MÉX: maleta) suitcase

pétalo ['petalo] nm petal

petardo [pe'tardo] nm firework, firecracker

petición [peti'θjon] nf (pedido) request, plea; (memorial) petition; (Jur) plea

peto ['peto] nm (ESP) dungarees pl,

overalls pl (US)

petróleo [pe'troleo] nm oil, petroleum; **petrolero, -a** adj petroleum cpd ▷ nm (oil) tanker

peyorativo, -a [pejora'tiβo, a] adj pejorative

pez [peθ] nm fish; **pez espada** swordfish

pezón [pe'θon] nm teat, nipple

pezuña [pe'θuɲa] nf hoof

pianista [pja'nista] nmf pianist

piano ['pjano] nm piano

piar [pjar] vi to cheep

pibe, -a ['piβe, a] (RPL) nm/f boy/girl

picadero [pika'ðero] nm riding school

picadillo [pika'ðiʎo] nm mince, minced meat

picado, -a [pi'kaðo, a] adj pricked, punctured; (Culin) minced, chopped; (mar) choppy; (diente) bad; (tabaco) cut; (enfadado) cross

picador [pika'ðor] nm (Taur) picador; (minero) faceworker

picadura [pika'ðura] nf (pinchazo) puncture; (de abeja) sting; (de mosquito) bite; (tabaco picado) cut tobacco

picante [pi'kante] adj hot; (comentario) racy, spicy

picaporte [pika'porte] nm (manija) doorhandle; (pestillo) latch

picar [pi'kar] vt (agujerear, perforar) to prick, puncture; (abeja) to sting; (mosquito, serpiente) to bite; (Culin) to mince, chop; (incitar) to incite, goad; (dañar, irritar) to annoy, bother; (quemar: lengua) to burn, sting ▷ vi (pez) to bite, take the bait; (sol) to burn, scorch; (abeja, Med) to sting; (mosquito) to bite; **picarse** vr (agriarse) to turn sour, go off; (ofenderse) to take offence

picardía [pikar'ðia] nf villainy; (astucia) slyness, craftiness; (una picardía) dirty trick; (palabra) rude/bad word o expression

pícaro, -a ['pikaro, a] adj (malicioso) villainous; (travieso) mischievous ▷ nm (astuto) crafty sort; (sinvergüenza) rascal, scoundrel

pichi ['pitʃi] nm (ESP) pinafore dress (BRIT), jumper (US)

pichón [pi'tʃon] nm young pigeon

pico ['piko] nm (de ave) beak; (punta) sharp point; (Tec) pick, pickaxe; (Geo) peak, summit; **y ~ and** a bit; **las seis y ~** six and a bit

picor [pi'kor] nm itch

picoso, -a [pi'koso, a] (MÉX) adj (comida) hot

picudo, -a [pi'kuðo, a] adj pointed, with a point

pidió etc vb V **pedir**

pido etc vb V **pedir**

pie [pje] (pl **~s**) nm foot; (fig: motivo) motive, basis; (: fundamento) foothold; **ir a ~** to go on foot, walk; **estar de ~** to be standing (up); **ponerse de ~** to stand up; **de ~s a cabeza** from top to bottom; **al ~ de la letra** (citar) literally, verbatim; (copiar) exactly, word for word; **en ~ de guerra** on a war footing; **dar ~ a** to give cause for; **hacer ~** (en el agua) to touch (the) bottom

piedad [pje'ðað] nf (lástima) pity, compassion; (clemencia) mercy; (devoción) piety, devotion

piedra ['pjeðra] nf stone; (roca) rock; (de mechero) flint; (Meteorología) hailstone; **piedra preciosa** precious stone

piel [pjel] nf (Anat) skin; (Zool) skin, hide, fur; (cuero) leather; (Bot) skin, peel

pienso etc vb V **pensar**

pierdo etc vb V **perder**

pierna ['pjerna] nf leg

pieza ['pjeθa] nf piece; (habitación) room; **pieza de recambio** o **repuesto** spare (part)

pigmeo, -a [piɣ'meo, a] adj, nm/f pigmy

pijama [pi'xama] nm pyjamas pl (BRIT), pajamas pl (US)

pila ['pila] nf (Elec) battery; (montón) heap, pile; (lavabo) sink

píldora ['pildora] nf pill; **la ~ (anticonceptiva)** the (contraceptive) pill

pileta [pi'leta] (RPL) nf (fregadero) (kitchen) sink; (piscina) swimming pool

pillar [pi'ʎar] vt (saquear) to pillage, plunder; (fam: coger) to catch; (: agarrar) to grasp, seize; (: entender) to grasp, catch on to; **pillarse** vr: **~se un dedo con la puerta** to catch one's finger in the door

pillo, -a ['piʎo, a] adj villainous; (astuto) sly, crafty ▷ nm/f rascal, rogue, scoundrel

piloto [pi'loto] nm pilot; (de aparato) (pilot) light; (Auto: luz) tail o rear light; (: conductor) driver; **piloto automático** automatic pilot

pimentón [pimen'ton] nm paprika

pimienta [pi'mjenta] nf pepper

pimiento [pi'mjento] nm pepper, pimiento

pin [pin] (pl **~s**) nm badge

pinacoteca [pinako'teka] nf art gallery

pinar [pi'nar] nm pine forest (BRIT), pine grove (US)

pincel [pin'θel] nm paintbrush

pinchadiscos [pintʃa'ðiskos] (ESP) nmf inv disc-jockey, DJ

pinchar [pin'tʃar] vt (perforar) to prick, pierce; (neumático) to puncture; (fig) to prod; (Inform) to click

pinchazo [pin'tʃaθo] nm (perforación) prick; (de neumático) puncture; (fig) prod

pincho ['pintʃo] nm savoury (snack); **pincho de tortilla** small slice of omelette; **pincho moruno** shish kebab

ping-pong ['pin'pon] nm table tennis

pingüino [pin'gwino] nm penguin

pino ['pino] nm pine (tree)

pinta ['pinta] nf spot; (de líquidos) spot, drop; (aspecto) appearance, look(s) (pl); **pintado, -a** adj spotted; (de colores) colourful; **pintadas** nfpl graffiti sg

pintalabios [pinta'laβjos] (ESP) nm inv lipstick

pintar [pin'tar] vt to paint ▷ vi to paint; (fam) to count, be important; **pintarse** vr to put on make-up

pintor, a [pin'tor, a] nm/f painter

pintoresco, -a [pinto'resko, a] adj picturesque

pintura [pin'tura] nf painting; **pintura al óleo** oil painting

pinza ['pinθa] nf (Zool) claw; (para colgar ropa) clothes peg; (Tec) pincers pl; **pinzas** nfpl (para depilar etc) tweezers pl

piña ['pina] nf (de pino) pine cone; (fruta) pineapple; (fig) group

piñata [pi'nata] nf container hung up at parties to be beaten with sticks until sweets or presents fall out

piñón [pi'non] nm (fruto) pine nut; (Tec) pinion

pío, -a ['pio, a] adj (devoto) pious, devout; (misericordioso) merciful

piojo ['pjoxo] nm louse

pipa ['pipa] nf pipe; **pipas** nfpl (Bot) (edible) sunflower seeds

pipí [pi'pi] (fam) nm: **hacer ~** to have a wee(-wee) (BRIT), have to go (wee-wee) (US)

pique ['pike] nm (resentimiento) pique, resentment; (rivalidad) rivalry, competition; **irse a ~** to sink; (esperanza, familia) to be ruined

piqueta [pi'keta] nf pick(axe)

piquete [pi'kete] nm (Mil) squad, party;

(de obreros) picket; (MÉX: de insecto) bite; **piquetear** (LAM) vt to picket

pirado, -a [pi'raðo, a] (fam) adj round the bend ▷ nm/f nutter

piragua [pi'raɣwa] nf canoe; **piragüismo** nm canoeing

pirámide [pi'ramiðe] nf pyramid

pirata [pi'rata] adj, nmf pirate; **pirata informático** hacker

Pirineo(s) [piri'neo(s)] nm(pl) Pyrenees pl

pirómano, -a [pi'romano, a] nm/f (Med, Jur) arsonist

piropo [pi'ropo] nm compliment, (piece of) flattery

pirueta [pi'rweta] nf pirouette

piruleta [piru'leta] (ESP) nf lollipop

pis [pis] (fam) nm pee, piss; **hacer ~** to have a pee; (para niños) to wee-wee

pisada [pi'saða] nf (paso) footstep; (huella) footprint

pisar [pi'sar] vt (caminar sobre) to walk on, tread on; (apretar con el pie) to press; (fig) to trample on, walk all over ▷ vi to tread, step, walk

piscina [pis'θina] nf swimming pool

Piscis [pis'θis] nm Pisces

piso [pi'so] nm (suelo, planta) floor; (ESP: apartamento) flat (BRIT), apartment; **primer ~** (ESP) first floor; (LAM: planta baja) ground floor

pisotear [pisote'ar] vt to trample (on o underfoot)

pista ['pista] nf track, trail; (indicio) clue; **pista de aterrizaje** runway; **pista de baile** dance floor; **pista de hielo** ice rink; **pista de tenis** (ESP) tennis court

pistola [pis'tola] nf pistol; (Tec) spray-gun

pistón [pis'ton] nm (Tec) piston; (Mús) key

pitar [pi'tar] vt (silbato) to blow; (rechiflar) to whistle at, boo ▷ vi to whistle; (Auto) to sound o toot one's horn; (LAM: fumar) to smoke

pitillo [pi'tiʎo] nm cigarette

pito ['pito] nm whistle; (de coche) horn

pitón [pi'ton] nm (Zool) python

pitonisa [pito'nisa] nf fortune-teller

pitorreo [pito'rreo] nm joke; **estar de ~** to be joking

píxel ['piksel] (pl pixels or ~es) nm pixel

piyama [pi'jama] (LAM) nm pyjamas pl (BRIT), pajamas pl (US)

pizarra [pi'θarra] nf (piedra) slate; (ESP: encerado) blackboard; **pizarra blanca** whiteboard; **pizarra interactiva** interactive whiteboard

pizarrón [piθa'rron] (LAM) nm blackboard

pizca ['piθka] nf pinch, spot; (fig) spot, speck; **ni ~** not a bit

placa ['plaka] nf plate; (distintivo) badge, insignia; **placa de matrícula** (LAM) number plate

placard [pla'kar] (RPL) nm cupboard

placer [pla'θer] nm pleasure ▷ vt to please

plaga ['plaɣa] nf pest; (Med) plague; (abundancia) abundance

plagio ['plaxjo] nm plagiarism

plan [plan] nm (esquema, proyecto) plan; (idea, intento) idea, intention; **tener ~** (fam) to have a date; **tener un ~** (fam) to have an affair; **en ~ económico** (fam) on the cheap; **vamos en ~ de turismo** we're going as tourists; **si te pones en ese ~ ...** if that's your attitude ...

plana ['plana] nf sheet (of paper), page; (Tec) trowel; **en primera ~** on the front page

plancha ['plantʃa] nf (para planchar) iron; (rótulo) plate, sheet; (Náut) gangway; **a la ~** (Culin) grilled; **planchar** vt to iron ▷ vi to do the ironing

planear [plane'ar] vt to plan ▷ vi to glide

planeta [pla'neta] nm planet

plano, -a ['plano, a] adj flat, level, even ▷ nm (Mat, Tec) plane; (Foto) shot; (Arq) plan; (Geo) map; (de ciudad) map, street plan; **primer ~** close-up

planta ['planta] nf (Bot, Tec) plant; (Anat) sole of the foot, foot; (piso) floor; (LAM: personal) staff; **planta baja** ground floor

plantar [plan'tar] vt (Bot) to plant; (levantar) to erect, set up; **plantarse** vr to stand firm; **~ a algn en la calle** to throw sb out; **dejar plantado a algn** (fam) to stand sb up

plantear [plante'ar] vt (problema) to pose; (dificultad) to raise

plantilla [plan'tiʎa] nf (de zapato) insole; (ESP: personal) personnel; **ser de ~** (ESP) to be on the staff

plantón [plan'ton] nm (Mil) guard, sentry; (fam) long wait; **dar (un) ~ a algn** to stand sb up

plasta ['plasta] (ESP: fam) adj inv boring ▷ nmf bore

plástico, -a ['plastiko, a] adj plastic ▷ nm plastic

Plastilina® [plasti'lina] nf Plasticine®

plata ['plata] nf (metal) silver; (cosas hechas de plata) silverware; (cs: dinero) cash, dough

plataforma [plata'forma] nf platform; **plataforma de lanzamiento/perforación** launch(ing) pad/drilling rig

plátano ['platano] nm (fruta) banana; (árbol) plane tree; banana tree

platea [pla'tea] nf (Teatro) pit

plática ['platika] nf talk, chat; **platicar** vi

to talk, chat

platillo [pla'tiʎo] nm saucer; **platillos** nmpl (Mús) cymbals; **platillo volante** flying saucer

platino [pla'tino] nm platinum; **platinos** nmpl (Auto) contact points

plato ['plato] nm plate, dish; (parte de comida) course; (comida) dish; **primer ~** first course; **plato combinado** set main course (served on one plate); **plato fuerte** main course

playa ['plaja] nf beach; (costa) seaside; **playa de estacionamiento** (cs) car park (BRIT), parking lot (US)

playera [pla'jera] nf (MÉX: camiseta) T-shirt; **playeras** nfpl (zapatos) canvas shoes

plaza ['plaθa] nf square; (mercado) market(place); (sitio) room, space; (de vehículo) seat, place; (colocación) post, job; **plaza de toros** bullring

plazo ['plaθo] nm (lapso de tiempo) time, period; (fecha de vencimiento) expiry date; (pago parcial) instalment; **a corto/largo ~** short-/long-term; **comprar algo a ~s** to buy sth on hire purchase (BRIT) o on time (US)

plazoleta [plaθo'leta] nf small square

plebeyo, -a [ple'βejo, a] adj plebeian; (pey) coarse, common

plegable [ple'ɣaβle] adj collapsible; (silla) folding

pleito ['pleito] nm (Jur) lawsuit, case; (fig) dispute, feud

plenitud [pleni'tuð] nf plenitude, fullness; (abundancia) abundance

pleno, -a ['pleno, a] adj full; (completo) complete ▷ nm plenum; **en ~ día** in broad daylight; **en ~ verano** at the height of summer; **en plena cara** full in the face

pliego etc ['pljeɣo] vb V **plegar** ▷ nm (hoja) sheet (of paper); (carta) sealed letter/ document; **pliego de condiciones** details pl, specifications pl

pliegue etc ['pljeɣe] vb V **plegar** ▷ nm fold, crease; (de vestido) pleat

plomería [plome'ria] (LAM) nf plumbing; **plomero** [plo'mero] nm plumber

plomo ['plomo] nm (metal) lead; (Elec) fuse; **sin ~** unleaded

pluma ['pluma] nf feather; (para escribir): ~ **(estilográfica)** (LAM) ink pen; ~ **fuente** (LAM) fountain pen

plumero [plu'mero] nm (para el polvo) feather duster

plumón [plu'mon] nm (de ave) down

plural [plu'ral] adj plural

pluriempleo [pluriem'pleo] nm having more than one job

plus [plus] nm bonus

población [poβla'θjon] nf population; (pueblo, ciudad) town, city

poblado, -a [po'βlaðo, a] adj inhabited ▷ nm (aldea) village; (pueblo) (small) town; **densamente ~** densely populated

poblador, a [poβla'ðor, a] nm/f settler, colonist

pobre ['poβre] adj poor ▷ nmf poor person; **pobreza** nf poverty

pocilga [po'θilɣa] nf pigsty

poco, -a ['poko, a] adj **1** (sg) little, not much; **poco tiempo** little o not much time; **de poco interés** of little interest, not very interesting; **poca cosa** not much

2 (pl) few, not many; **unos pocos** a few, some; **pocos niños comen lo que les conviene** few children eat what they should ▷ adv **1** little, not much; **cuesta poco** it doesn't cost much

2 (+ adj: negativo, antónimo): **poco amable/ inteligente** not very nice/intelligent

3: **por poco me caigo** I almost fell

4: **a poco: a poco de haberse casado** shortly after getting married

5: **poco a poco** little by little ▷ nm a little, a bit; **un poco triste/de dinero** a little sad/money

podar [po'ðar] vt to prune

poder [po'ðer] vi **1** (tener capacidad) can, be able to; **no puedo hacerlo** I can't do it, I'm unable to do it

2 (tener permiso) can, may, be allowed to; ¿**se puede?** may I (o we)?; **puedes irte ahora** you may go now; **no se puede fumar en este hospital** smoking is not allowed in this hospital

3 (tener posibilidad) may, might, could; **puede llegar mañana** he may o might arrive tomorrow; **pudiste haberte hecho daño** you might o could have hurt yourself; ¡**podías habérmelo dicho antes!** you might have told me before!

4: **puede ser** perhaps; **puede ser que lo sepa Tomás** Tomás may o might know

5: ¡**no puedo más!** I've had enough!; **es tonto a más no poder** he's as stupid as they come

6: **poder con: no puedo con este crío** this kid's too much for me

▷ *nm* power; **detentar** *o* **ocupar** *o*
estar en el poder to be in power; **poder**
adquisitivo/ejecutivo/legislativo
purchasing/executive/legislative power;
poder judicial judiciary

poderoso, -a [poðe'roso, a] *adj* (*político,*
país) powerful
podio ['poðjo] *nm* (*Deporte*) podium
podium ['poðjum] = **podio**
podrido, -a [po'ðriðo, a] *adj* rotten, bad;
(*fig*) rotten, corrupt
podrir [po'ðrir] = **pudrir**
poema [po'ema] *nm* poem
poesía [poe'sia] *nf* poetry
poeta [po'eta] *nmf* poet; **poético, -a** *adj*
poetic(al)
poetisa [poe'tisa] *nf* (woman) poet
póker ['poker] *nm* poker
polaco, -a [po'lako, a] *adj* Polish ▷ *nm/f*
Pole
polar [po'lar] *adj* polar
polea [po'lea] *nf* pulley
polémica [po'lemika] *nf* polemics *sg*; (*una*
polémica) controversy, polemic
polen ['polen] *nm* pollen
policía [poli'θia] *nmf* policeman/woman
▷ *nf* police; **policíaco, -a** *adj* police *cpd*;
novela policíaca detective story; **policial**
adj police *cpd*
polideportivo [poliðepor'tiβo] *nm* sports
centre *o* complex
polígono [po'liɣono] *nm* (*Mat*) polygon;
polígono industrial (*ESP*) industrial estate
polilla [po'liʎa] *nf* moth
polio ['poljo] *nf* polio
política [po'litika] *nf* politics *sg*;
(*económica, agraria etc*) policy; V *tb* **político**
político, -a [po'litiko, a] *adj* political;
(*discreto*) tactful; (*de familia*) ...-in-law ▷ *nm/f*
politician; **padre ~** father-in-law
póliza ['poliθa] *nf* certificate, voucher;
(*impuesto*) tax stamp; **póliza de seguro(s)**
insurance policy
polizón [poli'θon] *nm* stowaway
pollera [po'ʎera] (*cs*) *nf* skirt
pollo ['poʎo] *nm* chicken
polo ['polo] *nm* (*Geo, Elec*) pole; (*helado*) ice
lolly (*BRIT*), Popsicle® (*US*); (*Deporte*) polo;
(*suéter*) polo-neck; **polo Norte/Sur** North/
South Pole
Polonia [po'lonja] *nf* Poland
poltrona [pol'trona] *nf* easy chair
polución [polu'θjon] *nf* pollution
polvera [pol'βera] *nf* powder compact
polvo ['polβo] *nm* dust; (*Quím, Culin, Med*)
powder; **polvos** *nmpl* (*maquillaje*) powder
sg; **en ~** powdered; **quitar el ~** to dust; **estar**

hecho ~ (*fam*) to be worn out *o* exhausted;
polvos de talco talcum powder *sg*
pólvora ['polβora] *nf* gunpowder
polvoriento, -a [polβo'rjento, a] *adj*
(*superficie*) dusty; (*sustancia*) powdery
pomada [po'maða] *nf* cream, ointment
pomelo [po'melo] *nm* grapefruit
pómez ['pomeθ] *nf*: **piedra ~** pumice stone
pomo ['pomo] *nm* doorknob
pompa ['pompa] *nf* (*burbuja*) bubble;
(*bomba*) pump; (*esplendor*) pomp, splendour
pómulo ['pomulo] *nm* cheekbone
pon [pon] *vb* V **poner**
ponchadura [pontʃa'dura] (*MÉX*) *nf*
puncture (*BRIT*), flat (*US*); **ponchar** (*MÉX*) *vt*
(*llanta*) to puncture
ponche ['pontʃe] *nm* punch
poncho ['pontʃo] *nm* poncho
pondré *etc vb* V **poner**

○ **PALABRA CLAVE**

poner [po'ner] *vt* **1** (*colocar*) to put;
(*telegrama*) to send; (*obra de teatro*) to put on;
(*película*) to show; **ponlo más fuerte** turn it
up; **¿qué ponen en el Excelsior?** what's on
at the Excelsior?
2 (*tienda*) to open; (*instalar: gas etc*) to put in;
(*radio, TV*) to switch *o* turn on
3 (*suponer*): **pongamos que ...** let's suppose
that ...
4 (*contribuir*): **el gobierno ha puesto otro**
millón the government has contributed
another million
5 (*Tel*): **póngame con el Sr. López** can you
put me through to Mr. López?
6: **poner de: le han puesto de director**
general they've appointed him general
manager
7 (*+ adj*) to make; **me estás poniendo**
nerviosa you're making me nervous
8 (*dar nombre*): **al hijo le pusieron Diego**
they called their son Diego
▷ *vi* (*gallina*) to lay
ponerse *vr* **1** (*colocarse*): **se puso a mi lado**
he came and stood beside me; **tú ponte en**
esa silla you go and sit on that chair
2 (*vestido, cosméticos*) to put on; **¿por qué no**
te pones el vestido nuevo? why don't you
put on *o* wear your new dress?
3 (*+ adj*) to turn; to get, become; **se puso**
muy serio he got very serious; **después de**
lavarla la tela se puso azul after washing
it the material turned blue
4: **ponerse a: se puso a llorar** he started
to cry; **tienes que ponerte a estudiar** you
must get down to studying

pongo etc vb V **poner**
poniente [po'njente] nm (occidente) west; (viento) west wind
pontífice [pon'tifiθe] nm pope, pontiff
popa ['popa] nf stern
popote [po'pote] (MÉX) nm straw
popular [popu'lar] adj popular; (cultura) of the people, folk cpd; **popularidad** nf popularity

○ **PALABRA CLAVE**

por [por] prep **1** (objetivo) for; **luchar por la patria** to fight for one's country
2 (+ infin): **por no llegar tarde** so as not to arrive late; **por citar unos ejemplos** to give a few examples
3 (causa) out of, because of; **por escasez de fondos** through o for lack of funds
4 (tiempo): **por la mañana/noche** in the morning/at night; **se queda por una semana** she's staying (for) a week
5 (lugar): **pasar por Madrid** to pass through Madrid; **ir a Guayaquil por Quito** to go to Guayaquil via Quito; **caminar por la calle** to walk along the street; V tb **todo**
6 (cambio, precio): **te doy uno nuevo por el que tienes** I'll give you a new one (in return) for the one you've got
7 (valor distributivo): **6 euros por hora/cabeza** 6 euros an o per hour/a o per head
8 (modo, medio) by; **por correo/avión** by post/air; **entrar por la entrada principal** to go in through the main entrance
9: **10 por 10 son 100** 10 times 10 is 100
10 (en lugar de): **vino él por su jefe** he came instead of his boss
11: **por mí que revienten** as far as I'm concerned they can drop dead
12: **¿por qué?** why?; **¿por qué no?** why not?

porcelana [porθe'lana] nf porcelain; (china) china
porcentaje [porθen'taxe] nm percentage
porción [por'θjon] nf (parte) portion, share; (cantidad) quantity, amount
porfiar [por'fjar] vi to persist, insist; (disputar) to argue stubbornly
pormenor [porme'nor] nm detail, particular
pornografía [pornoɣra'fia] nf pornography
poro ['poro] nm pore
pororó [poro'ro] (RPL) nm popcorn
poroso, -a [po'roso, a] adj porous
poroto [po'roto] (CS) nm bean
porque ['porke] conj (a causa de) because; (ya que) since; (con el fin de) so that, in order

that
porqué [por'ke] nm reason, cause
porquería [porke'ria] nf (suciedad) filth, dirt; (acción) dirty trick; (objeto) small thing, trifle; (fig) rubbish
porra ['porra] (ESP) nf (arma) stick, club
porrazo [po'rraθo] nm blow, bump
porro ['porro] (fam) nm (droga) joint (fam)
porrón [po'rron] nm glass wine jar with a long spout
portaaviones [porta'(a)βjones] nm inv aircraft carrier
portada [por'taða] nf (de revista) cover
portador, a [porta'ðor, a] nm/f carrier, bearer; (Com) bearer, payee
portaequipajes [portaeki'paxes] nm inv (Auto: maletero) boot; (: baca) luggage rack
portafolio [porta'foljo] (LAM) nm briefcase
portal [por'tal] nm (entrada) vestibule, hall; (portada) porch, doorway; (puerta de entrada) main door; (Internet) portal; **portales** nmpl (LAM) arcade sg
portamaletas [portama'letas] nm inv (Auto: maletero) boot; (: baca) roof rack
portarse [por'tarse] vr to behave, conduct o.s.
portátil [por'tatil] adj portable
portavoz [porta'βoθ] nmf spokesman/woman
portazo [por'taθo] nm: **dar un ~** to slam the door
porte ['porte] nm (Com) transport; (precio) transport charges pl
portentoso, -a [porten'toso, a] adj marvellous, extraordinary
porteño, -a [por'teno, a] adj of o from Buenos Aires
portería [porte'ria] nf (oficina) porter's office; (Deporte) goal
portero, -a [por'tero, a] nm/f porter; (conserje) caretaker; (ujier) doorman; (Deporte) goalkeeper; **portero automático** (ESP) entry phone
pórtico ['portiko] nm (patio) portico, porch; (fig) gateway; (arcada) arcade
portorriqueño, -a [portorri'keno, a] adj Puerto Rican
Portugal [portu'ɣal] nm Portugal; **portugués, -esa** adj, nm/f Portuguese ▷ nm (Ling) Portuguese
porvenir [porβe'nir] nm future
pos [pos] prep: **en ~ de** after, in pursuit of
posaderas [posa'ðeras] nfpl backside sg, buttocks
posar [po'sar] vt (en el suelo) to lay down, put down; (la mano) to place, put gently ▷ vi (modelo) to sit, pose; **posarse** vr to settle;

p

(*pájaro*) to perch; (*avión*) to land, come down

posavasos [posa'basos] *nm inv* coaster; (*para cerveza*) beermat

posdata [pos'ðata] *nf* postscript

pose ['pose] *nf* pose

poseedor, a [posee'ðor, a] *nm/f* owner, possessor; (*de récord, puesto*) holder

poseer [pose'er] *vt* to possess, own; (*ventaja*) to enjoy; (*récord, puesto*) to hold

posesivo, -a [pose'siβo, a] *adj* possessive

posibilidad [posiβili'ðað] *nf* possibility; (*oportunidad*) chance; **posibilitar** *vt* to make possible; (*hacer realizable*) to make feasible

posible [po'siβle] *adj* possible; (*realizable*) feasible; **de ser ~** if possible; **en lo ~** as far as possible

posición [posi'θjon] *nf* position; (*rango social*) status

positivo, -a [posi'tiβo, a] *adj* positive

poso ['poso] *nm* sediment; (*heces*) dregs *pl*

posponer [pospo'ner] *vt* (*relegar*) to put behind/below; (*aplazar*) to postpone

posta ['posta] *nf*: **a ~** deliberately, on purpose

postal [pos'tal] *adj* postal ▷ *nf* postcard

poste ['poste] *nm* (*de telégrafos etc*) post, pole; (*columna*) pillar

póster ['poster] (*pl* **-es, ~s**) *nm* poster

posterior [poste'rjor] *adj* back, rear; (*siguiente*) following, subsequent; (*más tarde*) later

postgrado [post'graðo] *nm* = **posgrado**

postizo, -a [pos'tiθo, a] *adj* false, artificial ▷ *nm* hairpiece

postre ['postre] *nm* sweet, dessert

póstumo, -a ['postumo, a] *adj* posthumous

postura [pos'tura] *nf* (*del cuerpo*) posture, position; (*fig*) attitude, position

potable [po'taβle] *adj* drinkable; **agua ~** drinking water

potaje [po'taxe] *nm* thick vegetable soup

potencia [po'tenθja] *nf* power; **potencial** [poten'θjal] *adj, nm* potential

potente [po'tente] *adj* powerful

potro, -a ['potro, a] *nm/f* (*Zool*) colt/filly ▷ *nm* (*de gimnasia*) vaulting horse

pozo ['poθo] *nm* well; (*de río*) deep pool; (*de mina*) shaft

PP (ESP) *nm abr* = **Partido Popular**

práctica ['praktika] *nf* practice; (*método*) method; (*arte, capacidad*) skill; **en la ~** in practice

practicable [prakti'kaβle] *adj* practicable; (*camino*) passable

practicante [prakti'kante] *nmf* (*Med: ayudante de doctor*) medical assistant;

(*: enfermero*) nurse; (*quien practica algo*) practitioner ▷ *adj* practising

practicar [prakti'kar] *vt* to practise; (*Deporte*) to play; (*realizar*) to carry out, perform

práctico, -a ['praktiko, a] *adj* practical; (*instruído: persona*) skilled, expert

practique *etc vb* V **practicar**

pradera [pra'ðera] *nf* meadow; (*US etc*) prairie

prado ['praðo] *nm* (*campo*) meadow, field; (*pastizal*) pasture

Praga ['praxa] *n* Prague

pragmático, -a [prax'matiko, a] *adj* pragmatic

precario, -a [pre'karjo, a] *adj* precarious

precaución [prekau'θjon] *nf* (*medida preventiva*) preventive measure, precaution; (*prudencia*) caution, wariness

precedente [preθe'ðente] *adj* preceding; (*anterior*) former ▷ *nm* precedent

preceder [preθe'ðer] *vt, vi* to precede, go before, come before

precepto [pre'θepto] *nm* precept

precinto [pre'θinto] *nm* (*tb:* **~ de garantía**) seal

precio ['preθjo] *nm* price; (*costo*) cost; (*valor*) value, worth; (*de viaje*) fare; **precio al contado/de coste/de oportunidad** cash/cost/bargain price; **precio al por menor** retail price; **precio de ocasión** bargain price; **precio de venta al público** retail price; **precio tope** top price

preciosidad [preθjosi'ðað] *nf* (*valor*) (high) value, (great) worth; (*encanto*) charm; (*cosa bonita*) beautiful thing; **es una ~** it's lovely, it's really beautiful

precioso, -a [pre'θjoso, a] *adj* precious; (*de mucho valor*) valuable; (*fam*) lovely, beautiful

precipicio [preθi'piθjo] *nm* cliff, precipice; (*fig*) abyss

precipitación [preθipita'θjon] *nf* haste; (*lluvia*) rainfall

precipitado, -a [preθipi'taðo, a] *adj* (*conducta*) hasty, rash; (*salida*) hasty, sudden

precipitar [preθipi'tar] *vt* (*arrojar*) to hurl down, throw; (*apresurar*) to hasten; (*acelerar*) to speed up, accelerate; **precipitarse** *vr* to throw o.s.; (*apresurarse*) to rush; (*actuar sin pensar*) to act rashly

precisamente [preθisa'mente] *adv* precisely; (*exactamente*) precisely, exactly

precisar [preθi'sar] *vt* (*necesitar*) to need, require; (*fijar*) to determine exactly, fix; (*especificar*) to specify

precisión [preθi'sjon] *nf* (*exactitud*) precision

preciso, -a [pre'θiso, a] *adj* (*exacto*) precise; (*necesario*) necessary, essential

preconcebido, -a [prekonθe'βiðo, a] *adj* preconceived

precoz [pre'koθ] *adj* (*persona*) precocious; (*calvicie etc*) premature

predecir [preðe'θir] *vt* to predict, forecast

predestinado, -a [preðesti'naðo, a] *adj* predestined

predicar [preði'kar] *vt, vi* to preach

predicción [preðik'θjon] *nf* prediction

predilecto, -a [preði'lekto, a] *adj* favourite

predisposición [preðisposi'θjon] *nf* inclination; prejudice, bias

predominar [preðomi'nar] *vt* to dominate ▷ *vi* to predominate; (*prevalecer*) to prevail; **predominio** *nm* predominance; prevalence

preescolar [pre(e)sko'lar] *adj* preschool

prefabricado, -a [prefaβri'kaðo, a] *adj* prefabricated

prefacio [pre'faθjo] *nm* preface

preferencia [prefe'renθja] *nf* preference; **de ~** preferably, for preference

preferible [prefe'riβle] *adj* preferable

preferir [prefe'rir] *vt* to prefer

prefiero *etc* *vb* V **preferir**

prefijo [pre'fixo] *nm* (*Tel*) (dialling) code

pregunta [pre'ɣunta] *nf* question; **hacer una ~** to ask a question; **preguntas frecuentes** FAQs, frequently asked questions

preguntar [preɣun'tar] *vt* to ask; (*cuestionar*) to question ▷ *vi* to ask; **preguntarse** *vr* to wonder; **preguntar por algn** to ask for sb; **preguntón, -ona** [preɣun'ton, ona] *adj* inquisitive

prehistórico, -a [preis'toriko, a] *adj* prehistoric

prejuicio [pre'xwiθjo] *nm* (*acto*) prejudgement; (*idea preconcebida*) preconception; (*parcialidad*) prejudice, bias

preludio [pre'luðjo] *nm* prelude

prematuro, -a [prema'turo, a] *adj* premature

premeditar [premeði'tar] *vt* to premeditate

premiar [pre'mjar] *vt* to reward; (*en un concurso*) to give a prize to

premio ['premjo] *nm* reward; prize; (*Com*) premium

prenatal [prena'tal] *adj* antenatal, prenatal

prenda ['prenda] *nf* (*ropa*) garment, article of clothing; (*garantía*) pledge; **prendas** *nfpl* (*talentos*) talents, gifts

prender [pren'der] *vt* (*captar*) to catch, capture; (*detener*) to arrest; (*Costura*) to pin, attach; (*sujetar*) to fasten ▷ *vi* to catch; (*arraigar*) to take root; **prenderse** *vr* (*encenderse*) to catch fire

prendido, -a [pren'diðo, a] (*LAM*) *adj* (*luz etc*) on

prensa ['prensa] *nf* press; **la ~** the press

preñado, -a [pre'ɲaðo, a] *adj* pregnant; **~ de** pregnant with, full of

preocupación [preokupa'θjon] *nf* worry, concern; (*ansiedad*) anxiety

preocupado, -a [preoku'paðo, a] *adj* worried, concerned; (*ansioso*) anxious

preocupar [preoku'par] *vt* to worry; **preocuparse** *vr* to worry; **~se de algo** (*hacerse cargo*) to take care of sth

preparación [prepara'θjon] *nf* (*acto*) preparation; (*estado*) readiness; (*entrenamiento*) training

preparado, -a [prepa'raðo, a] *adj* (*dispuesto*) prepared; (*Culin*) ready (to serve) ▷ *nm* preparation

preparar [prepa'rar] *vt* (*disponer*) to prepare, get ready; (*Tec: tratar*) to prepare, process; (*entrenar*) to teach, train; **prepararse** *vr*: **~se a** *o* **para** to prepare to *o* for, get ready to *o* for; **preparativo, -a** *adj* preparatory, preliminary; **preparativos** *nmpl* preparations; **preparatoria** (*MÉX*) *nf* sixth-form college (*BRIT*), senior high school (*US*)

presa ['presa] *nf* (*cosa apresada*) catch; (*víctima*) victim; (*de animal*) prey; (*de agua*) dam

presagiar [presa'xjar] *vt* to presage, forebode; **presagio** *nm* omen

prescindir [presθin'dir] *vi*: **~ de** (*privarse de*) to do *o* go without; (*descartar*) to dispense with

prescribir [preskri'βir] *vt* to prescribe

presencia [pre'senθja] *nf* presence; **presenciar** *vt* to be present at; (*asistir a*) to attend; (*ver*) to see, witness

presentación [presenta'θjon] *nf* presentation; (*introducción*) introduction

presentador, a [presenta'ðor, a] *nm/f* presenter, compère

presentar [presen'tar] *vt* to present; (*ofrecer*) to offer; (*mostrar*) to show, display; (*a una persona*) to introduce; **presentarse** *vr* (*llegar inesperadamente*) to appear, turn up; (*ofrecerse: como candidato*) to run, stand; (*aparecer*) to show, appear; (*solicitar empleo*) to apply

presente [pre'sente] *adj* present ▷ *nm* present; **hacer ~** to state, declare; **tener ~** to remember, bear in mind

presentimiento [presenti'mjento] *nm*

premonition, presentiment

presentir [presen'tir] *vt* to have a premonition of

preservación [preserβa'θjon] *nf* protection, preservation

preservar [preser'βar] *vt* to protect, preserve; **preservativo** *nm* sheath, condom

presidencia [presi'ðenθja] *nf* presidency; *(de comité)* chairmanship

presidente [presi'ðente] *nmf* president; *(de comité)* chairman/woman

presidir [presi'ðir] *vt (dirigir)* to preside at, preside over; *(: comité)* to take the chair at; *(dominar)* to dominate, rule ▷ *vi* to preside; to take the chair

presión [pre'sjon] *nf* pressure; **presión atmosférica** atmospheric *o* air pressure; **presionar** *vt* to press; *(fig)* to press, put pressure on ▷ *vi*: **presionar para** to press for

preso, -a ['preso, a] *nm/f* prisoner; **tomar** *o* **llevar ~ a algn** to arrest sb, take sb prisoner

prestación [presta'θjon] *nf* service; *(subsidio)* benefit; **prestaciones** *nfpl (Tec, Auto)* performance features

prestado, -a [pres'taðo, a] *adj* on loan; **pedir ~** to borrow

prestamista [presta'mista] *nmf* moneylender

préstamo ['prestamo] *nm* loan; **préstamo hipotecario** mortgage

prestar [pres'tar] *vt* to lend, loan; *(atención)* to pay; *(ayuda)* to give

prestigio [pres'tixjo] *nm* prestige; **prestigioso, -a** *adj (honorable)* prestigious; *(famoso, renombrado)* renowned, famous

presumido, -a [presu'miðo, a] *adj (persona)* vain

presumir [presu'mir] *vt* to presume ▷ *vi (tener aires)* to be conceited; **presunto, -a** *adj (supuesto)* supposed, presumed; *(así llamado)* so-called; **presuntuoso, -a** *adj* conceited, presumptuous

presupuesto [presu'pwesto] *pp de* **presuponer** ▷ *nm (Finanzas)* budget; *(estimación: de costo)* estimate

pretencioso, -a [preten'θjoso, a] *adj* pretentious

pretender [preten'der] *vt (intentar)* to try to, seek to; *(reivindicar)* to claim; *(buscar)* to seek, try for; *(cortejar)* to woo, court; **~ que** to expect that

▌ No confundir **pretender** con la palabra inglesa *pretend*.

pretendiente *nmf (amante)* suitor; *(al trono)* pretender; **pretensión** *nf (aspiración)* aspiration; *(reivindicación)* claim; *(orgullo)*

pretension

pretexto [pre'teksto] *nm* pretext; *(excusa)* excuse

prevención [preβen'θjon] *nf* prevention; *(precaución)* precaution

prevenido, -a [preβe'niðo, a] *adj* prepared, ready; *(cauteloso)* cautious

prevenir [preβe'nir] *vt (impedir)* to prevent; *(predisponer)* to prejudice, bias; *(avisar)* to warn; *(preparar)* to prepare, get ready; **prevenirse** *vr* to get ready, prepare; **~se contra** to take precautions against; **preventivo, -a** *adj* preventive, precautionary

prever [pre'βer] *vt* to foresee

previo, -a ['preβjo, a] *adj (anterior)* previous; *(preliminar)* preliminary ▷ *prep*: **~ acuerdo de los otros** subject to the agreement of the others

previsión [preβi'sjon] *nf (perspicacia)* foresight; *(predicción)* forecast; **previsto, -a** *adj* anticipated, forecast

prima ['prima] *nf (Com)* bonus; *(de seguro)* premium; V *tb* **primo**

primario, -a [pri'marjo, a] *adj* primary

primavera [prima'βera] *nf* spring(-time)

primera [pri'mera] *nf (Auto)* first gear; *(Ferro: tb: **~ clase**)* first class; **de ~** *(fam)* first-class, first-rate

primero, -a [pri'mero, a] *(adj* **primer**) first; *(principal)* prime *adv* first; *(más bien)* sooner, rather; **primera plana** front page

primitivo, -a [primi'tiβo, a] *adj* primitive; *(original)* original

primo, -a ['primo, a] *adj* prime ▷ *nm/f* cousin; *(fam)* fool, idiot; **materias primas** raw materials; **primo hermano** first cousin

primogénito, -a [primo'xenito, a] *adj* first-born

primoroso, -a [primo'roso, a] *adj* exquisite, delicate

princesa [prin'θesa] *nf* princess

principal [prinθi'pal] *adj* principal, main ▷ *nm (jefe)* chief, principal

príncipe ['prinθipe] *nm* prince

principiante [prinθi'pjante] *nmf* beginner

principio [prin'θipjo] *nm (comienzo)* beginning, start; *(origen)* origin; *(primera etapa)* rudiment, basic idea; *(moral)* principle; **desde el ~** from the first; **en un ~** at first; **a ~s de** at the beginning of

pringue ['pringe] *nm (grasa)* grease, fat, dripping

prioridad [priori'ðað] *nf* priority

prisa ['prisa] *nf (apresuramiento)* hurry, haste; *(rapidez)* speed; *(urgencia)* (sense of) urgency; **a** *o* **de ~** quickly; **correr ~** to be urgent; **darse ~** to hurry up; **tener ~** to be in a hurry

prisión [pri'sjon] nf (*cárcel*) prison; (*período de cárcel*) imprisonment; **prisionero, -a** nm/f prisoner

prismáticos [pris'matikos] nmpl binoculars

privado, -a [pri'βaðo, a] adj private

privar [pri'βar] vt to deprive; **privativo, -a** adj exclusive

privilegiar [priβile'xjar] vt to grant a privilege to; (*favorecer*) to favour

privilegio [priβi'lexjo] nm privilege; (*concesión*) concession

pro [pro] nm o f profit, advantage ▷ prep: **asociación ~ ciegos** association for the blind ▷ prefijo: **~ americano** pro-American; **en ~ de** on behalf of, for; **los ~s y los contras** the pros and cons

proa ['proa] nf bow, prow; **de ~** bow cpd, fore

probabilidad [proβaβili'ðað] nf probability, likelihood; (*oportunidad, posibilidad*) chance, prospect; **probable** adj probable, likely

probador [proβa'ðor] nm (*en tienda*) fitting room

probar [pro'βar] vt (*demostrar*) to prove; (*someter a prueba*) to test, try out; (*ropa*) to try on; (*comida*) to taste ▷ vi to try; **~se un traje** to try on a suit

probeta [pro'βeta] nf test tube

problema [pro'βlema] nm problem

procedente [proθe'ðente] adj (*razonable*) reasonable; (*conforme a derecho*) proper, fitting; **~ de** coming from, originating in

proceder [proθe'ðer] vi (*avanzar*) to proceed; (*actuar*) to act; (*ser correcto*) to be right (and proper), be fitting ▷ nm (*comportamiento*) behaviour, conduct; **~ de** to come from, originate in; **procedimiento** nm procedure; (*proceso*) process; (*método*) means pl, method

procesador [proθesa'ðor] nm processor; **procesador de textos** word processor

procesar [proθe'sar] vt to try, put on trial

procesión [proθe'sjon] nf procession

proceso [pro'θeso] nm process; (*Jur*) trial

proclamar [prokla'mar] vt to proclaim

procrear [prokre'ar] vt, vi to procreate

procurador, a [prokura'ðor, a] nm/f attorney

procurar [proku'rar] vt (*intentar*) to try, endeavour; (*conseguir*) to get, obtain; (*asegurar*) to secure; (*producir*) to produce

prodigio [pro'ðixjo] nm prodigy; (*milagro*) wonder, marvel; **prodigioso, -a** adj prodigious, marvellous

pródigo, -a ['proðixo, a] adj: **hijo ~** prodigal son

producción [proðuk'θjon] nf (*gen*) production; (*producto*) output; **producción en serie** mass production

producir [proðu'θir] vt to produce; (*causar*) to cause, bring about; **producirse** vr (*cambio*) to come about; (*accidente*) to take place; (*problema etc*) to arise; (*hacerse*) to be produced, be made; (*estallar*) to break out

productividad [proðuktiβi'ðað] nf productivity; **productivo, -a** adj. productive; (*provechoso*) profitable

producto [pro'ðukto] nm product

productor, a [proðuk'tor, a] adj productive, producing ▷ nm/f producer

proeza [pro'eθa] nf exploit, feat

profano, -a [pro'fano, a] adj profane ▷ nm/f layman/woman

profecía [profe'θia] nf prophecy

profesión [profe'sjon] nf profession; (*en formulario*) occupation; **profesional** adj professional

profesor, a [profe'sor, a] nm/f teacher; **profesorado** nm teaching profession

profeta [pro'feta] nmf prophet

prófugo, -a ['profuxo, a] nm/f fugitive; (*Mil: desertor*) deserter

profundidad [profundi'ðað] nf depth; **profundizar** vi: **profundizar en** to go deeply into; **profundo, -a** adj deep; (*misterio, pensador*) profound

progenitor [proxeni'tor] nm ancestor; **progenitores** nmpl (*padres*) parents

programa [pro'xrama] nm programme (BRIT), program (US); **programa de estudios** curriculum, syllabus; **programación** nf programming; **programador, a** nm/f programmer; **programar** vt to program

progresar [proxre'sar] vi to progress, make progress; **progresista** adj, nmf progressive; **progresivo, -a** adj progressive; (*gradual*) gradual; (*continuo*) continuous; **progreso** nm progress

prohibición [proiβi'θjon] nf prohibition, ban

prohibir [proi'βir] vt to prohibit, ban, forbid; **prohibido o se prohibe fumar** no smoking; **"prohibido el paso"** "no entry"

prójimo, -a ['proximo, a] nm/f fellow man; (*vecino*) neighbour

prólogo ['proloxo] nm prologue

prolongar [prolon'xar] vt to extend; (*reunión etc*) to prolong; (*calle, tubo*) to extend

promedio [pro'meðjo] nm average; (*de distancia*) middle, mid-point

promesa [pro'mesa] nf promise

prometer [prome'ter] vt to promise ▷ vi

to show promise; **prometerse** vr (novios) to get engaged; **prometido, -a** adj promised; engaged ▷ nm/f fiancé/fiancée

prominente [promi'nente] adj prominent

promoción [promo'θjon] nf promotion

promotor [promo'tor] nm promoter; (instigador) instigator

promover [promo'βer] vt to promote; (causar) to cause; (instigar) to instigate, stir up

promulgar [promul'ɣar] vt to promulgate; (anunciar) to proclaim

pronombre [pro'nombre] nm pronoun

pronosticar [pronosti'kar] vt to predict, foretell, forecast; **pronóstico** nm prediction, forecast; **pronóstico del tiempo** weather forecast

pronto, -a ['pronto, a] adj (rápido) prompt, quick; (preparado) ready ▷ adv quickly, promptly; (en seguida) at once, right away; (dentro de poco) soon; (temprano) early ▷ nm: **tiene unos ~s muy malos** he gets ratty all of a sudden (inf); **de ~** suddenly; **por lo ~** meanwhile, for the present

pronunciación [pronunθja'θjon] nf pronunciation

pronunciar [pronun'θjar] vt to pronounce; (discurso) to make, deliver; **pronunciarse** vr to revolt, rebel; (declararse) to declare o.s.

propagación [propaɣa'θjon] nf propagation

propaganda [propa'ɣanda] nf (Pol) propaganda; (Com) advertising

propenso, -a [pro'penso, a] adj inclined to; **ser ~ a** to be inclined to, have a tendency to

propicio, -a [pro'piθjo, a] adj favourable, propitious

propiedad [propje'ðað] nf property; (posesión) possession, ownership; **propiedad particular** private property

propietario, -a [propje'tarjo, a] nm/f owner, proprietor

propina [pro'pina] nf tip

propio, -a ['propjo, a] adj own, of one's own; (característico) characteristic, typical; (debido) proper; (mismo) selfsame, very; **el ~ ministro** the minister himself; **¿tienes casa propia?** have you a house of your own?

proponer [propo'ner] vt to propose, put forward; (problema) to pose; **proponerse** vr to propose, intend

proporción [propor'θjon] nf proportion; (Mat) ratio; **proporciones** nfpl (dimensiones) dimensions; (fig) size sg; **proporcionado, -a** adj proportionate; (regular) medium,

middling; (justo) just right; **proporcionar** vt (dar) to give, supply, provide

proposición [proposi'θjon] nf proposition; (propuesta) proposal

propósito [pro'posito] nm purpose; (intento) aim, intention ▷ adv: **a ~** by the way, incidentally; (a posta) on purpose, deliberately; **a ~ de** about, with regard to

propuesta [pro'pwesta] vb V **proponer** ▷ nf proposal

propulsar [propul'sar] vt to drive, propel; (fig) to promote, encourage; **propulsión** nf propulsion; **propulsión a chorro** o **por reacción** jet propulsion

prórroga ['prorroɣa] nf extension; (Jur) stay; (Com) deferment; (Deporte) extra time; **prorrogar** vt (período) to extend; (decisión) to defer, postpone

prosa ['prosa] nf prose

proseguir [prose'ɣir] vt to continue, carry on ▷ vi to continue, go on

prospecto [pros'pekto] nm prospectus

prosperar [prospe'rar] vi to prosper, thrive, flourish; **prosperidad** nf prosperity; (éxito) success; **próspero, -a** adj prosperous, flourishing; (que tiene éxito) successful

prostíbulo [pros'tiβulo] nm brothel (BRIT), house of prostitution (US)

prostitución [prostitu'θjon] nf prostitution

prostituir [prosti'twir] vt to prostitute; **prostituirse** vr to prostitute o.s., become a prostitute

prostituta [prosti'tuta] nf prostitute

protagonista [protaɣo'nista] nmf protagonist

protección [protek'θjon] nf protection

protector, a [protek'tor, a] adj protective, protecting ▷ nm/f protector

proteger [prote'xer] vt to protect; **protegido, -a** nm/f protégé/protégée

proteína [prote'ina] nf protein

protesta [pro'testa] nf protest; (declaración) protestation

protestante [protes'tante] adj Protestant

protestar [protes'tar] vt to protest, declare ▷ vi to protest

protocolo [proto'kolo] nm protocol

prototipo [proto'tipo] nm prototype

provecho [pro'βetʃo] nm advantage, benefit; (Finanzas) profit; **¡buen ~!** bon appétit!; **en ~ de** to the benefit of; **sacar ~ de** to benefit from, profit by

provenir [proβe'nir] vi: **~ de** to come o stem from

proverbio [pro'βerβjo] nm proverb

providencia [proβi'ðenθja] *nf* providence
provincia [pro'βinθja] *nf* province
provisión [proβi'sjon] *nf* provision;
(*abastecimiento*) provision, supply; (*medida*)
measure, step
provisional [proβisjo'nal] *adj* provisional
provocar [proβo'kar] *vt* to provoke;
(*alentar*) to tempt, invite; (*causar*) to bring
about, lead to; (*promover*) to promote;
(*estimular*) to rouse, stimulate; **¿te provoca
un café?** (*CAM*) would you like a coffee?;
provocativo, -a *adj* provocative
proxeneta [prokse'neta] *nm* pimp
próximamente [proksima'mente] *adv*
shortly, soon
proximidad [proksimi'ðað] *nf* closeness,
proximity; **próximo, -a** *adj* near, close;
(*vecino*) neighbouring; (*siguiente*) next
proyectar [projek'tar] *vt* (*objeto*) to hurl,
throw; (*luz*) to cast, shed; (*Cine*) to screen,
show; (*planear*) to plan
proyectil [projek'til] *nm* projectile,
missile
proyecto [pro'jekto] *nm* plan; (*estimación
de costo*) detailed estimate
proyector [projek'tor] *nm* (*Cine*) projector
prudencia [pru'ðenθja] *nf* (*sabiduría*)
wisdom; (*cuidado*) care; **prudente** *adj*
sensible, wise; (*conductor*) careful
prueba *etc* ['prweβa] *vb* V **probar** ▷ *nf*
proof; (*ensayo*) test, trial; (*degustación*)
tasting, sampling; (*de ropa*) fitting; **a ~** on
trial; **a ~ de** proof against; **a ~ de agua/
fuego** waterproof/fireproof; **someter a ~** to
put to the test
psico... [siko] *prefijo* psycho...;
psicología *nf* psychology; **psicológico,
-a** *adj* psychological; **psicólogo, -a** *nm/f*
psychologist; **psicópata** *nmf* psychopath;
psicosis *nf inv* psychosis
psiquiatra [si'kjatra] *nmf* psychiatrist;
psiquiátrico, -a *adj* psychiatric
PSOE [pe'soe] (*ESP*) *nm abr* = **Partido
Socialista Obrero Español**
púa ['pua] *nf* (*Bot, Zool*) prickle, spine; (*para
guitarra*) plectrum (*BRIT*), pick (*US*); **alambre
de ~** barbed wire
pubertad [puβer'tað] *nf* puberty
publicación [puβlika'θjon] *nf*
publication
publicar [puβli'kar] *vt* (*editar*) to publish;
(*hacer público*) to publicize; (*divulgar*) to make
public, divulge
publicidad [puβliθi'ðað] *nf* publicity;
(*Com: propaganda*) advertising; **publicitario,
-a** *adj* publicity *cpd*; advertising *cpd*
público, -a ['puβliko, a] *adj* public ▷ *nm*
public; (*Teatro etc*) audience

puchero [pu'tʃero] *nm* (*Culin: guiso*) stew;
(: *olla*) cooking pot; **hacer ~s** to pout
pucho ['putʃo] (*CS: fam*) *nm* cigarette,
fag (*BRIT*)
pude *etc vb* V **poder**
pudiente [pu'ðjente] *adj* (*rico*) wealthy,
well-to-do
pudiera *etc vb* V **poder**
pudor [pu'ðor] *nm* modesty
pudrir [pu'ðrir] *vt* to rot; **pudrirse** *vr* to
rot, decay
pueblo ['pweβlo] *nm* people; (*nación*)
nation; (*aldea*) village
puedo *etc vb* V **poder**
puente ['pwente] *nm* bridge; **hacer ~**
(*fam*) to take extra days off work between 2
public holidays; to take a long weekend;
puente aéreo shuttle service; **puente
colgante** suspension bridge; **puente
levadizo** drawbridge

⬤ **HACER PUENTE**
⬤
⬤ When a public holiday in Spain falls on
⬤ a Tuesday or Thursday it is common
⬤ practice for employers to make the
⬤ Monday or Friday a holiday as well and
⬤ to give everyone a four-day weekend.
⬤ This is known as **hacer puente**. When
⬤ a named public holiday such as the **Día
de la Constitución** falls on a Tuesday
⬤ or Thursday, people refer to the whole
⬤ holiday period as e.g. the **puente de la
Constitución**.

puerco, -a ['pwerko, a] *nm/f* pig/
sow ▷ *adj* (*sucio*) dirty, filthy; (*obsceno*)
disgusting; **puerco espín** porcupine
pueril [pwe'ril] *adj* childish
puerro ['pwerro] *nm* leek
puerta ['pwerta] *nf* door; (*de jardín*) gate;
(*portal*) doorway; (*fig*) gateway; (*portería*)
goal; **a la ~** at the door; **a ~ cerrada** behind
closed doors; **puerta giratoria** revolving
door
puerto ['pwerto] *nm* port; (*paso*) pass; (*fig*)
haven, refuge
Puerto Rico [pwerto'riko] *nm* Puerto
Rico; **puertorriqueño, -a** *adj, nm/f* Puerto
Rican
pues [pwes] *adv* (*entonces*) then; (*bueno*)
well, well then; (*así que*) so ▷ *conj* (*ya que*)
since; **¡~ sí!** yes!, certainly!
puesta ['pwesta] *nf* (*apuesta*) bet, stake;
puesta al día updating; **puesta a punto**
fine tuning; **puesta de sol** sunset; **puesta
en marcha** starting
puesto, -a ['pwesto, a] *pp de* **poner**

P

▷ *adj*: **tener algo ~** to have sth on, be wearing sth ▷ *nm* (*lugar, posición*) place; (*trabajo*) post, job; (*Com*) stall ▷ *conj*: **~ que** since, as

púgil ['puxil] *nm* boxer

pulga ['pulɣa] *nf* flea

pulgada [pul'ɣaða] *nf* inch

pulgar [pul'ɣar] *nm* thumb

pulir [pu'lir] *vt* to polish; (*alisar*) to smooth; (*fig*) to polish up, touch up

pulmón [pul'mon] *nm* lung; **pulmonía** *nf* pneumonia

pulpa ['pulpa] *nf* pulp; (*de fruta*) flesh, soft part

pulpería [pulpe'ria] (*LAM*) *nf* (*tienda*) small grocery store

púlpito ['pulpito] *nm* pulpit

pulpo ['pulpo] *nm* octopus

pulque ['pulke] *nm* pulque

● **PULQUE**
●
● **Pulque** is a thick, white, alcoholic
● drink which is very popular in Mexico.
● In ancient times it was considered
● sacred by the Aztecs. It is produced by
● fermenting the juice of the **maguey**,
● a Mexican cactus similar to the agave.
● It can be drunk by itself or mixed with
● fruit or vegetable juice.

pulsación [pulsa'θjon] *nf* beat; **pulsaciones** pulse rate

pulsar [pul'sar] *vt* (*tecla*) to touch, tap; (*Mús*) to play; (*botón*) to press, push ▷ *vi* to pulsate; (*latir*) to beat, throb

pulsera [pul'sera] *nf* bracelet

pulso ['pulso] *nm* (*Anat*) pulse; (*fuerza*) strength; (*firmeza*) steadiness, steady hand

pulverizador [pulβeriθa'ðor] *nm* spray, spray gun

pulverizar [pulβeri'θar] *vt* to pulverize; (*líquido*) to spray

puna ['puna] (*CAM*) *nf* mountain sickness

punta ['punta] *nf* point, tip; (*extremo*) end; (*fig*) touch, trace; **horas ~** peak o rush hours; **sacar ~ a** to sharpen

puntada [pun'taða] *nf* (*Costura*) stitch

puntal [pun'tal] *nm* prop, support

puntapié [punta'pje] *nm* kick

puntería [punte'ria] *nf* (*de arma*) aim, aiming; (*destreza*) marksmanship

puntero, -a [pun'tero, a] *adj* leading ▷ *nm* (*palo*) pointer

puntiagudo, -a [puntja'ɣuðo, a] *adj* sharp, pointed

puntilla [pun'tiʎa] *nf* (*encaje*) lace edging o trim; (**andar**) **de ~s** (to walk) on tiptoe

punto ['punto] *nm* (*gen*) point; (*señal diminuta*) spot, dot; (*Costura, Med*) stitch; (*lugar*) spot, place; (*momento*) point, moment; **a ~** ready; **estar a ~ de** to be on the point of o about to; **en ~** on the dot; **hasta cierto ~** to some extent; **hacer ~** (*ESP: tejer*) to knit; **dos ~s** (*Ling*) colon; **punto de interrogación** question mark; **punto de vista** point of view, viewpoint; **punto final** full stop (*BRIT*), period (*US*); **punto muerto** dead center; (*Auto*) neutral (gear); **punto y aparte** (*en dictado*) full stop, new paragraph; **punto y coma** semicolon

puntocom [punto'kom] *adj inv, nf inv* dotcom

puntuación [puntwa'θjon] *nf* punctuation; (*puntos: en examen*) mark(s) (*pl*); (*Deporte*) score

puntual [pun'twal] *adj* (*a tiempo*) punctual; (*exacto*) exact, accurate; **puntualidad** *nf* punctuality; exactness, accuracy

puntuar [pun'twar] *vi* (*Deporte*) to score, count

punzante [pun'θante] *adj* (*dolor*) shooting, sharp; (*herramienta*) sharp

puñado [pu'ɲaðo] *nm* handful

puñal [pu'ɲal] *nm* dagger; **puñalada** *nf* stab

puñetazo [puɲe'taθo] *nm* punch

puño ['puɲo] *nm* (*Anat*) fist; (*cantidad*) fistful, handful; (*Costura*) cuff; (*de herramienta*) handle

pupila [pu'pila] *nf* pupil

pupitre [pu'pitre] *nm* desk

puré [pu're] *nm* purée; (*sopa*) (thick) soup; **puré de papas** (*LAM*) mashed potatoes; **puré de patatas** (*ESP*) mashed potatoes

purga ['purxa] *nf* purge; **purgante** *adj, nm* purgative

purgatorio [purxa'torjo] *nm* purgatory

purificar [purifi'kar] *vt* to purify; (*refinar*) to refine

puritano, -a [puri'tano, a] *adj* (*actitud*) puritanical; (*iglesia, tradición*) puritan ▷ *nm/f* puritan

puro, -a ['puro, a] *adj* pure; (*verdad*) simple, plain ▷ *nm* cigar

púrpura ['purpura] *nf* purple

pus [pus] *nm* pus

puse *etc vb* V **poder**

pusiera *etc vb* V **poder**

puta ['puta] (*fam!*) *nf* whore, prostitute

putrefacción [putrefak'θjon] *nf* rotting, putrefaction

PVP *nm abr* (= *precio de venta al público*) RRP

pyme, PYME ['pime] *nf abr* (= *Pequeña y Mediana Empresa*) SME

q

que [ke] *conj* **1** (*con oración subordinada: muchas veces no se traduce*) that; **dijo que vendría** he said (that) he would come; **espero que lo encuentres** I hope (that) you find it; V *tb* **el**

2 (*en oración independiente*): **¡que entre!** send him in; **¡que aproveche!** enjoy your meal!; **¡que se mejore tu padre!** I hope your father gets better

3 (*enfático*): **¿me quieres? – ¡que sí!** do you love me? – of course!

4 (*consecutivo: muchas veces no se traduce*) that; **es tan grande que no lo puedo levantar** it's so big (that) I can't lift it

5 (*comparaciones*) than; **yo que tú/él** if I were you/him; V *tb* **más, menos, mismo**

6 (*valor disyuntivo*): **que le guste o no** whether he likes it or not; **que venga o que no venga** whether he comes or not

7 (*porque*): **no puedo, que tengo que quedarme en casa** I can't, I've got to stay in ⊳ *pron* **1** (*cosa*) that, which; (+ *prep*) which; **el sombrero que te compraste** the hat (that *o* which) you bought; **la cama en que dormí** the bed (that *o* which) I slept in

2 (*persona: suj*) that, who; (*: objeto*) that, whom; **el amigo que me acompañó al museo** the friend that *o* who went to the museum with me; **la chica que invité** the girl (that *o* whom) I invited

qué [ke] *adj* what?, which? ⊳ *pron* what?; **¡~ divertido!** how funny!; **¿~ edad tienes?** how old are you?; **¿de ~ me hablas?** what are you saying to me?; **¿~ tal?** how are you?, how are things?; **¿~ hay (de nuevo)?** what's new?

quebrado, -a [ke'βraðo, a] *adj* (*roto*) broken ⊳ *nm/f* bankrupt ⊳ *nm* (*Mat*) fraction

quebrantar [keβran'tar] *vt* (*infringir*) to violate, transgress

quebrar [ke'βrar] *vt* to break, smash ⊳ *vi* to go bankrupt

quedar [ke'ðar] *vi* to stay, remain; (*encontrarse: sitio*) to be; (*haber aún*) to remain, be left; **quedarse** *vr* to remain, stay (behind); **~se (con) algo** to keep sth; **~ en** (*acordar*) to agree on/to; **~ en nada** to come to nothing; **~ por hacer** to be still to be done; **~ ciego/mudo** to be left blind/dumb; **no te queda bien ese vestido** that dress doesn't suit you; **eso queda muy lejos** that's a long way (away); **quedamos a las seis** we agreed to meet at six

quedo, -a ['keðo, a] *adj* still ⊳ *adv* softly, gently

quehacer [kea'θer] *nm* task, job; **quehaceres (domésticos)** *nmpl* household chores

queja ['kexa] *nf* complaint; **quejarse** *vr* (*enfermo*) to moan, groan; (*protestar*) to complain; **quejarse de que** to complain that; **quejido** *nm* moan

quemado, -a [ke'maðo, a] *adj* burnt

quemadura [kema'ðura] *nf* burn, scald

quemar [ke'mar] *vt* to burn; (*fig: malgastar*) to burn up, squander ⊳ *vi* to be burning hot; **quemarse** *vr* (*consumirse*) to burn (up); (*del sol*) to get sunburnt

quemarropa [kema'rropa]: **a ~** *adv* point-blank

quepo *etc vb* V **caber**

querella [ke'reʎa] *nf* (*Jur*) charge; (*disputa*) dispute

querer [ke'rer] *vt* **1** (*desear*) to want; **quiero más dinero** I want more money; **quisiera** *o* **querría un té** I'd like a tea; **sin querer** unintentionally; **quiero ayudar/que vayas** I want to help/you to go

2 (*preguntas: para pedir algo*): **¿quiere abrir la ventana?** could you open the window?; **¿quieres echarme una mano?** can you give me a hand?

3 (*amar*) to love; (*tener cariño a*) to be fond of; **te quiero** I love you; **quiere mucho a sus hijos** he's very fond of his children

4 le pedí que me dejara ir pero no quiso I asked him to let me go but he refused

querido, -a [ke'riðo, a] *adj* dear ⊳ *nm/f* darling; (*amante*) lover

queso ['keso] *nm* cheese; **queso crema** (*LAM*) cream cheese; **queso de untar** (*ESP*) cream cheese; **queso manchego** sheep's milk cheese made in La Mancha

quicio ['kiθjo] nm hinge; **sacar a algn de ~** to get on sb's nerves

quiebra ['kjeβra] nf break, split; (Com) bankruptcy; (Econ) slump

quiebro ['kjeβro] nm (del cuerpo) swerve

quien [kjen] pron who; **hay ~ piensa que** there are those who think that; **no hay ~ lo haga** no-one will do it

quién [kjen] pron who, whom; **¿~ es?** who's there?

quienquiera [kjen'kjera] (pl **quienesquiera**) pron whoever

quiero etc vb V **querer**

quieto, -a ['kjeto, a] adj still; (carácter) placid

> No confundir **quieto** con la palabra inglesa quiet.

quietud nf stillness

químico, -a ['kimiko, a] adj chemical ▷ nm/f chemist ▷ nf chemistry

quincalla [kin'kaʎa] nf hardware, ironmongery (BRIT)

quince ['kinθe] num fifteen; **~ días** a fortnight; **quinceañero, -a** nm/f teenager; **quincena** nf fortnight; (pago) fortnightly pay; **quincenal** adj fortnightly

quiniela [ki'njela] nf football pools pl; **quinielas** nfpl (impreso) pools coupon sg

quinientos, -as [ki'njentos, as] adj, num five hundred

quinto, -a ['kinto, a] adj fifth ▷ nf country house; (Mil) call-up, draft

quiosco ['kjosko] nm (de música) bandstand; (de periódicos) news stand

quirófano [ki'rofano] nm operating theatre

quirúrgico, -a [ki'rurxiko, a] adj surgical

quise etc vb V **querer**

quisiera etc vb V **querer**

quisquilloso, -a [kiski'ʎoso, a] adj (susceptible) touchy; (meticuloso) pernickety

quiste ['kiste] nm cyst

quitaesmalte [kitaes'malte] nm nail-polish remover

quitamanchas [kita'mantʃas] nm inv stain remover

quitanieves [kita'njeβes] nm inv snowplough (BRIT), snowplow (US)

quitar [ki'tar] vt to remove, take away; (ropa) to take off; (dolor) to relieve; **¡quita de ahí!** get away!; **quitarse** vr to withdraw; (ropa) to take off; **se quitó el sombrero** he took off his hat

Quito ['kito] n Quito

quizá(s) [ki'θa(s)] adv perhaps, maybe

rábano ['raβano] nm radish; **me importa un ~** I don't give a damn

rabia ['raβja] nf (Med) rabies sg; (ira) fury, rage; **rabiar** vi to have rabies; to rage, be furious; **rabiar por algo** to long for sth

rabieta [ra'βjeta] nf tantrum, fit of temper

rabino [ra'βino] nm rabbi

rabioso, -a [ra'βjoso, a] adj rabid; (fig) furious

rabo ['raβo] nm tail

racha ['ratʃa] nf gust of wind; **buena/ mala ~** spell of good/bad luck

racial [ra'θjal] adj racial, race cpd

racimo [ra'θimo] nm bunch

ración [ra'θjon] nf portion; **raciones** nfpl rations

racional [raθjo'nal] adj (razonable) reasonable; (lógico) rational

racionar [raθjo'nar] vt to ration (out)

racismo [ra'θismo] nm racism; **racista** adj, nm racist

radar [ra'ðar] nm radar

radiador [raðja'ðor] nm radiator

radiante [ra'ðjante] adj radiant

radical [raði'kal] adj, nmf radical

radicar [raði'kar] vi: **~ en** (dificultad, problema) to lie in; (solución) to consist in

radio ['raðjo] nf radio; (aparato) radio (set) ▷ nm (Mat) radius; (Quím) radium; **radioactividad** nf radioactivity; **radioactivo, -a** adj radioactive; **radiografía** nf X-ray; **radioterapia** nf radiotherapy; **radioyente** nmf listener

ráfaga ['rafaxa] nf gust; (de luz) flash; (de tiros) burst

raíz [ra'iθ] nf root; **a ~ de** as a result of; **raíz cuadrada** square root

raja ['raxa] nf (de melón etc) slice; (grieta) crack; **rajar** vt to split; (fam) to slash; **rajarse** vr to split, crack; **rajarse de** to back out of

rajatabla [raxa'taβla]: **a ~** adv (estrictamente) strictly, to the letter

rallador [raʎa'ðor] nm grater

rallar [ra'ʎar] vt to grate

rama ['rama] nf branch; **ramaje** nm branches pl, foliage; **ramal** nm (de cuerda) strand; (Ferro) branch line (BRIT); (Auto) branch (road) (BRIT)

rambla ['rambla] nf (avenida) avenue

ramo ['ramo] nm branch; (sección) department, section

rampa ['rampa] nf ramp; **rampa de acceso** entrance ramp

rana ['rana] nf frog; **salto de ~** leapfrog

ranchero [ran'tʃero] (MÉX) nm (hacendado) rancher; smallholder

rancho ['rantʃo] nm (grande) ranch; (pequeño) small farm

rancio, -a ['ranθjo, a] adj (comestibles) rancid; (vino) aged, mellow; (fig) ancient

rango ['rango] nm rank, standing

ranura [ra'nura] nf groove; (de teléfono etc) slot

rapar [ra'par] vt to shave; (los cabellos) to crop

rapaz [ra'paθ] (nf ~a) nmf young boy/girl ▷ adj (Zool) predatory

rape ['rape] nm (pez) monkfish; **al ~** cropped

rapé [ra'pe] nm snuff

rapidez [rapi'ðeθ] nf speed, rapidity; **rápido, -a** adj fast, quick ▷ adv quickly ▷ nm (Ferro) express; **rápidos** nmpl rapids

rapiña [ra'piɲa] nf robbery; **ave de ~** bird of prey

raptar [rap'tar] vt to kidnap; **rapto** nm kidnapping; (impulso) sudden impulse; (éxtasis) ecstasy, rapture

raqueta [ra'keta] nf racquet

raquítico, -a [ra'kitiko, a] adj stunted; (fig) poor, inadequate

rareza [ra'reθa] nf rarity; (fig) eccentricity

raro, -a ['raro, a] adj (poco común) rare; (extraño) odd, strange; (excepcional) remarkable

ras [ras] nm: **a ~ de** level with; **a ~ de tierra** at ground level

rasar [ra'sar] vt (igualar) to level

rascacielos [raska'θjelos] nm inv skyscraper

rascar [ras'kar] vt (con las uñas etc) to scratch; (raspar) to scrape; **rascarse** vr to scratch (o.s.)

rasgar [ras'ɣar] vt to tear, rip (up)

rasgo ['rasɣo] nm (con pluma) stroke; **rasgos** nmpl (facciones) features, characteristics; **a grandes ~s** in outline, broadly

rasguño [ras'ɣuɲo] nm scratch

raso, -a ['raso, a] adj (liso) flat, level; (a baja altura) very low ▷ nm satin; **cielo ~** clear sky

raspadura [raspa'ðura] nf (acto) scrape, scraping; (marca) scratch; **raspaduras** nfpl (de papel etc) scrapings

raspar [ras'par] vt to scrape; (arañar) to scratch; (limar) to file

rastra ['rastra] nf (Agr) rake; **a ~s** by dragging; (fig) unwillingly

rastrear [rastre'ar] vt (seguir) to track

rastrero, -a [ras'trero, a] adj (Bot, Zool) creeping; (fig) despicable, mean

rastrillo [ras'triʎo] nm rake

rastro ['rastro] nm (Agr) rake; (pista) track, trail; (vestigio) trace; **el R~** (ESP) the Madrid fleamarket

rasurado [rasu'raðo] (MÉX) nm shaving; **rasuradora** [rasura'ðora] (MÉX) nf electric shaver; **rasurar** [rasu'rar] (MÉX) vt to shave; **rasurarse** vr to shave

rata ['rata] nf rat

ratear [rate'ar] vt (robar) to steal

ratero, -a [ra'tero, a] adj light-fingered ▷ nm/f (carterista) pickpocket; (ladrón) petty thief

rato ['rato] nm while, short time; **a ~s** from time to time; **hay para ~** there's still a long way to go; **al poco ~** soon afterwards; **pasar el ~** to kill time; **pasar un buen/mal ~** to have a good/rough time; **en mis ~s libres** in my spare time

ratón [ra'ton] nm mouse; **ratonera** nf mousetrap

raudal [rau'ðal] nm torrent; **a ~es** in abundance

raya ['raja] nf line; (marca) scratch; (en tela) stripe; (de pelo) parting; (límite) boundary; (pez) ray; (puntuación) dash; **a ~s** striped; **pasarse de la ~** to go too far; **tener a ~** to keep in check; **rayar** vt to line; to scratch; (subrayar) to underline ▷ vi: **rayar en** o **con** to border on

rayo ['rajo] nm (del sol) ray, beam; (de luz) shaft; (en una tormenta) (flash of) lightning; **rayos X** X-rays

raza ['raθa] nf race; **raza humana** human race

razón [ra'θon] nf reason; (justicia) right, justice; (razonamiento) reasoning; (motivo) reason, motive; (Mat) ratio; **a ~ de 10 cada día** at the rate of 10 a day; **en ~ de** with regard to; **dar ~ a algn** to agree that sb is right; **tener ~** to be right; **razón de ser** raison d'être; **razón directa/inversa** direct/inverse proportion; **razonable** adj reasonable; (justo, moderado) fair; **razonamiento** nm (juicio) judg(e)ment;

(*argumento*) reasoning; **razonar** *vt, vi* to reason, argue

re [re] *nm* (*Mús*) D

reacción [reak'θjon] *nf* reaction; **avión a ~** jet plane; **reacción en cadena** chain reaction; **reaccionar** *vi* to react

reacio, -a [re'aθjo, a] *adj* stubborn

reactivar [reakti'βar] *vt* to revitalize

reactor [reak'tor] *nm* reactor

real [re'al] *adj* real; (*del rey, fig*) royal

realidad [reali'ðað] *nf* reality, fact; (*verdad*) truth

realista [rea'lista] *nmf* realist

realización [realiθa'θjon] *nf* fulfilment

realizador, a [realiθa'ðor, a] *nm/f* film-maker

realizar [reali'θar] *vt* (*objetivo*) to achieve; (*plan*) to carry out; (*viaje*) to make, undertake; **realizarse** *vr* to come about, come true

realmente [real'mente] *adv* really, actually

realzar [real'θar] *vt* to enhance; (*acentuar*) to highlight

reanimar [reani'mar] *vt* to revive; (*alentar*) to encourage; **reanimarse** *vr* to revive

reanudar [reanu'ðar] *vt* (*renovar*) to renew; (*historia, viaje*) to resume

reaparición [reapari'θjon] *nf* reappearance

rearme [re'arme] *nm* rearmament

rebaja [re'βaxa] *nf* (*Com*) reduction; (: *descuento*) discount; **rebajas** *nfpl* (*Com*) sale; **rebajar** *vt* (*bajar*) to lower; (*reducir*) to reduce; (*disminuir*) to lessen; (*humillar*) to humble

rebanada [reβa'naða] *nf* slice

rebañar [reβa'nar] *vt* (*comida*) to scrape up; (*plato*) to scrape clean

rebaño [re'βano] *nm* herd; (*de ovejas*) flock

rebatir [reβa'tir] *vt* to refute

rebeca [re'βeka] *nf* cardigan

rebelarse [reβe'larse] *vr* to rebel, revolt

rebelde [re'βelde] *adj* rebellious; (*niño*) unruly ▷ *nmf* rebel; **rebeldía** *nf* rebelliousness; (*desobediencia*) disobedience

rebelión [reβe'ljon] *nf* rebellion

reblandecer [reβlande'θer] *vt* to soften

rebobinar [reβoβi'nar] *vt* (*cinta, película de video*) to rewind

rebosante [reβo'sante] *adj* overflowing

rebosar [reβo'sar] *vi* (*líquido, recipiente*) to overflow; (*abundar*) to abound, be plentiful

rebotar [reβo'tar] *vt* to bounce; (*rechazar*) to repel ▷ *vi* (*pelota*) to bounce; (*bala*) to ricochet; **rebote** *nm* rebound; **de rebote** on the rebound

rebozado, -a [reβo'θaðo, a] *adj* fried in batter o breadcrumbs

rebozar [reβo'θar] *vt* to wrap up; (*Culin*) to fry in batter o breadcrumbs

rebuscado, -a [reβus'kaðo, a] *adj* (*amanerado*) affected; (*palabra*) recherché; (*idea*) far-fetched

rebuscar [reβus'kar] *vi*: **~ (en/por)** to search carefully (in/for)

recado [re'kaðo] *nm* (*mensaje*) message; (*encargo*) errand; **tomar un ~** (*Tel*) to take a message

recaer [reka'er] *vi* to relapse; **~ en** to fall to o on; (*criminal etc*) to fall back into, relapse into; **recaída** *nf* relapse

recalcar [rekal'kar] *vt* (*fig*) to stress, emphasize

recalentar [rekalen'tar] *vt* (*volver a calentar*) to reheat; (*calentar demasiado*) to overheat

recámara [re'kamara] (*MÉX*) *nf* bedroom

recambio [re'kambjo] *nm* spare; (*de pluma*) refill

recapacitar [rekapaθi'tar] *vi* to reflect

recargado, -a [rekar'xaðo, a] *adj* overloaded

recargar [rekar'xar] *vt* to overload; (*batería*) to recharge; **~ el saldo de** (*Tel*) to top up; **recargo** *nm* surcharge; (*aumento*) increase

recatado, -a [reka'taðo, a] *adj* (*modesto*) modest, demure; (*prudente*) cautious

recaudación [rekauða'θjon] *nf* (*acción*) collection; (*cantidad*) takings *pl*; (*en deporte*) gate; **recaudador, a** *nm/f* tax collector

recelar [reθe'lar] *vt*: **~ que ...** (*sospechar*) to suspect that ...; (*temer*) to fear that ... ▷ *vi*: **~ de** to distrust; **recelo** *nm* distrust, suspicion

recepción [reθep'θjon] *nf* reception; **recepcionista** *nmf* receptionist

receptor, a [reθep'tor, a] *nm/f* recipient ▷ *nm* (*Tel*) receiver

recesión [reθe'sjon] *nf* (*Com*) recession

receta [re'θeta] *nf* (*Culin*) recipe; (*Med*) prescription

▌ No confundir **receta** con la palabra inglesa *receipt*.

rechazar [retʃa'θar] *vt* to reject; (*oferta*) to turn down; (*ataque*) to repel

rechazo [re'tʃaθo] *nm* rejection

rechinar [retʃi'nar] *vi* to creak; (*dientes*) to grind

rechistar [retʃis'tar] *vi*: **sin ~** without a murmur

rechoncho, -a [re'tʃontʃo, a] (*fam*) *adj* thickset (*BRIT*), heavy-set (*US*)

rechupete [retʃu'pete]: **de ~** *adj* (*comida*)

delicious, scrumptious

recibidor [reθiβi'ðor] *nm* entrance hall

recibimiento [reθiβi'mjento] *nm* reception, welcome

recibir [reθi'βir] *vt* to receive; *(dar la bienvenida)* to welcome ▷ *vi* to entertain; **recibo** *nm* receipt

reciclable [reθi'klaβle] *adj* recyclable

reciclar [reθi'klar] *vt* to recycle

recién [re'θjen] *adv* recently, newly; **los ~ casados** the newly-weds; **el ~ llegado** the newcomer; **el ~ nacido** the newborn child

reciente [re'θjente] *adj* recent; *(fresco)* fresh

recinto [re'θinto] *nm* enclosure; *(área)* area, place

recio, -a ['reθjo, a] *adj* strong, tough; *(voz)* loud ▷ *adv* hard, loud(ly)

recipiente [reθi'pjente] *nm* receptacle

recíproco, -a [re'θiproco, a] *adj* reciprocal

recital [reθi'tal] *nm* (*Mús*) recital; (*Literatura*) reading

recitar [reθi'tar] *vt* to recite

reclamación [reklama'θjon] *nf* claim, demand; *(queja)* complaint

reclamar [rekla'mar] *vt* to claim, demand ▷ *vi*: **~ contra** to complain about; **reclamo** *nm* (*anuncio*) advertisement; (*tentación*) attraction

reclinar [rekli'nar] *vt* to recline, lean; **reclinarse** *vr* to lean back

reclusión [reklu'sjon] *nf* (*prisión*) prison; (*refugio*) seclusion

recluta [re'kluta] *nmf* recruit ▷ *nf* recruitment; **reclutar** *vt* (*datos*) to collect; (*dinero*) to collect up; **reclutamiento** *nm* recruitment

recobrar [reko'βrar] *vt* (*salud*) to recover; (*rescatar*) to get back; **recobrarse** *vr* to recover

recodo [re'koðo] *nm* (*de río, camino*) bend

recogedor [rekoxe'ðor] *nm* dustpan

recoger [reko'xer] *vt* to collect; (*Agr*) to harvest; (*levantar*) to pick up; (*juntar*) to gather; (*pasar a buscar*) to come for, get; (*dar asilo*) to give shelter to; (*faldas*) to gather up; (*pelo*) to put up; **recogerse** *vr* (*retirarse*) to retire; **recogido, -a** *adj* (*lugar*) quiet, secluded; (*pequeño*) small ▷ *nf* (*Correos*) collection; (*Agr*) harvest

recolección [rekolek'θjon] *nf* (*Agr*) harvesting; (*colecta*) collection

recomendación [rekomenda'θjon] *nf* (*sugerencia*) suggestion, recommendation; (*referencia*) reference

recomendar [rekomen'dar] *vt* to suggest, recommend; (*confiar*) to entrust

recompensa [rekom'pensa] *nf* reward, recompense; **recompensar** *vt* to reward, recompense

reconciliación [rekonθilja'θjon] *nf* reconciliation

reconciliar [rekonθi'ljar] *vt* to reconcile; **reconciliarse** *vr* to become reconciled

recóndito, -a [re'kondito, a] *adj* (*lugar*) hidden, secret

reconocer [rekono'θer] *vt* to recognize; (*registrar*) to search; (*Med*) to examine; **reconocido, -a** *adj* recognized; (*agradecido*) grateful; **reconocimiento** *nm* recognition; search; examination; gratitude; (*confesión*) admission

reconquista [rekon'kista] *nf* reconquest; **la R~** the Reconquest (of Spain)

reconstituyente [rekonstitu'jente] *nm* tonic

reconstruir [rekonstru'ir] *vt* to reconstruct

reconversión [rekonβer'sjon] *nf* (*reestructuración*) restructuring; **reconversión industrial** industrial rationalization

recopilación [rekopila'θjon] *nf* (*resumen*) summary; (*compilación*) compilation; **recopilar** *vt* to compile

récord ['rekorð] (*pl* **~s**) *adj inv*, *nm* record

recordar [rekor'ðar] *vt* (*acordarse de*) to remember; (*acordar a otro*) to remind ▷ *vi* to remember

> No confundir **recordar** con la palabra inglesa *record*.

recorrer [reko'rrer] *vt* (*país*) to cross, travel through; (*distancia*) to cover; (*registrar*) to search; (*repasar*) to look over; **recorrido** *nm* run, journey; **tren de largo recorrido** main-line train

recortar [rekor'tar] *vt* to cut out; **recorte** *nm* (*acción, de prensa*) cutting; (*de telas, chapas*) trimming; **recorte presupuestario** budget cut

recostar [rekos'tar] *vt* to lean; **recostarse** *vr* to lie down

recoveco [reko'βeko] *nm* (*de camino, río etc*) bend; (*en casa*) cubby hole

recreación [rekrea'θjon] *nf* recreation

recrear [rekre'ar] *vt* (*entretener*) to entertain; (*volver a crear*) to recreate; **recreativo, -a** *adj* recreational; **recreo** *nm* recreation; (*Escol*) break, playtime

recriminar [rekrimi'nar] *vt* to reproach ▷ *vi* to recriminate; **recriminarse** *vr* to reproach each other

recrudecer [rekruðe'θer] *vt, vi* to worsen; **recrudecerse** *vr* to worsen

recta ['rekta] *nf* straight line

rectángulo, -a [rek'tangulo, a] *adj*
rectangular ▷ *nm* rectangle

rectificar [rektifi'kar] *vt* to rectify;
(*volverse recto*) to straighten ▷ *vi* to correct
o.s.

rectitud [rekti'tuð] *nf* straightness

recto, -a ['rekto, a] *adj* straight; (*persona*)
honest, upright; **siga todo ~** go straight on
▷ *nm* rectum

rector, a [rek'tor, a] *adj* governing

recuadro [re'kwaðro] *nm* box; (*Tip*) inset

recubrir [reku'βrir] *vt*: **~ (con)** (*pintura,
crema*) to cover (with)

recuento [re'kwento] *nm* inventory;
hacer el ~ de to count *o* reckon up

recuerdo [re'kwerðo] *nm* souvenir;
recuerdos *nmpl* (*memorias*) memories;
¡~s a tu madre! give my regards to your
mother!

recular [reku'lar] *vi* to back down

recuperación [rekupera'θjon] *nf*
recovery

recuperar [rekupe'rar] *vt* to recover;
(*tiempo*) to make up; **recuperarse** *vr* to
recuperate

recurrir [reku'rrir] *vi* (*Jur*) to appeal; **~ a**
to resort to; (*persona*) to turn to; **recurso**
nm resort; (*medios*) means *pl*, resources *pl*;
(*Jur*) appeal

red [reð] *nf* net, mesh; (*Ferro etc*) network;
(*trampa*) trap; **la R~** (*Internet*) the Net

redacción [reðak'θjon] *nf* (*acción*) editing;
(*personal*) editorial staff; (*Escol*) essay,
composition

redactar [reðak'tar] *vt* to draw up, draft;
(*periódico*) to edit

redactor, a [reðak'tor, a] *nm/f* editor

redada [re'ðaða] *nf* (*de policía*) raid,
round-up

rededor [reðe'ðor] *nm*: **al** *o* **en ~** around,
round about

redoblar [reðo'βlar] *vt* to redouble ▷ *vi*
(*tambor*) to roll

redonda [re'ðonda] *nf*: **a la ~** around,
round about

redondear [reðonde'ar] *vt* to round,
round off

redondel [reðon'del] *nm* (*círculo*) circle;
(*Taur*) bullring, arena

redondo, -a [re'ðondo, a] *adj* (*circular*)
round; (*completo*) complete

reducción [reðuk'θjon] *nf* reduction

reducido, -a [reðu'θiðo, a] *adj* reduced;
(*limitado*) limited; (*pequeño*) small

reducir [reðu'θir] *vt* to reduce; to limit;
reducirse *vr* to diminish

redundancia [reðun'danθja] *nf*
redundancy

reembolsar [re(e)mbol'sar] *vt* (*persona*)
to reimburse; (*dinero*) to repay, pay back;
(*depósito*) to refund; **reembolso** *nm*
reimbursement; refund

reemplazar [re(e)mpla'θar] *vt* to
replace; **reemplazo** *nm* replacement; **de
reemplazo** (*Mil*) reserve

reencuentro [re(e)n'kwentro] *nm*
reunion

reescribible [reeskri'βiβle] *adj* rewritable

refacción [refak'θjon] (*MÉx*) *nf* spare
(part)

referencia [refe'renθja] *nf* reference; **con
~ a** with reference to

referéndum [refe'rendum] (*pl* **~s**) *nm*
referendum

referente [refe'rente] *adj*: **~ a** concerning,
relating to

réferi ['referi] (*LAM*) *nmf* referee

referir [refe'rir] *vt* (*contar*) to tell, recount;
(*relacionar*) to refer, relate; **referirse** *vr*: **~se
a** to refer to

refilón [refi'lon]: **de ~** *adv* obliquely

refinado, -a [refi'naðo, a] *adj* refined

refinar [refi'nar] *vt* to refine; **refinería**
nf refinery

reflejar [refle'xar] *vt* to reflect; **reflejo,
-a** *adj* reflected; (*movimiento*) reflex ▷ *nm*
reflection; (*Anat*) reflex

reflexión [reflek'sjon] *nf* reflection;
reflexionar *vt* to reflect on ▷ *vi* to reflect;
(*detenerse*) to pause (to think)

reflexivo, -a [reflek'siβo, a] *adj*
thoughtful; (*Ling*) reflexive

reforma [re'forma] *nf* reform; (*Arq etc*)
repair; **reforma agraria** agrarian reform

reformar [refor'mar] *vt* to reform;
(*modificar*) to change, alter; (*Arq*) to repair;
reformarse *vr* to mend one's ways

reformatorio [reforma'torjo] *nm*
reformatory

reforzar [refor'θar] *vt* to strengthen; (*Arq*)
to reinforce; (*fig*) to encourage

refractario, -a [refrak'tarjo, a] *adj* (*Tec*)
heat-resistant

refrán [re'fran] *nm* proverb, saying

refregar [refre'ɣar] *vt* to scrub

refrescante [refres'kante] *adj* refreshing,
cooling

refrescar [refres'kar] *vt* to refresh ▷ *vi* to
cool down; **refrescarse** *vr* to get cooler;
(*tomar aire fresco*) to go out for a breath of
fresh air; (*beber*) to have a drink

refresco [re'fresko] *nm* soft drink, cool
drink; **"~s"** "refreshments"

refriega [re'frjexa] *nf* scuffle, brawl

refrigeración [refrixera'θjon] *nf*
refrigeration; (*de sala*) air-conditioning

refrigerador [refrixera'ðor] *nm* refrigerator (BRIT); icebox (US)

refrigerar [refrixe'rar] *vt* to refrigerate; (*sala*) to air-condition

refuerzo [re'fwerθo] *nm* reinforcement; (*Tec*) support

refugiado, -a [refu'xjaðo, a] *nm/f* refugee

refugiarse [refu'xjarse] *vr* to take refuge, shelter

refugio [re'fuxjo] *nm* refuge; (*protección*) shelter

refunfuñar [refunfu'ɲar] *vi* to grunt, growl; (*quejarse*) to grumble

regadera [reɣa'ðera] *nf* watering can

regadío [reɣa'ðio] *nm* irrigated land

regalado, -a [reɣa'laðo, a] *adj* comfortable, luxurious; (*gratis*) free, for nothing

regalar [reɣa'lar] *vt* (*dar*) to give (as a present); (*entregar*) to give away; (*mimar*) to pamper, make a fuss of

regaliz [reɣa'liθ] *nm* liquorice

regalo [re'ɣalo] *nm* (*obsequio*) gift, present; (*gusto*) pleasure

regañadientes [reɣaɲa'ðjentes]: **a ~** *adv* reluctantly

regañar [reɣa'ɲar] *vt* to scold ▷ *vi* to grumble; **regañón, -ona** *adj* nagging

regar [re'ɣar] *vt* to water, irrigate; (*fig*) to scatter, sprinkle

regatear [reɣate'ar] *vt* (*Com*) to bargain over; (*escatimar*) to be mean with ▷ *vi* to bargain, haggle; (*Deporte*) to dribble; **regateo** *nm* bargaining; dribbling; (*del cuerpo*) swerve, dodge

regazo [re'ɣaθo] *nm* lap

regenerar [rexene'rar] *vt* to regenerate

régimen ['reximen] (*pl* **regímenes**) *nm* regime; (*Med*) diet

regimiento [rexi'mjento] *nm* regiment

regio, -a ['rexjo, a] *adj* royal, regal; (*fig: suntuoso*) splendid; (*cs: fam*) great, terrific

región [re'xjon] *nf* region

regir [re'xir] *vt* to govern, rule; (*dirigir*) to manage, run ▷ *vi* to apply, be in force

registrar [rexis'trar] *vt* (*buscar*) to search; (*: en cajón*) to look through; (*inspeccionar*) to inspect; (*anotar*) to register, record; (*Inform*) to log; **registrarse** *vr* to register; (*ocurrir*) to happen

registro [re'xistro] *nm* (*acto*) registration; (*Mús, libro*) register; (*inspección*) inspection, search; **registro civil** registry office

regla ['reɣla] *nf* (*ley*) rule, regulation; (*de medir*) ruler, rule; (*Med: período*) period; **en ~** in order

reglamentación [reɣlamenta'θjon] *nf* (*acto*) regulation; (*lista*) rules *pl*

reglamentar [reɣlamen'tar] *vt* to regulate; **reglamentario, -a** *adj* statutory; **reglamento** *nm* rules *pl*, regulations *pl*

regocijarse [reɣoθi'xarse] *vr* (*alegrarse*) to rejoice; **regocijo** *nm* joy, happiness

regrabadora [reɣraβa'ðora] *nf* rewriter; **regrabadora de DVD** DVD rewriter

regresar [reɣre'sar] *vi* to come back, go back, return; **regreso** *nm* return

reguero [re'ɣero] *nm* (*de sangre etc*) trickle; (*de humo*) trail

regulador [reɣula'ðor] *nm* regulator; (*de radio etc*) knob, control

regular [reɣu'lar] *adj* regular; (*normal*) normal, usual; (*común*) ordinary; (*organizado*) regular, orderly; (*mediano*) average; (*fam*) not bad, so-so ▷ *adv* so-so, alright ▷ *vt* (*controlar*) to control, regulate; (*Tec*) to adjust; **por lo ~** as a rule; **regularidad** *nf* regularity; **regularizar** *vt* to regularize

rehabilitación [reaβilita'θjon] *nf* rehabilitation; (*Arq*) restoration

rehabilitar [reaβili'tar] *vt* to rehabilitate; (*Arq*) to restore; (*reintegrar*) to reinstate

rehacer [rea'θer] *vt* (*reparar*) to mend, repair; (*volver a hacer*) to redo, repeat; **rehacerse** *vr* (*Med*) to recover

rehén [re'en] *nm* hostage

rehuir [reu'ir] *vt* to avoid, shun

rehusar [reu'sar] *vt, vi* to refuse

reina ['reina] *nf* queen; **reinado** *nm* reign

reinar [rei'nar] *vi* to reign

reincidir [reinθi'ðir] *vi* to relapse

reincorporarse [reinkorpo'rarse] *vr*: **~ a** to rejoin

reino ['reino] *nm* kingdom; **reino animal/ vegetal** animal/plant kingdom; **el Reino Unido** the United Kingdom

reintegrar [reinte'ɣrar] *vt* (*reconstituir*) to reconstruct; (*persona*) to reinstate; (*dinero*) to refund, pay back; **reintegrarse** *vr*: **~se a** to return to

reír [re'ir] *vi* to laugh; **reírse** *vr* to laugh; **~se de** to laugh at

reiterar [reite'rar] *vt* to reiterate

reivindicación [reiβindika'θjon] *nf* (*demanda*) claim, demand; (*justificación*) vindication

reivindicar [reiβindi'kar] *vt* to claim

reja ['rexa] *nf* (*de ventana*) grille, bars *pl*; (*en la calle*) grating

rejilla [re'xiʎa] *nf* grating, grille; (*muebles*) wickerwork; (*de ventilación*) vent; (*de coche etc*) luggage rack

rejoneador [rexonea'ðor] *nm* mounted bullfighter

rejuvenecer [rexuβene'θer] vt, vi to rejuvenate

relación [rela'θjon] nf relation, relationship; (Mat) ratio; (narración) report; **con ~ a, en ~ con** in relation to; **relaciones públicas** public relations; **relacionar** vt to relate, connect; **relacionarse** vr to be connected, be linked

relajación [relaxa'θjon] nf relaxation

relajar [rela'xar] vt to relax; **relajarse** vr to relax

relamerse [rela'merse] vr to lick one's lips

relámpago [re'lampaxo] nm flash of lightning; **visita ~** lightning visit

relatar [rela'tar] vt to tell, relate

relativo, -a [rela'tiβo, a] adj relative; **en lo ~ a** concerning

relato [re'lato] nm (narración) story, tale

relegar [rele'xar] vt to relegate

relevante [rele'βante] adj eminent, outstanding

relevar [rele'βar] vt (sustituir) to relieve; **relevarse** vr to relay; **~ a algn de un cargo** to relieve sb of his post

relevo [re'leβo] nm relief; **carrera de ~s** relay race

relieve [re'ljeβe] nm (Arte, Tec) relief; (fig) prominence, importance; **bajo ~** bas-relief

religión [reli'xjon] nf religion; **religioso, -a** adj religious ▷ nm/f monk/nun

relinchar [relin'tʃar] vi to neigh

reliquia [re'likja] nf relic; **reliquia de familia** heirloom

rellano [re'ʎano] nm (Arq) landing

rellenar [reʎe'nar] vt (llenar) to fill up; (Culin) to stuff; (Costura) to pad; **relleno, -a** adj full up; stuffed ▷ nm stuffing; (de tapicería) padding

reloj [re'lo(x)] nm clock; **poner el ~ (en hora)** to set one's watch (o the clock); **reloj (de pulsera)** wristwatch; **reloj despertador** alarm (clock); **reloj digital** digital watch; **relojero, -a** nm/f clockmaker; watchmaker

reluciente [relu'θjente] adj brilliant, shining

relucir [relu'θir] vi to shine; (fig) to excel

remachar [rema'tʃar] vt to rivet; (fig) to hammer home, drive home; **remache** nm rivet

remangar [reman'gar] vt to roll up

remanso [re'manso] nm pool

remar [re'mar] vi to row

rematado, -a [rema'taðo, a] adj complete, utter

rematar [rema'tar] vt to finish off; (Com) to sell off cheap ▷ vi to end, finish off; (Deporte) to shoot

remate [re'mate] nm end, finish; (punta) tip; (Deporte) shot; (Arq) top; **de o para ~** to crown it all (BRIT), to top it off

remedar [reme'ðar] vt to imitate

remediar [reme'ðjar] vt to remedy; (subsanar) to make good, repair; **de (evitar)** to avoid

remedio [re'meðjo] nm remedy; (alivio) relief, help; (Jur) recourse, remedy; **poner ~ a** to correct, stop; **no tener más ~** to have no alternative; **¡qué ~!** there's no choice!; **sin ~** hopeless

remendar [remen'dar] vt to repair; (con parche) to patch

remiendo [re'mjendo] nm mend; (con parche) patch; (cosido) darn

remilgado, -a [remil'xaðo, a] adj prim; (afectado) affected

remiso, -a [re'miso, a] adj slack, slow

remite [re'mite] nm (en sobre) name and address of sender

remitir [remi'tir] vt to remit, send ▷ vi to slacken; (en carta): **remite: X** sender: X; **remitente** nmf sender

remo ['remo] nm (de barco) oar; (Deporte) rowing

remojar [remo'xar] vt to steep, soak; (galleta etc) to dip, dunk

remojo [re'moxo] nm: **dejar la ropa en ~** to leave clothes to soak

remolacha [remo'latʃa] nf beet, beetroot

remolcador [remolka'ðor] nm (Náut) tug; (Auto) breakdown lorry

remolcar [remol'kar] vt to tow

remolino [remo'lino] nm eddy; (de agua) whirlpool; (de viento) whirlwind; (de gente) crowd

remolque [re'molke] nm tow, towing; (cuerda) towrope; **llevar a ~** to tow

remontar [remon'tar] vt to mend; **remontarse** vr to soar; **~se a** (Com) to amount to; **~ el vuelo** to soar

remorder [remor'ðer] vt to distress, disturb; **~le la conciencia a algn** to have a guilty conscience; **remordimiento** nm remorse

remoto, -a [re'moto, a] adj remote

remover [remo'βer] vt to stir; (tierra) to turn over; (objetos) to move round

remuneración [remunera'θjon] nf remuneration

remunerar [remune'rar] vt to remunerate; (premiar) to reward

renacer [rena'θer] vi to be reborn; (fig) to revive; **renacimiento** nm rebirth; **el Renacimiento** the Renaissance

renacuajo [rena'kwaxo] nm (Zool) tadpole

renal [re'nal] *adj* renal, kidney *cpd*

rencilla [ren'θiʎa] *nf* quarrel

rencor [ren'kor] *nm* rancour, bitterness;
rencoroso, -a *adj* spiteful

rendición [rendi'θjon] *nf* surrender

rendido, -a [ren'diðo, a] *adj* (*sumiso*)
submissive; (*cansado*) worn-out, exhausted

rendija [ren'dixa] *nf* (*hendedura*) crack,
cleft

rendimiento [rendi'mjento] *nm*
(*producción*) output; (*Tec, Com*) efficiency

rendir [ren'dir] *vt* (*vencer*) to defeat;
(*producir*) to produce; (*dar beneficio*) to yield;
(*agotar*) to exhaust ▷ *vi* to pay; **rendirse**
vr (*someterse*) to surrender; (*cansarse*) to
wear o.s. out; **~ homenaje** *o* **culto a** to pay
homage to

renegar [rene'xar] *vi* (*renunciar*) to
renounce; (*blasfemar*) to blaspheme;
(*quejarse*) to complain

RENFE ['renfe] *nf abr* (= *Red Nacional de los
Ferrocarriles Españoles*)

renglón [ren'glon] *nm* (*línea*) line; (*Com*)
item, article; **a ~ seguido** immediately after

renombre [re'nombre] *nm* renown

renovación [renoβa'θjon] *nf* (*de contrato*)
renewal; (*Arq*) renovation

renovar [reno'βar] *vt* to renew; (*Arq*) to
renovate

renta ['renta] *nf* (*ingresos*) income;
(*beneficio*) profit; (*alquiler*) rent; **renta
vitalicia** annuity; **rentable** *adj* profitable

renuncia [re'nunθja] *nf* resignation;
renunciar [renun'θjar] *vt* to renounce;
(*tabaco, alcohol etc*): **renunciar a** to give up;
(*oferta, oportunidad*) to turn down; (*puesto*) to
resign ▷ *vi* to resign

reñido, -a [re'ɲiðo, a] *adj* (*batalla*) bitter,
hard-fought; **estar ~ con algn** to be on bad
terms with sb

reñir [re'ɲir] *vt* (*regañar*) to scold ▷ *vi*
(*estar peleado*) to quarrel, fall out; (*combatir*)
to fight

reo ['reo] *nmf* culprit, offender; (*acusado*)
accused, defendant

reojo [re'oxo]: **de ~** *adv* out of the corner
of one's eye

reparación [repara'θjon] *nf* (*acto*)
mending, repairing; (*Tec*) repair; (*fig*)
amends *pl*, reparation

reparar [repa'rar] *vt* to repair; (*fig*) to
make amends for; (*observar*) to observe
▷ *vi*: **~ en** (*darse cuenta de*) to notice; (*prestar
atención a*) to pay attention to

reparo [re'paro] *nm* (*advertencia*)
observation; (*duda*) doubt; (*dificultad*)
difficulty; **poner ~s (a)** to raise objections
(to)

repartidor, a [reparti'ðor, a] *nm/f*
distributor

repartir [repar'tir] *vt* to distribute,
share out; (*Correos*) to deliver; **reparto** *nm*
distribution; delivery; (*Teatro, Cine*) cast;
(CAM: *urbanización*) housing estate (BRIT),
real estate development (US)

repasar [repa'sar] *vt* (*Escol*) to revise;
(*Mecánica*) to check, overhaul; (*Costura*)
to mend; **repaso** *nm* revision; overhaul;
checkup; mending

repecho [re'petʃo] *nm* steep incline

repelente [repe'lente] *adj* repellent,
repulsive

repeler [repe'ler] *vt* to repel

repente [re'pente] *nm*: **de ~** suddenly

repentino, -a [repen'tino, a] *adj* sudden

repercusión [reperku'sjon] *nf*
repercussion

repercutir [reperku'tir] *vi* (*objeto*) to
rebound; (*sonido*) to echo; **~ en** (*fig*) to have
repercussions on

repertorio [reper'torjo] *nm* list; (*Teatro*)
repertoire

repetición [repeti'θjon] *nf* repetition

repetir [repe'tir] *vt* to repeat; (*plato*) to
have a second helping of ▷ *vi* to repeat;
(*sabor*) to come back; **repetirse** *vr* (*volver
sobre un tema*) to repeat o.s.

repetitivo, -a [repeti'tiβo, a] *adj*
repetitive, repetitious

repique [re'pike] *nm* pealing, ringing;
repiqueteo *nm* pealing; (*de tambor*)
drumming

repisa [re'pisa] *nf* ledge, shelf; (*de ventana*)
windowsill; **la ~ de la chimenea** the
mantelpiece

repito *etc vb* V **repetir**

replantearse [replante'arse] *vr*: **~ un
problema** to reconsider a problem

repleto, -a [re'pleto, a] *adj* replete, full up

réplica ['replika] *nf* answer; (*Arte*) replica

replicar [repli'kar] *vi* to answer; (*objetar*)
to argue, answer back

repliegue [re'pljexe] *nm* (*Mil*) withdrawal

repoblación [repoβla'θjon] *nf*
repopulation; (*de río*) restocking;
repoblación forestal reafforestation

repoblar [repo'βlar] *vt* to repopulate; (*con
árboles*) to reafforest

repollito [repo'ʎito] (cs) *nm*: **~s de
Bruselas** (Brussels) sprouts

repollo [re'poʎo] *nm* cabbage

reponer [repo'ner] *vt* to replace, put back;
(*Teatro*) to revive; **reponerse** *vr* to recover;
~ que ... to reply that ...

reportaje [repor'taxe] *nm* report, article

reportero, -a [repor'tero, a] *nm/f*

reporter

reposacabezas [reposaka'βeθas] nm inv headrest

reposar [repo'sar] vi to rest, repose

reposera [repo'sera] (RPL) nf deck chair

reposición [reposi'θjon] nf replacement; (Cine) remake

reposo [re'poso] nm rest

repostar [repos'tar] vt to replenish; (Auto) to fill up (with petrol (BRIT) o gasoline (US))

repostería [reposte'ria] nf confectioner's (shop)

represa [re'presa] nf dam; (lago artificial) lake, pool

represalia [repre'salja] nf reprisal

representación [representa'θjon] nf representation; (Teatro) performance; **representante** nmf representative; performer

representar [represen'tar] vt to represent; (Teatro) to perform; (edad) to look; **representarse** vr to imagine; **representativo, -a** adj representative

represión [repre'sjon] nf repression

reprimenda [repri'menda] nf reprimand, rebuke

reprimir [repri'mir] vt to repress

reprobar [repro'βar] vt to censure, reprove

reprochar [repro'tʃar] vt to reproach; **reproche** nm reproach

reproducción [reproðuk'θjon] nf reproduction

reproducir [reproðu'θir] vt to reproduce; **reproducirse** vr to breed; (situación) to recur

reproductor, a [reproðuk'tor, a] adj reproductive ▷ nm player; **reproductor de CD** CD player

reptil [rep'til] nm reptile

república [re'puβlika] nf republic; **República Dominicana** Dominican Republic; **republicano, -a** adj, nm republican

repudiar [repu'ðjar] vt to repudiate; (fe) to renounce

repuesto [re'pwesto] nm (pieza de recambio) spare (part); (abastecimiento) supply; **rueda de ~** spare wheel

repugnancia [repuɣ'nanθja] nf repugnance; **repugnante** adj repugnant, repulsive

repugnar [repuɣ'nar] vt to disgust

repulsa [re'pulsa] nf rebuff

repulsión [repul'sjon] nf repulsion, aversion; **repulsivo, -a** adj repulsive

reputación [reputa'θjon] nf reputation

requerir [reke'rir] vt (pedir) to ask, request; (exigir) to require; (llamar) to send for, summon

requesón [reke'son] nm cottage cheese

requete... [re'kete] prefijo extremely

réquiem ['rekjem] (pl **~s**) nm requiem

requisito [reki'sito] nm requirement, requisite

res [res] nf beast, animal

resaca [re'saka] nf (de mar) undertow, undercurrent; (fam) hangover

resaltar [resal'tar] vi to project, stick out; (fig) to stand out

resarcir [resar'θir] vt to compensate; **resarcirse** vr to make up for

resbaladero [resβala'ðero] (MÉX) nm slide

resbaladizo, -a [resβala'ðiθo, a] adj slippery

resbalar [resβa'lar] vi to slip, slide; (fig) to slip (up); **resbalarse** vr to slip, slide; to slip (up); **resbalón** nm (acción) slip

rescatar [reska'tar] vt (salvar) to save, rescue; (objeto) to get back, recover; (cautivos) to ransom

rescate [res'kate] nm rescue; (de objeto) recovery; **pagar un ~** to pay a ransom

rescindir [resθin'dir] vt to rescind

rescisión [resθi'sjon] nf cancellation

resecar [rese'kar] vt to dry thoroughly; (Med) to cut out, remove; **resecarse** vr to dry up

reseco, -a [re'seko, a] adj very dry; (fig) skinny

resentido, -a [resen'tiðo, a] adj resentful

resentimiento [resenti'mjento] nm resentment, bitterness

resentirse [resen'tirse] vr (debilitarse: persona) to suffer; **~ de** (consecuencias) to feel the effects of; **~ de (o por) algo** to resent sth, be bitter about sth

reseña [re'seɲa] nf (cuenta) account; (informe) report; (Literatura) review

reseñar [rese'ɲar] vt to describe; (Literatura) to review

reserva [re'serβa] nf reserve; (reservación) reservation

reservado, -a [reser'βaðo, a] adj reserved; (retraído) cold, distant ▷ nm private room

reservar [reser'βar] vt (guardar) to keep; (habitación, entrada) to reserve; **reservarse** vr to save o.s.; (callar) to keep to o.s.

resfriado [resfri'aðo] nm cold; **resfriarse** vr to cool; (Med) to catch a cold

resguardar [resɣwar'ðar] vt to protect, shield; **resguardarse** vr: **~se de** to guard against; **resguardo** nm defence; (vale) voucher; (recibo) receipt, slip

residencia [resi'ðenθja] *nf* residence; **residencia de ancianos** residential home, old people's home; **residencia universitaria** hall of residence; **residencial** *nf* (*urbanización*) housing estate

residente [resi'ðente] *adj, nmf* resident

residir [resi'ðir] *vi* to reside, live; **~ en** to reside in, lie in

residuo [re'siðwo] *nm* residue

resignación [resiɣna'θjon] *nf* resignation; **resignarse** *vr*: **resignarse a** *o* **con** to resign o.s. to, be resigned to

resina [re'sina] *nf* resin

resistencia [resis'tenθja] *nf* (*dureza*) endurance, strength; (*oposición, Elec*) resistance; **resistente** *adj* strong, hardy; resistant

resistir [resis'tir] *vt* (*soportar*) to bear; (*oponerse a*) to resist, oppose; (*aguantar*) to put up with ▷ *vi* to resist; (*aguantar*) to last, endure; **resistirse** *vr*: **~se a** to refuse to, resist

resoluto, -a [reso'luto, a] *adj* resolute

resolver [resol'βer] *vt* to resolve; (*solucionar*) to solve, resolve; (*decidir*) to decide, settle; **resolverse** *vr* to make up one's mind

resonar [reso'nar] *vi* to ring, echo

resoplar [reso'plar] *vi* to snort; **resoplido** *nm* heavy breathing

resorte [re'sorte] *nm* spring; (*fig*) lever

resortera [resor'tera] (*MÉX*) *nf* catapult

respaldar [respal'dar] *vt* to back (up), support; **respaldarse** *vr* to lean back; **~se con** *o* **en** (*fig*) to take one's stand on; **respaldo** *nm* (*de sillón*) back; (*fig*) support, backing

respectivo, -a [respek'tiβo, a] *adj* respective; **en lo ~ a** with regard to

respecto [res'pekto] *nm*: **al ~** on this matter; **con ~ a, ~ de** with regard to, in relation to

respetable [respe'taβle] *adj* respectable

respetar [respe'tar] *vt* to respect; **respeto** *nm* respect; (*acatamiento*) deference; **respetos** *nmpl* respects; **respetuoso, -a** *adj* respectful

respingo [res'pingo] *nm* start, jump

respiración [respira'θjon] *nf* breathing; (*Med*) respiration; (*ventilación*) ventilation; **respiración asistida** artificial respiration (*by machine*)

respirar [respi'rar] *vi* to breathe; **respiratorio, -a** *adj* respiratory; **respiro** *nm* breathing; (*fig: descanso*) respite

resplandecer [resplande'θer] *vi* to shine; **resplandeciente** *adj* resplendent, shining; **resplandor** *nm* brilliance, brightness; (*de luz, fuego*) blaze

responder [respon'der] *vt* to answer ▷ *vi* to answer; (*fig*) to respond; (*pey*) to answer back; **~ de** *o* **por** to answer for; **respondón, -ona** *adj* cheeky

responsabilidad [responsaβili'ðað] *nf* responsibility

responsabilizarse [responsaβili'θarse] *vr* to make o.s. responsible, take charge

responsable [respon'saβle] *adj* responsible

respuesta [res'pwesta] *nf* answer, reply

resquebrajar [reskeβra'xar] *vt* to crack, split; **resquebrajarse** *vr* to crack, split

resquicio [res'kiθjo] *nm* chink; (*hendedura*) crack

resta ['resta] *nf* (*Mat*) remainder

restablecer [restaβle'θer] *vt* to re-establish, restore; **restablecerse** *vr* to recover

restante [res'tante] *adj* remaining; **lo ~** the remainder

restar [res'tar] *vt* (*Mat*) to subtract; (*fig*) to take away ▷ *vi* to remain, be left

restauración [restaura'θjon] *nf* restoration

restaurante [restau'rante] *nm* restaurant

restaurar [restau'rar] *vt* to restore

restituir [restitu'ir] *vt* (*devolver*) to return, give back; (*rehabilitar*) to restore

resto ['resto] *nm* (*residuo*) rest, remainder; (*apuesta*) stake; **restos** *nmpl* remains

restorán [resto'ran] *nm* (*Lam*) restaurant

restregar [restre'ɣar] *vt* to scrub, rub

restricción [restrik'θjon] *nf* restriction

restringir [restrin'xir] *vt* to restrict, limit

resucitar [resuθi'tar] *vt, vi* to resuscitate, revive

resuelto, -a [re'swelto, a] *pp de* **resolver** ▷ *adj* resolute, determined

resultado [resul'taðo] *nm* result; (*conclusión*) outcome; **resultante** *adj* resulting, resultant

resultar [resul'tar] *vi* (*ser*) to be; (*llegar a ser*) to turn out to be; (*salir bien*) to turn out well; (*Com*) to amount to; **~ de** to stem from; **me resulta difícil hacerlo** it's difficult for me to do it

resumen [re'sumen] (*pl* **resúmenes**) *nm* summary, résumé; **en ~** in short

resumir [resu'mir] *vt* to sum up; (*cortar*) to abridge, cut down; (*condensar*) to summarize

> No confundir **resumir** con la palabra inglesa *resume*.

resurgir [resur'xir] *vi* (*reaparecer*) to reappear

resurrección [resurre(k)'θjon] *nf* resurrection

retablo [re'taβlo] *nm* altarpiece

retaguardia [reta'ɣwarðja] *nf* rearguard

retahíla [reta'ila] *nf* series, string

retal [re'tal] *nm* remnant

retar [re'tar] *vt* to challenge; (*desafiar*) to defy, dare

retazo [re'taθo] *nm* snippet (BRIT), fragment

retención [reten'θjon] *nf* (*tráfico*) hold-up; **retención fiscal** deduction for tax purposes

retener [rete'ner] *vt* (*intereses*) to withhold

reticente [reti'θente] *adj* (*tono*) insinuating; (*postura*) reluctant; **ser ~ a hacer algo** to be reluctant *o* unwilling to do sth

retina [re'tina] *nf* retina

retintín [retin'tin] *nm* jangle, jingle

retirada [reti'raða] *nf* (Mil, *refugio*) retreat; (*de dinero*) withdrawal; (*de embajador*) recall; **retirado, -a** *adj* (*lugar*) remote; (*vida*) quiet; (*jubilado*) retired

retirar [reti'rar] *vt* to withdraw; (*quitar*) to remove; (*jubilar*) to retire, pension off; **retirarse** *vr* to retreat, withdraw; to retire; (*acostarse*) to retire, go to bed; **retiro** *nm* retreat; retirement; (*pago*) pension

reto ['reto] *nm* dare, challenge

retocar [reto'kar] *vt* (*fotografía*) to touch up, retouch

retoño [re'toɲo] *nm* sprout, shoot; (*fig*) offspring, child

retoque [re'toke] *nm* retouching

retorcer [retor'θer] *vt* to twist; (*manos, lavado*) to wring; **retorcerse** *vr* to become twisted; (*mover el cuerpo*) to writhe

retorcido, -a [retor'θiðo, a] *adj* (*persona*) devious

retorcijón [retorθi'jon] (LAM) *nm* (tb: **~ de tripas**) stomach cramp

retórica [re'torika] *nf* rhetoric; (*pey*) affectedness

retorno [re'torno] *nm* return

retortijón [retorti'xon] (ESP) *nm* (tb: **~ de tripas**) stomach cramp

retozar [reto'θar] *vi* (*juguetear*) to frolic, romp; (*saltar*) to gambol

retracción [retrak'θjon] *nf* retraction

retraerse [retra'erse] *vr* to retreat, withdraw; **retraído, -a** *adj* shy, retiring; **retraimiento** *nm* retirement; (*timidez*) shyness

retransmisión [retransmi'sjon] *nf* repeat (broadcast)

retransmitir [retransmi'tir] *vt* (*mensaje*) to relay; (TV *etc*) to repeat, retransmit; (: *en vivo*) to broadcast live

retrasado, -a [retra'saðo, a] *adj* late; (Med) mentally retarded; (*país etc*) backward, underdeveloped

retrasar [retra'sar] *vt* (*demorar*) to postpone, put off; (*retardar*) to slow down ▷ *vi* (*atrasarse*) to be late; (*reloj*) to be slow; (*producción*) to fall (off); (*quedarse atrás*) to lag behind; **retrasarse** *vr* to be late; to be slow; to fall (off); to lag behind

retraso [re'traso] *nm* (*demora*) delay; (*lentitud*) slowness; (*tardanza*) lateness; (*atraso*) backwardness; **retrasos** *nmpl* (Finanzas) arrears; **llegar con ~** to arrive late; **retraso mental** mental deficiency

retratar [retra'tar] *vt* (Arte) to paint the portrait of; (*fotografiar*) to photograph; (*fig*) to depict, describe; **retrato** *nm* portrait; (*fig*) likeness; **retrato-robot** (ESP) *nm* Identikit®

retrete [re'trete] *nm* toilet

retribuir [retri'βwir] *vt* (*recompensar*) to reward; (*pagar*) to pay

retro... [retro] *prefijo* retro...

retroceder [retroθe'ðer] *vi* (*echarse atrás*) to move back(wards); (*fig*) to back down

retroceso [retro'θeso] *nm* backward movement; (Med) relapse; (*fig*) backing down

retrospectivo, -a [retrospek'tiβo, a] *adj* retrospective

retrovisor [retroβi'sor] *nm* (tb: **espejo ~**) rear-view mirror

retumbar [retum'bar] *vi* to echo, resound

reúma [re'uma], **reuma** ['reuma] *nm* rheumatism

reunión [reu'njon] *nf* (*asamblea*) meeting; (*fiesta*) party

reunir [reu'nir] *vt* (*juntar*) to reunite, join (together); (*recoger*) to gather (together); (*personas*) to get together; (*cualidades*) to combine; **reunirse** *vr* (*personas: en asamblea*) to meet, gather

revalidar [reβali'ðar] *vt* (*ratificar*) to confirm, ratify

revalorizar [reβalori'θar] *vt* to revalue, reassess

revancha [re'βantʃa] *nf* revenge

revelación [reβela'θjon] *nf* revelation

revelado [reβe'laðo] *nm* developing

revelar [reβe'lar] *vt* to reveal; (Foto) to develop

reventa [re'βenta] *nf* (*de entradas: para concierto*) touting

reventar [reβen'tar] *vt* to burst, explode

reventón [reβen'ton] *nm* (Auto) blow-out (BRIT), flat (US)

reverencia [reβe'renθja] *nf* reverence; **reverenciar** *vt* to revere

reverendo, -a [reβe'rendo, a] *adj* reverend

reverente [reβe'rente] *adj* reverent

reversa [re'βersa] (*MÉX, CAM*) *nf* reverse (gear)

reversible [reβer'siβle] *adj* (*prenda*) reversible

reverso [re'βerso] *nm* back, other side; (*de moneda*) reverse

revertir [reβer'tir] *vi* to revert

revés [re'βes] *nm* back, wrong side; (*fig*) reverse, setback; (*Deporte*) backhand; **al ~** the wrong way round; (*de arriba abajo*) upside down; (*ropa*) inside out; **volver algo del ~** to turn sth round; (*ropa*) to turn sth inside out

revisar [reβi'sar] *vt* (*examinar*) to check; (*texto etc*) to revise; **revisión** *nf* revision; **revisión salarial** wage review

revisor, a [reβi'sor, a] *nm/f* inspector; (*Ferro*) ticket collector

revista [re'βista] *nf* magazine, review; (*Teatro*) revue; (*inspección*) inspection; **pasar ~ a** to review, inspect; **revista del corazón** *magazine featuring celebrity gossip and real-life romance stories*

revivir [reβi'βir] *vi* to revive

revolcarse [reβol'karse] *vr* to roll about

revoltijo [reβol'tixo] *nm* mess, jumble

revoltoso, -a [reβol'toso, a] *adj* (*travieso*) naughty, unruly

revolución [reβolu'θjon] *nf* revolution; **revolucionario, -a** *adj, nm/f* revolutionary

revolver [reβol'βer] *vt* (*desordenar*) to disturb, mess up; (*mover*) to move about ▷ *vi*: **~ en** to go through, rummage (about) in; **revolverse** *vr* (*volver contra*) to turn on *o* against

revólver [re'βolβer] *nm* revolver

revuelo [re'βwelo] *nm* fluttering; (*fig*) commotion

revuelta [re'βwelta] *nf* (*motín*) revolt; (*agitación*) commotion

revuelto, -a [re'βwelto, a] *pp de* **revolver** ▷ *adj* (*mezclado*) mixed-up, in disorder

rey [rei] *nm* king; **Día de R~es** Twelfth Night; **los R~es Magos** the Three Wise Men, the Magi

● the town by land or sea to the delight of
● the children.

reyerta [re'jerta] *nf* quarrel, brawl

rezagado, -a [reθa'γaðo, a] *nm/f* straggler

rezar [re'θar] *vi* to pray; **~ con** (*fam*) to concern, have to do with; **rezo** *nm* prayer

rezumar [reθu'mar] *vt* to ooze

ría ['ria] *nf* estuary

riada [ri'aða] *nf* flood

ribera [ri'βera] *nf* (*de río*) bank; (: *área*) riverside

ribete [ri'βete] *nm* (*de vestido*) border; (*fig*) addition

ricino [ri'θino] *nm*: **aceite de ~** castor oil

rico, -a ['riko, a] *adj* rich; (*adinerado*) wealthy, rich; (*lujoso*) luxurious; (*comida*) delicious; (*niño*) lovely, cute ▷ *nm/f* rich person

ridiculez [riðiku'leθ] *nf* absurdity

ridiculizar [riðikuli'θar] *vt* to ridicule

ridículo, -a [ri'ðikulo, a] *adj* ridiculous; **hacer el ~** to make a fool of o.s.; **poner a algn en ~** to make a fool of sb

riego ['rjeγo] *nm* (*aspersión*) watering; (*irrigación*) irrigation; **riego sanguíneo** blood flow *o* circulation

riel [rjel] *nm* rail

rienda ['rjenda] *nf* rein; **dar ~ suelta a** to give free rein to

riesgo ['rjesγo] *nm* risk; **correr el ~ de** to run the risk of

rifa ['rifa] *nf* (*lotería*) raffle; **rifar** *vt* to raffle

rifle ['rifle] *nm* rifle

rigidez [rixi'ðeθ] *nf* rigidity, stiffness; (*fig*) strictness; **rígido, -a** *adj* rigid, stiff; strict, inflexible

rigor [ri'γor] *nm* strictness, rigour; (*inclemencia*) harshness; **de ~** de rigueur, essential; **riguroso, -a** *adj* rigorous; harsh; (*severo*) severe

rimar [ri'mar] *vi* to rhyme

rimbombante [rimbom'bante] *adj* pompous

rímel ['rimel] *nm* mascara

rímmel ['rimel] *nm* = **rímel**

rin [rin] (*MÉX*) *nm* (wheel) rim

rincón [rin'kon] *nm* corner (*inside*)

rinoceronte [rinoθe'ronte] *nm* rhinoceros

riña ['riɲa] *nf* (*disputa*) argument; (*pelea*) brawl

riñón [ri'ɲon] *nm* kidney

río *etc* ['rio] *vb* V **reír** ▷ *nm* river; (*fig*) torrent, stream; **río abajo/arriba** downstream/upstream; **Río de la Plata** River Plate

rioja [ri'oxa] *nm* (*vino*) rioja (wine)
rioplatense [riopla'tense] *adj* of o from the River Plate region
riqueza [ri'keθa] *nf* wealth, riches *pl*; (*cualidad*) richness
risa ['risa] *nf* laughter; (*una risa*) laugh; **¡qué ~!** what a laugh!
risco ['risko] *nm* crag, cliff
ristra ['ristra] *nf* string
risueño, -a [ri'sweɲo, a] *adj* (*sonriente*) smiling; (*contento*) cheerful
ritmo ['ritmo] *nm* rhythm; **a ~ lento** slowly; **trabajar a ~ lento** to go slow; **ritmo cardíaco** heart rate
rito ['rito] *nm* rite
ritual [ri'twal] *adj, nm* ritual
rival [ri'βal] *adj, nmf* rival; **rivalidad** *nf* rivalry; **rivalizar** *vi*: **rivalizar con** to rival, vie with
rizado, -a [ri'θaðo, a] *adj* curly ▷ *nm* curls *pl*
rizar [ri'θar] *vt* to curl; **rizarse** *vr* (*pelo*) to curl; (*agua*) to ripple; **rizo** *nm* curl; ripple
RNE *nf abr* = **Radio Nacional de España**
robar [ro'βar] *vt* to rob; (*objeto*) to steal; (*casa etc*) to break into; (*Naipes*) to draw
roble ['roβle] *nm* oak; **robledal** *nm* oakwood
robo ['roβo] *nm* robbery, theft
robot [ro'βot] *nm* robot; **robot (de cocina)** (*ESP*) food processor
robustecer [roβuste'θer] *vt* to strengthen
robusto, -a [ro'βusto, a] *adj* robust, strong
roca ['roka] *nf* rock
roce ['roθe] *nm* (*caricia*) brush; (*Tec*) friction; (*en la piel*) graze; **tener ~ con** to be in close contact with
rociar [ro'θjar] *vt* to spray
rocín [ro'θin] *nm* nag, hack
rocío [ro'θio] *nm* dew
rocola [ro'kola] (*LAM*) *nf* jukebox
rocoso, -a [ro'koso, a] *adj* rocky
rodaballo [roða'βaʎo] *nm* turbot
rodaja [ro'ðaxa] *nf* slice
rodaje [ro'ðaxe] *nm* (*Cine*) shooting, filming; (*Auto*) **en ~** running in
rodar [ro'ðar] *vt* (*vehículo*) to wheel (along); (*escalera*) to roll down; (*viajar por*) to travel (over) ▷ *vi* to roll; (*coche*) to go, run; (*Cine*) to shoot, film
rodear [roðe'ar] *vt* to surround ▷ *vi* to go round; **rodearse** *vr*: **~se de amigos** to surround o.s. with friends
rodeo [ro'ðeo] *nm* (*ruta indirecta*) detour; (*evasión*) evasion; (*Deporte*) rodeo; **hablar sin ~s** to come to the point, speak plainly
rodilla [ro'ðiʎa] *nf* knee; **de ~s** kneeling;

ponerse de ~s to kneel (down)
rodillo [ro'ðiʎo] *nm* roller; (*Culin*) rolling-pin
roedor, a [roe'ðor, a] *adj* gnawing ▷ *nm* rodent
roer [ro'er] *vt* (*masticar*) to gnaw; (*corroer, fig*) to corrode
rogar [ro'ɣar] *vt, vi* (*pedir*) to ask for; (*suplicar*) to beg, plead; **se ruega no fumar** please do not smoke
rojizo, -a [ro'xiθo, a] *adj* reddish
rojo, -a ['roxo, a] *adj, nm* red; **al ~ vivo** red-hot
rol [rol] *nm* list, roll; (*papel*) role
rollito [ro'ʎito] *nm* (*tb*: **~ de primavera**) spring roll
rollizo, -a [ro'ʎiθo, a] *adj* (*objeto*) cylindrical; (*persona*) plump
rollo ['roʎo] *nm* roll; (*de cuerda*) coil; (*madera*) log; (*ESP: fam*) bore; **¡qué ~!** (*ESP: fam*) what a carry-on!
Roma ['roma] *n* Rome
romance [ro'manθe] *nm* (*amoroso*) romance; (*Literatura*) ballad
romano, -a [ro'mano, a] *adj, nm/f* Roman; **a la romana** in batter
romanticismo [romanti'θismo] *nm* romanticism
romántico, -a [ro'mantiko, a] *adj* romantic
rombo ['rombo] *nm* (*Geom*) rhombus
romería [rome'ria] *nf* (*Rel*) pilgrimage; (*excursión*) trip, outing

● **ROMERÍA**
●
●
● Originally a pilgrimage to a shrine or
● church to express devotion to the Virgin
● Mary or a local Saint, the **romería** has
● also become a rural festival which
● accompanies the pilgrimage. People
● come from all over to attend, bringing
● their own food and drink, and spend the
● day in celebration.

romero, -a [ro'mero, a] *nm/f* pilgrim ▷ *nm* rosemary
romo, -a ['romo, a] *adj* blunt; (*fig*) dull
rompecabezas [rompeka'βeθas] *nm inv* riddle, puzzle; (*juego*) jigsaw (puzzle)
rompehuelgas [rompe'welɣas] (*LAM*) *nm inv* strikebreaker, scab
rompeolas [rompe'olas] *nm inv* breakwater
romper [rom'per] *vt* to break; (*hacer pedazos*) to smash; (*papel, tela etc*) to tear, rip ▷ *vi* (*olas*) to break; (*sol, diente*) to break through; **romperse** *vr* to break; **~ un**

contrato to break a contract; **~ a** (empezar a) to start (suddenly) to; **~ a llorar** to burst into tears; **~ con algn** to fall out with sb
ron [ron] nm rum
roncar [ron'kar] vi to snore
ronco, -a ['ronko, a] adj (afónico) hoarse; (áspero) raucous
ronda ['ronda] nf (gen) round; (patrulla) patrol; **rondar** vt to patrol ▷ vi to patrol; (fig) to prowl round
ronquido [ron'kiðo] nm snore, snoring
ronronear [ronrone'ar] vi to purr
roña ['rona] nf (Veterinaria) mange; (mugre) dirt, grime; (óxido) rust
roñoso, -a [ro'noso, a] adj (mugriento) filthy; (tacaño) mean
ropa ['ropa] nf clothes pl, clothing; **ropa blanca** linen; **ropa de cama** bed linen; **ropa de color** coloureds pl; **ropa interior** underwear; **ropa sucia** dirty washing; **ropaje** nm gown, robes pl
ropero [ro'pero] nm linen cupboard; (guardarropa) wardrobe
rosa ['rosa] adj pink ▷ nf rose
rosado, -a [ro'saðo, a] adj pink ▷ nm rosé
rosal [ro'sal] nm rosebush
rosario [ro'sarjo] nm (Rel) rosary; **rezar el ~** to say the rosary
rosca ['roska] nf (de tornillo) thread; (de humo) coil, spiral; (pan, postre) ring-shaped roll/pastry
rosetón [rose'ton] nm rosette; (Arq) rose window
rosquilla [ros'kiʎa] nf doughnut-shaped fritter
rostro ['rostro] nm (cara) face
rotativo, -a [rota'tiβo, a] adj rotary
roto, -a ['roto, a] pp de **romper** ▷ adj broken
rotonda [ro'tonda] nf roundabout
rótula ['rotula] nf kneecap; (Tec) ball-and-socket joint
rotulador [rotula'ðor] nm felt-tip pen
rótulo ['rotulo] nm heading, title; label; (letrero) sign
rotundamente [rotunda'mente] adv (negar) flatly; (responder, afirmar) emphatically; **rotundo, -a** adj round; (enfático) emphatic
rotura [ro'tura] nf (acto) breaking; (Med) fracture
rozadura [roθa'ðura] nf abrasion, graze
rozar [ro'θar] vt (frotar) to rub; (arañar) to scratch; (tocar ligeramente) to shave, touch lightly; **rozarse** vr to rub (together); **~se con** (fam) to rub shoulders with
rte. abr (= remite, remitente) sender
RTVE nf abr = **Radiotelevisión Española**

rubí [ru'βi] nm ruby; (de reloj) jewel
rubio, -a ['ruβjo, a] adj fair-haired, blond(e) ▷ nm/f blond/blonde; **tabaco ~** Virginia tobacco
rubor [ru'βor] nm (sonrojo) blush; (timidez) bashfulness; **ruborizarse** vr to blush
rúbrica ['ruβrika] nf (de la firma) flourish; **rubricar** vt (firmar) to sign with a flourish; (concluir) to sign and seal
rudimentario, -a [ruðimen'tarjo, a] adj rudimentary
rudo, -a ['ruðo, a] adj (sin pulir) unpolished; (grosero) coarse; (violento) violent; (sencillo) simple
rueda ['rweða] nf wheel; (círculo) ring, circle; (rodaja) slice, round; **rueda de auxilio** (RPL) spare tyre; **rueda delantera/trasera/ de repuesto** front/back/spare wheel; **rueda de prensa** press conference; **rueda gigante** (LAM) big (BRIT) o Ferris (US) wheel
ruedo ['rweðo] nm (círculo) circle; (Taur) arena, bullring
ruego etc ['rwexo] vb V **rogar** ▷ nm request
rugby ['ruxβi] nm rugby
rugido [ru'xiðo] nm roar
rugir [ru'xir] vi to roar
rugoso, -a [ru'xoso, a] adj (arrugado) wrinkled; (áspero) rough; (desigual) ridged
ruido ['rwiðo] nm noise; (sonido) sound; (alboroto) racket, row; (escándalo) commotion, rumpus; **ruidoso, -a** adj noisy, loud; (fig) sensational
ruin [rwin] adj contemptible, mean
ruina ['rwina] nf ruin; (colapso) collapse; (de persona) ruin, downfall
ruinoso, -a [rwi'noso, a] adj ruinous; (destartalado) dilapidated, tumbledown; (Com) disastrous
ruiseñor [rwise'nor] nm nightingale
rulero [ru'lero] (RPL) nm roller
ruleta [ru'leta] nf roulette
rulo ['rulo] nm (para el pelo) curler
Rumanía [ruma'nia] nf Rumania
rumba ['rumba] nf rumba
rumbo ['rumbo] nm (ruta) route, direction; (ángulo de dirección) course, bearing; (fig) course of events; **ir con ~ a** to be heading for
rumiante [ru'mjante] nm ruminant
rumiar [ru'mjar] vt to chew; (fig) to chew over ▷ vi to chew the cud
rumor [ru'mor] nm (ruido sordo) low sound; (murmuración) murmur, buzz; **rumorearse** vr: **se rumorea que ...** it is rumoured that ...
rupestre [ru'pestre] adj rock cpd
ruptura [rup'tura] nf rupture
rural [ru'ral] adj rural

r

Rusia ['rusja] nf Russia; **ruso, -a** adj, nm/f
  Russian
rústico, -a ['rustiko, a] adj rustic;
  (ordinario) coarse, uncouth ▷ nm/f yokel
ruta ['ruta] nf route
rutina [ru'tina] nf routine

S

S abr (= santo, a) St; (= sur) S
s. abr (= siglo) C.; (= siguiente) foll
S.A. abr (= Sociedad Anónima) Ltd. (BRIT),
  Inc. (US)
sábado ['saβaðo] nm Saturday
sábana ['saβana] nf sheet
sabañón [saβa'non] nm chilblain
saber [sa'βer] vt to know; (llegar a conocer)
  to find out, learn; (tener capacidad de) to
  know how to ▷ vi: ~ **a** to taste of, taste like
  ▷ nm knowledge, learning; **a** ~ namely;
  ¿sabes conducir/nadar? can you drive/
  swim?; **¿sabes francés?** do you speak
  French?; ~ **de memoria** to know by heart;
  hacer ~ **algo a algn** to inform sb of sth, let
  sb know sth
sabiduría [saβiðu'ria] nf (conocimientos)
  wisdom; (instrucción) learning
sabiendas [sa'βjendas]: **a** ~ adv knowingly
sabio, -a ['saβjo,a] adj (docto) learned;
  (prudente) wise, sensible
sabor [sa'βor] nm taste, flavour; **saborear**
  vt to taste, savour; (fig) to relish
sabotaje [saβo'taxe] nm sabotage
sabré etc vb V **saber**
sabroso, -a [sa'βroso, a] adj tasty;
  (fig: fam) racy, salty
sacacorchos [saka'kortʃos] nm inv
  corkscrew
sacapuntas [saka'puntas] nm inv pencil
  sharpener
sacar [sa'kar] vt to take out; (fig: extraer)
  to get (out); (quitar) to remove, get out;
  (hacer salir) to bring out; (conclusión) to draw;
  (novela etc) to publish, bring out; (ropa) to
  take off; (obra) to make; (premio) to receive;
  (entradas) to get; (Tenis) to serve; ~ **adelante**
  (niño) to bring up; (negocio) to carry on, go on
  with; ~ **a algn a bailar** to get sb up to dance;
  ~ **una foto** to take a photo; ~ **la lengua** to
  stick out one's tongue; ~ **buenas/malas**

notas to get good/bad marks

sacarina [saka'rina] *nf* saccharin(e)

sacerdote [saθer'ðote] *nm* priest

saciar [sa'θjar] *vt* (*hambre, sed*) to satisfy; **saciarse** *vr* (*de comida*) to get full up

saco ['sako] *nm* bag; (*grande*) sack; (*su contenido*) bagful; (LAM: *chaqueta*) jacket; **saco de dormir** sleeping bag

sacramento [sakra'mento] *nm* sacrament

sacrificar [sakrifi'kar] *vt* to sacrifice; **sacrificio** *nm* sacrifice

sacristía [sakris'tia] *nf* sacristy

sacudida [saku'ðiða] *nf* (*agitación*) shake, shaking; (*sacudimiento*) jolt, bump; **sacudida eléctrica** electric shock

sacudir [saku'ðir] *vt* to shake; (*golpear*) to hit

Sagitario [saxi'tarjo] *nm* Sagittarius

sagrado, -a [sa'xraðo, a] *adj* sacred, holy

Sáhara ['saara] *nm*: **el ~** the Sahara (desert)

sal [sal] *vb* V **salir** ⊳ *nf* salt; **sales de baño** bath salts

sala ['sala] *nf* room; (*tb*: **~ de estar**) living room; (*Teatro*) house, auditorium; (*de hospital*) ward; **sala de espera** waiting room; **sala de estar** living room; **sala de fiestas** dance hall

salado, -a [sa'laðo, a] *adj* salty; (*fig*) witty, amusing; **agua salada** salt water

salar [sa'lar] *vt* to salt, add salt to

salario [sa'larjo] *nm* wage, pay

salchicha [sal'tʃitʃa] *nf* (*pork*) sausage; **salchichón** *nm* (salami-type) sausage

saldo ['saldo] *nm* (*pago*) settlement; (*de una cuenta*) balance; (*lo restante*) remnant(s) (*pl*), remainder; (*de móvil*) credit; **saldos** *nmpl* (*en tienda*) sale

saldré *etc vb* V **salir**

salero [sa'lero] *nm* salt cellar

salgo *etc vb* V **salir**

salida [sa'liða] *nf* (*puerta etc*) exit, way out; (*acto*) leaving, going out; (*de tren, Aviac*) departure; (*Tec*) output, production; (*fig*) way out; (*Com*) opening; (*Geo, válvula*) outlet; (*de gas*) leak; **calle sin ~** cul-de-sac; **salida de baño** (RPL) bathrobe; **salida de emergencia/incendios** emergency exit/ fire escape

○ **PALABRA CLAVE**

salir [sa'lir] *vi* **1** (*partir*: *tb*: **salir de**) to leave; **Juan ha salido** Juan's out; **salió de la cocina** he came out of the kitchen

2 (*aparecer*) to appear; (*disco, libro*) to come out; **anoche salió en la tele** she appeared *o* was on TV last night; **salió en todos los periódicos** it was in all the papers

3 (*resultar*): **la muchacha nos salió muy trabajadora** the girl turned out to be a very hard worker; **la comida te ha salido exquisita** the food was delicious; **sale muy caro** it's very expensive

4: **salirle a uno algo: la entrevista que hice me salió bien/mal** the interview I did went *o* turned out well/badly

5: **salir adelante: no sé como haré para salir adelante** I don't know how I'll get by

salirse *vr* (*líquido*) to spill; (*animal*) to escape

saliva [sa'liβa] *nf* saliva

salmo ['salmo] *nm* psalm

salmón [sal'mon] *nm* salmon

salmonete [salmo'nete] *nm* red mullet

salón [sa'lon] *nm* (*de casa*) living room, lounge; (*muebles*) lounge suite; **salón de baile** dance hall; **salón de belleza** beauty parlour

salpicadera [salpika'ðera] (MÉX) *nf* mudguard (BRIT), fender (US)

salpicadero [salpika'ðero] *nm* (*Auto*) dashboard

salpicar [salpi'kar] *vt* (*rociar*) to sprinkle, spatter; (*esparcir*) to scatter

salpicón [salpi'kon] *nm* (*tb*: **~ de marisco**) seafood salad

salsa ['salsa] *nf* sauce; (*con carne asada*) gravy; (*fig*) spice

saltamontes [salta'montes] *nm inv* grasshopper

saltar [sal'tar] *vt* to jump (over), leap (over); (*dejar de lado*) to skip, miss out ⊳ *vi* to jump, leap; (*pelota*) to bounce; (*al aire*) to fly up; (*quebrarse*) to break; (*al agua*) to dive; (*fig*) to explode, blow up

salto ['salto] *nm* jump, leap; (*al agua*) dive; **salto de agua** waterfall; **salto de altura/ longitud** high/long jump

salud [sa'luð] *nf* health; **¡(a su) ~!** cheers!, good health!; **saludable** *adj* (*de buena salud*) healthy; (*provechoso*) good, beneficial

saludar [salu'ðar] *vt* to greet; (*Mil*) to salute; **saludo** *nm* greeting; **"saludos"** (*en carta*) "best wishes", "regards"

salvación [salβa'θjon] *nf* salvation; (*rescate*) rescue

salvado [sal'βaðo] *nm* bran

salvaje [sal'βaxe] *adj* wild; (*tribu*) savage

salvamanteles [salβaman'teles] *nm inv* table mat

salvamento [salβa'mento] *nm* rescue

salvapantallas [salβapan'taʎas] *nm inv* screen saver

salvar [sal'βar] *vt* (*rescatar*) to save, rescue; (*resolver*) to overcome, resolve; (*cubrir*

distancias) to cover, travel; (*hacer excepción*) to except, exclude; (*barco*) to salvage
salvavidas [salβa'βiðas] *adj inv*: **bote/chaleco ~** lifeboat/life jacket
salvo, -a ['salβo, a] *adj* safe ▷ *adv* except (for), save; **a ~** out of danger; **~ que** unless
san [san] *adj* saint; **S~ Juan** St John
sanar [sa'nar] *vt* (*herida*) to heal; (*persona*) to cure ▷ *vi* (*persona*) to get well, recover; (*herida*) to heal
sanatorio [sana'torjo] *nm* sanatorium
sanción [san'θjon] *nf* sanction
sancochado, -a [sanko'tʃado, a] (*MÉX*) *adj* (*Culin*) underdone, rare
sandalia [san'dalja] *nf* sandal
sandía [san'dia] *nf* watermelon
sandwich ['sandwitʃ] (*pl* **~s, ~es**) *nm* sandwich
sanfermines [sanfer'mines] *nmpl* festivities in celebration of San Fermín (Pamplona)

● **SANFERMINES**
●
●
● The **Sanfermines** is a week-long
● festival in Pamplona made famous by
● Ernest Hemingway. From the 7th July,
● the feast of "San Fermín", crowds of
● mainly young people take to the streets
● drinking, singing and dancing. Early in
● the morning bulls are released along the
● narrow streets leading to the bullring,
● and young men risk serious injury to
● show their bravery by running out in
● front of them, a custom which is also
● typical of many Spanish villages.

sangrar [san'grar] *vt, vi* to bleed; **sangre** *nf* blood
sangría [san'gria] *nf* sangria, *sweetened drink of red wine with fruit*
sangriento, -a [san'grjento, a] *adj* bloody
sanguíneo, -a [san'gineo, a] *adj* blood cpd
sanidad [sani'ðað] *nf* (tb: **~ pública**) public health
San Isidro [sani'sidro] *nm* patron saint of Madrid

● **SAN ISIDRO**
●
●
● **San Isidro** is the patron saint of Madrid,
● and gives his name to the week-long
● festivities which take place around the
● 15th May. Originally an 18th-century
● trade fair, the **San Isidro** celebrations

now include music, dance, a famous
romería, theatre and bullfighting.

sanitario, -a [sani'tarjo, a] *adj* health cpd; **sanitarios** *nmpl* toilets (*BRIT*), washroom (*US*)
sano, -a ['sano, a] *adj* healthy; (*sin daños*) sound; (*comida*) wholesome; (*entero*) whole, intact; **~ y salvo** safe and sound

▌ No confundir **sano** con la palabra inglesa *sane*.

Santiago [san'tjaxo] *nm*: **~ (de Chile)** Santiago
santiamén [santja'men] *nm*: **en un ~** in no time at all
santidad [santi'ðað] *nf* holiness, sanctity
santiguarse [santi'ɣwarse] *vr* to make the sign of the cross
santo, -a ['santo, a] *adj* holy; (*fig*) wonderful, miraculous ▷ *nm/f* saint ▷ *nm* saint's day; **~ y seña** password
santuario [san'twarjo] *nm* sanctuary, shrine
sapo ['sapo] *nm* toad
saque ['sake] *nm* (*Tenis*) service, serve; (*Fútbol*) throw-in; **saque de esquina** corner (kick)
saquear [sake'ar] *vt* (*Mil*) to sack; (*robar*) to loot, plunder; (*fig*) to ransack
sarampión [saram'pjon] *nm* measles *sg*
sarcástico, -a [sar'kastiko, a] *adj* sarcastic
sardina [sar'ðina] *nf* sardine
sargento [sar'xento] *nm* sergeant
sarmiento [sar'mjento] *nm* (*Bot*) vine shoot
sarna ['sarna] *nf* itch; (*Med*) scabies
sarpullido [sarpu'ʎiðo] *nm* (*Med*) rash
sarro ['sarro] *nm* (*en dientes*) tartar, plaque
sartén [sar'ten] *nf* frying pan
sastre ['sastre] *nm* tailor; **sastrería** *nf* (*arte*) tailoring; (*tienda*) tailor's (shop)
Satanás [sata'nas] *nm* Satan
satélite [sa'telite] *nm* satellite
sátira ['satira] *nf* satire
satisfacción [satisfak'θjon] *nf* satisfaction
satisfacer [satisfa'θer] *vt* to satisfy; (*gastos*) to meet; (*pérdida*) to make good; **satisfacerse** *vr* to satisfy o.s., be satisfied; (*vengarse*) to take revenge; **satisfecho, -a** *adj* satisfied; (*contento*) content(ed), happy; (tb: **satisfecho de sí mismo**) self-satisfied, smug
saturar [satu'rar] *vt* to saturate; **saturarse** *vr* (*mercado, aeropuerto*) to reach saturation point
sauce ['sauθe] *nm* willow; **sauce llorón**

weeping willow

sauna ['sauna] *nf* sauna

savia ['saβja] *nf* sap

saxofón [sakso'fon] *nm* saxophone

sazonar [saθo'nar] *vt* to ripen; (*Culin*) to flavour, season

scooter [e'skuter] (*ESP*) *nf* scooter

Scotch® [skotʃ] (*LAM*) *nm* Sellotape® (*BRIT*), Scotch tape® (*US*)

SE *abr* (= *sudeste*) SE

○ **PALABRA CLAVE**

se [se] *pron* **1** (*reflexivo: sg: m*) himself; (*: f*) herself; (*: pl*) themselves; (*: cosa*) itself; (*: de Vd*) yourself; (*: de Vds*) yourselves; **se está preparando** she's preparing herself
2 (*con complemento indirecto*) to him; to her; to them; to it; to you; **a usted se lo dije ayer** I told you yesterday; **se compró un sombrero** he bought himself a hat; **se rompió la pierna** he broke his leg
3 (*uso recíproco*) each other, one another; **se miraron (el uno al otro)** they looked at each other o one another
4 (*en oraciones pasivas*): **se han vendido muchos libros** a lot of books have been sold
5 (*impers*): **se dice que ...** people say that ..., it is said that ...; **allí se come muy bien** the food there is very good, you can eat very well there

sé *etc* [se] *vb* V **saber; ser**

sea *etc* *vb* V **ser**

sebo ['seβo] *nm* fat, grease

secador [seka'ðor] *nm*: **~ de pelo** hairdryer

secadora [seka'ðora] *nf* tumble dryer

secar [se'kar] *vt* to dry; **secarse** *vr* to dry (off); (*río, planta*) to dry up

sección [sek'θjon] *nf* section

seco, -a ['seko, a] *adj* dry; (*carácter*) cold; (*respuesta*) sharp, curt; **parar en ~** to stop dead; **decir algo a secas** to say sth curtly

secretaría [sekreta'ria] *nf* secretariat

secretario, -a [sekre'tarjo, a] *nm/f* secretary

secreto, -a [se'kreto, a] *adj* secret; (*persona*) secretive ⊳ *nm* secret; (*calidad*) secrecy

secta ['sekta] *nf* sect

sector [sek'tor] *nm* sector

secuela [se'kwela] *nf* consequence

secuencia [se'kwenθja] *nf* sequence

secuestrar [sekwes'trar] *vt* to kidnap; (*bienes*) to seize, confiscate; **secuestro** *nm* kidnapping; seizure, confiscation

secundario, -a [sekun'darjo, a] *adj* secondary

sed [seð] *nf* thirst; **tener ~** to be thirsty

seda ['seða] *nf* silk

sedal [se'ðal] *nm* fishing line

sedán [se'ðan] (*LAM*) *nm* saloon (*BRIT*), sedan (*US*)

sedante [se'ðante] *nm* sedative

sede ['seðe] *nf* (*de gobierno*) seat; (*de compañía*) headquarters *pl*; **Santa S~** Holy See

sedentario, -a [seðen'tarjo, a] *adj* sedentary

sediento, -a [se'ðjento, a] *adj* thirsty

sedimento [seði'mento] *nm* sediment

seducción [seðuk'θjon] *nf* seduction

seducir [seðu'θir] *vt* to seduce; (*cautivar*) to charm, fascinate; (*atraer*) to attract; **seductor, a** *adj* seductive; charming, fascinating; attractive ⊳ *nm/f* seducer

segar [se'ɣar] *vt* (*mies*) to reap, cut; (*hierba*) to mow, cut

seglar [se'ɣlar] *adj* secular, lay

seguida [se'ɣiða] *nf*: **en ~** at once, right away

seguido, -a [se'ɣiðo, a] *adj* (*continuo*) continuous, unbroken; (*recto*) straight ⊳ *adv* (*directo*) straight (on); (*después*) after; (*LAM: a menudo*) often; **~s** consecutive, successive; **5 días ~s** 5 days running, 5 days in a row

seguir [se'ɣir] *vt* to follow; (*venir después*) to follow on, come after; (*proseguir*) to continue; (*perseguir*) to chase, pursue ⊳ *vi* (*gen*) to follow; (*continuar*) to continue, carry o go on; **seguirse** *vr* to follow; **sigo sin comprender** I still don't understand; **sigue lloviendo** it's still raining

según [se'ɣun] *prep* according to ⊳ *adv*: **¿irás? – ~** are you going? – it all depends ⊳ *conj* as; **~ caminamos** while we walk

segundo, -a [se'ɣundo, a] *adj* second ⊳ *nm* second ⊳ *nf* second meaning; **de segunda mano** second-hand; **segunda (clase)** second class; **segunda (marcha)** (*Auto*) second (gear)

seguramente [seɣura'mente] *adv* surely; (*con certeza*) for sure, with certainty

seguridad [seɣuri'ðað] *nf* safety; (*del estado, de casa etc*) security; (*certidumbre*) certainty; (*confianza*) confidence; (*estabilidad*) stability; **seguridad social** social security

seguro, -a [se'ɣuro, a] *adj* (*cierto*) sure, certain; (*fiel*) trustworthy; (*libre de peligro*) safe; (*bien defendido, firme*) secure ⊳ *adv* for sure, certainly ⊳ *nm* (*Com*) insurance; **seguro contra terceros/a todo riesgo** third party/comprehensive insurance;

seguros sociales social security *sg*

seis [seis] *num* six

seísmo [se'ismo] *nm* tremor, earthquake

selección [selek'θjon] *nf* selection; **seleccionar** *vt* to pick, choose, select

selectividad [selektiβi'ðað] (*ESP*) *nf* university entrance examination

selecto, -a [se'lekto, a] *adj* select, choice; (*escogido*) selected

sellar [se'ʎar] *vt* (*documento oficial*) to seal; (*pasaporte, visado*) to stamp

sello ['seʎo] *nm* stamp; (*precinto*) seal

selva ['selβa] *nf* (*bosque*) forest, woods *pl*; (*jungla*) jungle

semáforo [se'maforo] *nm* (*Auto*) traffic lights *pl*; (*Ferro*) signal

semana [se'mana] *nf* week; **entre ~** during the week; **Semana Santa** Holy Week; **semanal** *adj* weekly; **semanario** *nm* weekly magazine

- **SEMANA SANTA**
-
- In Spain celebrations for **Semana Santa** (Holy Week) are often spectacular. "Viernes Santo", "Sábado Santo" and "Domingo de Resurrección" (Good Friday, Holy Saturday, Easter Sunday) are all national public holidays, with additional days being given as local holidays. There are fabulous **procesiones** all over the country, with members of "cofradías" (brotherhoods) dressing in hooded robes and parading their "pasos" (religious floats and sculptures) through the streets. Seville has the most famous Holy Week processions.

sembrar [sem'brar] *vt* to sow; (*objetos*) to sprinkle, scatter about; (*noticias etc*) to spread

semejante [seme'xante] *adj* (*parecido*) similar ▷ *nm* fellow man, fellow creature; **~s** alike, similar; **nunca hizo cosa ~** he never did any such thing; **semejanza** *nf* similarity, resemblance

semejar [seme'xar] *vi* to seem like, resemble; **semejarse** *vr* to look alike, be similar

semen ['semen] *nm* semen

semestral [semes'tral] *adj* half-yearly, bi-annual

semicírculo [semi'θirkulo] *nm* semicircle

semidesnatado, -a [semiðesna'taðo, a] *adj* semi-skimmed

semifinal [semifi'nal] *nf* semifinal

semilla [se'miʎa] *nf* seed

seminario [semi'narjo] *nm* (*Rel*) seminary; (*Escol*) seminar

sémola ['semola] *nf* semolina

senado [se'naðo] *nm* senate; **senador, a** *nm/f* senator

sencillez [senθi'ʎeθ] *nf* simplicity; (*de persona*) naturalness; **sencillo, -a** *adj* simple; natural, unaffected

senda ['senda] *nf* path, track

senderismo [sende'rismo] *nm* hiking

sendero [sen'dero] *nm* path, track

sendos, -as ['sendos, as] *adj pl*: **les dio ~ golpes** he hit both of them

senil [se'nil] *adj* senile

seno ['seno] *nm* (*Anat*) bosom, bust; (*fig*) bosom; **~s** breasts

sensación [sensa'θjon] *nf* sensation; (*sentido*) sense; (*sentimiento*) feeling; **sensacional** *adj* sensational

sensato, -a [sen'sato, a] *adj* sensible

sensible [sen'sible] *adj* sensitive; (*apreciable*) perceptible, appreciable; (*pérdida*) considerable

⎪ No confundir **sensible** con la palabra inglesa *sensible*.

sensiblero, -a *adj* sentimental

sensitivo, -a [sensi'tiβo, a] *adj* sense *cpd*

sensorial [senso'rjal] *adj* sensory

sensual [sen'swal] *adj* sensual

sentada [sen'taða] *nf* sitting; (*protesta*) sit-in

sentado, -a [sen'taðo, a] *adj*: **estar ~** to sit, be sitting (down); **dar por ~** to take for granted, assume

sentar [sen'tar] *vt* to sit, seat; (*fig*) to establish ▷ *vi* (*vestido*) to suit; (*alimento*): **~ bien/mal a** to agree/disagree with; **sentarse** *vr* (*persona*) to sit, sit down; (*los depósitos*) to settle

sentencia [sen'tenθja] *nf* (*máxima*) maxim, saying; (*Jur*) sentence; **sentenciar** *vt* to sentence

sentido, -a [sen'tiðo, a] *adj* (*pérdida*) regrettable; (*carácter*) sensitive ▷ *nm* sense; (*sentimiento*) feeling; (*significado*) sense, meaning; (*dirección*) direction; **mi más ~ pésame** my deepest sympathy; **tener ~** to make sense; **sentido común** common sense; **sentido del humor** sense of humour; **sentido único** one-way (street)

sentimental [sentimen'tal] *adj* sentimental; **vida ~** love life

sentimiento [senti'mjento] *nm* feeling

sentir [sen'tir] *vt* to feel; (*percibir*) to perceive, sense; (*lamentar*) to regret, be sorry for ▷ *vi* (*tener la sensación*) to feel; (*lamentarse*) to feel sorry ▷ *nm* opinion, judgement; **~se bien/mal** to feel well/ill; **lo**

siento I'm sorry

seña ['seɲa] nf sign; (Mil) password; **señas** nfpl (dirección) address sg; **señas personales** personal description sg

señal [se'ɲal] nf sign; (síntoma) symptom; (Ferro, Tel) signal; (marca) mark; (Com) deposit; **en ~ de** as a token o sign of; **señalar** vt to mark; (indicar) to point out, indicate

señor [se'ɲor] nm (hombre) man; (caballero) gentleman; (dueño) owner, master; (trato: antes de nombre propio) Mr; (: hablando directamente) sir; **muy ~ mío** Dear Sir; **el ~ alcalde/presidente** the mayor/president

señora [se'ɲora] nf (dama) lady; (trato: antes de nombre propio) Mrs; (: hablando directamente) madam; (esposa) wife; **Nuestra S~** Our Lady

señorita [seɲo'rita] nf (con nombre y/o apellido) Miss; (mujer joven) young lady

señorito [seɲo'rito] nm young gentleman; (pey) rich kid

sepa etc vb V **saber**

separación [separa'θjon] nf separation; (división) division; (hueco) gap

separar [sepa'rar] vt to separate; (dividir) to divide; **separarse** vr (parte) to come away; (partes) to come apart; (persona) to leave, go away; (matrimonio) to separate; **separatismo** nm separatism

sepia ['sepja] nf cuttlefish

septentrional [septentrjo'nal] adj northern

septiembre [sep'tjembre] nm September

séptimo, -a ['septimo, a] adj, nm seventh

sepulcral [sepul'kral] adj (fig: silencio, atmósfera) deadly; **sepulcro** nm tomb, grave

sepultar [sepul'tar] vt to bury; **sepultura** nf (acto) burial; (tumba) grave, tomb

sequía [se'kia] nf drought

séquito ['sekito] nm (de rey etc) retinue; (seguidores) followers pl

○ **PALABRA CLAVE**

ser [ser] vi **1** (descripción) to be; **es médica/ muy alta** she's a doctor/very tall; **la familia es de Cuzco** his (o her etc) family is from Cuzco; **soy Ana** (Tel) Ana speaking o here

2 (propiedad): **es de Joaquín** it's Joaquín's, it belongs to Joaquín

3 (horas, fechas, números): **es la una** it's one o'clock; **son las seis y media** it's half-past six; **es el 1 de junio** it's the first of June; **somos/son seis** there are six of us/them

4 (en oraciones pasivas): **ha sido descubierto ya** it's already been discovered

5: **es de esperar que ...** it is to be hoped o I etc hope that ...

6 (locuciones con sub): **o sea** that is to say; **sea él sea su hermana** either him or his sister

7: **a no ser por él ...** but for him ...

8: **a no ser que: a no ser que tenga uno ya** unless he's got one already ▷ nm being; **ser humano** human being

sereno, -a [se'reno, a] adj (persona) calm, unruffled; (el tiempo) fine, settled; (ambiente) calm, peaceful ▷ nm night watchman

serial [ser'jal] nm serial

serie ['serje] nf series; (cadena) sequence, succession; **fuera de ~** out of order; (fig) special, out of the ordinary; **fabricación en ~** mass production

seriedad [serje'ðað] nf seriousness; (formalidad) reliability; **serio, -a** adj serious; reliable, dependable; grave, serious; **en serio** adv seriously

serigrafía [serixra'fia] nf silk-screen printing

sermón [ser'mon] nm (Rel) sermon

seropositivo, -a [seroposi'tiβo] adj HIV positive

serpentear [serpente'ar] vi to wriggle; (camino, río) to wind, snake

serpentina [serpen'tina] nf streamer

serpiente [ser'pjente] nf snake; **serpiente de cascabel** rattlesnake

serranía [serra'nia] nf mountainous area

serrar [se'rrar] vt = **aserrar**

serrín [se'rrin] nm sawdust

serrucho [se'rrutʃo] nm saw

service ['serβis] (RPL) nm (Auto) service

servicio [ser'βiθjo] nm service; (LAM Auto) service; **servicios** nmpl (ESP) toilet(s); **servicio incluido** service charge included; **servicio militar** military service

servidumbre [serβi'ðumbre] nf (sujeción) servitude; (criados) servants pl, staff

servil [ser'βil] adj servile

servilleta [serβi'ʎeta] nf serviette, napkin

servir [ser'βir] vt to serve ▷ vi to serve; (tener utilidad) to be of use, be useful; **servirse** vr to serve o help o.s.; **~se de algo** to make use of sth, use sth; **sírvase pasar** please come in

sesenta [se'senta] num sixty

sesión [se'sjon] nf (Pol) session, sitting; (Cine) showing

seso ['seso] nm brain; **sesudo, -a** adj sensible, wise

seta ['seta] nf mushroom; **seta venenosa** toadstool

setecientos, -as [sete'θjentos, as] adj, num seven hundred

setenta [se'tenta] num seventy

seto ['seto] nm hedge

severo, -a [se'βero, a] *adj* severe

Sevilla [se'βiλa] *n* Seville; **sevillano, -a** *adj* of o from Seville ▷ *nm/f* native o inhabitant of Seville

sexo ['sekso] *nm* sex

sexto, -a ['seksto, a] *adj, nm* sixth

sexual [sek'swal] *adj* sexual; **vida ~** sex life

si [si] *conj* if ▷ *nm* (*Mús*) B; **me pregunto ~ ...** I wonder if o whether ...

sí [si] *adv* yes ▷ *nm* consent ▷ *pron* (*uso impersonal*) oneself; (*sg: m*) himself; (*: f*) herself; (*: de cosa*) itself; (*de usted*) yourself; (*pl*) themselves; (*de ustedes*) yourselves; (*recíproco*) each other; **él no quiere pero yo ~** he doesn't want to but I do; **ella ~ vendrá** she will certainly come, she is sure to come; **claro que ~** of course; **creo que ~** I think so

siamés, -esa [sja'mes, esa] *adj, nm/f* Siamese

SIDA ['siða] *nm abr* (= *Síndrome de Inmunodeficiencia Adquirida*) AIDS

siderúrgico, -a [siðe'rurxiko, a] *adj* iron and steel *cpd*

sidra ['siðra] *nf* cider

siembra ['sjembra] *nf* sowing

siempre ['sjempre] *adv* always; (*todo el tiempo*) all the time; **~ que** (*cada vez*) whenever; (*dado que*) provided that; **como ~** as usual; **para ~** for ever

sien [sjen] *nf* temple

siento *etc* ['sjento] *vb* V **sentar; sentir**

sierra ['sjerra] *nf* (*Tec*) saw; (*cadena de montañas*) mountain range

siervo, -a ['sjerβo, a] *nm/f* slave

siesta ['sjesta] *nf* siesta, nap; **echar la ~** to have an afternoon nap o a siesta

siete ['sjete] *num* seven

sifón [si'fon] *nm* syphon

sigla ['siγla] *nf* abbreviation; acronym

siglo ['siγlo] *nm* century; (*fig*) age

significado [siγnifi'kaðo] *nm* (*de palabra etc*) meaning

significar [siγnifi'kar] *vt* to mean, signify; (*notificar*) to make known, express

signo ['siγno] *nm* sign; **signo de admiración o exclamación** exclamation mark; **signo de interrogación** question mark

sigo *etc vb* V **seguir**

siguiente [si'γjente] *adj* next, following

siguió *etc vb* V **seguir**

sílaba ['silaβa] *nf* syllable

silbar [sil'βar] *vt, vi* to whistle; **silbato** *nm* whistle; **silbido** *nm* whistle, whistling

silenciador [silenθja'ðor] *nm* silencer

silenciar [silen'θjar] *vt* (*persona*) to silence; (*escándalo*) to hush up; **silencio** *nm* silence, quiet; **silencioso, -a** *adj* silent, quiet

silla ['siλa] *nf* (*asiento*) chair; (*tb: ~ de montar*) saddle; **silla de ruedas** wheelchair

sillón [si'λon] *nm* armchair, easy chair

silueta [si'lweta] *nf* silhouette; (*de edificio*) outline; (*figura*) figure

silvestre [sil'βestre] *adj* wild

simbólico, -a [sim'boliko, a] *adj* symbolic(al)

simbolizar [simboli'θar] *vt* to symbolize

símbolo ['simbolo] *nm* symbol

similar [simi'lar] *adj* similar

simio ['simjo] *nm* ape

simpatía [simpa'tia] *nf* liking; (*afecto*) affection; (*amabilidad*) kindness; **simpático, -a** *adj* nice, pleasant; kind

▌ No confundir **simpático** con la palabra inglesa *sympathetic*.

simpatizante [simpati'θante] *nmf* sympathizer

simpatizar [simpati'θar] *vi*: **~ con** to get on well with

simple ['simple] *adj* simple; (*elemental*) simple, easy; (*mero*) mere; (*puro*) pure, sheer ▷ *nmf* simpleton; **simpleza** *nf* simpleness; (*necedad*) silly thing; **simplificar** *vt* to simplify

simposio [sim'posjo] *nm* symposium

simular [simu'lar] *vt* to simulate

simultáneo, -a [simul'taneo, a] *adj* simultaneous

sin [sin] *prep* without; **la ropa está ~ lavar** the clothes are unwashed; **~ que** without; **~ embargo** however, still

sinagoga [sina'γoγa] *nf* synagogue

sinceridad [sinθeri'ðað] *nf* sincerity; **sincero, -a** *adj* sincere

sincronizar [sinkroni'θar] *vt* to synchronize

sindical [sindi'kal] *adj* union *cpd*, trade-union *cpd*; **sindicalista** *adj, nmf* trade unionist

sindicato [sindi'kato] *nm* (*de trabajadores*) trade(s) union; (*de negociantes*) syndicate

síndrome ['sinðrome] *nm* (*Med*) syndrome; **síndrome de abstinencia** (*Med*) withdrawal symptoms; **síndrome de la clase turista** (*Med*) economy-class syndrome

sinfín [sin'fin] *nm*: **un ~ de** a great many, no end of

sinfonía [sinfo'nia] *nf* symphony

singular [singu'lar] *adj* singular; (*fig*) outstanding, exceptional; (*raro*) peculiar, odd

siniestro, -a [si'njestro, a] *adj* sinister ▷ *nm* (*accidente*) accident

sinnúmero [sin'numero] *nm* = **sinfín**

sino ['sino] nm fate, destiny ▷ conj (pero) but; (salvo) except, save

sinónimo, -a [si'nonimo, a] adj synonymous ▷ nm synonym

síntesis ['sintesis] nf synthesis; **sintético, -a** adj synthetic

sintió vb V **sentir**

síntoma ['sintoma] nm symptom

sintonía [sinto'nia] nf (Radio, Mús: de programa) tuning; **sintonizar** vt (Radio: emisora) to tune (in)

sinvergüenza [simber'xwenθa] nmf rogue, scoundrel; **¡es un ~!** he's got a nerve!

siquiera [si'kjera] conj even if, even though ▷ adv at least; **ni ~** not even

Siria ['sirja] nf Syria

sirviente, -a [sir'βjente, a] nm/f servant

sirvo etc vb V **servir**

sistema [sis'tema] nm system; (método) method; **sistema educativo** education system; **sistemático, -a** adj systematic

● **SISTEMA EDUCATIVO**
●
● The reform of the Spanish **sistema**
● **educativo** (education system) begun
● in the early 90s has replaced the
● courses **EGB**, **BUP** and **COU** with the
● following: "Primaria" a compulsory 6
● years; "Secundaria" a compulsory 4 years
● and "Bachillerato" an optional 2-year
● secondary school course, essential
● for those wishing to go on to higher
● education.

sitiar [si'tjar] vt to besiege, lay siege to

sitio ['sitjo] nm (lugar) place; (espacio) room, space; (Mil) siege; **sitio de taxis** (MÉX: parada) taxi stand o rank (BRIT); **sitio web** (Inform) website

situación [sitwa'θjon] nf situation, position; (estatus) position, standing

situado, -a [situ'aðo] adj situated, placed

situar [si'twar] vt to place, put; (edificio) to locate, situate

slip [slip] nm pants pl, briefs pl

smoking ['smokin, es'mokin] (pl ~s) nm dinner jacket (BRIT), tuxedo (US)

▌ No confundir **smoking** con la palabra inglesa smoking.

SMS nm (mensaje) text message, SMS message

snob [es'nob] = **esnob**

SO abr (= suroeste) SW

sobaco [so'βako] nm armpit

sobar [so'βar] vt (ropa) to rumple; (comida) to play around with

soberanía [soβera'nia] nf sovereignty;

soberano, -a adj sovereign; (fig) supreme ▷ nm/f sovereign

soberbia [so'βerβja] nf pride; haughtiness, arrogance; magnificence

soberbio, -a [so'βerβjo, a] adj (orgulloso) proud; (altivo) arrogant; (estupendo) magnificent, superb

sobornar [soβor'nar] vt to bribe; **soborno** nm bribe

sobra ['soβra] nf excess, surplus; **sobras** nfpl left-overs, scraps; **de ~** surplus, extra; **tengo de ~** I've more than enough; **¡es un ~!**

sobrado, -a adj (más que suficiente) more than enough; (superfluo) excessive; **sobrante** adj remaining, extra ▷ nm surplus, remainder

sobrar [so'βrar] vt to exceed, surpass ▷ vi (tener de más) to be more than enough; (quedar) to remain, be left (over)

sobrasada [soβra'saða] nf pork sausage spread

sobre ['soβre] prep (gen) on; (encima) on (top of); (por encima de, arriba de) over, above; (más que) more than; (además) in addition to, besides; (alrededor de) about ▷ nm envelope; **~ todo** above all

sobrecama [soβre'kama] nf bedspread

sobrecargar [soβrekar'xar] vt (camión) to overload; (Com) to surcharge

sobredosis [soβre'ðosis] nf inv overdose

sobreentender [soβre(e)nten'der] vt to deduce, infer; **sobreentenderse** vr: **se sobreentiende que ...** it is implied that ...

sobrehumano, -a [soβreu'mano, a] adj superhuman

sobrellevar [soβreʎe'βar] vt to bear, endure

sobremesa [soβre'mesa] nf: **durante la ~** after dinner

sobrenatural [soβrenatu'ral] adj supernatural

sobrenombre [soβre'nombre] nm nickname

sobrepasar [soβrepa'sar] vt to exceed, surpass

sobreponerse [soβrepo'nerse] vr: **~ a** to overcome

sobresaliente [soβresa'ljente] adj outstanding, excellent

sobresalir [soβresa'lir] vi to project, jut out; (fig) to stand out, excel

sobresaltar [soβresal'tar] vt (asustar) to scare, frighten; (sobrecoger) to startle; **sobresalto** nm (movimiento) start; (susto) scare; (turbación) sudden shock

sobretodo [soβre'toðo] nm overcoat

sobrevenir [soβreβe'nir] vi (ocurrir) to happen (unexpectedly); (resultar) to follow, ensue

sobrevivir [soβreβi'βir] *vi* to survive

sobrevolar [soβreβo'lar] *vt* to fly over

sobriedad [soβrje'ðað] *nf* sobriety, soberness; (*moderación*) moderation, restraint

sobrino, -a [so'βrino, a] *nm/f* nephew/ niece

sobrio, -a ['soβrjo, a] *adj* sober; (*moderado*) moderate, restrained

socarrón, -ona [soka'rron, ona] *adj* (*sarcástico*) sarcastic, ironic(al)

socavón [soka'βon] *nm* (*hoyo*) hole

sociable [so'θjaβle] *adj* (*persona*) sociable, friendly; (*animal*) social

social [so'θjal] *adj* social; (*Com*) company *cpd*

socialdemócrata [soθjalde'mokrata] *nmf* social democrat

socialista [soθja'lista] *adj, nm* socialist

socializar [soθjali'θar] *vt* to socialize

sociedad [soθje'ðað] *nf* society; (*Com*) company; **sociedad anónima** limited company; **sociedad de consumo** consumer society

socio, -a ['soθjo, a] *nm/f* (*miembro*) member; (*Com*) partner

sociología [soθjolo'xia] *nf* sociology; **sociólogo, -a** *nm/f* sociologist

socorrer [soko'rrer] *vt* to help; **socorrista** *nmf* first aider; (*en piscina, playa*) lifeguard; **socorro** *nm* (*ayuda*) help, aid; (*Mil*) relief; **¡socorro!** help!

soda ['soða] *nf* (*sosa*) soda; (*bebida*) soda (water)

sofá [so'fa] (*pl* **~s**) *nm* sofa, settee; **sofá-cama** *nm* studio couch; sofa bed

sofocar [sofo'kar] *vt* to suffocate; (*apagar*) to smother, put out; **sofocarse** *vr* to suffocate; (*fig*) to blush, feel embarrassed; **sofoco** *nm* suffocation; embarrassment

sofreír [sofre'ir] *vt* (*Culin*) to fry lightly

soga ['soxa] *nf* rope

sois *etc vb* V **ser**

soja ['soxa] *nf* soya

sol [sol] *nm* sun; (*luz*) sunshine, sunlight; (*Mús*) G; **hace ~** it's sunny

solamente [sola'mente] *adv* only, just

solapa [so'lapa] *nf* (*de chaqueta*) lapel; (*de libro*) jacket

solapado, -a [sola'paðo, a] *adj* (*intenciónes*) underhand; (*gestos, movimiento*) sly

solar [so'lar] *adj* solar, sun *cpd*

soldado [sol'daðo] *nm* soldier; **soldado raso** private

soldador [solda'ðor] *nm* soldering iron; (*persona*) welder

soldar [sol'dar] *vt* to solder, weld

soleado, -a [sole'aðo, a] *adj* sunny

soledad [sole'ðað] *nf* solitude; (*estado infeliz*) loneliness

solemne [so'lemne] *adj* solemn

soler [so'ler] *vi* to be in the habit of, be accustomed to; **suele salir a las ocho** she usually goes out at eight o'clock

solfeo [sol'feo] *nm* solfa

solicitar [soliθi'tar] *vt* (*permiso*) to ask for, seek; (*puesto*) to apply for; (*votos*) to canvass for; (*atención*) to attract

solícito, -a [so'liθito, a] *adj* (*diligente*) diligent; (*cuidadoso*) careful; **solicitud** *nf* (*calidad*) great care; (*petición*) request; (*a un puesto*) application

solidaridad [soliðari'ðað] *nf* solidarity; **solidario, -a** *adj* (*participación*) joint, common; (*compromiso*) mutually binding

sólido, -a [so'liðo, a] *adj* solid

soliloquio [soli'lokjo] *nm* soliloquy

solista [so'lista] *nmf* soloist

solitario, -a [soli'tarjo, a] *adj* (*persona*) lonely, solitary; (*lugar*) lonely, desolate ▷ *nm/f* (*recluso*) recluse; (*en la sociedad*) loner ▷ *nm* solitaire

sollozar [soλo'θar] *vi* to sob; **sollozo** *nm* sob

solo, -a ['solo, a] *adj* (*único*) single, sole; (*sin compañía*) alone; (*solitario*) lonely; **hay una sola dificultad** there is just one difficulty; **a solas** alone, by oneself

sólo ['solo] *adv* only, just

solomillo [solo'miλo] *nm* sirloin

soltar [sol'tar] *vt* (*dejar ir*) to let go of; (*desprender*) to unfasten, loosen; (*librar*) to release, set free; (*risa etc*) to let out

soltero, -a [sol'tero, a] *adj* single, unmarried ▷ *nm/f* bachelor/single woman; **solterón, -ona** *nm/f* old bachelor/spinster

soltura [sol'tura] *nf* looseness, slackness; (*de los miembros*) agility, ease of movement; (*en el hablar*) fluency, ease

soluble [so'luβle] *adj* (*Quím*) soluble; (*problema*) solvable; **~ en agua** soluble in water

solución [solu'θjon] *nf* solution; **solucionar** *vt* (*problema*) to solve; (*asunto*) to settle, resolve

solventar [solβen'tar] *vt* (*pagar*) to settle, pay; (*resolver*) to resolve; **solvente** *adj* (*Econ: empresa, persona*) solvent

sombra ['sombra] *nf* shadow; (*como protección*) shade; **sombras** *nfpl* (*oscuridad*) darkness *sg*, shadows; **tener buena/mala ~** to be lucky/unlucky

sombrero [som'brero] *nm* hat

sombrilla [som'briλa] *nf* parasol,

sunshade

sombrío, -a [som'brio, a] *adj* (*oscuro*) dark; (*triste*) sombre, sad; (*persona*) gloomy

someter [some'ter] *vt* (*país*) to conquer; (*persona*) to subject to one's will; (*informe*) to present, submit; **someterse** *vr* to give in, yield, submit; **~ a** to subject to

somier [so'mjer] (*pl* **~s**) *n* spring mattress

somnífero [som'nifero] *nm* sleeping pill

somos *vb* V **ser**

son [son] *vb* V **ser** ▷ *nm* sound

sonaja [so'naxa] (*MÉX*) *nf* = **sonajero**

sonajero [sona'xero] *nm* (baby's) rattle

sonambulismo [sonambu'lismo] *nm* sleepwalking; **sonámbulo, -a** *nm/f* sleepwalker

sonar [so'nar] *vt* to ring ▷ *vi* to sound; (*hacer ruido*) to make a noise; (*pronunciarse*) to be sounded, be pronounced; (*ser conocido*) to sound familiar; (*campana*) to ring; (*reloj*) to strike, chime; **sonarse** *vr*: **~se (las narices)** to blow one's nose; **me suena ese nombre** that name rings a bell

sonda ['sonda] *nf* (*Náut*) sounding; (*Tec*) bore, drill; (*Med*) probe

sondear [sonde'ar] *vt* to sound; to bore (into), drill; to probe, sound; (*fig*) to sound out; **sondeo** *nm* sounding, boring, drilling; (*fig*) poll, enquiry

sonido [so'niðo] *nm* sound

sonoro, -a [so'noro, a] *adj* sonorous; (*resonante*) loud, resonant

sonreír [sonre'ir] *vi* to smile; **sonreírse** *vr* to smile; **sonriente** *adj* smiling; **sonrisa** *nf* smile

sonrojarse [sonro'xarse] *vr* to blush, go red; **sonrojo** *nm* blush

soñador, a [soɲa'ðor, a] *nm/f* dreamer

soñar [so'ɲar] *vt, vi* to dream; **~ con** to dream about o of

soñoliento, -a [soɲo'ljento, a] *adj* sleepy, drowsy

sopa ['sopa] *nf* soup

soplar [so'plar] *vt* (*polvo*) to blow away, blow off; (*inflar*) to blow up; (*vela*) to blow out ▷ *vi* to blow; **soplo** *nm* blow, puff; (*de viento*) puff, gust

soplón, -ona [so'plon, ona] (*fam*) *nm/f* (*niño*) telltale; (*de policía*) grass (*fam*)

soporífero [sopo'rifero] *nm* sleeping pill

soportable [sopor'taβle] *adj* bearable

soportar [sopor'tar] *vt* to bear, carry; (*fig*) to bear, put up with

┃ No confundir **soportar** con la palabra inglesa *support*.

soporte *nm* support; (*fig*) pillar, support

soprano [so'prano] *nf* soprano

sorber [sor'βer] *vt* (*chupar*) to sip; (*absorber*)

to soak up, absorb

sorbete [sor'βete] *nm* iced fruit drink

sorbo ['sorβo] *nm* (*trago: grande*) gulp, swallow; (*: pequeño*) sip

sordera [sor'ðera] *nf* deafness

sórdido, -a ['sorðiðo, a] *adj* dirty, squalid

sordo, -a ['sorðo, a] *adj* (*persona*) deaf ▷ *nm/f* deaf person; **sordomudo, -a** *adj* deaf and dumb

sorna ['sorna] *nf* sarcastic tone

soroche [so'rotʃe] (*CAM*) *nm* mountain sickness

sorprendente [sorpren'dente] *adj* surprising

sorprender [sorpren'der] *vt* to surprise; **sorpresa** *nf* surprise

sortear [sorte'ar] *vt* to draw lots for; (*rifar*) to raffle; (*dificultad*) to avoid; **sorteo** *nm* (*en lotería*) draw; (*rifa*) raffle

sortija [sor'tixa] *nf* ring; (*rizo*) ringlet, curl

sosegado, -a [sose'ɣaðo, a] *adj* quiet, calm

sosiego [so'sjeɣo] *nm* quiet(ness), calm(ness)

soso, -a ['soso, a] *adj* (*Culin*) tasteless; (*aburrido*) dull, uninteresting

sospecha [sos'petʃa] *nf* suspicion; **sospechar** *vt* to suspect; **sospechoso, -a** *adj* suspicious; (*testimonio, opinión*) suspect ▷ *nm/f* suspect

sostén [sos'ten] *nm* (*apoyo*) support; (*sujetador*) bra; (*alimentación*) sustenance, food

sostener [soste'ner] *vt* to support; (*mantener*) to keep up, maintain; (*alimentar*) to sustain, keep going; **sostenerse** *vr* to support o.s.; (*seguir*) to continue, remain; **sostenido, -a** *adj* continuous, sustained; (*prolongado*) prolonged

sotana [so'tana] *nf* (*Rel*) cassock

sótano ['sotano] *nm* basement

soy [soi] *vb* V **ser**

soya ['soja] (*LAM*) *nf* soya (*BRIT*), soy (*US*)

Sr. *abr* (= *Señor*) Mr

Sra. *abr* (= *Señora*) Mrs

Sres. *abr* (= *Señores*) Messrs

Srta. *abr* (= *Señorita*) Miss

Sta. *abr* (= *Santa*) St

Sto. *abr* (= *Santo*) St

su [su] *pron* (*de él*) his; (*de ella*) her; (*de una cosa*) its; (*de ellos, ellas*) their; (*de usted, ustedes*) your

suave ['swaβe] *adj* gentle; (*superficie*) smooth; (*trabajo*) easy; (*música, voz*) soft, sweet; **suavidad** *nf* gentleness; smoothness; softness, sweetness; **suavizante** *nm* (*de ropa*) softener; (*del pelo*) conditioner; **suavizar** *vt* to soften; (*quitar*

s

la aspereza) to smooth (out)

subasta [su'βasta] *nf* auction; **subastar** *vt* to auction (off)

subcampeón, -ona [suβkampe'on, ona] *nm/f* runner-up

subconsciente [suβkon'sθjente] *adj, nm* subconscious

subdesarrollado, -a [suβðesarro'ʎaðo, a] *adj* underdeveloped

subdesarrollo [suβðesa'rroʎo] *nm* underdevelopment

subdirector, a [suβðirek'tor, a] *nm/f* assistant director

súbdito, -a ['suβðito, a] *nm/f* subject

subestimar [suβesti'mar] *vt* to underestimate, underrate

subida [su'βiða] *nf* (*de montaña etc*) ascent, climb; (*de precio*) rise, increase; (*pendiente*) slope, hill

subir [su'βir] *vt* (*objeto*) to raise, lift up; (*cuesta, calle*) to go up; (*colina, montaña*) to climb; (*precio*) to raise, put up ▷ *vi* to go up, come up; (*a un coche*) to get in; (*a un autobús, tren o avión*) to get on, board; (*precio*) to rise, go up; (*río, marea*) to rise; **subirse** *vr* to get up, climb

súbito, -a ['suβito, a] *adj* (*repentino*) sudden; (*imprevisto*) unexpected

subjetivo, -a [suβxe'tiβo, a] *adj* subjective

sublevar [suβle'βar] *vt* to rouse to revolt; **sublevarse** *vr* to revolt, rise

sublime [su'βlime] *adj* sublime

submarinismo [suβmari'nismo] *nm* scuba diving

submarino, -a [suβma'rino, a] *adj* underwater ▷ *nm* submarine

subnormal [suβnor'mal] *adj* subnormal ▷ *nmf* subnormal person

subordinado, -a [suβorði'naðo, a] *adj, nm/f* subordinate

subrayar [suβra'jar] *vt* to underline

subsanar [suβsa'nar] *vt* to rectify

subsidio [suβ'siðjo] *nm* (*ayuda*) aid, financial help; (*subvención*) subsidy, grant; (*de enfermedad, paro etc*) benefit, allowance

subsistencia [suβsis'tenθja] *nf* subsistence

subsistir [suβsis'tir] *vi* to subsist; (*sobrevivir*) to survive, endure

subte ['suβte] (RPL) *nm* underground (BRIT), subway (US)

subterráneo, -a [suβte'rraneo, a] *adj* underground, subterranean ▷ *nm* underpass, underground passage

subtítulo [suβ'titulo] *nm* (*Cine*) subtitle

suburbio [su'βurβjo] *nm* (*barrio*) slum quarter

subvención [suββen'θjon] *nf* (*Econ*) subsidy, grant; **subvencionar** *vt* to subsidize

sucedáneo, -a [suθe'ðaneo, a] *adj* substitute ▷ *nm* substitute (food)

suceder [suθe'ðer] *vt, vi* to happen; (*seguir*) to succeed, follow; **lo que sucede es que ...** the fact is that ...; **sucesión** *nf* succession; (*serie*) sequence, series

sucesivamente [suθesiβa'mente] *adv*: **y así ~** and so on

sucesivo, -a [suθe'siβo, a] *adj* successive, following; **en lo ~** in future, from now on

suceso [su'θeso] *nm* (*hecho*) event, happening; (*incidente*) incident

▎ No confundir **suceso** con la palabra inglesa *success*.

suciedad [suθje'ðað] *nf* (*estado*) dirtiness; (*mugre*) dirt, filth

sucio, -a ['suθjo, a] *adj* dirty

suculento, -a [suku'lento, a] *adj* succulent

sucumbir [sukum'bir] *vi* to succumb

sucursal [sukur'sal] *nf* branch (office)

sudadera [suða'ðera] *nf* sweatshirt

Sudáfrica [suð'afrika] *nf* South Africa

Sudamérica [suða'merika] *nf* South America; **sudamericano, -a** *adj, nm/f* South American

sudar [su'ðar] *vt, vi* to sweat

sudeste [su'ðeste] *nm* south-east

sudoeste [suðo'este] *nm* south-west

sudor [su'ðor] *nm* sweat; **sudoroso, -a** *adj* sweaty, sweating

Suecia ['sweθja] *nf* Sweden; **sueco, -a** *adj* Swedish ▷ *nm/f* Swede

suegro, -a ['swexro, a] *nm/f* father-/mother-in-law

suela ['swela] *nf* sole

sueldo ['sweldo] *nm* pay, wage(s) (pl)

suele *etc vb* V **soler**

suelo ['swelo] *nm* (*tierra*) ground; (*de casa*) floor

suelto, -a ['swelto, a] *adj* loose; (*libre*) free; (*separado*) detached; (*ágil*) quick, agile ▷ *nm* (loose) change, small change

sueñito [swe'ɲito] (LAM) *nm* nap

sueño *etc* [swe'ɲo] *vb* V **soñar** ▷ *nm* sleep; (*somnolencia*) sleepiness, drowsiness; (*lo soñado, fig*) dream; **tener ~** to be sleepy

suero ['swero] *nm* (*Med*) serum; (*de leche*) whey

suerte ['swerte] *nf* (*fortuna*) luck; (*azar*) chance; (*destino*) fate, destiny; (*especie*) sort, kind; **tener ~** to be lucky

suéter ['sweter] *nm* sweater

suficiente [sufi'θjente] *adj* enough, sufficient ▷ *nm* (*Escol*) pass

sufragio [su'fraxjo] nm (voto) vote; (derecho de voto) suffrage

sufrido, -a [su'friðo, a] adj (persona) tough; (paciente) long-suffering, patient

sufrimiento [sufri'mjento] nm (dolor) suffering

sufrir [su'frir] vt (padecer) to suffer; (soportar) to bear, put up with; (apoyar) to hold up, support ▷ vi to suffer

sugerencia [suxe'renθja] nf suggestion

sugerir [suxe'rir] vt to suggest; (sutilmente) to hint

sugestión [suxes'tjon] nf suggestion; (sutil) hint; **sugestionar** vt to influence

sugestivo, -a [suxes'tiβo, a] adj stimulating; (fascinante) fascinating

suicida [sui'θiða] adj suicidal ▷ nmf suicidal person; (muerto) suicide, person who has committed suicide; **suicidarse** vr to commit suicide, kill o.s.; **suicidio** nm suicide

Suiza ['swiθa] nf Switzerland; **suizo, -a** adj, nm/f Swiss

sujeción [suxe'θjon] nf subjection

sujetador [suxeta'ðor] nm (sostén) bra

sujetar [suxe'tar] vt (fijar) to fasten; (detener) to hold down; **sujetarse** vr to subject o.s.; **sujeto, -a** adj fastened, secure ▷ nm subject; (individuo) individual; **sujeto a** subject to

suma ['suma] nf (cantidad) total, sum; (de dinero) sum; (acto) adding (up), addition; **en ~** in short

sumamente [suma'mente] adv extremely, exceedingly

sumar [su'mar] vt to add (up) ▷ vi to add up

sumergir [sumer'xir] vt to submerge; (hundir) to sink

suministrar [sumini'strar] vt to supply, provide; **suministro** nm supply; (acto) supplying, providing

sumir [su'mir] vt to sink, submerge; (fig) to plunge

sumiso, -a [su'miso, a] adj submissive, docile

sumo, -a ['sumo, a] adj great, extreme; (autoridad) highest, supreme

suntuoso, -a [sun'twoso, a] adj sumptuous, magnificent

supe etc vb V **saber**

super... [super] prefijo super..., over...

superbueno, -a [super'bweno, a] adj great, fantastic

súper ['super] nf (gasolina) four-star (petrol)

superar [supe'rar] vt (sobreponerse a) to overcome; (rebasar) to surpass, do better

than; (pasar) to go beyond; **superarse** vr to excel o.s.

superficial [superfi'θjal] adj superficial; (medida) surface cpd, of the surface

superficie [super'fiθje] nf surface; (área) area

superfluo, -a [su'perflwo, a] adj superfluous

superior [supe'rjor] adj (piso, clase) upper; (temperatura, número, nivel) higher; (mejor: calidad, producto) superior, better ▷ nmf superior; **superioridad** nf superiority

supermercado [supermer'kaðo] nm supermarket

superponer [superpo'ner] vt to superimpose

superstición [supersti'θjon] nf superstition; **supersticioso, -a** adj superstitious

supervisar [superβi'sar] vt to supervise

supervivencia [superβi'βenθja] nf survival

superviviente [superβi'βjente] adj surviving

supiera etc vb V **saber**

suplantar [suplan'tar] vt to supplant

suplemento [suple'mento] nm supplement

suplente [su'plente] adj, nm substitute

supletorio, -a [suple'torjo, a] adj supplementary ▷ nm supplement; **teléfono ~** extension

súplica ['suplika] nf request; (Jur) petition

suplicar [supli'kar] vt (cosa) to beg (for), plead for; (persona) to beg, plead with

suplicio [su'pliθjo] nm torture

suplir [su'plir] vt (compensar) to make good, make up for; (reemplazar) to replace, substitute ▷ vi: **~ a** to take the place of, substitute for

supo etc vb V **saber**

suponer [supo'ner] vt to suppose; **suposición** nf supposition

suprimir [supri'mir] vt to suppress; (derecho, costumbre) to abolish; (palabra etc) to delete; (restricción) to cancel, lift

supuesto, -a [su'pwesto, a] pp de **suponer** ▷ adj (hipotético) supposed ▷ nm assumption, hypothesis; **~ que** since; **por ~** of course

sur [sur] nm south

surcar [sur'kar] vt to plough; **surco** nm (en metal, disco) groove; (Agr) furrow

surgir [sur'xir] vi to arise, emerge; (dificultad) to come up, crop up

suroeste [suro'este] nm south-west

surtido, -a [sur'tiðo, a] adj mixed,

assorted ▷ nm (*selección*) selection, assortment; (*abastecimiento*) supply, stock; **surtidor** nm (*tb:* **surtidor de gasolina**) petrol pump (BRIT), gas pump (US)

surtir [sur'tir] vt to supply, provide ▷ vi to spout, spurt

susceptible [susθep'tiβle] adj susceptible; (*sensible*) sensitive; **~ de** capable of

suscitar [susθi'tar] vt to cause, provoke; (*interés, sospechas*) to arouse

suscribir [suskri'βir] vt (*firmar*) to sign; (*respaldar*) to subscribe to, endorse; **suscribirse** vr to subscribe; **suscripción** nf subscription

susodicho, -a [suso'ðitʃo, a] adj above-mentioned

suspender [suspen'der] vt (*objeto*) to hang (up), suspend; (*trabajo*) to stop, suspend; (*Escol*) to fail; (*interrumpir*) to adjourn; (*atrasar*) to postpone

suspense [sus'pense] (ESP) nm suspense; **película/novela de ~** thriller

suspensión [suspen'sjon] nf suspension; (*fig*) stoppage, suspension

suspenso, -a [sus'penso, a] adj hanging, suspended; (ESP Escol) failed ▷ nm (ESP Escol) fail; **película** o **novela de ~** (LAM) thriller; **quedar** o **estar en ~** to be pending

suspicaz [suspi'kaθ] adj suspicious, distrustful

suspirar [suspi'rar] vi to sigh; **suspiro** nm sigh

sustancia [sus'tanθja] nf substance

sustento [sus'tento] nm support; (*alimento*) sustenance, food

sustituir [sustitu'ir] vt to substitute, replace; **sustituto, -a** nm/f substitute, replacement

susto ['susto] nm fright, scare

sustraer [sustra'er] vt to remove, take away; (*Mat*) to subtract

susurrar [susu'rrar] vi to whisper; **susurro** nm whisper

sutil [su'til] adj (*aroma, diferencia*) subtle; (*tenue*) thin; (*inteligencia, persona*) sharp

suyo, -a ['sujo, a] (*con artículo o después del verbo* **ser**) adj (*de él*) his; (*de ella*) hers; (*de ellos, ellas*) theirs; (*de Ud, Uds*) yours; **un amigo ~** a friend of his (o hers o theirs o yours)

t

Tabacalera [taβaka'lera] nf Spanish state tobacco monopoly

tabaco [ta'βako] nm tobacco; (ESP: fam) cigarettes pl

tabaquería [tabake'ria] (LAM) nf tobacconist's (shop) (BRIT), smoke shop (US); **tabaquero, -a** (LAM) nm/f tobacconist

taberna [ta'βerna] nf bar, pub (BRIT)

tabique [ta'βike] nm partition (wall)

tabla ['taβla] nf (*de madera*) plank; (*estante*) shelf; (*de vestido*) pleat; (*Arte*) panel; **tablas** nfpl: **estar** o **quedar en ~s** to draw; **tablado** nm (*plataforma*) platform; (*Teatro*) stage

tablao [ta'βlao] nm (tb: **~ flamenco**) flamenco show

tablero [ta'βlero] nm (*de madera*) plank, board; (*de ajedrez, damas*) board; **tablero de mandos** (LAM Auto) dashboard

tableta [ta'βleta] nf (*Med*) tablet; (*de chocolate*) bar

tablón [ta'βlon] nm (*de suelo*) plank; (*de techo*) beam; **tablón de anuncios** notice (BRIT) o bulletin (US) board

tabú [ta'βu] nm taboo

taburete [taβu'rete] nm stool

tacaño, -a [ta'kaɲo, a] adj mean

tacha ['tatʃa] nf flaw; (Tec) stud; **tachar** vt (*borrar*) to cross out; **tachar de** to accuse of

tacho ['tatʃo] (CS) nm (*balde*) bucket; **tacho de la basura** rubbish bin (BRIT), trash can (US)

taco ['tako] nm (Billar) cue; (*de billetes*) book; (CS: *de zapato*) heel; (*tarugo*) peg; (*palabrota*) swear word

tacón [ta'kon] nm heel; **de ~ alto** high-heeled

táctica ['taktika] nf tactics pl

táctico, -a ['taktiko, a] adj tactical

tacto ['takto] nm touch; (*fig*) tact

tajada [ta'xaða] nf slice

tajante [ta'xante] adj sharp

tajo ['taxo] nm (corte) cut; (Geo) cleft

tal [tal] adj such ⊳ pron (persona) someone, such a one; (cosa) something, such a thing ⊳ adv: **~ como** (igual) just as ⊳ conj: **con ~ de que** provided that; **~ cual** (como es) just as it is; **~ vez** perhaps; **~ como** such as; **~ para cual** (dos iguales) two of a kind; **¿qué ~?** how are things?; **¿qué ~ te gusta?** how do you like it?

taladrar [tala'ðrar] vt to drill; **taladro** nm drill

talante [ta'lante] nm (humor) mood; (voluntad) will, willingness

talar [ta'lar] vt (madera) to fell, cut down; (devastar) to devastate

talco ['talko] nm (polvos) talcum powder

talento [ta'lento] nm talent; (capacidad) ability

TALGO ['talxo] (ESP) nm abr (= tren articulado ligero Goicoechea-Oriol) ≈ HST (BRIT)

talismán [talis'man] nm talisman

talla ['taʎa] nf (estatura, fig, Med) height, stature; (palo) measuring rod; (Arte) carving; (medida) size

tallar [ta'ʎar] vt (madera) to carve; (metal etc) to engrave; (medir) to measure

tallarines [taʎa'rines] nmpl noodles

talle ['taʎe] nm (Anat) waist; (fig) appearance

taller [ta'ʎer] nm (Tec) workshop; (de artista) studio

tallo ['taʎo] nm (de planta) stem; (de hierba) blade; (brote) shoot

talón [ta'lon] nm (Anat) heel; (Com) counterfoil; (cheque) cheque (BRIT), check (US)

talonario [talo'narjo] nm (de cheques) chequebook (BRIT), checkbook (US); (de recibos) receipt book

tamaño, -a [ta'maɲo, a] adj (tan grande) such a big; (tan pequeño) such a small ⊳ nm size; **de ~ natural** full-size

tamarindo [tama'rindo] nm tamarind

tambalearse [tambale'arse] vr (persona) to stagger; (vehículo) to sway

también [tam'bjen] adv (igualmente) also, too, as well; (además) besides

tambor [tam'bor] nm drum; (Anat) eardrum; **tambor del freno** brake drum

tamizar [tami'θar] vt to sieve

tampoco [tam'poko] adv nor, neither; **yo ~ lo compré** I didn't buy it either

tampón [tam'pon] nm tampon

tan [tan] adv so; **~ es así que ...** so much so that

tanda ['tanda] nf (gen) series; (turno) shift

tangente [tan'xente] nf tangent

tangerina [tanxe'rina] (LAM) nf tangerine

tangible [tan'xiβle] adj tangible

tanque ['tanke] nm (cisterna, Mil) tank; (Auto) tanker

tantear [tante'ar] vt (calcular) to reckon (up); (medir) to take the measure of; (probar) to test, try out; (tomar la medida: persona) to take the measurements of; (situación) to weigh up; (persona: opinión) to sound out ⊳ vi (Deporte) to score; **tanteo** nm (cálculo) (rough) calculation; (prueba) test, trial; (Deporte) scoring

tanto, -a ['tanto, a] adj (cantidad) so much, as much ⊳ adv (cantidad) so much, as much; (tiempo) so long, as long ⊳ conj: **en ~ que** while ⊳ nm (suma) certain amount; (proporción) so much; (punto) point; (gol) goal; **un ~ perezoso** somewhat lazy ⊳ pron: **cada uno paga ~** each one pays so much; **~s** so many, as many; **20 y ~s** 20-odd; **hasta ~ (que)** until such time as; **~ tú como yo** both you and I; **~ como eso** as much as that; **~ más ... cuanto que** all the more ... because; **~ mejor/peor** so much the better/the worse; **~ si viene como si va** whether he comes or whether he goes; **~ es así que** so much so that; **por (lo) ~** therefore; **entre ~** meanwhile; **estar al ~** to be up to date; **me he vuelto ronco de o con ~ hablar** I have become hoarse with so much talking; **a ~s de agosto** on such and such a day in August

tapa ['tapa] nf (de caja, olla) lid; (de botella) top; (de libro) cover; (comida) snack

tapadera [tapa'ðera] nf lid, cover

tapar [ta'par] vt (cubrir) to cover; (envolver) to wrap o cover up; (la vista) to obstruct; (persona, falta) to conceal; (MÉX, CAM: diente) to fill; **taparse** vr to wrap o.s. up

taparrabo [tapa'rraβo] nm loincloth

tapete [ta'pete] nm table cover

tapia ['tapja] nf (garden) wall

tapicería [tapiθe'ria] nf tapestry; (para muebles) upholstery; (tienda) upholsterer's (shop)

tapiz [ta'piθ] nm (alfombra) carpet; (tela tejida) tapestry; **tapizar** vt (muebles) to upholster

tapón [ta'pon] nm (de botella) top; (de lavabo) plug; **tapón de rosca** screw-top

taquigrafía [takixra'fia] nf shorthand; **taquígrafo, -a** nm/f shorthand writer, stenographer

taquilla [ta'kiʎa] nf (donde se compra) booking office; (suma recogida) takings pl

tarántula [ta'rantula] nf tarantula

tararear [tarare'ar] vi to hum

tardar [tar'ðar] vi (tomar tiempo) to take a

long time; (*llegar tarde*) to be late; (*demorar*) to delay; **¿tarda mucho el tren?** does the train take (very) long?; **a más** at the latest; **no tardes en venir** come soon

tarde ['tarðe] *adv* late ▷ *nf* (*de día*) afternoon; (*al anochecer*) evening; **de ~ en ~** from time to time; **¡buenas ~s!** good afternoon!; **a** *o* **por la ~** in the afternoon; in the evening

tardío, -a [tar'ðio, a] *adj* (*retrasado*) late; (*lento*) slow (to arrive)

tarea [ta'rea] *nf* task; (*faena*) chore; (*Escol*) homework

tarifa [ta'rifa] *nf* (*lista de precios*) price list; (*precio*) tariff

tarima [ta'rima] *nf* (*plataforma*) platform

tarjeta [tar'xeta] *nf* card; **tarjeta de crédito/de Navidad/postal/telefónica** credit card/Christmas card/postcard/ phonecard; **tarjeta de embarque** boarding pass; **tarjeta de memoria** memory card; **tarjeta prepago** top-up card; **tarjeta SIM** SIM card

tarro ['tarro] *nm* jar, pot

tarta ['tarta] *nf* (*pastel*) cake; (*de base dura*) tart

tartamudear [tartamuðe'ar] *vi* to stammer; **tartamudo, -a** *adj* stammering ▷ *nm/f* stammerer

tártaro, -a ['tartaro, a] *adj*: **salsa tártara** tartar(e) sauce

tasa ['tasa] *nf* (*precio*) (fixed) price, rate; (*valoración*) valuation; (*medida, norma*) measure, standard; **tasa de cambio/ interés** exchange/interest rate; **tasas de aeropuerto** airport tax; **tasas universitarias** university fees

tasar [ta'sar] *vt* (*arreglar el precio*) to fix a price for; (*valorar*) to value, assess

tasca ['taska] *(fam)* *nf* pub

tatarabuelo, -a [tatara'βwelo, a] *nm/f* great-great-grandfather/mother

tatuaje [ta'twaxe] *nm* (*dibujo*) tattoo; (*acto*) tattooing

tatuar [ta'twar] *vt* to tattoo

taurino, -a [tau'rino, a] *adj* bullfighting *cpd*

Tauro ['tauro] *nm* Taurus

tauromaquia [tauro'makja] *nf* tauromachy, (art of) bullfighting

taxi ['taksi] *nm* taxi; **taxista** [tak'sista] *nmf* taxi driver

taza ['taθa] *nf* cup; (*de retrete*) bowl; **~ para café** coffee cup; **taza de café** cup of coffee; **tazón** *nm* (*taza grande*) mug, large cup; (*de fuente*) basin

te [te] *pron* (*complemento de objeto*) you; (*complemento indirecto*) (to) you; (*reflexivo*)

(to) yourself; **¿~ duele mucho el brazo?** does your arm hurt a lot?; **~ equivocas** you're wrong; **¡cálma~!** calm down!

té [te] *nm* tea

teatral [tea'tral] *adj* theatre *cpd*; (*fig*) theatrical

teatro [te'atro] *nm* theatre; (*Literatura*) plays *pl*, drama

tebeo [te'βeo] *nm* comic

techo ['tetʃo] *nm* (*externo*) roof; (*interno*) ceiling; **techo corredizo** sunroof

tecla ['tekla] *nf* key; **teclado** *nm* keyboard; **teclear** *vi* (*Mús*) to strum; (*con los dedos*) to tap ▷ *vt* (*Inform*) to key in

técnica ['teknika] *nf* technique; (*tecnología*) technology; *V tb* **técnico**

técnico, -a ['tekniko, a] *adj* technical ▷ *nm/f* technician; (*experto*) expert

tecnología [teknolo'xia] *nf* technology; **tecnológico, -a** *adj* technological

tecolote [teko'lote] *(MÉX)* *nm* owl

tedioso, -a [te'ðjoso, a] *adj* boring, tedious

teja ['texa] *nf* tile; (*Bot*) lime (tree); **tejado** *nm* (tiled) roof

tejemaneje [texema'nexe] *nm* (*lío*) fuss; (*intriga*) intrigue

tejer [te'xer] *vt* to weave; (*hacer punto*) to knit; (*fig*) to fabricate; **tejido** *nm* (*tela*) material, fabric; (*telaraña*) web; (*Anat*) tissue

tel [tel] *abr* (*=teléfono*) tel

tela ['tela] *nf* (*tejido*) material; (*telaraña*) web; (*en líquido*) skin; **telar** *nm* (*máquina*) loom

telaraña [tela'raɲa] *nf* cobweb

tele ['tele] *(fam)* *nf* telly (BRIT), tube (US)

tele... ['tele] *prefijo* tele...; **telebasura** *nf* trash TV; **telecomunicación** *nf* telecommunication; **telediario** *nm* television news; **teledirigido, -a** *adj* remote-controlled

teleférico [tele'feriko] *nm* (*de esquí*) ski-lift

telefonear [telefone'ar] *vi* to telephone

telefónico, -a [tele'foniko, a] *adj* telephone *cpd*

telefonillo [telefo'niʎo] *nm* (*de puerta*) intercom

telefonista [telefo'nista] *nmf* telephonist

teléfono [te'lefono] *nm* (tele)phone; **estar hablando al ~** to be on the phone; **llamar a algn por ~** to ring sb (up) *o* phone sb (up); **teléfono celular** (LAM) mobile phone; **teléfono con cámara** camera phone; **teléfono inalámbrico** cordless phone; **teléfono móvil** (ESP) mobile phone

telégrafo [te'leɣrafo] *nm* telegraph

telegrama [tele'ɣrama] *nm* telegram

tele: telenovela nf soap (opera);
teleobjetivo nm telephoto lens; **telepatía**
nf telepathy; **telepático, -a** adj telepathic;
telerrealidad nf reality TV; **telescopio**
nm telescope; **telesilla** nm chairlift;
telespectador, a nm/f viewer; **telesquí**
nm ski-lift; **teletarjeta** nf phonecard;
teletipo nm teletype; **teletrabajador,
a** nm/f teleworker; **teletrabajo** nm
teleworking; **televentas** nfpl telesales
televidente [teleβi'ðente] nmf viewer
televisar [teleβi'sar] vt to televise
televisión [teleβi'sjon] nf television;
televisión digital digital television
televisor [teleβi'sor] nm television set
télex ['teleks] nm inv telex
telón [te'lon] nm curtain; **telón de acero**
(Pol) iron curtain; **telón de fondo** backcloth,
background
tema ['tema] nm (asunto) subject, topic;
(Mús) theme; **temático, -a** adj thematic
temblar [tem'blar] vi to shake, tremble;
(por frío) to shiver; **temblor** nm trembling;
(de tierra) earthquake; **tembloroso, -a** adj
trembling
temer [te'mer] vt to fear ▷ vi to be afraid;
temo que llegue tarde I am afraid he may
be late
temible [te'miβle] adj fearsome
temor [te'mor] nm (miedo) fear; (duda)
suspicion
témpano ['tempano] nm (tb: ~ de hielo)
ice-floe
temperamento [tempera'mento] nm
temperament
temperatura [tempera'tura] nf
temperature
tempestad [tempes'tað] nf storm
templado, -a [tem'plaðo, a] adj
(moderado) moderate; (frugal) frugal; (agua)
lukewarm; (clima) mild; (Mús) well-tuned;
templanza nf moderation; mildness
templar [tem'plar] vt (moderar) to
moderate; (furia) to restrain; (calor) to
reduce; (afinar) to tune (up); (acero) to
temper; (tuerca) to tighten up; **temple**
nm (ajuste) tempering; (afinación) tuning;
(pintura) tempera
templo ['templo] nm (iglesia) church;
(pagano etc) temple
temporada [tempo'raða] nf time, period;
(estación) season
temporal [tempo'ral] adj (no permanente)
temporary ▷ nm storm
temprano, -a [tem'prano, a] adj early;
(demasiado pronto) too soon, too early
ten vb V **tener**
tenaces [te'naθes] adj pl V **tenaz**

tenaz [te'naθ] adj (material) tough;
(persona) tenacious; (creencia, resistencia)
stubborn
tenaza(s) [te'naθa(s)] nf(pl) (Med) forceps;
(Tec) pliers; (Zool) pincers
tendedero [tende'ðero] nm (para ropa)
drying place; (cuerda) clothes line
tendencia [ten'denθja] nf tendency;
tener ~ a to tend to, have a tendency to
tender [ten'der] vt (extender) to spread out;
(colgar) to hang out; (vía férrea, cable) to lay;
(estirar) to stretch ▷ vi: **~ a** to tend to, to have
a tendency towards; **tenderse** vr to lie
down; **~ la cama/mesa** (LAM) to make the
bed/lay (BRIT) o set (US) the table
tenderete [tende'rete] nm (puesto) stall;
(exposición) display of goods
tendero, -a [ten'dero, a] nm/f
shopkeeper
tendón [ten'don] nm tendon
tendré etc vb V **tener**
tenebroso, -a [tene'βroso, a] adj (oscuro)
dark; (fig) gloomy
tenedor [tene'ðor] nm (Culin) fork
tenencia [te'nenθja] nf (de casa) tenancy;
(de oficio) tenure; (de propiedad) possession

○ **PALABRA CLAVE**

tener [te'ner] vt **1** (poseer, gen) to have; (en
la mano) to hold; **¿tienes un boli?** have you
got a pen?; **va a tener un niño** she's going
to have a baby; **¡ten (o tenga)!, ¡aquí tienes
(o tiene)!** here you are!
2 (edad, medidas) to be; **tiene 7 años** she's 7
(years old); **tiene 15 cm de largo** it's 15 cm
long; V **calor; hambre** etc
3 (considerar): **lo tengo por brillante** I
consider him to be brilliant; **tener en
mucho a algn** to think very highly of sb
4 (+ pp: = pretérito): **tengo terminada ya la
mitad del trabajo** I've done half the work
already
5: **tener que hacer algo** to have to do sth;
tengo que acabar este trabajo hoy I have
to finish this job today
6: **¿qué tienes, estás enfermo?** what's the
matter with you, are you ill?
tenerse vr **1**: **tenerse en pie** to stand up
2: **tenerse por** to think o.s.

tengo etc vb V **tener**
tenia ['tenja] nf tapeworm
teniente [te'njente] nm (rango)
lieutenant; (ayudante) deputy
tenis ['tenis] nm tennis; **tenis de mesa**
table tennis; **tenista** nmf tennis player
tenor [te'nor] nm (sentido) meaning; (Mús)

t

tenor; **a ~ de** on the lines of

tensar [ten'sar] *vt* to tighten; (*arco*) to draw

tensión [ten'sjon] *nf* tension; (*Tec*) stress; **tener la ~ alta** to have high blood pressure; **tensión arterial** blood pressure

tenso, -a ['tenso, a] *adj* tense

tentación [tenta'θjon] *nf* temptation

tentáculo [ten'takulo] *nm* tentacle

tentador, a [tenta'ðor, a] *adj* tempting

tentar [ten'tar] *vt* (*seducir*) to tempt; (*atraer*) to attract

tentempié [tentem'pje] *nm* snack

tenue ['tenwe] *adj* (*delgado*) thin, slender; (*neblina*) light; (*lazo, vínculo*) slight

teñir [te'ɲir] *vt* to dye; (*fig*) to tinge; **teñirse** *vr* to dye; **~se el pelo** to dye one's hair

teología [teolo'xia] *nf* theology

teoría [teo'ria] *nf* theory; **en ~** in theory; **teórico, -a** *adj* theoretic(al) ▷ *nm/f* theoretician, theorist; **teorizar** *vi* to theorize

terapéutico, -a [tera'peutiko, a] *adj* therapeutic

terapia [te'rapja] *nf* therapy

tercer *adj* V **tercero**

tercermundista [terθermun'dista] *adj* Third World *cpd*

tercero, -a [ter'θero, a] (*delante de nmsg: tercer*) *adj* third ▷ *nm* (*Jur*) third party

terceto [ter'θeto] *nm* trio

terciar [ter'θjar] *vi* (*participar*) to take part; (*hacer de árbitro*) to mediate; **terciario, -a** *adj* tertiary

tercio ['terθjo] *nm* third

terciopelo [terθjo'pelo] *nm* velvet

terco, -a ['terko, a] *adj* obstinate

tergal® [ter'ɣal] *nm type of polyester*

tergiversar [terxiβer'sar] *vt* to distort

termal [ter'mal] *adj* thermal

termas ['termas] *nfpl* hot springs

térmico, -a ['termiko, a] *adj* thermal

terminal [termi'nal] *adj, nm, nf* terminal

terminante [termi'nante] *adj* (*final*) final, definitive; (*tajante*) categorical; **terminantemente** *adv*: **terminantemente prohibido** strictly forbidden

terminar [termi'nar] *vt* (*completar*) to complete, finish; (*concluir*) to end ▷ *vi* (*llegar a su fin*) to end; (*parar*) to stop; (*acabar*) to finish; **terminarse** *vr* to come to an end; **~ por hacer algo** to end up (by) doing sth

término ['termino] *nm* end, conclusion; (*parada*) terminus; (*límite*) boundary; **en último ~** (*a fin de cuentas*) in the last analysis; (*como último recurso*) as a last resort; **término medio** average; (*fig*) middle way

termómetro [ter'mometro] *nm* thermometer

termo(s)® ['termo(s)] *nm* Thermos®

termostato [termo'stato] *nm* thermostat

ternero, -a [ter'nero, a] *nm/f* (*animal*) calf ▷ *nf* (*carne*) veal

ternura [ter'nura] *nf* (*trato*) tenderness; (*palabra*) endearment; (*cariño*) fondness

terrado [te'rraðo] *nm* terrace

terraplén [terra'plen] *nm* embankment

terrateniente [terrate'njente] *nmf* landowner

terraza [te'rraθa] *nf* (*balcón*) balcony; (*tejado*) (flat) roof; (*Agr*) terrace

terremoto [terre'moto] *nm* earthquake

terrenal [terre'nal] *adj* earthly

terreno [te'rreno] *nm* (*tierra*) land; (*parcela*) plot; (*suelo*) soil; (*fig*) field; **un ~** a piece of land

terrestre [te'rrestre] *adj* terrestrial; (*ruta*) land *cpd*

terrible [te'rriβle] *adj* terrible, awful

territorio [terri'torjo] *nm* territory

terrón [te'rron] *nm* (*de azúcar*) lump; (*de tierra*) clod, lump

terror [te'rror] *nm* terror; **terrorífico, -a** *adj* terrifying; **terrorista** *adj, nmf* terrorist; **terrorista suicida** suicide bomber

terso, -a ['terso, a] *adj* (*liso*) smooth; (*pulido*) polished

tertulia [ter'tulja] *nf* (*reunión informal*) social gathering; (*grupo*) group, circle

tesis ['tesis] *nf inv* thesis

tesón [te'son] *nm* (*firmeza*) firmness; (*tenacidad*) tenacity

tesorero, -a [teso'rero, a] *nm/f* treasurer

tesoro [te'soro] *nm* treasure; (*Com, Pol*) treasury

testamento [testa'mento] *nm* will

testarudo, -a [testa'ruðo, a] *adj* stubborn

testículo [tes'tikulo] *nm* testicle

testificar [testifi'kar] *vt* to testify; (*fig*) to attest ▷ *vi* to give evidence

testigo [tes'tixo] *nmf* witness; **testigo de cargo/descargo** witness for the prosecution/defence; **testigo ocular** eye witness

testimonio [testi'monjo] *nm* testimony

teta ['teta] *nf* (*de biberón*) teat; (*Anat: fam*) breast

tétanos ['tetanos] *nm* tetanus

tetera [te'tera] *nf* teapot

tétrico, -a ['tetriko, a] *adj* gloomy, dismal

textil [teks'til] *adj* textile

texto ['teksto] *nm* text; **textual** *adj* textual

textura [teks'tura] nf (de tejido) texture

tez [teθ] nf (cutis) complexion

ti [ti] pron you; (reflexivo) yourself

tía ['tia] nf (pariente) aunt; (fam) chick, bird

tibio, -a ['tiβjo, a] adj lukewarm

tiburón [tiβu'ron] nm shark

tic [tik] nm (ruido) click; (de reloj) tick; (Med): **~ nervioso** nervous tic

tictac [tik'tak] nm (de reloj) tick tock

tiempo ['tjempo] nm time; (época, período) age, period; (Meteorología) weather; (Ling) tense; (Deporte) half; **a ~** in time; **a un** o **al mismo ~** at the same time; **al poco ~** very soon (after); **se quedó poco ~** he didn't stay very long; **hace poco ~** not long ago; **mucho ~** a long time; **de ~ en ~** from time to time; **hace buen/mal ~** the weather is fine/bad; **estar a ~** to be in time; **hace ~** some time ago; **hacer ~** to while away the time; **motor de 2 ~s** two-stroke engine; **primer ~** first half

tienda ['tjenda] nf shop, store; **tienda de abarrotes** (MÉX, CAM) grocer's (BRIT), grocery store (US); **tienda de alimentación** o **comestibles** grocer's (BRIT), grocery store (US); **tienda de campaña** tent

tienes etc vb V **tener**

tienta etc ['tjenta] vb V **tentar** ⊳ nf: **andar a ~s** to grope one's way along

tiento etc ['tjento] vb V **tentar** ⊳ nm (tacto) touch; (precaución) wariness

tierno, -a ['tjerno, a] adj (blando) tender; (fresco) fresh; (amable) sweet

tierra ['tjerra] nf earth; (suelo) soil; (mundo) earth, world; (país) country, land; **~ adentro** inland

tieso, -a ['tjeso, a] adj (rígido) rigid; (duro) stiff; (fam: orgulloso) conceited

tiesto ['tjesto] nm flowerpot

tifón [ti'fon] nm typhoon

tifus ['tifus] nm typhus

tigre ['tixre] nm tiger

tijera [ti'xera] nf scissors pl; (Zool) claw; **tijeras** nfpl scissors; (para plantas) shears

tila ['tila] nf lime blossom tea

tildar [til'dar] vt: **~ de** to brand as

tilde ['tilde] nf (Tip) tilde

tilín [ti'lin] nm tinkle

timar [ti'mar] vt (estafar) to swindle

timbal [tim'bal] nm small drum

timbre ['timbre] nm (sello) stamp; (campanilla) bell; (tono) timbre; (Com) stamp duty

timidez [timi'ðeθ] nf shyness; **tímido, -a** adj shy

timo ['timo] nm swindle

timón [ti'mon] nm helm, rudder; **timonel** nm helmsman

tímpano ['timpano] nm (Anat) eardrum; (Mús) small drum

tina ['tina] nf tub; (baño) bath(tub); **tinaja** nf large jar

tinieblas [ti'njeβlas] nfpl darkness sg; (sombras) shadows

tino ['tino] nm (habilidad) skill; (juicio) insight

tinta ['tinta] nf ink; (Tec) dye; (Arte) colour

tinte ['tinte] nm dye

tintero [tin'tero] nm inkwell

tinto ['tinto] nm red wine

tintorería [tintore'ria] nf dry cleaner's

tío ['tio] nm (pariente) uncle; (fam: individuo) bloke (BRIT), guy

tiovivo [tio'βiβo] nm merry-go-round

típico, -a ['tipiko, a] adj typical

tipo ['tipo] nm (clase) type, kind; (hombre) fellow; (Anat: de hombre) build; (: de mujer) figure; (Imprenta) type; **tipo bancario/de descuento/de interés/de cambio** bank/discount/interest/exchange rate

tipografía [tipoɣra'fia] nf printing cpd

tíquet ['tiket] (pl **~s**) nm ticket; (en tienda) cash slip

tiquismiquis [tikis'mikis] nm inv fussy person ⊳ nmpl (querellas) squabbling sg; (escrúpulos) silly scruples

tira ['tira] nf strip; (fig) abundance; **tira y afloja** give and take

tirabuzón [tiraβu'θon] nm (rizo) curl

tirachinas [tira'tʃinas] nm inv catapult

tirada [ti'raða] nf (acto) cast, throw; (serie) series; (Tip) printing, edition; **de una ~** at one go

tirado, -a [ti'raðo, a] adj (barato) dirt-cheap; (fam: fácil) very easy

tirador [tira'ðor] nm (mango) handle

tirano, -a [ti'rano, a] adj tyrannical ⊳ nm/f tyrant

tirante [ti'rante] adj (cuerda etc) tight, taut; (relaciónes) strained ⊳ nm (Arq) brace; (Tec) stay; **tirantes** nmpl (de pantalón) braces (BRIT), suspenders (US); **tirantez** nf tightness; (fig) tension

tirar [ti'rar] vt to throw; (dejar caer) to drop; (volcar) to upset; (derribar) to knock down o over; (desechar) to throw out o away; (dinero) to squander; (imprimir) to print ⊳ vi (disparar) to shoot; (de la puerta etc) to pull; (fam: andar) to go; (tender a, buscar realizar) to tend to; (Deporte) to shoot; **tirarse** vr to throw o.s.; **~ abajo** to bring down, destroy; **tira más a su padre** he takes more after his father; **ir tirando** to manage

tirita [ti'rita] nf (sticking) plaster (BRIT), Bandaid® (US)

tiritar [tiri'tar] vi to shiver

tiro ['tiro] nm (lanzamiento) throw; (disparo) shot; (Deporte) shot; (Golf, Tenis) drive; (alcance) range; **caballo de ~** cart-horse; **tiro al blanco** target practice

tirón [ti'ron] nm (sacudida) pull, tug; **de un ~** in one go, all at once

tiroteo [tiro'teo] nm exchange of shots, shooting

tisis ['tisis] nf inv consumption, tuberculosis

títere ['titere] nm puppet

titubear [tituβe'ar] vi to stagger; to stammer; (fig) to hesitate; **titubeo** nm staggering; stammering; hesitation

titulado, -a [titu'laðo, a] adj (libro) entitled; (persona) titled

titular [titu'lar] adj titular ▷ nmf holder ▷ nm headline ▷ vt to title; **titularse** vr to be entitled; **título** nm title; (de diario) headline; (certificado) professional qualification; (universitario) (university) degree; **a título de** in the capacity of

tiza ['tiθa] nf chalk

toalla [to'aʎa] nf towel

tobillo [to'βiʎo] nm ankle

tobogán [toβo'ɣan] nm (montaña rusa) roller-coaster; (de niños) chute, slide

tocadiscos [toka'ðiskos] nm inv record player

tocado, -a [to'kaðo, a] adj (fam) touched ▷ nm headdress

tocador [toka'ðor] nm (mueble) dressing table; (cuarto) boudoir; (fam) ladies' toilet (BRIT) o room (US)

tocar [to'kar] vt to touch; (Mús) to play; (referirse a) to allude to; (timbre) to ring ▷ vi (a la puerta) to knock (on o at the door); (ser de turno) to fall to, be the turn of; (ser hora) to be due; **tocarse** vr (cubrirse la cabeza) to cover one's head; (tener contacto) to touch (each other); **por lo que a mí me toca** as far as I am concerned; **te toca a ti** it's your turn

tocayo, -a [to'kajo, a] nm/f namesake

tocino [to'θino] nm bacon

todavía [toða'βia] adv (aun) even; (aún) still, yet; **~ más** yet more; **~ no** not yet

○ **PALABRA CLAVE**

todo, -a ['toðo, a] adj **1** (con artículo sg) all; **toda la carne** all the meat; **toda la noche** all night, the whole night; **todo el libro** the whole book; **toda una botella** a whole bottle; **todo lo contrario** quite the opposite; **está toda sucia** she's all dirty; **por todo el país** throughout the whole country

2 (con artículo pl) all; every; **todos los libros** all the books; **todas las noches** every night; **todos los que quieran salir** all those who want to leave

▷ pron **1** everything, all; **todos** everyone, everybody; **lo sabemos todo** we know everything; **todos querían más tiempo** everybody o everyone wanted more time; **nos marchamos todos** all of us left

2: **con todo: con todo él me sigue gustando** even so I still like him

▷ adv all; **vaya todo seguido** keep straight on o ahead

▷ nm: **como un todo** as a whole; **del todo: no me agrada del todo** I don't entirely like it

todopoderoso, -a [toðopoðe'roso, a] adj all powerful; (Rel) almighty

todoterreno [toðote'rreno] sm inv four-wheel drive, SUV (ESP US)

toga ['toɣa] nf toga; (Escol) gown

Tokio ['tokjo] n Tokyo

toldo ['toldo] nm (para el sol) sunshade (BRIT), parasol; (tienda) marquee

tolerancia [tole'ranθja] nf tolerance; **tolerante** adj (sociedad) liberal; (persona) open-minded

tolerar [tole'rar] vt to tolerate; (resistir) to endure

toma ['toma] nf (acto) taking; (Med) dose; **toma de corriente** socket; **toma de tierra** earth (wire); **tomacorriente** (LAM) nm socket

tomar [to'mar] vt to take; (aspecto) to take on; (beber) to drink ▷ vi to take; (LAM: beber) to drink; **tomarse** vr to take; **~se por** to consider o.s. to be; **~ a bien/mal** to take well/badly; **~ en serio** to take seriously; **~ el pelo a algn** to pull sb's leg; **-la con algn** to pick a quarrel with sb; **¡tome!** here you are!; **~ el sol** to sunbathe

tomate [to'mate] nm tomato

tomillo [to'miʎo] nm thyme

tomo ['tomo] nm (libro) volume

ton [ton] abr = **tonelada** ▷ nm: **sin ~ ni son** without rhyme or reason

tonalidad [tonali'ðað] nf tone

tonel [to'nel] nm barrel

tonelada [tone'laða] nf ton; **tonelaje** nm tonnage

tónica ['tonika] nf (Mús) tonic; (fig) keynote

tónico, -a ['toniko, a] adj tonic ▷ nm (Med) tonic

tono ['tono] nm tone; **fuera de ~** inappropriate

tontería [tonte'ria] nf (estupidez) foolishness; (cosa) stupid thing; (acto) foolish act; **tonterías** nfpl (disparates) rubbish sg, nonsense sg

tonto, -a ['tonto, a] adj stupid, silly ▷ nm/f fool

topar [to'par] vi: ~ **contra** o **en** to run into; ~ **con** to run up against

tope ['tope] adj maximum ▷ nm (fin) end; (límite) limit; (Ferro) buffer; (Auto) bumper; **al ~** end to end

tópico, -a ['topiko, a] adj topical ▷ nm platitude

topo ['topo] nm (Zool) mole; (fig) blunderer

toque etc ['toke] vb V **tocar** ▷ nm touch; (Mús) beat; (de campana) peal; **dar un ~ a** to warn; **toque de queda** curfew

toqué etc vb V **tocar**

toquetear [tokete'ar] vt to finger

toquilla [to'kiʎa] nf (pañuelo) headscarf; (chal) shawl

tórax ['toraks] nm thorax

torbellino [torbe'ʎino] nm whirlwind; (fig) whirl

torcedura [torθe'ðura] nf twist; (Med) sprain

torcer [tor'θer] vt to twist; (la esquina) to turn; (Med) to sprain ▷ vi (desviar) to turn off; **torcerse** vr (ladearse) to bend; (desviarse) to go astray; (fracasar) to go wrong; **torcido, -a** adj twisted; (fig) crooked ▷ nm curl

tordo, -a ['torðo, a] adj dappled ▷ nm thrush

torear [tore'ar] vt (fig: evadir) to avoid; (jugar con) to tease ▷ vi to fight bulls; **toreo** nm bullfighting; **torero, -a** nm/f bullfighter

tormenta [tor'menta] nf storm; (fig: confusión) turmoil

tormento [tor'mento] nm torture; (fig) anguish

tornar [tor'nar] vt (devolver) to return, give back; (transformar) to transform ▷ vi to go back

tornasolado, -a [tornaso'laðo, a] adj (brillante) iridescent; (reluciente) shimmering

torneo [tor'neo] nm tournament

tornillo [tor'niʎo] nm screw

torniquete [torni'kete] nm (Med) tourniquet

torno ['torno] nm (Tec) winch; (tambor) drum; **en ~ (a)** round, about

toro ['toro] nm bull; (fam) he-man; **los ~s** bullfighting

toronja [to'ronxa] nf grapefruit

torpe ['torpe] adj (poco hábil) clumsy, awkward; (necio) dim; (lento) slow

torpedo [tor'peðo] nm torpedo

torpeza [tor'peθa] nf (falta de agilidad) clumsiness; (lentitud) slowness; (error) mistake

torre ['torre] nf tower; (de petróleo) derrick

torrefacto, -a [torre'fakto, a] adj roasted

torrente [to'rrente] nm torrent

torrija [to'rrixa] nf French toast

torsión [tor'sjon] nf twisting

torso ['torso] nm torso

torta ['torta] nf cake; (fam) slap

tortícolis [tor'tikolis] nm inv stiff neck

tortilla [tor'tiʎa] nf omelette; (LAM: de maíz) maize pancake; **tortilla de papas** (LAM) potato omelette; **tortilla de patatas** (ESP) potato omelette; **tortilla francesa** (ESP) plain omelette

tórtola ['tortola] nf turtledove

tortuga [tor'tuxa] nf tortoise

tortuoso, -a [tor'twoso, a] adj winding

tortura [tor'tura] nf torture; **torturar** vt to torture

tos [tos] nf cough; **tos ferina** whooping cough

toser [to'ser] vi to cough

tostada [tos'taða] nf piece of toast; **tostado, -a** adj toasted; (por el sol) dark brown; (piel) tanned

tostador [tosta'ðor] (ESP) nm toaster; **tostadora** (LAM) nf = tostador

tostar [tos'tar] vt to toast; (café) to roast; (persona) to tan; **tostarse** vr to get brown

total [to'tal] adj total ▷ adv in short; (al fin y al cabo) when all is said and done ▷ nm total; **en ~** in all; ~ **que ...** to cut (BRIT) o make (US) a long story short ...

totalidad [totali'ðað] nf whole

totalitario, -a [totali'tarjo, a] adj totalitarian

tóxico, -a ['toksiko, a] adj toxic ▷ nm poison; **toxicómano, -a** nm/f drug addict

toxina [to'ksina] nf toxin

tozudo, -a [to'θuðo, a] adj obstinate

trabajador, a [traβaxa'ðor, a] adj hard-working o nm/f worker; **trabajador autónomo** o **por cuenta propia** self-employed person

trabajar [traβa'xar] vt to work; (Agr) to till; (empeñarse en) to work at; (convencer) to persuade ▷ vi to work; (esforzarse) to strive; **trabajo** nm work; (tarea) task; (Pol) labour; (fig) effort; **tomarse el trabajo de** to take the trouble to; **trabajo a destajo** piecework; **trabajo en equipo** teamwork; **trabajo por turnos** shift work; **trabajos forzados** hard labour sg

trabalenguas [traβa'lengwas] nm inv tongue twister

tracción [trak'θjon] nf traction; **tracción delantera/trasera** front-wheel/rear-wheel drive

tractor [trak'tor] nm tractor

tradición [traði'θjon] nf tradition; **tradicional** adj traditional

traducción [traðuk'θjon] nf translation

traducir [traðu'θir] vt to translate; **traductor, a** nm/f translator

traer [tra'er] vt to bring; (llevar) to carry; (llevar puesto) to wear; (incluir) to carry; (causar) to cause; **traerse** vr: **~se algo** to be up to sth

traficar [trafi'kar] vi to trade

tráfico ['trafiko] nm (Com) trade; (Auto) traffic

tragaluz [traɣa'luθ] nm skylight

tragamonedas [traɣamo'neðas] (LAM) nf inv slot machine

tragaperras [traɣa'perras] (ESP) nf inv slot machine

tragar [tra'ɣar] vt to swallow; (devorar) to devour, bolt down; **tragarse** vr. to swallow

tragedia [tra'xeðja] nf tragedy; **trágico, -a** adj tragic

trago ['traɣo] nm (líquido) drink; (bocado) gulp; (fam: de bebida) swig; (desgracia) blow; **echar un ~** to have a drink

traición [trai'θjon] nf treachery; (Jur) treason; (una traición) act of treachery; **traicionar** vt to betray

traidor, a [trai'ðor, a] adj treacherous ▷ nm/f traitor

traigo etc vb V **traer**

traje ['traxe] vb V **traer** ▷ nm (de hombre) suit; (de mujer) dress; (vestido típico) costume; **traje de baño/chaqueta** swimsuit/suit; **traje de etiqueta** dress suit; **traje de luces** bullfighter's costume

trajera etc vb V **traer**

trajín [tra'xin] nm (fam: movimiento) bustle; **trajinar** vi (moverse) to bustle about

trama ['trama] nf (intriga) plot; (de tejido) weft (BRIT), woof (US); **tramar** vt to plot; (Tec) to weave

tramitar [trami'tar] vt (asunto) to transact; (negociar) to negotiate

trámite ['tramite] nm (paso) step; (Jur) transaction; **trámites** nmpl (burocracia) procedure sg; (Jur) proceedings

tramo ['tramo] nm (de tierra) plot; (de escalera) flight; (de vía) section

trampa ['trampa] nf trap; (en el suelo) trapdoor; (truco) trick; (engaño) fiddle; **trampear** vt, vi to cheat

trampolín [trampo'lin] nm (de piscina etc) diving board

tramposo, -a [tram'poso, a] adj crooked, cheating ▷ nm/f crook, cheat

tranca ['tranka] nf (palo) stick; (de puerta, ventana) bar; **trancar** vt to bar

trance ['tranθe] nm (momento difícil) difficult moment o juncture; (estado hipnotizado) trance

tranquilidad [trankili'ðað] nf (calma) calmness, stillness; (paz) peacefulness

tranquilizar [trankili'θar] vt (calmar) to calm (down); (asegurar) to reassure; **tranquilizarse** vr. to calm down; **tranquilo, -a** adj (calmado) calm; (apacible) peaceful; (mar) calm; (mente) untroubled

transacción [transak'θjon] nf transaction

transbordador [transβorða'ðor] nm ferry

transbordo [trans'βorðo] nm transfer; **hacer ~** to change (trains etc)

transcurrir [transku'rrir] vi (tiempo) to pass; (hecho) to take place

transcurso [trans'kurso] nm: **~ del tiempo** lapse (of time)

transeúnte [transe'unte] nmf passer-by

transferencia [transfe'renθja] nf transference; (Com) transfer

transferir [transfe'rir] vt to transfer

transformador [transforma'ðor] nm (Elec) transformer

transformar [transfor'mar] vt to transform; (convertir) to convert

transfusión [transfu'sjon] nf transfusion

transgénico, -a [trans'xeniko, a] adj genetically modified, GM

transición [transi'θjon] nf transition

transigir [transi'xir] vi to compromise, make concessions

transitar [transi'tar] vi to go (from place to place); **tránsito** nm transit; (Auto) traffic; **transitorio, -a** adj transitory

transmisión [transmi'sjon] nf (Tec) transmission; (transferencia) transfer; **transmisión exterior/en directo** outside/live broadcast

transmitir [transmi'tir] vt to transmit; (Radio, TV) to broadcast

transparencia [transpa'renθja] nf transparency; (claridad) clearness, clarity; (foto) slide

transparentar [transparen'tar] vt to reveal ▷ vi to be transparent; **transparente** adj transparent; (claro) clear

transpirar [transpi'rar] vi to perspire

transportar [transpor'tar] vt to transport; (llevar) to carry; **transporte** nm transport; (Com) haulage

transversal [transβer'sal] adj transverse, cross

tranvía [tram'bia] nm tram

trapeador [trapea'ðor] (LAM) nm mop; **trapear** (LAM) vt to mop

trapecio [tra'peθjo] nm trapeze;
 trapecista nmf trapeze artist
trapero, -a [tra'pero, a] nm/f ragman
trapicheo [trapi'tʃeo] (fam) nm scheme,
 fiddle
trapo ['trapo] nm (tela) rag; (de cocina) cloth
tráquea ['trakea] nf windpipe
traqueteo [trake'teo] nm rattling
tras [tras] prep (detrás) behind; (después)
 after
trasatlántico [trasat'lantiko] nm (barco)
 (cabin) cruiser
trascendencia [trasθen'denθja] nf
 (importancia) importance; (Filosofía)
 transcendence
trascendental [trasθenden'tal] adj
 important; (Filosofía) transcendental
trasero, -a [tra'sero, a] adj back, rear
 ▷ nm (Anat) bottom
trasfondo [tras'fondo] nm background
trasgredir [trasɣre'ðir] vt to contravene
trashumante [trasu'mante] adj
 (animales) migrating
trasladar [trasla'ðar] vt to move;
 (persona) to transfer; (postergar) to postpone;
 (copiar) to copy; **trasladarse** vr (mudarse) to
 move; **traslado** nm move; (mudanza) move,
 removal
traslucir [traslu'θir] vt to show
trasluz [tras'luθ] nm reflected light; **al ~**
 against o up to the light
trasnochador, a [trasnotʃa'ðor, a] nm/f
 night owl
trasnochar [trasno'tʃar] vi (acostarse
 tarde) to stay up late
traspapelar [traspape'lar] vt (documento,
 carta) to mislay, misplace
traspasar [traspa'sar] vt (suj: bala etc)
 to pierce, go through; (propiedad) to sell,
 transfer; (calle) to cross over; (límites) to go
 beyond; (ley) to break; **traspaso** nm (venta)
 transfer, sale
traspatio [tras'patjo] (LAM) nm backyard
traspié [tras'pje] nm (tropezón) trip; (error)
 blunder
trasplantar [trasplan'tar] vt to
 transplant
traste ['traste] nm (Mús) fret; **dar al ~ con
 algo** to ruin sth
trastero [tras'tero] nm storage room
trastienda [tras'tjenda] nf back of shop
trasto ['trasto] (pey) nm (cosa) piece of
 junk; (persona) dead loss
trastornado, -a [trastor'naðo, a] adj
 (loco) mad, crazy
trastornar [trastor'nar] vt (fig: planes) to
 disrupt; (: nervios) to shatter; (: persona) to
 drive crazy; **trastornarse** vr (volverse loco)

to go mad o crazy; **trastorno** nm (acto)
 overturning; (confusión) confusion
tratable [tra'taβle] adj friendly
tratado [tra'taðo] nm (Pol) treaty; (Com)
 agreement
tratamiento [trata'mjento] nm
 treatment; **tratamiento de textos** (Inform)
 word processing cpd
tratar [tra'tar] vt (ocuparse de) to treat;
 (manejar, Tec) to handle; (Med) to treat;
 (dirigirse a: persona) to address ▷ vi: **~
 de** (hablar sobre) to deal with, be about;
 (intentar) to try to; **tratarse** vr to treat each
 other; **~ con** (Com) to trade in; (negociar) to
 negotiate with; (tener contactos) to have
 dealings with; **¿de qué se trata?** what's it
 about?; **trato** nm dealings pl; (relaciónes)
 relationship; (comportamiento) manner;
 (Com) agreement
trauma ['trauma] nm trauma
través [tra'βes] nm (fig) reverse; **al ~**
 across, crossways; **a ~ de** across; (sobre)
 over; (por) through
travesaño [traβe'saɲo] nm (Arq)
 crossbeam; (Deporte) crossbar
travesía [traβe'sia] nf (calle) cross-street;
 (Náut) crossing
travesura [traβe'sura] nf (broma) prank;
 (ingenio) wit
travieso, -a [tra'βjeso, a] adj (niño)
 naughty
trayecto [tra'jekto] nm (ruta) road, way;
 (viaje) journey; (tramo) stretch; **trayectoria**
 nf trajectory; (fig) path
traza ['traθa] nf (aspecto) looks pl; (señal)
 sign; **trazado, -a** adj: **bien trazado** shapely,
 well-formed ▷ nm (Arq) plan, design; (fig)
 outline
trazar [tra'θar] vt (Arq) to plan; (Arte) to
 sketch; (fig) to trace; (plan) to draw up; **trazo**
 nm (línea) line; (bosquejo) sketch
trébol ['treβol] nm (Bot) clover
trece ['treθe] num thirteen
trecho ['tretʃo] nm (distancia) distance;
 (tiempo) while
tregua ['treɣwa] nf (Mil) truce; (fig) respite
treinta ['treinta] num thirty
tremendo, -a [tre'mendo, a] adj (terrible)
 terrible; (imponente: cosa) imposing;
 (fam: fabuloso) tremendous
tren [tren] nm train; **tren de aterrizaje**
 undercarriage; **tren de cercanías** suburban
 train
trenca ['trenka] nf duffel coat
trenza ['trenθa] nf (de pelo) plait (BRIT),
 braid (US)
trepadora [trepa'ðora] nf (Bot) climber
trepar [tre'par] vt, vi to climb

t

tres [tres] *num* three

tresillo [tre'siʎo] *nm* three-piece suite; (*Mús*) triplet

treta ['treta] *nf* trick

triángulo ['trjangulo] *nm* triangle

tribu ['triβu] *nf* tribe

tribuna [tri'βuna] *nf* (*plataforma*) platform; (*Deporte*) (grand)stand

tribunal [triβu'nal] *nm* (*Jur*) court; (*comisión, fig*) tribunal; **~ popular** jury

tributo [tri'βuto] *nm* (*Com*) tax

trigal [tri'ɣal] *nm* wheatfield

trigo ['triɣo] *nm* wheat

trigueño, -a [tri'ɣeɲo, a] *adj* (*pelo*) corn-coloured

trillar [tri'ʎar] *vt* (*Agr*) to thresh

trimestral [trimes'tral] *adj* quarterly; (*Escol*) termly

trimestre [tri'mestre] *nm* (*Escol*) term

trinar [tri'nar] *vi* (*pájaros*) to sing; (*rabiar*) to fume, be angry

trinchar [trin'tʃar] *vt* to carve

trinchera [trin'tʃera] *nf* (*fosa*) trench

trineo [tri'neo] *nm* sledge

trinidad [trini'ðað] *nf* trio; (*Rel*): **la T~** the Trinity

tripa ['tripa] *nf* (*Anat*) intestine; (*fam: tb*: **~s**) insides *pl*

triple ['triple] *adj* triple

triplicado, -a [tripli'kaðo, a] *adj*: **por ~** in triplicate

tripulación [tripula'θjon] *nf* crew

tripulante [tripu'lante] *nmf* crewman/woman

tripular [tripu'lar] *vt* (*barco*) to man; (*Auto*) to drive

triquiñuela [triki'ɲwela] *nf* trick

tris [tris] *nm inv* crack

triste ['triste] *adj* sad; (*lamentable*) sorry, miserable; **tristeza** *nf* (*aflicción*) sadness; (*melancolía*) melancholy

triturar [tritu'rar] *vt* (*moler*) to grind; (*mascar*) to chew

triunfar [trjun'far] *vi* (*tener éxito*) to triumph; (*ganar*) to win; **triunfo** *nm* triumph

trivial [tri'βjal] *adj* trivial

triza ['triθa] *nf*: **hacer ~s** to smash to bits; (*papel*) to tear to shreds

trocear [troθe'ar] *vt* (*carne, manzana*) to cut up, cut into pieces

trocha ['trotʃa] *nf* short cut

trofeo [tro'feo] *nm* (*premio*) trophy; (*éxito*) success

tromba ['tromba] *nf* downpour

trombón [trom'bon] *nm* trombone

trombosis [trom'bosis] *nf inv* thrombosis

trompa ['trompa] *nf* horn; (*trompo*) humming top; (*hocico*) snout; (*fam*): **cogerse una ~** to get tight

trompazo [trom'paθo] *nm* bump, bang

trompeta [trom'peta] *nf* trumpet; (*clarín*) bugle

trompicón [trompi'kon]: **a trompicones** *adv* in fits and starts

trompo ['trompo] *nm* spinning top

trompón [trom'pon] *nm* bump

tronar [tro'nar] *vt* (*MÉX, CAM: fusilar*) to shoot; (*MÉX: examen*) to flunk ▷ *vi* to thunder; (*fig*) to rage

tronchar [tron'tʃar] *vt* (*árbol*) to chop down; (*fig: vida*) to cut short; (: *esperanza*) to shatter; (*persona*) to tire out; **troncharse** *vr* to fall down

tronco ['tronko] *nm* (*de árbol, Anat*) trunk

trono ['trono] *nm* throne

tropa ['tropa] *nf* (*Mil*) troop; (*soldados*) soldiers *pl*

tropezar [trope'θar] *vi* to trip, stumble; (*errar*) to slip up; **~ con** to run into; (*topar con*) to bump into; **tropezón** *nm* trip; (*fig*) blunder

tropical [tropi'kal] *adj* tropical

trópico ['tropiko] *nm* tropic

tropiezo [tro'pjeθo] *vb* V **tropezar** ▷ *nm* (*error*) slip, blunder; (*desgracia*) misfortune; (*obstáculo*) snag

trotamundos [trota'mundos] *nm inv* globetrotter

trotar [tro'tar] *vi* to trot; **trote** *nm* trot; (*fam*) travelling; **de mucho trote** hard-wearing

trozar [tro'θar] (*LAM*) *vt* to cut up, cut into pieces

trozo ['troθo] *nm* bit, piece

trucha ['trutʃa] *nf* trout

truco ['truko] *nm* (*habilidad*) knack; (*engaño*) trick

trueno ['trweno] *nm* thunder; (*estampido*) bang

trueque *etc* ['trweke] *vb* V **trocar** ▷ *nm* exchange; (*Com*) barter

trufa ['trufa] *nf* (*Bot*) truffle

truhán, -ana [tru'an, ana] *nm/f* rogue

truncar [trun'kar] *vt* (*cortar*) to truncate; (*fig: la vida etc*) to cut short; (: *el desarrollo*) to stunt

tu [tu] *adj* your

tú [tu] *pron* you

tubérculo [tu'βerkulo] *nm* (*Bot*) tuber

tuberculosis [tuβerku'losis] *nf inv* tuberculosis

tubería [tuβe'ria] *nf* pipes *pl*; (*conducto*) pipeline

tubo ['tuβo] *nm* tube, pipe; **tubo de ensayo** test tube; **tubo de escape** exhaust

(pipe)
tuerca ['twerka] nf nut
tuerto, -a ['twerto, a] adj blind in one eye
▷ nm/f one-eyed person
tuerza etc vb V **torcer**
tuétano ['twetano] nm marrow; (Bot) pith
tufo ['tufo] nm (hedor) stench
tul [tul] nm tulle
tulipán [tuli'pan] nm tulip
tullido, -a [tu'ʎiðo, a] adj crippled
tumba ['tumba] nf (sepultura) tomb
tumbar [tum'bar] vt to knock down;
tumbarse vr (echarse) to lie down;
(extenderse) to stretch out
tumbo ['tumbo] nm: **dar ~s** to stagger
tumbona [tum'bona] nf (butaca) easy
chair; (de playa) deckchair (BRIT), beach
chair (US)
tumor [tu'mor] nm tumour
tumulto [tu'multo] nm turmoil
tuna ['tuna] nf (Mús) student music group;
V tb **tuno**

● **TUNA**
●
● A **tuna** is a musical group made up of
● university students or former students
● who dress up in costumes from the
● "Edad de Oro", the Spanish Golden
● Age. These groups go through the
● town playing their guitars, lutes and
● tambourines and serenade the young
● ladies in the halls of residence or make
● impromptu appearances at weddings
● or parties singing traditional Spanish
● songs for a few coins.

tunante [tu'nante] nmf rascal
tunear [tune'ar] vt (Auto) to style, mod
(inf)
túnel ['tunel] nm tunnel
tuning ['tunin] nm (Auto) car styling,
modding (inf)
tuno, -a ['tuno, a] nm/f (fam) rogue ▷ nm
member of student music group
tupido, -a [tu'piðo, a] adj (denso) dense;
(tela) close-woven
turbante [tur'βante] nm turban
turbar [tur'βar] vt (molestar) to disturb;
(incomodar) to upset
turbina [tur'βina] nf turbine
turbio, -a ['turβjo, a] adj cloudy; (tema
etc) confused
turbulencia [turβu'lenθja] nf
turbulence; (fig) restlessness; **turbulento,
-a** adj turbulent; (fig: intranquilo) restless;
(: ruidoso) noisy
turco, -a ['turko, a] adj Turkish ▷ nm/f

Turk
turismo [tu'rismo] nm tourism; (coche)
car; **turista** nmf tourist; **turístico, -a** adj
tourist cpd
turnar [tur'nar] vi to take (it in) turns;
turnarse vr to take (it in) turns; **turno** nm
(de trabajo) shift; (en juegos etc) turn
turquesa [tur'kesa] nf turquoise
Turquía [tur'kia] nf Turkey
turrón [tu'rron] nm (dulce) nougat
tutear [tute'ar] vt to address as familiar
"tú"; **tutearse** vr to be on familiar terms
tutela [tu'tela] nf (legal) guardianship;
tutelar adj tutelary ▷ vt to protect
tutor, a [tu'tor, a] nm/f (legal) guardian;
(Escol) tutor
tuve etc vb V **tener**
tuviera etc vb V **tener**
tuyo, -a ['tujo, a] adj yours, of yours
▷ pron yours; **un amigo ~** a friend of yours;
los ~s (fam) your relations o family
TV nf abr (= televisión) TV
TVE nf abr = **Televisión Española**

u [u] *conj* or

ubicar [uβi'kar] *vt* to place, situate; (*LAM: encontrar*) to find; **ubicarse** *vr* (*LAM: encontrarse*) to lie, be located

ubre ['uβre] *nf* udder

UCI *nf abr* (= *Unidad de Cuidados Intensivos*) ICU

Ud(s) *abr* = **usted(es)**

UE *nf abr* (= *Unión Europea*) EU

ufanarse [ufa'narse] *vr* to boast; **ufano, -a** *adj* (*arrogante*) arrogant; (*presumido*) conceited

UGT (*ESP*) *nf abr* = **Unión General de Trabajadores**

úlcera ['ulθera] *nf* ulcer

ulterior [ulte'rjor] *adj* (*más allá*) farther, further; (*subsecuente, siguiente*) subsequent

últimamente ['ultimamente] *adv* (*recientemente*) lately, recently

ultimar [ulti'mar] *vt* to finish; (*finalizar*) to finalize; (*LAM: matar*) to kill

ultimátum [ulti'matum] (*pl* **~s**) *nm* ultimatum

último, -a ['ultimo, a] *adj* last; (*más reciente*) latest, most recent; (*más bajo*) bottom; (*más alto*) top; **en las últimas** on one's last legs; **por ~** finally

ultra ['ultra] *adj* ultra ▷ *nmf* extreme right-winger

ultraje [ul'traxe] *nm* outrage; insult

ultramar [ultra'mar] *nm*: **de** *o* **en ~** abroad, overseas

ultramarinos [ultrama'rinos] *nmpl* groceries; **tienda de ~** grocer's (shop)

ultranza [ul'tranθa]: **a ~** *adv* (*a todo trance*) at all costs; (*completo*) outright

umbral [um'bral] *nm* (*gen*) threshold

○ **PALABRA CLAVE**

un, una [un, 'una] *art indef* a; (*antes de vocal*) an; **una mujer/naranja** a woman/ an orange
▷ *adj*: **unos** (*o* **unas**): **hay unos regalos para ti** there are some presents for you; **hay unas cervezas en la nevera** there are some beers in the fridge

unánime [u'nanime] *adj* unanimous; **unanimidad** *nf* unanimity

undécimo, -a [un'deθimo, a] *adj* eleventh

ungir [un'xir] *vt* to anoint

ungüento [un'gwento] *nm* ointment

único, -a ['uniko, a] *adj* only, sole; (*sin par*) unique

unidad [uni'ðað] *nf* unity; (*Com, Tec etc*) unit

unido, -a [u'niðo, a] *adj* joined, linked; (*fig*) united

unificar [unifi'kar] *vt* to unite, unify

uniformar [unifor'mar] *vt* to make uniform, level up; (*persona*) to put into uniform

uniforme [uni'forme] *adj* uniform, equal; (*superficie*) even ▷ *nm* uniform

unilateral [unilate'ral] *adj* unilateral

unión [u'njon] *nf* union; (*acto*) uniting, joining; (*unidad*) unity; (*Tec*) joint; **Unión Europea** European Union

unir [u'nir] *vt* (*juntar*) to join, unite; (*atar*) to tie, fasten; (*combinar*) to combine; **unirse** *vr* to join together, unite; (*empresas*) to merge

unísono [u'nisono] *nm*: **al ~** in unison

universal [uniβer'sal] *adj* universal; (*mundial*) world *cpd*

universidad [uniβersi'ðað] *nf* university

universitario, -a [uniβersi'tarjo, a] *adj* university *cpd* ▷ *nm/f* (*profesor*) lecturer; (*estudiante*) (university) student; (*graduado*) graduate

universo [uni'βerso] *nm* universe

○ **PALABRA CLAVE**

uno, -a ['uno, a] *adj* one; **unos pocos** a few; **unos cien** about a hundred ▷ *pron*
1 one; **quiero sólo uno** I only want one; **uno de ellos** one of them
2 (*alguien*) somebody, someone; **conozco a uno que se te parece** I know somebody *o* someone who looks like you; **uno mismo** oneself; **unos querían quedarse** some (people) wanted to stay
3 (**los**) **unos ...** (**los**) **otros ...** some ... others
▷ *nf* one; **es la una** it's one o'clock
▷ *nm* (*number*) one

untar [un'tar] vt (*mantequilla*) to spread; (*engrasar*) to grease, oil

uña ['uɲa] nf (*Anat*) nail; (*garra*) claw; (*casco*) hoof; (*arrancaclavos*) claw

uranio [u'ranjo] nm uranium

urbanización [urβaniθa'θjon] nf (*barrio, colonia*) housing estate

urbanizar [urβani'θar] vt (*zona*) to develop, urbanize

urbano, -a [ur'βano, a] adj (*de ciudad*) urban; (*cortés*) courteous, polite

urbe ['urβe] nf large city

urdir [ur'ðir] vt to warp; (*complot*) to plot, contrive

urgencia [ur'xenθja] nf urgency; (*prisa*) haste, rush; (*emergencia*) emergency; **servicios de ~** emergency services; **"U~s"** "Casualty"; **urgente** adj urgent

urgir [ur'xir] vi to be urgent; **me urge** I'm in a hurry for it

urinario, -a [uri'narjo, a] adj urinary ▷ nm urinal

urna ['urna] nf urn; (*Pol*) ballot box

urraca [u'rraka] nf magpie

URSS [urs] nf (*Hist*): **la URSS** the USSR

Uruguay [uru'ɣwai] nm (*tb*: **el ~**) Uruguay; **uruguayo, -a** adj, nm/f Uruguayan

usado, -a [u'saðo, a] adj used; (*de segunda mano*) secondhand

usar [u'sar] vt to use; (*ropa*) to wear; (*tener costumbre*) to be in the habit of; **usarse** vr to be used; **uso** nm use; wear; (*costumbre*) usage, custom; (*moda*) fashion; **al uso** in keeping with custom; **al uso de** in the style of; **de uso externo** (*Med*) for external use

usted [us'teð] pron (*sg*) you *sg*; (*pl*): **~es** you *pl*

usual [u'swal] adj usual

usuario, -a [usu'arjo, a] nm/f user

usurpar [usur'par] vt to usurp

utensilio [uten'siljo] nm tool; (*Culin*) utensil

útero ['utero] nm uterus, womb

útil ['util] adj useful ▷ nm tool; **utilidad** nf usefulness; (*Com*) profit; **utilizar** vt to use, utilize

uva ['uβa] nf grape

v abr (= *voltio*) v

va vb V **ir**

vaca ['baka] nf (*animal*) cow; **carne de ~** beef

vacaciones [baka'θjones] nfpl holidays

vacante [ba'kante] adj vacant, empty ▷ nf vacancy

vaciar [ba'θjar] vt to empty out; (*ahuecar*) to hollow out; (*moldear*) to cast; **vaciarse** vr to empty

vacilar [baθi'lar] vi to be unsteady; (*al hablar*) to falter; (*dudar*) to hesitate, waver; (*memoria*) to fail

vacío, -a [ba'θio, a] adj empty; (*puesto*) vacant; (*desocupado*) idle; (*vano*) vain ▷ nm emptiness; (*Física*) vacuum; (*un vacío*) (empty) space

vacuna [ba'kuna] nf vaccine; **vacunar** vt to vaccinate

vacuno, -a [ba'kuno, a] adj cow *cpd*; **ganado ~** cattle

vadear [baðe'ar] vt (*río*) to ford; **vado** nm ford

vagabundo, -a [baɣa'βundo, a] adj wandering ▷ nm tramp

vagancia [ba'ɣanθja] nf (*pereza*) idleness, laziness

vagar [ba'ɣar] vi to wander; (*no hacer nada*) to idle

vagina [ba'xina] nf vagina

vago, -a ['baɣo, a] adj vague; (*perezoso*) lazy ▷ nm/f (*vagabundo*) tramp; (*flojo*) lazybones *sg*, idler

vagón [ba'ɣon] nm (*Ferro: de pasajeros*) carriage; (: *de mercancías*) wagon

vaho ['bao] nm (*vapor*) vapour, steam; (*respiración*) breath

vaina ['baina] nf sheath

vainilla [bai'niʎa] nf vanilla

vais vb V **ir**

vaivén [bai'βen] nm to-and-fro

movement; (*de tránsito*) coming and going;
vaivenes *nmpl* (*fig*) ups and downs
vajilla [ba'xiʎa] *nf* crockery, dishes *pl*;
(*juego*) service, set
valdré *etc vb* V **valer**
vale ['bale] *nm* voucher; (*recibo*) receipt;
(*pagaré*) IOU
valedero, -a [bale'ðero, a] *adj* valid
valenciano, -a [balen'θjano, a] *adj*
Valencian
valentía [balen'tia] *nf* courage, bravery
valer [ba'ler] *vt* to be worth; (*Mat*) to
equal; (*costar*) to cost ▷ *vi* (*ser útil*) to be
useful; (*ser válido*) to be valid; **valerse** *vr*
to take care of oneself; **~se de** to make
use of, take advantage of; **~ la pena** to be
worthwhile; **¿vale?** (*ESP*) OK?; **más vale que
nos vayamos** we'd better go; **¡eso a mí no
me vale!** (*MÉX: fam: no importar*) I couldn't
care less about that
valeroso, -a [bale'roso, a] *adj* brave,
valiant
valgo *etc vb* V **valer**
valía [ba'lia] *nf* worth, value
validar [bali'ðar] *vt* to validate; **validez** *nf*
validity; **válido, -a** *adj* valid
valiente [ba'ljente] *adj* brave, valiant
▷ *nm* hero
valija [ba'lixa] (*CS*) *nf* (suit)case
valioso, -a [ba'ljoso, a] *adj* valuable
valla ['baʎa] *nf* fence; (*Deporte*) hurdle;
valla publicitaria hoarding; **vallar** *vt* to
fence in
valle ['baʎe] *nm* valley
valor [ba'lor] *nm* value, worth; (*precio*)
price; (*valentía*) valour, courage; (*importancia*)
importance; **valores** *nmpl* (*Com*) securities;
valorar *vt* to value
vals [bals] *nm inv* waltz
válvula ['balβula] *nf* valve
vamos *vb* V **ir**
vampiro, -resa [bam'piro, 'resa] *nm/f*
vampire
van *vb* V **ir**
vanguardia [ban'gwardja] *nf* vanguard;
(*Arte etc*) avant-garde
vanidad [bani'ðað] *nf* vanity; **vanidoso,
-a** *adj* vain, conceited
vano, -a ['bano, a] *adj* vain
vapor [ba'por] *nm* vapour; (*vaho*) steam;
al ~ (*Culin*) steamed; **vapor de agua** water
vapour; **vaporizador** *nm* atomizer;
vaporizar *vt* to vaporize; **vaporoso, -a** *adj*
vaporous
vaquero, -a [ba'kero, a] *adj* cattle *cpd*
▷ *nm* cowboy; **vaqueros** *nmpl* (*pantalones*)
jeans
vaquilla [ba'kiʎa] *nf* (*Zool*) heifer

vara ['bara] *nf* stick; (*Tec*) rod
variable [ba'rjaβle] *adj, nf* variable
variación [barja'θjon] *nf* variation
variar [bar'jar] *vt* to vary; (*modificar*) to
modify; (*cambiar de posición*) to switch
around ▷ *vi* to vary
varicela [bari'θela] *nf* chickenpox
varices [ba'riθes] *nfpl* varicose veins
variedad [barje'ðað] *nf* variety
varilla [ba'riʎa] *nf* stick; (*Bot*) twig; (*Tec*)
rod; (*de rueda*) spoke
vario, -a ['barjo, a] *adj* varied; **~s** various,
several
varita [ba'rita] *nf* (*tb:* **~ mágica**) magic
wand
varón [ba'ron] *nm* male, man; **varonil** *adj*
manly, virile
Varsovia [bar'soβja] *n* Warsaw
vas *vb* V **ir**
vasco, -a ['basko, a] *adj, nm/f* Basque;
vascongado, -a [baskon'gaðo, a] *adj*
Basque; **las Vascongadas** the Basque
Country
vaselina [base'lina] *nf* Vaseline®
vasija [ba'sixa] *nf* container, vessel
vaso ['baso] *nm* glass, tumbler; (*Anat*)
vessel

> No confundir **vaso** con la palabra inglesa
> *vase*.

vástago ['bastaɣo] *nm* (*Bot*) shoot; (*Tec*)
rod; (*fig*) offspring
vasto, -a ['basto, a] *adj* vast, huge
Vaticano [bati'kano] *nm*: **el ~** the Vatican
vatio ['batjo] *nm* (*Elec*) watt
vaya *etc vb* V **ir**
Vd(s) *abr* = **usted(es)**
ve [be] *vb* V **ir; ver**
vecindad [beθin'dað] *nf* neighbourhood;
(*habitantes*) residents *pl*
vecindario [beθin'darjo] *nm*
neighbourhood; residents *pl*
vecino, -a [be'θino, a] *adj* neighbouring
▷ *nm/f* neighbour; (*residente*) resident
veda ['beða] *nf* prohibition; **vedar**
[be'ðar] *vt* (*prohibir*) to ban, prohibit;
(*impedir*) to stop, prevent
vegetación [bexeta'θjon] *nf* vegetation
vegetal [bexe'tal] *adj, nm* vegetable
vegetariano, -a [bexeta'rjano, a] *adj,
nm/f* vegetarian
vehículo [be'ikulo] *nm* vehicle; (*Med*)
carrier
veía *etc vb* V **ver**
veinte ['beinte] *num* twenty
vejar [be'xar] *vt* (*irritar*) to annoy, vex;
(*humillar*) to humiliate
vejez [be'xeθ] *nf* old age
vejiga [be'xiɣa] *nf* (*Anat*) bladder

vela ['bela] nf (de cera) candle; (Náut) sail; (insomnio) sleeplessness; (vigilia) vigil; (Mil) sentry duty; **estar a dos ~s** (fam: sin dinero) to be skint

velado, -a [be'laðo, a] adj veiled; (sonido) muffled; (Foto) blurred ▷ nf soirée

velar [be'lar] vt (vigilar) to keep watch over ▷ vi to stay awake; **~ por** to watch over, look after

velatorio [bela'torjo] nm (funeral) wake

velero [be'lero] nm (Náut) sailing ship; (Aviac) glider

veleta [be'leta] nf weather vane

veliz [be'lis] (MÉX) nm (suit)case

vello ['beʎo] nm down, fuzz

velo ['belo] nm veil

velocidad [beloθi'ðað] nf speed; (Tec, Auto) gear

velocímetro [belo'θimetro] nm speedometer

velorio [be'lorjo] (LAM) nm (funeral) wake

veloz [be'loθ] adj fast

ven vb V **venir**

vena ['bena] nf vein

venado [be'naðo] nm deer

vencedor, a [benθe'ðor, a] adj victorious ▷ nm/f victor, winner

vencer [ben'θer] vt (dominar) to defeat, beat; (derrotar) to vanquish; (superar, controlar) to overcome, master ▷ vi (triunfar) to win (through), triumph; (plazo) to expire; **vencido, -a** adj (derrotado) defeated, beaten; (Com) due ▷ adv: **pagar vencido** to pay in arrears

venda ['benda] nf bandage; **vendaje** nm bandage, dressing; **vendar** vt to bandage; **vendar los ojos** to blindfold

vendaval [benda'βal] nm (viento) gale

vendedor, a [bende'ðor, a] nm/f seller

vender [ben'der] vt to sell; **venderse** vr (estar a la venta) to be on sale; **~ al contado/ al por mayor/al por menor** to sell for cash/ wholesale/retail; **"se vende"** "for sale"

vendimia [ben'dimja] nf grape harvest

vendré etc vb V **venir**

veneno [be'neno] nm poison; (de serpiente) venom; **venenoso, -a** adj poisonous; venomous

venerable [bene'raβle] adj venerable; **venerar** vt (respetar) to revere; (adorar) to worship

venéreo, -a [be'nereo, a] adj: **enfermedad venérea** venereal disease

venezolano, -a [beneθo'lano, a] adj Venezuelan

Venezuela [beneˈθwela] nf Venezuela

venganza [ben'ganθa] nf vengeance, revenge; **vengar** vt to avenge; **vengarse**

vr to take revenge; **vengativo, -a** adj (persona) vindictive

vengo etc vb V **venir**

venia ['benja] nf (perdón) pardon; (permiso) consent

venial [be'njal] adj venial

venida [be'niða] nf (llegada) arrival; (regreso) return

venidero, -a [beni'ðero, a] adj coming, future

venir [be'nir] vi to come; (llegar) to arrive; (ocurrir) to happen; (fig): **~ de** to stem from; **~ bien/mal** to be suitable/unsuitable; **el año que viene** next year; **~se abajo** to collapse

venta ['benta] nf (Com) sale; **"en ~"** "for sale"; **estar a la o en ~** to be (up) for sale o on the market; **venta a domicilio** door-to-door selling; **venta a plazos** hire purchase; **venta al contado/al por mayor/al por menor** cash sale/wholesale/retail

ventaja [ben'taxa] nf advantage; **ventajoso, -a** adj advantageous

ventana [ben'tana] nf window; **ventanilla** nf (de taquilla) window (of booking office etc)

ventilación [bentila'θjon] nf ventilation; (corriente) draught

ventilador [bentila'ðor] nm fan

ventilar [benti'lar] vt to ventilate; (para secar) to put out to dry; (asunto) to air, discuss

ventisca [ben'tiska] nf blizzard

ventrílocuo, -a [ben'trilokwo, a] nm/f ventriloquist

ventura [ben'tura] nf (felicidad) happiness; (buena suerte) luck; (destino) fortune; **a la (buena) ~** at random; **venturoso, -a** adj happy; (afortunado) lucky, fortunate

veo etc vb V **ver**

ver [ber] vt to see; (mirar) to look at, watch; (entender) to understand; (investigar) to look into ▷ vi to see; to understand; **verse** vr (encontrarse) to meet; (dejarse ver) to be seen; (hallarse: en un apuro) to find o.s., be; **(vamos) a ~** let's see; **no tener nada que ~ con** to have nothing to do with; **a mi modo de ~** as I see it; **ya ~emos** we'll see

vera ['bera] nf edge, verge; (de río) bank

veranear [berane'ar] vi to spend the summer; **veraneo** nm summer holiday; **veraniego, -a** adj summer cpd

verano [be'rano] nm summer

veras ['beras] nfpl truth sg; **de ~** really, truly

verbal [ber'βal] adj verbal

verbena [ber'βena] nf (baile) open-air dance

v

verbo ['berβo] nm verb

verdad [ber'ðað] nf truth; (fiabilidad) reliability; **de ~** real, proper; **a decir ~** to tell the truth; **verdadero, -a** adj (veraz) true, truthful; (fiable) reliable; (fig) real

verde ['berðe] adj green; (chiste) blue, dirty ▷ nm green; **viejo ~** dirty old man; **verdear** vi to turn green; **verdor** nm greenness

verdugo [ber'ðuxo] nm executioner

verdulero, -a [berðu'lero, a] nm/f greengrocer

verduras [ber'ðuras] nfpl (Culin) greens

vereda [be'reða] nf path; (cs: acera) pavement (BRIT), sidewalk (US)

veredicto [bere'ðikto] nm verdict

vergonzoso, -a [berɣon'θoso, a] adj shameful; (tímido) timid, bashful

vergüenza [ber'ɣwenθa] nf shame, sense of shame; (timidez) bashfulness; (pudor) modesty; **me da ~** I'm ashamed

verídico, -a [be'riðiko, a] adj true, truthful

verificar [berifi'kar] vt to check; (corroborar) to verify; (llevar a cabo) to carry out; **verificarse** vr (predicción) to prove to be true

verja ['berxa] nf (cancela) iron gate; (valla) iron railings pl; (de ventana) grille

vermut [ber'mut] (pl **~s**) nm vermouth

verosímil [bero'simil] adj likely, probable; (relato) credible

verruga [be'rruɣa] nf wart

versátil [ber'satil] adj versatile

versión [ber'sjon] nf version

verso ['berso] nm verse; **un ~** a line of poetry

vértebra ['berteβra] nf vertebra

verter [ber'ter] vt (líquido: adrede) to empty, pour (out); (: sin querer) to spill; (basura) to dump ▷ vi to flow

vertical [berti'kal] adj vertical

vértice ['bertiθe] nm vertex, apex

vertidos [ber'tiðos] nmpl waste sg

vertiente [ber'tjente] nf slope; (fig) aspect

vértigo ['bertixo] nm vertigo; (mareo) dizziness

vesícula [be'sikula] nf blister

vespino® [bes'pino] nm o nf moped

vestíbulo [bes'tiβulo] nm hall; (de teatro) foyer

vestido [bes'tiðo] nm (ropa) clothes pl, clothing; (de mujer) dress, frock ▷ pp de **vestir**; **~ de azul/marinero** dressed in blue/as a sailor

vestidor [besti'ðor] (MÉX) nm (Deporte) changing (BRIT) o locker (US) room

vestimenta [besti'menta] nf clothing

vestir [bes'tir] vt (poner: ropa) to put on; (llevar: ropa) to wear; (proveer de ropa a) to clothe; (sastre) to make clothes for ▷ vi to dress; (verse bien) to look good; **vestirse** vr to get dressed, dress o.s.

vestuario [bes'twarjo] nm clothes pl, wardrobe; (Teatro: cuarto) dressing room; (Deporte) changing (BRIT) o locker (US) room

vetar [be'tar] vt to veto

veterano, -a [bete'rano, a] adj, nm veteran

veterinaria [beteri'narja] nf veterinary science; V tb **veterinario**

veterinario, -a [beteri'narjo, a] nm/f vet(erinary surgeon)

veto ['beto] nm veto

vez [beθ] nf time; (turno) turn; **a la ~ que** at the same time as; **a su ~** in its turn; **otra ~** again; **una ~** once; **de una ~** in one go; **de una ~ para siempre** once and for all; **en ~ de** instead of; **a o algunas veces** sometimes; **una y otra ~** repeatedly; **de ~ en cuando** from time to time; **7 veces 9** 7 times 9; **hacer las veces de** to stand in for; **tal ~** perhaps

vía ['bia] nf track, route; (Ferro) line; (fig) way; (Anat) passage, tube ▷ prep via, by way of; **por ~ judicial** by legal means; **en ~s de** in the process of; **vía aérea** airway; **Vía Láctea** Milky Way; **vía pública** public road o thoroughfare

viable ['bjaβle] adj (solución, plan, alternativa) feasible

viaducto [bja'ðukto] nm viaduct

viajante [bja'xante] nm commercial traveller

viajar [bja'xar] vi to travel; **viaje** nm journey; (gira) tour; (Náut) voyage; **estar de viaje** to be on a trip; **viaje de ida y vuelta** round trip; **viaje de novios** honeymoon; **viajero, -a** adj travelling; (Zool) migratory ▷ nm/f (quien viaja) traveller; (pasajero) passenger

víbora ['biβora] nf (Zool) viper; (: MÉX: venenoso) poisonous snake

vibración [biβra'θjon] nf vibration

vibrar [bi'βrar] vt, vi to vibrate

vicepresidente [biθepresi'ðente] nmf vice-president

viceversa [biθe'βersa] adv vice versa

vicio ['biθjo] nm vice; (mala costumbre) bad habit; **vicioso, -a** adj (muy malo) vicious; (corrompido) depraved ▷ nm/f depraved person

víctima ['biktima] nf victim

victoria [bik'torja] nf victory; **victorioso, -a** adj victorious

vid [bið] nf vine

vida ['biða] nf (gen) life; (duración) lifetime;

de por ~ for life; **en la** o **mi ~** never; **estar con ~** to be still alive; **ganarse la ~** to earn one's living

vídeo ['biðeo] nm video ▷ adj inv: **película de ~** video film; **videocámara** nf camcorder; **videocasete** nm video cassette, videotape; **videoclub** nm video club; **videojuego** nm video game; **videollamada** nf video call; **videoteléfono** nf videophone

vidrio ['biðrjo] nm glass

vieira ['bjeira] nf scallop

viejo, -a ['bjexo, a] adj old ▷ nm/f old man/woman; **hacerse ~** to get old

Viena ['bjena] n Vienna

vienes etc vb V **venir**

vienés, -esa [bje'nes, esa] adj Viennese

viento ['bjento] nm wind; **hacer ~** to be windy

vientre ['bjentre] nm belly; (matriz) womb

viernes ['bjernes] nm inv Friday; **Viernes Santo** Good Friday

Vietnam [bjet'nam] nm Vietnam; **vietnamita** adj Vietnamese

viga ['bixa] nf beam, rafter; (de metal) girder

vigencia [bi'xenθja] nf validity; **estar en ~** to be in force; **vigente** adj valid, in force; (imperante) prevailing

vigésimo, -a [bi'xesimo, a] adj twentieth

vigía [bi'xia] nm look-out

vigilancia [bixi'lanθja] nf: **tener a algn bajo ~** to keep watch on sb

vigilar [bixi'lar] vt to watch over ▷ vi (gen) to be vigilant; (hacer guardia) to keep watch; **~ por** to take care of

vigilia [vi'xilja] nf wakefulness, being awake; (Rel) fast

vigor [bi'xor] nm vigour, vitality; **en ~** in force; **entrar/poner en ~** to come/put into effect; **vigoroso, -a** adj vigorous

VIH nm abr (= virus de la inmunodeficiencia humana) HIV; **VIH negativo/positivo** HIV-negative/-positive

vil [bil] adj vile, low

villa ['biʎa] nf (casa) villa; (pueblo) small town; (municipalidad) municipality

villancico [biʎan'θiko] nm (Christmas) carol

vilo ['bilo]: **en ~** adv in the air, suspended; (fig) on tenterhooks, in suspense

vinagre [bi'naxre] nm vinegar

vinagreta [bina'xreta] nf vinaigrette, French dressing

vinculación [binkula'θjon] nf (lazo) link, bond; (acción) linking

vincular [binku'lar] vt to link, bind;

vínculo nm link, bond

vine etc vb V **venir**

vinicultura [binikul'tura] nf wine growing

viniera etc vb V **venir**

vino ['bino] vb V **venir** ▷ nm wine; **vino blanco/tinto** white/red wine

viña ['bina] nf vineyard; **viñedo** nm vineyard

viola ['bjola] nf viola

violación [bjola'θjon] nf violation; (sexual) rape

violar [bjo'lar] vt to violate; (sexualmente) to rape

violencia [bjo'lenθja] nf violence, force; (incomodidad) embarrassment; (acto injusto) unjust act; **violentar** vt to force; (casa) to break into; (agredir) to assault; (violar) to violate; **violento, -a** adj violent; (furioso) furious; (situación) embarrassing; (acto) forced, unnatural

violeta [bjo'leta] nf violet

violín [bjo'lin] nm violin

violón [bjo'lon] nm double bass

virar [bi'rar] vi to change direction

virgen ['birxen] adj, nf virgin

Virgo ['birxo] nm Virgo

viril [bi'ril] adj virile; **virilidad** nf virility

virtud [bir'tuð] nf virtue; **en ~ de** by virtue of; **virtuoso, -a** adj virtuous ▷ nm/f virtuoso

viruela [bi'rwela] nf smallpox

virulento, -a [biru'lento, a] adj virulent

virus ['birus] nm inv virus

visa ['bisa] (LAM) nf = **visado**

visado [bi'saðo] (ESP) nm visa

víscera ['bisθera] nf (Anat, Zool) gut, bowel; **vísceras** nfpl entrails

visceral [bisθe'ral] adj (odio) intense; **reacción ~** gut reaction

visera [bi'sera] nf visor

visibilidad [bisiβili'ðað] nf visibility; **visible** adj visible; (fig) obvious

visillos [bi'siʎos] nmpl lace curtains

visión [bi'sjon] nf (Anat) vision, (eye)sight; (fantasía) vision, fantasy

visita [bi'sita] nf call, visit; (persona) visitor; **hacer una ~** to pay a visit; **visitar** [bisi'tar] vt to visit, call on

visón [bi'son] nm mink

visor [bi'sor] nm (Foto) viewfinder

víspera ['bispera] nf: **la ~ de ...** the day before ...

vista ['bista] nf sight, vision; (capacidad de ver) (eye)sight; (mirada) look(s) (pl); **a primera ~** at first glance; **hacer la ~ gorda** to turn a blind eye; **volver la ~** to look back; **está a la ~ que** it's obvious that; **en ~ de** in view of; **en ~ de que** in view of the fact that; **¡hasta la ~!** so long!, see you!; **con ~s a** with a view to; **vistazo** *nm* glance; **dar o echar un vistazo a** to glance at

visto, -a ['bisto, a] *pp de* **ver** ▷ *vb* V *tb* **vestir** ▷ *adj* seen; (*considerado*) considered ▷ *nm*: **~ bueno** approval; **por lo ~** apparently; **está ~ que** it's clear that; **está bien/mal ~** it's acceptable/unacceptable; **~ que** since, considering that

vistoso, -a [bis'toso, a] *adj* colourful

visual [bi'swal] *adj* visual

vital [bi'tal] *adj* life *cpd*, living *cpd*; (*fig*) vital; (*persona*) lively, vivacious; **vitalicio, -a** *adj* for life; **vitalidad** *nf* (*de persona, negocio*) energy; (*de ciudad*) liveliness

vitamina [bita'mina] *nf* vitamin

vitorear [bitore'ar] *vt* to cheer, acclaim

vitrina [bi'trina] *nf* show case; (*LAM: escaparate*) shop window

viudo, -a ['bjuðo, a] *nm/f* widower/ widow

viva ['biβa] *excl* hurrah!; **¡~ el rey!** long live the king!

vivaracho, -a [biβa'ratʃo, a] *adj* jaunty, lively; (*ojos*) bright, twinkling

vivaz [bi'βaθ] *adj* lively

víveres ['biβeres] *nmpl* provisions

vivero [bi'βero] *nm* (*para plantas*) nursery; (*para peces*) fish farm; (*fig*) hotbed

viveza [bi'βeθa] *nf* liveliness; (*agudeza: mental*) sharpness

vivienda [bi'βjenda] *nf* housing; (*una vivienda*) house; (*piso*) flat (BRIT), apartment (US)

viviente [bi'βjente] *adj* living

vivir [bi'βir] *vt, vi* to live ▷ *nm* life, living

vivo, -a ['biβo, a] *adj* living, alive; (*fig: descripción*) vivid; (*persona: astuto*) smart, clever; **en ~** (*transmisión etc*) live

vocablo [bo'kaβlo] *nm* (*palabra*) word; (*término*) term

vocabulario [bokaβu'larjo] *nm* vocabulary

vocación [boka'θjon] *nf* vocation; **vocacional** (*LAM*) *nf* ≈ technical college

vocal [bo'kal] *adj* vocal ▷ *nf* vowel; **vocalizar** *vt* to vocalize

vocero [bo'θero] (*LAM*) *nmf* spokesman/ woman

voces ['boθes] *pl de* **voz**

vodka ['boðka] *nm o f* vodka

vol *abr* = **volumen**

volado [bo'laðo] (*MÉX*) *adv* in a rush, hastily

volador, a [bola'ðor, a] *adj* flying

volandas [bo'landas]: **en ~** *adv* in the air

volante [bo'lante] *adj* flying ▷ *nm* (*de coche*) steering wheel; (*de reloj*) balance

volar [bo'lar] *vt* (*edificio*) to blow up ▷ *vi* to fly

volátil [bo'latil] *adj* volatile

volcán [bol'kan] *nm* volcano; **volcánico, -a** *adj* volcanic

volcar [bol'kar] *vt* to upset, overturn; (*tumbar, derribar*) to knock over; (*vaciar*) to empty out ▷ *vi* to overturn; **volcarse** *vr* to tip over

voleibol [bolei'βol] *nm* volleyball

volqué *etc vb* V **volcar**

voltaje [bol'taxe] *nm* voltage

voltear [bolte'ar] *vt* to turn over; (*volcar*) to turn upside down

voltereta [bolte'reta] *nf* somersault

voltio ['boltjo] *nm* volt

voluble [bo'luβle] *adj* fickle

volumen [bo'lumen] (*pl* **volúmenes**) *nm* volume; **voluminoso, -a** *adj* voluminous; (*enorme*) massive

voluntad [bolun'tað] *nf* will; (*resolución*) willpower; (*deseo*) desire, wish

voluntario, -a [bolun'tarjo, a] *adj* voluntary ▷ *nm/f* volunteer

volver [bol'βer] *vt* (*gen*) to turn; (*dar vuelta a*) to turn (over); (*voltear*) to turn round, turn upside down; (*poner al revés*) to turn inside out; (*devolver*) to return ▷ *vi* to return, go back, come back; **volverse** *vr* to turn round; **~ la espalda** to turn one's back; **~ triste** *etc* **a algn** to make sb sad *etc*; **~ a hacer** to do again; **~ a sí** to come to; **~se insoportable/muy caro** to get o become unbearable/very expensive; **~se loco** to go mad

vomitar [bomi'tar] *vt, vi* to vomit; **vómito** *nm* vomit

voraz [bo'raθ] *adj* voracious

vos [bos] (*LAM*) *pron* you

vosotros, -as [bo'sotros, as] (*ESP*) *pron* you; (*reflexivo*): **entre/para ~** among/for yourselves

votación [bota'θjon] *nf* (*acto*) voting; (*voto*) vote

votar [bo'tar] *vi* to vote; **voto** *nm* vote; (*promesa*) vow; **votos** *nmpl* (good) wishes

voy *vb* V **ir**

voz [boθ] *nf* voice; (*grito*) shout; (*rumor*) rumour; (*Ling*) word; **dar voces** to shout, yell; **de viva ~** verbally; **en ~ alta** aloud; **en ~ baja** in a low voice, in a whisper; **voz de mando** command

vuelco ['bwelko] *vb* V **volcar** ▷ *nm* spill, overturning

vuelo ['bwelo] *vb* V **volar** ▷ *nm* flight; (*encaje*) lace, frill; **coger al ~** to catch in flight; **vuelo chárter/regular** charter/

scheduled flight; **vuelo libre** (*Deporte*)
hang-gliding

vuelque *etc vb* V **volcar**

vuelta ['bwelta] *nf* (*gen*) turn; (*curva*)
bend, curve; (*regreso*) return; (*revolución*)
revolution; (*de circuito*) lap; (*de papel, tela*)
reverse; (*cambio*) change; **a la ~** on one's
return; **a la ~ (de la esquina)** round the
corner; **a ~ de correo** by return of post; **dar
~s** (*cabeza*) to spin; **dar(se) la ~** (*volverse*) to
turn round; **dar ~s a una idea** to turn over
an idea (in one's head); **estar de ~** to be
back; **dar una ~** to go for a walk; (*en coche*)
to go for a drive; **vuelta ciclista** (*Deporte*)
(cycle) tour

vuelto ['bwelto] *pp de* **volver**

vuelvo *etc vb* V **volver**

vuestro, -a ['bwestro, a] *adj pos* your;
un amigo ~ a friend of yours ▷ *pron*: **el ~/la
vuestra, los ~s/las vuestras** yours

vulgar [bul'ɣar] *adj* (*ordinario*) vulgar;
(*común*) common; **vulgaridad** *nf*
commonness; (*acto*) vulgarity; (*expresión*)
coarse expression

vulnerable [bulne'raβle] *adj* vulnerable

vulnerar [bulne'rar] *vt* (*ley, acuerdo*) to
violate, breach; (*derechos, intimidad*) to
violate; (*reputación*) to damage

walkie-talkie [walki-'talki] (*pl* **~s**) *nm*
walkie-talkie

Walkman® ['walkman] *nm* Walkman®

wáter ['bater] *nm* (*taza*) toilet; (*LAM: lugar*)
toilet (*BRIT*), rest room (*US*)

web [web] *nm o f* (*página*) website; (*red*)
(World Wide) Web; **webcam** *nf* webcam;
webmaster *nmf* webmaster; **website** *nm*
website

western ['western] (*pl* **~s**) *nm* western

whisky ['wiski] *nm* whisky, whiskey

windsurf ['winsurf] *nm* windsurfing;
hacer ~ to go windsurfing

xenofobia [kseno'foβja] *nf* xenophobia
xilófono [ksi'lofono] *nm* xylophone
xocoyote, -a [ksoko'yote, a] (*MÉX*) *nm/f*
  baby of the family, youngest child

y [i] *conj* and
ya [ja] *adv* (*gen*) already; (*ahora*) now; (*en
  seguida*) at once; (*pronto*) soon ▷ *excl* all
  right! ▷ *conj* (*ahora que*) now that; **~ lo sé**
  I know; **~ que** ... since; **¡~ está bien!** that's
  (quite) enough!; **¡~ voy!** coming!
yacaré [jaka're] (*cs*) *nm* cayman
yacer [ja'θer] *vi* to lie
yacimiento [jaθi'mjento] *nm* (*de mineral*)
  deposit; (*arqueológico*) site
yanqui ['janki] *adj, nmf* Yankee
yate ['jate] *nm* yacht
yazco *etc vb V* **yacer**
yedra ['jeðra] *nf* ivy
yegua ['jeɣwa] *nf* mare
yema ['jema] *nf* (*del huevo*) yolk; (*Bot*) leaf
  bud; (*fig*) best part; **yema del dedo** fingertip
yerno ['jerno] *nm* son-in-law
yeso ['jeso] *nm* plaster
yo [jo] *pron* I; **soy ~** it's me
yodo ['joðo] *nm* iodine
yoga ['joɣa] *nm* yoga
yogur(t) [jo'ɣur(t)] *nm* yoghurt
yuca ['juka] *nf* (*alimento*) cassava, manioc
  root
Yugoslavia [juɣos'laβja] *nf* (*Hist*)
  Yugoslavia
yugular [juɣu'lar] *adj* jugular
yunque ['junke] *nm* anvil
yuyo ['jujo] (*RPL*) *nm* (*mala hierba*) weed

Z

zafar [θa'far] vt (soltar) to untie; (superficie) to clear; **zafarse** vr (escaparse) to escape; (Tec) to slip off

zafiro [θa'firo] nm sapphire

zaga ['θaɣa] nf: **a la ~** behind

zaguán [θa'ɣwan] nm hallway

zalamero, -a [θala'mero, a] adj flattering; (cobista) suave

zamarra [θa'marra] nf (chaqueta) sheepskin jacket

zambullirse [θambu'ʎirse] vr to dive

zampar [θam'par] vt to gobble down

zanahoria [θana'orja] nf carrot

zancadilla [θanka'ðiʎa] nf trip

zanco ['θanko] nm stilt

zanja ['θanxa] nf ditch; **zanjar** vt (resolver) to resolve

zapata [θa'pata] nf (Mecánica) shoe

zapatería [θapate'ria] nf (oficio) shoemaking; (tienda) shoe shop; (fábrica) shoe factory; **zapatero, -a** nm/f shoemaker

zapatilla [θapa'tiʎa] nf slipper; **zapatilla de deporte** training shoe

zapato [θa'pato] nm shoe

zapping ['θapin] nm channel-hopping; **hacer ~** to channel-hop

zar [θar] nm tsar, czar

zarandear [θarande'ar] (fam) vt to shake vigorously

zarpa ['θarpa] nf (garra) claw

zarpar [θar'par] vi to weigh anchor

zarza ['θarθa] nf (Bot) bramble; **zarzamora** nf blackberry

zarzuela [θar'θwela] nf Spanish light opera

zigzag [θiɣ'θaɣ] nm zigzag

zinc [θink] nm zinc

zíper ['θiper] (MÉX, CAM) nm zip (fastener) (BRIT), zipper (US)

zócalo ['θokalo] nm (Arq) plinth, base; (de pared) skirting board (BRIT), baseboard (US); (MÉX: plaza) main o public square

zoclo ['θoklo] (MÉX) nm skirting board (BRIT), baseboard (US)

zodíaco [θo'ðiako] nm zodiac

zona ['θona] nf zone; **zona fronteriza** border area; **zona roja** (LAM) red-light district

zonzo, -a (LAM: fam) ['θonθo, a] adj silly ▷ nm/f fool

zoo ['θoo] nm zoo

zoología [θoolo'xia] nf zoology; **zoológico, -a** adj zoological ▷ nm (tb: **parque zoológico**) zoo; **zoólogo, -a** nm/f zoologist

zoom [θum] nm zoom lens

zopilote [θopi'lote] (MÉX, CAM) nm buzzard

zoquete [θo'kete] nm (fam) blockhead

zorro, -a ['θorro, a] adj crafty ▷ nm/f fox/ vixen

zozobrar [θoθo'βrar] vi (hundirse) to capsize; (fig) to fail

zueco ['θweko] nm clog

zumbar [θum'bar] vt (golpear) to hit ▷ vi to buzz; **zumbido** nm buzzing

zumo ['θumo] nm juice

zurcir [θur'θir] vt (coser) to darn

zurdo, -a ['θurðo, a] adj left-handed

zurrar [θu'rrar] (fam) vt to wallop

a

A [eɪ] n (Mus) la m

○ **KEYWORD**

a [ə] (before vowel or silent h: an) indef art
1 un(a); **a book** un libro; **an apple** una manzana; **she's a doctor** (ella) es médica
2 (instead of the number "one") un(a); **a year ago** hace un año; **a hundred/thousand etc pounds** cien/mil etc libras
3 (in expressing ratios, prices etc): **3 a day/week** 3 al día/a la semana; **10 km an hour** 10 km por hora; **£5 a person** £5 por persona; **30p a kilo** 30p el kilo

A2 (BRIT: Scol) n segunda parte de los "A levels"
A.A. n abbr (BRIT: = Automobile Association) ≈ RACE m (SP); (= Alcoholics Anonymous) Alcohólicos Anónimos
A.A.A. (US) n abbr (= American Automobile Association) ≈ RACE m (SP)
aback [əˈbæk] adv: **to be taken ~** quedar desconcertado
abandon [əˈbændən] vt abandonar; (give up) renunciar a
abattoir [ˈæbətwɑː*] (BRIT) n matadero
abbey [ˈæbɪ] n abadía
abbreviation [əˈbriːvɪˈeɪʃən] n (short form) abreviatura
abdomen [ˈæbdəmən] n abdomen m
abduct [æbˈdʌkt] vt raptar, secuestrar
abide [əˈbaɪd] vt: **I can't ~ it/him** no lo/le puedo ver; **abide by** vt fus atenerse a
ability [əˈbɪlɪtɪ] n habilidad f, capacidad f; (talent) talento
able [ˈeɪbl] adj capaz; (skilled) hábil; **to be ~ to do sth** poder hacer algo
abnormal [æbˈnɔːməl] adj anormal
aboard [əˈbɔːd] adv a bordo ▷ prep a bordo de
abolish [əˈbɒlɪʃ] vt suprimir, abolir

abolition [æbəuˈlɪʃən] n supresión f, abolición f
abort [əˈbɔːt] vt, vi abortar; **abortion** [əˈbɔːʃən] n aborto; **to have an abortion** abortar, hacerse abortar

○ **KEYWORD**

about [əˈbaut] adv **1** (approximately) más o menos, aproximadamente; **about a hundred/thousand etc** unos(unas) cien/mil etc; **it takes about 10 hours** se tarda unas or más o menos 10 horas; **at about 2 o'clock** sobre las dos; **I've just about finished** casi he terminado
2 (referring to place) por todas partes; **to leave things lying about** dejar las cosas (tiradas) por ahí; **to run about** correr por todas partes; **to walk about** pasearse, ir y venir
3: **to be about to do sth** estar a punto de hacer algo
▷ prep **1** (relating to) de, sobre, acerca de; **a book about London** un libro sobre or acerca de Londres; **what is it about?** ¿de qué se trata?; **we talked about it** hablamos de eso or ello; **what or how about doing this?** ¿qué tal si hacemos esto?
2 (referring to place) por; **to walk about the town** caminar por la ciudad

above [əˈbʌv] adv encima, por encima, arriba ▷ prep encima de; (greater than: in number) más de; (: in rank) superior a; **mentioned ~** susodicho; **~ all** sobre todo
abroad [əˈbrɔːd] adv (to be) en el extranjero; (to go) al extranjero
abrupt [əˈbrʌpt] adj (sudden) brusco; (curt) áspero
abscess [ˈæbsɪs] n absceso
absence [ˈæbsəns] n ausencia
absent [ˈæbsənt] adj ausente; **absent-minded** adj distraído
absolute [ˈæbsəluːt] adj absoluto; **absolutely** [-ˈluːtlɪ] adv (totally) totalmente; (certainly!) ¡por supuesto (que sí)!
absorb [əbˈzɔːb] vt absorber; **to be ~ed in a book** estar absorto en un libro; **absorbent cotton** (US) n algodón m hidrófilo; **absorbing** adj absorbente
abstain [əbˈsteɪn] vi: **to ~ (from)** abstenerse (de)
abstract [ˈæbstrækt] adj abstracto
absurd [əbˈsɜːd] adj absurdo
abundance [əˈbʌndəns] n abundancia
abundant [əˈbʌndənt] adj abundante
abuse [n əˈbjuːs, vb əˈbjuːz] n (insults)

insultos *mpl*, injurias *fpl*; *(ill-treatment)* malos tratos *mpl*; *(misuse)* abuso ▷ *vt* insultar; maltratar; abusar de; **abusive** *adj* ofensivo

abysmal [ə'bɪzməl] *adj* pésimo; *(failure)* garrafal; *(ignorance)* supino

academic [ækə'dɛmɪk] *adj* académico, universitario; *(pej: issue)* puramente teórico ▷ *n* estudioso/a, profesor(a) *m/f* universitario/a; **academic year** *n* *(Univ)* año *m* académico; *(Scol)* año *m* escolar

academy [ə'kædəmɪ] *n* *(learned body)* academia; *(school)* instituto, colegio; **~ of music** conservatorio

accelerate [æk'sɛləreɪt] *vt, vi* acelerar; **acceleration** [æksɛlə'reɪʃən] *n* aceleración *f*; **accelerator** (BRIT) *n* acelerador *m*

accent ['æksɛnt] *n* acento; *(fig)* énfasis *m*

accept [ək'sɛpt] *vt* aceptar; *(responsibility, blame)* admitir; **acceptable** *adj* aceptable; **acceptance** *n* aceptación *f*

access ['æksɛs] *n* acceso; **to have ~ to** tener libre acceso a; **accessible** [-'sɛsəbl] *adj* *(place, person)* accesible; *(knowledge etc)* asequible

accessory [æk'sɛsərɪ] *n* accesorio; *(Law):* **~ to** cómplice de

accident ['æksɪdənt] *n* accidente *m*; *(chance event)* casualidad *f*; **by ~** *(unintentionally)* sin querer; *(by chance)* por casualidad; **accidental** [-'dɛntl] *adj* accidental, fortuito; **accidentally** [-'dɛntəlɪ] *adv* sin querer; por casualidad; **Accident and Emergency Department** *n* (BRIT) Urgencias *fpl*; **accident insurance** *n* seguro contra accidentes

acclaim [ə'kleɪm] *vt* aclamar, aplaudir ▷ *n* aclamación *f*, aplausos *mpl*

accommodate [ə'kɔmədeɪt] *vt* *(person)* alojar, hospedar; *(: car, hotel etc)* tener cabida para; *(oblige, help)* complacer

accommodation [əkɔmə'deɪʃən] (us **accommodations**) *n* alojamiento

accompaniment [ə'kʌmpənɪmənt] *n* acompañamiento

accompany [ə'kʌmpənɪ] *vt* acompañar

accomplice [ə'kʌmplɪs] *n* cómplice *mf*

accomplish [ə'kʌmplɪʃ] *vt* *(finish)* concluir; *(achieve)* lograr; **accomplishment** *n* *(skill: gen pl)* talento; *(completion)* realización *f*

accord [ə'kɔːd] *n* acuerdo ▷ *vt* conceder; **of his own ~** espontáneamente; **accordance** *n*: **in accordance with** de acuerdo con; **according** ▷ **according to** *prep* según; *(in accordance with)* conforme a; **accordingly** *adv* *(appropriately)* de acuerdo con esto; *(as a result)* en consecuencia

account [ə'kaunt] *n* *(Comm)* cuenta; *(report)* informe *m*; **accounts** *npl* *(Comm)* cuentas *fpl*; **of no ~** de ninguna importancia; **on ~** a cuenta; **on no ~** bajo ningún concepto; **on ~ of** a causa de, por motivo de; **to take into ~, take ~ of** tener en cuenta; **account for** *vt fus* *(explain)* explicar; *(represent)* representar; **accountable** *adj*: **accountable (to)** responsable (ante); **accountant** *n* contable *mf*, contador(a) *m/f*; **account number** *n* *(at bank etc)* número de cuenta

accumulate [ə'kjuːmjuleɪt] *vt* acumular ▷ *vi* acumularse

accuracy ['ækjurəsɪ] *n* *(of total)* exactitud *f*; *(of description etc)* precisión *f*

accurate ['ækjurɪt] *adj* *(total)* exacto; *(description)* preciso; *(person)* cuidadoso; *(device)* de precisión; **accurately** *adv* con precisión

accusation [ækju'zeɪʃən] *n* acusación *f*

accuse [ə'kjuːz] *vt*: **to ~ sb (of sth)** acusar a algn (de algo); **accused** *n* *(Law)* acusado/a

accustomed [ə'kʌstəmd] *adj*: **~ to** acostumbrado a

ace [eɪs] *n* as *m*

ache [eɪk] *n* dolor *m* ▷ *vi* doler; **my head ~s** me duele la cabeza

achieve [ə'tʃiːv] *vt* *(aim, result)* alcanzar; *(success)* lograr, conseguir; **achievement** *n* *(completion)* realización *f*; *(success)* éxito

acid ['æsɪd] *adj* ácido; *(taste)* agrio ▷ *n* *(Chem, inf: LSD)* ácido

acknowledge [ək'nɔlɪdʒ] *vt* *(letter: also:* **~ receipt of**) acusar recibo de; *(fact, situation, person)* reconocer; **acknowledgement** *n* acuse *m* de recibo

acne ['æknɪ] *n* acné *m*

acorn ['eɪkɔːn] *n* bellota

acoustic [ə'kuːstɪk] *adj* acústico

acquaintance [ə'kweɪntəns] *n* *(person)* conocido/a; *(with person, subject)* conocimiento

acquire [ə'kwaɪə*] *vt* adquirir; **acquisition** [ækwɪ'zɪʃən] *n* adquisición *f*

acquit [ə'kwɪt] *vt* absolver, exculpar; **to ~ o.s. well** salir con éxito

acre ['eɪkə*] *n* acre *m*

acronym ['ækrənɪm] *n* siglas *fpl*

across [ə'krɔs] *prep* *(on the other side of)* al otro lado de, del otro lado de; *(crosswise)* a través de ▷ *adv* de un lado a otro, de una parte a otra; a través, al través; *(measurement)*: **the road is 10m ~** la carretera tiene 10m de ancho; **to run/swim ~** atravesar corriendo/nadando; **~ from** enfrente de

acrylic [ə'krɪlɪk] *adj* acrílico ▷ *n* acrílica

act [ækt] n acto, acción f; (of play) acto; (in music hall etc) número; (Law) decreto, ley f ▷ vi (behave) comportarse; (have effect: drug, chemical) hacer efecto; (Theatre) actuar; (pretend) fingir; (take action) obrar ▷ vt (part) hacer el papel de; **in the ~ of: to catch sb in the ~ of ...** pillar a algn en el momento en que ...; **to ~ as** actuar or hacer de; **act up** (inf) vi (person) portarse mal; **acting** adj suplente ▷ n (activity) actuación f; (profession) profesión f de actor

action ['ækʃən] n acción f, acto; (Mil) acción f, batalla; (Law) proceso, demanda; **out of ~** (person) fuera de combate; (thing) estropeado; **to take ~** tomar medidas; **action replay** n (TV) repetición f

activate ['æktɪveɪt] vt activar

active ['æktɪv] adj activo, enérgico; (volcano) en actividad; **actively** adv (participate) activamente; (discourage, dislike) enérgicamente

activist ['æktɪvɪst] n activista m/f

activity [-'tɪvɪtɪ] n actividad f; **activity holiday** n vacaciones con actividades organizadas

actor ['æktə*] n actor m, actriz f

actress ['æktrɪs] n actriz f

actual ['æktjʊəl] adj verdadero, real; (emphatic use) propiamente dicho

> Be careful not to translate **actual** by the Spanish word actual.

actually ['æktjʊəlɪ] adv realmente, en realidad; (even) incluso

> Be careful not to translate **actually** by the Spanish word actualmente.

acupuncture ['ækjʊpʌŋktʃə*] n acupuntura

acute [ə'kjuːt] adj agudo

ad [æd] n abbr = **advertisement**

A.D. adv abbr = anno Domini) DC

adamant ['ædəmənt] adj firme, inflexible

adapt [ə'dæpt] vt adaptar ▷ vi: **to ~ (to)** adaptarse (a), ajustarse (a); **adapter** (us **adaptor**) n (Elec) adaptador m; (for several plugs) ladrón m

add [æd] vt añadir, agregar; **add up** vt (figures) sumar ▷ vi (fig): **it doesn't add up** no tiene sentido; **add up to** vt fus (Math) sumar, ascender a; (fig: mean) querer decir, venir a ser

addict ['ædɪkt] n adicto/a; (enthusiast) entusiasta mf; **addicted** [ə'dɪktɪd] adj: **to be addicted to** ser adicto a, ser fanático de; **addiction** [ə'dɪkʃən] n (to drugs etc) adicción f; **addictive** [ə'dɪktɪv] adj que causa adicción

addition [ə'dɪʃən] n (adding up) adición f; (thing added) añadidura, añadido; **in ~** además, por añadidura; **in ~ to** además de; **additional** adj adicional

additive ['ædɪtɪv] n aditivo

address [ə'drɛs] n dirección f, señas fpl; (speech) discurso ▷ vt (letter) dirigir; (speak to) dirigirse a, dirigir la palabra a; (problem) tratar; **address book** n agenda (de direcciones)

adequate ['ædɪkwɪt] adj (satisfactory) adecuado; (enough) suficiente

adhere [əd'hɪə*] vi: **to ~ to** (stick to) pegarse a; (fig: abide by) observar; (: belief etc) ser partidario de

adhesive [əd'hiːzɪv] n adhesivo; **adhesive tape** n (BRIT) cinta adhesiva; (US Med) esparadrapo

adjacent [ə'dʒeɪsənt] adj: **~ to** contiguo a, inmediato a

adjective ['ædʒɛktɪv] n adjetivo

adjoining [ə'dʒɔɪnɪŋ] adj contiguo, vecino

adjourn [ə'dʒəːn] vt aplazar ▷ vi suspenderse

adjust [ə'dʒʌst] vt (change) modificar; (clothing) arreglar; (machine) ajustar ▷ vi: **to ~ (to)** adaptarse (a); **adjustable** adj ajustable; **adjustment** n adaptación f; (to machine, prices) ajuste m

administer [əd'mɪnɪstə*] vt administrar; **administration** [-'treɪʃən] n (management) administración f; (government) gobierno; **administrative** [-trətɪv] adj administrativo

administrator [əd'mɪnɪstreɪtə*] n administrador(a) m/f

admiral ['ædmərəl] n almirante m

admiration [ædmə'reɪʃən] n admiración f

admire [əd'maɪə*] vt admirar; **admirer** n (fan) admirador(a) m/f

admission [əd'mɪʃən] n (to university, club) ingreso; (entry fee) entrada; (confession) confesión f

admit [əd'mɪt] vt (confess) confesar; (permit to enter) dejar entrar, dar entrada a; (to club, organization) admitir; (accept: defeat) reconocer; **to be ~ted to hospital** ingresar en el hospital; **admit to** vt fus confesarse culpable de; **admittance** n entrada; **admittedly** adv es cierto or verdad que

adolescent [ædəu'lɛsnt] adj, n adolescente mf

adopt [ə'dɔpt] vt adoptar; **adopted** adj adoptivo; **adoption** [ə'dɔpʃən] n adopción f

adore [ə'dɔː*] vt adorar

adorn [ə'dɔːn] vt adornar

Adriatic [eɪdrɪ'ætɪk] n: **the ~ (Sea)** el (Mar) Adriático

adrift [əˈdrɪft] *adv* a la deriva

adult [ˈædʌlt] *n* adulto/a ▷ *adj* (*grown-up*) adulto; (*for adults*) para adultos; **adult education** *n* educación *f* para adultos

adultery [əˈdʌltərɪ] *n* adulterio

advance [ədˈvɑːns] *n* (*progress*) adelanto, progreso; (*money*) anticipo, préstamo; (*Mil*) avance *m* ▷ *adj*: **~ booking** venta anticipada; **~ notice**, **~ warning** previo aviso ▷ *vt* (*money*) anticipar; (*theory, idea*) proponer (para la discusión) ▷ *vi* avanzar, adelantarse; **to make ~s (to sb)** hacer proposiciones (a algn); **in ~** por adelantado; **advanced** *adj* avanzado; (*Scol: studies*) adelantado

advantage [ədˈvɑːntɪdʒ] *n* (*also Tennis*) ventaja; **to take ~ of** (*person*) aprovecharse de; (*opportunity*) aprovechar

advent [ˈædvənt] *n* advenimiento; **A~** Adviento

adventure [ədˈventʃə*] *n* aventura; **adventurous** [-tʃərəs] *adj* atrevido; aventurero

adverb [ˈædvəːb] *n* adverbio

adversary [ˈædvəsərɪ] *n* adversario, contrario

adverse [ˈædvəːs] *adj* adverso, contrario

advert [ˈædvəːt] (BRIT) *n abbr* = **advertisement**

advertise [ˈædvətaɪz] *vi* (*in newspaper etc*) anunciar, hacer publicidad; **to ~ for** (*staff, accommodation etc*) buscar por medio de anuncios ▷ *vt* anunciar; **advertisement** [ədˈvəːtɪsmənt] *n* (*Comm*) anuncio; **advertiser** *n* anunciante *mf*; **advertising** *n* publicidad *f*, anuncios *mpl*; (*industry*) industria publicitaria

advice [ədˈvaɪs] *n* consejo, consejos *mpl*; (*notification*) aviso; **a piece of ~** un consejo; **to take legal ~** consultar con un abogado

advisable [ədˈvaɪzəbl] *adj* aconsejable, conveniente

advise [ədˈvaɪz] *vt* aconsejar; (*inform*): **to ~ sb of sth** informar a algn de algo; **to ~ sb against sth/doing sth** desaconsejar algo a algn/aconsejar a algn que no haga algo; **adviser, advisor** *n* consejero/a; (*consultant*) asesor(a) *m/f*; **advisory** *adj* consultivo

advocate [*vb* ˈædvəkeɪt, *n* -kɪt] *vt* abogar por ▷ *n* (*lawyer*) abogado/a; (*supporter*): **~ of** defensor(a) *m/f* de

Aegean [iːˈdʒiːən] *n*: **the ~ (Sea)** el (Mar) Egeo

aerial [ˈɛərɪəl] *n* antena ▷ *adj* aéreo

aerobics [ɛəˈrəubɪks] *n* aerobic *m*

aeroplane [ˈɛərəpleɪn] (BRIT) *n* avión *m*

aerosol [ˈɛərəsɔl] *n* aerosol *m*

affair [əˈfɛə*] *n* asunto; (*also*: **love ~**) aventura (amorosa)

affect [əˈfɛkt] *vt* (*influence*) afectar, influir en; (*afflict, concern*) afectar; (*move*) conmover; **affected** *adj* afectado;

affection *n* afecto, cariño; **affectionate** *adj* afectuoso, cariñoso

afflict [əˈflɪkt] *vt* afligir

affluent [ˈæfluənt] *adj* (*wealthy*) acomodado; **the ~ society** la sociedad opulenta

afford [əˈfɔːd] *vt* (*provide*) proporcionar; **can we ~ (to buy) it?** ¿tenemos bastante dinero para comprarlo?; **affordable** *adj* asequible

Afghanistan [æfˈgænɪstæn] *n* Afganistán *m*

afraid [əˈfreɪd] *adj*: **to be ~ of** (*person*) tener miedo a; (*thing*) tener miedo de; **to be ~ to** tener miedo de, temer; **I am ~ that** me temo que; **I am ~ not/so** lo siento, pero no/es así

Africa [ˈæfrɪkə] *n* África; **African** *adj*, *n* africano/a *m/f*; **African-American** *adj*, *n* afroamericano/a

after [ˈɑːftə*] *prep* (*time*) después de; (*place, order*) detrás de, tras ▷ *adv* después ▷ *conj* después (de) que; **what/who are you ~?** ¿qué/a quién busca usted?; **~ having done/ he left** después de haber hecho/después de que se marchó; **to name sb ~ sb** llamar a algn por algn; **it's twenty ~ eight** (US) son las ocho y veinte; **to ask ~ sb** preguntar por algn; **~ all** después de todo, al fin y al cabo; **~ you!** ¡pase usted!; **after-effects** *npl* consecuencias *fpl*, efectos *mpl*; **aftermath** *n* consecuencias *fpl*, resultados *mpl*; **afternoon** *n* tarde *f*; **after-shave (lotion)** *n* aftershave *m*; **aftersun (lotion/cream)** *n* loción *f*/crema para después del sol, aftersun *m*; **afterwards** (US **afterward**) *adv* después, más tarde

again [əˈgɛn] *adv* otra vez, de nuevo; **to do sth ~** volver a hacer algo; **~ and ~** una y otra vez

against [əˈgɛnst] *prep* (*in opposition to*) en contra de; (*leaning on, touching*) contra, junto a

age [eɪdʒ] *n* edad *f*; (*period*) época ▷ *vi* envejecer(se) ▷ *vt* envejecer; **she is 20 years of ~** tiene 20 años; **to come of ~** llegar a la mayoría de edad; **it's been ~s since I saw you** hace siglos que no te veo; **~d 10** de 10 años de edad; **age group** *n*: **to be in the same age group** tener la misma edad; **age limit** *n* edad *f* mínima (*or* máxima)

agency [ˈeɪdʒənsɪ] *n* agencia

agenda [əˈdʒɛndə] *n* orden *m* del día

■ Be careful not to translate **agenda** by the

Spanish word *agenda*.

agent ['eɪdʒənt] *n* agente *mf*;
(*Comm: holding concession*) representante *mf*,
delegado/a; (*Chem, fig*) agente *m*

aggravate ['ægrəveɪt] *vt* (*situation*)
agravar; (*person*) irritar

aggression [ə'greʃən] *n* agresión *f*

aggressive [ə'gresɪv] *adj* (*belligerent*)
agresivo; (*assertive*) enérgico

agile ['ædʒaɪl] *adj* ágil

agitated ['ædʒɪteɪtɪd] *adj* agitado

AGM *n abbr* (= *annual general meeting*)
asamblea anual

ago [ə'gəʊ] *adv*: **2 days ~** hace 2 días; **not
long ~** hace poco; **how long ~?** ¿hace cuánto
tiempo?

agony ['ægənɪ] *n* (*pain*) dolor *m* agudo;
(*distress*) angustia; **to be in ~** retorcerse
de dolor

agree [ə'griː] *vt* (*price, date*) acordar,
quedar en ▷ *vi* (*have same opinion*): **to ~
(with/that)** estar de acuerdo (con/que);
(*correspond*) coincidir, concordar; (*consent*)
acceder; **to ~ with** (*person*) estar de acuerdo
con, ponerse de acuerdo con; (: *food*) sentar
bien a; (*Ling*) concordar con; **to ~ to sth/
to do sth** consentir en algo/aceptar
hacer algo; **to ~ that** (*admit*) estar de
acuerdo en que; **agreeable** *adj* (*sensation*)
agradable; (*person*) simpático; (*willing*)
de acuerdo, conforme; **agreed** *adj* (*time,
place*) convenido; **agreement** *n* acuerdo;
(*contract*) contrato; **in agreement** de
acuerdo, conforme

agricultural [ægrɪ'kʌltʃərəl] *adj* agrícola

agriculture ['ægrɪkʌltʃə*] *n* agricultura

ahead [ə'hed] *adv* (*in front*) delante; (*into
the future*): **she had no time to think ~** no
tenía tiempo de hacer planes para el futuro;
~ of delante de; (*in advance of*) antes de; **~ of
time** antes de la hora; **go right** *or* **straight
~** (*direction*) siga adelante; (*permission*) hazlo
(or hágalo)

aid [eɪd] *n* ayuda, auxilio; (*device*) aparato
▷ *vt* ayudar, auxiliar; **in ~ of** a beneficio de

aide [eɪd] *n* (*person, also Mil*) ayudante *mf*

AIDS [eɪdz] *n abbr* (= *acquired immune
deficiency syndrome*) SIDA *m*

ailing ['eɪlɪŋ] *adj* (*person, economy*)
enfermizo

ailment ['eɪlmənt] *n* enfermedad *f*,
achaque *m*

aim [eɪm] *vt* (*gun, camera*) apuntar; (*missile,
remark*) dirigir; (*blow*) asestar ▷ *vi* (*also*: **take
~**) apuntar ▷ *n* (*in shooting: skill*) puntería;
(*objective*) propósito; meta; **to ~ at** (*with
weapon*) apuntar a; (*objective*) aspirar a,
pretender; **to ~ to do** tener la intención

de hacer

ain't [eɪnt] (*inf*) = **am not; aren't; isn't**

air [εə*] *n* aire *m*; (*appearance*) aspecto
▷ *vt* (*room*) ventilar; (*clothes, ideas*) airear
▷ *cpd* aéreo; **to throw sth into the ~**
(*ball etc*) lanzar algo al aire; **by ~** (*travel*)
en avión; **to be on the ~** (*Radio, TV*) estar
en antena; **airbag** *n* airbag *m inv*; **airbed**
(BRIT) *n* colchón *m* neumático; **airborne**
adj (*in the air*) en el aire; **as soon as the
plane was airborne** tan pronto como el
avión estuvo en el aire; **air-conditioned**
adj climatizado; **air conditioning** *n* aire
acondicionado; **aircraft** *n inv* avión *m*;
airfield *n* campo de aviación; **Air Force** *n*
fuerzas *fpl* aéreas, aviación *f*; **air hostess**
(BRIT) *n* azafata; **airing cupboard** *n* (BRIT)
armario *m* para oreo; **airlift** *n* puente
m aéreo; **airline** *n* línea aérea; **airliner**
n avión *m* de pasajeros; **airmail** *n*: **by
airmail** por avión; **airplane** (US) *n* avión *m*;
airport *n* aeropuerto; **air raid** *n* ataque *m*
aéreo; **airsick** *adj*: **to be airsick** marearse
(en avión); **airspace** *n* espacio aéreo;
airstrip *n* pista de aterrizaje; **air terminal**
n terminal *f*; **airtight** *adj* hermético;
air-traffic controller *n* controlador(a) *m/f*
aéreo/a; **airy** *adj* (*room*) bien ventilado;
(*fig: manner*) desenfadado

aisle [aɪl] *n* (*of church*) nave *f*; (*of theatre,
supermarket*) pasillo; **aisle seat** *n* (*on plane*)
asiento de pasillo

ajar [ə'dʒɑː*] *adj* entreabierto

à la carte [ælæ'kɑːt] *adv* a la carta

alarm [ə'lɑːm] *n* (*in shop, bank*) alarma;
(*anxiety*) inquietud *f* ▷ *vt* asustar, inquietar;
alarm call *n* (*in hotel etc*) alarma; **alarm
clock** *n* despertador *m*; **alarmed** *adj*
(*person*) alarmado, asustado; (*house, car etc*)
con alarma; **alarming** *adj* alarmante

Albania [æl'beɪnɪə] *n* Albania

albeit [ɔːl'biːɪt] *conj* aunque

album ['ælbəm] *n* álbum *m*; (*L.P.*) elepé *m*

alcohol ['ælkəhɒl] *n* alcohol *m*; **alcohol-
free** *adj* sin alcohol; **alcoholic** [-'hɒlɪk] *adj*,
n alcohólico/a *m/f*

alcove ['ælkəʊv] *n* nicho, hueco

ale [eɪl] *n* cerveza

alert [ə'lɜːt] *adj* (*attentive*) atento; (*to
danger, opportunity*) alerta ▷ *n* alerta *m*,
alarma ▷ *vt* poner sobre aviso; **to be on the
~** (*also Mil*) estar alerta *or* sobre aviso

algebra ['ældʒɪbrə] *n* álgebra

Algeria [æl'dʒɪərɪə] *n* Argelia

alias ['eɪlɪəs] *adv* alias, conocido por ▷ *n*
(*of criminal*) apodo; (*of writer*) seudónimo

alibi ['ælɪbaɪ] *n* coartada

alien ['eɪlɪən] *n* (*foreigner*) extranjero/a;

(*extraterrestrial*) extraterrestre *mf* ▷ *adj:* **~ to** ajeno a; **alienate** *vt* enajenar, alejar

alight [ə'laɪt] *adj* ardiendo; (*eyes*) brillante ▷ *vi* (*person*) apearse, bajar; (*bird*) posarse

align [ə'laɪn] *vt* alinear

alike [ə'laɪk] *adj* semejantes, iguales ▷ *adv* igualmente, del mismo modo; **to look ~** parecerse

alive [ə'laɪv] *adj* vivo; (*lively*) alegre

○ **KEYWORD**

all [ɔːl] *adj* (*sg*) todo/a; (*pl*) todos/as; **all day** todo el día; **all night** toda la noche; **all men** todos los hombres; **all five came** vinieron los cinco; **all the books** todos los libros; **all his life** toda su vida
▷ *pron* 1 todo; **I ate it all, I ate all of it** me lo comí todo; **all of us went** fuimos todos; **all the boys went** fueron todos los chicos; **is that all?** ¿eso es todo?, ¿algo más?; (*in shop*) ¿algo más?, ¿alguna cosa más?
2 (*in phrases*): **above all** sobre todo; por encima de todo; **after all** después de todo; **at all: not at all** (*in answer to question*) en absoluto; (*in answer to thanks*) ¡de nada!, ¡no hay de qué!; **I'm not at all tired** no estoy nada cansado/a; **anything at all will do** cualquier cosa viene bien; **all in all** a fin de cuentas
▷ *adv*: **all alone** completamente solo/a; **it's not as hard as all that** no es tan difícil como lo pintas; **all the more/the better** tanto más/mejor; **all but** casi; **the score is 2 all** están empatados a 2

Allah ['ælə] *n* Alá *m*

allegation [ælɪ'geɪʃən] *n* alegato

alleged [ə'ledʒd] *adj* supuesto, presunto; **allegedly** *adv* supuestamente, según se afirma

allegiance [ə'liːdʒəns] *n* lealtad *f*

allergic [ə'lə:dʒɪk] *adj:* **~ to** alérgico a

allergy ['ælədʒɪ] *n* alergia

alleviate [ə'liːvɪeɪt] *vt* aliviar

alley ['ælɪ] *n* callejuela

alliance [ə'laɪəns] *n* alianza

allied ['ælaɪd] *adj* aliado

alligator ['ælɪgeɪtə*] *n* (*Zool*) caimán *m*

all-in (*BRIT*) ['ɔːlɪn] *adj, adv* (*charge*) todo incluido

allocate ['æləkeɪt] *vt* (*money etc*) asignar

allot [ə'lɒt] *vt* asignar

all-out ['ɔːlaut] *adj* (*effort etc*) supremo

allow [ə'lau] *vt* permitir, dejar; (*a claim*) admitir; (*sum, time etc*) dar, conceder; (*concede*): **to ~ that** reconocer que; **to ~ sb to do** permitir a algn hacer; **he is ~ed to**

... se le permite ...; **allow for** *vt fus* tener en cuenta; **allowance** *n* subvención *f*; (*welfare payment*) subsidio, pensión *f*; (*pocket money*) dinero de bolsillo; (*tax allowance*) desgravación *f*; **to make allowances for** (*person*) disculpar a; (*thing*) tener en cuenta

all right *adv* bien; (*as answer*) ¡conforme!, ¡está bien!

ally ['ælaɪ] *n* aliado/a ▷ *vt:* **to ~ o.s. with** aliarse con

almighty [ɔːl'maɪtɪ] *adj* todopoderoso; (*row etc*) imponente

almond ['ɑːmənd] *n* almendra

almost ['ɔːlməust] *adv* casi

alone [ə'ləun] *adj, adv* solo; **to leave sb ~** dejar a algn en paz; **to leave sth ~** no tocar algo, dejar algo sin tocar; **let ~ ...** y mucho menos ...

along [ə'lɒŋ] *prep* a lo largo de, por
▷ *adv:* **is he coming ~ with us?** ¿viene con nosotros?; **he was limping ~** iba cojeando; **~ with** junto con; **all ~** (*all the time*) desde el principio; **alongside** *prep* al lado de ▷ *adv* al lado

aloof [ə'luːf] *adj* reservado ▷ *adv:* **to stand ~** mantenerse apartado

aloud [ə'laud] *adv* en voz alta

alphabet ['ælfəbet] *n* alfabeto

Alps [ælps] *npl:* **the ~** los Alpes

already [ɔːl'redɪ] *adv* ya

alright ['ɔːl'raɪt] (*BRIT*) *adv* = **all right**

also ['ɔːlsəu] *adv* también, además

altar ['ɔːltə*] *n* altar *m*

alter ['ɔːltə*] *vt* cambiar, modificar
▷ *vi* cambiar; **alteration** [ɔːltə'reɪʃən] *n* cambio; (*to clothes*) arreglo; (*to building*) arreglos *mpl*

alternate [*adj* ɔl'tə:nɪt, *vb* 'ɔːltə:neɪt] *adj* (*actions etc*) alternativo; (*events*) alterno; (*US*) = **alternative** ▷ *vi:* **to ~ (with)** alternar (con); **on ~ days** un día sí y otro no

alternative [ɔl'tə:nətɪv] *adj* alternativo ▷ *n* alternativa; **~ medicine** medicina alternativa; **alternatively** *adv:* **alternatively one could ...** por otra parte se podría ...

although [ɔːl'ðəu] *conj* aunque

altitude ['æltɪtjuːd] *n* altura

altogether [ɔːltə'geðə*] *adv* completamente, del todo; (*on the whole*) en total, en conjunto

aluminium [ælju'mɪnɪəm] (*BRIT*), **aluminum** [ə'luːmɪnəm] (*US*) *n* aluminio

always ['ɔːlweɪz] *adv* siempre

Alzheimer's (disease) ['æltshaɪməz-] *n* enfermedad *f* de Alzheimer

am [æm] *vb see* **be**

amalgamate [ə'mælgəmeɪt] *vi*

amalgamarse ▷ vt amalgamar, unir
amass [ə'mæs] vt amontonar, acumular
amateur ['æmətə*] n aficionado/a,
amateur mf
amaze [ə'meɪz] vt asombrar, pasmar; **to
be ~d (at)** quedar pasmado (de); **amazed**
adj asombrado; **amazement** n asombro,
sorpresa; **amazing** adj extraordinario;
(fantastic) increíble
Amazon ['æməzən] n (Geo) Amazonas m
ambassador [æm'bæsədə*] n
embajador(a) m/f
amber ['æmbə*] n ámbar m; **at ~** (BRIT Aut)
en el amarillo
ambiguous [æm'bɪgjuəs] adj ambiguo
ambition [æm'bɪʃən] n ambición f;
ambitious [-fəs] adj ambicioso
ambulance ['æmbjuləns] n ambulancia
ambush ['æmbuʃ] n emboscada ▷ vt
tender una emboscada a
amen [ɑː'mɛn] excl amén
amend [ə'mɛnd] vt enmendar; **to make
~s** dar cumplida satisfacción; **amendment**
n enmienda
amenities [ə'miːnɪtɪz] npl comodidades
fpl
America [ə'mɛrɪkə] n (USA) Estados mpl
Unidos; **American** adj, n norteamericano/a;
estadounidense mf; **American football** n
(BRIT) fútbol m americano
amicable ['æmɪkəbl] adj amistoso,
amigable
amid(st) [ə'mɪd(st)] prep entre, en medio
de
ammunition [æmju'nɪʃən] n municiones
fpl
amnesty ['æmnɪstɪ] n amnistía
among(st) [ə'mʌŋ(st)] prep entre, en
medio de
amount [ə'maunt] n (gen) cantidad f; (of
bill etc) suma, importe m ▷ vi: **to ~ to** sumar;
(be same as) equivaler a, significar
amp(ère) ['æmp(ɛə*)] n amperio
ample ['æmpl] adj (large) grande;
(abundant) abundante; (enough) bastante,
suficiente
amplifier ['æmplɪfaɪə*] n amplificador m
amputate ['æmpjuteɪt] vt amputar
Amtrak ['æmtræk] (US) n empresa nacional
de ferrocarriles de los EEUU
amuse [ə'mjuːz] vt divertir; (distract)
distraer, entretener; **amusement** n
diversión f; (pastime) pasatiempo; (laughter)
risa; **amusement arcade** n salón m de
juegos; **amusement park** n parque m de
atracciones
amusing [ə'mjuːzɪŋ] adj divertido
an [æn] indef art see **a**

anaemia [ə'niːmɪə] (US **anemia**) n
anemia
anaemic [ə'niːmɪk] (US **anemic**) adj
anémico; (fig) soso, insípido
anaesthetic [ænɪs'θɛtɪk] (US **anesthetic**)
n anestesia
analog(ue) ['ænələg] adj (computer,
watch) analógico
analogy [ə'nælədʒɪ] n analogía
analyse ['ænəlaɪz] (US **analyze**) vt
analizar; **analysis** [ə'næləsɪs] (pl **analyses**)
n análisis m inv; **analyst** [-lɪst] n (political
analyst, psychoanalyst) analista mf
analyze ['ænəlaɪz] (US) vt = **analyse**
anarchy ['ænəkɪ] n anarquía, desorden m
anatomy [ə'nætəmɪ] n anatomía
ancestor ['ænsɪstə*] n antepasado
anchor ['æŋkə*] n ancla, áncora ▷ vi
(also: **to drop ~**) anclar ▷ vt anclar; **to
weigh ~** levar anclas
anchovy ['æntʃəvɪ] n anchoa
ancient ['eɪnʃənt] adj antiguo
and [ænd] conj y; (before i-, hi- + consonant)
e; **men ~ women** hombres y mujeres;
father ~ son padre y hijo; **trees ~ grass**
árboles y hierba; **~ so on** sucesivamente, y así
sucesivamente; **try ~ come** procura venir;
he talked ~ talked habló sin parar; **better ~
better** cada vez mejor
Andes ['ændiːz] npl: **the ~** los Andes
Andorra [æn'dɔːrə] n Andorra
anemia etc [ə'niːmɪə] (US) = **anaemia** etc
anesthetic [ænɪs'θɛtɪk] (US) =
anaesthetic
angel ['eɪndʒəl] n ángel m
anger ['æŋgə*] n cólera
angina [æn'dʒaɪnə] n angina (del pecho)
angle ['æŋgl] n ángulo; **from their ~** desde
su punto de vista
angler ['æŋglə*] n pescador(a) m/f (de
caña)
Anglican ['æŋglɪkən] adj, n anglicano/a
m/f
angling ['æŋglɪŋ] n pesca con caña
angrily ['æŋgrɪlɪ] adv coléricamente,
airadamente
angry ['æŋgrɪ] adj enfadado, airado;
(wound) inflamado; **to be ~ with sb/at sth**
estar enfadado con algn/por algo; **to get ~**
enfadarse, enojarse
anguish ['æŋgwɪʃ] n (physical) tormentos
mpl; (mental) angustia
animal ['ænɪməl] n animal m; (pej: person)
bestia ▷ adj animal
animated [-meɪtɪd] adj animado
animation [ænɪ'meɪʃən] n animación f
aniseed ['ænɪsiːd] n anís m
ankle ['æŋkl] n tobillo

annex [n 'æneks, vb æ'neks] n (BRIT: also: **~e**: building) edificio anexo ▷ vt (territory) anexionar

anniversary [ænɪ'vəːsərɪ] n aniversario

announce [ə'nauns] vt anunciar; **announcement** n anuncio; (official) declaración f; **announcer** n (Radio) locutor(a) m/f; (TV) presentador(a) m/f

annoy [ə'nɔɪ] vt molestar, fastidiar; **don't get ~ed!** ¡no se enfade!; **annoying** adj molesto, fastidioso; (person) pesado

annual ['ænjuəl] adj anual ▷ n (Bot) anual m; (book) anuario; **annually** adv anualmente, cada año

annum ['ænəm] n see **per**

anonymous [ə'nɔnɪməs] adj anónimo

anorak ['ænəræk] n anorak m

anorexia [ænə'reksɪə] n (Med: also: ~ **nervosa**) anorexia

anorexic [ænə'reksɪk] adj, n anoréxico/a m/f

another [ə'nʌðə*] adj (one more, a different one) otro ▷ pron otro; see **one**

answer ['ɑːnsə*] n contestación f, respuesta; (to problem) solución f ▷ vi contestar, responder ▷ vt (reply to) contestar a, responder a; (problem) resolver; (prayer) escuchar; **in ~ to your letter** contestando or en contestación a su carta; **to ~ the phone** contestar or coger el teléfono; **to ~ the bell** or **the door** acudir a la puerta; **answer back** vi replicar, ser respondón/ona; **answerphone** n (esp BRIT) contestador m (automático)

ant [ænt] n hormiga

Antarctic [ænt'ɑːktɪk] n: **the ~** el Antártico

antelope ['æntɪləup] n antílope m

antenatal ['æntɪ'neɪtl] adj antenatal, prenatal

antenna [æn'tɛnə, pl -niː] (pl **antennae**) n antena

anthem ['ænθəm] n: **national ~** himno nacional

anthology [æn'θɔlədʒɪ] n antología

anthrax ['ænθræks] n ántrax m

anthropology [ænθrə'pɔlədʒɪ] n antropología

anti [æntɪ] prefix anti; **antibiotic** [-baɪ'ɔtɪk] n antibiótico; **antibody** ['æntɪbɔdɪ] n anticuerpo

anticipate [æn'tɪsɪpeɪt] vt prever; (expect) esperar, contar con; (look forward to) esperar con ilusión; (do first) anticiparse a, adelantarse a; **anticipation** [-'peɪʃən] n (expectation) previsión f; (eagerness) ilusión f, expectación f

anticlimax [æntɪ'klaɪmæks] n decepción f

anticlockwise [æntɪ'klɔkwaɪz] (BRIT) adv en dirección contraria a la de las agujas del reloj

antics ['æntɪks] npl gracias fpl

anti: antidote ['æntɪdəut] n antídoto; **antifreeze** ['æntɪfriːz] n anticongelante m; **antihistamine** [-'hɪstəmiːn] n antihistamínico; **antiperspirant** ['æntɪpəːspɪrənt] n antitranspirante m

antique [æn'tiːk] n antigüedad f ▷ adj antiguo; **antique shop** n tienda de antigüedades

antiseptic [æntɪ'septɪk] adj, n antiséptico

antisocial [æntɪ'səuʃəl] adj antisocial

antivirus [æntɪ'vaɪərəs] adj (program, software) antivirus inv

antlers ['æntləz] npl cuernas fpl, cornamenta sg

anxiety [æŋ'zaɪətɪ] n inquietud f; (Med) ansiedad f; **~ to do** deseo de hacer

anxious ['æŋkʃəs] adj inquieto, preocupado; (worrying) preocupante; (keen): **to be ~ to do** tener muchas ganas de hacer

○ **KEYWORD**

any ['enɪ] adj **1** (in questions etc) algún/alguna; **have you any butter/children?** ¿tienes mantequilla/hijos?; **if there are any tickets left** si quedan billetes, si queda algún billete

2 (with negative): **I haven't any money/books** no tengo dinero/libros

3 (no matter which) cualquier; **any excuse will do** valdrá or servirá cualquier excusa; **choose any book you like** escoge el libro que quieras

4 (in phrases): **in any case** de todas formas, en cualquier caso; **any day now** cualquier día (de estos); **at any moment** en cualquier momento, de un momento a otro; **at any rate** en todo caso; **any time: come (at) any time** ven cuando quieras; **he might come (at) any time** podría llegar de un momento a otro

▷ pron **1** (in questions etc): **have you got any?** ¿tienes alguno(s)/a(s)?; **can any of you sing?** ¿sabe cantar alguno de vosotros/ustedes?

2 (with negative): **I haven't any (of them)** no tengo ninguno

3 (no matter which one(s)): **take any of those books (you like)** toma el libro que quieras de ésos

▷ adv **1** (in questions etc): **do you want any**

more soup/sandwiches? ¿quieres más sopa/bocadillos?; **are you feeling any better?** ¿te sientes algo mejor? 2 (with negative): **I can't hear him any more** ya no le oigo; **don't wait any longer** no esperes más

any: anybody pron cualquiera; (in interrogative sentences) alguien; (in negative sentences): **I don't see anybody** no veo a nadie; **if anybody should phone ...** si llama alguien ...; **anyhow** adv (at any rate) de todos modos, de todas formas; (haphazard): **do it anyhow you like** hazlo como quieras; **she leaves things just anyhow** deja las cosas como quiera or de cualquier modo; **I shall go anyhow** de todos modos iré; **anyone** pron = **anybody**; **anything** pron (in questions etc) algo, alguna cosa; (with negative) nada; **can you see anything?** ¿ves algo?; **if anything happens to me ...** no importa cuándo, cuando quiera; **anyway** adv (at any rate) de todos modos, de todas formas; **I shall go anyway** iré de todos modos; (besides): **anyway, I couldn't come even if I wanted to** además, no podría venir aunque quisiera; **why are you phoning, anyway?** ¿entonces, por qué llamas?, ¿por qué llamas, pues?; **anywhere** adv (in questions etc): **can you see him anywhere?** ¿le ves por algún lado?; **are you going anywhere?** ¿vas a algún sitio?; (with negative): **I can't see him anywhere** no le veo por ninguna parte; **anywhere in the world** (no matter where) en cualquier parte (del mundo); **put the books down anywhere** deja los libros donde quieras

apart [ə'pɑːt] adv (aside) aparte; (situation): **~ (from)** separado (de); (movement): **to pull ~** separar; **10 miles ~** separados por 10 millas; **to take ~** desmontar; **~ from** prep aparte de

apartment [ə'pɑːtmənt] n (US) piso (SP), departamento (LAM), apartamento; (room) cuarto; **apartment building** (US) n edificio de apartamentos

apathy ['æpəθɪ] n apatía, indiferencia

ape [eɪp] n mono ⊳ vt imitar, remedar

aperitif [ə'pɛrɪtɪf] n aperitivo

aperture ['æpətʃjuə*] n rendija,

resquicio; (Phot) abertura

APEX ['eɪpɛks] n abbr (= Advanced Purchase Excursion Fare) tarifa f APEX

apologize [ə'pɒlədʒaɪz] vi: **to ~ (for sth to sb)** disculparse (con algn de algo)

apology [ə'pɒlədʒɪ] n disculpa, excusa

▌ Be careful not to translate **apology** by the Spanish word apología.

apostrophe [ə'pɒstrəfɪ] n apóstrofo

appal [ə'pɔːl] (US **appall**) vt horrorizar, espantar; **appalling** adj espantoso; (awful) pésimo

apparatus [æpə'reɪtəs] n (equipment) equipo; (organization) aparato; (in gymnasium) aparatos mpl

apparent [ə'pærənt] adj aparente; (obvious) evidente; **apparently** adv por lo visto, al parecer

appeal [ə'piːl] vi (Law) apelar ⊳ n (Law) apelación f; (request) llamamiento; (plea) petición f; (charm) atractivo; **to ~ for** reclamar; **to ~ to** (be attractive to) atraer; **it doesn't ~ to me** no me atrae, no me llama la atención; **appealing** adj (attractive) atractivo

appear [ə'pɪə*] vi aparecer, presentarse; (Law) comparecer; (publication) salir (a luz), publicarse; (seem) parecer; **to ~ on TV/in "Hamlet"** salir por la tele/hacer un papel en "Hamlet"; **it would ~ that** parecería que; **appearance** n aparición f; (look) apariencia, aspecto

appendices [ə'pɛndɪsiːz] npl of **appendix**

appendicitis [əpɛndɪ'saɪtɪs] n apendicitis f

appendix [ə'pɛndɪks] (pl **appendices**) n apéndice m

appetite ['æpɪtaɪt] n apetito; (fig) deseo, anhelo

appetizer ['æpɪtaɪzə*] n (drink) aperitivo; (food) tapas fpl (SP)

applaud [ə'plɔːd] vt, vi aplaudir

applause [ə'plɔːz] n aplausos mpl

apple ['æpl] n manzana; **apple pie** n pastel m de manzana, pay m de manzana (LAM)

appliance [ə'plaɪəns] n aparato

applicable [ə'plɪkəbl] adj (relevant): **to be ~ (to)** referirse (a)

applicant [ə'plɪkənt] n candidato/a; solicitante mf

application [æplɪ'keɪʃən] n aplicación f; (for a job etc) solicitud f, petición f; **application form** n solicitud f

apply [ə'plaɪ] vt (paint etc) poner; (law etc: put into practice) poner en vigor ⊳ vi: **to ~ to** (ask) dirigirse a; (be applicable) ser aplicable a; **to ~ for** (permit, grant, job) solicitar; **to ~ o.s. to** aplicarse a, dedicarse a

appoint [ə'pɔɪnt] *vt* (*to post*) nombrar a
▌Be careful not to translate **appoint** by the Spanish word *apuntar*.

appointment *n* (*with client*) cita; (*act*) nombramiento; (*post*) puesto; (*at hairdresser etc*): **to have an appointment** tener hora; **to make an appointment (with sb)** citarse (con algn)

appraisal [ə'preɪzl] *n* valoración *f*

appreciate [ə'priːʃɪeɪt] *vt* apreciar, tener en mucho; (*be grateful for*) agradecer; (*be aware*) comprender ▷ *vi* (*Comm*) aumentar(se) en valor; **appreciation** [-'eɪʃən] *n* apreciación *f*; (*gratitude*) reconocimiento, agradecimiento; (*Comm*) aumento en valor

apprehension [æprɪ'hɛnʃən] *n* (*fear*) aprensión *f*

apprehensive [æprɪ'hɛnsɪv] *adj* aprensivo

apprentice [ə'prɛntɪs] *n* aprendiz(a) *m/f*

approach [ə'prəʊtʃ] *vi* acercarse ▷ *vt* acercarse a; (*ask, apply to*) dirigirse a; (*situation, problem*) abordar ▷ *n* acercamiento; (*access*) acceso; (*to problem, situation*): **~ (to)** actitud *f* (ante)

appropriate [*adj* ə'prəʊprɪɪt, *vb* ə'prəʊprɪeɪt] *adj* apropiado, conveniente ▷ *vt* (*take*) apropiarse de

approval [ə'pruːvəl] *n* aprobación *f*, visto bueno; (*permission*) consentimiento; **on ~** (*Comm*) a prueba

approve [ə'pruːv] *vt* aprobar; **approve of** *vt fus* (*thing*) aprobar; (*person*): **they don't approve of her** (ella) no les parece bien

approximate [ə'prɒksɪmɪt] *adj* aproximado; **approximately** *adv* aproximadamente, más o menos

Apr. *abbr* (= *April*) abr

apricot ['eɪprɪkɒt] *n* albaricoque *m*, chabacano (*MEX*), damasco (*RPL*)

April ['eɪprəl] *n* abril *m*; **April Fools' Day** *n* el primero de abril, ≈ día *m* de los Inocentes (*28 December*)

apron ['eɪprən] *n* delantal *m*

apt [æpt] *adj* acertado, apropiado; (*likely*): **~ to do** propenso a hacer

aquarium [ə'kwɛərɪəm] *n* acuario

Aquarius [ə'kwɛərɪəs] *n* Acuario

Arab ['ærəb] *adj*, *n* árabe *mf*

Arabia [ə'reɪbɪə] *n* Arabia; **Arabian** *adj* árabe; **Arabic** ['ærəbɪk] *adj* árabe; (*numerals*) arábigo ▷ *n* árabe *m*

arbitrary ['ɑːbɪtrərɪ] *adj* arbitrario

arbitration [ɑːbɪ'treɪʃən] *n* arbitraje *m*

arc [ɑːk] *n* arco

arcade [ɑː'keɪd] *n* (*round a square*)

soportales *mpl*; (*shopping mall*) galería comercial

arch [ɑːtʃ] *n* arco; (*of foot*) arco del pie ▷ *vt* arquear

archaeology [ɑːkɪ'ɔlədʒɪ] (*us* **archeology**) *n* arqueología

archbishop [ɑːtʃ'bɪʃəp] *n* arzobispo

archeology [ɑːkɪ'ɔlədʒɪ] (*us*) = **archaeology**

architect ['ɑːkɪtɛkt] *n* arquitecto/a; **architectural** [ɑːkɪ'tɛktʃərəl] *adj* arquitectónico; **architecture** *n* arquitectura

archive ['ɑːkaɪv] *n* (*often pl: also Comput*) archivo

Arctic ['ɑːktɪk] *adj* ártico ▷ *n*: **the ~** el Ártico

are [ɑː*] *vb see* be

area ['ɛərɪə] *n* área, región *f*; (*part of place*) zona; (*Math etc*) área, superficie *f*; (*in room: e.g. dining area*) parte *f*; (*of knowledge, experience*) campo; **area code** (*us*) *n* (*Tel*) prefijo

arena [ə'riːnə] *n* estadio; (*of circus*) pista

aren't [ɑːnt] = **are not**

Argentina [ɑːdʒən'tiːnə] *n* Argentina; **Argentinian** [-'tɪnɪən] *adj*, *n* argentino/a *m/f*

arguably ['ɑːgjuəblɪ] *adv* posiblemente

argue ['ɑːgjuː] *vi* (*quarrel*) discutir, pelearse; (*reason*) razonar, argumentar; **to ~ that** sostener que

argument ['ɑːgjumənt] *n* discusión *f*, pelea; (*reasons*) argumento

Aries ['ɛərɪz] *n* Aries *m*

arise [ə'raɪz] (*pt* **arose**, *pp* **arisen**) *vi* surgir, presentarse

arithmetic [ə'rɪθmətɪk] *n* aritmética

arm [ɑːm] *n* brazo ▷ *vt* armar; **arms** *npl* armas *fpl*; **~ in ~** cogidos del brazo; **armchair** ['ɑːmtʃɛə*] *n* sillón *m*, butaca

armed [ɑːmd] *adj* armado; **armed robbery** *n* robo a mano armada

armour ['ɑːmə*] (*us* **armor**) *n* armadura; (*Mil: tanks*) blindaje *m*

armpit ['ɑːmpɪt] *n* sobaco, axila

armrest ['ɑːmrɛst] *n* apoyabrazos *m inv*

army ['ɑːmɪ] *n* ejército; (*fig*) multitud *f*

A road *n* (*BRIT*) ≈ carretera *f* nacional

aroma [ə'rəumə] *n* aroma *m*, fragancia; **aromatherapy** *n* aromaterapia

arose [ə'rəuz] *pt of* arise

around [ə'raund] *adv* alrededor; (*in the area*): **there is no one else ~** no hay nadie más por aquí ▷ *prep* alrededor de

arouse [ə'rauz] *vt* despertar; (*anger*) provocar

arrange [ə'reɪndʒ] *vt* arreglar, ordenar;

(*organize*) organizar; **to ~ to do sth** quedar
en hacer algo; **arrangement** n arreglo;
(*agreement*) acuerdo; **arrangements** npl
(*preparations*) preparativos mpl

array [əˈreɪ] n: **~ of** (*things*) serie f de;
(*people*) conjunto de

arrears [əˈrɪəz] npl atrasos mpl; **to be in ~
with one's rent** estar retrasado en el pago
del alquiler

arrest [əˈrest] vt detener; (*sb's attention*)
llamar ▷ n detención f; **under ~** detenido

arrival [əˈraɪvəl] n llegada; **new ~** recién
llegado/a; (*baby*) recién nacido

arrive [əˈraɪv] vi llegar; (*baby*) nacer; **arrive
at** vt fus (*decision, solution*) llegar a

arrogance [ˈærəgəns] n arrogancia,
prepotencia (LAM)

arrogant [ˈærəgənt] adj arrogante

arrow [ˈærəʊ] n flecha

arse [ɑːs] (BRIT: inf!) n culo, trasero

arson [ˈɑːsn] n incendio premeditado

art [ɑːt] n arte m; (*skill*) destreza; **art
college** n escuela f de Bellas Artes

artery [ˈɑːtərɪ] n arteria

art gallery n pinacoteca; (*saleroom*)
galería de arte

arthritis [ɑːˈθraɪtɪs] n artritis f

artichoke [ˈɑːtɪtʃəʊk] n alcachofa;
Jerusalem ~ aguaturma

article [ˈɑːtɪkl] n artículo

articulate [adj ɑːˈtɪkjʊlɪt, vb ɑːˈtɪkjuleɪt]
adj claro, bien expresado ▷ vt expresar

artificial [ɑːtɪˈfɪʃəl] adj artificial; (*affected*)
afectado

artist [ˈɑːtɪst] n artista mf; (Mus) intérprete
mf; **artistic** [ɑːˈtɪstɪk] adj artístico

art school n escuela de bellas artes

○ **KEYWORD**

as [æz] conj **1** (*referring to time*)
cuando, mientras; a medida que; **as the
years went by** con el paso de los años; **he
came in as I was leaving** entró cuando me
marchaba; **as
from tomorrow** desde or a partir de
mañana

2 (*in comparisons*): **as big as** tan grande
como; **twice as big as** el doble de grande
que; **as much money/many books as**
tanto dinero/tantos libros como; **as soon
as** en cuanto

3 (*since, because*) como, ya que; **he left
early as he had to be home by 10** se fue
temprano ya que tenía que estar en casa
a las 10

4 (*referring to manner, way*): **do as you wish**
haz lo que quieras; **as she said** como dijo;

he gave it to me as a present me lo dio
de regalo

5 (*in the capacity of*): **he works as a barman**
trabaja de barman; **as chairman of the
company, he ...** como presidente de la
compañía ...

6 (*concerning*): **as for** or **to that** por or en lo
que respecta a eso

7: **as if** or **though** como si; **he looked as
if he was ill** parecía como si estuviera
enfermo, tenía aspecto de enfermo; *see also*
long; **such**; **well**

a.s.a.p. abbr (= *as soon as possible*) cuanto
antes

asbestos [æzˈbestəs] n asbesto, amianto

ascent [əˈsent] n subida; (*slope*) cuesta,
pendiente f

ash [æʃ] n ceniza; (*tree*) fresno

ashamed [əˈʃeɪmd] adj avergonzado,
apenado (LAM); **to be ~ of** avergonzarse de

ashore [əˈʃɔː*] adv en tierra; (*swim etc*) a
tierra

ashtray [ˈæʃtreɪ] n cenicero

Ash Wednesday n miércoles m de Ceniza

Asia [ˈeɪʃə] n Asia; **Asian** adj, n asiático/a
m/f

aside [əˈsaɪd] adv a un lado ▷ n aparte m

ask [ɑːsk] vt (*question*) preguntar; (*invite*)
invitar; **to ~ sb sth/to do sth** preguntar
algo a algn/pedir a algn que haga algo; **to
~ sb about sth** preguntar algo a algn; **to
~ (sb) a question** hacer una pregunta (a
algn); **to ~ sb out to dinner** invitar a cenar a
algn; **ask for** vt fus pedir; (*trouble*) buscar

asleep [əˈsliːp] adj dormido; **to fall ~**
dormirse, quedarse dormido

asparagus [əsˈpærəgəs] n (*plant*)
espárrago; (*food*) espárragos mpl

aspect [ˈæspekt] n aspecto, apariencia;
(*direction in which a building etc faces*)
orientación f

aspirations [æspəˈreɪʃənz] npl
aspiraciones fpl; (*ambition*) ambición f

aspire [əsˈpaɪə*] vi: **to ~ to** aspirar a,
ambicionar

aspirin [ˈæsprɪn] n aspirina

ass [æs] n asno, burro; (*inf: idiot*) imbécil
mf; (US: inf!) culo, trasero

assassin [əˈsæsɪn] n asesino/a;
assassinate vt asesinar

assault [əˈsɔːlt] n asalto; (*Law*) agresión f
▷ vt asaltar, atacar; (*sexually*) violar

assemble [əˈsembl] vt reunir, juntar;
(*Tech*) montar ▷ vi reunirse, juntarse

assembly [əˈsemblɪ] n reunión f,
asamblea; (*parliament*) parlamento;
(*construction*) montaje m

assert [ə'sə:t] vt afirmar; (authority) hacer valer; **assertion** [-fən] n afirmación f

assess [ə'sɛs] vt valorar, calcular; (tax, damages) fijar; (for tax) gravar; **assessment** n valoración f; (for tax) gravamen m

asset ['æsɛt] n ventaja; **assets** npl (Comm) activo; (property, funds) fondos mpl

assign [ə'saɪn] vt: **to ~ (to)** (date) fijar (para); (task) asignar (a); (resources) destinar (a); **assignment** n tarea

assist [ə'sɪst] vt ayudar; **assistance** n ayuda, auxilio; **assistant** n ayudante mf; (BRIT: also: **shop assistant**) dependiente/a m/f

associate [adj, n ə'səʊʃɪɪt, vb ə'səʊʃɪeɪt] adj asociado ▷ n (at work) colega mf ▷ vt asociar; (ideas) relacionar ▷ vi: **to ~ with sb** tratar con algn

association [əsəʊsɪ'eɪʃən] n asociación f

assorted [ə'sɔ:tɪd] adj surtido, variado

assortment [ə'sɔ:tmənt] n (of shapes, colours) surtido; (of books) colección f; (of people) mezcla

assume [ə'sju:m] vt suponer; (responsibilities) asumir; (attitude) adoptar, tomar

assumption [ə'sʌmpʃən] n suposición f, presunción f; (of power etc) toma

assurance [ə'ʃuərəns] n garantía, promesa; (confidence) confianza, aplomo; (insurance) seguro

assure [ə'ʃuə*] vt asegurar

asterisk ['æstərɪsk] n asterisco

asthma ['æsmə] n asma

astonish [ə'stɒnɪʃ] vt asombrar, pasmar; **astonished** adj estupefacto, pasmado; **to be astonished (at)** asombrarse (de); **astonishing** adj asombroso, pasmoso; **I find it astonishing that ...** me asombra or pasma que ...; **astonishment** n asombro, sorpresa

astound [ə'staund] vt asombrar, pasmar

astray [ə'streɪ] adv: **to go ~** extraviarse; **to lead ~** (morally) llevar por mal camino

astrology [æs'trɒlədʒɪ] n astrología

astronaut ['æstrənɔ:t] n astronauta mf

astronomer [əs'trɒnəmə*] n astrónomo/a

astronomical [æstrə'nɒmɪkəl] adj astronómico

astronomy [əs'trɒnəmɪ] n astronomía

astute [əs'tju:t] adj astuto

asylum [ə'saɪləm] n (refuge) asilo; (mental hospital) manicomio

○ **KEYWORD**

at [æt] prep **1** (referring to position) en; (direction) a; **at the top** en lo

alto; **at home/school** en casa/la escuela; **to look at sth/sb** mirar algo/a algn

2 (referring to time): **at 4 o'clock** a las 4; **at night** por la noche; **at Christmas** en Navidad; **at times** a veces

3 (referring to rates, speed etc): **at £1 a kilo** a una libra el kilo; **two at a time** de dos en dos; **at 50 km/h** a 50 km/h

4 (referring to manner): **at a stroke** de un golpe; **at peace** en paz

5 (referring to activity): **to be at work** estar trabajando; (in the office etc) estar en el trabajo; **to play at cowboys** jugar a los vaqueros; **to be good at sth** ser bueno en algo

6 (referring to cause): **shocked/surprised/ annoyed at sth** asombrado/sorprendido/ fastidiado por algo; **I went at his suggestion** fui a instancias suyas

7 (symbol) arroba

ate [eɪt] pt of **eat**

atheist ['eɪθɪɪst] n ateo/a

Athens ['æθɪnz] n Atenas

athlete ['æθli:t] n atleta mf

athletic [æθ'lɛtɪk] adj atlético; **athletics** n atletismo

Atlantic [ət'læntɪk] adj atlántico ▷ n: **the ~ (Ocean)** el (Océano) Atlántico

atlas ['ætləs] n atlas m inv

A.T.M. n abbr (= automated telling machine) cajero automático

atmosphere ['ætməsfɪə*] n atmósfera; (of place) ambiente m

atom ['ætəm] n átomo; **atomic** [ə'tɒmɪk] adj atómico; **atom(ic) bomb** n bomba atómica

A to Z® n (map) callejero

atrocity [ə'trɒsɪtɪ] n atrocidad f

attach [ə'tætʃ] vt (fasten) atar; (join) unir, sujetar; (document, letter) adjuntar; (importance etc) dar, conceder; **to be ~ed to sb/sth** (to like) tener cariño a algn/ algo; **attachment** n (tool) accesorio; (Comput) archivo, documento adjunto; (love): **attachment (to)** apego (a)

attack [ə'tæk] vt (Mil) atacar; (criminal) agredir, asaltar; (criticize) criticar; (task) emprender ▷ n ataque m, asalto; (on sb's life) atentado; (fig: criticism) crítica; (of illness) ataque m; **heart ~** infarto (de miocardio); **attacker** n agresor(a) m/f, asaltante mf

attain [ə'teɪn] vt (also: **~ to**) alcanzar; (achieve) lograr, conseguir

attempt [ə'tɛmpt] n tentativa, intento; (attack) atentado ▷ vt intentar

attend [ə'tɛnd] vt asistir a; (patient)

atender; **attend to** vt fus ocuparse de;
(*customer, patient*) atender a; **attendance**
n asistencia, presencia; (*people present*)
concurrencia; **attendant** n ayudante mf;
(*in garage etc*) encargado/a ▷ adj (*dangers*)
concomitante

attention [ə'tɛnʃən] n atención f; (*care*)
atenciones fpl ▷ excl (*Mil*) ¡firme(s)!; **for the**
~ of ... (*Admin*) atención ...

attic ['ætɪk] n desván m

attitude ['ætɪtjuːd] n actitud f;
(*disposition*) disposición f

attorney [ə'tɜːnɪ] n (*lawyer*) abogado/a;
Attorney General n (*BRIT*) ≈ Presidente
m del Consejo del Poder Judicial (*SP*); (*US*) ≈
ministro de Justicia

attract [ə'trækt] vt atraer; (*sb's attention*)
llamar; **attraction** [ə'trækʃən] n encanto;
(*gen pl: amusements*) diversiones fpl; (*Physics*)
atracción f; (*fig: towards sb, sth*) atractivo;
attractive adj guapo; (*interesting*)
atrayente

attribute [n 'ætrɪbjuːt, vb ə'trɪbjuːt] n
atributo ▷ vt: **to ~ sth to** atribuir algo a

aubergine ['əubəʒiːn] (*BRIT*) n berenjena;
(*colour*) morado

auburn ['ɔːbən] adj color castaño rojizo

auction ['ɔːkʃən] n (*also: sale by ~*)
subasta ▷ vt subastar

audible ['ɔːdɪbl] adj audible, que se puede
oír

audience ['ɔːdɪəns] n público; (*Radio*)
radioescuchas mpl; (*TV*) telespectadores
mpl; (*interview*) audiencia

audit ['ɔːdɪt] vt revisar, intervenir

audition [ɔː'dɪʃən] n audición f

auditor ['ɔːdɪtə*] n interventor(a) m/f,
censor(a) m/f de cuentas

auditorium [ɔːdɪ'tɔːrɪəm] n auditorio

Aug. abbr (=August) ag

August ['ɔːgəst] n agosto

aunt [ɑːnt] n tía; **auntie** n diminutive of
aunt; aunty n diminutive of **aunt**

au pair ['əu'pɛə*] n (*also: ~ girl*) (chica)
au pair f

aura ['ɔːrə] n aura; (*atmosphere*) ambiente
m

austerity [ɔ'stɛrɪtɪ] n austeridad f

Australia [ɔs'treɪlɪə] n Australia;
Australian adj, n australiano/a m/f

Austria ['ɔstrɪə] n Austria; **Austrian** adj, n
austríaco/a m/f

authentic [ɔː'θɛntɪk] adj auténtico

author ['ɔːθə*] n autor(a) m/f

authority [ɔː'θɔrɪtɪ] n autoridad f; (*official*
permission) autorización f; **the authorities**
npl las autoridades

authorize ['ɔːθəraɪz] vt autorizar

auto ['ɔːtəu] (*US*) n coche m (*SP*), carro
(*LAM*), automóvil m

auto: autobiography [ɔːtəbaɪ'ɔgrəfɪ] n
autobiografía; **autograph**
['ɔːtəgrɑːf] n autógrafo ▷ vt (*photo etc*)
dedicar; (*programme*) firmar; **automatic**
[ɔːtə'mætɪk] adj automático ▷ n
(*gun*) pistola automática; (*car*) coche
m automático; **automatically** adv
automáticamente; **automobile**
['ɔːtəməbiːl] (*US*) n coche m (*SP*), carro
(*LAM*), automóvil m; **autonomous**
[ɔː'tɔnəməs] adj autónomo; **autonomy**
[ɔː'tɔnəmɪ] n autonomía

autumn ['ɔːtəm] n otoño

auxiliary [ɔːg'zɪlɪərɪ] adj, n auxiliar mf

avail [ə'veɪl] vt: **to ~ o.s. of** aprovechar(se)
de ▷ n: **to no ~** en vano, sin resultado

availability [əveɪlə'bɪlɪtɪ] n
disponibilidad f

available [ə'veɪləbl] adj disponible;
(*unoccupied*) libre; (*person: unattached*) soltero
y sin compromiso

avalanche ['ævəlɑːnʃ] n alud m,
avalancha

Ave. abbr =**avenue**

avenue ['ævənjuː] n avenida; (*fig*) camino

average ['ævərɪdʒ] n promedio, término
medio ▷ adj medio, de término medio;
(*ordinary*) regular, corriente ▷ vt sacar un
promedio de; **on ~** por regla general

avert [ə'vɜːt] vt prevenir; (*blow*) desviar;
(*one's eyes*) apartar

avid ['ævɪd] adj ávido

avocado [ævə'kɑːdəu] n (*also BRIT: ~ pear*)
aguacate m, palta (*SC*)

avoid [ə'vɔɪd] vt evitar, eludir

await [ə'weɪt] vt esperar, aguardar

awake [ə'weɪk] (*pt* awoke, *pp* awoken *or*
awaked) adj despierto ▷ vt despertar ▷ vi
despertarse; **to be ~** estar despierto

award [ə'wɔːd] n premio; (*Law: damages*)
indemnización f ▷ vt otorgar, conceder;
(*Law: damages*) adjudicar

aware [ə'wɛə*] adj: **~ (of)** consciente
(de); **to become ~ of/that** (*realize*) darse
cuenta de/de que; (*learn*) enterarse de/de
que; **awareness** n conciencia; (*knowledge*)
conocimiento

away [ə'weɪ] adv fuera; (*movement*): **she**
went ~ se marchó; **far ~** lejos; **two**
kilometres ~ a dos kilómetros de distancia;
two hours ~ by car a dos horas en coche;
the holiday was two weeks ~ faltaban
dos semanas para las vacaciones; **he's ~**
for a week estará ausente una semana;
to take ~ (from) quitar (a); (*subtract*)
substraer (de); **to work/pedal ~** seguir

trabajando/pedaleando; **to fade ~** (*colour*)
desvanecerse; (*sound*) apagarse
awe [ɔ:] *n* admiración f respetuosa;
awesome ['ɔ:səm] (*us*) *adj* (*excellent*)
formidable
awful ['ɔ:fəl] *adj* horroroso; (*quantity*): **an
~ lot (of)** cantidad (de); **awfully** *adv* (*very*)
terriblemente
awkward ['ɔ:kwəd] *adj* desmañado,
torpe; (*shape*) incómodo; (*embarrassing*)
delicado, difícil
awoke [ə'wəuk] *pt of* **awake**
awoken [ə'wəukən] *pp of* **awake**
axe [æks] (*us* **ax**) *n* hacha ▷ *vt* (*project*)
cortar; (*jobs*) reducir
axle ['æksl] *n* eje *m*, árbol *m*
ay(e) [aɪ] *excl* sí
azalea [ə'zeɪlɪə] *n* azalea

B [bi:] *n* (*Mus*) si *m*
B.A. *abbr* = **Bachelor of Arts**
baby ['beɪbɪ] *n* bebé *mf*; (*us: inf: darling*)
mi amor; **baby carriage** (*us*) *n* cochecito;
baby-sit *vi* hacer de canguro; **baby-sitter**
n canguro/a; **baby wipe** *n* toallita húmeda
(*para bebés*)
bachelor ['bætʃələ*] *n* soltero; **B~ of Arts/
Science** licenciado/a en Filosofía y Letras/
Ciencias
back [bæk] *n* (*of person*) espalda; (*of
animal*) lomo; (*of hand*) dorso; (*as opposed
to front*) parte f de atrás; (*of chair*) respaldo;
(*of page*) reverso; (*of book*) final *m*; (*Football*)
defensa *m*; (*of crowd*): **the ones at the ~**
los del fondo ▷ *vt* (*candidate: also:* **~ up**)
respaldar, apoyar; (*horse: at races*) apostar
a; (*car*) dar marcha atrás a or con ▷ *vi* (*car
etc*) ir (*or salir or entrar*) marcha atrás
▷ *adj* (*payment, rent*) atrasado; (*seats,
wheels*) de atrás ▷ *adv* (*not forward*) (hacia)
atrás; (*returned*): **he's ~** está de vuelta,
ha vuelto; **he ran ~** volvió corriendo;
(*restitution*): **throw the ball ~** devuelve la
pelota; **can I have it ~?** ¿me lo devuelve?;
(*again*): **he called ~** llamó de nuevo; **back
down** *vi* echarse atrás; **back out** *vi* (*of
promise*) volverse atrás; **back up** *vt* (*person*)
apoyar, respaldar; (*theory*) defender;
(*Comput*) hacer una copia preventiva
or de reserva; **backache** *n* dolor *m* de
espalda; **backbencher** (*BRIT*) *n* *miembro del
parlamento sin cargo relevante*; **backbone** *n*
columna vertebral; **back door** *n* puerta
f trasera; **backfire** *vi* (*Aut*) petardear;
(*plans*) fallar, salir mal; **backgammon** *n*
backgammon *m*; **background** *n* fondo; (*of
events*) antecedentes *mpl*; (*basic knowledge*)
bases *fpl*; (*experience*) conocimientos *mpl*,
educación *f*; **family background** origen *m*,
antecedentes *mpl*; **backing** *n* (*fig*) apoyo,

respaldo; **backlog** n: **backlog of work** trabajo atrasado; **backpack** n mochila; **backpacker** n mochilero/a; **backslash** n pleca, barra inversa; **backstage** adv entre bastidores; **backstroke** n espalda; **backup** adj suplementario; (Comput) de reserva ▷ n (support) apoyo; (also: **backup file**) copia preventiva or de reserva; **backward** adj (person, country) atrasado; **backwards** adv hacia atrás; (read a list) al revés; (fall) de espaldas; **backyard** n traspatio

bacon ['beɪkən] n tocino, beicon m

bacteria [bæk'tɪərɪə] npl bacterias fpl

bad [bæd] adj malo; (mistake, accident) grave; (food) podrido, pasado; **his ~ leg** su pierna lisiada; **to go ~** (food) pasarse

badge [bædʒ] n insignia; (policeman's) chapa, placa

badger ['bædʒə*] n tejón m

badly ['bædlɪ] adv mal; **to reflect ~ on sb** influir negativamente en la reputación de algn; **~ wounded** gravemente herido; **he needs it ~** le hace gran falta; **to be ~ off (for money)** andar mal de dinero

bad-mannered ['bæd'mænəd] adj mal educado

badminton ['bædmɪntən] n bádminton m

bad-tempered ['bæd'tempəd] adj de mal genio or carácter; (temporarily) de mal humor

bag [bæg] n bolsa; (handbag) bolso; (satchel) mochila; (case) maleta; **~s of** (inf) un montón de; **baggage** n equipaje m; **baggage allowance** n límite m de equipaje; **baggage reclaim** n recogida de equipajes; **baggy** adj amplio; **bagpipes** npl gaita

bail [beɪl] n fianza ▷ vt (prisoner: gen: grant bail to) poner en libertad bajo fianza; (boat: also: **~ out**) achicar; **on ~** (prisoner) bajo fianza; **to ~ sb out** obtener la libertad de algn bajo fianza

bait [beɪt] n cebo ▷ vt poner cebo en; (tease) tomar el pelo a

bake [beɪk] vt cocer (al horno) ▷ vi cocerse; **baked beans** npl judías fpl en salsa de tomate; **baked potato** n patata al horno; **baker** n panadero/a; **bakery** n panadería; (for cakes) pastelería; **baking** n (act) amasar m; (batch) hornada; **baking powder** n levadura (en polvo)

balance ['bæləns] n equilibrio; (Comm: sum) balance m; (remainder) resto; (scales) balanza ▷ vt equilibrar; (budget) nivelar; (account) saldar; (make equal) equilibrar; **~ of trade/payments** balanza de comercio/pagos; **balanced** adj (personality, diet) equilibrado; (report) objetivo; **balance sheet** n balance m

balcony ['bælkənɪ] n (open) balcón m; (closed) galería; (in theatre) anfiteatro

bald [bɔːld] adj calvo; (tyre) liso

Balearics [bælɪ'ærɪks] npl: **the ~** las Baleares

ball [bɔːl] n pelota; (football) balón m; (of wool, string) ovillo; (dance) baile m; **to play ~** (fig) cooperar

ballerina [bælə'riːnə] n bailarina

ballet ['bæleɪ] n ballet m; **ballet dancer** n bailarín/ina m/f

balloon [bə'luːn] n globo

ballot ['bælət] n votación f

ballpoint (pen) ['bɔːlpɔɪnt-] n bolígrafo

ballroom ['bɔːlrum] n salón m de baile

Baltic ['bɔːltɪk] n: **the ~ (Sea)** el (Mar) Báltico

bamboo [bæm'buː] n bambú m

ban [bæn] n prohibición f, proscripción f ▷ vt prohibir, proscribir

banana [bə'nɑːnə] n plátano, banana (LAM), banano (CAM)

band [bænd] n grupo; (strip) faja, tira; (stripe) lista; (Mus: jazz) orquesta; (: rock) grupo; (Mil) banda

bandage ['bændɪdʒ] n venda, vendaje m ▷ vt vendar

Band-Aid® ['bændeɪd] (US) n tirita

bandit ['bændɪt] n bandido

bang [bæŋ] n (of gun, exhaust) estallido, detonación f; (of door) portazo; (blow) golpe m ▷ vt (door) cerrar de golpe; (one's head) golpear ▷ vi estallar; (door) cerrar de golpe

Bangladesh [bɑːŋglə'deʃ] n Bangladesh m

bangle ['bæŋgl] n brazalete m, ajorca

bangs [bæŋz] (US) npl flequillo

banish ['bænɪʃ] vt desterrar

banister(s) ['bænɪstə(z)] n(pl) barandilla, pasamanos m inv

banjo ['bændʒəu] (pl **~es** or **~s**) n banjo

bank [bæŋk] n (Comm) banco; (of river, lake) ribera, orilla; (of earth) terraplén m ▷ vi (Aviat) ladearse; **bank on** vt fus contar con; **bank account** n cuenta de banco; **bank balance** n saldo; **bank card** n tarjeta bancaria; **bank charges** npl comisión fsg; **banker** n banquero; **bank holiday** n (BRIT) día m festivo or de fiesta; **banking** n banca; **bank manager** n director(a) m/f (de sucursal) de banco; **banknote** n billete m de banco

---

● **BANK HOLIDAY**
●
● El término **bank holiday** se aplica en el
● Reino Unido a todo día festivo oficial
● en el que cierran bancos y comercios.

● Los más importantes son en Navidad,
● Semana Santa, finales de mayo y
● finales de agosto y, al contrario que
● en los países de tradición católica, no
● coinciden necesariamente con una
● celebración religiosa.

bankrupt ['bæŋkrʌpt] *adj* quebrado,
insolvente; **to go ~** hacer bancarrota; **to be
~** estar en quiebra; **bankruptcy** *n* quiebra
bank statement *n* balance *m or* detalle
m de cuenta
banner ['bænə*] *n* pancarta
bannister(s) ['bænɪstə(z)] *n(pl)* =
banister(s)
banquet ['bæŋkwɪt] *n* banquete *m*
baptism ['bæptɪzəm] *n* bautismo; *(act)*
bautizo
baptize [bæp'taɪz] *vt* bautizar
bar [bɑ:*] *n (pub)* bar *m; (counter)* mostrador
m; (rod) barra; *(of window, cage)* reja; *(of soap)*
pastilla; *(of chocolate)* tableta; *(fig: hindrance)*
obstáculo; *(prohibition)* proscripción *f; (Mus)*
barra ▷ *vt (road)* obstruir; *(person)* excluir;
(activity) prohibir; **the B~** *(Law)* la abogacía;
behind ~s entre rejas; **~ none** sin excepción
barbaric [bɑ:'bærɪk] *adj* bárbaro
barbecue ['bɑ:bɪkju:] *n* barbacoa
barbed wire ['bɑ:bd-] *n* alambre *m* de
púas
barber ['bɑ:bə*] *n* peluquero, barbero;
barber's (shop) *(us* **barber (shop))** *n*
peluquería
bar code *n* código de barras
bare [bɛə*] *adj* desnudo; *(trees)* sin hojas;
(necessities etc) básico ▷ *vt* desnudar; *(teeth)*
enseñar; **barefoot** *adj, adv* descalzo; **barely**
adv apenas
bargain ['bɑ:gɪn] *n* pacto, negocio; *(good
buy)* ganga ▷ *vi* negociar; *(haggle)* regatear;
into the ~ además, por añadidura; **bargain
for** *vt fus*: **he got more than he bargained
for** le resultó peor de lo que esperaba
barge [bɑ:dʒ] *n* barcaza; **barge in**
vi irrumpir; *(interrupt: conversation)*
interrumpir
bark [bɑ:k] *n (of tree)* corteza; *(of dog)*
ladrido ▷ *vi* ladrar
barley ['bɑ:lɪ] *n* cebada
barmaid ['bɑ:meɪd] *n* camarera
barman ['bɑ:mən] *(irreg)* *n* camarero,
barman *m*
barn [bɑ:n] *n* granero
barometer [bə'rɔmɪtə*] *n* barómetro
baron ['bærən] *n* barón *m; (press baron etc)*
magnate *m;* **baroness** *n* baronesa
barracks ['bærəks] *npl* cuartel *m*
barrage ['bærɑ:ʒ] *n (Mil)* descarga,

bombardeo; *(dam)* presa; *(of criticism)* lluvia,
aluvión *m*
barrel ['bærəl] *n* barril *m; (of gun)* cañón *m*
barren ['bærən] *adj* estéril
barrette [bə'rɛt] *(us)* *n* pasador *m (LAM,
SP)*, broche *m (MEX)*
barricade [bærɪ'keɪd] *n* barricada
barrier ['bærɪə*] *n* barrera
barring ['bɑ:rɪŋ] *prep* excepto, salvo
barrister ['bærɪstə*] *(BRIT)* *n* abogado/a
barrow ['bærəu] *n (cart)* carretilla (de
mano)
bartender ['bɑ:tɛndə*] *(us)* *n* camarero,
barman *m*
base [beɪs] *n* base *f* ▷ *vt*: **to ~ sth on** basar
or fundar algo en ▷ *adj* bajo, infame
baseball ['beɪsbɔ:l] *n* béisbol *m;* **baseball
cap** *n* gorra *f* de béisbol
basement ['beɪsmənt] *n* sótano
bases[1] ['beɪsi:z] *npl of* **basis**
bases[2] ['beɪsɪz] *npl of* **base**
bash [bæʃ] *(inf)* *vt* golpear
basic ['beɪsɪk] *adj* básico; **basically** *adv*
fundamentalmente, en el fondo; *(simply)*
sencillamente; **basics** *npl*: **the basics** los
fundamentos
basil ['bæzl] *n* albahaca
basin ['beɪsn] *n* cuenco, tazón *m; (Geo)*
cuenca; *(also:* **wash~**) lavabo
basis ['beɪsɪs] *(pl* **bases**) *n* base *f;* **on a
part-time/trial ~** a tiempo parcial/a
prueba
basket ['bɑ:skɪt] *n* cesta, cesto; canasta;
basketball *n* baloncesto
bass [beɪs] *n (Mus: instrument)* bajo; *(double
bass)* contrabajo; *(singer)* bajo
bastard ['bɑ:stəd] *n* bastardo; *(inf!)* hijo
de puta (!)
bat [bæt] *n (Zool)* murciélago; *(for ball
games)* palo; *(BRIT: for table tennis)* pala
▷ *vt*: **he didn't ~ an eyelid** ni pestañeó
batch [bætʃ] *n (of bread)* hornada; *(of letters
etc)* lote *m*
bath [bɑ:θ, *pl* bɑ:ðz] *n (action)* baño;
(bathtub) bañera *(sp)*, tina *(LAM)*, bañadera
(RPL) ▷ *vt* bañar; **to have a ~** bañarse,
tomar un baño; *see also* **baths**
bathe [beɪð] *vi* bañarse ▷ *vt (wound)* lavar
bathing ['beɪðɪŋ] *n* el bañarse; **bathing
costume** *(us* **bathing suit)** *n* traje *m* de
baño
bath: bathrobe *n (man's)* batín *m;*
(woman's) bata; **bathroom** *n* (cuarto de)
baño; **baths** [bɑ:ðz] *npl (also:* **swimming
baths)** piscina; **bath towel** *n* toalla de
baño; **bathtub** *n* bañera
baton ['bætən] *n (Mus)* batuta; *(Athletics)*
testigo; *(weapon)* porra

batter ['bætə*] vt maltratar; (*rain etc*) azotar ▷ n masa (para rebozar); **battered** adj (*hat, pan*) estropeado

battery ['bætərɪ] n (*Aut*) batería; (*of torch*) pila; **battery farming** n cría intensiva

battle ['bætl] n batalla; (*fig*) lucha ▷ vi luchar; **battlefield** n campo m de batalla

bay [beɪ] n (*Geo*) bahía; **B~ of Biscay** = mar Cantábrico; **to hold sb at ~** mantener a algn a raya

bazaar [bə'zɑ:*] n bazar m; (*fete*) venta con fines benéficos

B. & B. n abbr = **bed and breakfast**; (*place*) pensión f; (*terms*) cama y desayuno

BBC n abbr (= British Broadcasting Corporation) cadena de radio y televisión estatal británica

B.C. adv abbr (= before Christ) a. de C.

○ **KEYWORD**

be [bi:] (*pt* **was, were**, *pp* **been**) aux vb
1 (*with present participle: forming continuous tenses*): **what are you doing?** ¿qué estás haciendo?, ¿qué haces?; **they're coming tomorrow** vienen mañana; **I've been waiting for you for hours** llevo horas esperándote

2 (*with pp: forming passives*) ser (*but often replaced by active or reflexive constructions*); **to be murdered** ser asesinado; **the box had been opened** habían abierto la caja; **the thief was nowhere to be seen** no se veía al ladrón por ninguna parte

3 (*in tag questions*): **it was fun, wasn't it?** fue divertido, ¿no? *or* ¿verdad?; **he's good-looking, isn't he?** es guapo, ¿no te parece?; **she's back again, is she?** entonces, ¿ha vuelto?

4 (+*to* +*infin*): **the house is to be sold** (*necessity*) hay que vender la casa; (*future*) van a vender la casa; **he's not to open it** no tiene que abrirlo ▷ vb +complement
1 (*with n or num complement, but see also 3, 4, 5 and impers vb below*) ser; **he's a doctor** es médico; **2 and 2 are 4** 2 y 2 son 4

2 (*with adj complement: expressing permanent or inherent quality*) ser; (: *expressing state seen as temporary or reversible*) estar; **I'm English** soy inglés/esa; **she's tall/pretty** es alta/bonita; **he's young** es joven; **be careful/good/quiet** ten cuidado/pórtate bien/cállate; **I'm tired** estoy cansado/a; **it's dirty** está sucio/a

3 (*of health*) estar; **how are you?** ¿cómo estás?; **he's very ill** está muy enfermo; **I'm better now** ya estoy mejor

4 (*of age*) tener; **how old are you?** ¿cuántos años tienes?; **I'm sixteen (years old)** tengo dieciséis años

5 (*cost*) costar; ser; **how much was the meal?** ¿cuánto fue *or* costó la comida?; **that'll be £5.75, please** son £5.75, por favor; **this shirt is £17** esta camisa cuesta £17 ▷ vi **1** (*exist, occur etc*) existir, haber; **the best singer that ever was** el mejor cantante que existió jamás; **is there a God?** ¿hay un Dios?, ¿existe Dios?; **be that as it may** sea como sea; **so be it** así sea

2 (*referring to place*) estar; **I won't be here tomorrow** no estaré aquí mañana

3 (*referring to movement*): **where have you been?** ¿dónde has estado? ▷ impers vb **1** (*referring to time*): **it's 5 o'clock** son las 5; **it's the 28th of April** estamos a 28 de abril

2 (*referring to distance*): **it's 10 km to the village** el pueblo está a 10 km

3 (*referring to the weather*): **it's too hot/cold** hace demasiado calor/frío; **it's windy today** hace viento hoy

4 (*emphatic*): **it's me** soy yo; **it was Maria who paid the bill** fue María la que pagó la cuenta

beach [bi:tʃ] n playa ▷ vt varar

beacon ['bi:kən] n (*lighthouse*) faro; (*marker*) guía

bead [bi:d] n cuenta; (*of sweat etc*) gota; **beads** npl (*necklace*) collar m

beak [bi:k] n pico

beam [bi:m] n (*Arch*) viga, travesaño; (*of light*) rayo, haz m de luz ▷ vi brillar; (*smile*) sonreír

bean [bi:n] n judía; **runner/broad ~** habichuela/haba; **coffee ~** grano de café; **beansprouts** npl brotes mpl de soja

bear [bɛə*] (*pt* **bore**, *pp* **borne**) n oso ▷ vt (*weight etc*) llevar; (*cost*) pagar; (*responsibility*) tener; (*endure*) soportar, aguantar; (*children*) parir, tener; (*fruit*) dar ▷ vi: **to ~ right/left** torcer a la derecha/izquierda

beard [bɪəd] n barba

bearer ['bɛərə*] n portador(a) m/f

bearing ['bɛərɪŋ] n porte m, comportamiento; (*connection*) relación f

beast [bi:st] n bestia; (*inf*) bruto, salvaje m

beat [bi:t] (*pt* **~**, *pp* **beaten**) n (*of heart*) latido; (*Mus*) ritmo, compás m; (*of policeman*) ronda ▷ vt pegar, golpear; (*eggs*) batir; (*defeat: opponent*) vencer, derrotar; (: *record*) sobrepasar ▷ vi (*heart*) latir; (*drum*) redoblar; (*rain, wind*) azotar; **off the ~en track** aislado; **to ~ it** (*inf*) largarse; **beat up** vt (*attack*) dar una paliza a; **beating** n paliza

beautiful ['bju:tɪful] adj precioso,

hermoso, bello; **beautifully** adv maravillosamente

beauty ['bju:tɪ] n belleza; **beauty parlour** (US **beauty parlor**) n salón m de belleza; **beauty salon** n salón m de belleza; **beauty spot** n (Tourism) lugar m pintoresco

beaver ['bi:və*] n castor m

became [bɪ'keɪm] pt of **become**

because [bɪ'kɔz] conj porque; **~ of** debido a, a causa de

beckon ['bɛkən] vt (also: **~ to**) llamar con señas

become [bɪ'kʌm] (pt **became**, pp **~**) vt (suit) favorecer, sentar bien a ▷ vi (+ n) hacerse, llegar a ser; (+ adj) ponerse, volverse; **to ~ fat** engordar

bed [bɛd] n cama; (of flowers) macizo; (of coal, clay) capa; (of river) lecho; (of sea) fondo; **to go to ~** acostarse; **bed and breakfast** n (place) pensión f; (terms) cama y desayuno; **bedclothes** npl ropa de cama; **bedding** n ropa de cama; **bed linen** n (BRIT) ropa f de cama

● **BED AND BREAKFAST**
●
● Se llama **bed and breakfast** a una forma
● de alojamiento, en el campo o la ciudad,
● que ofrece cama y desayuno a precios
● inferiores a los de un hotel. El servicio
● se suele anunciar con carteles en los
● que a menudo se usa únicamente la
● abreviatura **B. & B.**

bed: bedroom n dormitorio; **bedside** n: **at the bedside of** a la cabecera de; **bedside lamp** n lámpara de noche; **bedside table** n mesilla de noche; **bedsit(ter)** (BRIT)' n cuarto de alquiler; **bedspread** n cubrecama m, colcha; **bedtime** n hora de acostarse

bee [bi:] n abeja

beech [bi:tʃ] n haya

beef [bi:f] n carne f de vaca; **roast ~** rosbif m; **beefburger** n hamburguesa; **Beefeater** n alabardero de la Torre de Londres

been [bi:n] pp of **be**

beer [bɪə*] n cerveza; **beer garden** (BRIT) n terraza f de verano, jardín m (de un bar)

beet [bi:t] (US) n (also: **red ~**) remolacha

beetle ['bi:tl] n escarabajo

beetroot ['bi:tru:t] (BRIT) n remolacha

before [bɪ'fɔ:*] prep (of time) antes de; (of space) delante de ▷ conj antes (de) que ▷ adv antes, anteriormente; delante, adelante; **~ going** antes de marcharse; **~ she goes** antes de que se vaya; **the week**

~ la semana anterior; **I've never seen it ~** no lo he visto nunca; **beforehand** adv de antemano, con anticipación

beg [bɛg] vi pedir limosna ▷ vt pedir, rogar; (entreat) suplicar; **to ~ sb to do sth** rogar a algn que haga algo; see also **pardon**

began [bɪ'gæn] pt of **begin**

beggar ['bɛgə*] n mendigo/a

begin [bɪ'gɪn] (pt **began**, pp **begun**) vt, vi empezar, comenzar; **to ~ doing** or **to do sth** empezar a hacer algo; **beginner** n principiante mf; **beginning** n principio, comienzo

begun [bɪ'gʌn] pp of **begin**

behalf [bɪ'hɑ:f] n: **on ~ of** en nombre de, por; (for benefit of) en beneficio de; **on my/his ~** por mí/él

behave [bɪ'heɪv] vi (person) portarse, comportarse; (well: also: **~ o.s.**) portarse bien; **behaviour** (US **behavior**) n comportamiento, conducta

behind [bɪ'haɪnd] prep detrás de; (supporting): **to be ~ sb** apoyar a algn ▷ adv detrás, por detrás, atrás ▷ n trasero; **to be ~ (schedule)** ir retrasado; **~ the scenes** (fig) entre bastidores

beige [beɪʒ] adj color beige

Beijing ['beɪ'dʒɪŋ] n Pekín m

being ['bi:ɪŋ] n ser m; (existence): **in ~** existente; **to come into ~** aparecer

belated [bɪ'leɪtɪd] adj atrasado, tardío

belch [bɛltʃ] vi eructar ▷ vt (gen: belch out: smoke etc) arrojar

Belgian ['bɛldʒən] adj, n belga mf

Belgium ['bɛldʒəm] n Bélgica

belief [bɪ'li:f] n opinión f; (faith) fe f

believe [bɪ'li:v] vt, vi creer; **to ~ in** creer en; **believer** n partidario/a; (Rel) creyente mf, fiel mf

bell [bɛl] n campana; (small) campanilla; (on door) timbre m

bellboy ['bɛlbɔɪ] (BRIT) n botones m inv

bellhop ['bɛlhɔp] (US) n = **bellboy**

bellow ['bɛləu] vi bramar; (person) rugir

bell pepper n (esp US) pimiento, pimentón m (LAM)

belly ['bɛlɪ] n barriga, panza; **belly button** (inf) n ombligo

belong [bɪ'lɔŋ] vi: **to ~ to** pertenecer a; (club etc) ser socio de; **this book ~s here** este libro va aquí; **belongings** npl pertenencias fpl

beloved [bɪ'lʌvɪd] adj querido/a

below [bɪ'ləu] prep bajo, debajo de; (less than) inferior a ▷ adv abajo, (por) debajo; **see ~** véase más abajo

belt [bɛlt] n cinturón m; (Tech) correa, cinta ▷ vt (thrash) pegar con correa; **beltway** (US)

n (*Aut*) carretera de circunvalación
bemused [bɪ'mjuːzd] *adj* perplejo
bench [bɛntʃ] *n* banco; (*BRIT Pol*): **the Government/Opposition ~es** (los asientos de) los miembros del Gobierno/ de la Oposición; **the B~** (*Law: judges*) magistratura
bend [bɛnd] (*pt, pp* **bent**) *vt* doblar ▷ *vi* inclinarse ▷ *n* (*BRIT: in road, river*) curva; (*in pipe*) codo; **bend down** *vi* inclinarse, doblarse; **bend over** *vi* inclinarse
beneath [bɪ'niːθ] *prep* bajo, debajo de; (*unworthy*) indigno de ▷ *adv* abajo, (por) debajo
beneficial [bɛnɪ'fɪʃəl] *adj* beneficioso
benefit [ˈbɛnɪfɪt] *n* beneficio; (*allowance of money*) subsidio ▷ *vt* beneficiar ▷ *vi*: **he'll ~ from it** le sacará provecho
benign [bɪ'naɪn] *adj* benigno; (*smile*) afable
bent [bɛnt] *pt, pp of* **bend** ▷ *n* inclinación *f* ▷ *adj*: **to be ~ on** estar empeñado en
bereaved [bɪ'riːvd] *npl*: **the ~** los íntimos de una persona afligidos por su muerte
beret [ˈbɛreɪ] *n* boina
Berlin [bəːˈlɪn] *n* Berlín
Bermuda [bəːˈmjuːdə] *n* las Bermudas
berry [ˈbɛrɪ] *n* baya
berth [bəːθ] *n* (*bed*) litera; (*cabin*) camarote *m*; (*for ship*) amarradero *m* ▷ *vi* atracar, amarrar
beside [bɪ'saɪd] *prep* junto a, al lado de; **to be ~ o.s. with anger** estar fuera de sí; **that's ~ the point** eso no tiene nada que ver; **besides** *adv* además ▷ *prep* además de
best [bɛst] *adj* (el/la) mejor ▷ *adv* (lo) mejor; **the ~ part of** (*quantity*) la mayor parte de; **at ~** en el mejor de los casos; **to make the ~ of sth** sacar el mejor partido de algo; **to do one's ~** hacer todo lo posible; **to the ~ of my knowledge** que yo sepa; **to the ~ of my ability** como mejor puedo; **best-before date** *n* fecha de consumo preferente; **best man** (*irreg*) *n* padrino de boda; **bestseller** *n* éxito de librería, bestseller *m*
bet [bɛt] (*pt, pp ~ or ~ted*) *n* apuesta ▷ *vt*: **to ~ money on** apostar dinero por ▷ *vi* apostar; **to ~ sb sth** apostar algo a algn
betray [bɪ'treɪ] *vt* traicionar; (*trust*) faltar a
better [ˈbɛtə*] *adj, adv* mejor ▷ *vt* superar ▷ *n*: **to get the ~ of sb** quedar por encima de algn; **you had ~ do it** más vale que lo hagas; **he thought ~ of it** cambió de parecer; **to get ~** (*Med*) mejorar(se)
betting [ˈbɛtɪŋ] *n* juego, el apostar; **betting shop** (*BRIT*) *n* agencia de apuestas
between [bɪ'twiːn] *prep* entre ▷ *adv*

(*time*) mientras tanto; (*place*) en medio
beverage [ˈbɛvərɪdʒ] *n* bebida
beware [bɪ'wɛə*] *vi*: **to ~ (of)** tener cuidado (con); **"~ of the dog"** "perro peligroso"
bewildered [bɪ'wɪldəd] *adj* aturdido, perplejo
beyond [bɪ'jɔnd] *prep* más allá de; (*past: understanding*) fuera de; (*after: date*) después de, más allá de; (*above*) superior a ▷ *adv* (*in space*) más allá; (*in time*) posteriormente; **~ doubt** fuera de toda duda; **~ repair** irreparable
bias [ˈbaɪəs] *n* (*prejudice*) prejuicio, pasión *f*; (*preference*) predisposición *f*; **bias(s)ed** *adj* parcial
bib [bɪb] *n* babero
Bible [ˈbaɪbl] *n* Biblia
bicarbonate of soda [baɪˈkɑːbənɪt-] *n* bicarbonato sódico
biceps [ˈbaɪsɛps] *n* bíceps *m*
bicycle [ˈbaɪsɪkl] *n* bicicleta; **bicycle pump** *n* bomba de bicicleta
bid [bɪd] (*pt* **bade** *or ~*, *pp* **bidden** *or ~*) *n* oferta, postura; (*in tender*) licitación *f*; (*attempt*) tentativa, conato ▷ *vi* hacer una oferta ▷ *vt* (*offer*) ofrecer; **to ~ sb good day** dar a algn los buenos días; **bidder** *n*: **the highest bidder** el mejor postor
bidet [ˈbiːdeɪ] *n* bidet *m*
big [bɪg] *adj* grande; (*brother, sister*) mayor; **bigheaded** *adj* engreído; **big toe** *n* dedo gordo (del pie)
bike [baɪk] *n* bici *f*; **bike lane** *n* carril-bici *m*
bikini [bɪ'kiːnɪ] *n* bikini *m*
bilateral [baɪˈlætərl] *adj* (*agreement*) bilateral
bilingual [baɪˈlɪŋgwəl] *adj* bilingüe
bill [bɪl] *n* cuenta; (*invoice*) factura; (*Pol*) proyecto de ley; (*us: banknote*) billete *m*; (*of bird*) pico; (*of show*) programa *m*; **"post no ~s"** "prohibido fijar carteles"; **to fit** *or* **fill the ~** (*fig*) cumplir con los requisitos; **billboard** (*us*) *n* cartelera; **billfold** [ˈbɪlfəuld] (*us*) *n* cartera
billiards [ˈbɪljədz] *n* billar *m*
billion [ˈbɪljən] *n* (*BRIT*) billón *m* (*millón de millones*); (*us*) mil millones *mpl*
bin [bɪn] *n* (*for rubbish*) cubo *or* bote *m* (*MEX*) *or* tacho (*SC*) de la basura; (*container*) recipiente *m*
bind [baɪnd] (*pt, pp* **bound**) *vt* atar; (*book*) encuadernar; (*oblige*) obligar ▷ *n* (*inf: nuisance*) lata
binge [bɪndʒ] (*inf*) *n*: **to go on a ~** ir de juerga
bingo [ˈbɪŋgəu] *n* bingo *m*

binoculars [bɪ'nɔkjuləz] *npl* prismáticos *mpl*

bio... [baɪə'] *prefix*: **biochemistry** *n* bioquímica; **biodegradable** [baɪə udɪ'greɪdəbl] *adj* biodegradable; **biography** [baɪ'ɔgrəfɪ] *n* biografía; **biological** *adj* biológico; **biology** [baɪ'ɔlədʒɪ] *n* biología; **biometric** [baɪə'mɛtrɪk] *adj* biométrico

birch [bə:tʃ] *n* (*tree*) abedul *m*

bird [bə:d] *n* ave *f*, pájaro *m*; (*BRIT: inf: girl*) chica; **bird flu** *n* gripe *f* aviar; **bird of prey** *n* ave *f* de presa; **birdwatching** *n*: **he likes to go birdwatching on Sundays** los domingos le gusta ir a ver pájaros

Biro® ['baɪrəu] *n* boli

birth [bə:θ] *n* nacimiento; **to give ~ to** parir, dar a luz; **birth certificate** *n* partida de nacimiento; **birth control** *n* (*policy*) control *m* de natalidad; (*methods*) métodos *mpl* anticonceptivos; **birthday** *n* cumpleaños *m inv* ▷ *cpd* (*cake, card etc*) de cumpleaños; **birthmark** *n* antojo, marca de nacimiento; **birthplace** *n* lugar *m* de nacimiento

biscuit ['bɪskɪt] (*BRIT*) *n* galleta

bishop ['bɪʃəp] *n* obispo; (*Chess*) alfil *m*

bistro ['bi:strəu] *n* café-bar *m*

bit [bɪt] *pt of* **bite** ▷ *n* trozo, pedazo, pedacito; (*Comput*) bit *m*, bitio; (*for horse*) freno, bocado; **a ~ of** un poco de; **a ~ mad** un poco loco; **~ by ~** poco a poco

bitch [bɪtʃ] *n* perra; (*infl: woman*) zorra (!)

bite [baɪt] (*pt* **bit**, *pp* **bitten**) *vt, vi* morder; (*insect etc*) picar ▷ *n* (*insect bite*) picadura; (*mouthful*) bocado; **to ~ one's nails** comerse las uñas; **let's have a ~ (to eat)** (*inf*) vamos a comer algo

bitten ['bɪtn] *pp of* **bite**

bitter ['bɪtə*] *adj* amargo; (*wind*) cortante, penetrante; (*battle*) encarnizado ▷ *n* (*BRIT: beer*) cerveza típica británica a base de lúpulos

bizarre [bɪ'zɑ:*] *adj* raro, extraño

black [blæk] *adj* negro; (*tea, coffee*) solo ▷ *n* color *m* negro; (*person*): **B~** negro/a ▷ *vt* (*BRIT Industry*) boicotear; **to give sb a ~ eye** ponerle a algn el ojo morado; **~ and blue** (*bruised*) amoratado; **to be in the ~** (*bank account*) estar en números negros; **black out** *vi* (*faint*) desmayarse; **blackberry** *n* zarzamora; **blackbird** *n* mirlo; **blackboard** *n* pizarra; **black coffee** *n* café *m* solo; **blackcurrant** *n* grosella negra; **black ice** *n* hielo invisible en la carretera; **blackmail** *n* chantaje *m* ▷ *vt* chantajear; **black market** *n* mercado negro; **blackout** *n* (*Mil*) oscurecimiento; (*power cut*) apagón

m; (*TV, Radio*) interrupción *f* de programas; (*fainting*) desvanecimiento; **black pepper** *n* pimienta *f* negra; **black pudding** *n* morcilla; **Black Sea** *n*: **the Black Sea** el Mar Negro

bladder ['blædə*] *n* vejiga

blade [bleɪd] *n* hoja; (*of propeller*) paleta; **a ~ of grass** una brizna de hierba

blame [bleɪm] *n* culpa ▷ *vt*: **to ~ sb for sth** echar la culpa a algn de algo; **to be to ~ (for)** tener la culpa (de)

bland [blænd] *adj* (*music, taste*) soso

blank [blæŋk] *adj* en blanco; (*look*) sin expresión ▷ *n* (*of memory*): **my mind is a ~** no puedo recordar nada; (*on form*) blanco, espacio en blanco; (*cartridge*) cartucho sin bala *or* de fogueo

blanket ['blæŋkɪt] *n* manta (*SP*), cobija (*LAM*); (*of snow*) capa; (*of fog*) manto

blast [blɑ:st] *n* (*of wind*) ráfaga, soplo; (*of explosive*) explosión *f* ▷ *vt* (*blow up*) volar

blatant ['bleɪtənt] *adj* descarado

blaze [bleɪz] *n* (*fire*) fuego; (*fig: of colour*) despliegue *m*; (: *of glory*) esplendor *m* ▷ *vi* arder en llamas; (*fig*) brillar ▷ *vt*: **to ~ a trail** (*fig*) abrir (un) camino; **in a ~ of publicity** con gran publicidad

blazer ['bleɪzə*] *n* chaqueta de uniforme de colegial o de socio de club

bleach [bli:tʃ] *n* (*also*: **household ~**) lejía ▷ *vt* blanquear; **bleachers** (*US*) *npl* (*Sport*) gradas *fpl* al sol

bleak [bli:k] *adj* (*countryside*) desierto; (*prospect*) poco prometedor(a); (*weather*) crudo; (*smile*) triste

bled [bled] *pt, pp of* **bleed**

bleed [bli:d] (*pt, pp* **bled**) *vt, vi* sangrar; **my nose is ~ing** me está sangrando la nariz

blemish ['blemɪʃ] *n* marca, mancha; (*on reputation*) tacha

blend [blend] *n* mezcla ▷ *vt* mezclar; (*colours etc*) combinar, mezclar ▷ *vi* (*colours etc: also*: **~ in**) combinarse, mezclarse; **blender** *n* (*Culin*) batidora

bless [bles] (*pt, pp* **~ed** *or* **blest**) *vt* bendecir; **~ you!** (*after sneeze*) ¡Jesús!; **blessing** *n* (*approval*) aprobación *f*; (*godsend*) don *m* del cielo, bendición *f*; (*advantage*) beneficio, ventaja

blew [blu:] *pt of* **blow**

blight [blaɪt] *vt* (*hopes etc*) frustrar, arruinar

blind [blaɪnd] *adj* ciego; (*fig*): **~ (to)** ciego (a) ▷ *n* (*for window*) persiana ▷ *vt* (*dazzle*) deslumbrar; (*deceive*): **to ~ sb to ...** cegar a algn a ...; **the blind** *npl* los ciegos; **blind alley** *n* callejón *m* sin salida; **blindfold** *n* venda ▷ *adv* con los ojos

vendados ▷ vt vendar los ojos a
blink [blɪŋk] vi parpadear, pestañear;
(light) oscilar
bliss [blɪs] n felicidad f
blister ['blɪstə*] n ampolla ▷ vi (paint)
ampollarse
blizzard ['blɪzəd] n ventisca
bloated ['bləʊtɪd] adj hinchado;
(person: full) ahíto
blob [blɒb] n (drop) gota; (indistinct object)
bulto
block [blɒk] n bloque m; (in pipes)
obstáculo; (of buildings) manzana (SP),
cuadra (LAM) ▷ vt obstruir, cerrar; (progress)
estorbar; **~ of flats** (BRIT) bloque m de pisos;
mental ~ bloqueo mental; **block up** vt
tapar, obstruir; (pipe) atascar; **blockade**
[-'keɪd] n bloqueo ▷ vt bloquear; **blockage**
n estorbo, obstrucción f; **blockbuster** n
(book) bestseller m; (film) éxito de público;
block capitals npl mayúsculas fpl; **block
letters** npl mayúsculas fpl
blog [blɒg] n blog m
bloke [bləʊk] (BRIT: inf) n tipo, tío
blond(e) [blɒnd] adj, n rubio/a m/f
blood [blʌd] n sangre f; **blood donor**
n donante mf de sangre; **blood group**
n grupo sanguíneo; **blood poisoning**
n envenenamiento de la sangre; **blood
pressure** n presión f sanguínea;
bloodshed n derramamiento de sangre;
bloodshot adj inyectado en sangre;
bloodstream n corriente f sanguínea;
blood test n análisis m inv de sangre;
blood transfusion n transfusión f de
sangre; **blood type** n grupo sanguíneo;
blood vessel n vaso sanguíneo; **bloody**
adj sangriento; (nose etc) lleno de sangre;
(BRIT: inf!): **this bloody ...** este condenado o
puñetero ... (!) ▷ adv: **bloody strong/good**
(BRIT: inf!) terriblemente fuerte/bueno
bloom [bluːm] n flor f ▷ vi florecer
blossom ['blɒsəm] n flor f ▷ vi florecer
blot [blɒt] n borrón m; (fig) mancha ▷ vt
(stain) manchar
blouse [blaʊz] n blusa
blow [bləʊ] (pt **blew**, pp **blown**) n golpe
m; (with sword) espadazo ▷ vi soplar; (dust,
sand etc) volar; (fuse) fundirse ▷ vt (wind)
llevarse; (fuse) quemar; (instrument) tocar;
to ~ one's nose sonarse; **blow away** vt
llevarse, arrancar; **blow out** vi apagarse;
blow up vi estallar ▷ vt volar; (tyre) inflar;
(Phot) ampliar; **blow-dry** n moldeado (con
secador)
blown [bləʊn] pp of **blow**
blue [bluː] adj azul; (depressed) deprimido;
~ film/joke película/chiste m verde;

out of the ~ (fig) de repente; **bluebell** n
campanilla, campánula azul; **blueberry**
n arándano; **blue cheese** n queso azul;
blues npl: **the blues** (Mus) el blues; **to have
the blues** estar triste; **bluetit** n herrerillo
m (común)
bluff [blʌf] vi tirarse un farol, farolear ▷ n
farol m; **to call sb's ~** coger a algn la palabra
blunder ['blʌndə*] n patinazo, metedura
de pata ▷ vi cometer un error, meter la pata
blunt [blʌnt] adj (pencil) despuntado;
(knife) desafilado, romo; (person) franco,
directo
blur [blə:*] n (shape): **to become a ~**
hacerse borroso ▷ vt (vision) enturbiar;
(distinction) borrar; **blurred** adj borroso
blush [blʌʃ] vi ruborizarse, ponerse
colorado ▷ n rubor m; **blusher** n colorete
m
board [bɔːd] n (cardboard) cartón m;
(wooden) tabla, tablero; (on wall) tablón
m; (for chess etc) tablero; (committee)
junta, consejo; (in firm) mesa or junta
directiva; (Naut, Aviat): **on ~** a bordo ▷ vt
(ship) embarcarse en; (train) subir a; **full
~** (BRIT) pensión completa; **half ~** (BRIT)
media pensión; **to go by the ~** (fig) ser
abandonado or olvidado; **board game** n
juego de tablero; **boarding card** (BRIT) n
tarjeta de embarque; **boarding pass** (US)
n = **boarding card**; **boarding school** n
internado; **board room** n sala de juntas
boast [bəʊst] vi: **to ~ (about or of)** alardear
(de)
boat [bəʊt] n barco, buque m; (small)
barca, bote m
bob [bɒb] vi (also: **~ up and down**)
menearse, balancearse
bobby pin ['bɒbɪ-] (US) n horquilla
body ['bɒdɪ] n cuerpo; (corpse) cadáver m;
(of car) caja, carrocería; (fig: group) grupo;
(: organization) organismo; **body-building** n
culturismo; **bodyguard** n guardaespaldas
m inv; **bodywork** n carrocería
bog [bɒg] n pantano, ciénaga ▷ vt: **to get
~ged down** (fig) empantanarse, atascarse
bogus ['bəʊgəs] adj falso, fraudulento
boil [bɔɪl] vt (water) hervir; (eggs) pasar
por agua, cocer ▷ vi hervir; (fig: with anger)
estar furioso; (: with heat) asfixiarse ▷ n
(Med) furúnculo, divieso; **to come to the
~, to come to a ~** (US) comenzar a hervir;
to ~ down to (fig) reducirse a; **boil over** vi
salirse, rebosar; (anger etc) llegar al colmo;
boiled egg n (soft) huevo tibio (MEX) or
pasado por agua or a la copa (sc); (hard)
huevo duro; **boiled potatoes** npl patatas
fpl (SP) or papas fpl (LAM) cocidas; **boiler** n

caldera; **boiling** ['bɔɪlɪŋ] *adj*: **I'm boiling (hot)** (*inf*) estoy asado; **boiling point** *n* punto de ebullición

bold [bəuld] *adj* valiente, audaz; (*pej*) descarado; (*colour*) llamativo

Bolivia [bə'lɪvɪə] *n* Bolivia; **Bolivian** *adj*, *n* boliviano/a *m/f*

bollard ['bɔləd] (*BRIT*) *n* (*Aut*) poste *m*

bolt [bəult] *n* (*lock*) cerrojo; (*with nut*) perno, tornillo ▷ *adv*: **~ upright** rígido, erguido ▷ *vt* (*door*) echar el cerrojo a; (*also*: **~ together**) sujetar con tornillos; (*food*) engullir ▷ *vi* fugarse; (*horse*) desbocarse

bomb [bɔm] *n* bomba ▷ *vt* bombardear; **bombard** [bɔm'bɑːd] *vt* bombardear; (*fig*) asediar; **bomber** *n* (*Aviat*) bombardero; **bomb scare** *n* amenaza de bomba

bond [bɔnd] *n* (*promise*) fianza; (*Finance*) bono; (*link*) vínculo, lazo; (*Comm*): **in ~** en depósito bajo fianza; **bonds** *npl* (*chains*) cadenas *fpl*

bone [bəun] *n* hueso; (*of fish*) espina ▷ *vt* deshuesar; quitar las espinas a

bonfire ['bɔnfaɪə*] *n* hoguera, fogata

bonnet ['bɔnɪt] *n* gorra; (*BRIT*: *of car*) capó *m*

bonus ['bəunəs] *n* (*payment*) paga extraordinaria, plus *m*; (*fig*) bendición *f*

boo [buː] *excl* ¡uh! ▷ *vt* abuchear, rechiflar

book [buk] *n* libro; (*of tickets*) taco; (*of stamps etc*) librito ▷ *vt* (*ticket*) sacar; (*seat, room*) reservar; **books** *npl* (*Comm*) cuentas *fpl*, contabilidad *f*; **book in** *vi* (*at hotel*) registrarse; **book up** *vt*: **to be booked up** (*hotel*) estar completo; **bookcase** *n* librería, estante *m* para libros; **booking** *n* reserva; **booking office** *n* (*BRIT Rail*) despacho de billetes (*SP*) or boletos (*LAM*); (*Theatre*) taquilla (*SP*), boletería (*LAM*); **book-keeping** *n* contabilidad *f*; **booklet** *n* folleto; **bookmaker** *n* corredor *m* de apuestas; **bookmark** *n* (*also Comput*) marcador; **bookseller** *n* librero; **bookshelf** *n* estante *m* (para libros); **bookshop, book store** *n* librería

boom [buːm] *n* (*noise*) trueno, estampido; (*in prices etc*) alza rápida; (*Econ, in population*) boom *m* ▷ *vi* (*cannon*) hacer gran estruendo, retumbar; (*Econ*) estar en alza

boost [buːst] *n* estímulo, empuje *m* ▷ *vt* estimular, empujar

boot [buːt] *n* bota; (*BRIT*: *of car*) maleta, maletero ▷ *vt* (*Comput*) arrancar; **to ~** (*in addition*) además, por añadidura

booth [buːð] *n* (*telephone booth, voting booth*) cabina

booze [buːz] (*inf*) *n* bebida

border ['bɔːdə*] *n* borde *m*, margen *m*; (*of a country*) frontera; (*for flowers*) arriate *m* ▷ *vt* (*road*) bordear; (*another country*: *also*: **~ on**) lindar con; **borderline** *n*: **on the borderline** en el límite

bore [bɔː*] *pt of* **bear** ▷ *vt* (*hole*) hacer un agujero en; (*well*) perforar; (*person*) aburrir ▷ *n* (*person*) pelmazo, pesado; (*of gun*) calibre *m*; **bored** *adj* aburrido; **he's bored to tears** or **to death** or **stiff** está aburrido como una ostra, está muerto de aburrimiento; **boredom** *n* aburrimiento

boring ['bɔːrɪŋ] *adj* aburrido

born [bɔːn] *adj*: **to be ~** nacer; **I was ~ in 1960** nací en 1960

borne [bɔːn] *pp of* **bear**

borough ['bʌrə] *n* municipio

borrow ['bɔrəu] *vt*: **to ~ sth (from sb)** tomar algo prestado (a algn)

Bosnia(-Herzegovina) ['bɔːsnɪə(hɛrzə'gəuvɪːnə)] *n* Bosnia(-Herzegovina); **Bosnian** ['bɔznɪən] *adj*, *n* bosnio/a

bosom ['buzəm] *n* pecho

boss [bɔs] *n* jefe *m* ▷ *vt* (*also*: **~ about** or **around**) mangonear; **bossy** *adj* mandón/ona

both [bəuθ] *adj*, *pron* ambos/as, los dos (las dos); **~ of us went, we ~ went** fuimos los dos, ambos fuimos ▷ *adv*: **~ A and B** tanto A como B

bother ['bɔðə*] *vt* (*worry*) preocupar; (*disturb*) molestar, fastidiar ▷ *vi* (*also*: **~ o.s.**) molestarse ▷ *n* (*trouble*) dificultad *f*; (*nuisance*) molestia, lata; **to ~ doing** tomarse la molestia de hacer

bottle ['bɔtl] *n* botella; (*small*) frasco; (*baby's*) biberón *m* ▷ *vt* embotellar; **bottle bank** *n* contenedor *m* de vidrio; **bottle-opener** *n* abrebotellas *m inv*

bottom ['bɔtəm] *n* (*of box, sea*) fondo; (*buttocks*) trasero, culo; (*of page*) pie *m*; (*of list*) final *m*; (*of class*) último/a ▷ *adj* (*lowest*) más bajo; (*last*) último

bought [bɔːt] *pt, pp of* **buy**

boulder ['bəuldə*] *n* canto rodado

bounce [bauns] *vi* (*ball*) (re)botar; (*cheque*) ser rechazado ▷ *vt* hacer (re)botar ▷ *n* (*rebound*) (re)bote *m*; **bouncer** *n* (*inf*) gorila *m* (*que echa a los alborotadores de un bar, club etc*)

bound [baund] *pt, pp of* **bind** ▷ *n* (*leap*) salto; (*gen pl*: *limit*) límite *m* ▷ *vi* (*leap*) saltar ▷ *vt* (*border*) rodear ▷ *adj*: **~ by** rodeado de; **to be ~ to do sth** (*obliged*) tener el deber de hacer algo; **he's ~ to come** es seguro que vendrá; **out of ~s** prohibido el paso; **~ for** con destino a

boundary ['baundrɪ] *n* límite *m*

bouquet ['bukeɪ] n (of flowers) ramo
bourbon ['buəbən] (US) n (also: ~ whiskey) whisky m americano, bourbon m
bout [baut] n (of malaria etc) ataque m; (of activity) período; (Boxing etc) combate m, encuentro
boutique [bu:'ti:k] n boutique f, tienda de ropa
bow¹ [bəu] n (knot) lazo; (weapon, Mus) arco
bow² [bau] n (of the head) reverencia; (Naut: also: ~s) proa ▷ vi inclinarse, hacer una reverencia
bowels [bauəlz] npl intestinos mpl, vientre m; (fig) entrañas fpl
bowl [bəul] n tazón m, cuenco; (ball) bola ▷ vi (Cricket) arrojar la pelota; see also **bowls**
bowler n (Cricket) lanzador m (de la pelota); (BRIT: also: **bowler hat**) hongo, bombín m;
bowling n (game) bochas fpl, bolos mpl; **bowling alley** n bolera; **bowling green** n pista para bochas; **bowls** n juego de las bochas, bolos mpl
bow tie ['bəu-] n corbata de lazo, pajarita
box [bɒks] n (also: **cardboard ~**) caja, cajón m; (Theatre) palco ▷ vt encajonar ▷ vi (Sport) boxear; **boxer** ['bɒksə*] n (person) boxeador m; **boxer shorts** ['bɒksəʃɔːts] pl n bóxers; **a pair of boxer shorts** unos bóxers; **boxing** ['bɒksɪŋ] n (Sport) boxeo; **Boxing Day** (BRIT) n día en que se dan los aguinaldos, 26 de diciembre; **boxing gloves** npl guantes mpl de boxeo; **boxing ring** n ring m, cuadrilátero; **box office** n taquilla (SP), boletería (LAM)
boy [bɔɪ] n (young) niño; (older) muchacho, chico; (son) hijo; **boy band** n boy band m (grupo musical de chicos)
boycott ['bɔɪkɔt] n boicot m ▷ vt boicotear
boyfriend ['bɔɪfrɛnd] n novio
bra [brɑː] n sostén m, sujetador m
brace [breɪs] n (BRIT: also: ~s: on teeth) corrector m, aparato; (tool) berbiquí m ▷ vt (knees, shoulders) tensionar; **braces** npl (BRIT) tirantes mpl; **to ~ o.s.** (fig) prepararse
bracelet ['breɪslɪt] n pulsera, brazalete m
bracket ['brækɪt] n (Tech) soporte m, puntal m; (group) clase f, categoría; (also: **brace ~**) soporte m, abrazadera; (also: **round ~**) paréntesis m inv; (also: **square ~**) corchete m ▷ vt (word etc) poner entre paréntesis
brag [bræg] vi jactarse
braid [breɪd] n (trimming) galón m; (of hair) trenza
brain [breɪn] n cerebro; **brains** npl sesos mpl; **she's got ~s** es muy lista
braise [breɪz] vt cocer a fuego lento
brake [breɪk] n (on vehicle) freno ▷ vi

frenar; **brake light** n luz f de frenado
bran [bræn] n salvado
branch [brɑːntʃ] n rama; (Comm) sucursal f; **branch off** vi: **a small road branches off to the right** hay una carretera pequeña que sale hacia la derecha; **branch out** vi (fig) extenderse
brand [brænd] n marca; (fig: type) tipo ▷ vt (cattle) marcar con hierro candente; **brand name** n marca; **brand-new** adj flamante, completamente nuevo
brandy ['brændɪ] n coñac m
brash [bræʃ] adj (forward) descarado
brass [brɑːs] n latón m; **the ~** (Mus) los cobres; **brass band** n banda de metal
brat [bræt] (pej) n mocoso/a
brave [breɪv] adj valiente, valeroso ▷ vt (face up to) desafiar; **bravery** n valor m, valentía
brawl [brɔːl] n pelea, reyerta
Brazil [brə'zɪl] n (el) Brasil; **Brazilian** adj, n brasileño/a m/f
breach [briːtʃ] vt abrir brecha en ▷ n (gap) brecha; (breaking): **~ of contract** infracción f de contrato; **~ of the peace** perturbación f del órden público
bread [brɛd] n pan m; **breadbin** n panera; **breadbox** (US) n panera; **breadcrumbs** npl migajas fpl; (Culin) pan rallado
breadth [brɛtθ] n anchura; (fig) amplitud f
break [breɪk] (pt **broke**, pp **broken**) vt romper; (promise) faltar a; (law) violar, infringir; (record) batir ▷ vi romperse, quebrarse; (storm) estallar; (weather) cambiar; (dawn) despuntar; (news etc) darse a conocer ▷ n (gap) abertura; (fracture) fractura; (time) intervalo; (: at school) (período de) recreo; (chance) oportunidad f; **to ~ the news to sb** comunicar la noticia a algn; **break down** vt (figures, data) analizar, descomponer ▷ vi (machine) estropearse; (Aut) averiarse; (person) romper a llorar; (talks) fracasar; **break in** vt (horse etc) domar ▷ vi (burglar) forzar una entrada; (interrupt) interrumpir; **break into** vt fus (house) forzar; **break off** vi (speaker) pararse, detenerse; (branch) partir; **break out** vi estallar; (prisoner) escaparse; **to break out in spots** salirle a algn granos; **break up** vi (ship) hacerse pedazos; (crowd, meeting) disolverse; (marriage) deshacerse; (Scol) terminar (el curso); (line) cortarse ▷ vt (rocks etc) partir; (journey) partir; (fight etc) acabar con; **the line's** or **you're breaking up** se corta; **breakdown** n (Aut) avería; (in communications) interrupción f; (Med: also: **nervous breakdown**) colapso, crisis f nerviosa; (of marriage, talks) fracaso; (of

statistics) análisis *m inv*; **breakdown truck,**
breakdown van *n* (camión *m*) grúa

breakfast ['brɛkfəst] *n* desayuno

break: break-in *n* robo con allanamiento
de morada; **breakthrough** *n* (*also fig*)
avance *m*

breast [brɛst] *n* (*of woman*) pecho, seno;
(*chest*) pecho; (*of bird*) pechuga; **breast-feed**
(*pt, pp* **breast-fed**) *vt, vi* amamantar, criar
a los pechos; **breast-stroke** *n* braza (de
pecho)

breath [brɛθ] *n* aliento, respiración *f*; **to
take a deep ~** respirar hondo; **out of ~** sin
aliento, sofocado

Breathalyser® ['brɛθəlaɪzə*] (BRIT) *n*
alcoholímetro

breathe [bri:ð] *vt, vi* respirar; **breathe in**
vt, vi aspirar; **breathe out** *vt, vi* espirar;
breathing *n* respiración *f*

breath: breathless *adj* sin aliento,
jadeante; **breathtaking** *adj* imponente,
pasmoso; **breath test** *n* prueba de la
alcoholemia

bred [brɛd] *pt, pp of* **breed**

breed [bri:d] (*pt, pp* **bred**) *vt* criar ▷ *vi*
reproducirse, procrear ▷ *n* (*Zool*) raza,
casta; (*type*) tipo

breeze [bri:z] *n* brisa

breezy ['bri:zɪ] *adj* de mucho viento,
ventoso; (*person*) despreocupado

brew [bru:] *vt* (*tea*) hacer; (*beer*) elaborar
▷ *vi* (*fig: trouble*) prepararse; (*storm*)
amenazar; **brewery** *n* fábrica de cerveza,
cervecería

bribe [braɪb] *n* soborno ▷ *vt* sobornar,
cohechar; **bribery** *n* soborno, cohecho

bric-a-brac ['brɪkəbræk] *n inv* baratijas
fpl

brick [brɪk] *n* ladrillo; **bricklayer** *n* albañil
m

bride [braɪd] *n* novia; **bridegroom** *n*
novio; **bridesmaid** *n* dama de honor

bridge [brɪdʒ] *n* puente *m*; (*Naut*) puente
m de mando; (*of nose*) caballete *m*; (*Cards*)
bridge *m* ▷ *vt* (*fig*): **to ~ a gap** llenar un
vacío

bridle ['braɪdl] *n* brida, freno

brief [bri:f] *adj* breve, corto ▷ *n* (*Law*)
escrito; (*task*) cometido, encargo ▷ *vt*
informar; **briefs** *npl* (*for men*) calzoncillos
mpl; (*for women*) bragas *fpl*; **briefcase** *n*
cartera (*SP*), portafolio (*LAM*); **briefing**
n (*Press*) informe *m*; **briefly** *adv* (*glance*)
fugazmente; (*say*) en pocas palabras

brigadier [brɪgə'dɪə*] *n* general *m* de
brigada

bright [braɪt] *adj* brillante; (*room*)
luminoso; (*day*) de sol; (*person: clever*) listo,

inteligente; (*: lively*) alegre; (*colour*) vivo;
(*future*) prometedor(a)

brilliant ['brɪljənt] *adj* brillante; (*inf*)
fenomenal

brim [brɪm] *n* borde *m*; (*of hat*) ala

brine [braɪn] *n* (*Culin*) salmuera

bring [brɪŋ] (*pt, pp* **brought**) *vt* (*thing,
person: with you*) traer; (*: to sb*) llevar,
conducir; (*trouble, satisfaction*) causar;
bring about *vt* ocasionar, producir; **bring
back** *vt* volver a traer; (*return*) devolver;
bring down *vt* (*government, plane*) derribar;
(*price*) rebajar; **bring in** *vt* (*harvest*) recoger;
(*person*) hacer entrar or pasar; (*object*) traer;
(*Pol: bill, law*) presentar; (*produce: income*)
producir, rendir; **bring on** *vt* (*illness, attack*)
producir, causar; (*player, substitute*) sacar (de
la reserva), hacer salir; **bring out** *vt* sacar;
(*book etc*) publicar; (*meaning*) subrayar; **bring
up** *vt* subir; (*person*) educar, criar; (*question*)
sacar a colación; (*food: vomit*) devolver,
vomitar

brink [brɪŋk] *n* borde *m*

brisk [brɪsk] *adj* (*abrupt: tone*) brusco;
(*person*) enérgico, vigoroso; (*pace*) rápido;
(*trade*) activo

bristle ['brɪsl] *n* cerda ▷ *vi*: **to ~ in anger**
temblar de rabia

Brit [brɪt] *n abbr* (*inf*: = *British person*)
británico/a

Britain ['brɪtən] *n* (*also:* **Great ~**) Gran
Bretaña

British ['brɪtɪʃ] *adj* británico ▷ *npl*: **the ~**
los británicos; **British Isles** *npl*: **the British
Isles** las Islas Británicas

Briton ['brɪtən] *n* británico/a

brittle ['brɪtl] *adj* quebradizo, frágil

broad [brɔːd] *adj* ancho; (*range*) amplio;
(*smile*) abierto; (*general: outlines etc*) general;
(*accent*) cerrado; **in ~ daylight** en pleno día;
broadband *n* banda ancha; **broad bean**
n haba; **broadcast** (*pt, pp ~*) *n* emisión
f ▷ *vt* (*Radio*) emitir; (*TV*) transmitir ▷ *vi*
emitir; transmitir; **broaden** *vt* ampliar
▷ *vi* ensancharse; **to broaden one's mind**
hacer más tolerante a algn; **broadly** *adv*
en general; **broad-minded** *adj* tolerante,
liberal

broccoli ['brɔkəlɪ] *n* brécol *m*

brochure ['brəuʃjuə*] *n* folleto

broil [brɔɪl] *vt* (*Culin*) asar a la parrilla

broiler ['brɔɪlə*] *n* (*grill*) parrilla

broke [brəuk] *pt of* **break** ▷ *adj* (*inf*)
pelado, sin blanca

broken ['brəukən] *pp of* **break** ▷ *adj*
roto; (*machine: also: ~ down*) averiado; **~
leg** pierna rota; **in ~ English** en un inglés
imperfecto

broker ['brəukə*] n agente mf, bolsista mf; (insurance broker) agente de seguros
bronchitis [brɒŋ'kaɪtɪs] n bronquitis f
bronze [brɒnz] n bronce m
brooch [brəutʃ] n prendedor m, broche m
brood [bru:d] n camada, cría ▷ vi (person) dejarse obsesionar
broom [brum] n escoba; (Bot) retama
Bros. abbr (= Brothers) Hnos
broth [brɒθ] n caldo
brothel ['brɒθl] n burdel m
brother ['brʌðə*] n hermano; **brother-in-law** n cuñado
brought [brɔːt] pt, pp of **bring**
brow [brau] n (forehead) frente m; (eyebrow) ceja; (of hill) cumbre f
brown [braun] adj (colour) marrón; (hair) castaño; (tanned) bronceado, moreno ▷ n (colour) color m marrón or pardo ▷ vt (Culin) dorar; **brown bread** n pan integral
Brownie ['brauni] n niña exploradora
brown rice n arroz m integral
brown sugar n azúcar m terciado
browse [brauz] vi (through book) hojear; (in shop) mirar; **browser** n (Comput) navegador m
bruise [bru:z] n cardenal m (SP), moretón m ▷ vt magullar
brunette [bru:'net] n morena
brush [brʌʃ] n cepillo; (for painting, shaving etc) brocha; (artist's) pincel m; (with police etc) roce m ▷ vt (sweep) barrer; (groom) cepillar; (also: **~ against**) rozar al pasar
Brussels ['brʌslz] n Bruselas
Brussels sprout n col f de Bruselas
brutal ['bru:tl] adj brutal
B.Sc. abbr (= Bachelor of Science) licenciado en Ciencias
BSE n abbr (= bovine spongiform encephalopathy) encefalopatía espongiforme bovina
bubble ['bʌbl] n burbuja ▷ vi burbujear, borbotar; **bubble bath** n espuma para el baño; **bubble gum** n chicle m de globo; **bubblejet printer** ['bʌblʤɛt-] n impresora de inyección por burbujas
buck [bʌk] n (rabbit) conejo macho; (deer) gamo; (us: inf) dólar m ▷ vi corcovear; **to pass the ~ (to sb)** echar (a algn) el muerto
bucket ['bʌkɪt] n cubo, balde m
buckle ['bʌkl] n hebilla ▷ vt abrochar con hebilla ▷ vi combarse
bud [bʌd] n (of plant) brote m, yema; (of flower) capullo ▷ vi brotar, echar brotes
Buddhism ['budɪzm] n Budismo
Buddhist ['budɪst] adj, n budista m/f
buddy ['bʌdɪ] n (us) n compañero, compinche m

budge [bʌʤ] vt mover; (fig) hacer ceder ▷ vi moverse, ceder
budgerigar ['bʌʤərɪgɑ:*] n periquito
budget ['bʌʤɪt] n presupuesto ▷ vi: **to ~ for sth** presupuestar algo
budgie ['bʌʤɪ] n = **budgerigar**
buff [bʌf] adj (colour) color de ante ▷ n (inf: enthusiast) entusiasta mf
buffalo ['bʌfələu] (pl ~ or ~**es**) n (BRIT) búfalo; (us: bison) bisonte m
buffer ['bʌfə*] n (Comput) memoria intermedia; (Rail) tope m
buffet¹ ['bʌfɪt] vt golpear
buffet² ['bufeɪ] n (BRIT: in station) bar m, cafetería; (food) buffet m; **buffet car** (BRIT) n (Rail) coche-comedor m
bug [bʌg] n (esp us: insect) bicho, sabandija; (Comput) error m; (germ) microbio, bacilo; (spy device) micrófono oculto ▷ vt (inf: annoy) fastidiar; (room) poner micrófono oculto en
buggy ['bʌgi] n cochecito de niño
build [bɪld] (pt, pp **built**) n (of person) tipo ▷ vt construir, edificar; **build up** vt (morale, forces, production) acrecentar; (stocks) acumular; **builder** n (contractor) contratista mf; **building** n construcción f; (structure) edificio; **building site** n obra; **building society** (BRIT) n sociedad f inmobiliaria
built [bɪlt] pt, pp of **build**; **built-in** adj (cupboard) empotrado; (device) interior, incorporado; **built-up** adj (area) urbanizado
bulb [bʌlb] n (Bot) bulbo; (Elec) bombilla, foco (MEX), bujía (CAM), bombita (RPL)
Bulgaria [bʌl'geərɪə] n Bulgaria; **Bulgarian** adj, n búlgaro/a m/f
bulge [bʌlʤ] n bulto, protuberancia ▷ vi bombearse, pandearse; (pocket etc): **to ~ (with)** rebosar (de)
bulimia [bə'lɪmɪə] n bulimia
bulimic [bju:'lɪmɪk] adj, n bulímico/a m/f
bulk [bʌlk] n masa, mole f; **in ~** (Comm) a granel; **the ~ of** la mayor parte de; **bulky** adj voluminoso, abultado
bull [bul] n toro; (male elephant, whale) macho
bulldozer ['buldəuzə*] n bulldozer m
bullet ['bulɪt] n bala
bulletin ['bulɪtɪn] n anuncio, parte m; (journal) boletín m; **bulletin board** n (us) tablón m de anuncios; (Comput) tablero de noticias
bullfight ['bulfaɪt] n corrida de toros; **bullfighter** n torero; **bullfighting** n los toros, el toreo
bully ['buli] n valentón m, matón m ▷ vt

intimidar, tiranizar

bum [bʌm] n (inf: backside) culo; (esp US: tramp) vagabundo

bumblebee ['bʌmblbi:] n abejorro

bump [bʌmp] n (blow) tope m, choque m; (jolt) sacudida; (on road etc) bache m; (on head etc) chichón m ▷ vt (strike) chocar contra; **bump into** vt fus chocar contra, tropezar con; (person) topar con; **bumper** n (Aut) parachoques m inv ▷ adj: **bumper crop** or **harvest** cosecha abundante; **bumpy** adj (road) lleno de baches

bun [bʌn] n (BRIT: cake) pastel m; (US: bread) bollo; (of hair) moño

bunch [bʌntʃ] n (of flowers) ramo; (of keys) manojo; (of bananas) piña; (of people) grupo; **bunches** npl (in hair) coletas fpl

bundle ['bʌndl] n bulto, fardo; (of sticks) haz m; (of papers) legajo ▷ vt (also: ~ up) atar, envolver; **to ~ sth/sb into** meter algo/a algn precipitadamente en

bungalow ['bʌŋgələu] n bungalow m, chalé m

bungee jumping ['bʌndʒi:'dʒʌmpɪŋ] n puenting m, banyi m

bunion ['bʌnjən] n juanete m

bunk [bʌŋk] n litera; **bunk beds** npl literas fpl

bunker ['bʌŋkə*] n (coal store) carbonera; (Mil) refugio; (Golf) bunker m

bunny ['bʌnɪ] n (inf: also: ~ rabbit) conejito

buoy [bɔɪ] n boya; **buoyant** adj (ship) capaz de flotar; (economy) boyante; (person) optimista

burden ['bə:dn] n carga ▷ vt cargar

bureau [bjuə'rəu] (pl ~x) n (BRIT: writing desk) escritorio, buró m; (US: chest of drawers) cómoda; (office) oficina, agencia

bureaucracy [bjuə'rɔkrəsɪ] n burocracia

bureaucrat ['bjuərəkræt] n burócrata m/f

bureau de change [-də'ʃãʒ] (pl **bureaux de change**) n caja f de cambio

bureaux ['bjuərəuz] npl of **bureau**

burger ['bə:gə*] n hamburguesa

burglar ['bə:glə*] n ladrón/ona m/f; **burglar alarm** n alarma f antirrobo; **burglary** n robo con allanamiento, robo de una casa

burial ['berɪəl] n entierro

burn [bə:n] (pt, pp ~ed or ~t) vt quemar; (house) incendiar ▷ vi quemarse, arder; incendiarse; (sting) escocer ▷ n quemadura; **burn down** vt incendiar; **burn out** vt (writer etc): **to burn o.s. out** agotarse; **burning** adj (building etc) en llamas; (hot: sand etc) abrasador(a); (ambition) ardiente

Burns' Night [bə:nz-] n ver abajo

burnt [bə:nt] pt, pp of **burn**

burp [bə:p] (inf) n eructo ▷ vi eructar

burrow ['bʌrəu] n madriguera ▷ vi hacer una madriguera; (rummage) hurgar

burst [bə:st] (pt, pp ~) vt reventar; (river: banks etc) romper ▷ vi reventarse; (tyre) pincharse ▷ n (of gunfire) ráfaga; (also: ~ **pipe**) reventón m; **a ~ of energy/speed/ enthusiasm** una explosión de energía/ un ímpetu de velocidad/un arranque de entusiasmo; **to ~ into flames** estallar en llamas; **to ~ into tears** deshacerse en lágrimas; **to ~ out laughing** soltar la carcajada; **to ~ open** abrirse de golpe; **to be ~ing with** (container) estar lleno a rebosar de; (: person) reventar por or de; **burst into** vt fus (room etc) irrumpir en

bury ['berɪ] vt enterrar; (body) enterrar, sepultar

bus [bʌs] (pl ~es) n autobús m

bush [buʃ] n arbusto; (scrub land) monte m; **to beat about the ~** andar(se) con rodeos

business ['bɪznɪs] n (matter) asunto; (trading) comercio, negocios mpl; (firm) empresa, casa; (occupation) oficio; **to be away on ~** estar en viaje de negocios; **it's my ~ to ...** me toca or corresponde ...; **it's none of my ~** yo no tengo nada que ver; **he means ~** habla en serio; **business class** n (Aer) clase f preferente; **businesslike** adj eficiente; **businessman** (irreg) n hombre m de negocios; **business trip** n viaje m de negocios; **businesswoman** (irreg) n mujer f de negocios

busker ['bʌskə*] (BRIT) n músico/a ambulante

bus: bus pass n bonobús; **bus shelter** n parada cubierta; **bus station** n estación f de autobuses; **bus stop** n parada de autobús

bust [bʌst] n (Anat) pecho; (sculpture) busto

▷ *adj* (*inf: broken*) roto, estropeado; **to go ~** quebrar

bustling ['bʌslɪŋ] *adj* (*town*) animado, bullicioso

busy ['bɪzɪ] *adj* ocupado, atareado; (*shop, street*) concurrido, animado; (*Tel: line*) comunicando ▷*vt*: **to ~ o.s. with** ocuparse en; **busy signal** (*us*) *n* (*Tel*) señal *f* de comunicando

○ **KEYWORD**

but [bʌt] *conj* **1** pero; **he's not very bright, but he's hard-working** no es muy inteligente, pero es trabajador
2 (*in direct contradiction*) sino; **he's not English but French** no es inglés sino francés; **he didn't sing but he shouted** no cantó sino que gritó
3 (*showing disagreement, surprise etc*): **but that's far too expensive!** ¡pero eso es carísimo!; **but it does work!** ¡(pero) sí que funciona!
▷ *prep* (*apart from, except*) menos, salvo; **we've had nothing but trouble** no hemos tenido más que problemas; **no-one but him can do it** nadie más que él puede hacerlo; **who but a lunatic would do such a thing?** ¡sólo un loco haría una cosa así!; **but for you/your help** si no fuera por ti/tu ayuda; **anything but that** cualquier cosa menos eso
▷ *adv* (*just, only*): **she's but a child** no es más que una niña; **had I but known** si lo hubiera sabido; **I can but try** al menos lo puedo intentar; **it's all but finished** está casi acabado

butcher ['bʊtʃə*] *n* carnicero ▷*vt* hacer una carnicería con; (*cattle etc*) matar; **butcher's (shop)** *n* carnicería

butler ['bʌtlə*] *n* mayordomo

butt [bʌt] *n* (*barrel*) tonel *m*; (*of gun*) culata; (*of cigarette*) colilla; (*BRIT: fig: target*) blanco ▷*vt* dar cabezadas contra, top(et)ar

butter ['bʌtə*] *n* mantequilla ▷*vt* untar con mantequilla; **buttercup** *n* botón *m* de oro

butterfly ['bʌtəflaɪ] *n* mariposa; (*Swimming: also*: **~ stroke**) braza de mariposa

buttocks ['bʌtəks] *npl* nalgas *fpl*

button ['bʌtn] *n* botón *m*; (*us*) placa, chapa ▷*vt* (*also*: **~ up**) abotonar, abrochar ▷*vi* abrocharse

buy [baɪ] (*pt, pp* **bought**) *vt* comprar ▷*n* compra; **to ~ sb sth/sth from sb** comprarle algo a algn; **to ~ sb a drink** invitar a algn a tomar algo; **buy out** *vt* (*partner*) comprar

la parte de; **buy up** *vt* (*property*) acaparar; (*stock*) comprar todas las existencias de; **buyer** *n* comprador(a) *m/f*

buzz [bʌz] *n* zumbido; (*inf: phone call*) llamada (por teléfono) ▷*vi* zumbar; **buzzer** *n* timbre *m*

○ **KEYWORD**

by [baɪ] *prep* **1** (*referring to cause, agent*) por; de; **killed by lightning** muerto por un relámpago; **a painting by Picasso** un cuadro de Picasso
2 (*referring to method, manner, means*): **by bus/car/train** en autobús/coche/tren; **to pay by cheque** pagar con un cheque; **by moonlight/candlelight** a la luz de la luna/una vela; **by saving hard he …** ahorrando …
3 (*via, through*) por; **we came by Dover** vinimos por Dover
4 (*close to, past*): **the house by the river** la casa junto al río; **she rushed by me** pasó a mi lado como una exhalación; **I go by the post office every day** paso por delante de Correos todos los días
5 (*time: not later than*) para; (: *during*): **by daylight** de día; **by 4 o'clock** para las cuatro; **by this time tomorrow** mañana a estas horas; **by the time I got here it was too late** cuando llegué ya era demasiado tarde
6 (*amount*): **by the metre/kilo** por metro/kilo; **paid by the hour** pagado por hora
7 (*Math, measure*): **to divide/multiply by 3** dividir/multiplicar por 3; **a room 3 metres by 4** una habitación de 3 metros por 4; **it's broader by a metre** es un metro más ancho
8 (*according to*) según, de acuerdo con; **it's 3 o'clock by my watch** según mi reloj, son las tres; **it's all right by me** por mí, está bien
9: (**all**) **by oneself** *etc* todo solo; **he did it (all) by himself** lo hizo él solo; **he was standing (all) by himself in a corner** estaba de pie solo en un rincón
10: **by the way** a propósito, por cierto; **this wasn't my idea, by the way** pues, no fue idea mía
▷ *adv* **1** *see* **go; pass** *etc*
2: **by and by** finalmente; **they'll come back by and by** acabarán volviendo; **by and large** en líneas generales, en general

bye(-bye) ['baɪ('baɪ)] *excl* adiós, hasta luego

by-election (*BRIT*) *n* elección *f* parcial

bypass ['baɪpɑːs] *n* carretera de circunvalación; (*Med*) (operación *f* de) by-pass *f* ▷*vt* evitar

byte [baɪt] *n* (*Comput*) byte *m*, octeto

C

C [si:] n (Mus) do m
cab [kæb] n taxi m; (of truck) cabina
cabaret ['kæbəreɪ] n cabaret m
cabbage ['kæbɪdʒ] n col f, berza
cabin ['kæbɪn] n cabaña; (on ship) camarote m; (on plane) cabina; **cabin crew** n tripulación f de cabina
cabinet ['kæbɪnɪt] n (Pol) consejo de ministros; (furniture) armario; (also: **display ~**) vitrina; **cabinet minister** n ministro/a (del gabinete)
cable ['keɪbl] n cable m ▷ vt cablegrafiar; **cable car** n teleférico; **cable television** n televisión f por cable
cactus ['kæktəs] (pl **cacti**) n cacto
café ['kæfeɪ] n café m
cafeteria [kæfɪ'tɪərɪə] n cafetería
caffein(e) ['kæfi:n] n cafeína
cage [keɪdʒ] n jaula
cagoule [kə'gu:l] n chubasquero
cake [keɪk] n (Culin: large) tarta; (: small) pastel m; (of soap) pastilla
calcium ['kælsɪəm] n calcio
calculate ['kælkjuleɪt] vt calcular; **calculation** [-'leɪʃən] n cálculo, cómputo; **calculator** n calculadora
calendar ['kæləndə*] n calendario
calf [kɑ:f] (pl **calves**) n (of cow) ternero, becerro; (of other animals) cría; (also: **~skin**) piel f de becerro; (Anat) pantorrilla
calibre ['kælɪbə*] (US **caliber**) n calibre m
call [kɔ:l] vt llamar; (meeting) convocar ▷ vi (shout) llamar; (Tel) llamar (por teléfono); (visit: also: **~ in, ~ round**) hacer una visita ▷ n llamada; (of bird) canto; **to be ~ed** llamarse; **on ~** (on duty) de guardia; **call back** vi (return) volver; (Tel) volver a llamar; **call for** vt fus (demand) pedir, exigir; (fetch) pasar a recoger; **call in** vt (doctor, expert, police) llamar; **call off** vt (cancel: meeting, race) cancelar; (: deal) anular; (: strike)

desconvocar; **call on** vt fus (visit) visitar; (turn to) acudir a; **call out** vi gritar; **call up** vt (Mil) llamar al servicio militar; (Tel) llamar; **callbox** (BRIT) n cabina telefónica; **call centre** (US **call center**) n centro de atención al cliente; **caller** n visita; (Tel) usuario/a
callous ['kæləs] adj insensible, cruel
calm [kɑ:m] adj tranquilo; (sea) liso, en calma ▷ n calma, tranquilidad f ▷ vt calmar, tranquilizar; **calm down** vi calmarse, tranquilizarse ▷ vt calmar, tranquilizar; **calmly** ['kɑ:mlɪ] adv tranquilamente, con calma
Calor gas® ['kælə*-] n butano
calorie ['kælərɪ] n caloría
calves [kɑ:vz] npl of **calf**
camcorder ['kæmkɔ:də*] n videocámara
came [keɪm] pt of **come**
camel ['kæməl] n camello
camera ['kæmərə] n máquina fotográfica; (Cinema, TV) cámara; **in ~** (Law) a puerta cerrada; **cameraman** (irreg) n cámara m; **camera phone** n teléfono con cámara
camouflage ['kæməflɑ:ʒ] n camuflaje m ▷ vt camuflar
camp [kæmp] n campamento, camping m; (Mil) campamento; (for prisoners) campo; (fig: faction) bando ▷ vi acampar ▷ adj afectado, afeminado
campaign [kæm'peɪn] n (Mil, Pol etc) campaña ▷ vi hacer campaña; **campaigner** n: **campaigner for** defensor(a) m/f de
camp: campbed (BRIT) n cama de campaña; **camper** n campista mf; (vehicle) caravana; **campground** (US) n camping m, campamento; **camping** n camping m; **to go camping** hacer camping; **campsite** n camping m
campus ['kæmpəs] n ciudad f universitaria
can¹ [kæn] n (of oil, water) bidón m; (tin) lata, bote m ▷ vt enlatar

○ KEYWORD

can² [kæn] (negative **cannot, can't**, conditional and pt **could**) aux vb **1** (be able to) poder; **you can do it if you try** puedes hacerlo si lo intentas; **I can't see you** no te veo
2 (know how to) saber; **I can swim/play tennis/drive** sé nadar/jugar al tenis/conducir; **can you speak French?** ¿hablas o sabes hablar francés?
3 (may) poder; **can I use your phone?** ¿me dejas or puedo usar tu teléfono?
4 (expressing disbelief, puzzlement etc): **it can't**

be true! ¡no puede ser (verdad)!; **what CAN
he want?** ¿qué querrá?
5 (expressing possibility, suggestion etc): **he
could be in the library** podría estar en la
biblioteca; **she could have been delayed**
pudo haberse retrasado

Canada ['kænədə] n (el) Canadá;
Canadian [kə'neɪdɪən] adj, n canadiense
mf
canal [kə'næl] n canal m
canary [kə'nɛərɪ] n canario
Canary Islands [kə'nɛərɪ'aɪləndz]
npl: **the ~** las (Islas) Canarias
cancel ['kænsəl] vt cancelar; (train)
suprimir; (cross out) tachar, borrar;
cancellation [-'leɪʃən] n cancelación f,
supresión f
Cancer ['kænsə*] n (Astrology) Cáncer m
cancer ['kænsə*] n cáncer m
candidate ['kændɪdeɪt] n candidato/a
candle ['kændl] n vela; (in church) cirio;
candlestick n (single) candelero; (low)
palmatoria; (bigger, ornate) candelabro
candy ['kændɪ] n azúcar m cande; (us)
caramelo; **candy bar** (us) n barrita (dulce);
candyfloss (BRIT) n algodón m (azucarado)
cane [keɪn] n (Bot) caña; (stick) vara,
palmeta; (for furniture) mimbre f ▷ vt
(BRIT: Scol) castigar (con vara)
canister ['kænɪstə*] n bote m, lata; (of gas)
bombona
cannabis ['kænəbɪs] n marijuana
canned [kænd] adj en lata, de lata
cannon ['kænən] (pl **~** or **~s**) n cañón m
cannot ['kænɔt] = **can not**
canoe [kə'nu:] n canoa; (Sport) piragua;
canoeing n piragüismo
canon ['kænən] n (clergyman) canónigo;
(standard) canon m
can-opener ['kænəupnə*] n abrelatas
m inv
can't [kænt] = **can not**
canteen [kæn'ti:n] n (eating place)
cantina; (BRIT: of cutlery) juego
canter ['kæntə*] vi ir a medio galope
canvas ['kænvəs] n (material) lona;
(painting) lienzo; (Naut) velas fpl
canvass ['kænvəs] vi (Pol): **to ~ for**
solicitar votos por ▷ vt (Comm) sondear
canyon ['kænjən] n cañón m
cap [kæp] n (hat) gorra; (of pen) capuchón
m; (of bottle) tapa, tapón m; (contraceptive)
diafragma m; (for toy gun) cápsula ▷ vt
(outdo) superar; (limit) recortar
capability [keɪpə'bɪlɪtɪ] n capacidad f
capable ['keɪpəbl] adj capaz
capacity [kə'pæsɪtɪ] n capacidad f;

(position) calidad f
cape [keɪp] n capa; (Geo) cabo
caper ['keɪpə*] n (Culin: gen pl) alcaparra;
(prank) broma
capital ['kæpɪtl] n (also: **~ city**) capital f;
(money) capital m; (also: **~ letter**) mayúscula;
capitalism n capitalismo; **capitalist** adj, n
capitalista mf; **capital punishment** n pena
de muerte
Capitol ['kæpɪtl] n ver abajo

⬤ **CAPITOL**
⬤
⬤ El Capitolio **(Capitol)** es el edificio del
⬤ Congreso **(Congress)** de los Estados
⬤ Unidos, situado en la ciudad de
⬤ Washington. Por extensión, también
⬤ se suele llamar así al edificio en el que
⬤ tienen lugar las sesiones parlamentarias
⬤ de la cámara de representantes de
⬤ muchos de los estados.

Capricorn ['kæprɪkɔ:n] n Capricornio
capsize [kæp'saɪz] vt volcar, hacer
zozobrar ▷ vi volcarse, zozobrar
capsule ['kæpsju:l] n cápsula
captain ['kæptɪn] n capitán m
caption ['kæpʃən] n (heading) título; (to
picture) leyenda
captivity [kæp'tɪvɪtɪ] n cautiverio
capture ['kæptʃə*] vt prender, apresar;
(animal, Comput) capturar; (place) tomar;
(attention) captar, llamar ▷ n apresamiento;
captura; toma; (data capture) formulación
f de datos
car [kɑ:*] n coche m, carro (LAM), automóvil
m; (us Rail) vagón m
carafe [kə'ræf] n jarra
caramel ['kærəməl] n caramelo
carat ['kærət] n quilate m
caravan ['kærəvæn] n (BRIT) caravana,
ruló f; (in desert) caravana; **caravan site**
(BRIT) n camping m para caravanas
carbohydrate [kɑ:bəu'haɪdreɪt] n
hidrato de carbono; (food) fécula
carbon ['kɑ:bən] n carbono; **carbon
dioxide** n dióxido de carbono, anhídrido
carbónico; **carbon monoxide** n monóxido
de carbono
car boot sale n mercadillo organizado
en un aparcamiento, en el que se exponen las
mercancías en el maletero del coche
carburettor [kɑ:bju'retə*] (us
carburetor) n carburador m
card [kɑ:d] n (material) cartulina; (index
card etc) ficha; (playing card) carta, naipe
m; (visiting card, greetings card etc) tarjeta;
cardboard n cartón m; **card game** n

juego de naipes or cartas
cardigan ['kɑ:dɪɡən] n rebeca
cardinal ['kɑ:dɪnl] adj cardinal;
(importance, principal) esencial ▷ n cardenal m

cardphone ['kɑ:dfəun] n cabina que funciona con tarjetas telefónicas
care [kɛə*] n cuidado; (worry) inquietud f; (charge) cargo, custodia ▷ vi: **to ~ about** (person, animal) tener cariño a; (thing, idea) preocuparse por; **~ of** en casa de, al cuidado de; **in sb's ~** a cargo de algn; **to take ~ to** cuidarse de, tener cuidado de; **to take ~ of** cuidar; (problem etc) ocuparse de; **I don't ~** no me importa; **I couldn't ~ less** eso me trae sin cuidado; **care for** vt fus cuidar a; (like) querer

career [kə'rɪə*] n profesión f; (in work, school) carrera ▷ vi (also: **~ along**) correr a toda velocidad

care: carefree adj despreocupado; **careful** adj cuidadoso; (cautious) cauteloso; **(be) careful!** ¡tenga cuidado!; **carefully** adv con cuidado, cuidadosamente; con cautela; **caregiver** (us) n (professional) enfermero/a m/f; (unpaid) persona que cuida a un pariente o vecino; **careless** adj descuidado; (heedless) poco atento; **carelessness** n descuido, falta de atención; **carer** ['kɛərə*] n (professional) enfermero/a m/f; (unpaid) persona que cuida a un pariente o vecino; **caretaker** n portero/a, conserje mf

car-ferry ['kɑ:fɛrɪ] n transbordador m para coches
cargo ['kɑ:gəu] (pl **~es**) n cargamento, carga
car hire n alquiler m de automóviles
Caribbean [kærɪ'bi:ən] n: **the ~ (Sea)** el (Mar) Caribe
caring ['kɛərɪŋ] adj humanitario; (behaviour) afectuoso
carnation [kɑ:'neɪʃən] n clavel m
carnival ['kɑ:nɪvəl] n carnaval m; (us: funfair) parque m de atracciones
carol ['kærəl] n: **(Christmas) ~** villancico
carousel [kærə'sɛl] (us) n tiovivo, caballitos mpl
car park (BRIT) n aparcamiento, parking m
carpenter ['kɑ:pɪntə*] n carpintero/a
carpet ['kɑ:pɪt] n alfombra; (fitted) moqueta ▷ vt alfombrar
car rental (us) n alquiler m de coches
carriage ['kærɪdʒ] n (BRIT Rail) vagón m; (horse-drawn) coche m; (of goods) transporte m; (: cost) porte m, flete m; **carriageway** (BRIT) n (part of road) calzada
carrier ['kærɪə*] n (transport company) transportista, empresa de transportes;

(Med) portador(a) m/f; **carrier bag** (BRIT) n bolsa de papel or plástico
carrot ['kærət] n zanahoria
carry ['kærɪ] vt (person) llevar; (transport) transportar; (involve: responsibilities etc) entrañar, implicar; (Med) ser portador de ▷ vi (sound) oírse; **to get carried away** (fig) entusiasmarse; **carry on** vi (continue) seguir (adelante), continuar ▷ vt proseguir, continuar; **carry out** vt (orders) cumplir; (investigation) llevar a cabo, realizar
cart [kɑ:t] n carro, carreta ▷ vt (inf: transport) acarrear
carton ['kɑ:tən] n (box) caja (de cartón); (of milk etc) bote m; (of yogurt) tarrina
cartoon [kɑ:'tu:n] n (Press) caricatura; (comic strip) tira cómica; (film) dibujos mpl animados
cartridge ['kɑ:trɪdʒ] n cartucho; (of pen) recambio
carve [kɑ:v] vt (meat) trinchar; (wood, stone) cincelar, esculpir; (initials etc) grabar; **carving** n (object) escultura; (design) talla; (art) tallado
car wash n lavado de coches
case [keɪs] n (container) caja; (Med) caso; (for jewels etc) estuche m; (Law) causa, proceso; (BRIT: also: **suit~**) maleta; **in ~ of** en caso de; **in any ~** en todo caso; **just in ~** por si acaso
cash [kæʃ] n dinero en efectivo, dinero contante ▷ vt cobrar, hacer efectivo; **to pay (in) ~** pagar al contado; **~ on delivery** cóbrese al entregar; **cashback** n (discount) devolución f; (at supermarket etc) retirada de dinero en efectivo de un establecimiento donde se ha pagado con tarjeta; también dinero retirado; **cash card** n tarjeta f dinero; **cash desk** (BRIT) n caja; **cash dispenser** n cajero automático
cashew [kæ'ʃu:] n (also: **~ nut**) anacardo
cashier [kæ'ʃɪə*] n cajero/a
cashmere ['kæʃmɪə*] n cachemira
cash point n cajero automático
cash register n caja
casino [kə'si:nəu] n casino
casket ['kɑ:skɪt] n cofre m, estuche m; (us: coffin) ataúd m
casserole ['kæsərəul] n (food, pot) cazuela
cassette [kæ'sɛt] n casete f; **cassette player, cassette recorder** n casete m
cast [kɑ:st] (pt, pp **~**) vt (throw) echar, arrojar, lanzar; (glance, eyes) dirigir; (Theatre): **to ~ sb as Othello** dar a algn el papel de Otelo ▷ vi (Fishing) lanzar ▷ n (Theatre) reparto; (also: **plaster ~**) vaciado; **to ~ one's vote** votar; **to ~ doubt on** suscitar dudas acerca de; **cast off** vi (Naut)

desamarrar; (*Knitting*) cerrar (los puntos)
castanets [kæstə'nɛts] *npl* castañuelas
fpl
caster sugar ['kɑːstə*-] (BRIT) *n* azúcar
m extrafino
Castile [kæs'tiːl] *n* Castilla; **Castilian** *adj*,
n castellano/a *m/f*
cast-iron ['kɑːstaɪən] *adj* (*lit*) (hecho) de
hierro fundido; (*fig: case*) irrebatible
castle ['kɑːsl] *n* castillo; (*Chess*) torre *f*
casual ['kæʒjul] *adj* fortuito;
(*irregular: work etc*) eventual, temporero;
(*unconcerned*) despreocupado; (*clothes*)
informal

Be careful not to translate **casual** by the
Spanish word *casual*.

casualty ['kæʒjultɪ] *n* víctima, herido/a;
(*dead*) muerto/a; (*Med: department*)
urgencias *fpl*
cat [kæt] *n* gato; (*big cat*) felino
Catalan ['kætəlæn] *adj*, *n* catalán/ana *m/f*
catalogue ['kætəlɔg] (US **catalog**) *n*
catálogo ▷ *vt* catalogar
Catalonia [kætə'ləunɪə] *n* Cataluña
catalytic converter
[kætə'lɪtɪkkən'vəːtə*] *n* catalizador *m*
cataract ['kætərækt] *n* (*Med*) cataratas *fpl*
catarrh [kə'tɑː*] *n* catarro
catastrophe [kə'tæstrəfɪ] *n* catástrofe *f*
catch [kætʃ] (*pt, pp* **caught**) *vt* coger
(SP), agarrar (LAM); (*arrest*) detener; (*grasp*)
asir; (*breath*) contener; (*surprise: person*)
sorprender; (*attract: attention*) captar; (*hear*)
oír; (*Med*) contagiarse de, coger; (*also: ~ up*)
alcanzar ▷ *vi* (*fire*) encenderse; (*in branches
etc*) enredarse ▷ *n* (*fish etc*) pesca; (*act of
catching*) cogida; (*hidden problem*) dificultad *f*;
(*game*) pilla-pilla; (*of lock*) pestillo, cerradura;
to ~ fire encenderse; **to ~ sight of** divisar;
catch up *vi* (*fig*) ponerse al día; **catching**
['kætʃɪŋ] *adj* (*Med*) contagioso
category ['kætɪgərɪ] *n* categoría, clase *f*
cater ['keɪtə*] *vi*: **to ~ for** (BRIT) abastecer a;
(*needs*) atender a; (*Comm: parties etc*) proveer
comida a
caterpillar ['kætəpɪlə*] *n* oruga, gusano
cathedral [kə'θiːdrəl] *n* catedral *f*
Catholic ['kæθəlɪk] *adj*, *n* (*Rel*) católico/a
m/f
Catseye® ['kæts'aɪ] (BRIT) *n* (*Aut*) catafoto
cattle ['kætl] *npl* ganado
catwalk ['kætwɔːk] *n* pasarela
caught [kɔːt] *pt, pp* of **catch**
cauliflower ['kɔlɪflauə*] *n* coliflor *f*
cause [kɔːz] *n* causa, motivo, razón *f*;
(*principle: also Pol*) causa ▷ *vt* causar
caution ['kɔːʃən] *n* cautela, prudencia;
(*warning*) advertencia, amonestación *f*

▷ *vt* amonestar; **cautious** *adj* cauteloso,
prudente, precavido
cave [keɪv] *n* cueva, caverna; **cave in** *vi*
(*roof etc*) derrumbarse, hundirse
caviar(e) ['kævɪɑː*] *n* caviar *m*
cavity ['kævɪtɪ] *n* hueco, cavidad *f*
cc *abbr* (= *cubic centimetres*) c.c.; (= *carbon
copy*) copia hecha con papel del carbón
CCTV *n abbr* (= *closed-circuit television*)
circuito cerrado de televisión
CD *n abbr* (= *compact disc*) CD *m*; (*player*)
(reproductor *m* de) CD; **CD player** *n*
reproductor *m* de CD; **CD-ROM** [siːdiː'rɔm]
n abbr CD-ROM *m*; **CD writer** *n* grabadora
de CD
cease [siːs] *vt, vi* cesar; **ceasefire** *n* alto
m el fuego
cedar ['siːdə*] *n* cedro
ceilidh ['keɪlɪ] *n* baile con música y danzas
tradicionales escocesas o irlandesas
ceiling ['siːlɪŋ] *n* techo; (*fig*) límite *m*
celebrate ['sɛlɪbreɪt] *vt* celebrar ▷ *vi*
divertirse; **celebration** [-'breɪʃən] *n* fiesta,
celebración *f*
celebrity [sɪ'lɛbrɪtɪ] *n* celebridad *f*
celery ['sɛlərɪ] *n* apio
cell [sɛl] *n* celda; (*Biol*) célula; (*Elec*)
elemento
cellar ['sɛlə*] *n* sótano; (*for wine*) bodega
cello ['tʃɛləu] *n* violoncelo
Cellophane® ['sɛləfeɪn] *n* celofán *m*
cellphone ['sɛlfəun] *n* teléfono celular
Celsius ['sɛlsɪəs] *adj* centígrado
Celtic ['kɛltɪk] *adj* celta
cement [sə'mɛnt] *n* cemento
cemetery ['sɛmɪtrɪ] *n* cementerio
censor ['sɛnsə*] *n* censor *m* ▷ *vt* (*cut*)
censurar; **censorship** *n* censura
census ['sɛnsəs] *n* censo
cent [sɛnt] *n* (*unit of dollar*) centavo,
céntimo; (*unit of euro*) céntimo; *see also* **per**
centenary [sɛn'tiːnərɪ] *n* centenario
centennial [sɛn'tɛnɪəl] (US) *n* centenario
center ['sɛntə*] (US) = **centre**
centi... [sɛntɪ] *prefix*: **centigrade** *adj*
centígrado; **centimetre** (US **centimeter**)
n centímetro; **centipede** ['sɛntɪpiːd] *n*
ciempiés *m inv*
central ['sɛntrəl] *adj* central; (*of
house etc*) céntrico; **Central America**
n Centroamérica; **central heating** *n*
calefacción *f* central; **central reservation** *n*
(BRIT Aut) mediana
centre ['sɛntə*] (US **center**) *n* centro;
(*fig*) núcleo ▷ *vt* centrar; **centre-forward**
n (*Sport*) delantero centro; **centre-half** *n*
(*Sport*) medio centro
century ['sɛntjurɪ] *n* siglo; **20th ~** siglo

veinte

CEO n abbr = **chief executive officer**

ceramic [sɪ'ræmɪk] adj cerámico

cereal ['siːrɪəl] n cereal m

ceremony ['sɛrɪmənɪ] n ceremonia; **to stand on ~** hacer ceremonias, estar de cumplido

certain ['səːtən] adj seguro; (person): **a ~ Mr Smith** un tal Sr. Smith; (particular, some) cierto; **for ~** a ciencia cierta; **certainly** adv (undoubtedly) ciertamente; (of course) desde luego, por supuesto; **certainty** n certeza, certidumbre f, seguridad f; (inevitability) certeza

certificate [sə'tɪfɪkɪt] n certificado

certify ['səːtɪfaɪ] vt certificar; (award diploma to) conceder un diploma a; (declare insane) declarar loco

cf. abbr (= compare) cfr

CFC n abbr (= chlorofluorocarbon) CFC m

chain [tʃeɪn] n cadena; (of mountains) cordillera; (of events) sucesión f ▷ vt (also: ~ up) encadenar; **chain-smoke** vi fumar un cigarrillo tras otro

chair [tʃɛə*] n silla; (armchair) sillón m, butaca; (of university) cátedra; (of meeting etc) presidencia ▷ vt (meeting) presidir; **chairlift** n telesilla; **chairman** (irreg) n presidente m; **chairperson** n presidente/a m/f; **chairwoman** (irreg) n presidenta

chalet ['ʃæleɪ] n chalet m (de madera)

chalk [tʃɔːk] n (Geo) creta; (for writing) tiza, gis m (MEX); **chalkboard** (US) n pizarrón m (LAM), pizarra (SP)

challenge ['tʃælɪndʒ] n desafío, reto ▷ vt desafiar, retar; (statement, right) poner en duda; **to ~ sb to do sth** retar a algn a que haga algo; **challenging** adj exigente; (tone) de desafío

chamber ['tʃeɪmbə*] n cámara, sala; (Pol) cámara; (BRIT Law: gen pl) despacho; **~ of commerce** cámara de comercio; **chambermaid** n camarera

champagne [ʃæm'peɪn] n champaña m, champán m

champion ['tʃæmpɪən] n campeón/ona m/f; (of cause) defensor(a) m/f; **championship** n campeonato

chance [tʃɑːns] n (opportunity) ocasión f, oportunidad f; (likelihood) posibilidad f; (risk) riesgo ▷ vt arriesgar, probar ▷ adj fortuito, casual; **to ~ it** arriesgarse, intentarlo; **to take a ~** arriesgarse; **by ~** por casualidad

chancellor ['tʃɑːnsələ*] n canciller m; **Chancellor of the Exchequer** (BRIT) n Ministro de Hacienda

chandelier [ʃændə'lɪə*] n araña (de luces)

change [tʃeɪndʒ] vt cambiar; (replace) cambiar, reemplazar; (gear, clothes, job) cambiar de; (transform) transformar ▷ vi cambiar(se); (change trains) hacer transbordo; (traffic lights) cambiar de color; (be transformed): **to ~ into** transformarse en ▷ n cambio; (alteration) modificación f; (transformation) transformación f; (of clothes) muda; (coins) suelto, sencillo; (money returned) vuelta; **to ~ gear** (Aut) cambiar de marcha; **to ~ one's mind** cambiar de opinión or idea; **for a ~** para variar; **change over** vi (from sth to sth) cambiar; (players etc) cambiar(se) ▷ vt cambiar; **changeable** adj (weather) cambiable; **change machine** n máquina de cambio; **changing room** (BRIT) n vestuario

channel ['tʃænl] n (TV) canal m; (of river) cauce m; (groove) conducto; (fig: medium) medio ▷ vt (river etc) encauzar; **the (English) C~** el Canal (de la Mancha); **the C~ Islands** las Islas Normandas; **Channel Tunnel** n: **the Channel Tunnel** el túnel del Canal de la Mancha, el Eurotúnel

chant [tʃɑːnt] n (of crowd) gritos mpl; (Rel) canto ▷ vt (slogan, word) repetir a gritos

chaos ['keɪɔs] n caos m

chaotic [keɪ'ɔtɪk] adj caótico

chap [tʃæp] (BRIT: inf) n (man) tío, tipo

chapel ['tʃæpəl] n capilla

chapped [tʃæpt] adj agrietado

chapter ['tʃæptə*] n capítulo

character ['kærɪktə*] n carácter m, naturaleza, índole f; (moral strength, personality) carácter; (in novel, film) personaje m; **characteristic** [-'rɪstɪk] adj característico ▷ n característica; **characterize** ['kærɪktəraɪz] vt caracterizar

charcoal ['tʃɑːkəul] n carbón m vegetal; (Art) carboncillo

charge [tʃɑːdʒ] n (Law) cargo, acusación f; (cost) precio, coste m; (responsibility) cargo ▷ vt (Law): **to ~ (with)** acusar (de); (battery) cargar; (price) pedir; (customer) cobrar ▷ vi precipitarse; (Mil) cargar, atacar; **charge card** n tarjeta de cuenta; **charger** n (also: **battery charger**) cargador m (de baterías)

charismatic [kærɪz'mætɪk] adj carismático

charity ['tʃærɪtɪ] n caridad f; (organization) sociedad f benéfica; (money, gifts) limosnas fpl; **charity shop** n (BRIT) tienda de artículos de segunda mano que dedica su recaudación a causas benéficas

charm [tʃɑːm] n encanto, atractivo; (talisman) hechizo; (on bracelet) dije m ▷ vt encantar; **charming** adj encantador(a)

chart [tʃɑːt] n (diagram) cuadro; (graph) gráfica; (map) carta de navegación ▷ vt (course) trazar; (progress) seguir; **charts** npl (Top 40): **the ~s** los 40 principales (SP)

charter [ˈtʃɑːtə*] vt (plane) alquilar; (ship) fletar ▷ n (document) carta; (of university, company) estatutos mpl; **chartered accountant** (BRIT) n contable m/f diplomado/a; **charter flight** n vuelo chárter

chase [tʃeɪs] vt (pursue) perseguir; (also: ~ away) ahuyentar ▷ n persecución f

chat [tʃæt] vi (also: **have a ~**) charlar; (on Internet) chatear ▷ n charla; **chat up** vt (inf: girl) ligar con, enrollarse con; **chat room** n (Internet) chat m, canal m de charla; **chat show** (BRIT) n programa m de entrevistas

chatter [ˈtʃætə*] vi (person) charlar; (teeth) castañetear ▷ n (of birds) parloteo; (of people) charla, cháchara

chauffeur [ˈʃəʊfə*] n chófer m

chauvinist [ˈʃəʊvɪnɪst] n (male chauvinist) machista m; (nationalist) chovinista mf

cheap [tʃiːp] adj barato; (joke) de mal gusto; (poor quality) de mala calidad ▷ adv barato; **cheap day return** n billete de ida y vuelta el mismo día; **cheaply** adv barato, a bajo precio

cheat [tʃiːt] vi hacer trampa ▷ vt: **to ~ sb (out of sth)** estafar (algo) a algn ▷ n (person) tramposo/a; **cheat on** vt fus engañar

Chechnya [tʃɪtʃˈnjɑː] n Chechenia

check [tʃɛk] vt (examine) controlar; (facts) comprobar; (halt) parar, detener; (restrain) refrenar, restringir ▷ n (inspection) control m, inspección f; (curb) freno; (US: bill) nota, cuenta; (US) = **cheque**; (pattern: gen pl) cuadro; **check in** vi (at hotel) firmar el registro; (at airport) facturar el equipaje ▷ vt (luggage) facturar; **check off** vt (esp US: check) comprobar; (cross off) tachar; **check out** vi (of hotel) marcharse; **check up** vi: **to check up on sth** comprobar algo; **to check up on sb** investigar a algn; **checkbook** (US) = **chequebook**; **checked** adj a cuadros; **checkers** (US) n juego de damas; **check-in** n (also: **check-in desk**: at airport) mostrador m de facturación; **checking account** (US) n cuenta corriente; **checklist** n lista (de control); **checkmate** n jaque m mate; **checkout** n caja; **checkpoint** n (punto de) control m; **checkroom** (US) n consigna; **checkup** n (Med) reconocimiento general

cheddar [ˈtʃedə*] n (also: ~ **cheese**) queso m cheddar

cheek [tʃiːk] n mejilla; (impudence)

descaro; **what a ~!** ¡qué cara!; **cheekbone** n pómulo; **cheeky** adj fresco, descarado

cheer [tʃɪə*] vt vitorear, aplaudir; (gladden) alegrar, animar ▷ vi dar vivas ▷ n viva m; **cheer up** vi animarse ▷ vt alegrar, animar; **cheerful** adj alegre

cheerio [tʃɪərɪˈəʊ] (BRIT) excl ¡hasta luego!

cheerleader [ˈtʃɪəliːdə*] n animador(a) m/f

cheese [tʃiːz] n queso; **cheeseburger** n hamburguesa con queso; **cheesecake** n pastel m de queso

chef [ʃef] n jefe/a m/f de cocina

chemical [ˈkemɪkəl] adj químico ▷ n producto químico

chemist [ˈkemɪst] n (BRIT: pharmacist) farmacéutico/a; (scientist) químico/a; **chemistry** n química; **chemist's (shop)** (BRIT) n farmacia

cheque [tʃek] (US **check**) n cheque m; **chequebook** n talonario de cheques (SP), chequera (LAM); **cheque card** n tarjeta de cheque

cherry [ˈtʃerɪ] n cereza; (also: ~ **tree**) cerezo

chess [tʃes] n ajedrez m

chest [tʃest] n (Anat) pecho; (box) cofre m, cajón m

chestnut [ˈtʃesnʌt] n castaña; (also: ~ **tree**) castaño

chest of drawers n cómoda

chew [tʃuː] vt mascar, masticar; **chewing gum** n chicle m

chic [ʃiːk] adj elegante

chick [tʃɪk] n pollito, polluelo; (inf: girl) chica

chicken [ˈtʃɪkɪn] n gallina, pollo; (food) pollo; (inf: coward) gallina mf; **chicken out** (inf) vi rajarse; **chickenpox** n varicela

chickpea [ˈtʃɪkpiː] n garbanzo

chief [tʃiːf] n jefe/a m/f ▷ adj principal; **chief executive (officer)** n director(a) m/f general; **chiefly** adv principalmente

child [tʃaɪld] (pl ~ren) n niño/a; (offspring) hijo/a; **child abuse** n (with violence) malos tratos mpl a niños; (sexual) abuso m sexual de niños; **child benefit** n (BRIT) subsidio por cada hijo pequeño; **childbirth** n parto; **child-care** n cuidado de los niños; **childhood** n niñez f, infancia; **childish** adj pueril, aniñado; **child minder** (BRIT) n madre f de día; **children** [ˈtʃɪldrən] npl of **child**

Chile [ˈtʃɪlɪ] n Chile m; **Chilean** adj, n chileno/a m/f

chill [tʃɪl] n frío; (Med) resfriado ▷ vt enfriar; (Culin) congelar; **chill out** vi (esp US: inf) tranquilizarse

chil(l)i [ˈtʃɪlɪ] (BRIT) n chile m, ají m (SC)

chilly [ˈtʃɪlɪ] adj frío

chimney ['tʃɪmnɪ] n chimenea

chimpanzee [tʃɪmpæn'zi:] n chimpancé m

chin [tʃɪn] n mentón m, barbilla

China ['tʃaɪnə] n China

china ['tʃaɪnə] n porcelana; (crockery) loza

Chinese [tʃaɪ'ni:z] adj chino ▷ n inv chino/a m/f; (Ling) chino

chip [tʃɪp] n (gen pl: Culin: BRIT) patata (SP) or papa (LAM) frita; (: US: also: **potato** ~) patata or papa frita; (of wood) astilla; (of glass, stone) lasca; (at poker) ficha; (Comput) chip m ▷ vt (cup, plate) desconchar; **chip shop** n pescadería (donde se vende principalmente pescado rebozado y patatas fritas)

chiropodist [kɪ'rɔpədɪst] (BRIT) n pedicuro/a, callista m/f

chisel ['tʃɪzl] n (for wood) escoplo; (for stone) cincel m

chives [tʃaɪvz] npl cebollinos mpl

chlorine ['klɔ:ri:n] n cloro

choc-ice ['tʃɔkaɪs] n (BRIT) helado m cubierto de chocolate

chocolate ['tʃɔklɪt] n chocolate m; (sweet) bombón m

choice [tʃɔɪs] n elección f, selección f; (option) opción f; (preference) preferencia ▷ adj escogido

choir ['kwaɪə*] n coro

choke [tʃəuk] vi ahogarse; (on food) atragantarse ▷ vt estrangular, ahogar; (block): **to be ~d with** estar atascado de ▷ n (Aut) estárter m

cholesterol [kə'lestərul] n colesterol m

choose [tʃu:z] (pt **chose**, pp **chosen**) vt escoger, elegir; (team) seleccionar; **to ~ to do sth** optar por hacer algo

chop [tʃɔp] vt (wood) cortar, tajar; (Culin: also: ~ **up**) picar ▷ n (Culin) chuleta; **chop down** vt (tree) talar; **chop off** vt cortar (de un tajo); **chopsticks** ['tʃɔpstɪks] npl palillos mpl

chord [kɔ:d] n (Mus) acorde m

chore [tʃɔ:*] n faena, tarea; (routine task) trabajo rutinario

chorus ['kɔ:rəs] n coro; (repeated part of song) estribillo

chose [tʃəuz] pt of **choose**

chosen ['tʃəuzn] pp of **choose**

Christ [kraɪst] n Cristo

christen ['krɪsn] vt bautizar; **christening** n bautizo

Christian ['krɪstɪən] adj, n cristiano/a m/f; **Christianity** [-'ænɪtɪ] n cristianismo; **Christian name** n nombre m de pila

Christmas ['krɪsməs] n Navidad f; **Merry ~!** ¡Felices Pascuas!; **Christmas**

card n crismas m inv, tarjeta de Navidad; **Christmas carol** n villancico m; **Christmas Day** n día m de Navidad; **Christmas Eve** n Nochebuena; **Christmas pudding** n (esp BRIT) pudin m de Navidad; **Christmas tree** n árbol m de Navidad

chrome [krəum] n cromo

chronic ['krɔnɪk] adj crónico

chrysanthemum [krɪ'sænθəməm] n crisantemo

chubby ['tʃʌbɪ] adj regordete

chuck [tʃʌk] (inf) vt lanzar, arrojar; (BRIT: also: ~ **up**) abandonar; **chuck out** vt (person) echar (fuera); (rubbish etc) tirar

chuckle ['tʃʌkl] vi reírse entre dientes

chum [tʃʌm] n compañero/a

chunk [tʃʌŋk] n pedazo, trozo

church [tʃə:tʃ] n iglesia; **churchyard** n cementerio

churn [tʃə:n] n (for butter) mantequera; (for milk) lechera

chute [ʃu:t] n (also: **rubbish** ~) vertedero; (for coal etc) rampa de caída

chutney ['tʃʌtnɪ] n condimento a base de frutas de la India

CIA (US) n abbr (= Central Intelligence Agency) CIA f

CID (BRIT) n abbr (= Criminal Investigation Department) ≈ B.I.C. f (SP)

cider ['saɪdə*] n sidra

cigar [sɪ'gɑ:*] n puro

cigarette [sɪgə'ret] n cigarrillo; **cigarette lighter** n mechero

cinema ['sɪnəmə] n cine m

cinnamon ['sɪnəmən] n canela

circle ['sə:kl] n círculo; (in theatre) anfiteatro ▷ vi dar vueltas ▷ vt (surround) rodear, cercar; (move round) dar la vuelta a

circuit ['sə:kɪt] n circuito; (tour) gira; (track) pista; (lap) vuelta

circular ['sə:kjulə*] adj circular ▷ n circular f

circulate ['sə:kjuleɪt] vi circular; (person: at party etc) hablar con los invitados ▷ vt poner en circulación; **circulation** [-'leɪʃən] n circulación f; (of newspaper) tirada

circumstances ['sə:kəmstənsɪz] npl circunstancias fpl; (financial condition) situación f económica

circus ['sə:kəs] n circo

cite [saɪt] vt citar

citizen ['sɪtɪzn] n (Pol) ciudadano/a; (of city) vecino/a, habitante mf; **citizenship** n ciudadanía; (BRIT: Scol) civismo

citrus fruits ['sɪtrəs-] npl agrios mpl

city ['sɪtɪ] n ciudad f; **the C~** centro financiero de Londres; **city centre** (BRIT) n centro de la ciudad; **city technology college** n centro de formación profesional (*centro de enseñanza secundaria que da especial importancia a la ciencia y tecnología.*)

civic ['sɪvɪk] *adj* cívico; (*authorities*) municipal

civil ['sɪvɪl] *adj* civil; (*polite*) atento, cortés; **civilian** [sɪ'vɪlɪən] *adj* civil (*no militar*) ▷ *n* civil *mf*, paisano/a

civilization [sɪvɪlaɪ'zeɪʃən] *n* civilización *f*

civilized ['sɪvɪlaɪzd] *adj* civilizado

civil: civil law n derecho civil; **civil rights** *npl* derechos *mpl* civiles; **civil servant** n funcionario/a del Estado; **Civil Service** n administración *f* pública; **civil war** n guerra civil

CJD n abbr (= Creutzfeldt-Jakob disease) enfermedad de Creutzfeldt-Jakob

claim [kleɪm] *vt* exigir, reclamar; (*rights etc*) reivindicar; (*assert*) pretender ▷ *vi* (*for insurance*) reclamar ▷ *n* reclamación *f*; pretensión *f*; **claim form** n solicitud *f*

clam [klæm] n almeja

clamp [klæmp] n abrazadera, grapa ▷ *vt* (*two things together*) cerrar fuertemente; (*one thing on another*) afianzar (con abrazadera); (*Aut: wheel*) poner el cepo a

clan [klæn] n clan *m*

clap [klæp] *vi* aplaudir

claret ['klærət] n burdeos *m inv*

clarify ['klærɪfaɪ] *vt* aclarar

clarinet [klærɪ'nɛt] n clarinete *m*

clarity ['klærɪtɪ] n claridad *f*

clash [klæʃ] n enfrentamiento; choque *m*; desacuerdo; estruendo ▷ *vi* (*fight*) enfrentarse; (*beliefs*) chocar; (*disagree*) estar en desacuerdo; (*colours*) desentonar; (*two events*) coincidir

clasp [klɑːsp] n (*hold*) apretón *m*; (*of necklace, bag*) cierre *m* ▷ *vt* apretar; abrazar

class [klɑːs] n clase *f* ▷ *vt* clasificar

classic ['klæsɪk] *adj*, n clásico; **classical** *adj* clásico

classification [klæsɪfɪ'keɪʃən] n clasificación *f*

classify ['klæsɪfaɪ] *vt* clasificar

classmate ['klɑːsmeɪt] n compañero/a de clase

classroom ['klɑːsrum] n aula; **classroom assistant** n profesor(a) *m/f* de apoyo

classy ['klɑːsɪ] *adj* (*inf*) elegante, con estilo

clatter ['klætə*] n estrépito ▷ *vi* hacer ruido or estrépito

clause [klɔːz] n cláusula; (*Ling*) oración *f*

claustrophobic [klɔːstrə'fəʊbɪk] *adj* claustrofóbico; **I feel ~** me entra claustrofobia

claw [klɔː] n (*of cat*) uña; (*of bird of prey*)

garra; (*of lobster*) pinza

clay [kleɪ] n arcilla

clean [kliːn] *adj* limpio; (*record, reputation*) bueno, intachable; (*joke*) decente ▷ *vt* limpiar; (*hands etc*) lavar; **clean up** *vt* limpiar, asear; **cleaner** n (*person*) asistenta; (*substance*) producto para la limpieza; **cleaner's** n tintorería; **cleaning** n limpieza

cleanser ['klɛnzə*] n (*for face*) crema limpiadora

clear [klɪə*] *adj* claro; (*road, way*) libre; (*conscience*) limpio, tranquilo; (*skin*) terso; (*sky*) despejado ▷ *vt* (*space*) despejar, limpiar; (*Law: suspect*) absolver; (*obstacle*) salvar, saltar por encima de; (*cheque*) aceptar ▷ *vi* (*fog etc*) despejarse ▷ *adv*: **~ of** a distancia de; **to ~ the table** recoger or levantar la mesa; **clear away** *vt* (*things, clothes etc*) quitar (de en medio); (*dishes*) retirar; **clear up** *vt* limpiar; (*mystery*) aclarar, resolver; **clearance** n (*removal*) despeje *m*; (*permission*) acreditación *f*; **clear-cut** *adj* bien definido, nítido; **clearing** n (*in wood*) claro; **clearly** *adv* claramente; (*evidently*) sin duda; **clearway** (BRIT) n carretera donde no se puede parar

clench [klɛntʃ] *vt* apretar, cerrar

clergy ['klɜːdʒɪ] n clero

clerk [klɑːk, (US) klɜːrk] n (BRIT) oficinista *mf*; (US) dependiente/a *m/f*

clever ['klɛvə*] *adj* (*intelligent*) inteligente, listo; (*skilful*) hábil; (*device, arrangement*) ingenioso

cliché ['kliːʃeɪ] n cliché *m*, frase *f* hecha

click [klɪk] *vt* (*tongue*) chasquear; (*heels*) taconear ▷ *vi* (*Comput*) hacer clic; **to ~ on an icon** hacer clic en un icono

client ['klaɪənt] n cliente *m/f*

cliff [klɪf] n acantilado

climate ['klaɪmɪt] n clima *m*; **climate change** n cambio climático

climax ['klaɪmæks] n (*of battle, career*) apogeo; (*of film, book*) punto culminante; (*sexual*) orgasmo

climb [klaɪm] *vi* subir; (*plant*) trepar; (*move with effort*): **to ~ over a wall/into a car** trepar a una tapia/subir a un coche ▷ *vt* (*stairs*) subir; (*tree*) trepar a; (*mountain*) escalar ▷ *n* subida; **climb down** *vi* (*fig*) volverse atrás; **climber** n alpinista *mf* (SP, MEX), andinista *mf* (LAM); **climbing** n alpinismo (SP, MEX), andinismo (LAM)

clinch [klɪntʃ] *vt* (*deal*) cerrar; (*argument*) remachar

cling [klɪŋ] (*pt, pp* **clung**) *vi*: **to ~ to** agarrarse a; (*clothes*) pegarse a

Clingfilm® ['klɪŋfɪlm] n plástico

adherente
clinic ['klınık] n clínica
clip [klıp] n (for hair) horquilla; (also: **paper ~**) sujetapapeles m inv, clip m; (TV, Cinema) fragmento ▷ vt (cut) cortar; (also: **~ together**) unir; **clipping** n (newspaper) recorte m
cloak [kləuk] n capa, manto ▷ vt (fig) encubrir, disimular; **cloakroom** n guardarropa; (BRIT: WC) lavabo (SP), aseos mpl (SP), baño (LAM)
clock [klɒk] n reloj m; **clock in** or **on** vi (with card) fichar, picar; (start work) entrar a trabajar; **clock off** or **out** vi (with card) fichar or picar la salida; (leave work) salir del trabajar; **clockwise** adv en el sentido de las agujas del reloj; **clockwork** n aparato de relojería ▷ adj (toy) de cuerda
clog [klɒg] n zueco, chanclo ▷ vt atascar ▷ vi (also: **~ up**) atascarse
clone [kləun] n clon m ▷ vt clonar
close¹ [kləus] adj (near): **~ (to)** cerca (de); (friend) íntimo; (connection) estrecho; (examination) detallado, minucioso; (weather) bochornoso ▷ adv cerca; **~ by, ~ at hand** muy cerca; **to have a ~ shave** (fig) escaparse por un pelo
close² [kləuz] vt (shut) cerrar; (end) concluir, terminar ▷ vi (shop etc) cerrarse; (end) concluirse, terminarse ▷ n (end) fin m, final m, conclusión f; **close down** vi cerrarse definitivamente; **closed** adj (shop etc) cerrado
closely ['kləuslı] adv (study) con detalle; (watch) de cerca; (resemble) estrechamente
closet ['klɒzıt] n armario
close-up ['kləusʌp] n primer plano
closing time n hora de cierre
closure ['kləuʒə*] n cierre m
clot [klɒt] n (gen) coágulo; (inf: idiot) imbécil m/f ▷ vi (blood) coagularse
cloth [klɒθ] n (material) tela, paño; (rag) trapo
clothes [kləuðz] npl ropa; **clothes line** n cuerda (para tender la ropa); **clothes peg** (US **clothes pin**) n pinza
clothing ['kləuðıŋ] n = **clothes**
cloud [klaud] n nube f; **cloud over** vi (also fig) nublarse; **cloudy** adj nublado, nubloso; (liquid) turbio
clove [kləuv] n clavo; **~ of garlic** diente m de ajo
clown [klaun] n payaso ▷ vi (also: **~ about, ~ around**) hacer el payaso
club [klʌb] n (society) club m; (weapon) porra, cachiporra; (also: **golf ~**) palo ▷ vt aporrear ▷ vi: **to ~ together** (for gift) comprar entre todos; **clubs** npl (Cards)

tréboles mpl; **club class** n (Aviat) clase f preferente
clue [klu:] n pista; (in crosswords) indicación f; **I haven't a ~** no tengo ni idea
clump [klʌmp] n (of trees) grupo
clumsy ['klʌmzı] adj (person) torpe, desmañado; (tool) difícil de manejar; (movement) desgarbado
clung [klʌŋ] pt, pp of **cling**
cluster ['klʌstə*] n grupo ▷ vi agruparse, apiñarse
clutch [klʌtʃ] n (Aut) embrague m; (grasp): **~es** garras fpl ▷ vt asir; agarrar
cm abbr (= centimetre) cm
Co. abbr = **county; company**
c/o abbr (= care of) c/a, a/c
coach [kəutʃ] n autocar m (SP), coche m de línea; (horse-drawn) coche m; (of train) vagón m, coche m; (Sport) entrenador(a) m/f, instructor(a) m/f; (tutor) profesor(a) m/f particular ▷ vt (Sport) entrenar; (student) preparar, enseñar; **coach station** n (BRIT) estación f de autobuses etc; **coach trip** n excursión f en autocar
coal [kəul] n carbón m
coalition [kəuə'lıʃən] n coalición f
coarse [kɔ:s] adj basto, burdo; (vulgar) grosero, ordinario
coast [kəust] n costa, litoral m ▷ vi (Aut) ir en punto muerto; **coastal** adj costero, costanero; **coastguard** n guardacostas m inv; **coastline** n litoral m
coat [kəut] n abrigo; (of animal) pelaje m, lana; (of paint) mano f, capa ▷ vt cubrir, revestir; **coat hanger** n percha (SP), gancho (LAM); **coating** n capa, baño
coax [kəuks] vt engatusar
cob [kɒb] n see **corn**
cobbled ['kɒbld] adj: **~ street** calle f empedrada, calle f adoquinada
cobweb ['kɒbwɛb] n telaraña
cocaine [kə'keın] n cocaína
cock [kɒk] n (rooster) gallo; (male bird) macho ▷ vt (gun) amartillar; **cockerel** n gallito
cockney ['kɒknı] n habitante de ciertos barrios de Londres
cockpit ['kɒkpıt] n cabina
cockroach ['kɒkrəutʃ] n cucaracha
cocktail ['kɒkteıl] n coctel m, cóctel m
cocoa ['kəukəu] n cacao; (drink) chocolate m
coconut ['kəukənʌt] n coco
cod [kɒd] n bacalao
C.O.D. abbr (= cash on delivery) C.A.E.
code [kəud] n código; (cipher) clave f; (dialling code) prefijo; (post code) código postal

coeducational [kəuɛdju'keɪʃənl] *adj* mixto

coffee ['kɒfɪ] *n* café *m*; **coffee bar** (BRIT) *n* cafetería; **coffee bean** *n* grano de café; **coffee break** *n* descanso (para tomar café); **coffee maker** *n* máquina de hacer café, cafetera; **coffeepot** *n* cafetera; **coffee shop** *n* café *m*; **coffee table** *n* mesita (para servir el café)

coffin ['kɒfɪn] *n* ataúd *m*

cog [kɒg] *n* (wheel) rueda dentada; (tooth) diente *m*

cognac ['kɒnjæk] *n* coñac *m*

coherent [kəu'hɪərənt] *adj* coherente

coil [kɔɪl] *n* rollo; (Elec) bobina, carrete *m*; (contraceptive) espiral *f* ▷ *vt* enrollar

coin [kɔɪn] *n* moneda ▷ *vt* (word) inventar, idear

coincide [kəuɪn'saɪd] *vi* coincidir; (agree) estar de acuerdo; **coincidence** [kəu'ɪnsɪdəns] *n* casualidad *f*

Coke® [kəuk] *n* Coca-Cola®

coke [kəuk] *n* (coal) coque *m*

colander ['kɒləndə*] *n* colador *m*, escurridor *m*

cold [kəuld] *adj* frío ▷ *n* frío; (Med) resfriado; **it's ~** hace frío; **to be ~** (person) tener frío; **to catch (a) ~** resfriarse; **in ~ blood** a sangre fría; **cold sore** *n* herpes *mpl o fpl*

coleslaw ['kəulslɔ:] *n* especie de ensalada de col

colic ['kɒlɪk] *n* cólico

collaborate [kə'læbəreɪt] *vi* colaborar

collapse [kə'læps] *vi* hundirse, derrumbarse; (Med) sufrir un colapso ▷ *n* hundimiento, derrumbamiento; (Med) colapso

collar ['kɒlə*] *n* (of coat, shirt) cuello; (of dog etc) collar; **collarbone** *n* clavícula

colleague ['kɒli:g] *n* colega *mf*; (at work) compañero/a

collect [kə'lɛkt] *vt* (litter, mail etc) recoger; (as a hobby) coleccionar; (BRIT: call and pick up) recoger; (debts, subscriptions etc) recaudar ▷ *vi* reunirse; (dust) acumularse; **to call ~** (us Tel) llamar a cobro revertido; **collection** [kə'lɛkʃən] *n* colección *f*; (of mail, for charity) recogida; **collective** [kə'lɛktɪv] *adj* colectivo; **collector** *n* coleccionista *mf*

college ['kɒlɪdʒ] *n* colegio mayor; (of agriculture, technology) escuela universitaria

collide [kə'laɪd] *vi* chocar

collision [kə'lɪʒən] *n* choque *m*

cologne [kə'ləun] *n* (also: **eau de ~**) (agua de) colonia

Colombia [kə'lɒmbɪə] *n* Colombia; **Colombian** *adj, n* colombiano/a

colon ['kəulən] *n* (sign) dos puntos; (Med) colon *m*

colonel ['kə:nl] *n* coronel *m*

colonial [kə'ləunɪəl] *adj* colonial

colony ['kɒlənɪ] *n* colonia

colour *etc* ['kʌlə*] (us **color** etc) *n* color *m* ▷ *vt* color(e)ar; (dye) teñir; (fig: account) adornar; (: judgement) distorsionar ▷ *vi* (blush) sonrojarse; **colour in** *vt* colorear; **colour-blind** *adj* daltónico; **coloured** *adj* de color; (photo) en color; **colour film** *n* película en color; **colourful** *adj* lleno de color; (story) fantástico; (person) excéntrico; **colouring** *n* (complexion) tez *f*; (in food) colorante *m*; **colour television** *n* televisión *f* en color

column ['kɒləm] *n* columna

coma ['kəumə] *n* coma *m*

comb [kəum] *n* peine *m*; (ornamental) peineta ▷ *vt* (hair) peinar; (area) registrar a fondo

combat ['kɒmbæt] *n* combate *m* ▷ *vt* combatir

combination [kɒmbɪ'neɪʃən] *n* combinación *f*

combine [vb kəm'baɪn, n 'kɒmbaɪn] *vt* combinar; (qualities) reunir ▷ *vi* combinarse ▷ *n* (Econ) cartel *m*

○ **KEYWORD**

come [kʌm] (pt **came**, pp **come**) *vi*
1 (movement towards) venir; **to come running** venir corriendo
2 (arrive) llegar; **he's come here to work** ha venido aquí para trabajar; **to come home** volver a casa
3 (reach): **to come to** llegar a; **the bill came to £40** la cuenta ascendía a cuarenta libras
4 (occur): **an idea came to me** se me ocurrió una idea
5 (be, become): **to come loose/undone** etc aflojarse/desabrocharse/desatarse etc; **I've come to like him** por fin ha llegado a gustarme

come across *vt fus* (person) topar con; (thing) dar con

come along *vi* (BRIT: progress) ir

come back *vi* (return) volver

come down *vi* (price) bajar; (tree, building) ser derribado

come from *vt fus* (place, source) ser de

come in *vi* (visitor) entrar; (train, report) llegar; (fashion) ponerse de moda; (on deal etc) entrar

come off *vi* (button) soltarse, desprenderse; (attempt) salir bien

come on *vi* (pupil) progresar; (work, project)

desarrollarse; (*lights*) encenderse; (*electricity*) volver; **come on!** ¡vamos!
come out *vi* (*fact*) salir a la luz; (*book, sun*) salir; (*stain*) quitarse
come round *vi* (*after faint, operation*) volver en sí
come to *vi* (*wake*) volver en sí
come up *vi* (*sun*) salir; (*problem*) surgir; (*event*) aproximarse; (*in conversation*) mencionarse
come up with *vt fus* (*idea*) sugerir; (*money*) conseguir

comeback ['kʌmbæk] *n*: **to make a ~** (*Theatre*) volver a las tablas
comedian [kə'miːdɪən] *n* humorista *mf*
comedy ['kɒmɪdɪ] *n* comedia; (*humour*) comicidad *f*
comet ['kɒmɪt] *n* cometa *m*
comfort ['kʌmfət] *n* bienestar *m*; (*relief*) alivio ⊳ *vt* consolar; **comfortable** *adj* cómodo; (*financially*) acomodado; (*easy*) fácil; **comfort station** (*us*) *n* servicios *mpl*
comic ['kɒmɪk] *adj* (*also*: **~al**) cómico ⊳ *n* (*comedian*) cómico; (*BRIT: for children*) tebeo; (*BRIT: for adults*) comic *m*; **comic book** (*us*) *n* libro *m* de cómics; **comic strip** *n* tira cómica
comma ['kɒmə] *n* coma
command [kə'mɑːnd] *n* orden *f*, mandato; (*Mil: authority*) mando; (*mastery*) dominio ⊳ *vt* (*troops*) mandar; (*give orders to*): **to ~ sb to do** mandar *or* ordenar a algn hacer; **commander** *n* (*Mil*) comandante *mf*, jefe/a *m/f*
commemorate [kə'mɛməreɪt] *vt* conmemorar
commence [kə'mɛns] *vt, vi* comenzar, empezar; **commencement** (*us*) *n* (*Univ*) (ceremonia de) graduación *f*
commend [kə'mɛnd] *vt* elogiar, alabar; (*recommend*) recomendar
comment ['kɒmɛnt] *n* comentario ⊳ *vi*: **to ~ on** hacer comentarios sobre; **"no ~"** (*written*) "sin comentarios"; (*spoken*) "no tengo nada que decir"; **commentary** ['kɒməntərɪ] *n* comentario; **commentator** ['kɒmənteɪtə*] *n* comentarista *mf*
commerce ['kɒmɜːs] *n* comercio
commercial [kə'mɜːʃəl] *adj* comercial ⊳ *n* (*TV, Radio*) anuncio; **commercial break** *n* intermedio para publicidad
commission [kə'mɪʃən] *n* (*committee, fee*) comisión *f* ⊳ *vt* (*work of art*) encargar; **out of ~** fuera de servicio; **commissioner** *n* (*Police*) comisario de policía
commit [kə'mɪt] *vt* (*act*) cometer; (*resources*) dedicar; (*to sb's care*) entregar;

to ~ o.s. (to do) comprometerse (a hacer); **to ~ suicide** suicidarse; **commitment** *n* compromiso; (*to ideology etc*) entrega
committee [kə'mɪtɪ] *n* comité *m*
commodity [kə'mɒdɪtɪ] *n* mercancía
common ['kɒmən] *adj* común; (*pej*) ordinario ⊳ *n* campo común; **commonly** *adv* comúnmente; **commonplace** *adj* de lo más común; **Commons** (*BRIT*) *npl* (*Pol*): **the Commons** (la Cámara de) los Comunes; **common sense** *n* sentido común; **Commonwealth** *n*: **the Commonwealth** la Commonwealth
communal ['kɒmjuːnl] *adj* (*property*) comunal; (*kitchen*) común
commune [*n* 'kɒmjuːn, *vb* kə'mjuːn] *n* (*group*) comuna ⊳ *vi*: **to ~ with** comulgar *or* conversar con
communicate [kə'mjuːnɪkeɪt] *vt* comunicar ⊳ *vi*: **to ~ (with)** comunicarse (con); (*in writing*) estar en contacto (con)
communication [kəmjuːnɪ'keɪʃən] *n* comunicación *f*
communion [kə'mjuːnɪən] *n* (*also*: **Holy ~**) comunión *f*
communism ['kɒmjunɪzəm] *n* comunismo; **communist** *adj, n* comunista *mf*
community [kə'mjuːnɪtɪ] *n* comunidad *f*; (*large group*) colectividad *f*; **community centre** (*us* **community center**) *n* centro social; **community service** *n* trabajo *m* comunitario (*prestado en lugar de cumplir una pena de prisión*)
commute [kə'mjuːt] *vi* viajar a diario de la casa al trabajo ⊳ *vt* conmutar; **commuter** *n* persona que viaja a diario de la casa al trabajo
compact [*adj* kəm'pækt, *n* 'kɒmpækt] *adj* compacto ⊳ *n* (*also*: **powder ~**) polvera; **compact disc** *n* compact disc *m*; **compact disc player** *n* reproductor *m* de disco compacto, compact disc *m*
companion [kəm'pænɪən] *n* compañero/a
company ['kʌmpənɪ] *n* compañía; (*Comm*) sociedad *f*, compañía; **to keep sb ~** acompañar a algn; **company car** *n* coche *m* de la empresa; **company director** *n* director(a) *m/f* de empresa
comparable ['kɒmpərəbl] *adj* comparable
comparative [kəm'pærətɪv] *adj* relativo; (*study*) comparativo; **comparatively** *adv* (*relatively*) relativamente
compare [kəm'pɛə*] *vt*: **to ~ sth/sb with** *or* **to** comparar algo/a algn con ⊳ *vi*: **to ~ (with)** compararse (con); **comparison** [-'pærɪsn] *n* comparación *f*

compartment [kəm'pɑːtmənt] *n*
(*also: Rail*) compartim(i)ento

compass ['kʌmpəs] *n* brújula;
compasses *npl* (*Math*) compás *m*

compassion [kəm'pæʃən] *n* compasión *f*

compatible [kəm'pætɪbl] *adj* compatible

compel [kəm'pɛl] *vt* obligar; **compelling**
adj (*fig: argument*) convincente

compensate ['kɔmpənseɪt] *vt*
compensar ▷ *vi*: **to ~ for** compensar;
compensation [-'seɪʃən] *n* (*for loss*)
indemnización *f*

compete [kəm'piːt] *vi* (*take part*) tomar
parte, concurrir; (*vie with*): **to ~ with**
competir con, hacer competencia a

competent ['kɔmpɪtənt] *adj*
competente, capaz

competition [kɔmpɪ'tɪʃən] *n* (*contest*)
concurso; (*rivalry*) competencia

competitive [kəm'pɛtɪtɪv] *adj* (*Econ,
Sport*) competitivo

competitor [kəm'pɛtɪtə*] *n* (*rival*)
competidor(a) *m/f*; (*participant*) concursante
mf

complacent [kəm'pleɪsənt] *adj*
autocomplaciente

complain [kəm'pleɪn] *vi* quejarse; (*Comm*)
reclamar; **complaint** *n* queja; reclamación
f; (*Med*) enfermedad *f*

complement [*n* 'kɔmplɪmənt, *vb*
'kɔmplɪment] *n* complemento; (*esp
of ship's crew*) dotación *f* ▷ *vt* (*enhance*)
complementar; **complementary**
[kɔmplɪ'mɛntərɪ] *adj* complementario

complete [kəm'pliːt] *adj* (*full*) completo;
(*finished*) acabado ▷ *vt* (*fulfil*) completar;
(*finish*) acabar; (*a form*) llenar; **completely**
adv completamente; **completion**
[-'pliːʃən] *n* terminación *f*; (*of contract*)
realización *f*

complex ['kɔmplɛks] *adj, n* complejo

complexion [kəm'plɛkʃən] *n* (*of face*) tez
f, cutis *m*

compliance [kəm'plaɪəns] *n* (*submission*)
sumisión *f*; (*agreement*) conformidad *f*; **in ~
with** de acuerdo con

complicate ['kɔmplɪkeɪt] *vt* complicar;
complicated *adj* complicado;
complication [-'keɪʃən] *n* complicación *f*

compliment ['kɔmplɪmənt] *n* (*formal*)
cumplido ▷ *vt* felicitar; **complimentary**
[-'mɛntərɪ] *adj* lisonjero; (*free*) de favor

comply [kəm'plaɪ] *vi*: **to ~ with** cumplir
con

component [kəm'pəunənt] *adj*
componente ▷ *n* (*Tech*) pieza

compose [kəm'pəuz] *vt*: **to be ~d of**
componerse de; (*music etc*) componer;

to ~ o.s. tranquilizarse; **composer** *n*
(*Mus*) compositor(a) *m/f*; **composition**
[kɔmpə'zɪʃən] *n* composición *f*

composure [kəm'pəuʒə*] *n* serenidad
f, calma

compound ['kɔmpaund] *n* (*Chem*)
compuesto; (*Ling*) palabra compuesta;
(*enclosure*) recinto ▷ *adj* compuesto;
(*fracture*) complicado

comprehension [-'hɛnʃən] *n*
comprensión *f*

comprehensive [kɔmprɪ'hɛnsɪv] *adj*
exhaustivo; (*Insurance*) contra todo riesgo;
comprehensive (school) *n centro estatal de
enseñanza secundaria* ≈ Instituto Nacional de
Bachillerato (*SP*)

compress [*vb* kəm'prɛs, *n* 'kɔmprɛs] *vt*
comprimir; (*information*) condensar ▷ *n*
(*Med*) compresa

comprise [kəm'praɪz] *vt* (*also:* **be ~d
of**) comprender, constar de; (*constitute*)
constituir

compromise ['kɔmprəmaɪz] *n*
(*agreement*) arreglo ▷ *vt* comprometer ▷ *vi*
transigir

compulsive [kəm'pʌlsɪv] *adj* compulsivo;
(*viewing, reading*) obligado

compulsory [kəm'pʌlsərɪ] *adj*
obligatorio

computer [kəm'pjuːtə*] *n* ordenador *m*,
computador *m*, computadora; **computer
game** *n* juego para ordenador; **computer-
generated** *adj* realizado por ordenador,
creado por ordenador; **computerize** *vt*
(*data*) computerizar; (*system*) informatizar;
we're computerized now ya nos hemos
informatizado; **computer programmer**
n programador(a) *m/f*; **computer
programming** *n* programación *f*;
computer science *n* informática;
computer studies *npl* informática *fsg*,
computación *fsg* (*LAM*); **computing** [kəm-
'pjuːtɪŋ] *n* (*activity, science*) informática

con [kɔn] *vt* (*deceive*) engañar; (*cheat*)
estafar ▷ *n* estafa

conceal [kən'siːl] *vt* ocultar

concede [kən'siːd] *vt* (*point, argument*)
reconocer; (*territory*) ceder; **to ~ (defeat)**
darse por vencido; **to ~ that** admitir que

conceited [kən'siːtɪd] *adj* presumido

conceive [kən'siːv] *vt, vi* concebir

concentrate ['kɔnsəntreɪt] *vi*
concentrarse ▷ *vt* concentrar

concentration [kɔnsən'treɪʃən] *n*
concentración *f*

concept ['kɔnsɛpt] *n* concepto

concern [kən'səːn] *n* (*matter*) asunto;
(*Comm*) empresa; (*anxiety*) preocupación

f ▷ vt (*worry*) preocupar; (*involve*) afectar; (*relate to*) tener que ver con; **to be ~ed (about)** interesarse (por), preocuparse (por); **concerning** *prep* sobre, acerca de

concert ['kɔnsət] *n* concierto; **concert hall** *n* sala de conciertos

concerto [kən'tʃɔːtəu] *n* concierto

concession [kən'sɛʃən] *n* concesión *f*; **tax ~** privilegio fiscal

concise [kən'saɪs] *adj* conciso

conclude [kən'kluːd] *vt* concluir; (*treaty etc*) firmar; (*agreement*) llegar a; (*decide*) llegar a la conclusión de; **conclusion** [-'kluːʒən] *n* conclusión *f*; firma

concrete ['kɔnkriːt] *n* hormigón *m* ▷ *adj* de hormigón; (*fig*) concreto

concussion [kən'kʌʃən] *n* conmoción *f* cerebral

condemn [kən'dɛm] *vt* condenar; (*building*) declarar en ruina

condensation [kɔndən'seɪʃən] *n* condensación *f*

condense [kən'dɛns] *vi* condensarse ▷ *vt* condensar, abreviar

condition [kən'dɪʃən] *n* condición *f*, estado; (*requirement*) condición *f* ▷ *vt* condicionar; **on ~ that** a condición (de) que; **conditional** [kən'dɪʃənl] *adj* condicional; **conditioner** *n* suavizante

condo ['kɔndəu] (*US*) *n* (*inf*) = **condominium**

condom ['kɔndəm] *n* condón *m*

condominium [kɔndə'mɪnɪəm] (*US*) *n* (*building*) bloque *m* de pisos *or* apartamentos (*propiedad de quienes lo habitan*), condominio (*LAM*); (*apartment*) piso *or* apartamento (en propiedad), condominio (*LAM*)

condone [kən'dəun] *vt* condonar

conduct [*n* 'kɔndʌkt, *vb* kən'dʌkt] *n* conducta, comportamiento ▷ *vt* (*lead*) conducir; (*manage*) llevar a cabo, dirigir; (*Mus*) dirigir; **to ~ o.s.** comportarse; **conducted tour** (*BRIT*) *n* visita acompañada; **conductor** *n* (*of orchestra*) director *m*; (*US: on train*) revisor(a) *m/f*; (*on bus*) cobrador *m*; (*Elec*) conductor *m*

cone [kəun] *n* cono; (*pine cone*) piña; (*on road*) pivote *m*; (*for ice-cream*) cucurucho

confectionery [kən'fɛkʃənrɪ] *n* dulces *mpl*

confer [kən'fəː*] *vt*: **to ~ sth on** otorgar algo a ▷ *vi* conferenciar

conference ['kɔnfərns] *n* (*meeting*) reunión *f*; (*convention*) congreso

confess [kən'fɛs] *vt* confesar ▷ *vi* admitir; **confession** [-'fɛʃən] *n* confesión *f*

confide [kən'faɪd] *vi*: **to ~ in** confiar en

confidence ['kɔnfɪdns] *n* (*also*: **self-~**)

confianza; (*secret*) confidencia; **in ~** (*speak, write*) en confianza; **confident** *adj* seguro de sí mismo; (*certain*) seguro; **confidential** [kɔnfɪ'dɛnʃəl] *adj* confidencial

confine [kən'faɪn] *vt* (*limit*) limitar; (*shut up*) encerrar; **confined** *adj* (*space*) reducido

confirm [kən'fəːm] *vt* confirmar; **confirmation** [kɔnfə'meɪʃən] *n* confirmación *f*

confiscate ['kɔnfɪskeɪt] *vt* confiscar

conflict [*n* 'kɔnflɪkt, *vb* kən'flɪkt] *n* conflicto ▷ *vi* (*opinions*) chocar

conform [kən'fɔːm] *vi* conformarse; **to ~ to** ajustarse a

confront [kən'frʌnt] *vt* (*problems*) hacer frente a; (*enemy, danger*) enfrentarse con; **confrontation** [kɔnfrən'teɪʃən] *n* enfrentamiento

confuse [kən'fjuːz] *vt* (*perplex*) aturdir, desconcertar; (*mix up*) confundir; (*complicate*) complicar; **confused** *adj* confuso; (*person*) perplejo; **confusing** *adj* confuso; **confusion** [-'fjuːʒən] *n* confusión *f*

congestion [kən'dʒɛstʃən] *n* congestión *f*

congratulate [kən'grætjuleɪt] *vt*: **to ~ sb (on)** felicitar a algn (por); **congratulations** [-'leɪʃənz] *npl* felicitaciones *fpl*; **congratulations!** ¡enhorabuena!

congregation [-'geɪʃən] *n* (*of a church*) feligreses *mpl*

congress ['kɔngrɛs] *n* congreso; (*US*): **C~** Congreso; **congressman** (*irreg: US*) *n* miembro del Congreso; **congresswoman** (*irreg: US*) *n* diputada, miembro *f* del Congreso

conifer ['kɔnɪfə*] *n* conífera

conjugate ['kɔndʒugeɪt] *vt* conjugar

conjugation [kɔndʒə'geɪʃən] *n* conjugación *f*

conjunction [kən'dʒʌŋkʃən] *n* conjunción *f*; **in ~ with** junto con

conjure ['kʌndʒə*] *vi* hacer juegos de manos

connect [kə'nɛkt] *vt* juntar, unir; (*Elec*) conectar; (*Tel: subscriber*) poner; (*: caller*) poner al habla; (*fig*) relacionar, asociar ▷ *vi*: **to ~ with** (*train*) enlazar con; **to be ~ed with** (*associated*) estar relacionado con; **connecting flight** *n* vuelo *m* de enlace; **connection** [-ʃən] *n* juntura, unión *f*; (*Elec*) conexión *f*; (*Rail*) enlace *m*; (*Tel*) comunicación *f*; (*fig*) relación *f*

conquer ['kɔŋkə*] *vt* (*territory*) conquistar; (*enemy, feelings*) vencer

conquest ['kɔŋkwɛst] *n* conquista

cons [kɔnz] *npl see* **convenience; pro; mod**

conscience ['kɔnʃəns] n conciencia
conscientious [kɔnʃɪ'enʃəs] adj
concienzudo; (objection) de conciencia
conscious ['kɔnʃəs] adj (deliberate)
deliberado; (awake, aware) consciente;
consciousness n conciencia; (Med)
conocimiento
consecutive [kən'sɛkjutɪv] adj
consecutivo; **on 3 ~ occasions** en 3
ocasiones consecutivas
consensus [kən'sɛnsəs] n consenso
consent [kən'sɛnt] n consentimiento
▷ vi: **to ~ (to)** consentir (en)
consequence ['kɔnsɪkwəns] n
consecuencia; (significance) importancia
consequently ['kɔnsɪkwəntlɪ] adv por
consiguiente
conservation [kɔnsə'veɪʃən] n
conservación f
conservative [kən'sə:vətɪv] adj
conservador(a); (estimate etc) cauteloso;
Conservative (BRIT) adj, n (Pol)
conservador(a) m/f
conservatory [kən'sə:vətrɪ] n
invernadero; (Mus) conservatorio
consider [kən'sɪdə*] vt considerar;
(take into account) tener en cuenta;
(study) estudiar, examinar; **to ~ doing
sth** pensar en (la posibilidad de) hacer
algo; **considerable** adj considerable;
considerably adv notablemente;
considerate adj considerado;
consideration [-'reɪʃən] n consideración
f; (factor) factor m; **to give sth further
consideration** estudiar algo más a fondo;
considering prep teniendo en cuenta
consignment [kən'saɪnmənt] n envío
consist [kən'sɪst] vi: **to ~ of** consistir en
consistency [kən'sɪstənsɪ] n (of argument
etc) coherencia; consecuencia; (thickness)
consistencia
consistent [kən'sɪstənt] adj (person)
consecuente; (argument etc) coherente
consolation [kɔnsə'leɪʃən] n consuelo
console[1] [kən'səul] vt consolar
console[2] ['kɔnsəul] n consola
consonant ['kɔnsənənt] n consonante f
conspicuous [kən'spɪkjuəs] adj (visible)
visible
conspiracy [kən'spɪrəsɪ] n conjura,
complot m
constable ['kʌnstəbl] (BRIT) n policía m/f;
chief ~ ≈ jefe m de policía
constant ['kɔnstənt] adj constante;
constantly adv constantemente
constipated ['kɔnstɪpeɪtəd] adj
estreñido
⬛ Be careful not to translate **constipated**

⬛ by the Spanish word constipado.
constipation [kɔnstɪ'peɪʃən] n
estreñimiento
constituency [kən'stɪtjuənsɪ] n
(Pol: area) distrito electoral; (: electors)
electorado
constitute ['kɔnstɪtjuːt] vt constituir
constitution [kɔnstɪ'tjuːʃən] n
constitución f
constraint [kən'streɪnt] n obligación f;
(limit) restricción f
construct [kən'strʌkt] vt construir;
construction [-ʃən] n construcción f;
constructive adj constructivo
consul ['kɔnsl] n cónsul m/f; **consulate**
['kɔnsjulɪt] n consulado
consult [kən'sʌlt] vt consultar;
consultant n (BRIT Med) especialista m/f;
(other specialist) asesor(a) m/f; **consultation**
[kɔnsəl'teɪʃən] n consulta; **consulting
room** (BRIT) n consultorio
consume [kən'sjuːm] vt (eat) comerse;
(drink) beberse; (fire etc, Comm) consumir;
consumer n consumidor(a) m/f
consumption [kən'sʌmpʃən] n consumo
cont. abbr (=continued) sigue
contact ['kɔntækt] n contacto; (person)
contacto; (: pej) enchufe m ▷ vt ponerse en
contacto con; **contact lenses** npl lentes fpl
de contacto
contagious [kən'teɪdʒəs] adj contagioso
contain [kən'teɪn] vt contener; **to ~ o.s.**
contenerse; **container** n recipiente m; (for
shipping etc) contenedor m
contaminate [kən'tæmɪneɪt] vt
contaminar
cont'd abbr (=continued) sigue
contemplate ['kɔntəmpleɪt] vt
contemplar; (reflect upon) considerar
contemporary [kən'tɛmpərərɪ] adj, n
contemporáneo/a m/f
contempt [kən'tɛmpt] n desprecio; **~ of
court** (Law) desacato (a los tribunales)
contend [kən'tɛnd] vt (argue) afirmar
▷ vi: **to ~ with/for** luchar contra/por
content [adj, vb kən'tɛnt, n 'kɔntɛnt]
adj (happy) contento; (satisfied) satisfecho
▷ vt contentar; satisfacer ▷ n contenido;
contents npl contenido; **(table of) ~s**
índice m de materias; **contented** adj
contento; satisfecho
contest [n 'kɔntɛst, vb kən'tɛst] n lucha;
(competition) concurso ▷ vt (dispute)
impugnar; (Pol) presentarse como
candidato/a en
⬛ Be careful not to translate **contest** by the
⬛ Spanish word contestar.
contestant [kən'tɛstənt] n concursante

mf; *(in fight)* contendiente *mf*
context ['kɒntekst] *n* contexto
continent ['kɒntɪnənt] *n* continente
m; **the C~** (BRIT) el continente europeo;
continental [-'nentl] *adj* continental;
continental breakfast *n* desayuno
estilo europeo; **continental quilt** (BRIT) *n*
edredón *m*
continual [kən'tɪnjuəl] *adj* continuo;
continually *adv* constantemente
continue [kən'tɪnjuː] *vi*, *vt* seguir,
continuar
continuity [kɒntɪ'njuɪtɪ] *n* (*also Cine*)
continuidad *f*
continuous [kən'tɪnjuəs] *adj* continuo;
continuous assessment *n* (BRIT)
evaluación *f* continua; **continuously** *adv*
continuamente
contour ['kɒntuə*] *n* contorno; (*also:* ~
line) curva de nivel
contraception [kɒntrə'sepʃən] *n*
contracepción *f*
contraceptive [kɒntrə'septɪv] *adj, n*
anticonceptivo
contract [*n* 'kɒntrækt, *vb* kən'trækt]
n contrato ▷ *vi* (*Comm*): **to ~ to do sth**
comprometerse por contrato a hacer algo;
(*become smaller*) contraerse, encogerse ▷ *vt*
contraer; **contractor** *n* contratista *mf*
contradict [kɒntrə'dɪkt] *vt* contradecir;
contradiction [-ʃən] *n* contradicción *f*
contrary[1] ['kɒntrərɪ] *adj* contrario ▷ *n*
lo contrario; **on the ~** al contrario; **unless
you hear to the ~** a no ser que le digan lo
contrario
contrary[2] [kən'treərɪ] *adj* (*perverse*) terco
contrast [*n* 'kɒntrɑːst, *vt* kən'trɑːst] *n*
contraste *m* ▷ *vt* comparar; **in ~ to** en
contraste con
contribute [kən'trɪbjuːt] *vi* contribuir
▷ *vt*: **to ~ £10/an article to** contribuir con 10
libras/un artículo a; **to ~ to** (*charity*) donar
a; (*newspaper*) escribir para; (*discussion*)
intervenir en; **contribution** [kɒntrɪ'bjuː-
ʃən] *n* (*donation*) donativo; (BRIT: *for
social security*) cotización *f*; (*to debate*)
intervención *f*; (*to journal*) colaboración
f; **contributor** *n* contribuyente *mf*; (*to
newspaper*) colaborador(a) *m/f*
control [kən'trəul] *vt* controlar; (*process
etc*) dirigir; (*machinery*) manejar; (*temper*)
dominar; (*disease*) contener ▷ *n* control
m; **controls** *npl* (*of vehicle*) instrumentos
mpl de mando; (*of radio*) controles *mpl*;
(*governmental*) medidas *fpl* de control; **under
~** bajo control; **to be in ~ of** tener el mando
de; **the car went out of ~** se perdió el
control del coche; **control tower** *n* (*Aviat*)

torre *f* de control
controversial [kɒntrə'vəːʃl] *adj* polémico
controversy ['kɒntrəvəːsɪ] *n* polémica
convenience [kən'viːnɪəns] *n* (*easiness*)
comodidad *f*; (*suitability*) idoneidad *f*;
(*advantage*) ventaja; **at your ~** cuando le sea
conveniente; **all modern ~s, all mod cons**
(BRIT) todo confort
convenient [kən'viːnɪənt] *adj* (*useful*)
útil; (*place, time*) conveniente
convent ['kɒnvənt] *n* convento
convention [kən'venʃən] *n* convención
f; (*meeting*) asamblea; (*agreement*) convenio;
conventional *adj* convencional
conversation [kɒnvə'seɪʃən] *n*
conversación *f*
conversely [-'vəːslɪ] *adv* a la inversa
conversion [kən'vəːʃən] *n* conversión *f*
convert [*vb* kən'vəːt, *n* 'kɒnvəːt] *vt* (*Rel,
Comm*) convertir; (*alter*): **to ~ sth into/to**
transformar algo en/convertir algo a ▷ *n*
converso/a; **convertible** *adj* convertible
▷ *n* descapotable *m*
convey [kən'veɪ] *vt* llevar; (*thanks*)
comunicar; (*idea*) expresar; **conveyor belt** *n*
cinta transportadora
convict [*vb* kən'vɪkt, *n* 'kɒnvɪkt] *vt* (*find
guilty*) declarar culpable a ▷ *n* presidiario/a;
conviction [-ʃən] *n* condena; (*belief,
certainty*) convicción *f*
convince [kən'vɪns] *vt* convencer;
convinced *adj*: **convinced of/that**
convencido de/de que; **convincing** *adj*
convincente
convoy ['kɒnvɔɪ] *n* convoy *m*
cook [kuk] *vt* (*stew etc*) guisar; (*meal*)
preparar ▷ *vi* cocer; (*person*) cocinar ▷ *n*
cocinero/a; **cook book** *n* libro de cocina;
cooker *n* cocina; **cookery** *n* cocina;
cookery book (BRIT) *n* = **cook book; cookie**
(US) *n* galleta; **cooking** *n* cocina
cool [kuːl] *adj* fresco; (*not afraid*) tranquilo;
(*unfriendly*) frío ▷ *vt* enfriar ▷ *vi* enfriarse;
cool down *vi* enfriarse; (*fig: person,
situation*) calmarse; **cool off** *vi* (*become
calmer*) calmarse, apaciguarse; (*lose
enthusiasm*) perder (el) interés, enfriarse
cop [kɒp] (*inf*) *n* poli *mf* (SP), tira *mf* (MEX)
cope [kəup] *vi*: **to ~ with** (*problem*) hacer
frente a
copper ['kɒpə*] *n* (*metal*) cobre *m*; (BRIT: *inf*)
poli *mf*, tira *mf* (MEX)
copy ['kɒpɪ] *n* copia; (*of book etc*) ejemplar
m ▷ *vt* copiar; **copyright** *n* derechos *mpl*
de autor
coral ['kɒrəl] *n* coral *m*
cord [kɔːd] *n* cuerda; (*Elec*) cable *m*; (*fabric*)
pana; **cords** *npl* (*trousers*) pantalones *mpl* de

pana; **cordless** adj sin hilos

corduroy [ˈkɔːdərɔɪ] n pana

core [kɔː*] n centro, núcleo; (of fruit) corazón m; (of problem) meollo ▷ vt quitar el corazón de

coriander [kɒrɪˈændə*] n culantro

cork [kɔːk] n corcho; (tree) alcornoque m; **corkscrew** n sacacorchos m inv

corn [kɔːn] n (BRIT: cereal crop) trigo; (US: maize) maíz m; (on foot) callo; **~ on the cob** (Culin) mazorca, elote m (MEX), choclo (SC)

corned beef [ˈkɔːnd-] n carne f acecinada (en lata)

corner [ˈkɔːnə*] n (outside) esquina; (inside) rincón m; (in road) curva; (Football) córner m; (Boxing) esquina ▷ vt (trap) arrinconar; (Comm) acaparar ▷ vi (in car) tomar las curvas; **corner shop** (BRIT) tienda de la esquina

cornflakes [ˈkɔːnfleɪks] npl copos mpl de maíz, cornflakes mpl

cornflour [ˈkɔːnflauə*] (BRIT) n harina de maíz

cornstarch [ˈkɔːnstɑːtʃ] (US) n = **cornflour**

Cornwall [ˈkɔːnwəl] n Cornualles m

coronary [ˈkɒrənərɪ] n (also: **~ thrombosis**) infarto

coronation [kɒrəˈneɪʃən] n coronación f

coroner [ˈkɒrənə*] n juez mf de instrucción

corporal [ˈkɔːpərl] n cabo ▷ adj: **~ punishment** castigo corporal

corporate [ˈkɔːpərɪt] adj (action, ownership) colectivo; (finance, image) corporativo

corporation [kɔːpəˈreɪʃən] n (of town) ayuntamiento; (Comm) corporación f

corps [kɔː*, pl kɔːz] n inv cuerpo; **diplomatic ~** cuerpo diplomático; **press ~** gabinete m de prensa

corpse [kɔːps] n cadáver m

correct [kəˈrekt] adj justo, exacto; (proper) correcto ▷ vt corregir; (exam) corregir, calificar; **correction** [-ʃən] n (act) corrección f; (instance) rectificación f

correspond [kɒrɪsˈpɒnd] vi (write): **to ~ (with)** escribirse (con); (be equivalent to): **to ~ (to)** corresponder (a); (be in accordance): **to ~ (with)** corresponder (con); **correspondence** n correspondencia; **correspondent** n corresponsal mf; **corresponding** adj correspondiente

corridor [ˈkɒrɪdɔː*] n pasillo

corrode [kəˈrəud] vt corroer ▷ vi corroerse

corrupt [kəˈrʌpt] adj (person) corrupto; (Comput) corrompido ▷ vt corromper;

(Comput) degradar; **corruption** n corrupción f; (of data) alteración f

Corsica [ˈkɔːsɪkə] n Córcega

cosmetic [kɒzˈmetɪk] adj, n cosmético; **cosmetic surgery** n cirugía f estética

cosmopolitan [kɒzməˈpɒlɪtn] adj cosmopolita

cost [kɒst] (pt, pp **~**) n (price) precio ▷ vi costar, valer ▷ vt preparar el presupuesto de; **how much does it ~?** ¿cuánto cuesta?; **to ~ sb time/effort** costarle a algn tiempo/esfuerzo; **it ~ him his life** le costó la vida; **at all ~s** cueste lo que cueste; **costs** npl (Comm) costes mpl; (Law) costas fpl

co-star [ˈkəustɑː*] n coprotagonista mf

Costa Rica [ˈkɒstəˈriːkə] n Costa Rica; **Costa Rican** adj, n costarriqueño/a

costly [ˈkɒstlɪ] adj costoso

cost of living n costo or coste m (Sp) de la vida

costume [ˈkɒstjuːm] n traje m; (BRIT: also: **swimming ~**) traje de baño

cosy [ˈkəuzɪ] (US **cozy**) adj (person) cómodo; (room) acogedor(a)

cot [kɒt] n (BRIT: child's) cuna; (US: campbed) cama de campaña

cottage [ˈkɒtɪdʒ] n casita de campo; (rustic) barraca; **cottage cheese** n requesón m

cotton [ˈkɒtn] n algodón m; (thread) hilo; **cotton on** vi (inf): **to cotton on (to sth)** caer en la cuenta (de algo); **cotton bud** n (BRIT) bastoncillo m de algodón; **cotton candy** (US) n algodón m (azucarado); **cotton wool** (BRIT) n algodón m (hidrófilo)

couch [kautʃ] n sofá m; (doctor's etc) diván m

cough [kɒf] vi toser ▷ n tos f; **cough mixture** n jarabe m para la tos

could [kud] pt of **can²**; **couldn't** = **could not**

council [ˈkaunsl] n consejo; **city** or **town ~** consejo municipal; **council estate** (BRIT) n urbanización de viviendas municipales de alquiler; **council house** (BRIT) n vivienda municipal de alquiler; **councillor** (US **councilor**) n concejal(a) m/f; **council tax** n (BRIT) contribución f municipal (dependiente del valor de la vivienda)

counsel [ˈkaunsl] n (advice) consejo; (lawyer) abogado/a ▷ vt aconsejar; **counselling** (US **counseling**) n (Psych) asistencia f psicológica; **counsellor** (US **counselor**) n consejero/a, abogado/a

count [kaunt] vt contar; (include) incluir ▷ vi contar ▷ n cuenta; (of votes) escrutinio; (level) nivel m; (nobleman) conde m; **count in** (inf) vt: **to count sb in on sth** contar con

algn para algo; **count on** vt fus contar con;
countdown n cuenta atrás

counter ['kauntə*] n (in shop) mostrador
m; (in games) ficha ▷ vt contrarrestar
▷ adv: **to run ~ to** ser contrario a, ir en
contra de; **counter clockwise** (US) adv en
sentido contrario al de las agujas del reloj

counterfeit ['kauntəfɪt] n falsificación
f, simulación f ▷ vt falsificar ▷ adj falso,
falsificado

counterpart ['kauntəpɑːt] n
homólogo/a

countess ['kauntɪs] n condesa

countless ['kauntlɪs] adj innumerable

country ['kʌntrɪ] n país m; (native land)
patria; (as opposed to town) campo; (region)
región f, tierra; **country and western
(music)** n música country; **country house**
n casa de campo; **countryside** n campo

county ['kauntɪ] n condado

coup [kuː] (pl ~s) n (also: ~ d'état) golpe m
(de estado); (achievement) éxito

couple ['kʌpl] n (of things) par m; (of people)
pareja; (married couple) matrimonio; **a ~ of**
un par de

coupon ['kuːpɔn] n cupón m; (voucher)
valé m

courage ['kʌrɪdʒ] n valor m, valentía;
courageous [kə'reɪdʒəs] adj valiente

courgette [kuə'ʒɛt] (BRIT) n calabacín m,
calabacita (MEX)

courier ['kurɪə*] n mensajero/a; (for
tourists) guía mf (de turismo)

course [kɔːs] n (direction) dirección f;
(of river, Scol) curso; (process) transcurso;
(Med): ~ **of treatment** tratamiento; (of ship)
rumbo; (part of meal) plato; (Golf) campo; **of
~** desde luego, naturalmente; **of ~!** ¡claro!

court [kɔːt] n (royal) corte f; (Law) tribunal
m, juzgado; (Tennis etc) pista, cancha ▷ vt
(woman) cortejar a; **to take to ~** demandar

courtesy ['kɔːtəsɪ] n cortesía; **(by) ~ of**
por cortesía de; **courtesy bus, courtesy
coach** n autobús m gratuito

court: court-house ['kɔːthaus] (US) n
palacio de justicia; **courtroom** ['kɔːtrum]
n sala de justicia; **courtyard** ['kɔːtjɑːd]
n patio

cousin ['kʌzn] n primo/a; **first ~** primo/a
carnal, primo/a hermano/a

cover ['kʌvə*] vt cubrir; (feelings, mistake)
ocultar; (with lid) tapar; (book etc) forrar;
(distance) recorrer; (include) abarcar;
(protect: also: Insurance) cubrir; (Press)
investigar; (discuss) tratar ▷ n cubierta; (lid)
tapa; (for chair etc) funda; (envelope) sobre
m; (for book) forro; (of magazine) portada;
(shelter) abrigo; (Insurance) cobertura; (of

spy) cobertura; **covers** npl (on bed) sábanas;
mantas; **to take ~** (shelter) protegerse,
resguardarse; **under ~** (indoors) bajo techo;
under ~ of darkness al amparo de la
oscuridad; **under separate ~** (Comm) por
separado; **cover up** vi: **to cover up for sb**
encubrir a algn; **coverage** n (TV, Press)
cobertura; **cover charge** n precio del
cubierto; **cover-up** n encubrimiento

cow [kau] n vaca; (infl: woman) bruja ▷ vt
intimidar

coward ['kauəd] n cobarde mf; **cowardly**
adj cobarde

cowboy ['kaubɔɪ] n vaquero

cozy ['kəuzɪ] (US) adj = **cosy**

crab [kræb] n cangrejo

crack [kræk] n grieta; (noise) crujido; (drug)
crack m ▷ vt agrietar, romper; (nut) cascar;
(solve: problem) resolver; (: code) descifrar;
(whip etc) chasquear; (knuckles) crujir; (joke)
contar ▷ adj (expert) de primera; **crack
down on** vt fus adoptar fuertes medidas
contra; **cracked** adj (cup, window) rajado;
(wall) resquebrajado; **cracker** n (biscuit)
crácker m; (Christmas cracker) petardo
sorpresa

crackle ['krækl] vi crepitar

cradle ['kreɪdl] n cuna

craft [krɑːft] n (skill) arte m; (trade) oficio;
(cunning) astucia; (boat: pl inv) barco;
(plane: pl inv) avión m; **craftsman** (irreg)
n artesano; **craftsmanship** n (quality)
destreza

cram [kræm] vt (fill): **to ~ sth with** llenar
algo (a reventar) de; (put): **to ~ sth into**
meter algo a la fuerza en ▷ vi (for exams)
empollar

cramp [kræmp] n (Med) calambre m;
cramped adj apretado, estrecho

cranberry ['krænbərɪ] n arándano agrio

crane [kreɪn] n (Tech) grúa; (bird) grulla

crap [kræp] n (infl) mierda (!)

crash [kræʃ] n (noise) estrépito; (of cars
etc) choque m; (of plane) accidente m de
aviación; (Comm) quiebra ▷ vt (car, plane)
estrellar ▷ vi (car, plane) estrellarse; (two
cars) chocar; (Comm) quebrar; **crash course**
n curso acelerado; **crash helmet** n casco
(protector)

crate [kreɪt] n cajón m de embalaje; (for
bottles) caja

crave [kreɪv] vt, vi: **to ~ (for)** ansiar,
anhelar

crawl [krɔːl] vi (drag o.s.) arrastrarse; (child)
andar a gatas, gatear; (vehicle) avanzar
(lentamente) ▷ n (Swimming) crol m

crayfish ['kreɪfɪʃ] n inv (freshwater)
cangrejo de río; (saltwater) cigala

crayon ['kreiən] n lápiz m de color

craze [kreiz] n (fashion) moda

crazy ['kreizi] adj (person) loco; (idea) disparatado; (inf: keen): **~ about sb/sth** loco por algn/algo

creak [kri:k] vi (floorboard) crujir; (hinge etc) chirriar, rechinar

cream [kri:m] n (of milk) nata, crema; (lotion) crema; (fig) flor f y nata ▷ adj (colour) color crema; **cream cheese** n queso blanco; **creamy** adj cremoso; (colour) color crema

crease [kri:s] n (fold) pliegue m; (in trousers) raya; (wrinkle) arruga ▷ vt (wrinkle) arrugar ▷ vi (wrinkle up) arrugarse

create [kri:'eit] vt crear; **creation** [-ʃən] n creación f; **creative** adj creativo; **creator** n creador(a) m/f

creature ['kri:tʃə*] n (animal) animal m, bicho; (person) criatura

crèche [kreʃ] n guardería (infantil)

credentials [kri'denʃlz] npl (references) referencias fpl; (identity papers) documentos mpl de identidad

credibility [kredi'biliti] n credibilidad f

credible ['kredibl] adj creíble; (trustworthy) digno de confianza

credit ['kredit] n crédito; (merit) honor m, mérito ▷ vt (Comm) abonar; (believe: also: **give ~ to**) creer, prestar fe a ▷ adj crediticio; **credits** npl (Cinema) fichas fpl técnicas; **to be in ~** (person) tener saldo a favor; **to ~ sb with** (fig) reconocer a algn el mérito de; **credit card** n tarjeta de crédito

creek [kri:k] n cala, ensenada; (us) riachuelo

creep [kri:p] (pt, pp **crept**) vi arrastrarse

cremate [kri'meit] vt incinerar

crematorium [kremə'tɔ:riəm] (pl **crematoria**) n crematorio

crept [krept] pt, pp of **creep**

crescent ['kresnt] n media luna; (street) calle f (en forma de semicírculo)

cress [kres] n berro

crest [krest] n (of bird) cresta; (of hill) cima, cumbre f; (of coat of arms) blasón m

crew [kru:] n (of ship etc) tripulación f; (TV, Cinema) equipo; **crew-neck** n cuello a la caja

crib [krib] n cuna ▷ vt (inf) plagiar

cricket ['krikit] n (insect) grillo; (game) críquet m; **cricketer** n jugador(a) m/f de críquet

crime [kraim] n (no pl: illegal activities) crimen m; (illegal action) delito; **criminal** ['kriminl] n criminal mf, delincuente mf ▷ adj criminal; (illegal) delictivo; (law) penal

crimson ['krimzn] adj carmesí

cringe [krindʒ] vi agacharse, encogerse

cripple ['kripl] n lisiado/a, cojo/a ▷ vt lisiar, mutilar

crisis ['kraisis] (pl **crises**) n crisis f inv

crisp [krisp] adj fresco; (vegetables etc) crujiente; (manner) seco; **crispy** adj crujiente

criterion [krai'tiəriən] (pl **criteria**) n criterio

critic ['kritik] n crítico/a; **critical** adj crítico; (illness) grave; **criticism** ['kritisizm] n crítica; **criticize** ['kritisaiz] vt criticar

Croat ['krouæt] adj, n = **Croatian**

Croatia [krou'eiʃə] n Croacia; **Croatian** adj, n croata m/f ▷ n (Ling) croata m

crockery ['krɔkəri] n loza, vajilla

crocodile ['krɔkədail] n cocodrilo

crocus ['kroukəs] n croco, crocus m

croissant ['krwasŋ] n croissant m, medialuna (esp LAM)

crook [kruk] n ladrón/ona m/f; (of shepherd) cayado; **crooked** ['krukid] adj torcido; (dishonest) nada honrado

crop [krɔp] n (produce) cultivo; (amount produced) cosecha; (riding crop) látigo de montar ▷ vt cortar, recortar; **crop up** vi surgir, presentarse

cross [krɔs] n cruz f; (hybrid) cruce m ▷ vt (street etc) cruzar, atravesar ▷ adj de mal humor, enojado; **cross off** vt tachar; **cross out** vt tachar; **cross over** vi cruzar; **cross-Channel ferry** ['krɔs'tʃænl-] n transbordador m que cruza el Canal de la Mancha; **crosscountry (race)** n carrera a campo traviesa, cross m; **crossing** n (sea passage) travesía; (also: **pedestrian crossing**) paso para peatones; **crossing guard** (us) n persona encargada de ayudar a los niños a cruzar la calle; **crossroads** n cruce m, encrucijada; **crosswalk** (us) n paso de peatones; **crossword** n crucigrama m

crotch [krɔtʃ] n (Anat, of garment) entrepierna

crouch [krautʃ] vi agacharse, acurrucarse

crouton ['kru:tɔn] n cubito de pan frito

crow [krou] n (bird) cuervo; (of cock) canto, cacareo ▷ vi (cock) cantar

crowd [kraud] n muchedumbre f, multitud f ▷ vt (fill) llenar ▷ vi (gather): **to ~ round** reunirse en torno a; (cram): **to ~ in** entrar en tropel; **crowded** adj (full) atestado; (densely populated) superpoblado

crown [kraun] n corona; (of head) coronilla; (for tooth) funda; (of hill) cumbre f ▷ vt coronar; (fig) completar, rematar; **crown jewels** npl joyas fpl reales

crucial ['kru:ʃl] adj decisivo

crucifix ['kru:sifiks] n crucifijo

crude [kruːd] *adj* (*materials*) bruto; (*fig: basic*) tosco; (': *vulgar*) ordinario; **crude (oil)** *n* (petróleo) crudo

cruel ['kruəl] *adj* cruel; **cruelty** *n* crueldad *f*

cruise [kruːz] *n* crucero ▷ *vi* (*ship*) hacer un crucero; (*car*) ir a velocidad de crucero

crumb [krʌm] *n* miga, migaja

crumble ['krʌmbl] *vt* desmenuzar ▷ *vi* (*building, also fig*) desmoronarse

crumpet ['krʌmpɪt] *n* ≈ bollo para tostar

crumple ['krʌmpl] *vt* (*paper*) estrujar; (*material*) arrugar

crunch [krʌntʃ] *vt* (*with teeth*) mascar; (*underfoot*) hacer crujir ▷ *n* (*fig*) hora or momento de la verdad; **crunchy** *adj* crujiente

crush [krʌʃ] *n* (*crowd*) aglomeración *f*; (*infatuation*): **to have a ~ on sb** estar loco por algn; (*drink*): **lemon ~** limonada ▷ *vt* aplastar; (*paper*) estrujar; (*cloth*) arrugar; (*fruit*) exprimir; (*opposition*) aplastar; (*hopes*) destruir

crust [krʌst] *n* corteza; (*of snow, ice*) costra; **crusty** *adj* (*bread*) crujiente; (*person*) de mal carácter

crutch [krʌtʃ] *n* muleta

cry [kraɪ] *vi* llorar ▷ *n* (*shriek*) chillido; (*shout*) grito; **cry out** *vi* (*call out, shout*) lanzar un grito, echar un grito ▷ *vt* gritar

crystal ['krɪstl] *n* cristal *m*

cub [kʌb] *n* cachorro; (*also: ~ scout*) niño explorador

Cuba ['kjuːbə] *n* Cuba; **Cuban** *adj, n* cubano/a *m/f*

cube [kjuːb] *n* cubo ▷ *vt* (*Math*) cubicar

cubicle ['kjuːbɪkl] *n* (*at pool*) caseta; (*for bed*) cubículo

cuckoo ['kuku:] *n* cuco

cucumber ['kjuːkʌmbə*] *n* pepino

cuddle ['kʌdl] *vt* abrazar ▷ *vi* abrazarse

cue [kjuː] *n* (*snooker cue*) taco; (*Theatre etc*) señal *f*

cuff [kʌf] *n* (*of sleeve*) puño; (*us: of trousers*) vuelta; (*blow*) bofetada ▷ **off the ~** *adv* de improviso; **cufflinks** *npl* gemelos *mpl*

cuisine [kwɪ'ziːn] *n* cocina

cul-de-sac ['kʌldəsæk] *n* callejón *m* sin salida

cull [kʌl] *vt* (*idea*) sacar ▷ *n* (*of animals*) matanza selectiva

culminate ['kʌlmɪneɪt] *vi*: **to ~ in** terminar en

culprit ['kʌlprɪt] *n* culpable *mf*

cult [kʌlt] *n* culto

cultivate ['kʌltɪveɪt] *vt* cultivar

cultural ['kʌltʃərəl] *adj* cultural

culture ['kʌltʃə*] *n* (*also fig*) cultura; (*Biol*) cultivo

cumin ['kʌmɪn] *n* (*spice*) comino

cunning ['kʌnɪŋ] *n* astucia ▷ *adj* astuto

cup [kʌp] *n* taza; (*as prize*) copa

cupboard ['kʌbəd] *n* armario; (*in kitchen*) alacena

cup final *n* (*Football*) final *f* de copa

curator [kjuə'reɪtə*] *n* director(a) *m/f*

curb [kəːb] *vt* refrenar; (*person*) reprimir ▷ *n* freno; (*us*) bordillo

curdle ['kəːdl] *vi* cuajarse

cure [kjuə*] *vt* curar ▷ *n* cura, curación *f*; (*fig: solution*) remedio

curfew ['kəːfjuː] *n* toque *m* de queda

curiosity [kjuərɪ'ɔsɪtɪ] *n* curiosidad *f*

curious ['kjuərɪəs] *adj* curioso; (*person: interested*): **to be ~** sentir curiosidad

curl [kəːl] *n* rizo ▷ *vt* (*hair*) rizar ▷ *vi* rizarse; **curl up** *vi* (*person*) hacerse un ovillo; **curler** *n* rulo; **curly** *adj* rizado

currant ['kʌrnt] *n* pasa (de Corinto); (*blackcurrant, redcurrant*) grosella

currency ['kʌrnsɪ] *n* moneda; **to gain ~** (*fig*) difundirse

current ['kʌrnt] *n* corriente *f* ▷ *adj* (*accepted*) corriente; (*present*) actual; **current account** (*BRIT*) *n* cuenta corriente; **current affairs** *npl* noticias *fpl* de actualidad; **currently** *adv* actualmente

curriculum [kə'rɪkjuləm] (*pl ~s* or **curricula**) *n* plan *m* de estudios; **curriculum vitae** *n* currículum *m*

curry ['kʌrɪ] *n* curry *m* ▷ *vt*: **to ~ favour with** buscar favores con; **curry powder** *n* curry *m* en polvo

curse [kəːs] *vi* soltar tacos ▷ *vt* maldecir ▷ *n* maldición *f*; (*swearword*) palabrota, taco

cursor ['kəːsə*] *n* (*Comput*) cursor *m*

curt [kəːt] *adj* corto, seco

curtain ['kəːtn] *n* cortina; (*Theatre*) telón *m*

curve [kəːv] *n* curva ▷ *vi* (*road*) hacer una curva; (*line etc*) curvarse; **curved** *adj* curvo

cushion ['kuʃən] *n* cojín *m*; (*of air*) colchón *m* ▷ *vt* (*shock*) amortiguar

custard ['kʌstəd] *n* natillas *fpl*

custody ['kʌstədɪ] *n* custodia; **to take into ~** detener

custom ['kʌstəm] *n* costumbre *f*; (*Comm*) clientela

customer ['kʌstəmə*] *n* cliente *m/f*

customized ['kʌstəmaɪzd] *adj* (*car etc*) hecho a encargo

customs ['kʌstəmz] *npl* aduana; **customs officer** *n* aduanero/a

cut [kʌt] (*pt, pp ~*) *vt* cortar; (*price*) rebajar; (*text, programme*) acortar; (*reduce*) reducir ▷ *vi* cortar ▷ *n* (*of garment*) corte *m*; (*in skin*) cortadura; (*in salary etc*) rebaja; (*in spending*)

reducción f, recorte m; (slice of meat) tajada;
to ~ a tooth echar un diente; **to ~ and
paste** (Comput) cortar y pegar; **cut back**
vt (plants) podar; (production, expenditure)
reducir; **cut down** vt (tree) derribar; (reduce)
reducir; **cut off** vt cortar; (person, place)
aislar; (Tel) desconectar; **cut out** vt (shape)
recortar; (stop: activity etc) dejar; (remove)
quitar; **cut up** vt cortar (en pedazos);
cutback n reducción f
cute [kju:t] adj mono
cutlery ['kʌtlərɪ] n cubiertos mpl
cutlet ['kʌtlɪt] n chuleta; (nut etc cutlet)
plato vegetariano hecho con nueces y verdura en
forma de chuleta
cut-price ['kʌt'praɪs] (BRIT) adj a precio
reducido
cut-rate ['kʌt'reɪt] (US) adj = **cut-price**
cutting ['kʌtɪŋ] adj (remark) mordaz ⊳ n
(BRIT: from newspaper) recorte m; (from plant)
esqueje m
CV n abbr = **curriculum vitae**
cwt abbr = **hundredweight(s)**
cybercafé ['saɪbəkæfeɪ] n cibercafé m
cyberspace ['saɪbəspeɪs] n ciberespacio
cycle ['saɪkl] n ciclo; (bicycle) bicicleta ⊳ vi
ir en bicicleta; **cycle hire** n alquiler m de
bicicletas; **cycle lane** n carril-bici m; **cycle
path** n carril-bici m; **cycling** n ciclismo;
cyclist n ciclista mf
cyclone ['saɪkləun] n ciclón m
cylinder ['sɪlɪndə*] n cilindro; (of gas)
bombona
cymbal ['sɪmbl] n címbalo, platillo
cynical ['sɪnɪkl] adj cínico
Cypriot ['sɪprɪət] adj, n chipriota m/f
Cyprus ['saɪprəs] n Chipre f
cyst [sɪst] n quiste m; **cystitis** [-'taɪtɪs]
n cistitis f
czar [zɑ:*] n zar m
Czech [tʃɛk] adj, n checo/a m/f; **Czech
Republic** n: **the Czech Republic** la
República Checa

d

D [di:] n (Mus) re m
dab [dæb] vt (eyes, wound) tocar
(ligeramente); (paint, cream) poner un
poco de
dad [dæd] n = **daddy**
daddy ['dædɪ] n papá m
daffodil ['dæfədɪl] n narciso
daft [dɑ:ft] adj tonto
dagger ['dægə*] n puñal m, daga
daily ['deɪlɪ] adj diario, cotidiano ⊳ adv
todos los días, cada día
dairy ['dɛərɪ] n (shop) lechería; (on farm)
vaquería; **dairy produce** n productos mpl
lácteos
daisy ['deɪzɪ] n margarita
dam [dæm] n presa ⊳ vt construir una
presa sobre, represar
damage ['dæmɪdʒ] n lesión f; daño; (dents
etc) desperfectos mpl; (fig) perjuicio ⊳ vt
dañar, perjudicar; (spoil, break) estropear;
damages npl (Law) daños mpl y perjuicios
damn [dæm] vt condenar; (curse) maldecir
⊳ n (inf): **I don't give a ~** me importa un
pito ⊳ adj (inf: also: **~ed**) maldito; **~ (it)!**
¡maldito sea!
damp [dæmp] adj húmedo, mojado ⊳ n
humedad f ⊳ vt (also: **~en**: cloth, rag) mojar;
(: enthusiasm) enfriar
dance [dɑ:ns] n baile m ⊳ vi bailar;
dance floor n pista f de baile; **dancer** n
bailador(a) m/f; (professional) bailarín/ina
m/f; **dancing** n baile m
dandelion ['dændɪlaɪən] n diente m de
león
dandruff ['dændrəf] n caspa
Dane [deɪn] n danés/esa m/f
danger ['deɪndʒə*] n peligro; (risk) riesgo;
~! (on sign) ¡peligro de muerte!; **to be in ~ of**
correr riesgo de; **dangerous** adj peligroso
dangle ['dæŋgl] vt colgar ⊳ vi pender,
colgar

Danish ['deɪnɪʃ] *adj* danés/esa ▷ *n* (*Ling*) danés *m*

dare [dɛə*] *vt*: **to ~ sb to do** desafiar a algn a hacer ▷ *vi*: **to ~ (to) do sth** atreverse a hacer algo; **I ~ say** (*I suppose*) puede ser (que); **daring** *adj* atrevido, osado ▷ *n* atrevimiento, osadía

dark [dɑːk] *adj* oscuro; (*hair, complexion*) moreno ▷ *n*: **in the ~** a oscuras; **to be in the ~ about** (*fig*) no saber nada de; **after ~** después del anochecer; **darken** *vt* (*colour*) hacer más oscuro ▷ *vi* oscurecerse; **darkness** *n* oscuridad *f*; **darkroom** *n* cuarto oscuro

darling ['dɑːlɪŋ] *adj, n* querido/a *m/f*

dart [dɑːt] *n* dardo; (*in sewing*) sisa ▷ *vi* precipitarse; **dartboard** *n* diana; **darts** *n* (*game*) dardos *mpl*

dash [dæʃ] *n* (*small quantity: of liquid*) gota, chorrito; (*sign*) raya ▷ *vt* (*throw*) tirar; (*hopes*) defraudar ▷ *vi* precipitarse, ir de prisa

dashboard ['dæʃbɔːd] *n* (*Aut*) salpicadero

data ['deɪtə] *npl* datos *mpl*; **database** *n* base *f* de datos; **data processing** *n* proceso de datos

date [deɪt] *n* (*day*) fecha; (*with friend*) cita; (*fruit*) dátil *m* ▷ *vt* fechar; (*person*) salir con; **~ of birth** fecha de nacimiento; **to ~** *adv* hasta la fecha; **dated** *adj* anticuado

daughter ['dɔːtə*] *n* hija; **daughter-in-law** *n* nuera, hija política

daunting ['dɔːntɪŋ] *adj* desalentador(a)

dawn [dɔːn] *n* alba, amanecer *m*; (*fig*) nacimiento ▷ *vi* (*day*) amanecer; (*fig*): **it ~ed on him that ...** cayó en la cuenta de que ...

day [deɪ] *n* día *m*; (*working day*) jornada; (*heyday*) tiempos *mpl*, días *mpl*; **the ~ before/after** el día anterior/siguiente; **the ~ after tomorrow** pasado mañana; **the ~ before yesterday** anteayer; **the following ~** el día siguiente; **by ~** de día; **day-care centre** ['deɪkɛə-] *n* centro de día; (*for children*) guardería infantil; **daydream** *vi* soñar despierto; **daylight** *n* luz *f* (del día); **day return** (BRIT) *n* billete *m* de ida y vuelta (en un día); **daytime** *n* día *m*; **day-to-day** *adj* cotidiano; **day trip** *n* excursión *f* (de un día)

dazed [deɪzd] *adj* aturdido

dazzle ['dæzl] *vt* deslumbrar; **dazzling** *adj* (*light, smile*) deslumbrante; (*colour*) fuerte

DC *abbr* (= *direct current*) corriente *f* continua

dead [dɛd] *adj* muerto; (*limb*) dormido; (*telephone*) cortado; (*battery*) agotado ▷ *adv* (*completely*) totalmente; (*exactly*) exactamente; **to shoot sb ~** matar a algn a tiros; **~ tired** muerto (de cansancio); **to stop ~** parar en seco; **dead end** *n* callejón *m* sin salida; **deadline** *n* fecha (or hora) tope; **deadly** *adj* mortal, fatal; **Dead Sea** *n*: **the Dead Sea** el Mar Muerto

deaf [dɛf] *adj* sordo; **deafen** *vt* ensordecer; **deafening** *adj* ensordecedor/a

deal [diːl] (*pt, pp* **~t**) *n* (*agreement*) pacto, convenio; (*business deal*) trato ▷ *vt* dar; (*card*) repartir; **a great ~ (of)** bastante, mucho; **deal with** *vt fus* (*people*) tratar con; (*problem*) ocuparse de; (*subject*) tratar de; **dealer** *n* comerciante *m/f*; (*Cards*) mano *f*; **dealings** *npl* (*Comm*) transacciones *fpl*; (*relations*) relaciones *fpl*

dealt [dɛlt] *pt, pp* of **deal**

dean [diːn] *n* (*Rel*) deán *m*; (*Scol*: BRIT) decano; (: US) decano; rector *m*

dear [dɪə*] *adj* querido; (*expensive*) caro ▷ *n*: **my ~** mi querido/a ▷ *excl*: **~ me!** ¡Dios mío!; **D~ Sir/Madam** (*in letter*) Muy Señor Mío, Estimado Señor/Estimada Señora; **D~ Mr/Mrs X** Estimado/a Señor(a) X; **dearly** *adv* (*love*) mucho; (*pay*) caro

death [dɛθ] *n* muerte *f*; **death penalty** *n* pena de muerte; **death sentence** *n* condena a muerte

debate [dɪˈbeɪt] *n* debate *m* ▷ *vt* discutir

debit ['dɛbɪt] *n* debe *m* ▷ *vt*: **to ~ a sum to sb** or **to sb's account** cargar una suma en cuenta a algn; **debit card** *n* tarjeta *f* de débito

debris ['dɛbriː] *n* escombros *mpl*

debt [dɛt] *n* deuda; **to be in ~** tener deudas

debut ['deɪbjuː] *n* presentación *f*

Dec. *abbr* (= *December*) dic

decade ['dɛkeɪd] *n* decenio, década

decaffeinated [dɪˈkæfɪneɪtɪd] *adj* descafeinado

decay [dɪˈkeɪ] *n* (*of building*) desmoronamiento; (*of tooth*) caries *f inv* ▷ *vi* (*rot*) pudrirse

deceased [dɪˈsiːst] *n*: **the ~** el(la) difunto/a

deceit [dɪˈsiːt] *n* engaño; **deceive** [dɪˈsiːv] *vt* engañar

December [dɪˈsɛmbə*] *n* diciembre *m*

decency ['diːsənsɪ] *n* decencia

decent ['diːsənt] *adj* (*proper*) decente; (*person: kind*) amable, bueno

deception [dɪˈsɛpʃən] *n* engaño

deceptive [dɪˈsɛptɪv] *adj* engañoso

▌ Be careful not to translate **deception** by the Spanish word *decepción*.

decide [dɪˈsaɪd] *vt* (*person*) decidir; (*question, argument*) resolver ▷ *vi* decidir; **to ~ to do/that** decidir hacer/que; **to ~ on sth** decidirse por algo

decimal ['dɛsɪməl] *adj* decimal ▷ *n* decimal *m*

decision [dɪˈsɪʒən] n decisión f
decisive [dɪˈsaɪsɪv] adj decisivo; (person) decidido
deck [dɛk] n (Naut) cubierta; (of bus) piso; (record deck) platina; (of cards) baraja; **deckchair** n tumbona
declaration [dɛkləˈreɪʃən] n declaración f
declare [dɪˈklɛə*] vt declarar
decline [dɪˈklaɪn] n disminución f, descenso ▷ vt rehusar ▷ vi (person, business) decaer; (strength) disminuir
decorate [ˈdɛkəreɪt] vt (adorn): **to ~ (with)** adornar (de), decorar (de); (paint) pintar; (paper) empapelar; **decoration** [-ˈreɪʃən] n adorno; (act) decoración f; (medal) condecoración f; **decorator** n (workman) pintor m (decorador)
decrease [n ˈdiːkriːs, vb dɪˈkriːs] n: **~ (in)** disminución f (de) ▷ vt disminuir, reducir ▷ vi reducirse
decree [dɪˈkriː] n decreto
dedicate [ˈdɛdɪkeɪt] vt dedicar; **dedicated** adj dedicado; (Comput) especializado; **dedicated word processor** procesador m de textos especializado or dedicado; **dedication** [-ˈkeɪʃən] n (devotion) dedicación f; (in book) dedicatoria
deduce [dɪˈdjuːs] vt deducir
deduct [dɪˈdʌkt] vt restar; descontar; **deduction** [dɪˈdʌkʃən] n (amount deducted) descuento; (conclusion) deducción f, conclusión f
deed [diːd] n hecho, acto; (feat) hazaña; (Law) escritura
deem [diːm] vt (formal) juzgar, considerar
deep [diːp] adj profundo; (expressing measurements) de profundidad; (voice) bajo; (breath) profundo; (colour) intenso ▷ adv: **the spectators stood 20 ~** los espectadores se formaron de 20 en fondo; **to be 4 metres ~** tener 4 metros de profundidad; **deep-fry** vt freír en aceite abundante; **deeply** adv (breathe) a pleno pulmón; (interested, moved, grateful) profundamente, hondamente
deer [dɪə*] n inv ciervo
default [dɪˈfɔːlt] n: **by ~** (win) por incomparecencia ▷ adj (Comput) por defecto
defeat [dɪˈfiːt] n derrota ▷ vt derrotar, vencer
defect [n ˈdiːfɛkt, vb dɪˈfɛkt] n defecto ▷ vi: **to ~ to the enemy** pasarse al enemigo; **defective** [dɪˈfɛktɪv] adj defectuoso
defence [dɪˈfɛns] (us **defense**) n defensa
defend [dɪˈfɛnd] vt defender; **defendant** n acusado/a; (in civil case) demandado/a; **defender** n defensor(a) m/f; (Sport) defensa mf

defense [dɪˈfɛns] (us) = **defence**
defensive [dɪˈfɛnsɪv] adj defensivo ▷ n: **on the ~** a la defensiva
defer [dɪˈfəː*] vt aplazar
defiance [dɪˈfaɪəns] n desafío; **in ~ of** en contra de; **defiant** [dɪˈfaɪənt] adj (challenging) desafiante, retador(a)
deficiency [dɪˈfɪʃənsɪ] n (lack) falta; (defect) defecto; **deficient** [dɪˈfɪʃənt] adj deficiente
deficit [ˈdɛfɪsɪt] n déficit m
define [dɪˈfaɪn] vt (word etc) definir; (limits etc) determinar
definite [ˈdɛfɪnɪt] adj (fixed) determinado; (obvious) claro; (certain) indudable; **he was ~ about it** no dejó lugar a dudas (sobre ello); **definitely** adv desde luego, por supuesto
definition [dɛfɪˈnɪʃən] n definición f; (clearness) nitidez f
deflate [diːˈfleɪt] vt desinflar
deflect [dɪˈflɛkt] vt desviar
defraud [dɪˈfrɔːd] vt: **to ~ sb of sth** estafar algo a algn
defrost [diːˈfrɔst] vt descongelar
defuse [diːˈfjuːz] vt desactivar; (situation) calmar
defy [dɪˈfaɪ] vt (resist) oponerse a; (challenge) desafiar; (fig): **it defies description** resulta imposible describirlo
degree [dɪˈɡriː] n grado; (Scol) título; **to have a ~ in maths** tener una licenciatura en matemáticas; **by ~s** (gradually) poco a poco, por etapas; **to some ~** hasta cierto punto
dehydrated [diːhaɪˈdreɪtɪd] adj deshidratado; (milk) en polvo
de-icer [diːˈaɪsə*] n descongelador m
delay [dɪˈleɪ] vt demorar, aplazar; (person) entretener; (train) retrasar ▷ vi tardar ▷ n demora, retraso; **to be ~ed** retrasarse; **without ~** en seguida, sin tardar
delegate [n ˈdɛlɪɡət, vb ˈdɛlɪɡeɪt] n delegado/a ▷ vt (person) delegar en; (task) delegar
delete [dɪˈliːt] vt suprimir, tachar
deli [ˈdɛlɪ] n = **delicatessen**
deliberate [adj dɪˈlɪbərɪt, vb dɪˈlɪbəreɪt] adj (intentional) intencionado; (slow) pausado, lento ▷ vi deliberar; **deliberately** adv (on purpose) a propósito
delicacy [ˈdɛlɪkəsɪ] n delicadeza; (choice food) manjar m
delicate [ˈdɛlɪkɪt] adj delicado; (fragile) frágil
delicatessen [dɛlɪkəˈtɛsn] n ultramarinos mpl finos
delicious [dɪˈlɪʃəs] adj delicioso
delight [dɪˈlaɪt] n (feeling) placer m, deleite m; (person, experience etc) encanto,

delicia ▷ vt encantar, deleitar; **to take ~ in** deleitarse en; **delighted** adj: **delighted (at** or **with/to do)** encantado (con/de hacer); **delightful** adj encantador(a), delicioso

delinquent [dɪ'lɪŋkwənt] adj, n delincuente mf

deliver [dɪ'lɪvə*] vt (distribute) repartir; (hand over) entregar; (message) comunicar; (speech) pronunciar; (Med) asistir al parto de; **delivery** n reparto; entrega; (of speaker) modo de expresarse; (Med) parto, alumbramiento; **to take delivery of** recibir

delusion [dɪ'luːʒən] n ilusión f, engaño

de luxe [də'lʌks] adj de lujo

delve [dɛlv] vi: **to ~ into** hurgar en

demand [dɪ'mɑːnd] vt (gen) exigir; (rights) reclamar ▷ n exigencia; (claim) reclamación f; (Econ) demanda; **to be in ~** ser muy solicitado; **on ~** a solicitud; **demanding** adj (boss) exigente; (work) absorbente

demise [dɪ'maɪz] n (death) fallecimiento

demo ['dɛməu] (inf) n abbr (= demonstration) manifestación f

democracy [dɪ'mɔkrəsɪ] n democracia; **democrat** ['dɛməkræt] n demócrata mf; **democratic** [dɛmə'krætɪk] adj democrático; (us) demócrata

demolish [dɪ'mɔlɪʃ] vt derribar, demoler; (fig: argument) destruir

demolition [dɛmə'lɪʃən] n derribo, demolición f

demon ['diːmən] n (evil spirit) demonio

demonstrate ['dɛmənstreɪt] vt demostrar; (skill, appliance) mostrar ▷ vi manifestarse; **demonstration** [-'streɪʃən] n (Pol) manifestación f; (proof, exhibition) demostración f; **demonstrator** n (Pol) manifestante mf; (Comm) demostrador(a) m/f; vendedor(a) m/f

demote [dɪ'məut] vt degradar

den [dɛn] n (of animal) guarida; (room) habitación f

denial [dɪ'naɪəl] n (refusal) negativa; (of report etc) negación f

denim ['dɛnɪm] n tela vaquera; **denims** npl vaqueros mpl

Denmark ['dɛnmɑːk] n Dinamarca

denomination [dɪnɔmɪ'neɪʃən] n valor m; (Rel) confesión f

denounce [dɪ'nauns] vt denunciar

dense [dɛns] adj (crowd) denso; (thick) espeso; (: foliage etc) tupido; (inf: stupid) torpe

density ['dɛnsɪtɪ] n densidad f ▷ **single/ double-~ disk** n (Comput) disco de densidad sencilla/de doble densidad

dent [dɛnt] n abolladura ▷ vt (also: **make a ~ in**) abollar

dental ['dɛntl] adj dental; **dental floss** [-flɔs] n seda dental; **dental surgery** n clínica f dental, consultorio m dental

dentist ['dɛntɪst] n dentista mf

dentures ['dɛntʃəz] npl dentadura (postiza)

deny [dɪ'naɪ] vt negar; (charge) rechazar

deodorant [diː'əudərənt] n desodorante m

depart [dɪ'pɑːt] vi irse, marcharse; (train) salir; **to ~ from** (fig: differ from) apartarse de

department [dɪ'pɑːtmənt] n (Comm) sección f; (Scol) departamento; (Pol) ministerio; **department store** n gran almacén m

departure [dɪ'pɑːtʃə*] n partida, ida; (of train) salida; (of employee) marcha; **a new ~** un nuevo rumbo; **departure lounge** n (at airport) sala de embarque

depend [dɪ'pɛnd] vi: **to ~ on** depender de; (rely on) contar con; **it ~s** depende, según; **~ing on the result** según el resultado; **dependant** n dependiente mf; **dependent** adj: **to be dependent on** depender de ▷ n = **dependant**

depict [dɪ'pɪkt] vt (in picture) pintar; (describe) representar

deport [dɪ'pɔːt] vt deportar

deposit [dɪ'pɔzɪt] n depósito; (Chem) sedimento; (of ore, oil) yacimiento ▷ vt (gen) depositar; **deposit account** (BRIT) n cuenta de ahorros

depot ['dɛpəu] n (storehouse) depósito; (for vehicles) parque m; (us) estación f

depreciate [dɪ'priːʃɪeɪt] vi depreciarse, perder valor

depress [dɪ'prɛs] vt deprimir; (wages etc) hacer bajar; (press down) apretar; **depressed** adj deprimido; **depressing** adj deprimente; **depression** [dɪ'prɛʃən] n depresión f

deprive [dɪ'praɪv] vt: **to ~ sb of** privar a algn de; **deprived** adj necesitado

dept. abbr (= department) dto

depth [dɛpθ] n profundidad f; (of cupboard) fondo; **to be in the ~s of despair** sentir la mayor desesperación; **to be out of one's ~** (in water) no hacer pie; (fig) sentirse totalmente perdido

deputy ['dɛpjutɪ] adj: **~ head** subdirector(a) m/f ▷ n sustituto/a, suplente mf; (us Pol) diputado/a; (us: also: **sheriff**) agente m del sheriff

derail [dɪ'reɪl] vt: **to be ~ed** descarrilarse

derelict ['dɛrɪlɪkt] adj abandonado

derive [dɪ'raɪv] vt (benefit etc) obtener ▷ vi: **to ~ from** derivarse de

descend [dɪ'sɛnd] vt, vi descender, bajar;

to ~ from descender de; **to ~ to** rebajarse a; **descendant** n descendiente mf

descent [dɪ'sɛnt] n descenso; (origin) descendencia

describe [dɪs'kraɪb] vt describir; **description** [-'krɪpʃən] n descripción f; (sort) clase f, género

desert [n 'dɛzət, vb dɪ'zəːt] n desierto ▷ vt abandonar ▷ vi (Mil) desertar; **deserted** [dɪ'zəːtɪd] adj desierto

deserve [dɪ'zəːv] vt merecer, ser digno de

design [dɪ'zaɪn] n (sketch) bosquejo; (layout, shape) diseño; (pattern) dibujo; (intention) intención f ▷ vt diseñar; **design and technology** (BRIT: Scol) n ≈ dibujo y tecnología

designate [vb 'dɛzɪgneɪt, adj 'dɛzɪgnɪt] vt (appoint) nombrar; (destine) designar ▷ adj designado

designer [dɪ'zaɪnə*] n diseñador(a) m/f; (fashion designer) modisto/a, diseñador(a) m/f de moda

desirable [dɪ'zaɪərəbl] adj (proper) deseable; (attractive) atractivo

desire [dɪ'zaɪə*] n deseo ▷ vt desear

desk [dɛsk] n (in office) escritorio; (for pupil) pupitre m; (in hotel, at airport) recepción f; (BRIT: in shop, restaurant) caja; **desk-top publishing** ['dɛsktɔp-] n autoedición f

despair [dɪs'pɛə*] n desesperación f ▷ vi: **to ~ of** perder la esperanza de

despatch [dɪs'pætʃ] n, vt = **dispatch**

desperate ['dɛspərɪt] adj desesperado; (fugitive) peligroso; **to be ~ for sth/to do** necesitar urgentemente algo/hacer; **desperately** adv desesperadamente; (very) terriblemente, gravemente

desperation [dɛspə'reɪʃən] n desesperación f; **in (sheer) ~** (absolutamente) desesperado

despise [dɪs'paɪz] vt despreciar

despite [dɪs'paɪt] prep a pesar de, pese a

dessert [dɪ'zəːt] n postre m; **dessertspoon** n cuchara (de postre)

destination [dɛstɪ'neɪʃən] n destino

destined ['dɛstɪnd] adj: **~ for London** con destino a Londres

destiny ['dɛstɪnɪ] n destino

destroy [dɪs'trɔɪ] vt destruir; (animal) sacrificar

destruction [dɪs'trʌkʃən] n destrucción f

destructive [dɪs'trʌktɪv] adj destructivo, destructor(a)

detach [dɪ'tætʃ] vt separar; (unstick) despegar; **detached** adj (attitude) objetivo, imparcial; **detached house** n ≈ chalé m, ≈ chalet m

detail ['diːteɪl] n detalle m; (no pl; (: in picture etc) detalles mpl; (trifle) pequeñez f ▷ vt detallar; (Mil) destacar; **in ~** detalladamente; **detailed** adj detallado

detain [dɪ'teɪn] vt retener; (in captivity) detener

detect [dɪ'tɛkt] vt descubrir; (Med, Police) identificar; (Mil, Radar, Tech) detectar; **detection** [dɪ'tɛkʃən] n descubrimiento; identificación f; **detective** n detective mf; **detective story** n novela policíaca

detention [dɪ'tɛnʃən] n detención f, arresto; (Scol) castigo

deter [dɪ'təː*] vt (dissuade) disuadir

detergent [dɪ'təːdʒənt] n detergente m

deteriorate [dɪ'tɪərɪəreɪt] vi deteriorarse

determination [dɪtəːmɪ'neɪʃən] n resolución f

determine [dɪ'təːmɪn] vt determinar; **determined** adj (person) resuelto, decidido; **determined to do** resuelto a hacer

deterrent [dɪ'tɛrənt] n (Mil) fuerza de disuasión

detest [dɪ'tɛst] vt aborrecer

detour ['diːtuə*] n (gen, us Aut) desviación f

detract [dɪ'trækt] vt: **to ~ from** quitar mérito a, desvirtuar

detrimental [dɛtrɪ'mɛntl] adj: **~ (to)** perjudicial (a)

devastating ['dɛvəsteɪtɪŋ] adj devastador(a); (fig) arrollador(a)

develop [dɪ'vɛləp] vt desarrollar; (Phot) revelar; (disease) coger; (habit) adquirir; (fault) empezar a tener ▷ vi desarrollarse; (advance) progresar; (facts, symptoms) aparecer; **developing country** n país m en (vías de) desarrollo; **development** n desarrollo; (advance) progreso; (of affair, case) desenvolvimiento; (of land) urbanización f

device [dɪ'vaɪs] n (apparatus) aparato, mecanismo

devil ['dɛvl] n diablo, demonio

devious ['diːvɪəs] adj taimado

devise [dɪ'vaɪz] vt idear, inventar

devote [dɪ'vəut] vt: **to ~ sth to** dedicar algo a; **devoted** adj (loyal) leal, fiel; **to be devoted to sb** querer con devoción a algn; **the book is devoted to politics** el libro trata de la política; **devotion** n dedicación f; (Rel) devoción f

devour [dɪ'vauə*] vt devorar

devout [dɪ'vaut] adj devoto

dew [djuː] n rocío

diabetes [daɪə'biːtiːz] n diabetes f

diabetic [daɪə'bɛtɪk] adj, n diabético/a m/f

diagnose ['daɪəgnəuz] vt diagnosticar

diagnosis [daɪəg'nəusɪs] (pl **-ses**) n

diagnóstico

diagonal [daɪˈægənl] *adj, n* diagonal *f*

diagram [ˈdaɪəgræm] *n* diagrama *m*,
esquema *m*

dial [ˈdaɪəl] *n* esfera (SP), cara (LAM);
(*on radio etc*) dial *m*; (*of phone*) disco ▷ *vt*
(*number*) marcar

dialect [ˈdaɪəlɛkt] *n* dialecto

dialling code [ˈdaɪəlɪŋ-] *n* prefijo

dialling tone (US **dial tone**) *n* (BRIT) señal *f*
or tono de marcar

dialogue [ˈdaɪəlɔg] (US **dialog**) *n* diálogo

diameter [daɪˈæmɪtə*] *n* diámetro

diamond [ˈdaɪəmənd] *n* diamante *m*;
(*shape*) rombo; **diamonds** *npl* (*Cards*)
diamantes *mpl*

diaper [ˈdaɪəpə*] (US) *n* pañal *m*

diarrhoea [daɪəˈriːə] (US **diarrhea**) *n*
diarrea

diary [ˈdaɪərɪ] *n* (*daily account*) diario;
(*book*) agenda

dice [daɪs] *n inv* dados *mpl* ▷ *vt* (*Culin*)
cortar en cuadritos

dictate [dɪkˈteɪt] *vt* dictar; (*conditions*)
imponer; **dictation** [-ˈteɪʃən] *n* dictado;
(*giving of orders*) órdenes *fpl*

dictator [dɪkˈteɪtə*] *n* dictador *m*

dictionary [ˈdɪkʃənrɪ] *n* diccionario

did [dɪd] *pt of* **do**

didn't [ˈdɪdənt] = **did not**

die [daɪ] *vi* morir; (*fig: fade*) desvanecerse,
desaparecer; **to be dying for sth/to do sth**
morirse por algo/de ganas de hacer algo;
die down *vi* apagarse; (*wind*) amainar; **die
out** *vi* desaparecer

diesel [ˈdiːzəl] *n* vehículo con motor Diesel

diet [ˈdaɪət] *n* dieta; (*restricted food*)
régimen *m* ▷ *vi* (*also:* **be on a ~**) estar a
dieta, hacer régimen

differ [ˈdɪfə*] *vi:* **to ~ (from)** (*be different*)
ser distinto (a), diferenciarse (de); (*disagree*)
discrepar (de); **difference** *n* diferencia;
(*disagreement*) desacuerdo; **different**
adj diferente, distinto; **differentiate**
[-ˈrɛnʃɪeɪt] *vi:* **to differentiate (between)**
distinguir (entre); **differently** *adv* de otro
modo, en forma distinta

difficult [ˈdɪfɪkəlt] *adj* difícil; **difficulty** *n*
dificultad *f*

dig [dɪg] (*pt, pp* **dug**) *vt* (*hole, ground*)
cavar ▷ *n* (*prod*) empujón *m*; (*archaeological*)
excavación *f*; (*remark*) indirecta; **to ~ one's
nails into** clavar las uñas en; **dig up** *vt*
(*information*) desenterrar; (*plant*) desarraigar

digest [*vb* daɪˈdʒɛst, *n* ˈdaɪdʒɛst] *vt* (*food*)
digerir; (*facts*) asimilar ▷ *n* resumen *m*;
digestion [dɪˈdʒɛstʃən] *n* digestión *f*

digit [ˈdɪdʒɪt] *n* (*number*) dígito; (*finger*)

dedo; **digital** *adj* digital; **digital camera**
n cámara digital; **digital TV** *n* televisión
f digital

dignified [ˈdɪgnɪfaɪd] *adj* grave, solemne

dignity [ˈdɪgnɪtɪ] *n* dignidad *f*

digs [dɪgz] (BRIT: *inf*) *npl* pensión *f*,
alojamiento

dilemma [daɪˈlɛmə] *n* dilema *m*

dill [dɪl] *n* eneldo

dilute [daɪˈluːt] *vt* diluir

dim [dɪm] *adj* (*light*) débil; (*outline*)
indistinto; (*room*) oscuro; (*inf: stupid*) lerdo
▷ *vt* (*light*) bajar

dime [daɪm] (US) *n* moneda de diez centavos

dimension [dɪˈmɛnʃən] *n* dimensión *f*

diminish [dɪˈmɪnɪʃ] *vt, vi* disminuir

din [dɪn] *n* estruendo, estrépito

dine [daɪn] *vi* cenar; **diner** *n* (*person*)
comensal *mf*

dinghy [ˈdɪŋgɪ] *n* bote *m*; (*also:* **rubber ~**)
lancha (neumática)

dingy [ˈdɪndʒɪ] *adj* (*room*) sombrío; (*colour*)
sucio

dining car [ˈdaɪnɪŋ-] (BRIT) *n* (*Rail*) coche-
comedor *m*

dining room [ˈdaɪnɪŋ-] *n* comedor *m*

dining table *n* mesa *f* de comedor

dinner [ˈdɪnə*] *n* (*evening meal*) cena;
(*lunch*) comida; (*public*) cena, banquete *m*;
dinner jacket *n* smoking *m*; **dinner party**
n cena; **dinner time** *n* (*evening*) hora de
cenar; (*midday*) hora de comer

dinosaur [ˈdaɪnəsɔː*] *n* dinosaurio

dip [dɪp] *n* (*slope*) pendiente *m*; (*in sea*)
baño; (*Culin*) salsa ▷ *vt* (*in water*) mojar;
(*ladle etc*) meter; (BRIT *Aut*): **to ~ one's
lights** poner luces de cruce ▷ *vi* (*road etc*)
descender, bajar

diploma [dɪˈpləumə] *n* diploma *m*

diplomacy [dɪˈpləuməsɪ] *n* diplomacia

diplomat [ˈdɪpləmæt] *n* diplomático/a;
diplomatic [dɪpləˈmætɪk] *adj* diplomático

dipstick [ˈdɪpstɪk] (BRIT) *n* (*Aut*) varilla de
nivel (del aceite)

dire [daɪə*] *adj* calamitoso

direct [daɪˈrɛkt] *adj* directo; (*challenge*)
claro; (*person*) franco ▷ *vt* dirigir; (*order*): **to
~ sb to do sth** mandar a algn hacer algo
▷ *adv* derecho; **can you ~ me to ...?** ¿puede
indicarme dónde está ...?; **direct debit**
(BRIT) *n* domiciliación *f* bancaria de recibos

direction [dɪˈrɛkʃən] *n* dirección *f*; **sense
of ~** sentido de la dirección; **directions** *npl*
(*instructions*) instrucciones *fpl*; **~s for use**
modo de empleo

directly [dɪˈrɛktlɪ] *adv* (*in straight line*)
directamente; (*at once*) en seguida

director [dɪˈrɛktə*] *n* director(a) *m/f*

directory [dɪ'rɛktərɪ] n (Tel) guía (telefónica); (Comput) directorio; **directory enquiries** (us **directory assistance**) n (servicio de) información f

dirt [dəːt] n suciedad f; (earth) tierra; **dirty** adj sucio; (joke) verde, colorado (MEX) ▷ vt ensuciar; (stain) manchar

disability [dɪsə'bɪlɪtɪ] n incapacidad f

disabled [dɪs'eɪbld] adj: **to be physically ~** ser minusválido/a; **to be mentally ~** ser deficiente mental

disadvantage [dɪsəd'vɑːntɪdʒ] n desventaja, inconveniente m

disagree [dɪsə'griː] vi (differ) discrepar; **to ~ (with)** no estar de acuerdo (con); **disagreeable** adj desagradable; (person) antipático; **disagreement** n desacuerdo

disappear [dɪsə'pɪə*] vi desaparecer; **disappearance** n desaparición f

disappoint [dɪsə'pɔɪnt] vt decepcionar, defraudar; **disappointed** adj decepcionado; **disappointing** adj decepcionante; **disappointment** n decepción f

disapproval [dɪsə'pruːvəl] n desaprobación f

disapprove [dɪsə'pruːv] vi: **to ~ of** ver mal

disarm [dɪs'ɑːm] vt desarmar; **disarmament** [dɪs'ɑːməmənt] n desarme m

disaster [dɪ'zɑːstə*] n desastre m

disastrous [dɪ'zɑːstrəs] adj desastroso

disbelief [dɪsbə'liːf] n incredulidad f

disc [dɪsk] n disco; (Comput) = **disk**

discard [dɪs'kɑːd] vt (old things) tirar; (fig) descartar

discharge [vb dɪs'tʃɑːdʒ, n 'dɪstʃɑːdʒ] vt (task, duty) cumplir; (waste) verter; (patient) dar de alta; (employee) despedir; (soldier) licenciar; (defendant) poner en libertad ▷ n (Elec) descarga; (Med) supuración f; (dismissal) despedida; (of duty) desempeño; (of debt) pago, descargo

discipline ['dɪsɪplɪn] n disciplina ▷ vt disciplinar; (punish) castigar

disc jockey n pinchadiscos mf inv

disclose [dɪs'kləʊz] vt revelar

disco ['dɪskəʊ] n abbr discoteca

discoloured [dɪs'kʌləd] (us **discolored**) adj descolorido

discomfort [dɪs'kʌmfət] n incomodidad f; (unease) inquietud f; (physical) malestar m

disconnect [dɪskə'nɛkt] vt separar; (Elec etc) desconectar

discontent [dɪskən'tɛnt] n descontento

discontinue [dɪskən'tɪnjuː] vt interrumpir; (payments) suspender; **"~d"** (Comm) "ya no se fabrica"

discount [n 'dɪskaunt, vb dɪs'kaunt] n descuento ▷ vt descontar

discourage [dɪs'kʌrɪdʒ] vt desalentar; (advise against): **to ~ sb from doing** disuadir a algn de hacer

discover [dɪs'kʌvə*] vt descubrir; (error) darse cuenta de; **discovery** n descubrimiento

discredit [dɪs'krɛdɪt] vt desacreditar

discreet [dɪs'kriːt] adj (tactful) discreto; (careful) prudente

discrepancy [dɪs'krɛpənsɪ] n diferencia

discretion [dɪs'krɛʃən] n (tact) discreción f; **at the ~ of** a criterio de

discriminate [dɪs'krɪmɪneɪt] vi: **to ~ between** distinguir entre; **to ~ against** discriminar contra; **discrimination** [-'neɪʃən] n (discernment) perspicacia; (bias) discriminación f

discuss [dɪs'kʌs] vt discutir; (a theme) tratar; **discussion** [dɪs'kʌʃən] n discusión f

disease [dɪ'ziːz] n enfermedad f

disembark [dɪsɪm'baːk] vt, vi desembarcar

disgrace [dɪs'greɪs] n ignominia; (shame) vergüenza, escándalo ▷ vt deshonrar; **disgraceful** adj vergonzoso

disgruntled [dɪs'grʌntld] adj disgustado, descontento

disguise [dɪs'gaɪz] n disfraz m ▷ vt disfrazar; **in ~** disfrazado

disgust [dɪs'gʌst] n repugnancia ▷ vt repugnar, dar asco a

  ▌ Be careful not to translate **disgust** by the
  ▌ Spanish word disgustar.

disgusted [dɪs'gʌstɪd] adj indignado

  ▌ Be careful not to translate **disgusted** by
  ▌ the Spanish word disgustado.

disgusting [dɪs'gʌstɪŋ] adj repugnante, asqueroso; (behaviour etc) vergonzoso

dish [dɪʃ] n (gen) plato; **to do** or **wash the ~es** fregar los platos; **dishcloth** n estropajo

dishonest [dɪs'ɔnɪst] adj (person) poco honrado, tramposo; (means) fraudulento

dishtowel ['dɪʃtauəl] (us) n estropajo

dishwasher ['dɪʃwɔʃə*] n lavaplatos m inv

disillusion [dɪsɪ'luːʒən] vt desilusionar

disinfectant [dɪsɪn'fɛktənt] n desinfectante m

disintegrate [dɪs'ɪntɪgreɪt] vi disgregarse, desintegrarse

disk [dɪsk] n (esp us) = **disc**; (Comput) disco, disquete m; **single-/double-sided ~** disco de una cara/dos caras; **disk drive** n disc drive m; **diskette** n = **disk**

dislike [dɪs'laɪk] n antipatía, aversión f ▷ vt tener antipatía a

dislocate ['dɪsləkeɪt] vt dislocar

d

disloyal [dɪs'lɔɪəl] *adj* desleal

dismal ['dɪzml] *adj* (*gloomy*) deprimente, triste; (*very bad*) malísimo, fatal

dismantle [dɪs'mæntl] *vt* desmontar, desarmar

dismay [dɪs'meɪ] *n* consternación *f* ▷ *vt* consternar

dismiss [dɪs'mɪs] *vt* (*worker*) despedir; (*pupils*) dejar marchar; (*soldiers*) dar permiso para irse; (*idea, Law*) rechazar; (*possibility*) descartar; **dismissal** *n* despido

disobedient [dɪsə'biːdɪənt] *adj* desobediente

disobey [dɪsə'beɪ] *vt* desobedecer

disorder [dɪs'ɔːdə*] *n* desorden *m*; (*rioting*) disturbios *mpl*; (*Med*) trastorno

disorganized [dɪs'ɔːɡənaɪzd] *adj* desorganizado

disown [dɪs'əun] *vt* (*action*) renegar de; (*person*) negar cualquier tipo de relación con

dispatch [dɪs'pætʃ] *vt* enviar ▷ *n* (*sending*) envío; (*Press*) informe *m*; (*Mil*) parte *m*

dispel [dɪs'pɛl] *vt* disipar

dispense [dɪs'pɛns] *vt* (*medicines*) preparar; **dispense with** *vt fus* prescindir de; **dispenser** *n* (*container*) distribuidor *m* automático

disperse [dɪs'pəːs] *vt* dispersar ▷ *vi* dispersarse

display [dɪs'pleɪ] *n* (*in shop window*) escaparate *m*; (*exhibition*) exposición *f*; (*Comput*) visualización *f*; (*of feeling*) manifestación *f* ▷ *vt* exponer; manifestar; (*ostentatiously*) lucir

displease [dɪs'pliːz] *vt* (*offend*) ofender; (*annoy*) fastidiar

disposable [dɪs'pəuzəbl] *adj* desechable; (*income*) disponible

disposal [dɪs'pəuzl] *n* (*of rubbish*) destrucción *f*; **at one's ~** a su disposición

dispose [dɪs'pəuz] *vi*: **to ~ of** (*unwanted goods*) deshacerse de; (*problem etc*) resolver; **disposition** [dɪspə'zɪʃən] *n* (*nature*) temperamento; (*inclination*) propensión *f*

disproportionate [dɪsprə'pɔːʃənət] *adj* desproporcionado

dispute [dɪs'pjuːt] *n* disputa; (*also:* **industrial ~**) conflicto (laboral) ▷ *vt* (*argue*) disputar, discutir; (*question*) cuestionar

disqualify [dɪs'kwɔlɪfaɪ] *vt* (*Sport*) desclasificar; **to ~ sb for sth/from doing sth** incapacitar a algn para algo/hacer algo

disregard [dɪsrɪ'ɡɑːd] *vt* (*ignore*) no hacer caso de

disrupt [dɪs'rʌpt] *vt* (*plans*) desbaratar, trastornar; (*conversation*) interrumpir; **disruption** [dɪs'rʌpʃən] *n* trastorno, desbaratamiento; interrupción *f*

dissatisfaction [dɪssætɪs'fækʃən] *n* disgusto, descontento

dissatisfied [dɪs'sætɪsfaɪd] *adj* insatisfecho

dissect [dɪ'sɛkt] *vt* disecar

dissent [dɪ'sɛnt] *n* disensión *f*

dissertation [dɪsə'teɪʃən] *n* tesina

dissolve [dɪ'zɔlv] *vt* disolver ▷ *vi* disolverse; **to ~ in(to) tears** deshacerse en lágrimas

distance ['dɪstəns] *n* distancia; **in the ~** a lo lejos

distant ['dɪstənt] *adj* lejano; (*manner*) reservado, frío

distil [dɪs'tɪl] (*us* **distill**) *vt* destilar; **distillery** *n* destilería

distinct [dɪs'tɪŋkt] *adj* (*different*) distinto; (*clear*) claro; (*unmistakeable*) inequívoco; **as ~ from** a diferencia de; **distinction** [dɪs'tɪŋkʃən] *n* distinción *f*; (*honour*) honor *m*; (*in exam*) sobresaliente *m*; **distinctive** *adj* distintivo

distinguish [dɪs'tɪŋgwɪʃ] *vt* distinguir; **to ~ o.s.** destacarse; **distinguished** *adj* (*eminent*) distinguido

distort [dɪs'tɔːt] *vt* distorsionar; (*shape, image*) deformar

distract [dɪs'trækt] *vt* distraer; **distracted** *adj* distraído; **distraction** [dɪs'trækʃən] *n* distracción *f*; (*confusion*) aturdimiento

distraught [dɪs'trɔːt] *adj* loco de inquietud

distress [dɪs'trɛs] *n* (*anguish*) angustia, aflicción *f* ▷ *vt* afligir; **distressing** *adj* angustioso; doloroso

distribute [dɪs'trɪbjuːt] *vt* distribuir; (*share out*) repartir; **distribution** [-'bjuːʃən] *n* distribución *f*, reparto; **distributor** *n* (*Aut*) distribuidor *m*; (*Comm*) distribuidora

district ['dɪstrɪkt] *n* (*of country*) zona, región *f*; (*of town*) barrio; (*Admin*) distrito; **district attorney** (*us*) *n* fiscal *mf*

distrust [dɪs'trʌst] *n* desconfianza ▷ *vt* desconfiar de

disturb [dɪs'təːb] *vt* (*person: bother, interrupt*) molestar; (: *upset*) perturbar, inquietar; (*disorganize*) alterar; **disturbance** *n* (*upheaval*) perturbación *f*; (*political etc: gen pl*) disturbio; (*of mind*) trastorno; **disturbed** *adj* (*worried, upset*) preocupado, angustiado; **emotionally disturbed** trastornado; (*childhood*) inseguro; **disturbing** *adj* inquietante, perturbador(a)

ditch [dɪtʃ] *n* zanja; (*irrigation ditch*) acequia ▷ *vt* (*inf: partner*) deshacerse de; (: *plan, car etc*) abandonar

ditto ['dɪtəu] *adv* ídem, lo mismo

dive [daɪv] n (from board) salto; (underwater) buceo; (of submarine) sumersión f ▷ vi (swimmer: into water) saltar; (: under water) zambullirse, bucear; (fish, submarine) sumergirse; (bird) lanzarse en picado; **to ~ into** (bag etc) meter la mano en; (place) meterse de prisa en; **diver** n (underwater) buzo

diverse [daɪˈvəːs] adj diversos/as, varios/as

diversion [daɪˈvəːʃən] n (BRIT Aut) desviación f; (distraction, Mil) diversión f; (of funds) distracción f

diversity [daɪˈvəːsɪtɪ] n diversidad f

divert [daɪˈvəːt] vt (turn aside) desviar

divide [dɪˈvaɪd] vt (divir; (separate) separar ▷ vi dividirse; (road) bifurcarse; **divided highway** (US) n carretera de doble calzada

divine [dɪˈvaɪn] adj (also fig) divino

diving [ˈdaɪvɪŋ] n (Sport) salto; (underwater) buceo; **diving board** n trampolín m

division [dɪˈvɪʒən] n división f; (sharing out) reparto m; (disagreement) diferencias fpl; (Comm) sección f

divorce [dɪˈvɔːs] n divorcio ▷ vt divorciarse de; **divorced** adj divorciado; **divorcee** [-ˈsiː] n divorciado/a

D.I.Y. (BRIT) adj, n abbr = **do-it-yourself**

dizzy [ˈdɪzɪ] adj (spell) de mareo; **to feel ~** marearse

DJ n abbr = **disc jockey**

DNA n abbr (= deoxyribonucleic acid) ADN m

○ KEYWORD

do [duː] (pt **did**, pp **done**) n (inf: party etc): **we're having a little do on Saturday** damos una fiestecita el sábado; **it was rather a grand do** fue un acontecimiento a lo grande
▷ aux vb 1 (in negative constructions: not translated): **I don't understand** no entiendo
2 (to form questions: not translated): **didn't you know?** ¿no lo sabías?; **what do you think?** ¿qué opinas?
3 (for emphasis, in polite expressions): **people do make mistakes sometimes** sí que se cometen errores a veces; **she does seem rather late** a mí también me parece que se ha retrasado; **do sit down/help yourself** siéntate/sírvete por favor; **do take care!** ¡ten cuidado(, te pido)!
4 (used to avoid repeating vb): **she sings better than I do** canta mejor que yo; **do you agree? - yes, I do/no, I don't** ¿estás de acuerdo? - sí (lo estoy)/no (lo estoy); **she lives in Glasgow - so do I** vive en Glasgow

- yo también; **he didn't like it and neither did we** no le gustó a nosotros tampoco; **who made this mess? - I did** ¿quién hizo esta chapuza? - yo; **he asked me to help him and I did** me pidió que le ayudara y lo hice
5 (in question tags): **you like him, don't you?** te gusta, ¿verdad? or ¿no?; **I don't know him, do I?** creo que no le conozco
▷ vt 1 (gen, carry out, perform etc): **what are you doing tonight?** ¿qué haces esta noche?; **what can I do for you?** ¿en qué puedo servirle?; **to do the washing-up/cooking** fregar los platos/cocinar; **to do one's teeth/hair/nails** lavarse los dientes/arreglarse el pelo/arreglarse las uñas
2 (Aut etc): **the car was doing 100** el coche iba a 100; **we've done 200 km already** ya hemos hecho 200 km; **he can do 100 in that car** puede ir a 100 en ese coche
▷ vi 1 (act, behave) hacer; **do as I do** haz como yo
2 (get on, fare): **he's doing well/badly at school** va bien/mal en la escuela; **the firm is doing well** la empresa anda or va bien; **how do you do?** mucho gusto; (less formal) ¿qué tal?
3 (suit): **will it do?** ¿sirve?, ¿está or va bien?
4 (be sufficient) bastar; **will £10 do?** ¿será bastante con £10?; **that'll do** así está bien; **that'll do!** (in annoyance) ¡ya está bien!, ¡basta ya!; **to make do (with)** arreglárselas (con)

do up vt (laces) atar; (zip, dress, shirt) abrochar; (renovate: room, house) renovar

do with vt fus (need): **I could do with a drink/some help** no me vendría mal un trago/un poco de ayuda; (be connected) tener que ver con; **what has it got to do with you?** ¿qué tiene que ver contigo?

do without vi pasar sin; **if you're late for tea then you'll do without** si llegas tarde tendrás que quedarte sin cenar
▷ vt fus pasar sin; **I can do without a car** puedo pasar sin coche

dock [dɔk] n (Naut) muelle m; (Law) banquillo (de los acusados) ▷ vi (enter dock) atracar (la) muelle; (Space) acoplarse; **docks** npl (Naut) muelles mpl, puerto sg

doctor [ˈdɔktə*] n médico/a; (Ph.D. etc) doctor(a) m/f ▷ vt (drink etc) adulterar; **Doctor of Philosophy** n Doctor en Filosofía y Letras

document [ˈdɔkjumənt] n documento; **documentary** [-ˈmɛntərɪ] adj documental ▷ n documental m; **documentation** [-mɛnˈteɪʃən] n documentación f

dodge [dɔdʒ] n (fig) truco ▷ vt evadir; (blow) esquivar

dodgy ['dɔdʒɪ] adj (inf: uncertain) dudoso; (suspicious) sospechoso; (risky) arriesgado

does [dʌz] vb see **do**

doesn't ['dʌznt] = **does not**

dog [dɔg] n perro ▷ vt seguir los pasos de; (bad luck) perseguir; **doggy bag** ['dɔgɪ-] n bolsa para llevarse las sobras de la comida

do-it-yourself ['duːɪtjɔːˈsɛlf] n bricolaje m

dole [dəul] (BRIT) n (payment) subsidio de paro; **on the ~** parado

doll [dɔl] n muñeca; (US: inf: woman) muñeca, gachí f

dollar ['dɔlə*] n dólar m

dolphin ['dɔlfɪn] n delfín m

dome [dəum] n (Arch) cúpula

domestic [dəˈmɛstɪk] adj (animal, duty) doméstico; (flight, policy) nacional; **domestic appliance** n aparato m doméstico, aparato m de uso doméstico

dominant ['dɔmɪnənt] adj dominante

dominate ['dɔmɪneɪt] vt dominar

domino ['dɔmɪnəu] (pl **-es**) n ficha de dominó; **dominoes** n (game) dominó

donate [dəˈneɪt] vt donar; **donation** [dəˈneɪʃən] n donativo

done [dʌn] pp of **do**

donkey ['dɔŋkɪ] n burro

donor ['dəunə*] n donante mf; **donor card** n carnet m de donante

don't [dəunt] = **do not**

donut ['dəunʌt] (US) = **doughnut**

doodle ['duːdl] vi hacer dibujitos or garabatos

doom [duːm] n (fate) suerte f ▷ vt: **to be ~ed to failure** estar condenado al fracaso

door [dɔː*] n puerta; **doorbell** n timbre m; **door handle** n tirador m; (of car) manija; **doorknob** n pomo m de la puerta, manilla f (LAM); **doorstep** n peldaño; **doorway** n entrada, puerta

dope [dəup] n (inf: illegal drug) droga; (: person) imbécil mf ▷ vt (horse etc) drogar

dormitory ['dɔːmɪtrɪ] n (BRIT) dormitorio; (US) colegio mayor

DOS n abbr (= disk operating system) DOS m

dosage ['dəusɪdʒ] n dosis f inv

dose [dəus] n dosis f inv

dot [dɔt] n punto ▷ vt: **~ted with** salpicado de; **on the ~** en punto; **dotcom** [dɔtˈkɔm] n puntocom f inv; **dotted line** ['dɔtɪd-] n: **to sign on the dotted line** firmar

double ['dʌbl] adj doble ▷ adv (twice): **to cost ~** costar el doble ▷ n doble m ▷ vt doblar ▷ vi doblarse; **on the ~**, **at the ~** (BRIT) corriendo; **double back** vi (person)

volver sobre sus pasos; **double bass** n contrabajo; **double bed** n cama de matrimonio; **double-check** vt volver a revisar ▷ vi: **I'll double-check** voy a revisarlo otra vez; **double-click** vi (Comput) hacer doble clic; **double-cross** vt (trick) engañar; (betray) traicionar; **doubledecker** n autobús m de dos pisos; **double glazing** (BRIT) n doble acristalamiento; **double room** n habitación f doble; **doubles** n (Tennis) juego de dobles; **double yellow lines** npl (BRIT: Aut) línea doble amarilla de prohibido aparcar, ≈ línea f sg amarilla continua

doubt [daut] n duda ▷ vt dudar; (suspect) dudar de; **to ~ that** dudar que; **doubtful** adj dudoso; (person): **to be doubtful about sth** tener dudas sobre algo; **doubtless** adv sin duda

dough [dəu] n masa, pasta; **doughnut** (US **donut**) n ≈ rosquilla

dove [dʌv] n paloma

down [daun] n (feathers) plumón m, flojel m ▷ adv (downwards) abajo, hacia abajo; (on the ground) por or en tierra ▷ prep abajo ▷ vt (inf: drink) beberse; **~ with X!** ¡abajo X!; **down-and-out** n vagabundo/a; **downfall** n caída, ruina; **downhill** adv: **to go downhill** (also fig) ir cuesta abajo

Downing Street ['daunɪŋ-] n (BRIT) Downing Street f

down: download vt (Comput) bajar; **downright** adj (nonsense, lie) manifiesto; (refusal) terminante

Down's syndrome ['daunz-] n síndrome m de Down

down: downstairs adv (below) (en el piso de) abajo; (downwards) escaleras abajo; **down-to-earth** adj práctico; **downtown** adv en el centro de la ciudad; **down under** adv en Australia (or Nueva Zelanda); **downward** [-wəd] adj, adv hacia abajo; **downwards** [-wədz] adv hacia abajo

doz. abbr = **dozen**

doze [dəuz] vi dormitar

dozen ['dʌzn] n docena; **a ~ books** una docena de libros; **~s of** cantidad de

Dr. abbr = **doctor**; **drive**

drab [dræb] adj gris, monótono

draft [drɑːft] n (first copy) borrador m; (Pol: of bill) anteproyecto; (US: call-up) quinta ▷ vt (plan) preparar; (write roughly) hacer un borrador de; see also **draught**

drag [dræg] vt arrastrar; (river) dragar, rastrear ▷ vi (time) pasar despacio; (play, film etc) hacerse pesado ▷ n (inf) lata; (women's clothing): **in ~** vestido de travesti; **to ~ and drop** (Comput) arrastrar y soltar

dragon ['drægən] n dragón m
dragonfly ['drægənflaɪ] n libélula
drain [dreɪn] n desaguadero; (in street)
sumidero; (source of loss): **to be a ~ on**
consumir, agotar ▷ vt (land, marshes)
desaguar; (reservoir) desecar; (vegetables)
escurrir ▷ vi escurrirse; **drainage** n (act)
desagüe m; (Med, Agr) drenaje m; (sewage)
alcantarillado; **drainpipe** n tubo de
desagüe
drama ['drɑːmə] n (art) teatro; (play)
drama m; (excitement) emoción f; **dramatic**
[drə'mætɪk] adj dramático; (sudden,
marked) espectacular
drank [dræŋk] pt of **drink**
drape [dreɪp] vt (cloth) colocar; (flag)
colgar; **drapes** npl (us) cortinas fpl
drastic ['dræstɪk] adj (measure) severo;
(change) radical, drástico
draught [drɑːft] (us **draft**) n (of air)
corriente f de aire; (Naut) calado; **on ~** (beer)
de barril; **draught beer** n cerveza de barril;
draughts (BRIT) n (game) juego de damas
draw [drɔː] (pt **drew**, pp **drawn**) vt (picture)
dibujar; (cart) tirar de; (curtain) correr; (take
out) sacar; (attract) atraer; (money) retirar;
(wages) cobrar ▷ vi (Sport) empatar ▷ n
(Sport) empate m; (lottery) sorteo; **draw
out** vi (lengthen) alargarse ▷ vt sacar;
draw up vi (stop) pararse ▷ vt (chair)
acercar; (document) redactar; **drawback** n
inconveniente m, desventaja
drawer [drɔː*] n cajón m
drawing ['drɔːɪŋ] n dibujo; **drawing
pin** (BRIT) n chincheta; **drawing room** n
salón m
drawn [drɔːn] pp of **draw**
dread [drɛd] n pavor m, terror m ▷ vt
temer, tener miedo or pavor a; **dreadful** adj
horroroso
dream [driːm] (pt, pp **~ed** or **~t**) n sueño
▷ vt, vi soñar; **dreamer** n soñador(a) m/f
dreamt [drɛmt] pt, pp of **dream**
dreary ['drɪərɪ] adj monótono
drench [drɛntʃ] vt empapar
dress [drɛs] n vestido; (clothing) ropa
▷ vt vestir; (wound) vendar ▷ vi vestirse;
to get ~ed vestirse; **dress up** vi vestirse
de etiqueta; (in fancy dress) disfrazarse;
dress circle (BRIT) n principal m; **dresser**
n (furniture) aparador m; (: us) cómoda
(con espejo); **dressing** n (Med) vendaje m;
(Culin) aliño; **dressing gown** (BRIT) n bata;
dressing room n (Theatre) camarín m;
(Sport) vestuario; **dressing table** n tocador
m; **dressmaker** n modista, costurera
drew [druː] pt of **draw**
dribble ['drɪbl] vi (baby) babear ▷ vt (ball)

regatear
dried [draɪd] adj (fruit) seco; (milk) en polvo
drier ['draɪə*] n = **dryer**
drift [drɪft] n (of current etc) flujo; (of
snow) ventisquero; (meaning) significado
▷ vi (boat) ir a la deriva; (sand, snow)
amontonarse
drill [drɪl] n (drill bit) broca; (tool for DIY
etc) taladro; (of dentist) fresa; (for mining etc)
perforadora, barrena; (Mil) instrucción f
▷ vt perforar, taladrar; (troops) enseñar la
instrucción a ▷ vi (for oil) perforar
drink [drɪŋk] (pt **drank**, pp **drunk**) n
bebida; (sip) trago ▷ vt, vi beber; **to have a
~** tomar algo; tomar una copa or un trago; **a
~ of water** un trago de agua; **drink-driving**
n: **to be charged with drink-driving** ser
acusado de conducir borracho or en estado
de embriaguez; **drinker** n bebedor(a) m/f;
drinking water n agua potable
drip [drɪp] n (act) goteo; (one drip) gota;
(Med) gota a gota m ▷ vi gotear
drive [draɪv] (pt **drove**, pp **driven**) n
(journey) viaje m (en coche); (also: **~way**)
entrada; (energy) energía, vigor m;
(Comput: also: **disk ~**) drive m ▷ vt (car)
conducir (sp), manejar (LAM); (nail) clavar;
(push) empujar; (Tech: motor) impulsar ▷ vi
(Aut: at controls) conducir; (: travel) pasearse
en coche; **left-/right-hand ~** conducción f a
la izquierda/derecha; **to ~ sb mad** volverle
loco a algn; **drive out** vt (force out) expulsar,
echar; **drive-in** adj (esp us): **drive-in
cinema** autocine m
driven ['drɪvn] pp of **drive**
driver ['draɪvə*] n conductor(a) m/f (sp),
chofer mf (LAM); (of taxi, bus) chófer mf (sp),
chofer mf (LAM); **driver's license** (us) n
carnet m de conducir
driveway ['draɪvweɪ] n entrada
driving ['draɪvɪŋ] n el conducir (sp),
el manejar (LAM); **driving instructor**
n profesor(a) m/f de autoescuela (sp),
instructor(a) m/f de manejar (LAM); **driving
lesson** n clase f de conducir (sp) or manejar
(LAM); **driving licence** (BRIT) n licencia de
manejo (LAM), carnet m de conducir (sp);
driving test n examen de conducir (sp)
or manejar (LAM)
drizzle ['drɪzl] n llovizna
droop [druːp] vi (flower) marchitarse;
(shoulders) encorvarse; (head) inclinarse
drop [drɔp] n (of water) gota; (lessening)
baja; (fall) caída ▷ vt dejar caer; (voice, eyes,
price) bajar; (passenger) dejar; (omit) omitir
▷ vi (object) caer; (wind) amainar; **drop
in** vi (inf: visit): **to drop in (on)** pasar por
casa (de); **drop off** vi (sleep) dormirse ▷ vt

(*passenger*) dejar; **drop out** *vi* (*withdraw*) retirarse

drought [draut] *n* sequía

drove [drəuv] *pt of* **drive**

drown [draun] *vt* ahogar ▷ *vi* ahogarse

drowsy ['drauzɪ] *adj* soñoliento; **to be ~** tener sueño

drug [drʌg] *n* medicamento; (*narcotic*) droga ▷ *vt* drogar; **to be on ~s** drogarse; **drug addict** *n* drogadicto/a; **drug dealer** *n* traficante *mf* de drogas; **druggist** (*US*) *n* farmacéutico; **drugstore** (*US*) *n* farmacia

drum [drʌm] *n* tambor *m*; (*for oil, petrol*) bidón *m*; **drums** *npl* batería; **drummer** *n* tambor *m*

drunk [drʌŋk] *pp of* **drink** ▷ *adj* borracho ▷ *n* (*also:* **~ard**) borracho/a; **drunken** *adj* borracho; (*laughter, party*) de borrachos

dry [draɪ] *adj* seco; (*day*) sin lluvia; (*climate*) árido, seco ▷ *vt* secar; (*tears*) enjugarse ▷ *vi* secarse; **dry off** *vi* secarse ▷ *vt* secar; **dry up** *vi* (*river*) secarse; **dry-cleaner's** *n* tintorería; **dry-cleaning** *n* lavado en seco; **dryer** *n* (*for hair*) secador *m*; (*US: for clothes*) secadora

DSS *n abbr* = **Department of Social Security**

D & T (*BRIT: Scol*) *n abbr* (= *design and technology*) ≈ dibujo y tecnología

DTP *n abbr* (= *desk-top publishing*) autoedición *f*

dual ['djuəl] *adj* doble; **dual carriageway** (*BRIT*) *n* carretera de doble calzada

dubious ['djuːbɪəs] *adj* indeciso; (*reputation, company*) sospechoso

duck [dʌk] *n* pato ▷ *vi* agacharse

due [djuː] *adj* (*owed*) **he is ~ £10** se le deben 10 libras; (*expected: event*): **the meeting is ~ on Wednesday** la reunión tendrá lugar el miércoles; (: *arrival*): **the train is ~ at 8am** el tren tiene su llegada para las 8; (*proper*) debido ▷ *n*: **to give sb his** (*or* **her**) **~** ser justo con algn ▷ *adv*: **~ north** derecho al norte

duel ['djuəl] *n* duelo

duet [djuː'et] *n* dúo

dug [dʌg] *pt, pp of* **dig**

duke [djuːk] *n* duque *m*

dull [dʌl] *adj* (*light*) débil; (*stupid*) torpe; (*boring*) pesado; (*sound, pain*) sordo; (*weather, day*) gris ▷ *vt* (*pain, grief*) aliviar; (*mind, senses*) entorpecer

dumb [dʌm] *adj* mudo; (*pej: stupid*) estúpido

dummy ['dʌmɪ] *n* (*tailor's dummy*) maniquí *m*; (*mock-up*) maqueta; (*BRIT: for baby*) chupete *m* ▷ *adj* falso, postizo

dump [dʌmp] *n* (*also:* **rubbish ~**) basurero, vertedero; (*inf: place*) cuchitril *m* ▷ *vt* (*put down*) dejar; (*get rid of*) deshacerse de; (*Comput: data*) transferir

dumpling ['dʌmplɪŋ] *n* bola de masa hervida

dune [djuːn] *n* duna

dungarees [dʌŋgə'riːz] *npl* mono

dungeon ['dʌndʒən] *n* calabozo

duplex ['djuːpleks] *n* dúplex *m*

duplicate [*n* 'djuːplɪkət, *vb* 'djuːplɪkeɪt] *n* duplicado ▷ *vt* duplicar; (*photocopy*) fotocopiar; (*repeat*) repetir; **in ~** por duplicado

durable ['djuərəbl] *adj* duradero

duration [djuə'reɪʃən] *n* duración *f*

during ['djuərɪŋ] *prep* durante

dusk [dʌsk] *n* crepúsculo, anochecer *m*

dust [dʌst] *n* polvo ▷ *vt* quitar el polvo a, desempolvar; (*cake etc*): **to ~ with** espolvorear de; **dustbin** (*BRIT*) *n* cubo or bote *m* (*MEX*) or tacho (*SC*) de la basura; **duster** *n* paño, trapo; **dustman** (*BRIT: irreg*) *n* basurero; **dustpan** *n* cogedor *m*; **dusty** *adj* polvoriento

Dutch [dʌtʃ] *adj* holandés/esa ▷ *n* (*Ling*) holandés *m*; **the Dutch** *npl* los holandeses; **to go ~** (*inf*) pagar cada uno lo suyo; **Dutchman** (*irreg*) *n* holandés *m*; **Dutchwoman** (*irreg*) *n* holandésa

duty ['djuːtɪ] *n* deber *m*; (*tax*) derechos *mpl* de aduana; **on ~** de servicio; (*at night etc*) de guardia; **off ~** libre (de servicio); **duty-free** *adj* libre de impuestos

duvet ['duːveɪ] (*BRIT*) *n* edredón *m*

DVD *n abbr* (= *digital versatile or video disc*) DVD *m*; **DVD player** *n* lector *m* de DVD; **DVD writer** *n* grabadora de DVD

dwarf [dwɔːf] (*pl* **dwarves**) *n* enano/a ▷ *vt* empequeñecer

dwell [dwel] (*pt, pp* **dwelt**) *vi* morar; **dwell on** *vt fus* explayarse en

dwelt [dwelt] *pt, pp of* **dwell**

dwindle ['dwɪndl] *vi* disminuir

dye [daɪ] *n* tinte *m* ▷ *vt* teñir

dying ['daɪɪŋ] *adj* moribundo

dynamic [daɪ'næmɪk] *adj* dinámico

dynamite ['daɪnəmaɪt] *n* dinamita

dyslexia [dɪs'leksɪə] *n* dislexia

dyslexic [dɪs'leksɪk] *adj, n* disléxico/a *m/f*

e

E [iː] n (Mus) mi m

E111 n abbr (= form E111) impreso E111

each [iːtʃ] adj cada inv ▷ pron cada uno; **~ other** el uno al otro; **they hate ~ other** se odian (entre ellos or mutuamente); **they have 2 books ~** tienen 2 libros por persona

eager ['iːgə*] adj (keen) entusiasmado; **to be ~ to do sth** tener muchas ganas de hacer algo, impacientarse por hacer algo; **to be ~ for** tener muchas ganas de

eagle ['iːgl] n águila

ear [ɪə*] n oreja; oído; (of corn) espiga; **earache** n dolor m de oídos; **eardrum** n tímpano

earl [əːl] n conde m

earlier ['əːlɪə*] adj anterior ▷ adv antes

early ['əːlɪ] adv temprano; (before time) con tiempo, con anticipación ▷ adj temprano; (settlers etc) primitivo; (death, departure) prematuro; (reply) pronto; **to have an ~ night** acostarse temprano; **in the ~** or **~ in the spring/19th century** a principios de primavera/del siglo diecinueve; **early retirement** n jubilación f anticipada

earmark ['ɪəmaːk] vt: **to ~ (for)** reservar (para), destinar (a)

earn [əːn] vt (salary) percibir; (interest) devengar; (praise) merecerse

earnest ['əːnɪst] adj (wish) fervoroso; (person) serio, formal; **in ~** en serio

earnings ['əːnɪŋz] npl (personal) sueldo, ingresos mpl; (company) ganancias fpl

ear: earphones npl auriculares mpl; **earplugs** npl tapones mpl para los oídos; **earring** n pendiente m, arete m

earth [əːθ] n tierra; (BRIT Elec) cable m de toma de tierra ▷ vt (BRIT Elec) conectar a tierra; **earthquake** n terremoto

ease [iːz] n facilidad f; (comfort) comodidad f ▷ vt (lessen: problem) mitigar; (: pain) aliviar; (: tension) reducir; **to ~ sth in/out** meter/sacar algo con cuidado; **at ~!** (Mil) ¡descansen!

easily ['iːzɪlɪ] adv fácilmente

east [iːst] n este m ▷ adj del este, oriental; (wind) este ▷ adv al este, hacia el este; **the E~** el Oriente; (Pol) los países del Este; **eastbound** adj en dirección este

Easter ['iːstə*] n Pascua (de Resurrección); **Easter egg** n huevo de Pascua

eastern ['iːstən] adj del este, oriental; (oriental) oriental

Easter Sunday n Domingo de Resurrección

easy ['iːzɪ] adj fácil; (simple) sencillo; (comfortable) holgado, cómodo; (relaxed) tranquilo ▷ adv: **to take it** or **things ~** (not worry) tomarlo con calma; (rest) descansar; **easy-going** adj acomodadizo

eat [iːt] (pt **ate**, pp **eaten**) vt comer; **eat out** vi comer fuera

eavesdrop ['iːvzdrɔp] vi: **to ~ (on)** escuchar a escondidas

e-book ['iːbuk] n libro electrónico

e-business ['iːbɪznɪs] n (company) negocio electrónico; (commerce) comercio electrónico

EC n abbr (= European Community) CE f

eccentric [ɪk'sɛntrɪk] adj, n excéntrico/a m/f

echo ['ɛkəʊ] (pl **~es**) n eco ▷ vt (sound) repetir ▷ vi resonar, hacer eco

eclipse [ɪ'klɪps] n eclipse m

eco-friendly ['iːkəʊfrɛndlɪ] adj ecológico

ecological [iːkə'lɔdʒɪkl] adj ecológico

ecology [ɪ'kɔlədʒɪ] n ecología

e-commerce n abbr comercio electrónico

economic [iːkə'nɔmɪk] adj económico; (business etc) rentable; **economical** adj económico; **economics** n (Scol) economía ▷ npl (of project etc) rentabilidad f

economist [ɪ'kɔnəmɪst] n economista m/f

economize [ɪ'kɔnəmaɪz] vi economizar, ahorrar

economy [ɪ'kɔnəmɪ] n economía; **economy class** n (Aviat) clase f económica; **economy class syndrome** n síndrome m de la clase turista

ecstasy ['ɛkstəsɪ] n éxtasis m inv; (drug) éxtasis m inv; **ecstatic** [ɛks'tætɪk] adj extático

eczema ['ɛksɪmə] n eczema m

edge [ɛdʒ] n (of knife) filo; (of object) borde m; (of lake) orilla ▷ vt (Sewing) ribetear; **on ~** = **edgy**; **to ~ away from** alejarse poco a poco de

edgy ['ɛdʒɪ] adj nervioso, inquieto

edible ['ɛdɪbl] adj comestible

Edinburgh ['ɛdɪnbərə] n Edimburgo
edit ['ɛdɪt] vt (be editor of) dirigir; (text, report) corregir, preparar; **edition** [ɪ'dɪʃən] n edición f; **editor** n (of newspaper) director(a) m/f; (of column): **foreign/political editor** encargado de la sección de extranjero/política; (of book) redactor(a) m/f; **editorial** [-'tɔːrɪəl] adj editorial ▷ n editorial m
educate ['ɛdjukeɪt] vt (gen) educar; (instruct) instruir; **educated** ['ɛdjukeɪtɪd] adj culto
education [ɛdju'keɪʃən] n educación f; (schooling) enseñanza; (Scol) pedagogía; **educational** adj (policy etc) educacional; (experience) docente; (toy) educativo
eel [iːl] n anguila
eerie ['ɪərɪ] adj misterioso
effect [ɪ'fɛkt] n efecto ▷ vt efectuar, llevar a cabo; **to take ~** (law) entrar en vigor or vigencia; (drug) surtir efecto; **in ~** en realidad; **effects** npl (property) efectos mpl; **effective** adj eficaz; (actual) verdadero; **effectively** adv eficazmente; (in reality) efectivamente
efficiency [ɪ'fɪʃənsɪ] n eficiencia; rendimiento
efficient [ɪ'fɪʃənt] adj eficiente; (machine) de buen rendimiento; **efficiently** adv eficientemente, de manera eficiente
effort ['ɛfət] n esfuerzo; **effortless** adj sin ningún esfuerzo; (style) natural
e.g. adv abbr (= exempli gratia) p. ej.
egg [ɛg] n huevo; **hard-boiled/soft-boiled ~** huevo duro/pasado por agua; **eggcup** n huevera; **eggplant** (esp us) n berenjena; **eggshell** n cáscara de huevo; **egg white** n clara de huevo; **egg yolk** n yema de huevo
ego ['iːgəu] n ego
Egypt ['iːdʒɪpt] n Egipto; **Egyptian** [ɪ'dʒɪpʃən] adj, n egipcio/a m/f
eight [eɪt] num ocho; **eighteen** num diez y ocho, dieciocho; **eighteenth** adj decimoctavo; **the eighteenth floor** la planta dieciocho; **the eighteenth of August** el dieciocho de agosto; **eighth** num octavo; **eightieth** ['eɪtɪɪθ] adj octogésimo
eighty ['eɪtɪ] num ochenta
Eire ['ɛərə] n Eire m
either ['aɪðə*] adj cualquiera de los dos; (both, each) cada ▷ pron: **~ (of them)** cualquiera (de los dos) ▷ adv tampoco ▷ conj: **~ yes or no** o sí o no; **on ~ side** en ambos lados; **I don't like ~** no me gusta ninguno/a de los(las) dos; **no, I don't ~** no, yo tampoco
eject [ɪ'dʒɛkt] vt echar, expulsar; (tenant) desahuciar
elaborate [adj ɪ'læbərɪt, vb ɪ'læbəreɪt] adj (complex) complejo ▷ vt (expand) ampliar; (refine) refinar ▷ vi explicar con más detalles
elastic [ɪ'læstɪk] n elástico ▷ adj elástico; (fig) flexible; **elastic band** (BRIT) n gomita
elbow ['ɛlbəu] n codo
elder ['ɛldə*] adj mayor ▷ n (tree) saúco; (person) mayor; **elderly** adj de edad, mayor ▷ npl: **the elderly** los mayores
eldest ['ɛldɪst] adj, n el/la mayor
elect [ɪ'lɛkt] vt elegir ▷ adj: **the president ~** el presidente electo; **to ~ to do** optar por hacer; **election** n elección f; **electoral** adj electoral; **electorate** n electorado
electric [ɪ'lɛktrɪk] adj eléctrico; **electrical** adj eléctrico; **electric blanket** n manta eléctrica; **electric fire** n estufa eléctrica; **electrician** [ɪlɛk'trɪʃən] n electricista mf; **electricity** [ɪlɛk'trɪsɪtɪ] n electricidad f; **electric shock** n electrochoque m; **electrify** [ɪ'lɛktrɪfaɪ] vt (Rail) electrificar; (fig: audience) electrizar
electronic [ɪlɛk'trɔnɪk] adj electrónico; **electronic mail** n correo electrónico; **electronics** n electrónica
elegance ['ɛlɪgəns] n elegancia
elegant ['ɛlɪgənt] adj elegante
element ['ɛlɪmənt] n elemento; (of kettle etc) resistencia
elementary [ɛlɪ'mɛntərɪ] adj elemental; (primitive) rudimentario; **elementary school** (us) n escuela de enseñanza primaria
elephant ['ɛlɪfənt] n elefante m
elevate ['ɛlɪveɪt] vt (gen) elevar; (in rank) ascender
elevator ['ɛlɪveɪtə*] (us) n ascensor m; (in warehouse etc) montacargas m inv
eleven [ɪ'lɛvn] num once; **eleventh** num undécimo
eligible ['ɛlɪdʒəbl] adj: **an ~ young man/woman** un buen partido; **to be ~ for sth** llenar los requisitos para algo
eliminate [ɪ'lɪmɪneɪt] vt (suspect, possibility) descartar
elm [ɛlm] n olmo
eloquent ['ɛləkwənt] adj elocuente
else [ɛls] adv: **something ~** otra cosa; **somewhere ~** en otra parte; **everywhere ~** en todas partes menos aquí; **where ~?** ¿dónde más?, ¿en qué otra parte?; **there was little ~ to do** apenas quedaba otra cosa que hacer; **nobody ~ spoke** no habló nadie más; **elsewhere** adv (be) en otra parte; (go) a otra parte
elusive [ɪ'luːsɪv] adj esquivo; (quality) difícil de encontrar
e-mail ['iːmeɪl] n abbr (= electronic mail) correo electrónico, e-mail m; **e-mail**

address n dirección f electrónica, email m

embankment [ɪmˈbæŋkmənt] n terraplén m

embargo [ɪmˈbɑːgəu] (pl **-es**) n (Comm, Naut) embargo; (prohibition) prohibición f; **to put an ~ on sth** poner un embargo en algo

embark [ɪmˈbɑːk] vi embarcarse ▷vt embarcar; **to ~ on** (journey) emprender; (course of action) lanzarse a

embarrass [ɪmˈbærəs] vt avergonzar; (government etc) dejar en mal lugar; **embarrassed** adj (laugh, silence) embarazoso

> Be careful not to translate **embarrassed** by the Spanish word embarazada.

embarrassing adj (situation) violento; (question) embarazoso; **embarrassment** n (shame) vergüenza; (problem): **to be an embarrassment for sb** poner en un aprieto a algn

embassy [ˈembəsɪ] n embajada

embrace [ɪmˈbreɪs] vt abrazar, dar un abrazo a; (include) abarcar ▷vi abrazarse ▷n abrazo

embroider [ɪmˈbrɔɪdə*] vt bordar; **embroidery** n bordado

embryo [ˈembrɪəu] n embrión m

emerald [ˈemərəld] n esmeralda

emerge [ɪˈmɜːdʒ] vi salir; (arise) surgir

emergency [ɪˈmɜːdʒənsɪ] n crisis f inv; **in an ~** en caso de urgencia; **state of ~** estado de emergencia; **emergency brake** (us) n freno de mano; **emergency exit** n salida de emergencia; **emergency landing** n aterrizaje m forzoso; **emergency room** (us: Med) n sala f de urgencias; **emergency services** npl (fire, police, ambulance) servicios mpl de urgencia or emergencia

emigrate [ˈemɪgreɪt] vi emigrar; **emigration** [emɪˈgreɪʃən] n emigración f

eminent [ˈemɪnənt] adj eminente

emissions [ɪˈmɪʃənz] npl emisión f

emit [ɪˈmɪt] vt emitir; (smoke) arrojar; (smell) despedir; (sound) producir

emotion [ɪˈməuʃən] n emoción f; **emotional** adj (needs) emocional; (person) sentimental; (scene) conmovedor(a), emocionante; (speech) emocionado

emperor [ˈempərə*] n emperador m

emphasis [ˈemfəsɪs] (pl **-ses**) n énfasis m inv

emphasize [ˈemfəsaɪz] vt (word, point) subrayar, recalcar; (feature) hacer resaltar

empire [ˈempaɪə*] n imperio

employ [ɪmˈplɔɪ] vt emplear; **employee** [-ˈiː] n empleado/a; **employer** n patrón/ona m/f; empresario; **employment** n (work) trabajo; **employment agency** n

agencia de colocaciones

empower [ɪmˈpauə*] vt: **to ~ sb to do sth** autorizar a algn para hacer algo

empress [ˈempris] n emperatriz f

emptiness [ˈemptinis] n vacío; (of life etc) vaciedad f

empty [ˈemptɪ] adj vacío; (place) desierto; (house) desocupado; (threat) vano ▷vt vaciar; (place) dejar vacío ▷vi vaciarse; (house etc) quedar desocupado; **empty-handed** adj con las manos vacías

EMU n abbr (= European Monetary Union) UME f

emulsion [ɪˈmʌlʃən] n emulsión f; (also: ~ paint) pintura emulsión

enable [ɪˈneɪbl] vt: **to ~ sb to do sth** permitir a algn hacer algo

enamel [ɪˈnæməl] n esmalte m; (also: ~ paint) pintura esmaltada

enchanting [ɪnˈtʃɑːntɪŋ] adj encantador(a)

encl. abbr (= enclosed) adj

enclose [ɪnˈkləuz] vt (land) cercar; (letter etc) adjuntar; **please find ~d** le mandamos adjunto

enclosure [ɪnˈkləuʒə*] n cercado, recinto

encore [ɔŋˈkɔː*] excl ¡otra!, ¡bis! ▷n bis m

encounter [ɪnˈkauntə*] n encuentro ▷vt encontrar, encontrarse con; (difficulty) tropezar con

encourage [ɪnˈkʌrɪdʒ] vt alentar, animar; (activity) fomentar; (growth) estimular; **encouragement** n estímulo; (of industry) fomento

encouraging [ɪnˈkʌrɪdʒɪŋ] adj alentador(a)

encyclop(a)edia [ensaɪkləuˈpiːdɪə] n enciclopedia

end [end] n fin m; (of table) extremo; (of street) final m; (Sport) lado ▷vt terminar, acabar; (also: **bring to an ~, put an ~ to**) acabar con ▷vi terminar, acabar; **in the ~** al fin; **on ~** (object) de punta, de cabeza; **to stand on ~** (hair) erizarse; **for hours on ~** hora tras hora; **end up** vi: **to end up in** terminar en; (place) ir a parar en

endanger [ɪnˈdeɪndʒə*] vt poner en peligro; **an ~ed species** una especie en peligro de extinción

endearing [ɪnˈdɪərɪŋ] adj simpático, atractivo

endeavour [ɪnˈdevə*] (us **endeavor**) n esfuerzo; (attempt) tentativa ▷vi: **to ~ to do** esforzarse por hacer; (try) procurar hacer

ending [ˈendɪŋ] n (of book) desenlace m; (Ling) terminación f

endless [ˈendlɪs] adj interminable, inacabable

e

endorse [ɪnˈdɔːs] vt (cheque) endosar; (approve) aprobar; **endorsement** n (on driving licence) nota de inhabilitación

endurance [ɪnˈdjuərəns] n resistencia

endure [ɪnˈdjuə*] vt (bear) aguantar, soportar ▷ vi (last) durar

enemy [ˈɛnəmɪ] adj, n enemigo/a m/f

energetic [ɛnəˈdʒɛtɪk] adj enérgico

energy [ˈɛnədʒɪ] n energía

enforce [ɪnˈfɔːs] vt (Law) hacer cumplir

engaged [ɪnˈgeɪdʒd] adj (BRIT: busy, in use) ocupado; (betrothed) prometido; **to get ~** prometerse; **engaged tone** (BRIT) n (Tel) señal f de comunicando

engagement [ɪnˈgeɪdʒmənt] n (appointment) compromiso, cita; (booking) contratación f; (to marry) compromiso; (period) noviazgo; **engagement ring** n anillo de prometida

engaging [ɪnˈgeɪdʒɪŋ] adj atractivo

engine [ˈɛndʒɪn] n (Aut) motor m; (Rail) locomotora

engineer [ɛndʒɪˈnɪə*] n ingeniero; (BRIT: for repairs) mecánico; (on ship, US Rail) maquinista m; **engineering** n ingeniería

England [ˈɪŋglənd] n Inglaterra

English [ˈɪŋglɪʃ] adj inglés/esa ▷ n (Ling) inglés m; **the English** npl los ingleses mpl; **English Channel** n: **the English Channel** (el Canal de) la Mancha; **Englishman** (irreg) n inglés m; **Englishwoman** (irreg) n inglésa

engrave [ɪnˈgreɪv] vt grabar

engraving [ɪnˈgreɪvɪŋ] n grabado

enhance [ɪnˈhɑːns] vt (gen) aumentar; (beauty) realzar

enjoy [ɪnˈdʒɔɪ] vt (health, fortune) disfrutar de, gozar de; (like) gustarle a algn; **to ~ o.s.** divertirse; **enjoyable** adj agradable; (amusing) divertido; **enjoyment** n (joy) placer m; (activity) diversión f

enlarge [ɪnˈlɑːdʒ] vt aumentar; (broaden) extender; (Phot) ampliar ▷ vi: **to ~ on** (subject) tratar con más detalles; **enlargement** n (Phot) ampliación f

enlist [ɪnˈlɪst] vt alistar; (support) conseguir ▷ vi alistarse

enormous [ɪˈnɔːməs] adj enorme

enough [ɪˈnʌf] adj: **~ time/books** bastante tiempo/bastantes libros ▷ pron bastante(s) ▷ adv: **big ~** bastante grande; **he has not worked ~** no ha trabajado bastante; **have you got ~?** ¿tiene usted bastante(s)?; **~ to eat** (lo) suficiente or (lo) bastante para comer; **~!** ¡basta ya!; **that's ~, thanks** con eso basta, gracias; **I've had ~ of him** estoy harto de él; ... **which, funnily** or **oddly ~** ... ... lo que, por extraño que parezca ...

enquire [ɪnˈkwaɪə*] vt, vi = **inquire**

enquiry [ɪnˈkwaɪərɪ] n (official investigation) investigación

enrage [ɪnˈreɪdʒ] vt enfurecer

enrich [ɪnˈrɪtʃ] vt enriquecer

enrol [ɪnˈrəul] (US **enroll**) vt (members) inscribir; (Scol) matricular ▷ vi inscribirse; matricularse; **enrolment** (US **enrollment**) n inscripción f; matriculación f

en route [ɒnˈruːt] adv durante el viaje

en suite [ɒnˈswiːt] adj: **with ~ bathroom** con baño

ensure [ɪnˈʃuə*] vt asegurar

entail [ɪnˈteɪl] vt suponer

enter [ˈɛntə*] vt (room) entrar en; (club) hacerse socio de; (army) alistarse en; (sb for a competition) inscribir; (write down) anotar, apuntar; (Comput) meter ▷ vi entrar

enterprise [ˈɛntəpraɪz] n empresa; (spirit) iniciativa; **free ~** la libre empresa; **private ~** la iniciativa privada; **enterprising** adj emprendedor(a)

entertain [ɛntəˈteɪn] vt (amuse) divertir; (invite: guest) invitar (a casa); (idea) abrigar; **entertainer** n artista mf; **entertaining** adj divertido, entretenido; **entertainment** n (amusement) diversión f; (show) espectáculo

enthusiasm [ɪnˈθuːzɪæzəm] n entusiasmo

enthusiast [ɪnˈθuːzɪæst] n entusiasta mf; **enthusiastic** [-ˈæstɪk] adj entusiasta; **to be enthusiastic about** entusiasmarse por

entire [ɪnˈtaɪə*] adj entero; **entirely** adv totalmente

entitle [ɪnˈtaɪtl] vt: **to ~ sb to sth** dar a algn derecho a algo; **entitled** adj (book) titulado; **to be entitled to do** tener derecho a hacer

entrance [n ˈɛntrəns, vb ɪnˈtrɑːns] n entrada ▷ vt encantar, hechizar; **to gain ~ to** (university etc) ingresar en; **entrance examination** n examen m de ingreso; **entrance fee** n cuota; **entrance ramp** (US) n (Aut) rampa de acceso

entrant [ˈɛntrənt] n (in race, competition) participante mf; (in examination) candidato/a

entrepreneur [ɒntrəprəˈnəː] n empresario

entrust [ɪnˈtrʌst] vt: **to ~ sth to sb** confiar algo a algn

entry [ˈɛntrɪ] n entrada; (in competition) participación f; (in register) apunte m; (in account) partida; (in reference book) artículo; **"no ~"** "prohibido el paso"; (Aut) "dirección prohibida"; **entry phone** n portero automático

envelope [ˈɛnvələup] n sobre m

envious [ˈɛnvɪəs] adj envidioso; (look) de

envidia

environment [ɪn'vaɪərnmənt] n
(surroundings) entorno; (natural world):
the ~ el medio ambiente; **environmental**
[-'mɛntl] adj ambiental; medioambiental;
environmentally [-'mɛntəlɪ]
adv: **environmentally sound/friendly**
ecológico

envisage [ɪn'vɪzɪdʒ] vt prever

envoy ['ɛnvɔɪ] n enviado

envy ['ɛnvɪ] n envidia ▷ vt tener envidia a;
to ~ sb sth envidiar algo a algn

epic ['ɛpɪk] n épica ▷ adj épico

epidemic [ɛpɪ'dɛmɪk] n epidemia

epilepsy ['ɛpɪlɛpsɪ] n epilepsia

epileptic [ɛpɪ'lɛptɪk] adj, n epiléptico/a
m/f; **epileptic fit** [ɛpɪ'lɛptɪk-] n ataque m
de epilepsia, acceso m epiléptico

episode ['ɛpɪsəud] n episodio

equal ['iːkwl] adj igual; (treatment)
equitativo ▷ n igual mf ▷ vt ser igual a;
(fig) igualar; **to be ~ to** (task) estar a la altura
de; **equality** [iː'kwɔlɪtɪ] n igualdad f;
equalize vi (Sport) empatar; **equally** adv
igualmente; (share etc) a partes iguales

equation [ɪ'kweɪʒən] n (Math) ecuación f

equator [ɪ'kweɪtə*] n ecuador m

equip [ɪ'kwɪp] vt equipar; (person) proveer;
to be well ~ped estar bien equipado;
equipment n equipo; (tools) avíos mpl

equivalent [ɪ'kwɪvələnt] adj: **~ (to)**
equivalente (a) ▷ n equivalente m

ER abbr (BRIT: = Elizabeth Regina) la reina
Isabel; (us: Med) = **emergency room**

era ['ɪərə] n era, época

erase [ɪ'reɪz] vt borrar; **eraser** n goma
de borrar

erect [ɪ'rɛkt] adj erguido ▷ vt erigir,
levantar; (assemble) montar; **erection** [-ʃən]
n construcción f; (assembly) montaje m;
(Physiol) erección f

ERM n abbr (= Exchange Rate Mechanism) tipo
de cambio europeo

erode [ɪ'rəud] vt (Geo) erosionar; (metal)
corroer, desgastar; (fig) desgastar

erosion [ɪ'rəuʒən] n erosión f; desgaste m

erotic [ɪ'rɔtɪk] adj erótico

errand ['ɛrnd] n recado (SP), mandado
(LAM)

erratic [ɪ'rætɪk] adj desigual, poco
uniforme

error ['ɛrə*] n error m, equivocación f

erupt [ɪ'rʌpt] vi entrar en erupción; (fig)
estallar; **eruption** [ɪ'rʌpʃən] n erupción f;
(of war) estallido

escalate ['ɛskəleɪt] vi extenderse,
intensificarse

escalator ['ɛskəleɪtə*] n escalera móvil

escape [ɪ'skeɪp] n fuga ▷ vi escaparse;
(flee) huir, evadirse; (leak) fugarse
▷ vt (responsibility etc) evitar, eludir;
(consequences) escapar a; (elude): **his name
~s me** no me sale su nombre; **to ~ from**
(place) escaparse de; (person) escaparse a

escort [n 'ɛskɔːt, vb ɪ'skɔːt] n
acompañante mf; (Mil) escolta mf ▷ vt
acompañar

especially [ɪ'spɛʃlɪ] adv (above all)
sobre todo; (particularly) en particular,
especialmente

espionage [ɛspɪənɑːʒ] n espionaje m

essay ['ɛseɪ] n (Literature) ensayo;
(Scol: short) redacción f; (: long) trabajo

essence ['ɛsns] n esencia

essential [ɪ'sɛnʃl] adj (necessary)
imprescindible; (basic) esencial; **essentially**
adv esencialmente; **essentials** npl lo
imprescindible, lo esencial

establish [ɪ'stæblɪʃ] vt establecer;
(prove) demostrar; (relations) entablar;
(reputation) ganarse; **establishment** n
establecimiento; **the Establishment** la
clase dirigente

estate [ɪ'steɪt] n (land) finca, hacienda;
(inheritance) herencia; (BRIT: also: **housing
~**) urbanización f; **estate agent** (BRIT) n
agente mf inmobiliario/a; **estate car** (BRIT)
n furgoneta

estimate [n 'ɛstɪmət, vb 'ɛstɪmeɪt] n
estimación f, apreciación f; (assessment)
tasa, cálculo; (Comm) presupuesto ▷ vt
estimar, tasar; calcular

etc abbr (= et cetera) etc

eternal [ɪ'təːnl] adj eterno

eternity [ɪ'təːnɪtɪ] n eternidad f

ethical ['ɛθɪkl] adj ético; **ethics** ['ɛθɪks] n
ética ▷ npl moralidad f

Ethiopia [iːθɪ'əupɪə] n Etiopía

ethnic ['ɛθnɪk] adj étnico; **ethnic
minority** n minoría étnica

e-ticket ['iːtɪkɪt] n billete m electrónico
(SP), boleto electrónico (LAM)

etiquette ['ɛtɪkɛt] n etiqueta

EU n abbr (= European Union) UE f

euro n euro

Europe ['juərəp] n Europa; **European**
[-'piːən] adj, n europeo/a m/f; **European
Community** n Comunidad f Europea;
European Union n Unión f Europea

Eurostar® ['juərəustɑː*] n Eurostar® m

evacuate [ɪ'vækjueɪt] vt (people) evacuar;
(place) desocupar

evade [ɪ'veɪd] vt evadir, eludir

evaluate [ɪ'væljueɪt] vt evaluar; (value)
tasar; (evidence) interpretar

evaporate [ɪ'væpəreɪt] vi evaporarse; (fig)

desvanecerse

eve [i:v] *n*: **on the ~ of** en vísperas de

even ['i:vn] *adj* (*level*) llano; (*smooth*) liso; (*speed, temperature*) uniforme; (*number*) par ▷ *adv* hasta, incluso; (*introducing a comparison*) aún, todavía; **~ if, ~ though** aunque +*subjun*; **~ more** aun más; **~ so** aun así; **not ~** ni siquiera; **~ he was there** hasta él estuvo allí; **~ on Sundays** incluso los domingos; **to get ~ with sb** ajustar cuentas con algn

evening ['i:vnɪŋ] *n* tarde *f*; (*late*) noche *f*; **in the ~** por la tarde; **evening class** *n* clase *f* nocturna; **evening dress** *n* (*no pl: formal clothes*) traje *m* de etiqueta; (*woman's*) traje *m* de noche

event [ɪ'vɛnt] *n* suceso, acontecimiento; (*Sport*) prueba; **in the ~ of** en caso de; **eventful** *adj* (*life*) activo; (*day*) ajetreado

eventual [ɪ'vɛntʃuəl] *adj* final

▌Be careful not to translate **eventual** by the Spanish word *eventual*.

eventually *adv* (*finally*) finalmente; (*in time*) con el tiempo

ever ['ɛvə*] *adv* (*at any time*) nunca, jamás; (*at all times*) siempre; (*in question*): **why ~ not?** ¿y por qué no?; **the best ~** lo nunca visto; **have you ~ seen it?** ¿lo ha visto usted alguna vez?; **better than ~** mejor que nunca; **~ since** *adv* desde entonces ▷ *conj* después de que; **evergreen** *n* árbol *m* de hoja perenne

○ **KEYWORD**

every ['ɛvrɪ] *adj* **1** (*each*) cada; **every one of them** (*persons*) todos ellos/as; (*objects*) cada uno de ellos/as; **every shop in the town was closed** todas
las tiendas de la ciudad estaban cerradas
2 (*all possible*) todo/a; **I gave you every assistance** te di toda la ayuda posible; **I have every confidence in him** tiene toda mi confianza; **we wish you every success** te deseamos toda suerte de éxitos
3 (*showing recurrence*) todo/a; **every day/ week** todos los días/todas las semanas; **every other car had been broken into** habían forzado uno de cada dos coches; **she visits me every other/third day** me visita cada dos/tres días; **every now and then** de vez en cuando

every: **everybody** *pron* = **everyone**; **everyday** *adj* (*daily*) cotidiano, de todos los días; (*usual*) acostumbrado; **everyone** *pron* todos/as, todo el mundo; **everything** *pron* todo; **this shop sells everything**

esta tienda vende de todo; **everywhere** *adv*: **I've been looking for you everywhere** te he estado buscando por todas partes; **everywhere you go you meet ...** en todas partes encuentras ...

evict [ɪ'vɪkt] *vt* desahuciar

evidence ['ɛvɪdəns] *n* (*proof*) prueba; (*of witness*) testimonio; (*sign*) indicios *mpl*; **to give ~** prestar declaración, dar testimonio

evident ['ɛvɪdənt] *adj* evidente, manifiesto; **evidently** *adv* por lo visto

evil ['i:vl] *adj* malo; (*influence*) funesto ▷ *n* mal *m*

evoke [ɪ'vəuk] *vt* evocar

evolution [i:və'lu:ʃən] *n* evolución *f*

evolve [ɪ'vɔlv] *vt* desarrollar ▷ *vi* evolucionar, desarrollarse

ewe [ju:] *n* oveja

ex [ɛks] (*inf*) *n*: **my ~** mi ex

ex- [ɛks] *prefix* ex

exact [ɪg'zækt] *adj* exacto; (*person*) meticuloso ▷ *vt*: **to ~ sth (from)** exigir algo (de); **exactly** *adv* exactamente; (*indicating agreement*) exacto

exaggerate [ɪg'zædʒəreɪt] *vt, vi* exagerar; **exaggeration** [-'reɪʃən] *n* exageración *f*

exam [ɪg'zæm] *n abbr* (*Scol*) = **examination**

examination [ɪgzæmɪ'neɪʃən] *n* examen *m*; (*Med*) reconocimiento

examine [ɪg'zæmɪn] *vt* examinar; (*inspect*) inspeccionar, escudriñar; (*Med*) reconocer; **examiner** *n* examinador(a) *m/f*

example [ɪg'zɑ:mpl] *n* ejemplo; **for ~** por ejemplo

exasperated [ɪg'zɑ:spəreɪtɪd] *adj* exasperado

excavate ['ɛkskəveɪt] *vt* excavar

exceed [ɪk'si:d] *vt* (*amount*) exceder; (*number*) pasar de; (*speed limit*) sobrepasar; (*powers*) excederse en; (*hopes*) superar; **exceedingly** *adv* sumamente, sobremanera

excel [ɪk'sɛl] *vi* sobresalir; **to ~ o.s** lucirse

excellence ['ɛksələns] *n* excelencia

excellent ['ɛksələnt] *adj* excelente

except [ɪk'sɛpt] *prep* (*also*: **~ for, ~ing**) excepto, salvo ▷ *vt* exceptuar, excluir; **~ if/when** excepto si/cuando; **~ that** salvo que; **exception** [ɪk'sɛpʃən] *n* excepción *f*; **to take exception to** ofenderse por; **exceptional** [ɪk'sɛpʃənl] *adj* excepcional; **exceptionally** [ɪk'sɛpʃənəlɪ] *adv* excepcionalmente, extraordinariamente

excerpt ['ɛksə:pt] *n* extracto

excess [ɪk'sɛs] *n* exceso; **excess baggage** *n* exceso de equipaje; **excessive** *adj* excesivo

exchange [ɪks'tʃeɪndʒ] *n* intercambio; (*conversation*) diálogo; (*also*: **telephone ~**)

central f (telefónica) ▷ vt: **to ~ (for)** cambiar (por); **exchange rate** n tipo de cambio

excite [ɪkˈsaɪt] vt (*stimulate*) estimular; (*arouse*) excitar; **excited** adj: **to get excited** emocionarse; **excitement** n (*agitation*) excitación f; (*exhilaration*) emoción f; **exciting** adj emocionante

exclaim [ɪkˈskleɪm] vi exclamar; **exclamation** [ɛkskləˈmeɪʃən] n exclamación f; **exclamation mark** n punto de admiración; **exclamation point** (us) = **exclamation mark**

exclude [ɪkˈskluːd] vt excluir; exceptuar **excluding** [ɪksˈkluːdɪŋ] prep: **~ VAT** IVA no incluido

exclusion [ɪkˈskluːʒən] n exclusión f; **to the ~ of** con exclusión de

exclusive [ɪkˈskluːsɪv] adj exclusivo; (*club, district*) selecto; **~ of tax** excluyendo impuestos; **exclusively** adv únicamente

excruciating [ɪkˈskruːʃɪeɪtɪŋ] adj (*pain*) agudísimo, atroz; (*noise, embarrassment*) horrible

excursion [ɪkˈskəːʃən] n (*tourist excursion*) excursión f

excuse [n ɪkˈskjuːs, vb ɪkˈskjuːz] n disculpa, excusa; (*pretext*) pretexto ▷ vt (*justify*) justificar; (*forgive*) disculpar, perdonar; **to ~ sb from doing sth** dispensar a algn de hacer algo; **~ me!** (*attracting attention*) ¡por favor!; (*apologizing*) ¡perdón!; **if you will ~ me** con su permiso

ex-directory [ˈɛksdɪˈrɛktərɪ] (BRIT) adj que no consta en la guía

execute [ˈɛksɪkjuːt] vt (*plan*) realizar; (*order*) cumplir; (*person*) ajusticiar, ejecutar; **execution** [-ˈkjuːʃən] n realización f; cumplimiento; ejecución f

executive [ɪgˈzɛkjutɪv] n (*person, committee*) ejecutivo; (*Pol: committee*) poder m ejecutivo ▷ adj ejecutivo

exempt [ɪgˈzɛmpt] adj: **~ from** exento de ▷ vt: **to ~ sb from** eximir a algn de

exercise [ˈɛksəsaɪz] n ejercicio ▷ vt (*patience*) usar de; (*right*) valerse de; (*dog*) llevar de paseo; (*mind*) preocupar ▷ vi (*also*: **to take ~**) hacer ejercicio(s); **exercise book** n cuaderno

exert [ɪgˈzəːt] vt ejercer; **to ~ o.s.** esforzarse; **exertion** [-ʃən] n esfuerzo

exhale [eksˈheɪl] vt despedir ▷ vi exhalar

exhaust [ɪgˈzɔːst] n (Aut: also: **~ pipe**) escape m; (: *fumes*) gases mpl de escape ▷ vt agotar; **exhausted** adj agotado; **exhaustion** [ɪgˈzɔːstʃən] n agotamiento; **nervous exhaustion** postración f nerviosa

exhibit [ɪgˈzɪbɪt] n (Art) obra expuesta; (Law) objeto expuesto ▷ vt (show: *emotions*)

manifestar; (: *courage, skill*) demostrar; (*paintings*) exponer; **exhibition** [ɛksɪˈbɪʃən] n exposición f; (*of talent etc*) demostración f

exhilarating [ɪgˈzɪləreɪtɪŋ] adj estimulante, tónico

exile [ˈɛksaɪl] n exilio; (*person*) exiliado/a ▷ vt desterrar, exiliar

exist [ɪgˈzɪst] vi existir; (*live*) vivir; **existence** n existencia; **existing** adj existente, actual

exit [ˈɛksɪt] n salida ▷ vi (Theatre) hacer mutis; (Comput) salir (del sistema)

▌ Be careful not to translate **exit** by the Spanish word éxito.

exit ramp (us) n (Aut) vía de acceso

exotic [ɪgˈzɔtɪk] adj exótico

expand [ɪkˈspænd] vt ampliar; (*number*) aumentar ▷ vi (*population*) aumentar; (*trade etc*) expandirse; (*gas, metal*) dilatarse

expansion [ɪkˈspænʃən] n (*of population*) aumento; (*of trade*) expansión f

expect [ɪkˈspɛkt] vt esperar; (*require*) contar con; (*suppose*) suponer ▷ vi: **to be ~ing** (*pregnant woman*) estar embarazada; **expectation** [ɛkspɛkˈteɪʃən] n (*hope*) esperanza; (*belief*) expectativa

expedition [ɛkspəˈdɪʃən] n expedición f

expel [ɪkˈspɛl] vt arrojar; (*from place*) expulsar

expenditure [ɪksˈpɛndɪtʃə*] n gastos mpl, desembolso; consumo

expense [ɪkˈspɛns] n gasto, gastos mpl; (*high cost*) costa; **expenses** npl (Comm) gastos mpl; **at the ~ of** a costa de; **expense account** n cuenta de gastos

expensive [ɪkˈspɛnsɪv] adj caro, costoso

experience [ɪkˈspɪərɪəns] n experiencia ▷ vt experimentar; (*suffer*) sufrir; **experienced** adj experimentado

experiment [ɪkˈspɛrɪmənt] n experimento ▷ vi hacer experimentos; **experimental** [-ˈmɛntl] adj experimental; **the process is still at the experimental stage** el proceso está todavía en prueba

expert [ˈɛkspəːt] adj experto, perito ▷ n experto/a, perito/a; (*specialist*) especialista mf; **expertise** [-ˈtiːz] n pericia

expire [ɪkˈspaɪə*] vi caducar, vencer; **expiry** n vencimiento; **expiry date** n (*of medicine, food item*) fecha de caducidad

explain [ɪkˈspleɪn] vt explicar; **explanation** [ɛkspləˈneɪʃən] n explicación f

explicit [ɪkˈsplɪsɪt] adj explícito

explode [ɪkˈspləʊd] vi estallar, explotar; (*population*) crecer rápidamente; (*with anger*) reventar

exploit [n ˈɛksplɔɪt, vb ɪkˈsplɔɪt] n hazaña

▷ vt explotar; **exploitation** [-'teɪʃən] n explotación f

explore [ɪk'splɔ:*] vt explorar; (fig) examinar; investigar; **explorer** n explorador(a) m/f

explosion [ɪk'spləʊʒən] n explosión f; **explosive** [ɪks'pləʊsɪv] adj, n explosivo

export [vb ɛk'spɔ:t, n, cpd 'ɛkspɔ:t] vt exportar ▷ n (process) exportación f; (product) producto de exportación ▷ cpd de exportación; **exporter** n exportador m

expose [ɪk'spəʊz] vt exponer; (unmask) desenmascarar; **exposed** adj expuesto

exposure [ɪk'spəʊʒə*] n exposición f; (publicity) publicidad f; (Phot: speed) velocidad f de obturación; (: shot) fotografía; **to die from ~** (Med) morir de frío

express [ɪk'sprɛs] adj (definite) expreso, explícito; (BRIT: letter etc) urgente ▷ n (train) rápido ▷ vt expresar; **expression** [ɪk'sprɛʃən] n expresión f; (of actor etc) sentimiento; **expressway** (US) n (urban motorway) autopista

exquisite [ɛk'skwɪzɪt] adj exquisito

extend [ɪk'stɛnd] vt (visit, street) prolongar; (building) ampliar; (invitation) ofrecer ▷ vi (land) extenderse; (period of time) prolongarse

extension [ɪk'stɛnʃən] n extensión f; (building) ampliación f; (of time) prolongación f; (Tel: in private house) línea derivada; (: in office) extensión f; **extension lead** n alargador m, alargadera

extensive [ɪk'stɛnsɪv] adj extenso; (damage) importante; (knowledge) amplio

extent [ɪk'stɛnt] n (breadth) extensión f; (scope) alcance m; **to some ~** hasta cierto punto; **to the ~ of ...** hasta el punto de ...; **to such an ~ that ...** hasta tal punto que ...; **to what ~?** ¿hasta qué punto?

exterior [ɛk'stɪərɪə*] adj exterior, externo ▷ n exterior m

external [ɛk'stə:nl] adj externo

extinct [ɪk'stɪŋkt] adj (volcano) extinguido; (race) extinto; **extinction** n extinción f

extinguish [ɪk'stɪŋgwɪʃ] vt extinguir, apagar

extra ['ɛkstrə] adj adicional ▷ adv (in addition) de más ▷ n (luxury, addition) extra m; (Cinema, Theatre) extra mf, comparsa mf

extract [vb ɪk'strækt, n 'ɛkstrækt] vt sacar; (tooth) extraer; (money, promise) obtener ▷ n extracto

extradite ['ɛkstrədaɪt] vt extraditar

extraordinary [ɪk'strɔ:dnrɪ] adj extraordinario; (odd) raro

extravagance [ɪk'strævəgəns] n derroche m, despilfarro; (thing bought) extravagancia

extravagant [ɪk'strævəgənt] adj (lavish: person) pródigo; (: gift) (demasiado) caro; (wasteful) despilfarrador(a)

extreme [ɪk'stri:m] adj extremo, extremado ▷ n extremo; **extremely** adv sumamente, extremadamente

extremist [ɪk'stri:mɪst] adj, n extremista m/f

extrovert ['ɛkstrəvə:t] n extrovertido/a

eye [aɪ] n ojo ▷ vt mirar de soslayo, ojear; **to keep an ~ on** vigilar; **eyeball** n globo ocular; **eyebrow** n ceja; **eyedrops** npl gotas fpl para los ojos, colirio; **eyelash** n pestaña; **eyelid** n párpado; **eyeliner** n delineador m (de ojos); **eyeshadow** n sombreador m de ojos; **eyesight** n vista; **eye witness** n testigo mf presencial

f

F [ɛf] n (Mus) fa m

fabric ['fæbrɪk] n tejido, tela

 Be careful not to translate **fabric** by the Spanish word *fábrica*.

fabulous ['fæbjuləs] adj fabuloso

face [feɪs] n (Anat) cara, rostro; (of clock) esfera (SP), cara (LAM); (of mountain) cara, ladera; (of building) fachada ▷ vt (direction) estar de cara a; (situation) hacer frente a; (facts) aceptar; **~ down** (person, card) boca abajo; **to lose ~** desprestigiarse; **to make o pull a ~** hacer muecas; **in the ~ of** (difficulties etc) ante; **on the ~ of it** a primera vista; **~ to ~** cara a cara; **face up to** vt fus hacer frente a, arrostrar; **face cloth** (BRIT) n manopla; **face pack** n (BRIT) mascarilla

facial ['feɪʃəl] adj de la cara ▷ n (also: **beauty ~**) tratamiento facial, limpieza

facilitate [fə'sɪlɪteɪt] vt facilitar

facilities [fə'sɪlɪtɪz] npl (buildings) instalaciones fpl; (equipment) servicios mpl; **credit ~** facilidades fpl de crédito

fact [fækt] n hecho; **in ~** en realidad

faction ['fækʃən] n facción f

factor ['fæktə*] n factor m

factory ['fæktərɪ] n fábrica

factual ['fæktjuəl] adj basado en los hechos

faculty ['fækəltɪ] n facultad f; (US: teaching staff) personal m docente

fad [fæd] n novedad f, moda

fade [feɪd] vi desteñirse; (sound, smile) desvanecerse; (light) apagarse; (flower) marchitarse; (hope, memory) perderse; **fade away** vi (sound) apagarse

fag [fæg] (BRIT: inf) n (cigarette) pitillo (SP), cigarro

Fahrenheit ['fɑːrənhaɪt] n Fahrenheit m

fail [feɪl] vt (candidate, test) suspender (SP), reprobar (LAM); (memory etc) fallar a ▷ vi suspender (SP), reprobar (LAM); (be unsuccessful) fracasar; (strength, brakes) fallar; (light) acabarse; **to ~ to do sth** (neglect) dejar de hacer algo; (be unable) no poder hacer algo; **without ~** sin falta; **failing** n falta, defecto ▷ prep a falta de; **failure** ['feɪljə*] n fracaso; (person) fracasado/a; (mechanical etc) fallo

faint [feɪnt] adj débil; (recollection) vago; (mark) apenas visible ▷ n desmayo ▷ vi desmayarse; **to feel ~** estar mareado, marearse; **faintest** adj: **I haven't the faintest idea** no tengo la más remota idea; **faintly** adv débilmente; (vaguely) vagamente

fair [fɛə*] adj justo; (hair, person) rubio; (weather) bueno; (good enough) regular; (considerable) considerable ▷ adv (play) limpio ▷ n feria; (BRIT: funfair) parque m de atracciones; **fairground** n recinto ferial; **fair-haired** adj (person) rubio; **fairly** adv (justly) con justicia; (quite) bastante; **fair trade** n comercio justo; **fairway** n (Golf) calle f

fairy ['fɛərɪ] n hada; **fairy tale** n cuento de hadas

faith [feɪθ] n fe f; (trust) confianza; (sect) religión f; **faithful** adj (loyal: troops etc) leal; (spouse) fiel; (account) exacto; **faithfully** adv fielmente; **yours faithfully** (BRIT: in letters) le saluda atentamente

fake [feɪk] n (painting etc) falsificación f; (person) impostor(a) m/f ▷ adj falso ▷ vt fingir; (painting etc) falsificar

falcon ['fɔːlkən] n halcón m

fall [fɔːl] (pt fell, pp fallen) n caída; (in price etc) descenso; (US) otoño ▷ vi caer(se); (price) bajar, descender; **falls** npl (waterfall) cascada, salto de agua; **to ~ flat** (on one's face) caerse (boca abajo); (plan) fracasar; (joke, story) no hacer gracia; **fall apart** vi deshacerse; **fall down** vi (person) caerse; (building, hopes) derrumbarse; **fall for** vt fus (trick) dejarse engañar por; (person) enamorarse de; **fall off** vi (person) caerse; (diminish) disminuir; **fall out** vi (friends etc) reñir; (hair, teeth) caerse; **fall over** vi caer(se); **fall through** vi (plan, project) fracasar

fallen ['fɔːlən] pp of **fall**

fallout ['fɔːlaut] n lluvia radioactiva

false [fɔːls] adj falso; **under ~ pretences** con engaños; **false alarm** n falsa alarma; **false teeth** (BRIT) npl dentadura postiza

fame [feɪm] n fama

familiar [fə'mɪlɪə*] adj conocido, familiar; (tone) de confianza; **to be ~ with** (subject) conocer (bien); **familiarize** [fə'mɪlɪəraɪz] vt: **to familiarize o.s. with** familiarizarse con

family ['fæmɪlɪ] n familia; **family doctor** n médico/a de cabecera; **family planning** n planificación f familiar

famine ['fæmɪn] n hambre f, hambruna

famous ['feɪməs] adj famoso, célebre

fan [fæn] n abanico; (Elec) ventilador m; (of pop star) fan mf; (Sport) hincha mf ▷ vt abanicar; (fire, quarrel) atizar

fanatic [fə'nætɪk] n fanático/a

fan belt n correa del ventilador

fan club n club m de fans

fancy ['fænsɪ] n (whim) capricho, antojo; (imagination) imaginación f ▷ adj (luxury) lujoso, de lujo ▷ vt (feel like, want) tener ganas de; (imagine) imaginarse; (think) creer; **to take a ~ to sb** tomar cariño a algn; **he fancies her** (inf) le gusta (ella) mucho; **fancy dress** n disfraz m

fan heater n calefactor m de aire

fantasize ['fæntəsaɪz] vi fantasear, hacerse ilusiones

fantastic [fæn'tæstɪk] adj (enormous) enorme; (strange, wonderful) fantástico

fantasy ['fæntəzɪ] n (dream) sueño; (unreality) fantasía

fanzine ['fænziːn] n fanzine m

FAQs abbr (= frequently asked questions) preguntas frecuentes

far [fɑː*] adj (distant) lejano ▷ adv lejos; (much, greatly) mucho; **~ away, ~ off** (a lo) lejos; **~ better** mucho mejor; **~ from** lejos de; **by ~** con mucho; **go as ~ as the farm** vaya hasta la granja; **as ~ as I know** que yo sepa; **how ~?** ¿hasta dónde?; (fig) ¿hasta qué punto?

farce [fɑːs] n farsa

fare [fɛə*] n (on trains, buses) precio (del billete); (in taxi: cost) tarifa; (food) comida; **half ~** medio pasaje m; **full ~** pasaje completo

Far East n: **the ~** el Extremo Oriente

farewell [fɛə'wɛl] excl, n adiós m

farm [fɑːm] n cortijo (SP), hacienda (LAM), rancho (MEX), rancho (RPL) ▷ vt cultivar; **farmer** n granjero, hacendado (LAM), ranchero (MEX), estanciero (RPL); **farmhouse** n granja, casa del hacendado (LAM), rancho (MEX), casco de la estancia (RPL); **farming** n agricultura; (of crops) cultivo; (of animals) cría; **farmyard** n corral m

far-reaching [fɑː'riːtʃɪŋ] adj (reform, effect) de gran alcance

fart [fɑːt] (inf!) vi tirarse un pedo (!)

farther ['fɑːðə*] adv más lejos, más allá ▷ adj más lejano

farthest ['fɑːðɪst] superlative of **far**

fascinate ['fæsɪneɪt] vt fascinar;

fascinated adj fascinado

fascinating ['fæsɪneɪtɪŋ] adj fascinante

fascination [-'neɪʃən] n fascinación f

fascist ['fæʃɪst] adj, n fascista m/f

fashion ['fæʃən] n moda; (fashion industry) industria de la moda; (manner) manera ▷ vt formar; **in ~** a la moda; **out of ~** pasado de moda; **fashionable** adj de moda; **fashion show** n desfile m de modelos

fast [fɑːst] adj rápido; (dye, colour) resistente; (clock): **to be ~** estar adelantado ▷ adv rápidamente, de prisa; (stuck, held) firmemente ▷ n ayuno ▷ vi ayunar; **~ asleep** profundamente dormido

fasten ['fɑːsn] vt atar, sujetar; (coat, belt) abrochar ▷ vi atarse; abrocharse

fast food n comida rápida, platos mpl preparados

fat [fæt] adj gordo; (book) grueso; (profit) grande, pingüe ▷ n grasa; (on person) carnes fpl; (lard) manteca

fatal ['feɪtl] adj (mistake) fatal; (injury) mortal; **fatality** [fə'tælɪtɪ] n (road death etc) víctima; **fatally** adv fatalmente; mortalmente

fate [feɪt] n destino; (of person) suerte f

father ['fɑːðə*] n padre m; **Father Christmas** n Papá m Noel; **father-in-law** n suegro

fatigue [fə'tiːɡ] n fatiga, cansancio

fattening ['fætnɪŋ] adj (food) que hace engordar

fatty ['fætɪ] adj (food) graso ▷ n (inf) gordito/a, gordinflón/ona m/f

faucet ['fɔːsɪt] (US) n grifo (SP), llave f, canilla (RPL)

fault [fɔːlt] n (blame) culpa; (defect: in person, machine) defecto; (Geo) falla ▷ vt criticar; **it's my ~** es culpa mía; **to find ~ with** criticar, poner peros a; **at ~** culpable; **faulty** adj defectuoso

fauna ['fɔːnə] n fauna

favour etc ['feɪvə*] (US **favor** etc) n favor m; (approval) aprobación f ▷ vt (proposition) estar a favor de, aprobar; (assist) ser propicio a; **to do sb a ~** hacer un favor a algn; **to find ~ with sb** caer en gracia a algn; **in ~ of** a favor de; **favourable** adj favorable; **favourite** ['feɪvrɪt] adj, n favorito, preferido

fawn [fɔːn] n cervato ▷ adj (also: **~-coloured**) color de cervato, leonado ▷ vi: **to ~ (up)on** adular

fax [fæks] n (document) fax m; (machine) telefax m ▷ vt mandar por telefax

FBI (US) n abbr (= Federal Bureau of Investigation) ≈ BIC f (SP)

fear [fɪə*] n miedo, temor m ▷ vt tener

miedo de, temer; **for ~ of** por si; **fearful** adj temeroso, miedoso; (awful) terrible; **fearless** adj audaz

feasible ['fi:zəbl] adj factible

feast [fi:st] n banquete m; (Rel: also: ~ **day**) fiesta ▷ vi festejar

feat [fi:t] n hazaña

feather ['fɛðə*] n pluma

feature ['fi:tʃə*] n característica; (article) artículo de fondo ▷ vt (film) presentar ▷ vi: **to ~ in** tener un papel destacado en; **features** npl (of face) facciones fpl; **feature film** n largometraje m

Feb. abbr (= February) feb

February ['fɛbruərɪ] n febrero

fed [fɛd] pt, pp of **feed**

federal ['fɛdərəl] adj federal

federation [fɛdə'reɪʃən] n federación f

fed up [fɛd'ʌp] adj: **to be ~ (with)** estar harto (de)

fee [fi:] n pago; (professional) derechos mpl, honorarios mpl; (of club) cuota; **school ~s** matrícula

feeble ['fi:bl] adj débil; (joke) flojo

feed [fi:d] (pt, pp **fed**) n comida; (of animal) pienso; (on printer) dispositivo de alimentación ▷ vt alimentar; (BRIT: baby: breastfeed) dar el pecho a; (animal) dar de comer a; (data, information): **to ~ into** meter en; **feedback** n reacción f, feedback m

feel [fi:l] (pt, pp **felt**) n (sensation) sensación f; (sense of touch) tacto; (impression): **to have the ~ of** parecerse a ▷ vt tocar; (pain etc) sentir; (think, believe) creer; **to ~ hungry/ cold** tener hambre/frío; **to ~ lonely/ better** sentirse solo/mejor; **I don't ~ well** no me siento bien; **it ~s soft** es suave al tacto; **to ~ like** (want) tener ganas de; **feeling** n (physical) sensación f; (foreboding) presentimiento; (emotion) sentimiento

feet [fi:t] npl of **foot**

fell [fɛl] pt of **fall** ▷ vt (tree) talar

fellow ['fɛləu] n tipo, tío (SP); (comrade) compañero; (of learned society) socio/a; **fellow citizen** n conciudadano/a; **fellow countryman** (irreg) n compatriota m; **fellow men** npl semejantes mpl; **fellowship** n compañerismo; (grant) beca

felony ['fɛlənɪ] n crimen m

felt [fɛlt] pt, pp of **feel** ▷ n fieltro; **felt-tip** n (also: **felt-tip pen**) rotulador m

female ['fi:meɪl] n (pej: woman) mujer f, tía; (Zool) hembra ▷ adj femenino; hembra

feminine ['fɛmɪnɪn] adj femenino

feminist ['fɛmɪnɪst] n feminista

fence [fɛns] n valla, cerca ▷ vt (also: ~ **in**) cercar ▷ vi (Sport) hacer esgrima; **fencing**

n esgrima

fend [fɛnd] vi: **to ~ for o.s.** valerse por sí mismo; **fend off** vt (attack) rechazar; (questions) evadir

fender ['fɛndə*] (US) n guardafuego; (Aut) parachoques m inv

fennel ['fɛnl] n hinojo

ferment [vb fə'mɛnt, n 'fə:mɛnt] vi fermentar ▷ n (fig) agitación f

fern [fə:n] n helecho

ferocious [fə'rəuʃəs] adj feroz

ferret ['fɛrɪt] n hurón m

ferry ['fɛrɪ] n (small) barca (de pasaje), balsa; (large: also: ~**boat**) transbordador m, ferry m ▷ vt transportar

fertile ['fə:taɪl] adj fértil; (Biol) fecundo; **fertilize** ['fə:tɪlaɪz] vt (Biol) fecundar; (Agr) abonar; **fertilizer** n abono

festival ['fɛstɪvəl] n (Rel) fiesta; (Art, Mus) festival m

festive ['fɛstɪv] adj festivo; **the ~ season** (BRIT: Christmas) las Navidades

fetch [fɛtʃ] vt ir a buscar; (sell for) venderse por

fête [feɪt] n fiesta

fetus ['fi:təs] (US) n = **foetus**

feud [fju:d] n (hostility) enemistad f; (quarrel) disputa

fever ['fi:və*] n fiebre f; **feverish** adj febril

few [fju:] adj (not many) pocos ▷ pron pocos; algunos; **a ~** adj unos pocos, algunos; **fewer** adj menos; **fewest** adj los(las) menos

fiancé [fɪ'ɑ̃:ŋseɪ] n novio, prometido; **fiancée** n novia, prometida

fiasco [fɪ'æskəu] n fiasco

fib [fɪb] n mentirilla

fibre ['faɪbə*] (US **fiber**) n fibra; **fibreglass** (US **Fiberglass**®) n fibra de vidrio

fickle ['fɪkl] adj inconstante

fiction ['fɪkʃən] n ficción f; **fictional** adj novelesco

fiddle ['fɪdl] n (Mus) violín m; (cheating) trampa ▷ vt (BRIT: accounts) falsificar; **fiddle with** vt fus juguetear con

fidelity [fɪ'dɛlɪtɪ] n fidelidad f

field [fi:ld] n campo; (fig) campo, esfera; (Sport) campo (SP), cancha (LAM); **field marshal** n mariscal m

fierce [fɪəs] adj feroz; (wind, heat) fuerte; (fighting, enemy) encarnizado

fifteen [fɪf'ti:n] num quince; **fifteenth** adj decimoquinto; **the fifteenth floor** la planta quince; **the fifteenth of August** el quince de agosto

fifth [fɪfθ] num quinto

fiftieth ['fɪftɪθ] adj quincuagésimo

fifty ['fɪftɪ] num cincuenta; **fifty-fifty** adj

fig | 288

(*deal, split*) a medias ▷ *adv* a medias, mitad por mitad

fig [fɪg] *n* higo

fight [faɪt] (*pt, pp* **fought**) *n* (*gen*) pelea; (*Mil*) combate *m*; (*struggle*) lucha ▷ *vt* luchar contra; (*cancer, alcoholism*) combatir; (*election*) intentar ganar; (*emotion*) resistir ▷ *vi* pelear, luchar; **fight back** *vi* defenderse; (*after illness*) recuperarse ▷ *vt* (*tears*) contener; **fight off** *vt* (*attack, attacker*) rechazar; (*disease, sleep, urge*) luchar contra; **fighting** *n* combate *m*, pelea

figure ['fɪgə*] *n* (*Drawing, Geom*) figura, dibujo; (*number, cipher*) cifra; (*body, outline*) tipo; (*personality*) figura ▷ *vt* (*esp US*) imaginar ▷ *vi* (*appear*) figurar; **figure out** *vt* (*work out*) resolver

file [faɪl] *n* (*tool*) lima; (*dossier*) expediente *m*; (*folder*) carpeta; (*Comput*) fichero; (*row*) fila ▷ *vt* limar; (*Law: claim*) presentar; (*store*) archivar; **filing cabinet** *n* fichero, archivador *m*

Filipino [fɪlɪ'piːnəu] *adj* filipino ▷ *n* (*person*) filipino/a *m/f*; (*Ling*) tagalo

fill [fɪl] *vt* (*space*) **to ~ (with)** llenar (de); (*vacancy, need*) cubrir ▷ *n*: **to eat one's ~** llenarse; **fill in** *vt* rellenar; **fill out** *vt* (*form, receipt*) rellenar; **fill up** *vt* llenar (hasta el borde) ▷ *vi* (*Aut*) poner gasolina

fillet ['fɪlɪt] *n* filete *m*; **fillet steak** *n* filete *m* de ternera

filling ['fɪlɪŋ] *n* (*Culin*) relleno; (*for tooth*) empaste *m*; **filling station** *n* estación *f* de servicio

film [fɪlm] *n* película ▷ *vt* (*scene*) filmar ▷ *vi* rodar (una película); **film star** *n* astro, estrella de cine

filter ['fɪltə*] *n* filtro ▷ *vt* filtrar; **filter lane** (*BRIT*) *n* carril *m* de selección

filth [fɪlθ] *n* suciedad *f*; **filthy** *adj* sucio; (*language*) obsceno

fin [fɪn] *n* (*gen*) aleta

final ['faɪnl] *adj* (*last*) final, último; (*definitive*) definitivo, terminante ▷ *n* (*BRIT Sport*) final *f*; **finals** *npl* (*Scol*) examen *m* final; (*US Sport*) final *f*

finale [fɪ'nɑːlɪ] *n* final *m*

final: finalist *n* (*Sport*) finalista *mf*; **finalize** *vt* concluir, completar; **finally** *adv* (*lastly*) por último, finalmente; (*eventually*) por fin

finance [faɪ'næns] *n* (*money*) fondos *mpl* ▷ *vt* financiar; **finances** *npl* finanzas *fpl*; (*personal finances*) situación *f* económica; **financial** [-'nænʃəl] *adj* financiero; **financial year** *n* ejercicio (financiero)

find [faɪnd] (*pt, pp* **found**) *vt* encontrar, hallar; (*come upon*) descubrir ▷ *n* hallazgo; descubrimiento; **to ~ sb guilty** (*Law*)

declarar culpable a algn; **find out** *vt* averiguar; (*truth, secret*) descubrir; **to find out about** (*subject*) informarse sobre; (*by chance*) enterarse de; **findings** *npl* (*Law*) veredicto, fallo; (*of report*) recomendaciones *fpl*

fine [faɪn] *adj* excelente; (*thin*) fino ▷ *adv* (*well*) bien ▷ *n* (*Law*) multa ▷ *vt* (*Law*) multar; **to be ~** (*person*) estar bien; (*weather*) hacer buen tiempo; **fine arts** *npl* bellas artes *fpl*

finger ['fɪŋgə*] *n* dedo ▷ *vt* (*touch*) manosear; **little/index ~** (dedo) meñique *m*/índice *m*; **fingernail** *n* uña; **fingerprint** *n* huella dactilar; **fingertip** *n* yema del dedo

finish ['fɪnɪʃ] *n* (*end*) fin *m*; (*Sport*) meta; (*polish etc*) acabado ▷ *vt, vi* terminar; **to ~ doing sth** acabar de hacer algo; **to ~ third** llegar el tercero; **finish off** *vt* acabar, terminar; (*kill*) acabar con; **finish up** *vt* acabar, terminar ▷ *vi* ir a parar, terminar

Finland ['fɪnlənd] *n* Finlandia

Finn [fɪn] *n* finlandés/esa *m/f*; **Finnish** *adj* finlandés/esa ▷ *n* (*Ling*) finlandés *m*

fir [fəː*] *n* abeto

fire ['faɪə*] *n* fuego; (*in hearth*) lumbre *f*; (*accidental*) incendio; (*heater*) estufa ▷ *vt* (*gun*) disparar; (*interest*) despertar; (*inf: dismiss*) despedir ▷ *vi* (*shoot*) disparar; **on ~** ardiendo, en llamas; **fire alarm** *n* alarma de incendios; **firearm** *n* arma de fuego; **fire brigade** (*US* **fire department**) *n* (cuerpo de) bomberos *mpl*; **fire engine** (*BRIT*) *n* coche *m* de bomberos; **fire escape** *n* escalera de incendios; **fire exit** *n* salida de incendios; **fire extinguisher** *n* extintor *m* (de incendios); **fireman** (*irreg*) *n* bombero; **fireplace** *n* chimenea; **fire station** *n* parque *m* de bomberos; **firetruck** (*US*) *n* = **fire engine**; **firewall** *n* (*Internet*) firewall *m*; **firewood** *n* leña; **fireworks** *npl* fuegos *mpl* artificiales

firm [fəːm] *adj* firme; (*look, voice*) resuelto ▷ *n* firma, empresa; **firmly** *adv* firmemente; resueltamente

first [fəːst] *adj* primero ▷ *adv* (*before others*) primero; (*when listing reasons etc*) en primer lugar, primeramente ▷ *n* (*person: in race*) primero/a; (*Aut*) primera; (*BRIT Scol*) título de licenciado con calificación de sobresaliente; **at ~** al principio; **~ of all** ante todo; **first aid** *n* primera ayuda, primeros auxilios *mpl*; **first-aid kit** *n* botiquín *m*; **first-class** *adj* (*excellent*) de primera (categoría); (*ticket etc*) de primera clase; **first-hand** *adj* de primera mano; **first lady** *n* (*esp US*) primera dama; **firstly** *adv* en primer lugar; **first**

name n nombre m (de pila); **first-rate** adj estupendo

fiscal ['fɪskəl] adj fiscal; **fiscal year** n año fiscal, ejercicio

fish [fɪʃ] n inv pez m; (food) pescado ▷ vt, vi pescar; **to go ~ing** ir de pesca; **~ and chips** pescado frito con patatas fritas; **fisherman** (irreg) n pescador m; **fish fingers** (BRIT) npl croquetas fpl de pescado; **fishing** n pesca; **fishing boat** n barca de pesca; **fishing line** n sedal m; **fishmonger** n (BRIT) pescadero/a; **fishmonger's (shop)** (BRIT) n pescadería; **fish sticks** (US) npl = **fish fingers**; **fishy** (inf) adj sospechoso

fist [fɪst] n puño

fit [fɪt] adj (healthy) en (buena) forma; (proper) adecuado, apropiado ▷ vt (clothes) estar or sentar bien a; (instal) poner; (equip) proveer, dotar; (facts) cuadrar or corresponder con ▷ vi (clothes) sentar bien; (in space, gap) caber; (facts) coincidir ▷ n (Med) ataque m; **~ to** (ready) a punto de; **~ for** apropiado para; **a ~ of anger/pride** un arranque de cólera/orgullo; **this dress is a good ~** este vestido me sienta bien; **by ~s and starts** a rachas; **fit in** vi (fig: person) llevarse bien (con todos); **fitness** n (Med) salud f; **fitted** adj (jacket, shirt) entallado; (sheet) de cuatro picos; **fitted carpet** n moqueta; **fitted kitchen** n cocina amueblada; **fitting** adj apropiado ▷ n (of dress) prueba; (of piece of equipment) instalación f; **fitting room** n probador m; **fittings** npl instalaciones fpl

five [faɪv] num cinco; **fiver** (inf) n (BRIT) billete m de cinco libras; (US) billete m de cinco dólares

fix [fɪks] vt (secure) fijar, asegurar; (mend) arreglar; (prepare) preparar ▷ n: **to be in a ~** estar en un aprieto; **fix up** vt (meeting) arreglar; **to fix sb up with sth** proveer a algn de algo; **fixed** adj (prices etc) fijo; **fixture** n (Sport) encuentro

fizzy ['fɪzɪ] adj (drink) gaseoso

flag [flæg] n bandera; (stone) losa ▷ vi decaer ▷ vt: **to ~ sb down** hacer señas a algn para que se pare; **flagpole** n asta de bandera

flair [fleə*] n aptitud f especial

flak [flæk] n (Mil) fuego antiaéreo; (inf: criticism) lluvia de críticas

flake [fleɪk] n (of rust, paint) escama; (of snow, soap powder) copo ▷ vi (also: **~ off**) desconcharse

flamboyant [flæm'bɔɪənt] adj (dress) vistoso; (person) extravagante

flame [fleɪm] n llama

flamingo [flə'mɪŋgəu] n flamenco

flammable ['flæməbl] adj inflamable

flan [flæn] (BRIT) n tarta

■ Be careful not to translate **flan** by the Spanish word flan.

flank [flæŋk] n (of animal) ijar m; (of army) flanco ▷ vt flanquear

flannel ['flænl] n (BRIT: also: **face ~**) manopla; (fabric) franela

flap [flæp] n (of pocket, envelope) solapa ▷ vt (wings, arms) agitar ▷ vi (sail, flag) ondear

flare [fleə*] n llamarada; (Mil) bengala; (in skirt etc) vuelo; **flares** npl (trousers) pantalones mpl de campana; **flare up** vi encenderse; (fig: person) encolerizarse; (: revolt) estallar

flash [flæʃ] n relámpago; (also: **news ~**) noticias fpl de última hora; (Phot) flash m ▷ vt (light, headlights) lanzar un destello con; (news, message) transmitir; (smile) lanzar ▷ vi brillar; (hazard light etc) lanzar destellos; **in a ~** en un instante; **he ~ed by** or **past** pasó como un rayo; **flashback** n (Cinema) flashback m; **flashbulb** n bombilla fusible; **flashlight** n linterna

flask [flɑːsk] n frasco; (also: **vacuum ~**) termo

flat [flæt] adj llano; (smooth) liso; (tyre) desinflado; (battery) descargado; (beer) muerto; (refusal etc) rotundo; (Mus) desafinado; (rate) fijo ▷ n (BRIT: apartment) piso (SP), departamento (LAM); apartamento; (Aut) pinchazo; (Mus) bemol m; **to work ~ out** trabajar a toda mecha; **flatten** vt (also: **flatten out**) allanar; (smooth out) alisar; (building, plants) arrasar

flatter ['flætə*] vt adular, halagar; **flattering** adj halagüeño; (dress) qué favorece

flaunt [flɔːnt] vt ostentar, lucir

flavour etc (US **flavor** etc) n sabor m, gusto ▷ vt sazonar, condimentar; **strawberry-flavoured** con sabor a fresa; **flavouring** n (in product) aromatizante m

flaw [flɔː] n defecto; **flawless** adj impecable

flea [fliː] n pulga; **flea market** n rastro, mercadillo

flee [fliː] (pt, pp **fled**) vt huir de ▷ vi huir, fugarse

fleece [fliːs] n vellón m; (wool) lana; (top) forro polar ▷ vt (inf) desplumar

fleet [fliːt] n flota; (of lorries etc) escuadra

fleeting ['fliːtɪŋ] adj fugaz

Flemish ['flemɪʃ] adj flamenco

flesh [fleʃ] n carne f; (skin) piel f; (of fruit) pulpa

flew [fluː] pt of **fly**

flex [fleks] n cordón m ▷ vt (muscles)

tensar; **flexibility** n flexibilidad f; **flexible** adj flexible; **flexitime** (us **flextime**) n horario flexible

flick [flɪk] n capirotazo; chasquido ▷ vt (with hand) dar un capirotazo a; (whip etc) chasquear; (switch) accionar; **flick through** vt fus hojear

flicker ['flɪkə*] vi (light) parpadear; (flame) vacilar

flies [flaɪz] npl de **fly**

flight [flaɪt] n vuelo; (escape) huida, fuga; (also: ~ **of steps**) tramo (de escaleras); **flight attendant** n auxiliar mf de vuelo

flimsy ['flɪmzɪ] adj (thin) muy ligero; (building) endeble; (excuse) flojo

flinch [flɪntʃ] vi encogerse; **to ~ from** retroceder ante

fling [flɪŋ] (pt, pp **flung**) vt arrojar

flint [flɪnt] n pedernal m; (in lighter) piedra

flip [flɪp] vt dar la vuelta a; (switch: turn on) encender; (turn) apagar; (coin) echar a cara o cruz

flip-flops ['flɪpflɒps] npl (esp BRIT) chancletas fpl

flipper ['flɪpə*] n aleta

flirt [fləːt] vi coquetear, flirtear ▷ n coqueta

float [fləʊt] n flotador m; (in procession) carroza; (money) reserva ▷ vi flotar; (swimmer) hacer la plancha

flock [flɒk] n (of sheep) rebaño; (of birds) bandada ▷ vi: **to ~ to** acudir en tropel a

flood [flʌd] n inundación f; (of letters, imports etc) avalancha ▷ vt inundar ▷ vi (place) inundarse; (people): **to ~ into** inundar; **flooding** n inundaciones fpl; **floodlight** n foco

floor [flɔː*] n suelo; (storey) piso; (of sea) fondo ▷ vt (question) dejar sin respuesta; (: blow) derribar; **ground ~, first ~** (us) planta baja; **first ~, second ~** (us) primer piso; **floorboard** n tabla; **flooring** n suelo; (material) solería; **floor show** n cabaret m

flop [flɒp] n fracaso ▷ vi (fail) fracasar; (fall) derrumbarse; **floppy** adj flojo ▷ n (Comput: also: **floppy disk**) floppy m

flora ['flɔːrə] n flora

floral ['flɔːrl] adj (pattern) floreado

florist ['flɒrɪst] n florista mf; **florist's (shop)** n floristería

flotation [fləʊ'teɪʃən] n (of shares) emisión f; (of company) lanzamiento

flour ['flaʊə*] n harina

flourish ['flʌrɪʃ] vi florecer ▷ n ademán m, movimiento (ostentoso)

flow [fləʊ] n (movement) flujo; (of traffic) circulación f; (tide) corriente f ▷ vi (river, blood) fluir; (traffic) circular

flower ['flaʊə*] n flor f ▷ vi florecer; **flower bed** n macizo; **flowerpot** n tiesto

flown [fləʊn] pp de **fly**

fl. oz. abbr (= fluid ounce)

flu [fluː] n: **to have ~** tener la gripe

fluctuate ['flʌktjueɪt] vi fluctuar

fluent ['fluːənt] adj (linguist) que habla perfectamente; (speech) elocuente; **he speaks ~ French, he's ~ in French** domina el francés

fluff [flʌf] n pelusa; **fluffy** adj de pelo suave

fluid ['fluːɪd] adj (movement) fluido, líquido; (situation) inestable ▷ n fluido, líquido; **fluid ounce** n onza f líquida

fluke [fluːk] (inf) n chiripa

flung [flʌŋ] pt, pp de **fling**

fluorescent [fluə'resnt] adj fluorescente

fluoride ['fluəraɪd] n fluoruro

flurry ['flʌrɪ] n (of snow) temporal m; **~ of activity** frenesí m de actividad

flush [flʌʃ] n rubor m; (fig: of youth etc) resplandor m ▷ vt limpiar con agua ▷ vi ruborizarse ▷ adj: **~ with** a ras de; **to ~ the toilet** hacer funcionar la cisterna

flute [fluːt] n flauta

flutter ['flʌtə*] n (of wings) revoloteo, aleteo; (fig): **a ~ of panic/excitement** una oleada de pánico/excitación ▷ vi revolotear

fly [flaɪ] (pt **flew**, pp **flown**) n mosca; (on trousers: also: **flies**) bragueta ▷ vt (plane) pilot(e)ar; (cargo) transportar (en avión); (distances) recorrer (en avión) ▷ vi volar; (passengers) ir en avión; (escape) evadirse; (flag) ondear; **fly away, fly off** vi emprender el vuelo; **fly-drive** n: **fly-drive holiday** vacaciones que incluyen vuelo y alquiler de coche; **flying** n (activity) (el) volar; (action) vuelo ▷ adj: **flying visit** visita relámpago; **with flying colours** con lucimiento; **flying saucer** n platillo volante; **flyover** (BRIT) n paso a desnivel or superior

FM abbr (Radio) (= frequency modulation) FM

foal [fəʊl] n potro

foam [fəʊm] n espuma ▷ vi hacer espuma

focus ['fəʊkəs] (pl **~es**) n foco; (centre) centro ▷ vt (field glasses etc) enfocar ▷ vi: **to ~ (on)** enfocar (a); (issue etc) centrarse en; **in/out of ~** enfocado/desenfocado

foetus ['fiːtəs] (us **fetus**) n feto

fog [fɒg] n niebla; **foggy** adj: **it's foggy** hay niebla, está brumoso; **fog lamp** (us **fog light**) n (Aut) faro de niebla

foil [fɔɪl] vt frustrar ▷ n hoja; (kitchen foil) papel m (de) aluminio; (complement) complemento; (Fencing) florete m

fold [fəʊld] n (bend, crease) pliegue m; (Agr)

redil *m* ▷ *vt* doblar; (*arms*) cruzar; **fold up**
vi plegarse, doblarse; (*business*) quebrar
▷ *vt* (*map etc*) plegar; **folder** *n* (*for papers*)
carpeta; (*Comput*) directorio; **folding** *adj*
(*chair, bed*) plegable
foliage ['fəulɪɪdʒ] *n* follaje *m*
folk [fəuk] *npl* gente *f* ▷ *adj* popular,
folklórico; **folks** *npl* (*family*) familia *sg*,
parientes *mpl*; **folklore** ['fəuklɔ:*] *n*
folklore *m*; **folk music** *n* música folk; **folk
song** *n* canción *f* popular
follow ['fɔləu] *vt* seguir ▷ *vi* seguir;
(*result*) resultar; **to ~ suit** hacer lo mismo;
follow up *vt* (*letter, offer*) responder a; (*case*)
investigar; **follower** *n* (*of person, belief*)
partidario/a; **following** *adj* siguiente
▷ *n* afición *f*, partidarios *mpl*; **follow-up** *n*
continuación *f*
fond [fɔnd] *adj* (*memory, smile etc*) cariñoso;
(*hopes*) ilusorio; **to be ~ of** tener cariño a;
(*pastime, food*) ser aficionado a
food [fu:d] *n* comida; **food mixer** *n*
batidora; **food poisoning** *n* intoxicación
f alimenticia; **food processor** *n* robot *m*
de cocina; **food stamp** (*us*) *n* vale *m* para
comida
fool [fu:l] *n* tonto/a; (*Culin*) puré *m* de
frutas con nata ▷ *vt* engañar ▷ *vi* (*gen*)
bromear; **fool about, fool around** *vi*
hacer el tonto; **foolish** *adj* tonto; (*careless*)
imprudente; **foolproof** *adj* (*plan etc*)
infalible
foot [fut] (*pl* **feet**) *n* pie *m*; (*measure*) pie *m*
(=304 mm); (*of animal*) pata ▷ *vt* (*bill*) pagar;
on ~ a pie; **footage** *n* (*Cinema*) imágenes
fpl; **foot-and-mouth (disease)**
[futənd'mauθ-] *n* fiebre *f* aftosa; **football**
n balón *m*; (*game*: *BRIT*) fútbol *m*; (: *us*) fútbol
m americano; **footballer** *n* (*BRIT*) = **football
player**; **football match** *n* partido de
fútbol; **football player** *n* (*BRIT*) futbolista
mf; (*us*) jugador *m* de fútbol americano;
footbridge *n* puente *m* para peatones;
foothills *npl* estribaciones *fpl*; **foothold**
n pie *m* firme; **footing** *n* (*fig*) posición *f*; **to
lose one's footing** perder el pie; **footnote**
n nota (al pie de la página); **footpath**
n sendero; **footprint** *n* huella, pisada;
footstep *n* paso; **footwear** *n* calzado

○ **KEYWORD**

for [fɔ:] *prep* **1** (*indicating destination,
intention*) para; **the train for London** el
tren con destino a or de Londres; **he left for
Rome** marchó para Roma; **he went for the
paper** fue por el periódico; **is this for me?**
¿es esto para mí?; **it's time for lunch** es la

hora de comer
2 (*indicating purpose*) para; **what('s it) for?**
¿para qué (es)?; **to pray for peace** rezar
por la paz
3 (*on behalf of, representing*): **the MP for Hove**
el diputado por Hove; **he works for the
government/a local firm** trabaja para el
gobierno/en una empresa local; **I'll ask him
for you** se
lo pediré por ti; **G for George** G de Gerona
4 (*because of*) por esta razón; **for fear of
being criticized** por temor a ser criticado
5 (*with regard to*) para; **it's cold for July** hace
frío para julio; **he has a gift for languages**
tiene don de lenguas
6 (*in exchange for*) por; **I sold it for £5** lo vendí
por £5; **to pay 50 pence for a ticket** pagar
50 peniques por un billete
7 (*in favour of*) **are you for or against us?**
¿estás con nosotros o contra nosotros?; **I'm
all for it** estoy totalmente a favor; **vote for
X** vote (a) X
8 (*referring to distance*): **there are roadworks
for 5 km** hay obras en 5 km; **we walked for
miles** caminamos kilómetros y kilómetros
9 (*referring to time*): **he was away for two
years** estuvo fuera (durante) dos años; **it
hasn't rained for 3 weeks** no ha llovido
durante or en 3 semanas; **I have known her
for years** la conozco desde hace años; **can
you do it for tomorrow?** ¿lo podrás hacer
para mañana?
10 (*with infinitive clauses*): **it is not for me to
decide** la decisión no es cosa mía; **it would
be best for you to leave** sería mejor que
te fueras; **there is still time for you to do
it** todavía te queda tiempo para hacerlo;
for this to be possible ... para que esto sea
posible ...
11 (*in spite of*) a pesar de; **for all his
complaints** a pesar de sus quejas ▷ *conj*
(*since, as: rather formal*) puesto que

forbid [fə'bɪd] (*pt* **forbad(e)**, *pp* **forbidden**)
vt prohibir; **to ~ sb to do sth** prohibir a algn
hacer algo; **forbidden** *pt of* **forbid** ▷ *adj*
(*food, area*) prohibido; (*word, subject*) tabú
force [fɔ:s] *n* fuerza ▷ *vt* forzar; (*push*)
meter a la fuerza; **to ~ o.s. to do** hacer un
esfuerzo por hacer; **forced** *adj* forzado;
forceful *adj* enérgico
ford [fɔ:d] *n* vado
fore [fɔ:*] *n*: **to come to the ~** empezar
a destacar; **forearm** *n* antebrazo;
forecast (*pt, pp* **forecast**) *n* pronóstico
▷ *vt* pronosticar; **forecourt** *n* patio;
forefinger *n* (dedo) índice *m*; **forefront**
n: **in the forefront of** en la vanguardia de;

foreground n primer plano; **forehead** ['fɔrɪd] n frente f
foreign ['fɔrɪn] adj extranjero; (trade) exterior; (object) extraño; **foreign currency** n divisas fpl; **foreigner** n extranjero/a; **foreign exchange** n divisas fpl; **Foreign Office** (BRIT) n Ministerio de Asuntos Exteriores; **Foreign Secretary** (BRIT) n Ministro de Asuntos Exteriores
fore: foreman (irreg) n capataz m; (in construction) maestro de obras; **foremost** adj principal ▷ adv: **first and foremost** ante todo; **forename** n nombre m (de pila)
forensic [fə'rɛnsɪk] adj forense
foresee [fɔː'siː] (pt **foresaw**, pp **foreseen**) vt prever; **foreseeable** adj previsible
forest ['fɔrɪst] n bosque m; **forestry** n silvicultura
forever [fə'rɛvə*] adv para siempre; (endlessly) constantemente
foreword ['fɔːwəːd] n prefacio
forfeit ['fɔːfɪt] vt perder
forgave [fə'geɪv] pt of **forgive**
forge [fɔːdʒ] n herrería ▷ vt (signature, money) falsificar; (metal) forjar; **forger** n falsificador(a) m/f; **forgery** n falsificación f
forget [fə'gɛt] (pt **forgot**, pp **forgotten**) vt olvidar ▷ vi olvidarse; **forgetful** adj despistado
forgive [fə'gɪv] (pt **forgave**, pp **forgiven**) vt perdonar; **to ~ sb for sth** perdonar algo a algn
forgot [fə'gɔt] pt of **forget**
forgotten [fə'gɔtn] pp of **forget**
fork [fɔːk] n (for eating) tenedor m; (for gardening) horca; (of roads) bifurcación f ▷ vi (road) bifurcarse
forlorn [fə'lɔːn] adj (person) triste, melancólico; (place) abandonado; (attempt, hope) desesperado
form [fɔːm] n forma; (BRIT Scol) clase f; (document) formulario ▷ vt formar; (idea) concebir; (habit) adquirir; **in top ~** en plena forma; **to ~ a queue** hacer cola
formal ['fɔːməl] adj (offer, receipt) por escrito; (person etc) correcto; (occasion, dinner) de etiqueta; (dress) correcto; (garden) (de estilo) clásico; **formality** [-'mælɪtɪ] n (procedure) trámite m; corrección f; etiqueta
format ['fɔːmæt] n formato ▷ vt (Comput) formatear
formation [fɔː'meɪʃən] n formación f
former ['fɔːmə*] adj anterior; (earlier) antiguo; (ex) ex; **the ~ ... the latter ...** aquél ... éste ...; **formerly** adv antes
formidable ['fɔːmɪdəbl] adj formidable
formula ['fɔːmjulə] n fórmula
fort [fɔːt] n fuerte m

forthcoming [fɔː'θkʌmɪn] adj próximo, venidero; (help, information) disponible; (character) comunicativo
fortieth ['fɔːtɪɪθ] adj cuadragésimo
fortify ['fɔːtɪfaɪ] vt (city) fortificar; (person) fortalecer
fortnight ['fɔːtnaɪt] (BRIT) n quince días mpl; quincena; **fortnightly** adj de cada quince días, quincenal ▷ adv cada quince días, quincenalmente
fortress ['fɔːtrɪs] n fortaleza
fortunate ['fɔːtʃənɪt] adj afortunado; **it is ~ that ...** (es una) suerte que ...; **fortunately** adv afortunadamente
fortune ['fɔːtʃən] n suerte f; (wealth) fortuna; **fortune-teller** n adivino/a
forty ['fɔːtɪ] num cuarenta
forum ['fɔːrəm] n foro
forward ['fɔːwəd] adj (movement, position) avanzado; (front) delantero; (in time) adelantado; (not shy) atrevido ▷ n (Sport) delantero ▷ vt (letter) remitir; (career) promocionar; **to move ~** avanzar; **forwarding address** n destinatario; **forward(s)** adv (hacia) adelante; **forward slash** n barra diagonal
fossil ['fɔsl] n fósil m
foster ['fɔstə*] vt (child) acoger en una familia; fomentar; **foster child** n hijo/a adoptivo/a; **foster mother** n madre f adoptiva
fought [fɔːt] pt, pp of **fight**
foul [faul] adj sucio, puerco; (weather, smell etc) asqueroso; (language) grosero; (temper) malísimo ▷ n (Sport) falta ▷ vt (dirty) ensuciar; **foul play** n (Law) muerte f violenta
found [faund] pt, pp of **find** ▷ vt fundar; **foundation** [-'deɪʃən] n (act) fundación f; (basis) base f; (also: **foundation cream**) crema base; **foundations** npl (of building) cimientos mpl
founder ['faundə*] n fundador(a) m/f ▷ vi hundirse
fountain ['fauntɪn] n fuente f; **fountain pen** n (pluma) estilográfica (SP), pluma-fuente f (LAM)
four [fɔː*] num cuatro; **on all ~s** a gatas; **four-letter word** n taco; **four-poster** n (also: **four-poster bed**) cama de columnas; **fourteen** num catorce; **fourteenth** adj decimocuarto; **fourth** num cuarto; **four-wheel drive** n tracción f a las cuatro ruedas
fowl [faul] n ave f (de corral)
fox [fɔks] n zorro ▷ vt confundir
foyer ['fɔɪeɪ] n vestíbulo
fraction ['frækʃən] n fracción f
fracture ['fræktʃə*] n fractura

fragile ['frædʒaıl] adj frágil

fragment ['frægmənt] n fragmento

fragrance ['freıgrəns] n fragancia

frail [freıl] adj frágil; (person) débil

frame [freım] n (Tech) armazón m; (of person) cuerpo; (of picture, door etc) marco; (of spectacles: also: **~s**) montura ▷ vt enmarcar; **framework** n marco

France [frɑ:ns] n Francia

franchise ['fræntʃaız] n (Pol) derecho de votar, sufragio; (Comm) licencia, concesión f

frank [fræŋk] adj franco ▷ vt (letter) franquear; **frankly** adv francamente

frantic ['fræntık] adj (distraught) desesperado; (hectic) frenético

fraud [frɔ:d] n fraude m; (person) impostor(a) m/f

fraught [frɔ:t] adj: **~ with** lleno de

fray [freı] vi deshilacharse

freak [fri:k] n (person) fenómeno; (event) suceso anormal

freckle ['frɛkl] n peca

free [fri:] adj libre; (gratis) gratuito ▷ vt (prisoner etc) poner en libertad; (jammed object) soltar; **~ (of charge), for ~** gratis; **freedom** n libertad f; **Freefone®** n número gratuito; **free gift** n prima; **free kick** n tiro libre; **freelance** adj independiente ▷ adv por cuenta propia; **freely** adv libremente; (liberally) generosamente; **Freepost®** n porte m pagado; **free-range** adj (hen, eggs) de granja; **freeway** (US) n autopista; **free will** n libre albedrío; **of one's own free will** por su propia voluntad

freeze [fri:z] (pt **froze**, pp **frozen**) vi (weather) helar; (liquid, pipe, person) helarse, congelarse ▷ vt helar; (food, prices, salaries) congelar ▷ n helada; (on arms, wages) congelación f; **freezer** n congelador m, freezer m (SC)

freezing ['fri:zıŋ] adj helado; **three degrees below ~** tres grados bajo cero; **freezing point** n punto de congelación

freight [freıt] n (goods) carga; (money charged) flete m; **freight train** (US) n tren m de mercancías

French [frɛntʃ] adj francés/esa ▷ n (Ling) francés m; **the French** npl los franceses; **French bean** n judía verde; **French bread** n pan m francés; **French dressing** n (Culin) vinagreta; **French fried potatoes, French fries** (US) npl patatas fpl (SP) or papas fpl (LAM) fritas; **Frenchman** (irreg) n francés m; **Frenchwoman** (irreg) n francésa; **French stick** n barra de pan; **French window** n puerta de cristal

frenzy ['frɛnzı] n frenesí m

frequency ['fri:kwənsı] n frecuencia

frequent [adj 'fri:kwənt, vb frı'kwɛnt] adj frecuente ▷ vt frecuentar; **frequently** [-əntlı] adv frecuentemente, a menudo

fresh [frɛʃ] adj fresco; (bread) tierno; (new) nuevo; **freshen** vi (wind, air) soplar más recio; **freshen up** vi (person) arreglarse, lavarse; **fresher** (BRIT: inf) n (Univ) estudiante mf de primer año; **freshly** adv (made, painted etc) recién; **freshman** (US: irreg) n = **fresher**; **freshwater** adj (fish) de agua dulce

fret [frɛt] vi inquietarse

Fri abbr (= Friday) vier

friction ['frıkʃən] n fricción f

Friday ['fraıdı] n viernes m inv

fridge [frıdʒ] (BRIT) n frigorífico (SP), nevera (SP), refrigerador m (LAM), heladera (RPL)

fried [fraıd] adj frito

friend [frɛnd] n amigo/a; **friendly** adj simpático; (government) amigo; (place) acogedor(a); (match) amistoso; **friendship** n amistad f

fries [fraız] (esp US) npl = **French fried potatoes**

frigate ['frıgıt] n fragata

fright [fraıt] n (terror) terror m; (scare) susto; **to take ~** asustarse; **frighten** vt asustar; **frightened** adj asustado; **frightening** adj espantoso; **frightful** adj espantoso, horrible

frill [frıl] n volante m

fringe [frındʒ] n (BRIT: of hair) flequillo; (on lampshade etc) flecos mpl; (of forest etc) borde m, margen m

Frisbee® ['frızbı] n frisbee® m

fritter ['frıtə*] n buñuelo

frivolous ['frıvələs] adj frívolo

fro [frəu] see **to**

frock [frɔk] n vestido

frog [frɔg] n rana; **frogman** (irreg) n hombre-rana m

○ **KEYWORD**

from [frɔm] prep 1 (indicating starting place) de, desde; **where do you come from?** ¿de dónde eres?; **from London to Glasgow** de Londres a Glasgow; **to escape from sth/sb** escaparse de algo/algn

2 (indicating origin etc) de; **a letter/telephone call from my sister** una carta/llamada de mi hermana; **tell him from me that ...** dígale de mi parte que ...

3 (indicating time): **from one o'clock to** or **until** or **till two** de(sde) la una a or hasta las dos; **from January (on)** a partir de enero

f

4 (*indicating distance*) de; **the hotel is 1 km from the beach** el hotel está a 1 km de la playa
5 (*indicating price, number etc*) de; **prices range from £10 to £50** los precios van desde £10 a or hasta £50; **the interest rate was increased from 9% to 10%** el tipo de interés fue incrementado de un 9% a un 10%
6 (*indicating difference*) de; **he can't tell red from green** no sabe distinguir el rojo del verde; **to be different from sb/sth** ser diferente a algn/algo
7 (*because of, on the basis of*): **from what he says** por lo que dice; **weak from hunger** debilitado por el hambre

front [frʌnt] n (*foremost part*) parte f delantera; (*of house*) fachada; (*of dress*) delantero; (*promenade: also*: **sea ~**) paseo marítimo; (*Mil, Pol, Meteorology*) frente m; (*fig: appearances*) apariencias fpl ▷ adj (*wheel, leg*) delantero; (*row, line*) primero; **in ~ (of)** delante (de); **front door** n puerta principal; **frontier** ['frʌntɪə*] n frontera; **front page** n primera plana; **front-wheel drive** n tracción f delantera
frost [frɔst] n helada; (*also*: **hoar~**) escarcha; **frostbite** n congelación f; **frosting** n (*esp US: icing*) glaseado; **frosty** adj (*weather*) de helada; (*welcome etc*) glacial
froth [frɔθ] n espuma
frown [fraun] vi fruncir el ceño
froze [frəuz] pt of **freeze**
frozen ['frəuzn] pp of **freeze**
fruit [fruːt] n inv fruta; fruto; (*fig*) fruto; resultados mpl; **fruit juice** n zumo (SP) or jugo (LAM) de fruta; **fruit machine** (BRIT) n máquina f tragaperras; **fruit salad** n macedonia (SP) or ensalada (LAM) de frutas
frustrate [frʌs'treɪt] vt frustrar; **frustrated** adj frustrado
fry [fraɪ] (*pt, pp* **fried**) vt freír; **small ~** gente f menuda; **frying pan** n sartén f
ft. abbr = **foot; feet**
fudge [fʌdʒ] n (*Culin*) caramelo blando
fuel [fjuəl] n (*for heating*) combustible m; (*coal*) carbón m; (*wood*) leña; (*for engine*) carburante m; **fuel tank** n depósito (de combustible)
fulfil [ful'fɪl] vt (*function*) cumplir con; (*condition*) satisfacer; (*wish, desire*) realizar
full [ful] adj lleno; (*fig*) pleno; (*complete*) completo; (*maximum*) máximo; (*information*) detallado; (*price*) íntegro; (*skirt*) amplio ▷ adv: **to know ~ well that** saber perfectamente que; **I'm ~ (up)** no puedo más; **~ employment** pleno empleo; **a ~ two hours** dos horas completas; **at ~ speed** a

máxima velocidad; **in ~** (*reproduce, quote*) íntegramente; **full-length** adj (*novel etc*) entero; (*coat*) largo; (*portrait*) de cuerpo entero; **full moon** n luna llena; **full-scale** adj (*attack, war*) en gran escala; (*model*) de tamaño natural; **full stop** n punto; **full-time** adj (*work*) de tiempo completo ▷ adv: **to work full-time** trabajar a tiempo completo; **fully** adv completamente; (*at least*) por lo menos
fumble ['fʌmbl] vi: **to ~ with** manejar torpemente
fume [fjuːm] vi (*rage*) estar furioso; **fumes** npl humo, gases mpl
fun [fʌn] n (*amusement*) diversión f; **to have ~** divertirse; **for ~** en broma; **to make ~ of** burlarse de
function ['fʌŋkʃən] n función f ▷ vi funcionar
fund [fʌnd] n fondo; (*reserve*) reserva; **funds** npl (*money*) fondos mpl
fundamental [fʌndə'mɛntl] adj fundamental
funeral ['fjuːnərəl] n (*burial*) entierro; (*ceremony*) funerales mpl; **funeral director** n director(a) m/f de pompas fúnebres; **funeral parlour** (BRIT) n funeraria
funfair ['fʌnfɛə*] (BRIT) n parque m de atracciones
fungus ['fʌŋgəs] (*pl* **fungi**) n hongo; (*mould*) moho
funnel ['fʌnl] n embudo; (*of ship*) chimenea
funny ['fʌnɪ] adj gracioso, divertido; (*strange*) curioso, raro
fur [fəː*] n piel f; (BRIT: *in kettle etc*) sarro; **fur coat** n abrigo de pieles
furious ['fjuərɪəs] adj furioso; (*effort*) violento
furnish ['fəːnɪʃ] vt amueblar; (*supply*) suministrar; (*information*) facilitar; **furnishings** npl muebles mpl
furniture ['fəːnɪtʃə*] n muebles mpl; **piece of ~** mueble m
furry ['fəːrɪ] adj peludo
further ['fəːðə*] adj (*new*) nuevo, adicional ▷ adv (*more*) más; (*moreover*) además ▷ vt promover, adelantar; **further education** n educación f superior; **furthermore** adv además
furthest ['fəːðɪst] superlative of **far**
fury ['fjuərɪ] n furia
fuse [fjuːz] (US **fuze**) n fusible m; (*for bomb etc*) mecha ▷ vt (*metal*) fundir; (*fig*) fusionar ▷ vi fundirse; fusionarse; (BRIT *Elec*): **to ~ the lights** fundir los plomos; **fuse box** n caja de fusibles
fusion ['fjuːʒən] n fusión f

fuss [fʌs] n (excitement) conmoción f;
(trouble) alboroto; **to make a ~** armar un lío
or jaleo; **to make a ~ of sb** mimar a algn;
fussy adj (person) exigente; (too ornate)
recargado

future ['fjuːtʃə*] adj futuro; (coming)
venidero ▷ n futuro; (prospects) porvenir
m; **in ~** de ahora en adelante; **futures** npl
(Comm) operaciones fpl a término, futuros
mpl

fuze [fjuːz] (US) =**fuse**

fuzzy ['fʌzɪ] adj (Phot) borroso; (hair) muy
rizado

g

G [dʒiː] n (Mus) sol m
g. abbr (=gram(s)) gr.
gadget ['gædʒɪt] n aparato
Gaelic ['geɪlɪk] adj, n (Ling) gaélico
gag [gæg] n (on mouth) mordaza; (joke)
chiste m ▷ vt amordazar
gain [geɪn] n: **~ (in)** aumento (de);
(profit) ganancia ▷ vt ganar ▷ vi (watch)
adelantarse; **to ~ from/by sth** sacar
provecho de algo; **to ~ on sb** ganar terreno a
algn; **to ~ 3 lbs (in weight)** engordar 3 libras
gal. abbr =**gallon**
gala ['gaːlə] n fiesta
galaxy ['gæləksɪ] n galaxia
gale [geɪl] n (wind) vendaval m
gall bladder ['gɔːl-] n vesícula biliar
gallery ['gælərɪ] n (also: **art ~: public**)
pinacoteca; (: private) galería de arte; (for
spectators) tribuna
gallon ['gæln] n galón m (BRIT = 4,546 litros,
US = 3,785 litros)
gallop ['gæləp] n galope m ▷ vi galopar
gallstone ['gɔːlstəun] n cálculo biliario
gamble ['gæmbl] n (risk) riesgo ▷ vt
jugar, apostar ▷ vi (take a risk) jugárselas;
(bet) apostar; **to ~ on** apostar a; (success etc)
contar con; **gambler** n jugador(a) m/f;
gambling n juego
game [geɪm] n juego; (match) partido;
(of cards) partida; (Hunting) caza ▷ adj
(willing): **to be ~ for anything** atreverse
a todo; **big ~** caza mayor (contest) juegos;
(BRIT: Scol) deportes mpl; **games console**
[geɪmz-] n consola de juegos; **game show**
n programa m concurso m, concurso
gammon ['gæmən] n (bacon) tocino
ahumado; (ham) jamón m ahumado
gang [gæn] n (of criminals) pandilla; (of
friends etc) grupo; (of workmen) brigada
gangster ['gæŋstə*] n gángster m
gap [gæp] n vacío (SP), hueco (LAM);

(in trees, traffic) claro; (in time) intervalo; (difference): **~ (between)** diferencia (entre)

gape [ɡeɪp] vi mirar boquiabierto; (shirt etc) abrirse (completamente)

gap year n año sabático (antes de empezar a estudiar en la universidad)

garage ['ɡærɑːʒ] n garaje m; (for repairs) taller m; **garage sale** n venta de objetos usados (en el jardín de una casa particular)

garbage ['ɡɑːbɪdʒ] (us) n basura; (inf: nonsense) tonterías fpl; **garbage can** n cubo or bote m (MEX) or tacho (SC) de la basura; **garbage collector** (us) n basurero/a

garden ['ɡɑːdn] n jardín m; **gardens** npl (park) parque m; **garden centre** (BRIT) n centro de jardinería; **gardener** n jardinero/a; **gardening** n jardinería

garlic ['ɡɑːlɪk] n ajo

garment ['ɡɑːmənt] n prenda (de vestir)

garnish ['ɡɑːnɪʃ] vt (Culin) aderezar

garrison ['ɡærɪsn] n guarnición f

gas [ɡæs] n gas m; (fuel) combustible m; (us: gasoline) gasolina ▷ vt asfixiar con gas; **gas cooker** (BRIT) n cocina de gas; **gas cylinder** n bombona de gas; **gas fire** n estufa de gas

gasket ['ɡæskɪt] n (Aut) junta de culata

gasoline ['ɡæsəliːn] (us) n gasolina

gasp [ɡɑːsp] n boqueada; (of shock etc) grito sofocado ▷ vi (pant) jadear

gas: gas pedal n (esp us) acelerador m; **gas station** (us) n gasolinera; **gas tank** (us) n (Aut) depósito (de gasolina)

gate [ɡeɪt] n puerta; (iron gate) verja

gateau ['ɡætəu] (pl **~x**) n tarta

gatecrash ['ɡeɪtkræʃ] (BRIT) vt colarse en

gateway ['ɡeɪtweɪ] n puerta

gather ['ɡæðə*] vt (flowers, fruit) coger (SP), recoger; (assemble) reunir; (pick up) recoger; (Sewing) fruncir; (understand) entender ▷ vi (assemble) reunirse; **to ~ speed** ganar velocidad; **gathering** n reunión f, asamblea

gauge [ɡeɪdʒ] n (instrument) indicador m ▷ vt medir; (fig) juzgar

gave [ɡeɪv] pt of **give**

gay [ɡeɪ] adj (homosexual) gay; (joyful) alegre; (colour) vivo

gaze [ɡeɪz] n mirada fija ▷ vi: **to ~ at sth** mirar algo fijamente

GB abbr = **Great Britain**

GCSE (BRIT) n abbr (= General Certificate of Secondary Education) examen de reválida que se hace a los 16 años

gear [ɡɪə*] n equipo, herramientas fpl; (Tech) engranaje m; (Aut) velocidad f, marcha ▷ vt (fig: adapt): **to ~ sth to** adaptar

or ajustar algo a; **top** or **high** (us)**/low ~** cuarta/primera velocidad; **in ~** en marcha; **gear up** vi prepararse; **gear box** n caja de cambios; **gear lever** n palanca de cambio; **gear shift** (us) n = **gear lever**; **gear stick** n (BRIT) palanca de cambios

geese [ɡiːs] npl of **goose**

gel [dʒɛl] n gel m

gem [dʒɛm] n piedra preciosa

Gemini ['dʒɛmɪnaɪ] n Géminis m, Gemelos mpl

gender ['dʒɛndə*] n género

gene [dʒiːn] n gen(e) m

general ['dʒɛnərl] n general m ▷ adj general; **in ~** en general; **general anaesthetic** (us **general anesthetic**) n anestesia general; **general election** n elecciones fpl generales; **generalize** vi generalizar; **generally** adv generalmente, en general; **general practitioner** n médico general; **general store** n tienda (que vende de todo) (LAM, SP), almacén m (SC, SP)

generate ['dʒɛnəreɪt] vt (Elec) generar; (jobs, profits) producir

generation [dʒɛnə'reɪʃən] n generación f

generator ['dʒɛnəreɪtə*] n generador m

generosity [dʒɛnə'rɔsɪtɪ] n generosidad f

generous ['dʒɛnərəs] adj generoso

genetic [dʒɪ'nɛtɪk] adj: **~ engineering** ingeniería genética; **~ fingerprinting** identificación f genética; **genetically modified** adj transgénico; **genetics** n genética

genitals ['dʒɛnɪtlz] npl (órganos mpl) genitales mpl

genius ['dʒiːnɪəs] n genio

genome ['dʒiːnəum] n genoma m

gent [dʒɛnt] n abbr (BRIT inf) = **gentleman**

gentle ['dʒɛntl] adj apacible, dulce; (animal) manso; (breeze, curve etc) suave

■ Be careful not to translate **gentle** by the Spanish word gentil.

gentleman ['dʒɛntlmən] (irreg) n señor m; (well-bred man) caballero

gently ['dʒɛntlɪ] adv dulcemente; suavemente

gents [dʒɛnts] n aseos mpl (de caballeros)

genuine ['dʒɛnjuɪn] adj auténtico; (person) sincero; **genuinely** adv sinceramente

geographic(al) [dʒɪə'ɡræfɪk(l)] adj geográfico

geography [dʒɪ'ɔɡrəfɪ] n geografía

geology [dʒɪ'ɔlədʒɪ] n geología

geometry [dʒɪ'ɔmətrɪ] n geometría

geranium [dʒɪ'reɪnjəm] n geranio

geriatric [dʒɛrɪ'ætrɪk] adj, n geriátrico/a m/f

germ [dʒəːm] n (microbe) microbio, bacteria; (seed, fig) germen m

German ['dʒəːmən] adj alemán/ana ▷ n alemán/ana m/f; (Ling) alemán m; **German measles** n rubéola

Germany ['dʒəːmənɪ] n Alemania

gesture ['dʒɛstjə*] n gesto; (symbol) muestra

○ **KEYWORD**

get [gɛt] (pt, pp **got**, pp **gotten** (US)) vi
1 (become, be) ponerse, volverse; **to get old/ tired** envejecer/cansarse; **to get drunk** emborracharse; **to get dirty** ensuciarse; **to get married** casarse; **when do I get paid?** ¿cuándo me pagan or se me paga?; **it's getting late** se está haciendo tarde
2 (go): **to get to/from** llegar a/de; **to get home** llegar a casa
3 (begin) empezar a; **to get to know sb** (llegar a) conocer a algn; **I'm getting to like him** me está empezando a gustar; **let's get going** or **started** ¡vamos (a empezar)!
4 (modal aux vb): **you've got to do it** tienes que hacerlo
▷ vt 1: **to get sth done** (finish) terminar algo; (have done) mandar hacer algo; **to get one's hair cut** cortarse el pelo; **to get the car going** or **to go** arrancar el coche; **to get sb to do sth** conseguir or hacer que algn haga algo; **to get sth/sb ready** preparar algo/a algn
2 (obtain: money, permission, results) conseguir; (find: job, flat) encontrar; (fetch: person, doctor) buscar; (object) ir a buscar, traer; **to get sth for sb** conseguir algo para algn; **get me Mr Jones, please** (Tel) póngame (SP) or comuníqueme (LAM) con el Sr. Jones, por favor; **can I get you a drink?** ¿quieres algo de beber?
3 (receive: present, letter) recibir; (acquire: reputation) alcanzar; (: prize) ganar; **what did you get for your birthday?** ¿qué te regalaron por tu cumpleaños?; **how much did you get for the painting?** ¿cuánto sacaste por el cuadro?
4 (catch) coger (SP), agarrar (LAM); (hit: target etc) dar en; **to get sb by the arm/throat** coger or agarrar a algn por el brazo/cuello; **get him!** ¡cógelo! (SP), ¡atrápalo! (LAM); **the bullet got him in the leg** la bala le dio en la pierna
5 (take, move) llevar; **to get sth to sb** hacer llegar algo a algn; **do you think we'll get it through the door?** ¿crees que lo podremos meter por la puerta?
6 (catch, take: plane, bus etc) coger (SP),

tomar (LAM); **where do I get the train for Birmingham?** ¿dónde se coge or se toma el tren para Birmingham?
7 (understand) entender; (hear) oír; **I've got it!** ¡ya lo tengo!, ¡eureka!; **I don't get your meaning** no te entiendo; **I'm sorry, I didn't get your name** lo siento, no cogí tu nombre
8 (have, possess): **to have got** tener

get away vi marcharse; (escape) escaparse
get away with vt fus hacer impunemente
get back vi (return) volver ▷ vt recobrar
get in vi entrar; (train) llegar; (arrive home) volver a casa, regresar
get into vt fus entrar en; (vehicle) subir a; **to get into a rage** enfadarse
get off vi (from train etc) bajar; (depart: person, car) marcharse ▷ vt (remove) quitar ▷ vt fus (train, bus) bajar de
get on vi (at exam etc): **how are you getting on?** ¿cómo te va?; (agree): **to get on (with)** llevarse bien (con) ▷ vt fus subir a
get out vi salir; (of vehicle) bajar ▷ vt sacar
get out of vt fus salir de; (duty etc) escaparse de
get over vt fus (illness) recobrarse de
get through vi (Tel) (lograr) comunicarse
get up vi (rise) levantarse ▷ vt fus subir

getaway ['gɛtəweɪ] n fuga

Ghana ['gɑːnə] n Ghana

ghastly ['gɑːstlɪ] adj horrible

ghetto ['gɛtəu] n gueto

ghost [gəust] n fantasma m

giant ['dʒaɪənt] n gigante mf ▷ adj gigantesco, gigante

gift [gɪft] n regalo; (ability) talento; **gifted** adj dotado; **gift shop** (US **gift store**) n tienda de regalos; **gift token**, **gift voucher** n vale m canjeable por un regalo

gig [gɪg] n (inf: concert) actuación f

gigabyte ['dʒɪgəbaɪt] n gigabyte m

gigantic [dʒaɪ'gæntɪk] adj gigantesco

giggle ['gɪgl] vi reírse tontamente

gills [gɪlz] npl (of fish) branquias fpl, agallas fpl

gilt [gɪlt] adj, n dorado

gimmick ['gɪmɪk] n truco

gin [dʒɪn] n ginebra

ginger ['dʒɪndʒə*] n jengibre m

gipsy ['dʒɪpsɪ] n = **gypsy**

giraffe [dʒɪ'rɑːf] n jirafa

girl [gəːl] n (small) niña; (young woman) chica, joven f, muchacha; (daughter) hija; **an English ~** una (chica) inglesa; **girl band** n girl band m (grupo musical de chicas); **girlfriend** n (of girl) amiga; (of boy) novia; **Girl Scout** (US) n = **Girl Guide**

gist [dʒɪst] n lo esencial

give [gɪv] (*pt* **gave**, *pp* **given**) *vt* dar;
(*deliver*) entregar; (*as gift*) regalar ▷ *vi* (*break*)
romperse; (*stretch: fabric*) dar de sí; **to ~ sb
sth, ~ sth to sb** dar algo a algn; **give away**
vt (*give free*) regalar; (*betray*) traicionar;
(*disclose*) revelar; **give back** *vt* devolver;
give in *vi* ceder ▷ *vt* entregar; **give out**
vt distribuir; **give up** *vi* rendirse, darse
por vencido ▷ *vt* renunciar a; **to give up
smoking** dejar de fumar; **to give o.s. up**
entregarse

given ['gɪvn] *pp of* **give** ▷ *adj* (*fixed: time,
amount*) determinado ▷ *conj*: **~ (that) ...**
dado (que) ...; **~ the circumstances ...**
dadas las circunstancias ...

glacier ['glæsɪə*] *n* glaciar *m*

glad [glæd] *adj* contento; **gladly** ['-lɪ] *adv*
con mucho gusto

glamour ['glæmər] (*us* **glamor**) *n*
encanto, atractivo; **glamorous** *adj*
encantador(a), atractivo

glance [glɑːns] *n* ojeada, mirada ▷ *vi*: **to ~
at** echar una ojeada a

gland [glænd] *n* glándula

glare [glɛə*] *n* (*of anger*) mirada feroz; (*of
light*) deslumbramiento, brillo; **to be in
the ~ of publicity** ser el foco de la atención
pública ▷ *vi* deslumbrar; **to ~ at** mirar con
odio a; **glaring** *adj* (*mistake*) manifiesto

glass [glɑːs] *n* vidrio, cristal *m*; (*for
drinking*) vaso; (*: with stem*) copa; **glasses** *npl*
(*spectacles*) gafas *fpl*

glaze [gleɪz] *vt* (*window*) poner cristales a;
(*pottery*) vidriar ▷ *n* vidriado

gleam [gliːm] *vi* brillar

glen [glɛn] *n* cañada

glide [glaɪd] *vi* deslizarse; (*Aviat: birds*)
planear; **glider** *n* (*Aviat*) planeador *m*

glimmer ['glɪmə*] *n* luz *f* tenue; (*of
interest*) muestra; (*of hope*) rayo

glimpse [glɪmps] *n* vislumbre *m* ▷ *vt*
vislumbrar, entrever

glint [glɪnt] *vi* centellear

glisten ['glɪsn] *vi* relucir, brillar

glitter ['glɪtə*] *vi* relucir, brillar

global ['gləubl] *adj* mundial;
globalization *n* globalización *f*; **global
warming** *n* (re)calentamiento global *or*
de la tierra

globe [gləub] *n* globo; (*model*) globo
terráqueo

gloom [gluːm] *n* oscuridad *f*; (*sadness*)
tristeza; **gloomy** *adj* (*dark*) oscuro; (*sad*)
triste; (*pessimistic*) pesimista

glorious ['glɔːrɪəs] *adj* glorioso; (*weather
etc*) magnífico

glory ['glɔːrɪ] *n* gloria

gloss [glɔs] *n* (*shine*) brillo; (*paint*) pintura
de aceite

glossary ['glɔsərɪ] *n* glosario

glossy ['glɔsɪ] *adj* lustroso; (*magazine*)
de lujo

glove [glʌv] *n* guante *m*; **glove
compartment** *n* (*Aut*) guantera

glow [gləu] *vi* brillar

glucose ['gluːkəus] *n* glucosa

glue [gluː] *n* goma (de pegar), cemento
▷ *vt* pegar

GM *adj abbr* (= *genetically modified*)
transgénico

gm *abbr* (= *gram*) g

GMO *n abbr* (= *genetically modified organism*)
organismo transgénico

GMT *abbr* (= *Greenwich Mean Time*) GMT

gnaw [nɔː] *vt* roer

go [gəu] (*pt* **went**, *pp* **gone**, *pl* **~es**) *vi* ir;
(*travel*) viajar; (*depart*) irse, marcharse; (*work*)
funcionar, marchar; (*be sold*) venderse;
(*time*) pasar; (*fit, suit*): **to ~ with** hacer
juego con; (*become*) ponerse; (*break etc*)
estropearse, romperse ▷ *n*: **to have a ~
(at)** probar suerte (con); **to be on the ~** no
parar; **whose ~ is it?** ¿a quién le toca?; **he's
~ing to do it** va a hacerlo; **to ~ for a walk**
ir de paseo; **to ~ dancing** ir a bailar; **how
did it ~?** ¿qué tal salió or resultó?, ¿cómo ha
ido?; **to ~ round the back** pasar por detrás;
go ahead *vi* seguir adelante; **go away**
vi irse, marcharse; **go back** *vi* volver; **go
by** *vi* (*time*) pasar ▷ *vt fus* guiarse por;
go down *vi* bajar; (*ship*) hundirse; (*sun*)
ponerse ▷ *vt fus* bajar; **go for** *vt fus* (*fetch*)
ir por; (*like*) gustar; (*attack*) atacar; **go in** *vi*
entrar; **go into** *vt fus* entrar en; (*investigate*)
investigar; (*embark on*) dedicarse a; **go off**
vi irse, marcharse; (*food*) pasarse; (*explode*)
estallar; (*event*) realizarse ▷ *vt fus* dejar
de gustar; **I'm going off him/the idea**
ya no me gusta tanto él/la idea; **go on** *vi*
(*continue*) seguir, continuar; (*happen*) pasar,
ocurrir; **to go on doing sth** seguir haciendo
algo; **go out** *vi* salir; (*fire, light*) apagarse;
go over *vi* (*ship*) zozobrar ▷ *vt fus* (*check*)
revisar; **go past** *vi, vt fus* pasar; **go round**
vi (*circulate: news, rumour*) correr; (*suffice*)
alcanzar, bastar; (*revolve*) girar, dar vueltas;
(*visit*): **to go round (to sb's)** pasar a ver (a
algn); **to go round (by)** (*make a detour*) dar
la vuelta (por); **go through** *vt fus* (*town etc*)
atravesar; **go up** *vi, vt fus* subir; **go with**
vt fus (*accompany*) ir con, acompañar a; **go
without** *vt fus* pasarse sin

go-ahead ['gəuəhɛd] *adj* (*person*)
dinámico; (*firm*) innovador(a) ▷ *n* luz *f*
verde

goal [gəul] *n* meta; (*score*) gol *m*;

goalkeeper n portero; **goal-post** n poste m (de la portería)

goat [gəʊt] n cabra

gobble ['gɔbl] vt (also: ~ **down**, ~ **up**) tragarse, engullir

God [gɔd] n Dios m; **godchild** n ahijado/a; **goddaughter** n ahijada; **goddess** n diosa; **godfather** n padrino; **godmother** n madrina; **godson** n ahijado

goggles ['gɔglz] npl gafas fpl

going ['gəʊɪŋ] n (conditions) estado del terreno ▷ adj: **the ~ rate** la tarifa corriente or en vigor

gold [gəʊld] n oro ▷ adj de oro; **golden** adj (made of gold) de oro; (gold in colour) dorado; **goldfish** n pez m de colores; **goldmine** n (also fig) mina de oro; **gold-plated** adj chapado en oro

golf [gɔlf] n golf m; **golf ball** n (for game) pelota de golf; (on typewriter) esfera; **golf club** n club m de golf; (stick) palo (de golf); **golf course** n campo de golf; **golfer** n golfista mf

gone [gɔn] pp of **go**

gong [gɔŋ] n gong m

good [gʊd] adj bueno; (pleasant) agradable; (kind) bueno, amable; (well-behaved) educado ▷ n bien m, provecho; **goods** npl (Comm) mercancías fpl; **~!** ¡qué bien!; **to be ~ at** tener aptitud para; **to be ~ for** servir para; **it's ~ for you** te hace bien; **would you be ~ enough to …?** ¿podría hacerme el favor de …?, ¿sería tan amable de …?; **a ~ deal (of)** mucho; **a ~ many** muchos; **to make ~** reparar; **it's no ~ complaining** no vale la pena (de) quejarse; **for ~** para siempre, definitivamente; **~ morning/afternoon!** ¡buenos días/buenas tardes!; **~ evening!** ¡buenas noches!; **~ night!** ¡buenas noches!

goodbye [gʊd'baɪ] excl ¡adiós!; **to say ~ (to)** (person) despedirse (de)

good: Good Friday n Viernes m Santo; **good-looking** adj guapo; **good-natured** adj amable, simpático; **goodness** n (of person) bondad f; **for goodness sake!** ¡por Dios!; **goodness gracious!** ¡Dios mío!; **goods train** (BRIT) n tren m de mercancías; **goodwill** n buena voluntad f

Google® ['gu:gəl] n Google® m ▷ vi hacer búsquedas en Internet ▷ vt buscar información en Internet sobre

goose [gu:s] (pl **geese**) n ganso, oca

gooseberry ['gʊzbərɪ] n grosella espinosa; **to play ~** hacer de carabina

goose bumps, goose pimples npl carne f de gallina

gorge [gɔ:dʒ] n barranco ▷ vr: **to ~ o.s. (on)** atracarse (de)

gorgeous ['gɔ:dʒəs] adj (thing) precioso; (weather) espléndido; (person) guapísimo

gorilla [gə'rɪlə] n gorila m

gosh [gɔʃ] (inf) excl ¡cielos!

gospel ['gɔspl] n evangelio

gossip ['gɔsɪp] n (scandal) cotilleo, chismes mpl; (chat) charla; (scandalmonger) cotilla m/f, chismoso/a ▷ vi cotillear; **gossip column** n ecos mpl de sociedad

got [gɔt] pt, pp of **get**

gotten (US) ['gɔtn] pp of **get**

gourmet ['gʊəmeɪ] n gastrónomo/a m/f

govern ['gʌvən] vt gobernar; (influence) dominar; **government** n gobierno; **governor** n gobernador(a) m/f; (of school etc) miembro del consejo; (of jail) director(a) m/f

gown [gaʊn] n traje m; (of teacher, BRIT: of judge) toga

G.P. n abbr = **general practitioner**

grab [græb] vt coger (SP), agarrar (LAM), arrebatar ▷ vi: **to ~ at** intentar agarrar

grace [greɪs] n gracia ▷ vt honrar; (adorn) adornar; **5 days' ~** un plazo de 5 días; **graceful** adj grácil, ágil; (style, shape) elegante, gracioso; **gracious** ['greɪʃəs] adj amable

grade [greɪd] n (quality) clase f, calidad f; (in hierarchy) grado; (Scol: mark) nota; (US: school class) curso ▷ vt clasificar; **grade crossing** (US) n paso a nivel; **grade school** (US) n escuela primaria

gradient ['greɪdɪənt] n pendiente f

gradual ['grædjuəl] adj paulatino; **gradually** adv paulatinamente

graduate [n 'grædjuɪt, vb 'grædjueɪt] n (US: of high school) graduado/a; (of university) licenciado/a ▷ vi graduarse; licenciarse; **graduation** [-'eɪʃən] n (ceremony) entrega del título

graffiti [grə'fi:tɪ] n pintadas fpl

graft [grɑ:ft] n (Agr, Med) injerto; (BRIT: inf) trabajo duro; (bribery) corrupción f ▷ vt injertar

grain [greɪn] n (single particle) grano; (corn) granos mpl, cereales mpl; (of wood) fibra

gram [græm] n gramo

grammar ['græmə*] n gramática; **grammar school** (BRIT) n = instituto de segunda enseñanza, liceo (SP)

gramme [græm] n = **gram**

gran [græn] (inf) n (BRIT) abuelita

grand [grænd] adj magnífico, imponente; (wonderful) estupendo; (gesture etc) grandioso; **grandad** (inf) n = **granddad**; **grandchild** (pl **grandchildren**) n nieto/a m/f; **granddad** (inf) n yayo, abuelito;

granddaughter n nieta; **grandfather** n abuelo; **grandma** (inf) n yaya, abuelita; **grandmother** n abuela; **grandpa** (inf) n = **granddad**; **grandparents** npl abuelos mpl; **grand piano** n piano de cola; **Grand Prix** ['grãː'priː] n (Aut) gran premio, Grand Prix m; **grandson** n nieto

granite ['grænɪt] n granito

granny ['grænɪ] (inf) n abuelita, yaya

grant [grɑːnt] vt (concede) conceder; (admit) reconocer ⊳ n (Scol) beca; (Admin) subvención f; **to take sth/sb for ~ed** dar algo por sentado/no hacer ningún caso a algn

grape [greɪp] n uva

grapefruit ['greɪpfruːt] n pomelo (SP, SC), toronja (LAM)

graph [grɑːf] n gráfica; **graphic** ['græfɪk] adj gráfico; **graphics** n artes fpl gráficas ⊳ npl (drawings) dibujos mpl

grasp [grɑːsp] vt agarrar, asir; (understand) comprender ⊳ n (grip) asimiento; (understanding) comprensión f

grass [grɑːs] n hierba; (lawn) césped m; **grasshopper** n saltamontes m inv

grate [greɪt] n parrilla de chimenea ⊳ vi: **to ~ (on)** chirriar (sobre) ⊳ vt (Culin) rallar

grateful ['greɪtful] adj agradecido

grater ['greɪtə*] n rallador m

gratitude ['grætɪtjuːd] n agradecimiento

grave [greɪv] n tumba ⊳ adj serio, grave

gravel ['grævl] n grava

gravestone ['greɪvstəun] n lápida

graveyard ['greɪvjɑːd] n cementerio

gravity ['grævɪtɪ] n gravedad f

gravy ['greɪvɪ] n salsa de carne

gray [greɪ] adj = **grey**

graze [greɪz] vi pacer ⊳ vt (touch lightly) rozar; (scrape) raspar ⊳ n (Med) abrasión f

grease [griːs] n (fat) grasa; (lubricant) lubricante m ⊳ vt engrasar; lubrificar; **greasy** adj grasiento

great [greɪt] adj grande; (inf) magnífico, estupendo; **Great Britain** n Gran Bretaña; **great-grandfather** n bisabuelo; **great-grandmother** n bisabuela; **greatly** adv muy; (with verb) mucho

Greece [griːs] n Grecia

greed [griːd] n (also: **~iness**) codicia, avaricia; (for food) gula; (for power etc) avidez f; **greedy** adj avaro; (for food) glotón/ona

Greek [griːk] adj griego ⊳ n griego/a; (Ling) griego

green [griːn] adj (also Pol) verde; (inexperienced) novato ⊳ n verde m; (stretch of grass) césped m; (Golf) green; m **greens** npl (vegetables) verduras fpl; **green card**

n (Aut) carta verde; (US: work permit) permiso de trabajo para los extranjeros en EE. UU.; **greengage** n (ciruela) claudia; **greengrocer** (BRIT) n verdulero/a; **greenhouse** n invernadero; **greenhouse effect** n efecto invernadero

Greenland ['griːnlənd] n Groenlandia

green salad n ensalada f (de lechuga, pepino, pimiento verde, etc)

greet [griːt] vt (welcome) dar la bienvenida a; (receive: news) recibir; **greeting** n (welcome) bienvenida; **greeting(s) card** n tarjeta de felicitación

grew [gruː] pt of **grow**

grey [greɪ] (US **gray**) adj gris; (weather) sombrío; **grey-haired** adj canoso; **greyhound** n galgo

grid [grɪd] n reja; (Elec) red f; **gridlock** n (traffic jam) retención f

grief [griːf] n dolor m, pena

grievance ['griːvəns] n motivo de queja, agravio

grieve [griːv] vi afligirse, acongojarse ⊳ vt dar pena a; **to ~ for** llorar por

grill [grɪl] n (on cooker) parrilla; (also: **mixed ~**) parillada ⊳ vt (BRIT) asar a la parrilla; (inf: question) interrogar

grille [grɪl] n reja; (Aut) rejilla

grim [grɪm] adj (place) sombrío; (situation) triste; (person) ceñudo

grime [graɪm] n mugre f, suciedad f

grin [grɪn] n sonrisa abierta ⊳ vi sonreír abiertamente

grind [graɪnd] (pt, pp **ground**) vt (coffee, pepper etc) moler; (US: meat) picar; (make sharp) afilar ⊳ n (work) rutina

grip [grɪp] n (hold) asimiento; (control) control m, dominio; (of tyre etc): **to have a good/bad ~** agarrarse bien/mal; (handle) asidero; (holdall) maletín m ⊳ vt agarrar; (viewer, reader) fascinar; **to get to ~s with** enfrentarse con; **gripping** adj absorbente

grit [grɪt] n gravilla; (courage) valor m ⊳ vt (road) poner gravilla en; **to ~ one's teeth** apretar los dientes

grits [grɪts] (US) npl maíz msg a medio moler

groan [grəun] n gemido; quejido ⊳ vi gemir; quejarse

grocer ['grəusə*] n tendero (de ultramarinos (SP)); **groceries** npl comestibles mpl; **grocer's (shop)** n tienda de comestibles or (MEX, CAM) abarrotes, almacén (SC); **grocery** n (shop) tienda de ultramarinos

groin [grɔɪn] n ingle f

groom [gruːm] n mozo/a de cuadra; (also: **bride~**) novio ⊳ vt (horse) almohazar;

(fig): to ~ sb for preparar a algn para; **well-~ed** de buena presencia

groove [gruːv] n ranura, surco

grope [grəup] vi: **to ~ for** buscar a tientas

gross [grəus] adj (neglect, injustice) grave; (vulgar: behaviour) grosero; (: appearance) de mal gusto; (Comm) bruto; **grossly** adv (greatly) enormemente

grotesque [grə'tɛsk] adj grotesco

ground [graund] pt, pp of **grind** ▷ n suelo, tierra; (Sport) campo, terreno; (reason: gen pl) causa, razón f; (US: also: ~ **wire**) tierra ▷ vt (US) (plane) mantener en tierra; (US Elec) conectar con tierra; **grounds** npl (of coffee etc) poso; (gardens etc) jardines mpl, parque m; **on the ~** en el suelo; **to the ~** al suelo; **to gain/lose ~** ganar/perder terreno; **ground floor** n (BRIT) planta baja; **groundsheet** (BRIT) n tela impermeable; suelo; **groundwork** n preparación f

group [gruːp] n grupo; (musical) conjunto ▷ vt (also: ~ **together**) agrupar ▷ vi (also: ~ **together**) agruparse

grouse [graus] n inv (bird) urogallo ▷ vi (complain) quejarse

grovel ['grɒvl] vi (fig): **to ~ before** humillarse ante

grow [grəu] (pt **grew**, pp **grown**) vi crecer; (increase) aumentar; (expand) desarrollarse; (become) volverse; **to ~ rich/weak** enriquecerse/debilitarse ▷ vt cultivar; (hair, beard) dejar crecer; **grow on** vt fus: **that painting is growing on me** ese cuadro me gusta cada vez más; **grow up** vi crecer, hacerse hombre/mujer

growl [graul] vi gruñir

grown [grəun] pp of **grow**; **grown-up** n adulto/a, mayor mf

growth [grəuθ] n crecimiento, desarrollo; (what has grown) brote m; (Med) tumor m

grub [grʌb] n larva, gusano m; (inf: food) comida

grubby ['grʌbɪ] adj sucio, mugriento

grudge [grʌdʒ] n (motivo de) rencor m ▷ vt: **to ~ sb sth** dar algo a algn de mala gana; **to bear sb a ~** guardar rencor a algn

gruelling ['gruəlɪŋ] (US **grueling**) adj penoso, duro

gruesome ['gruːsəm] adj horrible

grumble ['grʌmbl] vi refunfuñar, quejarse

grumpy ['grʌmpɪ] adj gruñón/ona

grunt [grʌnt] vi gruñir

guarantee [gærən'tiː] n garantía ▷ vt garantizar

guard [gɑːd] n (squad) guardia; (one man) guardia mf; (BRIT Rail) jefe m de tren; (on machine) dispositivo de seguridad; (also: **fire~**) rejilla de protección ▷ vt guardar;

(prisoner) vigilar; **to be on one's ~** estar alerta; **guardian** n guardián/ana mf; (of minor) tutor(a) m/f

guerrilla [gə'rɪlə] n guerrillero/a

guess [gɛs] vi adivinar; (US) suponer ▷ vt adivinar; suponer ▷ n suposición f, conjetura; **to take** or **have a ~** tratar de adivinar

guest [gɛst] n invitado/a; (in hotel) huésped mf; **guest house** n casa de huéspedes, pensión f; **guest room** n cuarto de huéspedes

guidance ['gaɪdəns] n (advice) consejos mpl

guide [gaɪd] n (person) guía mf; (book, fig) guía; (also: **Girl ~**) guía ▷ vt (also: round museum etc) guiar; (lead) conducir; (direct) orientar; **guidebook** n guía; **guide dog** n perro m guía; **guided tour** n visita f con guía; **guidelines** npl (advice) directrices fpl

guild [gɪld] n gremio

guilt [gɪlt] n culpabilidad f; **guilty** adj culpable

guinea pig ['gɪnɪ-] n cobaya; (fig) conejillo de Indias

guitar [gɪ'tɑː*] n guitarra; **guitarist** n guitarrista m/f

gulf [gʌlf] n golfo; (abyss) abismo

gull [gʌl] n gaviota

gulp [gʌlp] vi tragar saliva ▷ vt (also: ~ **down**) tragarse

gum [gʌm] n (Anat) encía; (glue) goma, cemento; (sweet) caramelo de goma; (also: **chewing-~**) chicle m ▷ vt pegar con goma

gun [gʌn] n (small) pistola, revólver m; (shotgun) escopeta; (rifle) fusil m; (cannon) cañón m; **gunfire** n disparos mpl; **gunman** (irreg) n pistolero; **gunpoint** n: **at gunpoint** a mano armada; **gunpowder** n pólvora; **gunshot** n escopetazo

gush [gʌʃ] vi salir a raudales; (person) deshacerse en efusiones

gust [gʌst] n (of wind) ráfaga

gut [gʌt] n intestino; **guts** npl (Anat) tripas fpl; (courage) valor m

gutter ['gʌtə*] n (of roof) canalón m; (in street) cuneta

guy [gaɪ] n (also: ~**rope**) cuerda; (inf: man) tío (SP), tipo; (figure) monigote m

Guy Fawkes' Night [gaɪ'fɔːks-] n ver abajo

● **GUY FAWKES' NIGHT**
●
● La noche del cinco de noviembre, **Guy**
● **Fawkes' Night**, se celebra en el Reino
● Unido el fracaso de la conspiración de la
● pólvora ("Gunpowder Plot"), un intento

fallido de volar el parlamento de Jaime
I en 1605. Esa noche se lanzan fuegos
artificiales y se hacen hogueras en las
que se queman unos muñecos de trapo
que representan a **Guy Fawkes**, uno
de los cabecillas de la revuelta. Días
antes, los niños tienen por costumbre
pedir a los transeúntes "a penny for the
guy", dinero que emplean en comprar
cohetes y petardos.

gym [dʒɪm] n gimnasio; **gymnasium** n
gimnasio mf; **gymnast** n gimnasta mf;
gymnastics n gimnasia; **gym shoes** npl
zapatillas fpl (de deporte)
gynaecologist [gaɪnɪ'kɔlədʒɪst] (us
gynecologist) n ginecólogo/a
gypsy ['dʒɪpsɪ] n gitano/a

haberdashery [hæbə'dæʃərɪ] (BRIT) n
mercería
habit ['hæbɪt] n hábito, costumbre f; (drug
habit) adicción f; (costume) hábito
habitat ['hæbɪtæt] n hábitat m
hack [hæk] vt (cut) cortar; (slice) tajar ▷ n
(pej: writer) escritor(a) m/f a sueldo; **hacker**
n (Comput) pirata mf informático/a
had [hæd] pt, pp of **have**
haddock ['hædək] (pl ~ or ~**s**) n especie de
merluza
hadn't ['hædnt] = **had not**
haemorrhage ['hɛmərɪdʒ] (us
hemorrhage) n hemorragia
haemorrhoids ['hɛmərɔɪdz] (us
hemorrhoids) npl hemorroides fpl
haggle ['hægl] vi regatear
Hague [heɪg] n: The ~ La Haya
hail [heɪl] n granizo; (fig) lluvia ▷ vt
saludar; (taxi) llamar a; (acclaim) aclamar
▷ vi granizar; **hailstone** n (piedra de)
granizo
hair [hɛə*] n pelo, cabellos mpl; (one hair)
pelo, cabello; (on legs etc) vello; **to do one's**
~ arreglarse el pelo; **to have grey ~** tener
canas fpl; **hairband** n cinta; **hairbrush** n
cepillo (para el pelo); **haircut** n corte m (de
pelo); **hairdo** n peinado; **hairdresser** n
peluquero/a; **hairdresser's** n peluquería;
hair dryer n secador m de pelo; **hair gel**
n fijador; **hair spray** n laca; **hairstyle**
n peinado; **hairy** adj peludo; velludo;
(inf: frightening) espeluznante
hake [heɪk] (pl ~ or ~**s**) n merluza
half [hɑːf] (pl **halves**) n mitad f; (of beer)
≈ caña (sp), media pinta; (Rail, Bus) billete
m de niño ▷ adj medio ▷ adv medio, a
medias; **two and a ~** dos y media; **~ a dozen**
media docena; **~ a pound** media libra; **to
cut sth in ~** cortar algo por la mitad; **half
board** n (BRIT: in hotel) media pensión; **half-**

brother n hermanastro; **half day** n medio
día m, media jornada; **half fare** n medio
pasaje m; **half-hearted** adj indiferente,
poco entusiasta; **half-hour** n media hora;
half-price adj, adv a mitad de precio; **half
term** (BRIT) n (Scol) vacaciones de mediados
del trimestre; **half-time** n descanso;
halfway adv a medio camino; **halfway
through** a mitad de

hall [hɔːl] n (for concerts) sala; (entrance way)
hall m; vestíbulo

hallmark ['hɔːlmɑːk] n sello

hallo [hə'ləu] excl = **hello**

hall of residence (BRIT) n residencia

Hallowe'en [hæləu'iːn] n víspera de
Todos los Santos

● **HALLOWE'EN**
●
● La tradición anglosajona dice que en
● la noche del 31 de octubre, **Hallowe'en**,
● víspera de Todos los Santos, es posible
● ver a brujas y fantasmas. En este día los
● niños se disfrazan y van de puerta en
● puerta llevando un farol hecho con una
● calabaza en forma de cabeza humana.
● Cuando se les abre la puerta gritan "trick
● or treat", amenazando con gastar una
● broma a quien no les dé golosinas o algo
● de calderilla.

hallucination [həluːsɪ'neɪʃən] n
alucinación f

hallway ['hɔːlweɪ] n vestíbulo

halo ['heɪləu] n (of saint) halo, aureola

halt [hɔːlt] n (stop) alto, parada ▷ vt parar;
interrumpir ▷ vi pararse

halve [hɑːv] vt partir por la mitad

halves [hɑːvz] npl of **half**

ham [hæm] n jamón m (cocido)

hamburger ['hæmbəːgə*] n
hamburguesa

hamlet ['hæmlɪt] n aldea

hammer ['hæmə*] n martillo ▷ vt (nail)
clavar; (force): **to ~ an idea into sb/a
message home** meter una idea en la cabeza
a algn/machacar una idea ▷ vi dar golpes

hammock ['hæmək] n hamaca

hamper ['hæmpə*] vt estorbar ▷ n cesto

hamster ['hæmstə*] n hámster m

hamstring ['hæmstrɪŋ] n (Anat) tendón
m de la corva

hand [hænd] n mano f; (of clock) aguja;
(writing) letra; (worker) obrero ▷ vt dar,
pasar; **to give** or **lend sb a ~** echar una mano
a algn, ayudar a algn; **at ~** a mano; **in ~** (time)
libre; (job etc) entre manos; **on ~** (person,
services) a mano, al alcance; **to ~** (information

etc) a mano; **on the one ~ ...**, **on the other ~
...** por una parte ... por otra (parte) ...; **hand
down** vt pasar, bajar; (tradition) transmitir;
(heirloom) dejar en herencia; (us: sentence,
verdict) imponer; **hand in** vt entregar; **hand
out** vt distribuir; **hand over** vt (deliver)
entregar; **handbag** n bolso (SP), cartera
(LAM), bolsa (MEX); **hand baggage** n =
hand luggage; **handbook** n manual m;
handbrake n freno de mano; **handcuffs**
npl esposas fpl; **handful** n puñado

handicap ['hændɪkæp] n minusvalía;
(disadvantage) desventaja; (Sport) handicap
m ▷ vt estorbar; **to be mentally ~ped** ser
mentalmente m/f discapacitado; **to be
physically ~ped** ser minusválido/a

handkerchief ['hæŋkətʃɪf] n pañuelo

handle ['hændl] n (of door etc) tirador
m; (of cup etc) asa; (of knife etc) mango;
(for winding) manivela ▷ vt (touch) tocar;
(deal with) encargarse de; (treat: people)
manejar; **"~ with care"** "(manéjese) con
cuidado"; **to fly off the ~** perder los estribos;
handlebar(s) n(pl) manillar m

hand: hand luggage n equipaje m de
mano; **handmade** adj hecho a mano;
handout n (money etc) limosna; (leaflet)
folleto; **hands-free** adj (phone) manos
libres inv; **hands-free kit** n manos libres
m inv

handsome ['hænsəm] adj guapo;
(building) bello; (fig: profit) considerable

handwriting ['hændraɪtɪŋ] n letra

handy ['hændɪ] adj (close at hand) a la
mano; (tool etc) práctico; (skilful) hábil,
diestro

hang [hæŋ] (pt, pp **hung**) vt colgar;
(criminal: pt, pp **hanged**) ahorcar ▷ vi
(painting, coat etc) colgar; (hair, drapery) caer;
to get the ~ of sth (inf) lograr dominar algo;
hang about or **around** vi haraganear;
hang down vi colgar, pender; **hang on**
vi (wait) esperar; **hang out** vt (washing)
tender, colgar ▷ vi (inf: live) vivir; (spend
time) pasar el rato; **to hang out of sth**
colgar fuera de algo; **hang round** vi = **hang
around**; **hang up** vi (Tel) colgar ▷ vt colgar

hanger ['hæŋə*] n percha

hang-gliding ['-glaɪdɪŋ] n vuelo libre

hangover ['hæŋəuvə*] n (after drinking)
resaca

hankie, hanky ['hæŋkɪ] n abbr =
handkerchief

happen ['hæpən] vi suceder, ocurrir;
(chance): **he ~ed to hear/see** dió la
casualidad de que oyó/vió; **as it ~s** da la
casualidad de que

happily ['hæpɪlɪ] adv (luckily)

afortunadamente; (*cheerfully*) alegremente

happiness ['hæpɪnɪs] *n* felicidad *f*; (*cheerfulness*) alegría

happy ['hæpɪ] *adj* feliz; (*cheerful*) alegre; **to be ~ (with)** estar contento (con); **to be ~ to do** estar encantado de hacer; **~ birthday!** ¡feliz cumpleaños!

harass ['hærəs] *vt* acosar, hostigar; **harassment** *n* persecución *f*

harbour ['hɑ:bə*] (*US* **harbor**) *n* puerto ▷ *vt* (*fugitive*) dar abrigo a; (*hope etc*) abrigar

hard [hɑ:d] *adj* duro; (*difficult*) difícil; (*work*) arduo; (*person*) severo; (*fact*) innegable ▷ *adv* (*work*) mucho, duro; (*think*) profundamente; **to look ~ at** clavar los ojos en; **to try ~** esforzarse; **no ~ feelings!** ¡sin rencor(es)!; **to be ~ of hearing** ser duro de oído; **to be ~ done by** ser tratado injustamente; **hardback** *n* libro en cartoné; **hardboard** *n* aglomerado *m* (de madera); **hard disk** *n* (*Comput*) disco duro or rígido; **harden** *vt* endurecer; (*fig*) curtir ▷ *vi* endurecerse; curtirse

hardly ['hɑ:dlɪ] *adv* apenas; **~ ever** casi nunca

hard: hardship *n* privación *f*; **hard shoulder** (*BRIT*) *n* (*Aut*) arcén *m*; **hard-up** (*inf*) *adj* sin un duro (*SP*), pelado, sin un centavo (*MEX*), pato (*SC*); **hardware** *n* ferretería; (*Comput*) hardware *m*; (*Mil*) armamento; **hardware shop** (*US* **hardware store**) ferretería; **hard-working** *adj* trabajador(a)

hardy ['hɑ:dɪ] *adj* fuerte; (*plant*) resistente

hare [hɛə*] *n* liebre *f*

harm [hɑ:m] *n* daño, mal *m* ▷ *vt* (*person*) hacer daño a; (*health, interests*) perjudicar; (*thing*) dañar; **out of ~'s way** a salvo; **harmful** *adj* dañino; **harmless** *adj* (*person*) inofensivo; (*joke etc*) inocente

harmony ['hɑ:mənɪ] *n* armonía

harness ['hɑ:nɪs] *n* arreos *mpl*; (*for child*) arnés *m*; (*safety harness*) arneses *mpl* ▷ *vt* (*horse*) enjaezar; (*resources*) aprovechar

harp [hɑ:p] *n* arpa ▷ *vi*: **to ~ on (about)** machacar (con)

harsh [hɑ:ʃ] *adj* (*cruel*) duro, cruel; (*severe*) severo; (*sound*) áspero; (*light*) deslumbrador(a)

harvest ['hɑ:vɪst] *n* (*harvest time*) siega; (*of cereals etc*) cosecha; (*of grapes*) vendimia ▷ *vt* cosechar

has [hæz] *vb see* **have**

hasn't ['hæznt] = **has not**

hassle ['hæsl] (*inf*) *n* lata

haste [heɪst] *n* prisa; **hasten** ['heɪsn] *vt* acelerar ▷ *vi* darse prisa; **hastily** *adv* de prisa; precipitadamente; **hasty** *adj*

apresurado; (*rash*) precipitado

hat [hæt] *n* sombrero

hatch [hætʃ] *n* (*Naut: also*: **~way**) escotilla; (*also*: **service ~**) ventanilla ▷ *vi* (*bird*) salir del cascarón ▷ *vt* incubar; (*plot*) tramar; **5 eggs have ~ed** han salido 5 pollos

hatchback ['hætʃbæk] *n* (*Aut*) tres or cinco puertas *m*

hate [heɪt] *vt* odiar, aborrecer ▷ *n* odio; **hatred** ['heɪtrɪd] *n* odio

haul [hɔ:l] *vt* tirar ▷ *n* (*of fish*) redada; (*of stolen goods etc*) botín *m*

haunt [hɔ:nt] *vt* (*ghost*) aparecerse en; (*obsess*) obsesionar ▷ *n* guarida; **haunted** *adj* (*castle etc*) embrujado; (*look*) de angustia

○ **KEYWORD**

have [hæv] (*pt, pp* **had**) *aux vb* **1** (*gen*) haber; **to have arrived/eaten** haber llegado/comido; **having finished** or **when he had finished, he left** cuando hubo acabado, se fue

2 (*in tag questions*): **you've done it, haven't you?** lo has hecho, ¿verdad? or ¿no?

3 (*in short answers and questions*): **I haven't** no; **so I have** pues, es verdad; **we haven't paid – yes we have!** no hemos pagado – ¡sí que hemos pagado!; **I've been there before, have you?** he estado allí antes, ¿y tú?

▷ *modal aux vb* (*be obliged*): **to have (got) to do sth** tener que hacer algo; **you haven't to tell her** no hay que or no debes decírselo

▷ *vt* **1** (*possess*): **he has (got) blue eyes/ dark hair** tiene los ojos azules/el pelo negro

2 (*referring to meals etc*): **to have breakfast/ lunch/dinner** desayunar/comer/cenar; **to have a drink/a cigarette** tomar algo/ fumar un cigarrillo

3 (*receive*) recibir; (*obtain*) obtener; **may I have your address?** ¿puedes darme tu dirección?; **you can have it for £5** te lo puedes quedar por £5; **I must have it by tomorrow** lo necesito para mañana; **to have a baby** tener un niño or bebé

4 (*maintain, allow*): **I won't have it/this nonsense!** ¡no lo permitiré!/¡no permitiré estas tonterías!; **we can't have that** no podemos permitir eso

5 to have sth done hacer or mandar hacer algo; **to have one's hair cut** cortarse el pelo; **to have sb do sth** hacer que algn haga algo

6 (*experience, suffer*): **to have a cold/flu** tener un resfriado/la gripe; **she had her bag stolen/her arm broken** le robaron el bolso/se rompió un brazo; **to have an**

operation operarse
7 (+ *noun*): **to have a swim/walk/bath/
rest** nadar/dar un paseo/darse un baño/
descansar; **let's have a look** vamos a ver;
to have a meeting/party celebrar una
reunión/una fiesta; **let me have a try**
déjame intentarlo

haven ['heɪvn] *n* puerto; (*fig*) refugio
haven't ['hævnt] = **have not**
havoc ['hævək] *n* estragos *mpl*
Hawaii [hə'waɪiː] *n* (Islas *fpl*) Hawai *fpl*
hawk [hɔːk] *n* halcón *m*
hawthorn ['hɔːθɔːn] *n* espino
hay [heɪ] *n* heno; **hay fever** *n* fiebre *f* del
heno; **haystack** *n* almiar *m*
hazard ['hæzəd] *n* peligro ▷ *vt* aventurar;
hazardous *adj* peligroso; **hazard warning
lights** *npl* (*Aut*) señales *fpl* de emergencia
haze [heɪz] *n* neblina
hazel ['heɪzl] *n* (*tree*) avellano ▷ *adj* (*eyes*)
color *m* de avellano; **hazelnut** *n* avellana
hazy ['heɪzɪ] *adj* brumoso; (*idea*) vago
he [hiː] *pron* él; **~ who ...** él que ..., quien ...
head [hɛd] *n* cabeza; (*leader*) jefe/a *m/f*; (*of
school*) director(a) *m/f* ▷ *vt* (*list*) encabezar;
(*group*) capitanear; (*company*) dirigir; **~s
(or tails)** cara (o cruz); **~ first** de cabeza;
~ over heels (*in love*) perdidamente; **to ~
the ball** cabecear (la pelota); **head for** *vt
fus* dirigirse a; (*disaster*) ir camino de; **head
off** *vt* (*threat, danger*) evitar; **headache**
n dolor *m* de cabeza; **heading** *n* título;
headlamp (*BRIT*) *n* = **headlight**; **headlight**
n faro; **headline** *n* titular *m*; **head office** *n*
oficina central, central *f*; **headphones** *npl*
auriculares *mpl*; **headquarters** *npl* sede *f*
central; (*Mil*) cuartel *m* general; **headroom**
n (*in car*) altura interior; (*under bridge*)
(límite *m* de) altura; **headscarf** *n* pañuelo;
headset *n* cascos *mpl*; **headteacher** *n*
director(directora) *m*; **head waiter** *n* maître
m
heal [hiːl] *vt* curar ▷ *vi* cicatrizarse
health [hɛlθ] *n* salud *f*; **health care** *n*
asistencia sanitaria; **health centre** (*BRIT*) *n*
ambulatorio, centro médico; **health food**
n alimentos *mpl* orgánicos; **Health Service**
(*BRIT*) *n* el servicio de salud pública, ≈ el
Insalud (*SP*); **healthy** *adj* sano, saludable
heap [hiːp] *n* montón *m* ▷ *vt*: **to ~ (up)**
amontonar; **to ~ sth with** llenar algo hasta
arriba de; **~s of** un montón de
hear [hɪə*] (*pt, pp* **~d**) *vt* (*also Law*) oír;
(*news*) saber ▷ *vi* oír; **to ~ about** oír hablar
de; **to ~ from sb** tener noticias de algn
heard [həːd] *pt, pp of* **hear**
hearing ['hɪərɪŋ] *n* (*sense*) oído; (*Law*) vista;

hearing aid *n* audífono
hearse [həːs] *n* coche *m* fúnebre
heart [hɑːt] *n* corazón *m*; (*fig*) valor
m; (*of lettuce*) cogollo; **hearts** *npl*
(*Cards*) corazones *mpl*; **to lose/take ~**
descorazonarse/cobrar ánimo; **at ~** en
el fondo; **by ~** (*learn, know*) de memoria;
heart attack *n* infarto (de miocardio);
heartbeat *n* latido (del corazón);
heartbroken *adj*: **she was heartbroken
about it** esto le partió el corazón;
heartburn *n* acedía; **heart disease** *n*
enfermedad *f* cardíaca
hearth [hɑːθ] *n* (*fireplace*) chimenea
heartless ['hɑːtlɪs] *adj* despiadado
hearty ['hɑːtɪ] *adj* (*person*) campechano;
(*laugh*) sano; (*dislike, support*) absoluto
heat [hiːt] *n* calor *m*; (*Sport: also*:
qualifying ~) prueba eliminatoria ▷ *vt*
calentar; **heat up** *vi* calentarse ▷ *vt*
calentar; **heated** *adj* caliente; (*fig*)
acalorado; **heater** *n* estufa; (*in car*)
calefacción *f*
heather ['hɛðə*] *n* brezo
heating ['hiːtɪŋ] *n* calefacción *f*
heatwave ['hiːtweɪv] *n* ola de calor
heaven ['hɛvn] *n* cielo; (*fig*) una maravilla;
heavenly *adj* celestial; (*fig*) maravilloso
heavily ['hɛvɪlɪ] *adv* pesadamente;
(*drink, smoke*) con exceso; (*sleep, sigh*)
profundamente; (*depend*) mucho
heavy ['hɛvɪ] *adj* pesado; (*work, blow*)
duro; (*sea, rain, meal*) fuerte; (*drinker, smoker*)
grande; (*responsibility*) grave; (*schedule*)
ocupado; (*weather*) bochornoso
Hebrew ['hiːbruː] *adj, n* (*Ling*) hebreo
hectare ['hɛktɑː*] *n* (*BRIT*) hectárea
hectic ['hɛktɪk] *adj* agitado
he'd [hiːd] = **he would; he had**
hedge [hɛdʒ] *n* seto ▷ *vi* contestar con
evasivas; **to ~ one's bets** (*fig*) cubrirse
hedgehog ['hɛdʒhɔg] *n* erizo
heed [hiːd] *vt* (*also*: **take ~**: *pay attention to*)
hacer caso de
heel [hiːl] *n* talón *m*; (*of shoe*) tacón *m* ▷ *vt*
(*shoe*) poner tacón a
hefty ['hɛftɪ] *adj* (*person*) fornido; (*parcel,
profit*) gordo
height [haɪt] *n* (*of person*) estatura; (*of
building*) altura; (*high ground*) cerro; (*altitude*)
altitud *f*; (*fig: of season*): **at the ~ of summer**
en los días más calurosos del verano; (: *of
power etc*) cúspide *f*; (: *of stupidity etc*) colmo;
heighten *vt* elevar; (*fig*) aumentar
heir [ɛə*] *n* heredero; **heiress** *n* heredera
held [hɛld] *pt, pp of* **hold**
helicopter ['hɛlɪkɔptə*] *n* helicóptero
hell [hɛl] *n* infierno; **~!** (*inf*) ¡demonios!

he'll [hiːl] = **he will; he shall**

hello [hə'ləʊ] *excl* ¡hola!; (*to attract attention*) ¡oiga!; (*surprise*) ¡caramba!

helmet ['hɛlmɪt] *n* casco

help [hɛlp] *n* ayuda; (*cleaner etc*) criada, asistenta ▷ *vt* ayudar; **~!** ¡socorro!; **~ yourself** sírvete; **he can't ~ it** no es culpa suya; **help out** *vi* ayudar, echar una mano ▷ *vt*: **to help sb out** ayudar a algn, echar una mano a algn; **helper** *n* ayudante *mf*; **helpful** *adj* útil; (*person*) servicial; (*advice*) útil; **helping** *n* ración *f*; **helpless** *adj* (*incapable*) incapaz; (*defenceless*) indefenso; **helpline** *n* teléfono de asistencia al público

hem [hɛm] *n* dobladillo ▷ *vt* poner or coser el dobladillo de

hemisphere ['hɛmɪsfɪə*] *n* hemisferio

hemorrhage ['hɛmərɪdʒ] (*US*) *n* = **haemorrhage**

hemorrhoids ['hɛmərɔɪdz] (*US*) *npl* = **haemorrhoids**

hen [hɛn] *n* gallina; (*female bird*) hembra

hence [hɛns] *adv* (*therefore*) por lo tanto; **2 years ~** de aquí a 2 años

hen night, hen party *n* (*inf*) despedida de soltera

hepatitis [hɛpə'taɪtɪs] *n* hepatitis *f*

her [həː*] *pron* (*direct*) la; (*indirect*) le; (*stressed, after prep*) ella ▷ *adj* su; *see also* **me; my**

herb [həːb] *n* hierba; **herbal** *adj* de hierbas; **herbal tea** *n* infusión *f* de hierbas

herd [həːd] *n* rebaño

here [hɪə*] *adv* aquí; (*at this point*) en este punto; **~!** (*present*) ¡presente!; **~ is/are** aquí está/están; **~ she is** aquí está

hereditary [hɪ'rɛdɪtrɪ] *adj* hereditario

heritage ['hɛrɪtɪdʒ] *n* patrimonio

hernia ['həːnɪə] *n* hernia

hero ['hɪərəʊ] (*pl* **~es**) *n* héroe *m*; (*in book, film*) protagonista *m*; **heroic** [hɪ'rəʊɪk] *adj* heroico

heroin ['hɛrəʊɪn] *n* heroína

heroine ['hɛrəʊɪn] *n* heroína; (*in book, film*) protagonista

heron ['hɛrən] *n* garza

herring ['hɛrɪŋ] *n* arenque *m*

hers [həːz] *pron* (el) suyo/(la) suya) *etc*; *see also* **mine¹**

herself [həː'sɛlf] *pron* (*reflexive*) se; (*emphatic*) ella misma; (*after prep*) sí (misma); *see also* **oneself**

he's [hiːz] = **he is; he has**

hesitant ['hɛzɪtənt] *adj* vacilante

hesitate ['hɛzɪteɪt] *vi* vacilar; (*in speech*) titubear; (*be unwilling*) resistirse a; **hesitation** ['-teɪʃən] *n* indecisión *f*; titubeo; dudas *fpl*

heterosexual [hɛtərəʊ'sɛksjuəl] *adj* heterosexual

hexagon ['hɛksəgən] *n* hexágono

hey [heɪ] *excl* ¡oye!, ¡oiga!

heyday ['heɪdeɪ] *n*: **the ~ of** el apogeo de

HGV *n abbr* (= *heavy goods vehicle*) vehículo pesado

hi [haɪ] *excl* ¡hola!; (*to attract attention*) ¡oiga!

hibernate ['haɪbəneɪt] *vi* invernar

hiccough ['hɪkʌp] = **hiccup**

hiccup ['hɪkʌp] *vi* hipar

hid [hɪd] *pt of* **hide**

hidden ['hɪdn] *pp of* **hide** ▷ *adj*: **~ agenda** plan *m* encubierto

hide [haɪd] (*pt* **hid**, *pp* **hidden**) *n* (*skin*) piel *f* ▷ *vt* esconder, ocultar ▷ *vi*: **to ~ (from sb)** esconderse *or* ocultarse (de algn)

hideous ['hɪdɪəs] *adj* horrible

hiding ['haɪdɪŋ] *n* (*beating*) paliza; **to be in ~** (*concealed*) estar escondido

hi-fi ['haɪfaɪ] *n* estéreo, hifi *m* ▷ *adj* de alta fidelidad

high [haɪ] *adj* alto; (*speed, number*) grande; (*price*) elevado; (*wind*) fuerte; (*voice*) agudo ▷ *adv* alto, a gran altura; **it is 20 m ~** tiene 20 m de altura; **~ in the air** en las alturas; **highchair** *n* silla alta; **high-class** *adj* (*hotel*) de lujo; (*person*) distinguido, de categoría; (*food*) de alta categoría; **higher education** *n* educación *f* or enseñanza superior; **high heels** *npl* (*heels*) tacones *mpl* altos; (*shoes*) zapatos *mpl* de tacón; **high jump** *n* (*Sport*) salto de altura; **highlands** ['haɪləndz] *npl* tierras *fpl* altas; **the Highlands** (*in Scotland*) las Tierras Altas de Escocia; **highlight** *n* (*fig: of event*) punto culminante ▷ *vt* subrayar; **highlights** *npl* (*in hair*) reflejos *mpl*; **highlighter** *n* rotulador; **highly** *adv* (*paid*) muy bien; (*critical, confidential*) sumamente; (*a lot*): **to speak/think highly of** hablar muy bien de/tener en mucho a; **highness** *n* altura; **Her/His Highness** Su Alteza; **high-rise** *n* (*also*: **high-rise block, high-rise building**) torre *f* de pisos; **high school** *n* ≈ Instituto Nacional de Bachillerato (*SP*); **high season** (*BRIT*) *n* temporada alta; **high street** (*BRIT*) *n* calle *f* mayor; **high-tech** (*inf*) *adj* al-tec (*inf*), de alta tecnología; **highway** *n* carretera; (*US*) carretera nacional; autopista; **Highway Code** (*BRIT*) *n* código de la circulación

hijack ['haɪdʒæk] *vt* secuestrar; **hijacker** *n* secuestrador(a) *m/f*

hike [haɪk] *vi* (*go walking*) ir de excursión (a pie) ▷ *n* caminata; **hiker** *n* excursionista *mf*; **hiking** *n* senderismo

hilarious [hɪˈlɛərɪəs] *adj* divertidísimo

hill [hɪl] *n* colina; (*high*) montaña; (*slope*) cuesta; **hillside** *n* ladera; **hill walking** *n* senderismo (de montaña); **hilly** *adj* montañoso

him [hɪm] *pron* (*direct*) le, lo; (*indirect*) le; (*stressed, after prep*) él; *see also* **me**; **himself** *pron* (*reflexive*) se; (*emphatic*) él mismo; (*after prep*) sí (mismo); *see also* **oneself**

hind [haɪnd] *adj* posterior

hinder [ˈhɪndə*] *vt* estorbar, impedir

hindsight [ˈhaɪndsaɪt] *n*: **with ~** en retrospectiva

Hindu [ˈhɪnduː] *n* hindú *mf*; **Hinduism** *n* (*Rel*) hinduismo

hinge [hɪndʒ] *n* bisagra, gozne *m* ▷ *vi* (*fig*): **to ~ on** depender de

hint [hɪnt] *n* indirecta; (*advice*) consejo; (*sign*) dejo ▷ *vt*: **to ~ that** insinuar que ▷ *vi*: **to ~ at** hacer alusión a

hip [hɪp] *n* cadera

hippie [ˈhɪpɪ] *n* hippie *m/f*, jipi *m/f*

hippo [ˈhɪpəu] (*pl* **~s**) *n* hipopótamo

hippopotamus [hɪpəˈpɔtəməs] (*pl* **~es** or **hippopotami**) *n* hipopótamo

hippy [ˈhɪpɪ] *n* = **hippie**

hire [haɪə*] *vt* (*BRIT: car, equipment*) alquilar; (*worker*) contratar ▷ *n* alquiler *m*; **for ~** se alquila; (*taxi*) libre; **hire(d) car** (*BRIT*) *n* coche *m* de alquiler; **hire purchase** (*BRIT*) *n* compra a plazos

his [hɪz] *pron* (el) suyo/(la) suya) *etc* ▷ *adj* su; *see also* **mine¹**; **my**

Hispanic [hɪsˈpænɪk] *adj* hispánico

hiss [hɪs] *vi* silbar

historian [hɪˈstɔːrɪən] *n* historiador(a) *m/f*

historic(al) [hɪˈstɔrɪk(l)] *adj* histórico

history [ˈhɪstərɪ] *n* historia

hit [hɪt] (*pt, pp* **~**) *vt* (*strike*) golpear, pegar; (*reach: target*) alcanzar; (*collide with: car*) chocar contra; (*fig: affect*) afectar ▷ *n* golpe *m*; (*success*) éxito; (*on website*) visita; (*in web search*) correspondencia; **to ~ it off with sb** llevarse bien con algn; **hit back** *vi* defenderse; (*fig*) devolver golpe por golpe

hitch [hɪtʃ] *vt* (*fasten*) atar, amarrar; (*also:* ~ **up**) remangar ▷ *n* (*difficulty*) dificultad *f*; **to ~ a lift** hacer autostop

hitch-hike [ˈhɪtʃhaɪk] *vi* hacer autostop; **hitch-hiker** *n* autostopista *m/f*; **hitch-hiking** *n* autostop *m*

hi-tech [ˈhaɪˈtek] *adj* de alta tecnología

hitman [ˈhɪtmæn] (*irreg*) *n* asesino a sueldo

HIV *n abbr* (= *human immunodeficiency virus*) VIH *m*; **~-negative/positive** VIH negativo/positivo

hive [haɪv] *n* colmena

hoard [hɔːd] *n* (*treasure*) tesoro; (*stockpile*) provisión *f* ▷ *vt* acumular; (*goods in short supply*) acaparar

hoarse [hɔːs] *adj* ronco

hoax [həuks] *n* trampa

hob [hɔb] *n* quemador *m*

hobble [ˈhɔbl] *vi* cojear

hobby [ˈhɔbɪ] *n* pasatiempo, afición *f*

hobo [ˈhəubəu] (*US*) *n* vagabundo

hockey [ˈhɔkɪ] *n* hockey *m*; **hockey stick** *n* palo *m* de hockey

hog [hɔg] *n* cerdo, puerco ▷ *vt* (*fig*) acaparar; **to go the whole ~** poner toda la carne en el asador

Hogmanay [hɔgməˈneɪ] *n ver abajo*

> ### HOGMANAY
>
> La Nochevieja o "New Year's Eve" se conoce como "Hogmanay" en Escocia, donde se festeje de forma especial. La familia y los amigos se suelen juntar para oír las campanadas del reloj y luego se hace el "first-footing", costumbre que consiste en visitar a los amigos y vecinos llevando algo de beber (generalmente whisky) y un trozo de carbón que se supone que traerá buena suerte para el año entrante.

hoist [hɔɪst] *n* (*crane*) grúa ▷ *vt* levantar, alzar; (*flag, sail*) izar

hold [həuld] (*pt, pp* **held**) *vt* sostener; (*contain*) contener; (*have: power, qualification*) tener; (*keep back*) retener; (*believe*) sostener; (*consider*) considerar; (*keep in position*): **to ~ one's head up** mantener la cabeza alta; (*meeting*) celebrar ▷ *vi* (*withstand: pressure*) resistir; (*be valid*) valer ▷ *n* (*grasp*) asimiento; (*fig*) dominio; (*Tel*) ¡no cuelgue!; **to ~ one's own** (*fig*) defenderse; **to catch** or **get (a) ~ of** agarrarse or asirse de; **hold back** *vt* retener; (*secret*) ocultar; **hold on** *vi* agarrarse bien; (*wait*) esperar; **hold on!** (*Tel*) ¡(espere) un momento!; **hold out** *vt* ofrecer ▷ *vi* (*resist*) resistir; **hold up** *vt* (*raise*) levantar; (*support*) apoyar; (*delay*) retrasar; (*rob*) asaltar; **holdall** (*BRIT*) *n* bolsa; **holder** *n* (*container*) receptáculo; (*of ticket, record*) poseedor(a) *m/f*; (*of office, title etc*) titular *mf*

hole [həul] *n* agujero

holiday [ˈhɔlədɪ] *n* vacaciones *fpl*; (*public holiday*) (día *m* de) fiesta, día *m* feriado; **on ~** de vacaciones; **holiday camp** *n* (*BRIT: also:* **holiday centre**) centro de vacaciones; **holiday job** *n* (*BRIT*) trabajillo extra para las vacaciones; **holiday-maker** (*BRIT*) *n* turista *mf*; **holiday resort** *n* centro turístico

Holland ['hɔlənd] *n* Holanda

hollow ['hɔləu] *adj* hueco; (*claim*) vacío; (*eyes*) hundido; (*sound*) sordo ▷ *n* hueco; (*in ground*) hoyo ▷ *vt*: **to ~ out** excavar

holly ['hɔlı] *n* acebo

Hollywood ['hɔlıwud] *n* Hollywood *m*

holocaust ['hɔləkɔːst] *n* holocausto

holy ['həulı] *adj* santo, sagrado; (*water*) bendito

home [həum] *n* casa; (*country*) patria; (*institution*) asilo ▷ *cpd* (*domestic*) casero, de casa; (*Econ, Pol*) nacional ▷ *adv* (*direction*) a casa; (*right in: nail etc*) a fondo; **at ~** en casa; (*in country*) en el país; (*fig*) como pez en el agua; **to go/come ~** ir/volver a casa; **make yourself at ~** ¡estás en tu casa!; **home address** *n* domicilio; **homeland** *n* tierra natal; **homeless** *adj* sin hogar, sin casa; **homely** *adj* (*simple*) sencillo; **home-made** *adj* casero; **home match** *n* partido en casa; **Home Office** (*BRIT*) *n* Ministerio del Interior; **home owner** *n* propietario/a *m/f* de una casa; **home page** *n* página de inicio; **Home Secretary** (*BRIT*) *n* Ministro del Interior; **homesick** *adj*: **to be homesick** tener morriña, sentir nostalgia; **home town** *n* ciudad *f* natal; **homework** *n* deberes *mpl*

homicide ['hɔmɪsaɪd] (*US*) *n* homicidio

homoeopathic [həumɪə'pæθɪk] (*US* **homeopathic**) *adj* homeopático

homoeopathy [həumɪ'ɔpəθɪ] (*US* **homeopathy**) *n* homeopatía

homosexual [hɔməu'sɛksjuəl] *adj, n* homosexual *mf*

honest ['ɔnɪst] *adj* honrado; (*sincere*) franco, sincero; **honestly** *adv* honradamente; francamente; **honesty** *n* honradez *f*

honey ['hʌnɪ] *n* miel *f*; **honeymoon** *n* luna de miel; **honeysuckle** *n* madreselva

Hong Kong ['hɔŋ'kɔŋ] *n* Hong-Kong *m*

honorary ['ɔnərərɪ] *adj* (*member, president*) de honor; (*title*) honorífico; **~ degree** doctorado honoris causa

honour ['ɔnə*] (*US* **honor**) *vt* honrar; (*commitment, promise*) cumplir con ▷ *n* honor *m*, honra; **to graduate with ~s** ≈ licenciarse con matrícula (de honor); **honourable** (*US* **honorable**) *adj* honorable; **honours degree** *n* (*Scol*) título de licenciado con calificación alta

hood [hud] *n* capucha; (*BRIT Aut*) capota; (*US Aut*) capó *m*; (*of cooker*) campana de humos; **hoodie** *n* (*top*) jersey *m* con capucha

hoof [huːf] (*pl* **hooves**) *n* pezuña

hook [huk] *n* gancho; (*on dress*) corchete *m*, broche *m*; (*for fishing*) anzuelo ▷ *vt* enganchar; (*fish*) pescar

hooligan ['huːlɪgən] *n* gamberro

hoop [huːp] *n* aro

hooray [huː'reɪ] *excl* = **hurray**

hoot [huːt] (*BRIT*) *vi* (*Aut*) tocar el pito, pitar; (*siren*) (hacer) sonar; (*owl*) ulular

Hoover® ['huːvə*] (*BRIT*) *n* aspiradora ▷ *vt*: **to hoover** pasar la aspiradora por

hooves [huːvz] *npl of* **hoof**

hop [hɔp] *vi* saltar, brincar; (*on one foot*) saltar con un pie

hope [həup] *vt, vi* esperar ▷ *n* esperanza; **I ~ so/not** espero que sí/no; **hopeful** *adj* (*person*) optimista; (*situation*) prometedor(a); **hopefully** *adv* con esperanza; (*one hopes*): **hopefully he will recover** esperamos que se recupere; **hopeless** *adj* desesperado; (*person*): **to be hopeless** ser un desastre

hops [hɔps] *npl* lúpulo

horizon [hə'raɪzn] *n* horizonte *m*; **horizontal** [hɔrɪ'zɔntl] *adj* horizontal

hormone ['hɔːməun] *n* hormona

horn [hɔːn] *n* cuerno; (*Mus: also*: **French ~**) trompa; (*Aut*) pito, claxon *m*

horoscope ['hɔrəskəup] *n* horóscopo

horrendous [hɔ'rɛndəs] *adj* horrendo

horrible ['hɔrɪbl] *adj* horrible

horrid ['hɔrɪd] *adj* horrible, horroroso

horrific [hɔ'rɪfɪk] *adj* (*accident*) horroroso; (*film*) horripilante

horrifying ['hɔrɪfaɪɪŋ] *adj* horroroso

horror ['hɔrə*] *n* horror *m*; **horror film** *n* película de horror

hors d'œuvre [ɔː'dəːvrə] *n* entremeses *mpl*

horse [hɔːs] *n* caballo; **horseback** *n*: **on horseback** a caballo; **horse chestnut** *n* (*tree*) castaño de Indias; (*nut*) castaña de Indias; **horsepower** *n* caballo (de fuerza); **horse-racing** *n* carreras *fpl* de caballos; **horseradish** *n* rábano picante; **horse riding** *n* (*BRIT*) equitación *f*

hose [həuz] *n* manguera; **hosepipe** *n* manguera

hospital ['hɔspɪtl] *n* hospital *m*

hospitality [hɔspɪ'tælɪtɪ] *n* hospitalidad *f*

host [həust] *n* anfitrión *m*; (*TV, Radio*) presentador *m*; (*Rel*) hostia; (*large number*): **a ~ of** multitud de

hostage ['hɔstɪdʒ] *n* rehén *m*

hostel ['hɔstl] *n* hostal *m*; (**youth**) **~** albergue *m* juvenil

hostess ['həustɪs] *n* anfitriona; (*BRIT: air hostess*) azafata; (*TV, Radio*) presentadora

hostile ['hɔstaɪl] *adj* hostil

hostility [hɔ'stɪlɪtɪ] *n* hostilidad *f*

hot [hɔt] *adj* caliente; *(weather)* caluroso, de calor; *(as opposed to warm)* muy caliente; *(spicy)* picante; **to be ~** *(person)* tener calor; *(object)* estar caliente; *(weather)* hacer calor; **hot dog** *n* perro caliente

hotel [həu'tɛl] *n* hotel *m*

hot-water bottle [hɔt'wɔːtə*-] *n* bolsa de agua caliente

hound [haund] *vt* acosar ▷ *n* perro (de caza)

hour ['auə*] *n* hora; **hourly** *adj* (de) cada hora

house [*n* haus, *pl* 'hauzɪz, *vb* hauz] *n* (*gen, firm*) casa; (*Pol*) cámara; (*Theatre*) sala ▷ *vt* (*person*) alojar; (*collection*) albergar; **on the ~** *(fig)* la casa invita; **household** *n* familia; *(home)* casa; **householder** *n* propietario/a; *(head of house)* cabeza de familia; **housekeeper** *n* ama de llaves; **housekeeping** *n* *(work)* trabajos *mpl* domésticos; **housewife** *(irreg)* *n* ama de casa; **house wine** *n* vino *m* de la casa; **housework** *n* faenas *fpl* (de la casa)

housing ['hauzɪŋ] *n* *(act)* alojamiento; *(houses)* viviendas *fpl*; **housing development, housing estate** *(BRIT)* *n* urbanización *f*

hover ['hɔvə*] *vi* flotar (en el aire); **hovercraft** *n* aerodeslizador *m*

how [hau] *adv* *(in what way)* cómo; **~ are you?** ¿cómo estás?; **~ much milk/many people?** ¿cuánta leche/gente?; **~ much does it cost?** ¿cuánto cuesta?; **~ long have you been here?** ¿cuánto hace que estás aquí?; **~ old are you?** ¿cuántos años tienes?; **~ tall is he?** ¿cómo es de alto?; **~ is school?** ¿cómo (te) va (en) la escuela?; **~ was the film?** ¿qué tal la película?; **~ lovely/awful!** ¡qué bonito/horror!

however [hau'ɛvə*] *adv*: **~ I do it** lo haga como lo haga; **~ cold it is** por mucho frío que haga; **~ fast he runs** por muy rápido que corra; **~ did you do it?** ¿cómo lo hiciste? ▷ *conj* sin embargo, no obstante

howl [haul] *n* aullido ▷ *vi* aullar; *(person)* dar alaridos; *(wind)* ulular

H.P. *n abbr* = **hire purchase**

h.p. *abbr* = **horsepower**

HQ *n abbr* = **headquarters**

hr(s) *abbr* (= **hour(s)**) h

HTML *n abbr* (= *hypertext markup language*) lenguaje *m* de hipertexto

hubcap ['hʌbkæp] *n* tapacubos *m inv*

huddle ['hʌdl] *vi*: **to ~ together** acurrucarse

huff [hʌf] *n*: **in a ~** enojado

hug [hʌg] *vt* abrazar; *(thing)* apretar con los brazos

huge [hjuːdʒ] *adj* enorme

hull [hʌl] *n* *(of ship)* casco

hum [hʌm] *vt* tararear, canturrear ▷ *vi* tararear, canturrear; *(insect)* zumbar

human ['hjuːmən] *adj, n* humano

humane [hjuː'meɪn] *adj* humano, humanitario

humanitarian [hjuːmænɪ'tɛərɪən] *adj* humanitario

humanity [hjuː'mænɪtɪ] *n* humanidad *f*

human rights *npl* derechos *mpl* humanos

humble ['hʌmbl] *adj* humilde

humid ['hjuːmɪd] *adj* húmedo; **humidity** [-'mɪdɪtɪ] *n* humedad *f*

humiliate [hjuː'mɪlɪeɪt] *vt* humillar

humiliating [hjuː'mɪlɪeɪtɪŋ] *adj* humillante, vergonzoso

humiliation [hjuːmɪlɪ'eɪʃən] *n* humillación *f*

hummus ['huməs] *n* paté de garbanzos

humorous ['hjuːmərəs] *adj* gracioso, divertido

humour ['hjuːmə*] (*US* **humor**) *n* humorismo, sentido del humor; *(mood)* humor *m* ▷ *vt* *(person)* complacer

hump [hʌmp] *n* *(in ground)* montículo; *(camel's)* giba

hunch [hʌntʃ] *n* *(premonition)* presentimiento

hundred ['hʌndrəd] *num* ciento; *(before n)* cien; **~s of** centenares de; **hundredth** [-ɪdθ] *adj* centésimo

hung [hʌŋ] *pt, pp of* **hang**

Hungarian [hʌŋ'gɛərɪən] *adj, n* húngaro/a *m/f*

Hungary ['hʌŋgərɪ] *n* Hungría

hunger ['hʌŋgə*] *n* hambre *f* ▷ *vi*: **to ~ for** *(fig)* tener hambre de, anhelar

hungry ['hʌŋgrɪ] *adj*: **~ (for)** hambriento (de); **to be ~** tener hambre

hunt [hʌnt] *vt* *(seek)* buscar; *(Sport)* cazar ▷ *vi* *(search)*: **to ~ (for)** buscar; *(Sport)* cazar ▷ *n* búsqueda; caza, cacería; **hunter** *n* cazador(a) *m/f*; **hunting** *n* caza

hurdle ['həːdl] *n* *(Sport)* valla; *(fig)* obstáculo

hurl [həːl] *vt* lanzar, arrojar

hurrah [huː'rɑː] *excl* = **hurray**

hurray [hu'reɪ] *excl* ¡viva!

hurricane ['hʌrɪkən] *n* huracán *m*

hurry ['hʌrɪ] *n* prisa ▷ *vt* (*also:* **~ up**: *person*) dar prisa a; (: *work*) apresurar, hacer de prisa; **to be in a ~** tener prisa; **hurry up** *vi* darse prisa, apurarse (*LAM*)

hurt [həːt] (*pt, pp* **~**) *vt* hacer daño a ▷ *vi* doler ▷ *adj* lastimado

husband ['hʌzbənd] n marido

hush [hʌʃ] n silencio ▷vt hacer callar; **~!** ¡chitón!, ¡cállate!

husky ['hʌskɪ] adj ronco ▷n perro esquimal

hut [hʌt] n cabaña; (shed) cobertizo

hyacinth ['haɪəsɪnθ] n jacinto

hydrangea [haɪ'dreɪnʒə] n hortensia

hydrofoil ['haɪdrəfɔɪl] n aerodeslizador m

hydrogen ['haɪdrədʒən] n hidrógeno

hygiene ['haɪdʒiːn] n higiene f; **hygienic** [-'dʒiːnɪk] adj higiénico

hymn [hɪm] n himno

hype [haɪp] (inf) n bombardeo publicitario

hyphen ['haɪfn] n guión m

hypnotize ['hɪpnətaɪz] vt hipnotizar

hypocrite ['hɪpəkrɪt] n hipócrita mf

hypocritical [hɪpə'krɪtɪkl] adj hipócrita

hypothesis [haɪ'pɔθɪsɪs] (pl **hypotheses**) n hipótesis f inv

hysterical [hɪ'sterɪkl] adj histérico; (funny) para morirse de risa

hysterics [hɪ'sterɪks] npl histeria; **to be in ~** (fig) morirse de risa

I [aɪ] pron yo

ice [aɪs] n hielo; (ice cream) helado ▷vt (cake) alcorzar ▷vi (also: **~ over, ~ up**) helarse; **iceberg** n iceberg m; **ice cream** n helado; **ice cube** n cubito de hielo; **ice hockey** n hockey m sobre hielo

Iceland ['aɪslənd] n Islandia; **Icelander** n islandés/esa m/f; **Icelandic** [aɪs'lændɪk] adj islandés/esa ▷n (Ling) islandés m

ice: ice lolly (BRIT) n polo; **ice rink** n pista de hielo; **ice skating** n patinaje m sobre hielo

icing ['aɪsɪŋ] n (Culin) alcorza; **icing sugar** (BRIT) n azúcar m glas(eado)

icon ['aɪkɒn] n icono

ICT (BRIT: Scol) n abbr (= information and communications technology) informática

icy ['aɪsɪ] adj helado

I'd [aɪd] = **I would**; **I had**

ID card n (identity card) DNI m

idea [aɪ'dɪə] n idea

ideal [aɪ'dɪəl] n ideal m ▷adj ideal; **ideally** [-dɪəlɪ] adv idealmente; **they're ideally suited** hacen una pareja ideal

identical [aɪ'dentɪkl] adj idéntico

identification [aɪdentɪfɪ'keɪʃən] n identificación f; **(means of) ~** documentos mpl personales

identify [aɪ'dentɪfaɪ] vt identificar

identity [aɪ'dentɪtɪ] n identidad f; **identity card** n carnet m de identidad; **identity theft** n robo de identidad

ideology [aɪdɪ'ɔlədʒɪ] n ideología

idiom ['ɪdɪəm] n modismo; (style of speaking) lenguaje m

> ▌ Be careful not to translate **idiom** by the Spanish word idioma.

idiot ['ɪdɪət] n idiota mf

idle ['aɪdl] adj (inactive) ocioso; (lazy) holgazán/ana; (unemployed) parado, desocupado; (machinery etc) parado; (talk etc)

frívolo ▷ vi (machine) marchar en vacío
idol ['aɪdl] n ídolo
idyllic [ɪ'dɪlɪk] adj idílico
i.e. abbr (= that is) esto es
if [ɪf] conj sí; ~ **necessary** si fuera
necesario, si hiciese falta; ~ **I were you** yo
en tu lugar; ~ **so/not** de ser así/si no; ~ **only**
I could! ¡ojalá pudiera!; see also **as; even**
ignite [ɪg'naɪt] vt (set fire to) encender ▷ vi
encenderse
ignition [ɪg'nɪʃən] n (Aut: process) ignición
f; (: mechanism) encendido; **to switch on/off**
the ~ arrancar/apagar el motor
ignorance ['ɪgnərəns] n ignorancia
ignorant ['ɪgnərənt] adj ignorante; **to be**
~ **of** ignorar
ignore [ɪg'nɔ:*] vt (person, advice) no hacer
caso de; (fact) pasar por alto
I'll [aɪl] = **I will; I shall**
ill [ɪl] adj enfermo, malo ▷ n mal m ▷ adv
mal; **to be taken** ~ ponerse enfermo
illegal [ɪ'li:gl] adj ilegal
illegible [ɪ'ledʒɪbl] adj ilegible
illegitimate [ɪlɪ'dʒɪtɪmət] adj ilegítimo
ill health n mala salud f; **to be in** ~ estar
mal de salud
illiterate [ɪ'lɪtərət] adj analfabeto
illness ['ɪlnɪs] n enfermedad f
illuminate [ɪ'lu:mɪneɪt] vt (room, street)
iluminar, alumbrar
illusion [ɪ'lu:ʒən] n ilusión f; (trick) truco
illustrate ['ɪləstreɪt] vt ilustrar
illustration [ɪlə'streɪʃən] n (act of
illustrating) ilustración f; (example) ejemplo,
ilustración f; (in book) lámina
I'm [aɪm] = **I am**
image ['ɪmɪdʒ] n imagen f
imaginary [ɪ'mædʒɪnərɪ] adj imaginario
imagination [ɪmædʒɪ'neɪʃən] n
imaginación f; (inventiveness) inventiva
imaginative [ɪ'mædʒɪnətɪv] adj
imaginativo
imagine [ɪ'mædʒɪn] vt imaginarse
imbalance [ɪm'bæləns] n desequilibrio
imitate ['ɪmɪteɪt] vt imitar; **imitation**
[ɪmɪ'teɪʃən] n imitación f; (copy) copia
immaculate [ɪ'mækjulət] adj
inmaculado
immature [ɪmə'tjuə*] adj (person)
inmaduro
immediate [ɪ'mi:dɪət] adj inmediato;
(pressing) urgente, apremiante;
(nearest: family) próximo; (: neighbourhood)
inmediato; **immediately** adv (at once)
en seguida; (directly) inmediatamente;
immediately next to muy junto a
immense [ɪ'mɛns] adj inmenso, enorme;
(importance) enorme; **immensely** adv

enormemente
immerse [ɪ'mə:s] vt (submerge) sumergir;
to be ~d in (fig) estar absorto en
immigrant ['ɪmɪgrənt] n inmigrante mf;
immigration [ɪmɪ'greɪʃən] n inmigración
f
imminent ['ɪmɪnənt] adj inminente
immoral [ɪ'mɔrl] adj inmoral
immortal [ɪ'mɔ:tl] adj inmortal
immune [ɪ'mju:n] adj; ~ **(to)** inmune (a);
immune system n sistema m inmunitario
immunize ['ɪmjunaɪz] vt inmunizar
impact ['ɪmpækt] n impacto
impair [ɪm'pɛə*] vt perjudicar
impartial [ɪm'pɑ:ʃl] adj imparcial
impatience [ɪm'peɪʃəns] n impaciencia
impatient [ɪm'peɪʃənt] adj impaciente;
to get or **grow** ~ impacientarse
impeccable [ɪm'pɛkəbl] adj impecable
impending [ɪm'pɛndɪŋ] adj inminente
imperative [ɪm'pɛrətɪv] adj (tone)
imperioso; (need) imprescindible
imperfect [ɪm'pə:fɪkt] adj (goods etc)
defectuoso ▷ n (Ling: also: ~ **tense**)
imperfecto
imperial [ɪm'pɪərɪəl] adj imperial
impersonal [ɪm'pə:sənl] adj impersonal
impersonate [ɪm'pə:səneɪt] vt hacerse
pasar por; (Theatre) imitar
impetus ['ɪmpətəs] n ímpetu m; (fig)
impulso
implant [ɪm'plɑ:nt] vt (Med) injertar,
implantar; (fig: idea, principle) inculcar
implement [n 'ɪmplɪmənt, vb 'ɪmplɪment]
n herramienta; (for cooking) utensilio ▷ vt
(regulation) hacer efectivo; (plan) realizar
implicate ['ɪmplɪkeɪt] vt (compromise)
comprometer; **to ~ sb in sth** comprometer
a algn en algo
implication [ɪmplɪ'keɪʃən] n
consecuencia; **by** ~ indirectamente
implicit [ɪm'plɪsɪt] adj implícito; (belief,
trust) absoluto
imply [ɪm'plaɪ] vt (involve) suponer; (hint)
dar a entender que
impolite [ɪmpə'laɪt] adj mal educado
import [vb ɪm'pɔ:t, n 'ɪmpɔ:t] vt importar
▷ n (Comm) importación f; (: article)
producto importado; (meaning) significado,
sentido
importance [ɪm'pɔ:təns] n importancia
important [ɪm'pɔ:tənt] adj importante;
it's not ~ no importa, no tiene importancia
importer [ɪm'pɔ:tə*] n importador(a) m/f
impose [ɪm'pəuz] vt imponer ▷ vi: **to**
~ **on sb** abusar de algn; **imposing** adj
imponente, impresionante
impossible [ɪm'pɒsɪbl] adj imposible;

(*person*) insoportable
impotent ['ɪmpətənt] *adj* impotente
impoverished [ɪm'pɒvərɪʃt] *adj*
necesitado
impractical [ɪm'præktɪkl] *adj* (*person*,
plan) poco práctico
impress [ɪm'prɛs] *vt* impresionar; (*mark*)
estampar; **to ~ sth on sb** hacer entender
algo a algn
impression [ɪm'prɛʃən] *n* impresión f;
(*imitation*) imitación f; **to be under the ~
that** tener la impresión de que
impressive [ɪm'prɛsɪv] *adj*
impresionante
imprison [ɪm'prɪzn] *vt* encarcelar;
imprisonment *n* encarcelamiento; (*term of
imprisonment*) cárcel f
improbable [ɪm'prɒbəbl] *adj* improbable,
inverosímil
improper [ɪm'prɒpə*] *adj*
(*unsuitable: conduct etc*) incorrecto;
(*: activities*) deshonesto
improve [ɪm'pruːv] *vt* mejorar; (*foreign
language*) perfeccionar ▷ *vi* mejorarse;
improvement *n* mejoramiento;
perfección f; progreso
improvise ['ɪmprəvaɪz] *vt, vi* improvisar
impulse ['ɪmpʌls] *n* impulso; **to act on ~**
obrar sin reflexión; **impulsive** [ɪm'pʌlsɪv]
adj irreflexivo

○ **KEYWORD**

in [ɪn] *prep* **1** (*indicating place, position, with
place names*) en; **in the house/garden** en
(la) casa/el jardín; **in here/there** aquí/
ahí or allí dentro; **in London/England** en
Londres/Inglaterra
2 (*indicating time*) en; **in spring** en (la)
primavera; **in the afternoon** por la tarde;
at 4 o'clock in the afternoon a las 4 de la
tarde; **I did it in 3 hours/days** lo hice en 3
horas/días; **I'll see you in 2 weeks** *or* **in 2
weeks' time** te veré dentro de 2 semanas
3 (*indicating manner etc*) en; **in a loud/soft
voice** en voz alta/baja; **in pencil/ink** a
lápiz/bolígrafo; **the boy in the blue shirt** el
chico de la camisa azul
4 (*indicating circumstances*): **in the sun/
shade/rain** al sol/a la sombra/bajo la
lluvia; **a change in policy** un cambio de
política
5 (*indicating mood, state*): **in tears** en
lágrimas, llorando; **in anger/despair**
enfadado/desesperado; **to live in luxury**
vivir lujosamente
6 (*with ratios, numbers*): **1 in 10 households,
1 household in 10** una de cada 10 familias;

20 pence in the pound 20 peniques por
libra; **they lined up in twos** se alinearon de
dos en dos
7 (*referring to people, works*) en; entre;
the disease is common in children la
enfermedad es común entre los niños; **in
(the works of) Dickens** en (las obras de)
Dickens
8 (*indicating profession etc*): **to be in teaching**
estar en la enseñanza
9 (*after superlative*) de; **the best pupil in the
class** el(la) mejor alumno/a de la clase
10 (*with present participle*): **in saying this** al
decir esto
▷ *adv*: **to be in** (*person: at home*) estar en
casa; (*at work*) estar; (*train, ship, plane*) haber
llegado; (*in fashion*) estar de moda; **she'll be
in later today** llegará más tarde hoy; **to ask
sb in** hacer pasar a algn; **to run/limp** *etc* **in**
entrar corriendo/cojeando *etc*
▷ *n*: **the ins and outs** (*of proposal, situation
etc*) los detalles

inability [ɪnə'bɪlɪtɪ] *n*: **~ (to do)**
incapacidad f (de hacer)
inaccurate [ɪn'ækjurət] *adj* inexacto,
incorrecto
inadequate [ɪn'ædɪkwət] *adj* (*income,
reply etc*) insuficiente; (*person*) incapaz
inadvertently [ɪnəd'vəːtntlɪ] *adv* por
descuido
inappropriate [ɪnə'prəupriət] *adj*
inadecuado; (*improper*) poco oportuno
inaugurate [ɪ'nɔːɡjureɪt] *vt* inaugurar;
(*president, official*) investir
Inc. (*us*) *abbr* (*= incorporated*) S.A.
incapable [ɪn'keɪpəbl] *adj* incapaz
incense [*n* 'ɪnsɛns, *vb* ɪn'sɛns] *n* incienso
▷ *vt* (*anger*) indignar, encolerizar
incentive [ɪn'sɛntɪv] *n* incentivo,
estímulo
inch [ɪntʃ] *n* pulgada; **to be within an ~ of**
estar a dos dedos de; **he didn't give an ~** no
dio concesión alguna
incidence ['ɪnsɪdns] *n* (*of crime, disease*)
incidencia
incident ['ɪnsɪdnt] *n* incidente m
incidentally [ɪnsɪ'dɛntəlɪ] *adv* (*by the
way*) a propósito
inclination [ɪnklɪ'neɪʃən] *n* (*tendency*)
tendencia, inclinación f; (*desire*) deseo;
(*disposition*) propensión f
incline [*n* 'ɪnklaɪn, *vb* ɪn'klaɪn] *n*
pendiente m, cuesta ▷ *vt* (*head*) poner de
lado ▷ *vi* inclinarse; **to be ~d to** (*tend*) tener
tendencia a hacer algo
include [ɪn'kluːd] *vt* (*incorporate*) incluir;
(*in letter*) adjuntar; **including** *prep* incluso,

inclusive

inclusion [ɪnˈkluːʒən] n inclusión f

inclusive [ɪnˈkluːsɪv] adj inclusivo; **~ of tax** incluidos los impuestos

income [ˈɪŋkʌm] n (earned) ingresos mpl; (from property etc) renta; (from investment etc) rédito; **income support** n (BRIT) ≈ ayuda familiar; **income tax** n impuesto sobre la renta

incoming [ˈɪnkʌmɪŋ] adj (flight, government etc) entrante

incompatible [ɪnkəmˈpætɪbl] adj incompatible

incompetence [ɪnˈkɔmpɪtəns] n incompetencia

incompetent [ɪnˈkɔmpɪtənt] adj incompetente

incomplete [ɪnkəmˈpliːt] adj (partial: achievement etc) incompleto; (unfinished: painting etc) inacabado

inconsistent [ɪnkənˈsɪstənt] adj inconsecuente; (contradictory) incongruente; **~ with** (que) no concuerda con

inconvenience [ɪnkənˈviːnjəns] n inconvenientes mpl; (trouble) molestia, incomodidad f ▷ vt incomodar

inconvenient [ɪnkənˈviːnjənt] adj incómodo, poco práctico; (time, place, visitor) inoportuno

incorporate [ɪnˈkɔːpəreɪt] vt incorporar; (contain) comprender; (add) agregar

incorrect [ɪnkəˈrekt] adj incorrecto

increase n [ˈɪnkriːs, vb ɪnˈkriːs] n aumento ▷ vi aumentar; (grow) crecer; (price) subir ▷ vt aumentar; (price) subir; **increasingly** adv cada vez más, más y más

incredible [ɪnˈkredɪbl] adj increíble; **incredibly** adv increíblemente

incur [ɪnˈkəː*] vt (expenditure) incurrir; (loss) sufrir; (anger, disapproval) provocar

indecent [ɪnˈdiːsnt] adj indecente

indeed [ɪnˈdiːd] adv efectivamente, en realidad; (in fact) en efecto; (furthermore) es más; **yes ~!** ¡claro que sí!

indefinitely [ɪnˈdefɪnɪtlɪ] adv (wait) indefinidamente

independence [ɪndɪˈpendns] n independencia; **Independence Day** (US) n Día m de la Independencia

independent [ɪndɪˈpendənt] adj independiente; **independent school** n (BRIT) escuela f privada, colegio m privado

index [ˈɪndeks] (pl **-es**) n (in book) índice m; (: in library etc) catálogo; (pl **indices**: ratio, sign) exponente m

India [ˈɪndɪə] n la India; **Indian** adj, n indio/a; **Red Indian** piel roja mf

indicate [ˈɪndɪkeɪt] vt indicar; **indication** [-ˈkeɪʃən] n indicio, señal f; **indicative** [ɪnˈdɪkətɪv] adj: **to be indicative of** indicar; **indicator** n indicador m; (Aut) intermitente m

indices [ˈɪndɪsiːz] npl of **index**

indict [ɪnˈdaɪt] vt acusar; **indictment** n acusación f

indifference [ɪnˈdɪfrəns] n indiferencia

indifferent [ɪnˈdɪfrənt] adj indiferente; (mediocre) regular

indigenous [ɪnˈdɪdʒɪnəs] adj indígena

indigestion [ɪndɪˈdʒestʃən] n indigestión f

indignant [ɪnˈdɪɡnənt] adj: **to be ~ at sth/ with sb** indignarse por algo/con algn

indirect [ɪndɪˈrekt] adj indirecto

indispensable [ɪndɪˈspensəbl] adj indispensable, imprescindible

individual [ɪndɪˈvɪdjuəl] n individuo ▷ adj individual; (personal) personal; (particular) particular; **individually** adv (singly) individualmente

Indonesia [ɪndəˈniːzɪə] n Indonesia

indoor [ˈɪndɔː*] adj (swimming pool) cubierto; (plant) de interior; (sport) bajo cubierta; **indoors** [ɪnˈdɔːz] adv dentro

induce [ɪnˈdjuːs] vt inducir, persuadir; (bring about) producir; (labour) provocar

indulge [ɪnˈdʌldʒ] vt (whim) satisfacer; (person) complacer; (child) mimar ▷ vi: **to ~ in** darse el gusto de; **indulgent** adj indulgente

industrial [ɪnˈdʌstrɪəl] adj industrial; **industrial estate** (BRIT) n polígono (SP) or zona (LAM) industrial; **industrialist** n industrial mf; **industrial park** (US) n = **industrial estate**

industry [ˈɪndəstrɪ] n industria; (diligence) aplicación f

inefficient [ɪnɪˈfɪʃənt] adj ineficaz, ineficiente

inequality [ɪnɪˈkwɔlɪtɪ] n desigualdad f

inevitable [ɪnˈevɪtəbl] adj inevitable; **inevitably** adv inevitablemente

i

inexpensive [ɪnɪk'spɛnsɪv] *adj* económico

inexperienced [ɪnɪk'spɪərɪənst] *adj* inexperto

inexplicable [ɪnɪk'splɪkəbl] *adj* inexplicable

infamous ['ɪnfəməs] *adj* infame

infant ['ɪnfənt] *n* niño/a; (*baby*) niño/a pequeño/a, bebé *mf*; (*pej*) aniñado

infantry ['ɪnfəntrɪ] *n* infantería

infant school (*BRIT*) *n* parvulario

infect [ɪn'fɛkt] *vt* (*wound*) infectar; (*food*) contaminar; (*person, animal*) contagiar; **infection** [ɪn'fɛkʃən] *n* infección *f*; (*fig*) contagio; **infectious** [ɪn'fɛkʃəs] *adj* (*also fig*) contagioso

infer [ɪn'fə:*] *vt* deducir, inferir

inferior [ɪn'fɪərɪə*] *adj*, *n* inferior *mf*

infertile [ɪn'fə:taɪl] *adj* estéril; (*person*) infecundo

infertility [ɪnfə:'tɪlɪtɪ] *n* esterilidad *f*; infecundidad *f*

infested [ɪn'fɛstɪd] *adj*: **~ with** plagado de

infinite ['ɪnfɪnɪt] *adj* infinito; **infinitely** *adv* infinitamente

infirmary [ɪn'fə:mərɪ] *n* hospital *m*

inflamed [ɪn'fleɪmd] *adj*: **to become ~** inflamarse

inflammation [ɪnflə'meɪʃən] *n* inflamación *f*

inflatable [ɪn'fleɪtəbl] *adj* (*ball, boat*) inflable

inflate [ɪn'fleɪt] *vt* (*tyre, price etc*) inflar; (*fig*) hinchar; **inflation** [ɪn'fleɪʃən] *n* (*Econ*) inflación *f*

inflexible [ɪn'flɛksəbl] *adj* (*rule*) rígido; (*person*) inflexible

inflict [ɪn'flɪkt] *vt*: **to ~ sth on sb** infligir algo en algn

influence ['ɪnfluəns] *n* influencia ▷ *vt* influir en, influenciar; **under the ~ of alcohol** en estado de embriaguez; **influential** [-'ɛnʃl] *adj* influyente

influx ['ɪnflʌks] *n* afluencia

info (*inf*) ['ɪnfəu] *n* = **information**

inform [ɪn'fɔ:m] *vt*: **to ~ sb of sth** informar a algn sobre *or* de algo ▷ *vi*: **to ~ on sb** delatar a algn

informal [ɪn'fɔ:məl] *adj* (*manner, tone*) familiar; (*dress, interview, occasion*) informal; (*visit, meeting*) extraoficial

information [ɪnfə'meɪʃən] *n* información *f*; (*knowledge*) conocimientos *mpl*; **a piece of ~** un dato; **information office** *n* información *f*; **information technology** *n* informática

informative [ɪn'fɔ:mətɪv] *adj* informativo

infra-red [ɪnfrə'rɛd] *adj* infrarrojo

infrastructure ['ɪnfrəstrʌktʃə*] *n* (*of system etc*) infraestructura

infrequent [ɪn'fri:kwənt] *adj* infrecuente

infuriate [ɪn'fjuərɪeɪt] *vt*: **to become ~d** ponerse furioso

infuriating [ɪn'fjuərɪeɪtɪŋ] *adj* (*habit, noise*) enloquecedor(a)

ingenious [ɪn'dʒi:njəs] *adj* ingenioso

ingredient [ɪn'gri:dɪənt] *n* ingrediente *m*

inhabit [ɪn'hæbɪt] *vt* vivir en; **inhabitant** *n* habitante *mf*

inhale [ɪn'heɪl] *vt* inhalar ▷ *vi* (*breathe in*) aspirar; (*in smoking*) tragar; **inhaler** *n* inhalador *m*

inherent [ɪn'hɪərənt] *adj*: **~ in** *or* **to** inherente a

inherit [ɪn'hɛrɪt] *vt* heredar; **inheritance** *n* herencia; (*fig*) patrimonio

inhibit [ɪn'hɪbɪt] *vt* inhibir, impedir; **inhibition** [-'bɪʃən] *n* cohibición *f*

initial [ɪ'nɪʃl] *adj* primero ▷ *n* inicial *f* ▷ *vt* firmar con las iniciales; **initials** *npl* (*as signature*) iniciales *fpl*; (*abbreviation*) siglas *fpl*; **initially** *adv* al principio

initiate [ɪ'nɪʃɪeɪt] *vt* iniciar; **to ~ proceedings against sb** (*Law*) entablar proceso contra algn

initiative [ɪ'nɪʃətɪv] *n* iniciativa

inject [ɪn'dʒɛkt] *vt* inyectar; **to ~ sb with sth** inyectar algo a algn; **injection** [ɪn'dʒɛkʃən] *n* inyección *f*

injure ['ɪndʒə*] *vt* (*hurt*) herir, lastimar; (*fig: reputation etc*) perjudicar; **injured** *adj* (*person, arm*) herido, lastimado; **injury** *n* herida, lesión *f*; (*wrong*) perjuicio, daño

▌ Be careful not to translate **injury** by the Spanish word *injuria*.

injustice [ɪn'dʒʌstɪs] *n* injusticia

ink [ɪŋk] *n* tinta; **ink-jet printer** ['ɪŋkdʒɛt-] *n* impresora de chorro de tinta

inland [*adj* 'ɪnlənd, *adv* ɪn'lænd] *adj* (*waterway, port etc*) interior ▷ *adv* tierra adentro; **Inland Revenue** (*BRIT*) *n* departamento de impuestos ≈ Hacienda (*SP*)

in-laws ['ɪnlɔ:z] *npl* suegros *mpl*

inmate ['ɪnmeɪt] *n* (*in prison*) preso/a, presidiario/a; (*in asylum*) internado/a

inn [ɪn] *n* posada, mesón *m*

inner ['ɪnə*] *adj* (*courtyard, calm*) interior; (*feelings*) íntimo; **inner-city** *adj* (*schools, problems*) de las zonas céntricas pobres, de los barrios céntricos pobres

inning ['ɪnɪŋ] *n* (*us: Baseball*) inning *m*, entrada; **~s** (*Cricket*) entrada, turno

innocence ['ɪnəsns] *n* inocencia

innocent ['ɪnəsnt] *adj* inocente

innovation [ɪnəʊˈveɪʃən] n novedad f
innovative [ˈɪnəʊveɪtɪv] adj innovador
in-patient [ˈɪnpeɪʃənt] n paciente m/f
interno/a
input [ˈɪnpʊt] n entrada; (of resources)
inversión f; (Comput) entrada de datos
inquest [ˈɪnkwɛst] n (coroner's) encuesta
judicial
inquire [ɪnˈkwaɪə*] vi preguntar ▷ vt: **to
~ whether** preguntar si; **to ~ about** (person)
preguntar por; (fact) informarse de; **inquiry**
n pregunta; (investigation) investigación f,
pesquisa; **"Inquiries"** "Información"
ins. abbr = inches
insane [ɪnˈseɪn] adj loco; (Med) demente
insanity [ɪnˈsænɪtɪ] n demencia, locura
insect [ˈɪnsɛkt] n insecto; **insect
repellent** n loción f contra insectos
insecure [ɪnsɪˈkjʊə*] adj inseguro
insecurity [ɪnsɪˈkjʊərɪtɪ] n inseguridad f
insensitive [ɪnˈsɛnsɪtɪv] adj insensible
insert [vb ɪnˈsəːt, n ˈɪnsəːt] vt (into sth)
introducir ▷ n encarte m
inside [ˈɪnsaɪd] n interior m ▷ adj interior,
interno ▷ adv (be) (por) dentro; (go) hacia
dentro ▷ prep dentro de; (of time): **~ 10
minutes** en menos de 10 minutos; **inside
lane** n (Aut: in Britain) carril m izquierdo;
(: in US, Europe etc) carril m derecho; **inside
out** adv (turn) al revés; (know) a fondo
insight [ˈɪnsaɪt] n perspicacia
insignificant [ɪnsɪgˈnɪfɪknt] adj
insignificante
insincere [ɪnsɪnˈsɪə*] adj poco sincero
insist [ɪnˈsɪst] vi insistir; **to ~ on** insistir
en; **to ~ that** insistir en que; (claim) exigir
que; **insistent** adj insistente; (noise, action)
persistente
insomnia [ɪnˈsɔmnɪə] n insomnio
inspect [ɪnˈspɛkt] vt inspeccionar,
examinar; (troops) pasar revista a;
inspection [ɪnˈspɛkʃən] n inspección f,
examen m; (of troops) revista; **inspector**
n inspector(a) m/f; (BRIT: on buses, trains)
revisor(a) m/f
inspiration [ɪnspəˈreɪʃən] n inspiración
f; **inspire** [ɪnˈspaɪə*] vt inspirar; **inspiring**
adj inspirador(a)
instability [ɪnstəˈbɪlɪtɪ] n inestabilidad f
install [ɪnˈstɔːl] (US **instal**) vt instalar;
(official) nombrar; **installation** [ɪnstəˈleɪʃən]
n instalación f
instalment [ɪnˈstɔːlmənt] (US
installment) n plazo; (of story) entrega;
(of TV serial etc) capítulo; **in ~s** (pay, receive)
a plazos
instance [ˈɪnstəns] n ejemplo, caso; **for ~**
por ejemplo; **in the first ~** en primer lugar

instant [ˈɪnstənt] n instante m, momento
▷ adj inmediato; (coffee etc) instantáneo;
instantly adv en seguida; **instant
messaging** n mensajería instantánea
instead [ɪnˈstɛd] adv en cambio; **~ of** en
lugar de, en vez de
instinct [ˈɪnstɪŋkt] n instinto; **instinctive**
adj instintivo
institute [ˈɪnstɪtjuːt] n instituto;
(professional body) colegio ▷ vt (begin)
iniciar, empezar; (proceedings) entablar;
(system, rule) establecer
institution [ɪnstɪˈtjuːʃən] n institución
f; (Med: home) asilo; (: asylum) manicomio;
(of system etc) establecimiento; (of custom)
iniciación f
instruct [ɪnˈstrʌkt] vt: **to ~ sb in sth**
instruir a algn en or sobre algo; **to ~ sb to
do sth** dar instrucciones a algn de hacer
algo; **instruction** [ɪnˈstrʌkʃən] n (teaching)
instrucción f; **instructions** npl (orders)
órdenes fpl; **instructions (for use)** modo de
empleo; **instructor** n instructor(a) m/f
instrument [ˈɪnstrəmənt] n
instrumento; **instrumental** [-ˈmɛntl] adj
(Mus) instrumental; **to be instrumental in**
ser (el) artífice de
insufficient [ɪnsəˈfɪʃənt] adj insuficiente
insulate [ˈɪnsjuleɪt] vt aislar; **insulation**
[-ˈleɪʃən] n aislamiento
insulin [ˈɪnsjulɪn] n insulina
insult [n ˈɪnsʌlt, vb ɪnˈsʌlt] n insulto ▷ vt
insultar; **insulting** adj insultante
insurance [ɪnˈʃuərəns] n seguro; **fire/
life ~** seguro contra incendios/sobre la
vida; **insurance company** n compañía f
de seguros; **insurance policy** n póliza (de
seguros)
insure [ɪnˈʃuə*] vt asegurar
intact [ɪnˈtækt] adj íntegro; (unharmed)
intacto
intake [ˈɪnteɪk] n (of food) ingestión f; (of
air) consumo; (BRIT Scol): **an ~ of 200 a year**
200 matriculados al año
integral [ˈɪntɪgrəl] adj (whole) íntegro;
(part) integrante
integrate [ˈɪntɪgreɪt] vt integrar ▷ vi
integrarse
integrity [ɪnˈtɛgrɪtɪ] n honradez f,
rectitud f
intellect [ˈɪntəlɛkt] n intelecto;
intellectual [-ˈlɛktjuəl] adj, n intelectual
mf
intelligence [ɪnˈtɛlɪdʒəns] n inteligencia
intelligent [ɪnˈtɛlɪdʒənt] adj inteligente
intend [ɪnˈtɛnd] vt (gift etc): **to ~ sth
for** destinar algo a; **to ~ to do sth** tener
intención de or pensar hacer algo

intense [ɪn'tɛns] *adj* intenso

intensify [ɪn'tɛnsɪfaɪ] *vt* intensificar; (*increase*) aumentar

intensity [ɪn'tɛnsɪtɪ] *n* (*gen*) intensidad *f*

intensive [ɪn'tɛnsɪv] *adj* intensivo; **intensive care** *n*: **to be in intensive care** estar bajo cuidados intensivos; **intensive care unit** *n* unidad *f* de vigilancia intensiva

intent [ɪn'tɛnt] *n* propósito; (*Law*) premeditación *f* ▷ *adj* (*absorbed*) absorto; (*attentive*) atento; **to all ~s and purposes** prácticamente; **to be ~ on doing sth** estar resuelto a hacer algo

intention [ɪn'tɛnʃən] *n* intención *f*, propósito; **intentional** *adj* deliberado

interact [ɪntər'ækt] *vi* influirse mutuamente; **interaction** [ɪntər'ækʃən] *n* interacción *f*, acción *f* recíproca; **interactive** *adj* (*Comput*) interactivo

intercept [ɪntə'sɛpt] *vt* interceptar; (*stop*) detener

interchange ['ɪntətʃeɪndʒ] *n* intercambio; (*on motorway*) intersección *f*

intercourse ['ɪntəkɔːs] *n* (*sexual*) relaciones *fpl* sexuales

interest ['ɪntrɪst] *n* (*also Comm*) interés *m* ▷ *vt* interesar; **interested** *adj* interesado; **to be interested in** interesarse por; **interesting** *adj* interesante; **interest rate** *n* tipo or tasa de interés

interface ['ɪntəfeɪs] *n* (*Comput*) junción *f*

interfere [ɪntə'fɪə*] *vi*: **to ~ in** entrometerse en; **to ~ with** (*hinder*) estorbar; (*damage*) estropear

interference [ɪntə'fɪərəns] *n* intromisión *f*; (*Radio, TV*) interferencia

interim ['ɪntərɪm] *n*: **in the ~** en el ínterin ▷ *adj* provisional

interior [ɪn'tɪərɪə*] *n* interior *m* ▷ *adj* interior; **interior design** *n* interiorismo, decoración *f* de interiores

intermediate [ɪntə'miːdɪət] *adj* intermedio

intermission [ɪntə'mɪʃən] *n* intermisión *f*; (*Theatre*) descanso

intern [*vb* ɪn'tɜːn, *n* 'ɪntɜːn] (*US*) *vt* internar ▷ *n* interno/a

internal [ɪn'tɜːnl] *adj* (*layout, pipes, security*) interior; (*injury, structure, memo*) internal; **Internal Revenue Service** (*US*) *n* departamento de impuestos, ≈ Hacienda (*SP*)

international [ɪntə'næʃənl] *adj* internacional ▷ *n* (*BRIT: match*) partido internacional

Internet ['ɪntənɛt] *n*: **the ~** Internet *m* or *f*; **Internet café** *n* cibercafé *m*; **Internet Service Provider** *n* proveedor *m* de (acceso a) Internet; **Internet user** *n* internauta *mf*

interpret [ɪn'tɜːprɪt] *vt* interpretar; (*translate*) traducir; (*understand*) entender ▷ *vi* hacer de intérprete; **interpretation** [ɪntɜːprɪ'teɪʃən] *n* interpretación *f*; traducción *f*; **interpreter** *n* intérprete *mf*

interrogate [ɪn'tɛrəʊgeɪt] *vt* interrogar; **interrogation** [-'geɪʃən] *n* interrogatorio

interrogative [ɪntə'rɔgətɪv] *adj* interrogativo

interrupt [ɪntə'rʌpt] *vt, vi* interrumpir; **interruption** [-'rʌpʃən] *n* interrupción *f*

intersection [ɪntə'sɛkʃən] *n* (*of roads*) cruce *m*

interstate ['ɪntəsteɪt] (*US*) *n* carretera interestatal

interval ['ɪntəvl] *n* intervalo; (*BRIT Theatre, Sport*) descanso; (*Scol*) recreo; **at ~s** a ratos, de vez en cuando

intervene [ɪntə'viːn] *vi* intervenir; (*event*) interponerse; (*time*) transcurrir

interview ['ɪntəvjuː] *n* entrevista ▷ *vt* entrevistarse con; **interviewer** *n* entrevistador(a) *m/f*

intimate [*adj* 'ɪntɪmət, *vb* 'ɪntɪmeɪt] *adj* íntimo; (*friendship*) estrecho; (*knowledge*) profundo ▷ *vt* dar a entender

intimidate [ɪn'tɪmɪdeɪt] *vt* intimidar, amedrentar

intimidating [ɪn'tɪmɪdeɪtɪŋ] *adj* amedrentador, intimidante

into ['ɪntuː] *prep* en; (*towards*) a; (*inside*) hacia el interior de; **~ 3 pieces/French** en 3 pedazos/al francés

intolerant [ɪn'tɔlərənt] *adj*: **~ (of)** intolerante (con or para)

intranet ['ɪntrənɛt] *n* intranet *f*

intransitive [ɪn'trænsɪtɪv] *adj* intransitivo

intricate ['ɪntrɪkət] *adj* (*design, pattern*) intrincado

intrigue [ɪn'triːg] *n* intriga ▷ *vt* fascinar; **intriguing** *adj* fascinante

introduce [ɪntrə'djuːs] *vt* introducir, meter; (*speaker, TV show etc*) presentar; **to ~ sb (to sb)** presentar a algn (a algn); **to ~ sb to** (*pastime, technique*) introducir a algn a; **introduction** [-'dʌkʃən] *n* introducción *f*; (*of person*) presentación *f*; **introductory** [-'dʌktərɪ] *adj* introductorio; (*lesson, offer*) de introducción

intrude [ɪn'truːd] *vi* (*person*) entrometerse; **to ~ on** estorbar; **intruder** *n* intruso/a

intuition [ɪntjuː'ɪʃən] *n* intuición *f*

inundate ['ɪnʌndeɪt] *vt*: **to ~ with** inundar de

invade [ɪn'veɪd] *vt* invadir

invalid [n 'ɪnvəlɪd, adj ɪn'vælɪd] n (Med) minusválido/a ▷ adj (not valid) inválido, nulo

invaluable [ɪn'væljuəbl] adj inestimable

invariably [ɪn'vɛərɪəblɪ] adv sin excepción, siempre; **she is ~ late** siempre llega tarde

invasion [ɪn'veɪʒən] n invasión f

invent [ɪn'vɛnt] vt inventar; **invention** [ɪn'vɛnʃən] n invento; (lie) ficción f, mentira; **inventor** n inventor(a) m/f

inventory ['ɪnvəntrɪ] n inventario

inverted commas [ɪn'vəːtɪd-] npl comillas fpl

invest [ɪn'vɛst] vt invertir ▷ vi: **to ~ in** (company etc) invertir dinero en; (fig: sth useful) comprar

investigate [ɪn'vɛstɪɡeɪt] vt investigar; **investigation** [-'ɡeɪʃən] n investigación f, pesquisa

investigator [ɪn'vɛstɪɡeɪtə*] n investigador(a) m/f; **private ~** investigador(a) m/f privado/a

investment [ɪn'vɛstmənt] n inversión f

investor [ɪn'vɛstə*] n inversionista mf

invisible [ɪn'vɪzɪbl] adj invisible

invitation [ɪnvɪ'teɪʃən] n invitación f

invite [ɪn'vaɪt] vt invitar; (opinions etc) solicitar, pedir; **inviting** adj atractivo; (food) apetitoso

invoice ['ɪnvɔɪs] n factura ▷ vt facturar

involve [ɪn'vɔlv] vt suponer, implicar; tener que ver con; (concern, affect) corresponder; **to ~ sb (in sth)** comprometer a algn (con algo); **involved** adj complicado; **to be involved in** (take part) tomar parte en; (be engrossed) estar muy metido en; **involvement** n participación f; dedicación f

inward ['ɪnwəd] adj (movement) interior, interno; (thought, feeling) íntimo; **inward(s)** adv hacia dentro

iPod ® ['aɪpɔd] n iPod ® m

IQ n abbr (= intelligence quotient) cociente m intelectual

IRA n abbr (= Irish Republican Army) IRA m

Iran [ɪ'rɑːn] n Irán m; **Iranian** [ɪ'reɪnɪən] adj, n iraní mf

Iraq [ɪ'rɑːk] n Iraq; **Iraqi** adj, n iraquí mf

Ireland ['aɪələnd] n Irlanda

iris ['aɪrɪs] (pl **-es**) n (Anat) iris m; (Bot) lirio

Irish ['aɪrɪʃ] adj irlandés/esa ▷ npl: **the ~** los irlandeses; **Irishman** (irreg) n irlandés m; **Irishwoman** (irreg) n irlandésa

iron ['aɪən] n hierro; (for clothes) plancha ▷ cpd de hierro ▷ vt (clothes) planchar

ironic(al) [aɪ'rɔnɪk(l)] adj irónico; **ironically** adv irónicamente

ironing ['aɪənɪŋ] n (activity) planchadò; (clothes: ironed) ropa planchada; (: to be ironed) ropa por planchar; **ironing board** n tabla de planchar

irony ['aɪrənɪ] n ironía

irrational [ɪ'ræʃənl] adj irracional

irregular [ɪ'regjulə*] adj irregular; (surface) desigual; (action, event) anómalo; (behaviour) poco ortodoxo

irrelevant [ɪ'rɛləvənt] adj fuera de lugar, inoportuno

irresistible [ɪrɪ'zɪstɪbl] adj irresistible

irresponsible [ɪrɪ'spɔnsɪbl] adj (act) irresponsable; (person) poco serio

irrigation [ɪrɪ'ɡeɪʃən] n riego

irritable ['ɪrɪtəbl] adj (person) de mal humor

irritate ['ɪrɪteɪt] vt fastidiar; (Med) picar; **irritating** adj fastidioso; **irritation** [-'teɪʃən] n fastidio; enfado; picazón f

IRS (us) n abbr = **Internal Revenue Service**

is [ɪz] vb see **be**

ISDN n abbr (= Integrated Services Digital Network) RDSI f

Islam ['ɪzlɑːm] n Islam m; **Islamic** [ɪz'læmɪk] adj islámico

island ['aɪlənd] n isla; **islander** n isleño/a

isle [aɪl] n isla

isn't ['ɪznt] = **is not**

isolated ['aɪsəleɪtɪd] adj aislado

isolation [aɪsə'leɪʃən] n aislamiento

ISP n abbr = **Internet Service Provider**

Israel ['ɪzreɪl] n Israel m; **Israeli** [ɪz'reɪlɪ] adj, n israelí mf

issue ['ɪsjuː] n (problem, subject) cuestión f; (outcome) resultado; (of banknotes etc) emisión f; (of newspaper etc) edición f ▷ vt (rations, equipment) distribuir, repartir; (orders) dar; (certificate, passport) expedir; (decree) promulgar; (magazine) publicar; (cheques) extender; (banknotes, stamps) emitir; **at ~** en cuestión; **to take ~ with sb (over)** estar en desacuerdo con algn (sobre); **to make an ~ of sth** hacer una cuestión de algo

IT n abbr = **information technology**

○ **KEYWORD**

it [ɪt] pron **1** (specific subject: not generally translated) él (ella); (: direct object) lo, la; (: indirect object) le; (after prep) él (ella); (abstract concept) ello; **it's on the table** está en la mesa; **I can't find it** no lo (or la) encuentro; **give it to me** dámelo (or dámela); **I spoke to him about it** le hablé del asunto; **what did you learn from it?** ¿qué aprendiste de él (or ella)?; **did you go**

to it? (*party, concert etc*) ¿fuiste?
2 (*impersonal*): **it's raining** llueve, está
lloviendo; **it's 6 o'clock/the 10th of**
August son los 6/es el 10 de agosto; **how far**
is it? – it's 10 miles/2 hours on the train ¿a
qué distancia está? – a 10 millas/2 horas en
tren; **who is it? – it's me** ¿quién es? – soy yo

Italian [ɪ'tæljən] *adj* italiano ▷ *n*
italiano/a; (*Ling*) italiano
italics [ɪ'tælɪks] *npl* cursiva
Italy ['ɪtəlɪ] *n* Italia
itch [ɪtʃ] *n* picazón *f* ▷ *vi* (*part of body*)
picar; **to ~ to do sth** rabiar por hacer algo;
itchy *adj*: **my hand is itchy** me pica la
mano
it'd ['ɪtd] = **it would**; **it had**
item ['aɪtəm] *n* artículo; (*on agenda*)
asunto (a tratar); (*also*: **news ~**) noticia
itinerary [aɪ'tɪnərərɪ] *n* itinerario
it'll ['ɪtl] = **it will**; **it shall**
its [ɪts] *adj* su; sus *pl*
it's [ɪts] = **it is**; **it has**
itself [ɪt'sɛlf] *pron* (*reflexive*) sí mismo/a;
(*emphatic*) él mismo(ella misma)
ITV *n abbr* (BRIT: = *Independent Television*)
cadena de televisión comercial independiente
del Estado
I've [aɪv] = **I have**
ivory ['aɪvərɪ] *n* marfil *m*
ivy ['aɪvɪ] *n* (*Bot*) hiedra

J

jab [dʒæb] *vt*: **to ~ sth into sth** clavar algo
en algo ▷ *n* (*inf: Med*) pinchazo
jack [dʒæk] *n* (*Aut*) gato; (*Cards*) sota
jacket ['dʒækɪt] *n* chaqueta, americana
(SP), saco (LAM); (*of book*) sobrecubierta;
jacket potato *n* patata asada (con piel)
jackpot ['dʒækpɔt] *n* premio gordo
Jacuzzi® [dʒə'kuːzɪ] *n* jacuzzi® *m*
jagged ['dʒægɪd] *adj* dentado
jail [dʒeɪl] *n* cárcel *f* ▷ *vt* encarcelar; **jail**
sentence *n* pena *f* de cárcel
jam [dʒæm] *n* mermelada; (*also*: **traffic ~**)
embotellamiento; (*inf: difficulty*) apuro ▷ *vt*
(*passage etc*) obstruir; (*mechanism, drawer etc*)
atascar; (*Radio*) interferir ▷ *vi* atascarse,
trabarse; **to ~ sth into sth** meter algo a la
fuerza en algo
Jamaica [dʒə'meɪkə] *n* Jamaica
jammed [dʒæmd] *adj* atascado
Jan *abbr* (= *January*) ene
janitor ['dʒænɪtə*] *n* (*caretaker*) portero,
conserje *m*
January ['dʒænjuərɪ] *n* enero
Japan [dʒə'pæn] *n* (el) Japón; **Japanese**
[dʒæpə'niːz] *adj* japonés/esa ▷ *n inv*
japonés/esa *m/f*; (*Ling*) japonés *m*
jar [dʒɑː*] *n* tarro, bote *m* ▷ *vi* (*sound*)
chirriar; (*colours*) desentonar
jargon ['dʒɑːgən] *n* jerga
javelin ['dʒævlɪn] *n* jabalina
jaw [dʒɔː] *n* mandíbula
jazz [dʒæz] *n* jazz *m*
jealous ['dʒɛləs] *adj* celoso; (*envious*)
envidioso; **jealousy** *n* celos *mpl*; envidia
jeans [dʒiːnz] *npl* vaqueros *mpl*, tejanos *mpl*
Jello® ['dʒɛləu] (us) *n* gelatina
jelly ['dʒɛlɪ] *n* (*jam*) jalea; (*dessert etc*)
gelatina; **jellyfish** *n inv* medusa, aguaviva
(RPL)
jeopardize ['dʒɛpədaɪz] *vt* arriesgar,
poner en peligro

jerk [dʒəːk] n (jolt) sacudida; (wrench) tirón m; (inf) imbécil mf ▷ vt tirar bruscamente de ▷ vi (vehicle) traquetear

Jersey ['dʒəːzɪ] n Jersey m

jersey ['dʒəːzɪ] n jersey m; (fabric) (tejido de) punto

Jesus ['dʒiːzəs] n Jesús m

jet [dʒet] n (of gas, liquid) chorro; (Aviat) avión m a reacción; **jet lag** n desorientación f después de un largo vuelo; **jet-ski** vi practicar el motociclismo acuático

jetty ['dʒetɪ] n muelle m, embarcadero

Jew [dʒuː] n judío/a

jewel ['dʒuːəl] n joya; (in watch) rubí m; (jeweller (us jeweler) n joyero/a; **jeweller's (shop)** (us **jewelry store**) n joyería; **jewellery** (us **jewelry**) n joyas fpl, alhajas fpl

Jewish ['dʒuːɪʃ] adj judío

jigsaw ['dʒɪgsɔː] n (also: ~ **puzzle**) rompecabezas m inv, puzle m

job [dʒɔb] n (task) tarea; (post) empleo; **it's not my** ~ no me incumbe a mí; **it's a good ~ that ...** menos mal que ...; **just the** ~! ¡estupendo!; **job centre** (BRIT) n oficina estatal de colocaciones; **jobless** adj sin trabajo

jockey ['dʒɔkɪ] n jockey mf ▷ vi: **to ~ for position** maniobrar para conseguir una posición

jog [dʒɔg] vt empujar (ligeramente) ▷ vi (run) hacer footing; **to ~ sb's memory** refrescar la memoria a algn; **jogging** n footing m

join [dʒɔɪn] vt (things) juntar, unir; (club) hacerse socio de; (Pol: party) afiliarse a; (queue) ponerse en; (meet: people) reunirse con ▷ vi (roads) juntarse; (rivers) confluir ▷ n juntura; **join in** vi tomar parte, participar ▷ vt fus tomar parte or participar en; **join up** vi reunirse; (Mil) alistarse

joiner ['dʒɔɪnə*] (BRIT) n carpintero/a

joint [dʒɔɪnt] n (Tech) junta, unión f; (Anat) articulación f; (BRIT Culin) pieza de carne (para asar); (inf: place) tugurio; (: of cannabis) porro ▷ adj (common) común; (combined) combinado; **joint account** n (with bank etc) cuenta común; **jointly** adv (gen) en común; (together) conjuntamente

joke [dʒəuk] n chiste m; (also: **practical ~**) broma ▷ vi bromear; **to play a ~ on** gastar una broma a; **joker** n (Cards) comodín m

jolly ['dʒɔlɪ] adj (merry) alegre; (enjoyable) divertido ▷ adv (BRIT: inf) muy, terriblemente

jolt [dʒəult] n (jerk) sacudida; (shock) susto ▷ vt (physically) sacudir; (emotionally) asustar

Jordan ['dʒɔːdən] n (country) Jordania; (river) Jordán m

journal ['dʒəːnl] n (magazine) revista; (diary) periódico, diario; **journalism** n periodismo; **journalist** n periodista mf, reportero/a

journey ['dʒəːnɪ] n viaje m; (distance covered) trayecto

joy [dʒɔɪ] n alegría; **joyrider** n gamberro que roba un coche para dar una vuelta y luego abandonarlo; **joy stick** n (Aviat) palanca de mando; (Comput) palanca de control

Jr abbr = **junior**

judge [dʒʌdʒ] n juez mf; (fig: expert) perito ▷ vt juzgar; (consider) considerar

judo ['dʒuːdəu] n judo

jug [dʒʌg] n jarra

juggle ['dʒʌgl] vi hacer juegos malabares; **juggler** n malabarista mf

juice [dʒuːs] n zumo (SP), jugo (LAM); **juicy** adj jugoso

Jul abbr (= July) jul

July [dʒuː'laɪ] n julio

jumble ['dʒʌmbl] n revoltijo ▷ vt (also: ~ **up**) revolver; **jumble sale** (BRIT) n venta de objetos usados con fines benéficos

● **JUMBLE SALE**
●
● Los **jumble sales** son unos mercadillos
● que se organizan con fines benéficos
● en los locales de un colegio, iglesia u
● otro centro público. En ellos puede
● comprarse todo tipo de artículos
● baratos de segunda mano, sobre
● todo ropa, juguetes, libros, vajillas o
● muebles.

jumbo ['dʒʌmbəu] n (also: ~ **jet**) jumbo

jump [dʒʌmp] vi saltar, dar saltos; (with fear etc) pegar un bote; (increase) aumentar ▷ vt saltar ▷ n salto; aumento; **to ~ the queue** (BRIT) colarse

jumper ['dʒʌmpə*] n (BRIT: pullover) suéter m, jersey m; (US: dress) mandil m

jumper cables (US) npl = **jump leads**

jump leads (BRIT) npl cables mpl puente de batería

Jun. abbr = **junior**

junction ['dʒʌŋkʃən] n (BRIT: of roads) cruce m; (Rail) empalme m

June [dʒuːn] n junio

jungle ['dʒʌŋgl] n selva, jungla

junior ['dʒuːnɪə*] adj (in age) menor, más joven; (brother/sister etc): **seven years her ~** siete años menor que ella; (position) subalterno ▷ n menor mf, joven mf; **junior high school** (US) n centro de educación

secundaria; see also **high school**; **junior school** (BRIT) n escuela primaria

junk [dʒʌŋk] n (cheap goods) baratijas fpl; (rubbish) basura; **junk food** n alimentos preparados y envasados de escaso valor nutritivo

junkie ['dʒʌŋkɪ] (inf) n drogadicto/a, yonqui mf

junk mail n propaganda de buzón

Jupiter ['dʒuːpɪtə*] n (Mythology, Astrology) Júpiter m

jurisdiction [dʒuərɪs'dɪkʃən] n jurisdicción f; **it falls** or **comes within/ outside our ~** es/no es de nuestra competencia

jury ['dʒuərɪ] n jurado

just [dʒʌst] adj justo ▷ adv (exactly) exactamente; (only) sólo, solamente; **he's ~ done it/left** acaba de hacerlo/irse; **~ right** perfecto; **~ two o'clock** las dos en punto; **she's ~ as clever as you** (ella) es tan lista como tú; **~ as well that ...** menos mal que ...; **~ as he was leaving** en el momento en que se marchaba; **~ before/enough** justo antes/lo suficiente; **~ here** aquí mismo; **he ~ missed** ha fallado por poco; **~ listen to this** escucha esto un momento

justice ['dʒʌstɪs] n justicia; (US: judge) juez mf; **to do ~ to** (fig) hacer justicia a

justification [dʒʌstɪfɪ'keɪʃən] n justificación f

justify ['dʒʌstɪfaɪ] vt justificar; (text) alinear

jut [dʒʌt] vi (also: **~ out**) sobresalir

juvenile ['dʒuːvənaɪl] adj (court) de menores; (humour, mentality) infantil ▷ n menor m de edad

K abbr (= one thousand) mil; (= kilobyte) kilobyte m, kiloocteto

kangaroo [kæŋɡə'ruː] n canguro

karaoke [kɑːrɑ'əʊkɪ] n karaoke

karate [kə'rɑːtɪ] n karate m

kebab [kə'bæb] n pincho moruno

keel [kiːl] n quilla; **on an even ~** (fig) en equilibrio

keen [kiːn] adj (interest, desire) grande, vivo; (eye, intelligence) agudo; (competition) reñido; (edge) afilado; (eager) entusiasta; **to be ~ to do** or **on doing sth** tener muchas ganas de hacer algo; **to be ~ on sth/sb** interesarse por algo/algn

keep [kiːp] (pt, pp **kept**) vt (preserve, store) guardar; (hold back) quedarse con; (maintain) mantener; (detain) detener; (shop) ser propietario de; (feed: family etc) mantener; (promise) cumplir; (chickens, bees etc) criar; (accounts) llevar; (diary) escribir; (prevent): **to ~ sb from doing sth** impedir a algn hacer algo ▷ vi (food) conservarse; (remain) seguir, continuar ▷ n (of castle) torreón m; (food etc) comida, subsistencia; (inf): **for ~s** para siempre; **to ~ doing sth** seguir haciendo algo; **to ~ sb happy** tener a algn contento; **to ~ a place tidy** mantener un lugar limpio; **to ~ sth to o.s.** guardar algo para sí mismo; **to ~ sth (back) from sb** ocultar algo a algn; **to ~ time** (clock) mantener la hora exacta; **keep away** vt: **to keep sth/sb away from sb** mantener algo/a algn apartado de algn ▷ vi: **to keep away (from)** mantenerse apartado (de); **keep back** vt (crowd, tears) contener; (money) quedarse con; (conceal: information): **to keep sth back from sb** ocultar algo a algn ▷ vi hacerse a un lado; **keep off** vt (dog, person) mantener a distancia ▷ vi: **if the rain keeps off** so no llueve; **keep your hands off!** ¡no toques!; **"keep off the grass"** "prohibido pisar el césped"; **keep on** vi: **to keep on doing** seguir or continuar haciendo; **to keep on (about sth)** no parar de hablar (de algo); **keep out** vi (stay out) permanecer fuera; **"keep out"** "prohibida la entrada"; **keep up** vt mantener, conservar ▷ vi no retrasarse; **to keep up with** (pace) ir al paso de; (level) mantenerse a la altura de; **keeper** n guardián/ana m/f; **keeping** n (care) cuidado; **in keeping with** de acuerdo con

kennel ['kɛnl] n perrera; **kennels** npl residencia canina

Kenya ['kɛnjə] n Kenia

kept [kɛpt] pt, pp of **keep**

kerb [kə:b] (BRIT) n bordillo

kerosene ['kɛrəsi:n] n keroseno

ketchup ['kɛtʃəp] n salsa de tomate, catsup m

kettle ['kɛtl] n hervidor m de agua

key [ki:] n llave f; (Mus) tono; (of piano, typewriter) tecla ▷ adj (issue etc) clave inv ▷ vt (also: ~ **in**) teclear; **keyboard** n teclado; **keyhole** n ojo (de la cerradura); **keyring** n llavero

kg abbr (= kilogram) kg

khaki ['kɑ:kɪ] adj kaki

kick [kɪk] vt dar una patada or un puntapié a; (inf: habit) quitarse de ▷ vi (horse) dar coces ▷ n patada; puntapié m; (of animal) coz f; (thrill): **he does it for ~** s lo hace por pura diversión; **kick off** vi (Sport) hacer el saque inicial; **kick-off** n saque inicial; **the kick-off is at 10 o'clock** el partido empieza a las diez

kid [kɪd] n (inf: child) chiquillo/a; (animal) cabrito; (leather) cabritilla ▷ vi (inf) bromear

kidnap ['kɪdnæp] vt secuestrar; **kidnapping** n secuestro

kidney ['kɪdnɪ] n riñón m; **kidney bean** n judía, alubia

kill [kɪl] vt matar; (murder) asesinar ▷ n matanza; **to ~ time** matar el tiempo; **killer** n asesino/a; **killing** n (one) asesinato; (several) matanza; **to make a killing** (fig) hacer su agosto

kiln [kɪln] n horno

kilo ['ki:ləu] n kilo; **kilobyte** n (Comput) kilobyte m, kiloocteto; **kilogram(me)** n kilo, kilogramo; **kilometre** ['kɪləmi:tə*] (us **kilometer**) n kilómetro; **kilowatt** n kilovatio

kilt [kɪlt] n falda escocesa

kin [kɪn] n see **next-of-kin**

kind [kaɪnd] adj amable, atento ▷ n clase f, especie f; (species) género; **in ~** (Comm) en especie; **a ~ of** una especie de; **to be two of a ~** ser tal para cual

kindergarten ['kɪndəgɑ:tn] n jardín m de la infancia

kindly ['kaɪndlɪ] adj bondadoso; cariñoso ▷ adv bondadosamente, amablemente; **will you ~ ...** sea usted tan amable de ...

kindness ['kaɪndnɪs] n (quality) bondad f, amabilidad f; (act) favor m

king [kɪŋ] n rey m; **kingdom** n reino; **kingfisher** n martín m pescador; **king-size(d) bed** n cama de matrimonio extragrande

kiosk ['ki:ɔsk] n quiosco; (BRIT Tel) cabina

kipper ['kɪpə*] n arenque m ahumado

kiss [kɪs] n beso ▷ vt besar; **to ~ (each other)** besarse; **kiss of life** n respiración f boca a boca

kit [kɪt] n (equipment) equipo; (tools etc) (caja de) herramientas fpl; (assembly kit) juego de armar

kitchen ['kɪtʃɪn] n cocina

kite [kaɪt] n (toy) cometa

kitten ['kɪtn] n gatito/a

kiwi ['ki:wi:-] n (also: ~ **fruit**) kiwi m

km abbr (= kilometre) km

km/h abbr (= kilometres per hour) km/h

knack [næk] n: **to have the ~ of doing sth** tener el don de hacer algo

knee [ni:] n rodilla; **kneecap** n rótula

kneel [ni:l] (pt, pp knelt) vi (also: ~ **down**) arrodillarse

knelt [nɛlt] pt, pp of **kneel**

knew [nju:] pt of **know**

knickers ['nɪkəz] (BRIT) npl bragas fpl

knife [naɪf] (pl knives) n cuchillo ▷ vt acuchillar

knight [naɪt] n caballero; (Chess) caballo

knit [nɪt] vt tejer, tricotar ▷ vi hacer punto, tricotar; (bones) soldarse; **to ~ one's brows** fruncir el ceño; **knitting** n labor f de punto; **knitting needle** n aguja de hacer punto; **knitwear** n prendas fpl de punto

knives [naɪvz] npl of **knife**

knob [nɔb] n (of door) tirador m; (of stick) puño; (on radio, TV) botón m

knock [nɔk] vt (strike) golpear; (bump into) chocar contra; (inf) criticar ▷ vi (at door etc): **to ~ at/on** llamar a ▷ n golpe m; (on door) llamada; **knock down** vt atropellar; **knock off** (inf) vi (finish) salir del trabajo ▷ vt (from price) descontar; (inf: steal) birlar; **knock out** vt dejar sin sentido; (Boxing) poner fuera de combate, dejar K.O.; (in competition) eliminar; **knock over** vt (object) tirar; (person) atropellar; **knockout** n (Boxing) K.O. m, knockout m ▷ cpd (competition etc) eliminatorio

knot [nɔt] n nudo ▷ vt anudar

know [nəu] (pt knew, pp known) vt (facts) saber; (be acquainted with) conocer;

(*recognize*) reconocer, conocer; **to ~ how to swim** saber nadar; **to ~ about** *or* **of sb/sth** saber de algn/algo; **know-all** *n* sabelotodo *mf*; **know-how** *n* conocimientos *mpl*; **knowing** *adj* (*look*) de complicidad; **knowingly** *adv* (*purposely*) adrede; (*smile, look*) con complicidad; **know-it-all** (*US*) *n* = **know-all**

knowledge ['nɒlɪdʒ] *n* conocimiento; (*learning*) saber *m*, conocimientos *mpl*; **knowledgeable** *adj* entendido

known [nəun] *pp of* **know** ▷ *adj* (*thief, facts*) conocido; (*expert*) reconocido

knuckle ['nʌkl] *n* nudillo

koala [kəu'ɑ:lə] *n* (*also: ~ bear*) koala *m*

Koran [kɔ'rɑ:n] *n* Corán *m*

Korea [kə'rɪə] *n* Corea; **Korean** *adj, n* coreano/a *m/f*

kosher ['kəuʃə*] *adj* autorizado por la ley judía

Kosovar ['kɒsəvɑ*], **Kosovan** ['kɔ:səvən] *adj* kosovar

Kosovo ['kɒsəvəu] *n* Kosovo

Kremlin ['kremlɪn] *n*: **the ~** el Kremlin

Kuwait [ku'weɪt] *n* Kuwait *m*

L (*BRIT*) *abbr* = **learner driver**

l. *abbr* (= *litre*) l

lab [læb] *n abbr* = **laboratory**

label ['leɪbl] *n* etiqueta ▷ *vt* poner etiqueta a

labor *etc* ['leɪbə*] (*US*) = **labour** *etc*

laboratory [lə'bɒrətərɪ] *n* laboratorio

Labor Day (*US*) *n* día *m* de los trabajadores (*primer lunes de septiembre*)

labor union (*US*) *n* sindicato

labour ['leɪbə*] (*US* **labor**) *n* (*hard work*) trabajo; (*labour force*) mano f de obra; (*Med*): **to be in ~** estar de parto ▷ *vi*: **to ~ (at sth)** trabajar (en algo) ▷ *vt*: **to ~ a point** insistir en un punto; **L~, the L~ party** (*BRIT*) el partido laborista, los laboristas *mpl*; **labourer** *n* peón *m*; **farm labourer** peón *m*; (*day labourer*) jornalero

lace [leɪs] *n* encaje *m*; (*of shoe etc*) cordón *m* ▷ *vt* (*shoes: also: ~ up*) atarse (los zapatos)

lack [læk] *n* (*absence*) falta ▷ *vt* faltarle a algn, carecer de; **through** *or* **for ~ of** por falta de; **to be ~ing** faltar, no haber; **to be ~ing in sth** faltarle a algn algo

lacquer ['lækə*] *n* laca

lacy ['leɪsɪ] *adj* (*of lace*) de encaje; (*like lace*) como de encaje

lad [læd] *n* muchacho, chico

ladder ['lædə*] *n* escalera (de mano); (*BRIT: in tights*) carrera

ladle ['leɪdl] *n* cucharón *m*

lady ['leɪdɪ] *n* señora; (*dignified, graceful*) dama; **"ladies and gentlemen …"** "señoras y caballeros …"; **young ~** señorita; **the ladies' (room)** los servicios de señoras; **ladybird** (*US* **ladybug**) *n* mariquita

lag [læg] *n* retraso ▷ *vi* (*also: ~ behind*) retrasarse, quedarse atrás ▷ *vt* (*pipes*) revestir

lager ['lɑ:gə*] *n* cerveza (rubia)

lagoon [lə'gu:n] *n* laguna

laid [leɪd] pt, pp of **lay**; **laid back** (inf) adj
relajado

lain [leɪn] pp of **lie**

lake [leɪk] n lago

lamb [læm] n cordero; (meat) (carne f de)
cordero

lame [leɪm] adj cojo; (excuse) poco
convincente

lament [lə'mɛnt] n quejo ▷ vt
lamentarse de

lamp [læmp] n lámpara; **lamppost**
(BRIT) n (poste m de) farol m; **lampshade**
n pantalla

land [lænd] n tierra; (country) país m; (piece
of land) terreno; (estate) tierras fpl, finca ▷ vi
(from ship) desembarcar; (Aviat) aterrizar;
(fig: fall) caer, terminar ▷ vt (passengers,
goods) desembarcar; **to ~ sb with sth** (inf)
hacer cargar a algn con algo; **landing** n
aterrizaje m; (of staircase) rellano; **landing
card** n tarjeta de desembarque; **landlady**
n (of rented house, etc) dueña; **landlord** n
propietario; (of pub etc) patrón m; **landmark**
n lugar m conocido; **to be a landmark** (fig)
marcar un hito histórico; **landowner** n
terrateniente mf; **landscape** n paisaje m;
landslide n (Geo) corrimiento de tierras;
(fig: Pol) victoria arrolladora

lane [leɪn] n (in country) camino; (Aut) carril
m; (in race) calle f

language ['læŋgwɪdʒ] n lenguaje m;
(national tongue) idioma m, lengua; **bad ~**
palabrotas fpl; **language laboratory** n
laboratorio de idiomas; **language school** n
academia de idiomas

lantern ['læntn] n linterna, farol m

lap [læp] n (of track) vuelta; (of body) regazo
▷ vt (also: ~ **up**) beber a lengüetadas ▷ vi
(waves) chapotear; **to sit on sb's ~** sentarse
en las rodillas de algn

lapel [lə'pɛl] n solapa

lapse [læps] n fallo; (moral) desliz m; (of
time) intervalo ▷ vi (expire) caducar; (time)
pasar, transcurrir; **to ~ into bad habits** caer
en malos hábitos

laptop (computer) ['læptɔp-] n
(ordenador m) portátil m

lard [lɑːd] n manteca (de cerdo)

larder ['lɑːdə*] n despensa

large [lɑːdʒ] adj grande; **at ~** (free) en
libertad; (generally) en general

> Be careful not to translate **large** by the
> Spanish word largo.

largely adv (mostly) en su mayor parte;
(introducing reason) en gran parte; **large-
scale** adj (map) en gran escala; (fig)
importante

lark [lɑːk] n (bird) alondra; (joke) broma

laryngitis [lærɪn'dʒaɪtɪs] n laringitis f

lasagne [lə'zænjə] n lasaña

laser ['leɪzə*] n láser m; **laser printer** n
impresora (por) láser

lash [læʃ] n latigazo; (also: **eye~**) pestaña
▷ vt azotar; (tie): **to ~ to/together** atar
a/atar; **lash out** vi: **to lash out (at sb)**
(hit) arremeter (contra algn); **to lash out
against sb** lanzar invectivas contra algn

lass [læs] (BRIT) n chica

last [lɑːst] adj último; (end: of series etc)
final ▷ adv (most recently) la última vez;
(finally) por último ▷ vi durar; (continue)
continuar, seguir; **~ night** anoche; **~ week**
la semana pasada; **at ~** por fin; **~ but
one** penúltimo; **lastly** adv por último,
finalmente; **last-minute** adj de última
hora

latch [lætʃ] n pestillo; **latch onto** vt fus
(person, group) pegarse a; (idea) agarrarse a

late [leɪt] adj (far on: in time, process etc) al
final de; (not on time) tarde, atrasado; (dead)
fallecido ▷ adv tarde; (behind time, schedule)
con retraso; **of ~** últimamente; **~ at night**
a última hora de la noche; **in ~ May** hacia
fines de mayo; **the ~ Mr X** el difunto Sr X;
latecomer n recién llegado/a; **lately** adv
últimamente; **later** adj (date etc) posterior;
(version etc) más reciente ▷ adv más tarde,
después; **latest** ['leɪtɪst] adj último; **at the
latest** a más tardar

lather ['lɑːðə*] n espuma (de jabón) ▷ vt
enjabonar

Latin ['lætɪn] n latín m ▷ adj latino;
Latin America n América latina; **Latin
American** adj, n latinoamericano/a m/f

latitude ['lætɪtjuːd] n latitud f; (fig)
libertad f

latter ['lætə*] adj último; (of two) segundo
▷ n: **the ~** el último, éste

laugh [lɑːf] n risa ▷ vi reír(se); **(to do sth)
for a ~** (hacer algo) en broma; **laugh at** vt
fus reírse de; **laughter** n risa

launch [lɔːntʃ] n lanzamiento; (boat)
lancha ▷ vt (ship) botar; (rocket etc) lanzar;
(fig) comenzar; **launch into** vt fus lanzarse
a

launder ['lɔːndə*] vt lavar

Launderette® [lɔːn'drɛt] (BRIT) n
lavandería (automática)

Laundromat® ['lɔːndrəmæt] (US) n =
Launderette

laundry ['lɔːndrɪ] n (dirty) ropa sucia;
(clean) colada; (room) lavadero

lava ['lɑːvə] n lava

lavatory ['lævətərɪ] n wáter m

lavender ['lævəndə*] n lavanda

lavish ['lævɪʃ] adj (amount) abundante;

(*person*): **~ with** pródigo en ▷ *vt*: **to ~ sth on sb** colmar a algn de algo

law [lɔː] *n* ley *f*; (*Scol*) derecho; (*a rule*) regla; (*professions connected with law*) jurisprudencia; **lawful** *adj* legítimo, lícito; **lawless** *adj* (*action*) criminal

lawn [lɔːn] *n* césped *m*; **lawnmower** *n* cortacésped *m*

lawsuit ['lɔːsuːt] *n* pleito

lawyer ['lɔːjə*] *n* abogado/a; (*for sales, wills etc*) notario/a

lax [læks] *adj* laxo

laxative ['læksətɪv] *n* laxante *m*

lay [leɪ] (*pt, pp* **laid**) *pt of* **lie** ▷ *adj* laico; (*not expert*) lego ▷ *vt* (*place*) colocar; (*eggs, table*) poner; (*cable*) tender; (*carpet*) extender; **lay off** *vt* (*pen etc*) dejar; (*rules etc*) establecer; **to lay down the law** (*pej*) imponer las normas; **lay off** *vt* (*workers*) despedir; **lay on** *vt* (*meal, facilities*) proveer; **lay out** *vt* (*spread out*) disponer, exponer; **lay-by** *n* (*BRIT Aut*) área de aparcamiento

layer ['leɪə*] *n* capa

layman ['leɪmən] (*irreg*) *n* lego

layout ['leɪaut] *n* (*design*) plan *m*, trazado; (*Press*) composición *f*

lazy ['leɪzɪ] *adj* perezoso, vago; (*movement*) lento

lb. *abbr* = **pound** (*weight*)

lead¹ [liːd] (*pt, pp* **led**) *n* (*front position*) delantera; (*clue*) pista; (*Elec*) cable *m*; (*for dog*) correa; (*Theatre*) papel *m* principal ▷ *vt* (*walk etc in front*) ir a la cabeza de; (*guide*): **to ~ sb somewhere** conducir a algn a algún sitio; (*be leader*) dirigir; (*start, guide: activity*) protagonizar ▷ *vi* (*road, pipe etc*) conducir a; (*Sport*) ir primero; **to be in the ~** (*Sport*) llevar la delantera; (*fig*) ir a la cabeza; **to ~ the way** llevar la delantera; **lead up to** *vt fus* (*events*) conducir a; (*in conversation*) preparar el terreno para

lead² [lɛd] *n* (*metal*) plomo; (*in pencil*) mina

leader ['liːdə*] *n* jefe/a *m/f*, líder *mf*; (*Sport*) líder *mf*; **leadership** *n* dirección *f*; (*position*) mando; (*quality*) iniciativa

lead-free ['lɛdfriː] *adj* sin plomo

leading ['liːdɪŋ] *adj* (*main*) principal; (*first*) primero; (*front*) delantero

lead singer [liːd-] *n* cantante *mf*

leaf [liːf] (*pl* **leaves**) *n* hoja ▷ *vi*: **to ~ through** hojear; **to turn over a new ~** reformarse

leaflet ['liːflɪt] *n* folleto

league [liːg] *n* sociedad *f*; (*Football*) liga; **to be in ~ with** haberse confabulado con

leak [liːk] *n* (*of liquid, gas*) escape *m*, fuga; (*in pipe*) agujero; (*in roof*) gotera; (*in security*) filtración *f* ▷ *vi* (*shoes, ship*) hacer agua;

(*pipe*) tener (un) escape; (*roof*) gotear; (*liquid, gas*) escaparse, fugarse; (*fig*) divulgarse ▷ *vt* (*fig*) filtrar

lean [liːn] (*pt, pp* **~ed** *or* **~t**) *adj* (*thin*) flaco; (*meat*) magro ▷ *vt*: **to ~ sth on sth** apoyar algo en algo ▷ *vi* (*slope*) inclinarse; **to ~ against** apoyarse contra; **to ~ on** apoyarse en; **lean forward** *vi* inclinarse hacia adelante; **lean over** *vi* inclinarse; **leaning** *n*: **leaning (towards)** inclinación *f* (hacia)

leant [lɛnt] *pt, pp of* **lean**

leap [liːp] (*pt, pp* **~ed** *or* **~t**) *n* salto ▷ *vi* saltar

leapt [lɛpt] *pt, pp of* **leap**

leap year *n* año bisiesto

learn [ləːn] (*pt, pp* **~ed** *or* **~t**) *vt* aprender ▷ *vi* aprender; **to ~ about sth** enterarse de algo; **to ~ to do sth** aprender a hacer algo; **learner** *n* (*BRIT: also*: **learner driver**) principiante *mf*; **learning** *n* el saber *m*, conocimientos *mpl*

learnt [ləːnt] *pp of* **learn**

lease [liːs] *n* arriendo ▷ *vt* arrendar

leash [liːʃ] *n* correa

least [liːst] *adj*: **the ~** (*slightest*) el menor, el más pequeño; (*smallest amount of*) mínimo ▷ *adv* (+ *vb*) menos; (+ *adj*): **the ~ expensive** el (la) menos costoso/a; **the ~ possible effort** el menor esfuerzo posible; **at ~** por lo menos, al menos; **you could at ~ have written** por lo menos podías haber escrito; **not in the ~** en absoluto

leather ['lɛðə*] *n* cuero

leave [liːv] (*pt, pp* **left**) *vt* dejar; (*go away from*) abandonar; (*place etc: permanently*) salir de ▷ *vi* irse; (*train etc*) salir ▷ *n* permiso; **to ~ sth to sb** (*money etc*) legar algo a algn; (*responsibility etc*) encargar a algn de algo; **to be left** quedar, sobrar; **there's some milk left over** sobra *or* queda algo de leche; **on ~** de permiso; **leave behind** *vt* (*on purpose*) dejar; (*accidentally*) dejarse; **leave out** *vt* omitir

leaves [liːvz] *npl of* **leaf**

Lebanon ['lɛbənən] *n*: **the ~** el Líbano

lecture ['lɛktʃə*] *n* conferencia; (*Scol*) clase *f* ▷ *vi* dar una clase ▷ *vt* (*scold*): **to ~ sb on** *or* **about sth** echar una reprimenda a algn por algo; **to give a ~ on** dar una conferencia sobre; **lecture hall** *n* sala de conferencias; (*Univ*) aula; **lecturer** *n* conferenciante *mf*; (*BRIT: at university*) profesor(a) *m/f*; **lecture theatre** *n* = **lecture hall**

led [lɛd] *pt, pp of* **lead¹**

ledge [lɛdʒ] *n* repisa; (*of window*) alféizar *m*; (*of mountain*) saliente *m*

leek [liːk] *n* puerro

left [lɛft] *pt, pp of* **leave** ▷ *adj* izquierdo;

(remaining): **there are two ~** quedan dos ▷ *n* izquierda ▷ *adv* a la izquierda; **on** *or* **to the ~** a la izquierda; **the L~** (*Pol*) la izquierda; **left-hand** *adj*: **the left-hand side** la izquierda; **left-hand drive** *adj*: **a left-hand drive car** un coche con el volante a la izquierda; **left-handed** *adj* zurdo; **left-luggage locker** *n* (*BRIT*) consigna *f* automática; **left-luggage (office)** (*BRIT*) *n* consigna; **left-overs** *npl* sobras *fpl*; **left-wing** *adj* (*Pol*) de izquierdas, izquierdista

leg [lɛg] *n* pierna; (*of animal, chair*) pata; (*trouser leg*) pernera; (*Culin: of lamb*) pierna; (*: of chicken*) pata; (*of journey*) etapa

legacy ['lɛgəsɪ] *n* herencia

legal ['liːgl] *adj* (*permitted by law*) lícito; (*of law*) legal; **legal holiday** (*US*) *n* fiesta oficial; **legalize** *vt* legalizar; **legally** *adv* legalmente

legend ['lɛdʒənd] *n* (*also fig: person*) leyenda; **legendary** [-ərɪ] *adj* legendario

leggings ['lɛgɪŋz] *npl* mallas *fpl*, leggins *mpl*

legible ['lɛdʒəbl] *adj* legible

legislation [lɛdʒɪs'leɪʃən] *n* legislación *f*

legislative ['lɛdʒɪslətɪv] *adj* legislativo

legitimate [lɪ'dʒɪtɪmət] *adj* legítimo

leisure ['lɛʒə*] *n* ocio, tiempo libre; **at ~** con tranquilidad; **leisure centre** (*BRIT*) *n* centro de recreo; **leisurely** *adj* sin prisa; lento

lemon ['lɛmən] *n* limón *m*; **lemonade** *n* (*fizzy*) gaseosa; **lemon tea** *n* té *m* con limón

lend [lɛnd] (*pt, pp* **lent**) *vt*: **to ~ sth to sb** prestar algo a algn

length [lɛŋθ] *n* (*size*) largo, longitud *f*; (*distance*): **the ~ of** todo lo largo de; (*of swimming pool, cloth*) largo; (*of wood, string*) trozo; (*amount of time*) duración *f*; **at ~** (*at last*) por fin, finalmente; (*lengthily*) largamente; **lengthen** *vt* alargar ▷ *vi* alargarse; **lengthways** *adv* a lo largo; **lengthy** *adj* largo, extenso

lens [lɛnz] *n* (*of spectacles*) lente *f*; (*of camera*) objetivo

Lent [lɛnt] *n* Cuaresma

lent [lɛnt] *pt, pp of* **lend**

lentil ['lɛntɪl] *n* lenteja

Leo ['liːəu] *n* Leo

leopard ['lɛpəd] *n* leopardo

leotard ['liːətɑːd] *n* mallas *fpl*

leprosy ['lɛprəsɪ] *n* lepra

lesbian ['lɛzbɪən] *n* lesbiana

less [lɛs] *adj* (*in size, degree etc*) menor; (*in quality*) menos ▷ *pron, adv* menos ▷ *prep*: **~ tax/10% discount** menos impuestos/el 10 por ciento de descuento; **~ than half** menos de la mitad; **~ than ever** menos que

nunca; **~ and ~** cada vez menos; **the ~ he works ...** cuanto menos trabaja ...; **lessen** *vi* disminuir, reducirse ▷ *vt* disminuir, reducir; **lesser** ['lɛsə*] *adj* menor; **to a lesser extent** en menor grado

lesson ['lɛsn] *n* clase *f*; (*warning*) lección *f*

let [lɛt] (*pt, pp* ~) *vt* (*allow*) dejar, permitir; (*BRIT: lease*) alquilar; **to ~ sb do sth** dejar que algn haga algo; **to ~ sb know sth** comunicar algo a algn; **~'s go** ¡vamos!; **~ him come** que venga; **"to ~"** "se alquila"; **let down** *vt* (*tyre*) desinflar; (*disappoint*) defraudar; **let in** *vt* dejar entrar; (*visitor etc*) hacer pasar; **let off** *vt* (*culprit*) dejar escapar; (*gun*) disparar; (*bomb*) accionar; (*firework*) hacer estallar; **let out** *vt* dejar salir; (*sound*) soltar

lethal ['liːθl] *adj* (*weapon*) mortífero; (*poison, wound*) mortal

letter ['lɛtə*] *n* (*of alphabet*) letra; (*correspondence*) carta; **letterbox** (*BRIT*) *n* buzón *m*

lettuce ['lɛtɪs] *n* lechuga

leukaemia [luː'kiːmɪə] (*US* **leukemia**) *n* leucemia

level ['lɛvl] *adj* (*flat*) llano ▷ *adv*: **to draw ~ with** llegar a la altura de ▷ *n* nivel *m*; (*height*) altura ▷ *vt* nivelar; allanar; (*destroy: building*) derribar; (*: forest*) arrasar; **to be ~ with** estar a nivel de; **A ~s** (*BRIT*) ≈ exámenes *mpl* de bachillerato superior, B.U.P.; **AS ~** (*BRIT*) asignatura aprobada entre los "GCSEs" y los "A levels"; **on the ~** (*fig: honest*) serio; **level crossing** (*BRIT*) *n* paso a nivel

lever ['liːvə*] *n* (*also fig*) palanca ▷ *vt*: **to ~ up** levantar con palanca; **leverage** *n* (*using bar etc*) apalancamiento; (*fig: influence*) influencia

levy ['lɛvɪ] *n* impuesto ▷ *vt* exigir, recaudar

liability [laɪə'bɪlətɪ] *n* (*pej: person, thing*) estorbo, lastre *m*; (*Jur: responsibility*) responsabilidad *f*

liable ['laɪəbl] *adj* (*subject*): **~ to** sujeto a; (*responsible*): **~ for** responsable de; (*likely*): **~ to do** propenso a hacer

liaise [lɪ'eɪz] *vi*: **to ~ with** enlazar con

liar ['laɪə*] *n* mentiroso/a

liberal ['lɪbərəl] *adj* liberal; (*offer, amount etc*) generoso; **Liberal Democrat** *n* (*BRIT*) demócrata *m/f* liberal

liberate ['lɪbəreɪt] *vt* (*people: from poverty etc*) librar; (*prisoner*) libertar; (*country*) liberar

liberation [lɪbə'reɪʃən] *n* liberación *f*

liberty ['lɪbətɪ] *n* libertad *f*; **to be at ~** (*criminal*) estar en libertad; **to be at ~ to do** estar libre para hacer; **to take the ~ of doing sth** tomarse la libertad de hacer algo

Libra ['liːbrə] *n* Libra

librarian [laɪˈbrɛərɪən] n bibliotecario/a
library [ˈlaɪbrərɪ] n biblioteca
> Be careful not to translate **library** by the Spanish word *librería*.
Libya [ˈlɪbɪə] n Libia
lice [laɪs] npl of **louse**
licence [ˈlaɪsəns] (us **license**) n licencia; (*permit*) permiso; (*also:* **driving ~**) carnet m de conducir (sp), licencia de manejo (LAM)
license [ˈlaɪsəns] n (us) = **licence** ▷ vt autorizar, dar permiso a; **licensed** adj (*for alcohol*) autorizado para vender bebidas alcohólicas; (*car*) matriculado; **license plate** (us) n placa (de matrícula); **licensing hours** (BRIT) npl horas durante las cuales se permite la venta y consumo de alcohol (en un bar etc)
lick [lɪk] vt lamer; (*inf: defeat*) dar una paliza a; **to ~ one's lips** relamerse
lid [lɪd] n (*of box, case*) tapa; (*of pan*) tapadera
lie [laɪ] (*pt* **lay**, *pp* **lain**) vi (*rest*) estar echado, estar acostado; (*of object: be situated*) estar, encontrarse; (*tell lies: pt, pp* **lied**) mentir ▷ n mentira; **to ~ low** (*fig*) mantenerse a escondidas; **lie about** or **around** vi (*things*) estar tirado; (BRIT: *people*) estar tumbado; **lie down** vi echarse, tumbarse
Liechtenstein [ˈlɪktənstaɪn] n Liechtenstein m
lie-in [ˈlaɪɪn] (BRIT) n: **to have a ~** quedarse en la cama
lieutenant [lɛfˈtɛnənt, us luːˈtɛnənt] n (*Mil*) teniente mf
life [laɪf] (*pl* **lives**) n vida; **to come to ~** animarse; **life assurance** (BRIT) n seguro de vida; **lifeboat** n lancha de socorro; **lifeguard** n vigilante mf, socorrista mf; **life insurance** n = **life assurance**; **life jacket** n chaleco salvavidas; **lifelike** adj (*model etc*) que parece vivo; (*realistic*) realista; **life preserver** (us) n cinturón m/chaleco salvavidas; **life sentence** n cadena perpetua; **lifestyle** n estilo de vida; **lifetime** n (*of person*) vida; (*of thing*) período de vida
lift [lɪft] vt levantar; (*end: ban, rule*) levantar, suprimir ▷ vi (*fog*) disiparse ▷ n (BRIT: *machine*) ascensor m; **to give sb a ~** (BRIT) llevar a algn en el coche; **lift up** vt levantar; **lift-off** n despegue m
light [laɪt] (*pt, pp* **~ed** or **lit**) n luz f; (*lamp*) luz f, lámpara; (*Aut*) faro; (*for cigarette etc*): **have you got a ~?** ¿tienes fuego? ▷ vt (*candle, cigarette, fire*) encender (sp), prender (LAM); (*room*) alumbrar ▷ adj (*colour*) claro; (*not heavy, also fig*) ligero; (*room*) con mucha

luz; (*gentle, graceful*) ágil; **lights** npl (*traffic lights*) semáforos mpl; **to come to ~** salir a luz; **in the ~ of** (*new evidence etc*) a la luz de; **light up** vi (*smoke*) encender un cigarrillo; (*face*) iluminarse ▷ vt (*illuminate*) iluminar, alumbrar; (*set fire to*) encender; **light bulb** n bombilla (sp), foco (MEX), bujía (CAM), bombita (RPL); **lighten** vt (*make less heavy*) aligerar; **lighter** n (*also:* **cigarette lighter**) encendedor m, mechero; **light-hearted** adj (*person*) alegre; (*remark etc*) divertido; **lighthouse** n faro; **lighting** n (*system*) alumbrado; **lightly** adv ligeramente; (*not seriously*) con poca seriedad; **to get off lightly** ser castigado con poca severidad
lightning [ˈlaɪtnɪŋ] n relámpago, rayo
lightweight [ˈlaɪtweɪt] adj (*suit*) ligero ▷ n (*Boxing*) peso ligero
like [laɪk] vt gustarle a algn ▷ prep como ▷ adj parecido, semejante ▷ n: **and the ~** y otros por el estilo; **his ~s and dislikes** sus gustos y aversiones; **I would ~, I'd ~** me gustaría; (*for purchase*) quisiera; **would you ~ a coffee?** ¿te apetece un café?; **I ~ swimming** me gusta nadar; **she ~s apples** le gustan las manzanas; **to be** or **look ~ sb/sth** parecerse a algn/algo; **what does it look/taste/sound ~?** ¿cómo es/a qué sabe/cómo suena?; **that's just ~ him** es muy de él, es característico de él; **do it ~ this** hazlo así; **it is nothing ~ ...** no tiene parecido alguno con ...; **likeable** adj simpático, agradable
likelihood [ˈlaɪklɪhud] n probabilidad f
likely [ˈlaɪklɪ] adj probable; **he's ~ to leave** es probable que se vaya; **not ~!** ¡ni hablar!
likewise [ˈlaɪkwaɪz] adv igualmente; **to do ~** hacer lo mismo
liking [ˈlaɪkɪŋ] n: **~ (for)** (*person*) cariño (a); (*thing*) afición (a); **to be to sb's ~** ser del gusto de algn
lilac [ˈlaɪlək] n (*tree*) lilo; (*flower*) lila
Lilo® [ˈlaɪləu] n colchoneta inflable
lily [ˈlɪlɪ] n lirio, azucena; **~ of the valley** lirio de los valles
limb [lɪm] n miembro
limbo [ˈlɪmbəu] n: **to be in ~** (*fig*) quedar a la expectativa
lime [laɪm] n (*tree*) limero; (*fruit*) lima; (*Geo*) cal f
limelight [ˈlaɪmlaɪt] n: **to be in the ~** (*fig*) ser el centro de atención
limestone [ˈlaɪmstəun] n piedra caliza
limit [ˈlɪmɪt] n límite m ▷ vt limitar; **limited** adj limitado; **to be limited to** limitarse a
limousine [ˈlɪməziːn] n limusina
limp [lɪmp] n: **to have a ~** tener cojera ▷ vi

cojear ▷ adj flojo; (material) fláccido

line [laɪn] n línea; (rope) cuerda; (for fishing)
sedal m; (wire) hilo; (row, series) fila, hilera; (of
writing) renglón m, línea; (of song) verso; (on
face) arruga; (Rail) vía ▷ vt (road etc) llenar;
(Sewing) forrar; **to ~ the streets** llenar las
aceras; **in ~ with** alineado con; (according to)
de acuerdo con; **line up** vi hacer cola ▷ vt
alinear; (prepare) preparar; organizar

linear ['lɪnɪə*] adj lineal

linen ['lɪnɪn] n ropa blanca; (cloth) lino

liner ['laɪnə*] n vapor m de línea,
transatlántico; (for bin) bolsa (de basura)

line-up ['laɪnʌp] n (us: queue) cola; (Sport)
alineación f

linger ['lɪŋgə*] vi retrasarse, tardar en
marcharse; (smell, tradition) persistir

lingerie ['lænʒəriː] n lencería

linguist ['lɪŋgwɪst] n lingüista mf;
linguistic adj lingüístico

lining ['laɪnɪŋ] n forro; (Anat) (membrana)
mucosa

link [lɪŋk] n (of a chain) eslabón m;
(relationship) relación f, vínculo; (Internet)
link m, enlace m ▷ vt vincular, unir;
(associate): **to ~ with** or **to** relacionar con;
links npl (Golf) campo de golf; **link up** vt
acoplar ▷ vi unirse

lion ['laɪən] n león m; **lioness** n leona

lip [lɪp] n labio; **lipread** vi leer los labios;
lip salve n crema protectora para labios;
lipstick n lápiz m de labios, carmín m

liqueur [lɪ'kjuə*] n licor m

liquid ['lɪkwɪd] adj, n líquido; **liquidizer**
[-aɪzə*] n licuadora

liquor ['lɪkə*] n licor m, bebidas fpl
alcohólicas; **liquor store** (us) n bodega,
tienda de vinos y bebidas alcohólicas

Lisbon ['lɪzbən] n Lisboa

lisp [lɪsp] n ceceo ▷ vi cecear

list [lɪst] n lista ▷ vt (mention) enumerar;
(put on a list) poner en una lista

listen ['lɪsn] vi escuchar, oír; **to ~ to**
sb/sth escuchar a algn/algo; **listener** n
oyente mf; (Radio) radioyente mf

lit [lɪt] pt, pp of **light**

liter ['liːtə*] (us) n = **litre**

literacy ['lɪtərəsɪ] n capacidad f de leer
y escribir

literal ['lɪtərl] adj literal; **literally** adv
literalmente

literary ['lɪtərərɪ] adj literario

literate ['lɪtərət] adj que sabe leer y
escribir; (educated) culto

literature ['lɪtərɪtʃə*] n literatura;
(brochures etc) folletos mpl

litre ['liːtə*] (us **liter**) n litro

litter ['lɪtə*] n (rubbish) basura; (young

animals) camada, cría; **litter bin** (BRIT)
n papelera; **littered** adj: **littered with**
(scattered) lleno de

little ['lɪtl] adj (small) pequeño; (not much)
poco ▷ adv poco; **a ~** un poco (de); **~ house/**
bird casita/pajarito; **a ~ bit** un poquito;
~ by ~ poco a poco; **little finger** n dedo
meñique

live¹ [laɪv] adj (animal) vivo; (wire)
conectado; (broadcast) en directo; (shell)
cargado

live² [lɪv] vi vivir; **live together** vi vivir
juntos; **live up to** (fulfil) cumplir con

livelihood ['laɪvlɪhud] n sustento

lively ['laɪvlɪ] adj vivo; (interesting: place,
book etc) animado

liven up ['laɪvn-] vt animar ▷ vi animarse

liver ['lɪvə*] n hígado

lives [laɪvz] npl of **life**

livestock ['laɪvstɔk] n ganado

living ['lɪvɪŋ] adj (alive) vivo ▷ n: **to earn**
or **make a ~** ganarse la vida; **living room** n
sala (de estar)

lizard ['lɪzəd] n lagarto; (small) lagartija

load [ləud] n carga; (weight) peso ▷ vt
(Comput) cargar; (also: **~ up**): **to ~ (with)**
cargar (con or de); **a ~ of rubbish** (inf)
tonterías fpl; **a ~ of**, **~s of** (fig) (gran)
cantidad de, montones de; **loaded** adj
(vehicle): **to be loaded with** estar cargado de

loaf [ləuf] (pl **loaves**) n (barra de) pan m

loan [ləun] n préstamo ▷ vt prestar; **on**
~ prestado

loathe [ləuð] vt aborrecer; (person) odiar

loaves [ləuvz] npl of **loaf**

lobby ['lɔbɪ] n vestíbulo, sala de espera;
(Pol: pressure group) grupo de presión ▷ vt
presionar

lobster ['lɔbstə*] n langosta

local ['ləukl] adj local ▷ n (pub) bar m; **the**
locals npl los vecinos, los del lugar; **local**
anaesthetic n (Med) anestesia local; **local**
authority n municipio, ayuntamiento
(sp); **local government** n gobierno
municipal; **locally** [-kəlɪ] adv en la
vecindad; por aquí

locate [ləu'keɪt] vt (find) localizar;
(situate): **to be ~d in** estar situado en

location [ləu'keɪʃən] n situación f; **on ~**
(Cinema) en exteriores

loch [lɔx] n lago

lock [lɔk] n (of door, box) cerradura; (of
canal) esclusa; (of hair) mechón m ▷ vt
(with key) cerrar (con llave) ▷ vi (door etc)
cerrarse (con llave); (wheels) trabarse; **lock**
in vt encerrar; **lock out** vt (person) cerrar
la puerta a; **lock up** vt (criminal) meter en
la cárcel; (mental patient) encerrar; (house)

cerrar (con llave) ▷ vi echar la llave
locker ['lɔkə*] n casillero; **locker-room**
(us) n (Sport) vestuario
locksmith ['lɔksmɪθ] n cerrajero/a
locomotive [ləukə'məutɪv] n locomotora
lodge [lɔdʒ] n casita (del guarda) ▷ vi
(person): **to ~ (with)** alojarse (en casa de);
(bullet, bone) incrustarse ▷ vt presentar;
lodger n huésped mf
lodging ['lɔdʒɪŋ] n alojamiento,
hospedaje m
loft [lɔft] n desván m
log [lɔg] n (of wood) leño, tronco; (written
account) diario ▷ vt anotar; **log in, log on** vi
(Comput) entrar en el sistema; **log off, log out**
vi (Comput) salir del sistema
logic ['lɔdʒɪk] n lógica; **logical** adj lógico
logo ['ləugəu] n logotipo
lollipop ['lɔlɪpɔp] n pirulí m; **lollipop
man/lady** (BRIT: irreg) n persona encargada
de ayudar a los niños a cruzar la calle
lolly ['lɔlɪ] n (inf: ice cream) polo; (: lollipop)
piruleta; (: money) guita
London ['lʌndən] n Londres; **Londoner** n
londinense mf
lone [ləun] adj solitario
loneliness ['ləunlɪnɪs] n soledad f;
aislamiento
lonely ['ləunlɪ] adj (situation) solitario;
(person) solo; (place) aislado
long [lɔŋ] adj largo ▷ adv mucho tiempo,
largamente ▷ vi: **to ~ for sth** anhelar algo;
so or **as ~ as** mientras, con tal que; **don't
be ~!** ¡no tardes!, ¡vuelve pronto!; **how ~ is
the street?** ¿cuánto tiene la calle de largo?;
how ~ is the lesson? ¿cuánto dura la clase?;
6 metres ~ que mide 6 metros, de 6 metros
de largo; **6 months ~** que dura 6 meses,
de 6 meses de duración; **all night ~** toda
la noche; **he no ~er comes** ya no viene; **I
can't stand it any ~er** ya no lo aguanto
más; **~ before** mucho antes; **before ~**
(+ future) dentro de poco; (+ past) poco
tiempo después; **at ~ last** al fin, por fin;
long-distance adj (race) de larga distancia;
(call) interurbano; **long-haul** adj (flight) de
larga distancia; **longing** n anhelo, ansia;
(nostalgia) nostalgia ▷ adj anhelante
longitude ['lɔŋgɪtjuːd] n longitud f
long: long jump n salto de longitud;
long-life adj (batteries) de larga duración;
(milk) uperizado; **long-sighted** (BRIT) adj
présbita; **long-standing** adj de mucho
tiempo; **long-term** adj a largo plazo
loo [luː] (BRIT: inf) n wáter m
look [luk] vi mirar; (seem) parecer; (building
etc): **to ~ south/on to the sea** dar al sur/
al mar ▷ n (gen): **to have a ~** mirar; (glance)

mirada; (appearance) aire m, aspecto; **looks**
npl (good looks) belleza; **~ (here)!** (expressing
annoyance etc) ¡oye!; **~!** (expressing surprise)
¡mira!; **look after** vt fus (care for) cuidar a;
(deal with) encargarse de; **look around** vi
echar una mirada alrededor; **look at** vt fus
mirar; (read quickly) echar un vistazo a; **look
back** vi mirar hacia atrás; **look down on**
vt fus (fig) despreciar, mirar con desprecio;
look for vt fus buscar; **look forward to** vt
fus esperar con ilusión; (in letters): **we look
forward to hearing from you** quedamos
a la espera de sus gratas noticias; **look into**
vt investigar; **look out** vi (beware): **to look
out (for)** tener cuidado (de); **look out for**
vt fus (seek) buscar; (await) esperar; **look
round** vi volver la cabeza; **look through** vt
fus (examine) examinar; **look up** vi mirar
hacia arriba; (improve) mejorar ▷ vt (word)
buscar; **look up to** vt fus admirar; **lookout**
n (tower etc) puesto de observación; (person)
vigía mf; **to be on the lookout for sth** estar
al acecho de algo
loom [luːm] vi: **~ (up)** (threaten) surgir,
amenazar; (event: approach) aproximarse
loony ['luːnɪ] (inf) n, adj loco/a m/f
loop [luːp] n lazo ▷ vt: **to ~ sth round sth**
pasar algo alrededor de algo; **loophole** n
escapatoria
loose [luːs] adj suelto; (clothes) ancho;
(morals, discipline) relajado; **to be on the ~**
estar en libertad; **to be at a ~ end** or **at ~
ends** (us) no saber qué hacer; **loosely** adv
libremente, aproximadamente; **loosen** vt
aflojar
loot [luːt] n botín m ▷ vt saquear
lop-sided ['lɔp'saɪdɪd] adj torcido
lord [lɔːd] n señor m; **L~ Smith** Lord Smith;
the L~ el Señor; **my ~** (to bishop) Ilustrísima;
(to noble etc) Señor; **good L~!** ¡Dios mío!;
Lords npl (BRIT: Pol): **the (House of) Lords**
la Cámara de los Lores
lorry ['lɔrɪ] (BRIT) n camión m; **lorry driver**
(BRIT) n camionero/a
lose [luːz] (pt, pp lost) vt perder ▷ vi
perder, ser vencido; **to ~ (time)** (clock)
atrasarse; **lose out** vi salir perdiendo; **loser**
n perdedor(a) m/f
loss [lɔs] n pérdida; **heavy ~es** (Mil)
grandes pérdidas; **to be at a ~** no saber qué
hacer; **to make a ~** sufrir pérdidas
lost [lɔst] pt, pp of **lose** ▷ adj perdido; **lost
property** (US lost and found) n objetos mpl
perdidos
lot [lɔt] n (group: of things) grupo; (at
auctions) lote m; **the ~** el todo, todos; **a
~ (large number: of books etc)** muchos; (a
great deal) mucho, bastante; **a ~ of, ~s**

of mucho(s) *(pl)*; **I read a ~** leo bastante; **to draw ~s (for sth)** echar suertes (para decidir algo)

lotion ['ləʊʃən] *n* loción *f*

lottery ['lɒtərɪ] *n* lotería

loud [laʊd] *adj* (*voice, sound*) fuerte; (*laugh, shout*) estrepitoso; (*condemnation etc*) enérgico; (*gaudy*) chillón/ona ▷ *adv* (*speak etc*) fuerte; **out ~** en voz alta; **loudly** *adv* (*noisily*) fuerte; (*aloud*) en voz alta; **loudspeaker** *n* altavoz *m*

lounge [laʊndʒ] *n* salón *m*, sala (de estar); (*at airport etc*) sala; (BRIT: *also:* **~-bar**) salón-bar *m* ▷ *vi* (*also:* **~ about** *or* **around**) reposar, holgazanear

louse [laʊs] (*pl* **lice**) *n* piojo

lousy ['laʊzɪ] (*inf*) *adj* (*bad quality*) malísimo, asqueroso; (*ill*) fatal

love [lʌv] *n* (*romantic, sexual*) amor *m*; (*kind, caring*) cariño ▷ *vt* amar, querer; (*thing, activity*) encantarle a algn; **"~ from Anne"** (*on letter*) "un abrazo (de) Anne"; **to ~ to do** encantarle a algn hacer; **to ~ doing** encantarle a algn hacer; **to be/fall in ~ with** estar enamorado/enamorarse de; **to make ~** hacer el amor; **for the ~ of** por amor de; **"15 ~"** (*Tennis*) "15 a cero"; **I ~ you** te quiero; **I ~ paella** me encanta la paella; **love affair** *n* aventura sentimental; **love life** *n* vida sentimental

lovely ['lʌvlɪ] *adj* (*delightful*) encantador(a); (*beautiful*) precioso

lover ['lʌvə*] *n* amante *mf*; (*person in love*) enamorado; (*amateur*): **a ~ of** un(a) aficionado/a *or* un(a) amante de

loving ['lʌvɪŋ] *adj* amoroso, cariñoso; (*action*) tierno

low [ləʊ] *adj, adv* bajo ▷ *n* (*Meteorology*) área de baja presión; **to be ~ on** (*supplies etc*) andar mal de; **to feel ~** sentirse deprimido; **to turn (down) ~** bajar; **low-alcohol** *adj* de bajo contenido en alcohol; **low-calorie** *adj* bajo en calorías

lower ['ləʊə*] *adj* más bajo; (*less important*) menos importante ▷ *vt* bajar; (*reduce*) reducir ▷ *vr*: **to ~ o.s. to** (*fig*) rebajarse a

low-fat *adj* (*milk, yoghurt*) desnatado; (*diet*) bajo en calorías

loyal ['lɔɪəl] *adj* leal; **loyalty** *n* lealtad *f*; **loyalty card** *n* tarjeta cliente

L.P. *n abbr* (= *long-playing record*) elepé *m*

L-plates ['el-] (BRIT) *npl* placas *fpl* de aprendiz de conductor

● **L-PLATES**

● En el Reino Unido las personas que
● están aprendiendo a conducir deben
● llevar en la parte delantera y trasera de
● su vehículo unas placas blancas con una
● L en rojo conocidas como **L-Plates** (de
● **learner**). No es necesario que asistan
● a clases teóricas sino que, desde el
● principio, se le entrega un carnet de
● conducir provisional ("provisional
● driving licence") para que realicen sus
● prácticas, aunque no pueden circular
● por las autopistas y siempre deben ir
● acompañadas por un conductor con
● carnet definitivo ("full driving licence").

Lt *abbr* (= *lieutenant*) Tte.

Ltd *abbr* (= *limited company*) S.A.

luck [lʌk] *n* suerte *f*; **bad ~** mala suerte; **good ~!** ¡que tengas suerte!, ¡suerte!; **bad** *or* **hard** *or* **tough ~!** ¡qué pena!; **luckily** *adv* afortunadamente; **lucky** *adj* afortunado; (*at cards etc*) con suerte; (*object*) que trae suerte

lucrative ['lu:krətɪv] *adj* lucrativo

ludicrous ['lu:dɪkrəs] *adj* absurdo

luggage ['lʌɡɪdʒ] *n* equipaje *m*; **luggage rack** *n* (*on car*) baca, portaequipajes *m inv*

lukewarm ['lu:kwɔ:m] *adj* tibio

lull [lʌl] *n* tregua ▷ *vt*: **to ~ sb to sleep** arrullar a algn; **to ~ sb into a false sense of security** dar a algn una falsa sensación de seguridad

lullaby ['lʌləbaɪ] *n* nana

lumber ['lʌmbə*] *n* (*junk*) trastos *mpl* viejos; (*wood*) maderos *mpl*

luminous ['lu:mɪnəs] *adj* luminoso

lump [lʌmp] *n* (*swelling*) bulto ▷ *vt* (*also:* **~ together**) juntar; **lump sum** *n* suma global; **lumpy** *adj* (*sauce*) lleno de grumos; (*mattress*) lleno de bultos

lunatic ['lu:nətɪk] *adj* loco

lunch [lʌntʃ] *n* almuerzo, comida ▷ *vi* almorzar; **lunch break, lunch hour** *n* hora del almuerzo; **lunch time** *n* hora de comer

lung [lʌŋ] *n* pulmón *m*

lure [lʊə*] *n* (*attraction*) atracción *f* ▷ *vt* tentar

lurk [lə:k] *vi* (*person, animal*) estar al acecho; (*fig*) acechar

lush [lʌʃ] *adj* exuberante

lust [lʌst] *n* lujuria; (*greed*) codicia

Luxembourg ['lʌksəmbə:ɡ] *n* Luxemburgo

luxurious [lʌɡ'zjʊərɪəs] *adj* lujoso

luxury ['lʌkʃərɪ] *n* lujo ▷ *cpd* de lujo

Lycra® ['laɪkrə] *n* licra®

lying ['laɪɪŋ] *n* mentiras *fpl* ▷ *adj* mentiroso

lyrics ['lɪrɪks] *npl* (*of song*) letra

m

m. *abbr* = **metre; mile; million**

M.A. *abbr* = **Master of Arts**

ma *(inf)* [mɑ:] *n* mamá

mac [mæk] *(BRIT) n* impermeable *m*

macaroni [mækəˈrəuni] *n* macarrones *mpl*

Macedonia [mæsiˈdəuniə] *n* Macedonia; **Macedonian** [-ˈdəuniən] *adj* macedonio ▷ *n* macedonio/a; *(Ling)* macedonio

machine [məˈʃi:n] *n* máquina ▷ *vt (dress etc)* coser a máquina; *(Tech)* hacer a máquina; **machine gun** *n* ametralladora; **machinery** *n* maquinaria; *(fig)* mecanismo; **machine washable** *adj* lavable a máquina

macho [ˈmætʃəu] *adj* machista

mackerel [ˈmækrl] *n inv* caballa

mackintosh [ˈmækintɔʃ] *(BRIT) n* impermeable *m*

mad [mæd] *adj* loco; *(idea)* disparatado; *(angry)* furioso; *(keen)*: **to be ~ about sth** volverle loco a algn algo

Madagascar [mædəˈgæskə*] *n* Madagascar *m*

madam [ˈmædəm] *n* señora

mad cow disease *n* encefalopatía espongiforme bovina

made [meid] *pt, pp of* **make**; **made-to-measure** *(BRIT) adj* hecho a la medida; **made-up** [ˈmeidʌp] *adj (story)* ficticio

madly [ˈmædli] *adv* locamente

madman [ˈmædmən] *(irreg) n* loco

madness [ˈmædnis] *n* locura

Madrid [məˈdrid] *n* Madrid *m*

Mafia [ˈmæfiə] *n* Mafia

mag [mæg] *n abbr (BRIT inf)* = **magazine**

magazine [mægəˈzi:n] *n* revista; *(Radio, TV)* programa *m* magazina

maggot [ˈmægət] *n* gusano

magic [ˈmædʒik] *n* magia ▷ *adj* mágico; **magical** *adj* mágico; **magician** [məˈdʒiʃən] *n* mago/a; *(conjurer)* prestidigitador(a) *m/f*

magistrate [ˈmædʒistreit] *n* juez *mf* (municipal)

magnet [ˈmægnit] *n* imán *m*; **magnetic** [-ˈnetik] *adj* magnético; *(personality)* atrayente

magnificent [mægˈnifisənt] *adj* magnífico

magnify [ˈmægnifai] *vt (object)* ampliar; *(sound)* aumentar; **magnifying glass** *n* lupa

magpie [ˈmægpai] *n* urraca

mahogany [məˈhɔgəni] *n* caoba

maid [meid] *n* criada; **old ~** *(pej)* solterona

maiden name *n* nombre *m* de soltera

mail [meil] *n* correo; *(letters)* cartas *fpl* ▷ *vt* echar al correo; **mailbox** *(us) n* buzón *m*; **mailing list** *n* lista de direcciones; **mailman** *(us: irreg) n* cartero; **mail-order** *n* pedido postal

main [mein] *adj* principal, mayor ▷ *n (pipe)* cañería maestra; *(us)* red *f* eléctrica ▷ **the ~s** *npl (BRIT Elec)* la red eléctrica; **in the ~** en general; **main course** *n (Culin)* plato principal; **mainland** *n* tierra firme; **mainly** *adv* principalmente; **main road** *n* carretera; **mainstream** *n* corriente *f* principal; **main street** *n* calle *f* mayor

maintain [meinˈtein] *vt* mantener; **maintenance** [ˈmeintənəns] *n* mantenimiento; *(Law)* manutención *f*

maisonette [meizəˈnet] *n* dúplex *m*

maize [meiz] *(BRIT) n* maíz *m*, choclo *(sc)*

majesty [ˈmædʒisti] *n* majestad *f*; *(title)*: **Your M~** Su Majestad

major [ˈmeidʒə*] *n (Mil)* comandante *mf* ▷ *adj* principal; *(Mus)* mayor

Majorca [məˈjɔ:kə] *n* Mallorca

majority [məˈdʒɔriti] *n* mayoría

make [meik] *(pt, pp* **made**) *vt* hacer; *(manufacture)* fabricar; *(mistake)* cometer; *(speech)* pronunciar; *(cause to be)*: **to ~ sb sad** poner triste a algn; *(force)*: **to ~ sb do sth** obligar a algn a hacer algo; *(earn)* ganar; *(equal)*: **2 and 2 ~ 4** 2 y 2 son 4 ▷ *n* marca; **to ~ the bed** hacer la cama; **to ~ a fool of sb** poner a algn en ridículo; **to ~ a profit/loss** obtener ganancias/sufrir pérdidas; **to ~ it** *(arrive)* llegar; *(achieve sth)* tener éxito; **what time do you ~ it?** ¿qué hora tienes?; **to ~ do with** contentarse con; **make off** *vi* largarse; **make out** *vt (decipher)* descifrar; *(understand)* entender; *(see)* distinguir; *(cheque)* extender; **make up** *vt (invent)* inventar; *(prepare)* hacer; *(constitute)* constituir ▷ *vi* reconciliarse; *(with cosmetics)* maquillarse; **make up for** *vt*

fus compensar; **makeover** ['meɪkəʊvə*]
n (by beautician) sesión f de maquillaje y
peluquería; *(change of image)* lavado de cara;
maker *n* fabricante *mf*; *(of film, programme)*
autor(a) *m/f*; **makeshift** *adj* improvisado;
make-up *n* maquillaje *m*
making ['meɪkɪŋ] *n (fig)*: **in the ~** en vías
de formación; **to have the ~s of** *(person)*
tener madera de
malaria [mə'lɛərɪə] *n* malaria
Malaysia [mə'leɪzɪə] *n* Malasia, Malaysia
male [meɪl] *n (Biol)* macho ▷ *adj (sex,
attitude)* masculino; *(child etc)* varón
malicious [mə'lɪʃəs] *adj* malicioso;
rencoroso
malignant [mə'lɪgnənt] *adj (Med)*
maligno
mall [mɔ:l] *(us) n (also:* **shopping ~**) centro
comercial
mallet ['mælɪt] *n* mazo
malnutrition [mælnju:'trɪʃən] *n*
desnutrición f
malpractice [mæl'præktɪs] *n*
negligencia profesional
malt [mɔ:lt] *n* malta; *(whisky)* whisky *m*
de malta
Malta ['mɔ:ltə] *n* Malta; **Maltese** [-'ti:z]
adj, n inv maltés/esa *m/f*
mammal ['mæml] *n* mamífero
mammoth ['mæməθ] *n* mamut *m* ▷ *adj*
gigantesco
man [mæn] *(pl* **men**) *n* hombre *m*;
(mankind) el hombre ▷ *vt (Naut)* tripular;
(Mil) guarnecer; *(operate: machine)* manejar;
an old ~ un viejo; **~ and wife** marido y
mujer
manage ['mænɪdʒ] *vi* arreglárselas,
ir tirando ▷ *vt (be in charge of)* dirigir;
(control: person) manejar; *(: ship)*
gobernar; **manageable** *adj* manejable;
management *n* dirección f; **manager** *n*
director(a) *m/f*; *(of pop star)* mánager *mf*;
(Sport) entrenador(a) *m/f*; **manageress**
n directora; entrenadora; **managerial**
[-ə'dʒɪərɪəl] *adj* directivo; **managing
director** *n* director(a) *m/f* general
mandarin ['mændərɪn] *n (also:* **~ orange**)
mandarina; *(person)* mandarín *m*
mandate ['mændeɪt] *n* mandato
mandatory ['mændətərɪ] *adj* obligatorio
mane [meɪn] *n (of horse)* crin f; *(of lion)*
melena
maneuver [mə'nu:və*] *(us)* = **manoeuvre**
mangetout [mɔnʒ'tu:] *n* tirabeque *m*
mango ['mæŋgəʊ] *(pl* **~es**) *n* mango
man: manhole *n* agujero de acceso;
manhood *n* edad f viril; *(state)* virilidad f
mania ['meɪnɪə] *n* manía; **maniac**

['meɪnɪæk] *n* maníaco/a; *(fig)* maniático
manic ['mænɪk] *adj* frenético
manicure ['mænɪkjuə*] *n* manicura
manifest ['mænɪfɛst] *vt* manifestar,
mostrar ▷ *adj* manifiesto
manifesto [mænɪ'fɛstəʊ] *n* manifiesto
manipulate [mə'nɪpjuleɪt] *vt* manipular
man: mankind [mæn'kaɪnd] *n*
humanidad f, género humano; **manly** *adj*
varonil; **man-made** *adj* artificial
manner ['mænə*] *n* manera, modo;
(behaviour) conducta, manera de ser;
(type) **all ~ of things** toda clase de cosas;
manners *npl (behaviour)* modales *mpl*; **bad
~s** mala educación
manoeuvre [mə'nu:və*] *(us* **maneuver**)
vt, vi maniobrar ▷ *n* maniobra
manpower ['mænpauə*] *n* mano f de
obra
mansion ['mænʃən] *n* palacio, casa
grande
manslaughter ['mænslɔ:tə*] *n*
homicidio no premeditado
mantelpiece ['mæntlpi:s] *n* repisa,
chimenea
manual ['mænjuəl] *adj* manual ▷ *n*
manual *m*
manufacture [mænju'fæktʃə*] *vt*
fabricar ▷ *n* fabricación f; **manufacturer** *n*
fabricante *mf*
manure [mə'njuə*] *n* estiércol *m*
manuscript ['mænjuskrɪpt] *n*
manuscrito
many ['mɛnɪ] *adj, pron* muchos/as; **a
great ~** muchísimos, un buen número de; **~
a time** muchas veces
map [mæp] *n* mapa *m* ▷ **to ~ out** *vt*
proyectar
maple ['meɪpl] *n* arce *m*, maple *m (LAM)*
Mar *abbr (=March)* mar
mar [mɑ:*] *vt* estropear
marathon ['mærəθən] *n* maratón *m*
marble ['mɑ:bl] *n* mármol *m*; *(toy)* canica
March [mɑ:tʃ] *n* marzo
march [mɑ:tʃ] *vi (Mil)* marchar;
(demonstrators) manifestarse ▷ *n* marcha;
(demonstration) manifestación f
mare [mɛə*] *n* yegua
margarine [mɑ:dʒə'ri:n] *n* margarina
margin ['mɑ:dʒɪn] *n* margen *m*;
(Comm: profit margin) margen *m* de
beneficios; **marginal** *adj* marginal;
marginally *adv* ligeramente
marigold ['mærɪgəʊld] *n* caléndula
marijuana [mærɪ'wɑ:nə] *n* marijuana
marina [mə'ri:nə] *n* puerto deportivo
marinade [mærɪ'neɪd] *n* adobo
marinate ['mærɪneɪt] *vt* marinar

m

marine [məˈriːn] adj marino ▷ n soldado de marina

marital [ˈmærɪtl] adj matrimonial; **marital status** n estado m civil

maritime [ˈmærɪtaɪm] adj marítimo

marjoram [ˈmɑːdʒərəm] n mejorana

mark [mɑːk] n marca, señal f; (in snow, mud etc) huella; (stain) mancha; (BRIT Scol) nota ▷ vt marcar; manchar; (damage: furniture) rayar; (indicate: place etc) señalar; (BRIT Scol) calificar, corregir; **to ~ time** marcar el paso; (fig) marcar(se) un ritmo; **marked** adj (obvious) marcado, acusado; **marker** n (sign) marcador m; (bookmark) señal f (de libro)

market [ˈmɑːkɪt] n mercado ▷ vt (Comm) comercializar; **marketing** n márketing m; **marketplace** n mercado; **market research** n análisis m inv de mercados

marmalade [ˈmɑːməleɪd] n mermelada de naranja

maroon [məˈruːn] vt: **to be ~ed** quedar aislado; (fig) quedar abandonado ▷ n (colour) granate m

marquee [mɑːˈkiː] n entoldado

marriage [ˈmærɪdʒ] n (relationship, institution) matrimonio; (wedding) boda; (act) casamiento; **marriage certificate** n partida de casamiento

married [ˈmærɪd] adj casado; (life, love) conyugal

marrow [ˈmærəʊ] n médula; (vegetable) calabacín m

marry [ˈmærɪ] vt casarse con; (father, priest etc) casar ▷ vi (also: **get married**) casarse

Mars [mɑːz] n Marte m

marsh [mɑːʃ] n pantano; (salt marsh) marisma

marshal [ˈmɑːʃl] n (Mil) mariscal m; (at sports meeting etc) oficial m; (US: of police, fire department) jefe/a m/f ▷ vt (thoughts etc) ordenar; (soldiers) formar

martyr [ˈmɑːtə*] n mártir mf

marvel [ˈmɑːvl] n maravilla, prodigio ▷ vi: **to ~ (at)** maravillarse (de); **marvellous** (US **marvelous**) adj maravilloso

Marxism [ˈmɑːksɪzəm] n marxismo

Marxist [ˈmɑːksɪst] adj, n marxista mf

marzipan [ˈmɑːzɪpæn] n mazapán m

mascara [mæsˈkɑːrə] n rímel m

mascot [ˈmæskət] n mascota

masculine [ˈmæskjʊlɪn] adj masculino

mash [mæʃ] vt machacar; **mashed potato(es)** n(pl) puré m de patatas (SP) or papas (LAM)

mask [mɑːsk] n máscara ▷ vt (cover): **to ~ one's face** ocultarse la cara; (hide: feelings) esconder

mason [ˈmeɪsn] n (also: **stone~**) albañil m; (also: **free~**) masón m; **masonry** n (in building) mampostería

mass [mæs] n (people) muchedumbre f; (of air, liquid etc) masa; (of detail, hair etc) gran cantidad f; (Rel) misa ▷ cpd masivo ▷ vi reunirse; concentrarse; **the masses** npl las masas; **~es of** (inf) montones de

massacre [ˈmæsəkə*] n masacre f

massage [ˈmæsɑːʒ] n masaje m ▷ vt dar masaje en

massive [ˈmæsɪv] adj enorme; (support, changes) masivo

mass media npl medios mpl de comunicación

mass-produce [ˈmæsprəˈdjuːs] vt fabricar en serie

mast [mɑːst] n (Naut) mástil m; (Radio etc) torre f

master [ˈmɑːstə*] n (of servant) amo; (of situation) dueño, maestro; (in primary school) maestro; (in secondary school) profesor m; (title for boys): **M~ X** Señorito X ▷ vt dominar; **mastermind** n inteligencia superior ▷ vt dirigir, planear; **Master of Arts/Science** n licenciatura superior en Letras/Ciencias; **masterpiece** n obra maestra

masturbate [ˈmæstəbeɪt] vi masturbarse

mat [mæt] n estera; (also: **door~**) felpudo; (also: **table~**) salvamanteles m inv, posavasos m inv ▷ adj = **matt**

match [mætʃ] n cerilla, fósforo; (game) partido; (equal) igual m/f ▷ vt (go well with) hacer juego con; (equal) igualar; (correspond to) corresponderse con; (pair: also: **~ up**) casar con ▷ vi hacer juego; **to be a good ~** hacer juego; **matchbox** n caja de cerillas; **matching** adj que hace juego

mate [meɪt] n (workmate) colega mf; (inf: friend) amigo/a; (animal) macho/ hembra; (in merchant navy) segundo de a bordo ▷ vi acoplarse, aparearse ▷ vt aparear

material [məˈtɪərɪəl] n (substance) materia; (information) material m; (cloth) tela, tejido ▷ adj material; (important) esencial; **materials** npl materiales mpl

materialize [məˈtɪərɪəlaɪz] vi materializarse

maternal [məˈtɜːnl] adj maternal

maternity [məˈtɜːnɪtɪ] n maternidad f; **maternity hospital** n hospital m de maternidad; **maternity leave** n baja por maternidad

math [mæθ] (US) n = **mathematics**

mathematical [mæθəˈmætɪkl] adj matemático

mathematician [mæθəmə'tɪʃən] *n*
matemático/a
mathematics [mæθə'mætɪks] *n*
matemáticas *fpl*
maths [mæθs] (BRIT) *n* = **mathematics**
matinée ['mætɪneɪ] *n* sesión *f* de tarde
matron ['meɪtrən] *n* enfermera *f* jefe; (*in
school*) ama de llaves
matt [mæt] *adj* mate
matter ['mætə*] *n* cuestión *f*, asunto;
(*Physics*) sustancia, materia; (*reading matter*)
material *m*; (*Med: pus*) pus *m* ▷ *vi* importar;
matters *npl* (*affairs*) asuntos *mpl*, temas
mpl; **it doesn't ~** no importa; **what's the
~?** ¿qué pasa?; **no ~ what** pase lo que pase;
as a ~ of course por rutina; **as a ~ of fact**
de hecho
mattress ['mætrɪs] *n* colchón *m*
mature [mə'tjuə*] *adj* maduro ▷ *vi*
madurar; **mature student** *n estudiante de
más de 21 años*; **maturity** *n* madurez *f*
maul [mɔːl] *vt* magullar
mauve [məuv] *adj* de color malva (SP) or
guinda (LAM)
max *abbr* = **maximum**
maximize ['mæksɪmaɪz] *vt* (*profits etc*)
llevar al máximo; (*chances*) maximizar
maximum ['mæksɪməm] (*pl* **maxima**) *adj*
máximo ▷ *n* máximo
May [meɪ] *n* mayo
may [meɪ] (*conditional* **might**) *vi* (*indicating
possibility*): **he ~ come** puede que venga;
(*be allowed to*): **~ I smoke?** ¿puedo fumar?;
(*wishes*): **~ God bless you!** ¡que Dios le
bendiga!; **you ~ as well go** bien puedes irte
maybe ['meɪbiː] *adv* quizá(s)
May Day *n* el primero de Mayo
mayhem ['meɪhɛm] *n* caos *m* total
mayonnaise [meɪə'neɪz] *n* mayonesa
mayor [mɛə*] *n* alcalde *m*; **mayoress** *n*
alcaldesa
maze [meɪz] *n* laberinto
MD *n abbr* = **managing director**
me [miː] *pron* (*direct*) me; (*stressed, after
pron*) mí; **can you hear ~?** ¿me oyes?; **he
heard ME** ¡me oyó a mí!; **it's ~** soy yo; **give
them to ~** dámelos/las; **with/without ~**
conmigo/sin mí
meadow ['mɛdəu] *n* prado, pradera
meagre ['miːgə*] (US **meager**) *adj* escaso,
pobre
meal [miːl] *n* comida; (*flour*) harina;
mealtime *n* hora de comer
mean [miːn] (*pt, pp* **~t**) *adj* (*with money*)
tacaño; (*unkind*) mezquino, malo; (*shabby*)
humilde; (*average*) medio ▷ *vt* (*signify*)
querer decir, significar; (*refer to*) referirse
a; (*intend*): **to ~ to do sth** pensar or

pretender hacer algo ▷ *n* medio, término
medio; **means** *npl* (*way*) medio, manera;
(*money*) recursos *mpl*, medios *mpl*; **by ~s
of** mediante, por medio de; **by all ~s!**
¡naturalmente!, ¡claro que sí!; **do you ~ it?**
¿lo dices en serio?; **what do you ~?** ¿qué
quiere decir?; **to be ~t for sb/sth** ser para
algn/algo
meaning ['miːnɪŋ] *n* significado, sentido;
(*purpose*) sentido, propósito; **meaningful**
adj significativo; **meaningless** *adj* sin
sentido
meant [mɛnt] *pt, pp of* **mean**
meantime ['miːntaɪm] *adv* (*also*: **in the ~**)
mientras tanto
meanwhile ['miːnwaɪl] *adv* = **meantime**
measles ['miːzlz] *n* sarampión *m*
measure ['mɛʒə*] *vt, vi* medir ▷ *n*
medida; (*ruler*) regla; **measurement**
['mɛʒəmənt] *n* (*measure*) medida; (*act*)
medición *f*; **to take sb's measurements**
tomar las medidas a algn
meat [miːt] *n* carne *f*; **cold ~** fiambre *m*;
meatball *n* albóndiga
Mecca ['mɛkə] *n* La Meca
mechanic [mɪ'kænɪk] *n* mecánico/a;
mechanical *adj* mecánico
mechanism ['mɛkənɪzəm] *n* mecanismo
medal ['mɛdl] *n* medalla; **medallist** (US
medalist) *n* (*Sport*) medallista *mf*
meddle ['mɛdl] *vi*: **to ~ in** entrometerse en;
to ~ with sth manosear algo
media ['miːdɪə] *npl* medios *mpl* de
comunicación ▷ *npl of* **medium**
mediaeval [mɛdɪ'iːvl] *adj* = **medieval**
mediate ['miːdɪeɪt] *vi* mediar
medical ['mɛdɪkl] *adj* médico ▷ *n*
reconocimiento médico; **medical
certificate** *n* certificado *m* médico
medicated ['mɛdɪkeɪtɪd] *adj* medicinal
medication [mɛdɪ'keɪʃən] *n* medicación *f*
medicine ['mɛdsɪn] *n* medicina; (*drug*)
medicamento
medieval [mɛdɪ'iːvl] *adj* medieval
mediocre [miːdɪ'əukə*] *adj* mediocre
meditate ['mɛdɪteɪt] *vi* meditar
meditation [mɛdɪ'teɪʃən] *n* meditación *f*
Mediterranean [mɛdɪtə'reɪnɪən]
adj mediterráneo; **the ~ (Sea)** el (Mar)
Mediterráneo
medium ['miːdɪəm] (*pl* **media**) *adj*
mediano, regular ▷ *n* (*means*) medio; (*pl
mediums: person*) médium *mf*; **medium-
sized** *adj* de tamaño mediano; (*clothes*) de
(la) talla mediana; **medium wave** *n* onda
media
meek [miːk] *adj* manso, sumiso
meet [miːt] (*pt, pp* **met**) *vt* encontrar;

(*accidentally*) encontrarse con, tropezar con; (*by arrangement*) reunirse con; (*for the first time*) conocer; (*go and fetch*) ir a buscar; (*opponent*) enfrentarse con; (*obligations*) cumplir; (*encounter: problem*) hacer frente a; (*need*) satisfacer ▷ vi encontrarse; (*in session*) reunirse; (*join: objects*) unirse; (*for the first time*) conocerse; **meet up** vi: **to meet up with sb** reunirse con algn; **meet with** vt fus (*difficulty*) tropezar con; **to meet with success** tener éxito; **meeting** n encuentro; (*arranged*) cita, compromiso; (*business meeting*) reunión f; (*Pol*) mítin m; **meeting place** n lugar m de reunión or encuentro

megabyte ['mɛgəbaɪt] n (*Comput*) megabyte m, megaocteto

megaphone ['mɛgəfəun] n megáfono

megapixel ['mɛgəpɪksl] n megapíxel m

melancholy ['mɛlənkəlɪ] n melancolía ▷ adj melancólico

melody ['mɛlədɪ] n melodía

melon ['mɛlən] n melón m

melt [mɛlt] vi (*metal*) fundirse; (*snow*) derretirse ▷ vt fundir

member ['mɛmbə*] n (*gen, Anat*) miembro; (*of club*) socio/a; **Member of Congress** (us) n miembro mf del Congreso; **Member of Parliament** n (BRIT) diputado/a m/f, parlamentario/a m/f; **Member of the European Parliament** n diputado/a m/f del Parlamento Europeo, eurodiputado/a m/f; **Member of the Scottish Parliament** (BRIT) diputado/a del Parlamento escocés; **membership** n (*members*) número de miembros; (*state*) filiación f; **membership card** n carnet m de socio

memento [mə'mɛntəu] n recuerdo

memo ['mɛməu] n apunte m, nota

memorable ['mɛmərəbl] adj memorable

memorandum [mɛmə'rændəm] (pl **memoranda**) n apunte m, nota; (*official note*) acta

memorial [mɪ'mɔːrɪəl] n monumento conmemorativo ▷ adj conmemorativo

memorize ['mɛməraɪz] vt aprender de memoria

memory ['mɛmərɪ] n (*also: Comput*) memoria; (*instance*) recuerdo; (*of dead person*): **in ~ of** a la memoria de; **memory card** n (*for digital camera*) tarjeta de memoria

men [mɛn] npl of **man**

menace ['mɛnəs] n amenaza ▷ vt amenazar

mend [mɛnd] vt reparar, arreglar; (*darn*) zurcir ▷ vi reponerse ▷ n arreglo, reparación f zurcido ▷ n: **to be on the ~** ir mejorando; **to ~ one's ways** enmendarse

meningitis [mɛnɪn'dʒaɪtɪs] n meningitis f

menopause ['mɛnəupɔːz] n menopausia

men's room (us) n: **the ~** el servicio de caballeros

menstruation [mɛnstru'eɪʃən] n menstruación f

menswear ['mɛnzwɛə*] n confección f de caballero

mental ['mɛntl] adj mental; **mental hospital** n (*hospital m*) psiquiátrico; **mentality** [mɛn'tælɪtɪ] n mentalidad f; **mentally** adv: **to be mentally ill** tener una enfermedad mental

menthol ['mɛnθɒl] n mentol m

mention ['mɛnʃən] n mención f ▷ vt mencionar; (*speak*) hablar de; **don't ~ it!** ¡de nada!

menu ['mɛnjuː] n (*set menu*) menú m; (*printed*) carta; (*Comput*) menú m

MEP n abbr = **Member of the European Parliament**

mercenary ['məːsɪnərɪ] adj, n mercenario/a

merchandise ['məːtʃəndaɪz] n mercancías fpl

merchant ['məːtʃənt] n comerciante mf; **merchant navy** (us), **merchant marine** n marina mercante

merciless ['məːsɪlɪs] adj despiadado

mercury ['məːkjurɪ] n mercurio

mercy ['məːsɪ] n compasión f; (*Rel*) misericordia; **at the ~ of** a la merced de

mere [mɪə*] adj simple, mero; **merely** adv simplemente, sólo

merge [məːdʒ] vt (*join*) unir ▷ vi unirse; (*Comm*) fusionarse; (*colours etc*) fundirse; **merger** n (*Comm*) fusión f

meringue [mə'ræŋ] n merengue m

merit ['mɛrɪt] n mérito ▷ vt merecer

mermaid ['məːmeɪd] n sirena

merry ['mɛrɪ] adj alegre; **M~ Christmas!** ¡Felices Pascuas!; **merry-go-round** n tiovivo

mesh [mɛʃ] n malla

mess [mɛs] n (*muddle: of situation*) confusión f; (: *of room*) revoltijo; (*dirt*) porquería; (*Mil*) comedor m; **mess about** or **around** (*inf*) vi perder el tiempo; (*pass the time*) entretenerse; **mess up** vt (*spoil*) estropear; (*dirty*) ensuciar; **mess with** (*inf*) vt fus (*challenge, confront*) meterse con (*inf*); (*interfere with*) interferir con

message ['mɛsɪdʒ] n recado, mensaje m

messenger ['mɛsɪndʒə*] n mensajero/a

Messrs abbr (*on letters*) (= *Messieurs*) Sres

messy ['mɛsɪ] adj (*dirty*) sucio; (*untidy*) desordenado

met [mɛt] *pt, pp of* **meet**

metabolism [mɛ'tæbəlɪzəm] *n* metabolismo

metal ['mɛtl] *n* metal *m*; **metallic** [-'tælɪk] *adj* metálico

metaphor ['mɛtəfə*] *n* metáfora

meteor ['miːtɪə*] *n* meteoro; **meteorite** [-aɪt] *n* meteorito

meteorology [miːtɪɔ'rɔlədʒɪ] *n* meteorología

meter ['miːtə*] *n* (*instrument*) contador *m*; (*us: unit*) = **metre** ▷ *vt* (*US Post*) franquear

method ['mɛθəd] *n* método; **methodical** [mɪ'θɔdɪkl] *adj* metódico

meths [mɛθs] *n* (*BRIT*) alcohol *m* metilado or desnaturalizado

meticulous [mɛ'tɪkjuləs] *adj* meticuloso

metre ['miːtə*] (*us* **meter**) *n* metro

metric ['mɛtrɪk] *adj* métrico

metro ['mɛtrəu] *n* metro

metropolitan [mɛtrə'pɔlɪtən] *adj* metropolitano; **the M~ Police** (*BRIT*) la policía londinense

Mexican ['mɛksɪkən] *adj, n* mexicano/a , mejicano/a

Mexico ['mɛksɪkəu] *n* México, Méjico (*SP*)

mg *abbr* (= *milligram*) mg

mice [maɪs] *npl of* **mouse**

micro... [maɪkrəu] *prefix* micro...; **microchip** *n* microplaqueta; **microphone** *n* micrófono; **microscope** *n* microscopio; **microwave** *n* (*also:* **microwave oven**) horno microondas

mid [mɪd] *adj*: **in ~ May** a mediados de mayo; **in ~ afternoon** a media tarde; **in ~ air** en el aire; **midday** *n* mediodía *m*

middle ['mɪdl] *n* centro; (*half-way point*) medio; (*waist*) cintura ▷ *adj* de en medio; (*course, way*) intermedio; **in the ~ of the night** en plena noche; **middle-aged** *adj* de mediana edad; **Middle Ages** *npl*: **the Middle Ages** la Edad Media; **middle-class** *adj* de clase media; **the middle class(es)** la clase media; **Middle East** *n* Oriente *m* Medio; **middle name** *n* segundo nombre; **middle school** *n* (*US*) colegio para niños de doce a catorce años; (*BRIT*) colegio para niños de ocho o nueve a doce o trece años

midge [mɪdʒ] *n* mosquito

midget ['mɪdʒɪt] *n* enano/a

midnight ['mɪdnaɪt] *n* medianoche *f*

midst [mɪdst] *n*: **in the ~ of** (*crowd*) en medio de; (*situation, action*) en mitad de

midsummer [mɪd'sʌmə*] *n*: **in ~** en pleno verano

midway [mɪd'weɪ] *adj, adv*: **~ (between)** a medio camino (entre); **~ through** a la mitad (de)

midweek [mɪd'wiːk] *adv* entre semana

midwife ['mɪdwaɪf] (*irreg*) *n* comadrona, partera

midwinter [mɪd'wɪntə*] *n*: **in ~** en pleno invierno

might [maɪt] *vb see* **may** ▷ *n* fuerza, poder *m*; **mighty** *adj* fuerte, poderoso

migraine ['miːgreɪn] *n* jaqueca

migrant ['maɪgrənt] *n, adj* (*bird*) migratorio; (*worker*) emigrante

migrate [maɪ'greɪt] *vi* emigrar

migration [maɪ'greɪʃən] *n* emigración *f*

mike [maɪk] *n abbr* (= *microphone*) micro

mild [maɪld] *adj* (*person*) apacible; (*climate*) templado; (*slight*) ligero; (*taste*) suave; (*illness*) leve; **mildly** ['-lɪ] *adv* ligeramente; suavemente; **to put it mildly** para no decir más

mile [maɪl] *n* milla; **mileage** *n* número de millas ≈ kilometraje *m*; **mileometer** [maɪ'lɔmɪtə*] *n* ≈ cuentakilómetros *m inv*; **milestone** *n* mojón *m*

military ['mɪlɪtərɪ] *adj* militar

militia [mɪ'lɪʃə] *n* milicia

milk [mɪlk] *n* leche *f* ▷ *vt* (*cow*) ordeñar; (*fig*) chupar; **milk chocolate** *n* chocolate *m* con leche; **milkman** (*irreg*) *n* lechero; **milky** *adj* lechoso

mill [mɪl] *n* (*windmill etc*) molino; (*coffee mill*) molinillo; (*factory*) fábrica ▷ *vt* moler ▷ *vi* (*also:* **~ about**) arremolinarse

millennium [mɪ'lenɪəm] (*pl* **~s** *or* **millennia**) *n* milenio, milenario

milli... ['mɪlɪ] *prefix*: **milligram(me)** *n* miligramo; **millilitre** (*us* **milliliter**) ['mɪlɪliːtə*] *n* mililitro; **millimetre** (*us* **millimeter**) *n* milímetro

million ['mɪljən] *n* millón *m*; **a ~ times** un millón de veces; **millionaire** [-jə'nɛə*] *n* millonario/a; **millionth** [-θ] *adj* millonésimo

milometer [maɪ'lɔmɪtə*] (*BRIT*) *n* = **mileometer**

mime [maɪm] *n* mímica; (*actor*) mimo/a ▷ *vt* remedar ▷ *vi* actuar de mimo

mimic ['mɪmɪk] *n* imitador(a) *m/f* ▷ *adj* mímico ▷ *vt* remedar, imitar

min. *abbr* = **minimum; minute(s)**

mince [mɪns] *vt* picar ▷ *n* (*BRIT Culin*) carne *f* picada; **mincemeat** *n* conserva de fruta picada; (*us: meat*) carne *f* picada; **mince pie** *n* empanadilla rellena de fruta picada

mind [maɪnd] *n* mente *f*; (*intellect*) intelecto; (*contrasted with matter*) espíritu *m* ▷ *vt* (*attend to, look after*) ocuparse de, cuidar; (*be careful*) tener cuidado con; (*object to*): **I don't ~ the noise** no me molesta el ruido; **it is on my ~** me preocupa; **to bear**

sth in ~ tomar or tener algo en cuenta; **to make up one's ~** decidirse; **I don't ~** me es igual; **~ you ...** te advierto que ...; **never ~!** ¡es igual!, ¡no importa!; (*don't worry*) ¡no te preocupes!; **"~ the step"** "cuidado con el escalón"; **mindless** *adj* (*crime*) sin motivo; (*work*) de autómata

mine¹ [maɪn] *pron* el mío/la mía etc; **a friend of ~** un(a) amigo/a mío/mía ▷ *adj*: **this book is ~** este libro es mío

mine² [maɪn] *n* mina ▷ *vt* (*coal*) extraer; (*bomb: beach etc*) minar; **minefield** *n* campo de minas; **miner** *n* minero/a

mineral ['mɪnərəl] *adj* mineral ▷ *n* mineral *m*; **mineral water** *n* agua mineral

mingle ['mɪŋgl] *vi*: **to ~ with** mezclarse con

miniature ['mɪnətʃə*] *adj* (en) miniatura ▷ *n* miniatura

minibar ['mɪnɪbɑ:*] *n* minibar *m*

minibus ['mɪnɪbʌs] *n* microbús *m*

minicab ['mɪnɪkæb] *n* taxi *m* (*que sólo puede pedirse por teléfono*)

minimal ['mɪnɪml] *adj* mínimo

minimize ['mɪnɪmaɪz] *vt* minimizar; (*play down*) empequeñecer

minimum ['mɪnɪməm] (*pl* **minima**) *n*, *adj* mínimo

mining ['maɪnɪŋ] *n* explotación *f* minera

miniskirt ['mɪnɪskə:t] *n* minifalda

minister ['mɪnɪstə*] *n* (*BRIT Pol*) ministro/a (*SP*), secretario/a (*LAM*); (*Rel*) pastor *m* ▷ *vi*: **to ~ to** atender a

ministry ['mɪnɪstrɪ] *n* (*BRIT Pol*) ministerio, secretaría (*MEX*); (*Rel*) sacerdocio

minor ['maɪnə*] *adj* (*repairs, injuries*) leve; (*poet, planet*) menor; (*Mus*) menor ▷ *n* (*Law*) menor *m* de edad

Minorca [mɪ'nɔːkə] *n* Menorca

minority [maɪ'nɔrɪtɪ] *n* minoría

mint [mɪnt] *n* (*plant*) menta, hierbabuena; (*sweet*) caramelo de menta ▷ *vt* (*coins*) acuñar; **the (Royal) M~**, **the (US) M~** la Casa de la Moneda; **in ~ condition** en perfecto estado

minus ['maɪnəs] *n* (*also:* **~ sign**) signo de menos ▷ *prep* menos; **12 ~ 6 equals 6** 12 menos 6 son 6; **~ 24 °C** menos 24 grados

minute¹ ['mɪnɪt] *n* minuto; (*fig*) momento; **minutes** *npl* (*of meeting*) actas *fpl*; **at the last ~** a última hora

minute² [maɪ'njuːt] *adj* diminuto; (*search*) minucioso

miracle ['mɪrəkl] *n* milagro

miraculous [mɪ'rækjuləs] *adj* milagroso

mirage ['mɪrɑ:ʒ] *n* espejismo

mirror ['mɪrə*] *n* espejo; (*in car*) retrovisor *m*

misbehave [mɪsbɪ'heɪv] *vi* portarse mal

misc. *abbr* = **miscellaneous**

miscarriage ['mɪskærɪdʒ] *n* (*Med*) aborto; **~ of justice** error *m* judicial

miscellaneous [mɪsɪ'leɪnɪəs] *adj* varios/as, diversos/as

mischief ['mɪstʃɪf] *n* travesuras *fpl*, diabluras *fpl*; (*maliciousness*) malicia; **mischievous** [-ʃɪvəs] *adj* travieso

misconception [mɪskən'sepʃən] *n* idea equivocada; equivocación *f*

misconduct [mɪs'kɔndʌkt] *n* mala conducta; **professional ~** falta profesional

miser ['maɪzə*] *n* avaro/a

miserable ['mɪzərəbl] *adj* (*unhappy*) triste, desgraciado; (*unpleasant, contemptible*) miserable

misery ['mɪzərɪ] *n* tristeza; (*wretchedness*) miseria, desdicha

misfortune [mɪs'fɔ:tʃən] *n* desgracia

misgiving [mɪs'gɪvɪŋ] *n* (*apprehension*) presentimiento; **to have ~s about sth** tener dudas acerca de algo

misguided [mɪs'gaɪdɪd] *adj* equivocado

mishap ['mɪshæp] *n* desgracia, contratiempo

misinterpret [mɪsɪn'tə:prɪt] *vt* interpretar mal

misjudge [mɪs'dʒʌdʒ] *vt* juzgar mal

mislay [mɪs'leɪ] *vt* extraviar, perder

mislead [mɪs'li:d] *vt* llevar a conclusiones erróneas; **misleading** *adj* engañoso

misplace [mɪs'pleɪs] *vt* extraviar

misprint ['mɪsprɪnt] *n* errata, error *m* de imprenta

misrepresent [mɪsreprɪ'zent] *vt* falsificar

Miss [mɪs] *n* Señorita

miss [mɪs] *vt* (*train etc*) perder; (*fail to hit: target*) errar; (*regret the absence of*): **I ~ him** (yo) le echo de menos or a faltar; (*fail to see*): **you can't ~ it** no tiene pérdida ▷ *vi* fallar ▷ *n* (*shot*) tiro fallido or perdido; **miss out** (*BRIT*) *vt* omitir; **miss out on** *vt fus* (*fun, party, opportunity*) perderse

missile ['mɪsaɪl] *n* (*Aviat*) mísil *m*; (*object thrown*) proyectil *m*

missing ['mɪsɪŋ] *adj* (*pupil*) ausente; (*thing*) perdido; (*Mil*): **~ in action** desaparecido en combate

mission ['mɪʃən] *n* misión *f*; (*official representation*) delegación *f*; **missionary** *n* misionero/a

misspell [mɪs'spel] (*pt, pp* **misspelt** (*BRIT*) *or* **~ed**) *vt* escribir mal

mist [mɪst] *n* (*light*) neblina; (*heavy*) niebla; (*at sea*) bruma ▷ *vi* (*eyes: also:* **~ over**, **~ up**) llenarse de lágrimas; (*BRIT: windows: also:* **~**

over, ~ up) empañarse

mistake [mɪsˈteɪk] (vt: irreg) n error m
▷ vt entender mal; **by ~** por equivocación;
to make a ~ equivocarse; **to ~ A for B**
confundir A con B; **mistaken** pp of **mistake**
▷ adj equivocado; **to be mistaken**
equivocarse, engañarse

mister ['mɪstə*] (inf) n señor m; see **Mr**

mistletoe ['mɪsltəu] n muérdago

mistook [mɪsˈtuk] pt of **mistake**

mistress ['mɪstrɪs] n (lover) amante
f; (of house) señora (de la casa); (BRIT: in
primary school) maestra; (in secondary school)
profesora; (of situation) dueña

mistrust [mɪsˈtrʌst] vt desconfiar de

misty ['mɪstɪ] adj (day) de niebla; (glasses
etc) empañado

misunderstand [mɪsʌndəˈstænd] (irreg)
vt, vi entender mal; **misunderstanding** n
malentendido

misunderstood [mɪsʌndəˈstud] pt,
pp of **misunderstand** ▷ adj (person)
incomprendido

misuse [n mɪsˈjuːs, vb mɪsˈjuːz] n mal uso;
(of power) abuso; (of funds) malversación f
▷ vt abusar de; malversar

mitt(en) ['mɪt(n)] n manopla

mix [mɪks] vt mezclar; (combine) unir ▷ vi
mezclarse; (people) llevarse bien ▷ n mezcla;
mix up vt mezclar; (confuse) confundir;
mixed adj mixto; (feelings etc) encontrado;
mixed grill n (BRIT) parrillada mixta;
mixed salad n ensalada mixta; **mixed-up**
adj (confused) confuso, revuelto; **mixer** n
(for food) licuadora; (for drinks) coctelera;
(person): **he's a good mixer** tiene don de
gentes; **mixture** n mezcla; (also: **cough
mixture**) jarabe m; **mix-up** n confusión f

ml abbr (= millilitre(s)) ml

mm abbr (= millimetre) mm

moan [məun] n gemido ▷ vi gemir;
(inf: complain): **to ~ (about)** quejarse (de)

moat [məut] n foso

mob [mɔb] n multitud f ▷ vt acosar

mobile ['məubaɪl] adj móvil ▷ n móvil m;
mobile home n caravana; **mobile phone** n
teléfono móvil

mobility [məuˈbɪlɪtɪ] n movilidad f

mobilize ['məubɪlaɪz] vt movilizar

mock [mɔk] vt (ridicule) ridiculizar; (laugh
at) burlarse de ▷ adj fingido; **~ exam**
examen preparatorio antes de los exámenes
oficiales* (BRIT: Scol: inf) exámenes mpl de
prueba; **mockery** n burla

mod cons ['mɔdˈkɔnz] npl abbr (= modern
conveniences) see **convenience**

mode [məud] n modo

model ['mɔdl] n modelo; (fashion model,
artist's model) modelo mf ▷ adj modelo ▷ vt
(with clay etc) modelar; (copy): **to ~ o.s. on**
tomar como modelo a ▷ vi ser modelo; **to ~
clothes** pasar modelos, ser modelo

modem ['məudəm] n modem m

moderate [adj 'mɔdərət, vb 'mɔdəreɪt]
adj moderado/a ▷ vi moderarse, calmarse
▷ vt moderar

moderation [mɔdəˈreɪʃən] n moderación
f; **in ~** con moderación

modern ['mɔdən] adj moderno;
modernize vt modernizar; **modern
languages** npl lenguas fpl modernas

modest ['mɔdɪst] adj modesto; (small)
módico; **modesty** n modestia

modification [mɔdɪfɪˈkeɪʃən] n
modificación f

modify ['mɔdɪfaɪ] vt modificar

module ['mɔdjuːl] n (unit, component,
Space) módulo

mohair ['məuhɛə*] n mohair m

Mohammed [məˈhæmɛd] n Mahoma m

moist [mɔɪst] adj húmedo; **moisture**
['mɔɪstʃə*] n humedad f; **moisturizer**
['mɔɪstʃəraɪzə*] n crema hidratante

mold etc [məuld] (US) = **mould** etc

mole [məul] n (animal, spy) topo; (spot)
lunar m

molecule ['mɔlɪkjuːl] n molécula

molest [məuˈlɛst] vt importunar; (assault
sexually) abusar sexualmente de

▌Be careful not to translate **molest** by the
Spanish word molestar.

molten ['məultən] adj fundido; (lava)
líquido

mom [mɔm] (US) n = **mum**

moment ['məumənt] n momento; **at the
~** de momento, por ahora; **momentarily**
adv momentáneamente; (US: very soon)
de un momento a otro; **momentary** adj
momentáneo; **momentous** [-'mɛntəs] adj
trascendental, importante

momentum [məuˈmɛntəm] n momento;
(fig) ímpetu m; **to gather ~** cobrar
velocidad; (fig) ganar fuerza

mommy ['mɔmɪ] (US) n = **mummy**

Mon abbr (= Monday) lun

Monaco ['mɔnəkəu] n Mónaco

monarch ['mɔnək] n monarca mf;
monarchy n monarquía

monastery ['mɔnəstərɪ] n monasterio

Monday ['mʌndɪ] n lunes m inv

monetary ['mʌnɪtərɪ] adj monetario

money ['mʌnɪ] n dinero; (currency)
moneda; **to make ~** ganar dinero; **money
belt** n riñonera; **money order** n giro

mongrel ['mʌŋɡrəl] n (dog) perro mestizo

monitor ['mɔnɪtə*] n (Scol) monitor m;

(also: **television ~**) receptor m de control; (of computer) monitor m ▷ vt controlar
monk [mʌŋk] n monje m
monkey ['mʌŋkɪ] n mono
monologue ['mɒnələɡ] n monólogo
monopoly [mə'nɒpəlɪ] n monopolio
monosodium glutamate [mɒnə'səu-dɪəm'glu:təmeɪt] n glutamato monosódico
monotonous [mə'nɒtənəs] adj monótono
monsoon [mɒn'su:n] n monzón m
monster ['mɒnstə*] n monstruo
month [mʌnθ] n mes m; **monthly** adj mensual ▷ adv mensualmente
monument ['mɒnjumənt] n monumento
mood [mu:d] n humor m; (of crowd, group) clima m; **to be in a good/bad ~** estar de buen/mal humor; **moody** adj (changeable) de humor variable; (sullen) malhumorado
moon [mu:n] n luna; **moonlight** n luz f de la luna
moor [muə*] n páramo ▷ vt (ship) amarrar ▷ vi echar las amarras
moose [mu:s] n inv alce m
mop [mɒp] n fregona; (of hair) greña, melena ▷ vt fregar; **mop up** vt limpiar
mope [məup] vi estar or andar deprimido
moped ['məuped] n ciclomotor m
moral ['mɒrl] adj moral ▷ n moraleja; **morals** npl moralidad f, moral f
morale [mɒ'rɑ:l] n moral f
morality [mə'rælɪtɪ] n moralidad f
morbid ['mɔ:bɪd] adj (interest) morboso; (Med) mórbido

○ **KEYWORD**

more [mɔ:*] adj **1** (greater in number etc) más; **more people/work than before** más gente/trabajo que antes
2 (additional) más; **do you want (some) more tea?** ¿quieres más té?; **is there any more wine?** ¿queda vino?; **it'll take a few more weeks** tardará unas semanas más; **it's 2 kms more to the house** faltan 2 kms para la casa; **more time/letters than we expected** más tiempo del que/más cartas de las que esperábamos
▷ pron (greater amount, additional amount) más; **more than 10** más de 10; **it cost more than the other one/than we expected** costó más que el otro/más de lo que esperábamos; **is there any more?** ¿hay más?; **many/much more** muchos(as)/mucho(a) más
▷ adv más; **more dangerous/easily (than)**

más peligroso/fácilmente (que); **more and more expensive** cada vez más caro; **more or less** más o menos; **more than ever** más que nunca

moreover [mɔ:'rəuvə*] adv además, por otra parte
morgue [mɔ:ɡ] n depósito de cadáveres
morning ['mɔ:nɪŋ] n mañana; (early morning) madrugada ▷ cpd matutino, de la mañana; **in the ~** por la mañana; **7 o'clock in the ~** las 7 de la mañana; **morning sickness** n náuseas fpl matutinas
Moroccan [mə'rɒkən] adj, n marroquí m/f
Morocco [mə'rɒkəu] n Marruecos m
moron ['mɔ:rɒn] (inf) n imbécil mf
morphine ['mɔ:fi:n] n morfina
Morse [mɔ:s] n (also: **~ code**) (código) Morse
mortal ['mɔ:tl] adj, n mortal m
mortar ['mɔ:tə*] n argamasa
mortgage ['mɔ:ɡɪdʒ] n hipoteca ▷ vt hipotecar
mortician [mɔ:'tɪʃən] (us) n director/a m/f de pompas fúnebres
mortified ['mɔ:tɪfaɪd] adj: **I was ~** me dio muchísima vergüenza
mortuary ['mɔ:tjuərɪ] n depósito de cadáveres
mosaic [məu'zeɪɪk] n mosaico
Moslem ['mɒzləm] adj, n = **Muslim**
mosque [mɒsk] n mezquita
mosquito [mɒs'ki:təu] (pl **~es**) n mosquito (SP), zancudo (LAM)
moss [mɒs] n musgo
most [məust] adj la mayor parte de, la mayoría de ▷ pron la mayor parte, la mayoría ▷ adv el más; (very) muy; **the ~** (also: + adj) el más; **~ of them** la mayor parte de ellos; **I saw the ~** yo vi el que más; **at the (very) ~** a lo sumo, todo lo más; **to make the ~ of** aprovechar (al máximo); **a ~ interesting book** un libro interesantísimo; **mostly** adv en su mayor parte, principalmente
MOT (BRIT) n abbr = **Ministry of Transport**; **the ~ (test)** inspección (anual) obligatoria de coches y camiones
motel [məu'tel] n motel m
moth [mɒθ] n mariposa nocturna; (clothes moth) polilla
mother ['mʌðə*] n madre f ▷ adj materno ▷ vt (care for) cuidar (como una madre); **motherhood** n maternidad f; **mother-in-law** n suegra; **mother-of-pearl** n nácar m; **Mother's Day** n Día m de la Madre; **mother-to-be** n futura madre f; **mother tongue** n lengua materna

motif [mǝu'tiːf] n motivo

motion ['mǝuʃǝn] n movimiento; (gesture) ademán m, señal f; (at meeting) moción f ▷ vt, vi: **to ~ (to) sb to do sth** hacer señas a algn para que haga algo; **motionless** adj inmóvil; **motion picture** n película

motivate ['mǝutiveit] vt motivar

motivation [mǝuti'veiʃǝn] n motivación f

motive ['mǝutiv] n motivo

motor ['mǝutǝ*] n motor m; (BRIT: inf: vehicle) coche m (SP), carro (LAM), automóvil m ▷ adj motor (f: motora or motriz); **motorbike** n moto f; **motorboat** n lancha motora; **motorcar** (BRIT) n coche m, carro, automóvil m; **motorcycle** n motocicleta; **motorcyclist** n motociclista mf; **motoring** (BRIT) n automovilismo; **motorist** n conductor(a) m/f, automovilista mf; **motor racing** (BRIT) n carreras fpl de coches, automovilismo; **motorway** (BRIT) n autopista

motto ['mɔtǝu] (pl ~es) n lema m; (watchword) consigna

mould [mǝuld] (US **mold**) n molde m; (mildew) moho ▷ vt moldear; (fig) formar; **mouldy** adj enmohecido

mound [maund] n montón m, montículo

mount [maunt] n monte m ▷ vt montar, subir a; (jewel) engarzar; (picture) enmarcar; (exhibition etc) organizar ▷ vi (increase) aumentar; **mount up** vi aumentar

mountain ['mauntin] n montaña ▷ cpd de montaña; **mountain bike** n bicicleta de montaña; **mountaineer** n alpinista mf (SP, MEX), andinista mf (LAM); **mountaineering** n alpinismo (SP, MEX), andinismo (LAM); **mountainous** adj montañoso; **mountain range** n sierra

mourn [mɔːn] vt llorar, lamentar ▷ vi: **to ~ for** llorar la muerte de; **mourner** n doliente mf; dolorido/a; **mourning** n luto; **in mourning** de luto

mouse [maus] (pl **mice**) n (Zool, Comput) ratón m; **mouse mat** n (Comput) alfombrilla

moussaka [muˈsɑːkǝ] n musaca

mousse [muːs] n (Culin) crema batida; (for hair) espuma (moldeadora)

moustache [mǝsˈtɑːʃ] (US **mustache**) n bigote m

mouth [mauð, pl mauðz] n boca; (of river) desembocadura; **mouthful** n bocado; **mouth organ** n armónica; **mouthpiece** n (of musical instrument) boquilla; (spokesman) portavoz mf; **mouthwash** n enjuague m

move [muːv] n (movement) movimiento; (in game) jugada; (: turn to play) turno; (change: of house) mudanza; (: of job) cambio

de trabajo ▷ vt mover; (emotionally) conmover; (Pol: resolution etc) proponer ▷ vi moverse; (traffic) circular; (also: **~ house**) trasladarse, mudarse; **to ~ sb to do sth** mover a algn a hacer algo; **to get a ~ on** darse prisa; **move back** vi retroceder; **move in** vi (to a house) instalarse; (police, soldiers) intervenir; **move off** vi ponerse en camino; **move on** vi ponerse en camino; **move out** vi (of house) mudarse; **move over** vi apartarse, hacer sitio; **move up** vi (employee) ser ascendido; **movement** n movimiento

movie ['muːvi] n película; **to go to the ~s** ir al cine; **movie theater** (US) n cine m

moving ['muːviŋ] adj (emotional) conmovedor(a); (that moves) móvil

mow [mǝu] (pt ~**ed**, pp **mowed** or **mown**) vt (grass, corn) cortar, segar; **mower** n (also: **lawnmower**) cortacéspedes m inv

Mozambique [mǝuzæm'biːk] n Mozambique m

MP n abbr = **Member of Parliament**

MP3 n MP3; **MP3 player** n reproductor m (de) MP3

mpg n abbr = **miles per gallon**

m.p.h. abbr = **miles per hour** (60 m.p.h. = 96 k.p.h.)

Mr ['mistǝ*] (US **Mr.**) n: **~ Smith** (el) Sr. Smith

Mrs ['misiz] (US **Mrs.**) n: **~ Smith** (la) Sra. Smith

Ms [miz] (US **Ms.**) n = **Miss** or **Mrs**; **~ Smith** (la) Sr(t)a. Smith

MSP n abbr = **Member of the Scottish Parliament**

Mt abbr (Geo) (= **mount**) m

much [mʌtʃ] adj mucho ▷ adv mucho; (before pp) muy ▷ n or pron mucho; **how ~ is it?** ¿cuánto es?, ¿cuánto cuesta?; **too ~** demasiado; **it's not ~** no es mucho; **as ~ as** tanto como; **however ~ he tries** por mucho que se esfuerce

muck [mʌk] n suciedad f; **muck up** (inf) vt arruinar, estropear; **mucky** adj (dirty) sucio

mucus ['mjuːkǝs] n mucosidad f, moco

mud [mʌd] n barro, lodo

muddle ['mʌdl] n desorden m, confusión f; (mix-up) embrollo, lío ▷ vt (also: **~ up**) embrollar, confundir

muddy ['mʌdi] adj fangoso, cubierto de lodo

mudguard ['mʌdgɑːd] n guardabarros m inv

muesli ['mjuːzli] n muesli m

muffin ['mʌfin] n panecillo dulce

muffled ['mʌfld] adj (noise etc) amortiguado, apagado

muffler (US) ['mʌflə*] n (Aut) silenciador m

mug [mʌg] n taza grande (sin platillo); (for beer) jarra; (inf: face) jeta ▷ vt (assault) asaltar; **mugger** ['mʌgə*] n atracador(a) m/f; **mugging** n asalto

muggy ['mʌgɪ] adj bochornoso

mule [mju:l] n mula

multicoloured ['mʌltɪkʌləd] (US), **multicolored** adj multicolor

multimedia ['mʌltɪ'mi:dɪə] adj multimedia

multinational [mʌltɪ'næʃənl] n multinacional f ▷ adj multinacional

multiple ['mʌltɪpl] adj múltiple ▷ n múltiplo; **multiple choice (test)** n examen m de tipo test; **multiple sclerosis** n esclerosis f múltiple

multiplex cinema ['mʌltɪplɛks-] n multicines mpl

multiplication [mʌltɪplɪ'keɪʃən] n multiplicación f

multiply ['mʌltɪplaɪ] vt multiplicar ▷ vi multiplicarse

multistorey [mʌltɪ'stɔ:rɪ] (BRIT) adj de muchos pisos

mum [mʌm] (BRIT: inf) n mamá ▷ adj: **to keep ~** mantener la boca cerrada

mumble ['mʌmbl] vt, vi hablar entre dientes, refunfuñar

mummy ['mʌmɪ] n (BRIT: mother) mamá; (embalmed) momia

mumps [mʌmps] n paperas fpl

munch [mʌntʃ] vt, vi mascar

municipal [mju:'nɪsɪpl] adj municipal

mural ['mjuərl] n (pintura) mural m

murder ['mə:də*] n asesinato; (in law) homicidio ▷ vt asesinar, matar; **murderer** n asesino

murky ['mə:kɪ] adj (water) turbio; (street, night) lóbrego

murmur ['mə:mə*] n murmullo ▷ vt, vi murmurar

muscle ['mʌsl] n músculo; (fig: strength) garra, fuerza; **muscular** ['mʌskjulə*] adj muscular; (person) musculoso

museum [mju:'zɪəm] n museo

mushroom ['mʌʃrum] n seta, hongo; (Culin) champiñón m ▷ vi crecer de la noche a la mañana

music ['mju:zɪk] n música; **musical** adj musical; (sound) melodioso; (person) con talento musical ▷ n (show) comedia musical; **musical instrument** n instrumento musical; **musician** [-'zɪʃən] n músico/a

Muslim ['mʌzlɪm] adj, n musulmán/ ana m/f

muslin ['mʌzlɪn] n muselina

mussel ['mʌsl] n mejillón m

must [mʌst] aux vb (obligation): **I ~ do it** debo hacerlo, tengo que hacerlo; (probability): **he ~ be there by now** ya debe (de) estar allí ▷ n: **it's a ~** es imprescindible

mustache ['mʌstæʃ] (US) n = **moustache**

mustard ['mʌstəd] n mostaza

mustn't ['mʌsnt] = **must not**

mute [mju:t] adj, n mudo/a m/f

mutilate ['mju:tɪleɪt] vt mutilar

mutiny ['mju:tɪnɪ] n motín m ▷ vi amotinarse

mutter ['mʌtə*] vt, vi murmurar

mutton ['mʌtn] n carne f de cordero

mutual ['mju:tʃuəl] adj mutuo; (interest) común

muzzle ['mʌzl] n hocico; (for dog) bozal m; (of gun) boca ▷ vt (dog) poner un bozal a

my [maɪ] adj mi(s); **~ house/brother/ sisters** mi casa/mi hermano/mis hermanas; **I've washed ~ hair/cut ~ finger** me he lavado el pelo/cortado un dedo; **is this ~ pen or yours?** ¿es este bolígrafo mío o tuyo?

myself [maɪ'sɛlf] pron (reflexive) me; (emphatic) yo mismo; (after prep) mí (mismo); see also **oneself**

mysterious [mɪs'tɪərɪəs] adj misterioso

mystery ['mɪstərɪ] n misterio

mystical ['mɪstɪkl] adj místico

mystify ['mɪstɪfaɪ] vt (perplex) dejar perplejo

myth [mɪθ] n mito; **mythology** [mɪ'θɔlədʒɪ] n mitología

n

n/a *abbr* (= *not applicable*) no interesa

nag [næg] *vt* (*scold*) regañar

nail [neɪl] *n* (*human*) uña; (*metal*) clavo ▷ *vt* clavar; **to ~ sth to sth** clavar algo en algo; **to ~ sb down to doing sth** comprometer a algn a que haga algo; **nailbrush** *n* cepillo para las uñas; **nailfile** *n* lima para las uñas; **nail polish** *n* esmalte *m* or laca para las uñas; **nail polish remover** *n* quitaesmalte *m*; **nail scissors** *npl* tijeras *fpl* para las uñas; **nail varnish** (*BRIT*) *n* = **nail polish**

naïve [naɪˈiːv] *adj* ingenuo

naked [ˈneɪkɪd] *adj* (*nude*) desnudo; (*flame*) expuesto al aire

name [neɪm] *n* nombre *m*; (*surname*) apellido; (*reputation*) fama, renombre *m* ▷ *vt* (*child*) poner nombre a; (*criminal*) identificar; (*price, date etc*) fijar; **what's your ~?** ¿cómo se llama?; **by ~** de nombre; **in the ~ of** en nombre de; **to give one's ~ and address** dar sus señas; **namely** *adv* a saber

nanny [ˈnænɪ] *n* niñera

nap [næp] *n* (*sleep*) sueñecito, siesta

napkin [ˈnæpkɪn] *n* (*also:* **table ~**) servilleta

nappy [ˈnæpɪ] (*BRIT*) *n* pañal *m*

narcotics *npl* (*illegal drugs*) estupefacientes *mpl*, narcóticos *mpl*

narrative [ˈnærətɪv] *n* narrativa ▷ *adj* narrativo

narrator [nəˈreɪtə*] *n* narrador(a) *m/f*

narrow [ˈnærəu] *adj* estrecho, angosto; (*fig: majority etc*) corto; (: *ideas etc*) estrecho ▷ *vi* (*road*) estrecharse; (*diminish*) reducirse; **to have a ~ escape** escaparse por los pelos; **narrow down** *vt* (*search, investigation, possibilities*) restringir, limitar; (*list*) reducir; **narrowly** *adv* (*miss*) por poco; **narrow-minded** *adj* de miras estrechas

nasal [ˈneɪzl] *adj* nasal

nasty [ˈnɑːstɪ] *adj* (*remark*) feo; (*person*) antipático; (*revolting: taste, smell*) asqueroso; (*wound, disease etc*) peligroso, grave

nation [ˈneɪʃən] *n* nación *f*

national [ˈnæʃənl] *adj, n* nacional *m/f*; **national anthem** *n* himno nacional; **national dress** *n* vestido nacional; **National Health Service** (*BRIT*) *n* servicio nacional de salud pública ≈ Insalud *m* (*SP*); **National Insurance** (*BRIT*) *n* seguro social nacional; **nationalist** *adj, n* nacionalista *mf*; **nationality** [-ˈnælɪtɪ] *n* nacionalidad *f*; **nationalize** *vt* nacionalizar; **national park** (*BRIT*) *n* parque *m* nacional; **National Trust** *n* (*BRIT*) organización encargada de preservar el patrimonio histórico británico

nationwide [ˈneɪʃənwaɪd] *adj* en escala or a nivel nacional

native [ˈneɪtɪv] *n* (*local inhabitant*) natural *mf*, nacional *mf* ▷ *adj* (*indigenous*) indígena; (*country*) natal; (*innate*) natural, innato; **a ~ of Russia** un(a) natural *mf* de Rusia; **Native American** *adj, n* americano/a indígena, amerindio/a; **native speaker** *n* hablante *mf* nativo/a

NATO [ˈneɪtəu] *n abbr* (= *North Atlantic Treaty Organization*) OTAN *f*

natural [ˈnætʃrəl] *adj* natural; **natural gas** *n* gas *m* natural; **natural history** *n* historia natural; **naturally** *adv* (*speak etc*) naturalmente; (*of course*) desde luego, por supuesto; **natural resources** *npl* recursos *mpl* naturales

nature [ˈneɪtʃə*] *n* (*also:* **N~**) naturaleza *f*; (*group, sort*) género, clase *f*; (*character*) carácter *m*, genio; **by ~** por or de naturaleza; **nature reserve** *n* reserva natural

naughty [ˈnɔːtɪ] *adj* (*child*) travieso

nausea [ˈnɔːsɪə] *n* náuseas *fpl*

naval [ˈneɪvl] *adj* naval, de marina

navel [ˈneɪvl] *n* ombligo

navigate [ˈnævɪgeɪt] *vt* gobernar ▷ *vi* navegar; (*Aut*) ir de copiloto; **navigation** [-ˈgeɪʃən] *n* (*action*) navegación *f*; (*science*) náutica

navy [ˈneɪvɪ] *n* marina de guerra; (*ships*) armada, flota

Nazi [ˈnɑːtsɪ] *n* nazi *mf*

NB *abbr* (= *nota bene*) nótese

near [nɪə*] *adj* (*place, relation*) cercano; (*time*) próximo ▷ *adv* cerca ▷ *prep* (*also:* **~ to**: *space*) cerca de, junto a; (: *time*) cerca de ▷ *vt* acercarse a, aproximarse a; **nearby** [nɪəˈbaɪ] *adj* cercano, próximo ▷ *adv* cerca; **nearly** *adv* casi, por poco; **I nearly fell** por poco me caigo; **near-sighted** *adj* miope, corto de vista

neat [niːt] *adj* (*place*) ordenado, bien cuidado; (*person*) pulcro; (*plan*) ingenioso;

(spirits) solo; **neatly** adv (tidily) con esmero; (skilfully) ingeniosamente

necessarily ['nɛsɪsrɪlɪ] adv necesariamente

necessary ['nɛsɪsrɪ] adj necesario, preciso

necessity [nɪ'sɛsɪtɪ] n necesidad f

neck [nɛk] n (of person, garment, bottle) cuello; (of animal) pescuezo ▷ vi (inf) besuquearse; ~ **and** ~ parejos; **necklace** ['nɛklɪs] n collar m; **necktie** ['nɛktaɪ] n corbata

nectarine ['nɛktərɪn] n nectarina

need [niːd] n (lack) escasez f, falta; (necessity) necesidad f ▷ vt (require) necesitar; **I** ~ **to do it** tengo que or debo hacerlo; **you don't** ~ **to go** no hace falta que (te) vayas

needle ['niːdl] n aguja ▷ vt (fig: inf) picar, fastidiar

needless ['niːdlɪs] adj innecesario; ~ **to say** huelga decir que

needlework ['niːdlwəːk] n (activity) costura, labor f de aguja

needn't ['niːdnt] = need not

needy ['niːdɪ] adj necesitado

negative ['nɛgətɪv] n (Phot) negativo; (Ling) negación f ▷ adj negativo

neglect [nɪ'glɛkt] vt (one's duty) faltar a, no cumplir con; (child) descuidar, desatender ▷ n (of house, garden etc) abandono; (of child) desatención f; (of duty) incumplimiento

negotiate [nɪ'gəʊʃɪeɪt] vt (treaty, loan) negociar; (obstacle) franquear; (bend in road) tomar ▷ vi: **to** ~ **(with)** negociar (con)

negotiations [nɪgəʊʃɪ'eɪʃənz] pl n negociaciones

negotiator [nɪ'gəʊʃɪeɪtə*] n negociador(a) m/f

neighbour ['neɪbə*] (US **neighbor** etc) n vecino/a; **neighbourhood** n (place) vecindad f, barrio; (people) vecindario; **neighbouring** adj vecino

neither ['naɪðə*] adj ni ▷ conj: **I didn't move and ~ did John** no me he movido, ni Juan tampoco ▷ pron ninguno ▷ adv: ~ **good nor bad** ni bueno ni malo; ~ **is true** ninguno/a de los(las) dos es cierto/a

neon ['niːɔn] n neón m

Nepal [nɪ'pɔːl] n Nepal m

nephew ['nɛvjuː] n sobrino

nerve [nəːv] n (Anat) nervio; (courage) valor m; (impudence) descaro, frescura (nervousness) nerviosismo msg, nervios mpl; **a fit of ~s** un ataque de nervios

nervous ['nəːvəs] adj (anxious, Anat) nervioso; (timid) tímido, miedoso; **nervous breakdown** n crisis f nerviosa

nest [nɛst] n (of bird) nido; (wasps' nest) avispero ▷ vi anidar

net [nɛt] n (gen) red f; (fabric) tul m ▷ adj (Comm) neto, líquido ▷ vt coger (SP) or agarrar (LAM) con red; (Sport) marcar; **netball** n básquet m

Netherlands ['nɛðələndz] npl: **the ~** los Países Bajos

nett [nɛt] adj = net

nettle ['nɛtl] n ortiga

network ['nɛtwəːk] n red f

neurotic [njuə'rɔtɪk] adj neurótico/a

neuter ['njuːtə*] adj (Ling) neutro ▷ vt castrar, capar

neutral ['njuːtrəl] adj (person) neutral; (colour etc, Elec) neutro ▷ n (Aut) punto muerto

never ['nɛvə*] adv nunca, jamás; **I** ~ **went** no fui nunca; ~ **in my life** jamás en la vida; see also **mind**; **never-ending** adj interminable, sin fin; **nevertheless** [nɛvəðə'lɛs] adv sin embargo, no obstante

new [njuː] adj nuevo; (brand new) a estrenar; (recent) reciente; **New Age** n Nueva Era; **newborn** adj recién nacido; **newcomer** ['njuːkʌmə*] n recién venido/a or llegado/a; **newly** adv nuevamente, recién

news [njuːz] n noticias fpl; **a piece of ~** una noticia; **the ~** (Radio, TV) las noticias fpl; **news agency** n agencia de noticias; **newsagent** (BRIT) n vendedor(a) m/f de periódicos; **newscaster** n presentador(a) m/f, locutor(a) m/f; **news dealer** (US) n = **newsagent**; **newsletter** n hoja informativa, boletín m; **newspaper** n periódico, diario; **newsreader** n = **newscaster**

newt [njuːt] n tritón m

New Year n Año Nuevo; **New Year's Day** n Día m de Año Nuevo; **New Year's Eve** n Nochevieja

New Zealand [njuː'ziːlənd] n Nueva Zelanda; **New Zealander** n neozelandés/ esa m/f

next [nɛkst] adj (house, room) vecino; (bus stop, meeting) próximo; (following: page etc) siguiente ▷ adv después; **the ~ day** el día siguiente; ~ **time** la próxima vez; ~ **year** el año próximo or que viene; ~ **to** junto a, al lado de; ~ **to nothing** casi nada; ~ **please!** ¡el siguiente!; **next door** adv en la casa de al lado ▷ adj vecino, de al lado; **next-of-kin** n pariente m más cercano

NHS n abbr = **National Health Service**

nibble ['nɪbl] vt mordisquear, mordiscar

nice [naɪs] adj (likeable) simpático; (kind) amable; (pleasant) agradable;

(*attractive*) bonito, lindo (*LAM*); **nicely** *adv*
amablemente; bien

niche [ni:ʃ] *n* (*Arch*) nicho, hornacina

nick [nɪk] *n* (*wound*) rasguño; (*cut,
indentation*) mella, muesca ▷ *vt* (*inf*) birlar,
robar; **in the ~ of time** justo a tiempo

nickel ['nɪkl] *n* níquel *m*; (*us*) moneda de 5
centavos

nickname ['nɪkneɪm] *n* apodo, mote *m*
▷ *vt* apodar

nicotine ['nɪkəti:n] *n* nicotina

niece [ni:s] *n* sobrina

night [naɪt] *n* noche *f*; (*evening*) tarde *f*;
the ~ before last anteanoche; **at ~, by
~** de noche, por la noche; **night club** *n*
cabaret *m*; **nightdress** (*BRIT*) *n* camisón *m*;
nightie ['naɪtɪ] *n* = **nightdress**; **nightlife**
n vida nocturna; **nightly** *adj* de todas las
noches ▷ *adv* todas las noches, cada noche;
nightmare *n* pesadilla; **night school** *n*
clase(s) *f(pl)* nocturna(s); **night shift** *n*
turno nocturno *or* de noche; **night-time**
n noche *f*

nil [nɪl] (*BRIT*) *n* (*Sport*) cero, nada

nine [naɪn] *num* nueve; **nineteen** *num*
diecinueve, diez y nueve; **nineteenth**
[naɪn'ti:nθ] *adj* decimonoveno,
decimonono; **ninetieth** ['naɪntɪɪθ] *adj*
nonagésimo; **ninety** *num* noventa

ninth [naɪnθ] *adj* noveno

nip [nɪp] *vt* (*pinch*) pellizcar; (*bite*)
morder

nipple ['nɪpl] *n* (*Anat*) pezón *m*

nitrogen ['naɪtrədʒən] *n* nitrógeno

○ **KEYWORD**

no [nəu] (*pl* **noes**) *adv* (*opposite of "yes"*) no;
are you coming? – no (I'm not) ¿vienes? –
no; **would you like some more? – no thank
you** ¿quieres más? – no gracias ▷ *adj* (*not
any*): **I have no money/time/books** no
tengo dinero/tiempo/libros; **no other man
would have done it** ningún otro lo hubiera
hecho; **"no entry"** "prohibido el paso"; **"no
smoking"** "prohibido fumar"
▷ *n* no *m*

nobility [nəu'bɪlɪtɪ] *n* nobleza

noble ['nəubl] *adj* noble

nobody ['nəubədɪ] *pron* nadie

nod [nɔd] *vi* saludar con la cabeza; (*in
agreement*) decir que sí con la cabeza; (*doze*)
dar cabezadas ▷ *vt*: **to ~ one's head** inclinar
la cabeza ▷ *n* inclinación *f* de cabeza; **nod
off** *vi* dar cabezadas

noise [nɔɪz] *n* ruido; (*din*) escándalo,
estrépito; **noisy** *adj* ruidoso; (*child*)

escandaloso

nominal ['nɔmɪnl] *adj* nominal

nominate ['nɔmɪneɪt] *vt* (*propose*)
proponer; (*appoint*) nombrar;
nomination [nɔmɪ'neɪʃən] *n* propuesta;
nombramiento; **nominee** [-'ni:] *n*
candidato/a

none [nʌn] *pron* ninguno/a ▷ *adv* de
ninguna manera; **~ of you** ninguno
de vosotros; **I've ~ left** no me queda
ninguno/a; **he's ~ the worse for it** no le ha
hecho ningún mal

nonetheless [nʌnðə'lɛs] *adv* sin
embargo, no obstante

non-fiction [nɔn'fɪkʃən] *n* literatura no
novelesca

nonsense ['nɔnsəns] *n* tonterías *fpl*,
disparates *fpl*; **~!** ¡qué tonterías!

non: **non-smoker** *n* no fumador(a) *m/f*;
non-smoking *adj* (de) no fumador; **non-
stick** *adj* (*pan, surface*) antiadherente

noodles ['nu:dlz] *npl* tallarines *mpl*

noon [nu:n] *n* mediodía *m*

no-one ['nəuwʌn] *pron* = **nobody**

nor [nɔː*] *conj* = **neither** ▷ *adv see* **neither**

norm [nɔːm] *n* norma

normal ['nɔːml] *adj* normal; **normally** *adv*
normalmente

north [nɔːθ] *n* norte *m* ▷ *adj* del norte,
norteño ▷ *adv* al or hacia el norte; **North
America** *n* América del Norte; **North
American** *adj*, *n* norteamericano/a *m/f*;
northbound ['nɔːθbaund] *adj* (*traffic*)
que se dirige al norte; (*carriageway*) de
dirección norte; **north-east** *n* nor(d)este
m; **northeastern** *adj* nor(d)este, del nor(d)
este; **northern** ['nɔːðən] *adj* norteño,
del norte; **Northern Ireland** *n* Irlanda del
Norte; **North Korea** *n* Corea del Norte;
North Pole *n* Polo Norte; **North Sea** *n*
Mar *m* del Norte; **north-west** *n* nor(d)
oeste *m*; **northwestern**
['nɔːθ'westən] *adj* noroeste, del noroeste

Norway ['nɔːweɪ] *n* Noruega; **Norwegian**
[-'wi:dʒən] *adj* noruego/a ▷ *n* noruego/a;
(*Ling*) noruego

nose [nəuz] *n* (*Anat*) nariz *f*; (*Zool*) hocico;
(*sense of smell*) olfato ▷ *vi*: **to ~ about**
curiosear; **nosebleed** *n* hemorragia nasal;
nosey (*inf*) *adj* curioso, fisgón/ona

nostalgia [nɔs'tældʒɪə] *n* nostalgia

nostalgic [nɔs'tældʒɪk] *adj* nostálgico

nostril ['nɔstrɪl] *n* ventana de la nariz

nosy ['nəuzɪ] (*inf*) *adj* = **nosey**

not [nɔt] *adv* no; **~ that ...** no es que ...;
it's too late, isn't it? es demasiado tarde,
¿verdad or no?; **~ yet/now** todavía/ahora
no; **why ~?** ¿por qué no?; *see also* **all; only**

notable ['nəutəbl] *adj* notable; **notably** *adv* especialmente

notch [nɔtʃ] *n* muesca, corte *m*

note [nəut] *n* (Mus, record, letter) nota; (banknote) billete *m*; (tone) tono ▷ *vt* (observe) notar, observar; (write down) apuntar, anotar; **notebook** *n* libreta, cuaderno; **noted** ['nəutɪd] *adj* célebre, conocido; **notepad** *n* bloc *m*; **notepaper** *n* papel *m* para cartas

nothing ['nʌθɪŋ] *n* nada; (zero) cero; **he does ~** no hace nada; **~ new** nada nuevo; **~ much** no mucho; **for ~** (free) gratis, sin pago; (in vain) en balde

notice ['nəutɪs] *n* (announcement) anuncio; (warning) aviso; (dismissal) despido; (resignation) dimisión *f*; (period of time) plazo ▷ *vt* (observe) notar, observar; **to bring sth to sb's ~** (attention) llamar la atención de algn sobre algo; **to take ~ of** tomar nota de, prestar atención a; **at short ~** con poca anticipación; **until further ~** hasta nuevo aviso; **to hand in one's ~** dimitir

Be careful not to translate **notice** by the Spanish word *noticia*.

noticeable *adj* evidente, obvio

notify ['nəutɪfaɪ] *vt*: **to ~ sb (of sth)** comunicar (algo) a algn

notion ['nəuʃən] *n* idea; (opinion) opinión *f*; **notions** *npl* (US) mercería

notorious [nəu'tɔ:rɪəs] *adj* notorio

notwithstanding [nɔtwɪθ'stændɪŋ] *adv* no obstante, sin embargo; **~ this** a pesar de esto

nought [nɔ:t] *n* cero

noun [naun] *n* nombre *m*, sustantivo

nourish ['nʌrɪʃ] *vt* nutrir; (fig) alimentar; **nourishment** *n* alimento, sustento

Nov. *abbr* (= November) nov

novel ['nɔvl] *n* novela ▷ *adj* (new) nuevo, original; (unexpected) insólito; **novelist** *n* novelista *mf*; **novelty** *n* novedad *f*

November [nəu'vɛmbə*] *n* noviembre *m*

novice ['nɔvɪs] *n* (Rel) novicio/a

now [nau] *adv* (at the present time) ahora; (these days) actualmente, hoy día ▷ *conj*: **~ (that)** ya que, ahora que; **right ~** ahora mismo; **by ~** ya; **just ~** ahora mismo; **~ and then, ~ and again** de vez en cuando; **from ~ on** de ahora en adelante; **nowadays** ['nauədeɪz] *adv* hoy (en) día, actualmente

nowhere ['nəuwɛə*] *adv* (direction) a ninguna parte; (location) en ninguna parte

nozzle ['nɔzl] *n* boquilla

nr *abbr* (BRIT) = **near**

nuclear ['nju:klɪə*] *adj* nuclear

nucleus ['nju:klɪəs] (*pl* **nuclei**) *n* núcleo

nude [nju:d] *adj, n* desnudo/a *m/f*; **in the ~** desnudo

nudge [nʌdʒ] *vt* dar un codazo a

nudist ['nju:dɪst] *n* nudista *mf*

nudity ['nju:dɪtɪ] *n* desnudez *f*

nuisance ['nju:sns] *n* molestia, fastidio; (person) pesado, latoso; **what a ~!** ¡qué lata!

numb [nʌm] *adj*: **~ with cold/fear** entumecido por el frío/paralizado de miedo

number ['nʌmbə*] *n* número; (quantity) cantidad *f* ▷ *vt* (pages etc) numerar, poner número a; (amount to) sumar, ascender a; **to be ~ed among** figurar entre; **a ~ of** varios, algunos; **they were ten in ~** eran diez; **number plate** (BRIT) *n* matrícula, placa; **Number Ten** *n* (BRIT: 10 Downing Street) residencia del primer ministro

numerical [nju:'mɛrɪkl] *adj* numérico

numerous ['nju:mərəs] *adj* numeroso

nun [nʌn] *n* monja, religiosa

nurse [nə:s] *n* enfermero/a; (also: **~maid**) niñera ▷ *vt* (patient) cuidar, atender

nursery ['nə:sərɪ] *n* (institution) guardería infantil; (room) cuarto de los niños; (for plants) criadero, semillero; **nursery rhyme** *n* canción *f* infantil; **nursery school** *n* parvulario, escuela de párvulos; **nursery slope** (BRIT) *n* (Ski) cuesta para principiantes

nursing ['nə:sɪŋ] *n* (profession) profesión *f* de enfermera; (care) asistencia, cuidado; **nursing home** *n* clínica de reposo

nurture ['nə:tʃə*] *vt* (child, plant) alimentar, nutrir

nut [nʌt] *n* (Tech) tuerca; (Bot) nuez *f*

nutmeg ['nʌtmɛg] *n* nuez *f* moscada

nutrient ['nju:trɪənt] *adj* nutritivo ▷ *n* elemento nutritivo

nutrition [nju:'trɪʃən] *n* nutrición *f*, alimentación *f*

nutritious [nju:'trɪʃəs] *adj* nutritivo, alimenticio

nuts [nʌts] (inf) *adj* loco

NVQ *n abbr* (BRIT) = **National Vocational Qualification**

nylon ['naɪlɔn] *n* nilón *m* ▷ *adj* de nilón

O

oath [əuθ] *n* juramento; (*swear word*) palabrota; **on** (*BRIT*) *or* **under ~** bajo juramento

oak [əuk] *n* roble *m* ▷ *adj* de roble

O.A.P. (*BRIT*) *n, abbr* = **old-age pensioner**

oar [ɔː*] *n* remo

oasis [əu'eɪsɪs] (*pl* **oases**) *n* oasis *m inv*

oath [əuθ] *n* juramento; (*swear word*) palabrota; **on** (*BRIT*) *or* **under ~** bajo juramento

oatmeal ['əutmiːl] *n* harina de avena

oats [əuts] *npl* avena

obedience [ə'biːdɪəns] *n* obediencia

obedient [ə'biːdɪənt] *adj* obediente

obese [əu'biːs] *adj* obeso

obesity [əu'biːsɪtɪ] *n* obesidad *f*

obey [ə'beɪ] *vt* obedecer; (*instructions, regulations*) cumplir

obituary [ə'bɪtjuərɪ] *n* necrología

object *n* ['ɔbdʒɪkt, *vb* əb'dʒɛkt] *n* objeto; (*purpose*) objeto, propósito; (*Ling*) complemento ▷ *vi*: **to ~ to** estar en contra de; (*proposal*) oponerse a; **to ~ that** objetar que; **expense is no ~** no importa cuánto cuesta; **I ~!** ¡yo protesto!; **objection** [əb'dʒɛkʃən] *n* protesta; **I have no objection to ...** no tengo inconveniente en que ...; **objective** *adj, n* objetivo

obligation [ɔblɪ'geɪʃən] *n* obligación *f*; (*debt*) deber *m*; **without ~** sin compromiso

obligatory [ə'blɪgətərɪ] *adj* obligatorio

oblige [ə'blaɪdʒ] *vt* (*do a favour for*) complacer, hacer un favor a; **to ~ sb to do sth** forzar *or* obligar a algn a hacer algo; **to be ~d to sb for sth** estarle agradecido a algn por algo

oblique [ə'bliːk] *adj* oblicuo; (*allusion*) indirecto

obliterate [ə'blɪtəreɪt] *vt* borrar

oblivious [ə'blɪvɪəs] *adj*: **~ of** inconsciente de

oblong ['ɔblɔŋ] *adj* rectangular ▷ *n* rectángulo

obnoxious [əb'nɔkʃəs] *adj* odioso, detestable; (*smell*) nauseabundo

oboe ['əubəu] *n* oboe *m*

obscene [əb'siːn] *adj* obsceno

obscure [əb'skjuə*] *adj* oscuro ▷ *vt* oscurecer; (*hide: sun*) esconder

observant [əb'zəːvnt] *adj* observador(a)

observation [ɔbzə'veɪʃən] *n* observación *f*; (*Med*) examen *m*

observatory [əb'zəːvətrɪ] *n* observatorio

observe [əb'zəːv] *vt* observar; (*rule*) cumplir; **observer** *n* observador(a) *m/f*

obsess [əb'sɛs] *vt* obsesionar; **obsession** [əb'sɛʃən] *n* obsesión *f*; **obsessive** *adj* obsesivo; obsesionante

obsolete ['ɔbsəliːt] *adj*: **to be ~** estar en desuso

obstacle ['ɔbstəkl] *n* obstáculo; (*nuisance*) estorbo

obstinate ['ɔbstɪnɪt] *adj* terco, porfiado; (*determined*) obstinado

obstruct [əb'strʌkt] *vt* obstruir; (*hinder*) estorbar, obstaculizar; **obstruction** [əb'strʌkʃən] *n* (*action*) obstrucción *f*; (*object*) estorbo, obstáculo

obtain [əb'teɪn] *vt* obtener; (*achieve*) conseguir

obvious ['ɔbvɪəs] *adj* obvio, evidente; **obviously** *adv* evidentemente, naturalmente; **obviously not** por supuesto que no

occasion [ə'keɪʒən] *n* oportunidad *f*, ocasión *f*; (*event*) acontecimiento; **occasional** *adj* poco frecuente, ocasional; **occasionally** *adv* de vez en cuando

occult [ɔ'kʌlt] *adj* (*gen*) oculto

occupant ['ɔkjupənt] *n* (*of house*) inquilino/a; (*of car*) ocupante *mf*

occupation [ɔkju'peɪʃən] *n* ocupación *f*; (*job*) trabajo; (*pastime*) ocupaciones *fpl*

occupy ['ɔkjupaɪ] *vt* (*seat, post, time*) ocupar; (*house*) habitar; **to ~ o.s. in doing** pasar el tiempo haciendo

occur [ə'kəː*] *vi* pasar, suceder; **to ~ to sb** ocurrírsele a algn; **occurrence** [ə'kʌrəns] *n* acontecimiento; (*existence*) existencia

ocean ['əuʃən] *n* océano

o'clock [ə'klɔk] *adv*: **it is 5 ~** son las 5

Oct. *abbr* (= *October*) oct

October [ɔk'təubə*] *n* octubre *m*

octopus ['ɔktəpəs] *n* pulpo

odd [ɔd] *adj* extraño, raro; (*number*) impar; (*sock, shoe etc*) suelto; **60-~** 60 y pico; **at ~ times** de vez en cuando; **to be the ~ one out** estar de más; **oddly** *adv* curiosamente, extrañamente; *see also* **enough**; **odds** *npl*

(*in betting*) puntos *mpl* de ventaja; **it makes no odds** da lo mismo; **at odds** reñidos/as; **odds and ends** minucias *fpl*
odometer [ɔˈdɔmɪtə*] (*US*) *n* cuentakilómetros *m inv*
odour [ˈəʊdə*] (*US* **odor**) *n* olor *m*; (*unpleasant*) hedor *m*

○ **KEYWORD**

of [ɔv, əv] *prep* **1** (*gen*) de; **a friend of ours** un amigo nuestro; **a boy of 10** un chico de 10 años; **that was kind of you** eso fue muy amable por *or* de tu parte
2 (*expressing quantity, amount, dates etc*) de; **a kilo of flour** un kilo de harina; **there were three of them** había tres; **three of us went** tres de nosotros fuimos; **the 5th of July** el 5 de julio
3 (*from, out of*) de; **made of wood** (hecho) de madera

off [ɔf] *adj, adv* (*engine*) desconectado; (*light*) apagado; (*tap*) cerrado; (*BRIT: food: bad*) pasado, malo; (: *milk*) cortado; (*cancelled*) cancelado ▷ *prep* de; **to be ~** (*to leave*) irse, marcharse; **to be ~ sick** estar enfermo *or* de baja; **a day ~** un día libre *or* sin trabajar; **to have an ~ day** tener un día malo; **he had his coat ~** se había quitado el abrigo; **10% ~** (*Comm*) (con el) 10% de descuento; **5 km ~ (the road)** a 5 km (de la carretera); **~ the coast** frente a la costa; **I'm ~ meat** (*no longer eat/like it*) paso de la carne; **on the ~ chance** por si acaso; **~ and on** de vez en cuando

offence [əˈfɛns] (*US* **offense**) *n* (*crime*) delito; **to take ~ at** ofenderse por
offend [əˈfɛnd] *vt* (*person*) ofender; **offender** *n* delincuente *mf*
offense [əˈfɛns] (*US*) *n* = **offence**
offensive [əˈfɛnsɪv] *adj* ofensivo; (*smell etc*) repugnante ▷ *n* (*Mil*) ofensiva
offer [ˈɔfə*] *n* oferta, ofrecimiento; (*proposal*) propuesta ▷ *vt* ofrecer; (*opportunity*) facilitar; **"on ~"** (*Comm*) "en oferta"
offhand [ɔfˈhænd] *adj* informal ▷ *adv* de improviso
office [ˈɔfɪs] *n* (*place*) oficina; (*room*) despacho; (*position*) cargo, oficio; **doctor's ~** (*US*) consultorio; **to take ~** entrar en funciones; **office block** (*US*), **office building** *n* bloque *m* de oficinas; **office hours** *npl* horas *fpl* de oficina; (*US Med*) horas *fpl* de consulta
officer [ˈɔfɪsə*] *n* (*Mil etc*) oficial *mf*; (*also*: **police ~**) agente *mf* de policía; (*of*

organization) director(a) *m/f*
office worker *n* oficinista *mf*
official [əˈfɪʃl] *adj* oficial, autorizado ▷ *n* funcionario/a, oficial *mf*
off: **off-licence** (*BRIT*) *n* (*shop*) bodega **tienda de vinos y bebidas alcohólicas**; **off-line** *adj, adv* (*Comput*) fuera de línea; **off-peak** *adj* (*electricity*) de banda económica; (*ticket*) billete de precio reducido por viajar fuera de las horas punta; **off-putting** (*BRIT*) *adj* (*person*) asqueroso; (*remark*) desalentador(a); **off-season** *adj, adv* fuera de temporada

● **OFF-LICENCE**
●
● En el Reino Unido la venta de bebidas
● alcohólicas está estrictamente regulada
● y se necesita una licencia especial, con
● la que cuentan los bares, restaurantes
● y los establecimientos de **off-licence**,
● los únicos lugares en donde se pueden
● adquirir bebidas alcohólicas para su
● consumo fuera del local, de donde viene
● su nombre. También venden bebidas
● no alcohólicas, tabaco, chocolatinas,
● patatas fritas, etc. y a menudo forman
● parte de una cadena nacional.

offset [ˈɔfsɛt] *vt* contrarrestar, compensar
offshore [ɔfˈʃɔː*] *adj* (*breeze, island*) costera; (*fishing*) de bajura
offside [ˈɔfsaɪd] *adj* (*Sport*) fuera de juego; (*Aut: in UK*) del lado derecho; (: *in US, Europe etc*) del lado izquierdo
offspring [ˈɔfsprɪŋ] *n inv* descendencia
often [ˈɔfn] *adv* a menudo, con frecuencia; **how ~ do you go?** ¿cada cuánto vas?
oh [əʊ] *excl* ¡ah!
oil [ɔɪl] *n* aceite *m*; (*petroleum*) petróleo; (*for heating*) aceite *m* combustible ▷ *vt* engrasar; **oil filter** *n* (*Aut*) filtro de aceite; **oil painting** *n* pintura al óleo; **oil refinery** *n* refinería de petróleo; **oil rig** *n* torre *f* de perforación; **oil slick** *n* marea negra; **oil tanker** *n* petrolero; (*truck*) camión *m* cisterna; **oil well** *n* pozo (de petróleo); **oily** *adj* aceitoso; (*food*) grasiento
ointment [ˈɔɪntmənt] *n* ungüento
O.K., okay [ˈəʊˈkeɪ] *excl* ¡O.K.!, ¡está bien!, ¡vale! (*SP*) ▷ *adj* bien ▷ *vt* dar el visto bueno a
old [əʊld] *adj* viejo; (*former*) antiguo; **how ~ are you?** ¿cuántos años tienes?, ¿qué edad tienes?; **he's 10 years ~** tiene 10 años; **~er brother** hermano mayor; **old age** *n* vejez *f*, **old-age pension** *n* (*BRIT*) jubilación *f*, pensión *f*; **old-age pensioner** (*BRIT*) *n* jubilado/a; **old-fashioned** *adj* anticuado,

pasado de moda; **old people's home** n (esp BRIT) residencia f de ancianos

olive ['ɒlɪv] n (fruit) aceituna; (tree) olivo
▷ adj (also: **~-green**) verde oliva; **olive oil** n aceite m de oliva

Olympic [əu'lɪmpɪk] adj olímpico; **the ~ Games, the ~s** las Olimpiadas

omelet(te) ['ɒmlɪt] n tortilla francesa (SP), omelette f (LAM)

omen ['əumən] n presagio

ominous ['ɒmɪnəs] adj de mal agüero, amenazador(a)

omit [əu'mɪt] vt omitir

○ **KEYWORD**

on [ɒn] prep **1** (indicating position) en; sobre; **on the wall** en la pared; **it's on the table** está sobre o en la mesa; **on the left** a la izquierda
2 (indicating means, method, condition etc): **on foot** a pie; **on the train/plane** (go) en tren/avión; (be) en el tren/el avión; **on the radio/television/telephone** por o en la radio/televisión/al teléfono; **to be on drugs** drogarse; (Med) estar a tratamiento; **to be on holiday/business** estar de vacaciones/en viaje de negocios
3 (referring to time): **on Friday** el viernes; **on Fridays** los viernes; **on June 20th** el 20 de junio; **a week on Friday** del viernes en una semana; **on arrival** al llegar; **on seeing this** al ver esto
4 (about, concerning) sobre, acerca de; **a book on physics** un libro de o sobre física
▷ adv **1** (referring to dress): **to have one's coat on** tener o llevar el abrigo puesto; **she put her gloves on** se puso los guantes
2 (referring to covering): **"screw the lid on tightly"** "cerrar bien la tapa"
3 (further, continuously): **to walk** etc **on** seguir caminando etc
▷ adj **1** (functioning, in operation: machine, radio, TV, light) encendido/a (SP), prendido/a (LAM); (: tap) abierto/a; (: brakes) echado/a, puesto/a; **is the meeting still on?** (in progress) ¿todavía continúa la reunión?; (not cancelled) ¿va a haber reunión al fin?; **there's a good film on at the cinema** ponen una buena película en el cine
2 **that's not on!** (inf: not possible) ¡eso ni hablar!; (: not acceptable) ¡eso no se hace!

once [wʌns] adv una vez; (formerly) antiguamente ▷ conj una vez que; **~ he had left/it was done** una vez que se había marchado/se hizo; **at ~** en seguida, inmediatamente; (simultaneously) a la vez;

~ a week una vez por semana; **~ more** otra vez; **~ and for all** de una vez por todas; **~ upon a time** érase una vez

oncoming ['ɒnkʌmɪŋ] adj (traffic) que viene de frente

○ **KEYWORD**

one [wʌn] num un(o)/una; **one hundred and fifty** ciento cincuenta; **one by one** uno a uno
▷ adj **1** (sole) único; **the one book which** el único libro que; **the one man who** el único que
2 (same) mismo/a; **they came in the one car** vinieron en un solo coche
▷ pron **1** **this one** éste(ésta); **that one** ése(ésa); (more remote) aquél(aquella); **I've already got (a red) one** ya tengo uno/a rojo/a; **one by one** uno/a por uno/a
2 **one another** os (SP), se (+ el uno al otro, unos o otros etc); **do you two ever see one another?** ¿vosotros dos os veis alguna vez? (SP), ¿se ven ustedes dos alguna vez?; **the boys didn't dare look at one another** los chicos no se atrevieron a mirarse (el uno al otro); **they all kissed one another** se besaron unos a otros
3 (impers): **one never knows** nunca se sabe; **to cut one's finger** cortarse el dedo; **one needs to eat** hay que comer

one-off (BRIT: inf) n (event) acontecimiento único

oneself [wʌn'sɛlf] pron (reflexive) se; (after prep) sí; (emphatic) uno/a mismo/a; **to hurt ~** hacerse daño; **to keep sth for ~** guardarse algo; **to talk to ~** hablar solo

one: one-shot [wʌn'ʃɒt] (US) n = **one-off**; **one-sided** adj (argument) parcial; **one-to-one** adj (relationship) de dos; **one-way** adj (street) de sentido único

ongoing ['ɒngəuɪŋ] adj continuo

onion ['ʌnjən] n cebolla

on-line ['ɒnlaɪn] adj, adv (Comput) en línea

onlooker ['ɒnlukə*] n espectador(a) m/f

only ['əunlɪ] adv solamente, sólo ▷ adj único, solo ▷ conj solamente que, pero; **an ~ child** un hijo único; **not ~ ... but also ...** no sólo ... sino también ...

on-screen [ɒn'skri:n] adj (Comput etc) en pantalla; (romance, kiss) cinematográfico

onset ['ɒnsɛt] n comienzo

onto ['ɒntu] prep = **on to**

onward(s) ['ɒnwəd(z)] adv (move) (hacia) adelante; **from that time ~** desde entonces en adelante

oops [ups] excl (also: **~-a-daisy!**) ¡huy!

ooze [u:z] vi rezumar

opaque [əu'peɪk] adj opaco

open ['əupn] adj abierto; (car) descubierto; (road, view) despejado; (meeting) público; (admiration) manifiesto ▷ vt abrir ▷ vi abrirse; (book etc: commence) comenzar; **in the ~ (air)** al aire libre; **open up** vt abrir; (blocked road) despejar ▷ vi abrirse, empezar; **open-air** adj al aire libre; **opening** n abertura; (start) comienzo; (opportunity) oportunidad f; **opening hours** npl horario de apertura; **open learning** n enseñanza flexible a tiempo parcial; **openly** adv abiertamente; **open-minded** adj imparcial; **open-necked** adj (shirt) desabrochado; sin corbata; **open-plan** adj: **open-plan office** gran oficina sin particiones; **Open University** n (BRIT) ≈ Universidad f Nacional de Enseñanza a Distancia, UNED f

opera ['ɔpərə] n ópera; **opera house** n teatro de la ópera; **opera singer** n cantante m/f de ópera

operate ['ɔpəreɪt] vt (machine) hacer funcionar; (company) dirigir ▷ vi funcionar; **to ~ on sb** (Med) operar a algn

operating room ['ɔpəreɪtɪŋ-] (US) n quirófano, sala de operaciones

operating theatre (BRIT) n sala de operaciones

operation [ɔpə'reɪʃən] n operación f; (of machine) funcionamiento; **to be in ~** estar funcionando or en funcionamiento; **to have an ~** (Med) ser operado; **operational** adj operacional, en buen estado

operative ['ɔpərətɪv] adj en vigor

operator ['ɔpəreɪtə*] n (of machine) maquinista mf, operario/a; (Tel) operador(a) m/f, telefonista mf

opinion [ə'pɪnɪən] n opinión f; **in my ~** en mi opinión, a mi juicio; **opinion poll** n encuesta, sondeo

opponent [ə'pəunənt] n adversario/a, contrincante mf

opportunity [ɔpə'tju:nɪtɪ] n oportunidad f; **to take the ~ of doing** aprovechar la ocasión para hacer

oppose [ə'pəuz] vt oponerse a; **to be ~d to sth** oponerse a algo; **as ~d to** a diferencia de

opposite ['ɔpəzɪt] adj opuesto, contrario a; (house etc) de enfrente ▷ adv enfrente ▷ prep en frente de, frente a ▷ n lo contrario

opposition [ɔpə'zɪʃən] n oposición f

oppress [ə'prɛs] vt oprimir

opt [ɔpt] vi: **to ~ for** optar por; **to ~ to do** optar por hacer; **opt out** vi: **to opt out of** optar por no hacer

optician [ɔp'tɪʃn] n óptico m/f

optimism ['ɔptɪmɪzəm] n optimismo

optimist ['ɔptɪmɪst] n optimista mf; **optimistic** [-'mɪstɪk] adj optimista

optimum ['ɔptɪməm] adj óptimo

option ['ɔpʃən] n opción f; **optional** adj facultativo, discrecional

or [ɔ:*] conj o; (before o, ho) u; (with negative): **he hasn't seen ~ heard anything** no ha visto ni oído nada; **~ else** si no

oral ['ɔːrəl] adj oral ▷ n examen m oral

orange ['ɔrɪndʒ] n (fruit) naranja ▷ adj color naranja; **orange juice** n jugo m de naranja, zumo m de naranja (SP); **orange squash** n naranjada

orbit ['ɔ:bɪt] n órbita ▷ vt, vi orbitar

orchard ['ɔ:tʃəd] n huerto

orchestra ['ɔ:kɪstrə] n orquesta; (US: seating) platea

orchid ['ɔ:kɪd] n orquídea

ordeal [ɔ:'di:l] n experiencia horrorosa

order ['ɔ:də*] n orden m; (command) orden f; (good order) buen estado; (Comm) pedido ▷ vt (also: **put in ~**) arreglar, poner en orden; (Comm) pedir; (command) mandar, ordenar; **in ~** en orden; (of document) en regla; **in (working) ~** en funcionamiento; **in ~ to do/that** para hacer/que; **on ~** (Comm) pedido; **to be out of ~** estar desordenado; (not working) no funcionar; **to ~ sb to do sth** mandar a algn hacer algo; **order form** n hoja de pedido; **orderly** n (Mil) ordenanza m; (Med) enfermero/a (auxiliar) ▷ adj ordenado

ordinary ['ɔ:dnrɪ] adj corriente, normal; (pej) común y corriente; **out of the ~** fuera de lo común

ore [ɔ:*] n mineral m

oregano [ɔrɪ'gɑ:nəu] n orégano

organ ['ɔ:gən] n órgano; **organic** [ɔ:'gænɪk] adj orgánico; **organism** n organismo

organization [ɔ:gənaɪ'zeɪʃən] n organización f

organize ['ɔ:gənaɪz] vt organizar;

organized ['ɔːgənaizd] adj organizado;
organizer n organizador(a) m/f
orgasm ['ɔːgæzəm] n orgasmo
orgy ['ɔːdʒɪ] n orgía
oriental [ɔːrɪ'ɛntl] adj oriental
orientation [ɔːrɪen'teɪʃən] n orientación f
origin ['ɒrɪdʒɪn] n origen m
original [ə'rɪdʒɪnl] adj original; (first)
primero; (earlier) primitivo ⊳ n original m;
originally adv al principio
originate [ə'rɪdʒɪneɪt] vi: **to ~ from, to ~
in** surgir de, tener su origen en
Orkneys ['ɔːknɪz] npl: **the ~** (also: **the
Orkney Islands**) las Orcadas
ornament ['ɔːnəmənt] n adorno; (trinket)
chuchería; **ornamental** [-'mɛntl] adj
decorativo, de adorno
ornate [ɔː'neɪt] adj muy ornado, vistoso
orphan ['ɔːfn] n huérfano/a
orthodox ['ɔːθədɔks] adj ortodoxo
orthopaedic [ɔːθə'piːdɪk] (us **orthopedic**)
adj ortopédico
osteopath ['ɔstɪəpæθ] n osteópata mf
ostrich ['ɔstrɪtʃ] n avestruz m
other ['ʌðə*] adj otro ⊳ pron: **the ~ (one)**
el(la) otro/a ⊳ adv: **~ than** aparte de;
otherwise adv de otra manera ⊳ conj (if
not) si no
otter ['ɔtə*] n nutria
ouch [autʃ] excl ¡ay!
ought [ɔːt] (pt **~**) aux vb: **I ~ to do it** debería
hacerlo; **this ~ to have been corrected**
esto debiera haberse corregido; **he ~ to win**
(probability) debe or debiera ganar
ounce [auns] n onza (28.35g)
our ['auə*] adj nuestro; see also **my**; **ours**
pron (el) nuestro/(la) nuestra etc; see also
mine¹; **ourselves** pron pl (reflexive, after
prep) nosotros; (emphatic) nosotros mismos;
see also **oneself**
oust [aust] vt desalojar
out [aut] adv fuera, afuera; (not at home)
fuera (de casa); (light, fire) apagado; **~ there**
allí (fuera); **he's ~** (absent) no está, ha salido;
to be ~ in one's calculations equivocarse
(en sus cálculos); **to run ~** salir corriendo;
~ loud en alta voz; **~ of** (outside) fuera
de; (because of: anger etc) por; **~ of petrol**
sin gasolina; **"~ of order"** "no funciona";
outback n interior m; **outbound** adj
(flight) de salida; (flight: not return) de ida;
outbreak n (of war) comienzo; (of disease)
epidemia; (of violence etc) ola; **outburst** n
explosión f, arranque m; **outcast** n paria
mf; **outcome** n resultado; **outcry** n
protestas fpl; **outdated** adj anticuado,
fuera de moda; **outdoor** adj exterior, de
aire libre; (clothes) de calle; **outdoors** adv

al aire libre
outer ['autə*] adj exterior, externo; **outer
space** n espacio exterior
outfit ['autfɪt] n (clothes) conjunto
out: outgoing adj (character) extrovertido;
(retiring: president etc) saliente; **outgoings**
(BRIT) npl gastos mpl; **outhouse** n
dependencia
outing ['autɪŋ] n excursión f, paseo
out: outlaw n proscrito ⊳ vt proscribir;
outlay n inversión f; **outlet** n salida;
(of pipe) desagüe m; (us Elec) toma de
corriente; (also: **retail outlet**) punto de
venta; **outline** n (shape) contorno, perfil m;
(sketch, plan) esbozo ⊳ vt (plan etc) esbozar;
in outline (fig) a grandes rasgos; **outlook** n
(fig: prospects) perspectivas fpl; (: for weather)
pronóstico; **outnumber** vt superar
en número; **out-of-date** adj (passport)
caducado; (clothes) pasado de moda; **out-of-
doors** adv al aire libre; **out-of-the-way** adj
apartado; **out-of-town** adj (shopping centre
etc) en las afueras; **outpatient** n paciente
mf externo/a; **outpost** n puesto avanzado;
output n (volumen m de) producción m,
rendimiento; (Comput) salida
outrage ['autreɪdʒ] n escándalo; (atrocity)
atrocidad f ⊳ vt ultrajar; **outrageous**
[-'reɪdʒəs] adj monstruoso
outright [adv aut'raɪt, adj 'autraɪt]
adv (ask, deny) francamente; (refuse)
rotundamente; (win) de manera absoluta;
(be killed) en el acto ⊳ adj franco; rotundo
outset ['autsɛt] n principio
outside [aut'saɪd] n exterior m ⊳ adj
exterior, externo ⊳ adv fuera ⊳ prep fuera
de; (beyond) más allá de; **at the ~** (fig) a lo
sumo; **outside lane** n (Aut: in Britain) carril
m de la derecha; (: in US, Europe etc) carril m
de la izquierda; **outside line** n (Tel) línea
(exterior); **outsider** n (stranger) extraño,
forastero
out: outsize adj (clothes) de talla grande;
outskirts npl alrededores mpl, afueras fpl;
outspoken adj muy franco; **outstanding**
adj excepcional, destacado; (remaining)
pendiente
outward ['autwəd] adj externo; (journey)
de ida; **outwards** adv (esp BRIT) = **outward**
outweigh [aut'weɪ] vt pesar más que
oval ['əuvl] adj ovalado ⊳ n óvalo
ovary ['əuvərɪ] n ovario
oven ['ʌvn] n horno; **oven glove** n
guante m para el horno, manopla para el
horno; **ovenproof** adj resistente al horno;
oven-ready adj listo para el horno
over ['əuvə*] adv encima, por encima
⊳ adj or adv (finished) terminado; (surplus)

de sobra ▷ *prep* (por) encima de; (*above*) sobre; (*on the other side of*) al otro lado de; (*more than*) más de; (*during*) durante; **~ here** (por) aquí; **~ there** (por) allí or allá; **all ~** (*everywhere*) por todas partes; **~ and ~ (again)** una y otra vez; **~ and above** además de; **to ask sb ~** invitar a algn a casa; **to bend ~** inclinarse

overall [*adj, n* 'əuvərɔ:l, *adv* əuvə'rɔ:l] *adj* (*length etc*) total; (*study*) de conjunto ▷ *adv* en conjunto ▷ *n* (BRIT) guardapolvo; **overalls** *npl* (*boiler suit*) mono (SP) or overol *m* (LAM) (de trabajo)

overboard *adv* (*Naut*) por la borda

overcame [əuvə'keɪm] *pt of* **overcome**

overcast [əuvəka:st] *adj* encapotado

overcharge [əuvə'tʃɑ:dʒ] *vt*: **to ~ sb** cobrar un precio excesivo a algn

overcoat [əuvəkəut] *n* abrigo, sobretodo

overcome [əuvə'kʌm] *vt* vencer; (*difficulty*) superar

over: overcrowded *adj* atestado de gente; (*city, country*) superpoblado; **overdo** (*irreg*) *vt* exagerar; (*overcook*) cocer demasiado; **to overdo it** (*work etc*) pasarse; **overdone** [əuvə'dʌn] *adj* (*vegetables*) recocido; (*steak*) demasiado hecho; **overdose** *n* sobredosis *f inv*; **overdraft** *n* saldo deudor; **overdrawn** *adj* (*account*) en descubierto; **overdue** *adj* retrasado; **overestimate** *vt* sobreestimar

overflow [*vb* əuvə'fləu, *n* 'əuvəfləu] *vi* desbordarse ▷ *n* (*also*: **~ pipe**) (cañería de) desagüe *m*

overgrown [əuvə'grəun] *adj* (*garden*) invadido por la vegetación

overhaul [*vb* əuvə'hɔ:l, *n* 'əuvəhɔ:l] *vt* revisar, repasar ▷ *n* revisión *f*

overhead [*adv* əuvə'hɛd, *adj, n* 'əuvəhɛd] *adv* por arriba or encima ▷ *adj* (*cable*) aéreo ▷ *n* (US) = **overheads**; **overhead projector** *n* retroproyector; **overheads** *npl* (*expenses*) gastos *mpl* generales

over: overhear (*irreg*) *vt* oír por casualidad; **overheat** *vi* (*engine*) recalentarse; **overland** *adj, adv* por tierra; **overlap** [əuvə'læp] *vi* traslaparse; **overleaf** *adv* al dorso; **overload** *vt* sobrecargar; **overlook** *vt* (*have view of*) dar a, tener vistas a; (*miss: by mistake*) pasar por alto; (*excuse*) perdonar

overnight [əuvə'naɪt] *adv* durante la noche; (*fig*) de la noche a la mañana ▷ *adj* de noche; **to stay ~** pasar la noche; **overnight bag** *n* fin *m* de semana, neceser *m* de viaje

overpass (US) ['əuvəpɑ:s] *n* paso superior

overpower [əuvə'pauə*] *vt* dominar; (*fig*) embargar; **overpowering** *adj* (*heat*) agobiante; (*smell*) penetrante

over: overreact [əuvərɪ'ækt] *vi* reaccionar de manera exagerada; **overrule** *vt* (*decision*) anular; (*claim*) denegar; **overrun** (*irreg*) *vt* (*country*) invadir; (*time limit*) rebasar, exceder

overseas [əuvə'si:z] *adv* (*abroad: live*) en el extranjero; (*travel*) al extranjero ▷ *adj* (*trade*) exterior; (*visitor*) extranjero

oversee [əuvə'si:] (*irreg*) *vt* supervisar

overshadow [əuvə'ʃædəu] *vt*: **to be ~ed by** estar a la sombra de

oversight ['əuvəsaɪt] *n* descuido

oversleep [əuvə'sli:p] (*irreg*) *vi* quedarse dormido

overspend [əuvə'spɛnd] (*irreg*) *vi* gastar más de la cuenta; **we have overspent by 5 pounds** hemos excedido el presupuesto en 5 libras

overt [əu'və:t] *adj* abierto

overtake [əuvə'teɪk] (*irreg*) *vt* sobrepasar; (BRIT Aut) adelantar

over: overthrow (*irreg*) *vt* (*government*) derrocar; **overtime** *n* horas *fpl* extraordinarias

overtook [əuvə'tuk] *pt of* **overtake**

over: overturn *vt* volcar; (*fig: plan*) desbaratar; (: *government*) derrocar ▷ *vi* volcar; **overweight** *adj* demasiado gordo or pesado; **overwhelm** *vt* aplastar; (*emotion*) sobrecoger; **overwhelming** *adj* (*victory, defeat*) arrollador(a); (*feeling*) irresistible

ow [au] *excl* ¡ay!

owe [əu] *vt*: **to ~ sb sth, to ~ sth to sb** deber algo a algn; **owing to** *prep* debido a, por causa de

owl [aul] *n* búho, lechuza

own [əun] *vt* tener, poseer ▷ *adj* propio; **a room of my ~** una habitación propia; **to get one's ~ back** tomar revancha; **on one's ~** solo, a solas; **own up** *vi* confesar; **owner** *n* dueño/a; **ownership** *n* posesión *f*

ox [ɔks] (*pl* **~en**) *n* buey *m*

Oxbridge ['ɔksbrɪdʒ] *n* universidades de Oxford y Cambridge

oxen ['ɔksən] *npl of* **ox**

oxygen ['ɔksɪdʒən] *n* oxígeno

oyster ['ɔɪstə*] *n* ostra

oz. *abbr* = **ounce(s)**

ozone ['əuzəun] *n* ozono; **ozone friendly** *adj* que no daña la capa de ozono; **ozone layer** *n* capa *f* de ozono

p

p [pi:] *abbr* = **penny; pence**

P.A. *n abbr* = **personal assistant; public address system**

p.a. *abbr* = **per annum**

pace [peɪs] *n* paso ▷ *vi*: **to ~ up and down** pasearse de un lado a otro; **to keep ~ with** llevar el mismo paso que; **pacemaker** *n* (*Med*) regulador *m* cardíaco, marcapasos *m inv*; (*Sport: also:* **pacesetter**) liebre *f*

Pacific [pə'sɪfɪk] *n*: **the ~ (Ocean)** el (Océano) Pacífico

pacifier ['pæsɪfaɪə*] (*US*) *n* (*dummy*) chupete *m*

pack [pæk] *n* (*packet*) paquete *m*; (*of hounds*) jauría; (*of people*) manada, bando; (*of cards*) baraja; (*bundle*) fardo; (*US: of cigarettes*) paquete *m*; (*back pack*) mochila ▷ *vt* (*fill*) llenar; (*in suitcase etc*) meter, poner; (*cram*) llenar, atestar; **to ~ (one's bags)** hacerse la maleta; **to ~ sb off** despachar a algn; **pack in** *vi* (*watch, car*) estropearse ▷ *vt* (*inf*) dejar; **pack it in!** ¡para!, ¡basta ya!; **pack up** *vi* (*inf: machine*) estropearse; (*person*) irse ▷ *vt* (*belongings, clothes*) recoger; (*goods, presents*) empaquetar, envolver

package ['pækɪdʒ] *n* paquete *m*; (*bulky*) bulto; (*also:* **~ deal**) acuerdo global; **package holiday** *n* vacaciones *fpl* organizadas; **package tour** *n* viaje *m* organizado

packaging ['pækɪdʒɪŋ] *n* envase *m*

packed [pækt] *adj* abarrotado; **packed lunch** *n* almuerzo frío

packet ['pækɪt] *n* paquete *m*

packing ['pækɪŋ] *n* embalaje *m*

pact [pækt] *n* pacto

pad [pæd] *n* (*of paper*) bloc *m*; (*cushion*) cojinete *m*; (*inf: home*) casa ▷ *vt* rellenar; **padded** *adj* (*jacket*) acolchado; (*bra*) reforzado

paddle ['pædl] *n* (*oar*) canalete *m*; (*US: for table tennis*) paleta ▷ *vt* impulsar con canalete ▷ *vi* (*with feet*) chapotear; **paddling pool** (*BRIT*) *n* estanque *m* de juegos

paddock ['pædək] *n* corral *m*

padlock ['pædlɔk] *n* candado

paedophile ['pi:dəʊfaɪl] (*US* **pedophile**) *adj* de pedófilos ▷ *n* pedófilo/a

page [peɪdʒ] *n* (*of book*) página; (*of newspaper*) plana; (*also:* **~ boy**) paje *m* ▷ *vt* (*in hotel etc*) llamar por altavoz a

pager ['peɪdʒə*] *n* (*Tel*) busca *m*

paid [peɪd] *pt, pp of* **pay** ▷ *adj* (*work*) remunerado; (*holiday*) pagado; (*official etc*) a sueldo; **to put ~ to** (*BRIT*) acabar con

pain [peɪn] *n* dolor *m*; **to be in ~** sufrir; **to take ~s to do sth** tomarse grandes molestias en hacer algo; **painful** *adj* doloroso; (*difficult*) penoso; (*disagreeable*) desagradable; **painkiller** *n* analgésico; **painstaking** ['peɪnzteɪkɪŋ] *adj* (*person*) concienzudo, esmerado

paint [peɪnt] *n* pintura ▷ *vt* pintar; **to ~ the door blue** pintar la puerta de azul; **paintbrush** *n* (*of artist*) pincel *m*; (*of decorator*) brocha; **painter** *n* pintor(a) *m/f*; **painting** *n* pintura

pair [peə*] *n* (*of shoes, gloves etc*) par *m*; (*of people*) pareja; **a ~ of scissors** unas tijeras; **a ~ of trousers** unos pantalones, un pantalón

pajamas [pə'dʒɑːməz] (*US*) *npl* pijama *m*

Pakistan [pɑːkɪ'stɑːn] *n* Paquistán *m*; **Pakistani** *adj, n.* paquistaní *mf*

pal [pæl] (*inf*) *n* compinche *mf*, compañero/a

palace ['pæləs] *n* palacio

pale [peɪl] *adj* (*gen*) pálido; (*colour*) claro ▷ *n*: **to be beyond the ~** pasarse de la raya

Palestine ['pælɪstaɪn] *n* Palestina; **Palestinian** [-'tɪnɪən] *adj, n* palestino/a *m/f*

palm [pɑːm] *n* (*Anat*) palma; (*also:* **~ tree**) palmera, palma ▷ *vt*: **to ~ sth off on sb** (*inf*) encajar algo a algn

pamper ['pæmpə*] *vt* mimar

pamphlet ['pæmflət] *n* folleto

pan [pæn] *n* (*also:* **sauce~**) cacerola, cazuela, olla; (*also:* **frying ~**) sartén *f*

pancake ['pænkeɪk] *n* crepe *f*

panda ['pændə] *n* panda *m*

pane [peɪn] *n* cristal *m*

panel ['pænl] *n* (*of wood etc*) panel *m*; (*Radio, TV*) panel *m* de invitados

panhandler ['pænhændlə*] (*US*) *n* (*inf*) mendigo/a

panic ['pænɪk] *n* terror *m* pánico ▷ *vi* dejarse llevar por el pánico

panorama [pænə'rɑːmə] *n* panorama *m*

pansy ['pænzɪ] *n* (*Bot*) pensamiento; (*inf*,

pej) maricón *m*
pant [pænt] *vi* jadear
panther ['pænθə*] *n* pantera
panties ['pæntɪz] *npl* bragas *fpl*, pantis *mpl*
pantomime ['pæntəmaɪm] (*BRIT*) *n*
revista musical representada en Navidad, basada
en cuentos dehadas

● **PANTOMIME**
●
●
● En época navideña se ponen en escena
● en los teatros británicos las llamadas
● **pantomimes**, que son versiones libres
● de cuentos tradicionales como Aladino
● o El gato con botas. En ella nunca faltan
● personajes como la dama ("dame"),
● papel que siempre interpreta un actor,
● el protagonista joven ("principal boy"),
● normalmente interpretado por una
● actriz, y el malvado ("villain"). Es un
● espectáculo familiar en el que se anima
● al público a participar y aunque va
● dirigido principalmente a los niños,
● cuenta con grandes dosis de humor para
● adultos.

pants [pænts] *n* (*BRIT*: *underwear*: *woman's*)
bragas *fpl*; (: *man's*) calzoncillos *mpl*;
(*US*: *trousers*) pantalones *mpl*
paper ['peɪpə*] *n* papel *m*; (*also*: **news~**)
periódico, diario; (*academic essay*) ensayo;
(*exam*) examen *m* ▷ *adj* de papel ▷ *vt*
empapelar, tapizar (*MEX*); **papers** *npl*
(*also*: **identity ~s**) papeles *mpl*, documentos
mpl; **paperback** *n* libro en rústica; **paper
bag** *n* bolsa de papel; **paper clip** *n* clip *m*;
paper shop (*BRIT*) *n* tienda de periódicos;
paperwork *n* trabajo administrativo
paprika ['pæprɪkə] *n* pimentón *m*
par [pɑ:*] *n* par *f*; (*Golf*) par *m*; **to be on a ~
with** estar a la par con
paracetamol [pærə'si:təmɔl] (*BRIT*) *n*
paracetamol *m*
parachute ['pærəʃu:t] *n* paracaídas *m inv*
parade [pə'reɪd] *n* desfile *m* ▷ *vt* (*show*)
hacer alarde de ▷ *vi* desfilar; (*Mil*) pasar
revista
paradise ['pærədaɪs] *n* paraíso
paradox ['pærədɔks] *n* paradoja
paraffin ['pærəfɪn] (*BRIT*) *n* (*also*: **~ oil**)
parafina
paragraph ['pærəgrɑ:f] *n* párrafo
parallel ['pærəlɛl] *adj* en paralelo; (*fig*)
semejante ▷ *n* (*line*) paralela; (*fig*, *Geo*)
paralelo
paralysed ['pærəlaɪzd] *adj* paralizado
paralysis [pə'rælɪsɪs] *n* parálisis *f inv*
paramedic [pærə'mɛdɪk] *n* auxiliar *m/f*

sanitario/a
paranoid ['pærənɔɪd] *adj* (*person, feeling*)
paranoico
parasite ['pærəsaɪt] *n* parásito/a
parcel ['pɑ:sl] *n* paquete *m* ▷ *vt* (*also*: **~
up**) empaquetar, embalar
pardon ['pɑ:dn] *n* (*Law*) indulto ▷ *vt*
perdonar; **~ me!, I beg your ~!** (*I'm sorry!*)
¡perdone usted!; **(I beg your) ~?, ~ me?**
(*US*: *what did you say?*) ¿cómo?
parent ['pɛərənt] *n* (*mother*) madre *f*;
(*father*) padre *m*; **parents** *npl* padres *mpl*
▌ Be careful not to translate **parent** by the
Spanish word *pariente*.
parental [pə'rɛntl] *adj* paternal/maternal
Paris ['pærɪs] *n* París
parish ['pærɪʃ] *n* parroquia
Parisian [pə'rɪzɪən] *adj*, *n* parisiense *mf*
park [pɑ:k] *n* parque *m* ▷ *vt* aparcar,
estacionar ▷ *vi* aparcar, estacionarse
parking ['pɑ:kɪŋ] *n* aparcamiento,
estacionamiento; **"no ~"** "prohibido
estacionarse"; **parking lot** (*US*) *n* parking
m; **parking meter** *n* parquímetro; **parking
ticket** *n* multa de aparcamiento
parkway ['pɑ:kweɪ] (*US*) *n* alameda
parliament ['pɑ:ləmənt] *n* parlamento;
(*Spanish*) Cortes *fpl*; **parliamentary**
[-'mɛntərɪ] *adj* parlamentario

● **PARLIAMENT**
●
●
● El Parlamento británico (**Parliament**)
● tiene como sede el palacio de
● Westminster, también llamado "Houses
● of Parliament" y consta de dos cámaras.
● La Cámara de los Comunes ("House
● of Commons", compuesta por 650
● diputados (**Members of Parliament**)
● elegidos por sufragio universal en su
● respectiva circunscripción electoral
● (constituency), se reúne 175 días al año
● y sus sesiones son moderadas por el
● Presidente de la Cámara (**Speaker**). La
● cámara alta es la Cámara de los Lores
● ("House of Lords") y está formada por
● miembros que han sido nombrados
● por el monarca o que han heredado su
● escaño. Su poder es limitado, aunque
● actúa como tribunal supremo de
● apelación, excepto en Escocia.

Parmesan [pɑ:mɪ'zæn] *n* (*also*: **~ cheese**)
queso parmesano
parole [pə'rəʊl] *n*: **on ~** libre bajo palabra
parrot ['pærət] *n* loro, papagayo
parsley ['pɑ:slɪ] *n* perejil *m*
parsnip ['pɑ:snɪp] *n* chirivía

parson ['pɑːsn] n cura m

part [pɑːt] n (gen, Mus) parte f; (bit) trozo; (of machine) pieza; (Theatre etc) papel m; (of serial) entrega; (us: in hair) raya ▷ adv = **partly** ▷ vt separar ▷ vi (people) separarse; (crowd) apartarse; **to take ~ in** tomar parte or participar en; **to take sth in good ~** tomar algo en buena parte; **to take sb's ~** defender a algn; **for my ~** por mi parte; **for the most ~** en su mayor parte; **to ~ one's hair** hacerse la raya; **part with** vt fus ceder, entregar; (money) pagar; **part of speech** n parte f de la oración, categoría f gramatical

partial ['pɑːʃl] adj parcial; **to be ~ to** ser aficionado a

participant [pɑːˈtɪsɪpənt] n (in competition) concursante mf; (in campaign etc) participante mf

participate [pɑːˈtɪsɪpeɪt] vi: **to ~ in** participar en

particle ['pɑːtɪkl] n partícula; (of dust) grano

particular [pəˈtɪkjulə*] adj (special) particular; (concrete) concreto; (given) determinado; (fussy) quisquilloso; (demanding) exigente; **in ~** en particular; **particularly** adv (in particular) sobre todo; (difficult, good etc) especialmente; **particulars** npl (information) datos mpl; (details) pormenores mpl

parting ['pɑːtɪŋ] n (act) separación f; (farewell) despedida; (BRIT: in hair) raya ▷ adj de despedida

partition [pɑːˈtɪʃən] n (Pol) división f; (wall) tabique m

partly ['pɑːtlɪ] adv en parte

partner ['pɑːtnə*] n (Comm) socio/a; (Sport, at dance) pareja; (spouse) cónyuge mf; (lover) compañero/a; **partnership** n asociación f; (Comm) sociedad f

partridge ['pɑːtrɪdʒ] n perdiz f

part-time ['pɑːt'taɪm] adj, adv a tiempo parcial

party ['pɑːtɪ] n (Pol) partido; (celebration) fiesta; (group) grupo; (Law) parte f interesada ▷ cpd (Pol) de partido

pass [pɑːs] vt (time, object) pasar; (place) pasar por; (overtake) rebasar; (exam) aprobar; (approve) aprobar ▷ vi pasar; (Scol) aprobar, ser aprobado ▷ n (permit) permiso; (membership card) carnet m; (in mountains) puerto, desfiladero; (Sport) pase m; (Scol: also: **~ mark**): **to get a ~ in** aprobar en; **to ~ sth through sth** pasar algo por algo; **to make a ~ at sb** (inf) hacer proposiciones a algn; **pass away** vi fallecer; **pass by** vi pasar ▷ vt (ignore) pasar por alto; **pass on** vt transmitir; **pass out** vi desmayarse;

pass over vi, vt omitir, pasar por alto; **pass up** vt (opportunity) renunciar a; **passable** adj (road) transitable; (tolerable) pasable

passage ['pæsɪdʒ] n (also: **~way**) pasillo; (act of passing) tránsito; (fare, in book) pasaje m; (by boat) travesía; (Anat) tubo

passenger ['pæsɪndʒə*] n pasajero/a, viajero/a

passer-by [pɑːsəˈbaɪ] n transeúnte mf

passing place n (Aut) apartadero

passion ['pæʃən] n pasión f; **passionate** adj apasionado; **passion fruit** n fruta de la pasión, granadilla

passive ['pæsɪv] adj (gen, also Ling) pasivo

passport ['pɑːspɔːt] n pasaporte m; **passport control** n control m de pasaporte; **passport office** n oficina de pasaportes

password ['pɑːswəːd] n contraseña

past [pɑːst] prep (in front of) por delante de; (further than) más allá de; (later than) después de ▷ adj pasado; (president etc) antiguo ▷ n (time) pasado; (of person) antecedentes mpl; **he's ~ forty** tiene más de cuarenta años; **ten/quarter ~ eight** las ocho y diez/cuarto; **for the ~ few/3 days** durante los últimos días/últimos 3 días; **to run ~ sb** pasar a algn corriendo

pasta ['pæstə] n pasta

paste [peɪst] n pasta; (glue) engrudo ▷ vt pegar

pastel ['pæstl] adj pastel; (painting) al pastel

pasteurized ['pæstəraɪzd] adj pasteurizado

pastime ['pɑːstaɪm] n pasatiempo

pastor ['pɑːstə*] n pastor m

past participle [-'pɑːtɪsɪpl] n (Ling) participio m (de) pasado or (de) pretérito or pasivo

pastry ['peɪstrɪ] n (dough) pasta; (cake) pastel m

pasture ['pɑːstʃə*] n pasto

pasty¹ ['pæstɪ] n empanada

pasty² [peɪstɪ] adj (complexion) pálido

pat [pæt] vt dar una palmadita a; (dog etc) acariciar

patch [pætʃ] n (of material,: eye patch) parche m; (mended part) remiendo; (of land) terreno ▷ vt remendar; **(to go through) a bad ~** (pasar por) una mala racha; **patchy** adj desigual

pâté ['pæteɪ] n paté m

patent ['peɪtnt] n patente f ▷ vt patentar ▷ adj patente, evidente

paternal [pəˈtəːnl] adj paternal; (relation) paterno

paternity leave [pəˈtəːnɪtɪ-] n permiso m

por paternidad, licencia por paternidad

path [pɑ:θ] n camino, sendero; (trail, track) pista; (of missile) trayectoria

pathetic [pə'θetɪk] adj patético, lastimoso; (very bad) malísimo

pathway ['pɑ:θweɪ] n sendero, vereda

patience ['peɪʃns] n paciencia; (BRIT Cards) solitario

patient ['peɪʃnt] n paciente mf ▷ adj paciente, sufrido

patio ['pætɪəu] n patio

patriotic [pætrɪ'ɒtɪk] adj patriótico

patrol [pə'trəul] n patrulla ▷vt patrullar por; **patrol car** n coche m patrulla

patron ['peɪtrən] n (in shop) cliente mf; (of charity) patrocinador(a) m/f; ~ **of the arts** mecenas m

patronizing ['pætrənaɪzɪŋ] adj condescendiente

pattern ['pætən] n (Sewing) patrón m; (design) dibujo; **patterned** adj (material) estampado

pause [pɔ:z] n pausa ▷vi hacer una pausa

pave [peɪv] vt pavimentar; **to ~ the way for** preparar el terreno para

pavement ['peɪvmənt] (BRIT) n acera, banqueta (MEX), andén m (CAM), vereda (SC)

pavilion [pə'vɪlɪən] n (Sport) caseta

paving ['peɪvɪŋ] n pavimento, enlosado

paw [pɔ:] n pata

pawn [pɔ:n] n (Chess) peón m; (fig) instrumento ▷vt empeñar; **pawn broker** n prestamista mf

pay [peɪ] (pt, pp **paid**) n (wage etc) sueldo, salario ▷vt pagar ▷vi (be profitable) rendir; **to ~ attention (to)** prestar atención (a); **to ~ sb a visit** hacer una visita a algn; **to ~ one's respects to sb** presentar sus respetos a algn; **pay back** vt (money) reembolsar; (person) pagar; **pay for** vt fus pagar; **pay in** vt ingresar; **pay off** vt saldar ▷vi (scheme, decision) dar resultado; **pay out** vt (money) gastar, desembolsar; **pay up** vt pagar (de mala gana); **payable** adj: **payable to** pagadero a; **pay day** n día m de paga; **pay envelope** (US) n = **pay packet**; **payment** n pago; **monthly payment** mensualidad f; **payout** n pago; (in competition) premio en metálico; **pay packet** (BRIT) n sobre m (de paga); **pay phone** n teléfono público; **payroll** n nómina; **pay slip** n recibo de sueldo; **pay television** n televisión f de pago

PC n abbr = **personal computer**; (BRIT) (= police constable) policía mf ▷ adv abbr = **politically correct**

p.c. abbr = **per cent**

PDA n abbr (= personal digital assistant)

agenda electrónica

PE n abbr (= physical education) ed. física

pea [pi:] n guisante m (SP), arveja (LAM), chícharo (MEX, CAM)

peace [pi:s] n paz f; (calm) paz f, tranquilidad f; **peaceful** adj (gentle) pacífico; (calm) tranquilo, sosegado

peach [pi:tʃ] n melocotón m (SP), durazno (LAM)

peacock ['pi:kɔk] n pavo real

peak [pi:k] n (of mountain) cumbre f, cima; (of cap) visera; (fig) cumbre f; **peak hours** npl horas fpl punta

peanut ['pi:nʌt] n cacahuete m (SP), maní m (LAM), cacahuate m (MEX); **peanut butter** n manteca de cacahuete or maní

pear [peə*] n pera

pearl [pə:l] n perla

peasant ['peznt] n campesino/a

peat [pi:t] n turba

pebble ['pebl] n guijarro

peck [pek] vt (also: ~ at) picotear ▷n picotazo; (kiss) besito; **peckish** (BRIT: inf) adj: **I feel peckish** tengo ganas de picar algo

peculiar [pɪ'kju:lɪə*] adj (odd) extraño, raro; (typical) propio, característico; ~ **to** propio de

pedal ['pedl] n pedal m ▷ vi pedalear

pedalo ['pedələu] n patín m a pedal

pedestal ['pedəstl] n pedestal m

pedestrian [pɪ'destrɪən] n peatón/ona m/f ▷ adj pedestre; **pedestrian crossing** (BRIT) n paso de peatones; **pedestrianized** adj: **a pedestrianized street** una calle peatonal; **pedestrian precinct** (US) **pedestrian zone** n zona peatonal

pedigree ['pedɪgri:] n genealogía; (of animal) raza, pedigrí m ▷ cpd (animal) de raza, de casta

pedophile ['pi:dəufaɪl] (US) n = **paedophile**

pee [pi:] (inf) vi mear

peek [pi:k] vi mirar a hurtadillas

peel [pi:l] n piel f; (of orange, lemon) cáscara; (: removed) peladuras fpl ▷ vt pelar ▷ vi (paint etc) desconcharse; (wallpaper) despegarse, desprenderse; (skin) pelar

peep [pi:p] n (BRIT: look) mirada furtiva; (sound) pío ▷ vi (BRIT: look) mirar furtivamente

peer [pɪə*] vi: **to ~ at** esudriñar ▷ n (noble) par m; (equal) igual m; (contemporary) contemporáneo/a

peg [peg] n (for coat etc) gancho, colgadero; (BRIT: also: **clothes ~**) pinza

pelican ['pelɪkən] n pelícano; **pelican crossing** (BRIT) n (Aut) paso de peatones señalizado

pelt [pɛlt] vt: **to ~ sb with sth** arrojarle algo a algn ▷ vi (rain) llover a cántaros; (inf: run) correr ▷ n pellejo

pelvis ['pɛlvɪs] n pelvis f

pen [pɛn] n (fountain pen) pluma; (ballpoint pen) bolígrafo; (for sheep) redil m

penalty ['pɛnltɪ] n (gen) pena; (fine) multa

pence [pɛns] npl of **penny**

pencil ['pɛnsl] n lápiz m; **pencil in** vt (appointment) apuntar con carácter provisional; **pencil case** n estuche m; **pencil sharpener** n sacapuntas m inv

pendant ['pɛndnt] n pendiente m

pending ['pɛndɪŋ] prep antes de ▷ adj pendiente

penetrate ['pɛnɪtreɪt] vt penetrar

penfriend ['pɛnfrɛnd] (BRIT) n amigo/a por carta

penguin ['pɛŋgwɪn] n pingüino

penicillin [pɛnɪ'sɪlɪn] n penicilina

peninsula [pə'nɪnsjulə] n península

penis ['piːnɪs] n pene m

penitentiary [pɛnɪ'tɛnʃərɪ] (US) n cárcel f, presidio

penknife ['pɛnnaɪf] n navaja

penniless ['pɛnɪlɪs] adj sin dinero

penny ['pɛnɪ] (pl **pennies** or **pence**) (BRIT) n penique m; (US) centavo

penpal ['pɛnpæl] n amigo/a por carta

pension ['pɛnʃən] n (state benefit) jubilación f; **pensioner** (BRIT) n jubilado/a

pentagon ['pɛntəgən] (US) n: **the P~** (Pol) el Pentágono

⬤ **PENTAGON**
⬤
⬤ Se conoce como **Pentagon** al edificio
⬤ de planta pentagonal que acoge las
⬤ dependencias del Ministerio de Defensa
⬤ estadounidense ("Department of
⬤ Defense") en Arlington, Virginia. En
⬤ lenguaje periodístico se aplica también
⬤ a la dirección militar del país.

penthouse ['pɛnthaus] n ático de lujo

penultimate [pe'nʌltɪmət] adj penúltimo

people ['piːpl] npl gente f; (citizens) pueblo, ciudadanos mpl; (Pol): **the ~** el pueblo ▷ n (nation, race) pueblo, nación f; **several ~ came** vinieron varias personas; **~ say that ...** dice la gente que ...

pepper ['pɛpə*] n (spice) pimienta; (vegetable) pimiento ▷ vt: **to ~ with** (fig) salpicar de; **peppermint** n (sweet) pastilla de menta

per [pə:*] prep por; **~ day/~son** por día/persona; **~ annum** al año

perceive [pə'siːv] vt percibir; (realize) darse cuenta de

per cent n por ciento

percentage [pə'sɛntɪdʒ] n porcentaje m

perception [pə'sɛpʃən] n percepción f; (insight) perspicacia; (opinion etc) opinión f

perch [pə:tʃ] n (fish) perca; (for bird) percha ▷ vi: **to ~ (on)** (bird) posarse (en); (person) encaramarse (en)

percussion [pə'kʌʃən] n percusión f

perfect [adj, n 'pə:fɪkt, vb pə'fɛkt] adj perfecto ▷ n (also: **~ tense**) perfecto ▷ vt perfeccionar; **perfection** [pə'fɛkʃən] n perfección f; **perfectly** ['pə:fɪktlɪ] adv perfectamente

perform [pə'fɔːm] vt (carry out) realizar, llevar a cabo; (Theatre) representar; (piece of music) interpretar ▷ vi (well, badly) funcionar; **performance** n (of a play) representación f; (of actor, athlete etc) actuación f; (of car, engine, company) rendimiento; (of economy) resultados mpl; **performer** n (actor) actor m, actriz f

perfume ['pə:fjuːm] n perfume m

perhaps [pə'hæps] adv quizá(s), tal vez

perimeter [pə'rɪmɪtə*] n perímetro

period ['pɪərɪəd] n período; (Scol) clase f; (full stop) punto; (Med) regla ▷ adj (costume, furniture) de época; **periodical** [pɪərɪ'ɔdɪkl] n periódico; **periodically** adv de vez en cuando, cada cierto tiempo

perish ['pɛrɪʃ] vi perecer; (decay) echarse a perder

perjury ['pə:dʒərɪ] n (Law) perjurio

perk [pə:k] n extra m

perm [pə:m] n permanente f

permanent ['pə:mənənt] adj permanente; **permanently** adv (lastingly) para siempre, de modo definitivo; (all the time) permanentemente

permission [pə'mɪʃən] n permiso

permit [n 'pə:mɪt, vt pə'mɪt] n permiso, licencia ▷ vt permitir

perplex [pə'plɛks] vt dejar perplejo

persecute ['pə:sɪkjuːt] vt perseguir

persecution [pə:sɪ'kjuːʃən] n persecución f

persevere [pə:sɪ'vɪə*] vi persistir

Persian ['pə:ʃən] adj, n persa mf: **the ~ Gulf** el Golfo Pérsico

persist [pə'sɪst] vi: **to ~ (in doing sth)** persistir (en hacer algo); **persistent** adj persistente; (determined) porfiado

person ['pə:sn] n persona; **in ~** en persona; **personal** adj personal; individual; (visit) en persona; **personal assistant** n ayudante mf personal; **personal computer** n ordenador m personal; **personality**

P

[-'næliti] n personalidad f; **personally** adv
personalmente; (in person) en persona; **to
take sth personally** tomarse algo a mal;
personal organizer n agenda; **personal
stereo** n Walkman® m

personnel [pə:sə'nɛl] n personal m

perspective [pə'spɛktɪv] n perspectiva

perspiration [pə:spɪ'reɪʃən] n
transpiración f

persuade [pə'sweɪd] vt: **to ~ sb to do sth**
persuadir a algn para que haga algo

persuasion [pə'sweɪʒən] n persuasión f;
(persuasiveness) persuasiva

persuasive [pə'sweɪsɪv] adj persuasivo

perverse [pə'və:s] adj perverso; (wayward)
travieso

pervert [n 'pə:və:t, vb pə'və:t] n
pervertido/a ⊳vt pervertir; (truth, sb's
words) tergiversar

pessimism ['pɛsɪmɪzəm] n pesimismo

pessimist ['pɛsɪmɪst] n pesimista mf;
pessimistic [-'mɪstɪk] adj pesimista

pest [pɛst] n (insect) insecto nocivo; (fig)
lata, molestia

pester ['pɛstə*] vt molestar, acosar

pesticide ['pɛstɪsaɪd] n pesticida m

pet [pɛt] n animal m doméstico ⊳cpd
favorito ⊳vt acariciar; **teacher's ~**
favorito/a (del profesor); **~ hate** manía

petal ['pɛtl] n pétalo

petite [pə'ti:t] adj chiquita

petition [pə'tɪʃən] n petición f

petrified ['pɛtrɪfaɪd] adj horrorizado

petrol ['pɛtrəl] (BRIT) n gasolina

petroleum [pə'trəulɪəm] n petróleo

petrol: petrol pump (BRIT) n (in garage)
surtidor m de gasolina; **petrol station** (BRIT)
n gasolinera; **petrol tank** (BRIT) n depósito
(de gasolina)

petticoat ['pɛtɪkəut] n enaguas fpl

petty ['pɛtɪ] adj (mean) mezquino;
(unimportant) insignificante

pew [pju:] n banco

pewter ['pju:tə*] n peltre m

phantom ['fæntəm] n fantasma m

pharmacist ['fɑ:məsɪst] n
farmacéutico/a

pharmacy ['fɑ:məsɪ] n farmacia

phase [feɪz] n fase f; **phase in** vt
introducir progresivamente; **phase out** vt
(machinery, product) retirar progresivamente;
(job, subsidy) eliminar por etapas

Ph.D. abbr = **Doctor of Philosophy**

pheasant ['fɛznt] n faisán m

phenomena [fə'nɔmɪnə] npl of
phenomenon

phenomenal [fɪ'nɔmɪnl] adj fenomenal,
extraordinario

phenomenon [fə'nɔmɪnən] (pl
phenomena) n fenómeno

Philippines ['fɪlɪpi:nz] npl: **the ~** las
Filipinas

philosopher [fɪ'lɔsəfə*] n filósofo/a

philosophical [fɪlə'sɔfɪkl] adj filosófico

philosophy [fɪ'lɔsəfɪ] n filosofía

phlegm [flɛm] n flema

phobia ['fəubjə] n fobia

phone [fəun] n teléfono ⊳vt telefonear,
llamar por teléfono; **to be on the ~** tener
teléfono; (be calling) estar hablando por
teléfono; **phone back** vt, vi volver a llamar;
phone up, vi llamar por teléfono; **phone
book** n guía telefónica; **phone booth** n
cabina telefónica; **phone box** (BRIT) n =
phone booth; **phone call** n llamada
(telefónica); **phonecard** n teletarjeta;
phone number n número de teléfono

phonetics [fə'nɛtɪks] n fonética

phoney ['fəunɪ] adj falso

photo ['fəutəu] n foto f; **photo album**
n álbum m de fotos; **photocopier** n
fotocopiadora; **photocopy** n fotocopia
⊳vt fotocopiar

photograph ['fəutəgrɑ:f] n fotografía
⊳vt fotografiar; **photographer**
[fə'tɔgrəfə*] n fotógrafo; **photography**
[fə'tɔgrəfɪ] n fotografía

phrase [freɪz] n frase f ⊳vt expresar;
phrase book n libro de frases

physical ['fɪzɪkl] adj físico; **physical
education** n educación f física; **physically**
adv físicamente

physician [fɪ'zɪʃən] n médico/a

physicist ['fɪzɪsɪst] n físico/a

physics ['fɪzɪks] n física

physiotherapist [fɪzɪəu'θɛrəpɪst] n
fisioterapeuta

physiotherapy [fɪzɪəu'θɛrəpɪ] n
fisioterapia

physique [fɪ'zi:k] n físico

pianist ['pi:ənɪst] n pianista mf

piano [pɪ'ænəu] n piano

pick [pɪk] n (tool: also: **~-axe**) pico, piqueta
⊳vt (select) elegir, escoger; (gather) coger
(SP), recoger; (remove, take out) sacar,
quitar; (lock) abrir con ganzúa; **take your
~** escoja lo que quiera; **the ~ of** lo mejor
de; **to ~ one's nose/teeth** hurgarse las
narices/limpiarse los dientes; **to ~ a
quarrel with sb** meterse con algn; **pick
on** vt fus (person) meterse con; **pick out** vt
escoger; (distinguish) identificar; **pick up** vi
(improve: sales) ir mejor; (: patient) reponerse;
(Finance) recobrarse ⊳vt recoger; (learn)
aprender; (Police: arrest) detener; (person: for
sex) ligar; (Radio) captar; **to pick up speed**

acelerarse; **to pick o.s. up** levantarse

pickle ['pɪkl] n (also: **~s**: as condiment)
escabeche m; (fig: mess) apuro ▷ vt encurtir

pickpocket ['pɪkpɔkɪt] n carterista mf

pick-up ['pɪkʌp] n (also: **~ truck**)
furgoneta, camioneta

picnic ['pɪknɪk] n merienda ▷ vi ir de
merienda; **picnic area** n zona de picnic;
(Aut) área de descanso

picture ['pɪktʃə*] n cuadro; (painting)
pintura; (photograph) fotografía; (TV)
imagen f; (film) película; (fig: description)
descripción f; (: situation) situación f ▷ vt
(imagine) imaginar; **pictures** npl: **the ~s**
(BRIT) el cine; **picture frame** n marco;
picture messaging n (envío de) mensajes
con imágenes

picturesque [pɪktʃə'resk] adj pintoresco

pie [paɪ] n pastel m; (open) tarta; (small: of
meat) empanada

piece [piːs] n pedazo, trozo; (of cake) trozo;
(item): **a ~ of clothing/furniture/advice**
una prenda (de vestir)/un mueble/un
consejo ▷ vt: **to ~ together** juntar; (Tech)
armar; **to take to ~s** desmontar

pie chart n gráfico de sectores or tarta

pier [pɪə*] n muelle m, embarcadero

pierce [pɪəs] vt perforar; **pierced** adj: **I've
got pierced ears** tengo los agujeros hechos
en las orejas

pig [pɪg] n cerdo, chancho (LAM); (pej: unkind
person) asqueroso; (: greedy person) glotón/
ona m/f

pigeon ['pɪdʒən] n paloma; (as food)
pichón m

piggy bank ['pɪgɪ-] n hucha (en forma de
cerdito)

pigsty ['pɪgstaɪ] n pocilga

pigtail n (girl's) trenza

pike [paɪk] n (fish) lucio

pilchard ['pɪltʃəd] n sardina

pile [paɪl] n montón m; (of carpet, cloth)
pelo; **pile up** vi +adv (accumulate: work)
amontonarse, acumularse ▷ vt +adv (put
in a heap: books, clothes) apilar, amontonar;
(accumulate) acumular; **piles** npl (Med)
almorranas fpl, hemorroides mpl; **pile-up** n
(Aut) accidente m múltiple

pilgrimage ['pɪlgrɪmɪdʒ] n peregrinación
f, romería

pill [pɪl] n píldora; **the ~** la píldora

pillar ['pɪlə*] n pilar m

pillow ['pɪləʊ] n almohada; **pillowcase**
n funda

pilot ['paɪlət] n piloto ▷ cpd (scheme etc)
piloto ▷ vt pilotar; **pilot light** n piloto

pimple ['pɪmpl] n grano

PIN n abbr (= personal identification number)

número personal

pin [pɪn] n alfiler m ▷ vt prender (con
alfiler); **~s and needles** hormigueo; **to ~
sb down** (fig) hacer que algn concrete; **to ~
sth on sb** (fig) colgarle a algn el sambenito
de algo

pinafore ['pɪnəfɔ:*] n delantal m

pinch [pɪntʃ] n (of salt etc) pizca ▷ vt
pellizcar; (inf: steal) birlar; **at a ~** en caso
de apuro

pine [paɪn] n (also: **~ tree**) pino ▷ vi: **to ~
for** suspirar por

pineapple ['paɪnæpl] n piña, ananás m

ping [pɪŋ] n (noise) sonido agudo; **ping-
pong**® n pingpong® m

pink [pɪŋk] adj rosado, (color de) rosa ▷ n
(colour) rosa; (Bot) clavel m, clavellina

pinpoint ['pɪnpɔɪnt] vt precisar

pint [paɪnt] n pinta (BRIT = 568cc, US =
473cc); (BRIT: inf: of beer) pinta de cerveza ≈
jarra (SP)

pioneer [paɪə'nɪə*] n pionero/a

pious ['paɪəs] adj piadoso, devoto

pip [pɪp] n (seed) pepita; **the ~s** (BRIT) la
señal

pipe [paɪp] n tubo, caño; (for smoking) pipa
▷ vt conducir en cañerías; **pipeline** n (for
oil) oleoducto; (for gas) gasoducto; **piper** n
gaitero/a

pirate ['paɪərət] n pirata mf ▷ vt (cassette,
book) piratear

Pisces ['paɪsiːz] n Piscis m

piss [pɪs] (infl) vi mear; **pissed** (infl) adj
(drunk) borracho

pistol ['pɪstl] n pistola

piston ['pɪstən] n pistón m, émbolo

pit [pɪt] n hoyo; (also: **coal ~**) mina; (in
garage) foso de inspección; (also: **orchestra
~**) platea ▷ vt: **to ~ one's wits against sb**
medir fuerzas con algn

pitch [pɪtʃ] n (Mus) tono; (BRIT Sport)
campo, terreno; (fig) punto; (tar) brea ▷ vt
(throw) arrojar, lanzar ▷ vi (fall) caer(se); **to
~ a tent** montar una tienda (de campaña);
pitch-black adj negro como boca de lobo

pitfall ['pɪtfɔ:l] n riesgo

pith [pɪθ] n (of orange) médula

pitiful ['pɪtɪful] adj (touching) lastimoso,
conmovedor(a)

pity ['pɪtɪ] n compasión f, piedad f ▷ vt
compadecer(se de); **what a ~!** ¡qué pena!

pizza ['piːtsə] n pizza

placard ['plækɑːd] n letrero; (in march etc)
pancarta

place [pleɪs] n lugar m, sitio; (seat) plaza,
asiento; (post) puesto; (home): **at/to his ~**
en/a su casa; (role: in society etc) papel m ▷ vt
(object) poner, colocar; (identify) reconocer;

P

to take ~ tener lugar; **to be ~d** (in race, exam) colocarse; **out of ~** (not suitable) fuera de lugar; **in the first ~** en primer lugar; **to change ~s with sb** cambiarse de sitio con algn; **~ of birth** lugar m de nacimiento; **place mat** n (wooden etc) salvamanteles m inv; (linen etc) mantel m individual; **placement** n (positioning) colocación f; (at work) emplazamiento

placid ['plæsɪd] adj apacible

plague [pleɪg] n plaga; (Med) peste f ▷ vt (fig) acosar, atormentar

plaice [pleɪs] n inv platija

plain [pleɪn] adj (unpatterned) liso; (clear) claro, evidente; (simple) sencillo; (not handsome) poco atractivo ▷ adv claramente ▷ n llano, llanura; **plain chocolate** n chocolate m amargo; **plainly** adv claramente

plaintiff ['pleɪntɪf] n demandante mf

plait [plæt] n trenza

plan [plæn] n (drawing) plano; (scheme) plan m, proyecto ▷ vt proyectar, planificar ▷ vi hacer proyectos; **to ~ to do** pensar hacer

plane [pleɪn] n (Aviat) avión m; (Math, fig) plano; (also: **~ tree**) plátano; (tool) cepillo

planet ['plænɪt] n planeta m

plank [plæŋk] n tabla

planning ['plænɪŋ] n planificación f; **family ~** planificación familiar

plant [plɑːnt] n planta; (machinery) maquinaria; (factory) fábrica ▷ vt plantar; (field) sembrar; (bomb) colocar

plantation [plæn'teɪʃən] n plantación f; (estate) hacienda

plaque [plæk] n placa

plaster ['plɑːstə*] n (for walls) yeso; (also: **~ of Paris**) yeso mate, escayola (SP); (BRIT: also: **sticking ~**) tirita (SP), curita (LAM) ▷ vt enyesar; (cover): **to ~ with** llenar or cubrir de; **plaster cast** n (Med) escayola; (model, statue) vaciado de yeso

plastic ['plæstɪk] n plástico ▷ adj de plástico; **plastic bag** n bolsa de plástico; **plastic surgery** n cirujía plástica

plate [pleɪt] n (dish) plato; (metal, in book) lámina; (dental plate) placa de dentadura postiza

plateau ['plætəu] (pl **~s** or **~x**) n meseta, altiplanicie f

platform ['plætfɔːm] n (Rail) andén m; (stage, BRIT: on bus) plataforma; (at meeting) tribuna; (Pol) programa m (electoral)

platinum ['plætɪnəm] adj, n platino

platoon [plə'tuːn] n pelotón m

platter ['plætə*] n fuente f

plausible ['plɔːzɪbl] adj verosímil; (person) convincente

play [pleɪ] n (Theatre) obra, comedia ▷ vt (game) jugar; (compete against) jugar contra; (instrument) tocar; (part: in play etc) hacer el papel de; (tape, record) poner ▷ vi jugar; (band) tocar; (tape, record) sonar; **to ~ safe** ir a lo seguro; **play back** vt (tape) poner; **play up** vi (cause trouble to) dar guerra; **player** n jugador(a) m/f; (Theatre) actor(actriz) m/f; (Mus) músico/a; **playful** adj juguetón/ona; **playground** n (in school) patio de recreo; (in park) parque m infantil; **playgroup** n jardín m de niños; **playing card** n naipe m, carta; **playing field** n campo de deportes; **playschool** n = **playgroup**; **playtime** n (Scol) recreo; **playwright** n dramaturgo/a

plc abbr (= public limited company) ≈ S.A.

plea [pliː] n súplica, petición f; (Law) alegato, defensa

plead [pliːd] vt (Law): **to ~ sb's case** defender a algn; (give as excuse) poner como pretexto ▷ vi (Law) declararse; (beg): **to ~ with sb** suplicar or rogar a algn

pleasant ['plɛznt] adj agradable

please [pliːz] excl ¡por favor! ▷ vt (give pleasure to) dar gusto a, agradar ▷ vi (think fit): **do as you ~** haz lo que quieras; **~ yourself!** (inf) ¡haz lo que quieras!, ¡como quieras!; **pleased** adj (happy) alegre, contento; **pleased (with)** satisfecho (de); **pleased to meet you** ¡encantado!, ¡tanto gusto!

pleasure ['plɛʒə*] n placer m, gusto; **"it's a ~"** "el gusto es mío"

pleat [pliːt] n pliegue m

pledge [plɛdʒ] n (promise) promesa, voto ▷ vt prometer

plentiful ['plɛntɪful] adj copioso, abundante

plenty ['plɛntɪ] n: **~ of** mucho(s)/a(s)

pliers ['plaɪəz] npl alicates mpl, tenazas fpl

plight [plaɪt] n situación f difícil

plod [plɔd] vi caminar con paso pesado; (fig) trabajar laboriosamente

plonk [plɔŋk] (inf) n (BRIT: wine) vino peleón ▷ vt: **to ~ sth down** dejar caer algo

plot [plɔt] n (scheme) complot m, conjura; (of story, play) argumento; (of land) terreno ▷ vt (mark out) trazar; (conspire) tramar, urdir ▷ vi conspirar

plough [plau] (US **plow**) n arado ▷ vt (earth) arar; **to ~ money into** invertir dinero en; **ploughman's lunch** (BRIT) n almuerzo de pub a base de pan, queso y encurtidos

plow [plau] (US) = **plough**

ploy [plɔɪ] n truco, estratagema

pluck [plʌk] vt (fruit) coger (SP), recoger (LAM); (musical instrument) puntear; (bird) desplumar; (*eyebrows*) depilar; **to ~ up courage** hacer de tripas corazón

plug [plʌg] n tapón m; (*Elec*) enchufe m, clavija; (*Aut: also:* **spark(ing) ~**) bujía ▷ vt (*hole*) tapar; (*inf: advertise*) dar publicidad a; **plug in** vt (*Elec*) enchufar; **plughole** n desagüe m

plum [plʌm] n (*fruit*) ciruela

plumber ['plʌmə*] n fontanero/a (sp, cam), plomero/a (lam)

plumbing ['plʌmɪŋ] n (*trade*) fontanería, plomería; (*piping*) cañería

plummet ['plʌmɪt] vi: **to ~ (down)** caer a plomo

plump [plʌmp] adj rechoncho, rollizo ▷ vi: **to ~ for** (*inf: choose*) optar por

plunge [plʌndʒ] n zambullida ▷ vt sumergir, hundir ▷ vi (*fall*) caer; (*dive*) saltar; (*person*) arrojarse; **to take the ~** lanzarse

plural ['pluərl] adj plural ▷ n plural m

plus [plʌs] n (*also:* **~ sign**) signo más ▷ prep más, y, además de; **ten/twenty ~** más de diez/veinte

ply [plaɪ] vt (*a trade*) ejercer ▷ vi (*ship*) ir y venir ▷ n (*of wool, rope*) cabo; **to ~ sb with drink** insistir en ofrecer a algn muchas copas; **plywood** n madera contrachapada

P.M. n abbr = **Prime Minister**

p.m. adv abbr (= *post meridiem*) de la tarde or noche

PMS n abbr (= *premenstrual syndrome*) SPM m

PMT n abbr (= *premenstrual tension*) SPM m

pneumatic drill [nju:'mætɪk-] n martillo neumático

pneumonia [nju:'məunɪə] n pulmonía

poach [pəutʃ] vt (*cook*) escalfar; (*steal*) cazar (or pescar) en vedado ▷ vi cazar (or pescar) en vedado; **poached** adj escalfado

P.O. Box n abbr (= *Post Office Box*) apdo., aptdo.

pocket ['pɒkɪt] n bolsillo; (*fig: small area*) bolsa ▷ vt meter en el bolsillo; (*steal*) embolsar; **to be out of ~** (brit) salir perdiendo; **pocketbook** (us) n cartera; **pocket money** n asignación f

pod [pɒd] n vaina

podiatrist [pɒ'di:ətrɪst] (us) n pedicuro/a

podium ['pəudɪəm] n podio

poem ['pəuɪm] n poema m

poet ['pəuɪt] n poeta m/f; **poetic** [-'ɛtɪk] adj poético; **poetry** n poesía

poignant ['pɔɪnjənt] adj conmovedor(a)

point [pɔɪnt] n punto; (*tip*) punta; (*purpose*) fin m, propósito; (*use*) utilidad f; (*significant part*) lo significativo; (*moment*) momento; (*Elec*) toma (de corriente); (*also:* **decimal ~**): **2 ~ 3 (2.3)** dos coma tres (2,3) ▷ vt señalar; (*gun etc*): **to ~ sth at sb** apuntar

algo a algn ▷ vi: **to ~ at** señalar; **points** npl (*Aut*) contactos mpl; (*Rail*) agujas fpl; **to be on the ~ of doing sth** estar a punto de hacer algo; **to make a ~ of** poner empeño en; **to get/miss the ~** comprender/no comprender; **to come to the ~** ir al meollo; **there's no ~ (in doing)** no tiene sentido (hacer); **point out** vt señalar; **point-blank** adv (*say, refuse*) sin más hablar; (*also:* **at point-blank range**) a quemarropa; **pointed** adj (*shape*) puntiagudo, afilado; (*remark*) intencionado; **pointer** n (*needle*) aguja, indicador m; **pointless** adj sin sentido; **point of view** n punto de vista

poison ['pɔɪzn] n veneno ▷ vt envenenar; **poisonous** adj venenoso; (*fumes etc*) tóxico

poke [pəuk] vt (*jab with finger, stick etc*) empujar; (*put*): **to ~ sth in(to)** introducir algo en; **poke about** or **around** vi fisgonear; **poke out** vi (*stick out*) salir

poker ['pəukə*] n atizador m; (*Cards*) póker m

Poland ['pəulənd] n Polonia

polar ['pəulə*] adj polar; **polar bear** n oso polar

Pole [pəul] n polaco/a

pole [pəul] n palo; (*fixed*) poste m; (*Geo*) polo; **pole bean** (us) n ≈ judía verde; **pole vault** n salto con pértiga

police [pə'li:s] n policía ▷ vt vigilar; **police car** n coche-patrulla m; **police constable** (brit) n guardia m, policía m; **police force** n cuerpo de policía; **policeman** (*irreg*) n policía m, guardia m; **police officer** n guardia m, policía m; **police station** n comisaría; **policewoman** (*irreg*) n mujer f policía

policy ['pɒlɪsɪ] n política; (*also:* **insurance ~**) póliza

polio ['pəulɪəu] n polio f

Polish ['pəulɪʃ] adj polaco ▷ n (*Ling*) polaco

polish ['pɒlɪʃ] n (*for shoes*) betún m; (*for floor*) cera (de lustrar); (*shine*) brillo, lustre m; (*fig: refinement*) educación f ▷ vt (*shoes*) limpiar; (*make shiny*) pulir, sacar brillo a; **polish off** vt (*food*) despachar; **polished** adj (*fig: person*) elegante

polite [pə'laɪt] adj cortés, atento; **politeness** n cortesía

political [pə'lɪtɪkl] adj político; **politically** adv políticamente; **politically correct** políticamente correcto

politician [pɒlɪ'tɪʃən] n político/a

politics ['pɒlɪtɪks] n política

poll [pəul] n (*election*) votación f; (*also:* **opinion ~**) sondeo, encuesta ▷ vt encuestar; (*votes*) obtener

pollen ['pɒlən] n polen m

polling station ['pəʊlɪŋ-] n centro electoral

pollute [pə'luːt] vt contaminar

pollution [pə'luːʃən] n polución f, contaminación f del medio ambiente

polo ['pəʊləʊ] n (sport) polo; **polo-neck** adj de cuello vuelto ▷ n (sweater) suéter m de cuello vuelto; **polo shirt** n polo, niqui m

polyester [pɒlɪ'ɛstə*] n poliéster m

polystyrene [pɒlɪ'staɪriːn] n poliestireno

polythene ['pɒlɪθiːn] (BRIT) n politeno; **polythene bag** n bolsa de plástico

pomegranate ['pɒmɪgrænɪt] n granada

pompous ['pɒmpəs] adj pomposo

pond [pɒnd] n (natural) charca; (artificial) estanque m

ponder ['pɒndə*] vt meditar

pony ['pəʊnɪ] n poni m; **ponytail** n coleta; **pony trekking** (BRIT) n excursión f a caballo

poodle ['puːdl] n caniche m

pool [puːl] n (natural) charca; (also: **swimming ~**) piscina, alberca (MEX), pileta (RPL); (fig: of light etc) charco; (Sport) chapolín m ▷ vt juntar; **pools** npl quinielas fpl

poor [pʊə*] adj pobre; (bad) de mala calidad ▷ npl: **the ~** los pobres; **poorly** adj mal, enfermo ▷ adv mal

pop [pɒp] n (sound) ruido seco; (Mus) (música) pop m; (inf: father) papá m; (drink) gaseosa ▷ vt (put quickly) meter (de prisa) ▷ vi reventar; (cork) saltar; **pop in** vi entrar un momento; **pop out** vi salir un momento; **popcorn** n palomitas fpl

poplar ['pɒplə*] n álamo

popper ['pɒpə*] (BRIT) n automático

poppy ['pɒpɪ] n amapola

Popsicle® ['pɒpsɪkl] (US) n polo

pop star n estrella del pop

popular ['pɒpjʊlə*] adj popular; **popularity** [pɒpjʊ'lærɪtɪ] n popularidad f

population [pɒpjʊ'leɪʃən] n población f

pop-up ['pɒpʌp] (Comput) adj (menu, window) emergente ▷ n ventana emergente, (ventana f) pop-up f

porcelain ['pɔːslɪn] n porcelana

porch [pɔːtʃ] n pórtico, entrada; (US) veranda

pore [pɔː*] n poro ▷ vi: **to ~ over** engolfarse en

pork [pɔːk] n carne f de cerdo or (LAM) chancho; **pork chop** n chuleta de cerdo; **pork pie** n (BRIT: Culin) empanada de carne de cerdo

porn [pɔːn] adj (inf) porno inv ▷ n porno; **pornographic** [pɔːnə'græfɪk] adj pornográfico; **pornography** [pɔː'nɒgrəfɪ]

n pornografía

porridge ['pɒrɪdʒ] n gachas fpl de avena

port [pɔːt] n puerto; (Naut: left side) babor m; (wine) vino de Oporto; **~ of call** puerto de escala

portable ['pɔːtəbl] adj portátil

porter ['pɔːtə*] n (for luggage) maletero; (doorkeeper) portero/a, conserje m/f

portfolio [pɔːt'fəʊlɪəʊ] n cartera

portion ['pɔːʃən] n porción f; (of food) ración f

portrait ['pɔːtreɪt] n retrato

portray [pɔː'treɪ] vt retratar; (actor) representar

Portugal ['pɔːtjʊgl] n Portugal m

Portuguese [pɔːtjʊ'giːz] adj portugués/ esa ▷ n inv portugués/esa m/f; (Ling) portugués m

pose [pəʊz] n postura, actitud f ▷ vi (pretend): **to ~ as** hacerse pasar por ▷ vt (question) plantear; **to ~ for** posar para

posh [pɒʃ] (inf) adj elegante, de lujo

position [pə'zɪʃən] n posición f; (job) puesto; (situation) situación f ▷ vt colocar

positive ['pɒzɪtɪv] adj positivo; (certain) seguro; (definite) definitivo; **positively** adv (affirmatively, enthusiastically) de forma positiva; (inf: really) absolutamente

possess [pə'zɛs] vt poseer; **possession** [pə'zɛʃən] n posesión f; **possessions** npl (belongings) pertenencias fpl; **possessive** adj posesivo

possibility [pɒsɪ'bɪlɪtɪ] n posibilidad f

possible ['pɒsɪbl] adj posible; **as big as ~** lo más grande posible; **possibly** adv posiblemente; **I cannot possibly come** me es imposible venir

post [pəʊst] n (BRIT: system) correos mpl; (BRIT: letters, delivery) correo; (job, situation) puesto; (pole) poste m ▷ vt (BRIT: send by post) echar al correo; (BRIT: appoint): **to ~ to** enviar a; **postage** n porte m, franqueo; **postal** adj postal, de correos; **postal order** n giro postal; **postbox** (BRIT) n buzón m; **postcard** n tarjeta postal; **postcode** (BRIT) n código postal

poster ['pəʊstə*] n cartel m

postgraduate ['pəʊst'grædjuət] n posgraduado/a

postman ['pəʊstmən] (BRIT: irreg) n cartero

postmark ['pəʊstmɑːk] n matasellos m inv

post-mortem [-'mɔːtəm] n autopsia

post office n (building) (oficina de) correos m; (organization): **the Post Office** Correos m inv (SP), Dirección f General de Correos (LAM)

postpone [pəs'pəʊn] vt aplazar

posture ['pɒstʃə*] n postura, actitud f

postwoman ['pəustwumən] (BRIT: irreg) n cartera

pot [pɒt] n (for cooking) olla; (teapot) tetera; (coffeepot) cafetera; (for flowers) maceta; (for jam) tarro, pote m; (inf: marijuana) chocolate m ▷ vt (plant) poner en tiesto; **to go to ~** (inf) irse al traste

potato [pə'teɪtəu] (pl ~es) n patata (SP), papa (LAM); **potato peeler** n pelapatatas m inv

potent ['pəutnt] adj potente, poderoso; (drink) fuerte

potential [pə'tenʃl] adj potencial, posible ▷ n potencial m

pothole ['pɒthəul] n (in road) bache m; (BRIT: underground) gruta

pot plant ['pɒtplɑ:nt] n planta de interior

potter ['pɒtə*] n alfarero/a ▷ vi: **to ~ around** or **about** (BRIT) hacer trabajitos; **pottery** n cerámica; (factory) alfarería

potty ['pɒtɪ] n orinal m de niño

pouch [pautʃ] n (Zool) bolsa; (for tobacco) petaca

poultry ['pəultrɪ] n aves fpl de corral; (meat) pollo

pounce [pauns] vi: **to ~ on** precipitarse sobre

pound [paund] n libra (weight = 453g or 16oz; money = 100 pence) ▷ vt (beat) golpear; (crush) machacar ▷ vi (heart) latir; **pound sterling** n libra esterlina

pour [pɔ:*] vt echar; (tea etc) servir ▷ vi correr, fluir; **to ~ sb a drink** servirle a algn una copa; **pour in** vi (people) entrar en tropel; **pour out** vi salir en tropel ▷ vt (drink) echar, servir; (fig): **to pour out one's feelings** desahogarse; **pouring** adj: **pouring rain** lluvia torrencial

pout [paut] vi hacer pucheros

poverty ['pɒvətɪ] n pobreza, miseria

powder ['paudə*] n polvo; (also: face ~) polvos mpl ▷ vt polvorear; **to ~ one's face** empolvarse la cara; **powdered milk** n leche f en polvo

power ['pauə*] n poder m; (strength) fuerza; (nation, Tech) potencia; (drive) empuje m; (Elec) fuerza, energía ▷ vt impulsar; **to be in ~** (Pol) estar en el poder; **power cut** (BRIT) n apagón m; **power failure** n = power cut; **powerful** adj poderoso; (engine) potente; (speech etc) convincente; **powerless** adj: **powerless (to do)** incapaz (de hacer); **power point** (BRIT) n enchufe m; **power station** n central f eléctrica

p.p. abbr (= per procurationem); **p.p. J. Smith** p.p. (por poder de) J. Smith; (= pages) págs

PR n abbr = **public relations**

practical ['præktɪkl] adj práctico; **practical joke** n broma pesada; **practically** adv (almost) casi

practice ['præktɪs] n (habit) costumbre f; (exercise) práctica, ejercicio; (training) adiestramiento; (Med: of profession) práctica, ejercicio; (Med, Law: business) consulta ▷ vt, vi (us) = **practise**; **in ~** (in reality) en la práctica; **out of ~** desentrenado

practise ['præktɪs] (US **practice**) vt (carry out) practicar; (profession) ejercer; (train at) practicar ▷ vi ejercer; (train) practicar; **practising** adj (Christian etc) practicante; (lawyer) en ejercicio

practitioner [præk'tɪʃənə*] n (Med) médico/a

pragmatic [præg'mætɪk] adj pragmático

prairie ['preərɪ] n pampa

praise [preɪz] n alabanza(s) f(pl), elogio(s) m(pl) ▷ vt alabar, elogiar

pram [præm] (BRIT) n cochecito de niño

prank [præŋk] n travesura

prawn [prɔ:n] n gamba; **prawn cocktail** n cóctel m de gambas

pray [preɪ] vi rezar; **prayer** [preə*] n oración f, rezo; (entreaty) ruego, súplica

preach [pri:tʃ] vi predicar; **preacher** n predicador(a) m/f

precarious [prɪ'keərɪəs] adj precario

precaution [prɪ'kɔ:ʃən] n precaución f

precede [prɪ'si:d] vt, vi preceder; **precedent** ['presɪdənt] n precedente m; **preceding** [prɪ'si:dɪŋ] adj anterior

precinct ['pri:sɪŋkt] n recinto

precious ['preʃəs] adj precioso

precise [prɪ'saɪs] adj preciso, exacto; **precisely** adv precisamente, exactamente

precision [prɪ'sɪʒən] n precisión f

predator ['predətə*] n depredador m

predecessor ['pri:dɪsesə*] n antecesor(a) m/f

predicament [prɪ'dɪkəmənt] n apuro

predict [prɪ'dɪkt] vt pronosticar; **predictable** adj previsible; **prediction** [-'dɪkʃən] n predicción f

predominantly [prɪ'dɒmɪnəntlɪ] adv en su mayoría

preface ['prefəs] n prefacio

prefect ['pri:fekt] (BRIT) n (in school) monitor(a) m/f

prefer [prɪ'fə:*] vt preferir; **to ~ doing** or **to do** preferir hacer; **preferable** ['prefrəbl] adj preferible; **preferably** ['prefrəblɪ] adv de preferencia; **preference** ['prefrəns] n preferencia; (priority) prioridad f

prefix ['pri:fɪks] n prefijo

pregnancy ['pregnənsɪ] n (of woman) embarazo; (of animal) preñez f

pregnant ['prɛgnənt] adj (woman) embarazada; (animal) preñada
prehistoric [pri:hɪs'tɔrɪk] adj prehistórico
prejudice ['prɛdʒudɪs] n prejuicio; **prejudiced** adj (person) predispuesto
preliminary [prɪ'lɪmɪnəri] adj preliminar
prelude ['prɛlju:d] n preludio
premature ['prɛmətʃuə*] adj prematuro
premier ['prɛmɪə*] adj primero, principal ▷ n (Pol) primer(a) ministro/a
première ['prɛmɪɛə*] n estreno
Premier League [prɛmɪə'li:g] n primera división
premises ['prɛmɪsɪz] npl (of business etc) local m; **on the ~** en el lugar mismo
premium ['pri:mɪəm] n premio; (insurance) prima; **to be at a ~** ser muy solicitado
premonition [prɛmə'nɪʃən] n presentimiento
preoccupied [pri:'ɔkjupaɪd] adj ensimismado
prepaid [pri:'peɪd] adj porte pagado
preparation [prɛpə'reɪʃən] n preparación f; **preparations** npl preparativos mpl
preparatory school [prɪ'pærətərɪ-] n escuela preparatoria
prepare [prɪ'pɛə*] vt preparar, disponer; (Culin) preparar ▷ vi: **to ~ for** (action) prepararse o disponerse para; (event) hacer preparativos para; **~d to** dispuesto a; **~d for** listo para
preposition [prɛpə'zɪʃən] n preposición f
prep school [prɛp-] n = **preparatory school**
prerequisite [pri:'rɛkwɪzɪt] n requisito
preschool ['pri:'sku:l] adj preescolar
prescribe [prɪ'skraɪb] vt (Med) recetar
prescription [prɪ'skrɪpʃən] n (Med) receta
presence ['prɛzns] n presencia; **in sb's ~** en presencia de algn; **~ of mind** aplomo
present [adj, n 'prɛznt, vb prɪ'zɛnt] adj (in attendance) presente; (current) actual ▷ n (gift) regalo; (actuality): **the ~** la actualidad, el presente ▷ vt (introduce, describe) presentar; (expound) exponer; (give) presentar, dar, ofrecer; (Theatre) representar; **to give sb a ~** regalar algo a algn; **at ~** actualmente; **presentable** [prɪ'zɛntəbl] adj: **to make o.s. presentable** arreglarse; **presentation** [-'teɪʃən] n presentación f; (of report etc) exposición f; (formal ceremony) entrega de un regalo; **present-day** adj actual; **presenter** [prɪ'zɛntə*] n (Radio, TV) locutor(a) m/f; **presently** adv (soon) dentro de poco; (now) ahora; **present participle** n participio (de) presente

preservation [prɛzə'veɪʃən] n conservación f
preservative [prɪ'zə:vətɪv] n conservante m
preserve [prɪ'zə:v] vt (keep safe) preservar, proteger; (maintain) mantener; (food) conservar ▷ n (for game) coto, vedado; (often pl: jam) conserva, confitura
preside [prɪ'zaɪd] vi presidir
president ['prɛzɪdənt] n presidente m/f; **presidential** [-'dɛnʃl] adj presidencial
press [prɛs] n (newspapers): **the P~** la prensa; (printer's) imprenta; (of button) pulsación f ▷ vt empujar; (button etc) apretar; (clothes: iron) planchar; (put pressure on: person) presionar; (insist): **to ~ sth on sb** insistir en que algn acepte algo ▷ vi (squeeze) apretar; (pressurize): **to ~ for** presionar por; **we are ~ed for time/money** estamos apurados de tiempo/dinero; **press conference** n rueda de prensa; **pressing** adj apremiante; **press stud** (BRIT) n botón m de presión; **press-up** (BRIT) n plancha
pressure ['prɛʃə*] n presión f; **to put ~ on sb** presionar a algn; **pressure cooker** n olla a presión; **pressure group** n grupo de presión
prestige [prɛs'ti:ʒ] n prestigio
prestigious [prɛs'tɪdʒəs] adj prestigioso
presumably [prɪ'zju:məblɪ] adv es de suponer que, cabe presumir que
presume [prɪ'zju:m] vt: **to ~ (that)** presumir (que), suponer (que)
pretence [prɪ'tɛns] (us **pretense**) n fingimiento; **under false ~s** con engaños
pretend [prɪ'tɛnd] vt, vi (feign) fingir
> Be careful not to translate **pretend** by the Spanish word **pretender**.

pretense [prɪ'tɛns] (us) n = **pretence**
pretentious [prɪ'tɛnʃəs] adj presumido; (ostentatious) ostentoso, aparatoso
pretext ['pri:tɛkst] n pretexto
pretty ['prɪtɪ] adj bonito, lindo (LAM) ▷ adv bastante
prevail [prɪ'veɪl] vi (gain mastery) prevalecer; (be current) predominar; **prevailing** adj (dominant) predominante
prevalent ['prɛvələnt] adj (widespread) extendido
prevent [prɪ'vɛnt] vt: **to ~ sb from doing sth** impedir a algn hacer algo; **to ~ sth from happening** evitar que ocurra algo; **prevention** [prɪ'vɛnʃən] n prevención f; **preventive** adj preventivo
preview ['pri:vju:] n (of film) preestreno
previous ['pri:vɪəs] adj previo, anterior; **previously** adv antes
prey [preɪ] n presa ▷ vi: **to ~ on** (feed on)

alimentarse de; **it was ~ing on his mind** le preocupaba, le obsesionaba

price [praɪs] n precio ▷ vt (goods) fijar el precio de; **priceless** adj que no tiene precio; **price list** n tarifa

prick [prɪk] n (sting) picadura ▷ vt pinchar; (hurt) picar; **to ~ up one's ears** aguzar el oído

prickly ['prɪklɪ] adj espinoso; (fig: person) enojadizo

pride [praɪd] n orgullo; (pej) soberbia ▷ vt: **to ~ o.s. on** enorgullecerse de

priest [priːst] n sacerdote m

primarily ['praɪmərɪlɪ] adv ante todo

primary ['praɪmərɪ] adj (first in importance) principal ▷ n (US Pol) elección f primaria; **primary school** (BRIT) n escuela primaria

prime [praɪm] adj primero, principal; (excellent) selecto, de primera clase ▷ n: **in the ~ of life** en la flor de la vida ▷ vt (wood: fig) preparar; **~ example** ejemplo típico; **Prime Minister** n primer(a) ministro/a

primitive ['prɪmɪtɪv] adj primitivo; (crude) rudimentario

primrose ['prɪmrəuz] n primavera, prímula

prince [prɪns] n príncipe m

princess [prɪn'sɛs] n princesa

principal ['prɪnsɪpl] adj principal, mayor ▷ n director(a) m/f; **principally** adv principalmente

principle ['prɪnsɪpl] n principio; **in ~** en principio; **on ~** por principio

print [prɪnt] n (footprint) huella; (fingerprint) huella dactilar; (letters) letra de molde; (fabric) estampado; (Art) grabado; (Phot) impresión f ▷ vt imprimir; (cloth) estampar; (write in capitals) escribir en letras de molde; **out of ~** agotado; **print out** vt (Comput) imprimir; **printer** n (person) impresor(a) m/f; (machine) impresora; **printout** n (Comput) impresión f

prior ['praɪə*] adj anterior, previo; (more important) más importante; **~ to** antes de

priority [praɪ'ɔrɪtɪ] n prioridad f; **to have ~ (over)** tener prioridad (sobre)

prison ['prɪzn] n cárcel f, prisión f ▷ cpd carcelario; **prisoner** n (in prison) preso/a; (captured person) prisionero; **prisoner-of-war** n prisionero de guerra

pristine ['prɪstiːn] adj prístino

privacy ['prɪvəsɪ] n intimidad f

private ['praɪvɪt] adj (personal) particular; (property, industry, discussion etc) privado; (person) reservado; (place) tranquilo ▷ n soldado raso; **"~"** (on envelope) "confidencial"; (on door) "prohibido el paso";

in ~ en privado; **privately** adv en privado; (in o.s.) en secreto; **private property** n propiedad f privada; **private school** n colegio particular

privatize ['praɪvɪtaɪz] vt privatizar

privilege ['prɪvɪlɪdʒ] n privilegio; (prerogative) prerrogativa

prize [praɪz] n premio ▷ adj de primera clase ▷ vt apreciar, estimar; **prize-giving** n distribución f de premios; **prizewinner** n premiado/a

pro [prəu] n (Sport) profesional mf ▷ prep a favor de; **the ~s and cons** los pros y los contras

probability [prɔbə'bɪlɪtɪ] n probabilidad f; **in all ~** con toda probabilidad

probable ['prɔbəbl] adj probable

probably ['prɔbəblɪ] adv probablemente

probation [prə'beɪʃən] n: **on ~** (employee) a prueba; (Law) en libertad condicional

probe [prəub] n (Med, Space) sonda; (enquiry) encuesta, investigación f ▷ vt sondar; (investigate) investigar

problem ['prɔbləm] n problema m

procedure [prə'siːdʒə*] n procedimiento; (bureaucratic) trámites mpl

proceed [prə'siːd] vi (do afterwards): **to ~ to do sth** proceder a hacer algo; (continue): **to ~ (with)** continuar or seguir (con); **proceedings** npl acto(s) (pl); (Law) proceso; **proceeds** ['prəusiːdz] npl (money) ganancias fpl, ingresos mpl

process ['prəusɛs] n proceso ▷ vt tratar, elaborar

procession [prə'sɛʃən] n desfile m; **funeral ~** cortejo fúnebre

proclaim [prə'kleɪm] vt (announce) anunciar

prod [prɔd] vt empujar ▷ n empujón m

produce [n 'prɔdjuːs, vt prə'djuːs] n (Agr) productos mpl agrícolas ▷ vt producir; (play, film, programme) presentar; **producer** n productor(a) m/f; (of film, programme) director(a) m/f; (of record) productor(a) m/f

product ['prɔdʌkt] n producto; **production** [prə'dʌkʃən] n producción f; (Theatre) presentación f; **productive** [prə'dʌktɪv] adj productivo; **productivity** [prɔdʌk'tɪvɪtɪ] n productividad f

Prof. [prɔf] abbr (= professor) Prof

profession [prə'fɛʃən] n profesión f; **professional** adj profesional ▷ n profesional mf; (skilled person) perito

professor [prə'fɛsə*] n (BRIT) catedrático/a; (US, CANADA) profesor(a) m/f

profile ['prəufaɪl] n perfil m

profit ['prɔfɪt] n (Comm) ganancia ▷ vi: **to ~ by** or **from** aprovechar or sacar provecho

de; **profitable** adj (Econ) rentable
profound [prə'faund] adj profundo
programme ['prəʊgræm] (US **program**) n
programa m ▷ vt programar; **programmer**
(US **programer**) n programador(a)
m/f; **programming** (US **programing**) n
programación f
progress [n 'prəʊgrɛs, vi prə'grɛs]
n progreso; (development) desarrollo
▷ vi progresar, avanzar; **in ~** en curso;
progressive [-'grɛsɪv] adj progresivo;
(person) progresista
prohibit [prə'hɪbɪt] vt prohibir; **to ~ sb
from doing sth** prohibir a algn hacer algo
project [n 'prɒdʒɛkt, vb prə'dʒɛkt] n
proyecto ▷ vt proyectar ▷ vi (stick out) salir,
sobresalir; **projection** [prə'dʒɛkʃən]
n proyección f; (overhang) saliente m;
projector [prə'dʒɛktə*] n proyector m
prolific [prə'lɪfɪk] adj prolífico
prolong [prə'lɒŋ] vt prolongar, extender
prom [prɒm] n abbr = **promenade** (US: ball)
baile m de gala; **the P~s** ver abajo

● **PROM**
●
● El ciclo de conciertos de música clásica
● más conocido de Londres es el llamado
● **the Proms** (promenade concerts),
● que se celebra anualmente en el Royal
● Albert Hall. Su nombre se debe a que
● originalmente el público paseaba
● durante las actuaciones, costumbre que
● en la actualidad se mantiene de forma
● simbólica, permitiendo que parte de
● los asistentes permanezcan de pie. En
● Estados Unidos se llama **prom** a un
● baile de gala en un centro de educación
● secundaria o universitaria.

promenade [prɒmə'nɑːd] n (by sea) paseo
marítimo
prominent ['prɒmɪnənt] adj (standing out)
saliente; (important) eminente, importante
promiscuous [prə'mɪskjuəs] adj
(sexually) promiscuo
promise ['prɒmɪs] n promesa ▷ vt, vi
prometer; **promising** adj prometedor(a)
promote [prə'məʊt] vt (employee)
ascender; (product, pop star) hacer
propaganda por; (ideas) fomentar;
promotion [-'məʊʃən] n (advertising
campaign) campaña f de promoción; (in rank)
ascenso
prompt [prɒmpt] adj rápido ▷ adv: **at 6
o'clock ~** a las seis en punto ▷ n (Comput)
aviso ▷ vt (urge) mover, incitar; (when
talking) instar; (Theatre) apuntar; **to ~ sb to**

do sth instar a algn a hacer algo; **promptly**
adv rápidamente; (exactly) puntualmente
prone [prəʊn] adj (lying) postrado; **~ to**
propenso a
prong [prɒŋ] n diente m, punta
pronoun ['prəʊnaun] n pronombre m
pronounce [prə'nauns] vt pronunciar
pronunciation [prənʌnsɪ'eɪʃən] n
pronunciación f
proof [pruːf] n prueba ▷ adj: **~ against** a
prueba de
prop [prɒp] n apoyo; (fig) sostén m
accesorios mpl, at(t)rezzo msg; **prop up**
vt (roof, structure) apuntalar; (economy)
respaldar
propaganda [prɒpə'gændə] n
propaganda
propeller [prə'pɛlə*] n hélice f
proper ['prɒpə*] adj (suited, right) propio;
(exact) justo; (seemly) correcto, decente;
(authentic) verdadero; (referring to place): **the
village ~** el pueblo mismo; **properly** adv
(adequately) correctamente; (decently)
decentemente; **proper noun** n nombre
m propio
property ['prɒpətɪ] n propiedad f;
(personal) bienes mpl muebles
prophecy ['prɒfɪsɪ] n profecía
prophet ['prɒfɪt] n profeta m
proportion [prə'pɔːʃən] n proporción
f; (share) parte f; **proportions** npl
(size) dimensiones fpl; **proportional**
adj: **proportional (to)** en proporción (con)
proposal [prə'pəuzl] n (offer of marriage)
oferta de matrimonio; (plan) proyecto
propose [prə'pəuz] vt proponer ▷ vi
declararse; **to ~ to do** tener intención de
hacer
proposition [prɒpə'zɪʃən] n propuesta
proprietor [prə'praɪətə*] n propietario/a,
dueño/a
prose [prəuz] n prosa
prosecute ['prɒsɪkjuːt] vt (Law) procesar;
prosecution [-'kjuːʃən] n proceso, causa;
(accusing side) acusación f; **prosecutor** n
acusador(a) m/f; (also: **public prosecutor**)
fiscal mf
prospect [n 'prɒspɛkt, vb prə'spɛkt]
n (possibility) posibilidad f; (outlook)
perspectiva ▷ vi: **to ~ for** buscar; **prospects**
npl (for work etc) perspectivas fpl;
prospective [prə'spɛktɪv] adj futuro
prospectus [prə'spɛktəs] n prospecto
prosper ['prɒspə*] vi prosperar;
prosperity [-'spɛrɪtɪ] n prosperidad f;
prosperous adj próspero
prostitute ['prɒstɪtjuːt] n prostituta;
(male) hombre que se dedica a la prostitución

protect [prə'tɛkt] vt proteger; **protection** [-'tɛkʃən] n protección f; **protective** adj protector(a)

protein ['prəuti:n] n proteína

protest [n 'prəutɛst, vb prə'tɛst] n protesta ▷ vi: **to ~ about** or **at/against** protestar de/contra ▷ vt (insist): **to ~ (that)** insistir en (que)

Protestant ['prɒtɪstənt] adj, n protestante mf

protester [prə'tɛstə*] n manifestante mf

protractor [prə'træktə*] n (Geom) transportador m

proud [praud] adj orgulloso; (pej) soberbio, altanero

prove [pru:v] vt probar; (show) demostrar ▷ vi: **to ~ (to be) correct** resultar correcto; **to ~ o.s.** probar su valía

proverb ['prɒvə:b] n refrán m

provide [prə'vaɪd] vt proporcionar, dar; **to ~ sb with sth** proveer a algn de algo; **provide for** vt fus (person) mantener a; (problem etc) tener en cuenta; **provided** conj: **provided (that)** con tal de que, a condición de que; **providing** [prə'vaɪdɪŋ] conj: **providing (that)** a condición de que, con tal de que

province ['prɒvɪns] n provincia; (fig) esfera; **provincial** [prə'vɪnʃəl] adj provincial; (pej) provinciano

provision [prə'vɪʒən] n (supplying) suministro, abastecimiento; (of contract etc) disposición f; **provisions** npl (food) comestibles mpl; **provisional** adj provisional

provocative [prə'vɒkətɪv] adj provocativo

provoke [prə'vəuk] vt (cause) provocar, incitar; (anger) enojar

prowl [praul] vi (also: ~ **about**, ~ **around**) merodear ▷ n: **on the ~** de merodeo

proximity [prɒk'sɪmɪtɪ] n proximidad f

proxy ['prɒksɪ] n: **by ~** por poderes

prudent ['pru:dənt] adj prudente

prune [pru:n] n ciruela pasa ▷ vt podar

pry [praɪ] vi: **to ~ (into)** entrometerse (en)

PS n abbr (= postscript) P.D.

pseudonym ['sju:dəunɪm] n seudónimo

PSHE (BRIT: Scol) n abbr (= personal, social and health education) formación social y sanitaria

psychiatric [saɪkɪ'ætrɪk] adj psiquiátrico

psychiatrist [saɪ'kaɪətrɪst] n psiquiatra mf

psychic ['saɪkɪk] adj (also: ~al) psíquico

psychoanalysis [saɪkəuə'nælɪsɪs] n psicoanálisis m inv

psychological [saɪkə'lɒdʒɪkl] adj psicológico

psychologist [saɪ'kɒlədʒɪst] n psicólogo/a

psychology [saɪ'kɒlədʒɪ] n psicología

psychotherapy [saɪkəu'θɛrəpɪ] n psicoterapia

pt abbr = **pint(s)**; **point(s)**

PTO abbr (= please turn over) sigue

pub [pʌb] n abbr (= public house) pub m, bar m

puberty ['pju:bətɪ] n pubertad f

public ['pʌblɪk] adj público ▷ n: **the ~** el público; **in ~** en público; **to make ~** hacer público

publication [pʌblɪ'keɪʃən] n publicación f

public: public company n sociedad f anónima; **public convenience** (BRIT) n aseos mpl públicos (SP), sanitarios mpl (LAM); **public holiday** n (día m de) fiesta (SP), (día m) feriado (LAM); **public house** (BRIT) n bar m, pub m

publicity [pʌb'lɪsɪtɪ] n publicidad f

publicize ['pʌblɪsaɪz] vt publicitar

public: public limited company n sociedad f anónima (S.A.); **publicly** adv públicamente, en público; **public opinion** n opinión f pública; **public relations** n relaciones fpl públicas; **public school** n (BRIT) escuela privada; (US) instituto; **public transport** n transporte m público

publish ['pʌblɪʃ] vt publicar; **publisher** n (person) editor(a) m/f; (firm) editorial f; **publishing** n (industry) industria del libro

pub lunch n almuerzo que se sirve en un pub; **to go for a ~** almorzar o comer en un pub

pudding ['pudɪŋ] n pudín m; (BRIT: dessert) postre m; **black ~** morcilla

puddle ['pʌdl] n charco

Puerto Rico [pwɛ:təu'ri:kəu] n Puerto Rico

puff [pʌf] n soplo; (of smoke, air) bocanada; (of breathing) resoplido ▷ vt: **to ~ one's pipe** chupar la pipa ▷ vi (pant) jadear; **puff pastry** n hojaldre m

pull [pul] n (tug): **to give sth a ~** dar un tirón a algo ▷ vt tirar de; (press: trigger) apretar; (haul) tirar, arrastrar; (close: curtain) echar ▷ vi tirar; **to ~ to pieces** hacer pedazos; **not to ~ one's punches** no andarse con bromas; **to ~ one's weight** hacer su parte; **to ~ o.s. together** sobreponerse; **to ~ sb's leg** tomar el pelo a algn; **pull apart** vt (break) romper; **pull away** vi (vehicle: move off) salir, arrancar; (draw back) apartarse bruscamente; **pull back** vt (lever etc) tirar hacia sí; (curtains) descorrer ▷ vi (refrain) contenerse; (Mil: withdraw) retirarse; **pull down** vt (building) derribar; **pull in** vi (car etc) parar (junto a la acera); (train) llegar a la estación; **pull off** vt (deal etc) cerrar; **pull out** vi (car, train etc) salir ▷ vt sacar, arrancar; **pull over** vi (Aut) hacerse a un lado; **pull up** vi (stop) parar ▷ vt (raise) levantar; (uproot) arrancar, desarraigar

pulley ['pulɪ] n polea

pullover ['puləuvə*] n jersey m, suéter m

pulp [pʌlp] n (of fruit) pulpa

pulpit ['pulpɪt] n púlpito

pulse [pʌls] n (Anat) pulso; (rhythm) pulsación f; (Bot) legumbre f; **pulses** pl n legumbres

puma ['pju:mə] n puma m

pump [pʌmp] n bomba; (shoe) zapatilla ▷ vt sacar con una bomba; **pump up** vt inflar

pumpkin ['pʌmpkɪn] n calabaza

pun [pʌn] n juego de palabras

punch [pʌntʃ] n (blow) golpe m, puñetazo; (tool) punzón m; (drink) ponche m ▷ vt (hit): **to ~ sb/sth** dar un puñetazo or golpear a algn/algo; **punch-up** (BRIT: inf) n riña

punctual ['pʌŋktjuəl] adj puntual

punctuation [pʌŋktju'eɪʃən] n puntuación f

puncture ['pʌŋktʃə*] (BRIT) n pinchazo ▷ vt pinchar

punish ['pʌnɪʃ] vt castigar; **punishment** n castigo

punk [pʌŋk] n (also: ~ rocker) punki mf; (also: ~ rock) música punk; (US: inf: hoodlum) rufián m

pup [pʌp] n cachorro

pupil ['pju:pl] n alumno/a; (of eye) pupila

puppet ['pʌpɪt] n títere m

puppy ['pʌpɪ] n cachorro, perrito

purchase ['pə:tʃɪs] n compra ▷ vt comprar

pure [pjuə*] adj puro; **purely** adv puramente

purify ['pjuərɪfaɪ] vt purificar, depurar

purity ['pjuərɪtɪ] n pureza

purple ['pə:pl] adj purpúreo; morado

purpose ['pə:pəs] n propósito; **on ~** a propósito, adrede

purr [pə:*] vi ronronear

purse [pə:s] n monedero; (US: handbag) bolso (SP), cartera (LAM), bolsa (MEX) ▷ vt fruncir

pursue [pə'sju:] vt seguir

pursuit [pə'sju:t] n (chase) caza; (occupation) actividad f

pus [pʌs] n pus m

push [puʃ] n empuje m, empujón m; (of button) presión f; (drive) empuje m ▷ vt empujar; (button) apretar; (promote) promover ▷ vi empujar; (demand): **to ~ for** luchar por; **push in** vi colarse; **push off** (inf) vi largarse; **push on** vi seguir adelante; **push over** vt (cause to fall) hacer caer, derribar; (knock over) volcar; **push through** vi (crowd) abrirse paso a empujones ▷ vt (measure) despachar; **pushchair** (BRIT) n sillita de ruedas; **pusher** n (drug pusher) traficante mf de drogas; **push-up** (US) n plancha

pussy(-cat) ['pusɪ-] (inf) n minino (inf)

put [put] (pt, pp ~) vt (place) poner, colocar; (put into) meter; (say) expresar; (a question) hacer; (estimate) estimar; **put aside** vt (lay down: book etc) dejar or poner a un lado; (save) ahorrar; (in shop) guardar; **put away** vt (store) guardar; **put back** vt (replace) devolver a su lugar; (postpone) aplazar; **put by** vt (money) guardar; **put down** vt (on ground) poner en el suelo; (animal) sacrificar; (in writing) apuntar; (revolt etc) sofocar; (attribute): **to put sth down to** atribuir algo a; **put forward** vt (ideas) presentar, proponer; **put in** vt (complaint) presentar; (time) dedicar; **put off** vt (postpone) aplazar; (discourage) desanimar; **put on** vt ponerse; (light etc) encender; (play etc) presentar; (gain): **to put on weight** engordar; (brake) echar; (record, kettle etc) poner; (assume) adoptar; **put out** vt (fire, light) apagar; (rubbish etc) sacar; (cat etc) echar; (one's hand) alargar; (inf: person): **to be put out** alterarse; **put through** vt (Tel) poner; (plan etc) hacer aprobar; **put together** vt unir, reunir; (assemble: furniture) armar, montar; (meal) preparar; **put up** vt (raise) levantar, alzar; (hang) colgar; (build) construir; (increase) aumentar; (accommodate) alojar; **put up with** vt fus aguantar

putt [pʌt] n putt m, golpe m corto; **putting green** n green m; minigolf m

puzzle ['pʌzl] n rompecabezas m inv; (also: **crossword ~**) crucigrama m; (mystery) misterio ▷ vt dejar perplejo, confundir ▷ vi: **to ~ over sth** devanarse los sesos con algo; **puzzled** adj perplejo; **puzzling** adj misterioso, extraño

pyjamas [pɪ'dʒɑ:məz] (BRIT) npl pijama m

pylon ['paɪlən] n torre f de conducción eléctrica

pyramid ['pɪrəmɪd] n pirámide f

q

quack [kwæk] n graznido; (pej: doctor) curandero/a

quadruple [kwɔ'drupl] vt, vi cuadruplicar

quail [kweɪl] n codorniz f ▷ vi: **to ~ at** or **before** amedrentarse ante

quaint [kweɪnt] adj extraño; (picturesque) pintoresco

quake [kweɪk] vi temblar ▷ n abbr = **earthquake**

qualification [kwɔlɪfɪ'keɪʃən] n (ability) capacidad f; (often pl: diploma etc) título; (reservation) salvedad f

qualified ['kwɔlɪfaɪd] adj capacitado; (professionally) titulado; (limited) limitado

qualify ['kwɔlɪfaɪ] vt (make competent) capacitar; (modify) modificar ▷ vi (in competition): **to ~ (for)** calificarse (para); (pass examination(s): **to ~ (as)** calificarse (de), graduarse (en); (be eligible): **to ~ (for)** reunir los requisitos (para)

quality ['kwɔlɪtɪ] n calidad f; (of person) cualidad f

qualm [kwɑːm] n escrúpulo

quantify ['kwɔntɪfaɪ] vt cuantificar

quantity ['kwɔntɪtɪ] n cantidad f; **in ~** en grandes cantidades

quarantine ['kwɔrntiːn] n cuarentena

quarrel ['kwɔrl] n riña, pelea ▷ vi reñir, pelearse

quarry ['kwɔrɪ] n cantera

quart [kwɔːt] n ≈ litro

quarter ['kwɔːtə*] n cuarto, cuarta parte f; (us: coin) moneda de 25 centavos; (of year) trimestre m; (district) barrio ▷ vt dividir en cuartos; (Mil: lodge) alojar; **quarters** npl (barracks) cuartel m; (living quarters) alojamiento f; **a ~ of an hour** un cuarto de hora; **quarter final** n cuarto de final; **quarterly** adj trimestral ▷ adv cada 3 meses, trimestralmente

quartet(te) [kwɔː'tɛt] n cuarteto

quartz [kwɔːts] n cuarzo

quay [kiː] n (also: **~side**) muelle m

queasy ['kwiːzɪ] adj: **to feel ~** tener náuseas

queen [kwiːn] n reina; (Cards etc) dama

queer [kwɪə*] adj raro, extraño ▷ n (inf: highly offensive) maricón m

quench [kwɛntʃ] vt: **to ~ one's thirst** apagar la sed

query ['kwɪərɪ] n (question) pregunta ▷ vt dudar de

quest [kwɛst] n busca, búsqueda

question ['kwɛstʃən] n pregunta; (doubt) duda; (matter) asunto, cuestión f ▷ vt (doubt) dudar de; (interrogate) interrogar, hacer preguntas a; **beyond ~** fuera de toda duda; **out of the ~** imposible; ni hablar; **questionable** adj dudoso; **question mark** n punto de interrogación; **questionnaire** [-'neə*] n cuestionario

queue [kjuː] (BRIT) n cola ▷ vi (also: **~ up**) hacer cola

quiche [kiːʃ] n quiche m

quick [kwɪk] adj rápido; (agile) ágil; (mind) listo ▷ n: **cut to the ~** (fig) herido en lo vivo; **be ~!** ¡date prisa!; **quickly** adv rápidamente, de prisa

quid [kwɪd] (BRIT: inf) n inv libra

quiet ['kwaɪət] adj (voice, music etc) bajo; (person, place) tranquilo; (ceremony) íntimo ▷ n silencio; (calm) tranquilidad f ▷ vt, vi (US) = **quieten**

> Be careful not to translate **quiet** by the Spanish word *quieto*.

quietly adv tranquilamente; (silently) silenciosamente

quilt [kwɪlt] n edredón m

quirky ['kwɜːkɪ] adj raro, estrafalario

quit [kwɪt] (pt, pp = or **~ted**) vt dejar, abandonar; (premises) desocupar ▷ vi (give up) renunciar; (resign) dimitir

quite [kwaɪt] adv (rather) bastante; (entirely) completamente; **that's not ~ big enough** no acaba de ser lo bastante grande; **~ a few of them** un buen número de ellos; **~ (so)!** ¡así es!, ¡exactamente!

quits [kwɪts] adj: **~ (with)** en paz (con); **let's call it ~** dejémoslo en tablas

quiver ['kwɪvə*] vi estremecerse

quiz [kwɪz] n concurso ▷ vt interrogar

quota ['kwəʊtə] n cuota

quotation [kwəʊ'teɪʃən] n cita; (estimate) presupuesto; **quotation marks** npl comillas fpl

quote [kwəʊt] n cita; (estimate) presupuesto ▷ vt citar; (price) cotizar ▷ vi: **to ~ from** citar de; **quotes** npl (inverted commas) comillas fpl

q

r

rabbi ['ræbaɪ] n rabino
rabbit ['ræbɪt] n conejo
rabies ['reɪbiːz] n rabia
RAC (BRIT) n abbr (= Royal Automobile Club)
≈ RACE m
rac(c)oon [rə'kuːn] n mapache m
race [reɪs] n carrera; (species) raza ▷ vt
(horse) hacer correr; (engine) acelerar ▷ vi
(compete) competir; (run) correr; (pulse) latir
a ritmo acelerado; **race car** (US) = **racing
car**; **racecourse** n hipódromo; **racehorse**
n caballo de carreras; **racetrack** n pista;
(for cars) autódromo
racial ['reɪʃl] adj racial
racing ['reɪsɪŋ] n carreras fpl; **racing car**
(BRIT) n coche m de carreras; **racing driver**
(BRIT) n piloto mf de carreras
racism ['reɪsɪzəm] n racismo; **racist**
[-sɪst] adj, n racista mf
rack [ræk] n (also: **luggage ~**) rejilla;
(shelf) estante m; (also: **roof ~**) baca,
portaequipajes m inv; (dish rack)
escurreplatos m inv; (clothes rack) percha ▷ vt
atormentar; **to ~ one's brains** devanarse
los sesos
racket ['rækɪt] n (for tennis) raqueta; (noise)
ruido, estrépito; (swindle) estafa, timo
racquet ['rækɪt] n raqueta
radar ['reɪdɑː*] n radar m
radiation [reɪdɪ'eɪʃən] n radiación f
radiator ['reɪdɪeɪtə*] n radiador m
radical ['rædɪkl] adj radical
radio ['reɪdɪəu] n radio f; **on the ~** por
radio; **radioactive** adj radioactivo; **radio
station** n emisora
radish ['rædɪʃ] n rábano
RAF n abbr (= Royal Air Force) las Fuerzas
Aéreas Británicas
raffle ['ræfl] n rifa, sorteo
raft [rɑːft] n balsa; (also: **life ~**) balsa
salvavidas

rag [ræg] n (piece of cloth) trapo; (torn cloth)
harapo; (pej: newspaper) periodicucho; (for
charity) actividades estudiantiles benéficas;
rags npl (torn clothes) harapos mpl
rage [reɪdʒ] n rabia, furor m ▷ vi (person)
rabiar, estar furioso; (storm) bramar; **it's all
the ~** (very fashionable) está muy de moda
ragged ['rægɪd] adj (edge) desigual,
mellado; (appearance) andrajoso, harapiento
raid [reɪd] n (Mil) incursión f; (criminal)
asalto; (by police) redada ▷ vt invadir,
atacar; asaltar
rail [reɪl] n (on stair) barandilla, pasamanos
m inv; (on bridge, balcony) pretil m; (of ship)
barandilla; (also: **towel ~**) toallero; **railcard**
n (BRIT) tarjeta para obtener descuentos en el
tren; **railing(s)** n(pl) vallado; **railroad** (US)
n = **railway**; **railway** (BRIT) n ferrocarril
m, vía férrea; **railway line** (BRIT) n línea
(de ferrocarril); **railway station** (BRIT) n
estación f de ferrocarril
rain [reɪn] n lluvia ▷ vi llover; **in the
~** bajo la lluvia; **it's ~ing** llueve, está
lloviendo; **rainbow** n arco iris; **raincoat** n
impermeable m; **raindrop** n gota de lluvia;
rainfall n lluvia; (measured) cantidad de
agua caída; **rainforest** n selvas fpl
tropicales; **rainy** adj lluvioso
raise [reɪz] n aumento ▷ vt levantar;
(increase) aumentar; (improve: morale) subir;
(: standards) mejorar; (doubts) suscitar; (a
question) plantear; (cattle, family) criar; (crop)
cultivar; (army) reclutar; (loan) obtener; **to ~
one's voice** alzar la voz
raisin ['reɪzn] n pasa de Corinto
rake [reɪk] n (tool) rastrillo; (person)
libertino ▷ vt (garden) rastrillar
rally ['rælɪ] n (Pol etc) reunión f, mitin m;
(Aut) rallye m; (Tennis) peloteo ▷ vt reunir
▷ vi recuperarse
RAM [ræm] n abbr (= random access memory)
RAM f
ram [ræm] n carnero; (also: **battering ~**)
ariete m ▷ vt (crash into) dar contra, chocar
con; (push: fist etc) empujar con fuerza
Ramadan [ræmə'dæn] n ramadán m
ramble ['ræmbl] n caminata, excursión
f en el campo ▷ vi (pej: also: **~ on**) divagar;
rambler n excursionista mf; (Bot)
trepadora; **rambling** adj (speech) inconexo;
(house) laberíntico; (Bot) trepador(a)
ramp [ræmp] n rampa; **on/off ~** (US Aut)
vía de acceso/salida
rampage [ræm'peɪdʒ] n: **to be on the ~**
desmandarse ▷ vi: **they went rampaging
through the town** recorrieron la ciudad
armando alboroto
ran [ræn] pt of **run**
ranch [rɑːntʃ] n hacienda, estancia

random ['rændəm] *adj* fortuito, sin orden; (*Comput, Math*) aleatorio ▷ *n*: **at ~** al azar

rang [ræŋ] *pt of* **ring**

range [reɪndʒ] *n* (*of mountains*) cadena de montañas, cordillera; (*of missile*) alcance *m*; (*of voice*) registro; (*series*) serie *f*; (*of products*) surtido; (*Mil: also:* **shooting ~**) campo de tiro; (*also:* **kitchen ~**) fogón *m* ▷ *vt* (*place*) colocar; (*arrange*) arreglar ▷ *vi*: **to ~ over** (*extend*) extenderse por; **to ~ from ... to ...** oscilar entre ... y ...

ranger [reɪndʒə*] *n* guardabosques *mf inv*

rank [ræŋk] *n* (*row*) fila; (*Mil*) rango; (*status*) categoría; (BRIT: *also:* **taxi ~**) parada de taxis ▷ *vi*: **to ~ among** figurar entre ▷ *adj* fétido, rancio; **the ~ and file** (*fig*) la base

ransom ['rænsəm] *n* rescate *m*; **to hold to ~** (*fig*) hacer chantaje a

rant [rænt] *vi* divagar, desvariar

rap [ræp] *vt* golpear, dar un golpecito en ▷ *n* (*music*) rap *m*

rape [reɪp] *n* violación *f*; (*Bot*) colza ▷ *vt* violar

rapid ['ræpɪd] *adj* rápido; **rapidly** *adv* rápidamente; **rapids** *npl* (*Geo*) rápidos *mpl*

rapist ['reɪpɪst] *n* violador *m*

rapport [ræ'pɔː*] *n* simpatía

rare [rɛə*] *adj* raro, poco común; (*Culin: steak*) poco hecho; **rarely** *adv* pocas veces

rash [ræʃ] *adj* imprudente, precipitado ▷ *n* (*Med*) sarpullido, erupción *f* (cutánea); (*of events*) serie *f*

rasher ['ræʃə*] *n* lonja

raspberry ['rɑːzbərɪ] *n* frambuesa

rat [ræt] *n* rata

rate [reɪt] *n* (*ratio*) razón *f*; (*price*) precio; (: *of hotel etc*) tarifa; (*of interest*) tipo; (*speed*) velocidad *f* ▷ *vt* (*value*) tasar; (*estimate*) estimar; **rates** (BRIT: *property tax*) impuesto municipal; (*fees*) tarifa; **to ~ sth/ sb as** considerar algo/a algn como

rather ['rɑːðə*] *adv*: **it's ~ expensive** es algo caro; (*too much*) es demasiado caro; (*to some extent*) más bien; **there's ~ a lot** hay bastante; **I would** *or* **I'd ~ go** preferiría ir; **or ~** mejor dicho

rating ['reɪtɪŋ] *n* tasación *f*; (*score*) índice *m*; (*of ship*) clase *f*; **ratings** *npl* (*Radio, TV*) niveles *mpl* de audiencia

ratio ['reɪʃɪəʊ] *n* razón *f*; **in the ~ of 100 to 1** a razón de 100 a 1

ration ['ræʃən] *n* ración *f* ▷ *vt* racionar; **rations** *npl* víveres *mpl*

rational ['ræʃənl] *adj* (*solution, reasoning*) lógico, razonable; (*person*) cuerdo, sensato

rattle ['rætl] *n* golpeteo; (*of train etc*)

traqueteo; (*for baby*) sonaja, sonajero ▷ *vi* castañetear; (*car, bus*): **to ~ along** traquetear ▷ *vt* hacer sonar agitando

rave [reɪv] *vi* (*in anger*) encolerizarse; (*with enthusiasm*) entusiasmarse; (*Med*) delirar, desvariar ▷ *n* (*inf: party*) rave *m*

raven ['reɪvən] *n* cuervo

ravine [rə'viːn] *n* barranco

raw [rɔː] *adj* crudo; (*not processed*) bruto; (*sore*) vivo; (*inexperienced*) novato, inexperto; **~ materials** materias primas

ray [reɪ] *n* rayo; **~ of hope** (rayo de) esperanza

razor ['reɪzə*] *n* (*open*) navaja; (*safety razor*) máquina de afeitar; (*electric razor*) máquina (eléctrica) de afeitar; **razor blade** *n* hoja de afeitar

Rd *abbr* = **road**

RE *n abbr* (BRIT) = **religious education**

re [riː] *prep* con referencia a

reach [riːtʃ] *n* alcance *m*; (*of river etc*) extensión *f* entre dos recodos ▷ *vt* alcanzar, llegar a; (*achieve*) lograr ▷ *vi* extenderse; **within ~** al alcance (de la mano); **out of ~** fuera del alcance; **reach out** *vt* (*hand*) tender ▷ *vi*: **to reach out for sth** alargar *or* tender la mano para tomar algo

react [riː'ækt] *vi* reaccionar; **reaction** [-'ækʃən] *n* reacción *f*; **reactor** [riː'æktə*] *n* (*also:* **nuclear reactor**) reactor *m* (nuclear)

read [riːd, *pt, pp* rɛd] (*pt, pp ~*) *vi* leer ▷ *vt* leer; (*understand*) entender; (*study*) estudiar; **read out** *vt* leer en alta voz; **reader** *n* lector(a) *m/f*; (BRIT: *at university*) profesor(a) *m/f* adjunto/a

readily ['rɛdɪlɪ] *adv* (*willingly*) de buena gana; (*easily*) fácilmente; (*quickly*) en seguida

reading ['riːdɪŋ] *n* lectura; (*on instrument*) indicación *f*

ready ['rɛdɪ] *adj* listo, preparado; (*willing*) dispuesto; (*available*) disponible ▷ *adv*: **~-cooked** listo para comer ▷ *n*: **at the ~** (*Mil*) listo para tirar ▷ **to get ~** *vi* prepararse ▷ **to get ~** *vt* preparar; **ready-made** *adj* confeccionado

real [rɪəl] *adj* verdadero, auténtico; **in ~ terms** en términos reales; **real ale** *n* cerveza elaborada tradicionalmente; **real estate** *n* bienes *mpl* raíces; **realistic** [-'lɪstɪk] *adj* realista; **reality** [riː'ælɪtɪ] *n* realidad *f*; **reality TV** *n* telerrealidad *f*

realization [rɪəlaɪ'zeɪʃən] *n* comprensión *f*; (*fulfilment, Comm*) realización *f*

realize ['rɪəlaɪz] *vt* (*understand*) darse cuenta de

really ['rɪəlɪ] *adv* realmente; (*for emphasis*) verdaderamente; (*actually*): **what ~ happened** lo que pasó en realidad; **~?** ¿de

r

veras?; **~!** (annoyance) ¡vamos!, ¡por favor!

realm [rɛlm] n reino; (fig) esfera

realtor ['rɪəltɔ:*] (us) n agente mf inmobiliario/a

reappear [ri:ə'pɪə*] vi reaparecer

rear [rɪə*] adj trasero ▷ n parte f trasera ▷ vt (cattle, family) criar ▷ vi (also: ~ up: animal) encabritarse

rearrange [ri:ə'reɪndʒ] vt ordenar or arreglar de nuevo

rear: rear-view mirror n (Aut) (espejo) retrovisor m; **rear-wheel drive** n tracción f trasera

reason ['ri:zn] n razón f ▷ vi: **to ~ with sb** tratar de que algn entre en razón; **it stands to ~ that ...** es lógico que ...; **reasonable** adj razonable; (sensible) sensato; **reasonably** adv razonablemente; **reasoning** n razonamiento, argumentos mpl

reassurance [ri:ə'ʃuərəns] n consuelo

reassure [ri:ə'ʃuə*] vt tranquilizar, alentar; **to ~ sb that ...** tranquilizar a algn asegurando que ...

rebate ['ri:beɪt] n (on tax etc) desgravación f

rebel [n 'rɛbl, vi rɪ'bɛl] n rebelde mf ▷ vi rebelarse, sublevarse; **rebellion** [rɪ'bɛljən] n rebelión f, sublevación f; **rebellious** [rɪ'bɛljəs] adj rebelde; (child) revoltoso

rebuild [ri:'bɪld] vt reconstruir

recall [vb rɪ'kɔ:l, n 'ri:kɔl] vt (remember) recordar; (ambassador etc) retirar ▷ n recuerdo; retirada

rec'd abbr (= received) rbdo

receipt [rɪ'si:t] n (document) recibo; (for parcel etc) acuse m de recibo; (act of receiving) recepción f; **receipts** npl (Comm) ingresos mpl

▌Be careful not to translate **receipt** by the Spanish word receta.

receive [rɪ'si:v] vt recibir; (guest) acoger; (wound) sufrir; **receiver** n (Tel) auricular m; (Radio) receptor m; (of stolen goods) perista mf; (Comm) administrador m jurídico

recent ['ri:snt] adj reciente; **recently** adv recientemente; **recently arrived** recién llegado

reception [rɪ'sɛpʃən] n recepción f; (welcome) acogida; **reception desk** n recepción f; **receptionist** n recepcionista mf

recession [rɪ'sɛʃən] n recesión f

recharge [ri:'tʃɑ:dʒ] vt (battery) recargar

recipe ['rɛsɪpɪ] n receta; (for disaster, success) fórmula

recipient [rɪ'sɪpɪənt] n recibidor(a) m/f; (of letter) destinatario/a

recital [rɪ'saɪtl] n recital m

recite [rɪ'saɪt] vt (poem) recitar

reckless ['rɛkləs] adj temerario, imprudente; (driving, driver) peligroso

reckon ['rɛkən] vt calcular; (consider) considerar; (think): **I ~ that ...** me parece que ...

reclaim [rɪ'kleɪm] vt (land, waste) recuperar; (land: from sea) rescatar; (demand back) reclamar

recline [rɪ'klaɪn] vi reclinarse

recognition [rɛkəg'nɪʃən] n reconocimiento; **transformed beyond ~** irreconocible

recognize ['rɛkəgnaɪz] vt: **to ~ (by/as)** reconocer (por/como)

recollection [rɛkə'lɛkʃən] n recuerdo

recommend [rɛkə'mɛnd] vt recomendar; **recommendation** [rɛkəmɛn'deɪʃən] n recomendación f

reconcile ['rɛkənsaɪl] vt (two people) reconciliar; (two facts) compaginar; **to ~ o.s. to sth** conformarse a algo

reconsider [ri:kən'sɪdə*] vt repensar

reconstruct [ri:kən'strʌkt] vt reconstruir

record [n, adj 'rɛkɔ:d, vt rɪ'kɔ:d] n (Mus) disco; (of meeting etc) acta; (register) registro, partida; (file) archivo; (also: **criminal ~**) antecedentes mpl; (written) expediente m; (Sport, Comput) récord m ▷ adj récord, sin precedentes ▷ vt registrar; (Mus: song etc) grabar; **in ~ time** en un tiempo récord; **off the ~** adj no oficial ▷ adv confidencialmente; **recorded delivery** (BRIT) n (Post) entrega con acuse de recibo; **recorder** n (Mus) flauta de pico; **recording** n (Mus) grabación f; **record player** n tocadiscos m inv

recount [rɪ'kaunt] vt contar

recover [rɪ'kʌvə*] vt recuperar ▷ vi (from illness, shock) recuperarse; **recovery** n recuperación f

recreate [ri:krɪ'eɪt] vt recrear

recreation [rɛkrɪ'eɪʃən] n recreo; **recreational vehicle** (us) n caravan or rulota pequeña; **recreational drug** droga recreativa

recruit [rɪ'kru:t] n recluta mf ▷ vt reclutar; (staff) contratar; **recruitment** n reclutamiento

rectangle ['rɛktæŋgl] n rectángulo; **rectangular** [-'tæŋgjulə*] adj rectangular

rectify ['rɛktɪfaɪ] vt rectificar

rector ['rɛktə*] n (Rel) párroco

recur [rɪ'kə:*] vi repetirse; (pain, illness) producirse de nuevo; **recurring** adj (problem) repetido, constante

recyclable [ri:'saɪkləbl] adj reciclable

recycle [ri:'saɪkl] vt reciclar

recycling [riːˈsaɪklɪŋ] n reciclaje

red [rɛd] n rojo ▷ adj rojo; (hair) pelirrojo; (wine) tinto; **to be in the ~** (account) estar en números rojos; (business) tener un saldo negativo; **to give sb the ~ carpet treatment** recibir a algn con todos los honores; **Red Cross** n Cruz f Roja; **redcurrant** n grosella roja

redeem [rɪˈdiːm] vt redimir; (promises) cumplir; (sth in pawn) desempeñar; (fig, also Rel) rescatar

red: red-haired adj pelirrojo; **redhead** n pelirrojo/a; **red-hot** adj candente; **red light** n: **to go through a red light** (Aut) pasar la luz roja; **red-light district** n barrio chino

red meat n carne f roja

reduce [rɪˈdjuːs] vt reducir; **to ~ sb to tears** hacer llorar a algn; **"~ speed now"** (Aut) "reduzca la velocidad"; **reduced** adj (decreased) reducido, rebajado; **at a reduced price** con rebaja or descuento; **"greatly reduced prices"** "grandes rebajas"; **reduction** [rɪˈdʌkʃən] n reducción f; (of price) rebaja; (discount) descuento; (smaller-scale copy) copia reducida

redundancy [rɪˈdʌndənsɪ] n (dismissal) despido; (unemployment) desempleo

redundant [rɪˈdʌndnt] adj (BRIT: worker) parado, sin trabajo; (detail, object) superfluo; **to be made ~** quedar(se) sin trabajo

reed [riːd] n (Bot) junco, caña; (Mus) lengüeta

reef [riːf] n (at sea) arrecife m

reel [riːl] n carrete m, bobina; (of film) rollo; (dance) baile escocés ▷ vt (also: ~ up) devanar; (also: ~ in) sacar ▷ vi (sway) tambalear(se)

ref [rɛf] (inf) n abbr = **referee**

refectory [rɪˈfɛktərɪ] n comedor m

refer [rɪˈfəː*] vt (send: patient) referir; (: matter) remitir ▷ vi: **to ~ to** (allude to) referirse a, aludir a; (apply to) relacionarse con; (consult) consultar

referee [rɛfəˈriː] n árbitro; (BRIT: for job application): **to be a ~ for sb** proporcionar referencias a algn ▷ vt (match) arbitrar en

reference [ˈrɛfrəns] n referencia; (for job application: letter) carta de recomendación; **with ~ to** (Comm: in letter) me remito a; **reference number** n número de referencia

refill [vt riːˈfɪl, n ˈriːfɪl] vt rellenar ▷ n repuesto, recambio

refine [rɪˈfaɪn] vt refinar; **refined** adj (person) fino; **refinery** n refinería

reflect [rɪˈflɛkt] vt reflejar ▷ vi (think) reflexionar, pensar; **it ~s badly/well on him** le perjudica/le hace honor; **reflection** [-ˈflɛkʃən] n (act) reflexión f; (image) reflejo; (criticism) crítica; **on reflection** pensándolo bien

reflex [ˈriːflɛks] adj, n reflejo

reform [rɪˈfɔːm] n reforma ▷ vt reformar

refrain [rɪˈfreɪn] vi: **to ~ from doing** abstenerse de hacer ▷ n estribillo

refresh [rɪˈfrɛʃ] vt refrescar; **refreshing** adj refrescante; **refreshments** npl refrescos mpl

refrigerator [rɪˈfrɪdʒəreɪtə*] n frigorífico (SP), nevera (SP), refrigerador m (LAM), heladera (RPL)

refuel [riːˈfjuəl] vi repostar (combustible)

refuge [ˈrɛfjuːdʒ] n refugio, asilo; **to take ~ in** refugiarse en; **refugee** [rɛfjuˈdʒiː] n refugiado/a

refund [n ˈriːfʌnd, vb rɪˈfʌnd] n reembolso ▷ vt devolver, reembolsar

refurbish [riːˈfəːbɪʃ] vt restaurar, renovar

refusal [rɪˈfjuːzəl] n negativa; **to have first ~ on** tener la primera opción a

refuse¹ [ˈrɛfjuːs] n basura

refuse² [rɪˈfjuːz] vt rechazar; (invitation) declinar; (permission) denegar ▷ vi: **to ~ to do sth** negarse a hacer algo; (horse) rehusar

regain [rɪˈgeɪn] vt recobrar, recuperar

regard [rɪˈgɑːd] n mirada; (esteem) respeto; (attention) consideración f ▷ vt (consider) considerar; **to give one's ~s to** saludar de su parte a; **"with kindest ~s"** "con muchos recuerdos"; **as ~s, with ~ to** con respecto a, en cuanto a; **regarding** prep con respecto a, en cuanto a; **regardless** adv a pesar de todo; **regardless of** sin reparar en

regenerate [rɪˈdʒɛnəreɪt] vt regenerar

reggae [ˈrɛgeɪ] n reggae m

regiment [ˈrɛdʒɪmənt] n regimiento

region [ˈriːdʒən] n región f; **in the ~ of** (fig) alrededor de; **regional** adj regional

register [ˈrɛdʒɪstə*] n registro ▷ vt registrar; (birth) declarar; (car) matricular; (letter) certificar; (instrument) marcar, indicar ▷ vi (at hotel) registrarse; (as student) matricularse; (make impression) producir impresión; **registered** adj (letter, parcel) certificado

registrar [ˈrɛdʒɪstrɑː*] n secretario/a (del registro civil)

registration [rɛdʒɪsˈtreɪʃən] n (act) declaración f; (Aut: also: ~ number) matrícula

registry office [ˈrɛdʒɪstrɪ-] (BRIT) n registro civil; **to get married in a ~** casarse por lo civil

regret [rɪˈgrɛt] n sentimiento, pesar m ▷ vt sentir, lamentar; **regrettable** adj lamentable

regular [ˈrɛgjulə*] adj regular; (soldier)

profesional; (*usual*) habitual; (: *doctor*) de
cabecera ▷ *n* (*client etc*) cliente/a *m/f*
habitual; **regularly** *adv* con regularidad;
(*often*) repetidas veces
regulate ['rɛgjuleɪt] *vt* controlar;
regulation [-'leɪʃən] *n* (*rule*) regla,
reglamento
rehabilitation ['riːəbɪlɪ'teɪʃən] *n*
rehabilitación *f*
rehearsal [rɪ'həːsəl] *n* ensayo
rehearse [rɪ'həːs] *vt* ensayar
reign [reɪn] *n* reinado; (*fig*) predominio
▷ *vi* reinar; (*fig*) imperar
reimburse [riːɪm'bəːs] *vt* reembolsar
rein [reɪn] *n* (*for horse*) rienda
reincarnation [riːɪnkɑː'neɪʃən] *n*
reencarnación *f*
reindeer ['reɪndɪə*] *n inv* reno
reinforce [riːɪn'fɔːs] *vt* reforzar;
reinforcements *npl* (*Mil*) refuerzos *mpl*
reinstate [riːɪn'steɪt] *vt* reintegrar; (*tax,
law*) reinstaurar
reject [*n* 'riːdʒɛkt, *vb* rɪ'dʒɛkt] *n* (*thing*)
desecho ▷ *vt* rechazar; (*suggestion*)
descartar; (*coin*) expulsar; **rejection**
[rɪ'dʒɛkʃən] *n* rechazo
rejoice [rɪ'dʒɔɪs] *vi*: **to ~ at** or **over**
regocijarse or alegrarse de
relate [rɪ'leɪt] *vt* (*tell*) contar, relatar;
(*connect*) relacionar ▷ *vi* relacionarse;
related *adj* afín; (*person*) emparentado;
related to (*subject*) relacionado con;
relating to *prep* referente a
relation [rɪ'leɪʃən] *n* (*person*) familiar
mf, pariente *mf*; (*link*) relación *f*; **relations**
npl (*relatives*) familiares *mpl*; **relationship**
n relación *f*; (*personal*) relaciones *fpl*; (*also*:
family relationship) parentesco
relative ['rɛlətɪv] *n* pariente *mf*,
familiar *mf* ▷ *adj* relativo; **relatively** *adv*
(*comparatively*) relativamente
relax [rɪ'læks] *vi* descansar; (*unwind*)
relajarse ▷ *vt* (*one's grip*) soltar, aflojar;
(*control*) relajar; (*mind, person*) descansar;
relaxation [riːlæk'seɪʃən] *n* descanso; (*of
rule, control*) relajamiento; (*entertainment*)
diversión *f*; **relaxed** *adj* relajado; (*tranquil*)
tranquilo; **relaxing** *adj* relajante
relay ['riːleɪ] *n* (*race*) carrera de relevos ▷ *vt*
(*Radio, TV*) retransmitir
release [rɪ'liːs] *n* (*liberation*) liberación
f; (*from prison*) puesta en libertad; (*of
gas etc*) escape *m*; (*of film etc*) estreno;
(*of record*) lanzamiento ▷ *vt* (*prisoner*)
poner en libertad; (*gas*) despedir, arrojar;
(*from wreckage*) soltar; (*catch, spring etc*)
desenganchar; (*film*) estrenar; (*book*)
publicar; (*news*) difundir

relegate ['rɛləgeɪt] *vt* relegar; (BRIT
Sport) relegar a
relent [rɪ'lɛnt] *vi* ablandarse; **relentless**
adj implacable
relevant ['rɛləvənt] *adj* (*fact*) pertinente;
~ to relacionado con
reliable [rɪ'laɪəbl] *adj* (*person, firm*) de
confianza, de fiar; (*method, machine*) seguro;
(*source*) fidedigno
relic ['rɛlɪk] *n* (*Rel*) reliquia; (*of the past*)
vestigio
relief [rɪ'liːf] *n* (*from pain, anxiety*) alivio;
(*help, supplies*) socorro, ayuda; (*Art, Geo*)
relieve *m*
relieve [rɪ'liːv] *vt* (*pain*) aliviar; (*bring
help to*) ayudar, socorrer; (*take over from*)
sustituir; (: *guard*) relevar; **to ~ sb of sth**
quitar algo a algn; **to ~ o.s.** hacer sus
necesidades; **relieved** *adj*: **to be relieved**
sentir un gran alivio
religion [rɪ'lɪdʒən] *n* religión *f*
religious [rɪ'lɪdʒəs] *adj* religioso; **religious
education** *n* educación *f* religiosa
relish ['rɛlɪʃ] *n* (*Culin*) salsa; (*enjoyment*)
entusiasmo ▷ *vt* (*food etc*) saborear;
(*enjoy*): **to ~ sth** hacerle mucha ilusión a
algn algo
relocate [riːləu'keɪt] *vt* cambiar de lugar,
mudar ▷ *vi* mudarse
reluctance [rɪ'lʌktəns] *n* renuencia
reluctant [rɪ'lʌktənt] *adj* renuente;
reluctantly *adv* de mala gana
rely on [rɪ'laɪ-] *vt fus* depender de; (*trust*)
contar con
remain [rɪ'meɪn] *vi* (*survive*) quedar;
(*be left*) sobrar; (*continue*) quedar(se),
permanecer; **remainder** *n* resto;
remaining *adj* que queda(n); (*surviving*)
restante(s); **remains** *npl* restos *mpl*
remand [rɪ'mɑːnd] *n*: **on ~** detenido (bajo
custodia) ▷ *vt*: **to be ~ed in custody** quedar
detenido bajo custodia
remark [rɪ'mɑːk] *n* comentario ▷ *vt*
comentar; **remarkable** *adj* (*outstanding*)
extraordinario
remarry [riː'mærɪ] *vi* volver a casarse
remedy ['rɛmədɪ] *n* remedio ▷ *vt*
remediar, curar
remember [rɪ'mɛmbə*] *vt* recordar,
acordarse de; (*bear in mind*) tener presente;
(*send greetings to*): **~ me to him** dale
recuerdos de mi parte; **Remembrance Day**
n ≈ día en el que se recuerda a los caídos en
las dos guerras mundiales

● **REMEMBRANCE DAY**
●
● En el Reino Unido el domingo más

próximo al 11 de noviembre se conoce como **Remembrance Sunday** o **Remembrance Day**, aniversario de la firma del armisticio de 1918 que puso fin a la Primera Guerra Mundial. Ese día, a las once de la mañana (hora en que se firmó el armisticio), se recuerda a los que murieron en las dos guerras mundiales con dos minutos de silencio ante los monumentos a los caídos. Allí se colocan coronas de amapolas, flor que también se suele llevar prendida en el pecho tras pagar un donativo destinado a los inválidos de guerra.

remind [rɪ'maɪnd] vt: **to ~ sb to do sth** recordar a algn que haga algo; **to ~ sb of sth** (of fact) recordar algo a algn; **she ~s me of her mother** me recuerda a su madre; **reminder** n notificación f; (memento) recuerdo

reminiscent [rɛmɪ'nɪsnt] adj: **to be ~ of sth** recordar algo

remnant ['rɛmnənt] n resto; (of cloth) retal m

remorse [rɪ'mɔːs] n remordimientos mpl

remote [rɪ'məʊt] adj (distant) lejano; (person) distante; **remote control** n telecontrol m; **remotely** adv remotamente; (slightly) levemente

removal [rɪ'muːvəl] n (taking away) el quitar; (BRIT: from house) mudanza; (from office: dismissal) destitución f; (Med) extirpación f; **removal man** (irreg) n (BRIT) mozo de mudanzas; **removal van** (BRIT) n camión m de mudanzas

remove [rɪ'muːv] vt quitar; (employee) destituir; (name: from list) tachar, borrar; (doubt) disipar; (abuse) suprimir, acabar con; (Med) extirpar

Renaissance [rɪ'neɪsɑ̃s] n: **the ~** el Renacimiento

rename [riː'neɪm] vt poner nuevo nombre a

render ['rɛndə*] vt (thanks) dar; (aid) proporcionar, prestar; (make) **to ~ sth useless** hacer algo inútil

rendezvous ['rɔndɪvuː] n cita

renew [rɪ'njuː] vt renovar; (resume) reanudar; (loan etc) prorrogar

renovate ['rɛnəveɪt] vt renovar

renowned [rɪ'naʊnd] adj renombrado

rent [rɛnt] n (for house) arriendo, renta ▷ vt alquilar; **rental** n (for television, car) alquiler m

reorganize [riː'ɔːɡənaɪz] vt reorganizar

rep [rɛp] n abbr = **representative**

repair [rɪ'pɛə*] n reparación f, compostura

▷ vt reparar, componer; (shoes) remendar; **in good/bad ~** en buen/mal estado; **repair kit** n caja de herramientas

repay [riː'peɪ] vt (money) devolver, reembolsar; (person) pagar; (debt) liquidar; (sb's efforts) devolver, corresponder a; **repayment** n reembolso, devolución f; (sum of money) recompensa

repeat [rɪ'piːt] n (Radio, TV) reposición f ▷ vt repetir ▷ vi repetirse; **repeatedly** adv repetidas veces; **repeat prescription** n (BRIT) receta renovada

repellent [rɪ'pɛlənt] adj repugnante ▷ n: **insect ~** crema or loción f anti-insectos

repercussions [riːpə'kʌʃənz] npl consecuencias fpl

repetition [rɛpɪ'tɪʃən] n repetición f

repetitive [rɪ'pɛtɪtɪv] adj repetitivo

replace [rɪ'pleɪs] vt (put back) devolver a su sitio; (take the place) reemplazar, sustituir; **replacement** n (act) reposición f; (thing) recambio; (person) suplente mf

replay ['riːpleɪ] n (Sport) desempate m; (of tape, film) repetición f

replica ['rɛplɪkə] n copia, reproducción f (exacta)

reply [rɪ'plaɪ] n respuesta, contestación f ▷ vi contestar, responder

report [rɪ'pɔːt] n informe m; (Press etc) reportaje m; (BRIT: also: **school ~**) boletín m escolar; (of gun) estallido m ▷ vt informar de; (Press etc) hacer un reportaje sobre; (notify: accident, culprit) denunciar ▷ vi (make a report) presentar un informe; (present o.s.): **to ~ (to sb)** presentarse (ante algn); **report card** n (US, SCOTTISH) cartilla escolar; **reportedly** adv según se dice; **reporter** n periodista mf

represent [rɛprɪ'zɛnt] vt representar; (Comm) ser agente de; (describe): **to ~ sth as** describir algo como; **representation** [-'teɪʃən] n representación f; **representative** n representante mf; (US Pol) diputado/a m/f ▷ adj representativo

repress [rɪ'prɛs] vt reprimir; **repression** [-'prɛʃən] n represión f

reprimand ['rɛprɪmɑːnd] n reprimenda ▷ vt reprender

reproduce [riːprə'djuːs] vt reproducir ▷ vi reproducirse; **reproduction** [-'dʌkʃən] n reproducción f

reptile ['rɛptaɪl] n reptil m

republic [rɪ'pʌblɪk] n república; **republican** adj, n republicano/a m/f

reputable ['rɛpjutəbl] adj (make etc) de renombre

reputation [rɛpju'teɪʃən] n reputación f

request [rɪ'kwɛst] n petición f; (formal)

solicitud f ▷ vt: **to ~ sth of** or **from sb**
solicitar algo a algn; **request stop** (BRIT) n
parada discrecional
require [rɪ'kwaɪə*] vt (need: person)
necesitar, tener necesidad de; (: thing,
situation) exigir; (want) pedir; **to ~ sb
to do sth** pedir a algn que haga algo;
requirement n requisito; (need) necesidad
f
resat [riː'sæt] pt, pp of **resit**
rescue ['rɛskjuː] n rescate m ▷ vt rescatar
research [rɪ'səːtʃ] n investigaciones fpl
▷ vt investigar
resemblance [rɪ'zɛmbləns] n parecido
resemble [rɪ'zɛmbl] vt parecerse a
resent [rɪ'zɛnt] vt tomar a mal;
resentful adj resentido; **resentment** n
resentimiento
reservation [rɛzə'veɪʃən] n reserva;
reservation desk (US) n (in hotel) recepción
f
reserve [rɪ'zəːv] n reserva; (Sport) suplente
mf ▷ vt (seats etc) reservar; **reserved** adj
reservado
reservoir ['rɛzəvwɑː*] n (artificial lake)
embalse m, tank; (small) depósito
residence ['rɛzɪdəns] n (formal: home)
domicilio; (length of stay) permanencia;
residence permit (BRIT) n permiso de
permanencia
resident ['rɛzɪdənt] n (of area) vecino/a;
(in hotel) huésped mf ▷ adj (population)
permanente; (doctor) residente; **residential**
[-'dɛnʃəl] adj residencial
residue ['rɛzɪdjuː] n resto
resign [rɪ'zaɪn] vt renunciar a ▷ vi
dimitir; **to ~ o.s.** to (situation) resignarse a;
resignation [rɛzɪg'neɪʃən] n dimisión f;
(state of mind) resignación f
resin ['rɛzɪn] n resina
resist [rɪ'zɪst] vt resistir, oponerse a;
resistance n resistencia
resit ['riːsɪt] (BRIT) (pt, pp **resat**) vt (exam)
volver a presentarse a; (subject) recuperar,
volver a examinarse de (SP)
resolution [rɛzə'luːʃən] n resolución f
resolve [rɪ'zɔlv] n resolución f ▷ vt
resolver ▷ vi: **to ~ to do** resolver hacer
resort [rɪ'zɔːt] n (town) centro turístico;
(recourse) recurso ▷ vi: **to ~ to** recurrir a; **in
the last ~** como último recurso
resource [rɪ'sɔːs] n recurso; **resourceful**
adj despabilado, ingenioso
respect [rɪs'pɛkt] n respeto ▷ vt respetar;
respectable adj respetable; (large: amount)
apreciable; (passable) tolerable; **respectful**
adj respetuoso; **respective** adj respectivo;
respectively adv respectivamente

respite ['rɛspaɪt] n respiro
respond [rɪs'pɔnd] vi responder; (react)
reaccionar; **response** [-'pɔns] n respuesta;
reacción f
responsibility [rɪspɔnsɪ'bɪlɪtɪ] n
responsabilidad f
responsible [rɪs'pɔnsɪbl] adj (character)
serio, formal; (job) de confianza; (liable): ~
(for) responsable (de); **responsibly** adv con
seriedad
responsive [rɪs'pɔnsɪv] adj sensible
rest [rɛst] n descanso, reposo; (Mus, pause)
pausa, silencio; (support) apoyo; (remainder)
resto ▷ vi descansar; (be supported): **to ~ on**
descansar sobre ▷ vt: **to ~ sth on** or **against**
apoyar algo en or sobre/contra; **the ~ of
them** (people, objects) los demás; **it ~s with
him to ...** depende de él el que ...
restaurant ['rɛstərɔŋ] n restaurante m;
restaurant car (BRIT) n (Rail) coche-
comedor m
restless ['rɛstlɪs] adj inquieto
restoration [rɛstə'reɪʃən] n restauración
f; devolución f
restore [rɪ'stɔː*] vt (building) restaurar;
(sth stolen) devolver; (health) restablecer; (to
power) volver a poner a
restrain [rɪs'treɪn] vt (feeling) contener,
refrenar; (person): **to ~ (from doing)**
disuadir (de hacer); **restraint** n (restriction)
restricción f; (moderation) moderación f; (of
manner) reserva
restrict [rɪs'trɪkt] vt restringir, limitar;
restriction [-kʃən] n restricción f,
limitación f
rest room (US) n aseos mpl
restructure [riː'strʌktʃə*] vt
reestructurar
result [rɪ'zʌlt] n resultado ▷ vi: **to ~ in**
terminar en, tener por resultado; **as a ~ of** a
consecuencia de
resume [rɪ'zjuːm] vt reanudar ▷ vi
comenzar de nuevo

▌Be careful not to translate **resume** by the
▌Spanish word resumir.

résumé ['reɪzjuːmeɪ] n resumen m; (US)
currículum m
resuscitate [rɪ'sʌsɪteɪt] vt (Med) resucitar
retail ['riːteɪl] adj, adv al por menor;
retailer n detallista mf
retain [rɪ'teɪn] vt (keep) retener, conservar
retaliation [rɪtælɪ'eɪʃən] n represalias fpl
retarded [rɪ'tɑːdɪd] adj retrasado
retire [rɪ'taɪə*] vi (give up work) jubilarse;
(withdraw) retirarse; (go to bed) acostarse;
retired adj (person) jubilado; **retirement** n
(giving up work: state) retiro; (: act) jubilación
f

retort [rɪ'tɔːt] vi contestar
retreat [rɪ'triːt] n (place) retiro; (Mil) retirada ▷ vi retirarse
retrieve [rɪ'triːv] vt recobrar; (situation, honour) salvar; (Comput) recuperar; (error) reparar
retrospect ['rɛtrəspɛkt] n: **in ~** retrospectivamente; **retrospective** [-'spɛktɪv] adj retrospectivo; (law) retroactivo
return [rɪ'tɜːn] n (going or coming back) vuelta, regreso; (of sth stolen etc) devolución f; (Finance: from land, shares) ganancia, ingresos mpl ▷ cpd (journey) de regreso; (BRIT: ticket) de ida y vuelta; (match) de vuelta ▷ vi (person etc: come or go back) volver, regresar; (symptoms etc) reaparecer; (regain): **to ~ to** recuperar ▷ vt devolver; (favour, love etc) corresponder a; (verdict) pronunciar; (Pol: candidate) elegir; **returns** npl (Comm) ingresos mpl; **in ~ (for)** a cambio (de); **by ~ of post** a vuelta de correo; **many happy ~s (of the day)!** ¡feliz cumpleaños!; **return ticket** n (esp BRIT) billete m (SP) or boleto m (LAM) de ida y vuelta, billete m redondo (MEX)
reunion [riː'juːnɪən] n (of family) reunión f; (of two people, school) reencuentro
reunite [riːjuː'naɪt] vt reunir; (reconcile) reconciliar
revamp [riː'væmp] vt renovar
reveal [rɪ'viːl] vt revelar; **revealing** adj revelador(a)
revel ['rɛvl] vi: **to ~ in sth/in doing sth** gozar de algo/con hacer algo
revelation [rɛvə'leɪʃən] n revelación f
revenge [rɪ'vɛndʒ] n venganza; **to take ~ on** vengarse de
revenue ['rɛvənjuː] n ingresos mpl, rentas fpl
Reverend ['rɛvərənd] adj (in titles): **the ~ John Smith** (Anglican) el Reverendo John Smith; (Catholic) el Padre John Smith; (Protestant) el Pastor John Smith
reversal [rɪ'vɜːsl] n (of order) inversión f; (of direction, policy) cambio; (of decision) revocación f
reverse [rɪ'vɜːs] n (opposite) contrario; (back: of cloth) revés m; (: of coin) reverso; (: of paper) dorso; (Aut: also: **~ gear**) marcha atrás, revés m ▷ adj (order) inverso; (direction) contrario; (process) opuesto ▷ vt (decision, Aut) dar marcha atrás a; (position, function) invertir ▷ vi (BRIT Aut) dar marcha atrás; **reverse-charge call** (BRIT) n llamada a cobro revertido; **reversing lights** (BRIT) npl (Aut) luces fpl de retroceso
revert [rɪ'vɜːt] vi: **to ~ to** volver a

review [rɪ'vjuː] n (magazine, Mil) revista; (of book, film) reseña; (us: examination) repaso, examen m ▷ vt repasar, examinar; (Mil) pasar revista a; (book, film) reseñar
revise [rɪ'vaɪz] vt (manuscript) corregir; (opinion) modificar; (price, procedure) revisar ▷ vi (study) repasar; **revision** [rɪ'vɪʒən] n corrección f; modificación f; (for exam) repaso
revival [rɪ'vaɪvəl] n (recovery) reanimación f; (of interest) renacimiento; (Theatre) reestreno; (of faith) despertar m
revive [rɪ'vaɪv] vt resucitar; (custom) restablecer; (hope) despertar; (play) reestrenar ▷ vi (person) volver en sí; (business) reactivarse
revolt [rɪ'vəult] n rebelión f ▷ vi rebelarse, sublevarse ▷ vt dar asco a, repugnar; **revolting** adj asqueroso, repugnante
revolution [rɛvə'luːʃən] n revolución f; **revolutionary** adj, n revolucionario/a m/f
revolve [rɪ'vɔlv] vi dar vueltas, girar; (life, discussion): **to ~ (a)round** girar en torno a
revolver [rɪ'vɔlvə*] n revólver m
reward [rɪ'wɔːd] n premio, recompensa ▷ vt: **to ~ (for)** recompensar or premiar (por); **rewarding** adj (fig) valioso
rewind [riː'waɪnd] vt rebobinar
rewritable [riː'raɪtəbl] adj (CD, DVD) reescribible
rewrite [riː'raɪt] (pt **rewrote**, pp **rewritten**) vt reescribir
rheumatism ['ruːmətɪzəm] n reumatismo, reúma m
rhinoceros [raɪ'nɔsərəs] n rinoceronte m
rhubarb ['ruːbɑːb] n ruibarbo
rhyme [raɪm] n rima; (verse) poesía
rhythm ['rɪðm] n ritmo
rib [rɪb] n (Anat) costilla ▷ vt (mock) tomar el pelo a
ribbon ['rɪbən] n cinta; **in ~s** (torn) hecho trizas
rice [raɪs] n arroz m; **rice pudding** n arroz m con leche
rich [rɪtʃ] adj rico; (soil) fértil; (food) pesado; (: sweet) empalagoso; (abundant): **~ in** (minerals etc) rico en
rid [rɪd] (pt, pp **~**) vt: **to ~ sb of sth** librar a algn de algo; **to get ~ of** deshacerse or desembarazarse de
riddle ['rɪdl] n (puzzle) acertijo; (mystery) enigma m, misterio ▷ vt: **to be ~d with** ser lleno or plagado de
ride [raɪd] (pt **rode**, pp **ridden**) n paseo; (distance covered) viaje m, recorrido ▷ vi (as sport) montar; (go somewhere: on horse, bicycle) dar un paseo, pasearse; (travel: on bicycle, motorcycle, bus) viajar ▷ vt (a horse)

r

montar a; (*a bicycle, motorcycle*) andar en; (*distance*) recorrer; **to take sb for a ~** (*fig*) engañar a algn; **rider** n (*on horse*) jinete mf; (*on bicycle*) ciclista mf; (*on motorcycle*) motociclista mf

ridge [rɪdʒ] n (*of hill*) cresta; (*of roof*) caballete m; (*wrinkle*) arruga

ridicule ['rɪdɪkjuːl] n irrisión f, burla ▷ vt poner en ridículo, burlarse de; **ridiculous** [-'dɪkjʊləs] adj ridículo

riding ['raɪdɪŋ] n equitación f; **I like ~** me gusta montar a caballo; **riding school** n escuela de equitación

rife [raɪf] adj: **to be ~** ser muy común; **to be ~ with** abundar en

rifle ['raɪfl] n rifle m, fusil m ▷ vt saquear

rift [rɪft] n (*in clouds*) claro; (*fig: disagreement*) desavenencia

rig [rɪg] n (*also: oil ~: at sea*) plataforma petrolera ▷ vt (*election etc*) amañar

right [raɪt] adj (*correct*) correcto, exacto; (*suitable*) indicado, debido; (*proper*) apropiado; (*just*) justo; (*morally good*) bueno; (*not left*) derecho ▷ n bueno; (*title, claim*) derecho; (*not left*) derecha ▷ adv bien, correctamente; (*not left*) a la derecha; (*exactly*): **~ now** ahora mismo ▷ vt enderezar; (*correct*) corregir ▷ excl ¡bueno!, ¡está bien!; **to be ~** (*person*) tener razón; (*answer*) ser correcto; **is that the ~ time?** (*of clock*) ¿es esa la hora buena?; **by ~s** en justicia; **on the ~** a la derecha; **to be in the ~** tener razón; **~ away** en seguida; **~ in the middle** exactamente en el centro; **right angle** n ángulo recto; **rightful** adj legítimo; **right-hand** adj: **right-hand drive** conducción f por la derecha; **the right-hand side** derecha; **right-handed** adj diestro; **rightly** adv correctamente, debidamente; (*with reason*) con razón; **right of way** n (*on path etc*) derecho de paso; (*Aut*) prioridad f; **right-wing** adj (*Pol*) derechista

rigid ['rɪdʒɪd] adj rígido; (*person, ideas*) inflexible

rigorous ['rɪɡərəs] adj riguroso

rim [rɪm] n borde m; (*of spectacles*) aro; (*of wheel*) llanta

rind [raɪnd] n (*of bacon*) corteza; (*of lemon etc*) cáscara; (*of cheese*) costra

ring [rɪŋ] n (*pt* **rang**, *pp* **rung**) n (*of metal*) aro; (*on finger*) anillo; (*of people*) corro; (*of objects*) círculo; (*gang*) banda; (*for boxing*) cuadrilátero; (*of circus*) pista; (*bull ring*) ruedo, plaza; (*sound of bell*) toque m ▷ vi (*on telephone*) llamar por teléfono; (*bell*) repicar; (*doorbell, phone*) sonar; (*also: ~ out*) sonar; (*ears*) zumbar ▷ vt (BRIT Tel) llamar, telefonear; (*bell etc*) hacer sonar; (*doorbell*)

tocar; **to give sb a ~** (BRIT Tel) llamar or telefonear a algn; **ring back** (BRIT) vt, vi (Tel) devolver la llamada; **ring off** (BRIT) vi (Tel) colgar, cortar la comunicación; **ring up** (BRIT) vt (Tel) llamar, telefonear; **ringing tone** n (Tel) tono de llamada; **ringleader** n (*of gang*) cabecilla m; **ring road** (BRIT) n carretera periférica or de circunvalación; **ringtone** n (*on mobile*) tono de llamada

rink [rɪŋk] n (*also: ice ~*) pista de hielo

rinse [rɪns] n aclarado; (*dye*) tinte m ▷ vt aclarar; (*mouth*) enjuagar

riot ['raɪət] n motín m, disturbio ▷ vi amotinarse; **to run ~** desmandarse

rip [rɪp] n rasgón m, rasgadura ▷ vt rasgar, desgarrar ▷ vi rasgarse, desgarrarse; **rip off** vt (inf: cheat) estafar; **rip up** vt hacer pedazos

ripe [raɪp] adj maduro

rip-off ['rɪpɔf] n (inf): **it's a ~!** ¡es una estafa!, ¡es un timo!

ripple ['rɪpl] n onda, rizo; (*sound*) murmullo ▷ vi rizarse

rise [raɪz] (*pt* **rose**, *pp* **risen**) n (*slope*) cuesta, pendiente f; (*hill*) altura; (BRIT: in wages) aumento; (*in prices, temperature*) subida; (*fig: to power etc*) ascenso ▷ vi subir; (*waters*) crecer; (*sun, moon*) salir; (*person: from bed etc*) levantarse; (*also: ~ up: rebel*) sublevarse; (*in rank*) ascender; **to give ~ to** dar lugar or origen a; **to ~ to the occasion** ponerse a la altura de las circunstancias; **risen** ['rɪzn] pp of **rise**; **rising** adj (*increasing: number*) creciente; (: *prices*) en aumento or alza; (*tide*) creciente; (*sun, moon*) naciente

risk [rɪsk] n riesgo, peligro ▷ vt arriesgar; (*run the risk of*) exponerse a; **to take** or **run the ~ of doing** correr el riesgo de hacer; **at ~** en peligro; **at one's own ~** bajo su propia responsabilidad; **risky** adj arriesgado, peligroso

rite [raɪt] n rito; **last ~s** exequias fpl

ritual ['rɪtjʊəl] adj ritual ▷ n ritual m, rito

rival ['raɪvl] n rival mf; (*in business*) competidor(a) m/f ▷ adj rival, opuesto ▷ vt competir con; **rivalry** n competencia

river ['rɪvə*] n río ▷ cpd (*port*) de río; (*traffic*) fluvial; **up/down ~** río arriba/abajo; **riverbank** n orilla (del río)

rivet ['rɪvɪt] n roblón m, remache m ▷ vt (*fig*) captar

road [rəud] n camino; (*motorway etc*) carretera; (*in town*) calle f ▷ cpd (*accident*) de tráfico; **major/minor ~** carretera principal/secundaria; **roadblock** n barricada; **road map** n mapa m de carreteras; **road rage** n agresividad en la carretera; **road safety** n seguridad f vial; **roadside** n borde m (del camino); **roadsign** n señal f de tráfico; **road tax** n (BRIT) impuesto de rodaje; **roadworks** npl obras fpl

roam [rəum] vi vagar

roar [rɔ:*] n rugido; (of vehicle, storm) estruendo; (of laughter) carcajada ▷ vi rugir; hacer estruendo; **to ~ with laughter** reírse a carcajadas; **to do a ~ing trade** hacer buen negocio

roast [rəust] n carne f asada, asado ▷ vt asar; (coffee) tostar; **roast beef** n rosbif m

rob [rɒb] vt robar; **to ~ sb of sth** robar algo a algn; (fig: deprive) quitar algo a algn; **robber** n ladrón/ona m/f; **robbery** n robo

robe [rəub] n (for ceremony etc) toga; (also: **bath~**) albornoz m

robin ['rɒbɪn] n petirrojo

robot ['rəubɒt] n robot m

robust [rəu'bʌst] adj robusto, fuerte

rock [rɒk] n roca; (boulder) peña, peñasco; (US: small stone) piedrecita; (BRIT: sweet) ≈ pirulí ▷ vt (swing gently: cradle) balancear, mecer; (: child) arrullar; (shake) sacudir ▷ vi mecerse, balancearse; sacudirse; **on the ~s** (drink) con hielo; (marriage etc) en ruinas; **rock and roll** n rocanrol m; **rock climbing** n (Sport) escalada

rocket ['rɒkɪt] n cohete m; **rocking chair** ['rɒkɪŋ-] n mecedora

rocky ['rɒkɪ] adj rocoso

rod [rɒd] n vara, varilla; (also: **fishing ~**) caña

rode [rəud] pt of **ride**

rodent ['rəudnt] n roedor m

rogue [rəug] n pícaro, pillo

role [rəul] n papel m; **role-model** n modelo a imitar

roll [rəul] n rollo; (of bank notes) fajo; (also: **bread ~**) panecillo; (register, list) lista, nómina; (sound of drums etc) redoble m ▷ vt hacer rodar; (also: **~ up**: string) enrollar; (cigarette) liar; (also: **~ out**: pastry) aplanar; (flatten: road, lawn) apisonar ▷ vi rodar; (drum) redoblar; (ship) balancearse; **roll over** vi dar una vuelta; **roll up** vi (inf: arrive) aparecer ▷ vt (carpet) arrollar; (: sleeves) arremangar; **roller** n rodillo; (wheel) rueda; (for road) apisonadora; (for hair) rulo; **Rollerblades®** npl patines mpl en línea; **roller coaster** n montaña rusa; **roller skates** npl patines mpl de rueda; **roller-skating** n patinaje sobre ruedas; **to go roller-skating** ir a patinar (sobre ruedas); **rolling pin** n rodillo (de cocina)

ROM [rɒm] n abbr (Comput: = read only memory) ROM f

Roman ['rəumən] (irreg) adj romano/a;

Roman Catholic (irreg) adj, n católico/a m/f (romano/a)

romance [rə'mæns] n (love affair) amor m; (charm) lo romántico; (novel) novela de amor

Romania etc [ru:'meɪnɪə] n = **Rumania** etc

Roman numeral n número romano

romantic [rə'mæntɪk] adj romántico

Rome [rəum] n Roma

roof [ru:f] (pl ~s) n techo; (of house) techo, tejado ▷ vt techar, poner techo a; **the ~ of the mouth** el paladar; **roof rack** n (Aut) baca, portaequipajes m inv

rook [ruk] n (bird) graja; (Chess) torre f

room [ru:m] n cuarto, habitación f; (also: **bed~**) dormitorio, recámara (MEX), pieza (SC); (in school etc) sala; (space, scope) sitio, cabida; **roommate** n compañero/a de cuarto; **room service** n servicio de habitaciones; **roomy** adj espacioso; (garment) amplio

rooster ['ru:stə*] n gallo

root [ru:t] n raíz f ▷ vi arraigarse

rope [rəup] n cuerda; (Naut) cable m ▷ vt (tie) atar or amarrar con (una) cuerda; (climbers: also: **~ together**) encordarse; (an area: also: **~ off**) acordonar; **to know the ~s** (fig) conocer los trucos (del oficio)

rose [rəuz] pt of **rise** ▷ n rosa; (shrub) rosal m; (on watering can) roseta

rosé ['rəuzeɪ] n vino rosado

rosemary ['rəuzmərɪ] n romero

rosy ['rəuzɪ] adj rosado, sonrosado; **a ~ future** un futuro prometedor

rot [rɒt] n podredumbre f; (fig: pej) tonterías fpl ▷ vt pudrir ▷ vi pudrirse

rota ['rəutə] n (sistema m de) turnos m

rotate [rəu'teɪt] vt (revolve) hacer girar, dar vueltas a; (jobs) alternar ▷ vi girar, dar vueltas

rotten ['rɒtn] adj podrido; (dishonest) corrompido; (inf: bad) pocho; **to feel ~** (ill) sentirse fatal

rough [rʌf] adj (skin, surface) áspero; (terrain) quebrado; (road) desigual; (voice) bronco; (person, manner) tosco, grosero; (weather) borrascoso; (treatment) brutal; (sea) picado; (town, area) peligroso; (cloth) basto; (plan) preliminar; (guess) aproximado ▷ n (Golf): **in the ~** en las hierbas altas; **to ~ it** vivir sin comodidades; **to sleep ~** (BRIT) pasar la noche al raso; **roughly** adv (handle) torpemente; (make) toscamente; (speak) groseramente; (approximately) aproximadamente

roulette [ru:'let] n ruleta

round [raund] adj redondo ▷ n círculo; (BRIT: of toast) rebanada; (of policeman) ronda; (of milkman) recorrido; (of doctor) visitas *fpl*; (*game: of cards, in competition*) partida; (*of ammunition*) cartucho; (*Boxing*) asalto; (*of talks*) ronda ▷ *vt* (*corner*) doblar ▷ *prep* alrededor de; (*surrounding*): **~ his neck/the table** en su cuello/alrededor de la mesa; (*in a circular movement*): **to move ~ the room/sail ~ the world** dar una vuelta a la habitación/circunnavegar el mundo; (*in various directions*): **to move ~ a room/house** moverse por toda la habitación/casa; (*approximately*) alrededor de ▷ *adv*: **all ~** por todos lados; **the long way ~** por el camino menos directo; **all (the) year ~** durante todo el año; **it's just ~ the corner** (*fig*) está a la vuelta de la esquina; **~ the clock** *adv* las 24 horas; **to go ~ to sb's (house)** ir a casa de algn; **to go ~ the back** pasar por atrás; **enough to go ~** bastante (para todos); **a ~ of applause** una salva de aplausos; **a ~ of drinks/sandwiches** una ronda de bebidas/bocadillos; **round off** *vt* (*speech etc*) acabar, poner término a; **round up** *vt* (*cattle*) acorralar; (*people*) reunir; (*price*) redondear; **roundabout** (BRIT) *n* (Aut) isleta; (*at fair*) tiovivo ▷ *adj* (*route, means*) indirecto; **round trip** *n* viaje *m* de ida y vuelta; **roundup** *n* rodeo; (*of criminals*) redada; (*of news*) resumen *m*

rouse [rauz] *vt* (*wake up*) despertar; (*stir up*) suscitar

route [ruːt] *n* ruta, camino; (*of bus*) recorrido; (*of shipping*) derrota

routine [ruːˈtiːn] *adj* rutinario ▷ *n* rutina; (*Theatre*) número

row¹ [rəu] *n* (*line*) fila, hilera; (*Knitting*) pasada ▷ *vi* (*in boat*) remar ▷ *vt* conducir remando; **4 days in a ~** 4 días seguidos

row² [rau] *n* (*racket*) escándalo; (*dispute*) bronca, pelea; (*scolding*) regaño ▷ *vi* pelear(se)

rowboat ['rəubəut] (US) = **rowing boat**

rowing ['rəuɪŋ] *n* remo; **rowing boat** (BRIT) *n* bote *m* de remos

royal ['rɔɪəl] *adj* real; **royalty** *n* (*royal persons*) familia real; (*payment to author*) derechos *mpl* de autor

rpm *abbr* (= *revs per minute*) r.p.m.

R.S.V.P. *abbr* (= *répondez s'il vous plaît*) SRC

Rt. Hon. *abbr* (BRIT) (= *Right Honourable*) título honorífico de diputado

rub [rʌb] *vt* frotar; (*scrub*) restregar ▷ *n*: **to give sth a ~** frotar algo; **to ~ sb up** or **~ sb** (US) **the wrong way** entrarle algn por mal ojo; **rub in** *vt* (*ointment*) aplicar frotando; **rub off** *vi* borrarse; **rub out** *vt* borrar

rubber ['rʌbə*] *n* caucho, goma; (BRIT: *eraser*) goma de borrar; **rubber band** *n* goma, gomita; **rubber gloves** *npl* guantes

mpl de goma

rubbish ['rʌbɪʃ] (BRIT) *n* basura; (*waste*) desperdicios *mpl*; (*fig: pej*) tonterías *fpl*; (*junk*) pacotilla; **rubbish bin** (BRIT) *n* cubo or bote *m* (MEX) or tacho (SC) de la basura; **rubbish dump** (BRIT) *n* vertedero, basurero

rubble ['rʌbl] *n* escombros *mpl*

ruby ['ruːbɪ] *n* rubí *m*

rucksack ['rʌksæk] *n* mochila

rudder ['rʌdə*] *n* timón *m*

rude [ruːd] *adj* (*impolite: person*) mal educado; (*: word, manners*) grosero; (*crude*) crudo; (*indecent*) indecente

ruffle ['rʌfl] *vt* (*hair*) despeinar; (*clothes*) arrugar; **to get ~d** (*fig: person*) alterarse

rug [rʌg] *n* alfombra; (BRIT: *blanket*) manta

rugby ['rʌgbɪ] *n* rugby *m*

rugged ['rʌgɪd] *adj* (*landscape*) accidentado; (*features*) robusto

ruin ['ruːɪn] *n* ruina ▷ *vt* arruinar; (*spoil*) estropear; **ruins** *npl* ruinas *fpl*, restos *mpl*

rule [ruːl] *n* (*norm*) norma, costumbre *f*; (*regulation, ruler*) regla; (*government*) dominio ▷ *vt* (*country, person*) gobernar ▷ *vi* gobernar; (*Law*) fallar; **as a ~** por regla general; **rule out** *vt* excluir; **ruler** *n* (*sovereign*) soberano; (*for measuring*) regla; **ruling** *adj* (*party*) gobernante; (*class*) dirigente ▷ *n* (*Law*) fallo, decisión *f*

rum [rʌm] *n* ron *m*

Rumania [ruːˈmeɪnɪə] *n* Rumanía; **Rumanian** *adj* rumano/a ▷ *n* rumano/a *m/f*; (*Ling*) rumano

rumble ['rʌmbl] *n* (*noise*) ruido sordo ▷ *vi* retumbar, hacer un ruido sordo; (*stomach, pipe*) sonar

rumour ['ruːmə*] (US **rumor**) *n* rumor *m* ▷ *vt*: **it is ~ed that ...** se rumorea que ...

rump steak *n* filete *m* de lomo

run [rʌn] (*pt* **ran**, *pp* **run**) *n* (*fast pace*): **at a ~** corriendo; (*Sport, in tights*) carrera; (*outing*) paseo, excursión *f*; (*distance travelled*) trayecto; (*series*) serie *f*; (*Theatre*) temporada; (*Ski*) pista ▷ *vt* correr; (*operate: business*) dirigir; (*: competition, course*) organizar; (*: hotel, house*) administrar, llevar; (*Comput*) ejecutar; (*pass: hand*) pasar; (*Press: feature*) publicar ▷ *vi* correr; (*work: machine*) funcionar, marchar; (*bus, train: operate*) circular, ir; (*: travel*) ir; (*continue: play*) seguir; (*contract*) ser válido; (*flow: river*) fluir; (*colours, washing*) desteñirse; (*in election*) ser candidato; **there was a ~ on** (*meat, tickets*) hubo mucha demanda de; **in the long ~** a la larga; **on the ~** en fuga; **I'll ~ you to the station** te llevaré a la estación (en coche); **to ~ a risk** correr un riesgo; **to ~ a bath** llenar la bañera; **run after** *vt fus* (*to* *catch up*) correr tras; (*chase*) perseguir; **run away** *vi* huir; **run down** *vt* (*production*) ir reduciendo; (*factory*) ir restringiendo la producción en; (*car*) atropellar; (*criticize*) criticar; **to be run down** (*person: tired*) estar debilitado; **run into** *vt fus* (*meet: person, trouble*) tropezar con; (*collide with*) chocar con; **run off** *vt* (*water*) dejar correr; (*copies*) sacar ▷ *vi* huir corriendo; **run out** *vi* (*person*) salir corriendo; (*liquid*) irse; (*lease*) caducar, vencer; (*money etc*) acabarse; **run out of** *vt fus* quedar sin; **run over** *vt* (*Aut*) atropellar ▷ *vt fus* (*revise*) repasar; **run through** *vt fus* (*instructions*) repasar; **run up** *vt* (*debt*) contraer; **to run up against** (*difficulties*) tropezar con; **runaway** *adj* (*horse*) desbocado; (*truck*) sin frenos; (*child*) escapado de casa

rung [rʌŋ] *pp of* **ring** ▷ *n* (*of ladder*) escalón *m*, peldaño

runner ['rʌnə*] *n* (*in race: person*) corredor(a) *m/f*; (: *horse*) caballo; (*on sledge*) patín *m*; **runner bean** (BRIT) *n* ≈ judía verde; **runner-up** *n* subcampeón/ona *m/f*

running ['rʌnɪŋ] *n* (*sport*) atletismo; (*of business*) administración *f* ▷ *adj* (*water, costs*) corriente; (*commentary*) continuo; **to be in/out of the ~ for sth** tener/no tener posibilidades de ganar algo; **6 days ~** 6 días seguidos

runny ['rʌnɪ] *adj* fluido; (*nose, eyes*) gastante

run-up ['rʌnʌp] *n*: **~ to** (*election etc*) período previo a

runway ['rʌnweɪ] *n* (*Aviat*) pista de aterrizaje

rupture ['rʌptʃə*] *n* (*Med*) hernia ▷ *vt*: **to ~ o.s** causarse una hernia

rural ['ruərl] *adj* rural

rush [rʌʃ] *n* ímpetu *m*; (*hurry*) prisa; (*Comm*) demanda repentina; (*current*) corriente *f* fuerte; (*of feeling*) torrente *m*; (*Bot*) junco ▷ *vt* apresurar; (*work*) hacer de prisa ▷ *vi* correr, precipitarse; **rush hour** *n* horas *fpl* punta

Russia ['rʌʃə] *n* Rusia; **Russian** *adj* ruso/a ▷ *n* ruso/a *m/f*; (*Ling*) ruso

rust [rʌst] *n* herrumbre *f*, moho ▷ *vi* oxidarse

rusty ['rʌstɪ] *adj* oxidado

ruthless ['ruːθlɪs] *adj* despiadado

RV (*us*) *n abbr* = **recreational vehicle**

rye [raɪ] *n* centeno

S

Sabbath ['sæbəθ] *n* domingo; (*Jewish*) sábado

sabotage ['sæbətɑːʒ] *n* sabotaje *m* ▷ *vt* sabotear

saccharin(e) ['sækərɪn] *n* sacarina

sachet ['sæʃeɪ] *n* sobrecito

sack [sæk] *n* (*bag*) saco, costal *m* ▷ *vt* (*dismiss*) despedir; (*plunder*) saquear; **to get the ~** ser despedido

sacred ['seɪkrɪd] *adj* sagrado, santo

sacrifice ['sækrɪfaɪs] *n* sacrificio ▷ *vt* sacrificar

sad [sæd] *adj* (*unhappy*) triste; (*deplorable*) lamentable

saddle ['sædl] *n* silla (de montar); (*of cycle*) sillín *m* ▷ *vt* (*horse*) ensillar; **to be ~d with sth** (*inf*) quedar cargado con algo

sadistic [sə'dɪstɪk] *adj* sádico

sadly ['sædlɪ] *adv* lamentablemente; **to be ~ lacking in** estar por desgracia carente de

sadness ['sædnɪs] *n* tristeza

s.a.e. *abbr* (= *stamped addressed envelope*) sobre con las propias señas de uno y con sello

safari [sə'fɑːrɪ] *n* safari *m*

safe [seɪf] *adj* (*out of danger*) fuera de peligro; (*not dangerous, sure*) seguro; (*unharmed*) ileso ▷ *n* caja de caudales, caja fuerte; **~ and sound** sano y salvo; **(just) to be on the ~ side** para mayor seguridad; **safely** *adv* seguramente, con seguridad; **to arrive safely** llegar bien; **safe sex** *n* sexo seguro *or* sin riesgo

safety ['seɪftɪ] *n* seguridad *f*; **safety belt** *n* cinturón *m* (de seguridad); **safety pin** *n* imperdible *m*, seguro (MEX), alfiler *m* de gancho (sc)

saffron ['sæfrən] *n* azafrán *m*

sag [sæg] *vi* aflojarse

sage [seɪdʒ] *n* (*herb*) salvia; (*man*) sabio

Sagittarius [sædʒɪ'tɛərɪəs] *n* Sagitario

Sahara [sə'hɑːrə] *n*: **the ~ (Desert)** el

(desierto del) Sáhara

said [sɛd] pt, pp of **say**

sail [seɪl] n (on boat) vela; (trip): **to go for a ~** dar un paseo en barco ▷ vt (boat) gobernar ▷ vi (travel: ship) navegar; (Sport) hacer vela; (begin voyage) salir; **they ~ed into Copenhagen** arribaron a Copenhague; **sailboat** (US) n = **sailing boat**; **sailing** n (Sport) vela; **to go sailing** hacer vela; **sailing boat** n barco de vela; **sailor** n marinero, marino

saint [seɪnt] n santo

sake [seɪk] n: **for the ~ of** por

salad ['sæləd] n ensalada; **salad cream** (BRIT) n (especie f de) mayonesa; **salad dressing** n aliño

salami [sə'lɑːmɪ] n salami m, salchichón m

salary ['sælərɪ] n sueldo

sale [seɪl] n venta; (at reduced prices) liquidación f, saldo; (auction) subasta; **sales** npl (total amount sold) ventas fpl, facturación f; **"for ~"** "se vende"; **on ~** en venta; **on ~ or return** (goods) venta por reposición; **sales assistant** (US), **sales clerk** n dependiente/a m/f; **salesman/woman** (irreg) n (in shop) dependiente/a m/f; **salesperson** (irreg) n vendedor(a) m/f, dependiente/a m/f; **sales rep** n representante mf, agente mf comercial

saline ['seɪlaɪn] adj salino

saliva [sə'laɪvə] n saliva

salmon ['sæmən] n inv salmón m

salon ['sælɔn] n (hairdressing salon) peluquería; (beauty salon) salón m de belleza

saloon [sə'luːn] n (US) bar m, taberna; (BRIT Aut) coche m (de) turismo; (ship's lounge) cámara, salón m

salt [sɔlt] n sal f ▷ vt salar; (put salt on) poner sal en; **saltwater** adj de agua salada; **salty** adj salado

salute [sə'luːt] n saludo; (of guns) salva ▷ vt saludar

salvage ['sælvɪdʒ] n (saving) salvamento, recuperación f; (things saved) objetos mpl salvados ▷ vt salvar

Salvation Army [sæl'veɪʃən-] n Ejército de Salvación

same [seɪm] adj mismo ▷ pron: **the ~** el(la) mismo/a, los(las) mismos/as; **the ~ book as** el mismo libro que; **at the ~ time** (at the same moment) al mismo tiempo; (yet) sin embargo; **all** or **just the ~** sin embargo, aun así; **to do the ~ (as sb)** hacer lo mismo (que algn); **the ~ to you!** ¡igualmente!

sample ['sɑːmpl] n muestra ▷ vt (food) probar; (wine) catar

sanction ['sæŋkʃən] n aprobación f ▷ vt sancionar; aprobar; **sanctions** npl (Pol)

sanciones fpl

sanctuary ['sæŋktjuərɪ] n santuario; (refuge) asilo, refugio; (for wildlife) reserva

sand [sænd] n arena; (beach) playa ▷ vt (also: ~ down) lijar

sandal ['sændl] n sandalia

sand: **sandbox** (US) n = **sandpit**; **sandcastle** n castillo de arena; **sand dune** n duna; **sandpaper** n papel m de lija; **sandpit** n (for children) cajón m de arena; **sands** npl playa sg de arena; **sandstone** ['sændstəun] n piedra arenisca

sandwich ['sændwɪtʃ] n sandwich m ▷ vt intercalar; **~ed between** apretujado entre; **cheese/ham ~** sandwich de queso/jamón

sandy ['sændɪ] adj arenoso; (colour) rojizo

sane [seɪn] adj cuerdo; (sensible) sensato

▌ Be careful not to translate **sane** by the Spanish word sano.

sang [sæŋ] pt of **sing**

sanitary towel (US **sanitary napkin**) n paño higiénico, compresa

sanity ['sænɪtɪ] n cordura; (of judgment) sensatez f

sank [sæŋk] pt of **sink**

Santa Claus [sæntə'klɔːz] n San Nicolás, Papá Noel

sap [sæp] n (of plants) savia ▷ vt (strength) minar, agotar

sapphire ['sæfaɪə*] n zafiro

sarcasm ['sɑːkæzm] n sarcasmo

sarcastic [sɑː'kæstɪk] adj sarcástico

sardine [sɑː'diːn] n sardina

SASE (US) n abbr (= self-addressed stamped envelope) sobre con las propias señas de uno y con sello

Sat. abbr (= Saturday) sáb

sat [sæt] pt, pp of **sit**

satchel ['sætʃl] n (child's) mochila, cartera (SP)

satellite ['sætəlaɪt] n satélite m; **satellite dish** n antena de televisión por satélite; **satellite television** n televisión f vía satélite

satin ['sætɪn] n raso ▷ adj de raso

satire ['sætaɪə*] n sátira

satisfaction [sætɪs'fækʃən] n satisfacción f

satisfactory [sætɪs'fæktərɪ] adj satisfactorio

satisfied ['sætɪsfaɪd] adj satisfecho; **to be ~ (with sth)** estar satisfecho (de algo)

satisfy ['sætɪsfaɪ] vt satisfacer; (convince) convencer

Saturday ['sætədɪ] n sábado

sauce [sɔːs] n salsa; (sweet) crema; jarabe m; **saucepan** n cacerola, olla

saucer ['sɔːsə*] n platillo; **Saudi Arabia** n

Arabia Saudí or Saudita

sauna ['sɔːnə] n sauna

sausage ['sɔsɪdʒ] n salchicha; **sausage roll** n empanadita de salchicha

sautéed ['səuteɪd] adj salteado

savage ['sævɪdʒ] adj (cruel, fierce) feroz, furioso; (primitive) salvaje ▷ n salvaje mf ▷ vt (attack) embestir

save [seɪv] vt (rescue) salvar, rescatar; (money, time) ahorrar; (put by, keep: seat) guardar; (Comput) salvar (y guardar); (avoid: trouble) evitar; (Sport) parar ▷ vi (also: ~ up) ahorrar ▷ n (Sport) parada ▷ prep salvo, excepto

savings ['seɪvɪŋz] npl ahorros mpl; **savings account** n cuenta de ahorros; **savings and loan association** (us) n sociedad f de ahorro y préstamo

savoury ['seɪvərɪ] (us **savory**) adj sabroso; (dish: not sweet) salado

saw [sɔː] (pt **-ed**, pp **-ed** or **-n**) pt of **see** ▷ n (tool) sierra ▷ vt serrar; **sawdust** n (a) serrín m

sawn [sɔːn] pp of **saw**

saxophone ['sæksəfəun] n saxófono

say [seɪ] (pt, pp **said**) n: to have one's ~ expresar su opinión ▷ vt decir; **to have a** or **some ~ in sth** tener voz or tener que ver en algo; **to ~ yes/no** decir que sí/no; **could you ~ that again?** ¿podría repetir eso?; **that is to ~** es decir; **that goes without ~ing** ni que decir tiene; **saying** n dicho, refrán m

scab [skæb] n costra; (pej) esquirol m

scaffolding ['skæfəldɪŋ] n andamio, andamiaje m

scald [skɔːld] n escaldadura ▷ vt escaldar

scale [skeɪl] n (gen, Mus) escala; (of fish) escama; (of salaries, fees etc) escalafón m ▷ vt (mountain) escalar; (tree) trepar; **scales** npl (for weighing: small) balanza; (: large) báscula; **on a large ~** en gran escala; **~ of charges** tarifa, lista de precios

scallion ['skæljən] (us) n cebolleta

scallop ['skɔləp] n (Zool) venera; (Sewing) festón m

scalp [skælp] n cabellera ▷ vt escalpar

scalpel ['skælpl] n bisturí m

scam [skæm] n (inf) estafa, timo

scampi ['skæmpɪ] npl gambas fpl

scan [skæn] vt (examine) escudriñar; (glance at quickly) dar un vistazo a; (TV, Radar) explorar, registrar ▷ n (Med): **to have a ~** pasar por el escáner

scandal ['skændl] n escándalo; (gossip) chismes mpl

Scandinavia [skændɪ'neɪvɪə] n Escandinavia; **Scandinavian** adj, n escandinavo/a m/f

scanner ['skænə*] n (Radar, Med) escáner m

scapegoat ['skeɪpgəut] n cabeza de turco, chivo expiatorio

scar [skɑː] n cicatriz f; (fig) señal f ▷ vt dejar señales en

scarce [skɛəs] adj escaso; **to make o.s. ~** (inf) esfumarse; **scarcely** adv apenas

scare [skɛə*] n susto, sobresalto; (panic) pánico ▷ vt asustar, espantar; **to ~ sb stiff** dar a algn un susto de muerte; **bomb ~** amenaza de bomba; **scarecrow** n espantapájaros m inv; **scared** adj: **to be scared** estar asustado

scarf [skɑːf] (pl **~s** or **scarves**) n (long) bufanda; (square) pañuelo

scarlet ['skɑːlɪt] adj escarlata

scarves [skɑːvz] npl of **scarf**

scary ['skɛərɪ] (inf) adj espeluznante

scatter ['skætə*] vt (spread) esparcir, desparramar; (put to flight) dispersar ▷ vi desparramarse; dispersarse

scenario [sɪ'nɑːrɪəu] n (Theatre) argumento; (Cinema) guión m; (fig) escenario

scene [siːn] n (Theatre, fig etc) escena; (of crime etc) escenario; (view) panorama m; (fuss) escándalo; **scenery** n (Theatre) decorado; (landscape) paisaje m

> ▌ Be careful not to translate **scenery** by the
> Spanish word *escenario*.

scenic adj pintoresco

scent [sɛnt] n perfume m, olor m; (fig: track) rastro, pista

sceptical ['skɛptɪkl] adj escéptico

schedule ['ʃɛdjuːl] (us) ['skɛdjuːl] n (timetable) horario; (of events) programa m; (list) lista ▷ vt (visit) fijar la hora de; **to arrive on ~** llegar a la hora debida; **to be ahead of/behind ~** estar adelantado/en retraso; **scheduled flight** n vuelo regular

scheme [skiːm] n (plan) plan m, proyecto; (plot) intriga; (arrangement) disposición f; (pension scheme etc) sistema m ▷ vi (intrigue) intrigar

schizophrenic [skɪtzə'frɛnɪk] adj esquizofrénico

scholar ['skɔlə*] n (pupil) alumno/a; (learned person) sabio/a, erudito/a; **scholarship** n erudición f; (grant) beca

school [skuːl] n escuela, colegio; (in university) facultad f ▷ cpd escolar; **schoolbook** n libro de texto; **schoolboy** n alumno; **school children** npl alumnos mpl; **schoolgirl** n alumna; **schooling** n enseñanza; **schoolteacher** n (primary) maestro/a; (secondary) profesor(a) m/f

science ['saɪəns] n ciencia; **science**

fiction n ciencia-ficción f; **scientific**
[-'tɪfɪk] adj científico; **scientist** n
científico/a
sci-fi ['saɪfaɪ] n abbr (inf) = **science fiction**
scissors ['sɪzəz] npl tijeras fpl; **a pair of ~**
unas tijeras
scold [skəʊld] vt regañar
scone [skɒn] n pastel de pan
scoop [sku:p] n (for flour etc) pala; (Press)
exclusiva
scooter ['sku:tə*] n moto f; (toy) patinete
m
scope [skəʊp] n (of plan) ámbito; (of
person) competencia; (opportunity) libertad
f (de acción)
scorching ['skɔːtʃɪŋ] adj (heat, sun)
abrasador(a)
score [skɔː*] n (points etc) puntuación f;
(Mus) partitura; (twenty) veintena ▷ vt (goal,
point) ganar; (mark) rayar; (achieve: success)
conseguir ▷ vi marcar un tanto; (Football)
marcar (un) gol; (keep score) llevar el tanteo;
~s of (lots of) decenas de; **on that ~** en lo
que se refiere a eso; **to ~ 6 out of 10** obtener
una puntuación de 6 sobre 10; **score out** vt
tachar; **scoreboard** n marcador m; **scorer**
n marcador m; (keeping score) encargado/a
del marcador
scorn [skɔːn] n desprecio
Scorpio ['skɔːpɪəʊ] n Escorpión m
scorpion ['skɔːpɪən] n alacrán m
Scot [skɒt] n escocés/esa m/f
Scotch tape® (us) n cinta adhesiva, celo,
scotch® m
Scotland ['skɒtlənd] n Escocia
Scots [skɒts] adj escocés/esa; **Scotsman**
(irreg) n escocés; **Scotswoman** (irreg) n
escocésa; **Scottish** ['skɒtɪʃ] adj escocés/
esa; **Scottish Parliament** n Parlamento
escocés
scout [skaʊt] n (Mil: also: **boy ~**)
explorador m; **girl ~** (us) niña exploradora
scowl [skaʊl] vi fruncir el ceño; **to ~ at sb**
mirar con ceño a algn
scramble ['skræmbl] n (climb) subida
(difícil); (struggle) pelea ▷ vi: **to ~ through/
out** abrirse paso/salir con dificultad; **to ~
for** pelear por; **scrambled eggs** npl huevos
mpl revueltos
scrap [skræp] n (bit) pedacito; (fig) pizca;
(fight) riña, bronca; (also: **~ iron**) chatarra,
hierro viejo ▷ vt (discard) desechar,
descartar ▷ vi reñir, armar una bronca;
scraps npl (waste) sobras fpl, desperdicios
mpl; **scrapbook** n álbum m de recortes
scrape [skreɪp] n: **to get into a ~** meterse
en un lío ▷ vt raspar; (skin etc) rasguñar;
(scrape against) rozar ▷ vi: **to ~ through**

(exam) aprobar por los pelos; **scrap paper** n
pedazos mpl de papel
scratch [skrætʃ] n rasguño; (from claw)
arañazo ▷ vt (paint, car) rayar; (with claw,
nail) rasguñar, arañar; (rub: nose etc) rascarse
▷ vi rascarse; **to start from ~** partir de cero;
to be up to ~ cumplir con los requisitos;
scratch card n (BRIT) tarjeta f de "rasque
y gane"
scream [skriːm] n chillido ▷ vi chillar
screen [skriːn] n (Cinema, TV) pantalla;
(movable barrier) biombo ▷ vt (conceal)
tapar; (from the wind etc) proteger; (film)
proyectar; (candidates etc) investigar a;
screening n (Med) investigación f médica;
screenplay n guión m; **screen saver** n
(Comput) protector m de pantalla
screw [skruː] n tornillo ▷ vt (also: **~
in**) atornillar; **screw up** vt (paper etc)
arrugar; **to screw up one's eyes** arrugar el
entrecejo; **screwdriver** n destornillador m
scribble ['skrɪbl] n garabatos mpl ▷ vt, vi
garabatear
script [skrɪpt] n (Cinema etc) guión m;
(writing) escritura, letra
scroll [skrəʊl] n rollo
scrub [skrʌb] n (land) maleza ▷ vt fregar,
restregar; (inf: reject) cancelar, anular
scruffy ['skrʌfɪ] adj desaliñado, piojoso
scrum(mage) ['skrʌm(mɪdʒ)] n (Rugby)
melée f
scrutiny ['skruːtɪnɪ] n escrutinio, examen
m
scuba diving ['skuːbə'daɪvɪŋ] n
submarinismo
sculptor ['skʌlptə*] n escultor(a) m/f
sculpture ['skʌlptʃə*] n escultura
scum [skʌm] n (on liquid) espuma;
(pej: people) escoria
scurry ['skʌrɪ] vi correr; **to ~ off**
escabullirse
sea [siː] n mar m ▷ cpd de mar, marítimo;
by ~ (travel) en barco; **on the ~** (boat) en el
mar; (town) junto al mar; **to be all at ~** (fig)
estar despistado; **out to ~**, **at ~** en alta
mar; **seafood** n mariscos mpl; **sea front** n
paseo marítimo; **seagull** n gaviota
seal [siːl] n (animal) foca; (stamp) sello ▷ vt
(close) cerrar; **seal off** vt (area) acordonar
sea level n nivel m del mar
seam [siːm] n costura; (of metal) juntura;
(of coal) veta, filón m
search [sɜːtʃ] n (for person, thing) busca,
búsqueda; (Comput) búsqueda; (inspection: of
sb's home) registro ▷ vt (look in) buscar en;
(examine) examinar; (person, place) registrar
▷ vi: **to ~ for** buscar; **in ~ of** en busca de;
search engine n (Comput) buscador m;

search party n pelotón m de salvamento
sea: seashore n playa, orilla del mar;
seasick adj mareado; **seaside** n playa,
orilla del mar; **seaside resort** n centro
turístico costero
season ['siːzn] n (of year) estación f;
(sporting etc) temporada; (of films etc)
ciclo ⊳ vt (food) sazonar; **in/out of ~** en
sazón/fuera de temporada; **seasonal** adj
estacional; **seasoning** n condimento,
aderezo; **season ticket** n abono
seat [siːt] n (in bus, train) asiento; (chair)
silla; (Parliament) escaño; (buttocks) culo,
trasero; (of trousers) culera ⊳ vt sentar;
(have room for) tener cabida para; **to be
~ed** sentarse; **seat belt** n cinturón m de
seguridad; **seating** n asientos mpl
sea: sea water n agua del mar; **seaweed** n
alga marina
sec. abbr = **second(s)**
secluded [sɪ'kluːdɪd] adj retirado
second ['sɛkənd] adj segundo ⊳ adv en
segundo lugar ⊳ n segundo; (Aut: also:
~ gear) segunda; (Comm) artículo con
algún desperfecto; (BRIT Scol: degree) título
de licenciado con calificación de notable
⊳ vt (motion) apoyar; **secondary** adj
secundario; **secondary school** n escuela
secundaria; **second-class** adj de segunda
clase ⊳ adv (Rail) en segunda; **secondhand**
adj de segunda mano, usado; **secondly**
adv en segundo lugar; **second-rate** adj de
segunda categoría; **second thoughts**: **to
have second thoughts** cambiar de
opinión; **on second thoughts** or **thought**
(US) pensándolo bien
secrecy ['siːkrəsɪ] n secreto
secret ['siːkrɪt] adj, n secreto; **in ~** en
secreto
secretary ['sɛkrətərɪ] n secretario/a; **S~
of State (for)** (BRIT Pol) Ministro (de)
secretive ['siːkrətɪv] adj reservado,
sigiloso
secret service n servicio secreto
sect [sɛkt] n secta
section ['sɛkʃən] n sección f; (part) parte f;
(of document) artículo; (of opinion) sector m;
(cross-section) corte m transversal
sector ['sɛktə*] n sector m
secular ['sɛkjulə*] adj secular, seglar
secure [sɪ'kjuə*] adj seguro; (firmly fixed)
firme, fijo ⊳ vt (fix) asegurar, afianzar; (get)
conseguir
security [sɪ'kjuərɪtɪ] n seguridad f; (for
loan) fianza; (: object) prenda; **securities** npl
(Comm) valores mpl, títulos mpl; **security
guard** n guardia m/f de seguridad
sedan [sɪ'dæn] (US) n (Aut) sedán m

sedate [sɪ'deɪt] adj tranquilo ⊳ vt tratar
con sedantes
sedative ['sɛdɪtɪv] n sedante m, sedativo
seduce [sɪ'djuːs] vt seducir; **seductive**
[-'dʌktɪv] adj seductor(a)
see [siː] (pt **saw**, pp **seen**) vt ver;
(accompany): **to ~ sb to the door** acompañar
a algn a la puerta; (understand) ver,
comprender ⊳ vi ver ⊳ n (arz)obispado; **to
~ that** (ensure) asegurar que; **~ you soon!**
¡hasta pronto!; **see off** vt despedir; **see
out** vt (take to the door) acompañar hasta la
puerta; **see through** vt fus (fig) calar ⊳ vt
(plan) llevar a cabo; **see to** vt fus atender a,
encargarse de
seed [siːd] n semilla; (in fruit) pepita;
(fig: gen pl) germen m; (Tennis etc)
preseleccionado/a; **to go to ~** (plant)
granar; (fig) descuidarse
seeing ['siːɪŋ] conj: **~ (that)** visto que, en
vista de que
seek [siːk] (pt, pp **sought**) vt buscar; (post)
solicitar
seem [siːm] vi parecer; **there ~s to
be ...** parece que hay ...; **seemingly** adv
aparentemente, según parece
seen [siːn] pp of **see**
seesaw ['siːsɔː] n subibaja
segment ['sɛgmənt] n (part) sección f; (of
orange) gajo
segregate ['sɛgrɪgeɪt] vt segregar
seize [siːz] vt (grasp) agarrar, asir;
(take possession of) secuestrar; (: territory)
apoderarse de; (opportunity) aprovecharse de
seizure ['siːʒə*] n (Med) ataque m; (Law, of
power) incautación f
seldom ['sɛldəm] adv rara vez
select [sɪ'lɛkt] adj selecto, escogido
⊳ vt escoger, elegir; (Sport) seleccionar;
selection n selección f, elección f; (Comm)
surtido; **selective** adj selectivo
self [sɛlf] (pl **selves**) n uno mismo; **the
~** el yo ⊳ prefix auto...; **self-assured** adj
seguro de sí mismo; **self-catering** (BRIT)
adj (flat etc) con cocina; **self-centred** (US
self-centered) adj egocéntrico; **self-
confidence** n confianza en sí mismo;
self-confident adj seguro de sí (mismo),
lleno de confianza en sí mismo; **self-
conscious** adj cohibido; **self-contained**
(BRIT) adj (flat) con entrada particular;
self-control n autodominio; **self-defence**
(US **self-defense**) n defensa propia; **self-
drive** (BRIT) adj sin chófer or (SP) chófer;
self-employed adj que trabaja por cuenta
propia; **self-esteem** n amor m propio;
self-indulgent adj autocomplaciente;
self-interest n egoísmo; **selfish** adj

egoísta; **self-pity** n lástima de sí mismo;
self-raising [sɛlf'reɪzɪŋ] (US **self-rising**)
adj: **self-raising flour** harina con levadura;
self-respect n amor m propio; **self-service**
adj de autoservicio

sell [sɛl] (pt, pp **sold**) vt vender ⊳ vi
venderse; **to ~ at** or **for £10** venderse a 10
libras; **sell off** vt liquidar; **sell out** vi: **to
sell out of tickets/milk** vender todas las
entradas/toda la leche; **sell-by date** n
fecha de caducidad; **seller** n vendedor(a)
m/f

Sellotape® ['sɛləuteɪp] (BRIT) n celo (SP),
cinta Scotch® (LAM) o Dúrex® (MEX, ARG)

selves [sɛlvz] npl of **self**

semester [sɪ'mɛstə*] (US) n semestre m

semi... [sɛmɪ] prefix semi..., medio...;
semicircle n semicírculo; **semidetached
(house)** n (casa) semiseparada; **semi-final**
n semi-final m

seminar ['sɛmɪnɑ:*] n seminario

semi-skimmed [sɛmɪ'skɪmd] adj
semidesnatado; **semi-skimmed (milk)** n
leche semidesnatada

senate ['sɛnɪt] n senado; **the S~** (US) el
Senado; **senator** n senador(a) m/f

send [sɛnd] (pt, pp **sent**) vt mandar, enviar;
(signal) transmitir; **send back** vt devolver;
send for vt fus mandar traer; **send in** vt
(report, application, resignation) mandar; **send
off** vt (goods) despachar; (BRIT Sport: player)
expulsar; **send on** vt (letter, luggage)
remitir; (person) mandar; **send out** vt
(invitation) mandar; (signal) emitir; **send up**
vt (person, price) hacer subir; (BRIT: parody)
parodiar; **sender** n remitente mf; **send-off**
n: **a good send-off** una buena despedida

senile ['si:naɪl] adj senil

senior ['si:nɪə*] adj (older) mayor, más
viejo; (: on staff) de más antigüedad; (of
higher rank) superior; **senior citizen** n
persona de la tercera edad; **senior high
school** (US) n ≈ instituto de enseñanza
media; see also **high school**

sensation [sɛn'seɪʃən] n sensación f;
sensational adj sensacional

sense [sɛns] n (faculty, meaning) sentido;
(feeling) sensación f; (good sense) sentido
común, juicio ⊳ vt sentir, percibir; **it
makes ~** tiene sentido; **senseless** adj
estúpido, insensato; (unconscious) sin
conocimiento; **sense of humour** (BRIT) n
sentido del humor

sensible ['sɛnsɪbl] adj sensato; (reasonable)
razonable, lógico

▌Be careful not to translate **sensible** by
the Spanish word sensible.

sensitive ['sɛnsɪtɪv] adj sensible; (touchy)

susceptible

sensual ['sɛnsjuəl] adj sensual

sensuous ['sɛnsjuəs] adj sensual

sent [sɛnt] pt, pp of **send**

sentence ['sɛntns] n (Ling) oración f; (Law)
sentencia, fallo ⊳ vt: **to ~ sb to death/
to 5 years (in prison)** condenar a algn a
muerte/a 5 años de cárcel

sentiment ['sɛntɪmənt] n sentimiento;
(opinion) opinión f; **sentimental** [-'mɛntl]
adj sentimental

Sep. abbr (= September) sep., set.

separate [adj 'sɛprɪt, vb 'sɛpəreɪt] adj
separado; (distinct) distinto ⊳ vt separar;
(part) dividir ⊳ vi separarse; **separately**
adv por separado; **separates** npl (clothes)
coordinados mpl; **separation** [-'reɪʃən] n
separación f

September [sɛp'tɛmbə*] n se(p)tiembre
m

septic ['sɛptɪk] adj séptico; **septic tank** n
fosa séptica

sequel ['si:kwl] n consecuencia,
resultado; (of story) continuación f

sequence ['si:kwəns] n sucesión f, serie f;
(Cinema) secuencia

sequin ['si:kwɪn] n lentejuela

Serb [sə:b] adj, n = **Serbian**

Serbian ['sə:bɪən] adj serbio ⊳ n serbio/a;
(Ling) serbio

sergeant ['sɑ:dʒənt] n sargento

serial ['sɪərɪəl] n (TV) telenovela, serie
f televisiva; (Book) serie f; **serial killer** n
asesino a múltiple; **serial number** n
número de serie

series ['sɪəri:s] n inv serie f

serious ['sɪərɪəs] adj serio; (grave) grave;
seriously adv en serio; (ill, wounded etc)
gravemente

sermon ['sə:mən] n sermón m

servant ['sə:vənt] n servidor(a) m/f; (house
servant) criado/a

serve [sə:v] vt servir; (customer) atender;
(train) pasar por; (apprenticeship) hacer;
(prison term) cumplir ⊳ vi (at table) servir;
(Tennis) sacar; **to ~ as/for/to do** servir de/
para/para hacer ⊳ n (Tennis) saque m; **it ~s
him right** se lo tiene merecido; **server** n
(Comput) servidor m

service ['sə:vɪs] n servicio; (Rel) misa;
(Aut) mantenimiento; (dishes etc) juego
⊳ vt (car etc) revisar; (: repair) reparar; **to be
of ~ to sb** ser útil a algn; **~ included/not
included** servicio incluido/no incluido
(Econ: tertiary sector) sector m terciario or
(de) servicios; (BRIT: on motorway) área de
servicio; (Mil): **the S~s** las fuerzas armadas;
service area n (on motorway) área de

servicio; **service charge** (BRIT) n servicio;
serviceman (irreg) n militar m; **service
station** n estación f de servicio
serviette [sə:vɪ'ɛt] (BRIT) n servilleta
session ['sɛʃən] n sesión f; **to be in ~** estar
en sesión
set [sɛt] (pt, pp ~) n juego; (Radio) aparato;
(TV) televisor m; (of utensils) batería; (of
cutlery) cubierto; (of books) colección f;
(Tennis) set m; (group of people) grupo;
(Cinema) plató m; (Theatre) decorado;
(Hairdressing) marcado ▷ adj (fixed) fijo;
(ready) listo ▷ vt (place) poner, colocar; (fix)
fijar; (adjust) ajustar, arreglar; (decide: rules
etc) establecer, decidir ▷ vi (sun) ponerse;
(jam, jelly) cuajarse; (concrete) fraguar;
(bone) componerse; **to be ~ on doing
sth** estar empeñado en hacer algo; **to
~ to music** poner música a; **to ~ on fire**
incendiar, poner fuego a; **to ~ free** poner
en libertad; **to ~ sth going** poner algo en
marcha; **to ~ sail** zarpar, hacerse a la vela;
set aside vt poner aparte, dejar de lado;
(money, time) reservar; **set down** vt (bus,
train) dejar; **set in** vi (infection) declararse;
(complications) comenzar; **the rain has set
in for the day** parece que va a llover todo
el día; **set off** vi partir ▷ vt (bomb) hacer
estallar; (events) poner en marcha; (show
up well) hacer resaltar; **set out** vi partir
▷ vt (arrange) disponer; (state) exponer; **to
set out to do sth** proponerse hacer algo;
set up vt establecer; **setback** n revés m,
contratiempo; **set menu** n menú m
settee [sɛ'ti:] n sofá m
setting ['sɛtɪŋ] n (scenery) marco; (position)
disposición f; (of sun) puesta; (of jewel)
engaste m, montadura
settle ['sɛtl] vt (argument) resolver;
(accounts) ajustar, liquidar; (Med: calm)
calmar, sosegar ▷ vi (dust etc) depositarse;
(weather) serenarse; **to ~ for sth** convenir
en aceptar algo; **to ~ on sth** decidirse por
algo; **settle down** vi (get comfortable)
ponerse cómodo, acomodarse; (calm down)
calmarse, tranquilizarse; (live quietly) echar
raíces; **settle in** vi instalarse; **settle up**
vi: **to settle up with sb** ajustar cuentas con
algn; **settlement** n (payment) liquidación
f; (agreement) acuerdo, convenio; (village
etc) pueblo
setup ['sɛtʌp] n sistema m; (situation)
situación f
seven ['sɛvn] num siete; **seventeen**
num diez y siete, diecisiete; **seventeenth**
[sevn'ti:nθ] adj decimoséptimo; **seventh**
num séptimo; **seventieth** ['sɛvntɪɪθ] adj
septuagésimo; **seventy** num setenta

sever ['sɛvə*] vt cortar; (relations) romper
several ['sɛvərl] adj, pron varios/as m/fpl,
algunos/as m/fpl; **~ of us** varios de nosotros
severe [sɪ'vɪə*] adj severo; (serious) grave;
(hard) duro; (pain) intenso
sew [səu] (pt **~ed**, pp **~n**) vt, vi coser
sewage ['su:ɪdʒ] n aguas fpl residuales
sewer ['su:ə*] n alcantarilla, cloaca
sewing ['səuɪŋ] n costura; **sewing
machine** n máquina de coser
sewn [səun] pp of **sew**
sex [sɛks] n sexo; (lovemaking): **to have
~** hacer el amor; **sexism** ['sɛksɪzəm] n
sexismo; **sexist** adj, n sexista mf; **sexual**
['sɛksjuəl] adj sexual; **sexual intercourse**
n relaciones fpl sexuales; **sexuality**
[sɛksju'ælɪtɪ] n sexualidad f; **sexy** adj sexy
shabby ['ʃæbɪ] adj (person) desharrapado;
(clothes) raído, gastado; (behaviour) ruin inv
shack [ʃæk] n choza, chabola
shade [ʃeɪd] n sombra; (for lamp) pantalla;
(for eyes) visera; (of colour) matiz m, tonalidad
f; (small quantity): **a ~ (too big/more)** un
poquitín (grande/más) ▷ vt dar sombra a;
(eyes) proteger del sol; **in the ~** en la sombra;
shades npl (sunglasses) gafas fpl de sol
shadow ['ʃædəu] n sombra ▷ vt (follow)
seguir y vigilar; **shadow cabinet** (BRIT) n
(Pol) gabinete paralelo formado por el partido
de oposición
shady ['ʃeɪdɪ] adj sombreado;
(fig: dishonest) sospechoso; (: deal) turbio
shaft [ʃɑ:ft] n (of arrow, spear) astil m; (Aut,
Tech) eje m, árbol m; (of mine) pozo; (of lift)
hueco, caja; (of light) rayo
shake [ʃeɪk] (pt **shook**, pp **shaken**) vt
sacudir; (building) hacer temblar; (bottle,
cocktail) agitar ▷ vi (tremble) temblar; **to ~
one's head** (in refusal) negar con la cabeza;
(in dismay) mover or menear la cabeza,
incrédulo; **to ~ hands with sb** estrechar
la mano a algn; **shake off** vt sacudirse;
(fig) deshacerse de; **shake up** vt agitar;
(fig) reorganizar; **shaky** adj (hand, voice)
trémulo; (building) inestable
shall [ʃæl] aux vb: **~ I help you?** ¿quieres que
te ayude?; **I'll buy three, ~ I?** compro tres,
¿no te parece?
shallow ['ʃæləu] adj poco profundo; (fig)
superficial
sham [ʃæm] n fraude m, engaño
shambles ['ʃæmblz] n confusión f
shame [ʃeɪm] n vergüenza ▷ vt
avergonzar; **it is a ~ that/to do** es una
lástima que/hacer; **what a ~!** ¡qué lástima!;
shameful adj vergonzoso; **shameless** adj
desvergonzado
shampoo [ʃæm'pu:] n champú m ▷ vt

S

lavar con champú

shandy ['ʃændɪ] *n* mezcla de cerveza con gaseosa

shan't [ʃɑ:nt] = **shall not**

shape [ʃeɪp] *n* forma ▷ *vt* formar, dar forma a; (*sb's ideas*) formar; (*sb's life*) determinar; **to take ~** tomar forma

share [ʃeə*] *n* (*part*) parte f, porción f; (*contribution*) cuota; (*Comm*) acción f ▷ *vt* dividir; (*have in common*) compartir; **to ~ out (among** *or* **between)** repartir (entre); **shareholder** (BRIT) *n* accionista *mf*

shark [ʃɑ:k] *n* tiburón *m*

sharp [ʃɑ:p] *adj* (*blade, nose*) afilado; (*point*) puntiagudo; (*outline*) definido; (*pain*) intenso; (*Mus*) desafinado; (*contrast*) marcado; (*voice*) agudo; (*person: quick-witted*) astuto; (: *dishonest*) poco escrupuloso ▷ *n* (*Mus*) sostenido ▷ *adv*: **at 2 o'clock ~** a las 2 en punto; **sharpen** *vt* afilar; (*pencil*) sacar punta a; (*fig*) agudizar; **sharpener** *n* (*also*: **pencil sharpener**) sacapuntas *m inv*; **sharply** *adv* (*turn, stop*) bruscamente; (*stand out, contrast*) claramente; (*criticize, retort*) severamente

shatter ['ʃætə*] *vt* hacer añicos or pedazos; (*fig*: *ruin*) destruir, acabar con ▷ *vi* hacerse añicos; **shattered** *adj* (*grief-stricken*) destrozado, deshecho; (*exhausted*) agotado, hecho polvo

shave [ʃeɪv] *vt* afeitar, rasurar ▷ *vi* afeitarse, rasurarse ▷ *n*: **to have a ~** afeitarse; **shaver** *n* (*also*: **electric shaver**) máquina de afeitar (eléctrica)

shavings ['ʃeɪvɪŋz] *npl* (*of wood etc*) virutas *fpl*

shaving cream ['ʃeɪvɪŋ-] *n* crema de afeitar

shaving foam *n* espuma de afeitar

shawl [ʃɔ:l] *n* chal *m*

she [ʃi:] *pron* ella

sheath [ʃi:θ] *n* vaina; (*contraceptive*) preservativo

shed [ʃɛd] (*pt, pp ~*) *n* cobertizo ▷ *vt* (*skin*) mudar; (*tears, blood*) derramar; (*load*) derramar; (*workers*) despedir

she'd [ʃi:d] = **she had; she would**

sheep [ʃi:p] *n inv* oveja; **sheepdog** *n* perro pastor; **sheepskin** *n* piel f de carnero

sheer [ʃɪə*] *adj* (*utter*) puro, completo; (*steep*) escarpado; (*material*) diáfano ▷ *adv* verticalmente

sheet [ʃi:t] *n* (*on bed*) sábana; (*of paper*) hoja; (*of glass, metal*) lámina; (*of ice*) capa

sheik(h) [ʃeɪk] *n* jeque *m*

shelf [ʃɛlf] (*pl* **shelves**) *n* estante *m*

shell [ʃɛl] *n* (*on beach*) concha; (*of egg, nut etc*) cáscara; (*explosive*) proyectil *m*,

obús *m*; (*of building*) armazón f ▷ *vt* (*peas*) desenvainar; (*Mil*) bombardear

she'll [ʃi:l] = **she will; she shall**

shellfish ['ʃɛlfɪʃ] *n inv* crustáceo; (*as food*) mariscos *mpl*

shelter ['ʃɛltə*] *n* abrigo, refugio ▷ *vt* (*aid*) amparar, proteger; (*give lodging to*) abrigar ▷ *vi* abrigarse, refugiarse; **sheltered** *adj* (*life*) protegido; (*spot*) abrigado

shelves [ʃɛlvz] *npl of* **shelf**

shelving ['ʃɛlvɪŋ] *n* estantería

shepherd ['ʃɛpəd] *n* pastor *m* ▷ *vt* (*guide*) guiar, conducir; **shepherd's pie** (BRIT) *n* pastel de carne y patatas

sheriff ['ʃɛrɪf] (US) *n* sheriff *m*

sherry ['ʃɛrɪ] *n* jerez *m*

she's [ʃi:z] = **she is; she has**

Shetland ['ʃɛtlənd] *n* (*also*: **the ~s, the ~ Isles**) las Islas de Zetlandia

shield [ʃi:ld] *n* escudo; (*protection*) blindaje *m* ▷ *vt*: **to ~ (from)** proteger (de)

shift [ʃɪft] *n* (*change*) cambio; (*at work*) turno ▷ *vt* trasladar; (*remove*) quitar ▷ *vi* moverse

shin [ʃɪn] *n* espinilla

shine [ʃaɪn] (*pt, pp* **shone**) *n* brillo, lustre *m* ▷ *vi* brillar, relucir ▷ *vt* (*shoes*) lustrar, sacar brillo a; **to ~ a torch on sth** dirigir una linterna hacia algo

shingles ['ʃɪŋglz] *n* (*Med*) herpes *mpl* or *fpl*

shiny ['ʃaɪnɪ] *adj* brillante, lustroso

ship [ʃɪp] *n* buque *m*, barco ▷ *vt* (*goods*) embarcar; (*send*) transportar *or* enviar por vía marítima; **shipment** *n* (*goods*) envío; **shipping** *n* (*act*) embarque *m*; (*traffic*) buques *mpl*; **shipwreck** *n* naufragio ▷ *vt*: **to be shipwrecked** naufragar; **shipyard** *n* astillero

shirt [ʃə:t] *n* camisa; **in (one's) ~ sleeves** en mangas de camisa

shit [ʃɪt] (*infl*) *excl* ¡mierda! (!)

shiver ['ʃɪvə*] *n* escalofrío ▷ *vi* temblar, estremecerse; (*with cold*) tiritar

shock [ʃɔk] *n* (*impact*) choque *m*; (*Elec*) descarga (eléctrica); (*emotional*) conmoción f; (*start*) sobresalto, susto; (*Med*) postración f nerviosa ▷ *vt* dar un susto a; (*offend*) escandalizar; **shocking** *adj* (*awful*) espantoso; (*outrageous*) escandaloso

shoe [ʃu:] (*pt, pp* **shod**) *n* zapato; (*for horse*) herradura ▷ *vt* (*horse*) herrar; **shoelace** *n* cordón *m*; **shoe polish** *n* betún *m*; **shoeshop** *n* zapatería

shone [ʃɔn] *pt, pp of* **shine**

shook [ʃuk] *pt of* **shake**

shoot [ʃu:t] (*pt, pp* **shot**) *n* (*on branch, seedling*) retoño, vástago ▷ *vt* disparar; (*kill*) matar a tiros; (*wound*) pegar un tiro; (*execute*) fusilar; (film) rodar, filmar ▷ vi (Football) chutar; **shoot down** vt (plane) derribar; **shoot up** vi (prices) dispararse; **shooting** n (shots) tiros mpl; (Hunting) caza con escopeta

shop [ʃɔp] n tienda; (workshop) taller m ▷ vi (also: **go ~ping**) ir de compras; **shop assistant** (BRIT) n dependiente/a m/f; **shopkeeper** n tendero/a; **shoplifting** n mechería; **shopping** n (goods) compras fpl; **shopping bag** n bolsa (de compras); **shopping centre** (US **shopping center**) n centro comercial; **shopping mall** n centro comercial; **shopping trolley** n (BRIT) carrito de la compra; **shop window** n escaparate m (SP), vidriera (LAM)

shore [ʃɔː*] n orilla ▷ vt: **to ~ (up)** reforzar; **on ~** en tierra

short [ʃɔːt] adj corto; (in time) breve, de corta duración; (person) bajo; (curt) brusco, seco; (insufficient) insuficiente; **(a pair of) ~s** (unos) pantalones mpl cortos; **to be ~ of sth** estar falto de algo; **in ~** en pocas palabras; **~ of doing ...** fuera de hacer ...; **it is ~ for** es la forma abreviada de; **to cut ~** (speech, visit) interrumpir, terminar inesperadamente; **everything ~ of ...** todo menos ...; **to fall ~ of** no alcanzar; **to run ~ of** quedarle a algn poco; **to stop ~** parar en seco; **to stop ~ of** detenerse antes de; **shortage** n: **a shortage of** una falta de; **shortbread** n especie de mantecada; **shortcoming** n defecto, deficiencia; **short(crust) pastry** (BRIT) n pasta quebradiza; **shortcut** n atajo; **shorten** vt acortar; (visit) interrumpir; **shortfall** n déficit m; **shorthand** (BRIT) n taquigrafía; **short-lived** adj efímero; **shortly** adv en breve, dentro de poco; **shorts** npl pantalones mpl cortos; (US) calzoncillos mpl; **short-sighted** (BRIT) adj miope; (fig) imprudente; **short-sleeved** adj de manga corta; **short story** n cuento; **short-tempered** adj enojadizo; **short-term** adj (effect) a corto plazo

shot [ʃɔt] pt, pp of **shoot** ▷ n tiro, disparo; (try) tentativa; (injection) inyección f; (Phot) toma, fotografía; **to be a good/poor ~** (person) tener buena/mala puntería; **like a ~** (without any delay) como un rayo; **shotgun** n escopeta

should [ʃud] aux vb: **I ~ go now** debo irme ahora; **he ~ be there now** debe de haber llegado (ya); **I ~ go if I were you** yo en tu lugar me iría; **I ~ like to** me gustaría

shoulder ['ʃəuldə*] n hombro ▷ vt (fig) cargar con; **shoulder blade** n omóplato

shouldn't ['ʃudnt] = should not

shout [ʃaut] n grito ▷ vt gritar ▷ vi gritar, dar voces

shove [ʃʌv] n empujón m ▷ vt empujar; (inf: put): **to ~ sth in** meter algo a empellones

shovel ['ʃʌvl] n pala; (mechanical) excavadora ▷ vt mover con pala

show [ʃəu] (pt ~ed, pp ~n) n (of emotion) demostración f; (semblance) apariencia; (exhibition) exposición f; (Theatre) función f, espectáculo; (TV) show m ▷ vt mostrar, enseñar; (courage etc) mostrar, manifestar; (exhibit) exponer; (film) proyectar ▷ vi mostrarse; (appear) aparecer; **for ~** para impresionar; **on ~** (exhibits etc) expuesto; **show in** vt (person) hacer pasar; **show off** (pej) vi presumir ▷ vt (display) lucir; **show out** vt: **to show sb out** acompañar a algn a la puerta; **show up** vi (stand out) destacar; (inf: turn up) aparecer ▷ vt (unmask) desenmascarar; **show business** n mundo del espectáculo

shower ['ʃauə*] n (rain) chaparrón m, chubasco; (of stones etc) lluvia; (for bathing) ducha, regadera (MEX) ▷ vi llover ▷ vt (fig): **to ~ sb with sth** colmar a algn de algo; **to have a ~** ducharse; **shower cap** n gorro de baño; **shower gel** n gel m de ducha

showing ['ʃəuɪŋ] n (of film) proyección f

show jumping n hípica

shown [ʃəun] pp of **show**

show: show-off (inf) n (person) presumido/a; **showroom** n sala de muestras

shrank [ʃræŋk] pt of **shrink**

shred [ʃred] n (gen pl) triza, jirón m ▷ vt hacer trizas; (Culin) desmenuzar

shrewd [ʃruːd] adj astuto

shriek [ʃriːk] n chillido ▷ vi chillar

shrimp [ʃrɪmp] n camarón m

shrine [ʃraɪn] n santuario, sepulcro

shrink [ʃrɪŋk] (pt **shrank**, pp **shrunk**) vi encogerse; (be reduced) reducirse; (also: **~ away**) retroceder ▷ vt encoger ▷ n (inf, pej) loquero/a; **to ~ from (doing) sth** no atreverse a hacer algo

shrivel ['ʃrɪvl] (also: **~ up**) vt (dry) secar ▷ vi secarse

shroud [ʃraud] n sudario ▷ vt: **~ed in mystery** envuelto en el misterio

Shrove Tuesday ['ʃrəuv-] n martes m de carnaval

shrub [ʃrʌb] n arbusto

shrug [ʃrʌg] n encogimiento de hombros ▷ vt, vi: **to ~ (one's shoulders)** encogerse de hombros; **shrug off** vt negar importancia a

shrunk [ʃrʌŋk] pp of **shrink**

shudder ['ʃʌdə*] n estremecimiento, escalofrío ▷ vi estremecerse

shuffle ['ʃʌfl] vt (cards) barajar ▷ vi: **to ~**

(one's feet) arrastrar los pies

shun [ʃʌn] vt rehuir, esquivar

shut [ʃʌt] (pt, pp ~) vt cerrar ▷ vi cerrarse; **shut down** vt, vi cerrar; **shut up** vi (inf: keep quiet) callarse ▷ vt (close) cerrar; (silence) hacer callar; **shutter** n contraventana; (Phot) obturador m

shuttle ['ʃʌtl] n lanzadera; (also: ~ service) servicio rápido y continuo entre dos puntos; (Aviat) puente m aéreo; **shuttlecock** n volante m

shy [ʃaɪ] adj tímido

sibling ['sɪblɪŋ] n (formal) hermano/a

Sicily ['sɪsɪlɪ] n Sicilia

sick [sɪk] adj (ill) enfermo; (nauseated) mareado; (humour) negro; (vomiting): **to be ~** (BRIT) vomitar; **to feel ~** tener náuseas; **to be ~ of** (fig) estar harto de; **sickening** adj (fig) asqueroso; **sick leave** n baja por enfermedad; **sickly** adj enfermizo; (smell) nauseabundo; **sickness** n enfermedad f, mal m; (vomiting) náuseas fpl

side [saɪd] n (gen) lado; (of body) costado; (of lake) orilla; (of hill) ladera; (team) equipo ▷ adj (door, entrance) lateral ▷ vi: **to ~ with sb** tomar el partido de algn; **by the ~ of** al lado de; **~ by ~** juntos/as; **from ~ to ~** de un lado para otro; **from all ~s** de todos lados; **to take ~s (with)** tomar partido (con); **sideboard** n aparador m; **sideboards** (BRIT) npl = **sideburns**; **sideburns** npl patillas fpl; **sidelight** n (Aut) luz f lateral; **sideline** n (Sport) línea de banda; (fig) empleo suplementario; **side order** n plato de acompañamiento; **side road** n (BRIT) calle f lateral; **side street** n calle f lateral; **sidetrack** vt (fig) desviar (de su propósito); **sidewalk** (US) n acera; **sideways** adv de lado

siege [siːdʒ] n cerco, sitio

sieve [sɪv] n colador m ▷ vt cribar

sift [sɪft] vt cribar; (fig: information) escudriñar

sigh [saɪ] n suspiro ▷ vi suspirar

sight [saɪt] n (faculty) vista; (spectacle) espectáculo; (on gun) mira, alza ▷ vt divisar; **in ~** a la vista; **out of ~** fuera de (la) vista; **on ~** (shoot) sin previo aviso; **sightseeing** n excursionismo, turismo; **to go sightseeing** hacer turismo

sign [saɪn] n (with hand) señal f, seña; (trace) huella, rastro; (notice) letrero; (written) signo ▷ vt firmar; (Sport) fichar; **to ~ sth over to sb** firmar el traspaso de algo a algn; **sign for sb** vt fus (item) firmar el recibo de; **sign in** vi firmar el registro (al entrar); **sign on** vi (BRIT: as unemployed) registrarse como desempleado; (for course) inscribirse ▷ vt

(Mil) alistar; (employee) contratar; **sign up** vi (Mil) alistarse; (for course) inscribirse ▷ vt (player) fichar

signal ['sɪgnl] n señal f ▷ vi señalizar ▷ vt (person) hacer señas a; (message) comunicar por señales

signature ['sɪgnətʃə*] n firma

significance [sɪg'nɪfɪkəns] n (importance) trascendencia

significant [sɪg'nɪfɪkənt] adj significativo; (important) trascendente

signify ['sɪgnɪfaɪ] vt significar

sign language n lenguaje m para sordomudos

signpost ['saɪnpəʊst] n indicador m

Sikh [siːk] adj, n sij mf

silence ['saɪlns] n silencio ▷ vt acallar; (guns) reducir al silencio

silent ['saɪlnt] adj silencioso; (not speaking) callado; (film) mudo; **to remain ~** guardar silencio

silhouette [sɪluːˈet] n silueta

silicon chip ['sɪlɪkən-] n plaqueta de silicio

silk [sɪlk] n seda ▷ adj de seda

silly ['sɪlɪ] adj (person) tonto; (idea) absurdo

silver ['sɪlvə*] n plata; (money) moneda suelta ▷ adj de plata; (colour) plateado; **silver-plated** adj plateado

similar ['sɪmɪlə*] adj: **~ (to)** parecido or semejante (a); **similarity** [-'lærɪtɪ] n semejanza; **similarly** adv del mismo modo

simmer ['sɪmə*] vi hervir a fuego lento

simple ['sɪmpl] adj (easy) sencillo; (foolish, Comm: interest) simple; **simplicity** [-'plɪsɪtɪ] n sencillez f; **simplify** ['sɪmplɪfaɪ] vt simplificar; **simply** adv (live, talk) sencillamente; (just, merely) simplemente

simulate ['sɪmjuːleɪt] vt fingir, simular

simultaneous [sɪməl'teɪnɪəs] adj simultáneo; **simultaneously** adv simultáneamente

sin [sɪn] n pecado ▷ vi pecar

since [sɪns] adv desde entonces, después ▷ prep desde ▷ conj (time) desde que; (because) ya que, puesto que; **~ then, ever ~** desde entonces

sincere [sɪn'sɪə*] adj sincero; **sincerely** adv: **yours sincerely** (in letters) le saluda atentamente

sing [sɪŋ] (pt sang, pp sung) vt, vi cantar

Singapore [sɪŋə'pɔː*] n Singapur m

singer ['sɪŋə*] n cantante mf

singing ['sɪŋɪŋ] n canto

single ['sɪŋgl] adj único, solo; (unmarried) soltero; (not double) simple, sencillo ▷ n (BRIT: also: ~ ticket) billete m sencillo; (record) sencillo, single m; **singles** npl

(Tennis) individual m; **single out** vt (choose) escoger; **single bed** n cama individual; **single file** n: **in single file** en fila de uno; **single-handed** adv sin ayuda; **single-minded** adj resuelto, firme; **single parent** n padre m soltero, madre f soltera (o divorciado etc); **single parent family** familia monoparental; **single room** n cuarto individual

singular ['sɪŋɡjulə*] adj (odd) raro, extraño; (outstanding) excepcional ▷ n (Ling) singular m

sinister ['sɪnɪstə*] adj siniestro

sink [sɪŋk] (pt **sank**, pp **sunk**) n fregadero ▷ vt (ship) hundir, echar a pique; (foundations) excavar ▷ vi hundirse; **to ~ sth into** hundir algo en; **sink in** vi (fig) penetrar, calar

sinus ['saɪnəs] n (Anat) seno

sip [sɪp] n sorbo ▷ vt sorber, beber a sorbitos

sir [sə*] n señor m; **S~ John Smith** Sir John Smith; **yes ~** sí, señor

siren ['saɪərn] n sirena

sirloin ['sə:lɔɪn] n (also: **~ steak**) solomillo

sister ['sɪstə*] n hermana; (BRIT: nurse) enfermera jefe; **sister-in-law** n cuñada

sit [sɪt] (pt, pp **sat**) vi sentarse; (be sitting) estar sentado; (assembly) reunirse; (for painter) posar ▷ vt (exam) presentarse a; **sit back** vi (in seat) recostarse; **sit down** vi sentarse; **sit on** vt fus (jury, committee) ser miembro de, formar parte de; **sit up** vi incorporarse; (not go to bed) velar

sitcom ['sɪtkɔm] n abbr (= situation comedy) comedia de situación

site [saɪt] n sitio; (also: **building ~**) solar m ▷ vt situar

sitting ['sɪtɪŋ] n (of assembly etc) sesión f; (in canteen) turno; **sitting room** n sala de estar

situated ['sɪtjueɪtɪd] adj situado

situation [sɪtju'eɪʃən] n situación f; **"~s vacant"** (BRIT) "ofrecen trabajo"

six [sɪks] num seis; **sixteen** num diez y seis, dieciséis; **sixteenth** [sɪks'ti:nθ] adj decimosexto; **sixth** [sɪksθ] num sexto; **sixth form** n (BRIT) clase f de alumnos del sexto año (de 16 a 18 años de edad); **sixth-form college** n instituto m para alumnos de 16 a 18 años; **sixtieth** ['sɪkstɪɪθ] adj sexagésimo; **sixty** num sesenta

size [saɪz] n tamaño; (extent) extensión f; (of clothing) talla; (of shoes) número; **sizeable** adj importante, considerable

sizzle ['sɪzl] vi crepitar

skate [skeɪt] n patín m; (fish: pl inv) raya ▷ vi patinar; **skateboard** n monopatín m;

skateboarding n monopatín m; **skater** n patinador(a) m/f; **skating** n patinaje m; **skating rink** n pista de patinaje

skeleton ['skelɪtn] n esqueleto; (Tech) armazón f; (outline) esquema m

skeptical ['skeptɪkl] (US) = **sceptical**

sketch [sketʃ] n (drawing) dibujo; (outline) esbozo, bosquejo; (Theatre) sketch m ▷ vt dibujar; (plan etc: also: **~ out**) esbozar

skewer ['skju:ə*] n broqueta

ski [ski:] n esquí m ▷ vi esquiar; **ski boot** n bota de esquí

skid [skɪd] n patinazo ▷ vi patinar

ski: skier n esquiador(a) m/f; **skiing** n esquí m

skilful ['skɪlful] (US **skillful**) adj diestro, experto

ski lift n telesilla m, telesquí m

skill [skɪl] n destreza, pericia; técnica; **skilled** adj hábil, diestro; (worker) cualificado

skim [skɪm] vt (milk) desnatar; (glide over) rozar, rasar ▷ vi: **to ~ through** (book) hojear; **skimmed milk** (US **skim milk**) n leche f desnatada

skin [skɪn] n piel f; (complexion) cutis m ▷ vt (fruit etc) pelar; (animal) despellejar; **skinhead** n cabeza m/f rapada, skin(head) m/f; **skinny** adj flaco

skip [skɪp] n brinco, salto; (BRIT: container) contenedor m ▷ vi brincar; (with rope) saltar a la comba ▷ vt saltarse

ski: ski pass n forfait m (de esquí); **ski pole** n bastón m de esquiar

skipper ['skɪpə*] n (Naut, Sport) capitán m

skipping rope ['skɪpɪŋ-] (US **skip rope**) n comba

skirt [skə:t] n falda, pollera (SC) ▷ vt (go round) ladear

skirting board ['skə:tɪŋ-] (BRIT) n rodapié m

ski slope n pista de esquí

ski suit n traje m de esquiar

skull [skʌl] n calavera; (Anat) cráneo

skunk [skʌŋk] n mofeta

sky [skaɪ] n cielo; **skyscraper** n rascacielos m inv

slab [slæb] n (stone) bloque m; (flat) losa; (of cake) trozo

slack [slæk] adj (loose) flojo; (slow) de poca actividad; (careless) descuidado; **slacks** npl pantalones mpl

slain [sleɪn] pp of **slay**

slam [slæm] vt (throw) arrojar (violentamente); (criticize) criticar duramente ▷ vi (door) cerrarse de golpe; **to ~ the door** dar un portazo

slander ['slɑ:ndə*] n calumnia,

difamación f

slang [slæŋ] n argot m; (jargon) jerga

slant [slɑːnt] n sesgo, inclinación f; (fig) interpretación f

slap [slæp] n palmada; (in face) bofetada ▷ vt dar una palmada or bofetada a; (paint etc): **to ~ sth on sth** embadurnar algo con algo ▷ adv (directly) exactamente, directamente

slash [slæʃ] vt acuchillar; (fig: prices) fulminar

slate [sleɪt] n pizarra ▷ vt (fig: criticize) criticar duramente

slaughter ['slɔːtə*] n (of animals) matanza; (of people) carnicería ▷ vt matar; **slaughterhouse** n matadero

Slav [slɑːv] adj eslavo

slave [sleɪv] n esclavo/a ▷ vi (also: ~ away) sudar tinta; **slavery** n esclavitud f

slay [sleɪ] (pt **slew**, pp **slain**) vt matar

sleazy ['sliːzɪ] adj de mala fama

sled [sled] (US) = **sledge**

sledge [sledʒ] n trineo

sleek [sliːk] adj (shiny) lustroso; (car etc) elegante

sleep [sliːp] (pt, pp **slept**) n sueño ▷ vi dormir; **to go to ~** quedarse dormido; **sleep in** vi (oversleep) quedarse dormido; **sleep together** vi (have sex) acostarse juntos; **sleeper** n (person) durmiente mf; (BRIT Rail: on track) traviesa; (: train) coche-cama m; **sleeping bag** n saco de dormir; **sleeping car** n coche-cama m; **sleeping pill** n somnífero; **sleepover** n: **we're having a sleepover at Jo's** nos vamos a quedar a dormir en casa de Jo; **sleepwalk** vi caminar dormido; (habitually) ser sonámbulo; **sleepy** adj soñoliento; (place) soporífero

sleet [sliːt] n aguanieve f

sleeve [sliːv] n manga; (Tech) manguito; (of record) portada; **sleeveless** adj sin mangas

sleigh [sleɪ] n trineo

slender ['slendə*] adj delgado; (means) escaso

slept [slept] pt, pp of **sleep**

slew [sluː] pt of **slay** ▷ vi (BRIT: veer) torcerse

slice [slaɪs] n (of meat) tajada; (of bread) rebanada; (of lemon) rodaja; (utensil) pala ▷ vt cortar (en tajos), rebanar

slick [slɪk] adj (skilful) hábil, diestro; (clever) astuto ▷ n (also: **oil ~**) marea negra

slide [slaɪd] (pt, pp **slid**) n (movement) descenso, desprendimiento; (in playground) tobogán m; (Phot) diapositiva; (BRIT: also: **hair ~**) pasador m ▷ vt correr, deslizar ▷ vi

(slip) resbalarse; (glide) deslizarse; **sliding** adj (door) corredizo

slight [slaɪt] adj (slim) delgado; (frail) delicado; (pain etc) leve; (trivial) insignificante; (small) pequeño ▷ n desaire m ▷ vt (insult) ofender, desairar; **not in the ~est** en absoluto; **slightly** adv ligeramente, un poco

slim [slɪm] adj delgado, esbelto; (fig: chance) remoto ▷ vi adelgazar; **slimming** n adelgazamiento

slimy ['slaɪmɪ] adj cenagoso

sling [slɪŋ] (pt, pp **slung**) n (Med) cabestrillo; (weapon) honda ▷ vt tirar, arrojar

slip [slɪp] n (slide) resbalón m; (mistake) descuido; (underskirt) combinación f; (of paper) papelito ▷ vt (slide) deslizar ▷ vi deslizarse; (stumble) resbalar(se); (decline) decaer; (move smoothly): **to ~ into/out of** (room etc) introducirse en/salirse de; **to give sb the ~** eludir a algn; **a ~ of the tongue** un lapsus; **to ~ sth on/off** ponerse/quitarse algo; **slip up** vi (make mistake) equivocarse; meter la pata

slipper ['slɪpə*] n zapatilla, pantufla

slippery ['slɪpərɪ] adj resbaladizo; **slip road** (BRIT) n carretera de acceso

slit [slɪt] (pt, pp **~**) n raja; (cut) corte m ▷ vt rajar; cortar

slog [slɒg] (BRIT) vi sudar tinta; **it was a ~** costó trabajo (hacerlo)

slogan ['sləʊgən] n eslogan m, lema m

slope [sləʊp] n (up) cuesta, pendiente f; (down) declive m; (side of mountain) falda, vertiente m ▷ vi: **to ~ down** estar en declive; **to ~ up** inclinarse; **sloping** adj en pendiente; en declive; (writing) inclinado

sloppy ['slɒpɪ] adj (work) descuidado; (appearance) desaliñado

slot [slɒt] n ranura ▷ vt: **to ~ into** encajar en; **slot machine** n (BRIT: vending machine) distribuidor m automático; (for gambling) tragaperras m inv

Slovakia [sləʊ'vækɪə] n Eslovaquia

Slovene [sləʊ'viːn] adj esloveno ▷ n esloveno/a; (Ling) esloveno; **Slovenia** [sləʊ'viːnɪə] n Eslovenia; **Slovenian** adj, n = **Slovene**

slow [sləʊ] adj lento; (not clever) lerdo; (watch): **to be ~** atrasar ▷ adv lentamente, despacio ▷ vt, vi retardar; **"~"** (road sign) "disminuir velocidad"; **slow down** vi reducir la marcha; **slowly** adv lentamente, despacio; **slow motion** n: **in slow motion** a cámara lenta

slug [slʌg] n babosa; (bullet) posta; **sluggish** adj lento; (person) perezoso

slum [slʌm] n casucha

slump [slʌmp] n (economic) depresión f
▷ vi hundirse; (prices) caer en picado

slung [slʌŋ] pt, pp of **sling**

slur [sləː*] n: **to cast a ~ on** insultar ▷ vt
(speech) pronunciar mal

sly [slaɪ] adj astuto; (smile) taimado

smack [smæk] n bofetada ▷ vt dar con la
mano a; (child, on face) abofetear ▷ vi: **to ~ of**
saber a, oler a

small [smɔːl] adj pequeño; **small ads**
(BRIT) npl anuncios mpl por palabras; **small
change** n suelto, cambio

smart [smaːt] adj elegante; (clever) listo,
inteligente; (quick) rápido, vivo ▷ vi escocer,
picar; **smartcard** n tarjeta inteligente

smash [smæʃ] n (also: **~-up**) choque m;
(Mus) exitazo ▷ vt (break) hacer pedazos;
(car etc) estrellar; (Sport: record) batir
▷ vi hacerse pedazos; (against wall etc)
estrellarse; **smashing** (inf) adj estupendo

smear [smɪə*] n mancha; (Med) frotis m inv
▷ vt untar; **smear test** n (Med) citología,
frotis m inv (cervical)

smell [smɛl] (pt, pp **smelt** or **~ed**) n olor
m; (sense) olfato ▷ vt, vi oler; **smelly** adj
maloliente

smelt [smɛlt] pt, pp of **smell**

smile [smaɪl] n sonrisa ▷ vi sonreír

smirk [sməːk] n sonrisa falsa or afectada

smog [smɔg] n esmog m

smoke [sməuk] n humo ▷ vi fumar;
(chimney) echar humo ▷ vt (cigarettes)
fumar; **smoke alarm** n detector m de
humo, alarma contra incendios; **smoked**
adj (bacon, glass) ahumado; **smoker** n
fumador(a) m/f; (Rail) coche m fumador;
smoking n: "**no smoking**" "prohibido
fumar"

⏐ Be careful not to translate **smoking** by
the Spanish word smoking.

smoky adj (room) lleno de humo; (taste)
ahumado

smooth [smuːð] adj liso; (sea) tranquilo;
(flavour, movement) suave; (sauce) fino;
(person: pej) meloso ▷ vt (also: ~ **out**) alisar;
(creases, difficulties) allanar

smother ['smʌðə*] vt sofocar; (repress)
contener

SMS n abbr (= short message service) (servicio)
SMS; **SMS message** n (mensaje m) SMS

smudge [smʌdʒ] n mancha ▷ vt manchar

smug [smʌg] adj presumido; orondo

smuggle ['smʌgl] vt pasar de
contrabando; **smuggling** n contrabando

snack [snæk] n bocado; **snack bar** n
cafetería

snag [snæg] n problema m

snail [sneɪl] n caracol m

snake [sneɪk] n serpiente f

snap [snæp] n (sound) chasquido;
(photograph) foto f ▷ adj (decision)
instantáneo ▷ vt (break) quebrar; (fingers)
castañetear ▷ vi quebrarse; (fig: speak
sharply) contestar bruscamente; **to ~ shut**
cerrarse de golpe; **snap at** vt fus (dog)
intentar morder; **snap up** vt agarrar;
snapshot n foto f (instantánea)

snarl [snɑːl] vi gruñir

snatch [snætʃ] n (small piece) fragmento
▷ vt (snatch away) arrebatar; (fig) agarrar; **to
~ some sleep** encontrar tiempo para dormir

sneak [sniːk] (pt (US) **snuck**) vi: **to ~ in/out**
entrar/salir a hurtadillas ▷ n (inf) soplón/
ona m/f; **to ~ up on sb** aparecérsele de
improviso a algn; **sneakers** npl zapatos
mpl de lona

sneer [snɪə*] vi reír con sarcasmo;
(mock): **to ~ at** burlarse de

sneeze [sniːz] n (e)stornudo

sniff [snɪf] vi sollozar ▷ vt husmear, oler;
(drugs) esnifar

snigger ['snɪgə*] vi reírse con disimulo

snip [snɪp] n tijeretazo; (BRIT: inf: bargain)
ganga ▷ vt tijeretear

sniper ['snaɪpə*] n francotirador(a) m/f

snob [snɔb] n (e)snob m/f

snooker ['snuːkə*] n especie de billar

snoop [snuːp] vi: **to ~ about** fisgonear

snooze [snuːz] n siesta ▷ vi echar una
siesta

snore [snɔː*] n ronquido ▷ vi roncar

snorkel ['snɔːkl] n (tubo) respirador m

snort [snɔːt] n bufido ▷ vi bufar

snow [snəu] n nieve f ▷ vi nevar;
snowball n bola de nieve ▷ vi (fig)
agrandarse, ampliarse; **snowstorm** n
nevada, nevasca

snub [snʌb] vt (person) desairar ▷ n
desaire m, repulsa

snug [snʌg] adj (cosy) cómodo; (fitted)
ajustado

○ **KEYWORD**

so [səu] adv **1** (thus, likewise) así, de este
modo; **if so** de ser así; **I like swimming – so
do I** a mí me gusta nadar – a mí también;
I've got work to do – so has Paul tengo
trabajo que hacer – Paul también; **it's 5
o'clock – so it is!** son las cinco – ¡pues es
verdad!; **I hope/think so** espero/creo que
sí; **so far** hasta ahora; (in past) hasta este
momento

2 (in comparisons etc: to such a degree) tan;
so quickly (that) tan rápido (que); **so big**

(that) tan grande (que); **she's not so clever as her brother** no es tan lista como su hermano; **we were so worried** estábamos preocupadísimos

3: **so much** adj, adv tanto; **so many** tantos/as

4 (phrases): **10 or so** unos 10, 10 o así; **so long!** (inf: goodbye) ¡hasta luego!
▷ conj **1** (expressing purpose): **so as to do** para hacer; **so (that)** para que +subjun
2 (expressing result) así que; **so you see, I could have gone** así que ya ves, (yo) podría haber ido

soak [səuk] vt (drench) empapar; (steep in water) remojar ▷ vi remojarse, estar a remojo; **soak up** vt absorber; **soaking** adj (also: **soaking wet**) calado or empapado (hasta los huesos or el tuétano)
so-and-so ['səuənsəu] n (somebody) fulano/a de tal
soap [səup] n jabón m; **soap opera** n telenovela; **soap powder** n jabón m en polvo
soar [sɔ:*] vi (on wings) remontarse; (rocket: prices) dispararse; (building etc) elevarse
sob [sɔb] n sollozo ▷ vi sollozar
sober ['səubə*] adj (serious) serio; (not drunk) sobrio; (colour, style) discreto; **sober up** vt quitar la borrachera
so-called ['səu'kɔ:ld] adj así llamado
soccer ['sɔkə*] n fútbol m
sociable ['səuʃəbl] adj sociable
social ['səuʃl] adj social ▷ n velada, fiesta; **socialism** n socialismo; **socialist** adj, n socialista mf; **socialize** vi: **to socialize (with)** alternar (con); **social life** n vida social; **socially** adv socialmente; **social security** n seguridad f social; **social services** npl servicios mpl sociales; **social work** n asistencia social; **social worker** n asistente/a m/f social
society [sə'saɪətɪ] n sociedad f; (club) asociación f; (also: **high ~**) alta sociedad
sociology [səusɪ'ɔlədʒɪ] n sociología
sock [sɔk] n calcetín m
socket ['sɔkɪt] n cavidad f; (BRIT Elec) enchufe m
soda ['səudə] n (Chem) sosa; (also: **~ water**) soda; (US: also: **~ pop**) gaseosa
sodium ['səudɪəm] n sodio
sofa ['səufə] n sofá m; **sofa bed** n sofá-cama m
soft [sɔft] adj (lenient, not hard) blando; (gentle, not bright) suave; **soft drink** n bebida no alcohólica; **soft drugs** npl drogas fpl blandas; **soften** ['sɔfn] vt

ablandar; suavizar; (effect) amortiguar
▷ vi ablandarse; suavizarse; **softly** adv suavemente; (gently) delicadamente, con delicadeza; **software** n (Comput) software m
soggy ['sɔgɪ] adj empapado
soil [sɔɪl] n (earth) tierra, suelo ▷ vt ensuciar
solar ['səulə*] adj solar; **solar power** n energía solar; **solar system** n sistema m solar
sold [səuld] pt, pp of **sell**
soldier ['səuldʒə*] n soldado; (army man) militar m
sold out adj (Comm) agotado
sole [səul] n (of foot) planta; (of shoe) suela; (fish: pl inv) lenguado ▷ adj único; **solely** adv únicamente, sólo, solamente; **I will hold you solely responsible** le consideraré el único responsable
solemn ['sɔləm] adj solemne
solicitor [sə'lɪsɪtə*] (BRIT) n (for wills etc) ≈ notario/a; (in court) ≈ abogado/a
solid ['sɔlɪd] adj sólido; (gold etc) macizo ▷ n sólido
solitary ['sɔlɪtərɪ] adj solitario, solo
solitude ['sɔlɪtju:d] n soledad f
solo ['səuləu] n solo ▷ adv (fly) en solitario; **soloist** n solista m/f
soluble ['sɔlju:bl] adj soluble
solution [sə'lu:ʃən] n solución f
solve [sɔlv] vt resolver, solucionar
solvent ['sɔlvənt] adj (Comm) solvente ▷ n (Chem) solvente m
sombre ['sɔmbə*] (US **somber**) adj sombrío

○ **KEYWORD**

some [sʌm] adj **1** (a certain amount or number): **some tea/water/biscuits** té/agua/(unas) galletas; **there's some milk in the fridge** hay leche en el frigo; **there were some people outside** había algunas personas fuera; **I've got some money, but not much** tengo algo de dinero, pero no mucho
2 (certain: in contrasts) algunos/as; **some people say that ...** hay quien dice que ...; **some films were excellent, but most were mediocre** hubo películas excelentes, pero la mayoría fueron mediocres
3 (unspecified): **some woman was asking for you** una mujer estuvo preguntando por ti; **he was asking for some book (or other)** pedía un libro; **some day** algún día; **some day next week** un día de la semana que viene

▷ *pron* **1** (*a certain number*): **I've got some**
(*books etc*) tengo algunos/as
2 (*a certain amount*) algo; **I've got some**
(*money, milk*) tengo algo; **could I have some**
of that cheese? ¿me puede dar un poco de
ese queso?; **I've read some of the book** he
leído parte del libro
▷ *adv*: **some 10 people** unas 10 personas,
una decena de personas

some: somebody ['sʌmbədɪ] *pron* =
someone; somehow *adv* de alguna
manera; (*for some reason*) por una u otra
razón; **someone** *pron* alguien; **someplace**
(*US*) *adv* = **somewhere; something** *pron*
algo; **would you like something to eat/**
drink? ¿te gustaría cenar/tomar algo?;
sometime *adv* (*in future*) algún día, en
algún momento; (*in past*): **sometime last**
month durante el mes pasado; **sometimes**
adv a veces; **somewhat** *adv* algo;
somewhere *adv* (*be*) en alguna parte; (*go*) a
alguna parte; **somewhere else** (*be*) en otra
parte; (*go*) a otra parte

son [sʌn] *n* hijo
song [sɒŋ] *n* canción *f*
son-in-law ['sʌnɪnlɔː] *n* yerno
soon [suːn] *adv* pronto, dentro de poco;
~ afterwards poco después; *see also* **as**;
sooner *adv* (*time*) antes, más temprano;
(*preference: rather*): **I would sooner do that**
preferiría hacer eso; **sooner or later** tarde
o temprano
soothe [suːð] *vt* tranquilizar; (*pain*) aliviar
sophisticated [sə'fɪstɪkeɪtɪd] *adj*
sofisticado
sophomore ['sɒfəmɔː*] (*US*) *n* estudiante
mf de segundo año
soprano [sə'prɑːnəu] *n* soprano *f*
sorbet ['sɔːbeɪ] *n* sorbete *m*
sordid ['sɔːdɪd] *adj* (*place etc*) sórdido;
(*motive etc*) mezquino
sore [sɔː*] *adj* (*painful*) doloroso, que duele
▷ *n* llaga
sorrow ['sɒrəu] *n* pena, dolor *m*
sorry ['sɒrɪ] *adj* (*regretful*) arrepentido;
(*condition, excuse*) lastimoso; **~!** ¡perdón!,
¡perdone!; **~?** ¿cómo?; **to feel ~ for sb**
tener lástima a algn; **I feel ~ for him** me da
lástima
sort [sɔːt] *n* clase *f*, género, tipo; **sort out**
vt (*papers*) clasificar; (*organize*) ordenar,
organizar; (*resolve: problem, situation etc*)
arreglar, solucionar
SOS *n* SOS *m*
so-so ['səusəu] *adv* regular, así así
sought [sɔːt] *pt*, *pp of* **seek**
soul [səul] *n* alma

sound [saund] *n* (*noise*) sonido, ruido;
(*volume: on TV etc*) volumen *m*; (*Geo*) estrecho
▷ *adj* (*healthy*) sano; (*safe, not damaged*)
en buen estado; (*reliable: person*) digno de
confianza; (*sensible*) sensato, razonable;
(*secure: investment*) seguro ▷ *adv*: **~ asleep**
profundamente dormido ▷ *vt* (*alarm*) sonar
▷ *vi* sonar, resonar; (*fig: seem*) parecer; **to ~**
like sonar a; **soundtrack** *n* (*of film*) banda
sonora
soup [suːp] *n* (*thick*) sopa; (*thin*) caldo
sour ['sauə*] *adj* agrio; (*milk*) cortado; **it's ~**
grapes (*fig*) están verdes
source [sɔːs] *n* fuente *f*
south [sauθ] *n* sur *m* ▷ *adj* del sur,
sureño ▷ *adv* al sur, hacia el sur; **South**
Africa *n* África del Sur; **South African**
adj, n sudafricano/a *m/f*; **South America**
n América del Sur, Sudamérica; **South**
American *adj, n* sudamericano/a *m/f*;
southbound *adj* (con) rumbo al sur;
southeastern [sauθ'iːstən] *adj* sureste,
del sureste; **southern** ['sʌðən] *adj* del sur,
meridional; **South Korea** *n* Corea del Sur;
South Pole *n* Polo Sur; **southward(s)** *adv*
hacia el sur; **south-west** *n* suroeste *m*;
southwestern [sauθ'westən] *adj* suroeste
souvenir [suːvə'nɪə*] *n* recuerdo
sovereign ['sɒvrɪn] *adj, n* soberano/a *m/f*
sow¹ [səu] (*pt* **~ed**, *pp* **sown**) *vt* sembrar
sow² [sau] *n* cerda, puerca
soya ['sɔɪə] (*BRIT*) *n* soja
spa [spɑː] *n* balneario
space [speɪs] *n* espacio; (*room*) sitio
▷ *cpd* espacial ▷ *vt* (*also: ~ out*) espaciar;
spacecraft *n* nave *f* espacial; **spaceship** *n*
= **spacecraft**
spacious ['speɪʃəs] *adj* amplio
spade [speɪd] *n* (*tool*) pala, laya; **spades** *npl*
(*Cards: British*) picas *fpl*; (: *Spanish*) espadas *fpl*
spaghetti [spə'getɪ] *n* espaguetis *mpl*,
fideos *mpl*
Spain [speɪn] *n* España
spam [spæm] *n* (*junk e-mail*) spam *m*
span [spæn] *n* (*of bird, plane*) envergadura;
(*of arch*) luz *f*; (*in time*) lapso ▷ *vt* extenderse
sobre, cruzar; (*fig*) abarcar
Spaniard ['spænjəd] *n* español(a) *m/f*
Spanish ['spænɪʃ] *adj* español(a) ▷ *n*
(*Ling*) español *m*, castellano; **the Spanish**
npl los españoles
spank [spæŋk] *vt* zurrar
spanner ['spænə*] (*BRIT*) *n* llave *f* (inglesa)
spare [speə*] *adj* de reserva; (*surplus*)
sobrante, de más ▷ *n* = **spare part** ▷ *vt* (*do*
without) pasarse sin; (*refrain from hurting*)
perdonar; **to ~** (*surplus*) sobrante, de sobra;
spare part *n* pieza de repuesto; **spare**

s

room n cuarto de los invitados; **spare time**
n tiempo libre; **spare tyre** (us **spare tire**) n
(Aut) neumático or llanta (LAM) de recambio;
spare wheel n (Aut) rueda de recambio

spark [spɑːk] n chispa; (fig) chispazo;
spark(ing) plug n bujía

sparkle ['spɑːkl] n centelleo, destello ▷ vi
(shine) relucir, brillar

sparrow ['spærəʊ] n gorrión m

sparse [spɑːs] adj esparcido, escaso

spasm ['spæzəm] n (Med) espasmo

spat [spæt] pt, pp of **spit**

spate [speɪt] n (fig): **a ~ of** un torrente de

spatula ['spætjʊlə] n espátula

speak [spiːk] (pt **spoke**, pp **spoken**) vt
(language) hablar; (truth) decir ▷ vi hablar;
(make a speech) intervenir; **to ~ to sb/of**
or **about sth** hablar con algn/de or sobre
algo; **~ up!** ¡habla fuerte!; **speaker** n (in
public) orador(a) m/f; (also: **loudspeaker**)
altavoz m; (for stereo etc) bafle m; (Pol): **the
Speaker** (BRIT) el Presidente de la Cámara de
los Comunes; (US) el Presidente del Congreso

spear [spɪə*] n lanza ▷ vt alancear

special ['speʃl] adj especial; (edition etc)
extraordinario; (delivery) urgente; **special
delivery** n (Post): **by special delivery**
por entrega urgente; **special effects** npl
(Cine) efectos mpl especiales; **specialist** n
especialista mf; **speciality** [speʃɪ'ælɪtɪ]
(BRIT) n especialidad f; **specialize** vi: **to
specialize (in)** especializarse (en); **specially**
adv sobre todo, en particular; **special
needs** npl (BRIT): **children with special
needs** niños que requieren una atención
diferenciada; **special offer** n (Comm) oferta
especial; **special school** n (BRIT) colegio m
de educación especial; **specialty** (US) n =
speciality

species ['spiːʃiːz] n inv especie f

specific [spə'sɪfɪk] adj específico;
specifically adv específicamente

specify ['spesɪfaɪ] vt, vi especificar,
precisar

specimen ['spesɪmən] n ejemplar m;
(Med: of urine) espécimen m; (: of blood)
muestra

speck [spek] n grano, mota

spectacle ['spektəkl] n espectáculo;
spectacles npl (BRIT: glasses) gafas fpl (SP),
anteojos mpl; **spectacular** [-'tækjʊlə*] adj
espectacular; (success) impresionante

spectator [spek'teɪtə*] n espectador(a)
m/f

spectrum ['spektrəm] (pl **spectra**) n
espectro

speculate ['spekjʊleɪt] vi: **to ~ (on)**
especular (en)

sped [sped] pt, pp of **speed**

speech [spiːtʃ] n (faculty) habla; (formal
talk) discurso; (spoken language) lenguaje m;
speechless adj mudo, estupefacto

speed [spiːd] n velocidad f; (haste) prisa;
(promptness) rapidez f; **at full** or **top ~** a
máxima velocidad; **speed up** vi acelerarse
▷ vt acelerar; **speedboat** n lancha motora;
speeding n (Aut) exceso de velocidad;
speed limit n límite m de velocidad,
velocidad f máxima; **speedometer**
[spɪ'dɒmɪtə*] n velocímetro; **speedy** adj
(fast) veloz, rápido; (prompt) pronto

spell [spel] (pt, pp **spelt** (BRIT) or **~ed**) n
(also: **magic ~**) encanto, hechizo; (period
of time) rato, período ▷ vt deletrear; (fig)
anunciar, presagiar; **to cast a ~ on sb**
hechizar a algn; **he can't ~** pone faltas
de ortografía; **spell out** vt (explain): **to
spell sth out for sb** explicar algo a algn
en detalle; **spellchecker** ['speltʃekə*]
n corrector m ortográfico; **spelling** n
ortografía

spelt [spelt] pt, pp of **spell**

spend [spend] (pt, pp **spent**) vt (money)
gastar; (time) pasar; (life) dedicar; **spending**
n: **government spending** gastos mpl del
gobierno

spent [spent] pt, pp of **spend** ▷ adj
(cartridge, bullets, match) usado

sperm [spɜːm] n esperma

sphere [sfɪə*] n esfera

spice [spaɪs] n especia ▷ vt condimentar

spicy ['spaɪsɪ] adj picante

spider ['spaɪdə*] n araña

spike [spaɪk] n (point) punta; (Bot) espiga

spill [spɪl] (pt, pp **spilt** or **~ed**) vt derramar,
verter ▷ vi derramarse; **to ~ over**
desbordarse

spin [spɪn] (pt, pp **spun**) n (Aviat) barrena;
(trip in car) paseo (en coche); (on ball) efecto
▷ vt (wool etc) hilar; (ball etc) hacer girar ▷ vi
girar, dar vueltas

spinach ['spɪnɪtʃ] n espinaca; (as food)
espinacas fpl

spinal ['spaɪnl] adj espinal

spin doctor n informador(a) parcial al
servicio de un partido político etc

spin-dryer (BRIT) n secador m centrífugo

spine [spaɪn] n espinazo, columna
vertebral; (thorn) espina

spiral ['spaɪərl] n espiral f ▷ vi (fig: prices)
subir desorbitadamente

spire ['spaɪə*] n aguja, chapitel m

spirit ['spɪrɪt] n (soul) alma; (ghost)
fantasma m; (attitude, sense) espíritu m;
(courage) valor m, ánimo; **spirits** npl (drink)
licor(es) m(pl); **in good ~s** alegre, de buen

ánimo

spiritual ['spɪrɪtjuəl] *adj* espiritual ▷ *n* espiritual *m*

spit [spɪt] (*pt*, *pp* **spat**) *n* (*for roasting*) asador *m*, espetón *m*; (*saliva*) saliva ▷ *vi* escupir; (*sound*) chisporrotear; (*rain*) lloviznar

spite [spaɪt] *n* rencor *m*, ojeriza ▷ *vt* causar pena a, mortificar; **in ~ of** a pesar de, pese a; **spiteful** *adj* rencoroso, malévolo

splash [splæʃ] *n* (*sound*) chapoteo; (*of colour*) mancha ▷ *vt* salpicar ▷ *vi* (*also:* **~ about**) chapotear; **splash out** (*inf*) *vi* derrochar dinero

splendid ['splɛndɪd] *adj* espléndido

splinter ['splɪntə*] *n* (*of wood etc*) astilla; (*in finger*) espigón *m* ▷ *vi* astillarse, hacer astillas

split [splɪt] (*pt*, *pp* **~**) *n* hendedura, raja; (*fig*) división *f*; (*Pol*) escisión *f* ▷ *vt* partir, rajar; (*party*) dividir; (*share*) repartir ▷ *vi* dividirse, escindirse; **split up** *vi* (*couple*) separarse; (*meeting*) acabarse

spoil [spɔɪl] (*pt*, *pp* **~t** or **~ed**) *vt* (*damage*) dañar; (*mar*) estropear; (*child*) mimar, consentir

spoilt [spɔɪlt] *pt*, *pp* of **spoil** ▷ *adj* (*child*) mimado, consentido; (*ballot paper*) invalidado

spoke [spəʊk] *pt* of **speak** ▷ *n* rayo, radio

spoken ['spəʊkn] *pp* of **speak**

spokesman ['spəʊksmən] (*irreg*) *n* portavoz *m*

spokesperson ['spəʊkspɜːsn] (*irreg*) *n* portavoz *m/f*, vocero/a (*LAM*)

spokeswoman ['spəʊkswʊmən] (*irreg*) *n* portavoz *f*

sponge [spʌndʒ] *n* esponja; (*also:* **~ cake**) bizcocho ▷ *vt* (*wash*) lavar con esponja ▷ *vi:* **to ~ off** or **on sb** vivir a costa de algn; **sponge bag** (*BRIT*) *n* esponjera

sponsor ['sponsə*] *n* patrocinador(a) *m/f* ▷ *vt* (*applicant, proposal etc*) proponer; **sponsorship** *n* patrocinio

spontaneous [spon'teɪnɪəs] *adj* espontáneo

spooky ['spuːkɪ] (*inf*) *adj* espeluznante, horripilante

spoon [spuːn] *n* cuchara; **spoonful** *n* cucharada

sport [spɔːt] *n* deporte *m*; (*person*): **to be a good ~** ser muy majo ▷ *vt* (*wear*) lucir, ostentar; **sport jacket** (*US*) *n* = **sports jacket**; **sports car** *n* coche *m* deportivo; **sports centre** (*BRIT*) *n* polideportivo; **sports jacket** (*BRIT*) *n* chaqueta deportiva; **sportsman** (*irreg*) *n* deportista *m*; **sports utility vehicle** *n* todoterreno *m inv*;

sportswear *n* trajes *mpl* de deporte or sport; **sportswoman** (*irreg*) *n* deportista; **sporty** *adj* deportista

spot [spot] *n* sitio, lugar *m*; (*dot: on pattern*) punto, mancha; (*pimple*) grano; (*Radio, TV*) espacio publicitario; (*small amount*): **a ~ of** un poquito de ▷ *vt* (*notice*) notar, observar; **on the ~** allí mismo; **spotless** *adj* perfectamente limpio; **spotlight** *n* foco, reflector *m*; (*Aut*) faro auxiliar

spouse [spauz] *n* cónyuge *mf*

sprain [spreɪn] *n* torcedura ▷ *vt:* **to ~ one's ankle/wrist** torcerse el tobillo/la muñeca

sprang [spræŋ] *pt* of **spring**

sprawl [sprɔːl] *vi* tumbarse

spray [spreɪ] *n* rociada; (*of sea*) espuma; (*container*) atomizador *m*; (*paint etc*) pistola rociadora; (*of flowers*) ramita ▷ *vt* rociar; (*crops*) regar

spread [sprɛd] (*pt*, *pp* **~**) *n* extensión *f*; (*for bread etc*) pasta para untar; (*inf: food*) comilona ▷ *vt* extender; (*butter*) untar; (*wings, sails*) desplegar; (*work, wealth*) repartir; (*scatter*) esparcir ▷ *vi* (*also:* **~ out: stain**) extenderse; (*news*) diseminarse; **spread out** *vi* (*move apart*) separarse; **spreadsheet** *n* hoja electrónica or de cálculo

spree [spriː] *n:* **to go on a ~** ir de juerga

spring [sprɪŋ] (*pt* **sprang**, *pp* **sprung**) *n* (*season*) primavera; (*leap*) salto, brinco; (*coiled metal*) resorte *m*; (*of water*) fuente *f*, manantial *m* ▷ *vi* saltar, brincar; **spring up** *vi* (*thing: appear*) aparecer; (*problem*) surgir; **spring onion** *n* cebolleta

sprinkle ['sprɪŋkl] *vt* (*pour: liquid*) rociar; (*: salt, sugar*) espolvorear; **to ~ water etc on, ~ with water** *etc* rociar or salpicar de agua *etc*

sprint [sprɪnt] *n* esprint *m* ▷ *vi* esprintar

sprung [sprʌŋ] *pp* of **spring**

spun [spʌn] *pt*, *pp* of **spin**

spur [spɜː*] *n* espuela; (*fig*) estímulo, aguijón *m* ▷ *vt* (*also:* **~ on**) estimular, incitar; **on the ~ of the moment** de improviso

spurt [spɜːt] *n* chorro; (*of energy*) arrebato ▷ *vi* chorrear

spy [spaɪ] *n* espía *mf* ▷ *vi:* **to ~ on** espiar a ▷ *vt* (*see*) divisar, lograr ver

sq. *abbr* = **square**

squabble ['skwɔbl] *vi* reñir, pelear

squad [skwɔd] *n* (*Mil*) pelotón *m*; (*Police*) brigada; (*Sport*) equipo

squadron ['skwɔdrn] *n* (*Mil*) escuadrón *m*; (*Aviat, Naut*) escuadra

s

squander ['skwɔndə*] vt (money) derrochar, despilfarrar; (chances) desperdiciar

square [skwɛə*] n cuadro; (in town) plaza; (inf: person) carca m/f ▷ adj cuadrado; (inf: ideas, tastes) trasnochado ▷ vt (arrange) arreglar; (Math) cuadrar; (reconcile) compaginar; **all ~** igual(es); **to have a ~ meal** comer caliente; **2 metres ~** 2 metros en cuadro; **2 ~ metres** 2 metros cuadrados; **square root** n raíz f cuadrada

squash [skwɔʃ] n (BRIT: drink): **lemon/ orange ~** zumo (SP) or jugo (LAM) de limón/ naranja; (US Bot) calabacín m; (Sport) squash m ▷ vt aplastar

squat [skwɔt] adj achaparrado ▷ vi (also: ~ **down**) agacharse, sentarse en cuclillas; **squatter** n okupa mf(SP)

squeak [skwiːk] vi (hinge) chirriar, rechinar; (mouse) chillar

squeal [skwiːl] vi chillar, dar gritos agudos

squeeze [skwiːz] n presión f; (of hand) apretón m; (Comm) restricción f ▷ vt (hand, arm) apretar

squid [skwɪd] n inv calamar m; (Culin) calamares mpl

squint [skwɪnt] vi bizquear, ser bizco ▷ n (Med) estrabismo

squirm [skwəːm] vi retorcerse, revolverse

squirrel ['skwɪrəl] n ardilla

squirt [skwəːt] vi salir a chorros ▷ vt chiscar

Sr abbr = **senior**

Sri Lanka [srɪ'læŋkə] n Sri Lanka m

St abbr = **saint; street**

stab [stæb] n (with knife) puñalada; (of pain) pinchazo; (inf: try) **to have a ~ at (doing) sth** intentar (hacer) algo ▷ vt apuñalar

stability [stə'bɪlɪtɪ] n estabilidad f

stable ['steɪbl] adj estable ▷ n cuadra, caballeriza

stack [stæk] n montón m, pila ▷ vt amontonar, apilar

stadium ['steɪdɪəm] n estadio

staff [stɑːf] n (work force) personal m, plantilla; (BRIT Scol) cuerpo docente ▷ vt proveer de personal

stag [stæg] n ciervo, venado

stage [steɪdʒ] n escena; (point) etapa; (platform) plataforma; (profession): **the ~** el teatro ▷ vt (play) poner en escena, representar; (organize) montar, organizar; **in ~s** por etapas

stagger ['stægə*] vi tambalearse ▷ vt (amaze) asombrar; (hours, holidays) escalonar; **staggering** adj asombroso

stagnant ['stægnənt] adj estancado

stag night, stag party n despedida de soltero

stain [steɪn] n mancha; (colouring) tintura ▷ vt manchar; (wood) teñir; **stained glass** n vidrio m de color; **stainless steel** n acero inoxidable

staircase ['stɛəkeɪs] n = **stairway**

stairs [stɛəz] npl escaleras fpl

stairway ['stɛəweɪ] n escalera

stake [steɪk] n estaca, poste m; (Comm) interés m; (Betting) apuesta ▷ vt (money) apostar; (life) arriesgar; (reputation) poner en juego; (claim) presentar una reclamación; **to be at ~** estar en juego

stale [steɪl] adj (bread) duro; (food) pasado; (smell) rancio; (beer) agrio

stalk [stɔːk] n tallo, caña ▷ vt acechar, cazar al acecho

stall [stɔːl] n (in market) puesto; (in stable) casilla (de establo) ▷ vt (Aut) calar; (fig) dar largas a ▷ vi (Aut) calarse; (fig) andarse con rodeos

stamina ['stæmɪnə] n resistencia

stammer ['stæmə*] n tartamudeo ▷ vi tartamudear

stamp [stæmp] n sello (SP), estampilla (LAM), timbre m (MEX); (mark) marca, huella; (on document) timbre m ▷ vi (also: ~ **one's foot**) patear ▷ vt (mark) marcar; (letter) franquear; (with rubber stamp) sellar; **stamp out** vt (fire) apagar con el pie; (crime, opposition) acabar con; **stamped addressed envelope** n (BRIT) sobre m sellado con las señas propias

stampede [stæm'piːd] n estampida

stance [stæns] n postura

stand [stænd] (pt, pp **stood**) n (position) posición f, postura; (for taxis) parada; (hall stand) perchero; (music stand) atril m; (Sport) tribuna; (at exhibition) stand m ▷ vi (be) estar, encontrarse; (be on foot) estar de pie; (rise) levantarse; (remain) quedar en pie; (in election) presentar candidatura ▷ vt (place) poner, colocar; (withstand) aguantar, soportar; (invite to) invitar; **to make a ~** (fig) mantener una postura firme; **to ~ for parliament** (BRIT) presentarse (como candidato) a las elecciones; **stand back** vi retirarse; **stand by** vi (be ready) estar listo ▷ vt fus (opinion) aferrarse a; (person) apoyar; **stand down** vi (withdraw) ceder el puesto; **stand for** vt fus (signify) significar; (tolerate) aguantar, permitir; **stand in for** vt fus suplir a; **stand out** vi destacarse; **stand up** vi levantarse, ponerse de pie; **stand up for** vt fus defender; **stand up to** vt fus hacer frente a

standard ['stændəd] n patrón m, norma; (level) nivel m; (flag) estandarte m ▷ adj

(*size etc*) normal, corriente; (*text*) básico;
standards *npl* (*morals*) valores *mpl* morales;
standard of living *n* nivel *m* de vida
standing ['stændɪŋ] *adj* (*on foot*) de
pie, en pie; (*permanent*) permanente ▷ *n*
reputación *f*; **of many years' ~** que lleva
muchos años; **standing order** (BRIT) *n* (*at
bank*) orden *f* de pago permanente
stand: **standpoint** *n* punto de vista;
standstill *n*: **at a standstill** (*industry, traffic*)
paralizado; (*car*) parado; **to come to a
standstill** quedar paralizado; pararse
stank [stæŋk] *pt of* **stink**
staple ['steɪpl] *n* (*for papers*) grapa ▷ *adj*
(*food etc*) básico ▷ *vt* grapar
star [stɑː*] *n* estrella; (*celebrity*) estrella,
astro ▷ *vt* (*Theatre, Cinema*) ser el/la
protagonista de; **the stars** *npl* (*Astrology*)
el horóscopo
starboard ['stɑːbəd] *n* estribor *m*
starch [stɑːtʃ] *n* almidón *m*
stardom ['stɑːdəm] *n* estrellato
stare [steə*] *n* mirada fija ▷ *vi*: **to ~ at**
mirar fijo
stark [stɑːk] *adj* (*bleak*) severo, escueto
▷ *adv*: **~ naked** en cueros
start [stɑːt] *n* principio, comienzo;
(*departure*) salida; (*sudden movement*)
salto, sobresalto; (*advantage*) ventaja ▷ *vt*
empezar, comenzar; (*cause*) causar; (*found*)
fundar; (*engine*) poner en marcha ▷ *vi*
comenzar, empezar; (*with fright*) asustarse,
sobresaltarse; (*train etc*) salir; **to ~ doing** or
to do sth empezar a hacer algo; **start off**
vi empezar, comenzar; (*leave*) salir, ponerse
en camino; **start out** *vi* (*begin*) empezar;
(*set out*) partir, salir; **start up** *vi* comenzar;
(*car*) ponerse en marcha ▷ *vt* comenzar;
poner en marcha; **starter** *n* (*Aut*) botón *m*
de arranque; (*Sport: official*) juez *mf* de salida;
(BRIT Culin) entrante *m*; **starting point** *n*
punto de partida
startle ['stɑːtl] *vt* asustar, sobrecoger;
startling *adj* alarmante
starvation [stɑːˈveɪʃən] *n* hambre *f*
starve [stɑːv] *vi* tener mucha hambre; (*to
death*) morir de hambre ▷ *vt* hacer pasar
hambre
state [steɪt] *n* estado ▷ *vt* (*say, declare*)
afirmar; **the S~s** los Estados Unidos; **to
be in a ~** estar agitado; **statement** *n*
afirmación *f*; **state school** *n* escuela
or colegio estatal; **statesman** (*irreg*) *n*
estadista *m*
static ['stætɪk] *n* (Radio) parásitos *mpl*
▷ *adj* estático
station ['steɪʃən] *n* estación *f*; (Radio)
emisora; (*rank*) posición *f* social ▷ *vt*

colocar, situar; (*Mil*) apostar
stationary ['steɪʃnərɪ] *adj* estacionario,
fijo
stationer's (shop) (BRIT) *n* papelería
stationery [-nərɪ] *n* papel *m* de escribir,
artículos *mpl* de escritorio
station wagon (US) *n* ranchera
statistic [stəˈtɪstɪk] *n* estadística;
statistics *n* (*science*) estadística
statue ['stætjuː] *n* estatua
stature ['stætʃə*] *n* estatura; (*fig*) talla
status ['steɪtəs] *n* estado; (*reputation*)
estatus *m*; **status quo** *n* (e)statu quo *m*
statutory ['stætjutrɪ] *adj* estatutorio
staunch [stɔːntʃ] *adj* leal, incondicional
stay [steɪ] *n* estancia ▷ *vi* quedar(se);
(*as guest*) hospedarse; **to ~ put** seguir en el
mismo sitio; **to ~ the night/5 days** pasar
la noche/estar 5 días; **stay away** *vi* (*from
person, building*) no acercarse; (*from event*)
no acudir; **stay behind** *vi* quedar atrás;
stay in *vi* quedarse en casa; **stay on** *vi*
quedarse; **stay out** *vi* (*of house*) no volver a
casa; (*on strike*) permanecer en huelga; **stay
up** *vi* (*at night*) velar, no acostarse
steadily ['stedɪlɪ] *adv* constantemente;
(*firmly*) firmemente; (*work, walk*) sin parar;
(*gaze*) fijamente
steady ['stedɪ] *adj* (*firm*) firme; (*regular*)
regular; (*person, character*) sensato, juicioso;
(*boyfriend*) formal; (*look, voice*) tranquilo ▷ *vt*
(*stabilize*) estabilizar; (*nerves*) calmar
steak [steɪk] *n* filete *m*; (*beef*) bistec *m*
steal [stiːl] (*pt* **stole**, *pp* **stolen**) *vt* robar
▷ *vi* robar; (*move secretly*) andar a hurtadillas
steam [stiːm] *n* vapor *m*; (*mist*) vaho,
humo ▷ *vt* (Culin) cocer al vapor ▷ *vi* echar
vapor; **steam up** (*window*) empañarse;
to get steamed up about sth (*fig*) ponerse
negro por algo; **steamy** *adj* (*room*) lleno
de vapor; (*window*) empañado; (*heat,
atmosphere*) bochornoso
steel [stiːl] *n* acero ▷ *adj* de acero
steep [stiːp] *adj* escarpado, abrupto; (*stair*)
empinado; (*price*) exorbitante, excesivo ▷ *vt*
empapar, remojar
steeple ['stiːpl] *n* aguja
steer [stɪə*] *vt* (*car*) conducir (SP), manejar
(LAM); (*person*) dirigir ▷ *vi* conducir,
manejar; **steering** *n* (Aut) dirección *f*;
steering wheel *n* volante *m*
stem [stem] *n* (*of plant*) tallo; (*of glass*) pie
m ▷ *vt* detener; (*blood*) restañar
step [step] *n* paso; (*on stair*) peldaño,
escalón *m* ▷ *vi*: **to ~ forward/back** dar
un paso adelante/hacia atrás; **steps** *npl*
(BRIT) = **stepladder**; **in/out of ~ (with)**
acorde/en disonancia (con); **step down**

s

vi (*fig*) retirarse; **step in** *vi* entrar; (*fig*) intervenir; **step up** *vt* (*increase*) aumentar; **stepbrother** *n* hermanastro; **stepchild** (*pl* **stepchildren**) *n* hijastro/a *m/f*; **stepdaughter** *n* hijastra; **stepfather** *n* padrastro; **stepladder** *n* escalera doble *or* de tijera; **stepmother** *n* madrastra; **stepsister** *n* hermanastra; **stepson** *n* hijastro

stereo ['stɛrɪəu] *n* estéreo ▷ *adj* (*also*: **~phonic**) estéreo, estereofónico

stereotype ['stɪərɪətaɪp] *n* estereotipo ▷ *vt* estereotipar

sterile ['stɛraɪl] *adj* estéril; **sterilize** ['stɛrɪlaɪz] *vt* esterilizar

sterling ['stɜːlɪŋ] *adj* (*silver*) de ley ▷ *n* (*Econ*) libras *fpl* esterlinas *fpl*; **one pound ~** una libra esterlina

stern [stɜːn] *adj* severo, austero ▷ *n* (*Naut*) popa

steroid ['stɪərɔɪd] *n* esteroide *m*

stew [stjuː] *n* estofado, guiso ▷ *vt* estofar, guisar; (*fruit*) cocer

steward ['stjuːəd] *n* camarero; **stewardess** *n* (*esp on plane*) azafata

stick [stɪk] (*pt, pp* **stuck**) *n* palo; (*of dynamite*) barreno; (*as weapon*) porra; (*also*: **walking ~**) bastón *m* ▷ *vt* (*glue*) pegar; (*inf: put*) meter; (*: tolerate*) aguantar, soportar; (*thrust*): **to ~ sth into** clavar *or* hincar algo en ▷ *vi* pegarse; (*be unmoveable*) quedarse parado; (*in mind*) quedarse grabado; **stick out** *vi* sobresalir; **stick up** *vi* sobresalir; **stick up for** *vt fus* defender; **sticker** *n* (*label*) etiqueta engomada; (*with slogan*) pegatina; **sticking plaster** *n* esparadrapo; **stick shift** (*us*) *n* (*Aut*) palanca de cambios

sticky ['stɪkɪ] *adj* pegajoso; (*label*) engomado; (*fig*) difícil

stiff [stɪf] *adj* rígido, tieso; (*hard*) duro; (*manner*) estirado; (*difficult*) difícil; (*person*) inflexible; (*price*) exorbitante ▷ *adv*: **scared/bored ~** muerto de miedo/aburrimiento

stifling ['staɪflɪŋ] *adj* (*heat*) sofocante, bochornoso

stigma ['stɪgmə] *n* (*fig*) estigma *m*

stiletto [stɪ'lɛtəu] (*BRIT*) *n* (*also*: **~ heel**) tacón *m* de aguja

still [stɪl] *adj* inmóvil, quieto ▷ *adv* todavía; (*even*) aun; (*nonetheless*) sin embargo, aun así

stimulate ['stɪmjuleɪt] *vt* estimular

stimulus ['stɪmjuləs] (*pl* **stimuli**) *n* estímulo, incentivo

sting [stɪŋ] (*pt, pp* **stung**) *n* picadura; (*pain*) escozor *m*, picazón *f*; (*organ*) aguijón *m* ▷ *vt, vi* picar

stink [stɪŋk] (*pt* **stank**, *pp* **stunk**) *n* hedor *m*, tufo ▷ *vi* heder, apestar

stir [stɜː*] *n* (*fig: agitation*) conmoción *f* ▷ *vt* (*tea etc*) remover; (*fig: emotions*) provocar ▷ *vi* moverse; **stir up** *vt* (*trouble*) fomentar; **stir-fry** *vt* sofreír removiendo ▷ *n* plato preparado sofriendo y removiendo los ingredientes

stitch [stɪtʃ] *n* (*Sewing*) puntada; (*Knitting*) punto; (*Med*) punto (de sutura); (*pain*) punzada ▷ *vt* coser; (*Med*) suturar

stock [stɔk] *n* (*Comm: reserves*) existencias *fpl*, stock *m*; (*: selection*) surtido; (*Agr*) ganado, ganadería; (*Culin*) caldo; (*descent*) raza, estirpe *f*; (*Finance*) capital *m* ▷ *adj* (*fig: reply etc*) clásico ▷ *vt* (*have in stock*) tener existencias de; **~s and shares** acciones y valores; **in ~** en existencia *or* almacén; **out of ~** agotado; **to take ~ of** (*fig*) asesorar, examinar; **stockbroker** ['stɔkbrəukə*] *n* agente *mf* or corredor *mf* de bolsa(a); **stock cube** (*BRIT*) *n* pastilla de caldo; **stock exchange** *n* bolsa; **stockholder** ['stɔkhəuldə*] (*us*) *n* accionista *m/f*

stocking ['stɔkɪŋ] *n* media

stock market *n* bolsa (de valores)

stole [stəul] *pt of* **steal** ▷ *n* estola

stolen ['stəuln] *pp of* **steal**

stomach ['stʌmək] *n* (*Anat*) estómago; (*belly*) vientre *m* ▷ *vt* tragar, aguantar; **stomachache** *n* dolor *m* de estómago

stone [stəun] *n* piedra; (*in fruit*) hueso (= 6.348 *kg*; 14 *libras*) ▷ *adj* de piedra ▷ *vt* apedrear; (*fruit*) deshuesar

stood [stud] *pt, pp of* **stand**

stool [stuːl] *n* taburete *m*

stoop [stuːp] *vi* (*also*: **~ down**) doblarse, agacharse; (*also*: **have a ~**) ser cargado de espaldas

stop [stɔp] *n* parada; (*in punctuation*) punto ▷ *vt* parar, detener; (*break*) suspender; (*block: pay*) suspender; (*: cheque*) invalidar; (*also*: **put a ~ to**) poner término a ▷ *vi* pararse, detenerse; (*end*) acabarse; **to ~ doing sth** dejar de hacer algo; **stop by** *vi* pasar por; **stop off** *vi* interrumpir el viaje; **stopover** *n* parada; (*Aviat*) escala; **stoppage** *n* (*strike*) paro; (*blockage*) obstrucción *f*

storage ['stɔːrɪdʒ] *n* almacenaje *m*

store [stɔː*] *n* (*stock*) provisión *f*; (*depot*) (*BRIT: large shop*) almacén *m*; (*us*) tienda; (*reserve*) reserva, repuesto ▷ *vt* almacenar; **stores** *npl* víveres *mpl*; **to be in ~ for sb** (*fig*) esperarle a algn; **storekeeper** (*us*) *n* tendero/a

storey ['stɔːrɪ] (*us* **story**) *n* piso

storm [stɔːm] *n* tormenta; (*fig: of*

applause) salva; (: *of criticism*) nube *f* ▷ *vi* (*fig*) rabiar ▷ *vt* tomar por asalto; **stormy** *adj* tempestuoso

story ['stɔːrɪ] *n* historia; (*lie*) mentira; (*us*) = **storey**

stout [staut] *adj* (*strong*) sólido; (*fat*) gordo, corpulento; (*resolute*) resuelto ▷ *n* cerveza negra

stove [stəʊv] *n* (*for cooking*) cocina; (*for heating*) estufa

straight [streɪt] *adj* recto, derecho; (*frank*) franco, directo; (*simple*) sencillo ▷ *adv* derecho, directamente; (*drink*) sin mezcla; **to put** *or* **get sth ~** dejar algo en claro; **~ away**, **~ off** en seguida; **straighten** *vt* (*also*: **straighten out**) enderezar, poner derecho ▷ *vi* (*also*: **straighten up**) enderezarse, ponerse derecho; **straightforward** *adj* (*simple*) sencillo; (*honest*) honrado, franco

strain [streɪn] *n* tensión *f*; (*Tech*) presión *f*; (*Med*) torcedura; (*breed*) tipo, variedad *f* ▷ *vt* (*back etc*) torcerse; (*resources*) agotar; (*stretch*) estirar; (*food, tea*) colar; **strained** *adj* (*muscle*) torcido; (*laugh*) forzado; (*relations*) tenso; **strainer** *n* colador *m*

strait [streɪt] *n* (*Geo*) estrecho (*fig*): **to be in dire ~s** estar en un gran apuro

strand [strænd] *n* (*of thread*) hebra; (*of hair*) trenza; (*of rope*) ramal *m*; **stranded** *adj* (*person: without money*) desamparado; (: *without transport*) colgado

strange [streɪndʒ] *adj* (*not known*) desconocido; (*odd*) extraño, raro; **strangely** *adv* de un modo raro; **stranger** *n* desconocido/a; (*from another area*) forastero/a

▌ Be careful not to translate **stranger** by the Spanish word *extranjero*.

strangle ['stræŋgl] *vt* estrangular

strap [stræp] *n* correa; (*of slip, dress*) tirante *m*

strategic [strə'tiːdʒɪk] *adj* estratégico

strategy ['strætɪdʒɪ] *n* estrategia

straw [strɔː] *n* paja; (*drinking straw*) caña, pajita; **that's the last ~!** ¡eso es el colmo!

strawberry ['strɔːbərɪ] *n* fresa, frutilla (*sc*)

stray [streɪ] *adj* (*animal*) extraviado; (*bullet*) perdido; (*scattered*) disperso ▷ *vi* extraviarse, perderse

streak [striːk] *n* raya; (*in hair*) raya ▷ *vt* rayar ▷ *vi*: **to ~ past** pasar como un rayo

stream [striːm] *n* riachuelo, arroyo; (*of people, vehicles*) riada, caravana; (*of smoke, insults etc*) chorro ▷ *vt* (*Scol*) dividir en grupos por habilidad ▷ *vi* correr, fluir; **to ~ in/out** (*people*) entrar/salir en tropel

street [striːt] *n* calle *f*; **streetcar** (*us*) *n* tranvía *m*; **street light** *n* farol *m* (*LAm*), farola (*sp*); **street map** *n* plano (de la ciudad); **street plan** *n* plano

strength [strɛŋθ] *n* fuerza; (*of girder, knot etc*) resistencia; (*fig: power*) poder *m*; **strengthen** *vt* fortalecer, reforzar

strenuous ['strɛnjuəs] *adj* (*energetic, determined*) enérgico

stress [strɛs] *n* presión *f*; (*mental strain*) estrés *m*; (*accent*) acento ▷ *vt* subrayar, recalcar; (*syllable*) acentuar; **stressed** *adj* (*tense*) estresado, agobiado; (*syllable*) acentuado; **stressful** *adj* (*job*) estresante

stretch [strɛtʃ] *n* (*of sand etc*) trecho ▷ *vi* estirarse; (*extend*): **to ~ to** *or* **as far as** extenderse hasta ▷ *vt* extender, estirar; (*make demands*) exigir el máximo esfuerzo a; **stretch out** *vi* tenderse ▷ *vt* (*arm etc*) extender; (*spread*) estirar

stretcher ['strɛtʃə*] *n* camilla

strict [strɪkt] *adj* severo; (*exact*) estricto; **strictly** *adv* severamente; estrictamente

stride [straɪd] (*pt* **strode**, *pp* **stridden**) *n* zancada, tranco ▷ *vi* dar zancadas, andar a trancos

strike [straɪk] (*pt, pp* **struck**) *n* huelga; (*of oil etc*) descubrimiento; (*attack*) ataque *m* ▷ *vt* golpear, pegar; (*oil etc*) descubrir; (*bargain, deal*) cerrar ▷ *vi* declarar la huelga; (*attack*) atacar; (*clock*) dar la hora; **on ~** (*workers*) en huelga; **to ~ a match** encender un fósforo; **striker** *n* huelguista *mf*; (*Sport*) delantero; **striking** *adj* llamativo

string [strɪŋ] (*pt, pp* **strung**) *n* cuerda; (*row*) hilera ▷ *vt*: **to ~ together** ensartar; **to ~ out** extenderse; **the strings** *npl* (*Mus*) los instrumentos de cuerda; **to pull ~s** (*fig*) mover palancas

strip [strɪp] *n* tira; (*of land*) franja; (*of metal*) cinta, lámina ▷ *vt* desnudar; (*paint*) quitar; (*also*: **~ down**: *machine*) desmontar ▷ *vi* desnudarse; **strip off** *vt* (*paint etc*) quitar ▷ *vi* (*person*) desnudarse

stripe [straɪp] *n* raya; (*Mil*) galón *m*; **striped** *adj* a rayas, rayado

stripper ['strɪpə*] *n* artista *mf* de striptease

strip-search ['strɪpsɜːtʃ] *vt*: **to ~ sb** desnudar y registrar a algn

strive [straɪv] (*pt* **strove**, *pp* **striven**) *vi*: **to ~ for sth/to do sth** luchar por conseguir/ hacer algo

strode [strəʊd] *pt of* **stride**

stroke [strəʊk] *n* (*blow*) golpe *m*; (*Swimming*) brazada; (*Med*) apoplejía; (*of paintbrush*) toque *m* ▷ *vt* acariciar; **at a ~** de un solo golpe

s

stroll [strəʊl] n paseo, vuelta ▷ vi dar un paseo or una vuelta; **stroller** (us) n (for child) sillita de ruedas

strong [strɒŋ] adj fuerte; **they are 50 ~** son 50; **stronghold** n fortaleza; (fig) baluarte m; **strongly** adv fuertemente, con fuerza; (believe) firmemente

strove [strəʊv] pt of **strive**

struck [strʌk] pt, pp of **strike**

structure ['strʌktʃə*] n estructura; (building) construcción f

struggle ['strʌgl] n lucha ▷ vi luchar

strung [strʌŋ] pt, pp of **string**

stub [stʌb] n (of ticket etc) talón m; (of cigarette) colilla; **to ~ one's toe on sth** dar con el dedo (del pie) contra algo; **stub out** vt apagar

stubble ['stʌbl] n rastrojo; (on chin) barba (incipiente)

stubborn ['stʌbən] adj terco, testarudo

stuck [stʌk] pt, pp of **stick** ▷ adj (jammed) atascado

stud [stʌd] n (shirt stud) corchete m; (of boot) taco; (earring) pendiente m (de bolita); (also: ~ **farm**) caballeriza; (also: ~ **horse**) caballo semental ▷ vt (fig): **~ded with** salpicado de

student ['stjuːdənt] n estudiante mf ▷ adj estudiantil; **student driver** (us) n conductor(a) mf en prácticas; **students' union** n (building) centro de estudiantes; (BRIT: association) federación f de estudiantes

studio ['stjuːdɪəʊ] n estudio; (artist's) taller m; **studio flat** n estudio

study ['stʌdɪ] n estudio ▷ vt estudiar; (examine) examinar, investigar ▷ vi estudiar

stuff [stʌf] n materia; (substance) material m, sustancia; (things) cosas fpl ▷ vt llenar; (Culin) rellenar; (animals) disecar; (inf: push) meter; **stuffing** n relleno; **stuffy** adj (room) mal ventilado; (person) de miras estrechas

stumble ['stʌmbl] vi tropezar, dar un traspié; **to ~ across, ~ on** (fig) tropezar con

stump [stʌmp] n (of tree) tocón m; (of limb) muñón m ▷ vt: **to be ~ed for an answer** no saber qué contestar

stun [stʌn] vt dejar sin sentido

stung [stʌŋ] pt, pp of **sting**

stunk [stʌŋk] pp of **stink**

stunned [stʌnd] adj (dazed) aturdido, atontado; (amazed) pasmado; (shocked) anonadado

stunning ['stʌnɪŋ] adj (fig: news) pasmoso; (: outfit etc) sensacional

stunt [stʌnt] n (in film) escena peligrosa; (publicity stunt) truco publicitario

stupid ['stjuːpɪd] adj estúpido, tonto; **stupidity** [-'pɪdɪtɪ] n estupidez f

sturdy ['stɜːdɪ] adj robusto, fuerte

stutter ['stʌtə*] n tartamudeo ▷ vi tartamudear

style [staɪl] n estilo; **stylish** adj elegante, a la moda; **stylist** n (hair stylist) peluquero/a

sub... [sʌb] prefix sub...; **subconscious** adj subconsciente

subdued [səb'djuːd] adj (light) tenue; (person) sumiso, manso

subject [n 'sʌbdʒɪkt, vb səb'dʒɛkt] n súbdito; (Scol) asignatura; (matter) tema m; (Grammar) sujeto ▷ vt: **to ~ sb to sth** someter a algn a algo; **to be ~ to** (law) estar sujeto a; (person) ser propenso a; **subjective** [-'dʒɛktɪv] adj subjetivo; **subject matter** n (content) contenido

subjunctive [səb'dʒʌŋktɪv] adj, n subjuntivo

submarine [sʌbmə'riːn] n submarino

submission [səb'mɪʃən] n sumisión f

submit [səb'mɪt] vt someter ▷ vi: **to ~ to sth** someterse a algo

subordinate [sə'bɔːdɪnət] adj, n subordinado/a m/f

subscribe [səb'skraɪb] vi suscribir; **to ~ to** (opinion, fund) suscribir, aprobar; (newspaper) suscribirse a

subscription [səb'skrɪpʃən] n abono; (to magazine) subscripción f

subsequent ['sʌbsɪkwənt] adj subsiguiente, posterior; **subsequently** adv posteriormente, más tarde

subside [səb'saɪd] vi hundirse; (flood) bajar; (wind) amainar

subsidiary [səb'sɪdɪərɪ] adj secundario ▷ n sucursal f, filial f

subsidize ['sʌbsɪdaɪz] vt subvencionar

subsidy ['sʌbsɪdɪ] n subvención f

substance ['sʌbstəns] n sustancia

substantial [səb'stænʃl] adj sustancial, sustancioso; (fig) importante

substitute ['sʌbstɪtjuːt] n (person) suplente mf; (thing) sustituto ▷ vt: **to ~ A for B** sustituir A por B, reemplazar B por A; **substitution** n sustitución f

subtle ['sʌtl] adj sutil

subtract [səb'trækt] vt restar, sustraer

suburb ['sʌbəːb] n barrio residencial; **the ~s** las afueras (de la ciudad); **suburban** [sə'bəːbən] adj suburbano; (train etc) de cercanías

subway ['sʌbweɪ] n (BRIT) paso subterráneo or inferior; (us) metro

succeed [sək'siːd] vi (person) tener éxito; (plan) salir bien ▷ vt suceder a; **to ~ in**

doing lograr hacer
success [sək'sɛs] n éxito

> Be careful not to translate **success** by the Spanish word *suceso*.

successful adj exitoso; (business) próspero;
to be successful (in doing) lograr (hacer);
successfully adv con éxito
succession [sək'sɛʃən] n sucesión f, serie f
successive [sək'sɛsɪv] adj sucesivo, consecutivo
successor [sək'sɛsə*] n sucesor(a) m/f
succumb [sə'kʌm] vi sucumbir
such [sʌtʃ] adj tal, semejante; (of that kind): **~ a book** tal libro; (so much): **~ courage** tanto valor ▷ adv tan; **~ a long trip** un viaje tan largo; **~ a lot of** tanto(s)/a(s); **~ as** (like) tal como; **as ~** como tal; **such-and-such** adj tal o cual
suck [sʌk] vt chupar; (bottle) sorber; (breast) mamar
Sudan [su'dæn] n Sudán m
sudden ['sʌdn] adj (rapid) repentino, súbito; (unexpected) imprevisto; **all of a ~** de repente; **suddenly** adv de repente
sue [su:] vt demandar
suede [sweɪd] n ante m, gamuza
suffer ['sʌfə*] vt sufrir, padecer; (tolerate) aguantar, soportar ▷ vi sufrir; **to ~ from** (illness etc) padecer; **suffering** n sufrimiento
suffice [sə'faɪs] vi bastar, ser suficiente
sufficient [sə'fɪʃənt] adj suficiente, bastante
suffocate ['sʌfəkeɪt] vi ahogarse, asfixiarse
sugar ['ʃugə*] n azúcar m ▷ vt echar azúcar a, azucarar
suggest [sə'dʒɛst] vt sugerir; **suggestion** [-'dʒɛstʃən] n sugerencia
suicide ['suɪsaɪd] n suicidio; (person) suicida mf; see also **commit**; **suicide attack** n atentado suicida; **suicide bomber** n terrorista mf suicida; **suicide bombing** n atentado suicida
suit [su:t] n (man's) traje m; (woman's) conjunto; (Law) pleito; (Cards) palo ▷ vt convenir; (clothes) sentar a, ir bien a; (adapt): **to ~ sth to** adaptar or ajustar algo a; **well ~ed** (well matched: couple) hecho el uno para el otro; **suitable** adj conveniente; (apt) indicado; **suitcase** n maleta, valija (RPL)
suite [swi:t] n (of rooms, Mus) suite f; (furniture): **bedroom/dining room ~** (juego de) dormitorio/comedor; see also **three-piece suite**
sulfur ['sʌlfə*] (US) n = **sulphur**
sulk [sʌlk] vi estar de mal humor
sulphur ['sʌlfə*] (US **sulfur**) n azufre m

sultana [sʌl'tɑ:nə] n (fruit) pasa de Esmirna
sum [sʌm] n suma; (total) total m; **sum up** vt resumir ▷ vi hacer un resumen
summarize ['sʌməraɪz] vt resumir
summary ['sʌmərɪ] n resumen m ▷ adj (justice) sumario
summer ['sʌmə*] n verano ▷ cpd de verano; **in ~** en verano; **summer holidays** npl vacaciones fpl de verano; **summertime** n (season) verano
summit ['sʌmɪt] n cima, cumbre f; (also: **~ conference**, **~ meeting**) (conferencia) cumbre f
summon ['sʌmən] vt (person) llamar; (meeting) convocar; (Law) citar
Sun. abbr (= Sunday) dom
sun [sʌn] n sol m; **sunbathe** vi tomar el sol; **sunbed** n cama solar; **sunblock** n filtro solar; **sunburn** n (painful) quemadura; (tan) bronceado; **sunburned, sunburnt** adj (painfully) quemado por el sol; (tanned) bronceado
Sunday ['sʌndɪ] n domingo
sunflower ['sʌnflauə*] n girasol m
sung [sʌŋ] pp of **sing**
sunglasses ['sʌnglɑ:sɪz] npl gafas fpl (SP) or anteojos fpl (LAM) de sol
sunk [sʌŋk] pp of **sink**
sun: sunlight n luz f del sol; **sun lounger** n tumbona, perezosa (LAM); **sunny** adj soleado; (day) alegre; (fig) alegre; **sunrise** n salida del sol; **sun roof** n (Aut) techo corredizo; **sunscreen** n protector m solar; **sunset** n puesta del sol; **sunshade** n (over table) sombrilla; **sunshine** n sol m; **sunstroke** n insolación f; **suntan** n bronceado; **suntan lotion** n bronceador m; **suntan oil** n aceite m bronceador
super ['su:pə*] (inf) adj genial
superb [su:'pə:b] adj magnífico, espléndido
superficial [su:pə'fɪʃəl] adj superficial
superintendent [su:pərɪn'tɛndənt] n director(a) m/f; (Police) subjefe/a m/f
superior [su'pɪərɪə*] adj superior; (smug) desdeñoso ▷ n superior m
superlative [su'pə:lətɪv] n superlativo
supermarket ['su:pəmɑ:kɪt] n supermercado
supernatural [su:pə'nætʃərəl] adj sobrenatural ▷ n: **the ~** lo sobrenatural
superpower ['su:pəpauə*] n (Pol) superpotencia
superstition [su:pə'stɪʃən] n superstición f
superstitious [su:pə'stɪʃəs] adj supersticioso

S

superstore ['su:pəstɔ:*] n (BRIT)
hipermercado
supervise ['su:pəvaɪz] vt supervisar;
supervision [-'vɪʒən] n supervisión f;
supervisor n supervisor(a) m/f
supper ['sʌpə*] n cena
supple ['sʌpl] adj flexible
supplement [n 'sʌplɪmənt, vb sʌplɪ'mɛnt]
n suplemento ▷ vt suplir
supplier [sə'plaɪə*] n (Comm)
distribuidor(a) m/f
supply [sə'plaɪ] vt (provide) suministrar;
(equip): **to ~ (with)** proveer (de) ▷ n
provisión f; (of gas, water etc) suministro;
supplies npl (food) víveres mpl; (Mil)
pertrechos mpl
support [sə'pɔ:t] n apoyo; (Tech) soporte
m ▷ vt apoyar; (financially) mantener;
(uphold, Tech) sostener

> Be careful not to translate **support** by
> the Spanish word soportar.

supporter n (Pol etc) partidario/a; (Sport)
aficionado/a
suppose [sə'pəuz] vt suponer; (imagine)
imaginarse; (duty): **to be ~d to do sth** deber
hacer algo; **supposedly** [sə'pəuzɪdlɪ] adv
según cabe suponer; **supposing** conj en
caso de que
suppress [sə'prɛs] vt suprimir; (yawn)
ahogar
supreme [su'pri:m] adj supremo
surcharge ['sə:tʃɑ:dʒ] n sobretasa,
recargo
sure [ʃuə*] adj seguro; (definite, convinced)
cierto; **to make ~ of sth/that** asegurarse
de algo/asegurar que; **~!** (of course) ¡claro!,
¡por supuesto!; **~ enough** efectivamente;
surely adv (certainly) seguramente
surf [sə:f] n olas fpl ▷ vt: **to ~ the Net**
navegar por Internet
surface ['sə:fɪs] n superficie f ▷ vt (road)
revestir ▷ vi salir a la superficie; **by ~ mail**
por vía terrestre
surfboard ['sə:fbɔ:d] n tabla (de surf)
surfer ['sə:fə*] n (in sea) surfista mf; **web** or
net ~ internauta mf
surfing ['sə:fɪŋ] n surf m
surge [sə:dʒ] n oleada, oleaje m ▷ vi (wave)
romper; (people) avanzar en tropel
surgeon ['sə:dʒən] n cirujano/a
surgery ['sə:dʒərɪ] n cirugía; (BRIT: room)
consultorio
surname ['sə:neɪm] n apellido
surpass [sə:'pɑ:s] vt superar, exceder
surplus ['sə:pləs] n excedente m; (Comm)
superávit m ▷ adj excedente, sobrante
surprise [sə'praɪz] n sorpresa ▷ vt
sorprender; **surprised** adj (look, smile) de

sorpresa; **to be surprised** sorprenderse;
surprising adj sorprendente; **surprisingly**
adv: **it was surprisingly easy** me etc
sorprendió lo fácil que fue
surrender [sə'rɛndə*] n rendición f,
entrega ▷ vi rendirse, entregarse
surround [sə'raund] vt rodear,
circundar; (Mil etc) cercar; **surrounding**
adj circundante; **surroundings** npl
alrededores mpl, cercanías fpl
surveillance [sə:'veɪləns] n vigilancia
survey [n 'sə:veɪ, vb sə:'veɪ] n inspección
f, reconocimiento; (inquiry) encuesta ▷ vt
examinar, inspeccionar; (look at) mirar,
contemplar; **surveyor** n agrimensor(a) m/f
survival [sə'vaɪvl] n supervivencia
survive [sə'vaɪv] vi sobrevivir; (custom
etc) perdurar ▷ vt sobrevivir a; **survivor** n
superviviente mf
suspect [adj, n 'sʌspɛkt, vb səs'pɛkt] adj, n
sospechoso/a m/f ▷ vt (person) sospechar
de; (think) sospechar
suspend [səs'pɛnd] vt suspender;
suspended sentence n (Law) libertad f
condicional; **suspenders** npl (BRIT) ligas
fpl; (US) tirantes mpl
suspense [səs'pɛns] n incertidumbre f,
duda; (in film etc) suspense m; **to keep sb in
~** mantener a algn en suspense
suspension [səs'pɛnʃən] n (gen, Aut)
suspensión f; (of driving licence) privación f;
suspension bridge n puente m colgante
suspicion [səs'pɪʃən] n sospecha; (distrust)
recelo; **suspicious** adj receloso; (causing
suspicion) sospechoso
sustain [səs'teɪn] vt sostener, apoyar;
(suffer) sufrir, padecer
SUV (esp US) n abbr (= sports utility vehicle)
todoterreno m inv, 4x4 m
swallow ['swɔləu] n (bird) golondrina ▷ vt
tragar; (fig.: pride) tragarse
swam [swæm] pt of **swim**
swamp [swɔmp] n pantano, ciénaga
▷ vt (with water etc) inundar; (fig) abrumar,
agobiar
swan [swɔn] n cisne m
swap [swɔp] n canje m, intercambio
▷ vt: **to ~ (for)** cambiar (por)
swarm [swɔ:m] n (of bees) enjambre
m; (fig) multitud f ▷ vi (bees) formar un
enjambre; (people) pulular; **to be ~ing with**
ser un hervidero de
sway [sweɪ] vi mecerse, balancearse ▷ vt
(influence) mover, influir en
swear [swɛə*] (pt swore, pp sworn) vi
(curse) maldecir; (promise) jurar ▷ vt jurar;
swear in vt: **to be sworn in** prestar
juramento; **swearword** n taco, palabrota

sweat [swɛt] n sudor m ▷ vi sudar
sweater ['swɛtə*] n suéter m
sweatshirt ['swɛtʃəːt] n suéter m
sweaty ['swɛtɪ] adj sudoroso
Swede [swiːd] n sueco/a
swede [swiːd] (BRIT) n nabo
Sweden ['swiːdn] n Suecia; **Swedish** ['swiːdɪʃ] adj sueco ▷ n (Ling) sueco
sweep [swiːp] (pt, pp **swept**) n (act) barrido; (also: **chimney ~**) deshollinador(a) m/f ▷ vt barrer; (with arm) empujar; (current) arrastrar ▷ vi barrer; (arm etc) moverse rápidamente; (wind) soplar con violencia
sweet [swiːt] n (candy) dulce m, caramelo; (BRIT: pudding) postre m ▷ adj dulce; (fig: kind) dulce, amable; (: attractive) mono; **sweetcorn** n maíz m; **sweetener** ['swiːtnə*] n (Culin) edulcorante m; **sweetheart** n novio/a; **sweetshop** n (BRIT) confitería, bombonería
swell [swɛl] (pt **~ed**, pp **swollen** or **~ed**) n (of sea) marejada, oleaje m ▷ adj (US: inf: excellent) estupendo, fenomenal ▷ vt hinchar, inflar ▷ vi (also: **~ up**) hincharse; (numbers) aumentar; (sound, feeling) ir aumentando; **swelling** n (Med) hinchazón f
swept [swɛpt] pt, pp of **sweep**
swerve [swəːv] vi desviarse bruscamente
swift [swɪft] n (bird) vencejo ▷ adj rápido, veloz
swim [swɪm] (pt **swam**, pp **swum**) n: **to go for a ~** ir a nadar or a bañarse ▷ vi nadar; (head, room) dar vueltas ▷ vt nadar; (the Channel etc) cruzar a nado; **swimmer** n nadador(a) m/f; **swimming** n natación f; **swimming costume** (BRIT) n bañador m, traje m de baño; **swimming pool** n piscina, alberca (MEX), pileta (RPL); **swimming trunks** npl bañador m (de hombre); **swimsuit** n = **swimming costume**
swing [swɪŋ] (pt, pp **swung**) n (in playground) columpio; (movement) balanceo, vaivén m; (change of direction) viraje m; (rhythm) ritmo ▷ vt balancear; (also: **~ round**) voltear, girar ▷ vi balancearse, columpiarse; (also: **~ round**) dar media vuelta; **to be in full ~** estar en plena marcha
swipe card [swaɪp-] n tarjeta magnética deslizante, tarjeta swipe
swirl [swəːl] vi arremolinarse
Swiss [swɪs] adj, n inv suizo/a m/f
switch [swɪtʃ] n (for light etc) interruptor m; (change) cambio ▷ vt (change) cambiar de; **switch off** vt apagar; (engine) parar; **switch on** vt encender (SP), prender (LAM); (engine, machine) arrancar; **switchboard** n (Tel) centralita (SP), conmutador m (LAM)
Switzerland ['swɪtsələnd] n Suiza

swivel ['swɪvl] vi (also: **~ round**) girar
swollen ['swəʊlən] pp of **swell**
swoop [swuːp] n (by police etc) redada ▷ vi (also: **~ down**) calarse
swop [swɔp] = **swap**
sword [sɔːd] n espada; **swordfish** n pez m espada
swore [swɔː*] pt of **swear**
sworn [swɔːn] pp of **swear** ▷ adj (statement) bajo juramento; (enemy) implacable
swum [swʌm] pp of **swim**
swung [swʌŋ] pt, pp of **swing**
syllable ['sɪləbl] n sílaba
syllabus ['sɪləbəs] n programa m de estudios
symbol ['sɪmbl] n símbolo; **symbolic(al)** [sɪm'bɔlɪk(l)] adj simbólico; **to be symbolic(al) of sth** simbolizar algo
symmetrical [sɪ'mɛtrɪkl] adj simétrico
symmetry ['sɪmɪtrɪ] n simetría
sympathetic [sɪmpə'θɛtɪk] adj (understanding) comprensivo; (showing support): **~ to(wards)** bien dispuesto hacia

▌ Be careful not to translate **sympathetic** by the Spanish word simpático.

sympathize ['sɪmpəθaɪz] vi: **to ~ with** (person) compadecerse de; (feelings) comprender; (cause) apoyar
sympathy ['sɪmpəθɪ] n (pity) compasión f
symphony ['sɪmfənɪ] n sinfonía
symptom ['sɪmptəm] n síntoma m, indicio
synagogue ['sɪnəgɔg] n sinagoga
syndicate ['sɪndɪkɪt] n sindicato; (of newspapers) agencia (de noticias)
syndrome ['sɪndrəum] n síndrome m
synonym ['sɪnənɪm] n sinónimo
synthetic [sɪn'θɛtɪk] adj sintético
Syria ['sɪrɪə] n Siria
syringe [sɪ'rɪndʒ] n jeringa
syrup ['sɪrəp] n jarabe m; (also: **golden ~**) almíbar m
system ['sɪstəm] n sistema m; (Anat) organismo; **systematic** [-'mætɪk] adj sistemático, metódico; **systems analyst** n analista m/f de sistemas

s

t

ta [tɑː] (*BRIT: inf*) *excl* ¡gracias!
tab [tæb] *n* lengüeta; (*label*) etiqueta; **to keep ~s on** (*fig*) vigilar
table ['teɪbl] *n* mesa; (*of statistics etc*) cuadro, tabla ▷ *vt* (*BRIT: motion etc*) presentar; **to lay** *or* **set the ~** poner la mesa; **tablecloth** *n* mantel *m*; **table d'hôte** [tɑːbl'dəʊt] *adj* del menú; **table lamp** *n* lámpara de mesa; **tablemat** *n* (*for plate*) posaplatos *m inv*; (*for hot dish*) salvamantel *m*; **tablespoon** *n* cuchara de servir; (*also:* **tablespoonful**: *as measurement*) cucharada
tablet ['tæblɪt] *n* (*Med*) pastilla, comprimido; (*of stone*) lápida
table tennis *n* ping-pong *m*, tenis *m* de mesa
tabloid ['tæblɔɪd] *n* periódico popular sensacionalista

taboo [tə'buː] *adj*, *n* tabú *m*
tack [tæk] *n* (*nail*) tachuela; (*fig*) rumbo ▷ *vt* (*nail*) clavar con tachuelas; (*stitch*) hilvanar ▷ *vi* virar
tackle ['tækl] *n* (*fishing tackle*) aparejo (de pescar); (*for lifting*) aparejo ▷ *vt* (*difficulty*) enfrentarse con; (*challenge: person*) hacer frente a; (*grapple with*) agarrar; (*Football*) cargar; (*Rugby*) placar
tacky ['tækɪ] *adj* pegajoso; (*pej*) cutre
tact [tækt] *n* tacto, discreción *f*; **tactful** *adj* discreto, diplomático
tactics ['tæktɪks] *npl* táctica
tactless ['tæktlɪs] *adj* indiscreto
tadpole ['tædpəʊl] *n* renacuajo
taffy ['tæfɪ] (*US*) *n* melcocha
tag [tæg] *n* (*label*) etiqueta
tail [teɪl] *n* cola; (*of shirt, coat*) faldón *m* ▷ *vt* (*follow*) vigilar a; **tails** *npl* (*formal suit*) levita
tailor ['teɪlə*] *n* sastre *m*
Taiwan [taɪ'wɑːn] *n* Taiwán *m*; **Taiwanese** [taɪwə'niːz] *adj*, *n* taiwanés/esa *m/f*
take [teɪk] (*pt* **took**, *pp* **taken**) *vt* tomar; (*grab*) coger (*SP*), agarrar (*LAM*); (*gain: prize*) ganar; (*require: effort, courage*) exigir; (*tolerate: pain etc*) aguantar; (*hold: passengers etc*) tener cabida para; (*accompany, bring, carry*) llevar; (*exam*) presentarse a; **to ~ sth from** (*drawer etc*) sacar algo de; (*person*) quitar algo a; **I ~ it that ...** supongo que ...; **take after** *vt fus* parecerse a; **take apart** *vt* desmontar; **take away** *vt* (*remove*) quitar; (*carry*) llevar; (*Math*) restar; **take back** *vt* (*return*) devolver; (*one's words*) retractarse de; **take down** *vt* (*building*) derribar; (*letter etc*) apuntar; **take in** *vt* (*deceive*) engañar; (*understand*) entender; (*include*) abarcar; (*lodger*) acoger, recibir; **take off** *vi* (*Aviat*) despegar ▷ *vt* (*remove*) quitar; **take on** *vt* (*work*) aceptar; (*employee*) contratar; (*opponent*) desafiar; **take out** *vt* sacar; **take over** *vt* (*business*) tomar posesión de; (*country*) tomar el poder ▷ *vi*: **to take over from sb** reemplazar a algn; **take up** *vt* (*a dress*) acortar; (*occupy: time, space*) ocupar; (*engage in: hobby etc*) dedicarse a; (*accept*): **to take sb up on** aceptar algo de algn; **takeaway** (*BRIT*) *adj* (*food*) para llevar ▷ *n* tienda *or* restaurante *m* de comida para llevar; **taken** *pp of* **take**; **takeoff** *n* (*Aviat*) despegue *m*; **takeout** (*US*) *n* = **takeaway**; **takeover** *n* (*Comm*) absorción *f*; **takings** *npl* (*Comm*) ingresos *mpl*
talc [tælk] *n* (*also:* **~um powder**) (polvos de) talco
tale [teɪl] *n* (*story*) cuento; (*account*) relación *f*; **to tell ~s** (*fig*) chivarse
talent ['tælnt] *n* talento; **talented** *adj* de talento
talk [tɔːk] *n* charla; (*conversation*) conversación *f*; (*gossip*) habladurías *fpl*, chismes *mpl* ▷ *vi* hablar; **talks** *npl* (*Pol etc*) conversaciones *fpl*; **to ~ about** hablar de; **to ~ sb into doing sth** convencer a algn para que haga algo; **to ~ sb out of doing sth**

disuadir a algn de que haga algo; **to ~ shop** hablar del trabajo; **talk over** vt discutir; **talk show** n programa m de entrevistas

tall [tɔ:l] adj alto; (object) grande; **to be 6 feet ~** (person) ≈ medir 1 metro 80

tambourine [tæmbə'ri:n] n pandereta

tame [teɪm] adj domesticado; (fig) mediocre

tamper ['tæmpə*] vi: **to ~ with** tocar, andar con

tampon ['tæmpən] n tampón m

tan [tæn] n (also: **sun~**) bronceado ▷ vi ponerse moreno ▷ adj (colour) marrón

tandem ['tændəm] n tándem m

tangerine [tændʒə'ri:n] n mandarina

tangle ['tæŋgl] n enredo; **to get in(to) a ~** enredarse

tank [tæŋk] n (water tank) depósito, tanque m; (for fish) acuario; (Mil) tanque m

tanker ['tæŋkə*] n (ship) buque m, cisterna; (truck) camión m cisterna

tanned [tænd] adj (skin) moreno

tantrum ['tæntrəm] n rabieta

Tanzania [tænzə'nɪə] n Tanzania

tap [tæp] n (BRIT: on sink etc) grifo (SP), llave f, canilla (RPL); (gas tap) llave f; (gentle blow) golpecito ▷ vt (hit gently) dar golpecitos en; (resources) utilizar, explotar; (telephone) intervenir; **on ~** (fig: resources) a mano; **tap dancing** n claqué m

tape [teɪp] n (also: **magnetic ~**) cinta magnética; (cassette) cassette f, cinta; (sticky tape) cinta adhesiva; (for tying) cinta ▷ vt (record) grabar (en cinta); (stick with tape) pegar con cinta adhesiva; **tape measure** n cinta métrica, metro; **tape recorder** n grabadora

tapestry ['tæpɪstrɪ] n (object) tapiz m; (art) tapicería

tar [tɑ:] n alquitrán m, brea

target ['tɑ:gɪt] n blanco

tariff ['tærɪf] n (on goods) arancel m; (BRIT: in hotels etc) tarifa

tarmac ['tɑ:mæk] n (BRIT: on road) asfaltado; (Aviat) pista (de aterrizaje)

tarpaulin [tɑ:'pɔ:lɪn] n lona impermeabilizada

tarragon ['tærəgən] n estragón m

tart [tɑ:t] n (Culin) tarta; (BRIT: inf: prostitute) puta ▷ adj agrio, ácido

tartan ['tɑ:tn] n tejido escocés m

tartar(e) sauce ['tɑ:tə-] n salsa tártara

task [tɑ:sk] n tarea; **to take to ~** reprender

taste [teɪst] n (sense) gusto; (flavour) sabor m; (sample): **have a ~!** ¡prueba un poquito!; (fig) muestra, idea ▷ vt probar ▷ vi: **to ~ of** or **like** (fish, garlic etc) saber a; **you can ~ the garlic (in it)** se nota el sabor a ajo; **in**

good/bad ~ de buen/mal gusto; **tasteful** adj de buen gusto; **tasteless** adj (food) soso; (remark etc) de mal gusto; **tasty** adj sabroso, rico

tatters ['tætəz] npl: **in ~** hecho jirones

tattoo [tə'tu:] n tatuaje m; (spectacle) espectáculo militar ▷ vt tatuar

taught [tɔ:t] pt, pp of **teach**

taunt [tɔ:nt] n burla ▷ vt burlarse de

Taurus ['tɔ:rəs] n Tauro

taut [tɔ:t] adj tirante, tenso

tax [tæks] n impuesto ▷ vt gravar (con un impuesto); (fig: memory) poner a prueba; (: patience) agotar; **tax-free** adj libre de impuestos

taxi ['tæksɪ] n taxi m ▷ vi (Aviat) rodar por la pista; **taxi driver** n taxista mf; **taxi rank** (BRIT) n = **taxi stand; taxi stand** n parada de taxis

tax payer n contribuyente mf

TB n abbr = **tuberculosis**

tea [ti:] n té m; (BRIT: meal) ≈ merienda (SP); cena; **high ~** (BRIT) merienda-cena (SP); **tea bag** n bolsita de té; **tea break** (BRIT) n descanso para el té

teach [ti:tʃ] (pt, pp **taught**) vt: **to ~ sb sth, ~ sth to sb** enseñar algo a algn ▷ vi (be a teacher) ser profesor(a), enseñar; **teacher** n (in secondary school) profesor(a) m/f; (in primary school) maestro/a, profesor(a) de EGB; **teaching** n enseñanza

tea: tea cloth n (BRIT) paño de cocina, trapo de cocina (LAM); **teacup** n taza para el té

tea leaves npl hojas de té

team [ti:m] n equipo; (of horses) tiro; **team up** vi asociarse

teapot ['ti:pɔt] n tetera

tear¹ [tɪə*] n lágrima; **in ~s** llorando

tear² [tɛə*] (pt **tore**, pp **torn**) n rasgón m, desgarrón m ▷ vt romper, rasgar ▷ vi rasgarse; **tear apart** vt (also fig) hacer pedazos; **tear down** vt +adv (building, statue) derribar; (poster, flag) arrancar; **tear off** vt (sheet of paper etc) arrancar; (one's clothes) quitarse a tirones; **tear up** vt (sheet of paper etc) romper

tearful ['tɪəfəl] adj lloroso

tear gas ['tɪə-] n gas m lacrimógeno

tearoom ['ti:ru:m] n salón m de té

tease [ti:z] vt tomar el pelo a

tea: teaspoon n cucharita; (also: **teaspoonful**: as measurement) cucharadita; **teatime** n hora del té; **tea towel** (BRIT) n paño de cocina

technical ['tɛknɪkl] adj técnico

technician [tɛk'nɪʃn] n técnico/a

technique [tɛk'ni:k] n técnica

technology [tɛk'nɔlədʒɪ] n tecnología

teddy (bear) ['tɛdɪ-] n osito de felpa
tedious ['ti:dɪəs] adj pesado, aburrido
tee [ti:] n (Golf) tee m
teen [ti:n] adj = **teenage** ▷ n (US) = **teenager**
teenage ['ti:neɪdʒ] adj (fashions etc) juvenil; (children) quinceañero; **teenager** n adolescente mf
teens [ti:nz] npl: **to be in one's ~** ser adolescente
teeth [ti:θ] npl of **tooth**
teetotal [ti:'təutl] adj abstemio
telecommunications [tɛlɪkəmju:nɪ'keɪʃənz] n telecomunicaciones fpl
telegram ['tɛlɪɡræm] n telegrama m
telegraph pole ['tɛlɪɡrɑ:f-] n poste m telegráfico
telephone ['tɛlɪfəun] n teléfono ▷ vt llamar por teléfono, telefonear; (message) dar por teléfono; **to be on the ~** (talking) hablar por teléfono; (possessing telephone) tener teléfono; **telephone book** n guía f telefónica; **telephone booth, telephone box** (BRIT) n cabina telefónica; **telephone call** n llamada (telefónica); **telephone directory** n guía (telefónica); **telephone number** n número de teléfono
telesales ['tɛlɪseɪlz] npl televenta(s) (f(pl))
telescope ['tɛlɪskəup] n telescopio
televise ['tɛlɪvaɪz] vt televisar
television ['tɛlɪvɪʒən] n televisión f; **on ~** en la televisión; **television programme** n programa m de televisión
tell [tɛl] (pt, pp **told**) vt decir; (relate: story) contar; (distinguish): **to ~ sth from** distinguir algo de ▷ vi (talk): **to ~ (of)** contar; (have effect) tener efecto; **to ~ sb to do sth** mandar a algn hacer algo; **tell off** vt: **to tell sb off** regañar a algn; **teller** n (in bank) cajero/a
telly ['tɛlɪ] (BRIT: inf) n abbr (= television) tele f
temp [tɛmp] n abbr (BRIT) (= temporary) temporero/a
temper ['tɛmpə*] n (nature) carácter m; (mood) humor m; (bad temper) (mal) genio; (fit of anger) acceso de ira ▷ vt (moderate) moderar; **to be in a ~** estar furioso; **to lose one's ~** enfadarse, enojarse
temperament ['tɛmprəmənt] n (nature) temperamento; **temperamental** [tɛmprə'mɛntl] adj temperamental
temperature ['tɛmprətʃə*] n temperatura; **to have** or **run a ~** tener fiebre
temple ['tɛmpl] n (building) templo; (Anat) sien f
temporary ['tɛmpərərɪ] adj provisional;

(passing) transitorio; (worker) temporero; (job) temporal
tempt [tɛmpt] vt tentar; **to ~ sb into doing sth** tentar or inducir a algn a hacer algo; **temptation** n tentación f; **tempting** adj tentador(a); (food) apetitoso/a
ten [tɛn] num diez
tenant ['tɛnənt] n inquilino/a
tend [tɛnd] vt cuidar ▷ vi: **to ~ to do sth** tener tendencia a hacer algo; **tendency** ['tɛndənsɪ] n tendencia
tender ['tɛndə*] adj (person, care) tierno, cariñoso; (meat) tierno; (sore) sensible ▷ n (Comm: offer) oferta; (money): **legal ~** moneda de curso legal ▷ vt ofrecer
tendon ['tɛndən] n tendón m
tenner ['tɛnə*] n (inf) (billete m de) diez libras m
tennis ['tɛnɪs] n tenis m; **tennis ball** n pelota de tenis; **tennis court** n cancha de tenis; **tennis match** n partido de tenis; **tennis player** n tenista mf; **tennis racket** n raqueta de tenis
tenor ['tɛnə*] n (Mus) tenor m
tenpin bowling ['tɛnpɪn-] n (juego de los) bolos
tense [tɛns] adj (person) nervioso; (moment, atmosphere) tenso; (muscle) tenso, en tensión ▷ n (Ling) tiempo
tension ['tɛnʃən] n tensión f
tent [tɛnt] n tienda (de campaña) (SP), carpa (LAM)
tentative ['tɛntətɪv] adj (person, smile) indeciso; (conclusion, plans) provisional
tenth [tɛnθ] num décimo
tent: **tent peg** n clavija, estaca; **tent pole** n mástil m
tepid ['tɛpɪd] adj tibio
term [tə:m] n (word) término; (period) período; (Scol) trimestre m ▷ vt llamar; **terms** npl (conditions, Comm) condiciones fpl; **in the short/long ~** a corto/largo plazo; **to be on good ~s with sb** llevarse bien con algn; **to come to ~s with** (problem) aceptar
terminal ['tə:mɪnl] adj (disease) mortal; (patient) terminal ▷ n (Elec) borne m; (Comput) terminal m; (also: **air ~**) terminal f; (BRIT: also: **coach ~**) estación f terminal f
terminate ['tə:mɪneɪt] vt terminar
termini ['tə:mɪnaɪ] npl of **terminus**
terminology [tə:mɪ'nɔlədʒɪ] n terminología
terminus ['tə:mɪnəs] (pl **termini**) n término, (estación f) terminal f
terrace ['tɛrəs] n terraza; (BRIT: row of houses) hilera de casas adosadas; **the ~s** (BRIT Sport) las gradas fpl; **terraced** adj (garden) en terrazas; (house) adosado

terrain [tɛ'reɪn] n terreno
terrestrial [tɪ'rɛstrɪəl] adj (life) terrestre; (BRIT: channel) de transmisión (por) vía terrestre
terrible ['tɛrɪbl] adj terrible, horrible; (inf) atroz; **terribly** adv terriblemente; (very badly) malísimamente
terrier ['tɛrɪə*] n terrier m
terrific [tə'rɪfɪk] adj (very great) tremendo; (wonderful) fantástico, fenomenal
terrified ['tɛrɪfaɪd] adj aterrorizado
terrify ['tɛrɪfaɪ] vt aterrorizar; **terrifying** adj aterrador(a)
territorial [tɛrɪ'tɔːrɪəl] adj territorial
territory ['tɛrɪtərɪ] n territorio
terror ['tɛrə*] n terror m; **terrorism** n terrorismo; **terrorist** n terrorista mf; **terrorist attack** n atentado (terrorista)
test [tɛst] n (gen, Chem) prueba; (Med) examen m; (Scol) examen m, test m; (also: **driving ~**) examen m de conducir ▷ vt probar, poner a prueba; (Med, Scol) examinar
testicle ['tɛstɪkl] n testículo
testify ['tɛstɪfaɪ] vi (Law) prestar declaración; **to ~ to sth** atestiguar algo
testimony ['tɛstɪmənɪ] n (Law) testimonio
test: **test match** n (Cricket, Rugby) partido internacional; **test tube** n probeta
tetanus ['tɛtənəs] n tétano
text [tɛkst] n texto; (on mobile phone) mensaje m de texto ▷ vt: **to ~ sb** (inf) enviar un mensaje (de texto) or un SMS a algn; **textbook** n libro de texto
textile ['tɛkstaɪl] n textil m, tejido
text message n mensaje m de texto
text messaging [-'mɛsɪdʒɪn] n (envío de) mensajes mpl
texture ['tɛkstʃə*] n textura
Thai [taɪ] adj, n tailandés/esa m/f
Thailand ['taɪlænd] n Tailandia
than [ðæn] conj (in comparisons): **more ~ 10/once** más de 10/una vez; **I have more/less ~ you/Paul** tengo más/menos que tú/Paul; **she is older ~ you think** es mayor de lo que piensas
thank [θæŋk] vt dar las gracias a, agradecer; **~ you (very much)** muchas gracias; **~ God!** ¡gracias a Dios! ▷ excl (also: **many ~s, ~s a lot**) ¡gracias! ▷ **~s to** prep gracias a; **thanks** npl gracias fpl; **thankfully** adv (fortunately) afortunadamente; **Thanksgiving (Day)** n día m de Acción de Gracias

○ **KEYWORD**

that [ðæt] (pl **those**) adj (demonstrative) ese/a; (pl) esos/as; (more remote) aquel(aquella); (pl) aquellos/as; **leave those books on the table** deja esos libros sobre la mesa; **that one** ése(ésa); (more remote) aquél(aquélla); **that one over there** ése(ésa) de ahí; aquél(aquélla) de allí
▷ pron **1** (demonstrative) ése/a; (pl) ésos/as; (neuter) eso; (more remote) aquél(aquélla); (pl) aquéllos/as; (neuter) aquello; **what's that?** ¿qué es eso (or aquello)?; **who's that?** ¿quién es ése/a (or aquél (aquélla))?; **is that you?** ¿eres tú?; **will you eat all that?** ¿vas a comer todo eso?; **that's my house** ésa es mi casa; **that's what he said** eso es lo que dijo; **that is (to say)** es decir
2 (relative: subject, object) que; (with preposition) (el (la)) que etc, el(la) cual etc; **the book (that) I read** el libro que leí; **the books that are in the library** los libros que están en la biblioteca; **all (that) I have** todo lo que tengo; **the box (that) I put it in** la caja en la que or donde lo puse; **the people (that) I spoke to** la gente con la que hablé
3 (relative: of time) que; **the day (that) he came** el día (en) que vino
▷ conj que; **he thought that I was ill** creyó que yo estaba enfermo
▷ adv (demonstrative): **I can't work that much** no puedo trabajar tanto; **I didn't realise it was that bad** no creí que fuera tan malo; **that high** así de alto

thatched [θætʃt] adj (roof) de paja; (cottage) con tejado de paja
thaw [θɔː] n deshielo ▷ vi (ice) derretirse; (food) descongelarse ▷ vt (food) descongelar

○ **KEYWORD**

the [ðiː, ðə] def art **1** (gen) el f, la pl, los fpl, las (NB 'el' immediately before f n beginning with stressed (h)a; a+ el =al; de + el = del); **the boy/girl** el chico/la chica; **the books/flowers**

t

los libros/las flores; **to the postman/from the drawer** al cartero/del cajón; **I haven't the time/money** no tengo tiempo/dinero **2** (+adj to form n) los; lo; **the rich and the poor** los ricos y los pobres; **to attempt the impossible** intentar lo imposible **3** (in titles): **Elizabeth the First** Isabel primera; **Peter the Great** Pedro el Grande **4** (in comparisons): **the more he works the more he earns** cuanto más trabaja más gana

theatre ['θɪətə*] (us **theater**) n teatro; (also: **lecture ~**) aula; (Med: also: **operating ~**) quirófano

theft [θɛft] n robo

their [ðɛə*] adj su; **theirs** pron (el) suyo/(la) suya etc); see also **my**; **mine**[1]

them [ðɛm, ðəm] pron (direct) los/las; (indirect) les; (stressed, after prep) ellos(ellas); see also **me**

theme [θiːm] n tema m; **theme park** n parque de atracciones (en torno a un tema central)

themselves [ðəm'sɛlvz] pl pron (subject) ellos mismos(ellas mismas); (complement) se; (after prep) sí (mismos(as)); see also **oneself**

then [ðɛn] adv (at that time) entonces; (next) después; (later) luego, después; (and also) además ▷ conj (therefore) en ese caso, entonces ▷ adj: **the ~ president** el entonces presidente; **by ~** para entonces; **from ~ on** desde entonces

theology [θɪ'ɔlədʒɪ] n teología

theory ['θɪərɪ] n teoría

therapist ['θɛrəpɪst] n terapeuta mf

therapy ['θɛrəpɪ] n terapia

○ **KEYWORD**

there ['ðɛə*] adv **1 there is, there are** hay; **there is no-one here/no bread left** no hay nadie aquí/no queda pan; **there has been an accident** ha habido un accidente **2** (referring to place) ahí; (distant) allí; **it's there** está ahí; **put it in/on/up/down there** ponlo ahí dentro/encima/arriba/abajo; **I want that book there** quiero ese libro de ahí; **there he is!** ¡ahí está! **3 there, there** (esp to child) ea, ea

there: thereabouts adv por ahí; **thereafter** adv después; **thereby** adv así, de ese modo; **therefore** adv por lo tanto; **there's** = **there is; there has**

thermal ['θəːml] adj termal; (paper) térmico

thermometer [θə'mɔmɪtə*] n termómetro

thermostat ['θəːməustæt] n termostato

these [ðiːz] pl adj estos/as ▷ pl pron éstos/as

thesis ['θiːsɪs] (pl **theses**) n tesis f inv

they [ðeɪ] pl pron ellos(ellas); (stressed) ellos (mismos)(ellas (mismas)); **~ say that ...** (it is said that) se dice que ...; **they'd** = **they had; they would; they'll** = **they shall; they will; they're** = **they are; they've** = **they have**

thick [θɪk] adj (in consistency) espeso; (in size) grueso; (stupid) torpe ▷ n: **in the ~ of the battle** en lo más reñido de la batalla; **it's 20 cm ~** tiene 20 cm de espesor; **thicken** vi espesarse ▷ vt (sauce etc) espesar; **thickness** n espesor m; grueso

thief [θiːf] (pl **thieves**) n ladrón/ona m/f

thigh [θaɪ] n muslo

thin [θɪn] adj (person, animal) flaco; (in size) delgado; (in consistency) poco espeso; (hair, crowd) escaso ▷ vt: **to ~ (down)** diluir

thing [θɪŋ] n cosa; (object) objeto, artículo; (matter) asunto; (mania): **to have a ~ about sb/sth** estar obsesionado con algn/algo; **things** npl (belongings) efectos mpl (personales); **the best ~ would be to ...** lo mejor sería ...; **how are ~s?** ¿qué tal?

think [θɪŋk] (pt, pp **thought**) vi pensar ▷ vt pensar, creer; **what did you ~ of them?** ¿qué te parecieron?; **to ~ about sth/sb** pensar en algo/algn; **I'll ~ about it** lo pensaré; **to ~ of doing sth** pensar en hacer algo; **I ~ so/not** creo que sí/no; **to ~ well of sb** tener buen concepto de algn; **think over** vt reflexionar sobre, meditar; **think up** vt (plan etc) idear

third [θəːd] adj (before n) tercer(a); (following n) tercero/a ▷ n tercero/a; (fraction) tercio; (BRIT Scol: degree) título de licenciado con calificación de aprobado; **thirdly** adv en tercer lugar; **third party insurance** (BRIT) n seguro contra terceros; **Third World** n Tercer Mundo

thirst [θəːst] n sed f; **thirsty** adj (person, animal) sediento; (work) que da sed; **to be thirsty** tener sed

thirteen ['θəː'tiːn] num trece; **thirteenth** [-'tiːnθ] adj decimotercero

thirtieth ['θəːtɪəθ] adj trigésimo

thirty ['θəːtɪ] num treinta

○ **KEYWORD**

this [ðɪs] (pl **these**) adj (demonstrative) este/a pl; estos/as; (neuter) esto; **this man/woman** este hombre(esta mujer); **these children/flowers** estos chicos/estas flores;

this one (here) éste/a, esto (de aquí)
▷ pron (demonstrative) éste/a pl, éstos/as;
(neuter) esto; **who is this?** ¿quién es
éste/ésta?; **what is this?** ¿qué es esto?; **this
is where I live** aquí vivo; **this is what he
said** esto es lo que dijo; **this is Mr Brown**
(in introductions) le presento al Sr. Brown;
(photo) éste es el Sr. Brown; (on telephone)
habla el Sr. Brown
▷ adv (demonstrative): **this high/long** etc así
de alto/largo etc; **this far** hasta aquí

thistle ['θɪsl] n cardo
thorn [θɔ:n] n espina
thorough ['θʌrə] adj (search) minucioso;
(wash) a fondo; (knowledge, research)
profundo; (person) meticuloso; **thoroughly**
adv (search) minuciosamente; (study)
profundamente; (wash) a fondo; (utterly: bad,
wet etc) completamente, totalmente
those [ðəuz] pl adj esos(esas); (more
remote) aquellos/as
though [ðəu] conj aunque ▷ adv sin
embargo
thought [θɔ:t] pt, pp of **think** ▷ n
pensamiento; (opinion) opinión f;
thoughtful adj pensativo; (serious) serio;
(considerate) atento; **thoughtless** adj
desconsiderado
thousand ['θauzənd] num mil; **two ~**
dos mil; **~s of** miles de; **thousandth** num
milésimo
thrash [θræʃ] vt azotar; (defeat) derrotar
thread [θred] n hilo; (of screw) rosca ▷ vt
(needle) enhebrar
threat [θret] n amenaza; **threaten** vi
amenazar ▷ vt: **to threaten sb with/
to do** amenazar a algn con/con hacer;
threatening adj amenazador(a),
amenazante
three [θri:] num tres; **three-dimensional**
adj tridimensional; **three-piece suite** n
tresillo; **three-quarters** npl tres cuartas
partes; **three-quarters full** tres cuartas
partes lleno
threshold ['θreʃhəuld] n umbral m
threw [θru:] pt of **throw**
thrill [θrɪl] n (excitement) emoción f;
(shudder) estremecimiento ▷ vt emocionar;
to be ~ed (with gift etc) estar encantado;
thrilled adj: **I was thrilled** Estaba
emocionada; **thriller** n novela (or obra
or película) de suspense; **thrilling** adj
emocionante
thriving ['θraɪvɪŋ] adj próspero
throat [θrəut] n garganta; **to have a sore
~** tener dolor de garganta
throb [θrɒb] vi latir; dar punzadas; vibrar

throne [θrəun] n trono
through [θru:] prep por, a través de;
(time) durante; (by means of) por medio de,
mediante; (owing to) gracias a ▷ adj (ticket,
train) directo ▷ adv completamente, de
parte a parte; de principio a fin; **to put sb ~
to sb** (Tel) poner or pasar a algn con algn; **to
be ~** (Tel) tener comunicación; (have finished)
haber terminado; **"no ~ road"** (BRIT) "calle
sin salida"; **throughout** prep (place) por
todas partes de, por todo; (time) durante
todo ▷ adv por or en todas partes
throw [θrəu] (pt threw, pp thrown) n tiro;
(Sport) lanzamiento ▷ vt tirar, echar; (Sport)
lanzar; (rider) derribar; (fig) desconcertar;
to ~ a party dar una fiesta; **throw away**
vt tirar; (money) derrochar; **throw in** vt
(Sport: ball) sacar; (include) incluir; **throw
off** vt deshacerse de; **throw out** vt tirar;
(person) echar; expulsar; **throw up** vi
vomitar
thru [θru:] (us) = **through**
thrush [θrʌʃ] n zorzal m, tordo
thrust [θrʌst] (pt, pp ~) vt empujar con
fuerza
thud [θʌd] n golpe m sordo
thug [θʌg] n gamberro/a
thumb [θʌm] n (Anat) pulgar m; **to ~ a
lift** hacer autostop; **thumbtack** (us) n
chincheta (sp)
thump [θʌmp] n golpe m; (sound) ruido
seco or sordo ▷ vt golpear ▷ vi (heart etc)
palpitar
thunder ['θʌndə*] n trueno ▷ vi tronar;
(train etc): **to ~ past** pasar como un trueno;
thunderstorm n tormenta
Thur(s). abbr (= Thursday) juev
Thursday ['θə:zdɪ] n jueves m inv
thus [ðʌs] adv así, de este modo
thwart [θwɔ:t] vt frustrar
thyme [taɪm] n tomillo
Tibet [tɪ'bet] n el Tibet
tick [tɪk] n (sound: of clock) tictac m; (mark)
palomita (LAM); (Zool) garrapata; (BRIT: inf): **in
a ~** en un instante ▷ vi hacer tictac ▷ vt
marcar; **tick off** vt marcar; (person) reñir
ticket ['tɪkɪt] n billete m (sp), boleto
(LAM); (for cinema etc) entrada; (in shop: on
goods) etiqueta; (for raffle) papeleta; (for
library) tarjeta; (parking ticket) multa de
aparcamiento (sp) or por estacionamiento
(indebido) (LAM); **ticket barrier** n
(BRIT: Rail) barrera más allá de la cual se
necesita billete/boleto; **ticket collector**
n revisor(a) m/f; **ticket inspector** n
revisor(a) m/f, inspector(a) m/f de boletos
(LAM); **ticket machine** n máquina de
billetes (sp) or boletos (LAM); **ticket office** n

(*Theatre*) taquilla (*SP*), boletería (*LAM*); (*Rail*) mostrador *m* de billetes (*SP*) or boletos (*LAM*)

tickle ['tɪkl] *vt* hacer cosquillas a ▷ *vi* hacer cosquillas; **ticklish** *adj* (*person*) cosquilloso; (*problem*) delicado

tide [taɪd] *n* marea; (*fig: of events etc*) curso, marcha

tidy ['taɪdɪ] *adj* (*room etc*) ordenado; (*dress, work*) limpio; (*person*) (*bien*) arreglado ▷ *vt* (*also: ~ up*) poner en orden

tie [taɪ] *n* (*string etc*) atadura; (*BRIT: also:* **neck~**) corbata; (*fig: link*) vínculo, lazo; (*Sport etc: draw*) empate *m* ▷ *vt* atar ▷ *vi* (*Sport etc*) empatar; **to ~ in a bow** atar con un lazo; **to ~ a knot in sth** hacer un nudo en algo; **tie down** *vt* (*fig: person: restrict*) atar; (*: to price, date etc*) obligar a; **tie up** *vt* (*dog, person*) atar; (*arrangements*) concluir; **to be tied up** (*busy*) estar ocupado

tier [tɪə*] *n* grada; (*of cake*) piso

tiger ['taɪɡə*] *n* tigre *m*

tight [taɪt] *adj* (*rope*) tirante; (*money*) escaso; (*clothes*) ajustado; (*bend*) cerrado; (*shoes, schedule*) apretado; (*budget*) ajustado; (*security*) estricto; (*inf: drunk*) borracho ▷ *adv* (*squeeze*) muy fuerte; (*shut*) bien; **tighten** *vt* (*rope*) estirar; (*screw, grip*) apretar; (*security*) reforzar ▷ *vi* estirarse; apretarse; **tightly** *adv* (*grasp*) muy fuerte; **tights** (*BRIT*) *npl* panti *mpl*

tile [taɪl] *n* (*on roof*) teja; (*on floor*) baldosa; (*on wall*) azulejo

till [tɪl] *n* caja (registradora) ▷ *vt* (*land*) cultivar ▷ *prep, conj* = **until**

tilt [tɪlt] *vt* inclinar ▷ *vi* inclinarse

timber [tɪmbə*] *n* (*material*) madera

time [taɪm] *n* tiempo; (*epoch: often pl*) época; (*by clock*) hora; (*moment*) momento; (*occasion*) vez *f*; (*Mus*) compás *m* ▷ *vt* calcular or medir el tiempo de; (*race*) cronometrar; (*remark, visit etc*) elegir el momento para; **a long ~** mucho tiempo; **4 at a ~** de 4 en 4; 4 a la vez; **for the ~ being** de momento, por ahora; **from ~ to ~** de vez en cuando; **at ~s** a veces; **in ~** (*soon enough*) a tiempo; (*after some time*) con el tiempo; (*Mus*) al compás; **in a week's ~** dentro de una semana; **in no ~** en un abrir y cerrar de ojos; **any ~** cuando sea; **on ~** a la hora; **5 ~s 5** 5 por 5; **what ~ is it?** ¿qué hora es?; **to have a good ~** pasarlo bien, divertirse; **time limit** *n* plazo; **timely** *adj* oportuno; **timer** *n* (*in kitchen etc*) programador *m* horario; **time-share** *n* apartamento (or casa) a tiempo compartido; **timetable** *n* horario; **time zone** *n* huso horario

timid ['tɪmɪd] *adj* tímido

timing ['taɪmɪŋ] *n* (*Sport*) cronometraje *m*;

the ~ of his resignation el momento que eligió para dimitir

tin [tɪn] *n* estaño; (*also: ~ plate*) hojalata; (*BRIT: can*) lata; **tinfoil** *n* papel *m* de estaño

tingle ['tɪŋɡl] *vi* (*person*): **to ~ (with)** estremecerse (de); (*hands etc*) hormiguear

tinker ['tɪŋkə*]: **~ with** *vt fus* jugar con, tocar

tinned [tɪnd] (*BRIT*) *adj* (*food*) en lata, en conserva

tin opener [-əupnə*] (*BRIT*) *n* abrelatas *m inv*

tint [tɪnt] *n* matiz *m*; (*for hair*) tinte *m*; **tinted** *adj* (*hair*) teñido; (*glass, spectacles*) ahumado

tiny ['taɪnɪ] *adj* minúsculo, pequeñito

tip [tɪp] *n* (*end*) punta; (*gratuity*) propina; (*BRIT: for rubbish*) vertedero; (*advice*) consejo ▷ *vt* (*waiter*) dar una propina a; (*tilt*) inclinar; (*empty: also: ~ out*) vaciar, echar; (*overturn: also: ~ over*) volcar; **tip off** *vt* avisar, poner sobreaviso a

tiptoe ['tɪptəu] *n*: **on ~** de puntillas

tire ['taɪə*] *n* (*US*) = **tyre** ▷ *vt* cansar ▷ *vi* cansarse; (*become bored*) aburrirse; **tired** *adj* cansado; **to be tired of sth** estar harto de algo; **tire pressure** (*US*) = **tyre pressure**; **tiring** *adj* cansado

tissue ['tɪʃuː] *n* tejido; (*paper handkerchief*) pañuelo de papel, kleenex® *m*; **tissue paper** *n* papel *m* de seda

tit [tɪt] *n* (*bird*) herrerillo común; **to give ~ for tat** dar ojo por ojo

title ['taɪtl] *n* título

T-junction ['tiː'dʒʌŋkʃən] *n* cruce *m* en T

TM *abbr* = **trademark**

○ **KEYWORD**

to [tuː, tə] *prep* **1** (*direction*) a; **to go to France/London/school/the station** ir a Francia/Londres/al colegio/a la estación; **to go to Claude's/the doctor's** ir a casa de Claude/al médico; **the road to Edinburgh** la carretera de Edimburgo

2 (*as far as*) hasta, a; **from here to London** de aquí a or hasta Londres; **to count to 10** contar hasta 10; **from 40 to 50 people** entre 40 y 50 personas

3 (*with expressions of time*): **a quarter/twenty to 5** las 5 menos cuarto/veinte

4 (*for, of*): **the key to the front door** la llave de la puerta principal; **she is secretary to the director** es la secretaria del director; **a letter to his wife** una carta a or para su mujer

5 (*expressing indirect object*): **to give sth to sb** darle algo a algn; **to talk to sb** hablar con algn; **to be a danger to sb** ser un peligro para algn; **to carry out repairs to sth** hacer reparaciones en algo

6 (in relation to): **3 goals to 2** 3 goles a 2; **30 miles to the gallon** ≈ 94 litros a los cien (kms)

7 (purpose, result): **to come to sb's aid** venir en auxilio or ayuda de algn; **to sentence sb to death** condenar a algn a muerte; **to my great surprise** con gran sorpresa mía

▷ with vb **1** (simple infin): **to go/eat** ir/comer **2** (following another vb): **to want/try/start to do** querer/intentar/empezar a hacer **3** (with vb omitted): **I don't want to** no quiero **4** (purpose, result) para; **I did it to help you** lo hice para ayudarte; **he came to see you** vino a verte

5 (equivalent to relative clause): **I have things to do** tengo cosas que hacer; **the main thing is to try** lo principal es intentarlo

6 (after adj etc): **ready to go** listo para irse; **too old to ...** demasiado viejo (como) para ...

▷ adv: **pull/push the door to** tirar de/ empujar la puerta

toad [təud] n sapo; **toadstool** n hongo venenoso

toast [təust] n (Culin) tostada; (drink, speech) brindis m ▷ vt (Culin) tostar; (drink to) brindar por; **toaster** n tostador m

tobacco [tə'bækəu] n tabaco

toboggan [tə'bɔgən] n tobogán m

today [tə'deɪ] adv, n (also fig) hoy m

toddler ['tɔdlə*] n niño/a (que empieza a andar)

toe [təu] n dedo (del pie); (of shoe) punta; **to ~ the line** (fig) conformarse; **toenail** n uña del pie

toffee ['tɔfɪ] n toffee m

together [tə'geðə*] adv juntos; (at same time) al mismo tiempo, a la vez; **~ with** junto con

toilet ['tɔɪlət] n inodoro; (BRIT: room) (cuarto de) baño, servicio ▷ cpd (soap etc) de aseo; **toilet bag** n neceser m, bolsa de aseo; **toilet paper** n papel m higiénico; **toiletries** npl artículos mpl de tocador; **toilet roll** n rollo de papel higiénico

token ['təukən] n (sign) señal f, muestra; (souvenir) recuerdo; (disc) ficha ▷ adj (strike, payment etc) simbólico; **book/record ~** (BRIT) vale m para comprar libros/discos; **gift ~** (BRIT) vale-regalo

Tokyo ['təukjəu] n Tokio, Tokío

told [təuld] pt, pp of **tell**

tolerant ['tɔlərnt] adj: **~ of** tolerante con

tolerate ['tɔləreɪt] vt tolerar

toll [təul] n (of casualties) número de víctimas; (tax, charge) peaje m ▷ vi (bell) doblar; **toll call** n (US Tel) conferencia, llamada interurbana; **toll-free** (US) adj, adv gratis

tomato [tə'mɑːtəu] n (pl **~es**) tomate m; **tomato sauce** n salsa de tomate

tomb [tuːm] n tumba; **tombstone** n lápida

tomorrow [tə'mɔrəu] adv, n (also: fig) mañana; **the day after ~** pasado mañana; **~ morning** mañana por la mañana

ton [tʌn] n tonelada (BRIT = 1016 kg; US = 907 kg); (metric ton) tonelada métrica; **~s of** (inf) montones de

tone [təun] n tono ▷ vi (also: **~ in**) armonizar; **tone down** vt (criticism) suavizar; (colour) atenuar

tongs [tɔŋz] npl (for coal) tenazas fpl; (curling tongs) tenacillas fpl

tongue [tʌŋ] n lengua; **~ in cheek** irónicamente

tonic ['tɔnɪk] n (Med) tónico; (also: **~ water**) (agua) tónica

tonight [tə'naɪt] adv, n esta noche; esta tarde

tonne [tʌn] n tonelada (métrica) (1.000kg)

tonsil ['tɔnsl] n amígdala; **tonsillitis** [-'laɪtɪs] n amigdalitis f

too [tuː] adv (excessively) demasiado; (also) también; **~ much** demasiado; **~ many** demasiados/as

took [tuk] pt of **take**

tool [tuːl] n herramienta; **tool box** n caja de herramientas; **tool kit** n juego de herramientas

tooth [tuːθ] n (pl **teeth**) n (Anat, Tech) diente m; (molar) muela; **toothache** n dolor m de muelas; **toothbrush** n cepillo de dientes; **toothpaste** n pasta de dientes; **toothpick** n palillo

top [tɔp] n (of mountain) cumbre f, cima; (of tree) copa; (of head) coronilla; (of ladder, page) lo alto; (of table) superficie f; (of cupboard) parte f de arriba; (lid: of box) tapa; (: of bottle, jar) tapón m; (of list etc) cabeza; (toy) peonza; (garment) blusa; camiseta ▷ adj de arriba; (in rank) principal, primero; (best) mejor ▷ vt (exceed) exceder; (be first in) encabezar; **on ~ of** (above) sobre, encima de; (in addition to) además de; **from ~ to bottom** de pies a cabeza; **top up** vt llenar; (mobile phone) recargar (el saldo de); **top floor** n último piso; **top hat** n sombrero de copa

topic ['tɔpɪk] n tema m; **topical** adj actual

topless ['tɔplɪs] adj (bather, bikini) topless inv

topping ['tɔpɪŋ] n (Culin): **with a ~ of**

cream con nata por encima

topple ['tɔpl] vt derribar ▷ vi caerse

top-up card n (for mobile phone) tarjeta prepago

torch [tɔ:tʃ] n antorcha; (BRIT: electric) linterna

tore [tɔ:*] pt of **tear**²

torment [n 'tɔ:mɛnt, vt tɔ:'mɛnt] n tormento ▷ vt atormentar; (fig: annoy) fastidiar

torn [tɔ:n] pp of **tear**²

tornado [tɔ:'neɪdəʊ] (pl **~es**) n tornado

torpedo [tɔ:'pi:dəʊ] (pl **~es**) n torpedo

torrent ['tɔrnt] n torrente m; **torrential** [tɔ'rɛnʃl] adj torrencial

tortoise ['tɔ:təs] n tortuga

torture ['tɔ:tʃə*] n tortura ▷ vt torturar; (fig) atormentar

Tory ['tɔ:rɪ] (BRIT) adj, n (Pol) conservador(a) m/f

toss [tɔs] vt tirar, echar; (one's head) sacudir; **to ~ a coin** echar a cara o cruz; **to ~ up for sth** jugar a cara o cruz algo; **to ~ and turn** (in bed) dar vueltas

total ['təʊtl] adj total, entero; (emphatic: failure etc) completo, total ▷ n total m, suma ▷ vt (add up) sumar; (amount to) ascender a

totalitarian [təʊtælɪ'tɛərɪən] adj totalitario

totally ['təʊtəlɪ] adv totalmente

touch [tʌtʃ] n tacto; (contact) contacto ▷ vt tocar; (emotionally) conmover; **a ~ of** (fig) un poquito de; **to get in ~ with sb** ponerse en contacto con algn; **to lose ~** (friends) perder contacto; **touch down** vi (on land) aterrizar; **touchdown** n aterrizaje m; (on sea) amerizaje m; (us Football) ensayo; **touched** adj (moved) conmovido; **touching** adj (moving) conmovedor(a); **touchline** n (Sport) línea de banda; **touch-sensitive** adj sensible al tacto

tough [tʌf] adj (material) resistente; (meat) duro; (problem etc) difícil; (policy, stance) inflexible; (person) fuerte

tour ['tʊə*] n viaje m, vuelta; (also: **package ~**) viaje m todo comprendido; (of town, museum) visita; (by band etc) gira ▷ vt recorrer, visitar; **tour guide** n guía mf turístico/a

tourism ['tʊərɪzm] n turismo

tourist ['tʊərɪst] n turista mf ▷ cpd turístico; **tourist office** n oficina de turismo

tournament ['tʊənəmənt] n torneo

tour operator n touroperador(a) m/f, operador(a) m/f turístico/a

tow [təʊ] vt remolcar; **"on** or **in** (us) **~"**

(Aut) "a remolque"; **tow away** vt llevarse a remolque

toward(s) [tə'wɔ:d(z)] prep hacia; (attitude) respecto a, con; (purpose) para

towel ['taʊəl] n toalla; **towelling** n (fabric) felpa

tower ['taʊə*] n torre f; **tower block** (BRIT) n torre f (de pisos)

town [taʊn] n ciudad f; **to go to ~** ir a la ciudad; (fig) echar la casa por la ventana; **town centre** (BRIT) n centro de la ciudad; **town hall** n ayuntamiento

tow truck (us) n camión m grúa

toxic ['tɔksɪk] adj tóxico

toy [tɔɪ] n juguete m; **toy with** vt fus jugar con; (idea) acariciar; **toyshop** n juguetería

trace [treɪs] n rastro ▷ vt (draw) trazar, delinear; (locate) encontrar; (follow) seguir la pista de

track [træk] n (mark) huella, pista; (path: gen) camino, senda; (: of bullet etc) trayectoria; (: of suspect, animal) pista, rastro; (Rail) vía; (Sport) pista; (on tape, record) canción f ▷ vt seguir la pista de; **to keep ~ of** mantenerse al tanto de, seguir; **track down** vt (prey) seguir el rastro de; (sth lost) encontrar; **tracksuit** n chandal m

tractor ['træktə*] n tractor m

trade [treɪd] n comercio; (skill, job) oficio ▷ vi negociar, comerciar ▷ vt (exchange): **to ~ sth (for sth)** cambiar algo (por algo); **trade in** vt (old car etc) ofrecer como parte del pago; **trademark** n marca de fábrica; **trader** n comerciante mf; **tradesman** (irreg) n (shopkeeper) tendero; **trade union** n sindicato

trading ['treɪdɪŋ] n comercio

tradition [trə'dɪʃən] n tradición f; **traditional** adj tradicional

traffic ['træfɪk] n (gen, Aut) tráfico, circulación f ▷ vi: **to ~ in** (pej: liquor, drugs) traficar en; **traffic circle** (us) n isleta; **traffic island** n refugio, isleta; **traffic jam** n embotellamiento; **traffic lights** npl semáforo; **traffic warden** n guardia mf de tráfico

tragedy ['trædʒədɪ] n tragedia

tragic ['trædʒɪk] adj trágico

trail [treɪl] n (tracks) rastro, pista; (path) camino, sendero; (dust, smoke) estela ▷ vt (drag) arrastrar; (follow) seguir la pista de ▷ vi arrastrar; (in contest etc) ir perdiendo; **trailer** n (Aut) remolque m; (caravan) caravana; (Cinema) trailer m, avance m

train [treɪn] n tren m; (of dress) cola; (series) serie f ▷ vt (educate, teach skills to) formar; (sportsman) entrenar; (dog) adiestrar; (point: gun etc): **to ~ on** apuntar a ▷*vi* (*Sport*) entrenarse; (*learn a skill*): **to ~ as a teacher** *etc* estudiar para profesor *etc*; **one's ~ of thought** el razonamiento de algn; **trainee** *n* aprendiz(a) *m/f*; **trainer** *n* (*Sport: coach*) entrenador(a) *m/f*; (*of animals*) domador(a) *m/f*; **trainers** *npl* (*shoes*) zapatillas *fpl* (de deporte); **training** *n* formación *f*; entrenamiento; **to be in training** (*Sport*) estar entrenando; **training course** *n* curso de formación; **training shoes** *npl* zapatillas *fpl* (de deporte)

trait [treɪt] *n* rasgo

traitor ['treɪtə*] *n* traidor(a) *m/f*

tram [træm] (*BRIT*) *n* (*also:* **~car**) tranvía *m*

tramp [træmp] *n* (*person*) vagabundo/a; (*inf: pej: woman*) puta

trample ['træmpl] *vt*: **to ~ (underfoot)** pisotear

trampoline ['træmpəliːn] *n* trampolín *m*

tranquil ['træŋkwɪl] *adj* tranquilo; **tranquillizer** (*US* **tranquilizer**) *n* (*Med*) tranquilizante *m*

transaction [træn'zækʃən] *n* transacción *f*, operación *f*

transatlantic ['trænzət'læntɪk] *adj* transatlántico

transcript ['trænskrɪpt] *n* copia

transfer [*n* 'trænsfə:*, *vb* træns'fə:*] *n* (*of employees*) traslado; (*of money, power*) transferencia; (*Sport*) traspaso; (*picture, design*) calcomanía ▷*vt* trasladar; transferir; **to ~ the charges** (*BRIT Tel*) llamar a cobro revertido

transform [træns'fɔːm] *vt* transformar; **transformation** *n* transformación *f*

transfusion [træns'fjuːʒən] *n* transfusión *f*

transit ['trænzɪt] *n*: **in ~** en tránsito

transition [træn'zɪʃən] *n* transición *f*

transitive ['trænzɪtɪv] *adj* (*Ling*) transitivo

translate [trænz'leɪt] *vt* traducir; **translation** [-'leɪʃən] *n* traducción *f*; **translator** *n* traductor(a) *m/f*

transmission [trænz'mɪʃən] *n* transmisión *f*

transmit [trænz'mɪt] *vt* transmitir; **transmitter** *n* transmisor *m*

transparent [træns'pærnt] *adj* transparente

transplant ['trænsplɑːnt] *n* (*Med*) transplante *m*

transport [*n* 'trænspɔːt, *vt* træns'pɔːt] *n* transporte *m*; (*car*) coche *m* (*SP*), carro (*LAM*), automóvil *m* ▷*vt* transportar; **transportation** [-'teɪʃən] *n* transporte *m*

transvestite [trænz'vɛstaɪt] *n* travestí *mf*

trap [træp] *n* (*snare, trick*) trampa; (*carriage*) cabriolé *m* ▷*vt* coger (*SP*) or agarrar (*LAM*) (en una trampa); (*trick*) engañar; (*confine*) atrapar

trash [træʃ] *n* (*rubbish*) basura; (*nonsense*) tonterías *fpl*; (*pej*): **the book/film is ~** el libro/la película no vale nada; **trash can** (*US*) *n* cubo or bote *m* (*MEX*) or tacho (*SC*) de la basura

trauma ['trɔːmə] *n* trauma *m*; **traumatic** [trɔːˈmætɪk] *adj* traumático

travel ['trævl] *n* el viajar ▷*vi* viajar ▷*vt* (*distance*) recorrer; **travel agency** *n* agencia de viajes; **travel agent** *n* agente *mf* de viajes; **travel insurance** *n* seguro de viaje; **traveller** (*US* **traveler**) *n* viajero/a; **traveller's cheque** (*US* **traveler's check**) *n* cheque *m* de viajero; **travelling** (*US* **traveling**) *n* los viajes, el viajar; **travel-sick** *adj*: **to get travel-sick** marearse al viajar; **travel sickness** *n* mareo

tray [treɪ] *n* bandeja; (*on desk*) cajón *m*

treacherous ['trɛtʃərəs] *adj* traidor, traicionero; (*dangerous*) peligroso

treacle ['triːkl] (*BRIT*) *n* melaza

tread [trɛd] (*pt* **trod**, *pp* **trodden**) *n* (*step*) paso, pisada; (*sound*) ruido de pasos; (*of stair*) escalón *m*; (*of tyre*) banda de rodadura ▷*vi* pisar; **tread on** *vt fus* pisar

treasure ['trɛʒə*] *n* tesoro ▷*vt* (*value: object, friendship*) apreciar; (*: memory*) guardar; **treasurer** *n* tesorero/a

treasury ['trɛʒərɪ] *n*: **the T~** el Ministerio de Hacienda

treat [triːt] *n* (*present*) regalo ▷*vt* tratar; **to ~ sb to sth** invitar a algn a algo; **treatment** *n* tratamiento

treaty ['triːtɪ] *n* tratado

treble ['trɛbl] *adj* triple ▷*vt* triplicar ▷*vi* triplicarse

tree [triː] *n* árbol *m*; **~ trunk** tronco (de árbol)

trek [trɛk] *n* (*long journey*) viaje *m* largo y difícil; (*tiring walk*) caminata

tremble ['trɛmbl] *vi* temblar

tremendous [trɪ'mɛndəs] *adj* tremendo, enorme; (*excellent*) estupendo

trench [trɛntʃ] *n* zanja

trend [trɛnd] *n* (*tendency*) tendencia; (*of events*) curso; (*fashion*) moda; **trendy** *adj* de moda

trespass ['trɛspəs] *vi*: **to ~ on** entrar sin permiso en; **"no ~ing"** "prohibido el paso"

trial ['traɪəl] *n* (*Law*) juicio, proceso; (*test: of machine etc*) prueba; **trial period** *n* periodo de prueba

triangle ['traɪæŋgl] *n* (*Math, Mus*) triángulo

t

triangular [traɪ'æŋgjulə*] *adj* triangular

tribe [traɪb] *n* tribu *f*

tribunal [traɪ'bjuːnl] *n* tribunal *m*

tribute ['trɪbjuːt] *n* homenaje *m*, tributo; **to pay ~ to** rendir homenaje a

trick [trɪk] *n* (*skill, knack*) tino, truco; (*conjuring trick*) truco; (*joke*) broma; (*Cards*) baza ▷ *vt* engañar; **to play a ~ on sb** gastar una broma a algn; **that should do the ~** a ver si funciona así

trickle ['trɪkl] *n* (*of water etc*) goteo ▷ *vi* gotear

tricky ['trɪkɪ] *adj* difícil; delicado

tricycle ['traɪsɪkl] *n* triciclo

trifle ['traɪfl] *n* bagatela; (*Culin*) dulce de bizcocho borracho, gelatina, fruta y natillas ▷ *adv*: **a ~ long** un poquito largo

trigger ['trɪgə*] *n* (*of gun*) gatillo

trim [trɪm] *adj* (*house, garden*) en buen estado; (*person, figure*) esbelto ▷ *n* (*haircut etc*) recorte *m*; (*on car*) guarnición *f* ▷ *vt* (*neaten*) arreglar; (*cut*) recortar; (*decorate*) adornar; (*Naut: a sail*) orientar

trio ['triːəu] *n* trío

trip [trɪp] *n* viaje *m*; (*excursion*) excursión *f*; (*stumble*) traspié *m* ▷ *vi* (*stumble*) tropezar; (*go lightly*) andar a paso ligero; **on a ~** de viaje; **trip up** *vi* tropezar, caerse ▷ *vt* hacer tropezar or caer

triple ['trɪpl] *adj* triple

triplets ['trɪplɪts] *npl* trillizos/as *mpl/fpl*

tripod ['traɪpɔd] *n* trípode *m*

triumph ['traɪʌmf] *n* triunfo ▷ *vi*: **to ~ (over)** vencer; **triumphant** [traɪ'ʌmfənt] *adj* (*team etc*) vencedor(a); (*wave, return*) triunfal

trivial ['trɪvɪəl] *adj* insignificante; (*commonplace*) banal

trod [trɔd] *pt of* **tread**

trodden ['trɔdn] *pp of* **tread**

trolley ['trɔlɪ] *n* carrito; (*also:* **~ bus**) trolebús *m*

trombone [trɔm'bəun] *n* trombón *m*

troop [truːp] *n* grupo, banda; **troops** *npl* (*Mil*) tropas *fpl*

trophy ['trəufɪ] *n* trofeo

tropical ['trɔpɪkl] *adj* tropical

trot [trɔt] *n* trote *m* ▷ *vi* trotar; **on the ~** (*BRIT: fig*) seguidos/as

trouble ['trʌbl] *n* problema *m*, dificultad *f*; (*worry*) preocupación *f*; (*bother, effort*) molestia, esfuerzo; (*unrest*) inquietud *f*; (*Med*): **stomach** *etc* **~** problemas *mpl* gástricos *etc* ▷ *vt* (*disturb*) molestar; (*worry*) preocupar, inquietar ▷ *vi*: **to ~ to do sth** molestarse en hacer algo; **troubles** *npl* (*Pol etc*) conflictos *mpl*; (*personal*) problemas *mpl*; **to be in ~** estar en un apuro; **it's no ~!** ¡no

es molestia (ninguna)!; **what's the ~?** (*with broken TV etc*) ¿cuál es el problema?; (*doctor to patient*) ¿qué pasa?; **troubled** *adj* (*person*) preocupado; (*country, epoch, life*) agitado; **troublemaker** *n* agitador(a) *m/f*; (*child*) alborotador *m*; **troublesome** *adj* molesto

trough [trɔf] *n* (*also:* **drinking ~**) abrevadero; (*also:* **feeding ~**) comedero; (*depression*) depresión *f*

trousers ['trauzəz] *npl* pantalones *mpl*; **short ~** pantalones *mpl* cortos

trout [traut] *n inv* trucha

trowel ['trauəl] *n* (*of gardener*) palita; (*of builder*) paleta

truant ['truənt] *n*: **to play ~** (*BRIT*) hacer novillos

truce [truːs] *n* tregua

truck [trʌk] *n* (*lorry*) camión *m*; (*Rail*) vagón *m*; **truck driver** *n* camionero

true [truː] *adj* verdadero; (*accurate*) exacto; (*genuine*) auténtico; (*faithful*) fiel; **to come ~** realizarse

truly ['truːlɪ] *adv* (*really*) realmente; (*truthfully*) verdaderamente; (*faithfully*): **yours ~** (*in letter*) le saluda atentamente

trumpet ['trʌmpɪt] *n* trompeta

trunk [trʌŋk] *n* (*of tree, person*) tronco; (*of elephant*) trompa; (*case*) baúl *m*; (*us Aut*) maletero; **trunks** *npl* (*also:* **swimming ~s**) bañador *m* (de hombre)

trust [trʌst] *n* confianza; (*responsibility*) responsabilidad *f*; (*Law*) fideicomiso ▷ *vt* (*rely on*) tener confianza en; (*hope*) esperar; (*entrust*): **to ~ sth to sb** confiar algo a algn; **to take sth on ~** fiarse de algo; **trusted** *adj* de confianza; **trustworthy** *adj* digno de confianza

truth [truːθ, *pl* truːðz] *n* verdad *f*; **truthful** *adj* veraz

try [traɪ] *n* tentativa, intento; (*Rugby*) ensayo ▷ *vt* (*attempt*) intentar; (*test: also:* **~ out**) probar, someter a prueba; (*Law*) juzgar, procesar; (*strain: patience*) hacer perder ▷ *vi* probar; **to have a ~** probar suerte; **to ~ to do sth** intentar hacer algo; **~ again!** ¡vuelve a probar!; **~ harder!** ¡esfuérzate más!; **well, I tried** al menos lo intenté; **try on** *vt* (*clothes*) probarse; **trying** *adj* (*experience*) cansado; (*person*) pesado

T-shirt ['tiːʃəːt] *n* camiseta

tub [tʌb] *n* cubo (*SP*), cubeta (*SP, MEX*), balde *m* (*LAM*); (*bath*) bañera (*SP*), tina (*LAM*), bañadera (*RPL*)

tube [tjuːb] *n* tubo; (*BRIT: underground*) metro; (*for tyre*) cámara de aire

tuberculosis [tjubə:kjuːˈləusɪs] *n* tuberculosis *f inv*

tube station (BRIT) n estación f de metro
tuck [tʌk] vt (put) poner; **tuck away** vt (money) guardar; (building): **to be tucked away** esconderse, ocultarse; **tuck in** vt meter dentro; (child) arropar ▷ vi (eat) comer con apetito; **tuck shop** n (Scol) tienda ≈ bar m (del colegio) (SP)
Tue(s). abbr (= Tuesday) mart
Tuesday ['tjuːzdɪ] n martes m inv
tug [tʌg] n (ship) remolcador m ▷ vt tirar de
tuition [tjuːˈɪʃən] n (BRIT) enseñanza; (: private tuition) clases fpl particulares; (US: school fees) matrícula
tulip ['tjuːlɪp] n tulipán m
tumble ['tʌmbl] n (fall) caída ▷ vi caer; **to ~ to sth** (inf) caer en la cuenta de algo; **tumble dryer** (BRIT) n secadora
tumbler ['tʌmblə*] n (glass) vaso
tummy ['tʌmɪ] (inf) n barriga, tripa
tumour ['tjuːmə*] (US **tumor**) n tumor m
tuna ['tjuːnə] n inv (also: ~ **fish**) atún m
tune [tjuːn] n melodía ▷ vt (Mus) afinar; (Radio, TV, Aut) sintonizar; **to be in/out of ~** (instrument) estar afinado/desafinado; (singer) cantar afinadamente/desafinar; **to be in/out of ~ with** (fig) estar de acuerdo/ en desacuerdo con; **tune in** vi: **to tune in (to)** (Radio, TV) sintonizar (con); **tune up** vi (musician) afinar (su instrumento)
tunic ['tjuːnɪk] n túnica
Tunisia [tjuːˈnɪzɪə] n Túnez m
tunnel ['tʌnl] n túnel m; (in mine) galería ▷ vi construir un túnel/una galería
turbulence ['təːbjuləns] n (Aviat) turbulencia
turf [təːf] n césped m; (clod) tepe m ▷ vt cubrir con césped
Turk [təːk] n turco/a
Turkey ['təːkɪ] n Turquía
turkey ['təːkɪ] n pavo
Turkish ['təːkɪʃ] adj, n turco; (Ling) turco
turmoil ['təːmɔɪl] n: **in ~** revuelto
turn [təːn] n turno; (in road) curva; (of mind, events) rumbo; (Theatre) número; (Med) ataque m ▷ vt girar, volver; (collar, steak) dar la vuelta a; (page) pasar; (change): **to ~ sth into** convertir algo en ▷ vi volver; (person: look back) volverse; (reverse direction) dar la vuelta; (milk) cortarse; (become): **to ~ nasty/forty** ponerse feo/cumplir los cuarenta; **a good ~** un favor; **it gave me quite a ~** me dio un susto; **"no left ~"** (Aut) "prohibido girar a la izquierda"; **it's your ~** te toca a ti; **in ~** por turnos; **to take ~s (at)** turnarse (en); **turn around** vi (person) volverse, darse la vuelta ▷ vt (object) dar la vuelta a, voltear (LAM); **turn away** vi

apartar la vista ▷ vi rechazar; **turn back** vi volverse atrás ▷ vt hacer retroceder; (clock) retrasar; **turn down** vt (refuse) rechazar; (reduce) bajar; (fold) doblar; **turn in** vi (inf: go to bed) acostarse ▷ vt (fold) doblar hacia dentro; **turn off** vi (from road) desviarse ▷ vt (light, radio etc) apagar; (tap) cerrar; (engine) parar; **turn on** vt (light, radio etc) encender (SP), prender (LAM); (tap) abrir; (engine) poner en marcha; **turn out** vt (light, gas) apagar; (produce) producir ▷ vi (voters) concurrir; **to turn out to be ...** resultar ser ...; **turn over** vi (person) volverse ▷ vt (object) dar la vuelta a; (page) volver; **turn round** vi volverse; (rotate) girar; **turn to** vt fus: **to turn to sb** acudir a algn; **turn up** vi (person) llegar, presentarse; (lost object) aparecer ▷ vt (gen) subir; **turning** n (in road) vuelta; **turning point** n (fig) momento decisivo
turnip ['təːnɪp] n nabo
turn: turnout n concurrencia; **turnover** n (Comm: amount of money) volumen m de ventas; (: of goods) movimiento; **turnstile** n torniquete m; **turn-up** (BRIT) n (on trousers) vuelta
turquoise ['təːkwɔɪz] n (stone) turquesa ▷ adj color turquesa
turtle ['təːtl] n galápago; **turtleneck (sweater)** n jersey m de cuello vuelto
tusk [tʌsk] n colmillo
tutor ['tjuːtə*] n profesor(a) m/f; **tutorial** [-ˈtɔːrɪəl] n (Scol) seminario
tuxedo [tʌkˈsiːdəu] (US) n smóking m, esmoquin m
TV [tiːˈviː] n abbr (= television) tele f
tweed [twiːd] n tweed m
tweezers ['twiːzəz] npl pinzas fpl (de depilar)
twelfth [twelfθ] num duodécimo
twelve [twelv] num doce; **at ~ o'clock** (midday) a mediodía; (midnight) a medianoche
twentieth ['twentɪɪθ] adj vigésimo
twenty ['twentɪ] num veinte
twice [twaɪs] adv dos veces; **~ as much** dos veces más
twig [twɪg] n ramita
twilight ['twaɪlaɪt] n crepúsculo
twin [twɪn] adj, n gemelo/a m/f ▷ vt hermanar; **twin(-bedded) room** n habitación f doble; **twin beds** npl camas fpl gemelas
twinkle ['twɪŋkl] vi centellear; (eyes) brillar
twist [twɪst] n (action) torsión f; (in road, coil) vuelta; (in wire, flex) doblez f; (in story) giro ▷ vt torcer; (weave) trenzar; (roll around) enrollar; (fig) deformar ▷ vi serpentear

twit [twɪt] (*inf*) *n* tonto

twitch [twɪtʃ] *n* (*pull*) tirón *m*; (*nervous*) tic *m* ▷ *vi* crisparse

two [tu:] *num* dos; **to put ~ and ~ together** (*fig*) atar cabos

type [taɪp] *n* (*category*) tipo, género; (*model*) tipo; (*Typ*) tipo, letra ▷ *vt* (*letter etc*) escribir a máquina; **typewriter** *n* máquina de escribir

typhoid ['taɪfɔɪd] *n* tifoidea

typhoon [taɪ'fu:n] *n* tifón *m*

typical ['tɪpɪkl] *adj* típico; **typically** *adv* típicamente

typing ['taɪpɪŋ] *n* mecanografía

typist ['taɪpɪst] *n* mecanógrafo/a

tyre ['taɪə*] (*US* **tire**) *n* neumático, llanta (*LAM*); **tyre pressure** (*BRIT*) *n* presión *f* de los neumáticos

U

UFO ['ju:fəu] *n abbr* (= *unidentified flying object*) OVNI *m*

Uganda [ju:'gændə] *n* Uganda

ugly ['ʌglɪ] *adj* feo; (*dangerous*) peligroso

UHT *abbr* (= *UHT milk*) leche *f* UHT, leche *f* uperizada

UK *n abbr* = **United Kingdom**

ulcer ['ʌlsə*] *n* úlcera; (*mouth ulcer*) llaga

ultimate ['ʌltɪmət] *adj* último, final; (*greatest*) máximo; **ultimately** *adv* (*in the end*) por último, al final; (*fundamentally*) a or en fin de cuentas

ultimatum [ʌltɪ'meɪtəm] (*pl* **~s** or **ultimata**) *n* ultimátum *m*

ultrasound ['ʌltrəsaund] *n* (*Med*) ultrasonido

ultraviolet ['ʌltrə'vaɪəlɪt] *adj* ultravioleta

umbrella [ʌm'brɛlə] *n* paraguas *m inv*; (*for sun*) sombrilla

umpire ['ʌmpaɪə*] *n* árbitro

UN *n abbr* (= *United Nations*) NN. UU.

unable [ʌn'eɪbl] *adj*: **to be ~ to do sth** no poder hacer algo

unacceptable [ʌnək'sɛptəbl] *adj* (*proposal, behaviour, price*) inaceptable; **it's ~ that** no se puede aceptar que

unanimous [ju:'nænɪməs] *adj* unánime

unarmed [ʌn'ɑ:md] *adj* (*defenceless*) inerme; (*without weapon*) desarmado

unattended [ʌnə'tɛndɪd] *adj* desatendido

unattractive [ʌnə'træktɪv] *adj* poco atractivo

unavailable [ʌnə'veɪləbl] *adj* (*article, room, book*) no disponible; (*person*) ocupado

unavoidable [ʌnə'vɔɪdəbl] *adj* inevitable

unaware [ʌnə'wɛə*] *adj*: **to be ~ of** ignorar; **unawares** *adv*: **to catch sb unawares** pillar a algn desprevenido

unbearable [ʌn'bɛərəbl] *adj* insoportable

unbeatable [ʌn'bi:təbl] *adj* (*team*)

invencible; (*price*) inmejorable; (*quality*) insuperable

unbelievable [ʌnbɪ'liːvəbl] *adj* increíble

unborn [ʌn'bɔːn] *adj* que va a nacer

unbutton [ʌn'bʌtn] *vt* desabrochar

uncalled-for [ʌn'kɔːldfɔː*] *adj* gratuito, inmerecido

uncanny [ʌn'kænɪ] *adj* extraño

uncertain [ʌn'səːtn] *adj* incierto; (*indecisive*) indeciso; **uncertainty** *n* incertidumbre *f*

unchanged [ʌn'tʃeɪndʒd] *adj* igual, sin cambios

uncle ['ʌŋkl] *n* tío

unclear [ʌn'klɪə*] *adj* poco claro; **I'm still ~ about what I'm supposed to do** todavía no tengo muy claro lo que tengo que hacer

uncomfortable [ʌn'kʌmfətəbl] *adj* incómodo; (*uneasy*) inquieto

uncommon [ʌn'kɔmən] *adj* poco común, raro

unconditional [ʌnkən'dɪʃənl] *adj* incondicional

unconscious [ʌn'kɔnʃəs] *adj* sin sentido; (*unaware*): **to be ~ of** no darse cuenta de ▷ *n*: **the ~** el inconsciente

uncontrollable [ʌnkən'trəuləbl] *adj* (*child etc*) incontrolable; (*temper*) indomable; (*laughter*) incontenible

unconventional [ʌnkən'venʃənl] *adj* poco convencional

uncover [ʌn'kʌvə*] *vt* descubrir; (*take lid off*) destapar

undecided [ʌndɪ'saɪdd] *adj* (*character*) indeciso; (*question*) no resuelto

undeniable [ʌndɪ'naɪəbl] *adj* innegable

under ['ʌndə*] *prep* debajo de; (*less than*) menos de; (*according to*) según, de acuerdo con; (*sb's leadership*) bajo ▷ *adv* debajo, abajo; **~ there** allí abajo; **~ repair** en reparación; **undercover** *adj* clandestino; **underdone** *adj* (*Culin*) poco hecho; **underestimate** *vt* subestimar; **undergo** (*irreg*) *vt* sufrir; (*treatment*) recibir; **undergraduate** *n* estudiante *mf*; **underground** *n* (*BRIT*: *railway*) metro; (*Pol*) movimiento clandestino ▷ *adj* (*car park*) subterráneo ▷ *adv* (*work*) en la clandestinidad; **undergrowth** *n* maleza; **underline** *vt* subrayar; **undermine** *vt* socavar, minar; **underneath** [ʌndə'niːθ] *adv* debajo ▷ *prep* debajo de, bajo; **underpants** *npl* calzoncillos *mpl*; **underpass** (*BRIT*) *n* paso subterráneo; **underprivileged** *adj* desposeído; **underscore** *vt* subrayar; **undershirt** (*US*) *n* camiseta; **underskirt** (*BRIT*) *n* enaguas *fpl*

understand [ʌndə'stænd] *vt*, *vi* entender, comprender; (*assume*) tener entendido; **understandable** *adj* comprensible; **understanding** *adj* comprensivo ▷ *n* comprensión *f*, entendimiento; (*agreement*) acuerdo

understatement ['ʌndəsteɪtmənt] *n* modestia (excesiva); **that's an ~!** ¡eso es decir poco!

understood [ʌndə'stud] *pt*, *pp of* **understand** ▷ *adj* (*agreed*) acordado; (*implied*): **it is ~ that** se sobreentiende que

undertake [ʌndə'teɪk] (*irreg*) *vt* emprender; **to ~ to do sth** comprometerse a hacer algo

undertaker ['ʌndəteɪkə*] *n* director(a) *m/f* de pompas fúnebres

undertaking ['ʌndəteɪkɪŋ] *n* empresa; (*promise*) promesa

under: underwater *adv* bajo el agua ▷ *adj* submarino; **underway** *adj*: **to be underway** (*meeting*) estar en marcha; (*investigation*) estar llevándose a cabo; **underwear** *n* ropa interior; **underwent** *vb see* **undergo**; **underworld** *n* (*of crime*) hampa, inframundo

undesirable [ʌndɪ'zaɪrəbl] *adj* (*person*) indeseable; (*thing*) poco aconsejable

undisputed [ʌndɪ'spjuːtɪd] *adj* incontestable

undo [ʌn'duː] (*irreg*) *vt* (*laces*) desatar; (*button etc*) desabrochar; (*spoil*) deshacer

undone [ʌn'dʌn] *pp of* **undo** ▷ *adj*: **to come ~** (*clothes*) desabrocharse; (*parcel*) desatarse

undoubtedly [ʌn'dautɪdlɪ] *adv* indudablemente, sin duda

undress [ʌn'dres] *vi* desnudarse

unearth [ʌn'əːθ] *vt* desenterrar

uneasy [ʌn'iːzɪ] *adj* intranquilo, preocupado; (*feeling*) desagradable; (*peace*) inseguro

unemployed [ʌnɪm'plɔɪd] *adj* parado, sin trabajo ▷ *npl*: **the ~** los parados

unemployment [ʌnɪm'plɔɪmənt] *n* paro, desempleo; **unemployment benefit** *n* (*BRIT*) subsidio de desempleo *or* paro

unequal [ʌn'iːkwəl] *adj* (*unfair*) desigual; (*size*, *length*) distinto

uneven [ʌn'iːvn] *adj* desigual; (*road etc*) lleno de baches

unexpected [ʌnɪk'spektɪd] *adj* inesperado; **unexpectedly** *adv* inesperadamente

unfair [ʌn'fɛə*] *adj*: **~ (to sb)** injusto (con algn)

unfaithful [ʌn'feɪθful] *adj* infiel

unfamiliar [ʌnfə'mɪlɪə*] *adj* extraño, desconocido; **to be ~ with** desconocer

u

unfashionable [ʌnˈfæʃnəbl] *adj* pasado or fuera de moda

unfasten [ʌnˈfɑːsn] *vt* (*knot*) desatar; (*dress*) desabrochar; (*open*) abrir

unfavourable [ʌnˈfeɪvərəbl] (*us* **unfavorable**) *adj* desfavorable

unfinished [ʌnˈfɪnɪʃt] *adj* inacabado, sin terminar

unfit [ʌnˈfɪt] *adj* bajo de forma; (*incompetent*): ~ **(for)** incapaz (de); ~ **for work** no apto para trabajar

unfold [ʌnˈfəʊld] *vt* desdoblar ▷ *vi* abrirse

unforgettable [ʌnfəˈgetəbl] *adj* inolvidable

unfortunate [ʌnˈfɔːtʃnət] *adj* desgraciado; (*event, remark*) inoportuno; **unfortunately** *adv* desgraciadamente

unfriendly [ʌnˈfrendlɪ] *adj* antipático; (*behaviour, remark*) hostil, poco amigable

unfurnished [ʌnˈfɜːnɪʃt] *adj* sin amueblar

unhappiness [ʌnˈhæpɪnɪs] *n* tristeza, desdicha

unhappy [ʌnˈhæpɪ] *adj* (*sad*) triste; (*unfortunate*) desgraciado; (*childhood*) infeliz; ~ **about/with** (*arrangements etc*) poco contento con, descontento de

unhealthy [ʌnˈhelθɪ] *adj* (*place*) malsano; (*person*) enfermizo; (*fig: interest*) morboso

unheard-of [ʌnˈhɜːdɔv] *adj* inaudito, sin precedente

unhelpful [ʌnˈhelpful] *adj* (*person*) poco servicial; (*advice*) inútil

unhurt [ʌnˈhɜːt] *adj* ileso

unidentified [ʌnaɪˈdentɪfaɪd] *adj* no identificado, sin identificar; *see also* **UFO**

uniform [ˈjuːnɪfɔːm] *n* uniforme *m* ▷ *adj* uniforme

unify [ˈjuːnɪfaɪ] *vt* unificar, unir

unimportant [ʌnɪmˈpɔːtənt] *adj* sin importancia

uninhabited [ʌnɪnˈhæbɪtɪd] *adj* desierto

unintentional [ʌnɪnˈtenʃənəl] *adj* involuntario

union [ˈjuːnjən] *n* unión *f*; (*also:* **trade** ~) sindicato ▷ *cpd* sindical; **Union Jack** *n* bandera del Reino Unido

unique [juːˈniːk] *adj* único

unisex [ˈjuːnɪseks] *adj* unisex

unit [ˈjuːnɪt] *n* unidad *f*; (*section: of furniture etc*) elemento; (*team*) grupo; **kitchen** ~ módulo de cocina

unite [juːˈnaɪt] *vt* unir ▷ *vi* unirse; **united** *adj* unido; (*effort*) conjunto; **United Kingdom** *n* Reino Unido; **United Nations (Organization)** *n* Naciones *fpl* Unidas; **United States (of America)** *n* Estados *mpl* Unidos

unity [ˈjuːnɪtɪ] *n* unidad *f*

universal [juːnɪˈvɜːsl] *adj* universal

universe [ˈjuːnɪvɜːs] *n* universo

university [juːnɪˈvɜːsɪtɪ] *n* universidad *f*

unjust [ʌnˈdʒʌst] *adj* injusto

unkind [ʌnˈkaɪnd] *adj* poco amable; (*behaviour, comment*) cruel

unknown [ʌnˈnəʊn] *adj* desconocido

unlawful [ʌnˈlɔːful] *adj* ilegal, ilícito

unleaded [ʌnˈledɪd] *adj* (*petrol, fuel*) sin plombo

unleash [ʌnˈliːʃ] *vt* desatar

unless [ʌnˈles] *conj* a menos que; ~ **he comes** a menos que venga; ~ **otherwise stated** salvo indicación contraria

unlike [ʌnˈlaɪk] *adj* (*not alike*) distinto de o a; (*not like*) poco propio de ▷ *prep* a diferencia de

unlikely [ʌnˈlaɪklɪ] *adj* improbable; (*unexpected*) inverosímil

unlimited [ʌnˈlɪmɪtɪd] *adj* ilimitado

unlisted [ʌnˈlɪstɪd] (*us*) *adj* (*Tel*) que no consta en la guía

unload [ʌnˈləʊd] *vt* descargar

unlock [ʌnˈlɔk] *vt* abrir (con llave)

unlucky [ʌnˈlʌkɪ] *adj* desgraciado; (*object, number*) que da mala suerte; **to be** ~ tener mala suerte

unmarried [ʌnˈmærɪd] *adj* soltero

unmistak(e)able [ʌnmɪsˈteɪkəbl] *adj* inconfundible

unnatural [ʌnˈnætʃrəl] *adj* (*gen*) antinatural; (*manner*) afectado; (*habit*) perverso

unnecessary [ʌnˈnesəsərɪ] *adj* innecesario, inútil

UNO [ˈjuːnəʊ] *n abbr* (= *United Nations Organization*) ONU *f*

unofficial [ʌnəˈfɪʃl] *adj* no oficial; (*news*) sin confirmar

unpack [ʌnˈpæk] *vi* deshacer las maletas ▷ *vt* deshacer

unpaid [ʌnˈpeɪd] *adj* (*bill, debt*) sin pagar, impagado; (*Comm*) pendiente; (*holiday*) sin sueldo; (*work*) sin pago, voluntario

unpleasant [ʌnˈpleznt] *adj* (*disagreeable*) desagradable; (*person, manner*) antipático

unplug [ʌnˈplʌg] *vt* desenchufar, desconectar

unpopular [ʌnˈpɔpjulə*] *adj* impopular, poco popular

unprecedented [ʌnˈpresɪdəntɪd] *adj* sin precedentes

unpredictable [ʌnprɪˈdɪktəbl] *adj* imprevisible

unprotected [ˈʌnprəˈtektɪd] *adj* (*sex*) sin protección

unqualified [ʌnˈkwɔlɪfaɪd] *adj* sin título, no cualificado; (*success*) total

unravel [ʌnˈrævl] vt desenmarañar
unreal [ʌnˈrɪəl] adj irreal; (*extraordinary*) increíble
unrealistic [ʌnrɪəˈlɪstɪk] adj poco realista
unreasonable [ʌnˈriːznəbl] adj irrazonable; (*demand*) excesivo
unrelated [ʌnrɪˈleɪtɪd] adj sin relación; (*family*) no emparentado
unreliable [ʌnrɪˈlaɪəbl] adj (*person*) informal; (*machine*) poco fiable
unrest [ʌnˈrɛst] n inquietud f, malestar m; (*Pol*) disturbios mpl
unroll [ʌnˈrəul] vt desenrollar
unruly [ʌnˈruːlɪ] adj indisciplinado
unsafe [ʌnˈseɪf] adj peligroso
unsatisfactory [ˈʌnsætɪsˈfæktərɪ] adj poco satisfactorio
unscrew [ʌnˈskruː] vt destornillar
unsettled [ʌnˈsɛtld] adj inquieto, intranquilo; (*weather*) variable
unsettling [ʌnˈsɛtlɪŋ] adj perturbador(a), inquietante
unsightly [ʌnˈsaɪtlɪ] adj feo
unskilled [ʌnˈskɪld] adj (*work*) no especializado; (*worker*) no cualificado
unspoiled [ˈʌnˈspɔɪld], **unspoilt** [ˈʌnˈspɔɪlt] adj (*place*) que no ha perdido su belleza natural
unstable [ʌnˈsteɪbl] adj inestable
unsteady [ʌnˈstɛdɪ] adj inestable
unsuccessful [ʌnsəkˈsɛsful] adj (*attempt*) infructuoso; (*writer, proposal*) sin éxito; **to be ~** (*in attempting sth*) no tener éxito, fracasar
unsuitable [ʌnˈsuːtəbl] adj inapropiado; (*time*) inoportuno
unsure [ʌnˈʃuə*] adj inseguro, poco seguro
untidy [ʌnˈtaɪdɪ] adj (*room*) desordenado; (*appearance*) desaliñado
untie [ʌnˈtaɪ] vt desatar
until [ənˈtɪl] prep hasta ⊳ conj hasta que; **~ he comes** hasta que venga; **~ now** hasta ahora; **~ then** hasta entonces
untrue [ʌnˈtruː] adj (*statement*) falso
unused [ʌnˈjuːzd] adj sin usar
unusual [ʌnˈjuːʒuəl] adj insólito, poco común; (*exceptional*) inusitado; **unusually** adv (*exceptionally*) excepcionalmente; **he arrived unusually early** llegó más temprano que de costumbre
unveil [ʌnˈveɪl] vt (*statue*) descubrir
unwanted [ʌnˈwɒntɪd] adj (*clothing*) viejo; (*pregnancy*) no deseado
unwell [ʌnˈwɛl] adj: **to be/feel ~** estar indispuesto/sentirse mal
unwilling [ʌnˈwɪlɪŋ] adj: **to be ~ to do sth** estar poco dispuesto a hacer algo
unwind [ʌnˈwaɪnd] (*irreg*) vt desenvolver ⊳ vi (*relax*) relajarse

unwise [ʌnˈwaɪz] adj imprudente
unwittingly [ʌnˈwɪtɪŋlɪ] adv inconscientemente, sin darse cuenta
unwrap [ʌnˈræp] vt desenvolver
unzip [ʌnˈzɪp] vt abrir la cremallera de; (*Comput*) descomprimir

⊙ **KEYWORD**

up [ʌp] prep: **to go/be up sth** subir/estar subido en algo; **he went up the stairs/ the hill** subió las escaleras/la colina; **we walked/climbed up the hill** subimos la colina; **they live further up the street** viven más arriba en la calle; **go up that road and turn left** sigue por esa calle y gira a la izquierda
⊳ adv **1** (*upwards, higher*) más arriba; **up in the mountains** en lo alto (de la montaña); **put it a bit higher up** ponlo un poco más arriba or alto; **up there** ahí or allí arriba; **up above** en lo alto, por encima, arriba
2: **to be up** (*out of bed*) estar levantado; (*prices, level*) haber subido
3: **up to** (*as far as*) hasta; **up to now** hasta ahora or la fecha
4: **to be up to: it's up to you** (*depending on*) depende de ti; **he's not up to it** (*job, task etc*) no es capaz de hacerlo; **his work is not up to the required standard** su trabajo no da la talla; (*inf: be doing*): **what is he up to?** ¿que estará tramando?
⊳ n: **ups and downs** altibajos mpl

up-and-coming [ʌpəndˈkʌmɪŋ] adj prometedor(a)
upbringing [ˈʌpbrɪŋɪŋ] n educación f
update [ʌpˈdeɪt] vt poner al día
upfront [ʌpˈfrʌnt] adj claro, directo ⊳ adv a las claras; (*pay*) por adelantado; **to be ~ about sth** admitir algo claramente
upgrade [ʌpˈgreɪd] vt (*house*) modernizar; (*employee*) ascender
upheaval [ʌpˈhiːvl] n trastornos mpl; (*Pol*) agitación f
uphill [ʌpˈhɪl] adj cuesta arriba; (*fig: task*) penoso, difícil ⊳ adv: **to go ~** ir cuesta arriba
upholstery [ʌpˈhəulstərɪ] n tapicería
upmarket [ʌpˈmɑːkɪt] adj (*product*) de categoría
upon [əˈpɒn] prep sobre
upper [ˈʌpə*] adj superior, de arriba ⊳ n (*of shoe: also:* **~s**) empeine m; **upper-class** adj de clase alta
upright [ˈʌpraɪt] adj derecho; (*vertical*) vertical; (*fig*) honrado
uprising [ˈʌpraɪzɪŋ] n sublevación f
uproar [ˈʌprɔː*] n escándalo

upset [n 'ʌpsɛt, vb, adj ʌp'sɛt] n (to plan etc) revés m, contratiempo; (Med) trastorno ▷ vt irreg (glass etc) volcar; (plan) alterar; (person) molestar, disgustar ▷ adj molesto, disgustado; (stomach) revuelto

upside-down [ʌpsaɪd'daʊn] adv al revés; **to turn a place ~** (fig) revolverlo todo

upstairs [ʌp'stɛəz] adv arriba ▷ adj (room) de arriba ▷ n el piso superior

up-to-date ['ʌptə'deɪt] adj al día

uptown ['ʌptaʊn] (US) adv hacia las afueras ▷ adj exterior, de las afueras

upward ['ʌpwəd] adj ascendente; **upward(s)** adv hacia arriba; (more than): **upward(s) of** más de

uranium [juə'reɪnɪəm] n uranio

Uranus [juə'reɪnəs] n Urano

urban ['ɜːbən] adj urbano

urge [ɜːdʒ] n (desire) deseo ▷ vt: **to ~ sb to do sth** animar a algn a hacer algo

urgency ['ɜːdʒənsɪ] n urgencia

urgent ['ɜːdʒənt] adj urgente; (voice) perentorio

urinal ['juərɪnl] n (building) urinario; (vessel) orinal m

urinate ['juərɪneɪt] vi orinar

urine ['juərɪn] n orina, orines mpl

US n abbr (= United States) EE. UU.

us [ʌs] pron nos; (after prep) nosotros/as; see also **me**

USA n abbr (= United States (of America)) EE.UU.

use [n juːs, vb juːz] n uso, empleo; (usefulness) utilidad f ▷ vt usar, emplear; **she ~d to do it** (ella) solía or acostumbraba hacerlo; **in ~** en uso; **out of ~** en desuso; **to be of ~** servir; **it's no ~** (pointless) es inútil; (not useful) no sirve; **to be ~d to** estar acostumbrado a, acostumbrar; **use up** vt (food) consumir; (money) gastar; **used** [juːzd] adj (car) usado; **useful** adj útil; **useless** adj (unusable) inservible; (pointless) inútil; (person) inepto; **user** n usuario/a; **user-friendly** adj (computer) amistoso

usual ['juːʒuəl] adj normal, corriente; **as ~** como de costumbre; **usually** adv normalmente

utensil [juː'tɛnsl] n utensilio; **kitchen ~s** batería de cocina

utility [juː'tɪlɪtɪ] n utilidad f; (public utility) (empresa de) servicio público

utilize ['juːtɪlaɪz] vt utilizar

utmost ['ʌtməʊst] adj mayor ▷ n: **to do one's ~** hacer todo lo posible

utter ['ʌtə*] adj total, completo ▷ vt pronunciar, proferir; **utterly** adv completamente, totalmente

U-turn ['juː'tɜːn] n viraje m en redondo

v. abbr = **verse**; **versus**; (= volt) v; (= vide) véase

vacancy ['veɪkənsɪ] n (BRIT: job) vacante f; (room) habitación f libre; **"no vacancies"** "completo"

vacant ['veɪkənt] adj desocupado, libre; (expression) distraído

vacate [və'keɪt] vt (house, room) desocupar; (job) dejar (vacante)

vacation [və'keɪʃən] n vacaciones fpl; **vacationer** (US **vacationist**) n turista m/f

vaccination [væksɪ'neɪʃən] n vacunación f

vaccine ['væksiːn] n vacuna

vacuum ['vækjum] n vacío; **vacuum cleaner** n aspiradora

vagina [və'dʒaɪnə] n vagina

vague [veɪg] adj vago; (memory) borroso; (ambiguous) impreciso; (person: absent-minded) distraído; (: evasive): **to be ~** no decir las cosas claramente

vain [veɪn] adj (conceited) presumido; (useless) vano, inútil; **in ~** en vano

Valentine's Day ['væləntaɪnzdeɪ] n día de los enamorados

valid ['vælɪd] adj válido; (ticket) valedero; (law) vigente

valley ['vælɪ] n valle m

valuable ['væljuəbl] adj (jewel) de valor; (time) valioso; **valuables** npl objetos mpl de valor

value ['væljuː] n valor m; (importance) importancia ▷ vt (fix price of) tasar, valorar; (esteem) apreciar; **values** npl (principles) principios mpl

valve [vælv] n válvula

vampire ['væmpaɪə*] n vampiro

van [væn] n (Aut) furgoneta, camioneta

vandal ['vændl] n vándalo/a; **vandalism** n vandalismo; **vandalize** vt dañar, destruir

vanilla [və'nɪlə] n vainilla

vanish ['vænɪʃ] vi desaparecer

vanity ['vænɪtɪ] n vanidad f

vapour ['veɪpə*] (us **vapor**) n vapor m; (on breath, window) vaho

variable ['veərɪəbl] adj variable

variant ['veərɪənt] n variante f

variation [veərɪ'eɪʃən] n variación f

varied ['veərɪd] adj variado

variety [və'raɪətɪ] n (diversity) diversidad f; (type) variedad f

various ['veərɪəs] adj (several: people) varios/as; (reasons) diversos/as

varnish ['vɑːnɪʃ] n barniz m; (nail varnish) esmalte m ▷ vt barnizar; (nails) pintar (con esmalte)

vary ['veərɪ] vt variar; (change) cambiar ▷ vi variar

vase [vɑːz] n jarrón m

Be careful not to translate **vase** by the Spanish word vaso.

Vaseline® ['væsɪliːn] n vaselina®

vast [vɑːst] adj enorme

VAT [væt] (BRIT) n abbr (= value added tax) IVA m

vault [vɔːlt] n (of roof) bóveda; (tomb) panteón m; (in bank) cámara acorazada ▷ vt (also: ~ **over**) saltar (por encima de)

VCR n abbr = **video cassette recorder**

VDU n abbr (= visual display unit) UPV f

veal [viːl] n ternera

veer [vɪə*] vi (vehicle) virar; (wind) girar

vegan ['viːgən] n vegetariano/a estricto/a, vegetaliano/a

vegetable ['vedʒtəbl] n (Bot) vegetal m; (edible plant) legumbre f, hortaliza ▷ adj vegetal

vegetarian [vedʒɪ'teərɪən] adj, n vegetariano/a m/f

vegetation [vedʒɪ'teɪʃən] n vegetación f

vehicle ['viːɪkl] n vehículo; (fig) medio

veil [veɪl] n velo ▷ vt velar

vein [veɪn] n vena; (of ore etc) veta

Velcro® ['velkrəu] n velcro® m

velvet ['velvɪt] n terciopelo

vending machine ['vendɪŋ-] n distribuidor m automático

vendor ['vendə*] n vendedor(a) m/f; **street ~** vendedor(a) m/f callejero/a

vengeance ['vendʒəns] n venganza; **with a ~** (fig) con creces

venison ['venɪsn] n carne f de venado

venom ['venəm] n veneno; (bitterness) odio

vent [vent] n (in jacket) respiradero; (in wall) rejilla (de ventilación) ▷ vt (fig: feelings) desahogar

ventilation [ventɪ'leɪʃən] n ventilación f

venture ['ventʃə*] n empresa ▷ vt

(opinion) ofrecer ▷ vi arriesgarse, lanzarse; **business ~** empresa comercial

venue ['venjuː] n lugar m

Venus ['viːnəs] n Venus m

verb [vəːb] n verbo; **verbal** adj verbal

verdict ['vəːdɪkt] n veredicto, fallo; (fig) opinión f, juicio

verge [vəːdʒ] (BRIT) n borde m; "**soft ~s**" (Aut) "arcén m no asfaltado"; **to be on the ~ of doing sth** estar a punto de hacer algo

verify ['verɪfaɪ] vt comprobar, verificar

versatile ['vəːsətaɪl] adj (person) polifacético; (machine, tool etc) versátil

verse [vəːs] n poesía; (stanza) estrofa; (in bible) versículo

version ['vəːʃən] n versión f

versus ['vəːsəs] prep contra

vertical ['vəːtɪkl] adj vertical

very ['verɪ] adv muy ▷ adj: **the ~ book which** el mismo libro que; **the ~ last** el último de todos; **at the ~ least** al menos; **~ much** muchísimo

vessel ['vesl] n (ship) barco; (container) vasija; see **blood**

vest [vest] n (BRIT) camiseta; (US: waistcoat) chaleco

vet [vet] vt (candidate) investigar ▷ n abbr (BRIT) = **veterinary surgeon**

veteran ['vetərn] n excombatiente mf, veterano/a

veterinary surgeon ['vetrɪnərɪ-] (US **veterinarian**) n veterinario/a m/f

veto ['viːtəu] (pl **~es**) n veto ▷ vt prohibir, poner el veto a

via ['vaɪə] prep por, por medio de

viable ['vaɪəbl] adj viable

vibrate [vaɪ'breɪt] vi vibrar

vibration [vaɪ'breɪʃən] n vibración f

vicar ['vɪkə*] n párroco (de la Iglesia Anglicana)

vice [vaɪs] n (evil) vicio; (Tech) torno de banco; **vice-chairman** (irreg) n vicepresidente m

vice versa ['vaɪsɪ'vəːsə] adv viceversa

vicinity [vɪ'sɪnɪtɪ] n: **in the ~ (of)** cercano (a)

vicious ['vɪʃəs] adj (attack) violento; (words) cruel; (horse, dog) resabido

victim ['vɪktɪm] n víctima

victor ['vɪktə*] n vencedor(a) m/f

Victorian [vɪk'tɔːrɪən] adj victoriano

victorious [vɪk'tɔːrɪəs] adj vencedor(a)

victory ['vɪktərɪ] n victoria

video ['vɪdɪəu] n vídeo (SP), video (LAM); **video call** n videollamada; **video camera** n videocámara, cámara de vídeo; **video (cassette) recorder** n vídeo (SP), video (LAM); **video game** n videojuego;

videophone n videoteléfono; **video shop** n videoclub m; **video tape** n cinta de vídeo
vie [vaɪ] vi: **to ~ (with sb for sth)** competir (con algn por algo)
Vienna [vɪ'ɛnə] n Viena
Vietnam [vjɛt'næm] n Vietnam m; **Vietnamese** [-nə'miːz] n inv, adj vietnamita mf
view [vjuː] n vista; (outlook) perspectiva; (opinion) opinión f, criterio ▷ vt (look at) mirar; (fig) considerar; **on ~** (in museum etc) expuesto; **in full ~ (of)** en plena vista (de); **in ~ of the weather/the fact that** en vista del tiempo/del hecho de que; **in my ~** en mi opinión; **viewer** n espectador(a) m/f; (TV) telespectador(a) m/f; **viewpoint** n (attitude) punto de vista; (place) mirador m
vigilant ['vɪdʒɪlənt] adj vigilante
vigorous ['vɪgərəs] adj enérgico, vigoroso
vile [vaɪl] adj vil, infame; (smell) asqueroso; (temper) endemoniado
villa ['vɪlə] n (country house) casa de campo; (suburban house) chalet m
village ['vɪlɪdʒ] n aldea; **villager** n aldeano/a
villain ['vɪlən] n (scoundrel) malvado/a; (in novel) malo; (BRIT: criminal) maleante mf
vinaigrette [vɪneɪ'grɛt] n vinagreta
vine [vaɪn] n vid f
vinegar ['vɪnɪgə*] n vinagre m
vineyard ['vɪnjɑːd] n viña, viñedo
vintage ['vɪntɪdʒ] n (year) vendimia, cosecha ▷ cpd de época
vinyl ['vaɪnl] n vinilo
viola [vɪ'əʊlə] n (Mus) viola
violate ['vaɪəleɪt] vt violar
violation [vaɪə'leɪʃən] n violación f; **in ~ of sth** en violación de algo
violence ['vaɪələns] n violencia
violent ['vaɪələnt] adj violento; (intense) intenso
violet ['vaɪələt] adj violado, violeta ▷ n (plant) violeta
violin [vaɪə'lɪn] n violín m
VIP n abbr (= very important person) VIP m
virgin ['vəːdʒɪn] n virgen f
Virgo ['vəːgəʊ] n Virgo
virtual ['vəːtjʊəl] adj virtual; **virtually** adv prácticamente; **virtual reality** n (Comput) mundo or realidad f virtual
virtue ['vəːtjuː] n virtud f; (advantage) ventaja; **by ~ of** en virtud de
virus ['vaɪərəs] n (also Comput) virus m inv
visa ['viːzə] n visado (SP), visa (LAM)
vise [vaɪs] (US) n (Tech) = **vice**
visibility [vɪzɪ'bɪlɪtɪ] n visibilidad f
visible ['vɪzəbl] adj visible
vision ['vɪʒən] n (sight) vista; (foresight, in dream) visión f
visit ['vɪzɪt] n visita ▷ vt (person (US: also: ~ with)) visitar, hacer una visita a; (place) ir a, (ir a) conocer; **visiting hours** npl (in hospital etc) horas fpl de visita; **visitor** n (museum) visitante mf; (invited to house) visita; (tourist) turista mf; **visitor centre** (US **visitor center**) n centro m de información
visual ['vɪzjʊəl] adj visual; **visualize** vt imaginarse
vital ['vaɪtl] adj (essential) esencial; (dynamic) dinámico; (organ) vital
vitality [vaɪ'tælɪtɪ] n energía, vitalidad f
vitamin ['vɪtəmɪn] n vitamina
vivid ['vɪvɪd] adj (account) gráfico; (light) intenso; (imagination, memory) vivo
V-neck ['viːnɛk] n cuello de pico
vocabulary [vəʊ'kæbjʊlərɪ] n vocabulario
vocal ['vəʊkl] adj vocal; (articulate) elocuente
vocational [vəʊ'keɪʃənl] adj profesional
vodka ['vɒdkə] n vodka m
vogue [vəʊg] n: **in ~** en boga
voice [vɔɪs] n voz f ▷ vt expresar; **voice mail** n fonobuzón m
void [vɔɪd] n vacío; (hole) hueco ▷ adj (invalid) nulo, inválido; (empty): **~ of** carente or desprovisto de
volatile ['vɒlətaɪl] adj (situation) inestable; (person) voluble; (liquid) volátil
volcano [vɒl'keɪnəʊ] (pl **~es**) n volcán m
volleyball ['vɒlɪbɔːl] n vol(e)ibol m
volt [vəʊlt] n voltio; **voltage** n voltaje m
volume ['vɒljuːm] n (gen) volumen m; (book) tomo
voluntarily ['vɒləntrɪlɪ] adv libremente, voluntariamente
voluntary ['vɒləntərɪ] adj voluntario
volunteer [vɒlən'tɪə*] n voluntario/a ▷ vt (information) ofrecer ▷ vi ofrecerse (de voluntario); **to ~ to do** ofrecerse a hacer
vomit ['vɒmɪt] n vómito ▷ vt, vi vomitar
vote [vəʊt] n voto; (votes cast) votación f; (right to vote) derecho de votar; (franchise) sufragio ▷ vt (chairman) elegir; (propose): **to ~ that** proponer que ▷ vi votar, ir a votar; **~ of thanks** voto de gracias; **voter** n votante mf; **voting** n votación f
voucher ['vaʊtʃə*] n (for meal etc) vale m
vow [vaʊ] n voto ▷ vt: **to ~ to do/that** jurar hacer/que
vowel ['vaʊəl] n vocal f
voyage ['vɔɪɪdʒ] n viaje m
vulgar ['vʌlgə*] adj (rude) ordinario, grosero; (in bad taste) de mal gusto
vulnerable ['vʌlnərəbl] adj vulnerable
vulture ['vʌltʃə*] n buitre m

W

waddle ['wɔdl] vi anadear

wade [weɪd] vi: **to ~ through** (water) vadear; (fig: book) leer con dificultad

wafer ['weɪfə*] n galleta, barquillo

waffle ['wɔfl] n (Culin) gofre m ▷ vi dar el rollo

wag [wæg] vt menear, agitar ▷ vi moverse, menearse

wage [weɪdʒ] n (also: **~s**) sueldo, salario ▷ vt: **to ~ war** hacer la guerra

wag(g)on ['wægən] n (horse-drawn) carro; (BRIT Rail) vagón m

wail [weɪl] n gemido ▷ vi gemir

waist [weɪst] n cintura, talle m; **waistcoat** (BRIT) n chaleco

wait [weɪt] n (interval) pausa ▷ vi esperar; **to lie in ~ for** acechar a; **I can't ~ to** (fig) estoy deseando; **to ~ for** esperar (a); **wait on** vt fus servir a; **waiter** n camarero; **waiting list** n lista de espera; **waiting room** n sala de espera; **waitress** ['weɪtrɪs] n camarera

waive [weɪv] vt suspender

wake [weɪk] (pt **woke** or **~d**, pp **woken** or **~d**) vt (also: **~ up**) despertar ▷ vi (also: **~ up**) despertarse ▷ n (for dead person) vela, velatorio; (Naut) estela

Wales [weɪlz] n País m de Gales; **the Prince of ~** el príncipe de Gales

walk [wɔːk] n (stroll) paseo; (hike) excursión f a pie, caminata; (gait) paso, andar m; (in park etc) paseo, alameda ▷ vi andar, caminar; (for pleasure, exercise) pasear ▷ vt (distance) recorrer a pie, andar; (dog) pasear; **10 minutes' ~ from here** a 10 minutos de aquí andando; **people from all ~s of life** gente de todas las esferas; **walk out** vi (audience) salir; (workers) declararse en huelga; **walker** n (person) paseante mf, caminante mf; **walkie-talkie** ['wɔːkɪ'tɔːkɪ] n walkie-talkie m; **walking**

n el andar; **walking shoes** npl zapatos mpl para andar; **walking stick** n bastón m; **Walkman®** n Walkman® m; **walkway** n paseo

wall [wɔːl] n pared f; (exterior) muro; (city wall etc) muralla

wallet ['wɔlɪt] n cartera, billetera

wallpaper ['wɔːlpeɪpə*] n papel m pintado ▷ vt empapelar

walnut ['wɔːlnʌt] n nuez f; (tree) nogal m

walrus ['wɔːlrəs] (pl ~ or **~es**) n morsa

waltz [wɔːlts] n vals m ▷ vi bailar el vals

wand [wɔnd] n (also: **magic ~**) varita (mágica)

wander ['wɔndə*] vi (person) vagar; deambular; (thoughts) divagar ▷ vt recorrer, vagar por

want [wɔnt] vt querer, desear; (need) necesitar ▷ n: **for ~ of** por falta de; **wanted** adj (criminal) buscado; **"wanted"** (in advertisements) "se busca"

war [wɔː*] n guerra; **to make ~ (on)** declarar la guerra (a)

ward [wɔːd] n (in hospital) sala; (Pol) distrito electoral; (Law: child: also: **~ of court**) pupilo/a

warden ['wɔːdn] n (BRIT: of institution) director(a) m/f; (of park, game reserve) guardián/ana m/f; (BRIT: also: **traffic ~**) guardia mf

wardrobe ['wɔːdrəub] n armario, ropero; (clothes) vestuario

warehouse ['wɛəhaus] n almacén m, depósito

warfare ['wɔːfɛə*] n guerra

warhead ['wɔːhɛd] n cabeza armada

warm [wɔːm] adj caliente; (thanks) efusivo; (clothes etc) abrigado; (welcome, day) caluroso; **it's ~** hace calor; **I'm ~** tengo calor; **warm up** vi (room) calentarse; (person) entrar en calor; (athlete) hacer ejercicios de calentamiento ▷ vt calentar; **warmly** adv afectuosamente; **warmth** n calor m

warn [wɔːn] vt avisar, advertir; **warning** n aviso, advertencia; **warning light** n luz f de advertencia

warrant ['wɔrnt] n autorización f; (Law: to arrest) orden f de detención; (: to search) mandamiento de registro

warranty ['wɔrəntɪ] n garantía

warrior ['wɔrɪə*] n guerrero/a

Warsaw ['wɔːsɔː] n Varsovia

warship ['wɔːʃɪp] n buque m or barco de guerra

wart [wɔːt] n verruga

wartime ['wɔːtaɪm] n: **in ~** en tiempos de guerra, en la guerra

wary ['wɛərɪ] adj cauteloso

was [wɔz] *pt of* **be**
wash [wɔʃ] *vt* lavar ▷ *vi* lavarse; (*sea etc*): **to ~ against/over sth** llegar hasta/ cubrir algo ▷ *n* (*clothes etc*) lavado; (*of ship*) estela; **to have a ~** lavarse; **wash up** *vi* (BRIT) fregar los platos; (US) lavarse; **washbasin** (US) *n* lavabo; **wash cloth** (US) *n* manopla; **washer** *n* (*Tech*) arandela; **washing** *n* (*dirty*) ropa sucia; (*clean*) colada; **washing line** *n* cuerda de (colgar) la ropa; **washing machine** *n* lavadora; **washing powder** (BRIT) *n* detergente *m* (en polvo)
Washington ['wɔʃɪŋtən] *n* Washington *m*
wash: washing-up (BRIT) *n* fregado, platos *mpl* (para fregar); **washing-up liquid** (BRIT) *n* líquido lavavajillas; **washroom** (US) *n* servicios *mpl*
wasn't ['wɔznt] = **was not**
wasp [wɔsp] *n* avispa
waste [weɪst] *n* derroche *m*, despilfarro; (*of time*) pérdida; (*food*) sobras *fpl*; (*rubbish*) basura, desperdicios *mpl* ▷ *adj* (*material*) de desecho; (*left over*) sobrante; (*land*) baldío, descampado ▷ *vt* malgastar, derrochar; (*time*) perder; (*opportunity*) desperdiciar; **waste ground** (BRIT) *n* terreno baldío; **wastepaper basket** *n* papelera
watch [wɔtʃ] *n* (*also*: **wrist ~**) reloj *m*; (*Mil: group of guards*) centinela *m*; (*act*) vigilancia; (*Naut: spell of duty*) guardia ▷ *vt* (*look at*) mirar, observar; (: *match, programme*) ver; (*spy on, guard*) vigilar; (*be careful of*) cuidarse de, tener cuidado de ▷ *vi* ver, mirar; (*keep guard*) montar guardia; **watch out** *vi* cuidarse, tener cuidado; **watchdog** *n* perro guardián; (*fig*) *persona u organismo encargado de asegurarse de que las empresas actúan dentro de la legalidad*; **watch strap** *n* pulsera (de reloj)
water ['wɔːtə*] *n* agua ▷ *vt* (*plant*) regar ▷ *vi* (*eyes*) llorar; (*mouth*) hacerse la boca agua; **water down** *vt* (*milk etc*) aguar; (*fig: story*) dulcificar, diluir; **watercolour** (US **watercolor**) *n* acuarela; **watercress** *n* berro; **waterfall** *n* cascada, salto de agua; **watering can** *n* regadera; **watermelon** *n* sandía; **waterproof** *adj* impermeable; **water-skiing** *n* esquí *m* acuático
watt [wɔt] *n* vatio
wave [weɪv] *n* (*of hand*) señal *f* con la mano; (*on water*) ola; (*Radio, in hair*) onda; (*fig*) oleada ▷ *vi* agitar la mano; (*flag etc*) ondear ▷ *vt* (*handkerchief, gun*) agitar; **wavelength** *n* longitud *f* de onda
waver ['weɪvə*] *vi* (*voice, love etc*) flaquear; (*person*) vacilar
wavy ['weɪvɪ] *adj* ondulado
wax [wæks] *n* cera ▷ *vt* encerar ▷ *vi*

(*moon*) crecer
way [weɪ] *n* camino; (*distance*) trayecto, recorrido; (*direction*) dirección *f*, sentido; (*manner*) modo, manera; (*habit*) costumbre *f*; **which ~? - this ~** ¿por dónde? *or* ¿en qué dirección? - por aquí; **on the ~** (*en route*) en (el) camino; **to be on one's ~** estar en camino; **to be in the ~** bloquear el camino; (*fig*) estorbar; **to go out of one's ~ to do sth** desvivirse por hacer algo; **under ~** en marcha; **to lose one's ~** extraviarse; **in a ~** en cierto modo *or* sentido; **no ~!** (*inf*) ¡de eso nada!; **by the ~ ...** a propósito ...; **"~ in"** (BRIT) "entrada"; **"~ out"** (BRIT) "salida"; **the ~ back** el camino de vuelta; **"give ~"** (BRIT Aut) "ceda el paso"
W.C. *n* (BRIT) wáter *m*
we [wiː] *pl pron* nosotros/as
weak [wiːk] *adj* débil, flojo; (*tea etc*) claro; **weaken** *vi* debilitarse; (*give way*) ceder ▷ *vt* debilitar; **weakness** *n* debilidad *f*; (*fault*) punto débil; **to have a weakness for** tener debilidad por
wealth [welθ] *n* riqueza; (*of details*) abundancia; **wealthy** *adj* rico
weapon ['wepən] *n* arma; **~s of mass destruction** armas de destrucción masiva
wear [wɛə*] (*pt* **wore**, *pp* **worn**) *n* (*use*) uso; (*deterioration through use*) desgaste *m* ▷ *vt* (*clothes*) llevar; (*shoes*) calzar; (*damage: through use*) gastar, usar ▷ *vi* (*last*) durar; (*rub through etc*) desgastarse; **evening ~** ropa de etiqueta; **sports~/ baby~** ropa de deportes/de niños; **wear off** *vi* (*pain etc*) pasar, desaparecer; **wear out** *vt* desgastar; (*person, strength*) agotar
weary ['wɪərɪ] *adj* cansado; (*dispirited*) abatido ▷ *vi*: **to ~ of** cansarse de
weasel ['wiːzl] *n* (*Zool*) comadreja
weather ['wɛðə*] *n* tiempo ▷ *vt* (*storm, crisis*) hacer frente a; **under the ~** (*fig: ill*) indispuesto, pachucho; **weather forecast** *n* boletín *m* meteorológico
weave [wiːv] (*pt* **wove**, *pp* **woven**) *vt* (*cloth*) tejer; (*fig*) entretejer
web [web] *n* (*of spider*) telaraña; (*on duck's foot*) membrana; (*network*) red *f*; **the (World Wide) W~** la Red; **web address** *n* dirección *f* de Internet; **webcam** *n* webcam *f*; **web page** *n* (página) web *m or f*; **website** *n* sitio web
Wed. *abbr* (= *Wednesday*) miérc
wed [wed] (*pt, pp* **~ded**) *vt* casar ▷ *vi* casarse
we'd [wiːd] = **we had; we would**
wedding ['wedɪŋ] *n* boda, casamiento; **silver/golden ~ (anniversary)** bodas *fpl* de plata/de oro; **wedding anniversary** *n*

aniversario de boda; **wedding day** n día
m de la boda; **wedding dress** n traje m de
novia; **wedding ring** n alianza
wedge [wɛdʒ] n (of wood etc) cuña; (of cake)
trozo ▷ vt acuñar; (push) apretar
Wednesday ['wɛdnzdɪ] n miércoles m inv
wee [wi:] (SCOTTISH) adj pequeñito
weed [wi:d] n mala hierba, maleza
▷ vt escardar, desherbar; **weedkiller** n
herbicida m
week [wi:k] n semana; **a ~ today/
on Friday** de hoy/del viernes en ocho
días; **weekday** n día m laborable;
weekend n fin m de semana; **weekly**
adv semanalmente, cada semana ▷ adj
semanal ▷ n semanario
weep [wi:p] (pt, pp **wept**) vi, vt llorar
weigh [weɪ] vt, vi pesar; **to ~ anchor** levar
anclas; **weigh up** vt sopesar
weight [weɪt] n peso; (metal weight) pesa;
to lose/put on ~ adelgazar/engordar;
weightlifting n levantamiento de pesas
weir [wɪə*] n presa
weird [wɪəd] adj raro, extraño
welcome ['wɛlkəm] adj bienvenido ▷ n
bienvenida ▷ vt dar la bienvenida a; (be
glad of) alegrarse de; **thank you - you're**
**gracias - de nada
weld [wɛld] n soldadura ▷ vt soldar
welfare ['wɛlfɛə*] n bienestar m; (social
aid) asistencia social; **welfare state** n
estado del bienestar
well [wɛl] n fuente f, pozo ▷ adv bien
▷ adj: **to be ~** estar bien (de salud) ▷ excl
¡vaya!, ¡bueno!; **as ~** también; **as ~ as**
además de; **~ done!** ¡bien hecho!; **get ~**
soon! ¡que te mejores pronto!; **to do ~**
(business) ir bien; (person) tener éxito
we'll [wi:l] = **we will; we shall**
well: well-behaved adj bueno; **well-built**
adj (person) fornido; **well-dressed** adj bien
vestido
wellies ['wɛlɪz] (inf) npl (BRIT) botas de
goma
well: well-known adj (person) conocido;
well-off adj acomodado; **well-paid**
[wɛl'peɪd] adj bien pagado, bien retribuido
Welsh [wɛlʃ] adj galés/esa ▷ n (Ling)
galés m; **Welshman** (irreg) n galés m;
Welshwoman (irreg) n galesa
went [wɛnt] pt of **go**
wept [wɛpt] pt, pp of **weep**
were [wə:*] pt of **be**
we're [wɪə*] = **we are**
weren't [wə:nt] = **were not**
west [wɛst] n oeste m ▷ adj occidental,
del oeste ▷ adv al or hacia el oeste; **the**
W~ el Oeste, el Occidente; **westbound**

['wɛstbaund] adj (traffic, carriageway) con
rumbo al oeste; **western** adj occidental
▷ n (Cinema) película del oeste; **West Indian**
adj, n antillano/a m/f
wet [wɛt] adj (damp) húmedo; (soaked): **~**
through mojado; (rainy) lluvioso ▷ n
(BRIT: Pol) conservador(a) m/f moderado/a;
to get ~ mojarse; **"~ paint"** "recién
pintado"; **wetsuit** n traje m térmico
we've [wi:v] = **we have**
whack [wæk] vt dar un buen golpe a
whale [weɪl] n (Zool) ballena
wharf [wɔ:f] (pl **wharves**) n muelle m

○ **KEYWORD**

what [wɔt] adj **1** (in direct/indirect questions)
qué; **what size is he?** ¿qué talla usa?; **what**
colour/shape is it? ¿de qué color/forma es?
2 (in exclamations): **what a mess!** ¡qué
desastre!; **what a fool I am!** ¡qué tonto soy!
▷ pron **1** (interrogative) qué; **what are you**
doing? ¿qué haces or estás haciendo?; **what**
is happening? ¿qué pasa or está pasando?;
what is it called? ¿cómo se llama?; **what**
about me? ¿y yo qué?; **what about doing**
...? ¿qué tal si hacemos ...?
2 (relative) lo que; **I saw what you did/was**
on the table vi lo que hiciste/había en la
mesa
▷ excl (disbelieving) ¡cómo!; **what, no coffee!**
¡que no hay café!

whatever [wɔt'ɛvə*] adj: **~ book you**
choose cualquier libro que elijas ▷ pron: **do**
~ is necessary haga lo que sea necesario; **~**
happens pase lo que pase; **no reason ~** or
whatsoever ninguna razón sea la que sea;
nothing ~ nada en absoluto
whatsoever [wɔtsəu'ɛvə*] adj see
whatever
wheat [wi:t] n trigo
wheel [wi:l] n rueda; (Aut: also: **steering**
~) volante m; (Naut) timón m ▷ vt (pram
etc) empujar ▷ vi (also: **~ round**) dar la
vuelta, girar; **wheelbarrow** n carretilla;
wheelchair n silla de ruedas; **wheel clamp**
n (Aut) cepo
wheeze [wi:z] vi resollar

○ **KEYWORD**

when [wɛn] adv cuando; **when did it**
happen? ¿cuándo ocurrió?; **I know when it**
happened sé cuándo ocurrió
▷ conj **1** (at, during, after the time that)
cuando; **be careful when you cross the**
road ten cuidado al cruzar la calle; **that**

was when I needed you fue entonces que
te necesité
2 (on, at which): **on the day when I met him**
el día en qué le conocí
3 (whereas) cuando

whenever [wɛn'ɛvə*] conj cuando; (every
time that) cada vez que ▷ adv cuando sea
where [wɛə*] adv dónde ▷ conj donde;
this is ~ aquí es donde; **whereabouts**
adv dónde ▷ n: **nobody knows his
whereabouts** nadie conoce su paradero;
whereas conj visto que, mientras;
whereby pron por lo cual; **wherever** conj
dondequiera que; (interrogative) dónde
whether ['wɛðə*] conj si; **I don't know ~
to accept or not** no sé si aceptar o no; **~ you
go or not** vayas o no vayas

○ **KEYWORD**

which [wɪtʃ] adj **1** (interrogative: direct,
indirect) qué; **which picture(s) do you
want?** ¿qué cuadro(s) quieres?; **which one?**
¿cuál?
2 in which case en cuyo caso; **we got
there at 8 pm, by which time the cinema
was full** llegamos allí a las 8, cuando el cine
estaba lleno
▷ pron **1** (interrogative) cuál; **I don't mind
which** el/la que sea
2 (relative: replacing noun) que; (: replacing
clause) lo que; (: after preposition) (el)(la) que
etc el/la cual etc; **the apple which you
ate/which is on the table** la manzana que
comiste/que está en la mesa; **the chair on
which you are sitting** la silla en la que estás
sentado; **he said he knew, which is true/I
feared** dijo que lo sabía, lo cual or lo que es
cierto/me temía

whichever [wɪtʃ'ɛvə*] adj: **take ~ book
you prefer** coja (SP) el libro que prefiera; **~
book you take** cualquier libro que coja
while [waɪl] n rato, momento ▷ conj
mientras; (although) aunque; **for a ~** durante
algún tiempo
whilst [waɪlst] conj = **while**
whim [wɪm] n capricho
whine [waɪn] n (of pain) gemido; (of engine)
zumbido; (of siren) aullido ▷ vi gemir,
zumbar; (fig: complain) gimotear
whip [wɪp] n látigo; (Pol: person) encargado
de la disciplina partidaria en el parlamento
▷ vt azotar; (Culin) batir; (move quickly): **to ~
sth out/off** sacar/quitar algo de un tirón;
whipped cream n nata or crema montada
whirl [wə:l] vt hacer girar, dar vueltas

a ▷ vi girar, dar vueltas; (leaves etc)
arremolinarse
whisk [wɪsk] n (Culin) batidor m ▷ vt
(Culin) batir; **to ~ sb away** or **off** llevar
volando a algn
whiskers ['wɪskəz] npl (of animal) bigotes
mpl; (of man) patillas fpl
whiskey ['wɪskɪ] (US, IRELAND) n = **whisky**
whisky ['wɪskɪ] n whisky m
whisper ['wɪspə*] n susurro ▷ vi, vt
susurrar
whistle ['wɪsl] n (sound) silbido; (object)
silbato ▷ vi silbar
white [waɪt] adj blanco; (pale) pálido ▷ n
blanco; (of egg) clara; **whiteboard** n pizarra
blanca; **interactive whiteboard** pizarra
interactiva; **White House** (US) n Casa
Blanca; **whitewash** n (paint) jalbegue m,
cal f ▷ vt blanquear
whiting ['waɪtɪŋ] n inv (fish) pescadilla
Whitsun ['wɪtsn] n pentecostés m
whittle ['wɪtl] vt: **to ~ away, ~ down** ir
reduciendo
whizz [wɪz] vi: **to ~ past** or **by** pasar a toda
velocidad

○ **KEYWORD**

who [hu:] pron **1** (interrogative) quién; **who
is it?, who's there?** ¿quién es?; **who are
you looking for?** ¿a quién buscas?; **I told
her who I was** le dije quién era yo
2 (relative) que; **the man/woman who
spoke to me** el hombre/la mujer que habló
conmigo; **those who can swim** los que
saben or sepan nadar

whoever [hu:'ɛvə*] pron: **~ finds it**
cualquiera or quienquiera que lo encuentre;
ask ~ you like pregunta a quien quieras; **~
he marries** no importa con quién se case
whole [həʊl] adj (entire) todo, entero;
(not broken) intacto ▷ n todo; (all): **the
~ of the town** toda la ciudad, la ciudad
entera ▷ n (total) total m; (sum) conjunto;
on the ~, as a ~ en general; **wholefood(s)**
n(pl) alimento(s) m(pl) integral(es);
wholeheartedly [həʊl'hɑ:tɪdlɪ] adv con
entusiasmo; **wholemeal** adj integral;
wholesale n venta al por mayor ▷ adj al
por mayor; (fig: destruction) sistemático;
wholewheat adj = **wholemeal**; **wholly**
adv totalmente, enteramente

○ **KEYWORD**

whom [hu:m] pron **1** (interrogative):
whom did you see? ¿a quién viste?; **to**

whom did you give it? ¿a quién se lo diste?; **tell me from whom you received it** dígame de quién lo recibí
2 (relative) que; **to whom** a quien(es); **of whom** de quien(es), del/de la que etc; **the man whom I saw/to whom I wrote** el hombre que vi/a quien escribí; **the lady about/with whom I was talking** la señora de (la) que/con quien or (la) que hablaba

whore [hɔ:*] (inf, pej) n puta

○ KEYWORD

whose [hu:z] adj
1 (possessive: interrogative): **whose book is this?, whose is this book?** ¿de quién es este libro?; **whose pencil have you taken?** ¿de quién es el lápiz que has cogido?; **whose daughter are you?** ¿de quién eres hija?
2 (possessive: relative) cuyo/a, pl cuyos/ as; **the man whose son you rescued** el hombre cuyo hijo rescataste; **those whose passports I have** aquellas personas cuyos pasaportes tengo; **the woman whose car was stolen** la mujer a quien le robaron el coche ▷ pron de quién; **whose is this?** ¿de quién es esto?; **I know whose it is** sé de quién es

○ KEYWORD

why [waɪ] adv por qué; **why not?** ¿por qué no?; **why not do it now?** ¿por qué no lo haces (or hacemos etc) ahora? ▷ conj: **I wonder why he said that** me pregunto por qué dijo eso; **that's not why I'm here** no es por eso (por lo) que estoy aquí; **the reason why** la razón por la que
▷ excl (expressing surprise, shock, annoyance) ¡hombre!, ¡vaya!; (explaining): **why, it's you!** ¡hombre, eres tú!; **why, that's impossible** ¡pero sí eso es imposible!

wicked ['wɪkɪd] adj malvado, cruel
wicket ['wɪkɪt] n (Cricket: stumps) palos mpl; (: grass area) terreno de juego
wide [waɪd] adj ancho; (area, knowledge) vasto, grande; (choice) amplio ▷ adv: **to open ~** abrir de par en par; **to shoot ~** errar el tiro; **widely** adv (travelled) mucho; (spaced) muy; **it is widely believed/known that ...** mucha gente piensa/sabe que ...; **widen** vt ensanchar; (experience) ampliar ▷ vi ensancharse; **wide open** adj abierto de par en par; **widespread** adj extendido, general

widow ['wɪdəʊ] n viuda; **widower** n viudo
width [wɪdθ] n anchura; (of cloth) ancho
wield [wi:ld] vt (sword) blandir; (power) ejercer
wife [waɪf] (pl **wives**) n mujer f, esposa
wig [wɪg] n peluca
wild [waɪld] adj (animal) salvaje; (plant) silvestre; (person) furioso, violento; (idea) descabellado; (rough: sea) bravo; (: land) agreste; (: weather) muy revuelto; **wilderness** ['wɪldənɪs] n desierto; **wildlife** n fauna; **wildly** adv (behave) locamente; (lash out) a diestro y siniestro; (guess) a lo loco; (happy) a más no poder

○ KEYWORD

will [wɪl] aux vb **1** (forming future tense): **I will finish it tomorrow** lo terminaré or voy a terminar mañana; **I will have finished it by tomorrow** lo habré terminado para mañana; **will you do it? – yes I will/no I won't** ¿lo harás? – sí/no
2 (in conjectures, predictions): **he will** or **he'll be there by now** ya habrá or debe (de) haber llegado; **that will be the postman** será or debe ser el cartero
3 (in commands, requests, offers): **will you be quiet!** ¡quieres callarte?; **will you help me?** ¿quieres ayudarme?; **will you have a cup of tea?** ¿te apetece un té?; **I won't put up with it!** ¡no lo soporto! ▷ vt (pt, pp **willed**): **to will sb to do sth** desear que algn haga algo; **he willed himself to go on** con gran fuerza de voluntad, continuó
▷ n voluntad f; (testament) testamento

willing ['wɪlɪŋ] adj (with goodwill) de buena voluntad; (enthusiastic) entusiasta; **he's ~ to do it** está dispuesto a hacerlo; **willingly** adv con mucho gusto
willow ['wɪləʊ] n sauce m
willpower ['wɪlpaʊə*] n fuerza de voluntad
wilt [wɪlt] vi marchitarse
win [wɪn] (pt, pp **won**) n victoria, triunfo ▷ vt ganar; (obtain) conseguir, lograr ▷ vi ganar; **win over** vt convencer a
wince [wɪns] vi encogerse
wind¹ [wɪnd] n viento; (Med) gases mpl ▷ vt (take breath away from) dejar sin aliento a
wind² [waɪnd] (pt, pp **wound**) vt enrollar; (wrap) envolver; (clock, toy) dar cuerda a ▷ vi (road, river) serpentear; **wind down** vt (car window) bajar; (fig: production, business) disminuir; **wind up** vt (clock) dar cuerda a; (debate, meeting) concluir, terminar

windfall ['wɪndfɔːl] *n* golpe *m* de suerte

winding ['waɪndɪŋ] *adj* (*road*) tortuoso; (*staircase*) de caracol

windmill ['wɪndmɪl] *n* molino de viento

window ['wɪndəʊ] *n* ventana; (*in car, train*) ventanilla; (*in shop etc*) escaparate *m* (*SP*), vidriera (*LAM*); **window box** *n* jardinera de ventana; **window cleaner** *n* (*person*) limpiacristales *mf inv*; **window pane** *n* cristal *m*; **window seat** *n* asiento junto a la ventana; **windowsill** *n* alféizar *m*, repisa

windscreen ['wɪndskriːn] (*US* **windshield**) *n* parabrisas *m inv*; **windscreen wiper** (*US* **windshield wiper**) *n* limpiaparabrisas *m inv*

windsurfing ['wɪndsəːfɪŋ] *n* windsurf *m*

windy ['wɪndɪ] *adj* de mucho viento; **it's ~** hace viento

wine [waɪn] *n* vino; **wine bar** *n* enoteca; **wine glass** *n* copa (para vino); **wine list** *n* lista de vinos; **wine tasting** *n* degustación *f* de vinos

wing [wɪŋ] *n* ala; (*Aut*) aleta; **wing mirror** *n* (espejo) retrovisor *m*

wink [wɪŋk] *n* guiño, pestañeo ▷ *vi* guiñar, pestañear

winner ['wɪnə*] *n* ganador(a) *m/f*

winning ['wɪnɪŋ] *adj* (*team*) ganador(a); (*goal*) decisivo; (*smile*) encantador(a)

winter ['wɪntə*] *n* invierno ▷ *vi* invernar; **winter sports** *npl* deportes *mpl* de invierno; **wintertime** *n* invierno

wipe [waɪp] *n*: **to give sth a ~** pasar un trapo sobre algo ▷ *vt* limpiar; (*tape*) borrar; **wipe out** *vt* (*debt*) liquidar; (*memory*) borrar; (*destroy*) destruir; **wipe up** *vt* limpiar

wire ['waɪə*] *n* alambre *m*; (*Elec*) cable *m* (eléctrico); (*Tel*) telegrama *m* ▷ *vt* (*house*) poner la instalación eléctrica en; (*also*: **~ up**) conectar; (*person: telegram*) telegrafiar

wiring ['waɪərɪŋ] *n* instalación *f* eléctrica

wisdom ['wɪzdəm] *n* sabiduría, saber *m*; (*good sense*) cordura; **wisdom tooth** *n* muela del juicio

wise [waɪz] *adj* sabio; (*sensible*) juicioso

wish [wɪʃ] *n* deseo ▷ *vt* querer; **best ~es** (*on birthday etc*) felicidades *fpl*; **with best ~es** (*in letter*) saludos *mpl*, recuerdos *mpl*; **to ~ sb goodbye** despedirse de algn; **he ~ed me well** me deseó mucha suerte; **to ~ to do/sb to do sth** querer hacer/que algn haga algo; **to ~ for** desear

wistful ['wɪstful] *adj* pensativo

wit [wɪt] *n* ingenio, gracia; (*also*: **~s**) inteligencia; (*person*) chistoso/a

witch [wɪtʃ] *n* bruja

○ **KEYWORD**

with [wɪð, wɪθ] *prep* **1** (*accompanying, in the company of*) con (*con +mí, ti, sí = conmigo, contigo, consigo*); **I was with him** estaba con él; **we stayed with friends** nos quedamos en casa de unos amigos; **I'm (not) with you** (*don't understand*) (no) te entiendo; **to be with it** (*inf: person: up-to-date*) estar al tanto; (*: alert*) ser despabilado

2 (*descriptive, indicating manner etc*) con; de; **a room with a view** una habitación con vistas; **the man with blue eyes** el hombre de los ojos azules; **red with anger** rojo de ira; **to shake with fear** temblar de miedo; **to fill sth with water** llenar algo de agua

withdraw [wɪθ'drɔː] *vt* retirar, sacar ▷ *vi* retirarse; **to ~ money (from the bank)** retirar fondos (del banco); **withdrawal** *n* retirada; (*of money*) reintegro; **withdrawn** *pp of* **withdraw** ▷ *adj* (*person*) reservado, introvertido

withdrew [wɪθ'druː] *pt of* **withdraw**

wither ['wɪðə*] *vi* marchitarse

withhold [wɪθ'həʊld] *vt* (*money*) retener; (*decision*) aplazar; (*permission*) negar; (*information*) ocultar

within [wɪð'ɪn] *prep* dentro de ▷ *adv* dentro; **~ reach (of)** al alcance (de); **~ sight (of)** a la vista (de); **~ the week** antes de acabar la semana; **~ a mile (of)** a menos de una milla (de)

without [wɪð'aʊt] *prep* sin; **to go ~ sth** pasar sin algo

withstand [wɪθ'stænd] *vt* resistir a

witness ['wɪtnɪs] *n* testigo *mf* ▷ *vt* (*event*) presenciar; (*document*) atestiguar la veracidad de; **to bear ~ to** (*fig*) ser testimonio de

witty ['wɪtɪ] *adj* ingenioso

wives [waɪvz] *npl of* **wife**

wizard ['wɪzəd] *n* hechicero

wk *abbr* = **week**

wobble ['wɒbl] *vi* temblar; (*chair*) cojear

woe [wəʊ] *n* desgracia

woke [wəʊk] *pt of* **wake**

woken ['wəʊkən] *pp of* **wake**

wolf [wʊlf] *n* lobo

woman ['wʊmən] (*pl* **women**) *n* mujer *f*

womb [wuːm] *n* matriz *f*, útero

won [wʌn] *pt, pp of* **win**

wonder ['wʌndə*] *n* maravilla, prodigio; (*feeling*) asombro ▷ *vi*: **to ~ whether/why** preguntarse si/por qué; **to ~ at** asombrarse de; **to ~ about** pensar sobre or en; **it's no**

~ **(that)** no es de extrañarse (que +*subjun*);
wonderful *adj* maravilloso
won't [wəunt] = **will not**
wood [wud] *n* (*timber*) madera; (*forest*)
bosque *m*; **wooden** *adj* de madera;
woodwind *n* (*Mus*) instrumentos *mpl*
de viento de madera; **woodwork** *n*
carpintería
wool [wul] *n* lana; **to pull the ~ over sb's
eyes** (*fig*) engatusar a algn; **woollen** (*US*
woolen) *adj* de lana; **woolly** (*US* **wooly**) *adj*
lanudo, de lana; (*fig: ideas*) confuso
word [wə:d] *n* palabra; (*news*) noticia;
(*promise*) palabra (de honor) ▷ *vt* redactar;
in other ~s en otras palabras; **to break/
keep one's ~** faltar a la palabra/cumplir la
promesa; **to have ~s with sb** reñir con algn;
word processing *n* proceso de textos;
word processor *n* procesador *m* de textos
wore [wɔ:*] *pt of* **wear**
work [wə:k] *n* trabajo; (*job*) empleo,
trabajo; (*Art, Literature*) obra ▷ *vi* trabajar;
(*mechanism*) funcionar, marchar; (*medicine*)
ser eficaz, surtir efecto ▷ *vt* (*shape*)
trabajar; (*stone etc*) tallar; (*mine etc*) explotar;
(*machine*) manejar, hacer funcionar ▷ *npl*
(*of clock, machine*) mecanismo; **to be out
of ~** estar parado, no tener trabajo; **to ~
loose** (*part*) desprenderse; (*knot*) aflojarse;
works *n* (*BRIT: factory*) fábrica; **work out**
vi (*plans etc*) salir bien, funcionar; **works**
vt (*problem*) resolver; (*plan*) elaborar;
it works out at £100 suma 100 libras;
worker *n* trabajador(a) *m/f*, obrero/a;
work experience *n*: **I'm going to do my
work experience in a factory** voy a hacer
las prácticas en una fábrica; **workforce**
n mano de obra; **working class** *n* clase
f obrera ▷ *adj*: **working-class** obrero;
working week *n* semana laboral;
workman (*irreg*) *n* obrero; **work of art** *n*
obra de arte; **workout** *n* (*Sport*) sesión *f*
de ejercicios; **work permit** *n* permiso de
trabajo; **workplace** *n* lugar *m* de trabajo;
worksheet *n* (*Scol*) hoja de ejercicios;
workshop *n* taller *m*; **work station** *n*
puesto or estación *f* de trabajo; **work
surface** *n* encimera; **worktop** *n* encimera
world [wə:ld] *n* mundo ▷ *cpd* (*champion*)
del mundo; (*power, war*) mundial; **to think
the ~ of sb** (*fig*) tener un concepto muy alto
de algn; **World Cup** *n* (*Football*): **the World
Cup** el Mundial, los Mundiales; **world-wide**
adj mundial, universal; **World-Wide Web**
n: **the World-Wide Web** el World Wide Web
worm [wə:m] *n* (*also:* **earth ~**) lombriz *f*
worn [wɔ:n] *pp of* **wear** ▷ *adj* usado;
worn-out *adj* (*object*) gastado; (*person*)

rendido, agotado
worried ['wʌrɪd] *adj* preocupado
worry ['wʌrɪ] *n* preocupación *f* ▷ *vt*
preocupar, inquietar ▷ *vi* preocuparse;
worrying *adj* inquietante
worse [wə:s] *adj, adv* peor ▷ *n* lo peor;
a change for the ~ un empeoramiento;
worsen *vt, vi* empeorar; **worse off** *adj*
(*financially*): **to be worse off** tener menos
dinero; (*fig*): **you'll be worse off this way**
de esta forma estarás peor que nunca
worship ['wə:ʃɪp] *n* adoración *f* ▷ *vt*
adorar; **Your W~** (*BRIT: to mayor*) señor
alcalde; (: *to judge*) señor juez
worst [wə:st] *adj, adv* peor ▷ *n* lo peor; **at
~** en lo peor de los casos
worth [wə:θ] *n* valor *m* ▷ *adj*: **to be ~**
valer; **it's ~ it** vale or merece la pena; **to be ~
one's while (to do)** merecer la pena (hacer);
worthless *adj* sin valor; (*useless*) inútil;
worthwhile *adj* (*activity*) que merece la
pena; (*cause*) loable
worthy ['wə:ðɪ] *adj* respetable; (*motive*)
honesto; **~ of** digno de

○ **KEYWORD**

would [wud] *aux vb* **1** (*conditional tense*): **if
you asked him he would do it** si se lo
pidieras, lo haría; **if you had asked him
he would have done it** si se lo hubieras
pedido, lo habría or hubiera hecho
2 (*in offers, invitations, requests*): **would you
like a biscuit?** ¿quieres una galleta?; (*formal*)
¿querría una galleta?; **would you ask him
to come in?** ¿quiere hacerle pasar?; **would
you open the window please?** ¿quiere or
podría abrir la ventana, por favor?
3 (*in indirect speech*): **I said I would do it** dije
que lo haría
4 (*emphatic*): **it WOULD have to snow today!**
¡tenía que nevar precisamente hoy!
5 (*insistence*): **she wouldn't behave** no
quiso comportarse bien
6 (*conjecture*): **it would have been midnight**
sería medianoche; **it would seem so** parece
ser que sí
7 (*indicating habit*): **he would go there on
Mondays** iba allí los lunes

wouldn't ['wudnt] = **would not**
wound¹ [wu:nd] *n* herida ▷ *vt* herir
wound² [waund] *pt, pp of* **wind²**
wove [wəuv] *pt of* **weave**
woven ['wəuvən] *pp of* **weave**
wrap [ræp] *vt* (*also:* **~ up**) envolver;
(*gift*) envolver, abrigar ▷ *vi* (*dress warmly*)
abrigarse; **wrapper** *n* (*on chocolate*) papel

m; (BRIT: of book) sobrecubierta; **wrapping**
n envoltura, envase m; **wrapping paper**
n papel m de envolver; (fancy) papel m de
regalo

wreath [riːð, pl riːðz] n (funeral wreath)
corona

wreck [rɛk] n (ship: destruction) naufragio;
(: remains) restos mpl del barco; (pej: person)
ruina ▷vt (car etc) destrozar; (chances)
arruinar; **wreckage** n restos mpl; (of
building) escombros mpl

wren [rɛn] n (Zool) reyezuelo

wrench [rɛntʃ] n (Tech) llave f inglesa; (tug)
tirón m; (fig) dolor m ▷vt arrancar; **to ~
sth from sb** arrebatar algo violentamente
a algn

wrestle ['rɛsl] vi: **to ~ (with sb)** luchar (con
or contra algn); **wrestler** n luchador(a) m/f
(de lucha libre); **wrestling** n lucha libre

wretched ['rɛtʃɪd] adj miserable

wriggle ['rɪgl] vi (also: ~ **about**) menearse,
retorcerse

wring [rɪŋ] (pt, pp **wrung**) vt retorcer;
(wet clothes) escurrir; (fig): **to ~ sth out of sb**
sacar algo por la fuerza a algn

wrinkle ['rɪŋkl] n arruga ▷vt arrugar ▷vi
arrugarse

wrist [rɪst] n muñeca

writable ['raɪtəbl] adj (CD, DVD) escribible

write [raɪt] (pt **wrote**, pp **written**) vt
escribir; (cheque) extender ▷vi escribir;
write down vt escribir; (note) apuntar;
write off vt (debt) borrar (como
incobrable); (fig) desechar por inútil; **write
out** vt escribir; **write-off** n siniestro total;
writer n escritor(a) m/f

writing ['raɪtɪŋ] n escritura; (hand-writing)
letra; (of author) obras fpl; **in ~** por escrito;
writing paper n papel m de escribir

written ['rɪtn] pp of **write**

wrong [rɒŋ] adj (wicked) malo; (unfair)
injusto; (incorrect) equivocado, incorrecto;
(not suitable) inoportuno, inconveniente;
(reverse) del revés ▷adv equivocadamente
▷n injusticia ▷vt ser injusto con; **you
are ~ to do it** haces mal en hacerlo; **you
are ~ about that, you've got it ~** en eso
estás equivocado; **to be in the ~** no tener
razón, tener la culpa; **what's ~?** ¿qué pasa?;
to go ~ (person) equivocarse; (plan) salir
mal; (machine) estropearse; **wrongly** adv
mal, incorrectamente; (by mistake) por
error; **wrong number** n (Tel): **you've got
the wrong number** se ha equivocado de
número

wrote [raut] pt of **write**

wrung [rʌŋ] pt, pp of **wring**

WWW n abbr (= World Wide Web) WWW m

XL abbr = **extra large**

Xmas ['ɛksməs] n abbr = **Christmas**

X-ray ['ɛksreɪ] n radiografía ▷vt
radiografiar, sacar radiografías de

xylophone ['zaɪləfəun] n xilófono

Y

yacht [jɔt] n yate m; **yachting** n (sport) balandrismo

yard [jɑːd] n patio; (measure) yarda; **yard sale** (US) n venta de objetos usados (en el jardín de una casa particular)

yarn [jɑːn] n hilo; (tale) cuento, historia

yawn [jɔːn] n bostezo ▷ vi bostezar

yd. abbr (= yard) yda

yeah [jɛə] (inf) adv sí

year [jɪə*] n año; **to be 8 ~s old** tener 8 años; **an eight-~-old child** un niño de ocho años (de edad); **yearly** adj anual ▷ adv anualmente, cada año

yearn [jəːn] vi: **to ~ for sth** añorar algo, suspirar por algo

yeast [jiːst] n levadura

yell [jɛl] n grito, alarido ▷ vi gritar

yellow ['jɛləu] adj amarillo; **Yellow Pages**® npl páginas fpl amarillas

yes [jɛs] adv sí ▷ n sí m; **to say/answer ~** decir/contestar que sí

yesterday ['jɛstədɪ] adv ayer ▷ n ayer m; **~ morning/evening** ayer por la mañana/tarde; **all day ~** todo el día de ayer

yet [jɛt] adv ya; (negative) todavía ▷ conj sin embargo, a pesar de todo; **it is not finished ~** todavía no está acabado; **the best ~** el/la mejor hasta ahora; **as ~** hasta ahora, todavía

yew [juː] n tejo

Yiddish ['jɪdɪʃ] n yiddish m

yield [jiːld] n (Agr) cosecha; (Comm) rendimiento ▷ vt ceder; (results) producir, dar; (profit) rendir ▷ vi rendirse, ceder; (US Aut) ceder el paso

yob(bo) ['jɔb(bəu)] n (BRIT inf) gamberro

yoga ['jəugə] n yoga m

yog(h)ourt ['jəugət] n yogur m

yog(h)urt ['jəugət] n = **yog(h)ourt**

yolk [jəuk] n yema (de huevo)

○ **KEYWORD**

you [juː] pron **1** (subject: familiar) tú; (pl) vosotros/as (SP), ustedes (LAM); (polite) usted; (pl) ustedes; **you are very kind** eres/es etc muy amable; **you Spanish enjoy your food** a vosotros (or ustedes) los españoles os (or les) gusta la comida; **you and I will go** iremos tú y yo

2 (object: direct: familiar) te; (pl) os (SP), les (LAM); (polite) le; (pl) les; (f) la; (pl) las; **I know you** te/le etc conozco

3 (object: indirect: familiar) te; (pl) os (SP), les (LAM); (polite) le; (pl) les; **I gave the letter to you yesterday** te/os etc di la carta ayer

4 (stressed): **I told you to do it** te dije a ti que lo hicieras, es a ti a quien dije que lo hicieras; see also **3**; **5**

5 (after prep: NB: con +ti = contigo: familiar) ti; (pl) vosotros/as (SP), ustedes (LAM); (: polite) usted; (pl) ustedes; **it's for you** es para ti/vosotros etc

6 (comparisons: familiar) tú; (pl) vosotros/as (SP), ustedes (LAM); (: polite) usted; (pl) ustedes; **she's younger than you** es más joven que tú/vosotros etc

7 (impersonal one): **fresh air does you good** el aire puro (te) hace bien; **you never know** nunca se sabe; **you can't do that!** ¡eso no se hace!

you'd [juːd] = you had; you would

you'll [juːl] = you will; you shall

young [jʌŋ] adj joven ▷ npl (of animal) cría; (people): **the ~** los jóvenes, la juventud; **youngster** n joven mf

your [jɔː*] adj tu; (pl) vuestro; (formal) su; see also **my**

you're [juə*] = you are

yours [jɔːz] pron tuyo (pl), vuestro; (formal) suyo; see also **faithfully; mine¹** see also **sincerely**

yourself [jɔːˈsɛlf] pron tú mismo; (complement) te; (after prep) tí (mismo); (formal) usted mismo; (: complement) se; (: after prep) sí (mismo); **yourselves** pl pron vosotros mismos; (after prep) vosotros (mismos); (formal) ustedes (mismos); (: complement) se; (: after prep) sí mismos; see also **oneself**

youth [pl juːðz] n juventud f; (young man) joven m; **youth club** n club m juvenil; **youthful** adj juvenil; **youth hostel** n albergue m de juventud

you've [juːv] = you have

Z

zeal [ziːl] n celo, entusiasmo
zebra ['ziːbrə] n cebra; **zebra crossing**
 (BRIT) n paso de peatones
zero ['zɪərəu] n cero
zest [zɛst] n ánimo, vivacidad f; (of orange)
 piel f
zigzag ['zɪgzæg] n zigzag m ▷ vi
 zigzaguear, hacer eses
Zimbabwe [zɪmˈbɑːbwɪ] n Zimbabwe m
zinc [zɪŋk] n cinc m, zinc m
zip [zip] n (also: ~ fastener, (US) ~per)
 cremallera (SP), cierre (AM) m, zíper m (MEX,
 CAM) ▷ vt (also: ~ up) cerrar la cremallera
 de; (file) comprimir; **zip code** (US) n
 código postal; **zip file** n (Comput) archivo
 comprimido; **zipper** (US) n cremallera
zit [zit] n grano
zodiac ['zəudɪæk] n zodíaco
zone [zəun] n zona
zoo [zuː] n (jardín m) zoo m
zoology [zuˈɔlədʒɪ] n zoología
zoom [zuːm] vi: **to ~ past** pasar zumbando;
 zoom lens n zoom m
zucchini [zuːˈkiːnɪ] (US) n(pl)
 calabacín(ines) m(pl)